Demotech Performance
of
Title Insurance Companies

2008 EDITION

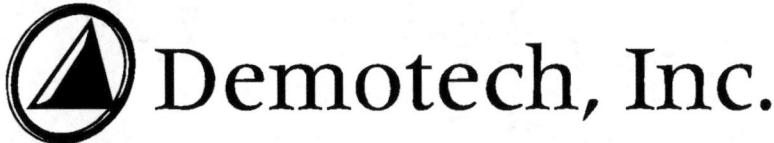

Published May 2008 by Demotech, Inc.
Editor: Joseph L. Petrelli, Jr.

Initial Print
ISBN 0-9675101-4-7

Published May 2008 by Demotech, Inc.

Technical Editor:	Paul D. Osborne
Assistant Editor:	Robert M. Warren
Contributing Analysts:	Brett Gissel
	Douglas A. Powell

Special thanks to the team at Demotech for their help and support.

Demotech, Inc.
2715 Tuller Parkway
Dublin, Ohio 43017-2310
Tel: (614) 761-8602
(800) 354-7207
Fax: (614) 761-0906
www.demotech.com
inquiry@demotech.com

TABLE OF CONTENTS

Publication Overview

Welcome to the twentieth edition of *Performance of Title Insurance Companies*, the Title industry's most complete and independent resource.

The Only Independent Source of Title Industry Information

Included in the 2008 publication are all publicly traded Title underwriters and most of the regional and local underwriters, representing more than 99% of the Title industry's Direct Premiums Written. Some Title underwriters are subsidiaries or affiliates of others, but each of the companies included in this publication is a licensed Title underwriter.

We are pleased to present comparative statutory operating results, as well as statutory financial positions of ninety-one Title underwriters.

Companies in the 2008 Edition

The 2008 edition includes data from a number of new companies. We excluded underwriters that are no longer actively writing business or whose data did not meet our reconciliation requirements. Some notable changes regarding the companies in the 2008 edition are as follows:

NEW COMPANIES

NAIC #	Company Name
12953	K.E.L. Title Insurance Group
12518	Public Title Insurance Company
12935	Titledge Insurance Company of New York

The following companies are not included in the statutory financial statements, market share reports and ratio analysis due to incomplete Form 9 Annual Statement data or balancing discrepancies at the time of publication. However, these companies will have corporate information, as well as Financial Stability Ratings® (FSRs) included in *Sections 1* and *4* of the publication.

COMPANIES EXCLUDED

NAIC #	Company Name
50164	The Bankers Guarantee Title & Trust Company
50199	First American Title Insurance of LA
N/A	Mortgage Guarantee & Title Company
N/A	Pilgrim Title Insurance Company

OTHER COMPANY CHANGES AND INFORMATION FOR THE 2008 EDITION

NAIC #	Company Name	Change
19640	Columbia National Title Insurance Company	Did not write any premium for the year 2007.
50822	Land Title Insurance Company	Has been absorbed by Lawyers Title Insurance Corporation (NAIC # 50024).
12551	Law Title Insurance Company	Is currently not writing business.
50000	North American Title Insurance Corporation	Has merged into North American Title Insurance Company (NAIC # 50130).

Publication Format

2008 Improvements

The 2008 edition continues our effort to evolve and improve this industry resource. This year's publication presents the following enhancements:

Intra-Group Ownership Structure - *Section 1 - Underwriter & NAIC Group Information* now includes *Intra-Group Ownership Structure* reports, which are designed to show Title underwriter ownership relationships within an NAIC Group. *Intra-Group Ownership Structure* reports are based on the information filed in Schedule Y of the Form 9 Annual Statements.

Inter-Report References - *Section 2 - Statutory Financial Statements* now cross-reference the financial statement line items to supporting detail and analysis included in *Section 5 - Financial Ratios and Analysis.*

Jurisdiction Dashboards - *Section 6 - Dashboards* now includes *Jurisdiction Dashboards.* *Jurisdiction Dashboards* consolidate reference data and reports regarding jurisdiction competition, market share and trends. These reports provide historical premium and loss activity, along with information related to the jurisdiction marketplace, including department of insurance contact information and associated Land Title Associations. As with *Underwriter Dashboards*, historical results are offered for key ratios and performance measures.

New Ratios and Analysis - *Section 5 - Financial Ratios and Analysis* includes two new ratios for more detailed analysis and market benchmarking.

Core Components of the Publication

Section 1 – Title Underwriter Information

Section 1 contains corporate information about the Title underwriters and NAIC Groups listed in the publication. This section presents information gathered primarily from the Jurat and General Interrogatories, such as the actuary providing the 2007 Statement of Actuarial Opinion, the accounting firm retained to conduct the 2007 annual audit, etc.

Additionally, Financial Stability Ratings® (FSRs) current as of the date of publication are presented. *Financial Stability Ratings®* *must be verified by visiting www.demotech.com.*

Section 1 also details the compositions of the NAIC Groups, which are essential to accurate competitive analysis, and in a rapidly changing market environment, are important considerations of the data contained in the publication. Note, unaffiliated organizations are consolidated as "Unaffiliated Companies." This is for presentation and summarization purposes, to reflect the role and impact of independent and regional underwriters. Designation as Unaffiliated Companies does not suggest any degree of partnership or other business coordination between these underwriters.

New for 2008, this section includes *Intra-Group Underwriter Ownership Structure*, which presents the relationships of Title underwriter ownership within an NAIC Group. While some groups have a number of holding companies, agencies and related businesses within their organizational structure, this report includes only those companies in the structure having direct ownership of a Title underwriter.

Intra-Group Ownership Structure reports are based on the information filed in Schedule Y of the Form 9 Annual Statements.

This section also lists the licensed jurisdictions for Title underwriters included in the publication, using data collected from the Schedule T. It does not necessarily reflect business activity within those areas. Licensed jurisdictions also are presented by NAIC Group, allowing perspective on the overall market coverage achieved through Group operations. Note, due to the nature of this report, Unaffiliated Companies are excluded to avoid misinterpretation.

Section 2 – Statutory Financial Statements

Section 2 presents the core statutory financial statements: Balance Sheet, Income Statement and Statement of Cash Flow. Each of these financial reports is presented with an industry composite, by NAIC Group as well as by individual underwriter. The Balance Sheet and Income Statement reports contained in *Section 2* are not identical to the statutory presentation, incorporating additional information from throughout the Form 9 Annual Statement. This detail is included using supporting exhibits and reports to enhance these references.

New for 2008 are *inter-report references within the Statutory Financial Statements.* These references facilitate enhanced review by cross-referencing associated material in *Section 5 - Financial Ratios and Analysis.* *Section 5* ratios offer expanded detail and analysis, allowing competitive benchmarking and historical analysis beyond the contents of the stand-alone financial statements

Statutory Financial Statements include *Consolidated Eliminations* for equity, as well as inter-company dividends by parent or affiliated underwriters. Special attention was given to fully reflect these eliminations in all summary financial reports. The composite Balance Sheet was adjusted to eliminate double counting the equity holdings of subsidiaries. The composite Income Statement and Statement of Cash Flow was adjusted to reflect the dividend distribution between affiliated organizations and to account for inter-company holdings, which decrease the aggregate policyholders' surplus.

See the *Publication Considerations* for additional information on *Consolidated Eliminations*.

Section 3 – Market Share Reports and Position Analysis

Section 3 contains premium information for each jurisdiction and reports each Title underwriter's market share for the presented category. The information is subdivided by operations: Direct, Non-Affiliated and Affiliated Agencies. Combined Losses Paid for each jurisdiction are also shown. The monoline separation of Title insurance activity allows the premium and loss data from Schedule T to be used for jurisdiction-by-jurisdiction market share comparisons.

Five-Year Trend reports provide graphical presentation of historical Direct Premiums Written activity by NAIC Group, individual underwriter and by jurisdiction.

Section 4 - Financial Stability Ratings® (FSRs) and Commercial Real Estate Recommendations (CRERs)

Section 4 contains Financial Stability Ratings® (FSRs) and Commercial Real Estate Recommendations (CRERs). FSRs are an assessment of an underwriter's on-going financial stability. Based on a predominantly quantitative analysis, an FSR provides an impartial perspective on financial stability, whether for a regional underwriter or one of the large, national underwriters. FSRs streamline the administrative process by addressing concerns related to the financial stability of an underwriter while simultaneously enhancing the image of well-rated underwriters.

Since 1992, FSRs have been an integral part of the Title insurance industry. No other organization reviews more underwriters or has been providing financial analysis longer than Demotech.

Additionally, Financial Stability Ratings® (FSRs) current as of the date of publication are presented. *Financial Stability Ratings® must be verified by visiting www.demotech.com.*

Section 5 – Financial Ratios and Analysis

Section 5 includes financial ratio and analysis reports with detailed results for each underwriter. The results are ranked and, where possible, compared with previous years to illustrate trends and changes. These ratios have been developed using Form 9 data as the sole source of input.

The ratios are intended to ease the work of analysts, whether at insurance departments, the NAIC, lenders or underwriters, who are interested in comparing Title underwriters within the industry. The ratios help establish baselines that determine results relevant to many worthwhile objectives.

To facilitate the review of company results, indices accompany ratios that are not sorted alphabetically. Also, stand-alone ratios used in the calculation of subsequent ratio results are noted. For instance, the *A.3 Loss Ratio* and the *A.5 Operating Expense Ratio*, which are separate ratio reports with current and historical results, are indicated as stand-alone ratios in the *A.6 Combined Ratio*. These cross-references facilitate recognition of the interaction between ratio details and also allow greater historical analysis using the details presented within the stand-alone reports.

New for 2008, two new ratios and analysis have been added, including an analysis of *B.8 - Implied Equity (Deficit) in the Statutory Premium Reserve (SPR)* and *C.11 - Loss Reserve Development to Policyholders Surplus (PHS)*. Further explanation of these important calculations are available in *Section 5*.

The ratios and analysis presented in *Section 5* are subdivided into *Measurements of Operating Results, Operating Position/ Situation* and *Losses and Ability to Meet Losses*. Each subdivision begins with ratio descriptions and explanations and reports summarizing the section's key results and ratios.

Where appropriate, ratios that present Composite results are <u>net</u> of *Consolidated Eliminations*. While best efforts were extended, the necessary information to discern the full historical consolidated eliminations was not available; therefore, *Consolidated Eliminations* are limited to 2005 to present.

See the *Publication Considerations* for additional information on *Consolidated Eliminations*.

Section 6 – Dashboards

Section 6 presents consolidated presentation of underwriter and jurisdiction information. The *Dashboard* reports are a single reference point for competitive comparisons and insight to the current position and trajectory of underwriter and jurisdiction performance.

Underwriter Dashboards consolidate metrics and historical perspective for presented underwriters. Dashboards provide key corporate information and observations, presenting up to five years of benchmarks, including underwriter corporate information, financial position, as well as operating and underwriting results.

New for 2008, *Jurisdiction Dashboards* present a consolidated reference point for jurisdiction resources, market share and trends, presenting historical results for key ratios and performance measures. These reports provide historical premium and loss activity, along with information regarding the jurisdiction marketplace, including department of insurance contact information and associated Land Title Association where available.

The 2008 Edition of
Demotech Performance of Title Insurance Companies

The contents of the publication reflect our commitment to the core information provided throughout the twenty-year history of this industry resource. The considerable amount of new and expanded content reflects our continued efforts to refine and enhance the publication.

Availability of Our *Form 9 Database* for Customized Analysis

The growing maturity of our proprietary *Form 9 Database* is a key component in the development of this publication. Just as your bookshelves have expanded to hold the annual releases of *Demotech Performance of Title Insurance Companies*, so has our *Form 9 Database*. The accumulation of our data allows the expansion of many reports beyond the data collected from the current Form 9 Annual Statement. For instance, the *Underwriter* and *Jurisdiction Dashboards*, *Five-Year Trend* and many ratios present five or more years of industry data, which is only possible due to our expanding Form 9 industry data repository. Demotech will leverage this asset as we continue to provide the most comprehensive Title industry coverage available.

The information within our *Form 9 Database* is available for customized analysis tailored to your specific needs.

Input and Suggestions

As always, we welcome your feedback as this publication is designed for our subscribers and we hope to continue refining it to meet your evolving needs. Comments can be sent to *PTIC@demotech.com*.

Thank you,

Joseph L. Petrelli, Jr., **Editor**   Paul Osborne, **Technical Editor**

Publication Considerations

Statutory Accounting and Form 9 Data

The data presented in this publication represents the Title underwriters' conformance with the reporting definitions established by the National Association of Insurance Commissioners (NAIC) with their Form 9 Annual Statement. This Form 9 data, which is the information source of this publication, is based upon Statutory Accounting Principles (SAP), which differs substantially from Generally Accepted Accounting Principles (GAAP). This information was provided to Demotech directly by each Title underwriter.

In most cases, publicly held companies engaged in the Title insurance business are holding companies owning one or more of the Title underwriters reported herein. As holding companies are not Title underwriters, they do not prepare Form 9 statements, and therefore are not included in this publication. Conclusions drawn from Form 9 data may not be consistent with conclusions based on GAAP financial statements.

Further explanation of the difference between GAAP and SAP is presented in Section 5.

Enhancements to the Presentation of Statutory Financial Statements

The Balance Sheet and Income Statement reports contained in Section 2 are not identical to the statutory presentation. It incorporates additional information from throughout the Form 9 Annual Statement, including supporting exhibits and reports to enhance these references.

The reports and analysis in this publication rely on both the summary and supporting schedules within the Form 9 Annual Statements. The figures presented in the ratio calculations presented in *Section 5 - Financial Ratios and Analysis* may differ slightly from figures presented in *Section 2 - Statutory Financial Statements* and other sections of the publication.

- Differences between results in *Section 2* and *Section 5* are due to discrepancies between summary and supporting Form 9 Annual Statement schedules, reported by the underwriters. These data discrepancies are inherent to the reported underwriter data and fall within the accepted error tolerances associated with Form 9 cross-checks and detail reporting. In some instances, the discrepancy in the underwriter statement and supporting schedules causes minor deviations in the *Composite* totals reported between sections.

- In general, the reports presented in *Section 2* extract figures from the supporting schedules, recalculating net and aggregate figures, where as the ratios presented in *Section 5* pull directly from the main financial reports.

Consolidated Eliminations

Our objective with *Consolidated Eliminations* is a simplified methodology to provide consistent calculations for each annual publication. To this end, we consider the equity position and inter-company dividends as the two primary considerations to facilitate and produce our eliminating adjustments.

Consolidated Eliminations affects Balance Sheet, Income Statement and Statement of Cash Flow items throughout the publication. We rely on Schedule Y and Schedule D, Part 6, Section 1 to determine the ownership structure of each NAIC Group. As changes to the NAIC Group structure occur, we update our documentation and incorporate these changes into the publication. If a company is included and it can be determined that another included company owns it, the companies will be consolidated and the appropriate eliminating entries will be made. If a company owns another company, either directly or indirectly, the companies will be consolidated to reflect the appropriate percent of ownership.

To produce the consolidated Balance Sheet for an NAIC Group, the equity position of each subsidiary is used to determine the amount to be eliminated from the invested assets of the parent. In the event the subsidiary is not a wholly owned subsidiary, the pro rata ownership is calculated to determine the amount of equity to eliminate.

For the Income Statement and Statement of Cash Flow, inter-company dividends are considered for the eliminating adjustments. As with the Balance Sheet, the source for determining the eliminating entries is the subsidiary company. The reference is the dividends paid or declared by the subsidiary company.

While we acknowledge that accounting practices for consolidation may include items other than subsidiary equity and inter-company dividends, we rely solely on the data available from the Form 9 filings to ensure the year to year consistency of the appropriate eliminating adjustments. Attempting to include other inter-company transactions would require reliance on other information resources. This reliance could potentially affect the consistency of the presented data.

Appropriate Interpretation of "Unaffiliated Companies"

Unaffiliated organizations are consolidated throughout the publication in summary NAIC Group reports as "Unaffiliated Companies." This is for presentation and summarization purposes to reflect the role and impact of independent and regional underwriters. Designation of Unaffiliated Companies does not suggest any degree of partnership or other business coordination between these underwriters.

Data Limitations

Demotech relies upon submitted Form 9 Annual Statements. As such, the information is subject to discrepancies and inconsistencies reported by and between underwriters. Demotech makes no warranties or statements as to the accuracy of this information.

Prior to inclusion in the publication, all underwriter data is analyzed and processed using established data validations. If possible, data discrepancies are researched and evaluated with the underwriters. However, in many cases, such discrepancies are not able to be resolved in a timely manner.

Demotech has full discretion in establishing data quality requirements. To the degree possible, consistent requirements are applied for the evaluation of all underwriters. Underwriter data deemed unacceptable is eliminated from the publication to avoid corruption of industry calculations. As a result, the Market Share Reports, Ratio Analysis and the Dashboard Reports are limited to underwriters with qualified data submissions.

The data and information is provided "as is" without warranty of any kind, express or implied, including, but not limited to, implied warranties of merchantability, fitness for a particular purpose, title or non-infringement.

In no event will Demotech be liable to any party for any direct, indirect, special, consequential or other damages for any use of or reliance upon the information in this publication, including, without limitation, lost profits, business interruption, loss of programs or other data, even if Demotech is expressly advised of the possibility of such damages.

S E C T I O N

UNDERWRITER & NAIC GROUP INFORMATION

UNDERWRITER CORPORATE INFORMATION AND FINANCIAL STABILITY RATINGS® (FSRs)

Underwriter Corporate Information and Financial Stability Ratings® (FSRs)

Alamo Title Insurance — ALAMO

601 Riverside Ave.
Jacksonville, FL 32204
(904) 854-8100
www.fnf.com

NAIC Number:	50598	Date of Incorporation:	10/1/1922
Group Number:	670	NAIC Group:	CHICAGO / FIDELITY
State of Domicile:			Texas

2007 Auditor: KPMG LLP
One Independent Dr., Ste. 2700
Independent Square
Jacksonville, FL 32202

2007 Actuary: Timothy L. Shilling, FCAS, MAAA
Fidelity National Title Group Inc.
601 Riverside Ave.
Jacksonville, FL 32204

A' Unsurpassed — Financial Stability Rating® — Demotech, Inc.

Alliance Title of America, Inc. — ALLIANCE

3401 W Cypress St., 2nd Fl.
Tampa, FL 33607
(813) 876-0619
www.stewart.com

NAIC Number:	50035	Date of Incorporation:	8/14/1996
Group Number:	340	NAIC Group:	STEWART
State of Domicile:			Florida

2007 Auditor: Hevia Beagles & Co., CPA
9400 Fourth St. N, Ste. 120
St. Petersburg, FL 33702

2007 Actuary: John Pierce, FCAS
John Pierce Consulting
1420 Renaissance Dr., Ste. 104
Park Ridge, IL 60068

A' Unsurpassed — Financial Stability Rating® — Demotech, Inc.

Alliant National Title Insurance Company — ALLIANT

2101 Ken Pratt Blvd., Ste. 102
Longmont, CO 80501
(303) 682-9800
www.alliantnational.com

Formerly Agents Title Insurance Company, Inc.

NAIC Number:	12309	Date of Incorporation:	7/27/2005
Group Number:		NAIC Group:	UNAFFILIATED COMPANIES
State of Domicile:			Colorado

2007 Auditor: Anton Collins & Mitchell LLP
303 E 17th Ave.
Denver, CO 80203

2007 Actuary: Mark W. Mulvaney FCAS, MAAA
Milliman Inc.
1099 18th St.
Denver, CO 80202-9131

A Exceptional — Financial Stability Rating® — Demotech, Inc.

American Eagle Title Insurance Company — AMERICAN EAGLE

1141 N Robinson, Ste. 100
Oklahoma City, OK 73103
(405) 232-6700
www.ameagletitle.com

NAIC Number:	50001	Date of Incorporation:	10/14/1994
Group Number:		NAIC Group:	UNAFFILIATED COMPANIES
State of Domicile:			Oklahoma

2007 Auditor:

2007 Actuary:

A' Exceptional — Financial Stability Rating® — Demotech, Inc.

American Guaranty Title Insurance Company — AMERICAN GUARANTY

4040 N Tulsa
Oklahoma City, OK 73112
(405) 942-4848
www.oldrepublictitle.com

NAIC Number:	51411	Date of Incorporation:	7/2/1979
Group Number:	150	NAIC Group:	OLD REPUBLIC
State of Domicile:			Oklahoma

2007 Auditor: PriceWaterhouseCoopers, LLP
225 S 6th St.
Minneapolis, MN 55402

2007 Actuary: J. Paul Cochran
Old Republic General Services Inc.
307 N Michigan Ave.
Chicago, IL 60601

A" Unsurpassed — Financial Stability Rating® — Demotech, Inc.

American Land and Aircraft Title Company — AMERICAN LAND & AIRCRAFT

Six NE 63rd St., Ste. 100
Oklahoma City, OK 73105
(405) 359-9472
www.alatc.com

NAIC Number:	11450	Date of Incorporation:	6/24/1998
Group Number:		NAIC Group:	UNAFFILIATED COMPANIES
State of Domicile:			Oklahoma

2007 Auditor:

2007 Actuary:

S Substantial — Financial Stability Rating® — Demotech, Inc.

American Security Title Insurance Company — AMERICAN SECURITY

1000 W 15th St.
Edmond, OK 73013
(405) 348-1248

NAIC Number:	51365	Date of Incorporation:	6/28/1978
Group Number:		NAIC Group:	UNAFFILIATED COMPANIES
State of Domicile:			Oklahoma

2007 Auditor: Grant Thornton, LLP
One Leadership Square, Ste. 1200
Oklahoma City, OK 73102

2007 Actuary: John Pierce, FCAS
John Pierce Consulting
1420 Renaissance Dr., Ste. 104
Park Ridge, IL 60068

A' Unsurpassed — Financial Stability Rating® — Demotech, Inc.

Arkansas Title Insurance Company — ARKANSAS TIC

17300 Chenal Pkwy.
Little Rock, AR 72223
(501) 228-8200
www.arkansastitle.com

NAIC Number:	50725	Date of Incorporation:	5/3/1982
Group Number:	340	NAIC Group:	STEWART
State of Domicile:			Arkansas

2007 Auditor: Blackman Kallick Bartelstein, LLP
10 S Riverside Plz., 9th Fl.
Chicago, IL 60606

2007 Actuary: Steve Osborn
Osborn Carreiro & Assoc., Inc.
124 W Capital Ave., Ste. 1690
1 Union National Plaza
Little Rock, AR 72201

A" Unsurpassed — Financial Stability Rating® — Demotech, Inc.

Important: Financial Stability Ratings® must be verified by visiting **www.demotech.com**

Underwriter Corporate Information and Financial Stability Ratings® (FSRs)

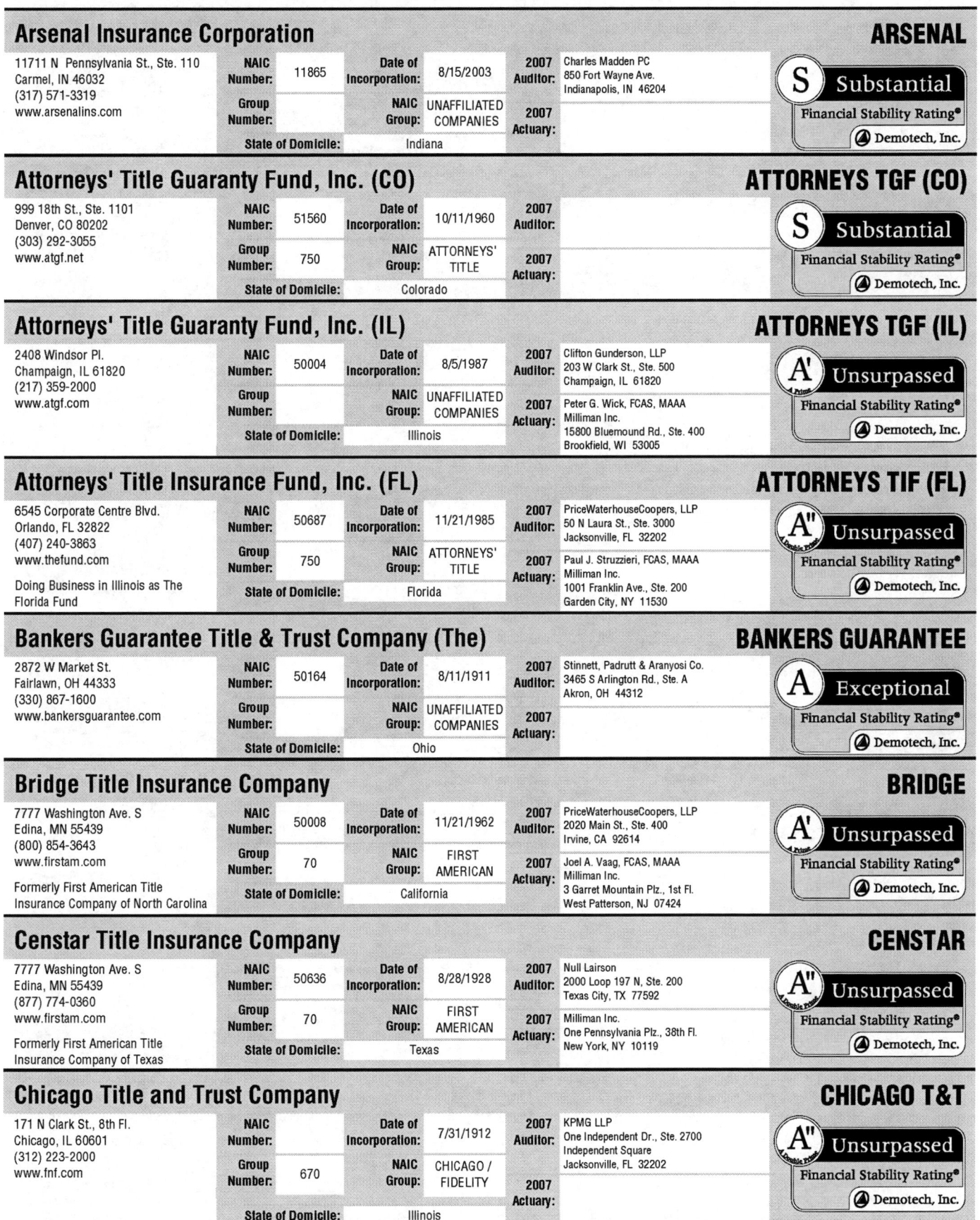

Arsenal Insurance Corporation — ARSENAL

11711 N Pennsylvania St., Ste. 110
Carmel, IN 46032
(317) 571-3319
www.arsenalins.com

NAIC Number:	11865
Group Number:	
State of Domicile:	Indiana

Date of Incorporation: 8/15/2003
NAIC Group: UNAFFILIATED COMPANIES

2007 Auditor: Charles Madden PC, 850 Fort Wayne Ave., Indianapolis, IN 46204
2007 Actuary:

S Substantial — Financial Stability Rating® — Demotech, Inc.

Attorneys' Title Guaranty Fund, Inc. (CO) — ATTORNEYS TGF (CO)

999 18th St., Ste. 1101
Denver, CO 80202
(303) 292-3055
www.atgf.net

NAIC Number:	51560
Group Number:	750
State of Domicile:	Colorado

Date of Incorporation: 10/11/1960
NAIC Group: ATTORNEYS' TITLE

2007 Auditor:
2007 Actuary:

S Substantial — Financial Stability Rating® — Demotech, Inc.

Attorneys' Title Guaranty Fund, Inc. (IL) — ATTORNEYS TGF (IL)

2408 Windsor Pl.
Champaign, IL 61820
(217) 359-2000
www.atgf.com

NAIC Number:	50004
Group Number:	
State of Domicile:	Illinois

Date of Incorporation: 8/5/1987
NAIC Group: UNAFFILIATED COMPANIES

2007 Auditor: Clifton Gunderson, LLP, 203 W Clark St., Ste. 500, Champaign, IL 61820
2007 Actuary: Peter G. Wick, FCAS, MAAA, Milliman Inc., 15800 Bluemound Rd., Ste. 400, Brookfield, WI 53005

A' Unsurpassed — Financial Stability Rating® — Demotech, Inc.

Attorneys' Title Insurance Fund, Inc. (FL) — ATTORNEYS TIF (FL)

6545 Corporate Centre Blvd.
Orlando, FL 32822
(407) 240-3863
www.thefund.com

Doing Business in Illinois as The Florida Fund

NAIC Number:	50687
Group Number:	750
State of Domicile:	Florida

Date of Incorporation: 11/21/1985
NAIC Group: ATTORNEYS' TITLE

2007 Auditor: PriceWaterhouseCoopers, LLP, 50 N Laura St., Ste. 3000, Jacksonville, FL 32202
2007 Actuary: Paul J. Struzzieri, FCAS, MAAA, Milliman Inc., 1001 Franklin Ave., Ste. 200, Garden City, NY 11530

A" Unsurpassed — Financial Stability Rating® — Demotech, Inc.

Bankers Guarantee Title & Trust Company (The) — BANKERS GUARANTEE

2872 W Market St.
Fairlawn, OH 44333
(330) 867-1600
www.bankersguarantee.com

NAIC Number:	50164
Group Number:	
State of Domicile:	Ohio

Date of Incorporation: 8/11/1911
NAIC Group: UNAFFILIATED COMPANIES

2007 Auditor: Stinnett, Padrutt & Aranyosi Co., 3465 S Arlington Rd., Ste. A, Akron, OH 44312
2007 Actuary:

A Exceptional — Financial Stability Rating® — Demotech, Inc.

Bridge Title Insurance Company — BRIDGE

7777 Washington Ave. S
Edina, MN 55439
(800) 854-3643
www.firstam.com

Formerly First American Title Insurance Company of North Carolina

NAIC Number:	50008
Group Number:	70
State of Domicile:	California

Date of Incorporation: 11/21/1962
NAIC Group: FIRST AMERICAN

2007 Auditor: PriceWaterhouseCoopers, LLP, 2020 Main St., Ste. 400, Irvine, CA 92614
2007 Actuary: Joel A. Vaag, FCAS, MAAA, Milliman Inc., 3 Garret Mountain Plz., 1st Fl., West Patterson, NJ 07424

A' Unsurpassed — Financial Stability Rating® — Demotech, Inc.

Censtar Title Insurance Company — CENSTAR

7777 Washington Ave. S
Edina, MN 55439
(877) 774-0360
www.firstam.com

Formerly First American Title Insurance Company of Texas

NAIC Number:	50636
Group Number:	70
State of Domicile:	Texas

Date of Incorporation: 8/28/1928
NAIC Group: FIRST AMERICAN

2007 Auditor: Null Lairson, 2000 Loop 197 N, Ste. 200, Texas City, TX 77592
2007 Actuary: Milliman Inc., One Pennsylvania Plz., 38th Fl., New York, NY 10119

A" Unsurpassed — Financial Stability Rating® — Demotech, Inc.

Chicago Title and Trust Company — CHICAGO T&T

171 N Clark St., 8th Fl.
Chicago, IL 60601
(312) 223-2000
www.fnf.com

NAIC Number:	
Group Number:	670
State of Domicile:	Illinois

Date of Incorporation: 7/31/1912
NAIC Group: CHICAGO / FIDELITY

2007 Auditor: KPMG LLP, One Independent Dr., Ste. 2700, Independent Square, Jacksonville, FL 32202
2007 Actuary:

A" Unsurpassed — Financial Stability Rating® — Demotech, Inc.

Important: Financial Stability Ratings® must be verified by visiting **www.demotech.com**

1

Underwriter Corporate Information and Financial Stability Ratings® (FSRs)

Chicago Title Insurance Company

CHICAGO TIC

601 Riverside Ave.
Jacksonville, FL 32204
(904) 854-8100
www.fnf.com

NAIC Number:	50229	Date of Incorporation:	8/30/1961
Group Number:	670	NAIC Group:	CHICAGO / FIDELITY
State of Domicile:			Nebraska

2007 Auditor: KPMG LLP
One Independent Dr., Ste. 2700
Independent Square
Jacksonville, FL 32202

2007 Actuary: Timothy L. Shilling, FCAS, MAAA
Fidelity National Title Group Inc.
601 Riverside Ave.
Jacksonville, FL 32204

A" Unsurpassed
Financial Stability Rating®
Demotech, Inc.

Chicago Title Insurance Company of Oregon

CHICAGO TIC (OR)

601 Riverside Ave.
Jacksonville, FL 32204
(904) 854-8100
www.fnf.com

NAIC Number:	50490	Date of Incorporation:	5/1/1970
Group Number:	670	NAIC Group:	CHICAGO / FIDELITY
State of Domicile:			Oregon

2007 Auditor: KPMG LLP
One Independent Dr., Ste. 2700
Independent Square
Jacksonville, FL 32202

2007 Actuary: Timothy L. Shilling, FCAS, MAAA
Fidelity National Title Group Inc.
601 Riverside Ave.
Jacksonville, FL 32204

A' Unsurpassed
Financial Stability Rating®
Demotech, Inc.

Columbian National Title Insurance Company

COLUMBIAN NATIONAL

2921 SW Wanamaker Dr., Ste. 100
Topeka, KS 66614
(785) 232-4365
www.columbiantitle.com

NAIC Number:	51373	Date of Incorporation:	6/9/1978
Group Number:	70	NAIC Group:	FIRST AMERICAN
State of Domicile:			Kansas

2007 Auditor: Mayer Hoffman McCann, PC
11440 Tomahawk Creek Pkwy.
Leawood, KS 66211

2007 Actuary:

A' Unsurpassed
Financial Stability Rating®
Demotech, Inc.

Commerce Title Insurance Company

COMMERCE

2828 N Harwood, 11th Fl.
Dallas, TX 75201
(214) 758-7204
www.commercetitleinsco.com

Formerly Benefit Land Title Insurance Company

NAIC Number:	50026	Date of Incorporation:	8/19/1993
Group Number:		NAIC Group:	UNAFFILIATED COMPANIES
State of Domicile:			California

2007 Auditor: White Nelson & Co.
2400 E Katella Ave., Ste. 900
Anaheim, CA 92806

2007 Actuary: Michael L. DeMattei
Milliman Inc.
70 S Lake Ave., 11th Fl.
Pasadena, CA 91101

A Exceptional
Financial Stability Rating®
Demotech, Inc.

Commonwealth Land Title Insurance Company

COMMONWEALTH LAND

5600 Cox Rd.
Glen Allen, VA 23060
(804) 267-8000
www.landam.com

Formerly Commonwealth Land Title Insurance Company Of Philadelphia (1929)

NAIC Number:	50083	Date of Incorporation:	3/31/1944
Group Number:	99	NAIC Group:	LAND AMERICA
State of Domicile:			Nebraska

2007 Auditor: Ernst & Young, LLP
901 E Cary St.
Richmond, VA 23219

2007 Actuary: Joel A. Vaag, FCAS, MAAA
Milliman Inc.
3 Garret Mountain Plz., 1st Fl.
West Patterson, NJ 07424

A" Unsurpassed
Financial Stability Rating®
Demotech, Inc.

Commonwealth Land Title Insurance Company of New Jersey

COMMONWEALTH LAND (NJ)

5600 Cox Rd.
Glen Allen, VA 23060
(804) 267-8000
www.landam.com

Formerly Continental Title Insurance Company

NAIC Number:	51195	Date of Incorporation:	3/6/1888
Group Number:	99	NAIC Group:	LAND AMERICA
State of Domicile:			New Jersey

2007 Auditor: Ernst & Young, LLP
901 E Cary St.
Richmond, VA 23219

2007 Actuary: Joel A. Vaag, FCAS, MAAA
Milliman Inc.
3 Garret Mountain Plz., 1st Fl.
West Patterson, NJ 07424

A" Unsurpassed
Financial Stability Rating®
Demotech, Inc.

Conestoga Title Insurance Co.

CONESTOGA

123 E King St.
Lancaster, PA 17602
(717) 299-4805
www.contitle.com

NAIC Number:	51209	Date of Incorporation:	10/11/1973
Group Number:		NAIC Group:	UNAFFILIATED COMPANIES
State of Domicile:			Pennsylvania

2007 Auditor: Buffamante Whipple Buttafaro, PC
100 E Fifth St.
Jamestown, NY 14702

2007 Actuary: Joseph L. Petrelli, MAAA, FCA, ACAS
2715 Tuller Pkwy.
Dublin, OH 43017

A' Unsurpassed
Financial Stability Rating®
Demotech, Inc.

Connecticut Attorneys Title Insurance Company

CT ATTORNEYS

101 Corporate Pl.
Rocky Hill, CT 06067
(860) 257-0606
www.caticaccess.com

NAIC Number:	51268	Date of Incorporation:	6/26/2001
Group Number:	4255	NAIC Group:	CATIC
State of Domicile:			Connecticut

2007 Auditor: Blum Shapiro & Co., PC
29 S Main St.
West Hartford, CT 06107

2007 Actuary: Peter G. Wick, FCAS, MAAA
Milliman Inc.
15800 Bluemound Rd., Ste. 400
Brookfield, WI 53005

A' Unsurpassed
Financial Stability Rating®
Demotech, Inc.

Important: Financial Stability Ratings® must be verified by visiting **www.demotech.com**

Underwriter Corporate Information and Financial Stability Ratings® (FSRs)

Dakota Homestead Title Insurance Company

DAKOTA HOMESTEAD

315 S Phillips Ave.
Sioux Falls, SD 57104
(605) 336-0388
www.dakotahomestead.com

NAIC Number:	50020	**Date of Incorporation:** 3/1/1993
Group Number:		**NAIC Group:** UNAFFILIATED COMPANIES
State of Domicile:		South Dakota

2007 Auditor: KMWF & Associates
301 E 4th St., Ste. 2
Dell Rapids, SD 57022

2007 Actuary: John Pierce, FCAS
John Pierce Consulting
1420 Renaissance Dr., Ste. 104
Park Ridge, IL 60068

A Exceptional
Financial Stability Rating®
Demotech, Inc.

Dreibelbiss Title Company, Inc.

DREIBELBISS

127 W Wayne St.
Fort Wayne, IN 46802-2503
(260) 422-8500
www.titlesbycd.com

NAIC Number:	51381	**Date of Incorporation:** 8/1/1916
Group Number:		**NAIC Group:** UNAFFILIATED COMPANIES
State of Domicile:		Indiana

2007 Auditor: BKD, LLP
200 E Main St., Ste. 700
Fort Wayne, IN 46802

2007 Actuary: John Pierce, FCAS
John Pierce Consulting
1420 Renaissance Dr., Ste. 104
Park Ridge, IL 60068

A Exceptional
Financial Stability Rating®
Demotech, Inc.

Equity National Title Insurance Company

EQUITY NATIONAL

401 Wampanoag Trl., Ste. 300
East Providence, RI 02228
(401) 434-5500
www.equitynational.com

NAIC Number:	12234	**Date of Incorporation:** 12/16/2004
Group Number:		**NAIC Group:** UNAFFILIATED COMPANIES
State of Domicile:		Massachusetts

2007 Auditor: BDO Seidman, LLP
330 Madison Ave.
New York, NY 01880

2007 Actuary: Milliman Inc.
289 Edgewater Dr.
Wakefield, MA

S Substantial
Financial Stability Rating®
Demotech, Inc.

Farmers National Title Insurance Company

FARMERS NATIONAL

1207 W Broadway, Ste. C
Columbia, MO 65203
(573) 442-3351
www.farmerstitle.com

NAIC Number:	12522	**Date of Incorporation:** 10/26/2005
Group Number:		**NAIC Group:** UNAFFILIATED COMPANIES
State of Domicile:		Missouri

2007 Auditor: Williams Keepers, LLC
3220 W Edgewood, Ste. E
Jefferson City, MO 65109

2007 Actuary: Osborn Carreiro & Assoc., Inc.
124 W Capital Ave., Ste. 1690
1 Union National Plaza
Little Rock, AR 72201

A Exceptional
Financial Stability Rating®
Demotech, Inc.

Fidelity National Title Insurance Company

FIDELITY NATIONAL

601 Riverside Ave.
Jacksonville, FL 32204
(904) 854-8100
www.fnf.com

NAIC Number:	51586	**Date of Incorporation:** 10/6/1981
Group Number:	670	**NAIC Group:** CHICAGO / FIDELITY
State of Domicile:		California

2007 Auditor: KPMG LLP
One Independent Dr., Ste. 2700
Independent Square
Jacksonville, FL 32202

2007 Actuary: Timothy L. Shilling, FCAS, MAAA
Fidelity National Title Group Inc.
601 Riverside Ave.
Jacksonville, FL 32204

A' Unsurpassed
Financial Stability Rating®
Demotech, Inc.

First American Title & Trust Company

FIRST AMERICAN T&T

133 NW 8th St.
Oklahoma City, OK 73102
(405) 236-2861
www.firstam.com

Formerly Southwest Title & Trust

NAIC Number:	50037	**Date of Incorporation:** 9/1/1960
Group Number:	70	**NAIC Group:** FIRST AMERICAN
State of Domicile:		Oklahoma

2007 Auditor: Hogan & Slovacek, PC

2007 Actuary: Milliman Inc.
1001 Franklin Ave., Ste. 200
Garden City, NY 11530

A' Unsurpassed
Financial Stability Rating®
Demotech, Inc.

First American Title Insurance Company

FIRST AMERICAN TIC

1 First American Way
Santa Ana, CA 92707
(714) 800-3000
www.firstam.com

NAIC Number:	50814	**Date of Incorporation:** 9/24/1968
Group Number:	70	**NAIC Group:** FIRST AMERICAN
State of Domicile:		California

2007 Auditor: PriceWaterhouseCoopers, LLP
350 S Grand Ave., 49th Fl.
Los Angeles, CA 90071

2007 Actuary: Milliman Inc.
One Pennsylvania Plz., 38th Fl.
New York, NY 10119

A" Unsurpassed
Financial Stability Rating®
Demotech, Inc.

First American Title Insurance Company of Kansas, Inc.

FIRST AMERICAN (KS)

1653 Larkin Williams Rd.
Fenton, MO 63026
(314) 821-5515
www.firstam.com

NAIC Number:	50043	**Date of Incorporation:** 5/22/1998
Group Number:	70	**NAIC Group:** FIRST AMERICAN
State of Domicile:		Kansas

2007 Auditor: PriceWaterhouseCoopers, LLP
350 S Grand Ave., 49th Fl.
Los Angeles, CA 90071

2007 Actuary: Milliman Inc.
1001 Franklin Ave., Ste. 200
Garden City, NY 11530

A Exceptional
Financial Stability Rating®
Demotech, Inc.

Important: Financial Stability Ratings® must be verified by visiting **www.demotech.com**

Underwriter Corporate Information and Financial Stability Ratings® (FSRs)

1

First American Title Insurance Company of Louisiana — FIRST AMERICAN (LA)

510 Bienville St.
New Orleans, LA 70130
(504) 588-9252
www.firstam.com

Formerly Greater Louisiana Title
Insurance Company

NAIC Number:	50199
Group Number:	70
State of Domicile:	Louisiana

Date of Incorporation:	9/21/1984
NAIC Group:	FIRST AMERICAN

2007 Auditor: Stephen K. Bellaire, CPA
510 Bienville St.
New Orleans, LA 70130

2007 Actuary: Paul J. Struzzieri, FCAS, MAAA
Milliman Inc.
1001 Franklin Ave., Ste. 200
Garden City, NY 11530

NR — Not Rated — Financial Stability Rating® — Demotech, Inc.

First American Title Insurance Company of New York — FIRST AMERICAN (NY)

633 Third Ave.
New York, NY 10017
(212) 922-9700
www.firstamny.com

NAIC Number:	51039
Group Number:	70
State of Domicile:	New York

Date of Incorporation:	9/14/1967
NAIC Group:	FIRST AMERICAN

2007 Auditor: BDO Seidman, LLP
330 Madison Ave.
New York, NY 10017-5001

2007 Actuary: Milliman Inc.
One Pennsylvania Plz., 38th Fl.
New York, NY 10019

A" — Unsurpassed — Financial Stability Rating® — Demotech, Inc.

First American Title Insurance Company of Oregon — FIRST AMERICAN (OR)

222 SW Columbia St., 4th Fl.
Portland, OR 97201
(503) 222-3651
www.firstam.com

Also Known As Title Insurance
Company Of Oregon

NAIC Number:	50504
Group Number:	70
State of Domicile:	Oregon

Date of Incorporation:	10/16/1937
NAIC Group:	FIRST AMERICAN

2007 Auditor: PriceWaterhouseCoopers, LLP
1300 SW Fifth Ave., Ste. 3100
Portland, OR 97201

2007 Actuary: Paul J. Struzzieri, FCAS, MAAA
Milliman Inc.
1001 Franklin Ave., Ste. 200
Garden City, NY 11530

A' — Unsurpassed — Financial Stability Rating® — Demotech, Inc.

First American Transportation Title Insurance Company — FIRST AMERICAN TRANS

510 Bienville St.
New Orleans, LA 70130
(504) 588-9252
www.firstam.com

Formerly Louisiana First Title
Insurance Company

NAIC Number:	51527
Group Number:	70
State of Domicile:	Louisiana

Date of Incorporation:	8/13/1980
NAIC Group:	FIRST AMERICAN

2007 Auditor: Stephen K. Bellaire, CPA
510 Bienville St.
New Orleans, LA 70130

2007 Actuary: Paul J. Struzzieri, FCAS, MAAA
Milliman Inc.
1001 Franklin Ave., Ste. 200
Garden City, NY 11530

A — Exceptional — Financial Stability Rating® — Demotech, Inc.

Founders Title Insurance — FOUNDERS

1814 Warren Ave.
Cheyenne, WY 82001
(307) 632-4414

NAIC Number:	11974
Group Number:	
State of Domicile:	Wyoming

Date of Incorporation:	12/31/2003
NAIC Group:	UNAFFILIATED COMPANIES

2007 Auditor:

2007 Actuary:

S — Substantial — Financial Stability Rating® — Demotech, Inc.

General Title & Trust Company — GENERAL T&T

24262 Broadway Ave.
Cleveland, OH 44146
(440) 232-5511
www.generaltitleandtrust.com

NAIC Number:	50172
Group Number:	
State of Domicile:	Ohio

Date of Incorporation:	3/25/1925
NAIC Group:	UNAFFILIATED COMPANIES

2007 Auditor: Hobe & Lucas CPAs, Inc.
4807 Rockside Rd.
Cleveland, OH 44131

2007 Actuary: Joseph L. Petrelli, MAAA, FCA, ACAS
2715 Tuller Pkwy.
Dublin, OH 43017

A — Exceptional — Financial Stability Rating® — Demotech, Inc.

Guarantee Title and Trust Company — GUARANTEE T&T

8230 Montgomery Rd., Ste. 200
Cincinnati, OH 45236
(513) 794-4020
www.gtitle.com

NAIC Number:	50180
Group Number:	3590
State of Domicile:	Ohio

Date of Incorporation:	4/29/1899
NAIC Group:	RELIANT HOLDING

2007 Auditor: Mayer Hoffman McCann, PC
11440 Tomahawk Creek Pkwy.
Leawood, KS 66211

2007 Actuary: Joseph L. Petrelli, MAAA, FCA, ACAS
2715 Tuller Pkwy.
Dublin, OH 43017

NR — Not Rated — Financial Stability Rating® — Demotech, Inc.

Guarantee Title Insurance Company — GUARANTEE

2 City Place Dr., Ste. 70
St. Louis, MO 63141
(314) 995-3940
www.gtitle.com

Formerly The Bar Plan Title Insurance
Company

NAIC Number:	50034
Group Number:	3590
State of Domicile:	Missouri

Date of Incorporation:	3/21/1995
NAIC Group:	RELIANT HOLDING

2007 Auditor: Mayer Hoffman McCann, PC
11440 Tomahawk Creek Pkwy.
Leawood, KS 66211

2007 Actuary: Joseph L. Petrelli, MAAA, FCA, ACAS
2715 Tuller Pkwy.
Dublin, OH 43017

NR — Not Rated — Financial Stability Rating® — Demotech, Inc.

Important: Financial Stability Ratings® must be verified by visiting **www.demotech.com**

Underwriter Corporate Information and Financial Stability Ratings® (FSRs)

1

Guardian National Title Insurance Company

4600 Rockside Rd., Ste. 104
Independence, OH 44131
(800) 362-2305
www.gtinsurance.com

NAIC Number:	51632	Date of Incorporation:	4/7/1978	2007 Auditor: Cohen & Co. 1350 Euclid Ave., Ste. 800 Cleveland, OH 44115
Group Number:		NAIC Group:	UNAFFILIATED COMPANIES	2007 Actuary: John Pierce Consulting 1420 Renaissance Dr., Ste. 104 Park Ridge, IL 60608
State of Domicile:			Ohio	

GUARDIAN NATIONAL

A' Unsurpassed
Financial Stability Rating®
Demotech, Inc.

Investors Title Insurance Company

121 N Columbia St.
Chapel Hill, NC 27514
(919) 968-2200
www.invtitle.com

NAIC Number:	50369	Date of Incorporation:	1/28/1972	2007 Auditor: Dixon Hughes, PLLC 1829 Eastchester Dr. High Point, NC 27265
Group Number:	627	NAIC Group:	INVESTORS	2007 Actuary: Joel A. Vaag, FCAS, MAAA Milliman Inc. 3 Garret Mountain Plz., 1st Fl. West Patterson, NJ 07424
State of Domicile:			North Carolina	

INVESTORS TIC

A" Unsurpassed
Financial Stability Rating®
Demotech, Inc.

K.E.L. Title Insurance Group

151 Wymore Rd., Ste. 2100
Altamonte Springs, FL 32714
(407) 513-1900
www.keltitle.com

NAIC Number:	12953	Date of Incorporation:	4/24/2007	2007 Auditor:
Group Number:		NAIC Group:	UNAFFILIATED COMPANIES	2007 Actuary: Casualty Actuarial Consultants, Inc. 7101 Executive Center Dr., #225 Brentwood, TN 37027
State of Domicile:			Florida	

K.E.L.

S Substantial
Financial Stability Rating®
Demotech, Inc.

Land Title Insurance Company (St. Louis)

1653 Larkin Williams Rd., Ste. 100
Fenton, MO 63026
(314) 821-5515
www.firstam.com

NAIC Number:	50237	Date of Incorporation:	12/31/1901	2007 Auditor: PriceWaterhouseCoopers, LLP 350 S Grand Ave., 49th Fl. Los Angeles, CA 90071
Group Number:	70	NAIC Group:	FIRST AMERICAN	2007 Actuary: Milliman Inc. One Pennsylvania Plz., 38th Fl. New York, NY 10119
State of Domicile:			Missouri	

LAND TIC (ST LOUIS)

A' Unsurpassed
Financial Stability Rating®
Demotech, Inc.

Land Title Insurance Corporation

3033 E First Ave., Ste. 708
Denver, CO 80206
(303) 331-6296

NAIC Number:	50002	Date of Incorporation:	6/30/1994	2007 Auditor: Ehrhardt Keefe Steiner & Hottman, PC 7979 E Tufts Ave., Ste. 400 Denver, CO 80237
Group Number:		NAIC Group:	UNAFFILIATED COMPANIES	2007 Actuary: Jan Lommele, FCAS, MCAA, FCA Deloitte Consulting, LLP 185 Asylum St., 33rd Fl. Cityplace I Hartford, CT 06103-3402
State of Domicile:			Colorado	

LAND CORP (CO)

A' Unsurpassed
Financial Stability Rating®
Demotech, Inc.

Lawyers Title Insurance Corporation

5600 Cox Rd.
Glen Allen, VA 23060
(804) 267-8000
www.landam.com

Merged with Land Title Insurance Company (NAIC # 50822)

NAIC Number:	50024	Date of Incorporation:	4/9/1925	2007 Auditor: Ernst & Young, LLP 901 E Cary St. Richmond, VA 23219
Group Number:	99	NAIC Group:	LAND AMERICA	2007 Actuary: Joel A. Vaag, FCAS, MAAA Milliman Inc. 3 Garret Mountain Plz., 1st Fl. West Patterson, NJ 07424
State of Domicile:			Nebraska	

LAWYERS

A' Unsurpassed
Financial Stability Rating®
Demotech, Inc.

Manito Title Insurance Company

100 W Market St.
West Chester, PA 19382
(610) 436-4767
www.manitotitle.com

NAIC Number:	51446	Date of Incorporation:	11/12/1979	2007 Auditor:
Group Number:		NAIC Group:	UNAFFILIATED COMPANIES	2007 Actuary:
State of Domicile:			Pennsylvania	

MANITO

A Exceptional
Financial Stability Rating®
Demotech, Inc.

Mason County Title Insurance Company

130 W Railroad
Shelton, WA 98584
(360) 701-6090
www.masoncountytitle.com

NAIC Number:	50962	Date of Incorporation:	9/7/1909	2007 Auditor:
Group Number:		NAIC Group:	UNAFFILIATED COMPANIES	2007 Actuary:
State of Domicile:			Washington	

MASON COUNTY

A Exceptional
Financial Stability Rating®
Demotech, Inc.

Important: Financial Stability Ratings® must be verified by visiting **www.demotech.com**

Underwriter Corporate Information and Financial Stability Ratings® (FSRs)

Mason Title Insurance Company · MASON

27544 Cashford Cir., Ste. 101
Wesley Chapel, FL 33544
(813) 286-2604
www.masontitle.com

NAIC Number:	12550
Group Number:	
State of Domicile:	Florida
Date of Incorporation:	2/21/2006
NAIC Group:	UNAFFILIATED COMPANIES

2007 Auditor: Hevia Beagles & Co., CPA, 9400 Fourth St. N, Ste. 120, St. Petersburg, FL 33702

2007 Actuary: Joseph L. Petrelli, MAAA, FCA, ACAS, 2715 Tuller Pkwy., Dublin, OH 43017

A Exceptional — Financial Stability Rating® — Demotech, Inc.

Massachusetts Title Insurance Company · MASSACHUSETTS TIC

101 Huntington Ave.
Boston, MA 02199
(617) 345-0088
www.firstamne.com

NAIC Number:	50989
Group Number:	70
State of Domicile:	Massachusetts
Date of Incorporation:	1/1/1885
NAIC Group:	FIRST AMERICAN

2007 Auditor:

2007 Actuary:

A Exceptional — Financial Stability Rating® — Demotech, Inc.

Mississippi Guaranty Title Insurance Company · MISSISSIPPI GUARANTY

1755 Lelia Dr., Ste. 102
Jackson, MS 39216
(601) 362-2010

NAIC Number:	50030
Group Number:	
State of Domicile:	Mississippi
Date of Incorporation:	7/2/1996
NAIC Group:	UNAFFILIATED COMPANIES

2007 Auditor:

2007 Actuary:

S Substantial — Financial Stability Rating® — Demotech, Inc.

Mississippi Valley Title Insurance Company · MISSISSIPPI VALLEY

315 Tombigbee St.
Jackson, MS 39201
(601) 969-0222
www.mvt.com

NAIC Number:	51004
Group Number:	150
State of Domicile:	Mississippi
Date of Incorporation:	5/30/1941
NAIC Group:	OLD REPUBLIC

2007 Auditor: PriceWaterhouseCoopers, LLP, 225 S 6th St., Minneapolis, MN 55402

2007 Actuary: J. Paul Cochran, Old Republic General Services Inc., 307 N Michigan Ave., Chicago, IL 60601

A" Unsurpassed — Financial Stability Rating® — Demotech, Inc.

Monroe Title Insurance Corporation · MONROE

47 W Main St.
Rochester, NY 14614-1499
(585) 232-2070
www.monroetitle.com

NAIC Number:	51063
Group Number:	340
State of Domicile:	New York
Date of Incorporation:	10/1/1922
NAIC Group:	STEWART

2007 Auditor: Bonadio & Co., LLP, 171 Sully's Trl., Pittsford, NY 14534-4557

2007 Actuary: Paul J. Struzzieri, FCAS, MAAA, Milliman Inc., 1001 Franklin Ave., Ste. 200, Garden City, NY 11530

A' Unsurpassed — Financial Stability Rating® — Demotech, Inc.

Mortgage Guarantee & Title Company · MORTGAGE GUARANTEE

450 Veterans Memorial Pkwy.
#700
East Providence, RI 02914
(401) 434-1000
www.firstamne.com

NAIC Number:	
Group Number:	70
State of Domicile:	Rhode Island
Date of Incorporation:	1/1/1921
NAIC Group:	FIRST AMERICAN

2007 Auditor:

2007 Actuary:

A Exceptional — Financial Stability Rating® — Demotech, Inc.

National Attorneys' Title Assurance Fund, Inc. · NATIONAL ATTORNEYS

306 W Pike St.
Vevay, IN 47043
(812) 427-9062
www.nataf.net

NAIC Number:	50938
Group Number:	750
State of Domicile:	Indiana
Date of Incorporation:	5/2/1958
NAIC Group:	ATTORNEYS' TITLE

2007 Auditor: Watermark CPA Group, LLC, 9265 Counselor's Row, Ste. 100, Indianapolis, IN 46240

2007 Actuary:

A Exceptional — Financial Stability Rating® — Demotech, Inc.

National Land Title Insurance Company · NATIONAL LAND

2800 W Higgins Road, Ste. 835
Hoffman Estates, IL 60169
(800) 533-6584
www.nltic.com

NAIC Number:	50156
Group Number:	340
State of Domicile:	Illinois
Date of Incorporation:	11/28/1970
NAIC Group:	STEWART

2007 Auditor: Blackman Kallick Bartelstein, LLP, 10 S Riverside Plz., 9th Fl., Chicago, IL 60606

2007 Actuary: Steve Osborn, Osborn Carriero & Assoc., Inc., 124 W Capital Ave., Ste. 1690, 1 Union National Plaza, Little Rock, AR 72201

A" Unsurpassed — Financial Stability Rating® — Demotech, Inc.

Important: Financial Stability Ratings® must be verified by visiting **www.demotech.com**

Underwriter Corporate Information and Financial Stability Ratings® (FSRs)

National Title Insurance Company

NATIONAL

151 SW 27th Ave.
Miami, FL 33135
(305) 642-6220
www.nationaltitleinsurance.com

NAIC Number:	50695
Group Number:	
State of Domicile:	Florida

Date of Incorporation:	7/31/1936
NAIC Group:	UNAFFILIATED COMPANIES

2007 Auditor: R & L Group CPA
16400 Loch Ness Ln.
Miami Lakes, FL 33014

2007 Actuary: John Pierce, FCAS
John Pierce Consulting
1420 Renaissance Dr., Ste. 104
Park Ridge, IL 60068

A Exceptional
Financial Stability Rating®
Demotech, Inc.

National Title Insurance of New York, Inc.

NATIONAL OF NY

601 Riverside Ave.
Jacksonville, FL 32204
(904) 854-8100
www.nationaltitleins.com

NAIC Number:	51020
Group Number:	
State of Domicile:	New York

Date of Incorporation:	3/14/1929
NAIC Group:	UNAFFILIATED COMPANIES

2007 Auditor: KPMG LLP
One Independent Dr., Ste. 2700
Independent Square
Jacksonville, FL 32202

2007 Actuary: Milliman Inc.
1325 Franklin Ave., Ste. 555
Garden City, NY 11530

A Exceptional
Financial Stability Rating®
Demotech, Inc.

Nations Title Insurance of New York, Inc.

NATIONS OF NY

601 Riverside Ave.
Jacksonville, FL 32204
(904) 854-8100
www.fnf.com

NAIC Number:	51101
Group Number:	670
State of Domicile:	New York

Date of Incorporation:	11/15/1927
NAIC Group:	CHICAGO / FIDELITY

2007 Auditor: KPMG LLP
One Independent Dr., Ste. 2700
Independent Square
Jacksonville, FL 32202

2007 Actuary: Timothy L. Shilling, FCAS, MAAA
Fidelity National Title Group Inc.
601 Riverside Ave.
Jacksonville, FL 32204

A Exceptional
Financial Stability Rating®
Demotech, Inc.

New Jersey Title Insurance Company

NEW JERSEY TIC

400 Lanidex Plz.
Parsippany, NJ 07054
(973) 952-0110
www.njtic.com

NAIC Number:	51187
Group Number:	4255
State of Domicile:	New Jersey

Date of Incorporation:	6/9/1937
NAIC Group:	CATIC

2007 Auditor: Blum Shapiro & Co., PC
29 S Main St.
West Hartford, CT 06107

2007 Actuary: Peter G. Wick, FCAS, MAAA
15800 W Bluemound Rd., Ste. 304
Brookfield, WI

A' Unsurpassed
Financial Stability Rating®
Demotech, Inc.

North American Title Insurance Company

NORTH AMERICAN

1855 Gateway Blvd., Ste. 600
Concord, CA 94520
(925) 935-5599
www.nat.com

Merged with North American Title Insurance Corporation (NAIC # 50000)

NAIC Number:	50130
Group Number:	
State of Domicile:	California

Date of Incorporation:	9/18/1958
NAIC Group:	UNAFFILIATED COMPANIES

2007 Auditor: Deloitte & Touche LLP
50 Fremont St.
San Francisco, CA 94109

2007 Actuary: Deloitte Consulting, LLP
350 Grand Ave., Ste. 2000
Los Angeles, CA 90071

A' Unsurpassed
Financial Stability Rating®
Demotech, Inc.

Northeast Investors Title Insurance Company

NORTHEAST INVESTORS

121 N Columbia St.
Chapel Hill, NC 27514
(919) 968-2200
www.invtitle.com

NAIC Number:	50377
Group Number:	627
State of Domicile:	South Carolina

Date of Incorporation:	2/23/1973
NAIC Group:	INVESTORS

2007 Auditor: Dixon Hughes, PLLC
1829 Eastchester Dr.
High Point, NC 27265

2007 Actuary: Joel A. Vaag, FCAS, MAAA
Milliman Inc.
3 Garret Mountain Plz., 1st Fl.
West Patterson, NJ 07424

A" Unsurpassed
Financial Stability Rating®
Demotech, Inc.

Ohio Bar Title Insurance Company

OHIO BAR

341 S Third St., Ste. 100
Columbus, OH 43215
(800) 628-4853
www.ohiobartitle.com

NAIC Number:	51330
Group Number:	70
State of Domicile:	Ohio

Date of Incorporation:	7/27/1953
NAIC Group:	FIRST AMERICAN

2007 Auditor: Battelle & Battelle, LLP
2000 W Dorothy Ln.
Dayton, OH 45439

2007 Actuary: Joel A. Vaag, FCAS, MAAA
Milliman Inc.
3 Garret Mountain Plz., 1st Fl.
West Patterson, NJ 07424

A Exceptional
Financial Stability Rating®
Demotech, Inc.

Old Republic General Title Insurance Corporation

OLD REPUBLIC GENERAL

400 Second Ave. S
Minneapolis, MN 55401-2499
(612) 371-1111
www.oldrepublictitle.com

NAIC Number:	50005
Group Number:	150
State of Domicile:	Ohio

Date of Incorporation:	8/3/1994
NAIC Group:	OLD REPUBLIC

2007 Auditor: PriceWaterhouseCoopers, LLP
225 S 6th St.
Minneapolis, MN 55402

2007 Actuary: J. Paul Cochran
Old Republic General Services Inc.
307 N Michigan Ave.
Chicago, IL 60601

A" Unsurpassed
Financial Stability Rating®
Demotech, Inc.

Important: Financial Stability Ratings® must be verified by visiting **www.demotech.com**

Underwriter Corporate Information and Financial Stability Ratings® (FSRs)

1

Old Republic National Title Insurance Company — OLD REPUBLIC NATIONAL

400 Second Ave. S
Minneapolis, MN 55401-2499
(612) 371-1111
www.oldrepublictitle.com

NAIC Number:	50520
Group Number:	150
Date of Incorporation:	8/20/1907
NAIC Group:	OLD REPUBLIC
State of Domicile:	Minnesota

2007 Auditor: PriceWaterhouseCoopers, LLP
225 S 6th St.
Minneapolis, MN 55402

2007 Actuary: J. Paul Cochran
Old Republic General Services Inc.
307 N Michigan Ave.
Chicago, IL 60601

A" Unsurpassed
Financial Stability Rating®
Demotech, Inc.

Olympic Title Insurance Company — OLYMPIC

555 S Front St., Ste. 400
Columbus, OH 43215
(614) 583-2414

Currently not writing business

NAIC Number:	50440
Group Number:	
Date of Incorporation:	11/29/1984
NAIC Group:	UNAFFILIATED COMPANIES
State of Domicile:	Ohio

2007 Auditor:

2007 Actuary:

NR Not Rated
Financial Stability Rating®
Demotech, Inc.

Pacific Northwest Title Insurance Company, Inc. — PACIFIC NORTHWEST

215 Columbia St.
Seattle, WA 98104-1511
(206) 622-1040
www.pnwt.com

NAIC Number:	50970
Group Number:	70
Date of Incorporation:	12/1/1926
NAIC Group:	FIRST AMERICAN
State of Domicile:	Washington

2007 Auditor: PriceWaterhouseCoopers, LLP
Seattle, WA

2007 Actuary: Paul J. Struzzieri, FCAS, MAAA
Milliman Inc.
1001 Franklin Ave., Ste. 200
Garden City, NY 11530

A" Unsurpassed
Financial Stability Rating®
Demotech, Inc.

Penn Attorneys Title Insurance Company — PENN ATTORNEYS

900 State St., Ste. 320
Erie, PA 16501
(814) 454-8278
www.pennattorneys.com

NAIC Number:	51497
Group Number:	70
Date of Incorporation:	12/1/1980
NAIC Group:	FIRST AMERICAN
State of Domicile:	Pennsylvania

2007 Auditor: Malin Bergquist & Co., LLP
2253 W Grandview Blvd.
Erie, PA 16506

2007 Actuary: Paul J. Struzzieri, FCAS, MAAA
Milliman Inc.
1001 Franklin Ave., Ste. 200
Garden City, NY 11530

A' Unsurpassed
Financial Stability Rating®
Demotech, Inc.

Pilgrim Title Insurance Company — PILGRIM

50 Park Row W, Ste. 102
Providence, RI 02903
(401) 274-9100
www.pilgrimtitle.com

NAIC Number:	
Group Number:	
Date of Incorporation:	3/11/1968
NAIC Group:	UNAFFILIATED COMPANIES
State of Domicile:	Rhode Island

2007 Auditor:

2007 Actuary:

A Exceptional
Financial Stability Rating®
Demotech, Inc.

Port Lawrence Title & Trust Company — PORT LAWRENCE

616 Madison Ave.
Toledo, OH 43604
(419) 244-4605
www.portlawrence.com

NAIC Number:	50202
Group Number:	70
Date of Incorporation:	8/7/1937
NAIC Group:	FIRST AMERICAN
State of Domicile:	Ohio

2007 Auditor: Battelle & Battelle, LLP
2000 W Dorothy Ln.
Dayton, OH 45439

2007 Actuary: Joel A. Vaag, FCAS, MAAA
Milliman Inc.
3 Garret Mountain Plz., 1st Fl.
West Patterson, NJ 07424

A Exceptional
Financial Stability Rating®
Demotech, Inc.

Public Title Insurance Company — PUBLIC

16 W Main St.
Rochester, NY 14614
(585) 987-4950
www.firstam.com

NAIC Number:	12518
Group Number:	70
Date of Incorporation:	4/15/2005
NAIC Group:	FIRST AMERICAN
State of Domicile:	New York

2007 Auditor:

2007 Actuary:

A Exceptional
Financial Stability Rating®
Demotech, Inc.

Seagate Title & Abstract Company, Inc. — SEAGATE

626 Madison Ave.
Toledo, OH 43604
(419) 248-4611

NAIC Number:	50270
Group Number:	
Date of Incorporation:	6/29/1984
NAIC Group:	UNAFFILIATED COMPANIES
State of Domicile:	Ohio

2007 Auditor:

2007 Actuary:

S Substantial
Financial Stability Rating®
Demotech, Inc.

Important: Financial Stability Ratings® must be verified by visiting **www.demotech.com**

Underwriter Corporate Information and Financial Stability Ratings® (FSRs)

Security Title Guarantee Corporation of Baltimore (The)

SECURITY TG (BALTIMORE)

6 S Calvert St.
Baltimore, MD 21202-1388
(410) 727-4456
www.esecuritytitle.com

NAIC Number:	50784
Group Number:	
State of Domicile:	Maryland

Date of Incorporation:	12/15/1952
NAIC Group:	UNAFFILIATED COMPANIES

2007 Auditor: Gorfine Schiller & Gardyn, PA
10045 Red Run Blvd., Ste. 250
Owings Mills, MD 21117

2007 Actuary: Paul J. Struzzieri, FCAS, MAAA
Milliman Inc.
1001 Franklin Ave., Ste. 200
Garden City, NY 11530

A' Unsurpassed
Financial Stability Rating®
Demotech, Inc.

Security Union Title Insurance Company

SECURITY UNION

601 Riverside Ave.
Jacksonville, FL 32204
(904) 854-8100
www.fnf.com

NAIC Number:	50857
Group Number:	670
State of Domicile:	California

Date of Incorporation:	3/5/1962
NAIC Group:	CHICAGO / FIDELITY

2007 Auditor: KPMG LLP
One Independent Dr., Ste. 2700
Independent Square
Jacksonville, FL 32202

2007 Actuary: Timothy L. Shilling, FCAS, MAAA
Fidelity National Title Group Inc.
601 Riverside Ave.
Jacksonville, FL 32204

A' Unsurpassed
Financial Stability Rating®
Demotech, Inc.

Sierra Title Insurance Guaranty Company

SIERRA

3409 N Tenth St.
McAllen, TX 78501
(956) 687-6294
www.sierratitle.com

NAIC Number:	12591
Group Number:	
State of Domicile:	Texas

Date of Incorporation:	6/2/2006
NAIC Group:	UNAFFILIATED COMPANIES

2007 Auditor: Richard Moore & Co.
501 W Nolana
McAllen, TX 78504

2007 Actuary: Charles I. Petit, FCAS, MAAA
Petit Actuarial Group, LLC
5737 Kanan Rd., #346
Agoura Hills, CA 91301

A Exceptional
Financial Stability Rating®
Demotech, Inc.

Southern Title Insurance Corporation

SOUTHERN TI CORP

1051 E Cary St., Ste. 700
Three James Ctr.
Richmond, VA 23219
(804) 648-6000
www.southerntitle.com

NAIC Number:	50792
Group Number:	228
State of Domicile:	Virginia

Date of Incorporation:	9/25/1925
NAIC Group:	OHIO FARMERS

2007 Auditor: KPMG LLP
191 W Nationwide Blvd., Ste. 500
Columbus, OH 43215-2568

2007 Actuary: Frank Tresco, FCAS, MAAA
KPMG LLP
100 Matsonford Rd.
Radnor, PA 19087

A' Unsurpassed
Financial Stability Rating®
Demotech, Inc.

Stewart Title Guaranty Company

STEWART TGC

1980 Post Oak Blvd.
PO Box 2029
Houston, TX 77056
(713) 625-8100
www.stewart.com

NAIC Number:	50121
Group Number:	340
State of Domicile:	Texas

Date of Incorporation:	2/20/1908
NAIC Group:	STEWART

2007 Auditor: KPMG LLP
700 Louisiana St.
Houston, TX 77002

2007 Actuary: Paul J. Struzzieri, FCAS, MAAA
Milliman Inc.
1001 Franklin Ave., Ste. 200
Garden City, NY 11530

A'' Unsurpassed
Financial Stability Rating®
Demotech, Inc.

Stewart Title Insurance Company

STEWART TIC

300 E 42nd St., 10th Fl.
New York, NY 10017
(212) 922-0050
www.stewart.com

NAIC Number:	51420
Group Number:	340
State of Domicile:	New York

Date of Incorporation:	10/26/1987
NAIC Group:	STEWART

2007 Auditor: KPMG LLP
757 Third Ave., 10th Fl.
New York, NY 10017

2007 Actuary: Paul J. Struzzieri, FCAS, MAAA
Milliman Inc.
1001 Franklin Ave., Ste. 200
Garden City, NY 11530

A'' Unsurpassed
Financial Stability Rating®
Demotech, Inc.

Stewart Title Insurance Company of Oregon

STEWART (OR)

1980 Post Oak Blvd.
PO Box 2029
Houston, TX 77056
(713) 625-8100
www.stewart.com

NAIC Number:	50036
Group Number:	340
State of Domicile:	Oregon

Date of Incorporation:	4/3/1997
NAIC Group:	STEWART

2007 Auditor: KPMG LLP
700 Louisiana St.
Houston, TX 77002

2007 Actuary: Paul J. Struzzieri, FCAS, MAAA
Milliman Inc.
1001 Franklin Ave., Ste. 200
Garden City, NY 11530

NR Not Rated
Financial Stability Rating®
Demotech, Inc.

T.A. Title Insurance Company

T.A. TITLE

620 Freedom Business Center Dr.
King of Prussia, PA 19406
(610) 892-8100
www.tatitle.com

NAIC Number:	51403
Group Number:	70
State of Domicile:	Pennsylvania

Date of Incorporation:	5/9/1979
NAIC Group:	FIRST AMERICAN

2007 Auditor: Rainer & Co.
2 Campus Blvd., Ste. 220
Newtown Square, PA 19073-3270

2007 Actuary: Joel A. Vaag, FCAS, MAAA
Milliman Inc.
3 Garret Mountain Plz., 1st Fl.
West Patterson, NJ 07424

A Exceptional
Financial Stability Rating®
Demotech, Inc.

Important: Financial Stability Ratings® must be verified by visiting **www.demotech.com**

Underwriter Corporate Information and Financial Stability Ratings® (FSRs)

1

Ticor Title Insurance Company
TICOR

601 Riverside Ave.
Jacksonville, FL 32204
(904) 854-8100
www.fnf.com

NAIC Number:	50067	Date of Incorporation:	11/18/1965
Group Number:	670	NAIC Group:	CHICAGO / FIDELITY
State of Domicile:		California	

2007 Auditor: KPMG LLP
One Independent Dr., Ste. 2700
Independent Square
Jacksonville, FL 32202

2007 Actuary: Timothy L. Shilling, FCAS, MAAA
Fidelity National Title Group Inc.
601 Riverside Ave.
Jacksonville, FL 32204

A' Unsurpassed
Financial Stability Rating®
Demotech, Inc.

Ticor Title Insurance Company of Florida
TICOR (FL)

601 Riverside Ave.
Jacksonville, FL 32204
(904) 854-8100
www.fnf.com

Formerly American Pioneer Title
Insurance Company

NAIC Number:	51535	Date of Incorporation:	2/4/1980
Group Number:	670	NAIC Group:	CHICAGO / FIDELITY
State of Domicile:		Nebraska	

2007 Auditor: KPMG LLP
One Independent Dr., Ste. 2700
Independent Square
Jacksonville, FL 32202

2007 Actuary: Timothy L. Shilling, FCAS, MAAA
Fidelity National Title Group Inc.
601 Riverside Ave.
Jacksonville, FL 32204

A Exceptional
Financial Stability Rating®
Demotech, Inc.

Title Guaranty and Trust Company of Chattanooga
TITLE G&TC

617 Walnut St.
Chattanooga, TN 37402
(423) 266-5751
www.titleguarantyandtrust.com

NAIC Number:	50261	Date of Incorporation:	12/31/1891
Group Number:		NAIC Group:	UNAFFILIATED COMPANIES
State of Domicile:		Tennessee	

2007 Auditor:

2007 Actuary:

S Substantial
Financial Stability Rating®
Demotech, Inc.

Title Guaranty Division of the Iowa Finance Authority
TITLE GUARANTY DIV (IA)

2015 Grand Ave.
Des Moines, IA 50312
(515) 725-4357
www.iowafinanceauthority.gov

NAIC Number:		Date of Incorporation:	7/1/1985
Group Number:		NAIC Group:	UNAFFILIATED COMPANIES
State of Domicile:		Iowa	

2007 Auditor:

2007 Actuary:

A' Unsurpassed
Financial Stability Rating®
Demotech, Inc.

Title Insurance Company of America
TITLE IC AMERICA

7557 Rambler Rd., Ste. 1200
Dallas, TX 75231
(888) 842-2545
www.landam.com

NAIC Number:	50245	Date of Incorporation:	1/30/1934
Group Number:	99	NAIC Group:	LAND AMERICA
State of Domicile:		Nebraska	

2007 Auditor: Ernst & Young, LLP
901 E Cary St.
Richmond, VA 23219

2007 Actuary: Joel A. Vaag, FCAS, MAAA
Milliman Inc.
3 Garret Mountain Plz., 1st Fl.
West Patterson, NJ 07424

A Exceptional
Financial Stability Rating®
Demotech, Inc.

Title Resources Guaranty Company
TITLE RESOURCES

8111 LBJ Freeway, Ste. 1200
Dallas, TX 75251
(972) 644-6500
www.trgctx.com

NAIC Number:	50016	Date of Incorporation:	3/14/1984
Group Number:		NAIC Group:	UNAFFILIATED COMPANIES
State of Domicile:		Texas	

2007 Auditor: Deloitte & Touche LLP
2200 Ross Ave., #1600
Dallas, TX 75201

2007 Actuary: Charles I. Petit, FCAS, MAAA
Petit Actuarial Group, LLC
5737 Kanan Rd., #346
Agoura Hills, CA 91301

A' Unsurpassed
Financial Stability Rating®
Demotech, Inc.

Titledge Insurance Company of New York
TITLEDGE

654 Sharrotts Rd.
Staten Island, NY 10309
(718) 701-6094
www.titledgeinsurancecompany.com

NAIC Number:	12935	Date of Incorporation:	8/22/2006
Group Number:		NAIC Group:	UNAFFILIATED COMPANIES
State of Domicile:		New York	

2007 Auditor: JH Cohn, LLP
1212 Avenue of the Americas
New York, NY 10036

2007 Actuary:

S Substantial
Financial Stability Rating®
Demotech, Inc.

Transnation Title Insurance Company
TRANSNATION

5600 Cox Rd.
Glen Allen, VA 23060
(804) 267-8000
www.landam.com

Formerly Transamerica Title
Insurance Company

NAIC Number:	50012	Date of Incorporation:	9/15/1992
Group Number:	99	NAIC Group:	LAND AMERICA
State of Domicile:		Nebraska	

2007 Auditor: Ernst & Young, LLP
901 E Cary St.
Richmond, VA 23219

2007 Actuary: Joel A. Vaag, FCAS, MAAA
Milliman Inc.
3 Garret Mountain Plz., 1st Fl.
West Patterson, NJ 07424

A Exceptional
Financial Stability Rating®
Demotech, Inc.

Important: Financial Stability Ratings® must be verified by visiting **www.demotech.com**

Underwriter Corporate Information and Financial Stability Ratings® (FSRs)

TransUnion National Title Insurance Company

TRANSUNION NATIONAL

2711 Middleburg Dr., Ste. 312
Columbia, SC 29204
(803) 799-4747

Formerly Atlantic Title Insurance
Company

NAIC Number:	51152
Group Number:	3889
State of Domicile:	South Carolina

Date of Incorporation:	6/18/1974
NAIC Group:	TRANSUNION

2007 Auditor: Grant Thornton, LLP
201 S College St., Ste. 2500
Charlotte, NC 28244

2007 Actuary: Godbold Malpere & Co.
570 W Crossville Rd., Ste. 204
Roswell, GA 30075

A' Unsurpassed
Financial Stability Rating®
Demotech, Inc.

TransUnion Title Insurance Company

TRANSUNION TIC

16700 Valley View Ave., Ste. 275
La Mirada, CA 90638
(626) 307-3180

Formerly Diversified Title Insurance
Company

NAIC Number:	50849
Group Number:	3889
State of Domicile:	California

Date of Incorporation:	12/22/1925
NAIC Group:	TRANSUNION

2007 Auditor: Grant Thornton, LLP
Charlotte, NC 28244

2007 Actuary: Godbold Malpere & Co.
570 W Crossville Rd., Ste. 204
Roswell, GA 30075

A Exceptional
Financial Stability Rating®
Demotech, Inc.

United Capital Title Insurance Company

UNITED CAPITAL

3250 Wilshire Ave., 18th Fl.
Los Angeles, CA 90010
(213) 385-3600
www.landam.com

NAIC Number:	50041
Group Number:	99
State of Domicile:	California

Date of Incorporation:	3/21/1991
NAIC Group:	LAND AMERICA

2007 Auditor: Ernst & Young, LLP
901 E Cary St.
Richmond, VA 23219

2007 Actuary: Joel A. Vaag, FCAS, MAAA
Milliman Inc.
3 Garret Mountain Plz., 1st Fl.
West Patterson, NJ 07424

A' Unsurpassed
Financial Stability Rating®
Demotech, Inc.

United General Title Insurance Company

UNITED GENERAL

8310 S Valley Hwy, Ste. 130
Engelwood, CO 80112
(303) 292-4848
www.ugtic.com

NAIC Number:	51624
Group Number:	70
State of Domicile:	California

Date of Incorporation:	9/2/1983
NAIC Group:	FIRST AMERICAN

2007 Auditor: PriceWaterhouseCoopers, LLP
2020 Main St., Ste. 400
Irvine, CA 92614

2007 Actuary: N. Terry Godbold ACAS, MAAA, FAC
Godbold Malpere & Co.
570 W Crossville Rd., Ste. 204
Roswell, GA 30075

A' Unsurpassed
Financial Stability Rating®
Demotech, Inc.

Washington Title Insurance Company

WASHINGTON TIC

31 Stewart St.
Floral Park, NY 11001
(516) 488-7100
www.washtitle.com

NAIC Number:	50029
Group Number:	
State of Domicile:	New York

Date of Incorporation:	10/14/1992
NAIC Group:	UNAFFILIATED COMPANIES

2007 Auditor: Hirshfield & Kantor, LLP
534 Broadhollow Rd., Ste. 302
Melville, NY 11747

2007 Actuary: Milliman Inc.
1001 Franklin Ave., Ste. 200
Garden City, NY 11520

S Substantial
Financial Stability Rating®
Demotech, Inc.

Westcor Land Title Insurance Company

WESTCOR

201 N New York Ave., Ste. 200
Winter Park, FL 32789
(407) 629-5842
www.wltic.com

Formerly Nevada Title Insurance
Company

NAIC Number:	50050
Group Number:	
State of Domicile:	California

Date of Incorporation:	1/11/1993
NAIC Group:	UNAFFILIATED COMPANIES

2007 Auditor: Deloitte & Touche LLP
200 S Orange Ave., Ste. 1800
Orlando, FL 32801

2007 Actuary: Milliman Inc.
One Pennsylvania Plz., 38th Fl.
New York, NY 10119

A' Unsurpassed
Financial Stability Rating®
Demotech, Inc.

Western National Title Insurance Company

WESTERN NATIONAL

560 S 300 East
Salt Lake City, UT 84111
(801) 578-8888
www.firstam.com

NAIC Number:	51225
Group Number:	70
State of Domicile:	Utah

Date of Incorporation:	11/5/1987
NAIC Group:	FIRST AMERICAN

2007 Auditor: David Start, PC
1015 Polly St.
Baytown, TX 77520

2007 Actuary: Bruce Ollodart
American Actuarial LLC
15 Cliffside Dr.
Wallinford, CT 06492

A Exceptional
Financial Stability Rating®
Demotech, Inc.

Important: Financial Stability Ratings® must be verified by visiting **www.demotech.com**

1

Notes

UNDERWRITERS AND NAIC GROUPS
INCLUDED IN THE 2008 PUBLICATION

Underwriters and NAIC Groups Included in the 2008 Publication

1

	GROUP NUMBER	GROUP NAME	NAIC NUMBER	COMPANY	COMPANY ABBREVIATION
1.	750	ATTORNEYS' TITLE	1. 51560	ATTORNEYS' TITLE GUARANTY FUND, INC. (CO)	ATTORNEYS TGF (CO)
2.			2. 50687	ATTORNEYS' TITLE INSURANCE FUND, INC. (FL)	ATTORNEYS TIF (FL)
3.			3. 50938	NATIONAL ATTORNEYS' TITLE ASSURANCE FUND, INC.	NATIONAL ATTORNEYS
4.	4255	CATIC	1. 51268	CONNECTICUT ATTORNEYS TITLE INSURANCE COMPANY	CT ATTORNEYS
5.			2. 51187	NEW JERSEY TITLE INSURANCE COMPANY	NEW JERSEY TIC
6.	670	CHICAGO / FIDELITY	1. 50598	ALAMO TITLE INSURANCE	ALAMO
7.			2.	CHICAGO TITLE AND TRUST COMPANY	CHICAGO T&T
8.			3. 50229	CHICAGO TITLE INSURANCE COMPANY	CHICAGO TIC
9.			4. 50490	CHICAGO TITLE INSURANCE COMPANY OF OREGON	CHICAGO TIC (OR)
10.			5. 51586	FIDELITY NATIONAL TITLE INSURANCE COMPANY	FIDELITY NATIONAL
11.			6. 51101	NATIONS TITLE INSURANCE OF NEW YORK, INC.	NATIONS OF NY
12.			7. 50857	SECURITY UNION TITLE INSURANCE COMPANY	SECURITY UNION
13.			8. 50067	TICOR TITLE INSURANCE COMPANY	TICOR
14.			9. 51535	TICOR TITLE INSURANCE COMPANY OF FLORIDA	TICOR (FL)
15.	70	FIRST AMERICAN	1. 50008	BRIDGE TITLE INSURANCE COMPANY	BRIDGE
16.			2. 50636	CENSTAR TITLE INSURANCE COMPANY	CENSTAR
17.			3. 51373	COLUMBIAN NATIONAL TITLE INSURANCE COMPANY	COLUMBIAN NATIONAL
18.			4. 50037	FIRST AMERICAN TITLE & TRUST COMPANY	FIRST AMERICAN T&T
19.			5. 50814	FIRST AMERICAN TITLE INSURANCE COMPANY	FIRST AMERICAN TIC
20.			6. 50043	FIRST AMERICAN TITLE INSURANCE COMPANY OF KANSAS, INC.	FIRST AMERICAN (KS)
21.			7. 50199	FIRST AMERICAN TITLE INSURANCE COMPANY OF LOUISIANA	FIRST AMERICAN (LA)
22.			8. 51039	FIRST AMERICAN TITLE INSURANCE COMPANY OF NEW YORK	FIRST AMERICAN (NY)
23.			9. 50504	FIRST AMERICAN TITLE INSURANCE COMPANY OF OREGON	FIRST AMERICAN (OR)
24.			10. 51527	FIRST AMERICAN TRANSPORTATION TITLE INSURANCE COMPANY	FIRST AMERICAN TRANS
25.			11. 50237	LAND TITLE INSURANCE COMPANY (ST. LOUIS)	LAND TIC (ST LOUIS)
26.			12. 50989	MASSACHUSETTS TITLE INSURANCE COMPANY	MASSACHUSETTS TIC
27.			13.	MORTGAGE GUARANTEE & TITLE COMPANY	MORTGAGE GUARANTEE
28.			14. 51330	OHIO BAR TITLE INSURANCE COMPANY	OHIO BAR
29.			15. 50970	PACIFIC NORTHWEST TITLE INSURANCE COMPANY, INC.	PACIFIC NORTHWEST
30.			16. 51497	PENN ATTORNEYS TITLE INSURANCE COMPANY	PENN ATTORNEYS
31.			17. 50202	PORT LAWRENCE TITLE & TRUST COMPANY	PORT LAWRENCE
32.			18. 12518	PUBLIC TITLE INSURANCE COMPANY	PUBLIC
33.			19. 51403	T.A. TITLE INSURANCE COMPANY	T.A. TITLE
34.			20. 51624	UNITED GENERAL TITLE INSURANCE COMPANY	UNITED GENERAL
35.			21. 51225	WESTERN NATIONAL TITLE INSURANCE COMPANY	WESTERN NATIONAL
36.	627	INVESTORS	1. 50369	INVESTORS TITLE INSURANCE COMPANY	INVESTORS TIC
37.			2. 50377	NORTHEAST INVESTORS TITLE INSURANCE COMPANY	NORTHEAST INVESTORS
38.	99	LAND AMERICA	1. 50083	COMMONWEALTH LAND TITLE INSURANCE COMPANY	COMMONWEALTH LAND
39.			2. 51195	COMMONWEALTH LAND TITLE INSURANCE COMPANY OF NEW JERSEY	COMMONWEALTH LAND (NJ)
40.			3. 50024	LAWYERS TITLE INSURANCE CORPORATION	LAWYERS
41.			4. 50245	TITLE INSURANCE COMPANY OF AMERICA	TITLE IC AMERICA
42.			5. 50012	TRANSNATION TITLE INSURANCE COMPANY	TRANSNATION
43.			6. 50041	UNITED CAPITAL TITLE INSURANCE COMPANY	UNITED CAPITAL
44.	228	OHIO FARMERS	1. 50792	SOUTHERN TITLE INSURANCE CORPORATION	SOUTHERN TI CORP
45.	150	OLD REPUBLIC	1. 51411	AMERICAN GUARANTY TITLE INSURANCE COMPANY	AMERICAN GUARANTY
46.			2. 51004	MISSISSIPPI VALLEY TITLE INSURANCE COMPANY	MISSISSIPPI VALLEY
47.			3. 50005	OLD REPUBLIC GENERAL TITLE INSURANCE CORPORATION	OLD REPUBLIC GENERAL
48.			4. 50520	OLD REPUBLIC NATIONAL TITLE INSURANCE COMPANY	OLD REPUBLIC NATIONAL
49.	3590	RELIANT HOLDING	1. 50180	GUARANTEE TITLE AND TRUST COMPANY	GUARANTEE T&T
50.			2. 50034	GUARANTEE TITLE INSURANCE COMPANY	GUARANTEE
51.	340	STEWART	1. 50035	ALLIANCE TITLE OF AMERICA, INC.	ALLIANCE
52.			2. 50725	ARKANSAS TITLE INSURANCE COMPANY	ARKANSAS TIC
53.			3. 51063	MONROE TITLE INSURANCE CORPORATION	MONROE
54.			4. 50156	NATIONAL LAND TITLE INSURANCE COMPANY	NATIONAL LAND
55.			5. 50121	STEWART TITLE GUARANTY COMPANY	STEWART TGC
56.			6. 51420	STEWART TITLE INSURANCE COMPANY	STEWART TIC
57.			7. 50036	STEWART TITLE INSURANCE COMPANY OF OREGON	STEWART (OR)
58.	3889	TRANSUNION	1. 51152	TRANSUNION NATIONAL TITLE INSURANCE COMPANY	TRANSUNION NATIONAL
59.			2. 50849	TRANSUNION TITLE INSURANCE COMPANY	TRANSUNION TIC
60.		UNAFFILIATED COMPANIES	1. 12309	ALLIANT NATIONAL TITLE INSURANCE COMPANY	ALLIANT
61.			2. 50001	AMERICAN EAGLE TITLE INSURANCE COMPANY	AMERICAN EAGLE
62.			3. 11450	AMERICAN LAND AND AIRCRAFT TITLE COMPANY	AMERICAN LAND & AIRCRAFT
63.			4. 51365	AMERICAN SECURITY TITLE INSURANCE COMPANY	AMERICAN SECURITY
64.			5. 11865	ARSENAL INSURANCE CORPORATION	ARSENAL
65.			6. 50004	ATTORNEYS' TITLE GUARANTY FUND, INC. (IL)	ATTORNEYS TGF (IL)
66.			7. 50164	BANKERS GUARANTEE TITLE & TRUST COMPANY (THE)	BANKERS GUARANTEE
67.			8. 50026	COMMERCE TITLE INSURANCE COMPANY	COMMERCE
68.			9. 51209	CONESTOGA TITLE INSURANCE CO.	CONESTOGA
69.			10. 50020	DAKOTA HOMESTEAD TITLE INSURANCE COMPANY	DAKOTA HOMESTEAD
70.			11. 51381	DREIBELBISS TITLE COMPANY, INC.	DREIBELBISS
71.			12. 12234	EQUITY NATIONAL TITLE INSURANCE COMPANY	EQUITY NATIONAL
72.			13. 12522	FARMERS NATIONAL TITLE INSURANCE COMPANY	FARMERS NATIONAL
73.			14. 11974	FOUNDERS TITLE INSURANCE	FOUNDERS
74.			15. 50172	GENERAL TITLE & TRUST COMPANY	GENERAL T&T
75.			16. 51632	GUARDIAN NATIONAL TITLE INSURANCE COMPANY	GUARDIAN NATIONAL
76.			17. 12953	K.E.L. TITLE INSURANCE GROUP	K.E.L.
77.			18. 50002	LAND TITLE INSURANCE CORPORATION	LAND CORP (CO)
78.			19. 51446	MANITO TITLE INSURANCE COMPANY	MANITO
79.			20. 50962	MASON COUNTY TITLE INSURANCE COMPANY	MASON COUNTY
80.			21. 12550	MASON TITLE INSURANCE COMPANY	MASON
81.			22. 50030	MISSISSIPPI GUARANTY TITLE INSURANCE COMPANY	MISSISSIPPI GUARANTY
82.			23. 50695	NATIONAL TITLE INSURANCE COMPANY	NATIONAL
83.			24. 51020	NATIONAL TITLE INSURANCE OF NEW YORK, INC.	NATIONAL OF NY
84.			25. 50130	NORTH AMERICAN TITLE INSURANCE COMPANY	NORTH AMERICAN
85.			26. 50440	OLYMPIC TITLE INSURANCE COMPANY	OLYMPIC
86.			27.	PILGRIM TITLE INSURANCE COMPANY	PILGRIM
87.			28. 50270	SEAGATE TITLE & ABSTRACT COMPANY, INC.	SEAGATE
88.			29. 50784	SECURITY TITLE GUARANTEE CORPORATION OF BALTIMORE (THE)	SECURITY TG (BALTIMORE)
89.			30. 12591	SIERRA TITLE INSURANCE GUARANTY COMPANY	SIERRA
90.			31. 50261	TITLE GUARANTY AND TRUST COMPANY OF CHATTANOOGA	TITLE G&TC
91.			32.	TITLE GUARANTY DIVISION OF THE IOWA FINANCE AUTHORITY	TITLE GUARANTY DIV (IA)
92.			33. 50016	TITLE RESOURCES GUARANTY COMPANY	TITLE RESOURCES
93.			34. 12935	TITLEDGE INSURANCE COMPANY OF NEW YORK	TITLEDGE
94.			35. 50029	WASHINGTON TITLE INSURANCE COMPANY	WASHINGTON TIC
95.			36. 50050	WESTCOR LAND TITLE INSURANCE COMPANY	WESTCOR

INTRA-GROUP UNDERWRITER OWNERSHIP STRUCTURE - *NEW!*

1

Overview of *Intra-Group Underwriter Ownership Structure*

The *Intra-Group Underwriter Ownership Structure* reports are designed to show Title underwriter ownership relationships within an NAIC Group. While some groups have a number of holding companies, agencies and related businesses within their organizational structure, this report includes only those companies in the structure having ownership interest in a Title underwriter.

Intra-Group Underwriter Ownership Structure reports are based on the information presented in Schedule Y of the Form 9 Annual Statements. While best efforts have been made to insure completeness and accuracy, the data is derived entirely from the statements submitted by the individual underwriters.

Chart Structure, Information and Elements

Each chart represents the ownership structure from the top downward. Each connecting line represents 100% ownership interest in the lower company unless otherwise marked. Title underwriters are identified with larger boxes, along with their NAIC Number. If an underwriter does not have an NAIC Number, "00000" is presented. Mid-level holding companies are represented with smaller boxes.

Intra-Group Underwriter Ownership Structure - New!

Attorneys' Title – *Group Number: 750*

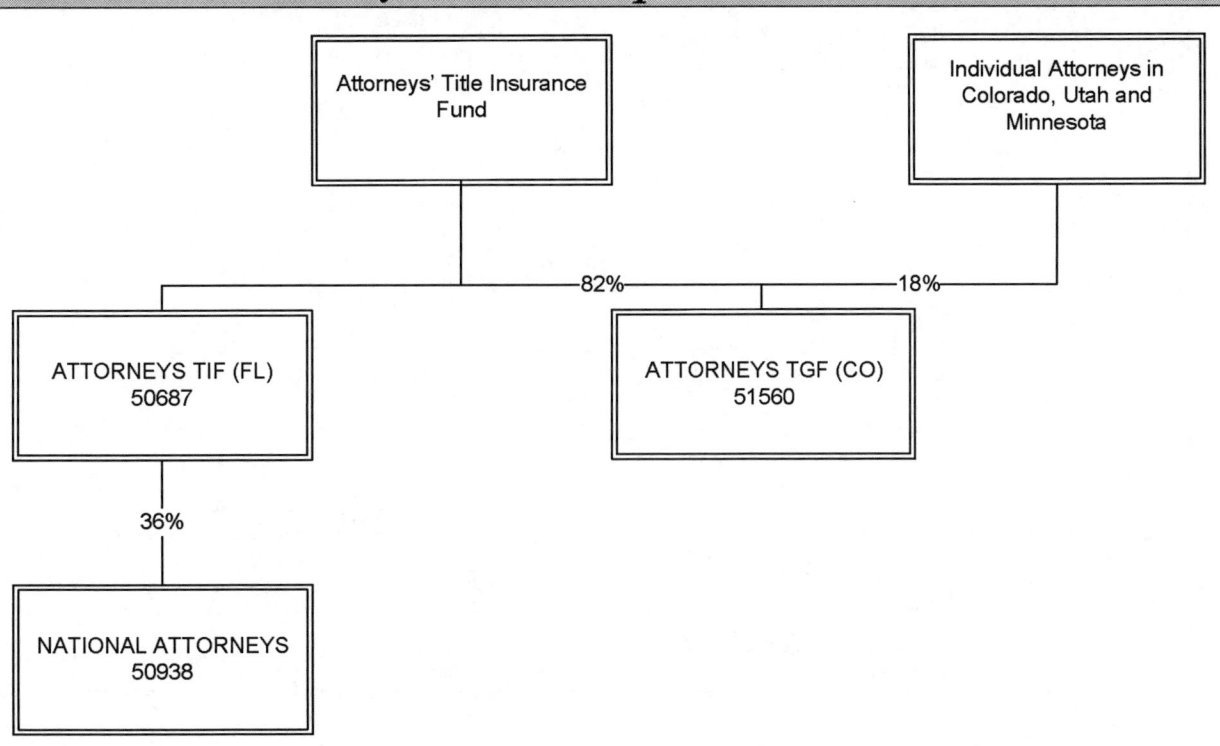

CATIC – *Group Number: 4255*

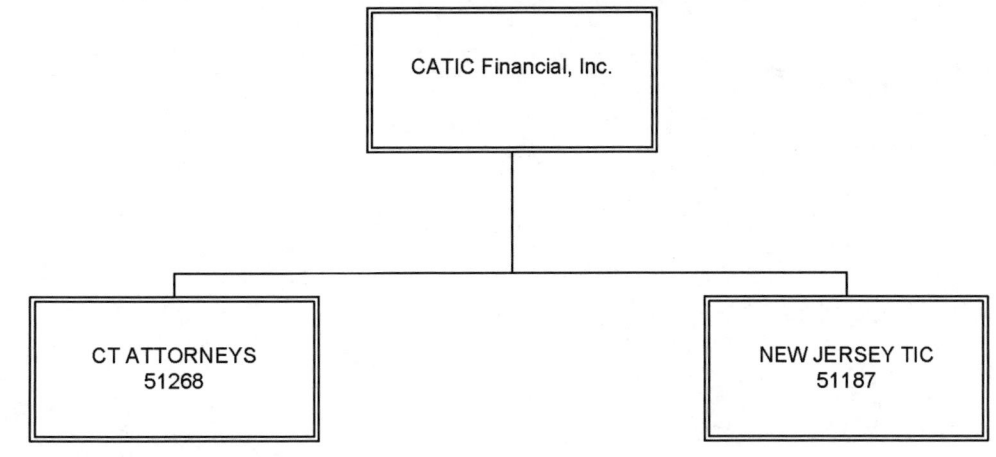

Intra-Group Underwriter Ownership Structure - New!

Chicago/Fidelity – *Group Number: 670*

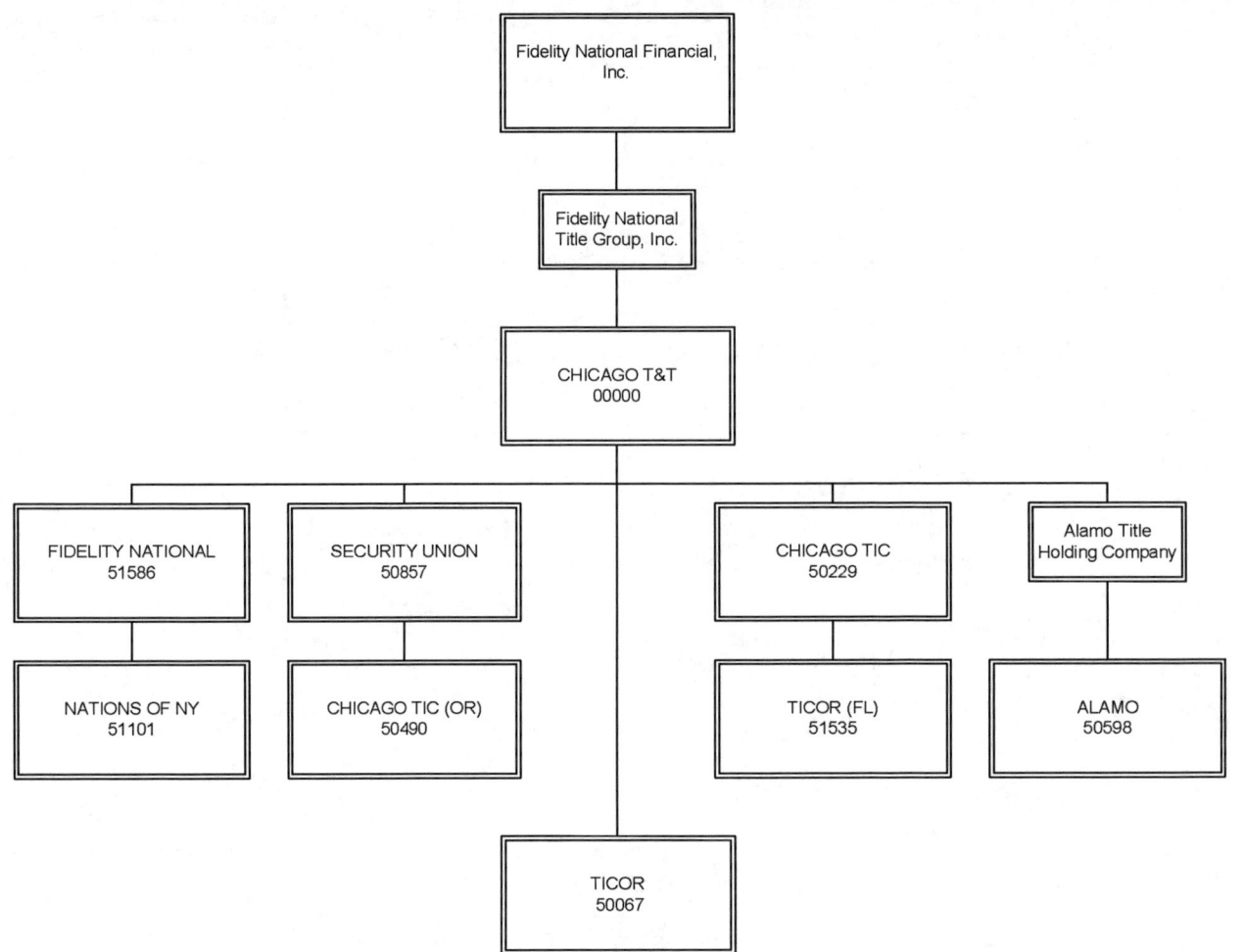

Intra-Group Underwriter Ownership Structure - New!

First American – *Group Number: 70*

1

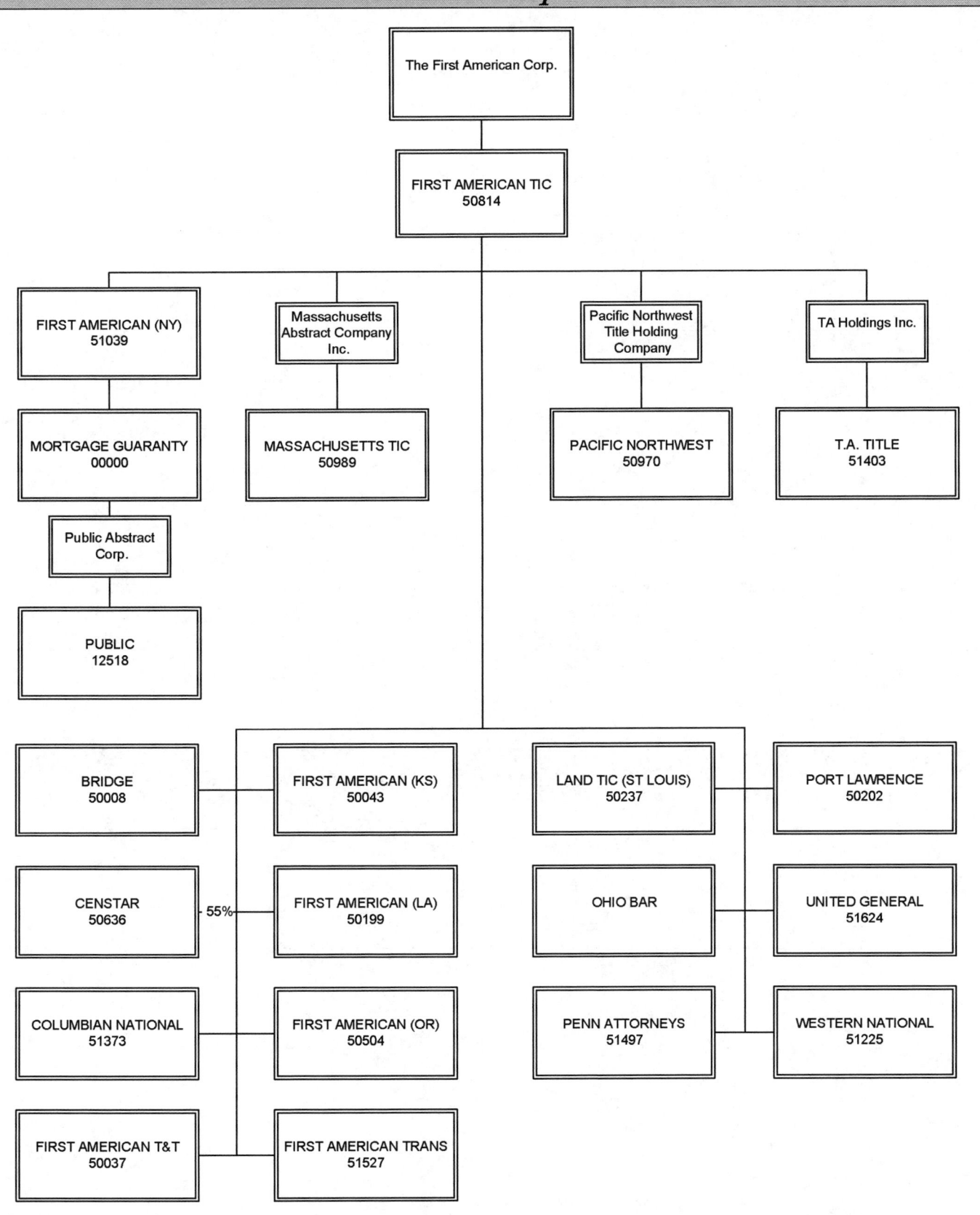

Intra-Group Underwriter Ownership Structure - New!

1

Investors – *Group Number: 627*

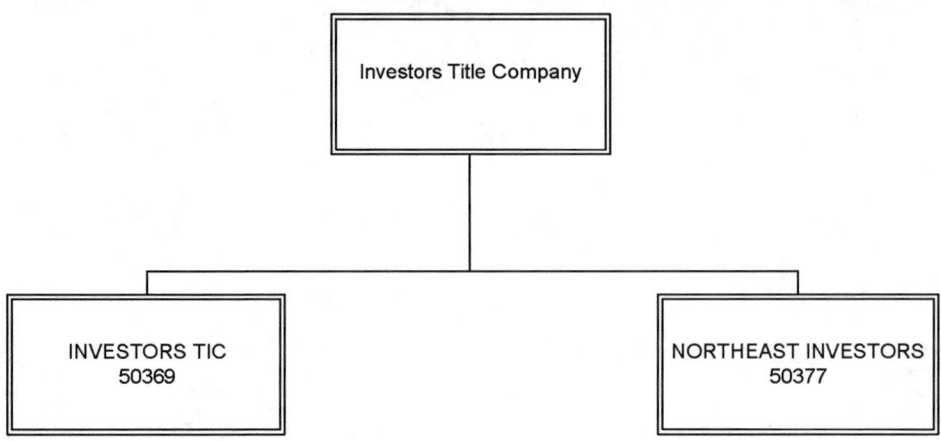

Land America – *Group Number: 99*

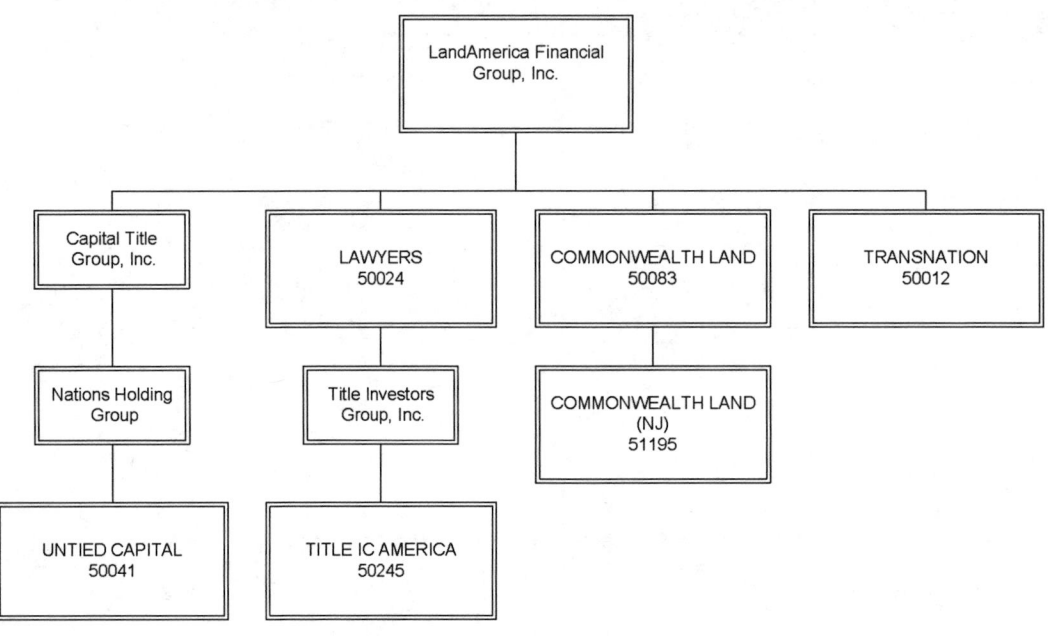

Intra-Group Underwriter Ownership Structure - New!

Old Republic - *Group Number: 150*

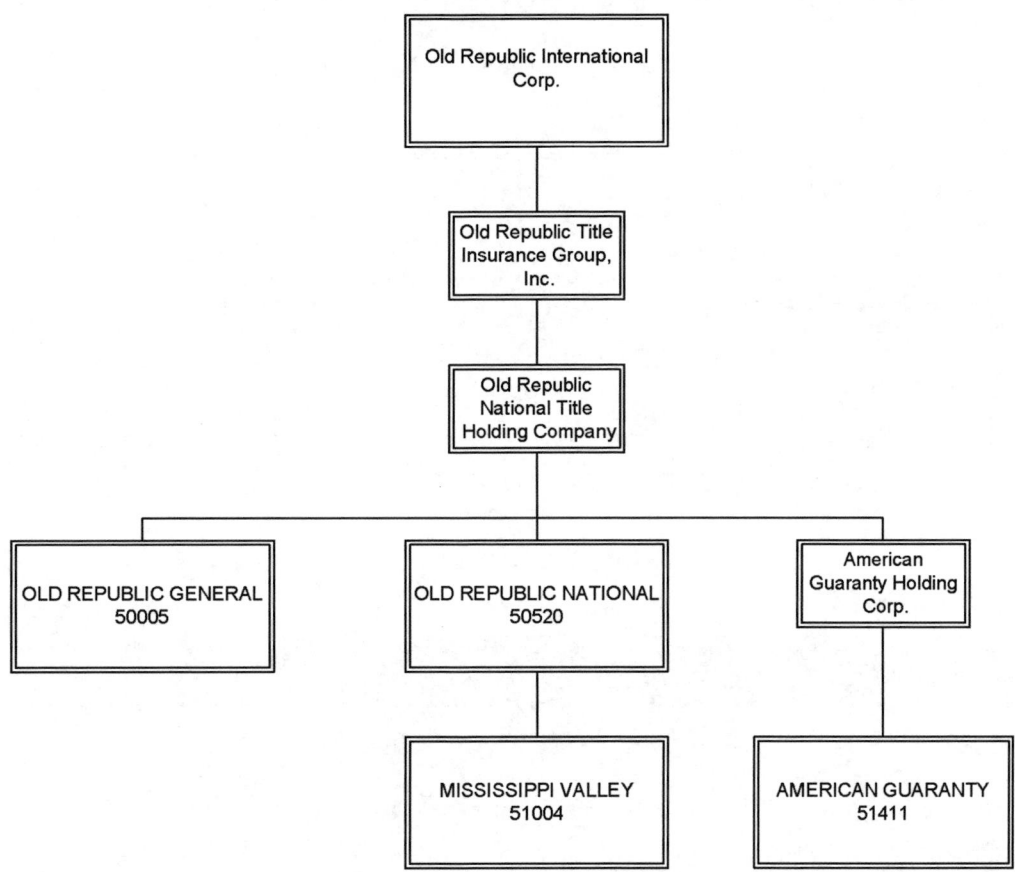

Ohio Farmers - *Group Number: 228*

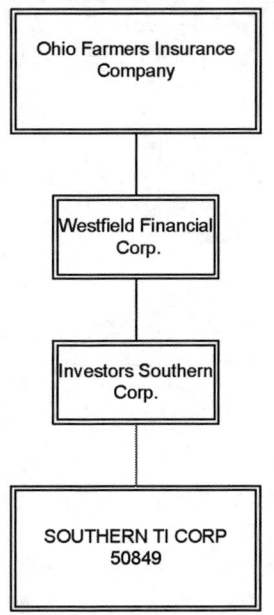

1

Reliant Holding – *Group Number: 3590*

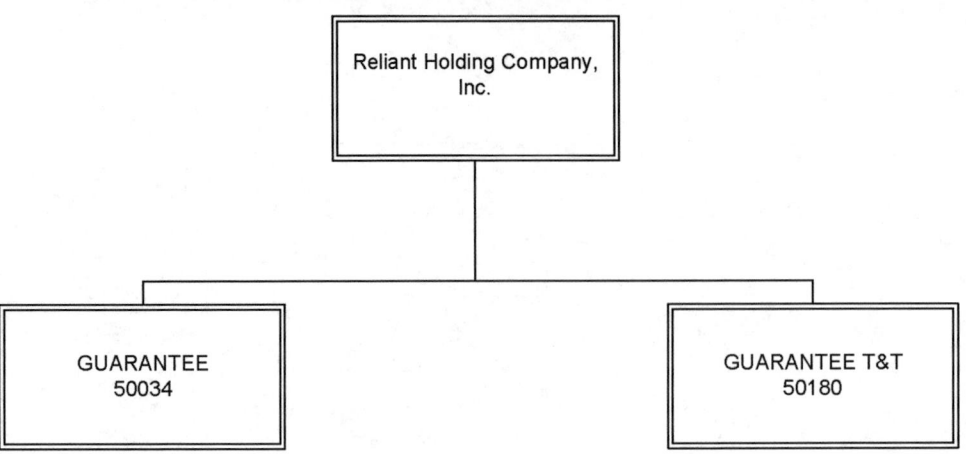

```
                    Reliant Holding Company,
                             Inc.
                              |
            ┌─────────────────┴─────────────────┐
      GUARANTEE                              GUARANTEE T&T
        50034                                   50180
```

Stewart – *Group Number: 340*

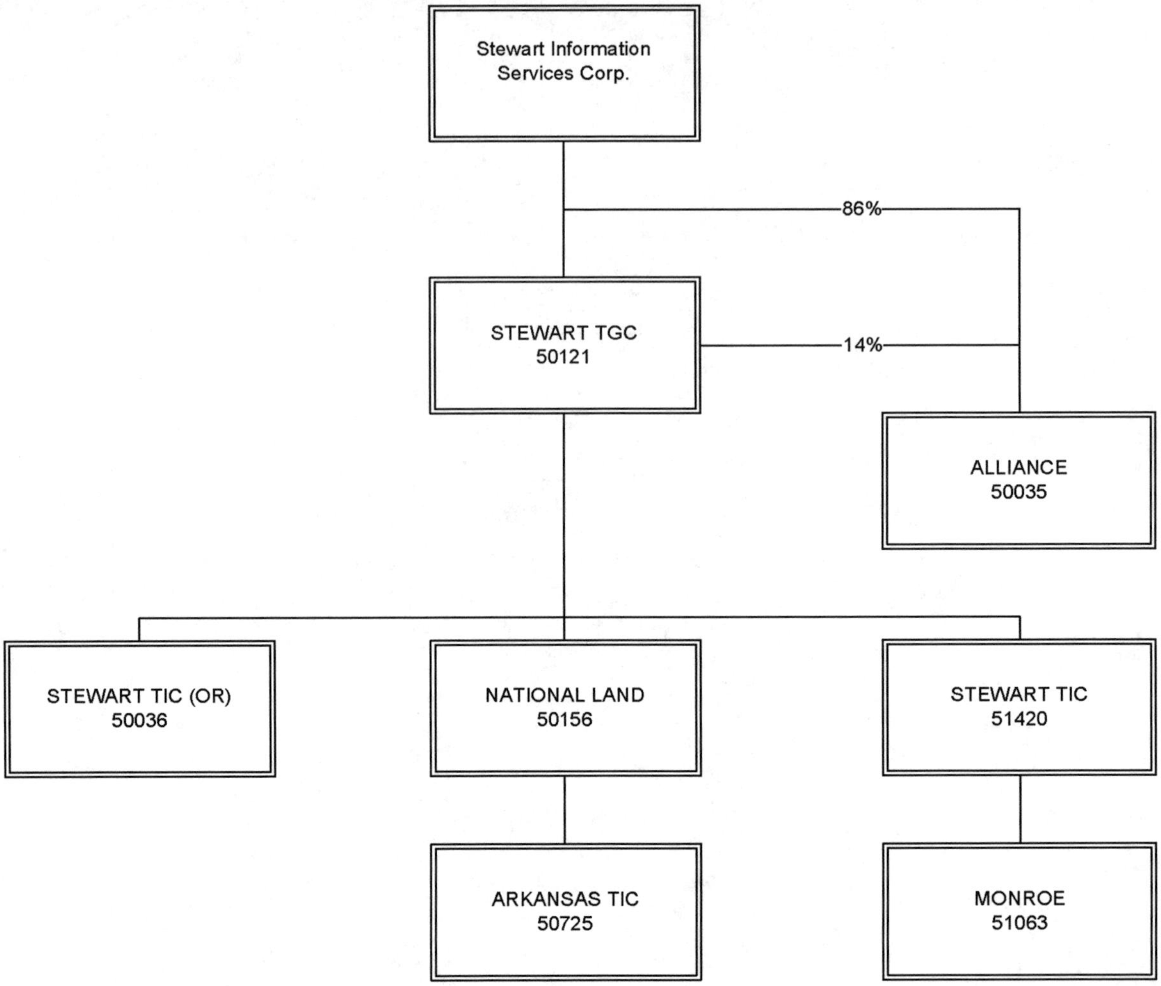

```
                    Stewart Information
                     Services Corp.
                           |
                           |──────────────86%──────────┐
                     STEWART TGC                        |
                       50121 ─────────14%───────────────┤
                           |                            |
                           |                        ALLIANCE
                           |                          50035
        ┌──────────────────┼──────────────────┐
  STEWART TIC (OR)    NATIONAL LAND        STEWART TIC
     50036               50156               51420
                           |                   |
                      ARKANSAS TIC          MONROE
                         50725              51063
```

Intra-Group Underwriter Ownership Structure - New!

TransUnion – *Group Number: 3889*

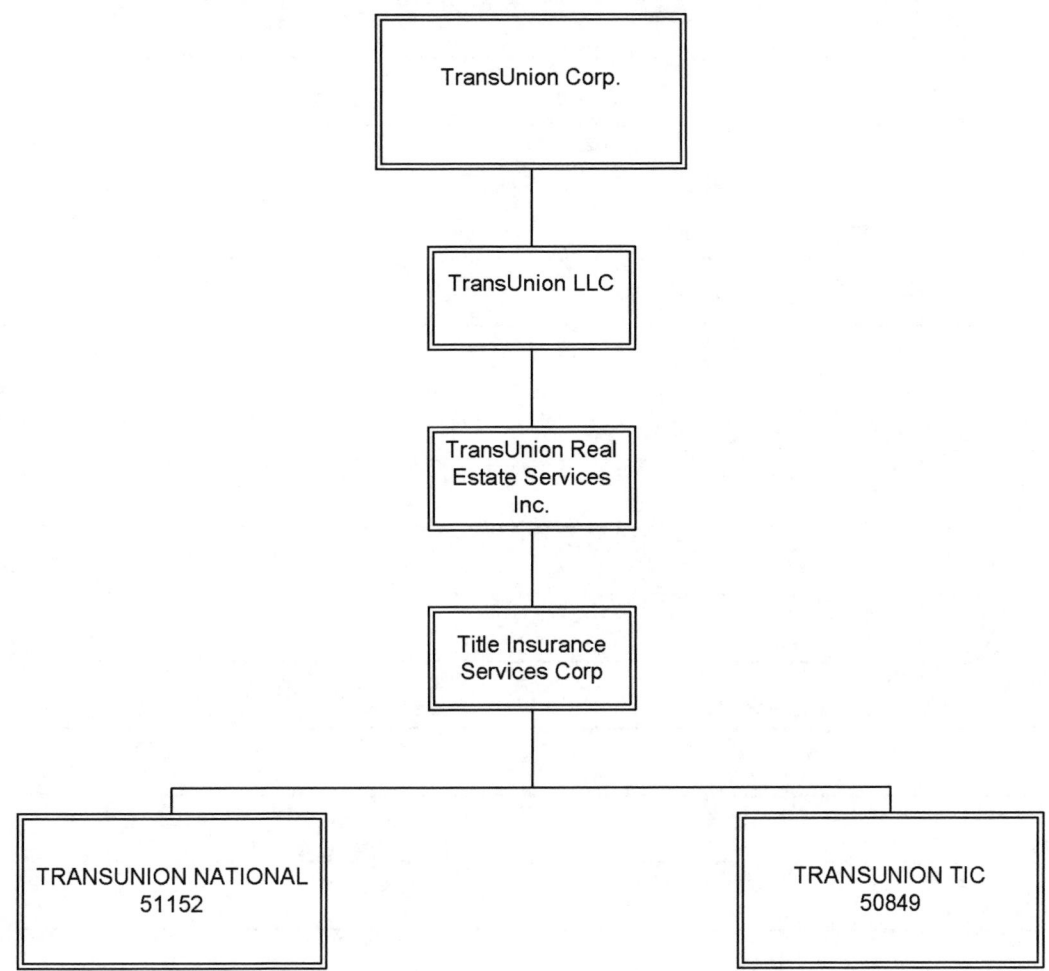

1

Notes

1

UNDERWRITER & NAIC GROUP INFORMATION - LICENSED JURISDICTIONS

NAIC Group Licensed Jurisdictions

	GROUP NUMBER	GROUP COUNT	AK	AL	AR	AZ	CA	CO	CT	DC	DE	FL	GA	HI	IA	ID	IL	IN	KS	KY	LA	MA	MD	ME	MI	MN	MO	MS	MT	NC	ND
1. ATTORNEYS' TITLE	750	3		✓	✓			✓				✓	✓			✓	✓						✓		✓	✓				✓	✓
2. CATIC	4255	2							✓														✓	✓							
3. CHICAGO / FIDELITY	670	9	✓	✓	✓	✓	✓	✓	✓	✓	✓	✓	✓	✓		✓	✓	✓	✓	✓	✓	✓	✓	✓	✓	✓	✓	✓	✓	✓	✓
4. FIRST AMERICAN	70	20	✓	✓	✓	✓	✓	✓	✓	✓	✓	✓	✓	✓		✓	✓	✓	✓	✓	✓	✓	✓	✓	✓	✓	✓	✓	✓	✓	✓
5. INVESTORS	627	2		✓	✓	✓		✓	✓	✓	✓	✓	✓			✓	✓	✓	✓	✓	✓	✓	✓	✓	✓	✓	✓	✓	✓	✓	✓
6. LAND AMERICA	99	6	✓	✓	✓	✓	✓	✓	✓	✓	✓	✓	✓	✓		✓	✓	✓	✓	✓	✓	✓	✓	✓	✓	✓	✓	✓	✓	✓	✓
7. OHIO FARMERS	228	1		✓	✓			✓			✓	✓	✓	✓								✓				✓				✓	
8. OLD REPUBLIC	150	4	✓	✓	✓	✓	✓	✓	✓	✓	✓	✓	✓	✓		✓	✓	✓	✓	✓	✓	✓	✓	✓	✓	✓	✓	✓	✓	✓	✓
9. RELIANT HOLDING	3590	2			✓	✓			✓							✓	✓	✓							✓	✓	✓	✓	✓		
10. STEWART	340	7	✓	✓	✓	✓	✓	✓		✓	✓	✓	✓			✓	✓	✓	✓	✓	✓	✓	✓		✓	✓	✓	✓	✓	✓	✓
11. TRANSUNION	3889	2		✓	✓	✓	✓		✓	✓	✓	✓	✓			✓	✓	✓	✓	✓	✓	✓	✓			✓		✓	✓	✓	✓
			11	21	23	21	17	20	17	20	21	22	21	14	0	17	22	25	19	21	19	19	23	16	20	20	20	21	19	21	16

NAIC Group Licensed Jurisdictions

COMPANY	GROUP NUMBER	NE	NH	NJ	NM	NV	NY	OH	OK	OR	PA	RI	SC	SD	TN	TX	UT	VA	VT	WA	WI	WV	WY	AS	GU	PR	VI	CN	MP	Total
1. ATTORNEYS' TITLE	750												✓				✓		✓							✓				16
2. CATIC	4255		✓	✓			✓				✓	✓						✓												10
3. CHICAGO / FIDELITY	670	✓	✓	✓	✓	✓	✓	✓	✓	✓	✓	✓	✓	✓	✓	✓	✓	✓	✓	✓	✓	✓	✓		✓	✓	✓	✓		272
4. FIRST AMERICAN	70	✓	✓	✓	✓	✓	✓	✓	✓	✓	✓	✓	✓	✓	✓	✓	✓	✓	✓	✓	✓	✓	✓		✓	✓	✓	✓		200
5. INVESTORS	627	✓	✓	✓	✓	✓	✓	✓	✓	✓	✓	✓	✓	✓	✓	✓	✓	✓	✓	✓		✓								65
6. LAND AMERICA	99	✓	✓	✓	✓	✓	✓	✓	✓	✓	✓	✓	✓	✓	✓	✓	✓	✓	✓	✓	✓	✓		✓		✓	✓	✓		188
7. OHIO FARMERS	228			✓	✓	✓		✓		✓			✓		✓	✓		✓				✓								21
8. OLD REPUBLIC	150	✓	✓	✓	✓	✓	✓	✓	✓	✓	✓	✓	✓	✓	✓	✓	✓	✓	✓	✓	✓	✓	✓		✓	✓				104
9. RELIANT HOLDING	3590							✓	✓	✓			✓	✓	✓		✓													18
10. STEWART	340	✓	✓	✓	✓	✓		✓	✓		✓	✓	✓	✓	✓	✓		✓	✓	✓	✓	✓	✓		✓	✓	✓	✓		73
11. TRANSUNION	3889				✓	✓		✓	✓				✓	✓	✓	✓	✓	✓				✓								32
		17	15	23	20	19	19	27	21	15	27	16	23	18	22	25	22	21	15	13	18	20	13	1	4	9	6	4	0	--

1

Underwriter Licensed Jurisdictions

	NAIC NUMBER	AK	AL	AR	AZ	CA	CO	CT	DC	DE	FL	GA	HI	IA	ID	IL	IN	KS	KY	LA	MA	MD	ME	MI	MN	MO	MS	MT	NC	ND
1. ALAMO	50598																													
2. ALLIANCE	50035										✓																			
3. ALLIANT	12309					✓																								
4. AMERICAN EAGLE	50001																													
5. AMERICAN GUARANTY	51411		✓	✓	✓	✓	✓	✓	✓	✓	✓	✓	✓			✓	✓	✓	✓	✓	✓	✓	✓	✓	✓	✓	✓	✓	✓	✓
6. AMERICAN LAND & AIRCRAFT	11450																													
7. AMERICAN SECURITY	51365																													
8. ARKANSAS TIC	50725			✓																										
9. ARSENAL	11865																✓													
10. ATTORNEYS TGF (CO)	51560						✓																							
11. ATTORNEYS TGF (IL)	50004															✓	✓													
12. ATTORNEYS TIF (FL)	50687		✓	✓						✓	✓											✓		✓	✓				✓	✓
13. BANKERS GUARANTEE	50164																													
14. BRIDGE	50008						✓					✓										✓							✓	
15. CENSTAR	50636		✓	✓	✓	✓	✓	✓	✓	✓	✓	✓				✓	✓					✓	✓		✓	✓	✓	✓	✓	✓
16. CHICAGO T&T														✓																
17. CHICAGO TIC	50229	✓	✓	✓	✓	✓	✓	✓	✓	✓	✓	✓	✓			✓	✓	✓	✓	✓	✓	✓	✓	✓	✓	✓	✓	✓	✓	✓
18. CHICAGO TIC (OR)	50490																	✓												
19. COLUMBIAN NATIONAL	51373			✓	✓	✓												✓							✓			✓		✓
20. COMMERCE	50026			✓	✓	✓	✓		✓	✓	✓	✓				✓	✓					✓		✓	✓	✓			✓	
21. COMMONWEALTH LAND	50083	✓	✓	✓	✓	✓	✓	✓	✓	✓	✓	✓	✓			✓	✓	✓	✓	✓	✓	✓	✓	✓	✓	✓	✓	✓	✓	✓
22. COMMONWEALTH LAND (NJ)	51195								✓	✓												✓								
23. CONESTOGA	51209		✓						✓	✓	✓	✓					✓			✓						✓				
24. CT ATTORNEYS	51268							✓													✓		✓							
25. DAKOTA HOMESTEAD	50020			✓		✓												✓							✓					✓
26. DREIBELBISS	51381																✓													
27. EQUITY NATIONAL	12234																					✓								
28. FARMERS NATIONAL	12522																									✓				
29. FIDELITY NATIONAL	51586	✓	✓	✓	✓	✓	✓	✓	✓	✓	✓	✓	✓			✓	✓	✓	✓	✓	✓	✓	✓	✓	✓	✓	✓	✓	✓	✓
30. FIRST AMERICAN (KS)	50043																	✓												
31. FIRST AMERICAN (LA)	50199																			✓										
32. FIRST AMERICAN (NY)	51039																	✓						✓						
33. FIRST AMERICAN (OR)	50504																							✓						
34. FIRST AMERICAN T&T	50037																													
35. FIRST AMERICAN TIC	50814	✓	✓	✓	✓	✓	✓	✓	✓	✓	✓	✓	✓			✓	✓	✓	✓	✓	✓	✓	✓	✓	✓	✓	✓	✓	✓	✓
36. FIRST AMERICAN TRANS	51527																					✓								
37. FOUNDERS	11974																													
38. GENERAL T&T	50172															✓														
39. GUARANTEE	50034																		✓							✓				
40. GUARANTEE T&T	50180			✓	✓			✓								✓	✓						✓	✓					✓	✓
41. GUARDIAN NATIONAL	51632				✓					✓	✓						✓		✓	✓							✓			
42. INVESTORS TIC	50369		✓	✓	✓		✓	✓	✓	✓	✓	✓				✓	✓	✓	✓	✓	✓	✓	✓	✓	✓	✓	✓	✓	✓	✓
43. K.E.L.	12953										✓																			
44. LAND CORP (CO)	50002			✓		✓																								
45. LAND TIC (ST LOUIS)	50237																									✓	✓			
46. LAWYERS	50024	✓	✓	✓	✓	✓	✓	✓	✓	✓	✓	✓	✓			✓	✓	✓	✓	✓	✓	✓	✓	✓	✓	✓	✓	✓	✓	✓
47. MANITO	51446																													
48. MASON	12550									✓																				
49. MASON COUNTY	50962																													
50. MASSACHUSETTS TIC	50989																				✓									
51. MISSISSIPPI GUARANTY	50030																										✓			
52. MISSISSIPPI VALLEY	51004		✓																								✓			
53. MONROE	51063																													
54. NATIONAL	50695		✓						✓	✓											✓						✓			
55. NATIONAL ATTORNEYS	50938																✓													
56. NATIONAL LAND	50156		✓													✓	✓	✓							✓	✓	✓	✓		✓
57. NATIONAL OF NY	51020			✓	✓	✓	✓	✓	✓	✓	✓	✓				✓	✓	✓		✓	✓	✓		✓		✓	✓	✓	✓	✓
58. NATIONS OF NY	51101					✓	✓	✓								✓	✓		✓		✓	✓		✓					✓	
59. NEW JERSEY TIC	51187																													
60. NORTH AMERICAN	50130			✓	✓	✓		✓	✓	✓						✓						✓		✓	✓				✓	
61. NORTHEAST INVESTORS	50377		✓					✓	✓	✓	✓						✓		✓			✓		✓	✓				✓	
62. OHIO BAR	51330															✓			✓											
63. OLD REPUBLIC GENERAL	50005						✓																							
64. OLD REPUBLIC NATIONAL	50520	✓	✓	✓	✓	✓	✓	✓	✓	✓	✓	✓	✓			✓	✓	✓	✓	✓	✓	✓	✓	✓	✓	✓	✓	✓	✓	✓
65. OLYMPIC	50440																													
66. PACIFIC NORTHWEST	50970	✓			✓											✓	✓	✓												
67. PENN ATTORNEYS	51497																													
68. PORT LAWRENCE	50202																													
69. SEAGATE	50270																													
70. SECURITY TG (BALTIMORE)	50784		✓	✓			✓		✓	✓		✓									✓	✓		✓	✓			✓		
71. SECURITY UNION	50857	✓	✓	✓	✓	✓	✓	✓		✓	✓	✓				✓	✓	✓	✓	✓	✓	✓	✓	✓	✓		✓	✓	✓	✓
72. SIERRA	12591																													
73. SOUTHERN TI CORP	50792		✓	✓			✓		✓	✓	✓	✓															✓		✓	
74. STEWART (OR)	50036																													
75. STEWART TGC	50121	✓	✓	✓	✓	✓	✓	✓	✓	✓	✓	✓				✓	✓	✓	✓	✓	✓	✓	✓	✓	✓	✓	✓	✓	✓	✓
76. STEWART TIC	51420					✓																								
77. T.A. TITLE	51403									✓												✓								
78. TICOR	50067	✓	✓	✓	✓	✓	✓	✓	✓	✓	✓	✓	✓			✓	✓	✓	✓	✓	✓	✓	✓	✓	✓	✓	✓	✓	✓	✓
79. TICOR (FL)	51535		✓	✓	✓	✓	✓	✓	✓	✓	✓	✓				✓	✓	✓	✓	✓	✓	✓	✓	✓	✓	✓	✓	✓	✓	✓
80. TITLE G&TC	50261																													
81. TITLE GUARANTY DIV (IA)														✓																
82. TITLE IC AMERICA	50245		✓	✓	✓		✓		✓	✓		✓				✓	✓	✓	✓	✓	✓	✓		✓	✓					
83. TITLE RESOURCES	50016			✓	✓		✓			✓									✓	✓	✓	✓				✓				
84. TITLEDGE	12935																													
85. TRANSNATION	50012		✓	✓	✓	✓	✓	✓	✓	✓	✓	✓				✓	✓	✓	✓	✓	✓	✓	✓	✓	✓	✓	✓	✓	✓	✓
86. TRANSUNION NATIONAL	51152		✓	✓	✓	✓	✓	✓	✓	✓	✓	✓				✓	✓	✓	✓	✓	✓	✓	✓	✓	✓	✓	✓	✓	✓	✓
87. TRANSUNION TIC	50849					✓																								
88. UNITED CAPITAL	50041				✓	✓					✓																			
89. UNITED GENERAL	51624	✓	✓	✓	✓	✓	✓	✓	✓	✓	✓	✓	✓			✓	✓	✓	✓	✓	✓	✓	✓	✓	✓	✓	✓	✓	✓	✓
90. WASHINGTON TIC	50029																													
91. WESTCOR	50050		✓		✓	✓	✓		✓		✓		✓			✓			✓			✓			✓			✓	✓	
92. WESTERN NATIONAL	51225																													
		11	25	25	29	21	29	18	26	26	31	27	15	1	18	26	34	23	25	23	23	30	19	21	25	24	28	21	23	18

Underwriter Licensed Jurisdictions

COMPANY	NAIC NUMBER	NE	NH	NJ	NM	NV	NY	OH	OK	OR	PA	RI	SC	SD	TN	TX	UT	VA	VT	WA	WI	WV	WY	AS	GU	PR	VI	CN	MP	Total
1. ALAMO	50598				✓											✓														2
2. ALLIANCE	50035																													1
3. ALLIANT	12309															✓														2
4. AMERICAN EAGLE	50001								✓																					1
5. AMERICAN GUARANTY	51411	✓		✓	✓	✓	✓	✓	✓	✓	✓	✓	✓	✓	✓	✓	✓	✓		✓	✓	✓	✓							47
6. AMERICAN LAND & AIRCRAFT	11450								✓																					1
7. AMERICAN SECURITY	51365								✓																					1
8. ARKANSAS TIC	50725																													1
9. ARSENAL	11865																													1
10. ATTORNEYS TGF (CO)	51560																✓													2
11. ATTORNEYS TGF (IL)	50004																			✓										3
12. ATTORNEYS TIF (FL)	50687												✓													✓				13
13. BANKERS GUARANTEE	50164						✓																							1
14. BRIDGE	50008												✓		✓			✓												8
15. CENSTAR	50636	✓		✓	✓	✓		✓	✓		✓									✓	✓									37
16. CHICAGO T&T																														1
17. CHICAGO TIC	50229	✓	✓	✓	✓	✓	✓	✓	✓	✓	✓	✓	✓	✓	✓	✓	✓	✓	✓	✓	✓	✓	✓			✓	✓	✓		53
18. CHICAGO TIC (OR)	50490									✓																				2
19. COLUMBIAN NATIONAL	51373			✓				✓					✓			✓	✓													12
20. COMMERCE	50026			✓	✓	✓		✓			✓		✓			✓	✓			✓										22
21. COMMONWEALTH LAND	50083	✓	✓	✓	✓	✓	✓	✓		✓	✓	✓	✓	✓	✓	✓	✓	✓	✓	✓	✓	✓	✓		✓	✓	✓			53
22. COMMONWEALTH LAND (NJ)	51195			✓																										5
23. CONESTOGA	51209			✓			✓	✓			✓		✓				✓													15
24. CT ATTORNEYS	51268		✓	✓							✓							✓												7
25. DAKOTA HOMESTEAD	50020	✓			✓									✓							✓									11
26. DREIBELBISS	51381																													1
27. EQUITY NATIONAL	12234																													1
28. FARMERS NATIONAL	12522																													1
29. FIDELITY NATIONAL	51586	✓	✓	✓	✓	✓	✓	✓	✓	✓	✓	✓	✓	✓	✓	✓	✓	✓	✓	✓	✓	✓	✓							50
30. FIRST AMERICAN (KS)	50043																													1
31. FIRST AMERICAN (LA)	50199																													1
32. FIRST AMERICAN (NY)	51039					✓	✓																							4
33. FIRST AMERICAN (OR)	50504									✓										✓										3
34. FIRST AMERICAN T&T	50037							✓																						1
35. FIRST AMERICAN TIC	50814	✓	✓	✓	✓	✓		✓	✓		✓	✓	✓	✓	✓	✓	✓	✓	✓	✓	✓	✓	✓		✓	✓	✓	✓		52
36. FIRST AMERICAN TRANS	51527								✓																					2
37. FOUNDERS	11974																					✓								1
38. GENERAL T&T	50172							✓																						2
39. GUARANTEE	50034							✓							✓															4
40. GUARANTEE T&T	50180						✓	✓			✓		✓	✓	✓		✓													14
41. GUARDIAN NATIONAL	51632			✓			✓	✓			✓		✓		✓		✓			✓										15
42. INVESTORS TIC	50369	✓	✓	✓	✓	✓	✓	✓	✓		✓	✓		✓	✓	✓	✓	✓	✓	✓		✓	✓	✓						45
43. K.E.L.	12953																													1
44. LAND CORP (CO)	50002																													2
45. LAND TIC (ST LOUIS)	50237																													2
46. LAWYERS	50024	✓	✓	✓	✓	✓	✓	✓	✓	✓	✓	✓	✓	✓	✓	✓	✓	✓	✓	✓	✓	✓	✓		✓	✓	✓			53
47. MANITO	51446					✓																								1
48. MASON	12550																													1
49. MASON COUNTY	50962																			✓										1
50. MASSACHUSETTS TIC	50989																													1
51. MISSISSIPPI GUARANTY	50030																													1
52. MISSISSIPPI VALLEY	51004														✓															3
53. MONROE	51063						✓																							1
54. NATIONAL	50695												✓		✓															7
55. NATIONAL ATTORNEYS	50938																													1
56. NATIONAL LAND	50156							✓			✓			✓																13
57. NATIONAL OF NY	51020	✓	✓	✓	✓	✓	✓	✓	✓		✓		✓		✓	✓		✓		✓		✓					✓			39
58. NATIONS OF NY	51101		✓	✓			✓				✓	✓	✓		✓	✓		✓	✓		✓	✓								23
59. NEW JERSEY TIC	51187			✓			✓				✓																			3
60. NORTH AMERICAN	50130			✓		✓			✓							✓				✓										19
61. NORTHEAST INVESTORS	50377	✓		✓				✓			✓		✓			✓		✓			✓									20
62. OHIO BAR	51330							✓																						4
63. OLD REPUBLIC GENERAL	50005							✓																						2
64. OLD REPUBLIC NATIONAL	50520	✓	✓	✓	✓	✓	✓	✓	✓	✓	✓	✓	✓	✓	✓	✓	✓	✓	✓	✓	✓	✓	✓		✓	✓				52
65. OLYMPIC	50440							✓																						1
66. PACIFIC NORTHWEST	50970								✓	✓							✓	✓		✓	✓									11
67. PENN ATTORNEYS	51497										✓																			1
68. PORT LAWRENCE	50202			✓				✓			✓																			3
69. SEAGATE	50270							✓																						1
70. SECURITY TG (BALTIMORE)	50784		✓	✓			✓	✓					✓		✓						✓									19
71. SECURITY UNION	50857	✓	✓	✓	✓	✓		✓	✓		✓		✓		✓	✓	✓	✓	✓	✓	✓									42
72. SIERRA	12591															✓														1
73. SOUTHERN TI CORP	50792			✓	✓								✓			✓		✓												21
74. STEWART (OR)	50036									✓																				1
75. STEWART TGC	50121	✓	✓	✓	✓	✓	✓	✓	✓	✓	✓	✓	✓	✓	✓	✓	✓	✓	✓	✓	✓	✓	✓		✓	✓	✓	✓		54
76. STEWART TIC	51420				✓	✓																								2
77. T.A. TITLE	51403			✓			✓				✓																			6
78. TICOR	50067	✓	✓	✓	✓	✓	✓	✓	✓	✓	✓	✓	✓	✓	✓	✓	✓	✓	✓	✓	✓	✓	✓		✓	✓	✓			53
79. TICOR (FL)	51535	✓	✓	✓	✓	✓	✓	✓	✓		✓	✓	✓	✓	✓	✓	✓	✓	✓	✓	✓	✓	✓							46
80. TITLE G&TC	50261														✓															1
81. TITLE GUARANTY DIV (IA)																														1
82. TITLE IC AMERICA	50245			✓	✓	✓		✓			✓		✓			✓	✓	✓												25
83. TITLE RESOURCES	50016			✓	✓	✓		✓	✓		✓					✓		✓												16
84. TITLEDGE	12935						✓																							1
85. TRANSNATION	50012	✓	✓	✓	✓	✓		✓	✓	✓	✓	✓				✓		✓		✓	✓		✓							45
86. TRANSUNION NATIONAL	51152			✓	✓			✓	✓		✓		✓	✓	✓	✓		✓		✓	✓									31
87. TRANSUNION TIC	50849																													1
88. UNITED CAPITAL	50041				✓	✓					✓					✓														7
89. UNITED GENERAL	51624	✓	✓	✓	✓	✓	✓	✓	✓	✓	✓	✓	✓		✓	✓	✓	✓		✓	✓		✓							50
90. WASHINGTON TIC	50029						✓																							1
91. WESTCOR	50050	✓		✓	✓	✓	✓				✓					✓	✓	✓												23
92. WESTERN NATIONAL	51225						✓									✓														
		20	17	29	26	24	25	38	28	15	36	16	30	20	28	32	25	26	16	15	21	22	16	1	4	9	7	4	0	--

1

Notes

S E C T I O N

STATUTORY FINANCIAL STATEMENTS

2

A.1 BALANCE SHEET
- INDUSTRY COMPOSITE

2

A.1 Balance Sheet - Industry Composite

ASSETS	Composite Value	% of Total
Bonds	$5,186,820,491	50.79%
Stocks:		
Preferred Stocks	$61,378,612	0.60%
Common Stocks	$1,268,197,289	12.42%
Mortgage Loans on Real Estate:		
First Liens	$71,886,078	0.70%
Other than First Liens	$0	0.00%
Real Estate:		
Properties Occupied by the Company	$131,437,431	1.29%
Properties Held for the Production of Income	$353,561	0.00%
Properties Held for Sale	$17,099,492	0.17%
Cash, Cash Equivalents and Short-Term Investments	$1,809,690,152	17.72%
Contract Loans	$0	0.00%
Other Invested Assets	$233,417,830	2.29%
Receivables for Securities	$5,462,193	0.05%
Aggregate Write-Ins for Invested Assets	$0	0.00%
Subtotals, Cash and Invested Assets	$8,785,743,129	86.03%
Title Plants	$284,268,151	2.78%
Investment Income Due and Accrued	$69,248,326	0.68%
Premiums and Considerations:		
Uncollected Premiums and Agents' Balances in the Course of Collection	$245,217,494	2.40%
Deferred Premiums, Agents' Balances & Installments Booked but Deferred & Not Yet Due	$0	0.00%
Accrued Retrospective Premiums	$0	0.00%
Reinsurance:		
Amounts Recoverable from Reinsurers	$706,358	0.01%
Funds Held by or Deposited with Reinsured Companies	$0	0.00%
Other Amounts Receivable Under Reinsurance Contracts	$4,945,211	0.05%
Amounts Receivable Relating to Uninsured Plans	$0	0.00%
Current Federal and Foreign Income Tax Recoverable and Interest Thereon	$81,750,224	0.80%
Net Deferred Tax Asset	$142,653,941	1.40%
Guaranty Funds Receivable or on Deposit	$25,760	0.00%
Electronic Data Processing Equipment and Software	$12,633,523	0.12%
Furniture and Equipment, Including Health Care Delivery Assets	$475,126	0.00%
Net Adjustment in Assets and Liabilities Due to Foreign Exchange Rates	$0	0.00%
Receivables from Parent, Subsidiaries and Affiliates	$470,500,138	4.61%
Health Care	$406,270	0.00%
Aggregate Write-Ins for Other than Invest Assets	$112,431,433	1.10%
Total Assets Excluding Separate Accounts, Segregated Accounts & Protected Cell Accounts	$10,211,005,084	99.99%
From Separate Accounts, Segregated Accounts and Protected Cell Accounts	$914,014	0.01%
TOTAL	$10,211,919,098	100.00%

LIABILITIES	Composite Value	% of Total
Known Claims Reserve (See Sec. 5, C.9)	$857,043,158	8.39%
Statutory Premium Reserve (See Sec. 5, C.9)	$4,475,895,184	43.83%
Aggregate of Other Reserves Required by Law (See Sec. 5, C.9)	$1,578,874	0.02%
Supplemental Reserve (See Sec. 5, C.9)	$118,987,761	1.17%
Commissions, Brokerage & Other Charges Due or Accrued to Attorneys, Agents & Real Estate Brokers	$1,858,797	0.02%
Other Expenses (Excluding Taxes, Licenses and Fees)	$555,155,217	5.44%
Taxes, Licenses and Fees (Excluding Federal and Foreign Income Taxes)	$69,073,410	0.68%
Current Federal and Foreign Income Taxes	$72,308,291	0.71%
Net Deferred Tax Liability	$13,222	0.00%
Borrowed Money and Interest Thereon	$8,156,101	0.08%
Dividends Declared and Unpaid	$2,004,082	0.02%
Premiums and Other Consideration Received in Advance	$27,394,822	0.27%
Unearned Interest and Real Estate Income Received in Advance	$12,950	0.00%
Funds Held by Company Under Reinsurance Treaties	$734,550	0.01%
Amounts Withheld or Retained by Company for Accounts of Others	$14,616,197	0.14%
Provision for Unauthorized Reinsurance	$0	0.00%
Net Adjustment in Assets and Liabilities Due to Foreign Exchange Rates	$10,304,820	0.10%
Drafts Outstanding	$0	0.00%
Payable to Parent, Subsidiaries and Affiliates	$152,450,599	1.49%
Payable for Securities	$705,880	0.01%
Aggregate Write-Ins for Other Liabilities	$1,065,008,471	10.43%
Total Liabilities (See Sec. 5, B.3)	$7,433,302,386	72.79%
Aggregate Write-Ins for Special Surplus Funds	$1,111,788	0.01%
Common Capital Stock	$413,407,164	4.05%
Preferred Capital Stock	$630,219	0.01%
Aggregate Write-Ins for Other than Special Surplus Funds	($65,000)	0.00%
Surplus Notes	$10,048,000	0.10%
Gross Paid In and Contributed Surplus	$1,953,687,054	19.13%
Unassigned Funds (Surplus)	$405,020,732	3.97%
Less Treasury Stock, at Cost:		
Shares Common	$4,507,545	0.04%
Shares Preferred	$715,700	0.01%
Surplus as Regards Policyholders (See Sec. 5, B.6, B.7, C.9, C.11)	$2,778,616,712	27.21%
TOTAL	$10,211,919,098	100.00%

CONSOLIDATED ELIMINATIONS

Investment in Parent, Subsidiary or Affiliated Title Underwriter

	EQUITY
ATTORNEYS' TITLE	$564,083
CHICAGO / FIDELITY	$652,643,330
FIRST AMERICAN	$256,658,111
LAND AMERICA	$33,132,445
OLD REPUBLIC	$9,683,618
STEWART	$43,058,340
TOTAL	**$995,739,927**

These adjustments remove the equity of investments in parent, subsidiary or affiliated Title underwriters, which are otherwise directly included in the composite data.

Some eliminations cannot be made because the shares of one underwriter, ultimately owned by another underwriter, are held by a subsidiary of the underwriter parent for which data is unavailable.

A.2 BALANCE SHEET
- BY NAIC GROUP

2

A.2 Balance Sheet - By NAIC Group

ASSETS	ATTORNEYS' TITLE Group Value	% of Total	CATIC Group Value	% of Total	CHICAGO / FIDELITY Group Value	% of Total	FIRST AMERICAN Group Value	% of Total
Bonds	$103,954,527	31.46%	$55,474,989	78.57%	$2,462,577,970	66.32%	$227,633,126	10.37%
Stocks:								
Preferred Stocks	$6,122,789	1.85%	$797,500	1.13%	$0	0.00%	$43,415,106	1.98%
Common Stocks	$130,242,733	39.41%	$5,429,164	7.69%	$133,008,720	3.58%	$353,383,409	16.10%
Mortgage Loans on Real Estate:								
First Liens	$192,847	0.06%	$0	0.00%	$25,534,961	0.69%	$42,527,880	1.94%
Other than First Liens	$0	0.00%	$0	0.00%	$0	0.00%	$0	0.00%
Real Estate:								
Properties Occupied by the Company	$7,290,739	2.21%	$0	0.00%	$1,067,674	0.03%	$110,995,697	5.06%
Properties Held for the Production of Income	$0	0.00%	$0	0.00%	$0	0.00%	$0	0.00%
Properties Held for Sale	$6,363,360	1.93%	$0	0.00%	$3,935,611	0.11%	$3,131,375	0.14%
Cash, Cash Equivalents and Short-Term Investments	$18,259,439	5.53%	$4,323,857	6.12%	$773,447,813	20.83%	$576,275,446	26.25%
Contract Loans	$0	0.00%	$0	0.00%	$0	0.00%	$0	0.00%
Other Invested Assets	$1,500	0.00%	$23,936	0.03%	$34,093,833	0.92%	$181,851,819	8.28%
Receivables for Securities	$647,429	0.20%	$0	0.00%	$1,683,721	0.05%	$0	0.00%
Aggregate Write-Ins for Invested Assets	$0	0.00%	$0	0.00%	$0	0.00%	$0	0.00%
Subtotals, Cash and Invested Assets	$273,075,363	82.63%	$66,049,446	93.54%	$3,435,350,303	92.51%	$1,539,213,858	70.11%
Title Plants	$4,888,211	1.48%	$810,376	1.15%	$94,254,025	2.54%	$97,071,422	4.42%
Investment Income Due and Accrued	$1,368,750	0.41%	$556,867	0.79%	$32,615,871	0.88%	$3,094,176	0.14%
Premiums and Considerations:								
Uncollected Premiums and Agents' Balances in the Course of Collection	$18,048,842	5.46%	$713,837	1.01%	$57,890,060	1.56%	$68,532,010	3.12%
Deferred Premiums, Agents' Balances & Installments Booked but Deferred & Not Yet Due	$0	0.00%	$0	0.00%	$0	0.00%	$0	0.00%
Accrued Retrospective Premiums	$0	0.00%	$0	0.00%	$0	0.00%	$0	0.00%
Reinsurance:								
Amounts Recoverable from Reinsurers	$0	0.00%	$0	0.00%	$0	0.00%	$0	0.00%
Funds Held by or Deposited with Reinsured Companies	$0	0.00%	$0	0.00%	$0	0.00%	$0	0.00%
Other Amounts Receivable Under Reinsurance Contracts	$82,038	0.02%	$0	0.00%	$0	0.00%	$4,284,792	0.20%
Amounts Receivable Relating to Uninsured Plans	$0	0.00%	$0	0.00%	$0	0.00%	$0	0.00%
Current Federal and Foreign Income Tax Recoverable and Interest Thereon	$12,761,797	3.86%	$801,331	1.13%	$9,060,350	0.24%	$14,934,667	0.68%
Net Deferred Tax Asset	$16,603,400	5.02%	$1,381,739	1.96%	$40,074,703	1.08%	$34,817,146	1.59%
Guaranty Funds Receivable or on Deposit	$0	0.00%	$0	0.00%	$0	0.00%	$0	0.00%
Electronic Data Processing Equipment and Software	$371,075	0.11%	$84,318	0.12%	$298,350	0.01%	$998,468	0.05%
Furniture and Equipment, Including Health Care Delivery Assets	$0	0.00%	$0	0.00%	$0	0.00%	$0	0.00%
Net Adjustment in Assets and Liabilities Due to Foreign Exchange Rates	$0	0.00%	$0	0.00%	$0	0.00%	$0	0.00%
Receivables from Parent, Subsidiaries and Affiliates	$0	0.00%	$38,234	0.05%	$43,606,595	1.17%	$362,899,199	16.53%
Health Care	$0	0.00%	$0	0.00%	$0	0.00%	$135,681	0.01%
Aggregate Write-Ins for Other than Invest Assets	$3,267,851	0.99%	$173,319	0.25%	$185,896	0.01%	$69,306,373	3.16%
Total Assets Excluding Separate Accounts, Segregated Accounts & Protected Cell Accounts	$330,467,327	100.00%	$70,609,467	100.00%	$3,713,336,153	100.00%	$2,195,287,792	100.00%
From Separate Accounts, Segregated Accounts and Protected Cell Accounts	$0	0.00%	$0	0.00%	$0	0.00%	$0	0.00%
TOTAL	$330,467,327	100.00%	$70,609,467	100.00%	$3,713,336,153	100.00%	$2,195,287,792	100.00%

LIABILITIES	Group Value	% of Total	Group Value	% of Total	Group Value	% of Total	Group Value	% of Total
Known Claims Reserve	$42,348,922	12.81%	$1,701,545	2.41%	$285,208,263	7.68%	$167,846,260	7.65%
Statutory Premium Reserve	$122,700,642	37.13%	$19,600,096	27.76%	$1,483,139,673	39.94%	$1,024,490,160	46.67%
Aggregate of Other Reserves Required by Law	$0	0.00%	$0	0.00%	$0	0.00%	$0	0.00%
Supplemental Reserve	$512,511	0.16%	$0	0.00%	$0	0.00%	$106,140,562	4.83%
Commissions, Brokerage & Other Charges Due or Accrued to Attorneys, Agents & Real Estate Brokers	$3,214	0.00%	$0	0.00%	$0	0.00%	$665,139	0.03%
Other Expenses (Excluding Taxes, Licenses and Fees)	$9,433,027	2.85%	$1,724,282	2.44%	$179,195,360	4.83%	$264,218,319	12.04%
Taxes, Licenses and Fees (Excluding Federal and Foreign Income Taxes)	$648,427	0.20%	$135,930	0.19%	$28,679,022	0.77%	$22,921,387	1.04%
Current Federal and Foreign Income Taxes	$0	0.00%	$440,000	0.62%	$44,544,357	1.20%	$16,192,170	0.74%
Net Deferred Tax Liability	$0	0.00%	$0	0.00%	$0	0.00%	$0	0.00%
Borrowed Money and Interest Thereon	$0	0.00%	$0	0.00%	$60,613	0.00%	$1,083,585	0.05%
Dividends Declared and Unpaid	$0	0.00%	$0	0.00%	$0	0.00%	$0	0.00%
Premiums and Other Consideration Received in Advance	$19,853	0.01%	$284,520	0.40%	$972,120	0.03%	$14,744,348	0.67%
Unearned Interest and Real Estate Income Received in Advance	$0	0.00%	$0	0.00%	$0	0.00%	$0	0.00%
Funds Held by Company Under Reinsurance Treaties	$0	0.00%	$0	0.00%	$0	0.00%	$12,348	0.00%
Amounts Withheld or Retained by Company for Accounts of Others	$350,123	0.11%	$0	0.00%	$9,930,168	0.27%	$3,313,062	0.15%
Provision for Unauthorized Reinsurance	$0	0.00%	$0	0.00%	$0	0.00%	$0	0.00%
Net Adjustment in Assets and Liabilities Due to Foreign Exchange Rates	$0	0.00%	$0	0.00%	$0	0.00%	$0	0.00%
Drafts Outstanding	$0	0.00%	$0	0.00%	$0	0.00%	$0	0.00%
Payable to Parent, Subsidiaries and Affiliates	$0	0.00%	$37,484	0.05%	$16,841,015	0.45%	$74,244,978	3.38%
Payable for Securities	$421,052	0.13%	$0	0.00%	$0	0.00%	$0	0.00%
Aggregate Write-Ins for Other Liabilities	$1,422,843	0.43%	$0	0.00%	$948,350,381	25.54%	$36,410,535	1.66%
Total Liabilities	$177,860,614	53.82%	$23,923,857	33.88%	$2,996,920,972	80.71%	$1,732,282,853	78.91%
Aggregate Write-Ins for Special Surplus Funds	$0	0.00%	$0	0.00%	$0	0.00%	$610,382	0.03%
Common Capital Stock	$3,543,912	1.07%	$1,000,000	1.42%	$118,424,552	3.19%	$224,141,099	10.21%
Preferred Capital Stock	$36,400	0.01%	$0	0.00%	$0	0.00%	$124,000	0.01%
Aggregate Write-Ins for Other than Special Surplus Funds	$0	0.00%	$0	0.00%	$0	0.00%	$0	0.00%
Surplus Notes	$5,650,000	1.71%	$1,500,000	2.12%	$0	0.00%	$0	0.00%
Gross Paid In and Contributed Surplus	$15,001,119	4.54%	$31,316,333	44.35%	$1,206,856,875	32.50%	$205,559,655	9.36%
Unassigned Funds (Surplus)	$128,375,280	38.85%	$12,869,277	18.23%	($608,866,249)	(16.40)%	$33,268,793	1.52%
Less Treasury Stock, at Cost:								
Shares Common	$0	0.00%	$0	0.00%	$0	0.00%	$698,990	0.03%
Shares Preferred	$0	0.00%	$0	0.00%	$0	0.00%	$0	0.00%
Surplus as Regards Policyholders	$152,606,711	46.18%	$46,685,610	66.12%	$716,415,178	19.29%	$463,004,939	21.09%
TOTAL	$330,467,325	100.00%	$70,609,467	100.00%	$3,713,336,150	100.00%	$2,195,287,792	100.00%

A.2 Balance Sheet - By NAIC Group

ASSETS	INVESTORS Group Value	% of Total	LAND AMERICA Group Value	% of Total	OHIO FARMERS Group Value	% of Total	OLD REPUBLIC Group Value	% of Total
Bonds	$71,655,068	64.08%	$1,094,064,346	68.59%	$17,083,173	73.05%	$513,538,922	79.00%
Stocks:								
Preferred Stocks	$419,646	0.38%	$10,338,339	0.65%	$0	0.00%	$0	0.00%
Common Stocks	$18,615,297	16.65%	$97,205,897	6.09%	$0	0.00%	$54,319,376	8.36%
Mortgage Loans on Real Estate:								
First Liens	$179,644	0.16%	$0	0.00%	$0	0.00%	$1,114,201	0.17%
Other than First Liens	$0	0.00%	$0	0.00%	$0	0.00%	$0	0.00%
Real Estate:								
Properties Occupied by the Company	$0	0.00%	$1,482,500	0.09%	$186,352	0.80%	$6,327,630	0.97%
Properties Held for the Production of Income	$0	0.00%	$0	0.00%	$0	0.00%	$5,600	0.00%
Properties Held for Sale	$278,477	0.25%	$655,800	0.04%	$145,750	0.62%	$495,000	0.08%
Cash, Cash Equivalents and Short-Term Investments	$9,622,628	8.60%	$110,651,003	6.94%	$2,307,156	9.87%	$29,921,262	4.60%
Contract Loans	$0	0.00%	$0	0.00%	$0	0.00%	$0	0.00%
Other Invested Assets	$351,532	0.31%	$10,264,070	0.64%	$0	0.00%	$2,500,000	0.38%
Receivables for Securities	$82,918	0.07%	$3,024,452	0.19%	$0	0.00%	$0	0.00%
Aggregate Write-Ins for Invested Assets	$0	0.00%	$0	0.00%	$0	0.00%	$0	0.00%
Subtotals, Cash and Invested Assets	$101,205,210	90.50%	$1,327,686,407	83.24%	$19,722,431	84.33%	$608,221,991	93.57%
Title Plants	$200,000	0.18%	$64,981,934	4.07%	$2,032,475	8.69%	$8,136,265	1.25%
Investment Income Due and Accrued	$1,021,268	0.91%	$12,999,390	0.82%	$215,960	0.92%	$7,530,847	1.16%
Premiums and Considerations:								
Uncollected Premiums and Agents' Balances in the Course of Collection	$5,888,594	5.27%	$36,623,081	2.30%	$145,439	0.62%	$11,399,884	1.75%
Deferred Premiums, Agents' Balances & Installments Booked but Deferred & Not Yet Due	$0	0.00%	$0	0.00%	$0	0.00%	$0	0.00%
Accrued Retrospective Premiums	$0	0.00%	$0	0.00%	$0	0.00%	$0	0.00%
Reinsurance:								
Amounts Recoverable from Reinsurers	$0	0.00%	$0	0.00%	$0	0.00%	$706,358	0.11%
Funds Held by or Deposited with Reinsured Companies	$0	0.00%	$0	0.00%	$0	0.00%	$0	0.00%
Other Amounts Receivable Under Reinsurance Contracts	$0	0.00%	$0	0.00%	$0	0.00%	$0	0.00%
Amounts Receivable Relating to Uninsured Plans	$0	0.00%	$0	0.00%	$0	0.00%	$0	0.00%
Current Federal and Foreign Income Tax Recoverable and Interest Thereon	$5,417	0.00%	$23,035,579	1.44%	$306,331	1.31%	$5,448,393	0.84%
Net Deferred Tax Asset	$2,146,936	1.92%	$27,471,732	1.72%	$354,988	1.52%	$6,737,451	1.04%
Guaranty Funds Receivable or on Deposit	$0	0.00%	$0	0.00%	$0	0.00%	$0	0.00%
Electronic Data Processing Equipment and Software	$1,112,738	1.00%	$6,235,480	0.39%	$28,630	0.12%	$1,750,537	0.27%
Furniture and Equipment, Including Health Care Delivery Assets	$0	0.00%	$0	0.00%	$0	0.00%	$0	0.00%
Net Adjustment in Assets and Liabilities Due to Foreign Exchange Rates	$0	0.00%	$0	0.00%	$0	0.00%	$0	0.00%
Receivables from Parent, Subsidiaries and Affiliates	$136,824	0.12%	$59,151,041	3.71%	$534,074	2.28%	$85,453	0.01%
Health Care	$0	0.00%	$0	0.00%	$0	0.00%	$0	0.00%
Aggregate Write-Ins for Other than Invest Assets	$110,911	0.10%	$36,832,482	2.31%	$46,194	0.20%	$0	0.00%
Total Assets Excluding Separate Accounts, Segregated Accounts & Protected Cell Accounts	$111,827,898	100.00%	$1,595,017,126	100.00%	$23,386,522	100.00%	$650,017,179	100.00%
From Separate Accounts, Segregated Accounts and Protected Cell Accounts	$0	0.00%	$0	0.00%	$0	0.00%	$0	0.00%
TOTAL	$111,827,898	100.00%	$1,595,017,126	100.00%	$23,386,522	100.00%	$650,017,179	100.00%

LIABILITIES	Group Value	% of Total	Group Value	% of Total	Group Value	% of Total	Group Value	% of Total
Known Claims Reserve	$3,927,050	3.51%	$165,038,543	10.35%	$3,274,516	14.00%	$73,124,745	11.25%
Statutory Premium Reserve	$39,878,656	35.66%	$826,022,242	51.79%	$11,001,692	47.04%	$356,117,758	54.79%
Aggregate of Other Reserves Required by Law	$0	0.00%	$0	0.00%	$0	0.00%	$70,000	0.01%
Supplemental Reserve	$0	0.00%	$9,601,900	0.60%	$0	0.00%	$0	0.00%
Commissions, Brokerage & Other Charges Due or Accrued to Attorneys, Agents & Real Estate Brokers	$250,408	0.22%	$0	0.00%	$0	0.00%	$640,912	0.10%
Other Expenses (Excluding Taxes, Licenses and Fees)	$1,594,700	1.43%	$45,506,614	2.85%	$458,772	1.96%	$15,519,879	2.39%
Taxes, Licenses and Fees (Excluding Federal and Foreign Income Taxes)	$39,014	0.03%	$8,427,963	0.53%	$385,051	1.65%	$1,366,218	0.21%
Current Federal and Foreign Income Taxes	$1,924,548	1.72%	$364,021	0.02%	$0	0.00%	$194,028	0.03%
Net Deferred Tax Liability	$0	0.00%	$0	0.00%	$0	0.00%	$0	0.00%
Borrowed Money and Interest Thereon	$18,265	0.02%	$5,250,000	0.33%	$0	0.00%	$0	0.00%
Dividends Declared and Unpaid	$0	0.00%	$0	0.00%	$0	0.00%	$0	0.00%
Premiums and Other Consideration Received in Advance	$0	0.00%	$5,841,248	0.37%	$533,079	2.28%	$2,707,181	0.42%
Unearned Interest and Real Estate Income Received in Advance	$0	0.00%	$0	0.00%	$0	0.00%	$0	0.00%
Funds Held by Company Under Reinsurance Treaties	$0	0.00%	$0	0.00%	$0	0.00%	$0	0.00%
Amounts Withheld or Retained by Company for Accounts of Others	$14,478	0.01%	$0	0.00%	$0	0.00%	$116,400	0.02%
Provision for Unauthorized Reinsurance	$0	0.00%	$0	0.00%	$0	0.00%	$0	0.00%
Net Adjustment in Assets and Liabilities Due to Foreign Exchange Rates	$0	0.00%	$0	0.00%	$0	0.00%	$0	0.00%
Drafts Outstanding	$0	0.00%	$0	0.00%	$0	0.00%	$0	0.00%
Payable to Parent, Subsidiaries and Affiliates	$244,642	0.22%	$35,361,209	2.22%	$17,806	0.08%	$12,331,328	1.90%
Payable for Securities	$0	0.00%	$284,828	0.02%	$0	0.00%	$0	0.00%
Aggregate Write-Ins for Other Liabilities	$8,292,900	7.42%	$53,170,773	3.33%	$0	0.00%	$14,134,286	2.17%
Total Liabilities	$56,184,661	50.24%	$1,154,869,341	72.40%	$15,670,916	67.01%	$476,322,735	73.28%
Aggregate Write-Ins for Special Surplus Funds	$0	0.00%	$0	0.00%	$0	0.00%	$0	0.00%
Common Capital Stock	$3,000,000	2.68%	$19,960,991	1.25%	$1,001,123	4.28%	$4,526,532	0.70%
Preferred Capital Stock	$0	0.00%	$0	0.00%	$0	0.00%	$0	0.00%
Aggregate Write-Ins for Other than Special Surplus Funds	$0	0.00%	$0	0.00%	$0	0.00%	$0	0.00%
Surplus Notes	$0	0.00%	$0	0.00%	$0	0.00%	$0	0.00%
Gross Paid In and Contributed Surplus	$1,825,610	1.63%	$169,690,914	10.64%	$5,975,338	25.55%	$90,024,788	13.85%
Unassigned Funds (Surplus)	$50,817,627	45.44%	$250,495,880	15.70%	$739,145	3.16%	$79,237,078	12.19%
Less Treasury Stock, at Cost:								
Shares Common	$0	0.00%	$0	0.00%	$0	0.00%	$93,954	0.01%
Shares Preferred	$0	0.00%	$0	0.00%	$0	0.00%	$0	0.00%
Surplus as Regards Policyholders	$55,643,237	49.76%	$440,147,785	27.60%	$7,715,606	32.99%	$173,694,444	26.72%
TOTAL	$111,827,898	100.00%	$1,595,017,126	100.00%	$23,386,522	100.00%	$650,017,179	100.00%

A.2 Balance Sheet - By NAIC Group

ASSETS	RELIANT HOLDING		STEWART		TRANSUNION		UNAFFILIATED COMPANIES	
	Group Value	% of Total	Group Value	% of Total	Group Value	% of Total	Group Value	% of Total
Bonds	$5,836,227	55.32%	$547,643,663	47.19%	$13,782,657	52.32%	$73,575,823	22.67%
Stocks:								
Preferred Stocks	$0	0.00%	$204,912	0.02%	$0	0.00%	$80,320	0.02%
Common Stocks	$391,245	3.71%	$448,511,788	38.65%	$2,188,800	8.31%	$24,900,860	7.67%
Mortgage Loans on Real Estate:								
First Liens	$200,000	1.90%	$1,575,077	0.14%	$0	0.00%	$561,468	0.17%
Other than First Liens	$0	0.00%	$0	0.00%	$0	0.00%	$0	0.00%
Real Estate:								
Properties Occupied by the Company	$0	0.00%	$1,359,386	0.12%	$0	0.00%	$2,727,453	0.84%
Properties Held for the Production of Income	$0	0.00%	$0	0.00%	$0	0.00%	$347,961	0.11%
Properties Held for Sale	$14,252	0.14%	$1,504,067	0.13%	$15,000	0.06%	$560,800	0.17%
Cash, Cash Equivalents and Short-Term Investments	$1,078,150	10.22%	$80,057,287	6.90%	$9,845,976	37.37%	$193,900,135	59.74%
Contract Loans	$0	0.00%	$0	0.00%	$0	0.00%	$0	0.00%
Other Invested Assets	$75,869	0.72%	$2,185,497	0.19%	$0	0.00%	$2,069,774	0.64%
Receivables for Securities	$0	0.00%	$0	0.00%	$0	0.00%	$23,673	0.01%
Aggregate Write-Ins for Invested Assets	$0	0.00%	$0	0.00%	$0	0.00%	$0	0.00%
Subtotals, Cash and Invested Assets	$7,595,743	72.00%	$1,083,041,677	93.33%	$25,832,433	98.06%	$298,748,267	92.04%
Title Plants	$542,050	5.14%	$5,722,039	0.49%	$114,022	0.43%	$5,515,332	1.70%
Investment Income Due and Accrued	$119,098	1.13%	$8,223,183	0.71%	$210,979	0.80%	$1,291,937	0.40%
Premiums and Considerations:								
Uncollected Premiums and Agents' Balances in the Course of Collection	$314,244	2.98%	$36,852,529	3.18%	$5,121	0.02%	$8,803,853	2.71%
Deferred Premiums, Agents' Balances & Installments Booked but Deferred & Not Yet Due	$0	0.00%	$0	0.00%	$0	0.00%	$0	0.00%
Accrued Retrospective Premiums	$0	0.00%	$0	0.00%	$0	0.00%	$0	0.00%
Reinsurance:								
Amounts Recoverable from Reinsurers	$0	0.00%	$0	0.00%	$0	0.00%	$0	0.00%
Funds Held by or Deposited with Reinsured Companies	$0	0.00%	$0	0.00%	$0	0.00%	$0	0.00%
Other Amounts Receivable Under Reinsurance Contracts	$0	0.00%	$578,381	0.05%	$0	0.00%	$0	0.00%
Amounts Receivable Relating to Uninsured Plans	$0	0.00%	$0	0.00%	$0	0.00%	$0	0.00%
Current Federal and Foreign Income Tax Recoverable and Interest Thereon	$0	0.00%	$11,548,025	1.00%	$51,421	0.20%	$3,796,913	1.17%
Net Deferred Tax Asset	$225,434	2.14%	$9,752,537	0.84%	$124,272	0.47%	$2,963,603	0.91%
Guaranty Funds Receivable or on Deposit	$0	0.00%	$0	0.00%	$0	0.00%	$25,760	0.01%
Electronic Data Processing Equipment and Software	$33,172	0.31%	$978,551	0.08%	$3,637	0.01%	$738,567	0.23%
Furniture and Equipment, Including Health Care Delivery Assets	$0	0.00%	$414,256	0.04%	$0	0.00%	$60,870	0.02%
Net Adjustment in Assets and Liabilities Due to Foreign Exchange Rates	$0	0.00%	$0	0.00%	$0	0.00%	$0	0.00%
Receivables from Parent, Subsidiaries and Affiliates	$825,624	7.83%	$1,940,128	0.17%	$0	0.00%	$1,282,966	0.40%
Health Care	$0	0.00%	$266,058	0.02%	$0	0.00%	$4,531	0.00%
Aggregate Write-Ins for Other than Invest Assets	$894,426	8.48%	$1,159,099	0.10%	$2,664	0.01%	$452,218	0.14%
Total Assets Excluding Separate Accounts, Segregated Accounts & Protected Cell Accounts	$10,549,791	100.00%	$1,160,476,463	100.00%	$26,344,549	100.00%	$323,684,817	99.72%
From Separate Accounts, Segregated Accounts and Protected Cell Accounts	$0	0.00%	$0	0.00%	$0	0.00%	$914,014	0.28%
TOTAL	$10,549,791	100.00%	$1,160,476,463	100.00%	$26,344,549	100.00%	$324,598,831	100.00%

LIABILITIES	Group Value	% of Total	Group Value	% of Total	Group Value	% of Total	Group Value	% of Total
Known Claims Reserve	$279,447	2.65%	$102,362,330	8.82%	$936,592	3.56%	$10,994,945	3.39%
Statutory Premium Reserve	$7,345,174	69.62%	$467,412,670	40.28%	$6,736,176	25.57%	$111,450,245	34.33%
Aggregate of Other Reserves Required by Law	$200,000	1.90%	$0	0.00%	$0	0.00%	$1,308,874	0.40%
Supplemental Reserve	$0	0.00%	$241,047	0.02%	$0	0.00%	$2,491,741	0.77%
Commissions, Brokerage & Other Charges Due or Accrued to Attorneys, Agents & Real Estate Brokers	$0	0.00%	$0	0.00%	$15,867	0.06%	$283,257	0.09%
Other Expenses (Excluding Taxes, Licenses and Fees)	$235,053	2.23%	$24,484,893	2.11%	$677,305	2.57%	$12,107,013	3.73%
Taxes, Licenses and Fees (Excluding Federal and Foreign Income Taxes)	$42,761	0.41%	$4,978,727	0.43%	$45,303	0.17%	$1,403,607	0.43%
Current Federal and Foreign Income Taxes	$0	0.00%	$4,424,037	0.38%	$0	0.00%	$4,225,130	1.30%
Net Deferred Tax Liability	$0	0.00%	$0	0.00%	$0	0.00%	$13,222	0.00%
Borrowed Money and Interest Thereon	$0	0.00%	$0	0.00%	$0	0.00%	$1,743,638	0.54%
Dividends Declared and Unpaid	$0	0.00%	$2,000,000	0.17%	$0	0.00%	$4,082	0.00%
Premiums and Other Consideration Received in Advance	$0	0.00%	$1,819,530	0.16%	$0	0.00%	$472,943	0.15%
Unearned Interest and Real Estate Income Received in Advance	$0	0.00%	$0	0.00%	$0	0.00%	$12,950	0.00%
Funds Held by Company Under Reinsurance Treaties	$0	0.00%	$554,242	0.05%	$0	0.00%	$167,960	0.05%
Amounts Withheld or Retained by Company for Accounts of Others	$0	0.00%	$0	0.00%	$0	0.00%	$891,966	0.27%
Provision for Unauthorized Reinsurance	$0	0.00%	$0	0.00%	$0	0.00%	$0	0.00%
Net Adjustment in Assets and Liabilities Due to Foreign Exchange Rates	$0	0.00%	$10,304,820	0.89%	$0	0.00%	$0	0.00%
Drafts Outstanding	$0	0.00%	$0	0.00%	$0	0.00%	$0	0.00%
Payable to Parent, Subsidiaries and Affiliates	$0	0.00%	$6,470,729	0.56%	$4,003,930	15.20%	$2,897,478	0.89%
Payable for Securities	$0	0.00%	$0	0.00%	$0	0.00%	$0	0.00%
Aggregate Write-Ins for Other Liabilities	$0	0.00%	$2,962,439	0.26%	$0	0.00%	$264,314	0.08%
Total Liabilities	$8,102,435	76.80%	$628,015,464	54.12%	$12,415,173	47.13%	$150,733,365	46.44%
Aggregate Write-Ins for Special Surplus Funds	$0	0.00%	$501,406	0.04%	$0	0.00%	$0	0.00%
Common Capital Stock	$2,250,000	21.33%	$11,465,425	0.99%	$2,500,000	9.49%	$21,593,530	6.65%
Preferred Capital Stock	$0	0.00%	$5,150	0.00%	$0	0.00%	$464,669	0.14%
Aggregate Write-Ins for Other than Special Surplus Funds	$0	0.00%	$0	0.00%	$0	0.00%	($65,000)	(0.02)%
Surplus Notes	$0	0.00%	$0	0.00%	$0	0.00%	$2,898,000	0.89%
Gross Paid In and Contributed Surplus	$12,648,179	119.89%	$146,050,927	12.59%	$21,335,400	80.99%	$47,401,916	14.60%
Unassigned Funds (Surplus)	($12,450,823)	(118.02)%	$375,291,334	32.34%	($9,906,024)	(37.60)%	$105,149,414	32.39%
Less Treasury Stock, at Cost:								
Shares Common	$0	0.00%	$137,543	0.01%	$0	0.00%	$3,577,058	1.10%
Shares Preferred	$0	0.00%	$715,700	0.06%	$0	0.00%	$0	0.00%
Surplus as Regards Policyholders	$2,447,356	23.20%	$532,460,999	45.88%	$13,929,376	52.87%	$173,865,471	53.56%
TOTAL	$10,549,791	100.00%	$1,160,476,463	100.00%	$26,344,549	100.00%	$324,598,836	100.00%

A.3 BALANCE SHEET
- BY INDIVIDUAL UNDERWRITER

2

A.3 Balance Sheet - By Individual Underwriter

ASSETS	ALAMO Company Value	% of Total	ALLIANCE Company Value	% of Total	ALLIANT Company Value	% of Total	AMERICAN EAGLE Company Value	% of Total
Bonds	$41,313,443	85.37%	$0	0.00%	$2,637,454	68.14%	$426,472	20.08%
Stocks:								
Preferred Stocks	$0	0.00%	$0	0.00%	$0	0.00%	$0	0.00%
Common Stocks	$725,821	1.50%	$0	0.00%	$0	0.00%	$0	0.00%
Mortgage Loans on Real Estate:								
First Liens	$0	0.00%	$0	0.00%	$0	0.00%	$0	0.00%
Other than First Liens	$0	0.00%	$0	0.00%	$0	0.00%	$0	0.00%
Real Estate:								
Properties Occupied by the Company	$0	0.00%	$0	0.00%	$0	0.00%	$0	0.00%
Properties Held for the Production of Income	$0	0.00%	$0	0.00%	$0	0.00%	$0	0.00%
Properties Held for Sale	$89,700	0.19%	$0	0.00%	$0	0.00%	$0	0.00%
Cash, Cash Equivalents and Short-Term Investments	$1,741,063	3.60%	$3,700,368	99.81%	$750,111	19.38%	$593,123	27.93%
Contract Loans	$0	0.00%	$0	0.00%	$0	0.00%	$0	0.00%
Other Invested Assets	$0	0.00%	$0	0.00%	$0	0.00%	$0	0.00%
Receivables for Securities	$146,953	0.30%	$0	0.00%	$0	0.00%	$0	0.00%
Aggregate Write-Ins for Invested Assets	$0	0.00%	$0	0.00%	$0	0.00%	$0	0.00%
Subtotals, Cash and Invested Assets	$44,016,980	90.95%	$3,700,368	99.81%	$3,387,565	87.52%	$1,019,595	48.02%
Title Plants	$1,685,119	3.48%	$0	0.00%	$0	0.00%	$915,000	43.09%
Investment Income Due and Accrued	$492,233	1.02%	$2,790	0.08%	$40,882	1.06%	$0	0.00%
Premiums and Considerations:								
Uncollected Premiums and Agents' Balances in the Course of Collection	$516,348	1.07%	$0	0.00%	$427,076	11.03%	$135,200	6.37%
Deferred Premiums, Agents' Balances & Installments Booked but Deferred & Not Yet Due	$0	0.00%	$0	0.00%	$0	0.00%	$0	0.00%
Accrued Retrospective Premiums	$0	0.00%	$0	0.00%	$0	0.00%	$0	0.00%
Reinsurance:								
Amounts Recoverable from Reinsurers	$0	0.00%	$0	0.00%	$0	0.00%	$0	0.00%
Funds Held by or Deposited with Reinsured Companies	$0	0.00%	$0	0.00%	$0	0.00%	$0	0.00%
Other Amounts Receivable Under Reinsurance Contracts	$0	0.00%	$0	0.00%	$0	0.00%	$0	0.00%
Amounts Receivable Relating to Uninsured Plans	$0	0.00%	$0	0.00%	$0	0.00%	$0	0.00%
Current Federal and Foreign Income Tax Recoverable and Interest Thereon	$1,234,306	2.55%	$0	0.00%	$0	0.00%	$0	0.00%
Net Deferred Tax Asset	$451,127	0.93%	$4,167	0.11%	$0	0.00%	$18,723	0.88%
Guaranty Funds Receivable or on Deposit	$0	0.00%	$0	0.00%	$0	0.00%	$0	0.00%
Electronic Data Processing Equipment and Software	$0	0.00%	$0	0.00%	$14,798	0.38%	$20,331	0.96%
Furniture and Equipment, Including Health Care Delivery Assets	$0	0.00%	$0	0.00%	$0	0.00%	$0	0.00%
Net Adjustment in Assets and Liabilities Due to Foreign Exchange Rates	$0	0.00%	$0	0.00%	$0	0.00%	$0	0.00%
Receivables from Parent, Subsidiaries and Affiliates	$0	0.00%	$0	0.00%	$0	0.00%	$14,522	0.68%
Health Care	$0	0.00%	$0	0.00%	$0	0.00%	$0	0.00%
Aggregate Write-Ins for Other than Invest Assets	$0	0.00%	$0	0.00%	$395	0.01%	$0	0.00%
Total Assets Excluding Separate Accounts, Segregated Accounts & Protected Cell Accounts	$48,396,113	100.00%	$3,707,325	100.00%	$3,870,716	100.00%	$2,123,371	100.00%
From Separate Accounts, Segregated Accounts and Protected Cell Accounts	$0	0.00%	$0	0.00%	$0	0.00%	$0	0.00%
TOTAL	$48,396,113	100.00%	$3,707,325	100.00%	$3,870,716	100.00%	$2,123,371	100.00%

LIABILITIES	ALAMO Company Value	% of Total	ALLIANCE Company Value	% of Total	ALLIANT Company Value	% of Total	AMERICAN EAGLE Company Value	% of Total
Known Claims Reserve (See Sec. 5, C.9)	$1,953,953	4.04%	$52,774	1.42%	$694,330	17.94%	$8,000	0.38%
Statutory Premium Reserve (See Sec. 5, C.9)	$17,966,320	37.12%	$283,953	7.66%	$522,995	13.51%	$416,000	19.59%
Aggregate of Other Reserves Required by Law (See Sec. 5, C.9)	$0	0.00%	$0	0.00%	$0	0.00%	$0	0.00%
Supplemental Reserve (See Sec. 5, C.9)	$0	0.00%	$241,047	6.50%	$50,000	1.29%	$0	0.00%
Commissions, Brokerage & Other Charges Due or Accrued to Attorneys, Agents & Real Estate Brokers	$0	0.00%	$0	0.00%	$0	0.00%	$0	0.00%
Other Expenses (Excluding Taxes, Licenses and Fees)	$622,114	1.29%	$0	0.00%	$221,481	5.72%	$342,710	16.14%
Taxes, Licenses and Fees (Excluding Federal and Foreign Income Taxes)	$475,149	0.98%	$3,037	0.08%	$0	0.00%	$455	0.02%
Current Federal and Foreign Income Taxes	$0	0.00%	$18,846	0.51%	$0	0.00%	$449,725	21.18%
Net Deferred Tax Liability	$0	0.00%	$0	0.00%	$0	0.00%	$0	0.00%
Borrowed Money and Interest Thereon	$0	0.00%	$0	0.00%	$0	0.00%	$185,619	8.74%
Dividends Declared and Unpaid	$0	0.00%	$0	0.00%	$0	0.00%	$4,082	0.19%
Premiums and Other Consideration Received in Advance	$0	0.00%	$0	0.00%	$0	0.00%	$0	0.00%
Unearned Interest and Real Estate Income Received in Advance	$0	0.00%	$0	0.00%	$0	0.00%	$0	0.00%
Funds Held by Company Under Reinsurance Treaties	$0	0.00%	$0	0.00%	$0	0.00%	$0	0.00%
Amounts Withheld or Retained by Company for Accounts of Others	$3,937	0.01%	$0	0.00%	$0	0.00%	$12	0.00%
Provision for Unauthorized Reinsurance	$0	0.00%	$0	0.00%	$0	0.00%	$0	0.00%
Net Adjustment in Assets and Liabilities Due to Foreign Exchange Rates	$0	0.00%	$0	0.00%	$0	0.00%	$0	0.00%
Drafts Outstanding	$0	0.00%	$0	0.00%	$0	0.00%	$0	0.00%
Payable to Parent, Subsidiaries and Affiliates	$1,148,045	2.37%	$0	0.00%	$0	0.00%	$0	0.00%
Payable for Securities	$0	0.00%	$0	0.00%	$0	0.00%	$0	0.00%
Aggregate Write-Ins for Other Liabilities	$0	0.00%	$5	0.00%	$27,357	0.71%	$0	0.00%
Total Liabilities (See Sec. 5, B.3)	$22,169,518	45.81%	$599,662	16.18%	$1,516,163	39.17%	$1,406,603	66.24%
Aggregate Write-Ins for Special Surplus Funds	$0	0.00%	$0	0.00%	$0	0.00%	$0	0.00%
Common Capital Stock	$3,103,590	6.41%	$15,425	0.42%	$1,000,000	25.84%	$500,000	23.55%
Preferred Capital Stock	$0	0.00%	$5,150	0.14%	$0	0.00%	$0	0.00%
Aggregate Write-Ins for Other than Special Surplus Funds	$0	0.00%	$0	0.00%	$0	0.00%	$0	0.00%
Surplus Notes	$0	0.00%	$0	0.00%	$600,000	15.50%	$0	0.00%
Gross Paid In and Contributed Surplus	$1,186,658	2.45%	$3,586,230	96.73%	$2,029,828	52.44%	$375,000	17.66%
Unassigned Funds (Surplus)	$21,936,344	45.33%	$354,101	9.55%	($1,275,275)	(32.95)%	($158,232)	(7.45)%
Less Treasury Stock, at Cost:								
Shares Common	$0	0.00%	$137,543	3.71%	$0	0.00%	$0	0.00%
Shares Preferred	$0	0.00%	$715,700	19.31%	$0	0.00%	$0	0.00%
Surplus as Regards Policyholders (See Sec. 5, B.6, B.7, C.9, C.11)	$26,226,592	54.19%	$3,107,663	83.82%	$2,354,553	60.83%	$716,768	33.76%
TOTAL	$48,396,110	100.00%	$3,707,325	100.00%	$3,870,716	100.00%	$2,123,371	100.00%

A.3 Balance Sheet - By Individual Underwriter

ASSETS	AMERICAN GUARANTY Company Value	% of Total	AMERICAN LAND & AIRCRAFT Company Value	% of Total	AMERICAN SECURITY Company Value	% of Total	ARKANSAS TIC Company Value	% of Total
Bonds	$10,733,232	75.14%	$0	0.00%	$0	0.00%	$0	0.00%
Stocks:								
Preferred Stocks	$0	0.00%	$0	0.00%	$0	0.00%	$0	0.00%
Common Stocks	$0	0.00%	$0	0.00%	$0	0.00%	$0	0.00%
Mortgage Loans on Real Estate:								
First Liens	$0	0.00%	$0	0.00%	$0	0.00%	$0	0.00%
Other than First Liens	$0	0.00%	$0	0.00%	$0	0.00%	$0	0.00%
Real Estate:								
Properties Occupied by the Company	$651,088	4.56%	$0	0.00%	$0	0.00%	$0	0.00%
Properties Held for the Production of Income	$0	0.00%	$0	0.00%	$0	0.00%	$0	0.00%
Properties Held for Sale	$0	0.00%	$0	0.00%	$0	0.00%	$0	0.00%
Cash, Cash Equivalents and Short-Term Investments	$2,575,221	18.03%	$804,060	99.59%	$8,480,294	97.69%	$4,708,359	94.37%
Contract Loans	$0	0.00%	$0	0.00%	$0	0.00%	$0	0.00%
Other Invested Assets	$0	0.00%	$0	0.00%	$0	0.00%	$0	0.00%
Receivables for Securities	$0	0.00%	$0	0.00%	$0	0.00%	$0	0.00%
Aggregate Write-Ins for Invested Assets	$0	0.00%	$0	0.00%	$0	0.00%	$0	0.00%
Subtotals, Cash and Invested Assets	$13,959,541	97.73%	$804,060	99.59%	$8,480,294	97.69%	$4,708,359	94.37%
Title Plants	$20,000	0.14%	$0	0.00%	$179,928	2.07%	$0	0.00%
Investment Income Due and Accrued	$154,678	1.08%	$2,465	0.31%	$0	0.00%	$0	0.00%
Premiums and Considerations:								
Uncollected Premiums and Agents' Balances in the Course of Collection	$1,737	0.01%	$0	0.00%	$0	0.00%	$224,638	4.50%
Deferred Premiums, Agents' Balances & Installments Booked but Deferred & Not Yet Due	$0	0.00%	$0	0.00%	$0	0.00%	$0	0.00%
Accrued Retrospective Premiums	$0	0.00%	$0	0.00%	$0	0.00%	$0	0.00%
Reinsurance:								
Amounts Recoverable from Reinsurers	$0	0.00%	$0	0.00%	$0	0.00%	$0	0.00%
Funds Held by or Deposited with Reinsured Companies	$0	0.00%	$0	0.00%	$0	0.00%	$0	0.00%
Other Amounts Receivable Under Reinsurance Contracts	$0	0.00%	$0	0.00%	$0	0.00%	$0	0.00%
Amounts Receivable Relating to Uninsured Plans	$0	0.00%	$0	0.00%	$0	0.00%	$0	0.00%
Current Federal and Foreign Income Tax Recoverable and Interest Thereon	$27,605	0.19%	$0	0.00%	$0	0.00%	$0	0.00%
Net Deferred Tax Asset	$34,932	0.24%	$0	0.00%	$0	0.00%	$26,220	0.53%
Guaranty Funds Receivable or on Deposit	$0	0.00%	$0	0.00%	$0	0.00%	$0	0.00%
Electronic Data Processing Equipment and Software	$0	0.00%	$823	0.10%	$6,657	0.08%	$0	0.00%
Furniture and Equipment, Including Health Care Delivery Assets	$0	0.00%	$0	0.00%	$0	0.00%	$0	0.00%
Net Adjustment in Assets and Liabilities Due to Foreign Exchange Rates	$0	0.00%	$0	0.00%	$0	0.00%	$0	0.00%
Receivables from Parent, Subsidiaries and Affiliates	$85,453	0.60%	$0	0.00%	$0	0.00%	$27,463	0.55%
Health Care	$0	0.00%	$0	0.00%	$0	0.00%	$0	0.00%
Aggregate Write-Ins for Other than Invest Assets	$0	0.00%	$0	0.00%	$13,600	0.16%	$2,605	0.05%
Total Assets Excluding Separate Accounts, Segregaled Accounts & Protected Cell Accounts	$14,283,946	100.00%	$807,348	100.00%	$8,680,479	100.00%	$4,989,285	100.00%
From Separate Accounts, Segregated Accounts and Protected Cell Accounts	$0	0.00%	$0	0.00%	$0	0.00%	$0	0.00%
TOTAL	$14,283,946	100.00%	$807,348	100.00%	$8,680,479	100.00%	$4,989,285	100.00%

LIABILITIES	Company Value	% of Total	Company Value	% of Total	Company Value	% of Total	Company Value	% of Total
Known Claims Reserve (See Sec. 5, C.9)	$74,000	0.52%	$0	0.00%	$0	0.00%	$316,110	6.34%
Statutory Premium Reserve (See Sec. 5, C.9)	$2,559,828	17.92%	$47,015	5.82%	$0	0.00%	$2,093,610	41.96%
Aggregate of Other Reserves Required by Law (See Sec. 5, C.9)	$0	0.00%	$0	0.00%	$0	0.00%	$0	0.00%
Supplemental Reserve (See Sec. 5, C.9)	$0	0.00%	$0	0.00%	$176,000	2.03%	$0	0.00%
Commissions, Brokerage & Other Charges Due or Accrued to Attorneys, Agents & Real Estate Brokers	$0	0.00%	$0	0.00%	$0	0.00%	$0	0.00%
Other Expenses (Excluding Taxes, Licenses and Fees)	$32,188	0.23%	$0	0.00%	$0	0.00%	$39,874	0.80%
Taxes, Licenses and Fees (Excluding Federal and Foreign Income Taxes)	$410	0.00%	$1,200	0.15%	$0	0.00%	$54,188	1.09%
Current Federal and Foreign Income Taxes	$0	0.00%	$0	0.00%	$0	0.00%	$87,653	1.76%
Net Deferred Tax Liability	$0	0.00%	$0	0.00%	$0	0.00%	$0	0.00%
Borrowed Money and Interest Thereon	$0	0.00%	$0	0.00%	$0	0.00%	$0	0.00%
Dividends Declared and Unpaid	$0	0.00%	$0	0.00%	$0	0.00%	$0	0.00%
Premiums and Other Consideration Received in Advance	$0	0.00%	$0	0.00%	$0	0.00%	$0	0.00%
Unearned Interest and Real Estate Income Received in Advance	$0	0.00%	$0	0.00%	$0	0.00%	$0	0.00%
Funds Held by Company Under Reinsurance Treaties	$0	0.00%	$16,617	2.06%	$0	0.00%	$0	0.00%
Amounts Withheld or Retained by Company for Accounts of Others	$0	0.00%	$0	0.00%	$0	0.00%	$0	0.00%
Provision for Unauthorized Reinsurance	$0	0.00%	$0	0.00%	$0	0.00%	$0	0.00%
Net Adjustment in Assets and Liabilities Due to Foreign Exchange Rates	$0	0.00%	$0	0.00%	$0	0.00%	$0	0.00%
Drafts Outstanding	$0	0.00%	$0	0.00%	$0	0.00%	$0	0.00%
Payable to Parent, Subsidiaries and Affiliates	$109,939	0.77%	$0	0.00%	$0	0.00%	$6,501	0.13%
Payable for Securities	$0	0.00%	$0	0.00%	$0	0.00%	$0	0.00%
Aggregate Write-Ins for Other Liabilities	$0	0.00%	$0	0.00%	$0	0.00%	$2,826	0.06%
Total Liabilities (See Sec. 5, B.3)	$2,776,365	19.44%	$64,832	8.03%	$176,000	2.03%	$2,600,762	52.13%
Aggregate Write-Ins for Special Surplus Funds	$0	0.00%	$0	0.00%	$0	0.00%	$0	0.00%
Common Capital Stock	$2,000,000	14.00%	$500,000	61.93%	$150,000	1.73%	$100,000	2.00%
Preferred Capital Stock	$0	0.00%	$0	0.00%	$0	0.00%	$0	0.00%
Aggregate Write-Ins for Other than Special Surplus Funds	$0	0.00%	$0	0.00%	$0	0.00%	$0	0.00%
Surplus Notes	$0	0.00%	$0	0.00%	$0	0.00%	$0	0.00%
Gross Paid In and Contributed Surplus	$2,498,390	17.49%	$250,000	30.97%	$75,000	0.86%	$145,000	2.91%
Unassigned Funds (Surplus)	$7,009,191	49.07%	($7,484)	(0.93)%	$8,279,479	95.38%	$2,143,523	42.96%
Less Treasury Stock, at Cost:								
Shares Common	$0	0.00%	$0	0.00%	$0	0.00%	$0	0.00%
Shares Preferred	$0	0.00%	$0	0.00%	$0	0.00%	$0	0.00%
Surplus as Regards Policyholders (See Sec. 5, B.6, B.7, C.9, C.11)	$11,507,581	80.56%	$742,516	91.97%	$8,504,479	97.97%	$2,388,523	47.87%
TOTAL	$14,283,946	100.00%	$807,348	100.00%	$8,680,479	100.00%	$4,989,285	100.00%

A.3 Balance Sheet - By Individual Underwriter

	ARSENAL		ATTORNEYS TGF (CO)		ATTORNEYS TGF (IL)		ATTORNEYS TIF (FL)	
ASSETS	Company Value	% of Total	Company Value	% of Total	Company Value	% of Total	Company Value	% of Total
Bonds	$0	0.00%	$924,617	19.24%	$1,022,960	3.45%	$102,729,910	31.68%
Stocks:								
Preferred Stocks	$0	0.00%	$0	0.00%	$0	0.00%	$6,122,789	1.89%
Common Stocks	$0	0.00%	$0	0.00%	$11,221,046	37.86%	$130,278,505	40.17%
Mortgage Loans on Real Estate:								
First Liens	$0	0.00%	$0	0.00%	$0	0.00%	$192,847	0.06%
Other than First Liens	$0	0.00%	$0	0.00%	$0	0.00%	$0	0.00%
Real Estate:								
Properties Occupied by the Company	$0	0.00%	$0	0.00%	$1,036,045	3.50%	$7,290,739	2.25%
Properties Held for the Production of Income	$0	0.00%	$0	0.00%	$0	0.00%	$0	0.00%
Properties Held for Sale	$0	0.00%	$1,437,390	29.91%	$100,000	0.34%	$4,925,970	1.52%
Cash, Cash Equivalents and Short-Term Investments	$593,238	99.91%	$1,214,186	25.27%	$12,615,446	42.56%	$16,401,367	5.06%
Contract Loans	$0	0.00%	$0	0.00%	$0	0.00%	$0	0.00%
Other Invested Assets	$0	0.00%	$1,500	0.03%	$171	0.00%	$0	0.00%
Receivables for Securities	$0	0.00%	$0	0.00%	$0	0.00%	$647,429	0.20%
Aggregate Write-Ins for Invested Assets	$0	0.00%	$0	0.00%	$0	0.00%	$0	0.00%
Subtotals, Cash and Invested Assets	$593,238	99.91%	$3,577,693	74.45%	$25,995,668	87.71%	$268,589,556	82.82%
Title Plants	$0	0.00%	$0	0.00%	$60,000	0.20%	$4,637,038	1.43%
Investment Income Due and Accrued	$0	0.00%	$7,608	0.16%	$45,525	0.15%	$1,359,972	0.42%
Premiums and Considerations:								
Uncollected Premiums and Agents' Balances in the Course of Collection	$507	0.09%	$892,080	18.56%	$211,542	0.71%	$16,962,181	5.23%
Deferred Premiums, Agents' Balances & Installments Booked but Deferred & Not Yet Due	$0	0.00%	$0	0.00%	$0	0.00%	$0	0.00%
Accrued Retrospective Premiums	$0	0.00%	$0	0.00%	$0	0.00%	$0	0.00%
Reinsurance:								
Amounts Recoverable from Reinsurers	$0	0.00%	$0	0.00%	$0	0.00%	$0	0.00%
Funds Held by or Deposited with Reinsured Companies	$0	0.00%	$0	0.00%	$0	0.00%	$0	0.00%
Other Amounts Receivable Under Reinsurance Contracts	$0	0.00%	$0	0.00%	$0	0.00%	$82,038	0.03%
Amounts Receivable Relating to Uninsured Plans	$0	0.00%	$0	0.00%	$0	0.00%	$0	0.00%
Current Federal and Foreign Income Tax Recoverable and Interest Thereon	$0	0.00%	$177,430	3.69%	$1,477,173	4.98%	$12,582,367	3.88%
Net Deferred Tax Asset	$0	0.00%	$90,069	1.87%	$878,640	2.96%	$16,513,331	5.09%
Guaranty Funds Receivable or on Deposit	$0	0.00%	$0	0.00%	$0	0.00%	$0	0.00%
Electronic Data Processing Equipment and Software	$0	0.00%	$60,583	1.26%	$263,592	0.89%	$310,492	0.10%
Furniture and Equipment, Including Health Care Delivery Assets	$0	0.00%	$0	0.00%	$0	0.00%	$0	0.00%
Net Adjustment in Assets and Liabilities Due to Foreign Exchange Rates	$0	0.00%	$0	0.00%	$0	0.00%	$0	0.00%
Receivables from Parent, Subsidiaries and Affiliates	$0	0.00%	$0	0.00%	$623,343	2.10%	$0	0.00%
Health Care	$0	0.00%	$0	0.00%	$0	0.00%	$0	0.00%
Aggregate Write-Ins for Other than Invest Assets	$0	0.00%	$0	0.00%	$83,497	0.28%	$3,267,851	1.01%
Total Assets Excluding Separate Accounts, Segregated Accounts & Protected Cell Accounts	$593,745	100.00%	$4,805,463	100.00%	$29,638,980	100.00%	$324,304,826	100.00%
From Separate Accounts, Segregated Accounts and Protected Cell Accounts	$0	0.00%	$0	0.00%	$0	0.00%	$0	0.00%
TOTAL	$593,745	100.00%	$4,805,463	100.00%	$29,638,980	100.00%	$324,304,826	100.00%

	Company Value	% of Total	Company Value	% of Total	Company Value	% of Total	Company Value	% of Total
LIABILITIES								
Known Claims Reserve (See Sec. 5, C.9)	$0	0.00%	$434,236	9.04%	$2,124,994	7.17%	$41,914,686	12.92%
Statutory Premium Reserve (See Sec. 5, C.9)	$50,000	8.42%	$1,834,898	38.18%	$7,963,611	26.87%	$120,815,744	37.25%
Aggregate of Other Reserves Required by Law (See Sec. 5, C.9)	$0	0.00%	$0	0.00%	$0	0.00%	$0	0.00%
Supplemental Reserve (See Sec. 5, C.9)	$0	0.00%	$362,511	7.54%	$1,892,395	6.38%	$0	0.00%
Commissions, Brokerage & Other Charges Due or Accrued to Attorneys, Agents & Real Estate Brokers	$0	0.00%	$0	0.00%	$0	0.00%	$0	0.00%
Other Expenses (Excluding Taxes, Licenses and Fees)	$0	0.00%	$123,938	2.58%	$7,877,398	26.58%	$9,309,089	2.87%
Taxes, Licenses and Fees (Excluding Federal and Foreign Income Taxes)	$0	0.00%	$3,551	0.07%	$0	0.00%	$602,501	0.19%
Current Federal and Foreign Income Taxes	$0	0.00%	$0	0.00%	$0	0.00%	$0	0.00%
Net Deferred Tax Liability	$0	0.00%	$0	0.00%	$0	0.00%	$0	0.00%
Borrowed Money and Interest Thereon	$0	0.00%	$0	0.00%	$0	0.00%	$0	0.00%
Dividends Declared and Unpaid	$0	0.00%	$0	0.00%	$0	0.00%	$0	0.00%
Premiums and Other Consideration Received in Advance	$0	0.00%	$19,853	0.41%	$14,493	0.05%	$0	0.00%
Unearned Interest and Real Estate Income Received in Advance	$0	0.00%	$0	0.00%	$0	0.00%	$0	0.00%
Funds Held by Company Under Reinsurance Treaties	$0	0.00%	$0	0.00%	$0	0.00%	$0	0.00%
Amounts Withheld or Retained by Company for Accounts of Others	$348	0.06%	$250,324	5.21%	$0	0.00%	$99,799	0.03%
Provision for Unauthorized Reinsurance	$0	0.00%	$0	0.00%	$0	0.00%	$0	0.00%
Net Adjustment in Assets and Liabilities Due to Foreign Exchange Rates	$0	0.00%	$0	0.00%	$0	0.00%	$0	0.00%
Drafts Outstanding	$0	0.00%	$0	0.00%	$0	0.00%	$0	0.00%
Payable to Parent, Subsidiaries and Affiliates	$59,236	9.98%	$0	0.00%	$11,613	0.04%	$0	0.00%
Payable for Securities	$0	0.00%	$0	0.00%	$0	0.00%	$421,052	0.13%
Aggregate Write-Ins for Other Liabilities	$0	0.00%	$0	0.00%	$0	0.00%	$1,314,211	0.41%
Total Liabilities (See Sec. 5, B.3)	$109,584	18.46%	$3,029,311	63.04%	$19,884,504	67.09%	$174,477,082	53.80%
Aggregate Write-Ins for Special Surplus Funds	$0	0.00%	$0	0.00%	$0	0.00%	$0	0.00%
Common Capital Stock	$500,000	84.21%	$1,321,062	27.49%	$0	0.00%	$2,000,000	0.62%
Preferred Capital Stock	$0	0.00%	$0	0.00%	$0	0.00%	$0	0.00%
Aggregate Write-Ins for Other than Special Surplus Funds	$0	0.00%	$0	0.00%	$0	0.00%	$0	0.00%
Surplus Notes	$0	0.00%	$5,650,000	117.57%	$0	0.00%	$0	0.00%
Gross Paid In and Contributed Surplus	$0	0.00%	$1,810,797	37.68%	$1,077,921	3.64%	$13,000,000	4.01%
Unassigned Funds (Surplus)	($15,839)	(2.67)%	($7,005,707)	(145.79)%	$8,676,555	29.27%	$134,827,744	41.57%
Less Treasury Stock, at Cost:								
Shares Common	$0	0.00%	$0	0.00%	$0	0.00%	$0	0.00%
Shares Preferred	$0	0.00%	$0	0.00%	$0	0.00%	$0	0.00%
Surplus as Regards Policyholders (See Sec. 5, B.6, B.7, C.9, C.11)	$484,161	81.54%	$1,776,152	36.96%	$9,754,476	32.91%	$149,827,744	46.20%
TOTAL	$593,745	100.00%	$4,805,463	100.00%	$29,638,980	100.00%	$324,304,826	100.00%

A.3 Balance Sheet - By Individual Underwriter

	BRIDGE		CENSTAR		CHICAGO T&T		CHICAGO TIC	
ASSETS	Company Value	% of Total	Company Value	% of Total	Company Value	% of Total	Company Value	% of Total
Bonds	$359,394	4.38%	$11,039,948	37.35%	$357,800,932	25.80%	$1,031,320,568	65.35%
Stocks:								
Preferred Stocks	$0	0.00%	$0	0.00%	$0	0.00%	$0	0.00%
Common Stocks	$0	0.00%	$0	0.00%	$652,683,327	47.06%	$65,145,855	4.13%
Mortgage Loans on Real Estate:								
First Liens	$0	0.00%	$0	0.00%	$0	0.00%	$20,231,215	1.28%
Other than First Liens	$0	0.00%	$0	0.00%	$0	0.00%	$0	0.00%
Real Estate:								
Properties Occupied by the Company	$0	0.00%	$0	0.00%	$0	0.00%	$298,573	0.02%
Properties Held for the Production of Income	$0	0.00%	$0	0.00%	$0	0.00%	$0	0.00%
Properties Held for Sale	$0	0.00%	$0	0.00%	$0	0.00%	$2,977,853	0.19%
Cash, Cash Equivalents and Short-Term Investments	$7,739,303	94.29%	$17,659,498	59.74%	$370,726,862	26.73%	$309,021,337	19.58%
Contract Loans	$0	0.00%	$0	0.00%	$0	0.00%	$0	0.00%
Other Invested Assets	$0	0.00%	$0	0.00%	$0	0.00%	$356,917	0.02%
Receivables for Securities	$0	0.00%	$0	0.00%	$376,589	0.03%	$346,155	0.02%
Aggregate Write-Ins for Invested Assets	$0	0.00%	$0	0.00%	$0	0.00%	$0	0.00%
Subtotals, Cash and Invested Assets	$8,098,697	98.67%	$28,699,446	97.08%	$1,381,587,710	99.61%	$1,429,698,473	90.59%
Title Plants	$0	0.00%	$0	0.00%	$0	0.00%	$38,408,467	2.43%
Investment Income Due and Accrued	$23,080	0.28%	$170,548	0.58%	$5,244,393	0.38%	$13,213,220	0.84%
Premiums and Considerations:								
Uncollected Premiums and Agents' Balances in the Course of Collection	$116	0.00%	$534,246	1.81%	$0	0.00%	$38,186,589	2.42%
Deferred Premiums, Agents' Balances & Installments Booked but Deferred & Not Yet Due	$0	0.00%	$0	0.00%	$0	0.00%	$0	0.00%
Accrued Retrospective Premiums	$0	0.00%	$0	0.00%	$0	0.00%	$0	0.00%
Reinsurance:								
Amounts Recoverable from Reinsurers	$0	0.00%	$0	0.00%	$0	0.00%	$0	0.00%
Funds Held by or Deposited with Reinsured Companies	$0	0.00%	$0	0.00%	$0	0.00%	$0	0.00%
Other Amounts Receivable Under Reinsurance Contracts	$0	0.00%	$0	0.00%	$0	0.00%	$0	0.00%
Amounts Receivable Relating to Uninsured Plans	$0	0.00%	$0	0.00%	$0	0.00%	$0	0.00%
Current Federal and Foreign Income Tax Recoverable and Interest Thereon	$69,717	0.85%	$128,594	0.43%	$0	0.00%	$0	0.00%
Net Deferred Tax Asset	$16,358	0.20%	$24,350	0.08%	$0	0.00%	$25,174,846	1.60%
Guaranty Funds Receivable or on Deposit	$0	0.00%	$0	0.00%	$0	0.00%	$0	0.00%
Electronic Data Processing Equipment and Software	$0	0.00%	$0	0.00%	$0	0.00%	$282,156	0.02%
Furniture and Equipment, Including Health Care Delivery Assets	$0	0.00%	$0	0.00%	$0	0.00%	$0	0.00%
Net Adjustment in Assets and Liabilities Due to Foreign Exchange Rates	$0	0.00%	$0	0.00%	$0	0.00%	$0	0.00%
Receivables from Parent, Subsidiaries and Affiliates	$0	0.00%	$3,457	0.01%	$0	0.00%	$33,194,492	2.10%
Health Care	$0	0.00%	$0	0.00%	$0	0.00%	$0	0.00%
Aggregate Write-Ins for Other than Invest Assets	$0	0.00%	$1,398	0.00%	$185,896	0.01%	$0	0.00%
Total Assets Excluding Separate Accounts, Segregated Accounts & Protected Cell Accounts	$8,207,968	100.00%	$29,562,039	100.00%	$1,387,017,999	100.00%	$1,578,158,243	100.00%
From Separate Accounts, Segregated Accounts and Protected Cell Accounts	$0	0.00%	$0	0.00%	$0	0.00%	$0	0.00%
TOTAL	$8,207,968	100.00%	$29,562,039	100.00%	$1,387,017,999	100.00%	$1,578,158,243	100.00%

	BRIDGE		CENSTAR		CHICAGO T&T		CHICAGO TIC	
LIABILITIES	Company Value	% of Total	Company Value	% of Total	Company Value	% of Total	Company Value	% of Total
Known Claims Reserve (See Sec. 5, C.9)	$8,466	0.10%	$93,076	0.31%	$0	0.00%	$131,009,849	8.30%
Statutory Premium Reserve (See Sec. 5, C.9)	$161,691	1.97%	$1,367,213	4.62%	$0	0.00%	$825,712,387	52.32%
Aggregate of Other Reserves Required by Law (See Sec. 5, C.9)	$0	0.00%	$0	0.00%	$0	0.00%	$0	0.00%
Supplemental Reserve (See Sec. 5, C.9)	$0	0.00%	$2,255,562	7.63%	$0	0.00%	$0	0.00%
Commissions, Brokerage & Other Charges Due or Accrued to Attorneys, Agents & Real Estate Brokers	$0	0.00%	$0	0.00%	$0	0.00%	$0	0.00%
Other Expenses (Excluding Taxes, Licenses and Fees)	$35,710	0.44%	$259,706	0.88%	$12,351,786	0.89%	$107,566,458	6.82%
Taxes, Licenses and Fees (Excluding Federal and Foreign Income Taxes)	$7,594	0.09%	$140,846	0.48%	$690,555	0.05%	$7,207,382	0.46%
Current Federal and Foreign Income Taxes	$0	0.00%	$0	0.00%	$13,284,927	0.96%	$10,469,034	0.66%
Net Deferred Tax Liability	$0	0.00%	$0	0.00%	$0	0.00%	$0	0.00%
Borrowed Money and Interest Thereon	$0	0.00%	$0	0.00%	$15,876	0.00%	$44,737	0.00%
Dividends Declared and Unpaid	$0	0.00%	$0	0.00%	$0	0.00%	$0	0.00%
Premiums and Other Consideration Received in Advance	$0	0.00%	$0	0.00%	$0	0.00%	$0	0.00%
Unearned Interest and Real Estate Income Received in Advance	$0	0.00%	$0	0.00%	$0	0.00%	$0	0.00%
Funds Held by Company Under Reinsurance Treaties	$0	0.00%	$0	0.00%	$0	0.00%	$0	0.00%
Amounts Withheld or Retained by Company for Accounts of Others	$0	0.00%	$0	0.00%	$818,846	0.06%	$5,688,902	0.36%
Provision for Unauthorized Reinsurance	$0	0.00%	$0	0.00%	$0	0.00%	$0	0.00%
Net Adjustment in Assets and Liabilities Due to Foreign Exchange Rates	$0	0.00%	$0	0.00%	$0	0.00%	$0	0.00%
Drafts Outstanding	$0	0.00%	$0	0.00%	$0	0.00%	$0	0.00%
Payable to Parent, Subsidiaries and Affiliates	$831	0.01%	$44,528	0.15%	$5,429,183	0.39%	$1,229,367	0.08%
Payable for Securities	$0	0.00%	$0	0.00%	$0	0.00%	$0	0.00%
Aggregate Write-Ins for Other Liabilities	$0	0.00%	$259,507	0.88%	$689,792,203	49.73%	$214,747,589	13.61%
Total Liabilities (See Sec. 5, B.3)	$214,292	2.61%	$4,420,438	14.95%	$722,383,376	52.08%	$1,303,675,705	82.61%
Aggregate Write-Ins for Special Surplus Funds	$0	0.00%	$0	0.00%	$0	0.00%	$0	0.00%
Common Capital Stock	$1,500,000	18.27%	$6,000,000	20.30%	$13,676,000	0.99%	$2,000,000	0.13%
Preferred Capital Stock	$0	0.00%	$0	0.00%	$0	0.00%	$0	0.00%
Aggregate Write-Ins for Other than Special Surplus Funds	$0	0.00%	$0	0.00%	$0	0.00%	$0	0.00%
Surplus Notes	$0	0.00%	$0	0.00%	$0	0.00%	$0	0.00%
Gross Paid In and Contributed Surplus	$4,823,060	58.76%	$2,450,000	8.29%	$907,836,635	65.45%	$104,916,792	6.65%
Unassigned Funds (Surplus)	$1,670,616	20.35%	$16,691,601	56.46%	($256,878,012)	(18.52)%	$167,565,746	10.62%
Less Treasury Stock, at Cost:								
Shares Common	$0	0.00%	$0	0.00%	$0	0.00%	$0	0.00%
Shares Preferred	$0	0.00%	$0	0.00%	$0	0.00%	$0	0.00%
Surplus as Regards Policyholders (See Sec. 5, B.6, B.7, C.9, C.11)	$7,993,676	97.39%	$25,141,601	85.05%	$664,634,623	47.92%	$274,482,538	17.39%
TOTAL	$8,207,968	100.00%	$29,562,039	100.00%	$1,387,017,999	100.00%	$1,578,158,243	100.00%

A.3 Balance Sheet - By Individual Underwriter

ASSETS	CHICAGO TIC (OR) Company Value	% of Total	COLUMBIAN NATIONAL Company Value	% of Total	COMMERCE Company Value	% of Total	COMMONWEALTH LAND Company Value	% of Total
Bonds	$23,231,311	83.07%	$158,930	4.36%	$4,326,755	19.41%	$523,301,582	70.22%
Stocks:								
Preferred Stocks	$0	0.00%	$0	0.00%	$0	0.00%	$8,453,506	1.13%
Common Stocks	$0	0.00%	$0	0.00%	$0	0.00%	$90,516,927	12.15%
Mortgage Loans on Real Estate:								
First Liens	$0	0.00%	$0	0.00%	$0	0.00%	$0	0.00%
Other than First Liens	$0	0.00%	$0	0.00%	$0	0.00%	$0	0.00%
Real Estate:								
Properties Occupied by the Company	$0	0.00%	$0	0.00%	$0	0.00%	$356,217	0.05%
Properties Held for the Production of Income	$0	0.00%	$0	0.00%	$0	0.00%	$0	0.00%
Properties Held for Sale	$0	0.00%	$0	0.00%	$0	0.00%	$0	0.00%
Cash, Cash Equivalents and Short-Term Investments	$3,028,961	10.83%	$3,406,579	93.54%	$16,857,473	75.62%	$32,891,679	4.41%
Contract Loans	$0	0.00%	$0	0.00%	$0	0.00%	$0	0.00%
Other Invested Assets	$160,874	0.58%	$0	0.00%	$0	0.00%	$3,603,620	0.48%
Receivables for Securities	$0	0.00%	$0	0.00%	$0	0.00%	$95,790	0.01%
Aggregate Write-Ins for Invested Assets	$0	0.00%	$0	0.00%	$0	0.00%	$0	0.00%
Subtotals, Cash and Invested Assets	$26,421,146	94.48%	$3,565,509	97.90%	$21,184,228	95.03%	$659,219,321	88.46%
Title Plants	$612,207	2.19%	$0	0.00%	$729,726	3.27%	$18,070,586	2.42%
Investment Income Due and Accrued	$298,120	1.07%	$5,036	0.14%	$23,556	0.11%	$6,367,149	0.85%
Premiums and Considerations:								
Uncollected Premiums and Agents' Balances in the Course of Collection	$143,305	0.51%	$0	0.00%	$1,665	0.01%	$13,387,083	1.80%
Deferred Premiums, Agents' Balances & Installments Booked but Deferred & Not Yet Due	$0	0.00%	$0	0.00%	$0	0.00%	$0	0.00%
Accrued Retrospective Premiums	$0	0.00%	$0	0.00%	$0	0.00%	$0	0.00%
Reinsurance:								
Amounts Recoverable from Reinsurers	$0	0.00%	$0	0.00%	$0	0.00%	$0	0.00%
Funds Held by or Deposited with Reinsured Companies	$0	0.00%	$0	0.00%	$0	0.00%	$0	0.00%
Other Amounts Receivable Under Reinsurance Contracts	$0	0.00%	$0	0.00%	$0	0.00%	$0	0.00%
Amounts Receivable Relating to Uninsured Plans	$0	0.00%	$0	0.00%	$0	0.00%	$0	0.00%
Current Federal and Foreign Income Tax Recoverable and Interest Thereon	$140,435	0.50%	$32,198	0.88%	$0	0.00%	$7,998,441	1.07%
Net Deferred Tax Asset	$349,870	1.25%	$106	0.00%	$105,211	0.47%	$8,318,245	1.12%
Guaranty Funds Receivable or on Deposit	$0	0.00%	$0	0.00%	$0	0.00%	$0	0.00%
Electronic Data Processing Equipment and Software	$0	0.00%	$0	0.00%	$0	0.00%	$439,478	0.06%
Furniture and Equipment, Including Health Care Delivery Assets	$0	0.00%	$0	0.00%	$0	0.00%	$0	0.00%
Net Adjustment in Assets and Liabilities Due to Foreign Exchange Rates	$0	0.00%	$0	0.00%	$0	0.00%	$0	0.00%
Receivables from Parent, Subsidiaries and Affiliates	$0	0.00%	$0	0.00%	$248,276	1.11%	$31,437,708	4.22%
Health Care	$0	0.00%	$0	0.00%	$0	0.00%	$0	0.00%
Aggregate Write-Ins for Other than Invest Assets	$0	0.00%	$39,160	1.08%	$0	0.00%	$0	0.00%
Total Assets Excluding Separate Accounts, Segregated Accounts & Protected Cell Accounts	$27,965,083	100.00%	$3,642,009	100.00%	$22,292,662	100.00%	$745,238,011	100.00%
From Separate Accounts, Segregated Accounts and Protected Cell Accounts	$0	0.00%	$0	0.00%	$0	0.00%	$0	0.00%
TOTAL	$27,965,083	100.00%	$3,642,009	100.00%	$22,292,662	100.00%	$745,238,011	100.00%

LIABILITIES	Company Value	% of Total	Company Value	% of Total	Company Value	% of Total	Company Value	% of Total
Known Claims Reserve (See Sec. 5, C.9)	$484,242	1.73%	$0	0.00%	$215,988	0.97%	$63,954,527	8.58%
Statutory Premium Reserve (See Sec. 5, C.9)	$10,648,750	38.08%	$0	0.00%	$11,245,480	50.44%	$361,541,447	48.51%
Aggregate of Other Reserves Required by Law (See Sec. 5, C.9)	$0	0.00%	$0	0.00%	$0	0.00%	$0	0.00%
Supplemental Reserve (See Sec. 5, C.9)	$0	0.00%	$0	0.00%	$0	0.00%	$0	0.00%
Commissions, Brokerage & Other Charges Due or Accrued to Attorneys, Agents & Real Estate Brokers	$0	0.00%	$0	0.00%	$0	0.00%	$0	0.00%
Other Expenses (Excluding Taxes, Licenses and Fees)	$1,809,149	6.47%	$111,297	3.06%	$407,982	1.83%	$14,579,261	1.96%
Taxes, Licenses and Fees (Excluding Federal and Foreign Income Taxes)	$345,230	1.23%	($7,810)	(0.21)%	$132,162	0.59%	$2,579,497	0.35%
Current Federal and Foreign Income Taxes	$0	0.00%	$0	0.00%	$1,479,138	6.64%	$0	0.00%
Net Deferred Tax Liability	$0	0.00%	$0	0.00%	$0	0.00%	$0	0.00%
Borrowed Money and Interest Thereon	$0	0.00%	$0	0.00%	$0	0.00%	$0	0.00%
Dividends Declared and Unpaid	$0	0.00%	$0	0.00%	$0	0.00%	$0	0.00%
Premiums and Other Consideration Received in Advance	$0	0.00%	$0	0.00%	$0	0.00%	$1,517,730	0.20%
Unearned Interest and Real Estate Income Received in Advance	$0	0.00%	$0	0.00%	$0	0.00%	$0	0.00%
Funds Held by Company Under Reinsurance Treaties	$0	0.00%	$0	0.00%	$0	0.00%	$0	0.00%
Amounts Withheld or Retained by Company for Accounts of Others	$749,053	2.68%	$0	0.00%	$0	0.00%	$0	0.00%
Provision for Unauthorized Reinsurance	$0	0.00%	$0	0.00%	$0	0.00%	$0	0.00%
Net Adjustment in Assets and Liabilities Due to Foreign Exchange Rates	$0	0.00%	$0	0.00%	$0	0.00%	$0	0.00%
Drafts Outstanding	$0	0.00%	$0	0.00%	$0	0.00%	$0	0.00%
Payable to Parent, Subsidiaries and Affiliates	$342,149	1.22%	$0	0.00%	$0	0.00%	$32,713,664	4.39%
Payable for Securities	$0	0.00%	$0	0.00%	$0	0.00%	$0	0.00%
Aggregate Write-Ins for Other Liabilities	$19,623	0.07%	$0	0.00%	$0	0.00%	$14,259,408	1.91%
Total Liabilities (See Sec. 5, B.3)	$14,398,196	51.49%	$103,487	2.84%	$13,480,750	60.47%	$491,145,534	65.90%
Aggregate Write-Ins for Special Surplus Funds	$0	0.00%	$0	0.00%	$0	0.00%	$0	0.00%
Common Capital Stock	$300,000	1.07%	$1,000,000	27.46%	$1,500,000	6.73%	$1,649,306	0.22%
Preferred Capital Stock	$0	0.00%	$0	0.00%	$0	0.00%	$0	0.00%
Aggregate Write-Ins for Other than Special Surplus Funds	$0	0.00%	$0	0.00%	$0	0.00%	$0	0.00%
Surplus Notes	$0	0.00%	$0	0.00%	$0	0.00%	$0	0.00%
Gross Paid In and Contributed Surplus	$2,433,152	8.70%	$4,899,770	134.53%	$4,631,662	20.78%	$58,584,448	7.86%
Unassigned Funds (Surplus)	$10,833,735	38.74%	($2,361,248)	(64.83)%	$2,680,250	12.02%	$193,858,723	26.01%
Less Treasury Stock, at Cost:								
Shares Common	$0	0.00%	$0	0.00%	$0	0.00%	$0	0.00%
Shares Preferred	$0	0.00%	$0	0.00%	$0	0.00%	$0	0.00%
Surplus as Regards Policyholders (See Sec. 5, B.6, B.7, C.9, C.11)	$13,566,887	48.51%	$3,538,522	97.16%	$8,811,912	39.53%	$254,092,477	34.10%
TOTAL	$27,965,083	100.00%	$3,642,009	100.00%	$22,292,662	100.00%	$745,238,011	100.00%

A.3 Balance Sheet - By Individual Underwriter

ASSETS	COMMONWEALTH LAND (NJ) Company Value	% of Total	CONESTOGA Company Value	% of Total	CT ATTORNEYS Company Value	% of Total	DAKOTA HOMESTEAD Company Value	% of Total
Bonds	$33,027,571	78.35%	$2,300,713	27.97%	$48,326,861	79.67%	$2,137,942	59.89%
Stocks:								
Preferred Stocks	$0	0.00%	$0	0.00%	$797,500	1.31%	$0	0.00%
Common Stocks	$0	0.00%	$1,253,660	15.24%	$5,429,164	8.95%	$306,196	8.58%
Mortgage Loans on Real Estate:								
First Liens	$0	0.00%	$174,191	2.12%	$0	0.00%	$0	0.00%
Other than First Liens	$0	0.00%	$0	0.00%	$0	0.00%	$0	0.00%
Real Estate:								
Properties Occupied by the Company	$0	0.00%	$1,048,050	12.74%	$0	0.00%	$0	0.00%
Properties Held for the Production of Income	$0	0.00%	$188,935	2.30%	$0	0.00%	$0	0.00%
Properties Held for Sale	$0	0.00%	$209,000	2.54%	$0	0.00%	$0	0.00%
Cash, Cash Equivalents and Short-Term Investments	$8,306,919	19.71%	$1,795,564	21.83%	$3,060,625	5.05%	$1,119,180	31.35%
Contract Loans	$0	0.00%	$0	0.00%	$0	0.00%	$0	0.00%
Other Invested Assets	$0	0.00%	$0	0.00%	$23,936	0.04%	$0	0.00%
Receivables for Securities	$0	0.00%	$0	0.00%	$0	0.00%	$0	0.00%
Aggregate Write-Ins for Invested Assets	$0	0.00%	$0	0.00%	$0	0.00%	$0	0.00%
Subtotals, Cash and Invested Assets	$41,334,490	98.06%	$6,970,113	84.74%	$57,638,086	95.02%	$3,563,318	99.82%
Title Plants	$0	0.00%	$265,000	3.22%	$306,463	0.51%	$0	0.00%
Investment Income Due and Accrued	$389,992	0.93%	$18,260	0.22%	$480,388	0.79%	$0	0.00%
Premiums and Considerations:								
Uncollected Premiums and Agents' Balances in the Course of Collection	$319,286	0.76%	$149,709	1.82%	$480,111	0.79%	$0	0.00%
Deferred Premiums, Agents' Balances & Installments Booked but Deferred & Not Yet Due	$0	0.00%	$0	0.00%	$0	0.00%	$0	0.00%
Accrued Retrospective Premiums	$0	0.00%	$0	0.00%	$0	0.00%	$0	0.00%
Reinsurance:								
Amounts Recoverable from Reinsurers	$0	0.00%	$0	0.00%	$0	0.00%	$0	0.00%
Funds Held by or Deposited with Reinsured Companies	$0	0.00%	$0	0.00%	$0	0.00%	$0	0.00%
Other Amounts Receivable Under Reinsurance Contracts	$0	0.00%	$0	0.00%	$0	0.00%	$0	0.00%
Amounts Receivable Relating to Uninsured Plans	$0	0.00%	$0	0.00%	$0	0.00%	$0	0.00%
Current Federal and Foreign Income Tax Recoverable and Interest Thereon	$0	0.00%	$351,206	4.27%	$463,331	0.76%	$5,000	0.14%
Net Deferred Tax Asset	$107,137	0.25%	$442,154	5.38%	$1,129,524	1.86%	$0	0.00%
Guaranty Funds Receivable or on Deposit	$0	0.00%	$0	0.00%	$0	0.00%	$0	0.00%
Electronic Data Processing Equipment and Software	$1,209	0.00%	$26,525	0.32%	$65,704	0.11%	$1,367	0.04%
Furniture and Equipment, Including Health Care Delivery Assets	$0	0.00%	$0	0.00%	$0	0.00%	$0	0.00%
Net Adjustment in Assets and Liabilities Due to Foreign Exchange Rates	$0	0.00%	$0	0.00%	$0	0.00%	$0	0.00%
Receivables from Parent, Subsidiaries and Affiliates	$0	0.00%	$0	0.00%	$38,234	0.06%	$0	0.00%
Health Care	$0	0.00%	$0	0.00%	$0	0.00%	$0	0.00%
Aggregate Write-Ins for Other than Invest Assets	$0	0.00%	$2,159	0.03%	$57,013	0.09%	$0	0.00%
Total Assets Excluding Separate Accounts, Segregated Accounts & Protected Cell Accounts	$42,152,114	100.00%	$8,225,126	100.00%	$60,658,854	100.00%	$3,569,685	100.00%
From Separate Accounts, Segregated Accounts and Protected Cell Accounts	$0	0.00%	$0	0.00%	$0	0.00%	$0	0.00%
TOTAL	$42,152,114	100.00%	$8,225,126	100.00%	$60,658,854	100.00%	$3,569,685	100.00%

LIABILITIES	Company Value	% of Total	Company Value	% of Total	Company Value	% of Total	Company Value	% of Total
Known Claims Reserve (See Sec. 5, C.9)	$1,779,428	4.22%	$332,350	4.04%	$1,361,851	2.25%	$337,000	9.44%
Statutory Premium Reserve (See Sec. 5, C.9)	$6,725,497	15.96%	$4,054,912	49.30%	$15,228,616	25.11%	$825,622	23.13%
Aggregate of Other Reserves Required by Law (See Sec. 5, C.9)	$0	0.00%	$0	0.00%	$0	0.00%	$0	0.00%
Supplemental Reserve (See Sec. 5, C.9)	$0	0.00%	$0	0.00%	$0	0.00%	$0	0.00%
Commissions, Brokerage & Other Charges Due or Accrued to Attorneys, Agents & Real Estate Brokers	$0	0.00%	$0	0.00%	$0	0.00%	$0	0.00%
Other Expenses (Excluding Taxes, Licenses and Fees)	$174,988	0.42%	$278,778	3.39%	$1,469,273	2.42%	$75,085	2.10%
Taxes, Licenses and Fees (Excluding Federal and Foreign Income Taxes)	$11,845	0.03%	$62,252	0.76%	$69,312	0.11%	$65,674	1.84%
Current Federal and Foreign Income Taxes	$295,051	0.70%	$0	0.00%	$440,000	0.73%	$0	0.00%
Net Deferred Tax Liability	$0	0.00%	$0	0.00%	$0	0.00%	$0	0.00%
Borrowed Money and Interest Thereon	$0	0.00%	$0	0.00%	$0	0.00%	$0	0.00%
Dividends Declared and Unpaid	$0	0.00%	$0	0.00%	$0	0.00%	$0	0.00%
Premiums and Other Consideration Received in Advance	$21,629	0.05%	$0	0.00%	$245,735	0.41%	$0	0.00%
Unearned Interest and Real Estate Income Received in Advance	$0	0.00%	$12,950	0.16%	$0	0.00%	$0	0.00%
Funds Held by Company Under Reinsurance Treaties	$0	0.00%	$0	0.00%	$0	0.00%	$0	0.00%
Amounts Withheld or Retained by Company for Accounts of Others	$0	0.00%	$0	0.00%	$0	0.00%	$0	0.00%
Provision for Unauthorized Reinsurance	$0	0.00%	$0	0.00%	$0	0.00%	$0	0.00%
Net Adjustment in Assets and Liabilities Due to Foreign Exchange Rates	$0	0.00%	$0	0.00%	$0	0.00%	$0	0.00%
Drafts Outstanding	$0	0.00%	$0	0.00%	$0	0.00%	$0	0.00%
Payable to Parent, Subsidiaries and Affiliates	$11,231	0.03%	$0	0.00%	$4,784	0.01%	$0	0.00%
Payable for Securities	$0	0.00%	$0	0.00%	$0	0.00%	$0	0.00%
Aggregate Write-Ins for Other Liabilities	$0	0.00%	$0	0.00%	$0	0.00%	$0	0.00%
Total Liabilities (See Sec. 5, B.3)	$9,019,669	21.40%	$4,741,242	57.64%	$18,819,571	31.03%	$1,303,381	36.51%
Aggregate Write-Ins for Special Surplus Funds	$0	0.00%	$0	0.00%	$0	0.00%	$0	0.00%
Common Capital Stock	$500,000	1.19%	$1,000,000	12.16%	$500,000	0.82%	$508,146	14.24%
Preferred Capital Stock	$0	0.00%	$0	0.00%	$0	0.00%	$0	0.00%
Aggregate Write-Ins for Other than Special Surplus Funds	$0	0.00%	$0	0.00%	$0	0.00%	$0	0.00%
Surplus Notes	$0	0.00%	$0	0.00%	$0	0.00%	$1,100,000	30.82%
Gross Paid In and Contributed Surplus	$3,150,068	7.47%	$1,778,123	21.62%	$27,936,333	46.05%	$554,527	15.53%
Unassigned Funds (Surplus)	$29,482,377	69.94%	$705,761	8.58%	$13,402,950	22.10%	$133,876	3.75%
Less Treasury Stock, at Cost:								
Shares Common	$0	0.00%	$0	0.00%	$0	0.00%	$30,243	0.85%
Shares Preferred	$0	0.00%	$0	0.00%	$0	0.00%	$0	0.00%
Surplus as Regards Policyholders (See Sec. 5, B.6, B.7, C.9, C.11)	$33,132,445	78.60%	$3,483,884	42.36%	$41,839,283	68.97%	$2,266,306	63.49%
TOTAL	$42,152,114	100.00%	$8,225,126	100.00%	$60,658,854	100.00%	$3,569,687	100.00%

A.3 Balance Sheet - By Individual Underwriter

	DREIBELBISS		EQUITY NATIONAL		FARMERS NATIONAL		FIDELITY NATIONAL	
ASSETS	Company Value	% of Total	Company Value	% of Total	Company Value	% of Total	Company Value	% of Total
Bonds	$10,904	0.37%	$0	0.00%	$420,000	33.96%	$670,229,900	77.86%
Stocks:								
Preferred Stocks	$80,320	2.71%	$0	0.00%	$0	0.00%	$0	0.00%
Common Stocks	$510,119	17.23%	$0	0.00%	$0	0.00%	$35,136,568	4.08%
Mortgage Loans on Real Estate:								
First Liens	$0	0.00%	$0	0.00%	$0	0.00%	$1,618,024	0.19%
Other than First Liens	$0	0.00%	$0	0.00%	$0	0.00%	$0	0.00%
Real Estate:								
Properties Occupied by the Company	$292,917	9.89%	$0	0.00%	$0	0.00%	$0	0.00%
Properties Held for the Production of Income	$0	0.00%	$0	0.00%	$0	0.00%	$0	0.00%
Properties Held for Sale	$0	0.00%	$0	0.00%	$0	0.00%	$665,108	0.08%
Cash, Cash Equivalents and Short-Term Investments	$1,878,546	63.45%	$1,585,635	99.99%	$693,268	56.05%	$65,463,142	7.61%
Contract Loans	$0	0.00%	$0	0.00%	$0	0.00%	$0	0.00%
Other Invested Assets	$0	0.00%	$0	0.00%	$0	0.00%	$32,468,603	3.77%
Receivables for Securities	$0	0.00%	$0	0.00%	$0	0.00%	$723,146	0.08%
Aggregate Write-Ins for Invested Assets	$0	0.00%	$0	0.00%	$0	0.00%	$0	0.00%
Subtotals, Cash and Invested Assets	**$2,772,806**	**93.65%**	**$1,585,635**	**99.99%**	**$1,113,268**	**90.01%**	**$806,304,491**	**93.67%**
Title Plants	$40,000	1.35%	$0	0.00%	$0	0.00%	$17,913,400	2.08%
Investment Income Due and Accrued	$7,149	0.24%	$0	0.00%	$6,127	0.50%	$8,558,527	0.99%
Premiums and Considerations:								
Uncollected Premiums and Agents' Balances in the Course of Collection	$60,840	2.05%	$0	0.00%	$78,291	6.33%	$13,427,181	1.56%
Deferred Premiums, Agents' Balances & Installments Booked but Deferred & Not Yet Due	$0	0.00%	$0	0.00%	$0	0.00%	$0	0.00%
Accrued Retrospective Premiums	$0	0.00%	$0	0.00%	$0	0.00%	$0	0.00%
Reinsurance:								
Amounts Recoverable from Reinsurers	$0	0.00%	$0	0.00%	$0	0.00%	$0	0.00%
Funds Held by or Deposited with Reinsured Companies	$0	0.00%	$0	0.00%	$0	0.00%	$0	0.00%
Other Amounts Receivable Under Reinsurance Contracts	$0	0.00%	$0	0.00%	$0	0.00%	$0	0.00%
Amounts Receivable Relating to Uninsured Plans	$0	0.00%	$0	0.00%	$0	0.00%	$0	0.00%
Current Federal and Foreign Income Tax Recoverable and Interest Thereon	$62,469	2.11%	$0	0.00%	$0	0.00%	$0	0.00%
Net Deferred Tax Asset	$0	0.00%	$0	0.00%	$0	0.00%	$7,612,185	0.88%
Guaranty Funds Receivable or on Deposit	$0	0.00%	$0	0.00%	$0	0.00%	$0	0.00%
Electronic Data Processing Equipment and Software	$17,629	0.60%	$0	0.00%	$19,702	1.59%	$14	0.00%
Furniture and Equipment, Including Health Care Delivery Assets	$0	0.00%	$0	0.00%	$0	0.00%	$0	0.00%
Net Adjustment in Assets and Liabilities Due to Foreign Exchange Rates	$0	0.00%	$0	0.00%	$0	0.00%	$0	0.00%
Receivables from Parent, Subsidiaries and Affiliates	$0	0.00%	$0	0.00%	$0	0.00%	$6,973,585	0.81%
Health Care	$0	0.00%	$221	0.01%	$0	0.00%	$0	0.00%
Aggregate Write-Ins for Other than Invest Assets	$0	0.00%	$0	0.00%	$19,401	1.57%	$0	0.00%
Total Assets Excluding Separate Accounts, Segregated Accounts & Protected Cell Accounts	**$2,960,893**	**100.00%**	**$1,585,856**	**100.00%**	**$1,236,789**	**100.00%**	**$860,789,383**	**100.00%**
From Separate Accounts, Segregated Accounts and Protected Cell Accounts	$0	0.00%	$0	0.00%	$0	0.00%	$0	0.00%
TOTAL	**$2,960,893**	**100.00%**	**$1,585,856**	**100.00%**	**$1,236,789**	**100.00%**	**$860,789,383**	**100.00%**

LIABILITIES	Company Value	% of Total	Company Value	% of Total	Company Value	% of Total	Company Value	% of Total
Known Claims Reserve (See Sec. 5, C.9)	$22,000	0.74%	$0	0.00%	$5,000	0.40%	$101,336,064	11.77%
Statutory Premium Reserve (See Sec. 5, C.9)	$50,000	1.69%	$111,701	7.04%	$152,975	12.37%	$424,888,225	49.36%
Aggregate of Other Reserves Required by Law (See Sec. 5, C.9)	$0	0.00%	$0	0.00%	$0	0.00%	$0	0.00%
Supplemental Reserve (See Sec. 5, C.9)	$130,300	4.40%	$0	0.00%	$0	0.00%	$0	0.00%
Commissions, Brokerage & Other Charges Due or Accrued to Attorneys, Agents & Real Estate Brokers	$0	0.00%	$0	0.00%	$0	0.00%	$0	0.00%
Other Expenses (Excluding Taxes, Licenses and Fees)	$31,843	1.08%	$0	0.00%	$98,501	7.96%	$35,328,106	4.10%
Taxes, Licenses and Fees (Excluding Federal and Foreign Income Taxes)	$26,500	0.90%	$0	0.00%	$12,420	1.00%	$11,015,295	1.28%
Current Federal and Foreign Income Taxes	$0	0.00%	$0	0.00%	$0	0.00%	$19,634,148	2.28%
Net Deferred Tax Liability	$0	0.00%	$0	0.00%	$0	0.00%	$0	0.00%
Borrowed Money and Interest Thereon	$0	0.00%	$0	0.00%	$0	0.00%	$0	0.00%
Dividends Declared and Unpaid	$0	0.00%	$0	0.00%	$0	0.00%	$0	0.00%
Premiums and Other Consideration Received in Advance	$0	0.00%	$0	0.00%	$562	0.05%	$0	0.00%
Unearned Interest and Real Estate Income Received in Advance	$0	0.00%	$0	0.00%	$0	0.00%	$0	0.00%
Funds Held by Company Under Reinsurance Treaties	$0	0.00%	$4,295	0.27%	$147,048	11.89%	$0	0.00%
Amounts Withheld or Retained by Company for Accounts of Others	$0	0.00%	$0	0.00%	$0	0.00%	$202,655	0.02%
Provision for Unauthorized Reinsurance	$0	0.00%	$0	0.00%	$0	0.00%	$0	0.00%
Net Adjustment in Assets and Liabilities Due to Foreign Exchange Rates	$0	0.00%	$0	0.00%	$0	0.00%	$0	0.00%
Drafts Outstanding	$0	0.00%	$0	0.00%	$0	0.00%	$0	0.00%
Payable to Parent, Subsidiaries and Affiliates	$0	0.00%	$28,260	1.78%	$3,076	0.25%	$423,976	0.05%
Payable for Securities	$0	0.00%	$0	0.00%	$0	0.00%	$0	0.00%
Aggregate Write-Ins for Other Liabilities	$49,811	1.68%	$3,460	0.22%	$0	0.00%	$30,278,810	3.52%
Total Liabilities (See Sec. 5, B.3)	**$310,454**	**10.49%**	**$147,716**	**9.31%**	**$419,582**	**33.93%**	**$623,107,279**	**72.39%**
Aggregate Write-Ins for Special Surplus Funds	$0	0.00%	$0	0.00%	$0	0.00%	$0	0.00%
Common Capital Stock	$117,000	3.95%	$0	0.00%	$400,000	32.34%	$35,826,800	4.16%
Preferred Capital Stock	$0	0.00%	$0	0.00%	$0	0.00%	$0	0.00%
Aggregate Write-Ins for Other than Special Surplus Funds	$0	0.00%	$0	0.00%	$0	0.00%	$0	0.00%
Surplus Notes	$0	0.00%	$0	0.00%	$0	0.00%	$0	0.00%
Gross Paid In and Contributed Surplus	$0	0.00%	$1,438,140	90.69%	$1,283,610	103.79%	$141,288,233	16.41%
Unassigned Funds (Surplus)	$2,533,439	85.56%	$0	0.00%	($866,403)	(70.05)%	$60,567,071	7.04%
Less Treasury Stock, at Cost:								
Shares Common	$0	0.00%	$0	0.00%	$0	0.00%	$0	0.00%
Shares Preferred	$0	0.00%	$0	0.00%	$0	0.00%	$0	0.00%
Surplus as Regards Policyholders (See Sec. 5, B.6, B.7, C.9, C.11)	**$2,650,439**	**89.51%**	**$1,438,140**	**90.69%**	**$817,207**	**66.07%**	**$237,682,104**	**27.61%**
TOTAL	**$2,960,893**	**100.00%**	**$1,585,856**	**100.00%**	**$1,236,789**	**100.00%**	**$860,789,383**	**100.00%**

A.3 Balance Sheet - By Individual Underwriter

	FIRST AMERICAN (KS)		FIRST AMERICAN (NY)		FIRST AMERICAN (OR)		FIRST AMERICAN T&T	
ASSETS	Company Value	% of Total	Company Value	% of Total	Company Value	% of Total	Company Value	% of Total
Bonds	$460,180	3.65%	$56,521,047	27.81%	$18,668,231	29.17%	$10,628,009	53.02%
Stocks:								
Preferred Stocks	$0	0.00%	$0	0.00%	$0	0.00%	$0	0.00%
Common Stocks	$7,432,853	58.97%	$9,671,270	4.76%	$4,192,114	6.55%	$1,632,489	8.14%
Mortgage Loans on Real Estate:								
First Liens	$0	0.00%	$0	0.00%	$4,239,068	6.62%	$0	0.00%
Other than First Liens	$0	0.00%	$0	0.00%	$0	0.00%	$0	0.00%
Real Estate:								
Properties Occupied by the Company	$0	0.00%	$0	0.00%	$76,777	0.12%	$322,262	1.61%
Properties Held for the Production of Income	$0	0.00%	$0	0.00%	$0	0.00%	$0	0.00%
Properties Held for Sale	$0	0.00%	$0	0.00%	$68,000	0.11%	$268,200	1.34%
Cash, Cash Equivalents and Short-Term Investments	$4,482,353	35.56%	$126,167,891	62.07%	$18,751,393	29.30%	$4,292,578	21.42%
Contract Loans	$0	0.00%	$0	0.00%	$0	0.00%	$0	0.00%
Other Invested Assets	$0	0.00%	$0	0.00%	$1,000,000	1.56%	$0	0.00%
Receivables for Securities	$0	0.00%	$0	0.00%	$0	0.00%	$0	0.00%
Aggregate Write-Ins for Invested Assets	$0	0.00%	$0	0.00%	$0	0.00%	$0	0.00%
Subtotals, Cash and Invested Assets	$12,375,386	98.19%	$192,360,208	94.64%	$46,995,583	73.43%	$17,143,538	85.53%
Title Plants	$134,514	1.07%	$0	0.00%	$9,783,095	15.29%	$1,730,158	8.63%
Investment Income Due and Accrued	$7,052	0.06%	$812,002	0.40%	$76,755	0.12%	$129,439	0.65%
Premiums and Considerations:								
Uncollected Premiums and Agents' Balances in the Course of Collection	$4,256	0.03%	$2,079,931	1.02%	$683,500	1.07%	$1,041,387	5.20%
Deferred Premiums, Agents' Balances & Installments Booked but Deferred & Not Yet Due	$0	0.00%	$0	0.00%	$0	0.00%	$0	0.00%
Accrued Retrospective Premiums	$0	0.00%	$0	0.00%	$0	0.00%	$0	0.00%
Reinsurance:								
Amounts Recoverable from Reinsurers	$0	0.00%	$0	0.00%	$0	0.00%	$0	0.00%
Funds Held by or Deposited with Reinsured Companies	$0	0.00%	$0	0.00%	$0	0.00%	$0	0.00%
Other Amounts Receivable Under Reinsurance Contracts	$0	0.00%	$0	0.00%	$0	0.00%	$0	0.00%
Amounts Receivable Relating to Uninsured Plans	$0	0.00%	$0	0.00%	$0	0.00%	$0	0.00%
Current Federal and Foreign Income Tax Recoverable and Interest Thereon	$0	0.00%	$0	0.00%	$1,107,057	1.73%	$0	0.00%
Net Deferred Tax Asset	$82,475	0.65%	$1,017,349	0.50%	$1,460,872	2.28%	$0	0.00%
Guaranty Funds Receivable or on Deposit	$0	0.00%	$0	0.00%	$0	0.00%	$0	0.00%
Electronic Data Processing Equipment and Software	$0	0.00%	$551,650	0.27%	$0	0.00%	$0	0.00%
Furniture and Equipment, Including Health Care Delivery Assets	$0	0.00%	$0	0.00%	$0	0.00%	$0	0.00%
Net Adjustment in Assets and Liabilities Due to Foreign Exchange Rates	$0	0.00%	$0	0.00%	$0	0.00%	$0	0.00%
Receivables from Parent, Subsidiaries and Affiliates	$0	0.00%	$2,364,332	1.16%	$1,386,324	2.17%	$0	0.00%
Health Care	$0	0.00%	$0	0.00%	$0	0.00%	$0	0.00%
Aggregate Write-Ins for Other than Invest Assets	$0	0.00%	$4,073,620	2.00%	$2,508,196	3.92%	$0	0.00%
Total Assets Excluding Separate Accounts, Segregated Accounts & Protected Cell Accounts	$12,603,683	100.00%	$203,259,092	100.00%	$64,001,382	100.00%	$20,044,522	100.00%
From Separate Accounts, Segregated Accounts and Protected Cell Accounts	$0	0.00%	$0	0.00%	$0	0.00%	$0	0.00%
TOTAL	$12,603,683	100.00%	$203,259,092	100.00%	$64,001,382	100.00%	$20,044,522	100.00%

LIABILITIES	Company Value	% of Total	Company Value	% of Total	Company Value	% of Total	Company Value	% of Total
Known Claims Reserve (See Sec. 5, C.9)	$257,303	2.04%	$9,669,601	4.76%	$2,405,104	3.76%	$38,551	0.19%
Statutory Premium Reserve (See Sec. 5, C.9)	$5,138,037	40.77%	$46,598,121	22.93%	$19,799,451	30.94%	$1,285,621	6.41%
Aggregate of Other Reserves Required by Law (See Sec. 5, C.9)	$0	0.00%	$0	0.00%	$0	0.00%	$0	0.00%
Supplemental Reserve (See Sec. 5, C.9)	$0	0.00%	$0	0.00%	$0	0.00%	$0	0.00%
Commissions, Brokerage & Other Charges Due or Accrued to Attorneys, Agents & Real Estate Brokers	$0	0.00%	$0	0.00%	$0	0.00%	$0	0.00%
Other Expenses (Excluding Taxes, Licenses and Fees)	$560,933	4.45%	$33,251,410	16.36%	$4,356,674	6.81%	$1,098,111	5.48%
Taxes, Licenses and Fees (Excluding Federal and Foreign Income Taxes)	$81,300	0.65%	$0	0.00%	$4,312,701	6.74%	$681	0.00%
Current Federal and Foreign Income Taxes	$591,838	4.70%	$6,353,790	3.13%	$0	0.00%	$1,200,000	5.99%
Net Deferred Tax Liability	$0	0.00%	$0	0.00%	$0	0.00%	$0	0.00%
Borrowed Money and Interest Thereon	$0	0.00%	$0	0.00%	$1,083,585	1.69%	$0	0.00%
Dividends Declared and Unpaid	$0	0.00%	$0	0.00%	$0	0.00%	$0	0.00%
Premiums and Other Consideration Received in Advance	$133,643	1.06%	$0	0.00%	$0	0.00%	$0	0.00%
Unearned Interest and Real Estate Income Received in Advance	$0	0.00%	$0	0.00%	$0	0.00%	$0	0.00%
Funds Held by Company Under Reinsurance Treaties	$0	0.00%	$0	0.00%	$0	0.00%	$0	0.00%
Amounts Withheld or Retained by Company for Accounts of Others	$0	0.00%	$0	0.00%	$2,592	0.00%	$8,470	0.04%
Provision for Unauthorized Reinsurance	$0	0.00%	$0	0.00%	$0	0.00%	$0	0.00%
Net Adjustment in Assets and Liabilities Due to Foreign Exchange Rates	$0	0.00%	$0	0.00%	$0	0.00%	$0	0.00%
Drafts Outstanding	$0	0.00%	$0	0.00%	$0	0.00%	$0	0.00%
Payable to Parent, Subsidiaries and Affiliates	$6,837	0.05%	$0	0.00%	$0	0.00%	$0	0.00%
Payable for Securities	$0	0.00%	$0	0.00%	$0	0.00%	$0	0.00%
Aggregate Write-Ins for Other Liabilities	$0	0.00%	$0	0.00%	$0	0.00%	$0	0.00%
Total Liabilities (See Sec. 5, B.3)	$6,769,891	53.71%	$95,872,922	47.17%	$31,960,107	49.94%	$3,631,434	18.12%
Aggregate Write-Ins for Special Surplus Funds	$0	0.00%	$0	0.00%	$610,382	0.95%	$0	0.00%
Common Capital Stock	$450,000	3.57%	$1,000,000	0.49%	$100,000	0.16%	$1,000,000	4.99%
Preferred Capital Stock	$0	0.00%	$0	0.00%	$0	0.00%	$0	0.00%
Aggregate Write-Ins for Other than Special Surplus Funds	$0	0.00%	$0	0.00%	$0	0.00%	$0	0.00%
Surplus Notes	$0	0.00%	$0	0.00%	$0	0.00%	$0	0.00%
Gross Paid In and Contributed Surplus	$1,511,000	11.99%	$93,463,402	45.98%	$4,772,222	7.46%	$14,424,612	71.96%
Unassigned Funds (Surplus)	$3,872,793	30.73%	$12,922,768	6.36%	$26,558,670	41.50%	$988,476	4.93%
Less Treasury Stock, at Cost:								
Shares Common	$0	0.00%	$0	0.00%	$0	0.00%	$0	0.00%
Shares Preferred	$0	0.00%	$0	0.00%	$0	0.00%	$0	0.00%
Surplus as Regards Policyholders (See Sec. 5, B.6, B.7, C.9, C.11)	$5,833,793	46.29%	$107,386,170	52.83%	$32,041,274	50.06%	$16,413,088	81.88%
TOTAL	$12,603,684	100.00%	$203,259,092	100.00%	$64,001,381	100.00%	$20,044,522	100.00%

A.3 Balance Sheet - By Individual Underwriter

	FIRST AMERICAN TIC		FIRST AMERICAN TRANS		FOUNDERS		GENERAL T&T	
ASSETS	Company Value	% of Total	Company Value	% of Total	Company Value	% of Total	Company Value	% of Total
Bonds	$40,588,983	2.17%	$0	0.00%	$0	0.00%	$4,635,232	68.41%
Stocks:								
Preferred Stocks	$41,391,064	2.21%	$0	0.00%	$0	0.00%	$0	0.00%
Common Stocks	$582,073,258	31.07%	$0	0.00%	$0	0.00%	$306,959	4.53%
Mortgage Loans on Real Estate:								
First Liens	$36,090,574	1.93%	$0	0.00%	$0	0.00%	$80,000	1.18%
Other than First Liens	$0	0.00%	$0	0.00%	$0	0.00%	$0	0.00%
Real Estate:								
Properties Occupied by the Company	$110,401,721	5.89%	$0	0.00%	$0	0.00%	$0	0.00%
Properties Held for the Production of Income	$0	0.00%	$0	0.00%	$0	0.00%	$159,026	2.35%
Properties Held for Sale	$2,795,175	0.15%	$0	0.00%	$0	0.00%	$166,800	2.46%
Cash, Cash Equivalents and Short-Term Investments	$295,870,894	15.79%	$2,078,017	92.65%	$823,832	98.52%	$1,107,848	16.35%
Contract Loans	$0	0.00%	$0	0.00%	$0	0.00%	$0	0.00%
Other Invested Assets	$180,851,819	9.65%	$0	0.00%	$0	0.00%	$0	0.00%
Receivables for Securities	$0	0.00%	$0	0.00%	$0	0.00%	$0	0.00%
Aggregate Write-Ins for Invested Assets	$0	0.00%	$0	0.00%	$0	0.00%	$0	0.00%
Subtotals, Cash and Invested Assets	**$1,290,063,488**	**68.87%**	**$2,078,017**	**92.65%**	**$823,832**	**98.52%**	**$6,455,865**	**95.28%**
Title Plants	$81,194,688	4.33%	$0	0.00%	$10,785	1.29%	$0	0.00%
Investment Income Due and Accrued	$836,169	0.04%	$0	0.00%	$1,565	0.19%	$64,727	0.96%
Premiums and Considerations:								
Uncollected Premiums and Agents' Balances in the Course of Collection	$56,926,130	3.04%	$30,861	1.38%	$0	0.00%	$46,835	0.69%
Deferred Premiums, Agents' Balances & Installments Booked but Deferred & Not Yet Due	$0	0.00%	$0	0.00%	$0	0.00%	$0	0.00%
Accrued Retrospective Premiums	$0	0.00%	$0	0.00%	$0	0.00%	$0	0.00%
Reinsurance:								
Amounts Recoverable from Reinsurers	$0	0.00%	$0	0.00%	$0	0.00%	$0	0.00%
Funds Held by or Deposited with Reinsured Companies	$0	0.00%	$0	0.00%	$0	0.00%	$0	0.00%
Other Amounts Receivable Under Reinsurance Contracts	$0	0.00%	$0	0.00%	$0	0.00%	$0	0.00%
Amounts Receivable Relating to Uninsured Plans	$0	0.00%	$0	0.00%	$0	0.00%	$0	0.00%
Current Federal and Foreign Income Tax Recoverable and Interest Thereon	$0	0.00%	$0	0.00%	$0	0.00%	$201,927	2.98%
Net Deferred Tax Asset	$29,100,181	1.55%	$3,405	0.15%	$0	0.00%	$0	0.00%
Guaranty Funds Receivable or on Deposit	$0	0.00%	$0	0.00%	$0	0.00%	$0	0.00%
Electronic Data Processing Equipment and Software	$0	0.00%	$0	0.00%	$0	0.00%	$0	0.00%
Furniture and Equipment, Including Health Care Delivery Assets	$0	0.00%	$0	0.00%	$0	0.00%	$6,387	0.09%
Net Adjustment in Assets and Liabilities Due to Foreign Exchange Rates	$0	0.00%	$0	0.00%	$0	0.00%	$0	0.00%
Receivables from Parent, Subsidiaries and Affiliates	$355,661,413	18.99%	$130,548	5.82%	$0	0.00%	$0	0.00%
Health Care	$0	0.00%	$0	0.00%	$0	0.00%	$0	0.00%
Aggregate Write-Ins for Other than Invest Assets	$59,498,486	3.18%	$0	0.00%	$0	0.00%	$0	0.00%
Total Assets Excluding Separate Accounts, Segregated Accounts & Protected Cell Accounts	**$1,873,280,555**	**100.00%**	**$2,242,831**	**100.00%**	**$836,182**	**100.00%**	**$6,775,741**	**100.00%**
From Separate Accounts, Segregated Accounts and Protected Cell Accounts	$0	0.00%	$0	0.00%	$0	0.00%	$0	0.00%
TOTAL	**$1,873,280,555**	**100.00%**	**$2,242,831**	**100.00%**	**$836,182**	**100.00%**	**$6,775,741**	**100.00%**

	Company Value	% of Total	Company Value	% of Total	Company Value	% of Total	Company Value	% of Total
LIABILITIES								
Known Claims Reserve (See Sec. 5, C.9)	$140,517,390	7.50%	$5,000	0.22%	$0	0.00%	$184,100	2.72%
Statutory Premium Reserve (See Sec. 5, C.9)	$847,535,313	45.24%	$470,908	21.00%	$25,068	3.00%	$4,789,975	70.69%
Aggregate of Other Reserves Required by Law (See Sec. 5, C.9)	$0	0.00%	$0	0.00%	$0	0.00%	$120,900	1.78%
Supplemental Reserve (See Sec. 5, C.9)	$103,885,000	5.55%	$0	0.00%	$0	0.00%	$0	0.00%
Commissions, Brokerage & Other Charges Due or Accrued to Attorneys, Agents & Real Estate Brokers	$0	0.00%	$0	0.00%	$0	0.00%	$0	0.00%
Other Expenses (Excluding Taxes, Licenses and Fees)	$214,383,183	11.44%	$94,484	4.21%	$4,119	0.49%	$72,773	1.07%
Taxes, Licenses and Fees (Excluding Federal and Foreign Income Taxes)	$16,582,113	0.89%	$5,437	0.24%	$1,679	0.20%	$0	0.00%
Current Federal and Foreign Income Taxes	$1,057,329	0.06%	$409,128	18.24%	$0	0.00%	$0	0.00%
Net Deferred Tax Liability	$0	0.00%	$0	0.00%	$0	0.00%	$0	0.00%
Borrowed Money and Interest Thereon	$0	0.00%	$0	0.00%	$0	0.00%	$0	0.00%
Dividends Declared and Unpaid	$0	0.00%	$0	0.00%	$0	0.00%	$0	0.00%
Premiums and Other Consideration Received in Advance	$12,121,506	0.65%	$2,101	0.09%	$0	0.00%	$11,000	0.16%
Unearned Interest and Real Estate Income Received in Advance	$0	0.00%	$0	0.00%	$0	0.00%	$0	0.00%
Funds Held by Company Under Reinsurance Treaties	$0	0.00%	$0	0.00%	$0	0.00%	$0	0.00%
Amounts Withheld or Retained by Company for Accounts of Others	$2,586,301	0.14%	$1,528	0.07%	$2,368	0.28%	$1,800	0.03%
Provision for Unauthorized Reinsurance	$0	0.00%	$0	0.00%	$0	0.00%	$0	0.00%
Net Adjustment in Assets and Liabilities Due to Foreign Exchange Rates	$0	0.00%	$0	0.00%	$0	0.00%	$0	0.00%
Drafts Outstanding	$0	0.00%	$0	0.00%	$0	0.00%	$0	0.00%
Payable to Parent, Subsidiaries and Affiliates	$72,009,520	3.84%	$0	0.00%	$0	0.00%	$0	0.00%
Payable for Securities	$0	0.00%	$0	0.00%	$0	0.00%	$0	0.00%
Aggregate Write-Ins for Other Liabilities	$36,075,657	1.93%	$0	0.00%	$2,826	0.34%	$0	0.00%
Total Liabilities (See Sec. 5, B.3)	$1,446,753,312	77.23%	$988,586	44.08%	$36,060	4.31%	$5,180,548	76.46%
Aggregate Write-Ins for Special Surplus Funds	$0	0.00%	$0	0.00%	$0	0.00%	$0	0.00%
Common Capital Stock	$200,000,000	10.68%	$50,000	2.23%	$500,000	59.80%	$255,960	3.78%
Preferred Capital Stock	$0	0.00%	$0	0.00%	$0	0.00%	$462,169	6.82%
Aggregate Write-Ins for Other than Special Surplus Funds	$0	0.00%	$0	0.00%	$0	0.00%	$0	0.00%
Surplus Notes	$0	0.00%	$0	0.00%	$0	0.00%	$0	0.00%
Gross Paid In and Contributed Surplus	$0	0.00%	$1,025,218	45.71%	$520,000	62.19%	$678,846	10.02%
Unassigned Funds (Surplus)	$226,527,243	12.09%	$179,027	7.98%	($219,878)	(26.30)%	$248,218	3.66%
Less Treasury Stock, at Cost:								
Shares Common	$0	0.00%	$0	0.00%	$0	0.00%	$50,000	0.74%
Shares Preferred	$0	0.00%	$0	0.00%	$0	0.00%	$0	0.00%
Surplus as Regards Policyholders (See Sec. 5, B.6, B.7, C.9, C.11)	**$426,527,243**	**22.77%**	**$1,254,245**	**55.92%**	**$800,122**	**95.69%**	**$1,595,193**	**23.54%**
TOTAL	**$1,873,280,555**	**100.00%**	**$2,242,831**	**100.00%**	**$836,182**	**100.00%**	**$6,775,741**	**100.00%**

A.3 Balance Sheet - By Individual Underwriter

	GUARANTEE		GUARANTEE T&T		GUARDIAN NATIONAL		INVESTORS TIC	
ASSETS	Company Value	% of Total	Company Value	% of Total	Company Value	% of Total	Company Value	% of Total
Bonds	$1,499,366	57.12%	$4,336,861	54.72%	$4,134,392	42.15%	$66,751,926	63.16%
Stocks:								
Preferred Stocks	$0	0.00%	$0	0.00%	$0	0.00%	$419,646	0.40%
Common Stocks	$235,355	8.97%	$155,890	1.97%	$0	0.00%	$18,374,601	17.39%
Mortgage Loans on Real Estate:								
First Liens	$0	0.00%	$200,000	2.52%	$0	0.00%	$179,644	0.17%
Other than First Liens	$0	0.00%	$0	0.00%	$0	0.00%	$0	0.00%
Real Estate:								
Properties Occupied by the Company	$0	0.00%	$0	0.00%	$0	0.00%	$0	0.00%
Properties Held for the Production of Income	$0	0.00%	$0	0.00%	$0	0.00%	$0	0.00%
Properties Held for Sale	$0	0.00%	$14,252	0.18%	$0	0.00%	$278,477	0.26%
Cash, Cash Equivalents and Short-Term Investments	$224,665	8.56%	$853,485	10.77%	$5,310,594	54.14%	$8,822,981	8.35%
Contract Loans	$0	0.00%	$0	0.00%	$0	0.00%	$0	0.00%
Other Invested Assets	$0	0.00%	$75,869	0.96%	$0	0.00%	$351,532	0.33%
Receivables for Securities	$0	0.00%	$0	0.00%	$0	0.00%	$82,918	0.08%
Aggregate Write-Ins for Invested Assets	$0	0.00%	$0	0.00%	$0	0.00%	$0	0.00%
Subtotals, Cash and Invested Assets	$1,959,386	74.65%	$5,636,357	71.12%	$9,444,986	96.28%	$95,261,725	90.14%
Title Plants	$0	0.00%	$542,050	6.84%	$0	0.00%	$200,000	0.19%
Investment Income Due and Accrued	$20,401	0.78%	$98,697	1.25%	$47,100	0.48%	$955,505	0.90%
Premiums and Considerations:								
Uncollected Premiums and Agents' Balances in the Course of Collection	$89,134	3.40%	$225,110	2.84%	$13,610	0.14%	$5,796,331	5.48%
Deferred Premiums, Agents' Balances & Installments Booked but Deferred & Not Yet Due	$0	0.00%	$0	0.00%	$0	0.00%	$0	0.00%
Accrued Retrospective Premiums	$0	0.00%	$0	0.00%	$0	0.00%	$0	0.00%
Reinsurance:								
Amounts Recoverable from Reinsurers	$0	0.00%	$0	0.00%	$0	0.00%	$0	0.00%
Funds Held by or Deposited with Reinsured Companies	$0	0.00%	$0	0.00%	$0	0.00%	$0	0.00%
Other Amounts Receivable Under Reinsurance Contracts	$0	0.00%	$0	0.00%	$0	0.00%	$0	0.00%
Amounts Receivable Relating to Uninsured Plans	$0	0.00%	$0	0.00%	$0	0.00%	$0	0.00%
Current Federal and Foreign Income Tax Recoverable and Interest Thereon	$0	0.00%	$0	0.00%	$0	0.00%	$0	0.00%
Net Deferred Tax Asset	$104,188	3.97%	$121,246	1.53%	$256,434	2.61%	$2,130,073	2.02%
Guaranty Funds Receivable or on Deposit	$0	0.00%	$0	0.00%	$0	0.00%	$0	0.00%
Electronic Data Processing Equipment and Software	$0	0.00%	$33,172	0.42%	$36,493	0.37%	$1,111,172	1.05%
Furniture and Equipment, Including Health Care Delivery Assets	$0	0.00%	$0	0.00%	$0	0.00%	$0	0.00%
Net Adjustment in Assets and Liabilities Due to Foreign Exchange Rates	$0	0.00%	$0	0.00%	$0	0.00%	$0	0.00%
Receivables from Parent, Subsidiaries and Affiliates	$35,000	1.33%	$790,624	9.98%	$0	0.00%	$130,673	0.12%
Health Care	$0	0.00%	$0	0.00%	$0	0.00%	$0	0.00%
Aggregate Write-Ins for Other than Invest Assets	$416,732	15.88%	$477,694	6.03%	$11,263	0.11%	$99,178	0.09%
Total Assets Excluding Separate Accounts, Segregated Accounts & Protected Cell Accounts	$2,624,841	100.00%	$7,924,950	100.00%	$9,809,886	100.00%	$105,684,657	100.00%
From Separate Accounts, Segregated Accounts and Protected Cell Accounts	$0	0.00%	$0	0.00%	$0	0.00%	$0	0.00%
TOTAL	$2,624,841	100.00%	$7,924,950	100.00%	$9,809,886	100.00%	$105,684,657	100.00%

LIABILITIES	Company Value	% of Total	Company Value	% of Total	Company Value	% of Total	Company Value	% of Total
Known Claims Reserve (See Sec. 5, C.9)	$133,699	5.09%	$145,748	1.84%	$327,553	3.34%	$3,924,050	3.71%
Statutory Premium Reserve (See Sec. 5, C.9)	$946,693	36.07%	$6,398,481	80.74%	$2,524,234	25.73%	$39,338,674	37.22%
Aggregate of Other Reserves Required by Law (See Sec. 5, C.9)	$200,000	7.62%	$0	0.00%	$0	0.00%	$0	0.00%
Supplemental Reserve (See Sec. 5, C.9)	$0	0.00%	$0	0.00%	$0	0.00%	$0	0.00%
Commissions, Brokerage & Other Charges Due or Accrued to Attorneys, Agents & Real Estate Brokers	$0	0.00%	$0	0.00%	$0	0.00%	$245,063	0.23%
Other Expenses (Excluding Taxes, Licenses and Fees)	$100,018	3.81%	$135,035	1.70%	$0	0.00%	$1,542,794	1.46%
Taxes, Licenses and Fees (Excluding Federal and Foreign Income Taxes)	$16,415	0.63%	$26,346	0.33%	$0	0.00%	$39,014	0.04%
Current Federal and Foreign Income Taxes	$0	0.00%	$0	0.00%	$44,250	0.45%	$1,924,548	1.82%
Net Deferred Tax Liability	$0	0.00%	$0	0.00%	$0	0.00%	$0	0.00%
Borrowed Money and Interest Thereon	$0	0.00%	$0	0.00%	$0	0.00%	$18,265	0.02%
Dividends Declared and Unpaid	$0	0.00%	$0	0.00%	$0	0.00%	$0	0.00%
Premiums and Other Consideration Received in Advance	$0	0.00%	$0	0.00%	$0	0.00%	$0	0.00%
Unearned Interest and Real Estate Income Received in Advance	$0	0.00%	$0	0.00%	$0	0.00%	$0	0.00%
Funds Held by Company Under Reinsurance Treaties	$0	0.00%	$0	0.00%	$0	0.00%	$0	0.00%
Amounts Withheld or Retained by Company for Accounts of Others	$0	0.00%	$0	0.00%	$0	0.00%	$14,478	0.01%
Provision for Unauthorized Reinsurance	$0	0.00%	$0	0.00%	$0	0.00%	$0	0.00%
Net Adjustment in Assets and Liabilities Due to Foreign Exchange Rates	$0	0.00%	$0	0.00%	$0	0.00%	$0	0.00%
Drafts Outstanding	$0	0.00%	$0	0.00%	$0	0.00%	$0	0.00%
Payable to Parent, Subsidiaries and Affiliates	$0	0.00%	$0	0.00%	$95,223	0.97%	$242,109	0.23%
Payable for Securities	$0	0.00%	$0	0.00%	$0	0.00%	$0	0.00%
Aggregate Write-Ins for Other Liabilities	$0	0.00%	$0	0.00%	$20,113	0.21%	$8,292,900	7.85%
Total Liabilities (See Sec. 5, B.3)	$1,396,825	53.22%	$6,705,610	84.61%	$3,011,373	30.70%	$55,581,895	52.59%
Aggregate Write-Ins for Special Surplus Funds	$0	0.00%	$0	0.00%	$0	0.00%	$0	0.00%
Common Capital Stock	$750,000	28.57%	$1,500,000	18.93%	$2,000,000	20.39%	$2,000,000	1.89%
Preferred Capital Stock	$0	0.00%	$0	0.00%	$0	0.00%	$0	0.00%
Aggregate Write-Ins for Other than Special Surplus Funds	$0	0.00%	$0	0.00%	$0	0.00%	$0	0.00%
Surplus Notes	$0	0.00%	$0	0.00%	$0	0.00%	$0	0.00%
Gross Paid In and Contributed Surplus	$2,866,608	109.21%	$9,781,571	123.43%	$4,432,700	45.19%	$550,110	0.52%
Unassigned Funds (Surplus)	($2,388,592)	(91.00%)	($10,062,231)	(126.97%)	$365,813	3.73%	$47,552,652	44.99%
Less Treasury Stock, at Cost:								
Shares Common	$0	0.00%	$0	0.00%	$0	0.00%	$0	0.00%
Shares Preferred	$0	0.00%	$0	0.00%	$0	0.00%	$0	0.00%
Surplus as Regards Policyholders (See Sec. 5, B.6, B.7, C.9, C.11)	$1,228,016	46.78%	$1,219,340	15.39%	$6,798,513	69.30%	$50,102,762	47.41%
TOTAL	$2,624,841	100.00%	$7,924,950	100.00%	$9,809,886	100.00%	$105,684,657	100.00%

A.3 Balance Sheet - By Individual Underwriter

	K.E.L.		LAND CORP (CO)		LAND TIC (ST LOUIS)		LAWYERS	
ASSETS	Company Value	% of Total	Company Value	% of Total	Company Value	% of Total	Company Value	% of Total
Bonds	$0	0.00%	$8,126,323	56.32%	$1,631,778	31.12%	$359,934,035	58.57%
Stocks:								
Preferred Stocks	$0	0.00%	$0	0.00%	$0	0.00%	$1,750,083	0.28%
Common Stocks	$0	0.00%	$1,466,301	10.16%	$0	0.00%	$38,885,660	6.33%
Mortgage Loans on Real Estate:								
First Liens	$0	0.00%	$0	0.00%	$0	0.00%	$0	0.00%
Other than First Liens	$0	0.00%	$0	0.00%	$0	0.00%	$0	0.00%
Real Estate:								
Properties Occupied by the Company	$0	0.00%	$0	0.00%	$0	0.00%	$110,491	0.02%
Properties Held for the Production of Income	$0	0.00%	$0	0.00%	$0	0.00%	$0	0.00%
Properties Held for Sale	$0	0.00%	$0	0.00%	$0	0.00%	$0	0.00%
Cash, Cash Equivalents and Short-Term Investments	$2,368,995	99.60%	$2,950,910	20.45%	$3,536,009	67.43%	$50,537,974	8.22%
Contract Loans	$0	0.00%	$0	0.00%	$0	0.00%	$0	0.00%
Other Invested Assets	$0	0.00%	$0	0.00%	$0	0.00%	$6,552,844	1.07%
Receivables for Securities	$0	0.00%	$0	0.00%	$0	0.00%	$237,475	0.04%
Aggregate Write-Ins for Invested Assets	$0	0.00%	$0	0.00%	$0	0.00%	$0	0.00%
Subtotals, Cash and Invested Assets	$2,368,995	99.60%	$12,543,534	86.93%	$5,167,787	98.55%	$458,008,562	74.52%
Title Plants	$0	0.00%	$1,198,000	8.30%	$0	0.00%	$39,869,634	6.49%
Investment Income Due and Accrued	$1,602	0.07%	$104,776	0.73%	$64,553	1.23%	$4,408,460	0.72%
Premiums and Considerations:								
Uncollected Premiums and Agents' Balances in the Course of Collection	$4,181	0.18%	$0	0.00%	$9,003	0.17%	$19,788,935	3.22%
Deferred Premiums, Agents' Balances & Installments Booked but Deferred & Not Yet Due	$0	0.00%	$0	0.00%	$0	0.00%	$0	0.00%
Accrued Retrospective Premiums	$0	0.00%	$0	0.00%	$0	0.00%	$0	0.00%
Reinsurance:								
Amounts Recoverable from Reinsurers	$0	0.00%	$0	0.00%	$0	0.00%	$0	0.00%
Funds Held by or Deposited with Reinsured Companies	$0	0.00%	$0	0.00%	$0	0.00%	$0	0.00%
Other Amounts Receivable Under Reinsurance Contracts	$0	0.00%	$0	0.00%	$0	0.00%	$0	0.00%
Amounts Receivable Relating to Uninsured Plans	$0	0.00%	$0	0.00%	$0	0.00%	$0	0.00%
Current Federal and Foreign Income Tax Recoverable and Interest Thereon	$3,633	0.15%	$19,290	0.13%	$0	0.00%	$6,939,985	1.13%
Net Deferred Tax Asset	$0	0.00%	$268,483	1.86%	$2,714	0.05%	$15,948,074	2.59%
Guaranty Funds Receivable or on Deposit	$0	0.00%	$0	0.00%	$0	0.00%	$0	0.00%
Electronic Data Processing Equipment and Software	$0	0.00%	$0	0.00%	$0	0.00%	$5,570,681	0.91%
Furniture and Equipment, Including Health Care Delivery Assets	$0	0.00%	$0	0.00%	$0	0.00%	$0	0.00%
Net Adjustment in Assets and Liabilities Due to Foreign Exchange Rates	$0	0.00%	$0	0.00%	$0	0.00%	$0	0.00%
Receivables from Parent, Subsidiaries and Affiliates	$0	0.00%	$295,039	2.04%	$0	0.00%	$27,217,485	4.43%
Health Care	$0	0.00%	$0	0.00%	$0	0.00%	$0	0.00%
Aggregate Write-Ins for Other than Invest Assets	$0	0.00%	$0	0.00%	$0	0.00%	$36,824,332	5.99%
Total Assets Excluding Separate Accounts, Segregated Accounts & Protected Cell Accounts	$2,378,411	100.00%	$14,429,122	100.00%	$5,244,057	100.00%	$614,576,148	100.00%
From Separate Accounts, Segregated Accounts and Protected Cell Accounts	$0	0.00%	$0	0.00%	$0	0.00%	$0	0.00%
TOTAL	$2,378,411	100.00%	$14,429,122	100.00%	$5,244,057	100.00%	$614,576,148	100.00%

LIABILITIES	Company Value	% of Total	Company Value	% of Total	Company Value	% of Total	Company Value	% of Total
Known Claims Reserve (See Sec. 5, C.9)	$0	0.00%	$162,568	1.13%	$0	0.00%	$75,773,461	12.33%
Statutory Premium Reserve (See Sec. 5, C.9)	$29,528	1.24%	$3,956,000	27.42%	$47,952	0.91%	$334,753,199	54.47%
Aggregate of Other Reserves Required by Law (See Sec. 5, C.9)	$0	0.00%	$0	0.00%	$0	0.00%	$0	0.00%
Supplemental Reserve (See Sec. 5, C.9)	$0	0.00%	$0	0.00%	$0	0.00%	$0	0.00%
Commissions, Brokerage & Other Charges Due or Accrued to Attorneys, Agents & Real Estate Brokers	$0	0.00%	$0	0.00%	$0	0.00%	$0	0.00%
Other Expenses (Excluding Taxes, Licenses and Fees)	$6,211	0.26%	$3,189	0.02%	$61,206	1.17%	$23,628,892	3.84%
Taxes, Licenses and Fees (Excluding Federal and Foreign Income Taxes)	$10,218	0.43%	$37,698	0.26%	$72,537	1.38%	$4,816,899	0.78%
Current Federal and Foreign Income Taxes	$0	0.00%	$0	0.00%	$44,148	0.84%	$0	0.00%
Net Deferred Tax Liability	$0	0.00%	$0	0.00%	$0	0.00%	$0	0.00%
Borrowed Money and Interest Thereon	$0	0.00%	$0	0.00%	$0	0.00%	$5,250,000	0.85%
Dividends Declared and Unpaid	$0	0.00%	$0	0.00%	$0	0.00%	$0	0.00%
Premiums and Other Consideration Received in Advance	$0	0.00%	$420,000	2.91%	$0	0.00%	$3,315,946	0.54%
Unearned Interest and Real Estate Income Received in Advance	$0	0.00%	$0	0.00%	$0	0.00%	$0	0.00%
Funds Held by Company Under Reinsurance Treaties	$0	0.00%	$0	0.00%	$0	0.00%	$0	0.00%
Amounts Withheld or Retained by Company for Accounts of Others	$0	0.00%	$0	0.00%	$0	0.00%	$0	0.00%
Provision for Unauthorized Reinsurance	$0	0.00%	$0	0.00%	$0	0.00%	$0	0.00%
Net Adjustment in Assets and Liabilities Due to Foreign Exchange Rates	$0	0.00%	$0	0.00%	$0	0.00%	$0	0.00%
Drafts Outstanding	$0	0.00%	$0	0.00%	$0	0.00%	$0	0.00%
Payable to Parent, Subsidiaries and Affiliates	$0	0.00%	$5,657	0.04%	$33,829	0.65%	$154,009	0.03%
Payable for Securities	$0	0.00%	$0	0.00%	$0	0.00%	$284,828	0.05%
Aggregate Write-Ins for Other Liabilities	$0	0.00%	$1,414	0.01%	$0	0.00%	$37,312,505	6.07%
Total Liabilities (See Sec. 5, B.3)	$45,957	1.93%	$4,586,526	31.79%	$259,672	4.95%	$485,289,739	78.96%
Aggregate Write-Ins for Special Surplus Funds	$0	0.00%	$0	0.00%	$0	0.00%	$0	0.00%
Common Capital Stock	$300	0.01%	$495,883	3.44%	$1,000,000	19.07%	$5,311,685	0.86%
Preferred Capital Stock	$0	0.00%	$0	0.00%	$0	0.00%	$0	0.00%
Aggregate Write-Ins for Other than Special Surplus Funds	$0	0.00%	$0	0.00%	$0	0.00%	$0	0.00%
Surplus Notes	$0	0.00%	$1,198,000	8.30%	$0	0.00%	$0	0.00%
Gross Paid In and Contributed Surplus	$2,499,700	105.10%	$0	0.00%	$1,130,796	21.56%	$63,600,223	10.35%
Unassigned Funds (Surplus)	($167,546)	(7.04)%	$8,148,713	56.47%	$2,853,589	54.42%	$60,374,501	9.82%
Less Treasury Stock, at Cost:								
Shares Common	$0	0.00%	$0	0.00%	$0	0.00%	$0	0.00%
Shares Preferred	$0	0.00%	$0	0.00%	$0	0.00%	$0	0.00%
Surplus as Regards Policyholders (See Sec. 5, B.6, B.7, C.9, C.11)	$2,332,454	98.07%	$9,842,596	68.21%	$4,984,385	95.05%	$129,286,409	21.04%
TOTAL	$2,378,411	100.00%	$14,429,122	100.00%	$5,244,057	100.00%	$614,576,148	100.00%

A.3 Balance Sheet - By Individual Underwriter

ASSETS	MANITO Company Value	% of Total	MASON Company Value	% of Total	MASON COUNTY Company Value	% of Total	MASSACHUSETTS TIC Company Value	% of Total
Bonds	$0	0.00%	$552,805	20.82%	$0	0.00%	$0	0.00%
Stocks:								
Preferred Stocks	$0	0.00%	$0	0.00%	$0	0.00%	$0	0.00%
Common Stocks	$0	0.00%	$0	0.00%	$0	0.00%	$2,262,405	87.56%
Mortgage Loans on Real Estate:								
First Liens	$0	0.00%	$0	0.00%	$0	0.00%	$0	0.00%
Other than First Liens	$0	0.00%	$0	0.00%	$0	0.00%	$0	0.00%
Real Estate:								
Properties Occupied by the Company	$0	0.00%	$0	0.00%	$0	0.00%	$0	0.00%
Properties Held for the Production of Income	$0	0.00%	$0	0.00%	$0	0.00%	$0	0.00%
Properties Held for Sale	$0	0.00%	$0	0.00%	$0	0.00%	$0	0.00%
Cash, Cash Equivalents and Short-Term Investments	$1,451,479	98.51%	$2,040,494	76.85%	$831,274	96.98%	$312,654	12.10%
Contract Loans	$0	0.00%	$0	0.00%	$0	0.00%	$0	0.00%
Other Invested Assets	$0	0.00%	$0	0.00%	$0	0.00%	$0	0.00%
Receivables for Securities	$0	0.00%	$0	0.00%	$0	0.00%	$0	0.00%
Aggregate Write-Ins for Invested Assets	$0	0.00%	$0	0.00%	$0	0.00%	$0	0.00%
Subtotals, Cash and Invested Assets	$1,451,479	98.51%	$2,593,299	97.67%	$831,274	96.98%	$2,575,059	99.66%
Title Plants	$0	0.00%	$0	0.00%	$0	0.00%	$0	0.00%
Investment Income Due and Accrued	$19,544	1.33%	$7,236	0.27%	$0	0.00%	$0	0.00%
Premiums and Considerations:								
Uncollected Premiums and Agents' Balances in the Course of Collection	$0	0.00%	$45,620	1.72%	$0	0.00%	$0	0.00%
Deferred Premiums, Agents' Balances & Installments Booked but Deferred & Not Yet Due	$0	0.00%	$0	0.00%	$0	0.00%	$0	0.00%
Accrued Retrospective Premiums	$0	0.00%	$0	0.00%	$0	0.00%	$0	0.00%
Reinsurance:								
Amounts Recoverable from Reinsurers	$0	0.00%	$0	0.00%	$0	0.00%	$0	0.00%
Funds Held by or Deposited with Reinsured Companies	$0	0.00%	$0	0.00%	$0	0.00%	$0	0.00%
Other Amounts Receivable Under Reinsurance Contracts	$0	0.00%	$0	0.00%	$0	0.00%	$0	0.00%
Amounts Receivable Relating to Uninsured Plans	$0	0.00%	$0	0.00%	$0	0.00%	$0	0.00%
Current Federal and Foreign Income Tax Recoverable and Interest Thereon	$2,437	0.17%	$0	0.00%	$0	0.00%	$8,763	0.34%
Net Deferred Tax Asset	$0	0.00%	$0	0.00%	$0	0.00%	$0	0.00%
Guaranty Funds Receivable or on Deposit	$0	0.00%	$0	0.00%	$0	0.00%	$0	0.00%
Electronic Data Processing Equipment and Software	$0	0.00%	$0	0.00%	$0	0.00%	$0	0.00%
Furniture and Equipment, Including Health Care Delivery Assets	$0	0.00%	$0	0.00%	$0	0.00%	$0	0.00%
Net Adjustment in Assets and Liabilities Due to Foreign Exchange Rates	$0	0.00%	$0	0.00%	$0	0.00%	$0	0.00%
Receivables from Parent, Subsidiaries and Affiliates	$0	0.00%	$0	0.00%	$0	0.00%	$0	0.00%
Health Care	$0	0.00%	$0	0.00%	$0	0.00%	$0	0.00%
Aggregate Write-Ins for Other than Invest Assets	$0	0.00%	$9,010	0.34%	$0	0.00%	$0	0.00%
Total Assets Excluding Separate Accounts, Segregated Accounts & Protected Cell Accounts	$1,473,460	100.00%	$2,655,165	100.00%	$831,274	96.98%	$2,583,822	100.00%
From Separate Accounts, Segregated Accounts and Protected Cell Accounts	$0	0.00%	$0	0.00%	$25,883	3.02%	$0	0.00%
TOTAL	$1,473,460	100.00%	$2,655,165	100.00%	$857,157	100.00%	$2,583,822	100.00%

LIABILITIES	MANITO Company Value	% of Total	MASON Company Value	% of Total	MASON COUNTY Company Value	% of Total	MASSACHUSETTS TIC Company Value	% of Total
Known Claims Reserve (See Sec. 5, C.9)	$12,050	0.82%	$12,000	0.45%	$0	0.00%	$0	0.00%
Statutory Premium Reserve (See Sec. 5, C.9)	$181,732	12.33%	$62,433	2.35%	$883	0.10%	$100,000	3.87%
Aggregate of Other Reserves Required by Law (See Sec. 5, C.9)	$0	0.00%	$0	0.00%	$25,000	2.92%	$0	0.00%
Supplemental Reserve (See Sec. 5, C.9)	$0	0.00%	$0	0.00%	$0	0.00%	$0	0.00%
Commissions, Brokerage & Other Charges Due or Accrued to Attorneys, Agents & Real Estate Brokers	$0	0.00%	$0	0.00%	$0	0.00%	$0	0.00%
Other Expenses (Excluding Taxes, Licenses and Fees)	$0	0.00%	$26,245	0.99%	$8,587	1.00%	$0	0.00%
Taxes, Licenses and Fees (Excluding Federal and Foreign Income Taxes)	$18,321	1.24%	$0	0.00%	$0	0.00%	$772	0.03%
Current Federal and Foreign Income Taxes	$0	0.00%	$0	0.00%	$0	0.00%	$0	0.00%
Net Deferred Tax Liability	$0	0.00%	$0	0.00%	$0	0.00%	$0	0.00%
Borrowed Money and Interest Thereon	$0	0.00%	$0	0.00%	$0	0.00%	$0	0.00%
Dividends Declared and Unpaid	$0	0.00%	$0	0.00%	$0	0.00%	$0	0.00%
Premiums and Other Consideration Received in Advance	$0	0.00%	$2,855	0.11%	$0	0.00%	$0	0.00%
Unearned Interest and Real Estate Income Received in Advance	$0	0.00%	$0	0.00%	$0	0.00%	$0	0.00%
Funds Held by Company Under Reinsurance Treaties	$0	0.00%	$0	0.00%	$0	0.00%	$0	0.00%
Amounts Withheld or Retained by Company for Accounts of Others	$0	0.00%	$991	0.04%	$0	0.00%	$0	0.00%
Provision for Unauthorized Reinsurance	$0	0.00%	$0	0.00%	$0	0.00%	$0	0.00%
Net Adjustment in Assets and Liabilities Due to Foreign Exchange Rates	$0	0.00%	$0	0.00%	$0	0.00%	$0	0.00%
Drafts Outstanding	$0	0.00%	$0	0.00%	$0	0.00%	$0	0.00%
Payable to Parent, Subsidiaries and Affiliates	$0	0.00%	$0	0.00%	$0	0.00%	$16,000	0.62%
Payable for Securities	$0	0.00%	$0	0.00%	$0	0.00%	$0	0.00%
Aggregate Write-Ins for Other Liabilities	$4,666	0.32%	$4,599	0.17%	$0	0.00%	$1,500	0.06%
Total Liabilities (See Sec. 5, B.3)	$216,769	14.71%	$109,123	4.11%	$34,470	4.02%	$118,272	4.58%
Aggregate Write-Ins for Special Surplus Funds	$0	0.00%	$0	0.00%	$0	0.00%	$0	0.00%
Common Capital Stock	$500,000	33.93%	$1,000,000	37.66%	$5,000	0.58%	$16,932	0.66%
Preferred Capital Stock	$0	0.00%	$0	0.00%	$0	0.00%	$124,000	4.80%
Aggregate Write-Ins for Other than Special Surplus Funds	$0	0.00%	$0	0.00%	$0	0.00%	$0	0.00%
Surplus Notes	$0	0.00%	$0	0.00%	$0	0.00%	$0	0.00%
Gross Paid In and Contributed Surplus	$250,000	16.97%	$2,000,000	75.32%	$18,208	2.12%	$59,830	2.32%
Unassigned Funds (Surplus)	$506,691	34.39%	($453,958)	(17.10)%	$799,479	93.27%	$2,266,528	87.72%
Less Treasury Stock, at Cost:								
Shares Common	$0	0.00%	$0	0.00%	$0	0.00%	$1,740	0.07%
Shares Preferred	$0	0.00%	$0	0.00%	$0	0.00%	$0	0.00%
Surplus as Regards Policyholders (See Sec. 5, B.6, B.7, C.9, C.11)	$1,256,691	85.29%	$2,546,042	95.89%	$822,687	95.98%	$2,465,550	95.42%
TOTAL	$1,473,460	100.00%	$2,655,165	100.00%	$857,157	100.00%	$2,583,822	100.00%

A.3 Balance Sheet - By Individual Underwriter

ASSETS	MISSISSIPPI GUARANTY Company Value	% of Total	MISSISSIPPI VALLEY Company Value	% of Total	MONROE Company Value	% of Total	NATIONAL Company Value	% of Total
Bonds	$0	0.00%	$40,059,896	87.70%	$9,262,563	44.53%	$0	0.00%
Stocks:								
Preferred Stocks	$0	0.00%	$0	0.00%	$0	0.00%	$0	0.00%
Common Stocks	$0	0.00%	$450,772	0.99%	$4,625,613	22.24%	$4,047,211	75.62%
Mortgage Loans on Real Estate:								
First Liens	$0	0.00%	$0	0.00%	$0	0.00%	$0	0.00%
Other than First Liens	$0	0.00%	$0	0.00%	$0	0.00%	$0	0.00%
Real Estate:								
Properties Occupied by the Company	$0	0.00%	$0	0.00%	$1,359,386	6.53%	$227,250	4.25%
Properties Held for the Production of Income	$0	0.00%	$0	0.00%	$0	0.00%	$0	0.00%
Properties Held for Sale	$0	0.00%	$0	0.00%	$0	0.00%	$0	0.00%
Cash, Cash Equivalents and Short-Term Investments	$833,121	94.09%	$3,583,400	7.84%	$3,385,766	16.28%	$425,378	7.95%
Contract Loans	$0	0.00%	$0	0.00%	$0	0.00%	$0	0.00%
Other Invested Assets	$0	0.00%	$0	0.00%	$246,706	1.19%	$0	0.00%
Receivables for Securities	$0	0.00%	$0	0.00%	$0	0.00%	$0	0.00%
Aggregate Write-Ins for Invested Assets	$0	0.00%	$0	0.00%	$0	0.00%	$0	0.00%
Subtotals, Cash and Invested Assets	$833,121	94.09%	$44,094,068	96.53%	$18,880,034	90.76%	$4,699,839	87.81%
Title Plants	$0	0.00%	$290,245	0.64%	$799,949	3.85%	$267,212	4.99%
Investment Income Due and Accrued	$0	0.00%	$594,230	1.30%	$106,775	0.51%	$0	0.00%
Premiums and Considerations:								
Uncollected Premiums and Agents' Balances in the Course of Collection	$48,493	5.48%	$210,723	0.46%	$686,139	3.30%	$0	0.00%
Deferred Premiums, Agents' Balances & Installments Booked but Deferred & Not Yet Due	$0	0.00%	$0	0.00%	$0	0.00%	$0	0.00%
Accrued Retrospective Premiums	$0	0.00%	$0	0.00%	$0	0.00%	$0	0.00%
Reinsurance:								
Amounts Recoverable from Reinsurers	$0	0.00%	$0	0.00%	$0	0.00%	$0	0.00%
Funds Held by or Deposited with Reinsured Companies	$0	0.00%	$0	0.00%	$0	0.00%	$0	0.00%
Other Amounts Receivable Under Reinsurance Contracts	$0	0.00%	$0	0.00%	$0	0.00%	$0	0.00%
Amounts Receivable Relating to Uninsured Plans	$0	0.00%	$0	0.00%	$0	0.00%	$0	0.00%
Current Federal and Foreign Income Tax Recoverable and Interest Thereon	$0	0.00%	$0	0.00%	$0	0.00%	$0	0.00%
Net Deferred Tax Asset	$0	0.00%	$470,186	1.03%	$197,221	0.95%	$0	0.00%
Guaranty Funds Receivable or on Deposit	$0	0.00%	$0	0.00%	$0	0.00%	$0	0.00%
Electronic Data Processing Equipment and Software	$3,795	0.43%	$19,582	0.04%	$112,544	0.54%	$265,116	4.95%
Furniture and Equipment, Including Health Care Delivery Assets	$0	0.00%	$0	0.00%	$0	0.00%	$13,943	0.26%
Net Adjustment in Assets and Liabilities Due to Foreign Exchange Rates	$0	0.00%	$0	0.00%	$0	0.00%	$0	0.00%
Receivables from Parent, Subsidiaries and Affiliates	$0	0.00%	$0	0.00%	$19,759	0.09%	$0	0.00%
Health Care	$0	0.00%	$0	0.00%	$0	0.00%	$0	0.00%
Aggregate Write-Ins for Other than Invest Assets	$0	0.00%	$0	0.00%	$0	0.00%	$106,155	1.98%
Total Assets Excluding Separate Accounts, Segregated Accounts & Protected Cell Accounts	$885,409	100.00%	$45,679,034	100.00%	$20,802,421	100.00%	$5,352,265	100.00%
From Separate Accounts, Segregated Accounts and Protected Cell Accounts	$0	0.00%	$0	0.00%	$0	0.00%	$0	0.00%
TOTAL	$885,409	100.00%	$45,679,034	100.00%	$20,802,421	100.00%	$5,352,265	100.00%

LIABILITIES	Company Value	% of Total	Company Value	% of Total	Company Value	% of Total	Company Value	% of Total
Known Claims Reserve (See Sec. 5, C.9)	$0	0.00%	$3,868,087	8.47%	$802,300	3.86%	$7,500	0.14%
Statutory Premium Reserve (See Sec. 5, C.9)	$506,777	57.24%	$31,106,574	68.10%	$6,040,094	29.04%	$418,127	7.81%
Aggregate of Other Reserves Required by Law (See Sec. 5, C.9)	$50,000	5.65%	$0	0.00%	$0	0.00%	$0	0.00%
Supplemental Reserve (See Sec. 5, C.9)	$0	0.00%	$0	0.00%	$0	0.00%	$0	0.00%
Commissions, Brokerage & Other Charges Due or Accrued to Attorneys, Agents & Real Estate Brokers	$12,494	1.41%	$315,000	0.69%	$0	0.00%	$0	0.00%
Other Expenses (Excluding Taxes, Licenses and Fees)	$11,485	1.30%	$317,539	0.70%	$523,293	2.52%	$269,661	5.04%
Taxes, Licenses and Fees (Excluding Federal and Foreign Income Taxes)	$4,553	0.51%	$45,539	0.10%	$320	0.00%	$48,723	0.91%
Current Federal and Foreign Income Taxes	$0	0.00%	$194,028	0.42%	$117,915	0.57%	$0	0.00%
Net Deferred Tax Liability	$0	0.00%	$0	0.00%	$0	0.00%	$0	0.00%
Borrowed Money and Interest Thereon	$0	0.00%	$0	0.00%	$0	0.00%	$1,558,019	29.11%
Dividends Declared and Unpaid	$0	0.00%	$0	0.00%	$0	0.00%	$0	0.00%
Premiums and Other Consideration Received in Advance	$0	0.00%	$0	0.00%	$1,819,530	8.75%	$0	0.00%
Unearned Interest and Real Estate Income Received in Advance	$0	0.00%	$0	0.00%	$0	0.00%	$0	0.00%
Funds Held by Company Under Reinsurance Treaties	$0	0.00%	$0	0.00%	$0	0.00%	$0	0.00%
Amounts Withheld or Retained by Company for Accounts of Others	$0	0.00%	$0	0.00%	$0	0.00%	$0	0.00%
Provision for Unauthorized Reinsurance	$0	0.00%	$0	0.00%	$0	0.00%	$0	0.00%
Net Adjustment in Assets and Liabilities Due to Foreign Exchange Rates	$0	0.00%	$0	0.00%	$0	0.00%	$0	0.00%
Drafts Outstanding	$0	0.00%	$0	0.00%	$0	0.00%	$0	0.00%
Payable to Parent, Subsidiaries and Affiliates	$0	0.00%	$86,005	0.19%	$98	0.00%	$0	0.00%
Payable for Securities	$0	0.00%	$0	0.00%	$0	0.00%	$0	0.00%
Aggregate Write-Ins for Other Liabilities	$0	0.00%	$62,644	0.14%	$0	0.00%	$0	0.00%
Total Liabilities (See Sec. 5, B.3)	$585,309	66.11%	$35,995,416	78.80%	$9,303,550	44.72%	$2,302,030	43.01%
Aggregate Write-Ins for Special Surplus Funds	$0	0.00%	$0	0.00%	$0	0.00%	$0	0.00%
Common Capital Stock	$208,600	23.56%	$500,098	1.09%	$250,000	1.20%	$789,400	14.75%
Preferred Capital Stock	$1,500	0.17%	$0	0.00%	$0	0.00%	$0	0.00%
Aggregate Write-Ins for Other than Special Surplus Funds	$0	0.00%	$0	0.00%	$0	0.00%	$0	0.00%
Surplus Notes	$0	0.00%	$0	0.00%	$0	0.00%	$0	0.00%
Gross Paid In and Contributed Surplus	$786,900	88.87%	$1,347,508	2.95%	$610,139	2.93%	$235,600	4.40%
Unassigned Funds (Surplus)	($696,900)	(78.71)%	$7,929,966	17.36%	$10,638,732	51.14%	$2,025,235	37.84%
Less Treasury Stock, at Cost:								
Shares Common	$0	0.00%	$93,954	0.21%	$0	0.00%	$0	0.00%
Shares Preferred	$0	0.00%	$0	0.00%	$0	0.00%	$0	0.00%
Surplus as Regards Policyholders (See Sec. 5, B.6, B.7, C.9, C.11)	$300,100	33.89%	$9,683,618	21.20%	$11,498,871	55.28%	$3,050,235	56.99%
TOTAL	$885,409	100.00%	$45,679,034	100.00%	$20,802,421	100.00%	$5,352,265	100.00%

2

A.3 Balance Sheet - By Individual Underwriter

ASSETS	NATIONAL ATTORNEYS Company Value	% of Total	NATIONAL LAND Company Value	% of Total	NATIONAL OF NY Company Value	% of Total	NATIONS OF NY Company Value	% of Total
Bonds	$300,000	15.62%	$3,221,848	46.28%	$10,162,031	63.79%	$18,810,423	90.44%
Stocks:								
Preferred Stocks	$0	0.00%	$0	0.00%	$0	0.00%	$0	0.00%
Common Stocks	$528,311	27.50%	$2,388,523	34.31%	$0	0.00%	$124,305	0.60%
Mortgage Loans on Real Estate:								
First Liens	$0	0.00%	$0	0.00%	$0	0.00%	$30,956	0.15%
Other than First Liens	$0	0.00%	$0	0.00%	$0	0.00%	$0	0.00%
Real Estate:								
Properties Occupied by the Company	$0	0.00%	$0	0.00%	$0	0.00%	$0	0.00%
Properties Held for the Production of Income	$0	0.00%	$0	0.00%	$0	0.00%	$0	0.00%
Properties Held for Sale	$0	0.00%	$0	0.00%	$0	0.00%	$0	0.00%
Cash, Cash Equivalents and Short-Term Investments	$643,886	33.52%	$1,276,808	18.34%	$5,511,112	34.60%	$1,427,890	6.87%
Contract Loans	$0	0.00%	$0	0.00%	$0	0.00%	$0	0.00%
Other Invested Assets	$0	0.00%	$0	0.00%	$0	0.00%	$0	0.00%
Receivables for Securities	$0	0.00%	$0	0.00%	$23,673	0.15%	$21,322	0.10%
Aggregate Write-Ins for Invested Assets	$0	0.00%	$0	0.00%	$0	0.00%	$0	0.00%
Subtotals, Cash and Invested Assets	$1,472,197	76.63%	$6,887,179	98.92%	$15,696,816	98.54%	$20,414,896	98.15%
Title Plants	$251,173	13.07%	$0	0.00%	$0	0.00%	$86,730	0.42%
Investment Income Due and Accrued	$1,170	0.06%	$27,515	0.40%	$139,966	0.88%	$249,061	1.20%
Premiums and Considerations:								
Uncollected Premiums and Agents' Balances in the Course of Collection	$194,581	10.13%	$17,052	0.24%	$0	0.00%	$5,455	0.03%
Deferred Premiums, Agents' Balances & Installments Booked but Deferred & Not Yet Due	$0	0.00%	$0	0.00%	$0	0.00%	$0	0.00%
Accrued Retrospective Premiums	$0	0.00%	$0	0.00%	$0	0.00%	$0	0.00%
Reinsurance:								
Amounts Recoverable from Reinsurers	$0	0.00%	$0	0.00%	$0	0.00%	$0	0.00%
Funds Held by or Deposited with Reinsured Companies	$0	0.00%	$0	0.00%	$0	0.00%	$0	0.00%
Other Amounts Receivable Under Reinsurance Contracts	$0	0.00%	$0	0.00%	$0	0.00%	$0	0.00%
Amounts Receivable Relating to Uninsured Plans	$0	0.00%	$0	0.00%	$0	0.00%	$0	0.00%
Current Federal and Foreign Income Tax Recoverable and Interest Thereon	$2,000	0.10%	$0	0.00%	$0	0.00%	$0	0.00%
Net Deferred Tax Asset	$0	0.00%	$15,683	0.23%	$93,078	0.58%	$43,352	0.21%
Guaranty Funds Receivable or on Deposit	$0	0.00%	$0	0.00%	$0	0.00%	$0	0.00%
Electronic Data Processing Equipment and Software	$0	0.00%	$0	0.00%	$0	0.00%	$0	0.00%
Furniture and Equipment, Including Health Care Delivery Assets	$0	0.00%	$0	0.00%	$0	0.00%	$0	0.00%
Net Adjustment in Assets and Liabilities Due to Foreign Exchange Rates	$0	0.00%	$0	0.00%	$0	0.00%	$0	0.00%
Receivables from Parent, Subsidiaries and Affiliates	$0	0.00%	$13,948	0.20%	$0	0.00%	$0	0.00%
Health Care	$0	0.00%	$0	0.00%	$0	0.00%	$0	0.00%
Aggregate Write-Ins for Other than Invest Assets	$0	0.00%	$855	0.01%	$0	0.00%	$0	0.00%
Total Assets Excluding Separate Accounts, Segregated Accounts & Protected Cell Accounts	$1,921,121	100.00%	$6,962,232	100.00%	$15,929,860	100.00%	$20,799,494	100.00%
From Separate Accounts, Segregated Accounts and Protected Cell Accounts	$0	0.00%	$0	0.00%	$0	0.00%	$0	0.00%
TOTAL	$1,921,121	100.00%	$6,962,232	100.00%	$15,929,860	100.00%	$20,799,494	100.00%

LIABILITIES	Company Value	% of Total	Company Value	% of Total	Company Value	% of Total	Company Value	% of Total
Known Claims Reserve (See Sec. 5, C.9)	$0	0.00%	$91,167	1.31%	$2,793,736	17.54%	$471,872	2.27%
Statutory Premium Reserve (See Sec. 5, C.9)	$50,000	2.60%	$1,117,693	16.05%	$3,924,691	24.64%	$4,230,527	20.34%
Aggregate of Other Reserves Required by Law (See Sec. 5, C.9)	$0	0.00%	$0	0.00%	$0	0.00%	$0	0.00%
Supplemental Reserve (See Sec. 5, C.9)	$150,000	7.81%	$0	0.00%	$0	0.00%	$0	0.00%
Commissions, Brokerage & Other Charges Due or Accrued to Attorneys, Agents & Real Estate Brokers	$3,214	0.17%	$0	0.00%	$0	0.00%	$0	0.00%
Other Expenses (Excluding Taxes, Licenses and Fees)	$0	0.00%	$94,918	1.36%	$15,330	0.10%	$906,915	4.36%
Taxes, Licenses and Fees (Excluding Federal and Foreign Income Taxes)	$42,375	2.21%	$12,625	0.18%	$352,214	2.21%	$35,052	0.17%
Current Federal and Foreign Income Taxes	$0	0.00%	$0	0.00%	$2,130,525	13.37%	$1,156,248	5.56%
Net Deferred Tax Liability	$0	0.00%	$0	0.00%	$0	0.00%	$0	0.00%
Borrowed Money and Interest Thereon	$0	0.00%	$0	0.00%	$0	0.00%	$0	0.00%
Dividends Declared and Unpaid	$0	0.00%	$0	0.00%	$0	0.00%	$0	0.00%
Premiums and Other Consideration Received in Advance	$0	0.00%	$0	0.00%	$0	0.00%	$0	0.00%
Unearned Interest and Real Estate Income Received in Advance	$0	0.00%	$0	0.00%	$0	0.00%	$0	0.00%
Funds Held by Company Under Reinsurance Treaties	$0	0.00%	$0	0.00%	$0	0.00%	$0	0.00%
Amounts Withheld or Retained by Company for Accounts of Others	$0	0.00%	$0	0.00%	$0	0.00%	$0	0.00%
Provision for Unauthorized Reinsurance	$0	0.00%	$0	0.00%	$0	0.00%	$0	0.00%
Net Adjustment in Assets and Liabilities Due to Foreign Exchange Rates	$0	0.00%	$0	0.00%	$0	0.00%	$0	0.00%
Drafts Outstanding	$0	0.00%	$0	0.00%	$0	0.00%	$0	0.00%
Payable to Parent, Subsidiaries and Affiliates	$0	0.00%	$11,997	0.17%	$0	0.00%	$73,688	0.35%
Payable for Securities	$0	0.00%	$0	0.00%	$0	0.00%	$0	0.00%
Aggregate Write-Ins for Other Liabilities	$108,632	5.65%	$400,055	5.75%	$0	0.00%	$1,298,000	6.24%
Total Liabilities (See Sec. 5, B.3)	$354,221	18.44%	$1,728,455	24.83%	$9,216,496	57.86%	$8,172,302	39.29%
Aggregate Write-Ins for Special Surplus Funds	$0	0.00%	$0	0.00%	$0	0.00%	$0	0.00%
Common Capital Stock	$222,850	11.60%	$1,000,000	14.36%	$1,007,258	6.32%	$1,268,162	6.10%
Preferred Capital Stock	$36,400	1.89%	$0	0.00%	$0	0.00%	$0	0.00%
Aggregate Write-Ins for Other than Special Surplus Funds	$0	0.00%	$0	0.00%	$0	0.00%	$0	0.00%
Surplus Notes	$0	0.00%	$0	0.00%	$0	0.00%	$0	0.00%
Gross Paid In and Contributed Surplus	$190,322	9.91%	$4,447,240	63.88%	$9,995,736	62.75%	$14,650,005	70.43%
Unassigned Funds (Surplus)	$1,117,326	58.16%	($213,463)	(3.07)%	($4,119,015)	(25.86)%	($3,290,975)	(15.82)%
Less Treasury Stock, at Cost:								
Shares Common	$0	0.00%	$0	0.00%	$170,615	1.07%	$0	0.00%
Shares Preferred	$0	0.00%	$0	0.00%	$0	0.00%	$0	0.00%
Surplus as Regards Policyholders (See Sec. 5, B.6, B.7, C.9, C.11)	$1,566,898	81.56%	$5,233,777	75.17%	$6,713,364	42.14%	$12,627,192	60.71%
TOTAL	$1,921,119	100.00%	$6,962,232	100.00%	$15,929,860	100.00%	$20,799,494	100.00%

A.3 Balance Sheet - By Individual Underwriter

ASSETS	NEW JERSEY TIC Company Value	% of Total	NORTH AMERICAN Company Value	% of Total	NORTHEAST INVESTORS Company Value	% of Total	OHIO BAR Company Value	% of Total
Bonds	$7,148,128	71.84%	$7,252,356	8.73%	$4,903,142	79.81%	$23,762,656	88.07%
Stocks:								
Preferred Stocks	$0	0.00%	$0	0.00%	$0	0.00%	$0	0.00%
Common Stocks	$0	0.00%	$0	0.00%	$240,696	3.92%	$299,788	1.11%
Mortgage Loans on Real Estate:								
First Liens	$0	0.00%	$162,948	0.20%	$0	0.00%	$0	0.00%
Other than First Liens	$0	0.00%	$0	0.00%	$0	0.00%	$0	0.00%
Real Estate:								
Properties Occupied by the Company	$0	0.00%	$0	0.00%	$0	0.00%	$0	0.00%
Properties Held for the Production of Income	$0	0.00%	$0	0.00%	$0	0.00%	$0	0.00%
Properties Held for Sale	$0	0.00%	$0	0.00%	$0	0.00%	$0	0.00%
Cash, Cash Equivalents and Short-Term Investments	$1,263,232	12.70%	$72,439,602	87.22%	$799,647	13.02%	$2,421,852	8.98%
Contract Loans	$0	0.00%	$0	0.00%	$0	0.00%	$0	0.00%
Other Invested Assets	$0	0.00%	$910,000	1.10%	$0	0.00%	$0	0.00%
Receivables for Securities	$0	0.00%	$0	0.00%	$0	0.00%	$0	0.00%
Aggregate Write-Ins for Invested Assets	$0	0.00%	$0	0.00%	$0	0.00%	$0	0.00%
Subtotals, Cash and Invested Assets	$8,411,360	84.53%	$80,764,906	97.24%	$5,943,485	96.75%	$26,484,296	98.16%
Title Plants	$503,913	5.06%	$1,350,000	1.63%	$0	0.00%	$0	0.00%
Investment Income Due and Accrued	$76,479	0.77%	$406,722	0.49%	$65,763	1.07%	$260,130	0.96%
Premiums and Considerations:								
Uncollected Premiums and Agents' Balances in the Course of Collection	$233,726	2.35%	$240,775	0.29%	$92,263	1.50%	$59,893	0.22%
Deferred Premiums, Agents' Balances & Installments Booked but Deferred & Not Yet Due	$0	0.00%	$0	0.00%	$0	0.00%	$0	0.00%
Accrued Retrospective Premiums	$0	0.00%	$0	0.00%	$0	0.00%	$0	0.00%
Reinsurance:								
Amounts Recoverable from Reinsurers	$0	0.00%	$0	0.00%	$0	0.00%	$0	0.00%
Funds Held by or Deposited with Reinsured Companies	$0	0.00%	$0	0.00%	$0	0.00%	$0	0.00%
Other Amounts Receivable Under Reinsurance Contracts	$0	0.00%	$0	0.00%	$0	0.00%	$0	0.00%
Amounts Receivable Relating to Uninsured Plans	$0	0.00%	$0	0.00%	$0	0.00%	$0	0.00%
Current Federal and Foreign Income Tax Recoverable and Interest Thereon	$338,000	3.40%	$0	0.00%	$5,417	0.09%	$0	0.00%
Net Deferred Tax Asset	$252,215	2.53%	$295,627	0.36%	$16,863	0.27%	$177,000	0.66%
Guaranty Funds Receivable or on Deposit	$0	0.00%	$0	0.00%	$0	0.00%	$0	0.00%
Electronic Data Processing Equipment and Software	$18,614	0.19%	$0	0.00%	$1,566	0.03%	$0	0.00%
Furniture and Equipment, Including Health Care Delivery Assets	$0	0.00%	$0	0.00%	$0	0.00%	$0	0.00%
Net Adjustment in Assets and Liabilities Due to Foreign Exchange Rates	$0	0.00%	$0	0.00%	$0	0.00%	$0	0.00%
Receivables from Parent, Subsidiaries and Affiliates	$0	0.00%	$0	0.00%	$6,151	0.10%	$0	0.00%
Health Care	$0	0.00%	$0	0.00%	$0	0.00%	$0	0.00%
Aggregate Write-Ins for Other than Invest Assets	$116,306	1.17%	$0	0.00%	$11,733	0.19%	$0	0.00%
Total Assets Excluding Separate Accounts, Segregated Accounts & Protected Cell Accounts	$9,950,613	100.00%	$83,058,030	100.00%	$6,143,241	100.00%	$26,981,319	100.00%
From Separate Accounts, Segregated Accounts and Protected Cell Accounts	$0	0.00%	$0	0.00%	$0	0.00%	$0	0.00%
TOTAL	$9,950,613	100.00%	$83,058,030	100.00%	$6,143,241	100.00%	$26,981,319	100.00%

LIABILITIES	Company Value	% of Total	Company Value	% of Total	Company Value	% of Total	Company Value	% of Total
Known Claims Reserve (See Sec. 5, C.9)	$339,694	3.41%	$687,616	0.83%	$3,000	0.05%	$510,817	1.89%
Statutory Premium Reserve (See Sec. 5, C.9)	$4,371,480	43.93%	$28,451,816	34.26%	$539,982	8.79%	$14,766,195	54.73%
Aggregate of Other Reserves Required by Law (See Sec. 5, C.9)	$0	0.00%	$0	0.00%	$0	0.00%	$0	0.00%
Supplemental Reserve (See Sec. 5, C.9)	$0	0.00%	$0	0.00%	$0	0.00%	$0	0.00%
Commissions, Brokerage & Other Charges Due or Accrued to Attorneys, Agents & Real Estate Brokers	$0	0.00%	$0	0.00%	$5,345	0.09%	$0	0.00%
Other Expenses (Excluding Taxes, Licenses and Fees)	$255,009	2.56%	$413,062	0.50%	$51,906	0.84%	$98,930	0.37%
Taxes, Licenses and Fees (Excluding Federal and Foreign Income Taxes)	$66,618	0.67%	$54,355	0.07%	$0	0.00%	$180,299	0.67%
Current Federal and Foreign Income Taxes	$0	0.00%	$139,225	0.17%	$0	0.00%	$2,156,300	7.99%
Net Deferred Tax Liability	$0	0.00%	$0	0.00%	$0	0.00%	$0	0.00%
Borrowed Money and Interest Thereon	$0	0.00%	$0	0.00%	$0	0.00%	$0	0.00%
Dividends Declared and Unpaid	$0	0.00%	$0	0.00%	$0	0.00%	$0	0.00%
Premiums and Other Consideration Received in Advance	$38,785	0.39%	$0	0.00%	$0	0.00%	$93,586	0.35%
Unearned Interest and Real Estate Income Received in Advance	$0	0.00%	$0	0.00%	$0	0.00%	$0	0.00%
Funds Held by Company Under Reinsurance Treaties	$0	0.00%	$0	0.00%	$0	0.00%	$0	0.00%
Amounts Withheld or Retained by Company for Accounts of Others	$0	0.00%	$0	0.00%	$0	0.00%	$0	0.00%
Provision for Unauthorized Reinsurance	$0	0.00%	$0	0.00%	$0	0.00%	$0	0.00%
Net Adjustment in Assets and Liabilities Due to Foreign Exchange Rates	$0	0.00%	$0	0.00%	$0	0.00%	$0	0.00%
Drafts Outstanding	$0	0.00%	$0	0.00%	$0	0.00%	$0	0.00%
Payable to Parent, Subsidiaries and Affiliates	$32,700	0.33%	$2,412,664	2.90%	$2,533	0.04%	$148,350	0.55%
Payable for Securities	$0	0.00%	$0	0.00%	$0	0.00%	$0	0.00%
Aggregate Write-Ins for Other Liabilities	$0	0.00%	$0	0.00%	$0	0.00%	$0	0.00%
Total Liabilities (See Sec. 5, B.3)	$5,104,286	51.30%	$32,158,738	38.72%	$602,766	9.81%	$17,954,477	66.54%
Aggregate Write-Ins for Special Surplus Funds	$0	0.00%	$0	0.00%	$0	0.00%	$0	0.00%
Common Capital Stock	$500,000	5.02%	$2,700,000	3.25%	$1,000,000	16.28%	$1,000,000	3.71%
Preferred Capital Stock	$0	0.00%	$0	0.00%	$0	0.00%	$0	0.00%
Aggregate Write-Ins for Other than Special Surplus Funds	$0	0.00%	$0	0.00%	$0	0.00%	$0	0.00%
Surplus Notes	$1,500,000	15.07%	$0	0.00%	$0	0.00%	$0	0.00%
Gross Paid In and Contributed Surplus	$3,380,000	33.97%	$5,771,391	6.95%	$1,275,500	20.76%	$6,147,722	22.79%
Unassigned Funds (Surplus)	($533,673)	(5.36)%	$42,427,901	51.08%	$3,264,975	53.15%	$1,879,120	6.96%
Less Treasury Stock, at Cost:								
Shares Common	$0	0.00%	$0	0.00%	$0	0.00%	$0	0.00%
Shares Preferred	$0	0.00%	$0	0.00%	$0	0.00%	$0	0.00%
Surplus as Regards Policyholders (See Sec. 5, B.6, B.7, C.9, C.11)	$4,846,327	48.70%	$50,899,292	61.28%	$5,540,475	90.19%	$9,026,842	33.46%
TOTAL	$9,950,613	100.00%	$83,058,030	100.00%	$6,143,241	100.00%	$26,981,319	100.00%

A.3 Balance Sheet - By Individual Underwriter

ASSETS	OLD REPUBLIC GENERAL Company Value	% of Total	OLD REPUBLIC NATIONAL Company Value	% of Total	OLYMPIC Company Value	% of Total	PACIFIC NORTHWEST Company Value	% of Total
Bonds	$93,932,247	81.44%	$368,813,547	76.14%	$0	0.00%	$15,358,547	50.02%
Stocks:								
Preferred Stocks	$0	0.00%	$0	0.00%	$0	0.00%	$1,668,923	5.44%
Common Stocks	$11,886,949	10.31%	$51,665,273	10.67%	$0	0.00%	$0	0.00%
Mortgage Loans on Real Estate:								
First Liens	$135,712	0.12%	$978,489	0.20%	$0	0.00%	$2,198,238	7.16%
Other than First Liens	$0	0.00%	$0	0.00%	$0	0.00%	$0	0.00%
Real Estate:								
Properties Occupied by the Company	$0	0.00%	$5,676,542	1.17%	$0	0.00%	$0	0.00%
Properties Held for the Production of Income	$0	0.00%	$5,600	0.00%	$0	0.00%	$0	0.00%
Properties Held for Sale	$0	0.00%	$495,000	0.10%	$0	0.00%	$0	0.00%
Cash, Cash Equivalents and Short-Term Investments	$1,253,315	1.09%	$22,509,326	4.65%	$326,224	91.50%	$8,473,681	27.60%
Contract Loans	$0	0.00%	$0	0.00%	$0	0.00%	$0	0.00%
Other Invested Assets	$0	0.00%	$2,500,000	0.52%	$0	0.00%	$0	0.00%
Receivables for Securities	$0	0.00%	$0	0.00%	$0	0.00%	$0	0.00%
Aggregate Write-Ins for Invested Assets	$0	0.00%	$0	0.00%	$0	0.00%	$0	0.00%
Subtotals, Cash and Invested Assets	$107,208,223	92.95%	$452,643,777	93.44%	$326,224	91.50%	$27,699,389	90.21%
Title Plants	$0	0.00%	$7,826,020	1.62%	$0	0.00%	$1,525,000	4.97%
Investment Income Due and Accrued	$1,400,130	1.21%	$5,381,809	1.11%	$4,338	1.22%	$136,766	0.45%
Premiums and Considerations:								
Uncollected Premiums and Agents' Balances in the Course of Collection	$4,822,528	4.18%	$6,364,896	1.31%	$0	0.00%	$1,137,110	3.70%
Deferred Premiums, Agents' Balances & Installments Booked but Deferred & Not Yet Due	$0	0.00%	$0	0.00%	$0	0.00%	$0	0.00%
Accrued Retrospective Premiums	$0	0.00%	$0	0.00%	$0	0.00%	$0	0.00%
Reinsurance:								
Amounts Recoverable from Reinsurers	$0	0.00%	$706,358	0.15%	$0	0.00%	$0	0.00%
Funds Held by or Deposited with Reinsured Companies	$0	0.00%	$0	0.00%	$0	0.00%	$0	0.00%
Other Amounts Receivable Under Reinsurance Contracts	$0	0.00%	$0	0.00%	$0	0.00%	$0	0.00%
Amounts Receivable Relating to Uninsured Plans	$0	0.00%	$0	0.00%	$0	0.00%	$0	0.00%
Current Federal and Foreign Income Tax Recoverable and Interest Thereon	$1,071,979	0.93%	$4,348,809	0.90%	$0	0.00%	$0	0.00%
Net Deferred Tax Asset	$831,063	0.72%	$5,401,270	1.12%	$0	0.00%	$201,258	0.66%
Guaranty Funds Receivable or on Deposit	$0	0.00%	$0	0.00%	$0	0.00%	$0	0.00%
Electronic Data Processing Equipment and Software	$0	0.00%	$1,730,955	0.36%	$0	0.00%	$0	0.00%
Furniture and Equipment, Including Health Care Delivery Assets	$0	0.00%	$0	0.00%	$0	0.00%	$0	0.00%
Net Adjustment in Assets and Liabilities Due to Foreign Exchange Rates	$0	0.00%	$0	0.00%	$0	0.00%	$0	0.00%
Receivables from Parent, Subsidiaries and Affiliates	$0	0.00%	$0	0.00%	$25,972	7.28%	$5,268	0.02%
Health Care	$0	0.00%	$0	0.00%	$0	0.00%	$0	0.00%
Aggregate Write-Ins for Other than Invest Assets	$0	0.00%	$0	0.00%	$0	0.00%	$1,000	0.00%
Total Assets Excluding Separate Accounts, Segregated Accounts & Protected Cell Accounts	$115,333,923	100.00%	$484,403,894	100.00%	$356,534	100.00%	$30,705,791	100.00%
From Separate Accounts, Segregated Accounts and Protected Cell Accounts	$0	0.00%	$0	0.00%	$0	0.00%	$0	0.00%
TOTAL	$115,333,923	100.00%	$484,403,894	100.00%	$356,534	100.00%	$30,705,791	100.00%

LIABILITIES	Company Value	% of Total	Company Value	% of Total	Company Value	% of Total	Company Value	% of Total
Known Claims Reserve (See Sec. 5, C.9)	$7,866,727	6.82%	$61,315,931	12.66%	$10,377	2.91%	$636,604	2.07%
Statutory Premium Reserve (See Sec. 5, C.9)	$60,548,499	52.50%	$261,902,857	54.07%	$0	0.00%	$12,118,349	39.47%
Aggregate of Other Reserves Required by Law (See Sec. 5, C.9)	$0	0.00%	$70,000	0.01%	$0	0.00%	$0	0.00%
Supplemental Reserve (See Sec. 5, C.9)	$0	0.00%	$0	0.00%	$0	0.00%	$0	0.00%
Commissions, Brokerage & Other Charges Due or Accrued to Attorneys, Agents & Real Estate Brokers	$0	0.00%	$325,912	0.07%	$0	0.00%	$420,916	1.37%
Other Expenses (Excluding Taxes, Licenses and Fees)	$27,301	0.02%	$15,142,851	3.13%	$10,006	2.81%	$57,283	0.19%
Taxes, Licenses and Fees (Excluding Federal and Foreign Income Taxes)	$0	0.00%	$1,320,269	0.27%	$0	0.00%	$218,301	0.71%
Current Federal and Foreign Income Taxes	$0	0.00%	$0	0.00%	$0	0.00%	$2,032,514	6.62%
Net Deferred Tax Liability	$0	0.00%	$0	0.00%	$0	0.00%	$0	0.00%
Borrowed Money and Interest Thereon	$0	0.00%	$0	0.00%	$0	0.00%	$0	0.00%
Dividends Declared and Unpaid	$0	0.00%	$0	0.00%	$0	0.00%	$0	0.00%
Premiums and Other Consideration Received in Advance	$0	0.00%	$2,707,181	0.56%	$0	0.00%	$0	0.00%
Unearned Interest and Real Estate Income Received in Advance	$0	0.00%	$0	0.00%	$0	0.00%	$0	0.00%
Funds Held by Company Under Reinsurance Treaties	$0	0.00%	$0	0.00%	$0	0.00%	$12,348	0.04%
Amounts Withheld or Retained by Company for Accounts of Others	$0	0.00%	$116,400	0.02%	$0	0.00%	$0	0.00%
Provision for Unauthorized Reinsurance	$0	0.00%	$0	0.00%	$0	0.00%	$0	0.00%
Net Adjustment in Assets and Liabilities Due to Foreign Exchange Rates	$0	0.00%	$0	0.00%	$0	0.00%	$0	0.00%
Drafts Outstanding	$0	0.00%	$0	0.00%	$0	0.00%	$0	0.00%
Payable to Parent, Subsidiaries and Affiliates	$0	0.00%	$12,135,384	2.51%	$0	0.00%	$52,633	0.17%
Payable for Securities	$0	0.00%	$0	0.00%	$0	0.00%	$0	0.00%
Aggregate Write-Ins for Other Liabilities	$706,358	0.61%	$13,365,284	2.76%	$0	0.00%	$0	0.00%
Total Liabilities (See Sec. 5, B.3)	$69,148,885	59.96%	$368,402,069	76.05%	$20,383	5.72%	$15,548,948	50.64%
Aggregate Write-Ins for Special Surplus Funds	$0	0.00%	$0	0.00%	$0	0.00%	$0	0.00%
Common Capital Stock	$500,000	0.43%	$1,526,434	0.32%	$45,000	12.62%	$4,943,200	16.10%
Preferred Capital Stock	$0	0.00%	$0	0.00%	$0	0.00%	$0	0.00%
Aggregate Write-Ins for Other than Special Surplus Funds	$0	0.00%	$0	0.00%	$0	0.00%	$0	0.00%
Surplus Notes	$0	0.00%	$0	0.00%	$0	0.00%	$0	0.00%
Gross Paid In and Contributed Surplus	$27,410,981	23.77%	$58,767,909	12.13%	$357,129	100.17%	$1,832,371	5.97%
Unassigned Funds (Surplus)	$18,274,057	15.84%	$55,707,482	11.50%	($65,978)	(18.51)%	$8,381,272	27.30%
Less Treasury Stock, at Cost:								
Shares Common	$0	0.00%	$0	0.00%	$0	0.00%	$0	0.00%
Shares Preferred	$0	0.00%	$0	0.00%	$0	0.00%	$0	0.00%
Surplus as Regards Policyholders (See Sec. 5, B.6, B.7, C.9, C.11)	$46,185,038	40.04%	$116,001,825	23.95%	$336,151	94.28%	$15,156,843	49.36%
TOTAL	$115,333,923	100.00%	$484,403,894	100.00%	$356,534	100.00%	$30,705,791	100.00%

A.3 Balance Sheet - By Individual Underwriter

	PENN ATTORNEYS		PORT LAWRENCE		PUBLIC		SEAGATE	
ASSETS	Company Value	% of Total	Company Value	% of Total	Company Value	% of Total	Company Value	% of Total
Bonds	$6,459,023	63.41%	$11,904,916	53.08%	$0	0.00%	$0	0.00%
Stocks:								
Preferred Stocks	$0	0.00%	$0	0.00%	$0	0.00%	$0	0.00%
Common Stocks	$0	0.00%	$39,806	0.18%	$0	0.00%	$0	0.00%
Mortgage Loans on Real Estate:								
First Liens	$0	0.00%	$0	0.00%	$0	0.00%	$0	0.00%
Other than First Liens	$0	0.00%	$0	0.00%	$0	0.00%	$0	0.00%
Real Estate:								
Properties Occupied by the Company	$0	0.00%	$194,937	0.87%	$0	0.00%	$0	0.00%
Properties Held for the Production of Income	$0	0.00%	$0	0.00%	$0	0.00%	$0	0.00%
Properties Held for Sale	$0	0.00%	$0	0.00%	$0	0.00%	$0	0.00%
Cash, Cash Equivalents and Short-Term Investments	$3,497,188	34.33%	$6,323,017	28.19%	$1,038,244	100.00%	$574,200	85.63%
Contract Loans	$0	0.00%	$0	0.00%	$0	0.00%	$0	0.00%
Other Invested Assets	$0	0.00%	$0	0.00%	$0	0.00%	$0	0.00%
Receivables for Securities	$0	0.00%	$0	0.00%	$0	0.00%	$0	0.00%
Aggregate Write-Ins for Invested Assets	$0	0.00%	$0	0.00%	$0	0.00%	$0	0.00%
Subtotals, Cash and Invested Assets	$9,956,211	97.74%	$18,462,676	82.32%	$1,038,244	100.00%	$574,200	85.63%
Title Plants	$0	0.00%	$1,698,967	7.57%	$0	0.00%	$0	0.00%
Investment Income Due and Accrued	$56,013	0.55%	$113,626	0.51%	$0	0.00%	$0	0.00%
Premiums and Considerations:								
Uncollected Premiums and Agents' Balances in the Course of Collection	$174,193	1.71%	$5,490	0.02%	$0	0.00%	$96,348	14.37%
Deferred Premiums, Agents' Balances & Installments Booked but Deferred & Not Yet Due	$0	0.00%	$0	0.00%	$0	0.00%	$0	0.00%
Accrued Retrospective Premiums	$0	0.00%	$0	0.00%	$0	0.00%	$0	0.00%
Reinsurance:								
Amounts Recoverable from Reinsurers	$0	0.00%	$0	0.00%	$0	0.00%	$0	0.00%
Funds Held by or Deposited with Reinsured Companies	$0	0.00%	$0	0.00%	$0	0.00%	$0	0.00%
Other Amounts Receivable Under Reinsurance Contracts	$0	0.00%	$0	0.00%	$0	0.00%	$0	0.00%
Amounts Receivable Relating to Uninsured Plans	$0	0.00%	$0	0.00%	$0	0.00%	$0	0.00%
Current Federal and Foreign Income Tax Recoverable and Interest Thereon	$0	0.00%	$0	0.00%	$0	0.00%	$0	0.00%
Net Deferred Tax Asset	$0	0.00%	$122,000	0.54%	$0	0.00%	$0	0.00%
Guaranty Funds Receivable or on Deposit	$0	0.00%	$0	0.00%	$0	0.00%	$0	0.00%
Electronic Data Processing Equipment and Software	$0	0.00%	$0	0.00%	$0	0.00%	$0	0.00%
Furniture and Equipment, Including Health Care Delivery Assets	$0	0.00%	$0	0.00%	$0	0.00%	$0	0.00%
Net Adjustment in Assets and Liabilities Due to Foreign Exchange Rates	$0	0.00%	$0	0.00%	$0	0.00%	$0	0.00%
Receivables from Parent, Subsidiaries and Affiliates	$0	0.00%	$1,890,521	8.43%	$0	0.00%	$0	0.00%
Health Care	$0	0.00%	$135,681	0.60%	$0	0.00%	$0	0.00%
Aggregate Write-Ins for Other than Invest Assets	$0	0.00%	$0	0.00%	$0	0.00%	$0	0.00%
Total Assets Excluding Separate Accounts, Segregated Accounts & Protected Cell Accounts	$10,186,417	100.00%	$22,428,961	100.00%	$1,038,244	100.00%	$670,548	100.00%
From Separate Accounts, Segregated Accounts and Protected Cell Accounts	$0	0.00%	$0	0.00%	$0	0.00%	$0	0.00%
TOTAL	$10,186,417	100.00%	$22,428,961	100.00%	$1,038,244	100.00%	$670,548	100.00%

LIABILITIES	Company Value	% of Total	Company Value	% of Total	Company Value	% of Total	Company Value	% of Total
Known Claims Reserve (See Sec. 5, C.9)	$177,062	1.74%	$34,542	0.15%	$0	0.00%	$0	0.00%
Statutory Premium Reserve (See Sec. 5, C.9)	$994,645	9.76%	$5,615,478	25.04%	$0	0.00%	$192,675	28.73%
Aggregate of Other Reserves Required by Law (See Sec. 5, C.9)	$0	0.00%	$0	0.00%	$0	0.00%	$0	0.00%
Supplemental Reserve (See Sec. 5, C.9)	$0	0.00%	$0	0.00%	$0	0.00%	$0	0.00%
Commissions, Brokerage & Other Charges Due or Accrued to Attorneys, Agents & Real Estate Brokers	$0	0.00%	$0	0.00%	$0	0.00%	$0	0.00%
Other Expenses (Excluding Taxes, Licenses and Fees)	$132,639	1.30%	$232,523	1.04%	$0	0.00%	$0	0.00%
Taxes, Licenses and Fees (Excluding Federal and Foreign Income Taxes)	$0	0.00%	$78,267	0.35%	$0	0.00%	$0	0.00%
Current Federal and Foreign Income Taxes	$290,396	2.85%	$1,711,600	7.63%	$0	0.00%	$0	0.00%
Net Deferred Tax Liability	$0	0.00%	$0	0.00%	$0	0.00%	$0	0.00%
Borrowed Money and Interest Thereon	$0	0.00%	$0	0.00%	$0	0.00%	$0	0.00%
Dividends Declared and Unpaid	$0	0.00%	$0	0.00%	$0	0.00%	$0	0.00%
Premiums and Other Consideration Received in Advance	$0	0.00%	$82,811	0.37%	$0	0.00%	$0	0.00%
Unearned Interest and Real Estate Income Received in Advance	$0	0.00%	$0	0.00%	$0	0.00%	$0	0.00%
Funds Held by Company Under Reinsurance Treaties	$0	0.00%	$0	0.00%	$0	0.00%	$0	0.00%
Amounts Withheld or Retained by Company for Accounts of Others	$0	0.00%	$0	0.00%	$0	0.00%	($1,684)	(0.25)%
Provision for Unauthorized Reinsurance	$0	0.00%	$0	0.00%	$0	0.00%	$0	0.00%
Net Adjustment in Assets and Liabilities Due to Foreign Exchange Rates	$0	0.00%	$0	0.00%	$0	0.00%	$0	0.00%
Drafts Outstanding	$0	0.00%	$0	0.00%	$0	0.00%	$0	0.00%
Payable to Parent, Subsidiaries and Affiliates	$240,004	2.36%	$0	0.00%	$0	0.00%	$5,000	0.75%
Payable for Securities	$0	0.00%	$0	0.00%	$0	0.00%	$0	0.00%
Aggregate Write-Ins for Other Liabilities	$0	0.00%	$0	0.00%	$0	0.00%	$0	0.00%
Total Liabilities (See Sec. 5, B.3)	$1,834,746	18.01%	$7,755,221	34.58%	$0	0.00%	$195,991	29.23%
Aggregate Write-Ins for Special Surplus Funds	$0	0.00%	$0	0.00%	$0	0.00%	$0	0.00%
Common Capital Stock	$500,000	4.91%	$1,000,000	4.46%	$500,000	48.16%	$120,000	17.90%
Preferred Capital Stock	$0	0.00%	$0	0.00%	$0	0.00%	$1,000	0.15%
Aggregate Write-Ins for Other than Special Surplus Funds	$0	0.00%	$0	0.00%	$0	0.00%	($65,000)	(9.69)%
Surplus Notes	$0	0.00%	$0	0.00%	$0	0.00%	$0	0.00%
Gross Paid In and Contributed Surplus	$251,377	2.47%	$2,684,372	11.97%	$500,000	48.16%	$180,000	26.84%
Unassigned Funds (Surplus)	$7,600,294	74.61%	$10,989,368	49.00%	$38,244	3.68%	$238,557	35.58%
Less Treasury Stock, at Cost:								
Shares Common	$0	0.00%	$0	0.00%	$0	0.00%	$0	0.00%
Shares Preferred	$0	0.00%	$0	0.00%	$0	0.00%	$0	0.00%
Surplus as Regards Policyholders (See Sec. 5, B.6, B.7, C.9, C.11)	$8,351,671	81.99%	$14,673,740	65.42%	$1,038,244	100.00%	$474,557	70.77%
TOTAL	$10,186,417	100.00%	$22,428,961	100.00%	$1,038,244	100.00%	$670,548	100.00%

A.3 Balance Sheet - By Individual Underwriter

ASSETS	SECURITY TG (BALTIMORE) Company Value	% of Total	SECURITY UNION Company Value	% of Total	SIERRA Company Value	% of Total	SOUTHERN TI CORP Company Value	% of Total
Bonds	$6,132,533	43.83%	$38,430,615	45.76%	$2,022,976	66.35%	$17,083,173	73.05%
Stocks:								
Preferred Stocks	$0	0.00%	$0	0.00%	$0	0.00%	$0	0.00%
Common Stocks	$2,212,475	15.81%	$18,086,859	21.54%	$0	0.00%	$0	0.00%
Mortgage Loans on Real Estate:								
First Liens	$144,329	1.03%	$217,075	0.26%	$0	0.00%	$0	0.00%
Other than First Liens	$0	0.00%	$0	0.00%	$0	0.00%	$0	0.00%
Real Estate:								
Properties Occupied by the Company	$0	0.00%	$0	0.00%	$0	0.00%	$186,352	0.80%
Properties Held for the Production of Income	$0	0.00%	$0	0.00%	$0	0.00%	$0	0.00%
Properties Held for Sale	$0	0.00%	$0	0.00%	$0	0.00%	$145,750	0.62%
Cash, Cash Equivalents and Short-Term Investments	$2,659,079	19.00%	$7,805,923	9.29%	$688,196	22.57%	$2,307,156	9.87%
Contract Loans	$0	0.00%	$0	0.00%	$0	0.00%	$0	0.00%
Other Invested Assets	$288,594	2.06%	$0	0.00%	$0	0.00%	$0	0.00%
Receivables for Securities	$0	0.00%	$20,514	0.02%	$0	0.00%	$0	0.00%
Aggregate Write-Ins for Invested Assets	$0	0.00%	$0	0.00%	$0	0.00%	$0	0.00%
Subtotals, Cash and Invested Assets	$11,437,010	81.74%	$64,560,986	76.87%	$2,711,172	88.92%	$19,722,431	84.33%
Title Plants	$362,031	2.59%	$14,613,343	17.40%	$0	0.00%	$2,032,475	8.69%
Investment Income Due and Accrued	$60,454	0.43%	$479,132	0.57%	$26,259	0.86%	$215,960	0.92%
Premiums and Considerations:								
Uncollected Premiums and Agents' Balances in the Course of Collection	$1,347,414	9.63%	$524,046	0.62%	$309,342	10.15%	$145,439	0.62%
Deferred Premiums, Agents' Balances & Installments Booked but Deferred & Not Yet Due	$0	0.00%	$0	0.00%	$0	0.00%	$0	0.00%
Accrued Retrospective Premiums	$0	0.00%	$0	0.00%	$0	0.00%	$0	0.00%
Reinsurance:								
Amounts Recoverable from Reinsurers	$0	0.00%	$0	0.00%	$0	0.00%	$0	0.00%
Funds Held by or Deposited with Reinsured Companies	$0	0.00%	$0	0.00%	$0	0.00%	$0	0.00%
Other Amounts Receivable Under Reinsurance Contracts	$0	0.00%	$0	0.00%	$0	0.00%	$0	0.00%
Amounts Receivable Relating to Uninsured Plans	$0	0.00%	$0	0.00%	$0	0.00%	$0	0.00%
Current Federal and Foreign Income Tax Recoverable and Interest Thereon	$535,256	3.83%	$2,449,207	2.92%	$0	0.00%	$306,331	1.31%
Net Deferred Tax Asset	$82,000	0.59%	$732,030	0.87%	$2,170	0.07%	$354,988	1.52%
Guaranty Funds Receivable or on Deposit	$0	0.00%	$0	0.00%	$0	0.00%	$0	0.00%
Electronic Data Processing Equipment and Software	$10,919	0.08%	$290	0.00%	$0	0.00%	$28,630	0.12%
Furniture and Equipment, Including Health Care Delivery Assets	$0	0.00%	$0	0.00%	$0	0.00%	$0	0.00%
Net Adjustment in Assets and Liabilities Due to Foreign Exchange Rates	$0	0.00%	$0	0.00%	$0	0.00%	$0	0.00%
Receivables from Parent, Subsidiaries and Affiliates	$58,709	0.42%	$626,572	0.75%	$0	0.00%	$534,074	2.28%
Health Care	$0	0.00%	$0	0.00%	$0	0.00%	$0	0.00%
Aggregate Write-Ins for Other than Invest Assets	$98,713	0.71%	$0	0.00%	$0	0.00%	$46,194	0.20%
Total Assets Excluding Separate Accounts, Segregated Accounts & Protected Cell Accounts	$13,992,506	100.00%	$83,985,606	100.00%	$3,048,943	100.00%	$23,386,522	100.00%
From Separate Accounts, Segregated Accounts and Protected Cell Accounts	$0	0.00%	$0	0.00%	$0	0.00%	$0	0.00%
TOTAL	$13,992,506	100.00%	$83,985,606	100.00%	$3,048,943	100.00%	$23,386,522	100.00%

LIABILITIES	Company Value	% of Total	Company Value	% of Total	Company Value	% of Total	Company Value	% of Total
Known Claims Reserve (See Sec. 5, C.9)	$1,562,323	11.17%	$9,847,553	11.73%	$0	0.00%	$3,274,516	14.00%
Statutory Premium Reserve (See Sec. 5, C.9)	$8,544,849	61.07%	$22,542,602	26.84%	$43,490	1.43%	$11,001,692	47.04%
Aggregate of Other Reserves Required by Law (See Sec. 5, C.9)	$0	0.00%	$0	0.00%	$0	0.00%	$0	0.00%
Supplemental Reserve (See Sec. 5, C.9)	$0	0.00%	$0	0.00%	$6,628	0.22%	$0	0.00%
Commissions, Brokerage & Other Charges Due or Accrued to Attorneys, Agents & Real Estate Brokers	$0	0.00%	$0	0.00%	$262,935	8.62%	$0	0.00%
Other Expenses (Excluding Taxes, Licenses and Fees)	$97,210	0.69%	$1,633,827	1.95%	$0	0.00%	$458,772	1.96%
Taxes, Licenses and Fees (Excluding Federal and Foreign Income Taxes)	$0	0.00%	$2,988,022	3.56%	$12,565	0.41%	$385,051	1.65%
Current Federal and Foreign Income Taxes	$0	0.00%	$0	0.00%	$65,763	2.16%	$0	0.00%
Net Deferred Tax Liability	$0	0.00%	$0	0.00%	$0	0.00%	$0	0.00%
Borrowed Money and Interest Thereon	$0	0.00%	$0	0.00%	$0	0.00%	$0	0.00%
Dividends Declared and Unpaid	$0	0.00%	$0	0.00%	$0	0.00%	$0	0.00%
Premiums and Other Consideration Received in Advance	$24,033	0.17%	$0	0.00%	$0	0.00%	$533,079	2.28%
Unearned Interest and Real Estate Income Received in Advance	$0	0.00%	$0	0.00%	$0	0.00%	$0	0.00%
Funds Held by Company Under Reinsurance Treaties	$0	0.00%	$0	0.00%	$0	0.00%	$0	0.00%
Amounts Withheld or Retained by Company for Accounts of Others	$0	0.00%	$396,877	0.47%	$0	0.00%	$0	0.00%
Provision for Unauthorized Reinsurance	$0	0.00%	$0	0.00%	$0	0.00%	$0	0.00%
Net Adjustment in Assets and Liabilities Due to Foreign Exchange Rates	$0	0.00%	$0	0.00%	$0	0.00%	$0	0.00%
Drafts Outstanding	$0	0.00%	$0	0.00%	$0	0.00%	$0	0.00%
Payable to Parent, Subsidiaries and Affiliates	$0	0.00%	$11,542	0.01%	$0	0.00%	$17,806	0.08%
Payable for Securities	$0	0.00%	$0	0.00%	$0	0.00%	$0	0.00%
Aggregate Write-Ins for Other Liabilities	$0	0.00%	$0	0.00%	$0	0.00%	$0	0.00%
Total Liabilities (See Sec. 5, B.3)	$10,228,415	73.10%	$37,420,423	44.56%	$391,381	12.84%	$15,670,916	67.01%
Aggregate Write-Ins for Special Surplus Funds	$0	0.00%	$0	0.00%	$0	0.00%	$0	0.00%
Common Capital Stock	$1,507,693	10.78%	$30,250,000	36.02%	$1,000,000	32.80%	$1,001,123	4.28%
Preferred Capital Stock	$0	0.00%	$0	0.00%	$0	0.00%	$0	0.00%
Aggregate Write-Ins for Other than Special Surplus Funds	$0	0.00%	$0	0.00%	$0	0.00%	$0	0.00%
Surplus Notes	$0	0.00%	$0	0.00%	$0	0.00%	$0	0.00%
Gross Paid In and Contributed Surplus	$0	0.00%	$12,777,384	15.21%	$1,530,000	50.18%	$5,975,338	25.55%
Unassigned Funds (Surplus)	$2,256,398	16.13%	$3,537,799	4.21%	$127,562	4.18%	$739,145	3.16%
Less Treasury Stock, at Cost:								
Shares Common	$0	0.00%	$0	0.00%	$0	0.00%	$0	0.00%
Shares Preferred	$0	0.00%	$0	0.00%	$0	0.00%	$0	0.00%
Surplus as Regards Policyholders (See Sec. 5, B.6, B.7, C.9, C.11)	$3,764,091	26.90%	$46,565,183	55.44%	$2,657,562	87.16%	$7,715,606	32.99%
TOTAL	$13,992,506	100.00%	$83,985,606	100.00%	$3,048,943	100.00%	$23,386,522	100.00%

A.3 Balance Sheet - By Individual Underwriter

ASSETS	STEWART (OR) Company Value	% of Total	STEWART TGC Company Value	% of Total	STEWART TIC Company Value	% of Total	T.A. TITLE Company Value	% of Total
Bonds	$3,551,979	66.92%	$471,732,412	43.60%	$59,874,861	75.09%	$2,254,290	18.64%
Stocks:								
Preferred Stocks	$0	0.00%	$204,912	0.02%	$0	0.00%	$0	0.00%
Common Stocks	$0	0.00%	$473,057,121	43.72%	$11,498,871	14.42%	$873,276	7.22%
Mortgage Loans on Real Estate:								
First Liens	$0	0.00%	$1,575,077	0.15%	$0	0.00%	$0	0.00%
Other than First Liens	$0	0.00%	$0	0.00%	$0	0.00%	$0	0.00%
Real Estate:								
Properties Occupied by the Company	$0	0.00%	$0	0.00%	$0	0.00%	$0	0.00%
Properties Held for the Production of Income	$0	0.00%	$0	0.00%	$0	0.00%	$0	0.00%
Properties Held for Sale	$0	0.00%	$1,504,067	0.14%	$0	0.00%	$0	0.00%
Cash, Cash Equivalents and Short-Term Investments	$1,538,969	28.99%	$62,968,304	5.82%	$2,478,713	3.11%	$7,462,687	61.72%
Contract Loans	$0	0.00%	$0	0.00%	$0	0.00%	$0	0.00%
Other Invested Assets	$0	0.00%	$1,938,791	0.18%	$0	0.00%	$0	0.00%
Receivables for Securities	$0	0.00%	$0	0.00%	$0	0.00%	$0	0.00%
Aggregate Write-Ins for Invested Assets	$0	0.00%	$0	0.00%	$0	0.00%	$0	0.00%
Subtotals, Cash and Invested Assets	$5,090,948	95.91%	$1,012,980,684	93.62%	$73,852,445	92.62%	$10,590,253	87.58%
Title Plants	$27,097	0.51%	$3,481,193	0.32%	$1,413,800	1.77%	$0	0.00%
Investment Income Due and Accrued	$41,550	0.78%	$7,204,582	0.67%	$839,971	1.05%	$0	0.00%
Premiums and Considerations:								
Uncollected Premiums and Agents' Balances in the Course of Collection	$117,002	2.20%	$34,353,138	3.17%	$1,454,560	1.82%	$27,269	0.23%
Deferred Premiums, Agents' Balances & Installments Booked but Deferred & Not Yet Due	$0	0.00%	$0	0.00%	$0	0.00%	$0	0.00%
Accrued Retrospective Premiums	$0	0.00%	$0	0.00%	$0	0.00%	$0	0.00%
Reinsurance:								
Amounts Recoverable from Reinsurers	$0	0.00%	$0	0.00%	$0	0.00%	$0	0.00%
Funds Held by or Deposited with Reinsured Companies	$0	0.00%	$0	0.00%	$0	0.00%	$0	0.00%
Other Amounts Receivable Under Reinsurance Contracts	$0	0.00%	$254,311	0.02%	$324,070	0.41%	$0	0.00%
Amounts Receivable Relating to Uninsured Plans	$0	0.00%	$0	0.00%	$0	0.00%	$0	0.00%
Current Federal and Foreign Income Tax Recoverable and Interest Thereon	$0	0.00%	$11,548,025	1.07%	$0	0.00%	$0	0.00%
Net Deferred Tax Asset	$30,532	0.58%	$8,439,075	0.78%	$1,039,639	1.30%	$16,660	0.14%
Guaranty Funds Receivable or on Deposit	$0	0.00%	$0	0.00%	$0	0.00%	$0	0.00%
Electronic Data Processing Equipment and Software	$0	0.00%	$683,207	0.06%	$182,800	0.23%	$0	0.00%
Furniture and Equipment, Including Health Care Delivery Assets	$0	0.00%	$414,256	0.04%	$0	0.00%	$0	0.00%
Net Adjustment in Assets and Liabilities Due to Foreign Exchange Rates	$0	0.00%	$0	0.00%	$0	0.00%	$0	0.00%
Receivables from Parent, Subsidiaries and Affiliates	$1,000	0.02%	$1,877,861	0.17%	$97	0.00%	$1,457,336	12.05%
Health Care	$0	0.00%	$266,058	0.02%	$0	0.00%	$0	0.00%
Aggregate Write-Ins for Other than Invest Assets	$0	0.00%	$522,156	0.05%	$633,483	0.79%	$0	0.00%
Total Assets Excluding Separate Accounts, Segregated Accounts & Protected Cell Accounts	$5,308,129	100.00%	$1,082,024,546	100.00%	$79,740,865	100.00%	$12,091,518	100.00%
From Separate Accounts, Segregated Accounts and Protected Cell Accounts	$0	0.00%	$0	0.00%	$0	0.00%	$0	0.00%
TOTAL	$5,308,129	100.00%	$1,082,024,546	100.00%	$79,740,865	100.00%	$12,091,518	100.00%

LIABILITIES	Company Value	% of Total	Company Value	% of Total	Company Value	% of Total	Company Value	% of Total
Known Claims Reserve (See Sec. 5, C.9)	$0	0.00%	$91,456,109	8.45%	$9,643,870	12.09%	$166,537	1.38%
Statutory Premium Reserve (See Sec. 5, C.9)	$2,274,776	42.85%	$428,407,949	39.59%	$27,194,595	34.10%	$4,710,958	38.96%
Aggregate of Other Reserves Required by Law (See Sec. 5, C.9)	$0	0.00%	$0	0.00%	$0	0.00%	$0	0.00%
Supplemental Reserve (See Sec. 5, C.9)	$0	0.00%	$0	0.00%	$0	0.00%	$0	0.00%
Commissions, Brokerage & Other Charges Due or Accrued to Attorneys, Agents & Real Estate Brokers	$0	0.00%	$0	0.00%	$0	0.00%	$0	0.00%
Other Expenses (Excluding Taxes, Licenses and Fees)	$3,000	0.06%	$20,013,762	1.85%	$3,810,046	4.78%	$254,194	2.10%
Taxes, Licenses and Fees (Excluding Federal and Foreign Income Taxes)	$0	0.00%	$4,914,690	0.45%	($6,133)	(0.01)%	$111,363	0.92%
Current Federal and Foreign Income Taxes	$93,173	1.76%	$0	0.00%	$4,106,450	5.15%	$345,127	2.85%
Net Deferred Tax Liability	$0	0.00%	$0	0.00%	$0	0.00%	$0	0.00%
Borrowed Money and Interest Thereon	$0	0.00%	$0	0.00%	$0	0.00%	$0	0.00%
Dividends Declared and Unpaid	$0	0.00%	$2,000,000	0.18%	$0	0.00%	$0	0.00%
Premiums and Other Consideration Received in Advance	$0	0.00%	$0	0.00%	$0	0.00%	$0	0.00%
Unearned Interest and Real Estate Income Received in Advance	$0	0.00%	$0	0.00%	$0	0.00%	$0	0.00%
Funds Held by Company Under Reinsurance Treaties	$0	0.00%	$554,242	0.05%	$0	0.00%	$0	0.00%
Amounts Withheld or Retained by Company for Accounts of Others	$0	0.00%	$0	0.00%	$0	0.00%	$0	0.00%
Provision for Unauthorized Reinsurance	$0	0.00%	$0	0.00%	$0	0.00%	$0	0.00%
Net Adjustment in Assets and Liabilities Due to Foreign Exchange Rates	$0	0.00%	$10,304,820	0.95%	$0	0.00%	$0	0.00%
Drafts Outstanding	$0	0.00%	$0	0.00%	$0	0.00%	$0	0.00%
Payable to Parent, Subsidiaries and Affiliates	$26,721	0.50%	$6,425,412	0.59%	$0	0.00%	$0	0.00%
Payable for Securities	$0	0.00%	$0	0.00%	$0	0.00%	$0	0.00%
Aggregate Write-Ins for Other Liabilities	$36,468	0.69%	$2,046,547	0.19%	$476,538	0.60%	$0	0.00%
Total Liabilities (See Sec. 5, B.3)	$2,434,138	45.86%	$566,123,531	52.32%	$45,225,366	56.72%	$5,588,179	46.22%
Aggregate Write-Ins for Special Surplus Funds	$0	0.00%	$501,406	0.05%	$0	0.00%	$0	0.00%
Common Capital Stock	$500,000	9.42%	$8,500,000	0.79%	$1,100,000	1.38%	$1,000,800	8.28%
Preferred Capital Stock	$0	0.00%	$0	0.00%	$0	0.00%	$0	0.00%
Aggregate Write-Ins for Other than Special Surplus Funds	$0	0.00%	$0	0.00%	$0	0.00%	$0	0.00%
Surplus Notes	$0	0.00%	$0	0.00%	$0	0.00%	$0	0.00%
Gross Paid In and Contributed Surplus	$2,544,359	47.93%	$110,952,424	10.25%	$23,765,535	29.80%	$830,098	6.87%
Unassigned Funds (Surplus)	($170,368)	(3.21)%	$395,947,185	36.59%	$9,649,964	12.10%	$4,672,441	38.64%
Less Treasury Stock, at Cost:								
Shares Common	$0	0.00%	$0	0.00%	$0	0.00%	$0	0.00%
Shares Preferred	$0	0.00%	$0	0.00%	$0	0.00%	$0	0.00%
Surplus as Regards Policyholders (See Sec. 5, B.6, B.7, C.9, C.11)	$2,873,991	54.14%	$515,901,015	47.68%	$34,515,499	43.28%	$6,503,339	53.78%
TOTAL	$5,308,129	100.00%	$1,082,024,546	100.00%	$79,740,865	100.00%	$12,091,518	100.00%

A.3 Balance Sheet - By Individual Underwriter

	TICOR		TICOR (FL)		TITLE G&TC		TITLE GUARANTY DIV (IA)	
ASSETS	Company Value	% of Total	Company Value	% of Total	Company Value	% of Total	Company Value	% of Total
Bonds	$181,124,297	76.10%	$100,316,481	82.99%	$119,867	8.27%	$0	0.00%
Stocks:								
Preferred Stocks	$0	0.00%	$0	0.00%	$0	0.00%	$0	0.00%
Common Stocks	$13,739,315	5.77%	$10,000	0.01%	$0	0.00%	$0	0.00%
Mortgage Loans on Real Estate:								
First Liens	$3,437,691	1.44%	$0	0.00%	$0	0.00%	$0	0.00%
Other than First Liens	$0	0.00%	$0	0.00%	$0	0.00%	$0	0.00%
Real Estate:								
Properties Occupied by the Company	$28,932	0.01%	$740,169	0.61%	$123,191	8.50%	$0	0.00%
Properties Held for the Production of Income	$0	0.00%	$0	0.00%	$0	0.00%	$0	0.00%
Properties Held for Sale	$48,600	0.02%	$154,350	0.13%	$0	0.00%	$0	0.00%
Cash, Cash Equivalents and Short-Term Investments	$11,935,844	5.02%	$2,296,791	1.90%	$1,044,756	72.12%	$6,191,804	99.78%
Contract Loans	$0	0.00%	$0	0.00%	$0	0.00%	$0	0.00%
Other Invested Assets	$1,107,439	0.47%	$0	0.00%	$0	0.00%	$0	0.00%
Receivables for Securities	$18,769	0.01%	$30,273	0.03%	$0	0.00%	$0	0.00%
Aggregate Write-Ins for Invested Assets	$0	0.00%	$0	0.00%	$0	0.00%	$0	0.00%
Subtotals, Cash and Invested Assets	$211,440,887	88.84%	$103,548,064	85.67%	$1,287,814	88.90%	$6,191,804	99.78%
Title Plants	$13,349,432	5.61%	$7,585,327	6.28%	$0	0.00%	$0	0.00%
Investment Income Due and Accrued	$2,712,183	1.14%	$1,369,002	1.13%	$886	0.06%	$0	0.00%
Premiums and Considerations:								
Uncollected Premiums and Agents' Balances in the Course of Collection	$2,469,658	1.04%	$2,617,478	2.17%	$7,850	0.54%	$0	0.00%
Deferred Premiums, Agents' Balances & Installments Booked but Deferred & Not Yet Due	$0	0.00%	$0	0.00%	$0	0.00%	$0	0.00%
Accrued Retrospective Premiums	$0	0.00%	$0	0.00%	$0	0.00%	$0	0.00%
Reinsurance:								
Amounts Recoverable from Reinsurers	$0	0.00%	$0	0.00%	$0	0.00%	$0	0.00%
Funds Held by or Deposited with Reinsured Companies	$0	0.00%	$0	0.00%	$0	0.00%	$0	0.00%
Other Amounts Receivable Under Reinsurance Contracts	$0	0.00%	$0	0.00%	$0	0.00%	$0	0.00%
Amounts Receivable Relating to Uninsured Plans	$0	0.00%	$0	0.00%	$0	0.00%	$0	0.00%
Current Federal and Foreign Income Tax Recoverable and Interest Thereon	$2,161,660	0.91%	$3,074,742	2.54%	$41,529	2.87%	$0	0.00%
Net Deferred Tax Asset	$3,033,542	1.27%	$2,677,751	2.22%	$0	0.00%	$0	0.00%
Guaranty Funds Receivable or on Deposit	$0	0.00%	$0	0.00%	$0	0.00%	$25,760	0.42%
Electronic Data Processing Equipment and Software	$15,890	0.01%	$0	0.00%	$22,901	1.58%	$0	0.00%
Furniture and Equipment, Including Health Care Delivery Assets	$0	0.00%	$0	0.00%	$0	0.00%	$40,540	0.65%
Net Adjustment in Assets and Liabilities Due to Foreign Exchange Rates	$0	0.00%	$0	0.00%	$0	0.00%	$0	0.00%
Receivables from Parent, Subsidiaries and Affiliates	$2,811,946	1.18%	$0	0.00%	$0	0.00%	($52,724)	(0.85%)
Health Care	$0	0.00%	$0	0.00%	$0	0.00%	$0	0.00%
Aggregate Write-Ins for Other than Invest Assets	$0	0.00%	$0	0.00%	$87,671	6.05%	$0	0.00%
Total Assets Excluding Separate Accounts, Segregated Accounts & Protected Cell Accounts	$237,995,198	100.00%	$120,872,364	100.00%	$1,448,651	100.00%	$6,205,380	100.00%
From Separate Accounts, Segregated Accounts and Protected Cell Accounts	$0	0.00%	$0	0.00%	$0	0.00%	$0	0.00%
TOTAL	$237,995,198	100.00%	$120,872,364	100.00%	$1,448,651	100.00%	$6,205,380	100.00%

	Company Value	% of Total	Company Value	% of Total	Company Value	% of Total	Company Value	% of Total
LIABILITIES								
Known Claims Reserve (See Sec. 5, C.9)	$21,961,002	9.23%	$18,143,728	15.01%	$0	0.00%	$340,218	5.48%
Statutory Premium Reserve (See Sec. 5, C.9)	$113,187,091	47.56%	$63,963,771	52.92%	$246,463	17.01%	$3,669,317	59.13%
Aggregate of Other Reserves Required by Law (See Sec. 5, C.9)	$0	0.00%	$0	0.00%	$100,000	6.90%	$1,000,000	16.12%
Supplemental Reserve (See Sec. 5, C.9)	$0	0.00%	$0	0.00%	$0	0.00%	$0	0.00%
Commissions, Brokerage & Other Charges Due or Accrued to Attorneys, Agents & Real Estate Brokers	$0	0.00%	$0	0.00%	$7,828	0.54%	$0	0.00%
Other Expenses (Excluding Taxes, Licenses and Fees)	$17,757,537	7.46%	$1,219,468	1.01%	$163,822	11.31%	$456,141	7.35%
Taxes, Licenses and Fees (Excluding Federal and Foreign Income Taxes)	$5,090,933	2.14%	$831,404	0.69%	$9,709	0.67%	$0	0.00%
Current Federal and Foreign Income Taxes	$0	0.00%	$0	0.00%	$0	0.00%	$0	0.00%
Net Deferred Tax Liability	$0	0.00%	$0	0.00%	$13,222	0.91%	$0	0.00%
Borrowed Money and Interest Thereon	$0	0.00%	$0	0.00%	$0	0.00%	$0	0.00%
Dividends Declared and Unpaid	$0	0.00%	$0	0.00%	$0	0.00%	$0	0.00%
Premiums and Other Consideration Received in Advance	$0	0.00%	$972,120	0.80%	$0	0.00%	$0	0.00%
Unearned Interest and Real Estate Income Received in Advance	$0	0.00%	$0	0.00%	$0	0.00%	$0	0.00%
Funds Held by Company Under Reinsurance Treaties	$0	0.00%	$0	0.00%	$0	0.00%	$0	0.00%
Amounts Withheld or Retained by Company for Accounts of Others	$2,069,898	0.87%	$0	0.00%	$0	0.00%	$0	0.00%
Provision for Unauthorized Reinsurance	$0	0.00%	$0	0.00%	$0	0.00%	$0	0.00%
Net Adjustment in Assets and Liabilities Due to Foreign Exchange Rates	$0	0.00%	$0	0.00%	$0	0.00%	$0	0.00%
Drafts Outstanding	$0	0.00%	$0	0.00%	$0	0.00%	$0	0.00%
Payable to Parent, Subsidiaries and Affiliates	$179,899	0.08%	$8,003,166	6.62%	$0	0.00%	$0	0.00%
Payable for Securities	$0	0.00%	$0	0.00%	$0	0.00%	$0	0.00%
Aggregate Write-Ins for Other Liabilities	$10,061,925	4.23%	$2,152,231	1.78%	$0	0.00%	$0	0.00%
Total Liabilities (See Sec. 5, B.3)	$170,308,285	71.56%	$95,285,888	78.83%	$541,044	37.35%	$5,465,676	88.08%
Aggregate Write-Ins for Special Surplus Funds	$0	0.00%	$0	0.00%	$0	0.00%	$0	0.00%
Common Capital Stock	$30,000,000	12.61%	$2,000,000	1.65%	$200,000	13.81%	$0	0.00%
Preferred Capital Stock	$0	0.00%	$0	0.00%	$0	0.00%	$0	0.00%
Aggregate Write-Ins for Other than Special Surplus Funds	$0	0.00%	$0	0.00%	$0	0.00%	$0	0.00%
Surplus Notes	$0	0.00%	$0	0.00%	$0	0.00%	$0	0.00%
Gross Paid In and Contributed Surplus	$16,123,418	6.77%	$5,644,598	4.67%	$17,733	1.22%	$0	0.00%
Unassigned Funds (Surplus)	$21,563,495	9.06%	$17,941,878	14.84%	$689,874	47.62%	$739,705	11.92%
Less Treasury Stock, at Cost:								
Shares Common	$0	0.00%	$0	0.00%	$0	0.00%	$0	0.00%
Shares Preferred	$0	0.00%	$0	0.00%	$0	0.00%	$0	0.00%
Surplus as Regards Policyholders (See Sec. 5, B.6, B.7, C.9, C.11)	$67,686,913	28.44%	$25,586,476	21.17%	$907,607	62.65%	$739,705	11.92%
TOTAL	$237,995,198	100.00%	$120,872,364	100.00%	$1,448,651	100.00%	$6,205,381	100.00%

A.3 Balance Sheet - By Individual Underwriter

ASSETS	TITLE IC AMERICA Company Value	% of Total	TITLE RESOURCES Company Value	% of Total	TITLEDGE Company Value	% of Total	TRANSNATION Company Value	% of Total
Bonds	$13,037,624	84.58%	$1,778,516	4.44%	$752,574	96.08%	$126,708,473	79.40%
Stocks:								
Preferred Stocks	$0	0.00%	$0	0.00%	$0	0.00%	$0	0.00%
Common Stocks	$0	0.00%	$0	0.00%	$0	0.00%	$935,755	0.59%
Mortgage Loans on Real Estate:								
First Liens	$0	0.00%	$0	0.00%	$0	0.00%	$0	0.00%
Other than First Liens	$0	0.00%	$0	0.00%	$0	0.00%	$0	0.00%
Real Estate:								
Properties Occupied by the Company	$0	0.00%	$0	0.00%	$0	0.00%	$1,015,792	0.64%
Properties Held for the Production of Income	$0	0.00%	$0	0.00%	$0	0.00%	$0	0.00%
Properties Held for Sale	$0	0.00%	$85,000	0.21%	$0	0.00%	$0	0.00%
Cash, Cash Equivalents and Short-Term Investments	$1,590,032	10.32%	$33,966,806	84.79%	$408	0.05%	$9,192,210	5.76%
Contract Loans	$0	0.00%	$0	0.00%	$0	0.00%	$0	0.00%
Other Invested Assets	$0	0.00%	$31,483	0.08%	$0	0.00%	$107,606	0.07%
Receivables for Securities	$100,000	0.65%	$0	0.00%	$0	0.00%	$2,380,187	1.49%
Aggregate Write-Ins for Invested Assets	$0	0.00%	$0	0.00%	$0	0.00%	$0	0.00%
Subtotals, Cash and Invested Assets	$14,727,656	95.55%	$35,861,805	89.52%	$752,982	96.13%	$140,340,023	87.94%
Title Plants	$476,895	3.09%	$0	0.00%	$0	0.00%	$6,564,819	4.11%
Investment Income Due and Accrued	$145,054	0.94%	$63,129	0.16%	$6,563	0.84%	$1,236,847	0.78%
Premiums and Considerations:								
Uncollected Premiums and Agents' Balances in the Course of Collection	$33,014	0.21%	$3,628,371	9.06%	$1,183	0.15%	$3,053,654	1.91%
Deferred Premiums, Agents' Balances & Installments Booked but Deferred & Not Yet Due	$0	0.00%	$0	0.00%	$0	0.00%	$0	0.00%
Accrued Retrospective Premiums	$0	0.00%	$0	0.00%	$0	0.00%	$0	0.00%
Reinsurance:								
Amounts Recoverable from Reinsurers	$0	0.00%	$0	0.00%	$0	0.00%	$0	0.00%
Funds Held by or Deposited with Reinsured Companies	$0	0.00%	$0	0.00%	$0	0.00%	$0	0.00%
Other Amounts Receivable Under Reinsurance Contracts	$0	0.00%	$0	0.00%	$0	0.00%	$0	0.00%
Amounts Receivable Relating to Uninsured Plans	$0	0.00%	$0	0.00%	$0	0.00%	$0	0.00%
Current Federal and Foreign Income Tax Recoverable and Interest Thereon	$0	0.00%	$291,093	0.73%	$0	0.00%	$5,198,821	3.26%
Net Deferred Tax Asset	$31,321	0.20%	$172,417	0.43%	$0	0.00%	$2,731,599	1.71%
Guaranty Funds Receivable or on Deposit	$0	0.00%	$0	0.00%	$0	0.00%	$0	0.00%
Electronic Data Processing Equipment and Software	$0	0.00%	$21,738	0.05%	$0	0.00%	$224,112	0.14%
Furniture and Equipment, Including Health Care Delivery Assets	$0	0.00%	$0	0.00%	$0	0.00%	$0	0.00%
Net Adjustment in Assets and Liabilities Due to Foreign Exchange Rates	$0	0.00%	$0	0.00%	$0	0.00%	$0	0.00%
Receivables from Parent, Subsidiaries and Affiliates	$0	0.00%	$0	0.00%	$22,555	2.88%	$227,818	0.14%
Health Care	$0	0.00%	$0	0.00%	$0	0.00%	$0	0.00%
Aggregate Write-Ins for Other than Invest Assets	$0	0.00%	$20,354	0.05%	$0	0.00%	$0	0.00%
Total Assets Excluding Separate Accounts, Segregated Accounts & Protected Cell Accounts	$15,413,940	100.00%	$40,058,907	100.00%	$783,283	100.00%	$159,577,693	100.00%
From Separate Accounts, Segregated Accounts and Protected Cell Accounts	$0	0.00%	$0	0.00%	$0	0.00%	$0	0.00%
TOTAL	$15,413,940	100.00%	$40,058,907	100.00%	$783,283	100.00%	$159,577,693	100.00%

LIABILITIES	Company Value	% of Total	Company Value	% of Total	Company Value	% of Total	Company Value	% of Total
Known Claims Reserve (See Sec. 5, C.9)	$326,405	2.12%	$413,706	1.03%	$0	0.00%	$19,021,314	11.92%
Statutory Premium Reserve (See Sec. 5, C.9)	$3,046,160	19.76%	$13,035,201	32.54%	$7,275	0.93%	$95,928,536	60.11%
Aggregate of Other Reserves Required by Law (See Sec. 5, C.9)	$0	0.00%	$12,974	0.03%	$0	0.00%	$0	0.00%
Supplemental Reserve (See Sec. 5, C.9)	$0	0.00%	$0	0.00%	$6,040	0.77%	$9,601,900	6.02%
Commissions, Brokerage & Other Charges Due or Accrued to Attorneys, Agents & Real Estate Brokers	$0	0.00%	$0	0.00%	$0	0.00%	$0	0.00%
Other Expenses (Excluding Taxes, Licenses and Fees)	$46,199	0.30%	$534,124	1.33%	$11,199	1.43%	$6,897,975	4.32%
Taxes, Licenses and Fees (Excluding Federal and Foreign Income Taxes)	$197,193	1.28%	$53,578	0.13%	$4,095	0.52%	$795,006	0.50%
Current Federal and Foreign Income Taxes	$68,970	0.45%	$0	0.00%	$1,589	0.20%	$0	0.00%
Net Deferred Tax Liability	$0	0.00%	$0	0.00%	$0	0.00%	$0	0.00%
Borrowed Money and Interest Thereon	$0	0.00%	$0	0.00%	$0	0.00%	$0	0.00%
Dividends Declared and Unpaid	$0	0.00%	$0	0.00%	$0	0.00%	$0	0.00%
Premiums and Other Consideration Received in Advance	$0	0.00%	$0	0.00%	$0	0.00%	$985,943	0.62%
Unearned Interest and Real Estate Income Received in Advance	$0	0.00%	$0	0.00%	$0	0.00%	$0	0.00%
Funds Held by Company Under Reinsurance Treaties	$0	0.00%	$0	0.00%	$0	0.00%	$0	0.00%
Amounts Withheld or Retained by Company for Accounts of Others	$0	0.00%	$0	0.00%	$0	0.00%	$0	0.00%
Provision for Unauthorized Reinsurance	$0	0.00%	$0	0.00%	$0	0.00%	$0	0.00%
Net Adjustment in Assets and Liabilities Due to Foreign Exchange Rates	$0	0.00%	$0	0.00%	$0	0.00%	$0	0.00%
Drafts Outstanding	$0	0.00%	$0	0.00%	$0	0.00%	$0	0.00%
Payable to Parent, Subsidiaries and Affiliates	$62,438	0.41%	$198,454	0.50%	$0	0.00%	$2,419,867	1.52%
Payable for Securities	$0	0.00%	$0	0.00%	$0	0.00%	$0	0.00%
Aggregate Write-Ins for Other Liabilities	$0	0.00%	$99,266	0.25%	$0	0.00%	$1,592,370	1.00%
Total Liabilities (See Sec. 5, B.3)	$3,747,365	24.31%	$14,347,303	35.82%	$30,198	3.86%	$137,242,911	86.00%
Aggregate Write-Ins for Special Surplus Funds	$0	0.00%	$0	0.00%	$0	0.00%	$0	0.00%
Common Capital Stock	$1,500,000	9.73%	$1,000,000	2.50%	$500,000	63.83%	$10,000,000	6.27%
Preferred Capital Stock	$0	0.00%	$0	0.00%	$0	0.00%	$0	0.00%
Aggregate Write-Ins for Other than Special Surplus Funds	$0	0.00%	$0	0.00%	$0	0.00%	$0	0.00%
Surplus Notes	$0	0.00%	$0	0.00%	$0	0.00%	$0	0.00%
Gross Paid In and Contributed Surplus	$4,775,488	30.98%	$1,477,452	3.69%	$250,000	31.92%	$36,580,687	22.92%
Unassigned Funds (Surplus)	$5,391,087	34.98%	$26,560,352	66.30%	$3,085	0.39%	($24,245,905)	(15.19%)
Less Treasury Stock, at Cost:								
Shares Common	$0	0.00%	$3,326,200	8.30%	$0	0.00%	$0	0.00%
Shares Preferred	$0	0.00%	$0	0.00%	$0	0.00%	$0	0.00%
Surplus as Regards Policyholders (See Sec. 5, B.6, B.7, C.9, C.11)	$11,666,575	75.69%	$25,711,604	64.18%	$753,085	96.14%	$22,334,782	14.00%
TOTAL	$15,413,940	100.00%	$40,058,907	100.00%	$783,283	100.00%	$159,577,693	100.00%

A.3 Balance Sheet - By Individual Underwriter

ASSETS	TRANSUNION NATIONAL Company Value	% of Total	TRANSUNION TIC Company Value	% of Total	UNITED CAPITAL Company Value	% of Total	UNITED GENERAL Company Value	% of Total
Bonds	$6,320,913	40.58%	$7,461,744	69.29%	$38,055,061	74.34%	$27,635,673	23.20%
Stocks:								
Preferred Stocks	$0	0.00%	$0	0.00%	$134,750	0.26%	$0	0.00%
Common Stocks	$2,188,800	14.05%	$0	0.00%	$0	0.00%	$1,564,261	1.31%
Mortgage Loans on Real Estate:								
First Liens	$0	0.00%	$0	0.00%	$0	0.00%	$0	0.00%
Other than First Liens	$0	0.00%	$0	0.00%	$0	0.00%	$0	0.00%
Real Estate:								
Properties Occupied by the Company	$0	0.00%	$0	0.00%	$0	0.00%	$0	0.00%
Properties Held for the Production of Income	$0	0.00%	$0	0.00%	$0	0.00%	$0	0.00%
Properties Held for Sale	$15,000	0.10%	$0	0.00%	$655,800	1.28%	$0	0.00%
Cash, Cash Equivalents and Short-Term Investments	$6,866,625	44.09%	$2,979,351	27.67%	$8,132,189	15.89%	$58,680,182	49.27%
Contract Loans	$0	0.00%	$0	0.00%	$0	0.00%	$0	0.00%
Other Invested Assets	$0	0.00%	$0	0.00%	$0	0.00%	$0	0.00%
Receivables for Securities	$0	0.00%	$0	0.00%	$211,000	0.41%	$0	0.00%
Aggregate Write-Ins for Invested Assets	$0	0.00%	$0	0.00%	$0	0.00%	$0	0.00%
Subtotals, Cash and Invested Assets	$15,391,338	98.82%	$10,441,095	96.95%	$47,188,800	92.18%	$87,880,116	73.79%
Title Plants	$0	0.00%	$114,022	1.06%	$0	0.00%	$1,005,000	0.84%
Investment Income Due and Accrued	$93,216	0.60%	$117,763	1.09%	$451,888	0.88%	$403,007	0.34%
Premiums and Considerations:								
Uncollected Premiums and Agents' Balances in the Course of Collection	$711	0.00%	$4,410	0.04%	$41,109	0.08%	$5,818,625	4.89%
Deferred Premiums, Agents' Balances & Installments Booked but Deferred & Not Yet Due	$0	0.00%	$0	0.00%	$0	0.00%	$0	0.00%
Accrued Retrospective Premiums	$0	0.00%	$0	0.00%	$0	0.00%	$0	0.00%
Reinsurance:								
Amounts Recoverable from Reinsurers	$0	0.00%	$0	0.00%	$0	0.00%	$0	0.00%
Funds Held by or Deposited with Reinsured Companies	$0	0.00%	$0	0.00%	$0	0.00%	$0	0.00%
Other Amounts Receivable Under Reinsurance Contracts	$0	0.00%	$0	0.00%	$0	0.00%	$4,284,792	3.60%
Amounts Receivable Relating to Uninsured Plans	$0	0.00%	$0	0.00%	$0	0.00%	$0	0.00%
Current Federal and Foreign Income Tax Recoverable and Interest Thereon	$51,421	0.33%	$0	0.00%	$2,898,332	5.66%	$13,502,740	11.34%
Net Deferred Tax Asset	$32,514	0.21%	$91,758	0.85%	$335,356	0.66%	$2,575,779	2.16%
Guaranty Funds Receivable or on Deposit	$0	0.00%	$0	0.00%	$0	0.00%	$0	0.00%
Electronic Data Processing Equipment and Software	$3,637	0.02%	$0	0.00%	$0	0.00%	$446,818	0.38%
Furniture and Equipment, Including Health Care Delivery Assets	$0	0.00%	$0	0.00%	$0	0.00%	$0	0.00%
Net Adjustment in Assets and Liabilities Due to Foreign Exchange Rates	$0	0.00%	$0	0.00%	$0	0.00%	$0	0.00%
Receivables from Parent, Subsidiaries and Affiliates	$0	0.00%	$0	0.00%	$268,030	0.52%	$0	0.00%
Health Care	$0	0.00%	$0	0.00%	$0	0.00%	$0	0.00%
Aggregate Write-Ins for Other than Invest Assets	$2,664	0.02%	$0	0.00%	$8,150	0.02%	$3,184,513	2.67%
Total Assets Excluding Separate Accounts, Segregated Accounts & Protected Cell Accounts	$15,575,501	100.00%	$10,769,048	100.00%	$51,191,665	100.00%	$119,101,390	100.00%
From Separate Accounts, Segregated Accounts and Protected Cell Accounts	$0	0.00%	$0	0.00%	$0	0.00%	$0	0.00%
TOTAL	$15,575,501	100.00%	$10,769,048	100.00%	$51,191,665	100.00%	$119,101,390	100.00%

LIABILITIES	Company Value	% of Total	Company Value	% of Total	Company Value	% of Total	Company Value	% of Total
Known Claims Reserve (See Sec. 5, C.9)	$788,340	5.06%	$148,252	1.38%	$4,183,408	8.17%	$13,277,853	11.15%
Statutory Premium Reserve (See Sec. 5, C.9)	$3,515,209	22.57%	$3,220,967	29.91%	$24,027,403	46.94%	$62,615,939	52.57%
Aggregate of Other Reserves Required by Law (See Sec. 5, C.9)	$0	0.00%	$0	0.00%	$0	0.00%	$0	0.00%
Supplemental Reserve (See Sec. 5, C.9)	$0	0.00%	$0	0.00%	$0	0.00%	$0	0.00%
Commissions, Brokerage & Other Charges Due or Accrued to Attorneys, Agents & Real Estate Brokers	$15,867	0.10%	$0	0.00%	$0	0.00%	$244,223	0.21%
Other Expenses (Excluding Taxes, Licenses and Fees)	$145,502	0.93%	$531,803	4.94%	$179,299	0.35%	$9,229,588	7.75%
Taxes, Licenses and Fees (Excluding Federal and Foreign Income Taxes)	$36,270	0.23%	$9,033	0.08%	$27,523	0.05%	$1,135,937	0.95%
Current Federal and Foreign Income Taxes	$0	0.00%	$0	0.00%	$0	0.00%	$0	0.00%
Net Deferred Tax Liability	$0	0.00%	$0	0.00%	$0	0.00%	$0	0.00%
Borrowed Money and Interest Thereon	$0	0.00%	$0	0.00%	$0	0.00%	$0	0.00%
Dividends Declared and Unpaid	$0	0.00%	$0	0.00%	$0	0.00%	$0	0.00%
Premiums and Other Consideration Received in Advance	$0	0.00%	$0	0.00%	$0	0.00%	$2,310,701	1.94%
Unearned Interest and Real Estate Income Received in Advance	$0	0.00%	$0	0.00%	$0	0.00%	$0	0.00%
Funds Held by Company Under Reinsurance Treaties	$0	0.00%	$0	0.00%	$0	0.00%	$0	0.00%
Amounts Withheld or Retained by Company for Accounts of Others	$0	0.00%	$0	0.00%	$0	0.00%	$714,171	0.60%
Provision for Unauthorized Reinsurance	$0	0.00%	$0	0.00%	$0	0.00%	$0	0.00%
Net Adjustment in Assets and Liabilities Due to Foreign Exchange Rates	$0	0.00%	$0	0.00%	$0	0.00%	$0	0.00%
Drafts Outstanding	$0	0.00%	$0	0.00%	$0	0.00%	$0	0.00%
Payable to Parent, Subsidiaries and Affiliates	$1,025,781	6.59%	$2,978,149	27.65%	$0	0.00%	$1,524,835	1.28%
Payable for Securities	$0	0.00%	$0	0.00%	$0	0.00%	$0	0.00%
Aggregate Write-Ins for Other Liabilities	$0	0.00%	$0	0.00%	$6,490	0.01%	$73,871	0.06%
Total Liabilities (See Sec. 5, B.3)	$5,526,969	35.49%	$6,888,204	63.96%	$28,424,123	55.52%	$91,127,118	76.51%
Aggregate Write-Ins for Special Surplus Funds	$0	0.00%	$0	0.00%	$0	0.00%	$0	0.00%
Common Capital Stock	$1,500,000	9.63%	$1,000,000	9.29%	$1,000,000	1.95%	$2,010,000	1.69%
Preferred Capital Stock	$0	0.00%	$0	0.00%	$0	0.00%	$0	0.00%
Aggregate Write-Ins for Other than Special Surplus Funds	$0	0.00%	$0	0.00%	$0	0.00%	$0	0.00%
Surplus Notes	$0	0.00%	$0	0.00%	$0	0.00%	$0	0.00%
Gross Paid In and Contributed Surplus	$11,309,905	72.61%	$10,025,495	93.10%	$3,000,000	5.86%	$64,753,805	54.37%
Unassigned Funds (Surplus)	($2,761,373)	(17.73)%	($7,144,651)	(66.34)%	$18,767,542	36.66%	($38,789,533)	(32.57)%
Less Treasury Stock, at Cost:								
Shares Common	$0	0.00%	$0	0.00%	$0	0.00%	$0	0.00%
Shares Preferred	$0	0.00%	$0	0.00%	$0	0.00%	$0	0.00%
Surplus as Regards Policyholders (See Sec. 5, B.6, B.7, C.9, C.11)	$10,048,532	64.51%	$3,880,844	36.04%	$22,767,542	44.48%	$27,974,272	23.49%
TOTAL	$15,575,501	100.00%	$10,769,048	100.00%	$51,191,665	100.00%	$119,101,390	100.00%

A.3 Balance Sheet - By Individual Underwriter

	WASHINGTON TIC		WESTCOR		WESTERN NATIONAL	
ASSETS	Company Value	% of Total	Company Value	% of Total	Company Value	% of Total
Bonds	$299,947	7.60%	$14,323,071	59.52%	$201,521	4.25%
Stocks:						
Preferred Stocks	$0	0.00%	$0	0.00%	$355,119	7.49%
Common Stocks	$0	0.00%	$3,576,893	14.86%	$0	0.00%
Mortgage Loans on Real Estate:						
First Liens	$0	0.00%	$0	0.00%	$0	0.00%
Other than First Liens	$0	0.00%	$0	0.00%	$0	0.00%
Real Estate:						
Properties Occupied by the Company	$0	0.00%	$0	0.00%	$0	0.00%
Properties Held for the Production of Income	$0	0.00%	$0	0.00%	$0	0.00%
Properties Held for Sale	$0	0.00%	$0	0.00%	$0	0.00%
Cash, Cash Equivalents and Short-Term Investments	$2,616,188	66.32%	$1,971,897	8.19%	$4,081,426	86.10%
Contract Loans	$0	0.00%	$0	0.00%	$0	0.00%
Other Invested Assets	$0	0.00%	$839,526	3.49%	$0	0.00%
Receivables for Securities	$0	0.00%	$0	0.00%	$0	0.00%
Aggregate Write-Ins for Invested Assets	$0	0.00%	$0	0.00%	$0	0.00%
Subtotals, Cash and Invested Assets	$2,916,135	73.92%	$20,711,387	86.07%	$4,638,066	97.84%
Title Plants	$0	0.00%	$137,650	0.57%	$0	0.00%
Investment Income Due and Accrued	$8,156	0.21%	$184,950	0.77%	$0	0.00%
Premiums and Considerations:						
Uncollected Premiums and Agents' Balances in the Course of Collection	$126,457	3.21%	$1,822,544	7.57%	$0	0.00%
Deferred Premiums, Agents' Balances & Installments Booked but Deferred & Not Yet Due	$0	0.00%	$0	0.00%	$0	0.00%
Accrued Retrospective Premiums	$0	0.00%	$0	0.00%	$0	0.00%
Reinsurance:						
Amounts Recoverable from Reinsurers	$0	0.00%	$0	0.00%	$0	0.00%
Funds Held by or Deposited with Reinsured Companies	$0	0.00%	$0	0.00%	$0	0.00%
Other Amounts Receivable Under Reinsurance Contracts	$0	0.00%	$0	0.00%	$0	0.00%
Amounts Receivable Relating to Uninsured Plans	$0	0.00%	$0	0.00%	$0	0.00%
Current Federal and Foreign Income Tax Recoverable and Interest Thereon	$0	0.00%	$805,900	3.35%	$85,598	1.81%
Net Deferred Tax Asset	$0	0.00%	$348,666	1.45%	$16,639	0.35%
Guaranty Funds Receivable or on Deposit	$0	0.00%	$0	0.00%	$0	0.00%
Electronic Data Processing Equipment and Software	$6,181	0.16%	$0	0.00%	$0	0.00%
Furniture and Equipment, Including Health Care Delivery Assets	$0	0.00%	$0	0.00%	$0	0.00%
Net Adjustment in Assets and Liabilities Due to Foreign Exchange Rates	$0	0.00%	$0	0.00%	$0	0.00%
Receivables from Parent, Subsidiaries and Affiliates	$0	0.00%	$47,274	0.20%	$0	0.00%
Health Care	$0	0.00%	$4,310	0.02%	$0	0.00%
Aggregate Write-Ins for Other than Invest Assets	$0	0.00%	$0	0.00%	$0	0.00%
Total Assets Excluding Separate Accounts, Segregated Accounts & Protected Cell Accounts	$3,056,929	77.49%	$24,062,681	100.00%	$4,740,303	100.00%
From Separate Accounts, Segregated Accounts and Protected Cell Accounts	$888,131	22.51%	$0	0.00%	$0	0.00%
TOTAL	$3,945,060	100.00%	$24,062,681	100.00%	$4,740,303	100.00%

	Company Value	% of Total	Company Value	% of Total	Company Value	% of Total
LIABILITIES						
Known Claims Reserve (See Sec. 5, C.9)	$147,409	3.74%	$594,127	2.47%	$48,354	1.02%
Statutory Premium Reserve (See Sec. 5, C.9)	$1,906,622	48.33%	$13,492,778	56.07%	$1,164,289	24.56%
Aggregate of Other Reserves Required by Law (See Sec. 5, C.9)	$0	0.00%	$0	0.00%	$0	0.00%
Supplemental Reserve (See Sec. 5, C.9)	$230,378	5.84%	$0	0.00%	$0	0.00%
Commissions, Brokerage & Other Charges Due or Accrued to Attorneys, Agents & Real Estate Brokers	$0	0.00%	$0	0.00%	$0	0.00%
Other Expenses (Excluding Taxes, Licenses and Fees)	$30,921	0.78%	$639,150	2.66%	$448	0.01%
Taxes, Licenses and Fees (Excluding Federal and Foreign Income Taxes)	($66,050)	(1.67)%	$561,286	2.33%	$1,049	0.02%
Current Federal and Foreign Income Taxes	($85,085)	(2.16)%	$0	0.00%	$0	0.00%
Net Deferred Tax Liability	$0	0.00%	$0	0.00%	$0	0.00%
Borrowed Money and Interest Thereon	$0	0.00%	$0	0.00%	$0	0.00%
Dividends Declared and Unpaid	$0	0.00%	$0	0.00%	$0	0.00%
Premiums and Other Consideration Received in Advance	$0	0.00%	$0	0.00%	$0	0.00%
Unearned Interest and Real Estate Income Received in Advance	$0	0.00%	$0	0.00%	$0	0.00%
Funds Held by Company Under Reinsurance Treaties	$0	0.00%	$0	0.00%	$0	0.00%
Amounts Withheld or Retained by Company for Accounts of Others	$888,131	22.51%	$0	0.00%	$0	0.00%
Provision for Unauthorized Reinsurance	$0	0.00%	$0	0.00%	$0	0.00%
Net Adjustment in Assets and Liabilities Due to Foreign Exchange Rates	$0	0.00%	$0	0.00%	$0	0.00%
Drafts Outstanding	$0	0.00%	$0	0.00%	$0	0.00%
Payable to Parent, Subsidiaries and Affiliates	$0	0.00%	$78,295	0.33%	$167,611	3.54%
Payable for Securities	$0	0.00%	$0	0.00%	$0	0.00%
Aggregate Write-Ins for Other Liabilities	$16,237	0.41%	$34,565	0.14%	$0	0.00%
Total Liabilities (See Sec. 5, B.3)	$3,068,563	77.78%	$15,400,201	64.00%	$1,381,751	29.15%
Aggregate Write-Ins for Special Surplus Funds	$0	0.00%	$0	0.00%	$0	0.00%
Common Capital Stock	$500,000	12.67%	$1,083,290	4.50%	$1,070,167	22.58%
Preferred Capital Stock	$0	0.00%	$0	0.00%	$0	0.00%
Aggregate Write-Ins for Other than Special Surplus Funds	$0	0.00%	$0	0.00%	$0	0.00%
Surplus Notes	$0	0.00%	$0	0.00%	$0	0.00%
Gross Paid In and Contributed Surplus	$420,346	10.65%	$2,486,364	10.33%	$0	0.00%
Unassigned Funds (Surplus)	($43,849)	(1.11)%	$5,092,828	21.16%	$2,985,635	62.98%
Less Treasury Stock, at Cost:						
Shares Common	$0	0.00%	$0	0.00%	$697,250	14.71%
Shares Preferred	$0	0.00%	$0	0.00%	$0	0.00%
Surplus as Regards Policyholders (See Sec. 5, B.6, B.7, C.9, C.11)	$876,497	22.22%	$8,662,482	36.00%	$3,358,552	70.85%
TOTAL	$3,945,060	100.00%	$24,062,683	100.00%	$4,740,303	100.00%

B.1 INCOME STATEMENT
- INDUSTRY COMPOSITE

2

B.1   Income Statement - Industry Composite

REVENUE	Composite Value	% Total Oper. Inc.
Premiums Written - Direct	$2,516,267,899	16.53%
Premiums Written - Non-Affiliated Agency	$8,571,639,324	56.30%
Premiums Written - Affiliated Agency	$2,973,364,482	19.53%
Premiums - Reinsurance Assumed	$90,470,183	0.59%
Premiums - Reinsurance Ceded	($93,569,869)	(0.61)%
Net Premiums Written (See Sec. 5, B.4)	$14,058,172,019	92.34%
Net Premiums Earned	$13,860,587,794	91.04%
PLUS:		
Title Examinations	$268,528,641	1.76%
Searches & Abstracts	$245,026,158	1.61%
Surveys	$865,325	0.01%
Escrow & Settlement Fees	$552,971,867	3.63%
Other Service Charges	$275,095,724	1.81%
Other Operating Income	$21,752,437	0.14%
Total Operating Income (See Sec. 5, A.2, A.3, A.5)	$15,224,827,946	100.00%
LESS:		
Amounts Retained By Agents (See Sec. 5, B.9)	$9,454,264,921	
NET OPERATING REVENUE	$5,770,563,025	

OPERATING EXPENSE	Composite Value	% Net Oper. Rev.
Total Personnel Costs	$2,443,558,231	42.35%
Production Services	$411,338,663	7.13%
Advertising	$39,681,250	0.69%
Boards, Bureaus & Associations	$8,588,630	0.15%
Title Plant Rent & Maintenance	$45,619,696	0.79%
Claim Adjustment Services	$99,873	0.00%
Amount Charged Off, Net	$54,466,013	0.94%
Marketing & Promotional Expense	$72,538,728	1.26%
Insurance	$20,898,584	0.36%
Directors' Fees	$2,320,655	0.04%
Travel & Related Expenses	$118,748,739	2.06%
Rent and Rent Items	$293,545,600	5.09%
Equipment	$110,205,102	1.91%
Cost/Depreciation, EDP Equipment & Software	$149,881,009	2.60%
Print, Stationery, etc.	$68,784,684	1.19%
Postage, Telephone, Express	$120,592,958	2.09%
Legal & Auditing	$226,224,431	3.92%
Taxes, Licenses & Fees	$231,140,020	4.01%
Real Estate Expenses	$13,367,323	0.23%
Real Estate Taxes	$979,310	0.02%
Miscellaneous	$129,428,083	2.24%
Other Operating Expense Incurred	$4,562,007,582	79.06%
TOTAL OPERATING EXPENSE INCURRED (AGENT RETENTION + OTHER OPERATING EXPENSE INCURRED)	$14,016,272,503	--
Aggregate Write-ins for Operating Deductions	$22,081	0.00%
Operating Profit (Loss) Before Losses (See Sec. 5, A.7)	$1,208,533,362	20.94%
Losses & Loss Adjustment Expense Incurred (See Sec. 5, C.2 - C.7)		
Direct Operations (See Sec. 5, C.7)	$337,830,542	5.85%
Agency Operations (See Sec. 5, C.7)	$959,138,551	16.62%
NET OPERATING GAIN (LOSS) (See Sec. 5, A.10)	($88,435,731)	(1.53)%

INVESTMENT INCOME	Composite Value	% Total Assets
Net Investment Income Earned (See Sec. 5, A.8)	$566,010,993	5.05%
Net Realized Capital Gains (Losses) less Capital Gains Tax	($25,332,367)	(0.23)%
NET INVESTMENT GAIN (LOSS) (See Sec. 5, A.9)	$540,678,626	4.82%

OTHER INCOME	Composite Value	% Total Assets
Other Income (Loss)	$3,363,300	0.03%
Net Income Before Taxes (See Sec. 5, A.11)	$455,606,195	4.07%
Federal & Foreign Income Taxes Incurred	$132,344,752	1.18%
NET INCOME (See Sec. 5, A.12)	$323,261,443	2.88%

CAPITAL AND SURPLUS ACCOUNT	Composite Value	% Total Assets
POLICYHOLDER SURPLUS - BEGINNING	$3,555,012,599	31.72%
Net Income	$323,261,443	2.88%
Change in Net Unrealized Capital Gains (Losses) less Capital Gains Tax	($415,449,393)	(3.71)%
Change in Net Unrealized Foreign Exchange Capital Gain (Loss)	$11,459,933	0.10%
Change in Net Deferred Income Tax	$113,279,339	1.01%
Change in Nonadmitted Assets	($311,442,999)	(2.78)%
Change in Provision for Unauthorized Reinsurance	$0	0.00%
Change in Supplemental Reserves	($105,554,502)	(0.94)%
Change in Surplus Notes	$600,000	0.01%
Cumulative Effect of Changes in Accounting Principles	$1,785,146	0.02%
Capital Changes	$17,801,781	0.16%
Surplus Adjustments	$56,652,032	0.51%
Dividends to Stockholders	($569,599,028)	(5.08)%
Change in Treasury Stock	($50,000)	0.00%
Aggregate Write-ins for Gains and Losses in Surplus	$100,861,644	0.90%
Net Change - Policyholder Surplus	($776,395,892)	(6.93)%
POLICYHOLDER SURPLUS - ENDING (See Sec. 5, B.6, B.7, C.9, C.11)	$2,778,616,706	24.79%

CONSOLIDATED ELIMINATIONS

Dividends to Parent, Subsidiary or Affiliated Title Underwriter

	DIVIDENDS
CHICAGO / FIDELITY	$250,244,936
FIRST AMERICAN	$20,938,663
OLD REPUBLIC	$900,000
STEWART	$6,000,000
TOTAL	**$278,083,599**

These adjustments remove the reported dividend contributions to parent, subsidiary or affiliated Title underwriters, which are otherwise directly included in the composite data.

Some eliminations cannot be made because the shares of one underwriter, ultimately owned by another underwriter, are held by a subsidiary of the underwriter parent for which data is unavailable.

B.2 INCOME STATEMENT - BY NAIC GROUP

2

B.2 Income Statement - By NAIC Group

	ATTORNEYS' TITLE		CATIC		CHICAGO / FIDELITY		FIRST AMERICAN	
REVENUE	Group Value	% Total Oper. Inc.	Group Value	% Total Oper. Inc.	Group Value	% Total Oper. Inc.	Group Value	% Total Oper. Inc.
Premiums Written - Direct	$831,940	0.22%	$0	0.00%	$805,518,501	19.22%	$794,964,527	17.66%
Premiums Written - Non-Affiliated Agency	$355,109,429	94.52%	$68,383,428	95.74%	$2,099,348,646	50.10%	$2,473,684,409	54.96%
Premiums Written - Affiliated Agency	$0	0.00%	$0	0.00%	$851,311,601	20.32%	$835,309,222	18.56%
Premiums - Reinsurance Assumed	$1,373,845	0.37%	$13,165	0.02%	$6,918,570	0.17%	$26,922,654	0.60%
Premiums - Reinsurance Ceded	($2,173,164)	(0.58)%	($59,738)	(0.08)%	($14,690,178)	(0.35)%	($28,215,135)	(0.63)%
Net Premiums Written	$355,142,050	94.53%	$68,336,855	95.67%	$3,748,407,140	89.46%	$4,102,665,677	91.15%
Net Premiums Earned	$359,428,677	95.67%	$67,392,963	94.35%	$3,663,562,734	87.43%	$4,026,001,742	89.45%
PLUS:								
Title Examinations	$0	0.00%	$0	0.00%	$47,836,545	1.14%	$125,823,973	2.80%
Searches & Abstracts	$496,686	0.13%	$2,020,146	2.83%	$94,921,747	2.27%	$114,462,833	2.54%
Surveys	$0	0.00%	$0	0.00%	$628,103	0.01%	$0	0.00%
Escrow & Settlement Fees	$76,620	0.02%	$0	0.00%	$216,697,367	5.17%	$226,095,386	5.02%
Other Service Charges	$30,352	0.01%	$531,506	0.74%	$166,529,841	3.97%	$8,929,324	0.20%
Other Operating Income	$15,652,083	4.17%	$1,482,140	2.08%	$0	0.00%	($466,282)	(0.01)%
Total Operating Income	$375,684,418	100.00%	$71,426,755	100.00%	$4,190,176,337	100.00%	$4,500,846,976	100.00%
LESS:								
Amounts Retained By Agents	$250,753,109		$48,702,639		$2,381,520,405		$2,755,211,852	
NET OPERATING REVENUE	$124,931,309		$22,724,116		$1,808,655,932		$1,745,635,124	
OPERATING EXPENSE	Group Value	% Net Oper. Rev.	Group Value	% Net Oper. Rev.	Group Value	% Net Oper. Rev.	Group Value	% Net Oper. Rev.
Total Personnel Costs	$67,976,721	54.41%	$10,950,384	48.19%	$708,330,906	39.16%	$778,918,595	44.62%
Production Services	$2,263,190	1.81%	$2,255,111	9.92%	$120,287,763	6.65%	$104,196,007	5.97%
Advertising	$6,442,318	5.16%	$681,320	3.00%	$9,292,051	0.51%	$10,597,140	0.61%
Boards, Bureaus & Associations	$372,891	0.30%	$258,900	1.14%	$1,178,413	0.07%	$3,650,563	0.21%
Title Plant Rent & Maintenance	$47,161	0.04%	$0	0.00%	$14,130,976	0.78%	$18,905,985	1.08%
Claim Adjustment Services	$0	0.00%	$0	0.00%	$0	0.00%	$0	0.00%
Amount Charged Off, Net	$631,078	0.51%	$0	0.00%	$3,367,153	0.19%	$31,327,172	1.79%
Marketing & Promotional Expense	$1,889,174	1.51%	$584,246	2.57%	$5,664,435	0.31%	$18,120,950	1.04%
Insurance	$769,955	0.62%	$675,239	2.97%	$5,183,156	0.29%	$5,423,180	0.31%
Directors' Fees	$404,732	0.32%	$92,000	0.40%	$0	0.00%	$26,432	0.00%
Travel & Related Expenses	$2,058,574	1.65%	$318,985	1.40%	$43,461,992	2.40%	$21,906,488	1.25%
Rent and Rent Items	$6,972,036	5.58%	$897,904	3.95%	$84,721,182	4.68%	$104,139,225	5.97%
Equipment	$5,071,791	4.06%	$496,716	2.19%	$43,825,853	2.42%	$34,995,676	2.00%
Cost/Depreciation, EDP Equipment & Software	$6,139,405	4.91%	$147,428	0.65%	$51,225,320	2.83%	$17,610,903	1.01%
Print, Stationery, etc.	$1,287,868	1.03%	$293,790	1.29%	$25,399,715	1.40%	$21,422,337	1.23%
Postage, Telephone, Express	$3,156,920	2.53%	$313,682	1.38%	$37,593,466	2.08%	$34,662,882	1.99%
Legal & Auditing	$11,300,627	9.05%	$532,435	2.34%	$51,903,836	2.87%	$111,885,907	6.41%
Taxes, Licenses & Fees	$1,260,070	1.01%	$1,143,563	5.03%	$64,618,075	3.57%	$64,005,725	3.67%
Real Estate Expenses	$1,338,482	1.07%	$0	0.00%	$0	0.00%	$11,835,385	0.68%
Real Estate Taxes	$212,558	0.17%	$0	0.00%	$0	0.00%	$603,167	0.03%
Miscellaneous	$622,979	0.50%	($10,812)	(0.05)%	$83,401,033	4.61%	$11,712,674	0.67%
Other Operating Expense Incurred	$120,218,530	96.23%	$19,630,891	86.39%	$1,353,585,325	74.84%	$1,405,946,393	80.54%
TOTAL OPERATING EXPENSE INCURRED (AGENT RETENTION + OTHER OPERATING EXPENSE INCURRED)	$370,971,639	--	$68,333,530	--	$3,735,105,730	--	$4,161,158,245	--
Aggregate Write-ins for Operating Deductions	$0	0.00%	$0	0.00%	$0	0.00%	($507)	0.00%
Operating Profit (Loss) Before Losses	$4,712,779	3.77%	$3,093,225	13.61%	$455,070,607	25.16%	$339,689,238	19.46%
Losses & Loss Adjustment Expense Incurred								
Direct Operations	$267,150	0.21%	$0	0.00%	$146,888,884	8.12%	$89,724,575	5.14%
Agency Operations	$44,635,936	35.73%	$5,302,463	23.33%	$225,733,548	12.48%	$330,281,768	18.92%
NET OPERATING GAIN (LOSS)	($40,190,307)	(32.17)%	($2,209,238)	(9.72)%	$82,448,175	4.56%	($80,317,105)	(4.60)%
INVESTMENT INCOME	Group Value	% Total Assets	Group Value	% Total Assets	Group Value	% Total Assets	Group Value	% Total Assets
Net Investment Income Earned	$7,432,576	2.25%	$2,778,751	3.94%	$217,849,004	4.99%	$198,624,923	8.10%
Net Realized Capital Gains (Losses) less Capital Gains Tax	$10,269,248	3.10%	$54,587	0.08%	$7,109,818	0.16%	($57,025,957)	(2.33)%
NET INVESTMENT GAIN (LOSS)	$17,701,824	5.35%	$2,833,338	4.01%	$224,958,822	5.15%	$141,598,966	5.77%
OTHER INCOME	Group Value	% Total Assets	Group Value	% Total Assets	Group Value	% Total Assets	Group Value	% Total Assets
Other Income (Loss)	$0	0.00%	($75,390)	(0.11)%	$518,026	0.01%	$15,856	0.00%
Net Income Before Taxes	($22,488,483)	(6.79)%	$548,710	0.78%	$307,925,023	7.05%	$61,297,717	2.50%
Federal & Foreign Income Taxes Incurred	($16,467,150)	(4.97)%	$110,564	0.16%	$63,473,422	1.45%	$51,964,069	2.12%
NET INCOME	($6,021,333)	(1.82)%	$438,146	0.62%	$244,451,601	5.60%	$9,333,648	0.38%
CAPITAL AND SURPLUS ACCOUNT	Group Value	% Total Assets	Group Value	% Total Assets	Group Value	% Total Assets	Group Value	% Total Assets
POLICYHOLDER SURPLUS - BEGINNING	$161,054,404	48.65%	$46,349,322	65.64%	$976,309,359	22.36%	$787,353,449	32.11%
Net Income	($6,021,333)	(1.82)%	$438,146	0.62%	$244,451,601	5.60%	$9,333,648	0.38%
Change in Net Unrealized Capital Gains (Losses) less Capital Gains Tax	($581,869)	(0.18)%	($201,138)	(0.28)%	($323,325,350)	(7.41)%	$7,548,590	0.31%
Change in Net Unrealized Foreign Exchange Capital Gain (Loss)	$0	0.00%	$0	0.00%	$0	0.00%	$1,289,403	0.05%
Change in Net Deferred Income Tax	($1,055,390)	(0.32)%	$169,529	0.24%	$22,641,125	0.52%	$84,851,712	3.46%
Change in Nonadmitted Assets	$3,118,774	0.94%	($70,247)	(0.10)%	($75,192,741)	(1.72)%	($279,374,549)	(11.39)%
Change in Provision for Unauthorized Reinsurance	$0	0.00%	$0	0.00%	$0	0.00%	$0	0.00%
Change in Supplemental Reserves	($6,823)	0.00%	$0	0.00%	$0	0.00%	($105,483,586)	(4.30)%
Change in Surplus Notes	$0	0.00%	$0	0.00%	$0	0.00%	$0	0.00%
Cumulative Effect of Changes in Accounting Principles	$0	0.00%	$0	0.00%	$0	0.00%	$0	0.00%
Capital Changes	($2,180)	0.00%	$0	0.00%	$0	0.00%	$8,090,407	0.33%
Surplus Adjustments	($2,195)	0.00%	$0	0.00%	$50,000	0.00%	$32,184,446	1.31%
Dividends to Stockholders	($3,950,000)	(1.19)%	$0	0.00%	($345,200,000)	(7.91)%	($36,261,084)	(1.48)%
Change in Treasury Stock	$0	0.00%	$0	0.00%	$0	0.00%	$0	0.00%
Aggregate Write-ins for Gains and Losses in Surplus	$53,324	0.02%	$0	0.00%	$216,681,211	4.96%	($46,527,235)	(1.90)%
Net Change - Policyholder Surplus	($8,447,693)	(2.55)%	$336,290	0.48%	($259,894,182)	(5.95)%	($324,348,514)	(13.23)%
POLICYHOLDER SURPLUS - ENDING	$152,606,711	46.10%	$46,685,612	66.12%	$716,415,177	16.41%	$463,004,934	18.88%

B.2   Income Statement - By NAIC Group

	INVESTORS		LAND AMERICA		OHIO FARMERS		OLD REPUBLIC	
REVENUE	Group Value	% Total Oper. Inc.	Group Value	% Total Oper. Inc.	Group Value	% Total Oper. Inc.	Group Value	% Total Oper. Inc.
Premiums Written - Direct	$29,790,883	43.02%	$643,344,121	21.82%	$1,173,787	2.20%	$14,562,733	1.79%
Premiums Written - Non-Affiliated Agency	$33,877,911	48.92%	$1,737,306,728	58.93%	$49,984,569	93.60%	$630,499,863	77.40%
Premiums Written - Affiliated Agency	$6,291,704	9.08%	$371,071,355	12.59%	$3,022,358	5.66%	$133,876,250	16.43%
Premiums - Reinsurance Assumed	$117,450	0.17%	$24,095,019	0.82%	$0	0.00%	$17,310,543	2.13%
Premiums - Reinsurance Ceded	($338,811)	(0.49)%	($21,089,708)	(0.72)%	($359,707)	(0.67)%	($13,983,727)	(1.72)%
Net Premiums Written	$69,739,137	100.70%	$2,754,727,515	93.44%	$53,821,007	100.78%	$782,265,662	96.03%
Net Premiums Earned	$67,968,084	98.14%	$2,729,095,481	92.57%	$52,180,887	97.71%	$789,088,823	96.87%
PLUS:								
Title Examinations	$0	0.00%	$66,371,199	2.25%	$0	0.00%	$584,651	0.07%
Searches & Abstracts	$595,512	0.86%	$5,239,654	0.18%	$549,656	1.03%	$4,950,072	0.61%
Surveys	$0	0.00%	$237,222	0.01%	$0	0.00%	$0	0.00%
Escrow & Settlement Fees	$429,070	0.62%	$99,006,826	3.36%	$45,437	0.09%	$4,161,656	0.51%
Other Service Charges	$127,304	0.18%	$48,224,888	1.64%	$187,410	0.35%	$15,746,206	1.93%
Other Operating Income	$136,802	0.20%	$0	0.00%	$440,858	0.83%	$80,554	0.01%
Total Operating Income	$69,256,772	100.00%	$2,948,175,270	100.00%	$53,404,248	100.00%	$814,611,962	100.00%
LESS:								
Amounts Retained By Agents	$28,424,960		$1,728,173,689		$41,851,861		$615,055,520	
NET OPERATING REVENUE	$40,831,812		$1,220,001,581		$11,552,387		$199,556,442	

	INVESTORS		LAND AMERICA		OHIO FARMERS		OLD REPUBLIC	
OPERATING EXPENSE	Group Value	% Net Oper. Rev.	Group Value	% Net Oper. Rev.	Group Value	% Net Oper. Rev.	Group Value	% Net Oper. Rev.
Total Personnel Costs	$18,506,752	45.32%	$575,413,566	47.16%	$5,746,011	49.74%	$62,605,332	31.37%
Production Services	$0	0.00%	$100,810,634	8.26%	$345,000	2.99%	$11,112,662	5.57%
Advertising	$81,850	0.20%	$8,957,380	0.73%	$125,742	1.09%	$218,469	0.11%
Boards, Bureaus & Associations	$148,667	0.36%	$1,101,712	0.09%	$0	0.00%	$739,945	0.37%
Title Plant Rent & Maintenance	$0	0.00%	$10,351,237	0.85%	$0	0.00%	$1,223,155	0.61%
Claim Adjustment Services	$0	0.00%	$0	0.00%	$0	0.00%	$0	0.00%
Amount Charged Off, Net	$0	0.00%	$14,611,177	1.20%	$93,876	0.81%	$1,647,633	0.83%
Marketing & Promotional Expense	$1,425,181	3.49%	$21,854,607	1.79%	$0	0.00%	$4,432,127	2.22%
Insurance	$273,231	0.67%	$4,666,181	0.38%	$110,944	0.96%	$1,401,890	0.70%
Directors' Fees	$3,000	0.01%	$970,396	0.08%	$7,999	0.07%	$111,512	0.06%
Travel & Related Expenses	$784,194	1.92%	$31,745,734	2.60%	$429,860	3.72%	$4,197,983	2.10%
Rent and Rent Items	$1,671,852	4.09%	$64,328,294	5.27%	$665,134	5.76%	$6,456,987	3.24%
Equipment	$890,305	2.18%	$19,509,594	1.60%	$77,623	0.67%	$1,933,792	0.97%
Cost/Depreciation, EDP Equipment & Software	$754,273	1.85%	$39,348,435	3.23%	$115,007	1.00%	$2,552,698	1.28%
Print, Stationery, etc.	$669,007	1.64%	$9,698,183	0.79%	$352,297	3.05%	$1,397,208	0.70%
Postage, Telephone, Express	$1,252,111	3.07%	$32,838,690	2.69%	$178,170	1.54%	$2,094,583	1.05%
Legal & Auditing	$329,538	0.81%	$18,276,711	1.50%	$256,533	2.22%	$5,985,001	3.00%
Taxes, Licenses & Fees	$1,858,148	4.55%	$48,847,234	4.00%	$1,354,501	11.72%	$14,618,098	7.33%
Real Estate Expenses	$0	0.00%	$0	0.00%	$23,729	0.21%	$0	0.00%
Real Estate Taxes	$0	0.00%	$0	0.00%	$7,964	0.07%	$21,263	0.01%
Miscellaneous	$668,200	1.64%	$21,459,130	1.76%	$117,192	1.01%	$5,538,576	2.78%
Other Operating Expense Incurred	$29,316,309	71.80%	$1,024,788,895	84.00%	$10,007,582	86.63%	$128,288,914	64.29%
TOTAL OPERATING EXPENSE INCURRED (AGENT RETENTION + OTHER OPERATING EXPENSE INCURRED)	$57,741,269	--	$2,752,962,584	--	$51,859,443	--	$743,344,434	--
Aggregate Write-ins for Operating Deductions	$0	0.00%	$0	0.00%	$0	0.00%	$0	0.00%
Operating Profit (Loss) Before Losses	$11,515,503	28.20%	$195,212,686	16.00%	$1,544,805	13.37%	$71,267,528	35.71%
Losses & Loss Adjustment Expense Incurred								
Direct Operations	$7,237,616	17.73%	$54,863,632	4.50%	$21,545	0.19%	$3,094,357	1.55%
Agency Operations	$1,886,770	4.62%	$161,233,410	13.22%	$3,715,778	32.16%	$65,474,603	32.81%
NET OPERATING GAIN (LOSS)	$2,391,117	5.86%	($20,884,356)	(1.71)%	($2,192,518)	(18.98)%	$2,698,568	1.35%

	INVESTORS		LAND AMERICA		OHIO FARMERS		OLD REPUBLIC	
INVESTMENT INCOME	Group Value	% Total Assets	Group Value	% Total Assets	Group Value	% Total Assets	Group Value	% Total Assets
Net Investment Income Earned	$4,247,444	3.80%	$63,082,946	3.87%	$913,640	3.91%	$28,090,133	4.26%
Net Realized Capital Gains (Losses) less Capital Gains Tax	$338,746	0.30%	$9,680,101	0.59%	$8,609	0.04%	$688,024	0.10%
NET INVESTMENT GAIN (LOSS)	$4,586,190	4.10%	$72,763,047	4.47%	$922,249	3.94%	$28,778,157	4.36%

	INVESTORS		LAND AMERICA		OHIO FARMERS		OLD REPUBLIC	
OTHER INCOME	Group Value	% Total Assets	Group Value	% Total Assets	Group Value	% Total Assets	Group Value	% Total Assets
Other Income (Loss)	$0	0.00%	$0	0.00%	$0	0.00%	$0	0.00%
Net Income Before Taxes	$6,977,307	6.24%	$51,878,691	3.19%	($1,270,269)	(5.43)%	$31,476,725	4.77%
Federal & Foreign Income Taxes Incurred	$1,670,494	1.49%	$14,268,580	0.88%	($249,268)	(1.07)%	$9,954,463	1.51%
NET INCOME	$5,306,813	4.75%	$37,610,111	2.31%	($1,021,001)	(4.37)%	$21,522,262	3.26%

	INVESTORS		LAND AMERICA		OHIO FARMERS		OLD REPUBLIC	
CAPITAL AND SURPLUS ACCOUNT	Group Value	% Total Assets	Group Value	% Total Assets	Group Value	% Total Assets	Group Value	% Total Assets
POLICYHOLDER SURPLUS - BEGINNING	$59,956,675	53.62%	$628,504,970	38.60%	$8,660,765	37.03%	$178,651,831	27.08%
Net Income	$5,306,813	4.75%	$37,610,111	2.31%	($1,021,001)	(4.37)%	$21,522,262	3.26%
Change in Net Unrealized Capital Gains (Losses) less Capital Gains Tax	($3,842,410)	(3.44)%	($75,106,282)	(4.61)%	$71,990	0.31%	($3,401,153)	(0.52)%
Change in Net Unrealized Foreign Exchange Capital Gain (Loss)	$0	0.00%	$374,119	0.02%	$0	0.00%	$0	0.00%
Change in Net Deferred Income Tax	($94,458)	(0.08)%	$3,326,305	0.20%	$243,442	1.04%	($1,777,100)	(0.27)%
Change in Nonadmitted Assets	$5,049,339	4.52%	$33,860,189	2.08%	$166,523	0.71%	$6,036,610	0.92%
Change in Provision for Unauthorized Reinsurance	$0	0.00%	$0	0.00%	$0	0.00%	$0	0.00%
Change in Supplemental Reserves	$0	0.00%	($507,465)	(0.03)%	$0	0.00%	$0	0.00%
Change in Surplus Notes	$0	0.00%	$0	0.00%	$0	0.00%	$0	0.00%
Cumulative Effect of Changes in Accounting Principles	$0	0.00%	$1,785,146	0.11%	$0	0.00%	$0	0.00%
Capital Changes	$0	0.00%	$5,063,554	0.31%	$0	0.00%	$0	0.00%
Surplus Adjustments	$0	0.00%	$0	0.00%	$0	0.00%	$0	0.00%
Dividends to Stockholders	($10,732,722)	(9.60)%	($126,250,000)	(7.75)%	($406,115)	(1.74)%	($30,000,000)	(4.55)%
Change in Treasury Stock	$0	0.00%	$0	0.00%	$0	0.00%	$0	0.00%
Aggregate Write-ins for Gains and Losses in Surplus	$0	0.00%	($68,512,865)	(4.21)%	$0	0.00%	$2,661,994	0.40%
Net Change - Policyholder Surplus	($4,313,438)	(3.86)%	($188,357,185)	(11.57)%	($945,159)	(4.04)%	($4,957,387)	(0.75)%
POLICYHOLDER SURPLUS - ENDING	$55,643,237	49.76%	$440,147,785	27.03%	$7,715,606	32.99%	$173,694,444	26.33%

B.2 Income Statement - By NAIC Group

	RELIANT HOLDING		STEWART		TRANSUNION		UNAFFILIATED COMPANIES	
REVENUE	Group Value	% Total Oper. Inc.	Group Value	% Total Oper. Inc.	Group Value	% Total Oper. Inc.	Group Value	% Total Oper. Inc.
Premiums Written - Direct	$204,520	1.18%	$202,827,066	11.84%	$992,350	19.12%	$22,057,471	4.73%
Premiums Written - Non-Affiliated Agency	$3,657,096	21.19%	$945,981,765	55.24%	$2,344,872	45.18%	$171,460,608	36.77%
Premiums Written - Affiliated Agency	$10,054,884	58.26%	$503,488,197	29.40%	$1,458,631	28.11%	$257,480,280	55.21%
Premiums - Reinsurance Assumed	$0	0.00%	$13,699,292	0.80%	$0	0.00%	$19,645	0.00%
Premiums - Reinsurance Ceded	($198,680)	(1.15)%	($8,454,361)	(0.49)%	($152,887)	(2.95)%	($3,853,773)	(0.83)%
Net Premiums Written	$13,717,820	79.48%	$1,657,541,959	96.79%	$4,642,966	89.46%	$447,164,231	95.89%
Net Premiums Earned	$13,355,816	77.38%	$1,642,855,376	95.94%	$5,148,767	99.21%	$444,508,444	95.32%
PLUS:								
Title Examinations	$0	0.00%	$26,919,500	1.57%	$41,137	0.79%	$951,636	0.20%
Searches & Abstracts	$3,108,107	18.01%	$11,162,062	0.65%	$0	0.00%	$7,519,683	1.61%
Surveys	$0	0.00%	$0	0.00%	$0	0.00%	$0	0.00%
Escrow & Settlement Fees	$795,839	4.61%	$2,377,269	0.14%	$0	0.00%	$3,286,397	0.70%
Other Service Charges	$0	0.00%	$25,758,117	1.50%	$0	0.00%	$9,030,776	1.94%
Other Operating Income	$0	0.00%	$3,387,733	0.20%	$0	0.00%	$1,038,549	0.22%
Total Operating Income	$17,259,762	100.00%	$1,712,460,057	100.00%	$5,189,904	100.00%	$466,335,485	100.00%
LESS:								
Amounts Retained By Agents	$10,421,117		$1,228,837,665		$2,660,897		$362,651,207	
NET OPERATING REVENUE	$6,838,645		$483,622,392		$2,529,007		$103,684,278	
OPERATING EXPENSE	Group Value	% Net Oper. Rev.	Group Value	% Net Oper. Rev.	Group Value	% Net Oper. Rev.	Group Value	% Net Oper. Rev.
Total Personnel Costs	$2,319,467	33.92%	$169,927,822	35.14%	$1,645,388	65.06%	$41,217,287	39.75%
Production Services	$2,124,000	31.06%	$63,835,485	13.20%	$87,710	3.47%	$4,021,101	3.88%
Advertising	$0	0.00%	$2,382,973	0.49%	$298	0.01%	$901,709	0.87%
Boards, Bureaus & Associations	$29,323	0.43%	$531,857	0.11%	$26,160	1.03%	$550,199	0.53%
Title Plant Rent & Maintenance	$0	0.00%	$351,550	0.07%	$0	0.00%	$609,632	0.59%
Claim Adjustment Services	$0	0.00%	$0	0.00%	$0	0.00%	$99,873	0.10%
Amount Charged Off, Net	($195,817)	(2.86)%	$2,554,785	0.53%	($16,488)	(0.65)%	$445,444	0.43%
Marketing & Promotional Expense	$21,335	0.31%	$16,899,756	3.49%	$1,207	0.05%	$1,645,710	1.59%
Insurance	$107,007	1.56%	$1,457,969	0.30%	$500	0.02%	$829,332	0.80%
Directors' Fees	$0	0.00%	$74,748	0.02%	$0	0.00%	$629,836	0.61%
Travel & Related Expenses	$102,526	1.50%	$11,722,907	2.42%	$100,496	3.97%	$1,919,000	1.85%
Rent and Rent Items	$419,399	6.13%	$18,815,822	3.89%	$270,031	10.68%	$4,187,734	4.04%
Equipment	$155,128	2.27%	$1,659,136	0.34%	$17,286	0.68%	$1,572,202	1.52%
Cost/Depreciation, EDP Equipment & Software	$34,484	0.50%	$30,389,313	6.28%	$0	0.00%	$1,563,743	1.51%
Print, Stationery, etc.	$78,624	1.15%	$6,378,771	1.32%	$18,516	0.73%	$1,788,368	1.72%
Postage, Telephone, Express	$108,701	1.59%	$6,437,805	1.33%	$96,232	3.81%	$1,859,716	1.79%
Legal & Auditing	$465,229	6.80%	$21,109,396	4.36%	$156,108	6.17%	$4,023,110	3.88%
Taxes, Licenses & Fees	$192,125	2.81%	$27,053,288	5.59%	$187,495	7.41%	$6,001,698	5.79%
Real Estate Expenses	$0	0.00%	$0	0.00%	$0	0.00%	$169,727	0.16%
Real Estate Taxes	$0	0.00%	$0	0.00%	$0	0.00%	$134,358	0.13%
Miscellaneous	$318,504	4.66%	$1,194,634	0.25%	$21,782	0.86%	$4,384,191	4.23%
Other Operating Expense Incurred	$6,280,035	91.83%	$382,778,017	79.15%	$2,612,721	103.31%	$78,553,970	75.76%
TOTAL OPERATING EXPENSE INCURRED (AGENT RETENTION + OTHER OPERATING EXPENSE INCURRED)	$16,701,152	--	$1,611,615,682	--	$5,273,618	--	$441,205,177	--
Aggregate Write-ins for Operating Deductions	$0	0.00%	$0	0.00%	$0	0.00%	$22,588	0.02%
Operating Profit (Loss) Before Losses	$558,610	8.17%	$100,844,375	20.85%	($83,714)	(3.31)%	$25,107,720	24.22%
Losses & Loss Adjustment Expense Incurred								
Direct Operations	$249,694	3.65%	$32,983,821	6.82%	$96,031	3.80%	$2,403,237	2.32%
Agency Operations	$2,198,655	32.15%	$105,202,984	21.75%	$1,140,869	45.11%	$12,331,767	11.89%
NET OPERATING GAIN (LOSS)	($1,889,739)	(27.63)%	($37,342,430)	(7.72)%	($1,320,614)	(52.22)%	$10,372,716	10.00%
INVESTMENT INCOME	Group Value	% Total Assets	Group Value	% Total Assets	Group Value	% Total Assets	Group Value	% Total Assets
Net Investment Income Earned	$96,471	0.91%	$29,181,791	2.42%	$954,947	3.62%	$12,758,367	3.93%
Net Realized Capital Gains (Losses) less Capital Gains Tax	$1,760	0.02%	$3,781,201	0.31%	$10,850	0.04%	($249,354)	(0.08)%
NET INVESTMENT GAIN (LOSS)	$98,231	0.93%	$32,962,992	2.74%	$965,797	3.67%	$12,509,013	3.85%
OTHER INCOME	Group Value	% Total Assets	Group Value	% Total Assets	Group Value	% Total Assets	Group Value	% Total Assets
Other Income (Loss)	$768	0.01%	$3,514,702	0.29%	$0	0.00%	($610,662)	(0.19)%
Net Income Before Taxes	($1,790,740)	(16.97)%	($864,736)	(0.07)%	($354,817)	(1.35)%	$22,271,067	6.86%
Federal & Foreign Income Taxes Incurred	$0	0.00%	($771,847)	(0.06)%	($256,854)	(0.97)%	$8,648,279	2.66%
NET INCOME	($1,790,740)	(16.97)%	($92,889)	(0.01)%	($97,963)	(0.37)%	$13,622,788	4.20%
CAPITAL AND SURPLUS ACCOUNT	Group Value	% Total Assets	Group Value	% Total Assets	Group Value	% Total Assets	Group Value	% Total Assets
POLICYHOLDER SURPLUS - BEGINNING	$4,033,376	38.23%	$526,934,327	43.78%	$14,125,347	53.62%	$163,078,774	50.24%
Net Income	($1,790,740)	(16.97)%	($92,889)	(0.01)%	($97,963)	(0.37)%	$13,622,788	4.20%
Change in Net Unrealized Capital Gains (Losses) less Capital Gains Tax	$53,025	0.50%	($15,856,821)	(1.32)%	($19,814)	(0.08)%	($788,161)	(0.24)%
Change in Net Unrealized Foreign Exchange Capital Gain (Loss)	$0	0.00%	$9,796,411	0.81%	$0	0.00%	$0	0.00%
Change in Net Deferred Income Tax	$717,171	6.80%	$3,438,305	0.29%	($140,633)	(0.53)%	$959,331	0.30%
Change in Nonadmitted Assets	($754,854)	(7.16)%	($4,257,188)	(0.35)%	$62,440	0.24%	($87,295)	(0.03)%
Change in Provision for Unauthorized Reinsurance	$0	0.00%	$0	0.00%	$0	0.00%	$0	0.00%
Change in Supplemental Reserves	$0	0.00%	$87,110	0.01%	$0	0.00%	$356,262	0.11%
Change in Surplus Notes	$0	0.00%	$0	0.00%	$0	0.00%	$600,000	0.18%
Cumulative Effect of Changes in Accounting Principles	$0	0.00%	$0	0.00%	$0	0.00%	$0	0.00%
Capital Changes	$200,000	1.90%	$0	0.00%	$0	0.00%	$4,450,000	1.37%
Surplus Adjustments	$0	0.00%	$21,283,384	1.77%	$0	0.00%	$3,136,397	0.97%
Dividends to Stockholders	$0	0.00%	($5,225,000)	(0.43)%	$0	0.00%	($11,574,107)	(3.57)%
Change in Treasury Stock	$0	0.00%	$0	0.00%	$0	0.00%	($50,000)	(0.02)%
Aggregate Write-ins for Gains and Losses in Surplus	$0	0.00%	($3,646,639)	(0.30)%	$0	0.00%	$151,854	0.05%
Net Change - Policyholder Surplus	($1,586,021)	(15.03)%	$5,526,672	0.46%	($195,973)	(0.74)%	$10,786,699	3.32%
POLICYHOLDER SURPLUS - ENDING	$2,447,355	23.20%	$532,460,998	44.24%	$13,929,374	52.87%	$173,865,473	53.56%

B.3 INCOME STATEMENT
- BY INDIVIDUAL UNDERWRITER

2

B.3 Income Statement - By Individual Underwriter

	ALAMO		ALLIANCE		ALLIANT		AMERICAN EAGLE	
REVENUE	Company Value	% Total Oper. Inc.	Company Value	% Total Oper. Inc.	Company Value	% Total Oper. Inc.	Company Value	% Total Oper. Inc.
Premiums Written - Direct	$0	0.00%	$0	0.00%	$0	0.00%	$1,906,376	25.29%
Premiums Written - Non-Affiliated Agency	$42,145,575	44.43%	$1,196	2.20%	$13,990,651	102.97%	$1,142,793	15.16%
Premiums Written - Affiliated Agency	$52,072,753	54.89%	$0	0.00%	$0	0.00%	$0	0.00%
Premiums - Reinsurance Assumed	$73,105	0.08%	$0	0.00%	$0	0.00%	$0	0.00%
Premiums - Reinsurance Ceded	($126,328)	(0.13)%	($749)	(1.38)%	($107,390)	(0.79)%	($53,711)	(0.71)%
Net Premiums Written (See Sec. 5, B.4)	$94,165,105	99.26%	$447	0.82%	$13,883,261	102.18%	$2,995,458	39.74%
Net Premiums Earned	$94,868,291	100.00%	$54,338	100.00%	$13,587,506	100.00%	$2,992,458	39.70%
PLUS:								
Title Examinations	$0	0.00%	$0	0.00%	$0	0.00%	$523,700	6.95%
Searches & Abstracts	$0	0.00%	$0	0.00%	$0	0.00%	$2,994,259	39.72%
Surveys	$0	0.00%	$0	0.00%	$0	0.00%	$0	0.00%
Escrow & Settlement Fees	$0	0.00%	$0	0.00%	$0	0.00%	$1,027,921	13.64%
Other Service Charges	$57	0.00%	$0	0.00%	$0	0.00%	$0	0.00%
Other Operating Income	$0	0.00%	$0	0.00%	$0	0.00%	$0	0.00%
Total Operating Income (See Sec. 5, A.2, A.3, A.5)	$94,868,348	100.00%	$54,338	100.00%	$13,587,506	100.00%	$7,538,338	100.00%
LESS:								
Amounts Retained By Agents (See Sec. 5, B.9)	$80,095,646		$838		$11,897,217		$916,270	
NET OPERATING REVENUE	$14,772,702		$53,500		$1,690,289		$6,622,068	
OPERATING EXPENSE	Company Value	% Net Oper. Rev.	Company Value	% Net Oper. Rev.	Company Value	% Net Oper. Rev.	Company Value	% Net Oper. Rev.
Total Personnel Costs	$2,599,918	17.60%	$0	0.00%	$854,068	50.53%	$3,558,803	53.74%
Production Services	$21	0.00%	$0	0.00%	$22,731	1.34%	$186,403	2.81%
Advertising	$158,310	1.07%	$0	0.00%	$0	0.00%	$57,210	0.86%
Boards, Bureaus & Associations	$0	0.00%	$3,009	5.62%	$27,105	1.60%	$13,625	0.21%
Title Plant Rent & Maintenance	($63,506)	(0.43)%	$0	0.00%	$0	0.00%	$97,524	1.47%
Claim Adjustment Services	$0	0.00%	$0	0.00%	$96,873	5.73%	$0	0.00%
Amount Charged Off, Net	$33,087	0.22%	($4,553)	(8.51)%	$0	0.00%	$216,992	3.28%
Marketing & Promotional Expense	$136,261	0.92%	$0	0.00%	$104,368	6.17%	$147,639	2.23%
Insurance	$38,827	0.26%	$0	0.00%	$17,550	1.04%	$40,361	0.61%
Directors' Fees	$0	0.00%	$0	0.00%	$665	0.04%	$0	0.00%
Travel & Related Expenses	$717,295	4.86%	$0	0.00%	$99,025	5.86%	$35,991	0.54%
Rent and Rent Items	$339,436	2.30%	$0	0.00%	$46,249	2.74%	$421,143	6.36%
Equipment	$519,740	3.52%	$0	0.00%	$3,135	0.19%	$100,744	1.52%
Cost/Depreciation, EDP Equipment & Software	$1,142,475	7.73%	$2,300	4.30%	$17,105	1.01%	$23,692	0.36%
Print, Stationery, etc.	$340,816	2.31%	$3,666	6.85%	$20,735	1.23%	$224,786	3.39%
Postage, Telephone, Express	$416,260	2.82%	$0	0.00%	$24,253	1.43%	$185,106	2.80%
Legal & Auditing	$949,509	6.43%	$99,830	186.60%	$43,197	2.56%	$101,488	1.53%
Taxes, Licenses & Fees	$1,567,254	10.61%	$6,566	12.27%	$167,455	9.91%	$70,721	1.07%
Real Estate Expenses	$0	0.00%	$0	0.00%	$0	0.00%	$0	0.00%
Real Estate Taxes	$0	0.00%	$0	0.00%	$0	0.00%	$13,368	0.20%
Miscellaneous	$237,462	1.61%	$5,688	10.63%	$10,938	0.65%	$789,196	11.92%
Other Operating Expense Incurred	$9,133,165	61.82%	$116,506	217.77%	$1,555,452	92.02%	$6,284,792	94.91%
TOTAL OPERATING EXPENSE INCURRED (AGENT RETENTION + OTHER OPERATING EXPENSE INCURRED)	$89,228,811	--	$117,344	--	$13,452,669	--	$7,201,062	--
Aggregate Write-ins for Operating Deductions	$0	0.00%	$0	0.00%	$0	0.00%	$0	0.00%
Operating Profit (Loss) Before Losses (See Sec. 5, A.7)	$5,639,537	38.18%	($63,006)	(117.77)%	$134,837	7.98%	$337,276	5.09%
Losses & Loss Adjustment Expense Incurred (See Sec. 5, C.2 - C.7)								
Direct Operations (See Sec. 5, C.7)	$0	0.00%	$0	0.00%	$0	0.00%	$30,838	0.47%
Agency Operations (See Sec. 5, C.7)	$4,542,653	30.75%	$66,579	124.45%	$974,113	57.63%	$0	0.00%
NET OPERATING GAIN (LOSS) (See Sec. 5, A.10)	$1,096,884	7.43%	($129,585)	(242.21)%	($839,276)	(49.65)%	$306,438	4.63%
INVESTMENT INCOME	Company Value	% Total Assets	Company Value	% Total Assets	Company Value	% Total Assets	Company Value	% Total Assets
Net Investment Income Earned (See Sec. 5, A.8)	$1,958,503	4.05%	$172,226	4.65%	$116,880	3.02%	$65,709	3.09%
Net Realized Capital Gains (Losses) less Capital Gains Tax	$920,620	1.90%	$0	0.00%	$944	0.02%	$0	0.00%
NET INVESTMENT GAIN (LOSS) (See Sec. 5, A.9)	$2,879,123	5.95%	$172,226	4.65%	$117,824	3.04%	$65,709	3.09%
OTHER INCOME	Company Value	% Total Assets	Company Value	% Total Assets	Company Value	% Total Assets	Company Value	% Total Assets
Other Income (Loss)	$0	0.00%	$0	0.00%	$0	0.00%	$35,680	1.68%
Net Income Before Taxes (See Sec. 5, A.11)	$3,976,007	8.22%	$42,641	1.15%	($721,452)	(18.64)%	$407,827	19.21%
Federal & Foreign Income Taxes Incurred	$677,100	1.40%	$6,471	0.17%	$0	0.00%	$257,092	12.11%
NET INCOME (See Sec. 5, A.12)	$3,298,907	6.82%	$36,170	0.98%	($721,452)	(18.64)%	$150,735	7.10%
CAPITAL AND SURPLUS ACCOUNT	Company Value	% Total Assets	Company Value	% Total Assets	Company Value	% Total Assets	Company Value	% Total Assets
POLICYHOLDER SURPLUS - BEGINNING	$37,138,910	76.74%	$2,985,582	80.53%	$2,517,038	65.03%	$1,356,111	63.87%
Net Income	$3,298,907	6.82%	$36,170	0.98%	($721,452)	(18.64)%	$150,735	7.10%
Change in Net Unrealized Capital Gains (Losses) less Capital Gains Tax	($1,500,982)	(3.10)%	$0	0.00%	$0	0.00%	$0	0.00%
Change in Net Unrealized Foreign Exchange Capital Gain (Loss)	$0	0.00%	$0	0.00%	$0	0.00%	$0	0.00%
Change in Net Deferred Income Tax	$597,601	1.23%	($5,218)	(0.14)%	$397,900	10.28%	$93,450	4.40%
Change in Nonadmitted Assets	($62,905)	(0.13)%	$4,020	0.11%	($408,933)	(10.56)%	($153,120)	(7.21)%
Change in Provision for Unauthorized Reinsurance	$0	0.00%	$0	0.00%	$0	0.00%	$0	0.00%
Change in Supplemental Reserves	$0	0.00%	$87,110	2.35%	($30,000)	(0.78)%	$0	0.00%
Change in Surplus Notes	$0	0.00%	$0	0.00%	$600,000	15.50%	$0	0.00%
Cumulative Effect of Changes in Accounting Principles	$0	0.00%	$0	0.00%	$0	0.00%	$0	0.00%
Capital Changes	$0	0.00%	$0	0.00%	$0	0.00%	$0	0.00%
Surplus Adjustments	$0	0.00%	$0	0.00%	$0	0.00%	$0	0.00%
Dividends to Stockholders	($13,244,936)	(27.37)%	$0	0.00%	$0	0.00%	($730,408)	(34.40)%
Change in Treasury Stock	$0	0.00%	$0	0.00%	$0	0.00%	$0	0.00%
Aggregate Write-ins for Gains and Losses in Surplus	$0	0.00%	$0	0.00%	$0	0.00%	$0	0.00%
Net Change - Policyholder Surplus	($10,912,318)	(22.55)%	$122,081	3.29%	($162,485)	(4.20)%	($639,343)	(30.11)%
POLICYHOLDER SURPLUS - ENDING (See Sec. 5, B.6, B.7, C.9, C.11)	$26,226,592	54.19%	$3,107,663	83.82%	$2,354,553	60.83%	$716,768	33.76%

B.3 Income Statement - By Individual Underwriter

	AMERICAN GUARANTY		AMERICAN LAND & AIRCRAFT		AMERICAN SECURITY		ARKANSAS TIC	
REVENUE	Company Value	% Total Oper. Inc.	Company Value	% Total Oper. Inc.	Company Value	% Total Oper. Inc.	Company Value	% Total Oper. Inc.
Premiums Written - Direct	$26,366	0.79%	$0	0.00%	$0	0.00%	$0	0.00%
Premiums Written - Non-Affiliated Agency	$546,233	16.36%	$126,906	21.34%	$2,940,198	99.98%	$7,269,128	89.97%
Premiums Written - Affiliated Agency	$2,917,327	87.37%	$532,250	89.50%	$0	0.00%	$1,017,272	12.59%
Premiums - Reinsurance Assumed	$0	0.00%	$0	0.00%	$0	0.00%	$0	0.00%
Premiums - Reinsurance Ceded	$0	0.00%	($65,292)	(10.98)%	$0	0.00%	($72,424)	(0.90)%
Net Premiums Written (See Sec. 5, B.4)	$3,489,926	104.52%	$593,864	99.86%	$2,940,198	99.98%	$8,213,976	101.67%
Net Premiums Earned	$3,338,923	100.00%	$594,713	100.00%	$2,940,198	99.98%	$8,026,817	99.35%
PLUS:								
Title Examinations	$0	0.00%	$0	0.00%	$0	0.00%	$0	0.00%
Searches & Abstracts	$0	0.00%	$0	0.00%	$0	0.00%	$0	0.00%
Surveys	$0	0.00%	$0	0.00%	$0	0.00%	$0	0.00%
Escrow & Settlement Fees	$0	0.00%	$0	0.00%	$0	0.00%	$0	0.00%
Other Service Charges	$35	0.00%	$0	0.00%	$0	0.00%	$0	0.00%
Other Operating Income	$0	0.00%	$0	0.00%	$500	0.02%	$52,298	0.65%
Total Operating Income (See Sec. 5, A.2, A.3, A.5)	$3,338,958	100.00%	$594,713	100.00%	$2,940,698	100.00%	$8,079,115	100.00%
LESS:								
Amounts Retained By Agents (See Sec. 5, B.9)	$2,815,249		$458,218		$2,106,598		$6,364,268	
NET OPERATING REVENUE	$523,709		$136,495		$834,100		$1,714,847	
OPERATING EXPENSE	Company Value	% Net Oper. Rev.	Company Value	% Net Oper. Rev.	Company Value	% Net Oper. Rev.	Company Value	% Net Oper. Rev.
Total Personnel Costs	$0	0.00%	$45,064	33.02%	$0	0.00%	$490,653	28.61%
Production Services	$17,613	3.36%	$16,500	12.09%	$0	0.00%	$24,000	1.40%
Advertising	$0	0.00%	$4,206	3.08%	$5,258	0.63%	$0	0.00%
Boards, Bureaus & Associations	$150	0.03%	$2,414	1.77%	$0	0.00%	$5,496	0.32%
Title Plant Rent & Maintenance	$43,930	8.39%	$0	0.00%	$0	0.00%	$0	0.00%
Claim Adjustment Services	$0	0.00%	$0	0.00%	$0	0.00%	$0	0.00%
Amount Charged Off, Net	$0	0.00%	$0	0.00%	$0	0.00%	$41	0.00%
Marketing & Promotional Expense	$3,000	0.57%	$0	0.00%	$0	0.00%	$93,554	5.46%
Insurance	$0	0.00%	$1,158	0.85%	$0	0.00%	$3,757	0.22%
Directors' Fees	$0	0.00%	$0	0.00%	$0	0.00%	$6,300	0.37%
Travel & Related Expenses	$0	0.00%	$267	0.20%	$27,960	3.35%	$59,786	3.49%
Rent and Rent Items	$10,000	1.91%	$28,501	20.88%	$0	0.00%	$28,204	1.64%
Equipment	$1,250	0.24%	$0	0.00%	$751	0.09%	$12,974	0.76%
Cost/Depreciation, EDP Equipment & Software	$0	0.00%	$755	0.55%	$3,389	0.41%	$10,531	0.61%
Print, Stationery, etc.	$0	0.00%	$2,812	2.06%	$23,283	2.79%	$54,624	3.19%
Postage, Telephone, Express	$6,668	1.27%	$4,242	3.11%	$2,264	0.27%	$35,996	2.10%
Legal & Auditing	$43,219	8.25%	$3,770	2.76%	$59,808	7.17%	$98,666	5.75%
Taxes, Licenses & Fees	$170,773	32.61%	$16,363	11.99%	$60,932	7.31%	$228,427	13.32%
Real Estate Expenses	$0	0.00%	$0	0.00%	$0	0.00%	$0	0.00%
Real Estate Taxes	$0	0.00%	$0	0.00%	$0	0.00%	$0	0.00%
Miscellaneous	$190,465	36.37%	$56,998	41.76%	$9,870	1.18%	$32,105	1.87%
Other Operating Expense Incurred	$487,068	93.00%	$183,050	134.11%	$193,515	23.20%	$1,185,114	69.11%
TOTAL OPERATING EXPENSE INCURRED (AGENT RETENTION + OTHER OPERATING EXPENSE INCURRED)	$3,302,317	--	$641,268	--	$2,300,113	--	$7,549,382	--
Aggregate Write-ins for Operating Deductions	$0	0.00%	$0	0.00%	$0	0.00%	$0	0.00%
Operating Profit (Loss) Before Losses (See Sec. 5, A.7)	$36,641	7.00%	($46,555)	(34.11)%	$640,585	76.80%	$529,733	30.89%
Losses & Loss Adjustment Expense Incurred (See Sec. 5, C.2 - C.7)								
Direct Operations (See Sec. 5, C.7)	$87,168	16.64%	$5,858	4.29%	$0	0.00%	$0	0.00%
Agency Operations (See Sec. 5, C.7)	$40,323	7.70%	$0	0.00%	$2,283	0.27%	$155,822	9.09%
NET OPERATING GAIN (LOSS) (See Sec. 5, A.10)	($90,850)	(17.35)%	($52,413)	(38.40)%	$638,302	76.53%	$373,911	21.80%
INVESTMENT INCOME	Company Value	% Total Assets	Company Value	% Total Assets	Company Value	% Total Assets	Company Value	% Total Assets
Net Investment Income Earned (See Sec. 5, A.8)	$1,553,637	10.88%	$40,829	5.06%	$367,143	4.23%	$220,890	4.43%
Net Realized Capital Gains (Losses) less Capital Gains Tax	$0	0.00%	$0	0.00%	$0	0.00%	$0	0.00%
NET INVESTMENT GAIN (LOSS) (See Sec. 5, A.9)	$1,553,637	10.88%	$40,829	5.06%	$367,143	4.23%	$220,890	4.43%
OTHER INCOME	Company Value	% Total Assets	Company Value	% Total Assets	Company Value	% Total Assets	Company Value	% Total Assets
Other Income (Loss)	$0	0.00%	$0	0.00%	$0	0.00%	$0	0.00%
Net Income Before Taxes (See Sec. 5, A.11)	$1,462,787	10.24%	($11,584)	(1.43)%	$1,005,445	11.58%	$594,801	11.92%
Federal & Foreign Income Taxes Incurred	$167,867	1.18%	$0	0.00%	$146,222	1.68%	$223,492	4.48%
NET INCOME (See Sec. 5, A.12)	$1,294,920	9.07%	($11,584)	(1.43)%	$859,223	9.90%	$371,309	7.44%
CAPITAL AND SURPLUS ACCOUNT	Company Value	% Total Assets	Company Value	% Total Assets	Company Value	% Total Assets	Company Value	% Total Assets
POLICYHOLDER SURPLUS - BEGINNING	$10,212,253	71.49%	$756,330	93.68%	$7,483,940	86.22%	$2,258,577	45.27%
Net Income	$1,294,920	9.07%	($11,584)	(1.43)%	$859,223	9.90%	$371,309	7.44%
Change in Net Unrealized Capital Gains (Losses) less Capital Gains Tax	$0	0.00%	$0	0.00%	$0	0.00%	$0	0.00%
Change in Net Unrealized Foreign Exchange Capital Gain (Loss)	$0	0.00%	$0	0.00%	$0	0.00%	$0	0.00%
Change in Net Deferred Income Tax	$1,196	0.01%	$0	0.00%	$0	0.00%	$17,854	0.36%
Change in Nonadmitted Assets	($788)	(0.01)%	($2,054)	(0.25)%	$11,318	0.13%	($34,217)	(0.69)%
Change in Provision for Unauthorized Reinsurance	$0	0.00%	$0	0.00%	$0	0.00%	$0	0.00%
Change in Supplemental Reserves	$0	0.00%	$0	0.00%	$0	0.00%	$0	0.00%
Change in Surplus Notes	$0	0.00%	$0	0.00%	$0	0.00%	$0	0.00%
Cumulative Effect of Changes in Accounting Principles	$0	0.00%	$0	0.00%	$0	0.00%	$0	0.00%
Capital Changes	$0	0.00%	$0	0.00%	$0	0.00%	$0	0.00%
Surplus Adjustments	$0	0.00%	$0	0.00%	$0	0.00%	$0	0.00%
Dividends to Stockholders	$0	0.00%	$0	0.00%	$0	0.00%	($225,000)	(4.51)%
Change in Treasury Stock	$0	0.00%	$0	0.00%	$0	0.00%	$0	0.00%
Aggregate Write-ins for Gains and Losses in Surplus	$0	0.00%	$178	0.02%	$149,998	1.73%	$0	0.00%
Net Change - Policyholder Surplus	$1,295,328	9.07%	($13,814)	(1.71)%	$1,020,539	11.76%	$129,946	2.60%
POLICYHOLDER SURPLUS - ENDING (See Sec. 5, B.6, B.7, C.9, C.11)	$11,507,581	80.56%	$742,516	91.97%	$8,504,479	97.97%	$2,388,523	47.87%

B.3 Income Statement - By Individual Underwriter

	ARSENAL		ATTORNEYS TGF (CO)		ATTORNEYS TGF (IL)		ATTORNEYS TIF (FL)	
REVENUE	Company Value	% Total Oper. Inc.	Company Value	% Total Oper. Inc.	Company Value	% Total Oper. Inc.	Company Value	% Total Oper. Inc.
Premiums Written - Direct	$0	0.00%	$0	0.00%	$10,998,779	54.55%	$0	0.00%
Premiums Written - Non-Affiliated Agency	$1,583,908	99.67%	$9,268,076	67.20%	$0	0.00%	$345,841,353	95.92%
Premiums Written - Affiliated Agency	$0	0.00%	$0	0.00%	$0	0.00%	$0	0.00%
Premiums - Reinsurance Assumed	$0	0.00%	$0	0.00%	$0	0.00%	$1,373,845	0.38%
Premiums - Reinsurance Ceded	$0	0.00%	($527,596)	(3.83)%	($345,794)	(1.72)%	($1,547,064)	(0.43)%
Net Premiums Written (See Sec. 5, B.4)	$1,583,908	99.67%	$8,740,480	63.38%	$10,652,985	52.84%	$345,668,134	95.87%
Net Premiums Earned	$1,583,908	99.67%	$8,935,625	64.79%	$10,535,492	52.25%	$349,759,615	97.01%
PLUS:								
Title Examinations	$0	0.00%	$0	0.00%	$0	0.00%	$0	0.00%
Searches & Abstracts	$0	0.00%	$0	0.00%	$2,591,955	12.86%	$0	0.00%
Surveys	$0	0.00%	$0	0.00%	$0	0.00%	$0	0.00%
Escrow & Settlement Fees	$0	0.00%	$0	0.00%	$279,902	1.39%	$0	0.00%
Other Service Charges	$0	0.00%	$0	0.00%	$6,754,393	33.50%	$0	0.00%
Other Operating Income	$5,315	0.33%	$4,855,900	35.21%	$0	0.00%	$10,796,183	2.99%
Total Operating Income (See Sec. 5, A.2, A.3, A.5)	$1,589,223	100.00%	$13,791,525	100.00%	$20,161,742	100.00%	$360,555,798	100.00%
LESS:								
Amounts Retained By Agents (See Sec. 5, B.9)	$1,253,313		$9,549,160		$0		$241,203,949	
NET OPERATING REVENUE	$335,910		$4,242,365		$20,161,742		$119,351,849	

OPERATING EXPENSE	Company Value	% Net Oper. Rev.	Company Value	% Net Oper. Rev.	Company Value	% Net Oper. Rev.	Company Value	% Net Oper. Rev.
Total Personnel Costs	$327,009	97.35%	$2,220,745	52.35%	$10,742,820	53.28%	$65,134,616	54.57%
Production Services	$0	0.00%	$841,780	19.84%	$1,036,922	5.14%	$981,335	0.82%
Advertising	$440	0.13%	$6,357	0.15%	$66,587	0.33%	$6,430,416	5.39%
Boards, Bureaus & Associations	$6,035	1.80%	$0	0.00%	$118,478	0.59%	$361,051	0.30%
Title Plant Rent & Maintenance	$0	0.00%	$0	0.00%	$0	0.00%	$0	0.00%
Claim Adjustment Services	$0	0.00%	$0	0.00%	$0	0.00%	$0	0.00%
Amount Charged Off, Net	$0	0.00%	$30,930	0.73%	($38,800)	(0.19)%	$600,000	0.50%
Marketing & Promotional Expense	$4,172	1.24%	$92,586	2.18%	$341,258	1.69%	$1,796,588	1.51%
Insurance	$3,157	0.94%	$40,102	0.95%	$299,016	1.48%	$723,982	0.61%
Directors' Fees	$0	0.00%	$43,232	1.02%	$517,859	2.57%	$361,500	0.30%
Travel & Related Expenses	$0	0.00%	$33,025	0.78%	$169,886	0.84%	$2,008,889	1.68%
Rent and Rent Items	$11,400	3.39%	$295,967	6.98%	$1,651,804	8.19%	$6,598,321	5.53%
Equipment	$11,571	3.44%	$36,735	0.87%	$650,776	3.23%	$5,022,617	4.21%
Cost/Depreciation, EDP Equipment & Software	$861	0.26%	$62,333	1.47%	$859,077	4.26%	$6,077,072	5.09%
Print, Stationery, etc.	$454	0.14%	$56,318	1.33%	$399,800	1.98%	$1,219,427	1.02%
Postage, Telephone, Express	$2,778	0.83%	$71,138	1.68%	$673,947	3.34%	$3,055,990	2.56%
Legal & Auditing	$6,873	2.05%	$388,394	9.16%	$350,530	1.74%	$10,879,178	9.12%
Taxes, Licenses & Fees	($17,205)	(5.12)%	$42,169	0.99%	$23,325	0.12%	$1,236,121	1.04%
Real Estate Expenses	$0	0.00%	$0	0.00%	$0	0.00%	$1,338,482	1.12%
Real Estate Taxes	$0	0.00%	$0	0.00%	$0	0.00%	$212,558	0.18%
Miscellaneous	$0	0.00%	$49,153	1.16%	$2,305,597	11.44%	$521,773	0.44%
Other Operating Expense Incurred	$357,545	106.44%	$4,310,964	101.62%	$20,168,882	100.04%	$114,559,916	95.99%
TOTAL OPERATING EXPENSE INCURRED (AGENT RETENTION + OTHER OPERATING EXPENSE INCURRED)	$1,610,858	--	$13,860,124	--	$20,168,882	--	$355,763,865	--
Aggregate Write-ins for Operating Deductions	$0	0.00%	$0	0.00%	$0	0.00%	$0	0.00%
Operating Profit (Loss) Before Losses (See Sec. 5, A.7)	($21,635)	(6.44)%	($68,599)	(1.62)%	($7,140)	(0.04)%	$4,791,933	4.01%
Losses & Loss Adjustment Expense Incurred (See Sec. 5, C.2 - C.7)								
Direct Operations (See Sec. 5, C.7)	$0	0.00%	$0	0.00%	$1,811,083	8.98%	$0	0.00%
Agency Operations (See Sec. 5, C.7)	$649	0.19%	$357,311	8.42%	$0	0.00%	$44,278,625	37.10%
NET OPERATING GAIN (LOSS) (See Sec. 5, A.10)	($22,284)	(6.63)%	($425,910)	(10.04)%	($1,818,223)	(9.02)%	($39,486,692)	(33.08)%

INVESTMENT INCOME	Company Value	% Total Assets	Company Value	% Total Assets	Company Value	% Total Assets	Company Value	% Total Assets
Net Investment Income Earned (See Sec. 5, A.8)	$25,816	4.35%	$45,252	0.94%	$1,656,985	5.59%	$7,300,683	2.25%
Net Realized Capital Gains (Losses) less Capital Gains Tax	$0	0.00%	$85,805	1.79%	$194,964	0.66%	$10,177,378	3.14%
NET INVESTMENT GAIN (LOSS) (See Sec. 5, A.9)	$25,816	4.35%	$131,057	2.73%	$1,851,949	6.25%	$17,478,061	5.39%

OTHER INCOME	Company Value	% Total Assets	Company Value	% Total Assets	Company Value	% Total Assets	Company Value	% Total Assets
Other Income (Loss)	$0	0.00%	$0	0.00%	$0	0.00%	$0	0.00%
Net Income Before Taxes (See Sec. 5, A.11)	$3,532	0.59%	($294,853)	(6.14)%	$33,726	0.11%	($22,008,631)	(6.79)%
Federal & Foreign Income Taxes Incurred	$36,298	6.11%	($217,091)	(4.52)%	$164,369	0.55%	($16,167,808)	(4.99)%
NET INCOME (See Sec. 5, A.12)	($32,766)	(5.52)%	($77,762)	(1.62)%	($130,643)	(0.44)%	($5,840,823)	(1.80)%

CAPITAL AND SURPLUS ACCOUNT	Company Value	% Total Assets	Company Value	% Total Assets	Company Value	% Total Assets	Company Value	% Total Assets
POLICYHOLDER SURPLUS - BEGINNING	$514,254	86.61%	$1,294,052	26.93%	$7,575,600	25.56%	$158,662,740	48.92%
Net Income	($32,766)	(5.52)%	($77,762)	(1.62)%	($130,643)	(0.44)%	($5,840,823)	(1.80)%
Change in Net Unrealized Capital Gains (Losses) less Capital Gains Tax	$0	0.00%	($7,701)	(0.16)%	$613,012	2.07%	($567,732)	(0.18)%
Change in Net Unrealized Foreign Exchange Capital Gain (Loss)	$0	0.00%	$0	0.00%	$0	0.00%	$0	0.00%
Change in Net Deferred Income Tax	$0	0.00%	($334,460)	(6.96)%	$181,700	0.61%	($720,930)	(0.22)%
Change in Nonadmitted Assets	$2,673	0.45%	$862,971	17.96%	$1,398,146	4.72%	$2,244,489	0.69%
Change in Provision for Unauthorized Reinsurance	$0	0.00%	$0	0.00%	$0	0.00%	$0	0.00%
Change in Supplemental Reserves	$0	0.00%	$43,177	0.90%	$213,011	0.72%	$0	0.00%
Change in Surplus Notes	$0	0.00%	$0	0.00%	$0	0.00%	$0	0.00%
Cumulative Effect of Changes in Accounting Principles	$0	0.00%	$0	0.00%	$0	0.00%	$0	0.00%
Capital Changes	$0	0.00%	($1,980)	(0.04)%	$0	0.00%	$0	0.00%
Surplus Adjustments	$0	0.00%	($2,145)	(0.04)%	($96,350)	(0.33)%	$0	0.00%
Dividends to Stockholders	$0	0.00%	$0	0.00%	$0	0.00%	($3,950,000)	(1.22)%
Change in Treasury Stock	$0	0.00%	$0	0.00%	$0	0.00%	$0	0.00%
Aggregate Write-ins for Gains and Losses in Surplus	$0	0.00%	$0	0.00%	$0	0.00%	$0	0.00%
Net Change - Policyholder Surplus	($30,093)	(5.07)%	$482,100	10.03%	$2,178,876	7.35%	($8,834,996)	(2.72)%
POLICYHOLDER SURPLUS - ENDING (See Sec. 5, B6, B7, C9, C11)	$484,161	81.54%	$1,776,152	36.96%	$9,754,476	32.91%	$149,827,744	46.20%

B.3 Income Statement - By Individual Underwriter

	BRIDGE		CENSTAR		CHICAGO T&T		CHICAGO TIC	
REVENUE	Company Value	% Total Oper. Inc.	Company Value	% Total Oper. Inc.	Company Value	% Total Oper. Inc.	Company Value	% Total Oper. Inc.
Premiums Written - Direct	$0	0.00%	$0	0.00%	$0	0.00%	$477,816,470	22.66%
Premiums Written - Non-Affiliated Agency	$462	2.36%	$39,460,039	104.07%	$0	0.00%	$1,033,035,988	49.00%
Premiums Written - Affiliated Agency	$0	0.00%	$0	0.00%	$0	0.00%	$376,443,234	17.85%
Premiums - Reinsurance Assumed	$0	0.00%	$0	0.00%	$178,675	0.39%	$3,442,321	0.16%
Premiums - Reinsurance Ceded	$0	0.00%	($1,212,751)	(3.20)%	$0	0.00%	($6,212,780)	(0.29)%
Net Premiums Written *(See Sec. 5, B.4)*	$462	2.36%	$38,247,288	100.88%	$178,675	0.39%	$1,884,525,233	89.38%
Net Premiums Earned	$19,541	100.00%	$37,718,672	99.48%	$178,675	0.39%	$1,806,353,030	85.67%
PLUS:								
Title Examinations	$0	0.00%	$0	0.00%	$0	0.00%	$42,689,191	2.02%
Searches & Abstracts	$0	0.00%	$0	0.00%	$76,768	0.17%	$52,744,018	2.50%
Surveys	$0	0.00%	$0	0.00%	$0	0.00%	$601,739	0.03%
Escrow & Settlement Fees	$0	0.00%	$0	0.00%	$45,503,268	98.84%	$111,308,296	5.28%
Other Service Charges	$0	0.00%	$0	0.00%	$279,234	0.61%	$94,741,036	4.49%
Other Operating Income	$0	0.00%	$196,439	0.52%	$0	0.00%	$0	0.00%
Total Operating Income *(See Sec. 5, A.2, A.3, A.5)*	$19,541	100.00%	$37,915,111	100.00%	$46,037,945	100.00%	$2,108,437,310	100.00%
LESS:								
Amounts Retained By Agents *(See Sec. 5, B.9)*	$346		$31,798,359		$0		$1,121,133,282	
NET OPERATING REVENUE	$19,195		$6,116,752		$46,037,945		$987,304,028	

	Company Value	% Net Oper. Rev.	Company Value	% Net Oper. Rev.	Company Value	% Net Oper. Rev.	Company Value	% Net Oper. Rev.
OPERATING EXPENSE								
Total Personnel Costs	$0	0.00%	$608,813	9.95%	$25,895,966	56.25%	$379,191,940	38.41%
Production Services	$0	0.00%	$0	0.00%	$1,867,191	4.06%	$82,334,098	8.34%
Advertising	$0	0.00%	$199	0.00%	($303,001)	(0.66)%	$2,553,267	0.26%
Boards, Bureaus & Associations	$0	0.00%	$29,625	0.48%	$0	0.00%	$892,828	0.09%
Title Plant Rent & Maintenance	$0	0.00%	$0	0.00%	$0	0.00%	$8,980,905	0.91%
Claim Adjustment Services	$0	0.00%	$0	0.00%	$0	0.00%	$0	0.00%
Amount Charged Off, Net	$3,493	18.20%	$0	0.00%	$0	0.00%	$1,231,132	0.12%
Marketing & Promotional Expense	$0	0.00%	$0	0.00%	$312,864	0.68%	$3,740,650	0.38%
Insurance	$0	0.00%	$52,812	0.86%	$687,235	1.49%	$2,211,857	0.22%
Directors' Fees	$0	0.00%	$0	0.00%	$0	0.00%	$0	0.00%
Travel & Related Expenses	$0	0.00%	$5,925	0.10%	$630,786	1.37%	$21,583,417	2.19%
Rent and Rent Items	$0	0.00%	$72,439	1.18%	$3,942,843	8.56%	$46,937,429	4.75%
Equipment	$0	0.00%	$9,348	0.15%	$1,380,425	3.00%	$22,616,352	2.29%
Cost/Depreciation, EDP Equipment & Software	$1,775	9.25%	$0	0.00%	($55,137)	(0.12)%	$26,553,729	2.69%
Print, Stationery, etc.	$2,456	12.79%	$15,247	0.25%	$735,702	1.60%	$13,474,615	1.36%
Postage, Telephone, Express	$361	1.88%	$31,757	0.52%	$118,821	0.26%	$21,335,036	2.16%
Legal & Auditing	$33,185	172.88%	$29,784	0.49%	$381,773	0.83%	$24,030,706	2.43%
Taxes, Licenses & Fees	$67,288	350.55%	$617,508	10.10%	$1,853,624	4.03%	$32,073,330	3.25%
Real Estate Expenses	$0	0.00%	$0	0.00%	$0	0.00%	$0	0.00%
Real Estate Taxes	$0	0.00%	$0	0.00%	$0	0.00%	$0	0.00%
Miscellaneous	$0	0.00%	$560,173	9.16%	$577,243	1.25%	$63,690,616	6.45%
Other Operating Expense Incurred	$108,558	565.55%	$2,033,630	33.25%	$38,026,335	82.60%	$753,431,907	76.31%
TOTAL OPERATING EXPENSE INCURRED (AGENT RETENTION + OTHER OPERATING EXPENSE INCURRED)	$108,904	--	$33,831,989	--	$38,026,335	--	$1,874,565,189	--
Aggregate Write-ins for Operating Deductions	$0	0.00%	$0	0.00%	$0	0.00%	$0	0.00%
Operating Profit (Loss) Before Losses *(See Sec. 5, A.7)*	($89,363)	(465.55)%	$4,083,122	66.75%	$8,011,610	17.40%	$233,872,121	23.69%
Losses & Loss Adjustment Expense Incurred *(See Sec. 5, C.2 - C.7)*								
Direct Operations *(See Sec. 5, C.7)*	$0	0.00%	$0	0.00%	$0	0.00%	$114,016,898	11.55%
Agency Operations *(See Sec. 5, C.7)*	$180,404	939.85%	$356,768	5.83%	$0	0.00%	$80,166,480	8.12%
NET OPERATING GAIN (LOSS) *(See Sec. 5, A.10)*	($269,767)	(1,405.40)%	$3,726,354	60.92%	$8,011,610	17.40%	$39,688,743	4.02%

	Company Value	% Total Assets	Company Value	% Total Assets	Company Value	% Total Assets	Company Value	% Total Assets
INVESTMENT INCOME								
Net Investment Income Earned *(See Sec. 5, A.8)*	$85,682	1.04%	$679,761	2.30%	$290,461,654	20.94%	$115,113,277	7.29%
Net Realized Capital Gains (Losses) less Capital Gains Tax	$0	0.00%	($1,362)	0.00%	$27,093	0.00%	$7,212,799	0.46%
NET INVESTMENT GAIN (LOSS) *(See Sec. 5, A.9)*	$85,682	1.04%	$678,399	2.29%	$290,488,747	20.94%	$122,326,076	7.75%

	Company Value	% Total Assets	Company Value	% Total Assets	Company Value	% Total Assets	Company Value	% Total Assets
OTHER INCOME								
Other Income (Loss)	$0	0.00%	$0	0.00%	$0	0.00%	$0	0.00%
Net Income Before Taxes *(See Sec. 5, A.11)*	($184,085)	(2.24)%	$4,404,753	14.90%	$298,500,357	21.52%	$162,014,819	10.27%
Federal & Foreign Income Taxes Incurred	($66,914)	(0.82)%	$1,171,735	3.96%	$8,586,833	0.62%	$32,768,138	2.08%
NET INCOME *(See Sec. 5, A.12)*	($117,171)	(1.43)%	$3,233,018	10.94%	$289,913,524	20.90%	$129,246,681	8.19%

	Company Value	% Total Assets	Company Value	% Total Assets	Company Value	% Total Assets	Company Value	% Total Assets
CAPITAL AND SURPLUS ACCOUNT								
POLICYHOLDER SURPLUS - BEGINNING	$8,110,976	98.82%	$23,537,586	79.62%	$920,680,679	66.38%	$429,467,367	27.21%
Net Income	($117,171)	(1.43)%	$3,233,018	10.94%	$289,913,524	20.90%	$129,246,681	8.19%
Change in Net Unrealized Capital Gains (Losses) less Capital Gains Tax	$0	0.00%	$0	0.00%	($207,664,345)	(14.97)%	($64,234,389)	(4.07)%
Change in Net Unrealized Foreign Exchange Capital Gain (Loss)	$0	0.00%	$0	0.00%	$0	0.00%	$0	0.00%
Change in Net Deferred Income Tax	($5,456)	(0.07)%	($53,170)	(0.18)%	$0	0.00%	$27,907,305	1.77%
Change in Nonadmitted Assets	$5,327	0.06%	$22,753	0.08%	$1,200,118	0.09%	($104,527,531)	(6.62)%
Change in Provision for Unauthorized Reinsurance	$0	0.00%	$0	0.00%	$0	0.00%	$0	0.00%
Change in Supplemental Reserves	$0	0.00%	($1,598,586)	(5.41)%	$0	0.00%	$0	0.00%
Change in Surplus Notes	$0	0.00%	$0	0.00%	$0	0.00%	$0	0.00%
Cumulative Effect of Changes in Accounting Principles	$0	0.00%	$0	0.00%	$0	0.00%	$0	0.00%
Capital Changes	$0	0.00%	$0	0.00%	$0	0.00%	$0	0.00%
Surplus Adjustments	$0	0.00%	$0	0.00%	$50,000	0.00%	$0	0.00%
Dividends to Stockholders	$0	0.00%	$0	0.00%	($340,000,000)	(24.51)%	($146,000,000)	(9.25)%
Change in Treasury Stock	$0	0.00%	$0	0.00%	$0	0.00%	$0	0.00%
Aggregate Write-ins for Gains and Losses in Surplus	$0	0.00%	$0	0.00%	$454,647	0.03%	$2,623,117	0.17%
Net Change - Policyholder Surplus	($117,300)	(1.43)%	$1,604,015	5.43%	($256,046,056)	(18.46)%	($154,984,829)	(9.82)%
POLICYHOLDER SURPLUS - ENDING *(See Sec. 5, B.6, B.7, C.9, C.11)*	$7,993,676	97.39%	$25,141,601	85.05%	$664,634,623	47.92%	$274,482,538	17.39%

B.3 Income Statement - By Individual Underwriter

	CHICAGO TIC (OR)		COLUMBIAN NATIONAL		COMMERCE		COMMONWEALTH LAND	
REVENUE	Company Value	% Total Oper. Inc.	Company Value	% Total Oper. Inc.	Company Value	% Total Oper. Inc.	Company Value	% Total Oper. Inc.
Premiums Written - Direct	$13,707,383	41.21%	$0	--	$43,152	0.10%	$220,717,997	18.17%
Premiums Written - Non-Affiliated Agency	$12,576,501	37.81%	$0	--	$1,532,096	3.60%	$808,458,154	66.55%
Premiums Written - Affiliated Agency	$0	0.00%	$0	--	$41,997,283	98.79%	$123,342,178	10.15%
Premiums - Reinsurance Assumed	$1,497	0.00%	$0	--	$0	0.00%	$10,500,643	0.86%
Premiums - Reinsurance Ceded	($62,427)	(0.19)%	$0	--	($663,855)	(1.56)%	($8,901,626)	(0.73)%
Net Premiums Written *(See Sec. 5, B.4)*	$26,222,954	78.84%	$0	--	$42,908,676	100.93%	$1,154,117,346	95.00%
Net Premiums Earned	$26,265,761	78.97%	$0	--	$42,512,147	100.00%	$1,164,353,355	95.84%
PLUS:								
Title Examinations	$0	0.00%	$0	--	$0	0.00%	$23,241,406	1.91%
Searches & Abstracts	$106,270	0.32%	$0	--	$0	0.00%	$226,656	0.02%
Surveys	$13,414	0.04%	$0	--	$0	0.00%	$4,653	0.00%
Escrow & Settlement Fees	$5,519,830	16.60%	$0	--	$0	0.00%	$13,057,252	1.07%
Other Service Charges	$1,353,941	4.07%	$0	--	$0	0.00%	$14,010,988	1.15%
Other Operating Income	$0	0.00%	$0	--	$0	0.00%	$0	0.00%
Total Operating Income *(See Sec. 5, A.2, A.3, A.5)*	$33,259,216	100.00%	$0	--	$42,512,147	100.00%	$1,214,894,310	100.00%
LESS:								
Amounts Retained By Agents *(See Sec. 5, B.9)*	$11,287,905		$0		$36,674,307		$760,409,081	
NET OPERATING REVENUE	$21,971,311		$0		$5,837,840		$454,485,229	

	Company Value	% Net Oper. Rev.	Company Value	% Net Oper. Rev.	Company Value	% Net Oper. Rev.	Company Value	% Net Oper. Rev.
OPERATING EXPENSE								
Total Personnel Costs	$11,902,638	54.17%	$0	--	$677,199	11.60%	$170,828,689	37.59%
Production Services	$28,815	0.13%	$1,917	--	$0	0.00%	$27,445,275	6.04%
Advertising	$65,794	0.30%	$0	--	$0	0.00%	$2,563,456	0.56%
Boards, Bureaus & Associations	$6,975	0.03%	$0	--	$0	0.00%	$453,783	0.10%
Title Plant Rent & Maintenance	$159,799	0.73%	$0	--	$0	0.00%	$4,036,422	0.89%
Claim Adjustment Services	$0	0.00%	$0	--	$0	0.00%	$0	0.00%
Amount Charged Off, Net	$3,443	0.02%	$0	--	$0	0.00%	$2,862,566	0.63%
Marketing & Promotional Expense	$63,861	0.29%	$0	--	$17,101	0.29%	$5,973,449	1.31%
Insurance	$91,033	0.41%	$0	--	$11,148	0.19%	$1,626,789	0.36%
Directors' Fees	$0	0.00%	$0	--	$0	0.00%	$562,390	0.12%
Travel & Related Expenses	$585,340	2.66%	$0	--	$47,815	0.82%	$10,208,707	2.25%
Rent and Rent Items	$1,210,708	5.51%	$4,800	--	$122,210	2.09%	$21,079,814	4.64%
Equipment	$592,329	2.70%	$1,099	--	$18,904	0.32%	$9,053,121	1.99%
Cost/Depreciation, EDP Equipment & Software	$366,575	1.67%	$2,157	--	$124,635	2.13%	$15,753,891	3.47%
Print, Stationery, etc.	$388,908	1.77%	$1,882	--	$17,372	0.30%	$2,834,387	0.62%
Postage, Telephone, Express	$732,946	3.34%	$2,415	--	$17,220	0.29%	$9,280,296	2.04%
Legal & Auditing	$575,620	2.62%	$17,953	--	$216,801	3.71%	$3,898,844	0.86%
Taxes, Licenses & Fees	$61,269	0.28%	$8,579	--	$664,036	11.37%	$22,145,634	4.87%
Real Estate Expenses	$0	0.00%	$0	--	$0	0.00%	$0	0.00%
Real Estate Taxes	$0	0.00%	$0	--	$0	0.00%	$0	0.00%
Miscellaneous	$205,869	0.94%	$98,514	--	($205,883)	(3.53)%	$12,500,226	2.75%
Other Operating Expense Incurred	$17,041,922	77.56%	$139,316	--	$1,728,558	29.61%	$323,107,739	71.09%
TOTAL OPERATING EXPENSE INCURRED (AGENT RETENTION + OTHER OPERATING EXPENSE INCURRED)	$28,329,827	--	$139,316	--	$38,402,865	--	$1,083,516,820	--
Aggregate Write-ins for Operating Deductions	$0	0.00%	$0	--	$0	0.00%	$0	0.00%
Operating Profit (Loss) Before Losses *(See Sec. 5, A.7)*	$4,929,389	22.44%	($139,316)	--	$4,109,282	70.39%	$131,377,490	28.91%
Losses & Loss Adjustment Expense Incurred *(See Sec. 5, C.2 - C.7)*								
Direct Operations *(See Sec. 5, C.7)*	$415,182	1.89%	$0	--	$0	0.00%	$19,511,239	4.29%
Agency Operations *(See Sec. 5, C.7)*	$239,937	1.09%	$0	--	$456,599	7.82%	$60,478,344	13.31%
NET OPERATING GAIN (LOSS) *(See Sec. 5, A.10)*	$4,274,270	19.45%	($139,316)	--	$3,652,683	62.57%	$51,387,907	11.31%

	Company Value	% Total Assets	Company Value	% Total Assets	Company Value	% Total Assets	Company Value	% Total Assets
INVESTMENT INCOME								
Net Investment Income Earned *(See Sec. 5, A.8)*	$1,152,795	4.12%	$38,289	1.05%	$626,185	2.81%	$29,461,702	3.95%
Net Realized Capital Gains (Losses) less Capital Gains Tax	($1,358)	0.00%	$0	0.00%	$0	0.00%	$3,028,893	0.41%
NET INVESTMENT GAIN (LOSS) *(See Sec. 5, A.9)*	$1,151,437	4.12%	$38,289	1.05%	$626,185	2.81%	$32,490,595	4.36%

	Company Value	% Total Assets	Company Value	% Total Assets	Company Value	% Total Assets	Company Value	% Total Assets
OTHER INCOME								
Other Income (Loss)	$0	0.00%	$608	0.02%	$0	0.00%	$0	0.00%
Net Income Before Taxes *(See Sec. 5, A.11)*	$5,425,707	19.40%	($100,419)	(2.76)%	$4,278,868	19.19%	$83,878,502	11.26%
Federal & Foreign Income Taxes Incurred	$1,512,478	5.41%	($32,112)	(0.88)%	$1,479,138	6.64%	$21,093,822	2.83%
NET INCOME *(See Sec. 5, A.12)*	$3,913,229	13.99%	($68,307)	(1.88)%	$2,799,730	12.56%	$62,784,680	8.42%

	Company Value	% Total Assets	Company Value	% Total Assets	Company Value	% Total Assets	Company Value	% Total Assets
CAPITAL AND SURPLUS ACCOUNT								
POLICYHOLDER SURPLUS - BEGINNING	$13,987,712	50.02%	$3,723,535	102.24%	$8,566,084	38.43%	$313,773,809	42.10%
Net Income	$3,913,229	13.99%	($68,307)	(1.88)%	$2,799,730	12.56%	$62,784,680	8.42%
Change in Net Unrealized Capital Gains (Losses) less Capital Gains Tax	($66,081)	(0.24)%	$0	0.00%	($495,839)	(2.22)%	($30,690,181)	(4.12)%
Change in Net Unrealized Foreign Exchange Capital Gain (Loss)	$0	0.00%	$0	0.00%	$0	0.00%	$0	0.00%
Change in Net Deferred Income Tax	($393,926)	(1.41)%	$110,178	3.03%	$1,384	0.01%	($1,364,441)	(0.18)%
Change in Nonadmitted Assets	$699,682	2.50%	($226,884)	(6.23)%	$338,443	1.52%	$2,582,117	0.35%
Change in Provision for Unauthorized Reinsurance	$0	0.00%	$0	0.00%	$0	0.00%	$0	0.00%
Change in Supplemental Reserves	$0	0.00%	$0	0.00%	$0	0.00%	$0	0.00%
Change in Surplus Notes	$0	0.00%	$0	0.00%	$0	0.00%	$0	0.00%
Cumulative Effect of Changes in Accounting Principles	$0	0.00%	$0	0.00%	$0	0.00%	$0	0.00%
Capital Changes	$0	0.00%	$0	0.00%	$0	0.00%	$5,063,554	0.68%
Surplus Adjustments	$0	0.00%	$0	0.00%	$0	0.00%	$0	0.00%
Dividends to Stockholders	($5,200,000)	(18.59)%	$0	0.00%	($2,400,000)	(10.77)%	($80,000,000)	(10.73)%
Change in Treasury Stock	$0	0.00%	$0	0.00%	$0	0.00%	$0	0.00%
Aggregate Write-ins for Gains and Losses in Surplus	$626,272	2.24%	$0	0.00%	$0	0.00%	($18,057,061)	(2.42)%
Net Change - Policyholder Surplus	($420,825)	(1.50)%	($185,013)	(5.08)%	$245,828	1.10%	($59,681,332)	(8.01)%
POLICYHOLDER SURPLUS - ENDING *(See Sec. 5, B.6, B.7, C.9, C.11)*	$13,566,887	48.51%	$3,538,522	97.16%	$8,811,912	39.53%	$254,092,477	34.10%

B.3 Income Statement - By Individual Underwriter

	COMMONWEALTH LAND (NJ)		CONESTOGA		CT ATTORNEYS		DAKOTA HOMESTEAD	
REVENUE	Company Value	% Total Oper. Inc.	Company Value	% Total Oper. Inc.	Company Value	% Total Oper. Inc.	Company Value	% Total Oper. Inc.
Premiums Written - Direct	$5,109,506	14.43%	$201,980	1.42%	$0	0.00%	$244,546	6.06%
Premiums Written - Non-Affiliated Agency	$30,277,935	85.53%	$13,366,327	94.28%	$51,258,956	94.76%	$3,869,021	95.90%
Premiums Written - Affiliated Agency	$0	0.00%	$376,063	2.65%	$0	0.00%	$0	0.00%
Premiums - Reinsurance Assumed	$25,900	0.07%	$0	0.00%	$13,165	0.02%	$0	0.00%
Premiums - Reinsurance Ceded	($1,712,749)	(4.84)%	($188,774)	(1.33)%	($55,943)	(0.10)%	($221,248)	(5.48)%
Net Premiums Written (See Sec. 5, B.4)	$33,700,592	95.20%	$13,755,596	97.03%	$51,216,178	94.68%	$3,892,319	96.47%
Net Premiums Earned	$33,610,559	94.95%	$13,907,911	98.10%	$50,593,631	93.53%	$3,850,567	95.44%
PLUS:								
Title Examinations	$848,184	2.40%	$0	0.00%	$0	0.00%	$0	0.00%
Searches & Abstracts	$25	0.00%	$0	0.00%	$2,020,146	3.73%	$0	0.00%
Surveys	$0	0.00%	$0	0.00%	$0	0.00%	$0	0.00%
Escrow & Settlement Fees	$350,325	0.99%	$0	0.00%	$0	0.00%	$0	0.00%
Other Service Charges	$589,959	1.67%	$268,991	1.90%	$0	0.00%	$0	0.00%
Other Operating Income	$0	0.00%	$0	0.00%	$1,482,140	2.74%	$183,978	4.56%
Total Operating Income (See Sec. 5, A.2, A.3, A.5)	$35,399,052	100.00%	$14,176,902	100.00%	$54,095,917	100.00%	$4,034,545	100.00%
LESS:								
Amounts Retained By Agents (See Sec. 5, B.9)	$25,866,635		$10,429,015		$33,564,663		$2,952,933	
NET OPERATING REVENUE	$9,532,417		$3,747,887		$20,531,254		$1,081,612	

OPERATING EXPENSE	Company Value	% Net Oper. Rev.	Company Value	% Net Oper. Rev.	Company Value	% Net Oper. Rev.	Company Value	% Net Oper. Rev.
Total Personnel Costs	$3,165,380	33.21%	$2,229,736	59.49%	$9,661,981	47.06%	$366,520	33.89%
Production Services	$214,966	2.26%	$94,543	2.52%	$2,236,359	10.89%	$0	0.00%
Advertising	$60,771	0.64%	$86,504	2.31%	$646,531	3.15%	$24,631	2.28%
Boards, Bureaus & Associations	$2,939	0.03%	$50,588	1.35%	$181,075	0.88%	$18,222	1.68%
Title Plant Rent & Maintenance	$3,293	0.03%	$0	0.00%	$0	0.00%	$0	0.00%
Claim Adjustment Services	$0	0.00%	$0	0.00%	$0	0.00%	$0	0.00%
Amount Charged Off, Net	$18,800	0.20%	$0	0.00%	$0	0.00%	$49,811	4.61%
Marketing & Promotional Expense	$66,220	0.69%	$52,976	1.41%	$584,246	2.85%	$19,652	1.82%
Insurance	$31,416	0.33%	$87,367	2.33%	$623,820	3.04%	$4,429	0.41%
Directors' Fees	$11,018	0.12%	$23,100	0.62%	$77,000	0.38%	$0	0.00%
Travel & Related Expenses	$144,872	1.52%	$155,665	4.15%	$239,595	1.17%	$40,131	3.71%
Rent and Rent Items	$421,689	4.42%	$231,000	6.16%	$792,159	3.86%	$22,524	2.08%
Equipment	$168,592	1.77%	$75,349	2.01%	$398,520	1.94%	$0	0.00%
Cost/Depreciation, EDP Equipment & Software	$184,099	1.93%	$67,988	1.81%	$130,339	0.63%	$19,410	1.79%
Print, Stationery, etc.	$70,416	0.74%	$84,992	2.27%	$236,639	1.15%	$35,570	3.29%
Postage, Telephone, Express	$134,961	1.42%	$73,182	1.95%	$286,114	1.39%	$12,120	1.12%
Legal & Auditing	$35,120	0.37%	$215,848	5.76%	$356,926	1.74%	$135,584	12.54%
Taxes, Licenses & Fees	$382,026	4.01%	$375,540	10.02%	$1,048,169	5.11%	$122,420	11.32%
Real Estate Expenses	$0	0.00%	$55,338	1.48%	$0	0.00%	$0	0.00%
Real Estate Taxes	$0	0.00%	$25,966	0.69%	$0	0.00%	$0	0.00%
Miscellaneous	$206,370	2.16%	$130,756	3.49%	($52,840)	(0.26)%	$0	0.00%
Other Operating Expense Incurred	$5,322,948	55.84%	$4,116,438	109.83%	$17,446,633	84.98%	$871,024	80.53%
TOTAL OPERATING EXPENSE INCURRED (AGENT RETENTION + OTHER OPERATING EXPENSE INCURRED)	$31,189,583	--	$14,545,453	--	$51,011,296	--	$3,823,957	--
Aggregate Write-ins for Operating Deductions	$0	0.00%	$0	0.00%	$0	0.00%	$0	0.00%
Operating Profit (Loss) Before Losses (See Sec. 5, A.7)	$4,209,469	44.16%	($368,551)	(9.83)%	$3,084,621	15.02%	$210,588	19.47%
Losses & Loss Adjustment Expense Incurred (See Sec. 5, C.2 - C.7)								
Direct Operations (See Sec. 5, C.7)	$383,394	4.02%	$12,755	0.34%	$0	0.00%	$0	0.00%
Agency Operations (See Sec. 5, C.7)	$1,516,743	15.91%	$979,151	26.13%	$4,086,369	19.90%	$251,953	23.29%
NET OPERATING GAIN (LOSS) (See Sec. 5, A.10)	$2,309,332	24.23%	($1,360,457)	(36.30)%	($1,001,748)	(4.88)%	($41,365)	(3.82)%

INVESTMENT INCOME	Company Value	% Total Assets	Company Value	% Total Assets	Company Value	% Total Assets	Company Value	% Total Assets
Net Investment Income Earned (See Sec. 5, A.8)	$1,825,496	4.33%	$337,732	4.11%	$2,404,707	3.96%	$79,714	2.23%
Net Realized Capital Gains (Losses) less Capital Gains Tax	$5,457	0.01%	$0	0.00%	$29,473	0.05%	$18,355	0.51%
NET INVESTMENT GAIN (LOSS) (See Sec. 5, A.9)	$1,830,953	4.34%	$337,732	4.11%	$2,434,180	4.01%	$98,069	2.75%

OTHER INCOME	Company Value	% Total Assets	Company Value	% Total Assets	Company Value	% Total Assets	Company Value	% Total Assets
Other Income (Loss)	$0	0.00%	$809	0.01%	($75,390)	(0.12)%	$0	0.00%
Net Income Before Taxes (See Sec. 5, A.11)	$4,140,285	9.82%	($1,021,916)	(12.42)%	$1,357,042	2.24%	$56,704	1.59%
Federal & Foreign Income Taxes Incurred	$1,165,287	2.76%	($380,714)	(4.63)%	$513,377	0.85%	$0	0.00%
NET INCOME (See Sec. 5, A.12)	$2,974,998	7.06%	($641,202)	(7.80)%	$843,665	1.39%	$56,704	1.59%

CAPITAL AND SURPLUS ACCOUNT	Company Value	% Total Assets	Company Value	% Total Assets	Company Value	% Total Assets	Company Value	% Total Assets
POLICYHOLDER SURPLUS - BEGINNING	$30,229,744	71.72%	$4,054,246	49.29%	$41,145,521	67.83%	$2,086,514	58.45%
Net Income	$2,974,998	7.06%	($641,202)	(7.80)%	$843,665	1.39%	$56,704	1.59%
Change in Net Unrealized Capital Gains (Losses) less Capital Gains Tax	$0	0.00%	$18,712	0.23%	($201,138)	(0.33)%	($26,277)	(0.74)%
Change in Net Unrealized Foreign Exchange Capital Gain (Loss)	$0	0.00%	$0	0.00%	$0	0.00%	$0	0.00%
Change in Net Deferred Income Tax	($60,305)	(0.14)%	$18,000	0.22%	$10,736	0.02%	$0	0.00%
Change in Nonadmitted Assets	($11,991)	(0.03)%	($143,996)	(1.75)%	$40,500	0.07%	$149,366	4.18%
Change in Provision for Unauthorized Reinsurance	$0	0.00%	$0	0.00%	$0	0.00%	$0	0.00%
Change in Supplemental Reserves	$0	0.00%	$0	0.00%	$0	0.00%	$0	0.00%
Change in Surplus Notes	$0	0.00%	$0	0.00%	$0	0.00%	$0	0.00%
Cumulative Effect of Changes in Accounting Principles	$0	0.00%	$0	0.00%	$0	0.00%	$0	0.00%
Capital Changes	$0	0.00%	$0	0.00%	$0	0.00%	$0	0.00%
Surplus Adjustments	$0	0.00%	$178,123	2.17%	$0	0.00%	$0	0.00%
Dividends to Stockholders	$0	0.00%	$0	0.00%	$0	0.00%	$0	0.00%
Change in Treasury Stock	$0	0.00%	$0	0.00%	$0	0.00%	$0	0.00%
Aggregate Write-ins for Gains and Losses in Surplus	$0	0.00%	$0	0.00%	$0	0.00%	$0	0.00%
Net Change - Policyholder Surplus	$2,902,701	6.89%	($570,363)	(6.93)%	$693,763	1.14%	$179,793	5.04%
POLICYHOLDER SURPLUS - ENDING (See Sec. 5, B.6, B.7, C.9, C.11)	$33,132,445	78.60%	$3,483,883	42.36%	$41,839,284	68.97%	$2,266,307	63.49%

B.3 Income Statement - By Individual Underwriter

	DREIBELBISS		EQUITY NATIONAL		FARMERS NATIONAL		FIDELITY NATIONAL	
REVENUE	Company Value	% Total Oper. Inc.	Company Value	% Total Oper. Inc.	Company Value	% Total Oper. Inc.	Company Value	% Total Oper. Inc.
Premiums Written - Direct	$517,581	29.34%	$280,228	13.55%	$0	0.00%	$251,405,363	18.36%
Premiums Written - Non-Affiliated Agency	$115,399	6.54%	$0	0.00%	$1,138,404	141.73%	$673,800,566	49.21%
Premiums Written - Affiliated Agency	$0	0.00%	$0	0.00%	$0	0.00%	$348,876,279	25.48%
Premiums - Reinsurance Assumed	$0	0.00%	$0	0.00%	$0	0.00%	$2,201,548	0.16%
Premiums - Reinsurance Ceded	($51,104)	(2.90)%	($43,366)	(2.10)%	($211,146)	(26.29)%	($6,584,780)	(0.48)%
Net Premiums Written (See Sec. 5, B.4)	$581,876	32.99%	$236,862	11.45%	$927,258	115.45%	$1,269,698,976	92.72%
Net Premiums Earned	$581,876	32.99%	$208,883	10.10%	$802,423	99.90%	$1,257,995,188	91.87%
PLUS:								
Title Examinations	$0	0.00%	$0	0.00%	$0	0.00%	$41,095	0.00%
Searches & Abstracts	$561,618	31.84%	$0	0.00%	$770	0.10%	$23,252,515	1.70%
Surveys	$0	0.00%	$0	0.00%	$0	0.00%	$0	0.00%
Escrow & Settlement Fees	$0	0.00%	$1,795,211	86.79%	$0	0.00%	$28,484,038	2.08%
Other Service Charges	$570,286	32.33%	$0	0.00%	$0	0.00%	$59,587,776	4.35%
Other Operating Income	$50,138	2.84%	$64,258	3.11%	$0	0.00%	$0	0.00%
Total Operating Income (See Sec. 5, A.2, A.3, A.5)	$1,763,918	100.00%	$2,068,352	100.00%	$803,193	100.00%	$1,369,360,612	100.00%
LESS:								
Amounts Retained By Agents (See Sec. 5, B.9)	$82,722		$0		$460,097		$840,562,038	
NET OPERATING REVENUE	$1,681,196		$2,068,352		$343,096		$528,798,574	

	DREIBELBISS		EQUITY NATIONAL		FARMERS NATIONAL		FIDELITY NATIONAL	
OPERATING EXPENSE	Company Value	% Net Oper. Rev.	Company Value	% Net Oper. Rev.	Company Value	% Net Oper. Rev.	Company Value	% Net Oper. Rev.
Total Personnel Costs	$1,082,764	64.40%	$0	0.00%	$295,003	85.98%	$208,224,931	39.38%
Production Services	$210,422	12.52%	$1,913,629	92.52%	$1,952	0.57%	$20,883,859	3.95%
Advertising	$12,975	0.77%	$750	0.04%	$14,818	4.32%	$6,049,528	1.14%
Boards, Bureaus & Associations	$3,071	0.18%	$0	0.00%	$10,113	2.95%	$59,846	0.01%
Title Plant Rent & Maintenance	$0	0.00%	$0	0.00%	$0	0.00%	$4,228,189	0.80%
Claim Adjustment Services	$0	0.00%	$0	0.00%	$0	0.00%	$0	0.00%
Amount Charged Off, Net	$54,113	3.22%	$0	0.00%	$11,559	3.37%	$257,027	0.05%
Marketing & Promotional Expense	$0	0.00%	$0	0.00%	$29,890	8.71%	$537,628	0.10%
Insurance	$32,044	1.91%	$3,788	0.18%	$7,171	2.09%	$1,418,376	0.27%
Directors' Fees	$0	0.00%	$0	0.00%	$6,622	1.93%	$0	0.00%
Travel & Related Expenses	$42,240	2.51%	$0	0.00%	$50,982	14.86%	$14,455,831	2.73%
Rent and Rent Items	$37,598	2.24%	$17,106	0.83%	$26,752	7.80%	$22,280,514	4.21%
Equipment	$37,325	2.22%	$0	0.00%	$41,070	11.97%	$11,708,720	2.21%
Cost/Depreciation, EDP Equipment & Software	$0	0.00%	$12,609	0.61%	$26,272	7.66%	$16,763,146	3.17%
Print, Stationery, etc.	$36,254	2.16%	$8,174	0.40%	$188	0.05%	$7,460,644	1.41%
Postage, Telephone, Express	$20,680	1.23%	$0	0.00%	$20,848	6.08%	$9,830,086	1.86%
Legal & Auditing	$74,496	4.43%	$28,785	1.39%	$44,197	12.88%	$18,023,675	3.41%
Taxes, Licenses & Fees	$0	0.00%	$0	0.00%	$26,631	7.76%	$21,462,156	4.06%
Real Estate Expenses	$61,946	3.68%	$0	0.00%	$0	0.00%	$0	0.00%
Real Estate Taxes	$29,245	1.74%	$0	0.00%	$0	0.00%	$0	0.00%
Miscellaneous	$115,653	6.88%	$248,245	12.00%	$25,065	7.31%	$16,862,717	3.19%
Other Operating Expense Incurred	$1,850,826	110.09%	$2,233,086	107.96%	$639,133	186.28%	$380,506,873	71.96%
TOTAL OPERATING EXPENSE INCURRED (AGENT RETENTION + OTHER OPERATING EXPENSE INCURRED)	$1,933,548	--	$2,233,086	--	$1,099,230	--	$1,221,068,911	--
Aggregate Write-ins for Operating Deductions	$0	0.00%	$0	0.00%	$0	0.00%	$0	0.00%
Operating Profit (Loss) Before Losses (See Sec. 5, A.7)	($169,630)	(10.09)%	($164,734)	(7.96)%	($296,037)	(86.28)%	$148,291,701	28.04%
Losses & Loss Adjustment Expense Incurred (See Sec. 5, C.2 - C.7)								
Direct Operations (See Sec. 5, C.7)	$216,747	12.89%	$0	0.00%	$0	0.00%	$16,952,424	3.21%
Agency Operations (See Sec. 5, C.7)	$0	0.00%	$0	0.00%	$68,819	20.06%	$89,020,790	16.83%
NET OPERATING GAIN (LOSS) (See Sec. 5, A.10)	($386,377)	(22.98)%	($164,734)	(7.96)%	($364,856)	(106.34)%	$42,318,487	8.00%

	DREIBELBISS		EQUITY NATIONAL		FARMERS NATIONAL		FIDELITY NATIONAL	
INVESTMENT INCOME	Company Value	% Total Assets	Company Value	% Total Assets	Company Value	% Total Assets	Company Value	% Total Assets
Net Investment Income Earned (See Sec. 5, A.8)	$163,001	5.51%	$230,044	14.51%	$41,556	3.36%	$36,388,258	4.23%
Net Realized Capital Gains (Losses) less Capital Gains Tax	$4,653	0.16%	$0	0.00%	$0	0.00%	$3,043,736	0.35%
NET INVESTMENT GAIN (LOSS) (See Sec. 5, A.9)	$167,654	5.66%	$230,044	14.51%	$41,556	3.36%	$39,431,994	4.58%

	DREIBELBISS		EQUITY NATIONAL		FARMERS NATIONAL		FIDELITY NATIONAL	
OTHER INCOME	Company Value	% Total Assets	Company Value	% Total Assets	Company Value	% Total Assets	Company Value	% Total Assets
Other Income (Loss)	$0	0.00%	$0	0.00%	$10,167	0.82%	($359,416)	(0.04)%
Net Income Before Taxes (See Sec. 5, A.11)	($218,723)	(7.39)%	$65,310	4.12%	($313,133)	(25.32)%	$81,391,065	9.46%
Federal & Foreign Income Taxes Incurred	($124,733)	(4.21)%	$33,611	2.12%	$0	0.00%	$23,293,807	2.71%
NET INCOME (See Sec. 5, A.12)	($93,990)	(3.17)%	$31,699	2.00%	($313,133)	(25.32)%	$58,097,258	6.75%

	DREIBELBISS		EQUITY NATIONAL		FARMERS NATIONAL		FIDELITY NATIONAL	
CAPITAL AND SURPLUS ACCOUNT	Company Value	% Total Assets	Company Value	% Total Assets	Company Value	% Total Assets	Company Value	% Total Assets
POLICYHOLDER SURPLUS - BEGINNING	$2,546,712	86.01%	$1,393,151	87.85%	$750,858	60.71%	$273,989,612	31.83%
Net Income	($93,990)	(3.17)%	$31,699	2.00%	($313,133)	(25.32)%	$58,097,258	6.75%
Change in Net Unrealized Capital Gains (Losses) less Capital Gains Tax	($16,145)	(0.55)%	$0	0.00%	$0	0.00%	($31,474,186)	(3.66)%
Change in Net Unrealized Foreign Exchange Capital Gain (Loss)	$0	0.00%	$0	0.00%	$0	0.00%	$0	0.00%
Change in Net Deferred Income Tax	$0	0.00%	$0	0.00%	$135,383	10.95%	$67,224	0.01%
Change in Nonadmitted Assets	$213,862	7.22%	$13,290	0.84%	($214,901)	(17.38)%	$16,302,198	1.89%
Change in Provision for Unauthorized Reinsurance	$0	0.00%	$0	0.00%	$0	0.00%	$0	0.00%
Change in Supplemental Reserves	$0	0.00%	$0	0.00%	$0	0.00%	$0	0.00%
Change in Surplus Notes	$0	0.00%	$0	0.00%	$0	0.00%	$0	0.00%
Cumulative Effect of Changes in Accounting Principles	$0	0.00%	$0	0.00%	$0	0.00%	$0	0.00%
Capital Changes	$0	0.00%	$0	0.00%	$0	0.00%	$0	0.00%
Surplus Adjustments	$0	0.00%	$0	0.00%	$459,000	37.11%	$0	0.00%
Dividends to Stockholders	$0	0.00%	$0	0.00%	$0	0.00%	($79,300,000)	(9.21)%
Change in Treasury Stock	$0	0.00%	$0	0.00%	$0	0.00%	$0	0.00%
Aggregate Write-ins for Gains and Losses in Surplus	$0	0.00%	$0	0.00%	$0	0.00%	$0	0.00%
Net Change - Policyholder Surplus	$103,727	3.50%	$44,989	2.84%	$66,349	5.36%	($36,307,508)	(4.22)%
POLICYHOLDER SURPLUS - ENDING (See Sec. 5, B.6, B.7, C.9, C.11)	$2,650,439	89.51%	$1,438,140	90.69%	$817,207	66.07%	$237,682,104	27.61%

B.3 Income Statement - By Individual Underwriter

	FIRST AMERICAN (KS)		FIRST AMERICAN (NY)		FIRST AMERICAN (OR)		FIRST AMERICAN T&T	
REVENUE	Company Value	% Total Oper. Inc.	Company Value	% Total Oper. Inc.	Company Value	% Total Oper. Inc.	Company Value	% Total Oper. Inc.
Premiums Written - Direct	$1,550,799	10.82%	$96,485,318	35.49%	$42,031,597	47.49%	$6,291,430	24.77%
Premiums Written - Non-Affiliated Agency	$5,813,820	40.55%	$131,671,357	48.43%	$13,032,270	14.72%	$0	0.00%
Premiums Written - Affiliated Agency	$7,399,061	51.60%	$11,099,012	4.08%	$0	0.00%	$0	0.00%
Premiums - Reinsurance Assumed	$0	0.00%	$463,933	0.17%	$6,316,032	7.14%	$0	0.00%
Premiums - Reinsurance Ceded	($250,057)	(1.74)%	($1,688,958)	(0.62)%	($359,054)	(0.41)%	$0	0.00%
Net Premiums Written *(See Sec. 5, B.4)*	$14,513,623	101.22%	$238,030,662	87.55%	$61,020,845	68.94%	$6,291,430	24.77%
Net Premiums Earned	$13,915,416	97.05%	$233,124,439	85.74%	$59,893,994	67.67%	$6,121,430	24.10%
PLUS:								
Title Examinations	$158,630	1.11%	$0	0.00%	$1,579,658	1.78%	$1,197,643	4.71%
Searches & Abstracts	$85,780	0.60%	$38,481,892	14.15%	$3,012,106	3.40%	$14,293,419	56.26%
Surveys	$0	0.00%	$0	0.00%	$0	0.00%	$0	0.00%
Escrow & Settlement Fees	$177,361	1.24%	$275,577	0.10%	$22,946,061	25.92%	$2,570,354	10.12%
Other Service Charges	$835	0.01%	$0	0.00%	$1,080,286	1.22%	$117,947	0.46%
Other Operating Income	$0	0.00%	$0	0.00%	$0	0.00%	$1,103,608	4.34%
Total Operating Income *(See Sec. 5, A.2, A.3, A.5)*	$14,338,022	100.00%	$271,881,908	100.00%	$88,512,105	100.00%	$25,404,401	100.00%
LESS:								
Amounts Retained By Agents *(See Sec. 5, B.9)*	$11,211,094		$121,059,713		$11,789,024		$1,227,400	
NET OPERATING REVENUE	$3,126,928		$150,822,195		$76,723,081		$24,177,001	
OPERATING EXPENSE	Company Value	% Net Oper. Rev.	Company Value	% Net Oper. Rev.	Company Value	% Net Oper. Rev.	Company Value	% Net Oper. Rev.
Total Personnel Costs	$1,163,907	37.22%	$88,910,592	58.95%	$44,574,400	58.10%	$11,969,973	49.51%
Production Services	$6,281	0.20%	$8,044,932	5.33%	$1,797,224	2.34%	$313,184	1.30%
Advertising	$868	0.03%	$6,701,881	4.44%	$772,920	1.01%	$27,009	0.11%
Boards, Bureaus & Associations	$0	0.00%	$721,226	0.48%	$8,462	0.01%	$0	0.00%
Title Plant Rent & Maintenance	$11,611	0.37%	$0	0.00%	$1,503,207	1.96%	$264,304	1.09%
Claim Adjustment Services	$0	0.00%	$0	0.00%	$0	0.00%	$0	0.00%
Amount Charged Off, Net	$22,441	0.72%	$552,011	0.37%	$122,209	0.16%	$528,369	2.19%
Marketing & Promotional Expense	$10,683	0.34%	$0	0.00%	$427,409	0.56%	$51,348	0.21%
Insurance	$2,931	0.09%	$368,469	0.24%	$243,301	0.32%	$43,158	0.18%
Directors' Fees	$0	0.00%	$5,700	0.00%	$1,500	0.00%	$0	0.00%
Travel & Related Expenses	$30,459	0.97%	$944,940	0.63%	$1,789,342	2.33%	$195,363	0.81%
Rent and Rent Items	$33,790	1.08%	$2,805,065	1.86%	$7,069,484	9.21%	$1,089,232	4.51%
Equipment	$11,490	0.37%	$1,963,472	1.30%	$1,260,727	1.64%	$219,734	0.91%
Cost/Depreciation, EDP Equipment & Software	$0	0.00%	$216,432	0.14%	$2,372,180	3.09%	$0	0.00%
Print, Stationery, etc.	$9,922	0.32%	$1,555,887	1.03%	$730,337	0.95%	$1,506,137	6.23%
Postage, Telephone, Express	$9,708	0.31%	$1,730,023	1.15%	$2,700,350	3.52%	$623,064	2.58%
Legal & Auditing	($3,117)	(0.10)%	$544,489	0.36%	$809,000	1.05%	$320,269	1.32%
Taxes, Licenses & Fees	$212,291	6.79%	$6,499,349	4.31%	$818,038	1.07%	$125,239	0.52%
Real Estate Expenses	$19,264	0.62%	$320,898	0.21%	$17,046	0.02%	$0	0.00%
Real Estate Taxes	$829	0.03%	$0	0.00%	$109,808	0.14%	$0	0.00%
Miscellaneous	$0	0.00%	$8,185,407	5.43%	($581,177)	(0.76)%	$1,944,003	8.04%
Other Operating Expense Incurred	$1,543,358	49.36%	$130,070,773	86.24%	$66,545,767	86.74%	$19,220,386	79.50%
TOTAL OPERATING EXPENSE INCURRED (AGENT RETENTION + OTHER OPERATING EXPENSE INCURRED)	$12,754,452	--	$251,130,486	--	$78,334,791	--	$20,447,786	--
Aggregate Write-ins for Operating Deductions	$0	0.00%	$0	0.00%	($507)	0.00%	$0	0.00%
Operating Profit (Loss) Before Losses *(See Sec. 5, A.7)*	$1,583,570	50.64%	$20,751,422	13.76%	$10,177,821	13.27%	$4,956,615	20.50%
Losses & Loss Adjustment Expense Incurred *(See Sec. 5, C.2 - C.7)*								
Direct Operations *(See Sec. 5, C.7)*	$128,072	4.10%	$2,933,200	1.94%	$1,475,918	1.92%	$217,877	0.90%
Agency Operations *(See Sec. 5, C.7)*	$628,581	20.10%	$7,057,846	4.68%	$1,443,867	1.88%	$0	0.00%
NET OPERATING GAIN (LOSS) *(See Sec. 5, A.10)*	$826,917	26.45%	$10,760,376	7.13%	$7,258,036	9.46%	$4,738,738	19.60%
INVESTMENT INCOME	Company Value	% Total Assets	Company Value	% Total Assets	Company Value	% Total Assets	Company Value	% Total Assets
Net Investment Income Earned *(See Sec. 5, A.8)*	$351,141	2.79%	$10,940,548	5.38%	$1,590,147	2.48%	$1,107,891	5.53%
Net Realized Capital Gains (Losses) less Capital Gains Tax	$0	0.00%	$271,625	0.13%	$168,650	0.26%	$0	0.00%
NET INVESTMENT GAIN (LOSS) *(See Sec. 5, A.9)*	$351,141	2.79%	$11,212,173	5.52%	$1,758,797	2.75%	$1,107,891	5.53%
OTHER INCOME	Company Value	% Total Assets	Company Value	% Total Assets	Company Value	% Total Assets	Company Value	% Total Assets
Other Income (Loss)	$0	0.00%	$0	0.00%	$0	0.00%	$15,248	0.08%
Net Income Before Taxes *(See Sec. 5, A.11)*	$1,178,058	9.35%	$21,972,549	10.81%	$9,016,833	14.09%	$5,861,877	29.24%
Federal & Foreign Income Taxes Incurred	$544,190	4.32%	$8,524,707	4.19%	$3,038,625	4.75%	$1,765,687	8.81%
NET INCOME *(See Sec. 5, A.12)*	$633,868	5.03%	$13,447,842	6.62%	$5,978,208	9.34%	$4,096,190	20.44%
CAPITAL AND SURPLUS ACCOUNT	Company Value	% Total Assets	Company Value	% Total Assets	Company Value	% Total Assets	Company Value	% Total Assets
POLICYHOLDER SURPLUS - BEGINNING	$5,292,674	41.99%	$90,145,277	44.35%	$33,010,673	51.58%	$11,218,295	55.97%
Net Income	$633,868	5.03%	$13,447,842	6.62%	$5,978,208	9.34%	$4,096,190	20.44%
Change in Net Unrealized Capital Gains (Losses) less Capital Gains Tax	$0	0.00%	($1,565,235)	(0.77)%	$277,788	0.43%	$0	0.00%
Change in Net Unrealized Foreign Exchange Capital Gain (Loss)	$0	0.00%	$0	0.00%	$0	0.00%	$0	0.00%
Change in Net Deferred Income Tax	$93,400	0.74%	$259,374	0.13%	($1,318,372)	(2.06)%	$0	0.00%
Change in Nonadmitted Assets	($200,828)	(1.59)%	($782,655)	(0.39)%	$3,674,414	5.74%	($5,085,576)	(25.37)%
Change in Provision for Unauthorized Reinsurance	$0	0.00%	$0	0.00%	$0	0.00%	$0	0.00%
Change in Supplemental Reserves	$0	0.00%	$0	0.00%	$0	0.00%	$0	0.00%
Change in Surplus Notes	$0	0.00%	$0	0.00%	$0	0.00%	$0	0.00%
Cumulative Effect of Changes in Accounting Principles	$0	0.00%	$0	0.00%	$0	0.00%	$0	0.00%
Capital Changes	$0	0.00%	$7,875,230	3.87%	$0	0.00%	$0	0.00%
Surplus Adjustments	$0	0.00%	$0	0.00%	$0	0.00%	$12,184,446	60.79%
Dividends to Stockholders	$0	0.00%	($1,993,663)	(0.98)%	($10,144,000)	(15.85)%	($6,000,000)	(29.93)%
Change in Treasury Stock	$0	0.00%	$0	0.00%	$0	0.00%	$0	0.00%
Aggregate Write-ins for Gains and Losses in Surplus	$14,676	0.12%	$0	0.00%	$562,563	0.88%	$0	0.00%
Net Change - Policyholder Surplus	$541,116	4.29%	$17,240,893	8.48%	($969,399)	(1.51)%	$5,194,790	25.92%
POLICYHOLDER SURPLUS - ENDING *(See Sec. 5, B.6, B.7, C.9, C.11)*	$5,833,790	46.29%	$107,386,170	52.83%	$32,041,274	50.06%	$16,413,085	81.88%

2

B.3 Income Statement - By Individual Underwriter

	FIRST AMERICAN TIC		FIRST AMERICAN TRANS		FOUNDERS		GENERAL T&T	
REVENUE	Company Value	% Total Oper. Inc.	Company Value	% Total Oper. Inc.	Company Value	% Total Oper. Inc.	Company Value	% Total Oper. Inc.
Premiums Written - Direct	$622,912,926	17.16%	$108,501	7.58%	$178,276	80.41%	$0	0.00%
Premiums Written - Non-Affiliated Agency	$1,936,771,199	53.34%	$1,474,514	102.95%	$0	0.00%	$2,510,539	90.28%
Premiums Written - Affiliated Agency	$752,682,458	20.73%	$0	0.00%	$0	0.00%	$266,652	9.59%
Premiums - Reinsurance Assumed	$13,696,134	0.38%	$0	0.00%	$0	0.00%	$0	0.00%
Premiums - Reinsurance Ceded	($24,360,429)	(0.67)%	$0	0.00%	($2,272)	(1.02)%	($100,820)	(3.63)%
Net Premiums Written (See Sec. 5, B.4)	$3,301,702,288	90.93%	$1,583,015	110.52%	$176,004	79.38%	$2,676,371	96.25%
Net Premiums Earned	$3,249,306,457	89.49%	$1,431,515	99.94%	$168,403	75.96%	$2,684,245	96.53%
PLUS:								
Title Examinations	$122,884,613	3.38%	$0	0.00%	$0	0.00%	$0	0.00%
Searches & Abstracts	$57,539,045	1.58%	$0	0.00%	$0	0.00%	$0	0.00%
Surveys	$0	0.00%	$0	0.00%	$0	0.00%	$0	0.00%
Escrow & Settlement Fees	$195,150,870	5.37%	$800	0.06%	$37,766	17.03%	$0	0.00%
Other Service Charges	$5,960,171	0.16%	$0	0.00%	$15,544	7.01%	$1,500	0.05%
Other Operating Income	$0	0.00%	$0	0.00%	$0	0.00%	$94,995	3.42%
Total Operating Income (See Sec. 5, A.2, A.3, A.5)	$3,630,841,156	100.00%	$1,432,315	100.00%	$221,713	100.00%	$2,780,740	100.00%
LESS:								
Amounts Retained By Agents (See Sec. 5, B.9)	$2,248,120,236		$736,408		$0		$2,112,834	
NET OPERATING REVENUE	$1,382,720,920		$695,907		$221,713		$667,906	
OPERATING EXPENSE	Company Value	% Net Oper. Rev.	Company Value	% Net Oper. Rev.	Company Value	% Net Oper. Rev.	Company Value	% Net Oper. Rev.
Total Personnel Costs	$575,017,676	41.59%	$402,763	57.88%	$177,654	80.13%	$732,631	109.69%
Production Services	$90,517,725	6.55%	$2,902	0.42%	$0	0.00%	$0	0.00%
Advertising	$2,093,345	0.15%	$15,125	2.17%	$906	0.41%	$593	0.09%
Boards, Bureaus & Associations	$2,603,531	0.19%	$12,324	1.77%	$0	0.00%	$0	0.00%
Title Plant Rent & Maintenance	$16,966,773	1.23%	$0	0.00%	$0	0.00%	$0	0.00%
Claim Adjustment Services	$0	0.00%	$0	0.00%	$0	0.00%	$0	0.00%
Amount Charged Off, Net	$27,769,774	2.01%	$0	0.00%	$0	0.00%	$0	0.00%
Marketing & Promotional Expense	$16,911,690	1.22%	$9,014	1.30%	$0	0.00%	$10,386	1.56%
Insurance	$4,455,008	0.32%	$2,400	0.34%	$752	0.34%	$11,474	1.72%
Directors' Fees	$7,032	0.00%	$0	0.00%	$0	0.00%	$0	0.00%
Travel & Related Expenses	$15,557,754	1.13%	$79,736	11.46%	$1,229	0.55%	$47,738	7.15%
Rent and Rent Items	$86,696,233	6.27%	$6,000	0.86%	$28,800	12.99%	$73,472	11.00%
Equipment	$30,412,706	2.20%	$4,044	0.58%	$7,655	3.45%	$19,323	2.89%
Cost/Depreciation, EDP Equipment & Software	$13,515,879	0.98%	$4,458	0.64%	$11,127	5.02%	$4,767	0.71%
Print, Stationery, etc.	$16,538,544	1.20%	$13,008	1.87%	$13,915	6.28%	$25,477	3.81%
Postage, Telephone, Express	$27,658,174	2.00%	$11,052	1.59%	$9,675	4.36%	$12,184	1.82%
Legal & Auditing	$108,659,980	7.86%	$25,988	3.73%	$44,244	19.96%	$43,188	6.47%
Taxes, Licenses & Fees	$48,066,988	3.48%	$40,225	5.78%	$4,815	2.17%	$11,851	1.77%
Real Estate Expenses	$11,478,177	0.83%	$0	0.00%	$0	0.00%	$0	0.00%
Real Estate Taxes	$471,852	0.03%	$0	0.00%	$0	0.00%	$17,025	2.55%
Miscellaneous	$0	0.00%	$16,786	2.41%	$8,217	3.71%	$55,320	8.28%
Other Operating Expense Incurred	$1,095,398,841	79.22%	$645,825	92.80%	$308,989	139.36%	$1,065,429	159.52%
TOTAL OPERATING EXPENSE INCURRED (AGENT RETENTION + OTHER OPERATING EXPENSE INCURRED)	$3,343,519,077	--	$1,382,233	--	$308,989	--	$3,178,263	--
Aggregate Write-ins for Operating Deductions	$0	0.00%	$0	0.00%	$0	0.00%	$0	0.00%
Operating Profit (Loss) Before Losses (See Sec. 5, A.7)	$287,322,079	20.78%	$50,082	7.20%	($87,276)	(39.36)%	($397,523)	(59.52)%
Losses & Loss Adjustment Expense Incurred (See Sec. 5, C.2 - C.7)								
Direct Operations (See Sec. 5, C.7)	$83,223,223	6.02%	$0	0.00%	$0	0.00%	$0	0.00%
Agency Operations (See Sec. 5, C.7)	$291,390,403	21.07%	($16,063)	(2.31)%	$0	0.00%	$457,564	68.51%
NET OPERATING GAIN (LOSS) (See Sec. 5, A.10)	($87,291,547)	(6.31)%	$66,145	9.50%	($87,276)	(39.36)%	($855,087)	(128.03)%
INVESTMENT INCOME	Company Value	% Total Assets	Company Value	% Total Assets	Company Value	% Total Assets	Company Value	% Total Assets
Net Investment Income Earned (See Sec. 5, A.8)	$195,715,802	10.45%	$92,479	4.12%	$41,264	4.93%	$267,819	3.95%
Net Realized Capital Gains (Losses) less Capital Gains Tax	($56,889,509)	(3.04)%	$0	0.00%	$0	0.00%	$60,573	0.89%
NET INVESTMENT GAIN (LOSS) (See Sec. 5, A.9)	$138,826,293	7.41%	$92,479	4.12%	$41,264	4.93%	$328,392	4.85%
OTHER INCOME	Company Value	% Total Assets	Company Value	% Total Assets	Company Value	% Total Assets	Company Value	% Total Assets
Other Income (Loss)	$0	0.00%	$0	0.00%	$0	0.00%	$0	0.00%
Net Income Before Taxes (See Sec. 5, A.11)	$51,534,746	2.75%	$158,624	7.07%	($46,012)	(5.50)%	($526,695)	(7.77)%
Federal & Foreign Income Taxes Incurred	$39,452,314	2.11%	$77,264	3.44%	$0	0.00%	($195,443)	(2.88)%
NET INCOME (See Sec. 5, A.12)	$12,082,432	0.64%	$81,360	3.63%	($46,012)	(5.50)%	($331,252)	(4.89)%
CAPITAL AND SURPLUS ACCOUNT	Company Value	% Total Assets	Company Value	% Total Assets	Company Value	% Total Assets	Company Value	% Total Assets
POLICYHOLDER SURPLUS - BEGINNING	$753,711,632	40.23%	$1,169,316	52.14%	$836,118	99.99%	$1,994,547	29.44%
Net Income	$12,082,432	0.64%	$81,360	3.63%	($46,012)	(5.50)%	($331,252)	(4.89)%
Change in Net Unrealized Capital Gains (Losses) less Capital Gains Tax	$9,206,664	0.49%	$0	0.00%	$0	0.00%	($28,824)	(0.43)%
Change in Net Unrealized Foreign Exchange Capital Gain (Loss)	$1,289,403	0.07%	$0	0.00%	$0	0.00%	$0	0.00%
Change in Net Deferred Income Tax	$82,599,773	4.41%	$2,613	0.12%	$0	0.00%	$0	0.00%
Change in Nonadmitted Assets	($272,934,996)	(14.57)%	$955	0.04%	$10,016	1.20%	$10,721	0.16%
Change in Provision for Unauthorized Reinsurance	$0	0.00%	$0	0.00%	$0	0.00%	$0	0.00%
Change in Supplemental Reserves	($103,885,000)	(5.55)%	$0	0.00%	$0	0.00%	$0	0.00%
Change in Surplus Notes	$0	0.00%	$0	0.00%	$0	0.00%	$0	0.00%
Cumulative Effect of Changes in Accounting Principles	$0	0.00%	$0	0.00%	$0	0.00%	$0	0.00%
Capital Changes	$0	0.00%	$0	0.00%	$0	0.00%	$0	0.00%
Surplus Adjustments	$0	0.00%	$0	0.00%	$0	0.00%	$0	0.00%
Dividends to Stockholders	($35,000,000)	(1.87)%	$0	0.00%	$0	0.00%	$0	0.00%
Change in Treasury Stock	$0	0.00%	$0	0.00%	$0	0.00%	($50,000)	(0.74)%
Aggregate Write-ins for Gains and Losses in Surplus	($20,542,664)	(1.10)%	$0	0.00%	$0	0.00%	$0	0.00%
Net Change - Policyholder Surplus	($327,184,387)	(17.47)%	$84,928	3.79%	($35,996)	(4.30)%	($399,354)	(5.89)%
POLICYHOLDER SURPLUS - ENDING (See Sec. 5, B.6, B.7, C.9, C.11)	$426,527,245	22.77%	$1,254,244	55.92%	$800,122	95.69%	$1,595,193	23.54%

2

B.3 Income Statement - By Individual Underwriter

	GUARANTEE		GUARANTEE T&T		GUARDIAN NATIONAL		INVESTORS TIC	
REVENUE	Company Value	% Total Oper. Inc.	Company Value	% Total Oper. Inc.	Company Value	% Total Oper. Inc.	Company Value	% Total Oper. Inc.
Premiums Written - Direct	$0	0.00%	$204,520	1.36%	$0	0.00%	$29,790,883	44.56%
Premiums Written - Non-Affiliated Agency	$1,125,386	49.75%	$2,531,710	16.88%	$3,445,031	95.84%	$31,463,285	47.06%
Premiums Written - Affiliated Agency	$1,472,208	65.08%	$8,582,676	57.23%	$428,862	11.93%	$6,291,704	9.41%
Premiums - Reinsurance Assumed	$0	0.00%	$0	0.00%	$0	0.00%	$74,074	0.11%
Premiums - Reinsurance Ceded	($161,473)	(7.14)%	($37,207)	(0.25)%	($144,538)	(4.02)%	($303,739)	(0.45)%
Net Premiums Written (See Sec. 5, B.4)	$2,436,121	107.70%	$11,281,699	75.22%	$3,729,355	103.75%	$67,316,207	100.69%
Net Premiums Earned	$2,262,039	100.00%	$11,093,777	73.97%	$3,594,472	100.00%	$65,565,455	98.07%
PLUS:								
Title Examinations	$0	0.00%	$0	0.00%	$0	0.00%	$0	0.00%
Searches & Abstracts	$0	0.00%	$3,108,107	20.72%	$0	0.00%	$595,512	0.89%
Surveys	$0	0.00%	$0	0.00%	$0	0.00%	$0	0.00%
Escrow & Settlement Fees	$0	0.00%	$795,839	5.31%	$0	0.00%	$428,143	0.64%
Other Service Charges	$0	0.00%	$0	0.00%	$0	0.00%	$127,301	0.19%
Other Operating Income	$0	0.00%	$0	0.00%	$0	0.00%	$136,802	0.20%
Total Operating Income (See Sec. 5, A.2, A.3, A.5)	$2,262,039	100.00%	$14,997,723	100.00%	$3,594,472	100.00%	$66,853,213	100.00%
LESS:								
Amounts Retained By Agents (See Sec. 5, B.9)	$1,337,903		$9,083,214		$3,124,113		$26,489,262	
NET OPERATING REVENUE	$924,136		$5,914,509		$470,359		$40,363,951	
OPERATING EXPENSE	Company Value	% Net Oper. Rev.	Company Value	% Net Oper. Rev.	Company Value	% Net Oper. Rev.	Company Value	% Net Oper. Rev.
Total Personnel Costs	$190,736	20.64%	$2,128,731	35.99%	$351,459	74.72%	$18,387,383	45.55%
Production Services	$135	0.01%	$2,123,865	35.91%	$3,317	0.71%	$80,406	0.00%
Advertising	$0	0.00%	$0	0.00%	$331	0.07%	$142,067	0.20%
Boards, Bureaus & Associations	$4,322	0.47%	$25,001	0.42%	$0	0.00%	$142,067	0.35%
Title Plant Rent & Maintenance	$0	0.00%	$0	0.00%	$0	0.00%	$0	0.00%
Claim Adjustment Services	$0	0.00%	$0	0.00%	$0	0.00%	$0	0.00%
Amount Charged Off, Net	($488)	(0.05)%	($195,329)	(3.30)%	$0	0.00%	$0	0.00%
Marketing & Promotional Expense	$63	0.01%	$21,272	0.36%	$8,918	1.90%	$1,342,202	3.33%
Insurance	$9,502	1.03%	$97,505	1.65%	$1,454	0.31%	$273,231	0.68%
Directors' Fees	$0	0.00%	$0	0.00%	$6,000	1.28%	$0	0.00%
Travel & Related Expenses	$6,207	0.67%	$96,319	1.63%	$22,009	4.68%	$767,229	1.90%
Rent and Rent Items	$13,953	1.51%	$405,446	6.86%	$27,139	5.77%	$1,661,150	4.12%
Equipment	$10,832	1.17%	$144,296	2.44%	$8,526	1.81%	$879,662	2.18%
Cost/Depreciation, EDP Equipment & Software	$3,302	0.36%	$31,182	0.53%	$36,925	7.85%	$754,273	1.87%
Print, Stationery, etc.	$15,757	1.71%	$62,867	1.06%	$13,697	2.91%	$663,647	1.64%
Postage, Telephone, Express	$5,067	0.55%	$103,634	1.75%	$14,400	3.06%	$1,242,737	3.08%
Legal & Auditing	$79,281	8.58%	$385,948	6.53%	$376,634	80.07%	$309,883	0.77%
Taxes, Licenses & Fees	$33,805	3.66%	$158,320	2.68%	$22,700	4.83%	$1,785,533	4.42%
Real Estate Expenses	$0	0.00%	$0	0.00%	$0	0.00%	$0	0.00%
Real Estate Taxes	$0	0.00%	$0	0.00%	$0	0.00%	$0	0.00%
Miscellaneous	$299,076	32.36%	$19,428	0.33%	$21,188	4.50%	$654,977	1.62%
Other Operating Expense Incurred	$671,550	72.67%	$5,608,485	94.83%	$914,697	194.47%	$28,944,380	71.71%
TOTAL OPERATING EXPENSE INCURRED (AGENT RETENTION + OTHER OPERATING EXPENSE INCURRED)	$2,009,453	--	$14,691,699	--	$4,038,810	--	$55,433,642	--
Aggregate Write-ins for Operating Deductions	$0	0.00%	$0	0.00%	$0	0.00%	$0	0.00%
Operating Profit (Loss) Before Losses (See Sec. 5, A.7)	$252,586	27.33%	$306,024	5.17%	($444,338)	(94.47)%	$11,419,571	28.29%
Losses & Loss Adjustment Expense Incurred (See Sec. 5, C.2 - C.7)								
Direct Operations (See Sec. 5, C.7)	$0	0.00%	$249,694	4.22%	$0	0.00%	$7,237,616	17.93%
Agency Operations (See Sec. 5, C.7)	$873,275	94.50%	$1,325,380	22.41%	($76,380)	(16.24)%	$1,737,442	4.30%
NET OPERATING GAIN (LOSS) (See Sec. 5, A.10)	($620,689)	(67.16)%	($1,269,050)	(21.46)%	($367,958)	(78.23)%	$2,444,513	6.06%
INVESTMENT INCOME	Company Value	% Total Assets	Company Value	% Total Assets	Company Value	% Total Assets	Company Value	% Total Assets
Net Investment Income Earned (See Sec. 5, A.8)	$98,999	3.77%	($2,528)	(0.03)%	$306,371	3.12%	$4,009,684	3.79%
Net Realized Capital Gains (Losses) less Capital Gains Tax	$0	0.00%	$1,760	0.02%	$210,417	2.14%	$344,666	0.33%
NET INVESTMENT GAIN (LOSS) (See Sec. 5, A.9)	$98,999	3.77%	($768)	(0.01)%	$516,788	5.27%	$4,354,350	4.12%
OTHER INCOME	Company Value	% Total Assets	Company Value	% Total Assets	Company Value	% Total Assets	Company Value	% Total Assets
Other Income (Loss)	$768	0.03%	$0	0.00%	$0	0.00%	$0	0.00%
Net Income Before Taxes (See Sec. 5, A.11)	($520,922)	(19.85)%	($1,269,818)	(16.02)%	$148,830	1.52%	$6,798,863	6.43%
Federal & Foreign Income Taxes Incurred	$0	0.00%	$0	0.00%	$27,350	0.28%	$1,672,444	1.58%
NET INCOME (See Sec. 5, A.12)	($520,922)	(19.85)%	($1,269,818)	(16.02)%	$121,480	1.24%	$5,126,419	4.85%
CAPITAL AND SURPLUS ACCOUNT	Company Value	% Total Assets	Company Value	% Total Assets	Company Value	% Total Assets	Company Value	% Total Assets
POLICYHOLDER SURPLUS - BEGINNING	$1,700,002	64.77%	$2,333,374	29.44%	$1,773,938	18.08%	$54,651,055	51.71%
Net Income	($520,922)	(19.85)%	($1,269,818)	(16.02)%	$121,480	1.24%	$5,126,419	4.85%
Change in Net Unrealized Capital Gains (Losses) less Capital Gains Tax	$8,404	0.32%	$44,621	0.56%	($150,068)	(1.53)%	($3,873,008)	(3.66)%
Change in Net Unrealized Foreign Exchange Capital Gain (Loss)	$0	0.00%	$0	0.00%	$0	0.00%	$0	0.00%
Change in Net Deferred Income Tax	$254,638	9.70%	$462,533	5.84%	$50,738	0.52%	($87,648)	(0.08)%
Change in Nonadmitted Assets	($414,108)	(15.78)%	($340,746)	(4.30)%	$2,425	0.02%	$5,018,666	4.75%
Change in Provision for Unauthorized Reinsurance	$0	0.00%	$0	0.00%	$0	0.00%	$0	0.00%
Change in Supplemental Reserves	$0	0.00%	$0	0.00%	$0	0.00%	$0	0.00%
Change in Surplus Notes	$0	0.00%	$0	0.00%	$0	0.00%	$0	0.00%
Cumulative Effect of Changes in Accounting Principles	$0	0.00%	$0	0.00%	$0	0.00%	$0	0.00%
Capital Changes	$200,000	7.62%	$0	0.00%	$1,200,000	12.23%	$0	0.00%
Surplus Adjustments	$0	0.00%	$0	0.00%	$3,800,000	38.74%	$0	0.00%
Dividends to Stockholders	$0	0.00%	$0	0.00%	$0	0.00%	($10,732,722)	(10.16)%
Change in Treasury Stock	$0	0.00%	$0	0.00%	$0	0.00%	$0	0.00%
Aggregate Write-ins for Gains and Losses in Surplus	$0	0.00%	$0	0.00%	$0	0.00%	$0	0.00%
Net Change - Policyholder Surplus	($471,986)	(17.98)%	($1,114,035)	(14.06)%	$5,024,575	51.22%	($4,548,293)	(4.30)%
POLICYHOLDER SURPLUS - ENDING (See Sec. 5, B.6, B.7, C.9, C.11)	$1,228,016	46.78%	$1,219,339	15.39%	$6,798,513	69.30%	$50,102,762	47.41%

B.3 Income Statement - By Individual Underwriter

	K.E.L.		LAND CORP (CO)		LAND TIC (ST LOUIS)		LAWYERS	
REVENUE	Company Value	% Total Oper. Inc.	Company Value	% Total Oper. Inc.	Company Value	% Total Oper. Inc.	Company Value	% Total Oper. Inc.
Premiums Written - Direct	$0	0.00%	$0	0.00%	$0	0.00%	$345,666,888	26.09%
Premiums Written - Non-Affiliated Agency	$8,460	1.53%	$0	0.00%	$2,257,316	100.37%	$762,376,163	57.54%
Premiums Written - Affiliated Agency	$575,455	103.80%	$19,602,608	98.93%	$0	0.00%	$107,567,639	8.12%
Premiums - Reinsurance Assumed	$0	0.00%	$0	0.00%	$0	0.00%	$11,078,528	0.84%
Premiums - Reinsurance Ceded	$0	0.00%	($22,397)	(0.11)%	($10,000)	(0.44)%	($9,705,881)	(0.73)%
Net Premiums Written (See Sec. 5, B.4)	$583,915	105.33%	$19,580,211	98.82%	$2,247,316	99.93%	$1,216,983,337	91.85%
Net Premiums Earned	$554,387	100.00%	$19,721,211	99.53%	$2,248,965	100.00%	$1,199,933,194	90.57%
PLUS:								
Title Examinations	$0	0.00%	$0	0.00%	$0	0.00%	$36,828,621	2.78%
Searches & Abstracts	$0	0.00%	$0	0.00%	$0	0.00%	$4,993,849	0.38%
Surveys	$0	0.00%	$0	0.00%	$0	0.00%	$232,004	0.02%
Escrow & Settlement Fees	$0	0.00%	$0	0.00%	$0	0.00%	$54,399,742	4.11%
Other Service Charges	$0	0.00%	$0	0.00%	$0	0.00%	$28,521,875	2.15%
Other Operating Income	$0	0.00%	$92,844	0.47%	$25	0.00%	$0	0.00%
Total Operating Income (See Sec. 5, A.2, A.3, A.5)	$554,387	100.00%	$19,814,055	100.00%	$2,248,990	100.00%	$1,324,909,285	100.00%
LESS:								
Amounts Retained By Agents (See Sec. 5, B.9)	$408,740		$17,250,295		$1,141,423		$700,268,473	
NET OPERATING REVENUE	$145,647		$2,563,760		$1,107,567		$624,640,812	
OPERATING EXPENSE	Company Value	% Net Oper. Rev.	Company Value	% Net Oper. Rev.	Company Value	% Net Oper. Rev.	Company Value	% Net Oper. Rev.
Total Personnel Costs	$152,196	104.50%	$446,020	17.40%	$69,488	6.27%	$312,499,783	50.03%
Production Services	$0	0.00%	$0	0.00%	$14,035	1.27%	$71,020,765	11.37%
Advertising	$14,993	10.29%	$0	0.00%	$3,171	0.29%	$5,134,223	0.82%
Boards, Bureaus & Associations	$0	0.00%	$3,129	0.12%	$2,028	0.18%	$550,288	0.09%
Title Plant Rent & Maintenance	$0	0.00%	$0	0.00%	$0	0.00%	$4,140,160	0.66%
Claim Adjustment Services	$0	0.00%	$0	0.00%	$0	0.00%	$0	0.00%
Amount Charged Off, Net	$0	0.00%	$0	0.00%	$1,519,364	137.18%	$11,277,170	1.81%
Marketing & Promotional Expense	$0	0.00%	$0	0.00%	$0	0.00%	$15,261,944	2.44%
Insurance	$568	0.39%	$3,607	0.14%	$137	0.01%	$2,256,811	0.36%
Directors' Fees	$0	0.00%	$13,500	0.53%	$0	0.00%	$131,414	0.02%
Travel & Related Expenses	$7,061	4.85%	$18,370	0.72%	$50	0.00%	$19,267,475	3.08%
Rent and Rent Items	$49,446	33.95%	$30,060	1.17%	$673	0.06%	$30,285,526	4.85%
Equipment	$0	0.00%	$0	0.00%	$1,530	0.14%	$4,639,881	0.74%
Cost/Depreciation, EDP Equipment & Software	$0	0.00%	$2,575	0.10%	$0	0.00%	$17,037,689	2.73%
Print, Stationery, etc.	$6,299	4.32%	$43,837	1.71%	$7,578	0.68%	$5,067,927	0.81%
Postage, Telephone, Express	$5,882	4.04%	$12	0.00%	$10,421	0.94%	$17,104,634	2.74%
Legal & Auditing	$0	0.00%	$58,661	2.29%	$28,912	2.61%	$11,255,324	1.80%
Taxes, Licenses & Fees	$10,218	7.02%	$62,139	2.42%	$145,310	13.12%	$22,405,589	3.59%
Real Estate Expenses	$0	0.00%	$0	0.00%	$0	0.00%	$0	0.00%
Real Estate Taxes	$0	0.00%	$0	0.00%	$0	0.00%	$0	0.00%
Miscellaneous	$121,928	83.71%	$122,856	4.79%	$5,355	0.48%	$6,942,799	1.11%
Other Operating Expense Incurred	$368,591	253.07%	$804,766	31.39%	$1,808,052	163.25%	$556,279,402	89.06%
TOTAL OPERATING EXPENSE INCURRED (AGENT RETENTION + OTHER OPERATING EXPENSE INCURRED)	$777,331	--	$18,055,061	--	$2,949,475	--	$1,256,547,875	--
Aggregate Write-ins for Operating Deductions	$0	0.00%	$0	0.00%	$0	0.00%	$0	0.00%
Operating Profit (Loss) Before Losses (See Sec. 5, A.7)	($222,944)	(153.07)%	$1,758,994	68.61%	($700,485)	(63.25)%	$68,361,410	10.94%
Losses & Loss Adjustment Expense Incurred (See Sec. 5, C.2 - C.7)								
Direct Operations (See Sec. 5, C.7)	$0	0.00%	$0	0.00%	$0	0.00%	$20,651,853	3.31%
Agency Operations (See Sec. 5, C.7)	$0	0.00%	$272,282	10.62%	$0	0.00%	$68,804,586	11.02%
NET OPERATING GAIN (LOSS) (See Sec. 5, A.10)	($222,944)	(153.07)%	$1,486,712	57.99%	($700,485)	(63.25)%	($21,095,029)	(3.38)%
INVESTMENT INCOME	Company Value	% Total Assets	Company Value	% Total Assets	Company Value	% Total Assets	Company Value	% Total Assets
Net Investment Income Earned (See Sec. 5, A.8)	$55,398	2.33%	$436,317	3.02%	$243,373	4.64%	$22,168,287	3.61%
Net Realized Capital Gains (Losses) less Capital Gains Tax	$0	0.00%	$31,740	0.22%	$0	0.00%	$6,258,207	1.02%
NET INVESTMENT GAIN (LOSS) (See Sec. 5, A.9)	$55,398	2.33%	$468,057	3.24%	$243,373	4.64%	$28,426,494	4.63%
OTHER INCOME	Company Value	% Total Assets	Company Value	% Total Assets	Company Value	% Total Assets	Company Value	% Total Assets
Other Income (Loss)	$0	0.00%	$28,315	0.20%	$0	0.00%	$0	0.00%
Net Income Before Taxes (See Sec. 5, A.11)	($167,546)	(7.04)%	$1,983,084	13.74%	($457,112)	(8.72)%	$7,331,465	1.19%
Federal & Foreign Income Taxes Incurred	$0	0.00%	$624,360	4.33%	$97,172	1.85%	$5,360,072	0.87%
NET INCOME (See Sec. 5, A.12)	($167,546)	(7.04)%	$1,358,724	9.42%	($554,284)	(10.57)%	$1,971,393	0.32%
CAPITAL AND SURPLUS ACCOUNT	Company Value	% Total Assets	Company Value	% Total Assets	Company Value	% Total Assets	Company Value	% Total Assets
POLICYHOLDER SURPLUS - BEGINNING	$0	0.00%	$10,266,967	71.15%	$4,863,151	92.74%	$218,001,231	35.47%
Net Income	($167,546)	(7.04)%	$1,358,724	9.42%	($554,284)	(10.57)%	$1,971,393	0.32%
Change in Net Unrealized Capital Gains (Losses) less Capital Gains Tax	$0	0.00%	($483)	0.00%	$0	0.00%	($40,887,517)	(6.65)%
Change in Net Unrealized Foreign Exchange Capital Gain (Loss)	$0	0.00%	$0	0.00%	$0	0.00%	$374,119	0.06%
Change in Net Deferred Income Tax	$0	0.00%	$10,848	0.08%	($41,943)	(0.80)%	$1,936,994	0.32%
Change in Nonadmitted Assets	$0	0.00%	($2,313)	(0.02)%	$35,455	0.68%	$31,387,935	5.11%
Change in Provision for Unauthorized Reinsurance	$0	0.00%	$0	0.00%	$0	0.00%	$0	0.00%
Change in Supplemental Reserves	$0	0.00%	$0	0.00%	$0	0.00%	$0	0.00%
Change in Surplus Notes	$0	0.00%	$0	0.00%	$0	0.00%	$0	0.00%
Cumulative Effect of Changes in Accounting Principles	$0	0.00%	$0	0.00%	$0	0.00%	$0	0.00%
Capital Changes	$2,500,000	105.11%	$0	0.00%	$0	0.00%	$0	0.00%
Surplus Adjustments	$0	0.00%	$0	0.00%	$0	0.00%	$0	0.00%
Dividends to Stockholders	$0	0.00%	($1,791,147)	(12.41)%	$0	0.00%	($40,000,000)	(6.51)%
Change in Treasury Stock	$0	0.00%	$0	0.00%	$0	0.00%	$0	0.00%
Aggregate Write-ins for Gains and Losses in Surplus	$0	0.00%	$0	0.00%	$682,006	13.01%	($43,497,749)	(7.08)%
Net Change - Policyholder Surplus	$2,332,454	98.07%	($424,371)	(2.94)%	$121,234	2.31%	($88,714,822)	(14.44)%
POLICYHOLDER SURPLUS - ENDING (See Sec. 5, B.6, B.7, C.9, C.11)	$2,332,454	98.07%	$9,842,596	68.21%	$4,984,385	95.05%	$129,286,409	21.04%

2

B.3 Income Statement - By Individual Underwriter

	MANITO		MASON		MASON COUNTY		MASSACHUSETTS TIC	
REVENUE	Company Value	% Total Oper. Inc.	Company Value	% Total Oper. Inc.	Company Value	% Total Oper. Inc.	Company Value	% Total Oper. Inc.
Premiums Written - Direct	$0	0.00%	$120,217	7.91%	$0	--	($254)	100.00%
Premiums Written - Non-Affiliated Agency	$97,958	13.24%	$0	0.00%	$0	--	$0	0.00%
Premiums Written - Affiliated Agency	$690,518	93.30%	$1,432,065	94.26%	$0	--	$0	0.00%
Premiums - Reinsurance Assumed	$0	0.00%	$0	0.00%	$0	--	$0	0.00%
Premiums - Reinsurance Ceded	($53,387)	(7.21)%	($32,301)	(2.13)%	$0	--	$0	0.00%
Net Premiums Written *(See Sec. 5, B.4)*	$735,089	99.32%	$1,519,981	100.05%	$0	--	($254)	100.00%
Net Premiums Earned	$740,110	100.00%	$1,474,582	97.06%	$0	--	($254)	100.00%
PLUS:								
Title Examinations	$0	0.00%	$1,925	0.13%	$0	--	$0	0.00%
Searches & Abstracts	$0	0.00%	$8,425	0.55%	$0	--	$0	0.00%
Surveys	$0	0.00%	$0	0.00%	$0	--	$0	0.00%
Escrow & Settlement Fees	$0	0.00%	$14,085	0.93%	$0	--	$0	0.00%
Other Service Charges	$0	0.00%	$20,235	1.33%	$0	--	$0	0.00%
Other Operating Income	$0	0.00%	$0	0.00%	$0	--	$0	0.00%
Total Operating Income *(See Sec. 5, A.2, A.3, A.5)*	$740,110	100.00%	$1,519,252	100.00%	$0	--	($254)	100.00%
LESS:								
Amounts Retained By Agents *(See Sec. 5, B.9)*	$647,875		$1,002,433		$0		$0	
NET OPERATING REVENUE	$92,235		$516,819		$0		($254)	
OPERATING EXPENSE	Company Value	% Net Oper. Rev.	Company Value	% Net Oper. Rev.	Company Value	% Net Oper. Rev.	Company Value	% Net Oper. Rev.
Total Personnel Costs	$0	0.00%	$635,736	123.01%	$0	--	$0	0.00%
Production Services	$0	0.00%	$20,318	3.93%	$0	--	$0	0.00%
Advertising	$0	0.00%	$1,100	0.21%	$0	--	$0	0.00%
Boards, Bureaus & Associations	$6,764	7.33%	$2,382	0.46%	$0	--	$0	0.00%
Title Plant Rent & Maintenance	$0	0.00%	$0	0.00%	$0	--	$0	0.00%
Claim Adjustment Services	$0	0.00%	$0	0.00%	$0	--	$0	0.00%
Amount Charged Off, Net	$0	0.00%	$0	0.00%	$0	--	$0	0.00%
Marketing & Promotional Expense	$0	0.00%	$19,695	3.81%	$0	--	$0	0.00%
Insurance	$0	0.00%	$0	0.00%	$0	--	$0	0.00%
Directors' Fees	$0	0.00%	$0	0.00%	$0	--	$700	(275.59)%
Travel & Related Expenses	$0	0.00%	$42,204	8.17%	$0	--	$0	0.00%
Rent and Rent Items	$12,000	13.01%	$61,148	11.83%	$0	--	$0	0.00%
Equipment	$0	0.00%	$4,038	0.78%	$0	--	$0	0.00%
Cost/Depreciation, EDP Equipment & Software	$0	0.00%	$9,817	1.90%	$0	--	$0	0.00%
Print, Stationery, etc.	$3,787	4.11%	$13,621	2.64%	$864	--	$0	0.00%
Postage, Telephone, Express	$0	0.00%	$21,296	4.12%	$15	--	$0	0.00%
Legal & Auditing	$14,566	15.79%	$35,793	6.93%	$5,589	--	$0	0.00%
Taxes, Licenses & Fees	$19,511	21.15%	$15,535	3.01%	$1,070	--	$19,877	(7,825.59)%
Real Estate Expenses	$0	0.00%	$0	0.00%	$0	--	$0	0.00%
Real Estate Taxes	$0	0.00%	$0	0.00%	$0	--	$0	0.00%
Miscellaneous	$80,000	86.73%	$42,168	8.16%	$0	--	$26,766	(10,537.80)%
Other Operating Expense Incurred	$136,628	148.13%	$924,851	178.95%	$7,538	--	$47,343	(18,638.98)%
TOTAL OPERATING EXPENSE INCURRED (AGENT RETENTION + OTHER OPERATING EXPENSE INCURRED)	$784,503	--	$1,927,284	--	$7,538	--	$47,343	--
Aggregate Write-ins for Operating Deductions	$0	0.00%	$0	0.00%	$0	--	$0	0.00%
Operating Profit (Loss) Before Losses *(See Sec. 5, A.7)*	($44,393)	(48.13)%	($408,032)	(78.95)%	($7,538)	--	($47,597)	18,738.98%
Losses & Loss Adjustment Expense Incurred *(See Sec. 5, C.2 - C.7)*								
Direct Operations *(See Sec. 5, C.7)*	$0	0.00%	$200	0.04%	$0	--	$0	0.00%
Agency Operations *(See Sec. 5, C.7)*	$39,324	42.63%	$12,000	2.32%	$0	--	$0	0.00%
NET OPERATING GAIN (LOSS) *(See Sec. 5, A.10)*	($83,717)	(90.76)%	($420,232)	(81.31)%	($7,538)	--	($47,597)	18,738.98%
INVESTMENT INCOME	Company Value	% Total Assets	Company Value	% Total Assets	Company Value	% Total Assets	Company Value	% Total Assets
Net Investment Income Earned *(See Sec. 5, A.8)*	$67,685	4.59%	$160,175	6.03%	$31,231	3.64%	$57,813	2.24%
Net Realized Capital Gains (Losses) less Capital Gains Tax	$0	0.00%	$18,849	0.71%	$0	0.00%	$1,180	0.05%
NET INVESTMENT GAIN (LOSS) *(See Sec. 5, A.9)*	$67,685	4.59%	$179,024	6.74%	$31,231	3.64%	$58,993	2.28%
OTHER INCOME	Company Value	% Total Assets	Company Value	% Total Assets	Company Value	% Total Assets	Company Value	% Total Assets
Other Income (Loss)	$0	0.00%	$0	0.00%	$0	0.00%	$0	0.00%
Net Income Before Taxes *(See Sec. 5, A.11)*	($16,032)	(1.09)%	($241,208)	(9.08)%	$23,693	2.76%	$11,396	0.44%
Federal & Foreign Income Taxes Incurred	$0	0.00%	$0	0.00%	$3,402	0.40%	($8,664)	(0.34)%
NET INCOME *(See Sec. 5, A.12)*	($16,032)	(1.09)%	($241,208)	(9.08)%	$20,291	2.37%	$20,060	0.78%
CAPITAL AND SURPLUS ACCOUNT	Company Value	% Total Assets	Company Value	% Total Assets	Company Value	% Total Assets	Company Value	% Total Assets
POLICYHOLDER SURPLUS - BEGINNING	$1,272,722	86.38%	$2,797,057	105.34%	$800,718	93.42%	$2,138,306	82.76%
Net Income	($16,032)	(1.09)%	($241,208)	(9.08)%	$20,291	2.37%	$20,060	0.78%
Change in Net Unrealized Capital Gains (Losses) less Capital Gains Tax	$0	0.00%	$0	0.00%	$0	0.00%	$308,126	11.93%
Change in Net Unrealized Foreign Exchange Capital Gain (Loss)	$0	0.00%	$0	0.00%	$0	0.00%	$0	0.00%
Change in Net Deferred Income Tax	$0	0.00%	$0	0.00%	$0	0.00%	$0	0.00%
Change in Nonadmitted Assets	$0	0.00%	($9,807)	(0.37)%	$0	0.00%	$2,404	0.09%
Change in Provision for Unauthorized Reinsurance	$0	0.00%	$0	0.00%	$0	0.00%	$0	0.00%
Change in Supplemental Reserves	$0	0.00%	$0	0.00%	$0	0.00%	$0	0.00%
Change in Surplus Notes	$0	0.00%	$0	0.00%	$0	0.00%	$0	0.00%
Cumulative Effect of Changes in Accounting Principles	$0	0.00%	$0	0.00%	$0	0.00%	$0	0.00%
Capital Changes	$0	0.00%	$0	0.00%	$0	0.00%	$0	0.00%
Surplus Adjustments	$0	0.00%	$0	0.00%	$0	0.00%	$0	0.00%
Dividends to Stockholders	$0	0.00%	$0	0.00%	$0	0.00%	($3,984)	(0.15)%
Change in Treasury Stock	$0	0.00%	$0	0.00%	$0	0.00%	$0	0.00%
Aggregate Write-ins for Gains and Losses in Surplus	$0	0.00%	$0	0.00%	$1,678	0.20%	$638	0.02%
Net Change - Policyholder Surplus	($16,032)	(1.09)%	($251,015)	(9.45)%	$21,969	2.56%	$327,244	12.67%
POLICYHOLDER SURPLUS - ENDING *(See Sec. 5, B.6, B.7, C.9, C.11)*	$1,256,690	85.29%	$2,546,042	95.89%	$822,687	95.98%	$2,465,550	95.42%

B.3 Income Statement - By Individual Underwriter

	MISSISSIPPI GUARANTY		MISSISSIPPI VALLEY		MONROE		NATIONAL	
REVENUE	Company Value	% Total Oper. Inc.	Company Value	% Total Oper. Inc.	Company Value	% Total Oper. Inc.	Company Value	% Total Oper. Inc.
Premiums Written - Direct	$56,517	18.90%	$488,573	1.92%	$5,556,612	28.06%	$127,106	3.43%
Premiums Written - Non-Affiliated Agency	$253,129	84.67%	$25,433,321	100.09%	$7,075,703	35.73%	$3,347,151	90.36%
Premiums Written - Affiliated Agency	$0	0.00%	$0	0.00%	$364,364	1.84%	$199,659	5.39%
Premiums - Reinsurance Assumed	$0	0.00%	$5,707	0.02%	$16,558	0.08%	$0	0.00%
Premiums - Reinsurance Ceded	($20,147)	(6.74)%	($539,057)	(2.12)%	($63,779)	(0.32)%	($173,772)	(4.69)%
Net Premiums Written *(See Sec. 5, B.4)*	$289,499	96.83%	$25,388,544	99.91%	$12,949,458	65.40%	$3,500,144	94.49%
Net Premiums Earned	$260,012	86.97%	$24,055,698	94.67%	$12,853,104	64.91%	$3,452,525	93.20%
PLUS:								
Title Examinations	$38,960	13.03%	$0	0.00%	$0	0.00%	$70,169	1.89%
Searches & Abstracts	$0	0.00%	$1,220,628	4.80%	$6,058,151	30.60%	$0	0.00%
Surveys	$0	0.00%	$0	0.00%	$0	0.00%	$0	0.00%
Escrow & Settlement Fees	$0	0.00%	$24,615	0.10%	$0	0.00%	$5,317	0.14%
Other Service Charges	$0	0.00%	$109,225	0.43%	$522,924	2.64%	$84,850	2.29%
Other Operating Income	$0	0.00%	$0	0.00%	$366,872	1.85%	$91,470	2.47%
Total Operating Income *(See Sec. 5, A.2, A.3, A.5)*	$298,972	100.00%	$25,410,166	100.00%	$19,801,051	100.00%	$3,704,331	100.00%
LESS:								
Amounts Retained By Agents *(See Sec. 5, B.9)*	$181,277		$17,911,771		$6,120,596		$2,467,634	
NET OPERATING REVENUE	$117,695		$7,498,395		$13,680,455		$1,236,697	
OPERATING EXPENSE	Company Value	% Net Oper. Rev.	Company Value	% Net Oper. Rev.	Company Value	% Net Oper. Rev.	Company Value	% Net Oper. Rev.
Total Personnel Costs	$113,720	96.62%	$3,491,817	46.57%	$8,130,118	59.43%	$725,899	58.70%
Production Services	$20,517	17.43%	$237,691	3.17%	$2,497,142	18.25%	$14,416	1.17%
Advertising	$3,741	3.18%	$14,317	0.19%	$110,366	0.81%	$61,498	4.97%
Boards, Bureaus & Associations	$2,000	1.70%	$33,681	0.45%	$17,599	0.13%	$18,894	1.53%
Title Plant Rent & Maintenance	$0	0.00%	$90,000	1.20%	$0	0.00%	$178,882	14.46%
Claim Adjustment Services	$0	0.00%	$0	0.00%	$0	0.00%	$0	0.00%
Amount Charged Off, Net	$0	0.00%	$50,000	0.67%	$73,635	0.54%	$0	0.00%
Marketing & Promotional Expense	$0	0.00%	$145,224	1.94%	$113,318	0.83%	$0	0.00%
Insurance	$8,981	7.63%	$57,869	0.77%	$58,531	0.43%	$19,186	1.55%
Directors' Fees	$0	0.00%	$24,750	0.33%	$0	0.00%	$0	0.00%
Travel & Related Expenses	$6,509	5.53%	$179,689	2.40%	$212,335	1.55%	$48,028	3.88%
Rent and Rent Items	$19,560	16.62%	$225,189	3.00%	$572,746	4.19%	$82,912	6.70%
Equipment	$7,200	6.12%	$32,962	0.44%	$461,502	3.37%	$33,406	2.70%
Cost/Depreciation, EDP Equipment & Software	$3,380	2.87%	$21,516	0.29%	$127,306	0.93%	$10,404	0.84%
Print, Stationery, etc.	$95	0.08%	$117,081	1.56%	$228,105	1.67%	$66,206	5.35%
Postage, Telephone, Express	$5,171	4.39%	$80,800	1.08%	$556,970	4.07%	$48,340	3.91%
Legal & Auditing	$26,773	22.75%	$127,145	1.70%	$102,362	0.75%	$93,413	7.55%
Taxes, Licenses & Fees	$7,375	6.27%	$726,671	9.69%	$343,179	2.51%	$79,478	6.43%
Real Estate Expenses	$0	0.00%	$0	0.00%	$0	0.00%	$6,300	0.51%
Real Estate Taxes	$0	0.00%	$0	0.00%	$0	0.00%	$38,462	3.11%
Miscellaneous	$26,182	22.25%	$185,614	2.48%	$26,452	0.19%	$36,869	2.98%
Other Operating Expense Incurred	$251,204	213.44%	$5,842,016	77.91%	$13,631,666	99.64%	$1,562,593	126.35%
TOTAL OPERATING EXPENSE INCURRED (AGENT RETENTION + OTHER OPERATING EXPENSE INCURRED)	$432,481	--	$23,753,787	--	$19,752,262	--	$4,030,227	--
Aggregate Write-ins for Operating Deductions	$0	0.00%	$0	0.00%	$0	0.00%	$0	0.00%
Operating Profit (Loss) Before Losses *(See Sec. 5, A.7)*	($133,509)	(113.44)%	$1,656,379	22.09%	$48,789	0.36%	($325,896)	(26.35)%
Losses & Loss Adjustment Expense Incurred *(See Sec. 5, C.2 - C.7)*								
Direct Operations *(See Sec. 5, C.7)*	$0	0.00%	$304,285	4.06%	$474,023	3.46%	$0	0.00%
Agency Operations *(See Sec. 5, C.7)*	$0	0.00%	$3,141,450	41.89%	$103,605	0.76%	($9,014)	(0.73)%
NET OPERATING GAIN (LOSS) *(See Sec. 5, A.10)*	($133,509)	(113.44)%	($1,789,356)	(23.86)%	($528,839)	(3.87)%	($316,882)	(25.62)%
INVESTMENT INCOME	Company Value	% Total Assets	Company Value	% Total Assets	Company Value	% Total Assets	Company Value	% Total Assets
Net Investment Income Earned *(See Sec. 5, A.8)*	$17,107	1.93%	$1,900,667	4.16%	$503,477	2.42%	$57,222	1.07%
Net Realized Capital Gains (Losses) less Capital Gains Tax	$0	0.00%	$10,925	0.02%	$327,125	1.57%	$104,776	1.96%
NET INVESTMENT GAIN (LOSS) *(See Sec. 5, A.9)*	$17,107	1.93%	$1,911,592	4.18%	$830,602	3.99%	$161,998	3.03%
OTHER INCOME	Company Value	% Total Assets	Company Value	% Total Assets	Company Value	% Total Assets	Company Value	% Total Assets
Other Income (Loss)	$0	0.00%	$0	0.00%	$0	0.00%	$0	0.00%
Net Income Before Taxes *(See Sec. 5, A.11)*	($116,402)	(13.15)%	$122,236	0.27%	$301,763	1.45%	($154,884)	(2.89)%
Federal & Foreign Income Taxes Incurred	$0	0.00%	($112,034)	(0.25)%	($145,209)	(0.70)%	$0	0.00%
NET INCOME *(See Sec. 5, A.12)*	($116,402)	(13.15)%	$234,270	0.51%	$446,972	2.15%	($154,884)	(2.89)%
CAPITAL AND SURPLUS ACCOUNT	Company Value	% Total Assets	Company Value	% Total Assets	Company Value	% Total Assets	Company Value	% Total Assets
POLICYHOLDER SURPLUS - BEGINNING	$416,502	47.04%	$10,157,366	22.24%	$13,957,721	67.10%	$2,903,330	54.24%
Net Income	($116,402)	(13.15)%	$234,270	0.51%	$446,972	2.15%	($154,884)	(2.89)%
Change in Net Unrealized Capital Gains (Losses) less Capital Gains Tax	$0	0.00%	($93,871)	(0.21)%	$20,672	0.10%	$355,511	6.64%
Change in Net Unrealized Foreign Exchange Capital Gain (Loss)	$0	0.00%	$0	0.00%	$0	0.00%	$0	0.00%
Change in Net Deferred Income Tax	$0	0.00%	($123,214)	(0.27)%	$501,182	2.41%	$0	0.00%
Change in Nonadmitted Assets	$0	0.00%	$409,067	0.90%	($427,676)	(2.06)%	$1,150,651	21.50%
Change in Provision for Unauthorized Reinsurance	$0	0.00%	$0	0.00%	$0	0.00%	$0	0.00%
Change in Supplemental Reserves	$0	0.00%	$0	0.00%	$0	0.00%	$0	0.00%
Change in Surplus Notes	$0	0.00%	$0	0.00%	$0	0.00%	$0	0.00%
Cumulative Effect of Changes in Accounting Principles	$0	0.00%	$0	0.00%	$0	0.00%	$0	0.00%
Capital Changes	$0	0.00%	$0	0.00%	$0	0.00%	$0	0.00%
Surplus Adjustments	$0	0.00%	$0	0.00%	$0	0.00%	($1,204,376)	(22.50)%
Dividends to Stockholders	$0	0.00%	($900,000)	(1.97)%	($3,000,000)	(14.42)%	$0	0.00%
Change in Treasury Stock	$0	0.00%	$0	0.00%	$0	0.00%	$0	0.00%
Aggregate Write-ins for Gains and Losses in Surplus	$0	0.00%	$0	0.00%	$0	0.00%	$0	0.00%
Net Change - Policyholder Surplus	($116,401)	(13.15)%	($473,748)	(1.04)%	($2,458,851)	(11.82)%	$146,905	2.74%
POLICYHOLDER SURPLUS - ENDING *(See Sec. 5, B.6, B.7, C.9, C.11)*	$300,101	33.89%	$9,683,618	21.20%	$11,498,870	55.28%	$3,050,235	56.99%

B.3 Income Statement - By Individual Underwriter

	NATIONAL ATTORNEYS		NATIONAL LAND		NATIONAL OF NY		NATIONS OF NY	
REVENUE	Company Value	% Total Oper. Inc.	Company Value	% Total Oper. Inc.	Company Value	% Total Oper. Inc.	Company Value	% Total Oper. Inc.
Premiums Written - Direct	$831,940	62.22%	$0	0.00%	$2,257,917	20.17%	$0	0.00%
Premiums Written - Non-Affiliated Agency	$0	0.00%	$2,494,729	99.71%	$4,027	0.04%	$0	0.00%
Premiums Written - Affiliated Agency	$0	0.00%	$0	0.00%	$9,776,776	87.34%	$0	0.00%
Premiums - Reinsurance Assumed	$0	0.00%	$0	0.00%	$2,484	0.02%	$19,007	2.12%
Premiums - Reinsurance Ceded	($98,504)	(7.37)%	($9,037)	(0.36)%	$0	0.00%	$0	0.00%
Net Premiums Written *(See Sec. 5, B.4)*	$733,436	54.85%	$2,485,692	99.35%	$12,041,204	107.56%	$19,007	2.12%
Net Premiums Earned	$733,437	54.85%	$2,497,933	99.84%	$11,194,386	100.00%	$895,124	100.00%
PLUS:								
Title Examinations	$0	0.00%	$0	0.00%	$0	0.00%	$0	0.00%
Searches & Abstracts	$496,686	37.15%	$0	0.00%	$0	0.00%	$0	0.00%
Surveys	$0	0.00%	$0	0.00%	$0	0.00%	$0	0.00%
Escrow & Settlement Fees	$76,620	5.73%	$0	0.00%	$0	0.00%	$0	0.00%
Other Service Charges	$30,352	2.27%	$0	0.00%	$0	0.00%	$0	0.00%
Other Operating Income	$0	0.00%	$4,110	0.16%	$0	0.00%	$0	0.00%
Total Operating Income *(See Sec. 5, A.2, A.3, A.5)*	$1,337,095	100.00%	$2,502,043	100.00%	$11,194,386	100.00%	$895,124	100.00%
LESS:								
Amounts Retained By Agents *(See Sec. 5, B.9)*	$0		$2,074,570		$8,674,820		$0	
NET OPERATING REVENUE	$1,337,095		$427,473		$2,519,566		$895,124	
OPERATING EXPENSE	Company Value	% Net Oper. Rev.	Company Value	% Net Oper. Rev.	Company Value	% Net Oper. Rev.	Company Value	% Net Oper. Rev.
Total Personnel Costs	$621,360	46.47%	$667,811	156.22%	$555,352	22.04%	$4,717	0.53%
Production Services	$440,075	32.91%	$0	0.00%	$406,648	16.14%	$6	0.00%
Advertising	$5,545	0.41%	$12,067	2.82%	$51	0.00%	$0	0.00%
Boards, Bureaus & Associations	$11,840	0.89%	$5,461	1.28%	$0	0.00%	$0	0.00%
Title Plant Rent & Maintenance	$47,161	3.53%	$0	0.00%	$84,449	3.35%	$211,905	23.67%
Claim Adjustment Services	$0	0.00%	$0	0.00%	$0	0.00%	$0	0.00%
Amount Charged Off, Net	$148	0.01%	$4	0.00%	$7,715	0.31%	$0	0.00%
Marketing & Promotional Expense	$0	0.00%	$15,077	3.53%	$4	0.00%	$0	0.00%
Insurance	$5,871	0.44%	$3,757	0.88%	$4,623	0.18%	$24	0.00%
Directors' Fees	$0	0.00%	$0	0.00%	$0	0.00%	$0	0.00%
Travel & Related Expenses	$16,660	1.25%	$47,057	11.01%	$5,141	0.20%	$125	0.01%
Rent and Rent Items	$77,748	5.81%	$46,631	10.91%	$48,312	1.92%	$648	0.07%
Equipment	$12,439	0.93%	$7,753	1.81%	$11,723	0.47%	$83	0.01%
Cost/Depreciation, EDP Equipment & Software	$0	0.00%	$19,985	4.68%	$101,675	4.04%	$30	0.00%
Print, Stationery, etc.	$12,123	0.91%	$39,638	9.27%	$24,438	0.97%	$4,955	0.55%
Postage, Telephone, Express	$29,792	2.23%	$15,880	3.71%	$55,030	2.18%	$107	0.01%
Legal & Auditing	$33,055	2.47%	$83,087	19.44%	$95,495	3.79%	$39,836	4.45%
Taxes, Licenses & Fees	($18,220)	(1.36)%	$60,756	14.21%	$293,732	11.66%	$33,515	3.74%
Real Estate Expenses	$0	0.00%	$0	0.00%	$0	0.00%	$0	0.00%
Real Estate Taxes	$0	0.00%	$0	0.00%	$0	0.00%	$0	0.00%
Miscellaneous	$52,053	3.89%	$72,038	16.85%	$21,539	0.85%	$1,864	0.21%
Other Operating Expense Incurred	$1,347,650	100.79%	$1,097,002	256.62%	$1,715,927	68.10%	$297,815	33.27%
TOTAL OPERATING EXPENSE INCURRED (AGENT RETENTION + OTHER OPERATING EXPENSE INCURRED)	$1,347,650	--	$3,171,572	--	$10,390,747	--	$297,815	--
Aggregate Write-ins for Operating Deductions	$0	0.00%	$0	0.00%	$0	0.00%	$0	0.00%
Operating Profit (Loss) Before Losses *(See Sec. 5, A.7)*	($10,555)	(0.79)%	($669,529)	(156.62)%	$803,639	31.90%	$597,309	66.73%
Losses & Loss Adjustment Expense Incurred *(See Sec. 5, C.2 - C.7)*								
Direct Operations *(See Sec. 5, C.7)*	$267,150	19.98%	$0	0.00%	$111,590	4.43%	$3,052	0.34%
Agency Operations *(See Sec. 5, C.7)*	$0	0.00%	$67,550	15.80%	$951,022	37.75%	$468,281	52.31%
NET OPERATING GAIN (LOSS) *(See Sec. 5, A.10)*	($277,705)	(20.77)%	($737,079)	(172.43)%	($258,973)	(10.28)%	$125,976	14.07%
INVESTMENT INCOME	Company Value	% Total Assets	Company Value	% Total Assets	Company Value	% Total Assets	Company Value	% Total Assets
Net Investment Income Earned *(See Sec. 5, A.8)*	$86,641	4.51%	$396,943	5.70%	$620,283	3.89%	$725,966	3.49%
Net Realized Capital Gains (Losses) less Capital Gains Tax	$6,065	0.32%	$0	0.00%	$0	0.00%	($1,938)	(0.01)%
NET INVESTMENT GAIN (LOSS) *(See Sec. 5, A.9)*	$92,706	4.83%	$396,943	5.70%	$620,283	3.89%	$724,028	3.48%
OTHER INCOME	Company Value	% Total Assets	Company Value	% Total Assets	Company Value	% Total Assets	Company Value	% Total Assets
Other Income (Loss)	$0	0.00%	$0	0.00%	$0	0.00%	$0	0.00%
Net Income Before Taxes *(See Sec. 5, A.11)*	($184,999)	(9.63)%	($340,136)	(4.89)%	$361,310	2.27%	$850,004	4.09%
Federal & Foreign Income Taxes Incurred	($82,251)	(4.28)%	$0	0.00%	$215,153	1.35%	($15,562)	(0.07)%
NET INCOME *(See Sec. 5, A.12)*	($102,748)	(5.35)%	($340,136)	(4.89)%	$146,157	0.92%	$865,566	4.16%
CAPITAL AND SURPLUS ACCOUNT	Company Value	% Total Assets	Company Value	% Total Assets	Company Value	% Total Assets	Company Value	% Total Assets
POLICYHOLDER SURPLUS - BEGINNING	$1,715,019	89.27%	$5,496,677	78.95%	$8,712,163	54.69%	$11,782,979	56.65%
Net Income	($102,748)	(5.35)%	($340,136)	(4.89)%	$146,157	0.92%	$865,566	4.16%
Change in Net Unrealized Capital Gains (Losses) less Capital Gains Tax	($6,436)	(0.34)%	$129,946	1.87%	$0	0.00%	$17,755	0.09%
Change in Net Unrealized Foreign Exchange Capital Gain (Loss)	$0	0.00%	$0	0.00%	$0	0.00%	$0	0.00%
Change in Net Deferred Income Tax	$0	0.00%	$208,707	3.00%	$130,784	0.82%	($229,420)	(1.10)%
Change in Nonadmitted Assets	$11,314	0.59%	($261,417)	(3.75)%	($2,275,740)	(14.29)%	$190,313	0.91%
Change in Provision for Unauthorized Reinsurance	$0	0.00%	$0	0.00%	$0	0.00%	$0	0.00%
Change in Supplemental Reserves	($50,000)	(2.60)%	$0	0.00%	$0	0.00%	$0	0.00%
Change in Surplus Notes	$0	0.00%	$0	0.00%	$0	0.00%	$0	0.00%
Cumulative Effect of Changes in Accounting Principles	$0	0.00%	$0	0.00%	$0	0.00%	$0	0.00%
Capital Changes	($200)	(0.01)%	$0	0.00%	$0	0.00%	$0	0.00%
Surplus Adjustments	($50)	0.00%	$0	0.00%	$0	0.00%	$0	0.00%
Dividends to Stockholders	$0	0.00%	$0	0.00%	$0	0.00%	$0	0.00%
Change in Treasury Stock	$0	0.00%	$0	0.00%	$0	0.00%	$0	0.00%
Aggregate Write-ins for Gains and Losses in Surplus	$0	0.00%	$0	0.00%	$0	0.00%	$0	0.00%
Net Change - Policyholder Surplus	($148,121)	(7.71)%	($262,900)	(3.78)%	($1,998,799)	(12.55)%	$844,213	4.06%
POLICYHOLDER SURPLUS - ENDING *(See Sec. 5, B.6, B.7, C.9, C.11)*	$1,566,898	81.56%	$5,233,777	75.17%	$6,713,364	42.14%	$12,627,192	60.71%

2

B.3 Income Statement - By Individual Underwriter

	NEW JERSEY TIC		NORTH AMERICAN		NORTHEAST INVESTORS		OHIO BAR	
REVENUE	Company Value	% Total Oper. Inc.	Company Value	% Total Oper. Inc.	Company Value	% Total Oper. Inc.	Company Value	% Total Oper. Inc.
Premiums Written - Direct	$0	0.00%	$0	0.00%	$0	0.00%	$0	0.00%
Premiums Written - Non-Affiliated Agency	$17,124,472	98.81%	$438,203	0.40%	$2,414,626	100.46%	$13,072,886	100.76%
Premiums Written - Affiliated Agency	$0	0.00%	$107,933,280	98.93%	$0	0.00%	$0	0.00%
Premiums - Reinsurance Assumed	$0	0.00%	$0	0.00%	$43,376	1.80%	$0	0.00%
Premiums - Reinsurance Ceded	($3,795)	(0.02)%	($3,800)	0.00%	($35,072)	(1.46)%	$0	0.00%
Net Premiums Written (See Sec. 5, B.4)	$17,120,677	98.79%	$108,367,683	99.33%	$2,422,930	100.81%	$13,072,886	100.76%
Net Premiums Earned	$16,799,332	96.93%	$109,101,307	100.00%	$2,402,629	99.96%	$12,961,750	99.90%
PLUS:								
Title Examinations	$0	0.00%	$0	0.00%	$0	0.00%	$0	0.00%
Searches & Abstracts	$0	0.00%	$0	0.00%	$0	0.00%	$0	0.00%
Surveys	$0	0.00%	$0	0.00%	$0	0.00%	$0	0.00%
Escrow & Settlement Fees	$0	0.00%	$0	0.00%	$927	0.04%	$0	0.00%
Other Service Charges	$531,506	3.07%	$0	0.00%	$3	0.00%	$0	0.00%
Other Operating Income	$0	0.00%	$0	0.00%	$0	0.00%	$13,010	0.10%
Total Operating Income (See Sec. 5, A.2, A.3, A.5)	$17,330,838	100.00%	$109,101,307	100.00%	$2,403,559	100.00%	$12,974,760	100.00%
LESS:								
Amounts Retained By Agents (See Sec. 5, B.9)	$15,137,976		$94,289,365		$1,935,698		$10,149,102	
NET OPERATING REVENUE	$2,192,862		$14,811,942		$467,861		$2,825,658	
OPERATING EXPENSE	Company Value	% Net Oper. Rev.	Company Value	% Net Oper. Rev.	Company Value	% Net Oper. Rev.	Company Value	% Net Oper. Rev.
Total Personnel Costs	$1,288,403	58.75%	$2,093,056	14.13%	$119,369	25.51%	$280,788	9.94%
Production Services	$18,752	0.86%	$114,531	0.77%	$0	0.00%	$0	0.00%
Advertising	$34,789	1.59%	$192,479	1.30%	$1,444	0.31%	$17,748	0.63%
Boards, Bureaus & Associations	$77,825	3.55%	$0	0.00%	$6,600	1.41%	$11,082	0.39%
Title Plant Rent & Maintenance	$0	0.00%	$1,026	0.01%	$0	0.00%	$0	0.00%
Claim Adjustment Services	$0	0.00%	$0	0.00%	$0	0.00%	$0	0.00%
Amount Charged Off, Net	$0	0.00%	$0	0.00%	$0	0.00%	$479,329	16.96%
Marketing & Promotional Expense	$0	0.00%	$0	0.00%	$82,979	17.74%	$120,525	4.27%
Insurance	$51,419	2.34%	$5,725	0.04%	$0	0.00%	$412	0.01%
Directors' Fees	$15,000	0.68%	$0	0.00%	$3,000	0.64%	$0	0.00%
Travel & Related Expenses	$79,390	3.62%	$82,049	0.55%	$16,965	3.63%	$12,770	0.45%
Rent and Rent Items	$105,745	4.82%	$218,292	1.47%	$10,702	2.29%	$105,875	3.75%
Equipment	$98,196	4.48%	$22,258	0.15%	$10,643	2.27%	$510	0.02%
Cost/Depreciation, EDP Equipment & Software	$17,089	0.78%	$37,601	0.25%	$0	0.00%	$15,415	0.55%
Print, Stationery, etc.	$57,151	2.61%	$139,142	0.94%	$5,360	1.15%	$49,526	1.75%
Postage, Telephone, Express	$27,568	1.26%	$31,018	0.21%	$9,374	2.00%	$28,855	1.02%
Legal & Auditing	$175,509	8.00%	$115,078	0.78%	$19,655	4.20%	$19,850	0.70%
Taxes, Licenses & Fees	$95,394	4.35%	$775,198	5.23%	$72,615	15.52%	$181,268	6.42%
Real Estate Expenses	$0	0.00%	$0	0.00%	$0	0.00%	$0	0.00%
Real Estate Taxes	$0	0.00%	$0	0.00%	$0	0.00%	$0	0.00%
Miscellaneous	$42,028	1.92%	$85,132	0.57%	$13,223	2.83%	$98,067	3.47%
Other Operating Expense Incurred	$2,184,258	99.61%	$3,912,585	26.42%	$371,929	79.50%	$1,422,020	50.33%
TOTAL OPERATING EXPENSE INCURRED (AGENT RETENTION + OTHER OPERATING EXPENSE INCURRED)	$17,322,234	--	$98,201,950	--	$2,307,627	--	$11,571,122	--
Aggregate Write-ins for Operating Deductions	$0	0.00%	$0	0.00%	$0	0.00%	$0	0.00%
Operating Profit (Loss) Before Losses (See Sec. 5, A.7)	$8,604	0.39%	$10,899,357	73.58%	$95,932	20.50%	$1,403,638	49.67%
Losses & Loss Adjustment Expense Incurred (See Sec. 5, C.2 - C.7)								
Direct Operations (See Sec. 5, C.7)	$0	0.00%	$0	0.00%	$0	0.00%	$0	0.00%
Agency Operations (See Sec. 5, C.7)	$1,216,094	55.46%	$2,424,736	16.37%	$149,328	31.92%	$1,445,381	51.15%
NET OPERATING GAIN (LOSS) (See Sec. 5, A.10)	($1,207,490)	(55.06)%	$8,474,621	57.21%	($53,396)	(11.41)%	($41,743)	(1.48)%
INVESTMENT INCOME	Company Value	% Total Assets	Company Value	% Total Assets	Company Value	% Total Assets	Company Value	% Total Assets
Net Investment Income Earned (See Sec. 5, A.8)	$374,044	3.76%	$3,642,852	4.39%	$237,760	3.87%	$1,242,982	4.61%
Net Realized Capital Gains (Losses) less Capital Gains Tax	$25,114	0.25%	$0	0.00%	($5,920)	(0.10)%	$2,136	0.01%
NET INVESTMENT GAIN (LOSS) (See Sec. 5, A.9)	$399,158	4.01%	$3,642,852	4.39%	$231,840	3.77%	$1,245,118	4.61%
OTHER INCOME	Company Value	% Total Assets	Company Value	% Total Assets	Company Value	% Total Assets	Company Value	% Total Assets
Other Income (Loss)	$0	0.00%	$333,580	0.40%	$0	0.00%	$0	0.00%
Net Income Before Taxes (See Sec. 5, A.11)	($808,332)	(8.12)%	$12,451,053	14.99%	$178,444	2.90%	$1,203,375	4.46%
Federal & Foreign Income Taxes Incurred	($402,813)	(4.05)%	$4,172,462	5.02%	($1,950)	(0.03)%	$356,300	1.32%
NET INCOME (See Sec. 5, A.12)	($405,519)	(4.08)%	$8,278,591	9.97%	$180,394	2.94%	$847,075	3.14%
CAPITAL AND SURPLUS ACCOUNT	Company Value	% Total Assets	Company Value	% Total Assets	Company Value	% Total Assets	Company Value	% Total Assets
POLICYHOLDER SURPLUS - BEGINNING	$5,203,801	52.30%	$42,573,217	51.26%	$5,305,620	86.37%	$8,192,661	30.36%
Net Income	($405,519)	(4.08)%	$8,278,591	9.97%	$180,394	2.94%	$847,075	3.14%
Change in Net Unrealized Capital Gains (Losses) less Capital Gains Tax	$0	0.00%	$0	0.00%	$30,598	0.50%	$11,786	0.04%
Change in Net Unrealized Foreign Exchange Capital Gain (Loss)	$0	0.00%	$0	0.00%	$0	0.00%	$0	0.00%
Change in Net Deferred Income Tax	$158,793	1.60%	($186,301)	(0.22)%	($6,810)	(0.11)%	($57,000)	(0.21)%
Change in Nonadmitted Assets	($110,747)	(1.11)%	$233,610	0.28%	$30,673	0.50%	$452,320	1.68%
Change in Provision for Unauthorized Reinsurance	$0	0.00%	$0	0.00%	$0	0.00%	$0	0.00%
Change in Supplemental Reserves	$0	0.00%	$0	0.00%	$0	0.00%	$0	0.00%
Change in Surplus Notes	$0	0.00%	$0	0.00%	$0	0.00%	$0	0.00%
Cumulative Effect of Changes in Accounting Principles	$0	0.00%	$0	0.00%	$0	0.00%	$0	0.00%
Capital Changes	$0	0.00%	$0	0.00%	$0	0.00%	$0	0.00%
Surplus Adjustments	$0	0.00%	$0	0.00%	$0	0.00%	$0	0.00%
Dividends to Stockholders	$0	0.00%	$0	0.00%	$0	0.00%	($420,000)	(1.56)%
Change in Treasury Stock	$0	0.00%	$0	0.00%	$0	0.00%	$0	0.00%
Aggregate Write-ins for Gains and Losses in Surplus	$0	0.00%	$0	0.00%	$0	0.00%	$0	0.00%
Net Change - Policyholder Surplus	($357,473)	(3.59)%	$8,326,075	10.02%	$234,855	3.82%	$834,181	3.09%
POLICYHOLDER SURPLUS - ENDING (See Sec. 5, B.6, B.7, C.9, C.11)	$4,846,328	48.70%	$50,899,292	61.28%	$5,540,475	90.19%	$9,026,842	33.46%

B.3 Income Statement - By Individual Underwriter

	OLD REPUBLIC GENERAL		OLD REPUBLIC NATIONAL		OLYMPIC		PACIFIC NORTHWEST	
REVENUE	Company Value	% Total Oper. Inc.	Company Value	% Total Oper. Inc.	Company Value	% Total Oper. Inc.	Company Value	% Total Oper. Inc.
Premiums Written - Direct	$0	0.00%	$14,047,794	1.82%	$0	--	$0	0.00%
Premiums Written - Non-Affiliated Agency	$0	0.00%	$604,520,309	78.46%	$0	--	$16,794,834	27.91%
Premiums Written - Affiliated Agency	$0	0.00%	$130,958,923	17.00%	$0	--	$41,667,730	69.25%
Premiums - Reinsurance Assumed	$14,067,656	91.44%	$3,237,180	0.42%	$0	--	$11,592	0.02%
Premiums - Reinsurance Ceded	$0	0.00%	($13,444,670)	(1.74)%	$0	--	($171,753)	(0.29)%
Net Premiums Written *(See Sec. 5, B.4)*	$14,067,656	91.44%	$739,319,536	95.96%	$0	--	$58,302,403	96.90%
Net Premiums Earned	$15,384,796	100.00%	$746,309,406	96.86%	$0	--	$60,092,709	99.88%
PLUS:								
Title Examinations	$0	0.00%	$584,651	0.08%	$0	--	$0	0.00%
Searches & Abstracts	$0	0.00%	$3,729,444	0.48%	$0	--	$0	0.00%
Surveys	$0	0.00%	$0	0.00%	$0	--	$0	0.00%
Escrow & Settlement Fees	$0	0.00%	$4,137,041	0.54%	$0	--	$0	0.00%
Other Service Charges	$0	0.00%	$15,636,946	2.03%	$0	--	$0	0.00%
Other Operating Income	$0	0.00%	$80,554	0.01%	$0	--	$75,000	0.12%
Total Operating Income *(See Sec. 5, A.2, A.3, A.5)*	$15,384,796	100.00%	$770,478,042	100.00%	$0	--	$60,167,709	100.00%
LESS:								
Amounts Retained By Agents *(See Sec. 5, B.9)*	$0		$594,328,500		$0		$52,730,302	
NET OPERATING REVENUE	$15,384,796		$176,149,542		$0		$7,437,407	
OPERATING EXPENSE	Company Value	% Net Oper. Rev.	Company Value	% Net Oper. Rev.	Company Value	% Net Oper. Rev.	Company Value	% Net Oper. Rev.
Total Personnel Costs	$0	0.00%	$59,113,515	33.56%	$0	--	$1,061,335	14.27%
Production Services	$0	0.00%	$10,857,358	6.16%	$0	--	$250,344	3.37%
Advertising	$1,030	0.01%	$203,122	0.12%	$0	--	$0	0.00%
Boards, Bureaus & Associations	$42,563	0.28%	$663,551	0.38%	$1,000	--	$29,014	0.39%
Title Plant Rent & Maintenance	($1,093)	(0.01)%	$1,090,318	0.62%	$0	--	$3,402	0.05%
Claim Adjustment Services	$0	0.00%	$0	0.00%	$0	--	$0	0.00%
Amount Charged Off, Net	$0	0.00%	$1,597,633	0.91%	$0	--	$0	0.00%
Marketing & Promotional Expense	$0	0.00%	$4,283,903	2.43%	$72	--	$1,408	0.02%
Insurance	$76,507	0.50%	$1,267,514	0.72%	$923	--	$0	0.00%
Directors' Fees	$28,640	0.19%	$58,122	0.03%	$0	--	$11,500	0.15%
Travel & Related Expenses	$0	0.00%	$4,018,294	2.28%	$0	--	$1,553	0.02%
Rent and Rent Items	$0	0.00%	$6,221,798	3.53%	$7,200	--	$40,200	0.54%
Equipment	$0	0.00%	$1,899,580	1.08%	$0	--	$763	0.01%
Cost/Depreciation, EDP Equipment & Software	$1,250	0.01%	$2,529,932	1.44%	$2,300	--	$0	0.00%
Print, Stationery, etc.	$5,947	0.04%	$1,274,180	0.72%	$200	--	$104,401	1.40%
Postage, Telephone, Express	$3,349	0.02%	$2,003,766	1.14%	$24	--	$8,100	0.11%
Legal & Auditing	$101,411	0.66%	$5,713,226	3.24%	$5,755	--	$152,455	2.05%
Taxes, Licenses & Fees	$881,067	5.73%	$12,839,587	7.29%	$1,793	--	$280,790	3.78%
Real Estate Expenses	$0	0.00%	$0	0.00%	$0	--	$0	0.00%
Real Estate Taxes	$0	0.00%	$21,263	0.01%	$0	--	$0	0.00%
Miscellaneous	$1,891,555	12.29%	$3,270,942	1.86%	$365	--	$4,597	0.06%
Other Operating Expense Incurred	$3,032,226	19.71%	$118,927,604	67.52%	$19,632	--	$1,949,862	26.22%
TOTAL OPERATING EXPENSE INCURRED (AGENT RETENTION + OTHER OPERATING EXPENSE INCURRED)	$3,032,226	--	$713,256,104	--	$19,632	--	$54,680,164	--
Aggregate Write-ins for Operating Deductions	$0	0.00%	$0	0.00%	$0	--	$0	0.00%
Operating Profit (Loss) Before Losses *(See Sec. 5, A.7)*	$12,352,570	80.29%	$57,221,938	32.48%	($19,632)	--	$5,487,545	73.78%
Losses & Loss Adjustment Expense Incurred *(See Sec. 5, C.2 - C.7)*								
Direct Operations *(See Sec. 5, C.7)*	$0	0.00%	$2,702,904	1.53%	$26,670	--	$277,652	3.73%
Agency Operations *(See Sec. 5, C.7)*	$8,609,260	55.96%	$53,683,570	30.48%	$0	--	$1,459,553	19.62%
NET OPERATING GAIN (LOSS) *(See Sec. 5, A.10)*	$3,743,310	24.33%	$835,464	0.47%	($46,302)	--	$3,750,340	50.43%
INVESTMENT INCOME	Company Value	% Total Assets	Company Value	% Total Assets	Company Value	% Total Assets	Company Value	% Total Assets
Net Investment Income Earned *(See Sec. 5, A.8)*	$5,016,179	4.35%	$20,519,650	4.24%	$10,677	2.99%	$1,489,812	4.85%
Net Realized Capital Gains (Losses) less Capital Gains Tax	$35,514	0.03%	$641,585	0.13%	$5,388	1.51%	($59,411)	(0.19)%
NET INVESTMENT GAIN (LOSS) *(See Sec. 5, A.9)*	$5,051,693	4.38%	$21,161,235	4.37%	$16,065	4.51%	$1,430,401	4.66%
OTHER INCOME	Company Value	% Total Assets	Company Value	% Total Assets	Company Value	% Total Assets	Company Value	% Total Assets
Other Income (Loss)	$0	0.00%	$0	0.00%	$0	0.00%	$0	0.00%
Net Income Before Taxes *(See Sec. 5, A.11)*	$8,795,003	7.63%	$21,996,699	4.54%	($30,237)	(8.48)%	$5,180,741	16.87%
Federal & Foreign Income Taxes Incurred	$2,583,677	2.24%	$7,314,953	1.51%	$0	0.00%	$1,737,425	5.66%
NET INCOME *(See Sec. 5, A.12)*	$6,211,326	5.39%	$14,681,746	3.03%	($30,237)	(8.48)%	$3,443,316	11.21%
CAPITAL AND SURPLUS ACCOUNT	Company Value	% Total Assets	Company Value	% Total Assets	Company Value	% Total Assets	Company Value	% Total Assets
POLICYHOLDER SURPLUS - BEGINNING	$49,245,695	42.70%	$119,193,883	24.61%	$366,389	102.76%	$12,038,747	39.21%
Net Income	$6,211,326	5.39%	$14,681,746	3.03%	($30,237)	(8.48)%	$3,443,316	11.21%
Change in Net Unrealized Capital Gains (Losses) less Capital Gains Tax	($805,255)	(0.70)%	($2,502,027)	(0.52)%	$0	0.00%	$0	0.00%
Change in Net Unrealized Foreign Exchange Capital Gain (Loss)	$0	0.00%	$0	0.00%	$0	0.00%	$0	0.00%
Change in Net Deferred Income Tax	($130,661)	(0.11)%	($1,524,421)	(0.31)%	$0	0.00%	$0	0.00%
Change in Nonadmitted Assets	($336,067)	(0.29)%	$5,964,398	1.23%	$0	0.00%	($50,298)	(0.16)%
Change in Provision for Unauthorized Reinsurance	$0	0.00%	$0	0.00%	$0	0.00%	$0	0.00%
Change in Supplemental Reserves	$0	0.00%	$0	0.00%	$0	0.00%	$0	0.00%
Change in Surplus Notes	$0	0.00%	$0	0.00%	$0	0.00%	$0	0.00%
Cumulative Effect of Changes in Accounting Principles	$0	0.00%	$0	0.00%	$0	0.00%	$0	0.00%
Capital Changes	$0	0.00%	$0	0.00%	$0	0.00%	$215,177	0.70%
Surplus Adjustments	$0	0.00%	$0	0.00%	$0	0.00%	$0	0.00%
Dividends to Stockholders	($8,000,000)	(6.94)%	($22,000,000)	(4.54)%	$0	0.00%	($490,100)	(1.60)%
Change in Treasury Stock	$0	0.00%	$0	0.00%	$0	0.00%	$0	0.00%
Aggregate Write-ins for Gains and Losses in Surplus	$0	0.00%	$2,188,246	0.45%	$0	0.00%	$0	0.00%
Net Change - Policyholder Surplus	($3,060,657)	(2.65)%	($3,192,058)	(0.66)%	($30,238)	(8.48)%	$3,118,096	10.15%
POLICYHOLDER SURPLUS - ENDING *(See Sec. 5, B.6, B.7, C.9, C.11)*	$46,185,038	40.04%	$116,001,825	23.95%	$336,151	94.28%	$15,156,843	49.36%

B.3 Income Statement - By Individual Underwriter

	PENN ATTORNEYS		PORT LAWRENCE		PUBLIC		SEAGATE	

REVENUE	Company Value	% Total Oper. Inc.	Company Value	% Total Oper. Inc.	Company Value	% Total Oper. Inc.	Company Value	% Total Oper. Inc.
Premiums Written - Direct	$1,777,598	97.50%	$2,836,725	41.80%	$0	--	$186,090	97.74%
Premiums Written - Non-Affiliated Agency	$0	0.00%	$2,437,031	35.91%	$0	--	$0	0.00%
Premiums Written - Affiliated Agency	$0	0.00%	$316,748	4.67%	$0	--	$0	0.00%
Premiums - Reinsurance Assumed	$0	0.00%	$0	0.00%	$0	--	$0	0.00%
Premiums - Reinsurance Ceded	($52,198)	(2.86)%	$0	0.00%	$0	--	$0	0.00%
Net Premiums Written (See Sec. 5, B.4)	$1,725,400	94.64%	$5,590,504	82.38%	$0	--	$186,090	97.74%
Net Premiums Earned	$1,710,517	93.82%	$5,437,029	80.12%	$0	--	$190,389	100.00%
PLUS:								
Title Examinations	$0	0.00%	$0	0.00%	$0	--	$0	0.00%
Searches & Abstracts	$0	0.00%	$591,773	8.72%	$0	--	$0	0.00%
Surveys	$0	0.00%	$0	0.00%	$0	--	$0	0.00%
Escrow & Settlement Fees	$0	0.00%	$723,859	10.67%	$0	--	$0	0.00%
Other Service Charges	$112,606	6.18%	$33,257	0.49%	$0	--	$0	0.00%
Other Operating Income	$0	0.00%	$0	0.00%	$0	--	$0	0.00%
Total Operating Income (See Sec. 5, A.2, A.3, A.5)	$1,823,123	100.00%	$6,785,918	100.00%	$0	--	$190,389	100.00%
LESS:								
Amounts Retained By Agents (See Sec. 5, B.9)	$0		$1,968,650		$0		$111,654	
NET OPERATING REVENUE	$1,823,123		$4,817,268		$0		$78,735	

OPERATING EXPENSE	Company Value	% Net Oper. Rev.	Company Value	% Net Oper. Rev.	Company Value	% Net Oper. Rev.	Company Value	% Net Oper. Rev.
Total Personnel Costs	$697,530	38.26%	$2,864,313	59.46%	$0	--	$35,797	45.47%
Production Services	$72,123	3.96%	$58,154	1.21%	$0	--	$0	0.00%
Advertising	$21,199	1.16%	$55,145	1.14%	$0	--	$0	0.00%
Boards, Bureaus & Associations	$6,214	0.34%	$15,742	0.33%	$5,000	--	$3,500	4.45%
Title Plant Rent & Maintenance	$0	0.00%	$0	0.00%	$0	--	$0	0.00%
Claim Adjustment Services	$0	0.00%	$0	0.00%	$0	--	$0	0.00%
Amount Charged Off, Net	($1,099)	(0.06)%	($44,698)	(0.93)%	$0	--	$0	0.00%
Marketing & Promotional Expense	$2,662	0.15%	$133,540	2.77%	$0	--	$0	0.00%
Insurance	$1,625	0.09%	$4,121	0.09%	$0	--	$20,767	26.38%
Directors' Fees	$0	0.00%	$0	0.00%	$0	--	$0	0.00%
Travel & Related Expenses	$3,526	0.19%	$114,217	2.37%	$0	--	$0	0.00%
Rent and Rent Items	$52,938	2.90%	$476,561	9.89%	$0	--	$0	0.00%
Equipment	$11,546	0.63%	$28,164	0.58%	$0	--	$0	0.00%
Cost/Depreciation, EDP Equipment & Software	$0	0.00%	$138,744	2.88%	$0	--	$0	0.00%
Print, Stationery, etc.	$3,200	0.18%	$80,853	1.68%	$0	--	$0	0.00%
Postage, Telephone, Express	$52,258	2.87%	$119,221	2.47%	$0	--	$0	0.00%
Legal & Auditing	$18,681	1.02%	$17,772	0.37%	$2,000	--	$0	0.00%
Taxes, Licenses & Fees	$67,938	3.73%	$104,858	2.18%	$247	--	$1,414	1.80%
Real Estate Expenses	$0	0.00%	$0	0.00%	$0	--	$0	0.00%
Real Estate Taxes	$0	0.00%	$20,481	0.43%	$0	--	$0	0.00%
Miscellaneous	$162,818	8.93%	$524,763	10.89%	$0	--	$2,388	3.03%
Other Operating Expense Incurred	$1,173,159	64.35%	$4,711,951	97.81%	$7,247	--	$63,866	81.12%
TOTAL OPERATING EXPENSE INCURRED (AGENT RETENTION + OTHER OPERATING EXPENSE INCURRED)	$1,173,159	--	$6,680,601	--	$7,247	--	$175,520	--
Aggregate Write-ins for Operating Deductions	$0	0.00%	$0	0.00%	$0	--	$0	0.00%
Operating Profit (Loss) Before Losses (See Sec. 5, A.7)	$649,964	35.65%	$105,317	2.19%	($7,247)	--	$14,869	18.88%
Losses & Loss Adjustment Expense Incurred (See Sec. 5, C.2 - C.7)								
Direct Operations (See Sec. 5, C.7)	$44,947	2.47%	$35,011	0.73%	$0	--	$0	0.00%
Agency Operations (See Sec. 5, C.7)	$0	0.00%	$0	0.00%	$0	--	$0	0.00%
NET OPERATING GAIN (LOSS) (See Sec. 5, A.10)	$605,017	33.19%	$70,306	1.46%	($7,247)	--	$14,869	18.88%

INVESTMENT INCOME	Company Value	% Total Assets	Company Value	% Total Assets	Company Value	% Total Assets	Company Value	% Total Assets
Net Investment Income Earned (See Sec. 5, A.8)	$459,407	4.51%	$1,071,905	4.78%	$35,090	3.38%	$24,229	3.61%
Net Realized Capital Gains (Losses) less Capital Gains Tax	$0	0.00%	($176,554)	(0.79)%	$0	0.00%	$0	0.00%
NET INVESTMENT GAIN (LOSS) (See Sec. 5, A.9)	$459,407	4.51%	$895,351	3.99%	$35,090	3.38%	$24,229	3.61%

OTHER INCOME	Company Value	% Total Assets	Company Value	% Total Assets	Company Value	% Total Assets	Company Value	% Total Assets
Other Income (Loss)	$0	0.00%	$0	0.00%	$0	0.00%	$0	0.00%
Net Income Before Taxes (See Sec. 5, A.11)	$1,064,424	10.45%	$965,657	4.31%	$27,843	2.68%	$39,098	5.83%
Federal & Foreign Income Taxes Incurred	$372,537	3.66%	$365,520	1.63%	$0	0.00%	$0	0.00%
NET INCOME (See Sec. 5, A.12)	$691,887	6.79%	$600,137	2.68%	$27,843	2.68%	$39,098	5.83%

CAPITAL AND SURPLUS ACCOUNT	Company Value	% Total Assets	Company Value	% Total Assets	Company Value	% Total Assets	Company Value	% Total Assets
POLICYHOLDER SURPLUS - BEGINNING	$8,451,243	82.97%	$15,367,935	68.52%	$1,010,401	97.32%	$500,459	74.63%
Net Income	$691,887	6.79%	$600,137	2.68%	$27,843	2.68%	$39,098	5.83%
Change in Net Unrealized Capital Gains (Losses) less Capital Gains Tax	$0	0.00%	$81,736	0.36%	$0	0.00%	$0	0.00%
Change in Net Unrealized Foreign Exchange Capital Gain (Loss)	$0	0.00%	$0	0.00%	$0	0.00%	$0	0.00%
Change in Net Deferred Income Tax	$0	0.00%	($27,000)	(0.12)%	$0	0.00%	$0	0.00%
Change in Nonadmitted Assets	$53,541	0.53%	$186,932	0.83%	$0	0.00%	($65,000)	(9.69)%
Change in Provision for Unauthorized Reinsurance	$0	0.00%	$0	0.00%	$0	0.00%	$0	0.00%
Change in Supplemental Reserves	$0	0.00%	$0	0.00%	$0	0.00%	$0	0.00%
Change in Surplus Notes	$0	0.00%	$0	0.00%	$0	0.00%	$0	0.00%
Cumulative Effect of Changes in Accounting Principles	$0	0.00%	$0	0.00%	$0	0.00%	$0	0.00%
Capital Changes	$0	0.00%	$0	0.00%	$0	0.00%	$0	0.00%
Surplus Adjustments	$0	0.00%	$0	0.00%	$0	0.00%	$0	0.00%
Dividends to Stockholders	($845,000)	(8.30)%	($1,536,000)	(6.85)%	$0	0.00%	$0	0.00%
Change in Treasury Stock	$0	0.00%	$0	0.00%	$0	0.00%	$0	0.00%
Aggregate Write-ins for Gains and Losses in Surplus	$0	0.00%	$0	0.00%	$0	0.00%	$0	0.00%
Net Change - Policyholder Surplus	($99,572)	(0.98)%	($694,195)	(3.10)%	$27,843	2.68%	($25,902)	(3.86)%
POLICYHOLDER SURPLUS - ENDING (See Sec. 5, B.6, B.7, C.9, C.11)	$8,351,671	81.99%	$14,673,740	65.42%	$1,038,244	100.00%	$474,557	70.77%

B.3 Income Statement - By Individual Underwriter

	SECURITY TG (BALTIMORE)		SECURITY UNION		SIERRA		SOUTHERN TI CORP	
REVENUE	Company Value	% Total Oper. Inc.	Company Value	% Total Oper. Inc.	Company Value	% Total Oper. Inc.	Company Value	% Total Oper. Inc.
Premiums Written - Direct	$413,934	1.79%	$11,530,727	17.31%	$0	0.00%	$1,173,787	2.20%
Premiums Written - Non-Affiliated Agency	$20,943,251	90.48%	$36,182,556	54.31%	$1,966,565	102.26%	$49,984,569	93.60%
Premiums Written - Affiliated Agency	$568,301	2.46%	$15,844,405	23.78%	$0	0.00%	$3,022,358	5.66%
Premiums - Reinsurance Assumed	$0	0.00%	$245,130	0.37%	$0	0.00%	$0	0.00%
Premiums - Reinsurance Ceded	($124,727)	(0.54)%	($153,636)	(0.23)%	$0	0.00%	($359,707)	(0.67)%
Net Premiums Written (See Sec. 5, B.4)	$21,800,759	94.18%	$63,649,182	95.54%	$1,966,565	102.26%	$53,821,007	100.78%
Net Premiums Earned	$22,255,342	96.14%	$64,329,252	96.56%	$1,923,075	100.00%	$52,180,887	97.71%
PLUS:								
Title Examinations	$143,246	0.62%	$5,930	0.01%	$0	0.00%	$0	0.00%
Searches & Abstracts	$57,536	0.25%	$23,081	0.03%	$0	0.00%	$549,656	1.03%
Surveys	$0	0.00%	$0	0.00%	$0	0.00%	$0	0.00%
Escrow & Settlement Fees	$31,845	0.14%	$1,021,865	1.53%	$0	0.00%	$45,437	0.09%
Other Service Charges	$660,099	2.85%	$1,241,629	1.86%	$0	0.00%	$187,410	0.35%
Other Operating Income	$0	0.00%	$0	0.00%	$0	0.00%	$440,858	0.83%
Total Operating Income (See Sec. 5, A.2, A.3, A.5)	$23,148,068	100.00%	$66,621,757	100.00%	$1,923,075	100.00%	$53,404,248	100.00%
LESS:								
Amounts Retained By Agents (See Sec. 5, B.9)	$17,165,336		$43,306,336		$1,671,695		$41,851,861	
NET OPERATING REVENUE	$5,982,732		$23,315,421		$251,380		$11,552,387	
OPERATING EXPENSE	Company Value	% Net Oper. Rev.	Company Value	% Net Oper. Rev.	Company Value	% Net Oper. Rev.	Company Value	% Net Oper. Rev.
Total Personnel Costs	$3,391,952	56.70%	$10,095,914	43.30%	$0	0.00%	$5,746,011	49.74%
Production Services	$211	0.00%	$1,394,371	5.98%	$0	0.00%	$345,000	2.99%
Advertising	$173,722	2.90%	$40,444	0.17%	$0	0.00%	$125,742	1.09%
Boards, Bureaus & Associations	$57,782	0.97%	$23,015	0.10%	$793	0.32%	$0	0.00%
Title Plant Rent & Maintenance	$0	0.00%	$10,432	0.04%	$0	0.00%	$0	0.00%
Claim Adjustment Services	$0	0.00%	$0	0.00%	$0	0.00%	$0	0.00%
Amount Charged Off, Net	$11,657	0.19%	$135,531	0.58%	$0	0.00%	$93,876	0.81%
Marketing & Promotional Expense	$158,207	2.64%	$106,434	0.46%	$0	0.00%	$0	0.00%
Insurance	$56,833	0.95%	$68,670	0.29%	$0	0.00%	$110,944	0.96%
Directors' Fees	$58,690	0.98%	$0	0.00%	$0	0.00%	$7,999	0.07%
Travel & Related Expenses	$414,906	6.94%	$980,942	4.21%	$0	0.00%	$429,860	3.72%
Rent and Rent Items	$300,604	5.02%	$878,471	3.77%	$36,000	14.32%	$665,134	5.76%
Equipment	$65,746	1.10%	$535,836	2.30%	$0	0.00%	$77,623	0.67%
Cost/Depreciation, EDP Equipment & Software	$73,100	1.22%	$942,670	4.04%	$0	0.00%	$115,007	1.00%
Print, Stationery, etc.	$165,542	2.77%	$409,973	1.76%	$6,514	2.59%	$352,297	3.05%
Postage, Telephone, Express	$169,896	2.84%	$1,188,855	5.10%	$0	0.00%	$178,170	1.54%
Legal & Auditing	$265,506	4.44%	$1,106,655	4.75%	$60,175	23.94%	$256,533	2.22%
Taxes, Licenses & Fees	$494,843	8.27%	$967,881	4.15%	$21,391	8.51%	$1,354,501	11.72%
Real Estate Expenses	$0	0.00%	$0	0.00%	$0	0.00%	$23,729	0.21%
Real Estate Taxes	$0	0.00%	$0	0.00%	$0	0.00%	$7,964	0.07%
Miscellaneous	$4,947	0.08%	$134,702	0.58%	$65,709	26.14%	$117,192	1.01%
Other Operating Expense Incurred	$5,864,144	98.02%	$19,020,796	81.58%	$190,582	75.81%	$10,007,582	86.63%
TOTAL OPERATING EXPENSE INCURRED (AGENT RETENTION + OTHER OPERATING EXPENSE INCURRED)	$23,029,480	--	$62,327,132	--	$1,862,277	--	$51,859,443	--
Aggregate Write-ins for Operating Deductions	$0	0.00%	$0	0.00%	$0	0.00%	$0	0.00%
Operating Profit (Loss) Before Losses (See Sec. 5, A.7)	$118,588	1.98%	$4,294,625	18.42%	$60,798	24.19%	$1,544,805	13.37%
Losses & Loss Adjustment Expense Incurred (See Sec. 5, C.2 - C.7)								
Direct Operations (See Sec. 5, C.7)	$7,125	0.12%	$4,987,809	21.39%	$0	0.00%	$21,545	0.19%
Agency Operations (See Sec. 5, C.7)	$1,636,530	27.35%	$5,063,410	21.72%	$0	0.00%	$3,715,778	32.16%
NET OPERATING GAIN (LOSS) (See Sec. 5, A.10)	($1,525,067)	(25.49)%	($5,756,594)	(24.69)%	$60,798	24.19%	($2,192,518)	(18.98)%
INVESTMENT INCOME	Company Value	% Total Assets	Company Value	% Total Assets	Company Value	% Total Assets	Company Value	% Total Assets
Net Investment Income Earned (See Sec. 5, A.8)	$493,989	3.53%	$7,368,227	8.77%	$140,652	4.61%	$913,640	3.91%
Net Realized Capital Gains (Losses) less Capital Gains Tax	($33,925)	(0.24)%	$868,864	1.03%	$0	0.00%	$8,609	0.04%
NET INVESTMENT GAIN (LOSS) (See Sec. 5, A.9)	$460,064	3.29%	$8,237,091	9.81%	$140,652	4.61%	$922,249	3.94%
OTHER INCOME	Company Value	% Total Assets	Company Value	% Total Assets	Company Value	% Total Assets	Company Value	% Total Assets
Other Income (Loss)	$1,721	0.01%	$0	0.00%	$0	0.00%	$0	0.00%
Net Income Before Taxes (See Sec. 5, A.11)	($1,063,282)	(7.60)%	$2,480,497	2.95%	$201,450	6.61%	($1,270,269)	(5.43)%
Federal & Foreign Income Taxes Incurred	($435,000)	(3.11)%	($1,130,923)	(1.35)%	$60,964	2.00%	($249,268)	(1.07)%
NET INCOME (See Sec. 5, A.12)	($628,282)	(4.49)%	$3,611,420	4.30%	$140,486	4.61%	($1,021,001)	(4.37)%
CAPITAL AND SURPLUS ACCOUNT	Company Value	% Total Assets	Company Value	% Total Assets	Company Value	% Total Assets	Company Value	% Total Assets
POLICYHOLDER SURPLUS - BEGINNING	$4,488,445	32.08%	$66,803,268	79.54%	$2,523,704	82.77%	$8,660,765	37.03%
Net Income	($628,282)	(4.49)%	$3,611,420	4.30%	$140,486	4.61%	($1,021,001)	(4.37)%
Change in Net Unrealized Capital Gains (Losses) less Capital Gains Tax	($403,923)	(2.89)%	($20,154,158)	(24.00)%	$0	0.00%	$71,990	0.31%
Change in Net Unrealized Foreign Exchange Capital Gain (Loss)	$0	0.00%	$0	0.00%	$0	0.00%	$0	0.00%
Change in Net Deferred Income Tax	($81,000)	(0.58)%	($141,845)	(0.17)%	$0	0.00%	$243,442	1.04%
Change in Nonadmitted Assets	$388,853	2.78%	$218,297	0.26%	$0	0.00%	$166,523	0.71%
Change in Provision for Unauthorized Reinsurance	$0	0.00%	$0	0.00%	$0	0.00%	$0	0.00%
Change in Supplemental Reserves	$0	0.00%	$0	0.00%	($6,628)	(0.22)%	$0	0.00%
Change in Surplus Notes	$0	0.00%	$0	0.00%	$0	0.00%	$0	0.00%
Cumulative Effect of Changes in Accounting Principles	$0	0.00%	$0	0.00%	$0	0.00%	$0	0.00%
Capital Changes	$0	0.00%	$0	0.00%	$0	0.00%	$0	0.00%
Surplus Adjustments	$0	0.00%	$0	0.00%	$0	0.00%	$0	0.00%
Dividends to Stockholders	$0	0.00%	($5,000,000)	(5.95)%	$0	0.00%	($406,115)	(1.74)%
Change in Treasury Stock	$0	0.00%	$0	0.00%	$0	0.00%	$0	0.00%
Aggregate Write-ins for Gains and Losses in Surplus	$0	0.00%	$1,228,211	1.46%	$0	0.00%	$0	0.00%
Net Change - Policyholder Surplus	($724,354)	(5.18)%	($20,238,085)	(24.10)%	$133,858	4.39%	($945,159)	(4.04)%
POLICYHOLDER SURPLUS - ENDING (See Sec. 5, B.6, B.7, C.9, C.11)	$3,764,091	26.90%	$46,565,183	55.44%	$2,657,562	87.16%	$7,715,606	32.99%

B.3 Income Statement - By Individual Underwriter

	STEWART (OR)		STEWART TGC		STEWART TIC		T.A. TITLE	
REVENUE	Company Value	% Total Oper. Inc.	Company Value	% Total Oper. Inc.	Company Value	% Total Oper. Inc.	Company Value	% Total Oper. Inc.
Premiums Written - Direct	$567,888	5.77%	$157,750,939	10.52%	$38,951,627	22.57%	$0	0.00%
Premiums Written - Non-Affiliated Agency	$10,237,613	104.08%	$796,976,776	53.15%	$121,926,620	70.65%	$13,742,041	81.54%
Premiums Written - Affiliated Agency	$0	0.00%	$500,732,921	33.39%	$1,373,640	0.80%	$3,297,800	19.57%
Premiums - Reinsurance Assumed	$0	0.00%	$11,941,780	0.80%	$1,740,954	1.01%	$0	0.00%
Premiums - Reinsurance Ceded	($671,490)	(6.83)%	($2,721,339)	(0.18)%	($4,915,543)	(2.85)%	($48,885)	(0.29)%
Net Premiums Written (See Sec. 5, B.4)	$10,134,011	103.02%	$1,464,681,077	97.67%	$159,077,298	92.17%	$16,990,956	100.82%
Net Premiums Earned	$9,836,516	100.00%	$1,453,129,953	96.90%	$156,456,715	90.66%	$16,770,422	99.51%
PLUS:								
Title Examinations	$0	0.00%	$26,669,673	1.78%	$249,827	0.14%	$3,429	0.02%
Searches & Abstracts	$0	0.00%	$3,951,503	0.26%	$1,152,408	0.67%	$0	0.00%
Surveys	$0	0.00%	$0	0.00%	$0	0.00%	$0	0.00%
Escrow & Settlement Fees	$0	0.00%	$2,252,266	0.15%	$125,003	0.07%	$0	0.00%
Other Service Charges	$0	0.00%	$10,981,116	0.73%	$14,254,077	8.26%	$78,770	0.47%
Other Operating Income	$0	0.00%	$2,620,195	0.17%	$344,258	0.20%	$0	0.00%
Total Operating Income (See Sec. 5, A.2, A.3, A.5)	$9,836,516	100.00%	$1,499,604,706	100.00%	$172,582,288	100.00%	$16,852,621	100.00%
LESS:								
Amounts Retained By Agents (See Sec. 5, B.9)	$9,221,086		$1,099,768,492		$105,287,815		$14,655,368	
NET OPERATING REVENUE	$615,430		$399,836,214		$67,294,473		$2,197,253	

	STEWART (OR)		STEWART TGC		STEWART TIC		T.A. TITLE	
OPERATING EXPENSE	Company Value	% Net Oper. Rev.	Company Value	% Net Oper. Rev.	Company Value	% Net Oper. Rev.	Company Value	% Net Oper. Rev.
Total Personnel Costs	$143,745	23.36%	$132,322,691	33.09%	$28,172,804	41.86%	$716,861	32.63%
Production Services	$332,799	54.08%	$56,440,184	14.12%	$4,541,360	6.75%	$185,025	8.42%
Advertising	$0	0.00%	$2,220,786	0.56%	$39,754	0.06%	$1,464	0.07%
Boards, Bureaus & Associations	$3,926	0.64%	$262,730	0.07%	$233,636	0.35%	$0	0.00%
Title Plant Rent & Maintenance	$1,225	0.20%	$350,325	0.09%	$0	0.00%	$0	0.00%
Claim Adjustment Services	$0	0.00%	$0	0.00%	$0	0.00%	$0	0.00%
Amount Charged Off, Net	$0	0.00%	$2,485,658	0.62%	$0	0.00%	$0	0.00%
Marketing & Promotional Expense	$5,203	0.85%	$10,327,722	2.58%	$6,344,882	9.43%	$60,790	2.77%
Insurance	$911	0.15%	$1,271,135	0.32%	$119,878	0.18%	$61,869	2.82%
Directors' Fees	$0	0.00%	$54,905	0.01%	$13,543	0.02%	$0	0.00%
Travel & Related Expenses	$12,715	2.07%	$10,659,787	2.67%	$731,227	1.09%	$39,573	1.80%
Rent and Rent Items	$14,400	2.34%	$15,940,663	3.99%	$2,213,178	3.29%	$31,386	1.43%
Equipment	$12,051	1.96%	$778,502	0.19%	$386,354	0.57%	$24,665	1.12%
Cost/Depreciation, EDP Equipment & Software	$0	0.00%	$29,939,287	7.49%	$289,904	0.43%	$24,980	1.14%
Print, Stationery, etc.	$15,054	2.45%	$5,653,857	1.41%	$383,827	0.57%	$21,275	0.97%
Postage, Telephone, Express	$2,476	0.40%	$5,015,269	1.25%	$811,214	1.21%	$22,196	1.01%
Legal & Auditing	$12,979	2.11%	$20,316,415	5.08%	$396,057	0.59%	$33,916	1.54%
Taxes, Licenses & Fees	$21,226	3.45%	$21,934,775	5.49%	$4,458,359	6.63%	$222,474	10.13%
Real Estate Expenses	$0	0.00%	$0	0.00%	$0	0.00%	$0	0.00%
Real Estate Taxes	$0	0.00%	$0	0.00%	$0	0.00%	$0	0.00%
Miscellaneous	$13	0.00%	$645,715	0.16%	$412,623	0.61%	$0	0.00%
Other Operating Expense Incurred	$578,723	94.04%	$316,620,406	79.19%	$49,548,600	73.63%	$1,446,474	65.83%
TOTAL OPERATING EXPENSE INCURRED (AGENT RETENTION + OTHER OPERATING EXPENSE INCURRED)	$9,799,809	--	$1,416,388,898	--	$154,836,415	--	$16,101,842	--
Aggregate Write-ins for Operating Deductions	$0	0.00%	$0	0.00%	$0	0.00%	$0	0.00%
Operating Profit (Loss) Before Losses (See Sec. 5, A.7)	$36,707	5.96%	$83,215,808	20.81%	$17,745,873	26.37%	$750,779	34.17%
Losses & Loss Adjustment Expense Incurred (See Sec. 5, C.2 - C.7)								
Direct Operations (See Sec. 5, C.7)	$0	0.00%	$32,516,708	8.13%	($6,910)	(0.01)%	$0	0.00%
Agency Operations (See Sec. 5, C.7)	$0	0.00%	$99,331,533	24.84%	$5,477,895	8.14%	$544,743	24.79%
NET OPERATING GAIN (LOSS) (See Sec. 5, A.10)	$36,707	5.96%	($48,632,433)	(12.16)%	$12,274,888	18.24%	$206,036	9.38%

	STEWART (OR)		STEWART TGC		STEWART TIC		T.A. TITLE	
INVESTMENT INCOME	Company Value	% Total Assets	Company Value	% Total Assets	Company Value	% Total Assets	Company Value	% Total Assets
Net Investment Income Earned (See Sec. 5, A.8)	$175,981	3.32%	$28,137,696	2.60%	$5,574,578	6.99%	$516,884	4.27%
Net Realized Capital Gains (Losses) less Capital Gains Tax	$0	0.00%	$3,445,843	0.32%	$8,233	0.01%	$475,814	3.94%
NET INVESTMENT GAIN (LOSS) (See Sec. 5, A.9)	$175,981	3.32%	$31,583,539	2.92%	$5,582,811	7.00%	$992,698	8.21%

	STEWART (OR)		STEWART TGC		STEWART TIC		T.A. TITLE	
OTHER INCOME	Company Value	% Total Assets	Company Value	% Total Assets	Company Value	% Total Assets	Company Value	% Total Assets
Other Income (Loss)	$0	0.00%	$3,514,702	0.32%	$0	0.00%	$0	0.00%
Net Income Before Taxes (See Sec. 5, A.11)	$212,688	4.01%	($13,534,192)	(1.25)%	$17,857,699	22.39%	$1,198,734	9.91%
Federal & Foreign Income Taxes Incurred	$85,398	1.61%	($7,075,535)	(0.65)%	$6,133,536	7.69%	$419,212	3.47%
NET INCOME (See Sec. 5, A.12)	$127,290	2.40%	($6,458,657)	(0.60)%	$11,724,163	14.70%	$779,522	6.45%

	STEWART (OR)		STEWART TGC		STEWART TIC		T.A. TITLE	
CAPITAL AND SURPLUS ACCOUNT	Company Value	% Total Assets	Company Value	% Total Assets	Company Value	% Total Assets	Company Value	% Total Assets
POLICYHOLDER SURPLUS - BEGINNING	$2,607,381	49.12%	$508,508,698	47.00%	$30,832,501	38.67%	$7,674,814	63.47%
Net Income	$127,290	2.40%	($6,458,657)	(0.60)%	$11,724,163	14.70%	$779,522	6.45%
Change in Net Unrealized Capital Gains (Losses) less Capital Gains Tax	$0	0.00%	($13,517,277)	(1.25)%	($2,490,162)	(3.12)%	$68,423	0.57%
Change in Net Unrealized Foreign Exchange Capital Gain (Loss)	$0	0.00%	$9,796,411	0.91%	$0	0.00%	$0	0.00%
Change in Net Deferred Income Tax	$10,167	0.19%	$2,328,445	0.22%	$377,168	0.47%	($140,008)	(1.16)%
Change in Nonadmitted Assets	$29,153	0.55%	($3,939,989)	(0.36)%	$372,938	0.47%	($1,112,412)	(9.20)%
Change in Provision for Unauthorized Reinsurance	$0	0.00%	$0	0.00%	$0	0.00%	$0	0.00%
Change in Supplemental Reserves	$0	0.00%	$0	0.00%	$0	0.00%	$0	0.00%
Change in Surplus Notes	$0	0.00%	$0	0.00%	$0	0.00%	$0	0.00%
Cumulative Effect of Changes in Accounting Principles	$0	0.00%	$0	0.00%	$0	0.00%	$0	0.00%
Capital Changes	$0	0.00%	$0	0.00%	$0	0.00%	$0	0.00%
Surplus Adjustments	$100,000	1.88%	$21,183,384	1.96%	$0	0.00%	$0	0.00%
Dividends to Stockholders	$0	0.00%	($2,000,000)	(0.18)%	($6,000,000)	(7.52)%	($767,000)	(6.34)%
Change in Treasury Stock	$0	0.00%	$0	0.00%	$0	0.00%	$0	0.00%
Aggregate Write-ins for Gains and Losses in Surplus	$0	0.00%	$0	0.00%	($301,109)	(0.38)%	$0	0.00%
Net Change - Policyholder Surplus	$266,610	5.02%	$7,392,317	0.68%	$3,682,998	4.62%	($1,171,475)	(9.69)%
POLICYHOLDER SURPLUS - ENDING (See Sec. 5, B.6, B.7, C.9, C.11)	$2,873,991	54.14%	$515,901,015	47.68%	$34,515,499	43.28%	$6,503,339	53.78%

B.3 Income Statement - By Individual Underwriter

	TICOR		TICOR (FL)		TITLE G&TC		TITLE GUARANTY DIV (IA)	
REVENUE	Company Value	% Total Oper. Inc.	Company Value	% Total Oper. Inc.	Company Value	% Total Oper. Inc.	Company Value	% Total Oper. Inc.
Premiums Written - Direct	$51,058,558	13.54%	$0	0.00%	$260,893	15.49%	$3,724,743	102.10%
Premiums Written - Non-Affiliated Agency	$218,064,012	57.83%	$83,543,448	89.25%	$0	0.00%	$0	0.00%
Premiums Written - Affiliated Agency	$58,074,930	15.40%	$0	0.00%	$0	0.00%	$0	0.00%
Premiums - Reinsurance Assumed	$668,661	0.18%	$88,626	0.09%	$0	0.00%	$0	0.00%
Premiums - Reinsurance Ceded	($1,239,651)	(0.33)%	($310,576)	(0.33)%	$0	0.00%	($38,518)	(1.06)%
Net Premiums Written (See Sec. 5, B.4)	$326,626,510	86.62%	$83,321,498	89.01%	$260,893	15.49%	$3,686,225	101.04%
Net Premiums Earned	$326,846,416	86.68%	$85,830,997	91.70%	$257,994	15.32%	$3,590,882	98.43%
PLUS:								
Title Examinations	$5,098,729	1.35%	$1,600	0.00%	$173,636	10.31%	$0	0.00%
Searches & Abstracts	$11,455,068	3.04%	$7,264,027	7.76%	$267,583	15.89%	$0	0.00%
Surveys	$12,950	0.00%	$0	0.00%	$0	0.00%	$0	0.00%
Escrow & Settlement Fees	$24,857,220	6.59%	$2,850	0.00%	$0	0.00%	$0	0.00%
Other Service Charges	$8,821,017	2.34%	$505,151	0.54%	$544,422	32.33%	$42,395	1.16%
Other Operating Income	$0	0.00%	$0	0.00%	$440,111	26.14%	$14,940	0.41%
Total Operating Income (See Sec. 5, A.2, A.3, A.5)	$377,091,400	100.00%	$93,604,625	100.00%	$1,683,746	100.00%	$3,648,217	100.00%
LESS:								
Amounts Retained By Agents (See Sec. 5, B.9)	$221,138,248		$63,996,950		$0		$0	
NET OPERATING REVENUE	$155,953,152		$29,607,675		$1,683,746		$3,648,217	
OPERATING EXPENSE	Company Value	% Net Oper. Rev.	Company Value	% Net Oper. Rev.	Company Value	% Net Oper. Rev.	Company Value	% Net Oper. Rev.
Total Personnel Costs	$57,701,274	37.00%	$12,713,608	42.94%	$1,060,761	63.00%	$1,338,719	36.70%
Production Services	$12,605,043	8.08%	$1,174,359	3.97%	$0	0.00%	$0	0.00%
Advertising	$587,343	0.38%	$140,366	0.47%	$31,672	1.88%	$126,128	3.46%
Boards, Bureaus & Associations	$169,226	0.11%	$26,523	0.09%	$15,341	0.91%	$0	0.00%
Title Plant Rent & Maintenance	$272,727	0.17%	$330,525	1.12%	$0	0.00%	$0	0.00%
Claim Adjustment Services	$0	0.00%	$0	0.00%	$0	0.00%	$0	0.00%
Amount Charged Off, Net	$171,331	0.11%	$1,535,602	5.19%	$0	0.00%	$0	0.00%
Marketing & Promotional Expense	$642,999	0.41%	$123,738	0.42%	$0	0.00%	$0	0.00%
Insurance	$446,066	0.29%	$221,068	0.75%	$43,183	2.56%	$0	0.00%
Directors' Fees	$0	0.00%	$0	0.00%	$3,400	0.20%	$0	0.00%
Travel & Related Expenses	$3,584,854	2.30%	$923,402	3.12%	$74,361	4.42%	$27,993	0.77%
Rent and Rent Items	$7,023,113	4.50%	$2,108,020	7.12%	$39,225	2.33%	$24,080	0.66%
Equipment	$3,757,724	2.41%	$2,714,644	9.17%	$79,192	4.70%	$12,364	0.34%
Cost/Depreciation, EDP Equipment & Software	$4,080,199	2.62%	$1,431,633	4.84%	$14,923	0.89%	$0	0.00%
Print, Stationery, etc.	$2,073,309	1.33%	$510,793	1.73%	$37,145	2.21%	$67,479	1.85%
Postage, Telephone, Express	$3,100,747	1.99%	$870,608	2.94%	$55,224	3.28%	$17,180	0.47%
Legal & Auditing	$3,871,523	2.48%	$2,924,539	9.88%	$18,393	1.09%	$825,617	22.63%
Taxes, Licenses & Fees	$5,364,730	3.44%	$1,234,316	4.17%	$32,400	1.92%	$0	0.00%
Real Estate Expenses	$0	0.00%	$0	0.00%	$45,090	2.68%	$0	0.00%
Real Estate Taxes	$0	0.00%	$0	0.00%	$10,292	0.61%	$0	0.00%
Miscellaneous	$1,403,093	0.90%	$287,467	0.97%	$36,128	2.15%	$19,336	0.53%
Other Operating Expense Incurred	$106,855,301	68.52%	$29,271,211	98.86%	$1,596,730	94.83%	$2,458,896	67.40%
TOTAL OPERATING EXPENSE INCURRED (AGENT RETENTION + OTHER OPERATING EXPENSE INCURRED)	$327,993,549	--	$93,268,161	--	$1,596,730	--	$2,458,896	--
Aggregate Write-ins for Operating Deductions	$0	0.00%	$0	0.00%	$0	0.00%	$22,588	0.62%
Operating Profit (Loss) Before Losses (See Sec. 5, A.7)	$49,097,851	31.48%	$336,464	1.14%	$87,016	5.17%	$1,166,733	31.98%
Losses & Loss Adjustment Expense Incurred (See Sec. 5, C.2 - C.7)								
Direct Operations (See Sec. 5, C.7)	$10,184,090	6.53%	$329,429	1.11%	$1,500	0.09%	$0	0.00%
Agency Operations (See Sec. 5, C.7)	$21,717,214	13.93%	$24,514,783	82.80%	$0	0.00%	$0	0.00%
NET OPERATING GAIN (LOSS) (See Sec. 5, A.10)	$17,196,547	11.03%	($24,507,748)	(82.77)%	$85,516	5.08%	$1,166,733	31.98%
INVESTMENT INCOME	Company Value	% Total Assets	Company Value	% Total Assets	Company Value	% Total Assets	Company Value	% Total Assets
Net Investment Income Earned (See Sec. 5, A.8)	$10,885,620	4.57%	$4,039,640	3.34%	$38,802	2.68%	$0	0.00%
Net Realized Capital Gains (Losses) less Capital Gains Tax	($5,044,091)	(2.12)%	$84,093	0.07%	$0	0.00%	$0	0.00%
NET INVESTMENT GAIN (LOSS) (See Sec. 5, A.9)	$5,841,529	2.45%	$4,123,733	3.41%	$38,802	2.68%	$0	0.00%
OTHER INCOME	Company Value	% Total Assets	Company Value	% Total Assets	Company Value	% Total Assets	Company Value	% Total Assets
Other Income (Loss)	($4,884)	0.00%	$882,326	0.73%	$0	0.00%	($1,021,000)	(16.45)%
Net Income Before Taxes (See Sec. 5, A.11)	$23,033,192	9.68%	($19,501,689)	(16.13)%	$124,318	8.58%	$145,733	2.35%
Federal & Foreign Income Taxes Incurred	$6,358,849	2.67%	($8,577,298)	(7.10)%	$49,169	3.39%	$0	0.00%
NET INCOME (See Sec. 5, A.12)	$16,674,343	7.01%	($10,924,391)	(9.04)%	$75,149	5.19%	$145,733	2.35%
CAPITAL AND SURPLUS ACCOUNT	Company Value	% Total Assets	Company Value	% Total Assets	Company Value	% Total Assets	Company Value	% Total Assets
POLICYHOLDER SURPLUS - BEGINNING	$52,898,518	22.23%	$29,857,989	24.70%	$853,479	58.92%	$593,992	9.57%
Net Income	$16,674,343	7.01%	($10,924,391)	(9.04)%	$75,149	5.19%	$145,733	2.35%
Change in Net Unrealized Capital Gains (Losses) less Capital Gains Tax	$1,751,036	0.74%	$0	0.00%	$100	0.01%	$0	0.00%
Change in Net Unrealized Foreign Exchange Capital Gain (Loss)	$0	0.00%	$0	0.00%	$0	0.00%	$0	0.00%
Change in Net Deferred Income Tax	($3,848,949)	(1.62)%	($1,316,865)	(1.09)%	($2,790)	(0.19)%	$0	0.00%
Change in Nonadmitted Assets	$2,817,344	1.18%	$7,969,743	6.59%	($6,053)	(0.42)%	$0	0.00%
Change in Provision for Unauthorized Reinsurance	$0	0.00%	$0	0.00%	$0	0.00%	$0	0.00%
Change in Supplemental Reserves	$0	0.00%	$0	0.00%	$0	0.00%	$0	0.00%
Change in Surplus Notes	$0	0.00%	$0	0.00%	$0	0.00%	$0	0.00%
Cumulative Effect of Changes in Accounting Principles	$0	0.00%	$0	0.00%	$0	0.00%	$0	0.00%
Capital Changes	$0	0.00%	$0	0.00%	$0	0.00%	$0	0.00%
Surplus Adjustments	$0	0.00%	$0	0.00%	$0	0.00%	$0	0.00%
Dividends to Stockholders	($6,700,000)	(2.82)%	$0	0.00%	($20,000)	(1.38)%	$0	0.00%
Change in Treasury Stock	$0	0.00%	$0	0.00%	$0	0.00%	$0	0.00%
Aggregate Write-ins for Gains and Losses in Surplus	$4,094,619	1.72%	$0	0.00%	$0	0.00%	$0	0.00%
Net Change - Policyholder Surplus	$14,788,395	6.21%	($4,271,514)	(3.53)%	$54,128	3.74%	$145,713	2.35%
POLICYHOLDER SURPLUS - ENDING (See Sec. 5, B.6, B.7, C.9, C.11)	$67,686,913	28.44%	$25,586,475	21.17%	$907,607	62.65%	$739,705	11.92%

B.3 Income Statement - By Individual Underwriter

	TITLE IC AMERICA		TITLE RESOURCES		TITLEDGE		TRANSNATION	
REVENUE	Company Value	% Total Oper. Inc.	Company Value	% Total Oper. Inc.	Company Value	% Total Oper. Inc.	Company Value	% Total Oper. Inc.
Premiums Written - Direct	$0	0.00%	$0	0.00%	$78,917	45.28%	$69,584,981	23.23%
Premiums Written - Non-Affiliated Agency	$11,954,125	102.93%	$64,857,278	62.90%	$102,655	58.90%	$124,240,351	41.47%
Premiums Written - Affiliated Agency	$0	0.00%	$38,990,484	37.81%	$0	0.00%	$81,004,543	27.04%
Premiums - Reinsurance Assumed	$0	0.00%	$14,000	0.01%	$0	0.00%	$2,489,948	0.83%
Premiums - Reinsurance Ceded	($57,189)	(0.49)%	($231,897)	(0.22)%	$0	0.00%	($712,263)	(0.24)%
Net Premiums Written *(See Sec. 5, B.4)*	$11,896,936	102.43%	$103,629,865	100.50%	$181,572	104.17%	$276,607,560	92.33%
Net Premiums Earned	$11,614,622	100.00%	$103,117,424	100.00%	$174,297	100.00%	$257,711,742	86.02%
PLUS:								
Title Examinations	$0	0.00%	$0	0.00%	$0	0.00%	$5,442,798	1.82%
Searches & Abstracts	$0	0.00%	$0	0.00%	$0	0.00%	$19,124	0.01%
Surveys	$0	0.00%	$0	0.00%	$0	0.00%	$565	0.00%
Escrow & Settlement Fees	$0	0.00%	$0	0.00%	$0	0.00%	$31,199,507	10.41%
Other Service Charges	($428)	0.00%	$0	0.00%	$0	0.00%	$5,216,091	1.74%
Other Operating Income	$0	0.00%	$0	0.00%	$0	0.00%	$0	0.00%
Total Operating Income *(See Sec. 5, A.2, A.3, A.5)*	$11,614,194	100.00%	$103,117,424	100.00%	$174,297	100.00%	$299,589,827	100.00%
LESS:								
Amounts Retained By Agents *(See Sec. 5, B.9)*	$10,137,288		$89,704,496		$153,755		$178,625,661	
NET OPERATING REVENUE	$1,476,906		$13,412,928		$20,542		$120,964,166	

	Company Value	% Net Oper. Rev.	Company Value	% Net Oper. Rev.	Company Value	% Net Oper. Rev.	Company Value	% Net Oper. Rev.
OPERATING EXPENSE								
Total Personnel Costs	$760,533	51.50%	$2,372,743	17.69%	$0	0.00%	$87,226,312	72.11%
Production Services	($3,279)	(0.22)%	$0	0.00%	$0	0.00%	$1,699,202	1.40%
Advertising	$16,940	1.15%	$0	0.00%	$0	0.00%	$1,181,891	0.98%
Boards, Bureaus & Associations	$7,812	0.53%	$41,748	0.31%	$0	0.00%	$74,207	0.06%
Title Plant Rent & Maintenance	$1,626	0.11%	$7,383	0.06%	$0	0.00%	$2,169,230	1.79%
Claim Adjustment Services	$0	0.00%	$0	0.00%	$3,000	14.60%	$0	0.00%
Amount Charged Off, Net	$19,931	1.35%	$3,547	0.03%	$0	0.00%	$428,908	0.35%
Marketing & Promotional Expense	$6,397	0.43%	$348,414	2.60%	$0	0.00%	$546,597	0.45%
Insurance	$25,897	1.75%	$0	0.00%	$933	4.54%	$725,268	0.60%
Directors' Fees	$9,115	0.62%	$0	0.00%	$0	0.00%	$256,459	0.21%
Travel & Related Expenses	$44,897	3.04%	$146,723	1.09%	$0	0.00%	$2,077,183	1.72%
Rent and Rent Items	$46,845	3.17%	$146,379	1.09%	$0	0.00%	$12,479,005	10.32%
Equipment	$77,676	5.26%	$253,521	1.89%	$0	0.00%	$5,547,702	4.59%
Cost/Depreciation, EDP Equipment & Software	$136,715	9.26%	$12,173	0.09%	$0	0.00%	$6,223,483	5.14%
Print, Stationery, etc.	$17,289	1.17%	$158,800	1.18%	$0	0.00%	$1,652,352	1.37%
Postage, Telephone, Express	$23,453	1.59%	$83,620	0.62%	$0	0.00%	$6,271,662	5.18%
Legal & Auditing	$181,012	12.26%	$211,632	1.58%	$6,300	30.67%	$2,333,124	1.93%
Taxes, Licenses & Fees	$107,459	7.28%	$1,322,571	9.86%	$28,457	138.53%	$3,357,313	2.78%
Real Estate Expenses	$0	0.00%	$1,053	0.01%	$0	0.00%	$0	0.00%
Real Estate Taxes	$0	0.00%	$0	0.00%	$0	0.00%	$0	0.00%
Miscellaneous	$11,869	0.80%	$61,476	0.46%	$0	0.00%	$349,636	0.29%
Other Operating Expense Incurred	$1,492,187	101.03%	$5,171,783	38.56%	$38,690	188.35%	$134,599,534	111.27%
TOTAL OPERATING EXPENSE INCURRED (AGENT RETENTION + OTHER OPERATING EXPENSE INCURRED)	$11,629,475	--	$94,876,279	--	$192,445	--	$313,225,195	--
Aggregate Write-ins for Operating Deductions	$0	0.00%	$0	0.00%	$0	0.00%	$0	0.00%
Operating Profit (Loss) Before Losses *(See Sec. 5, A.7)*	($15,281)	(1.03)%	$8,241,145	61.44%	($18,148)	(88.35)%	($13,635,368)	(11.27)%
Losses & Loss Adjustment Expense Incurred *(See Sec. 5, C.2 - C.7)*								
Direct Operations *(See Sec. 5, C.7)*	$0	0.00%	$0	0.00%	$0	0.00%	$14,317,146	11.84%
Agency Operations *(See Sec. 5, C.7)*	$211,989	14.35%	$2,723,051	20.30%	$0	0.00%	$21,755,938	17.99%
NET OPERATING GAIN (LOSS) *(See Sec. 5, A.10)*	($227,270)	(15.39)%	$5,518,094	41.14%	($18,148)	(88.35)%	($49,708,452)	(41.09)%

	Company Value	% Total Assets	Company Value	% Total Assets	Company Value	% Total Assets	Company Value	% Total Assets
INVESTMENT INCOME								
Net Investment Income Earned *(See Sec. 5, A.8)*	$638,482	4.14%	$1,697,987	4.24%	$28,862	3.68%	$6,656,185	4.17%
Net Realized Capital Gains (Losses) less Capital Gains Tax	$1,835	0.01%	$0	0.00%	$0	0.00%	$494,234	0.31%
NET INVESTMENT GAIN (LOSS) *(See Sec. 5, A.9)*	$640,317	4.15%	$1,697,987	4.24%	$28,862	3.68%	$7,150,419	4.48%

	Company Value	% Total Assets	Company Value	% Total Assets	Company Value	% Total Assets	Company Value	% Total Assets
OTHER INCOME								
Other Income (Loss)	$0	0.00%	$66	0.00%	$0	0.00%	$0	0.00%
Net Income Before Taxes *(See Sec. 5, A.11)*	$413,047	2.68%	$7,216,147	18.01%	$10,714	1.37%	($42,558,033)	(26.67)%
Federal & Foreign Income Taxes Incurred	$64,533	0.42%	$2,568,080	6.41%	$1,589	0.20%	($13,030,817)	(8.17)%
NET INCOME *(See Sec. 5, A.12)*	$348,514	2.26%	$4,648,067	11.60%	$9,125	1.16%	($29,527,216)	(18.50)%

	Company Value	% Total Assets	Company Value	% Total Assets	Company Value	% Total Assets	Company Value	% Total Assets
CAPITAL AND SURPLUS ACCOUNT								
POLICYHOLDER SURPLUS - BEGINNING	$9,145,238	59.33%	$27,728,428	69.22%	$0	0.00%	$62,836,418	39.38%
Net Income	$348,514	2.26%	$4,648,067	11.60%	$9,125	1.16%	($29,527,216)	(18.50)%
Change in Net Unrealized Capital Gains (Losses) less Capital Gains Tax	$0	0.00%	$0	0.00%	$0	0.00%	($3,500,862)	(2.19)%
Change in Net Unrealized Foreign Exchange Capital Gain (Loss)	$0	0.00%	$0	0.00%	$0	0.00%	$0	0.00%
Change in Net Deferred Income Tax	($810,652)	(5.26)%	$56,837	0.14%	$0	0.00%	$5,360,616	3.36%
Change in Nonadmitted Assets	$839,173	5.44%	($89,172)	(0.22)%	$0	0.00%	($1,662,200)	(1.04)%
Change in Provision for Unauthorized Reinsurance	$0	0.00%	$0	0.00%	$0	0.00%	$0	0.00%
Change in Supplemental Reserves	$359,155	2.33%	$0	0.00%	($6,040)	(0.77)%	($866,620)	(0.54)%
Change in Surplus Notes	$0	0.00%	$0	0.00%	$0	0.00%	$0	0.00%
Cumulative Effect of Changes in Accounting Principles	$1,785,146	11.58%	$0	0.00%	$0	0.00%	$0	0.00%
Capital Changes	$0	0.00%	$0	0.00%	$750,000	95.75%	$0	0.00%
Surplus Adjustments	$0	0.00%	$0	0.00%	$0	0.00%	$0	0.00%
Dividends to Stockholders	$0	0.00%	($6,632,552)	(16.56)%	$0	0.00%	($6,250,000)	(3.92)%
Change in Treasury Stock	$0	0.00%	$0	0.00%	$0	0.00%	$0	0.00%
Aggregate Write-ins for Gains and Losses in Surplus	$0	0.00%	$0	0.00%	$0	0.00%	($4,055,354)	(2.54)%
Net Change - Policyholder Surplus	$2,521,337	16.36%	($2,016,824)	(5.03)%	$753,085	96.14%	($40,501,636)	(25.38)%
POLICYHOLDER SURPLUS - ENDING *(See Sec. 5, B.6, B.7, C.9, C.11)*	$11,666,575	75.69%	$25,711,604	64.18%	$753,085	96.14%	$22,334,782	14.00%

B.3 Income Statement - By Individual Underwriter

	TRANSUNION NATIONAL		TRANSUNION TIC		UNITED CAPITAL		UNITED GENERAL	
REVENUE	Company Value	% Total Oper. Inc.	Company Value	% Total Oper. Inc.	Company Value	% Total Oper. Inc.	Company Value	% Total Oper. Inc.
Premiums Written - Direct	$109,890	3.02%	$882,460	56.81%	$2,264,749	3.67%	$20,969,887	6.37%
Premiums Written - Non-Affiliated Agency	$2,344,872	64.48%	$0	0.00%	$0	0.00%	$297,148,060	90.26%
Premiums Written - Affiliated Agency	$1,458,631	40.11%	$0	0.00%	$59,156,995	95.77%	$18,484,272	5.61%
Premiums - Reinsurance Assumed	$0	0.00%	$0	0.00%	$0	0.00%	$6,434,963	1.95%
Premiums - Reinsurance Ceded	($152,887)	(4.20)%	$0	0.00%	$0	0.00%	($61,050)	(0.02)%
Net Premiums Written (See Sec. 5, B.4)	$3,760,506	103.41%	$882,460	56.81%	$61,421,744	99.44%	$342,976,132	104.19%
Net Premiums Earned	$3,631,141	99.85%	$1,517,626	97.70%	$61,872,009	100.17%	$324,795,874	98.66%
PLUS:								
Title Examinations	$5,442	0.15%	$35,695	2.30%	$10,190	0.02%	$0	0.00%
Searches & Abstracts	$0	0.00%	$0	0.00%	$0	0.00%	$458,818	0.14%
Surveys	$0	0.00%	$0	0.00%	$0	0.00%	$0	0.00%
Escrow & Settlement Fees	$0	0.00%	$0	0.00%	$0	0.00%	$4,250,504	1.29%
Other Service Charges	$0	0.00%	$0	0.00%	($113,597)	(0.18)%	$1,545,452	0.47%
Other Operating Income	$0	0.00%	$0	0.00%	$0	0.00%	($1,854,364)	(0.56)%
Total Operating Income (See Sec. 5, A.2, A.3, A.5)	$3,636,583	100.00%	$1,553,321	100.00%	$61,768,602	100.00%	$329,196,284	100.00%
LESS:								
Amounts Retained By Agents (See Sec. 5, B.9)	$2,660,897		$0		$52,866,551		$248,281,918	
NET OPERATING REVENUE	$975,686		$1,553,321		$8,902,051		$80,914,366	
OPERATING EXPENSE	Company Value	% Net Oper. Rev.	Company Value	% Net Oper. Rev.	Company Value	% Net Oper. Rev.	Company Value	% Net Oper. Rev.
Total Personnel Costs	$623,547	63.91%	$1,021,841	65.78%	$932,869	10.48%	$50,548,074	62.47%
Production Services	($271)	(0.03)%	$87,981	5.66%	$433,705	4.87%	$2,932,161	3.62%
Advertising	$0	0.00%	$298	0.02%	$99	0.00%	$887,066	1.10%
Boards, Bureaus & Associations	$12,020	1.23%	$14,140	0.91%	$12,683	0.14%	$206,315	0.25%
Title Plant Rent & Maintenance	$0	0.00%	$0	0.00%	$506	0.01%	$156,688	0.19%
Claim Adjustment Services	$0	0.00%	$0	0.00%	$0	0.00%	$0	0.00%
Amount Charged Off, Net	$0	0.00%	($16,488)	(1.06)%	$3,802	0.04%	$375,979	0.46%
Marketing & Promotional Expense	$1,207	0.12%	$0	0.00%	$0	0.00%	$391,881	0.48%
Insurance	$500	0.05%	$0	0.00%	$0	0.00%	$186,937	0.23%
Directors' Fees	$0	0.00%	$0	0.00%	$0	0.00%	$0	0.00%
Travel & Related Expenses	$75,576	7.75%	$24,920	1.60%	$2,600	0.03%	$3,131,280	3.87%
Rent and Rent Items	$62,612	6.42%	$207,419	13.35%	$15,415	0.17%	$5,652,481	6.99%
Equipment	$13,092	1.34%	$4,194	0.27%	$22,622	0.25%	$1,045,468	1.29%
Cost/Depreciation, EDP Equipment & Software	$0	0.00%	$0	0.00%	$12,558	0.14%	$1,318,883	1.63%
Print, Stationery, etc.	$14,452	1.48%	$4,064	0.26%	$55,812	0.63%	$781,526	0.97%
Postage, Telephone, Express	$19,259	1.97%	$76,973	4.96%	$23,684	0.27%	$1,654,927	2.05%
Legal & Auditing	$72,667	7.45%	$83,441	5.37%	$573,287	6.44%	$1,141,222	1.41%
Taxes, Licenses & Fees	$153,134	15.70%	$34,361	2.21%	$449,213	5.05%	$6,525,614	8.06%
Real Estate Expenses	$0	0.00%	$0	0.00%	$0	0.00%	$0	0.00%
Real Estate Taxes	$0	0.00%	$0	0.00%	$0	0.00%	$0	0.00%
Miscellaneous	$13,696	1.40%	$8,086	0.52%	$1,448,230	16.27%	$666,602	0.82%
Other Operating Expense Incurred	$1,061,491	108.79%	$1,551,230	99.87%	$3,987,085	44.79%	$77,603,104	95.91%
TOTAL OPERATING EXPENSE INCURRED (AGENT RETENTION + OTHER OPERATING EXPENSE INCURRED)	$3,722,388	--	$1,551,230	--	$56,853,636	--	$325,885,022	--
Aggregate Write-ins for Operating Deductions	$0	0.00%	$0	0.00%	$0	0.00%	$0	0.00%
Operating Profit (Loss) Before Losses (See Sec. 5, A.7)	($85,805)	(8.79)%	$2,091	0.13%	$4,914,966	55.21%	$3,311,262	4.09%
Losses & Loss Adjustment Expense Incurred (See Sec. 5, C.2 - C.7)								
Direct Operations (See Sec. 5, C.7)	$0	0.00%	$96,031	6.18%	$0	0.00%	$1,388,675	1.72%
Agency Operations (See Sec. 5, C.7)	$1,156,258	118.51%	($15,389)	(0.99)%	$8,465,810	95.10%	$25,856,042	31.95%
NET OPERATING GAIN (LOSS) (See Sec. 5, A.10)	($1,242,063)	(127.30)%	($78,551)	(5.06)%	($3,550,844)	(39.89)%	($23,933,455)	(29.58)%
INVESTMENT INCOME	Company Value	% Total Assets	Company Value	% Total Assets	Company Value	% Total Assets	Company Value	% Total Assets
Net Investment Income Earned (See Sec. 5, A.8)	$650,881	4.18%	$304,066	2.82%	$2,332,794	4.56%	$3,724,034	3.13%
Net Realized Capital Gains (Losses) less Capital Gains Tax	$0	0.00%	$10,850	0.10%	($108,525)	(0.21)%	($818,526)	(0.69)%
NET INVESTMENT GAIN (LOSS) (See Sec. 5, A.9)	$650,881	4.18%	$314,916	2.92%	$2,224,269	4.34%	$2,905,508	2.44%
OTHER INCOME	Company Value	% Total Assets	Company Value	% Total Assets	Company Value	% Total Assets	Company Value	% Total Assets
Other Income (Loss)	$0	0.00%	$0	0.00%	$0	0.00%	$0	0.00%
Net Income Before Taxes (See Sec. 5, A.11)	($591,182)	(3.80)%	$236,365	2.19%	($1,326,575)	(2.59)%	($21,027,947)	(17.66)%
Federal & Foreign Income Taxes Incurred	($193,838)	(1.24)%	($63,016)	(0.59)%	($384,317)	(0.75)%	($5,885,149)	(4.94)%
NET INCOME (See Sec. 5, A.12)	($397,344)	(2.55)%	$299,381	2.78%	($942,258)	(1.84)%	($15,142,798)	(12.71)%
CAPITAL AND SURPLUS ACCOUNT	Company Value	% Total Assets	Company Value	% Total Assets	Company Value	% Total Assets	Company Value	% Total Assets
POLICYHOLDER SURPLUS - BEGINNING	$10,488,021	67.34%	$3,637,326	33.78%	$24,748,274	48.34%	$23,927,855	20.09%
Net Income	($397,344)	(2.55)%	$299,381	2.78%	($942,258)	(1.84)%	($15,142,798)	(12.71)%
Change in Net Unrealized Capital Gains (Losses) less Capital Gains Tax	($19,814)	(0.13)%	$0	0.00%	($27,722)	(0.05)%	($840,698)	(0.71)%
Change in Net Unrealized Foreign Exchange Capital Gain (Loss)	$0	0.00%	$0	0.00%	$0	0.00%	$0	0.00%
Change in Net Deferred Income Tax	$6,675	0.04%	($147,308)	(1.37)%	($1,735,907)	(3.39)%	$3,450,832	2.90%
Change in Nonadmitted Assets	($29,004)	(0.19)%	$91,444	0.85%	$725,155	1.42%	($3,420,921)	(2.87)%
Change in Provision for Unauthorized Reinsurance	$0	0.00%	$0	0.00%	$0	0.00%	$0	0.00%
Change in Supplemental Reserves	$0	0.00%	$0	0.00%	$0	0.00%	$0	0.00%
Change in Surplus Notes	$0	0.00%	$0	0.00%	$0	0.00%	$0	0.00%
Cumulative Effect of Changes in Accounting Principles	$0	0.00%	$0	0.00%	$0	0.00%	$0	0.00%
Capital Changes	$0	0.00%	$0	0.00%	$0	0.00%	$0	0.00%
Surplus Adjustments	$0	0.00%	$0	0.00%	$0	0.00%	$20,000,000	16.79%
Dividends to Stockholders	$0	0.00%	$0	0.00%	$0	0.00%	$0	0.00%
Change in Treasury Stock	$0	0.00%	$0	0.00%	$0	0.00%	$0	0.00%
Aggregate Write-ins for Gains and Losses in Surplus	$0	0.00%	$0	0.00%	$0	0.00%	$0	0.00%
Net Change - Policyholder Surplus	($439,489)	(2.82)%	$243,516	2.26%	($1,980,732)	(3.87)%	$4,046,417	3.40%
POLICYHOLDER SURPLUS - ENDING (See Sec. 5, B.6, B.7, C.9, C.11)	$10,048,532	64.51%	$3,880,842	36.04%	$22,767,542	44.48%	$27,974,272	23.49%

2

B.3 Income Statement - By Individual Underwriter

	WASHINGTON TIC		WESTCOR		WESTERN NATIONAL	
REVENUE	Company Value	% Total Oper. Inc.	Company Value	% Total Oper. Inc.	Company Value	% Total Oper. Inc.
Premiums Written - Direct	$172,102	1.13%	$288,117	0.55%	$0	0.00%
Premiums Written - Non-Affiliated Agency	$12,559,065	82.69%	$21,121,593	40.64%	$8,580	1.89%
Premiums Written - Affiliated Agency	$2,893,006	19.05%	$31,217,018	60.07%	$362,141	79.90%
Premiums - Reinsurance Assumed	$0	0.00%	$3,161	0.01%	$0	0.00%
Premiums - Reinsurance Ceded	($295,955)	(1.95)%	($657,562)	(1.27)%	$0	0.00%
Net Premiums Written (See Sec. 5, B.4)	$15,328,218	100.93%	$51,972,327	100.01%	$370,721	81.79%
Net Premiums Earned	$15,135,803	99.66%	$50,819,516	97.79%	$453,266	100.00%
PLUS:						
Title Examinations	$0	0.00%	$0	0.00%	$0	0.00%
Searches & Abstracts	$0	0.00%	$1,037,537	2.00%	$0	0.00%
Surveys	$0	0.00%	$0	0.00%	$0	0.00%
Escrow & Settlement Fees	$51,790	0.34%	$42,560	0.08%	$0	0.00%
Other Service Charges	$0	0.00%	$68,061	0.13%	$0	0.00%
Other Operating Income	$0	0.00%	$0	0.00%	$0	0.00%
Total Operating Income (See Sec. 5, A.2, A.3, A.5)	$15,187,593	100.00%	$51,967,674	100.00%	$453,266	100.00%
LESS:						
Amounts Retained By Agents (See Sec. 5, B.9)	$13,090,616		$43,363,579		$342,509	
NET OPERATING REVENUE	$2,096,977		$8,604,095		$110,757	
OPERATING EXPENSE	Company Value	% Net Oper. Rev.	Company Value	% Net Oper. Rev.	Company Value	% Net Oper. Rev.
Total Personnel Costs	$1,145,313	54.62%	$5,709,293	66.36%	$32,082	28.97%
Production Services	($250,507)	(11.95)%	$208,548	2.42%	$0	0.00%
Advertising	$1,608	0.08%	$19,508	0.23%	$0	0.00%
Boards, Bureaus & Associations	$65,203	3.11%	$82,012	0.95%	$0	0.00%
Title Plant Rent & Maintenance	$0	0.00%	$240,368	2.79%	$0	0.00%
Claim Adjustment Services	$0	0.00%	$0	0.00%	$0	0.00%
Amount Charged Off, Net	$0	0.00%	$128,850	1.50%	$0	0.00%
Marketing & Promotional Expense	$245,979	11.73%	$136,979	1.59%	$0	0.00%
Insurance	$3,952	0.19%	$139,182	1.62%	$0	0.00%
Directors' Fees	$0	0.00%	$0	0.00%	$0	0.00%
Travel & Related Expenses	$12,144	0.58%	$292,573	3.40%	$0	0.00%
Rent and Rent Items	$38,472	1.83%	$328,346	3.82%	$2,068	1.87%
Equipment	$9,147	0.44%	$98,478	1.14%	$410	0.37%
Cost/Depreciation, EDP Equipment & Software	$13,245	0.63%	$73,938	0.86%	$0	0.00%
Print, Stationery, etc.	$36,337	1.73%	$110,553	1.28%	$558	0.50%
Postage, Telephone, Express	$9,475	0.45%	$284,634	3.31%	$0	0.00%
Legal & Auditing	$201,322	9.60%	$237,599	2.76%	$33,568	30.31%
Taxes, Licenses & Fees	$443,079	21.13%	$841,910	9.78%	$1,844	1.66%
Real Estate Expenses	$0	0.00%	$0	0.00%	$0	0.00%
Real Estate Taxes	$0	0.00%	$0	0.00%	$197	0.18%
Miscellaneous	$27,897	1.33%	$58,111	0.68%	$0	0.00%
Other Operating Expense Incurred	$2,002,666	95.50%	$8,990,882	104.50%	$70,727	63.86%
TOTAL OPERATING EXPENSE INCURRED (AGENT RETENTION + OTHER OPERATING EXPENSE INCURRED)	$15,093,282	--	$52,354,461	--	$413,236	--
Aggregate Write-ins for Operating Deductions	$0	0.00%	$0	0.00%	$0	0.00%
Operating Profit (Loss) Before Losses (See Sec. 5, A.7)	$94,311	4.50%	($386,787)	(4.50)%	$40,030	36.14%
Losses & Loss Adjustment Expense Incurred (See Sec. 5, C.2 - C.7)						
Direct Operations (See Sec. 5, C.7)	$22,599	1.08%	$156,272	1.82%	$0	0.00%
Agency Operations (See Sec. 5, C.7)	$411,321	19.61%	$755,764	8.78%	($65,757)	(59.37)%
NET OPERATING GAIN (LOSS) (See Sec. 5, A.10)	($339,609)	(16.20)%	($1,298,823)	(15.10)%	$105,787	95.51%
INVESTMENT INCOME	Company Value	% Total Assets	Company Value	% Total Assets	Company Value	% Total Assets
Net Investment Income Earned (See Sec. 5, A.8)	$142,825	3.62%	$725,026	3.01%	$120,546	2.54%
Net Realized Capital Gains (Losses) less Capital Gains Tax	$1,299	0.03%	($867,387)	(3.60)%	$0	0.00%
NET INVESTMENT GAIN (LOSS) (See Sec. 5, A.9)	$144,124	3.65%	($142,361)	(0.59)%	$120,546	2.54%
OTHER INCOME	Company Value	% Total Assets	Company Value	% Total Assets	Company Value	% Total Assets
Other Income (Loss)	$0	0.00%	$0	0.00%	$0	0.00%
Net Income Before Taxes (See Sec. 5, A.11)	($195,485)	(4.96)%	($1,441,184)	(5.99)%	$226,333	4.77%
Federal & Foreign Income Taxes Incurred	($85,085)	(2.16)%	$29,995	0.12%	$34,220	0.72%
NET INCOME (See Sec. 5, A.12)	($110,400)	(2.80)%	($1,471,179)	(6.11)%	$192,113	4.05%
CAPITAL AND SURPLUS ACCOUNT	Company Value	% Total Assets	Company Value	% Total Assets	Company Value	% Total Assets
POLICYHOLDER SURPLUS - BEGINNING	$802,405	20.34%	$11,273,356	46.85%	$3,182,028	67.13%
Net Income	($110,400)	(2.80)%	($1,471,179)	(6.11)%	$192,113	4.05%
Change in Net Unrealized Capital Gains (Losses) less Capital Gains Tax	$0	0.00%	($653,937)	(2.72)%	$0	0.00%
Change in Net Unrealized Foreign Exchange Capital Gain (Loss)	$0	0.00%	$0	0.00%	$0	0.00%
Change in Net Deferred Income Tax	$0	0.00%	$152,398	0.63%	($21,509)	(0.45)%
Change in Nonadmitted Assets	($1,427)	(0.04)%	($638,153)	(2.65)%	$5,920	0.12%
Change in Provision for Unauthorized Reinsurance	$0	0.00%	$0	0.00%	$0	0.00%
Change in Supplemental Reserves	$185,919	4.71%	$0	0.00%	$0	0.00%
Change in Surplus Notes	$0	0.00%	$0	0.00%	$0	0.00%
Cumulative Effect of Changes in Accounting Principles	$0	0.00%	$0	0.00%	$0	0.00%
Capital Changes	$0	0.00%	$0	0.00%	$0	0.00%
Surplus Adjustments	$0	0.00%	$0	0.00%	$0	0.00%
Dividends to Stockholders	$0	0.00%	$0	0.00%	$0	0.00%
Change in Treasury Stock	$0	0.00%	$0	0.00%	$0	0.00%
Aggregate Write-ins for Gains and Losses in Surplus	$0	0.00%	$0	0.00%	$0	0.00%
Net Change - Policyholder Surplus	$74,092	1.88%	($2,610,872)	(10.85)%	$176,524	3.72%
POLICYHOLDER SURPLUS - ENDING (See Sec. 5, B.6, B.7, C.9, C.11)	$876,497	22.22%	$8,662,484	36.00%	$3,358,552	70.85%

C.1 STATEMENT OF CASH FLOW
- INDUSTRY COMPOSITE

2

C.1   Statement of Cash Flow - Industry Composite

BEGINNING CASH, CASH EQUIVALENTS & SHORT-TERM INVESTMENTS	$2,235,920,111	

CASH FROM OPERATIONS

	Composite Value	%
Premiums Collected Net of Reinsurance	$14,211,411,713	88.28%
Net Investment Income	$627,629,304	3.90%
Miscellaneous Income	$1,258,623,157	7.82%
Total	$16,097,664,174	100.00%
Benefit and Loss Related Payments	$1,094,316,194	7.12%
Net Transfers to Separate, Segregated Accounts & Protected Cell Accounts	$60,093	0.00%
Commissions, Expenses Paid and Aggregate Write-Ins for Deductions	$14,026,846,857	91.27%
Dividends Paid to Policyholders	$0	0.00%
Federal and Foreign Income Taxes Paid (Recovered), Net Tax on Capital Gains (Losses)	$247,286,649	1.61%
Total	$15,368,509,793	100.00%
NET CASH FROM OPERATIONS	$729,154,381	

CASH FROM INVESTMENTS

	Composite Value	%
Proceeds from Investments Sold, Matured or Repaid:		
Bonds	$4,835,890,331	79.59%
Stocks	$1,154,776,550	19.01%
Mortgage Loans	$7,830,425	0.13%
Real Estate	$18,403,590	0.30%
Other Invested Assets	$50,479,869	0.83%
Net Gains or (Losses) on Cash, Cash Equivalents & Short-Term Investments	$272,430	0.00%
Miscellaneous Proceeds	$8,224,656	0.14%
Total Investment Proceeds	$6,075,877,851	100.00%
Cost of Investments Acquired (Long-Term Only):		
Bonds	$4,801,484,437	78.46%
Stocks	$1,123,852,645	18.37%
Mortgage Loans	$13,506,238	0.22%
Real Estate	$6,473,687	0.11%
Other Invested Assets	$161,377,730	2.64%
Miscellaneous Applications	$12,723,006	0.21%
Total Investments Acquired	$6,119,417,743	100.00%
Net Increase (Decrease) in Contract Loans and Premium Notes	$0	
NET CASH FROM INVESTMENTS	($43,539,892)	

CASH FROM FINANCING AND MISCELLANEOUS SOURCES

	Composite Value
Cash Provided (Applied):	
Surplus Notes, Capital Notes	$1,700,000
Capital and paid in Surplus, Less Treasury Stock	$60,365,797
Borrowed Funds	($5,298,835)
Net Deposits on Deposit-Type Contracts & Other Insurance Liabilities	$0
Dividends to Stockholders	$567,784,307
Other Cash Provided (Applied)	($600,798,125)
NET CASH FROM FINANCING AND MISCELLANEOUS SOURCES	($1,111,815,470)

NET CHANGE IN CASH, CASH EQUIVALENTS & SHORT-TERM INVESTMENTS	($426,200,981)
ENDING CASH, CASH EQUIVALENTS & SHORT-TERM INVESTMENTS	$1,809,719,130

CONSOLIDATED ELIMINATIONS

Dividends to Parent, Subsidiary or Affiliated Title Underwriter

	DIVIDENDS
CHICAGO / FIDELITY	$250,244,936
FIRST AMERICAN	$20,938,663
OLD REPUBLIC	$900,000
STEWART	$6,000,000
TOTAL	$278,083,599

These adjustments remove the reported dividend contributions to parent, subsidiary or affiliated Title underwriters, which are otherwise directly included in the composite data.

Some eliminations cannot be made because the shares of one underwriter, ultimately owned by another underwriter, are held by a subsidiary of the underwriter parent for which data is unavailable.

C.2 STATEMENT OF CASH FLOW - BY NAIC GROUP

2

C.2 Statement of Cash Flow - By NAIC Group

	ATTORNEYS' TITLE		CATIC		CHICAGO / FIDELITY		FIRST AMERICAN	
BEGINNING CASH, CASH EQUIVALENTS & SHORT-TERM INVESTMENTS	$19,974,282		$6,836,936		$1,114,664,275		$643,061,637	
CASH FROM OPERATIONS	Group Value	%	Group Value	%	Group Value	%	Group Value	%
Premiums Collected Net of Reinsurance	$377,683,358	93.89%	$70,480,004	93.63%	$3,766,645,673	83.00%	$4,160,593,352	87.10%
Net Investment Income	$8,258,491	2.05%	$2,785,063	3.70%	$244,590,423	5.39%	$207,214,517	4.34%
Miscellaneous Income	$16,298,820	4.05%	$2,013,646	2.67%	$527,131,628	11.62%	$409,083,703	8.56%
Total	$402,240,669	100.00%	$75,278,713	100.00%	$4,538,367,724	100.00%	$4,776,891,572	100.00%
Benefit and Loss Related Payments	$31,344,459	7.76%	$5,054,716	6.86%	$361,191,871	8.61%	$284,087,118	6.25%
Net Transfers to Separate, Segregated Accounts & Protected Cell Accounts	$0	0.00%	$0	0.00%	$0	0.00%	$0	0.00%
Commissions, Expenses Paid and Aggregate Write-Ins for Deductions	$374,059,309	92.56%	$68,366,119	92.77%	$3,766,017,547	89.76%	$4,145,679,910	91.23%
Dividends Paid to Policyholders	$0	0.00%	$0	0.00%	$0	0.00%	$0	0.00%
Federal and Foreign Income Taxes Paid (Recovered), Net Tax on Capital Gains (Losses)	($1,295,845)	(0.32)%	$276,902	0.38%	$68,538,645	1.63%	$114,335,277	2.52%
Total	$404,107,923	100.00%	$73,697,737	100.00%	$4,195,748,063	100.00%	$4,544,102,305	100.00%
NET CASH FROM OPERATIONS	($1,867,254)		$1,580,976		$342,619,661		$232,789,267	
CASH FROM INVESTMENTS	Group Value	%	Group Value	%	Group Value	%	Group Value	%
Proceeds from Investments Sold, Matured or Repaid:								
Bonds	$84,673,670	43.00%	$17,892,867	90.57%	$3,898,435,991	81.34%	$53,486,557	51.77%
Stocks	$110,695,243	56.21%	$1,495,253	7.57%	$836,183,210	17.45%	$36,785,536	35.60%
Mortgage Loans	$52,651	0.03%	$0	0.00%	$2,090,257	0.04%	$869,273	0.84%
Real Estate	$0	0.00%	$0	0.00%	$6,441,432	0.13%	$8,696,640	8.42%
Other Invested Assets	$719,444	0.37%	$367,069	1.86%	$44,405,929	0.93%	$3,194,003	3.09%
Net Gains or (Losses) on Cash, Cash Equivalents & Short-Term Investments	($6)	0.00%	$0	0.00%	$0	0.00%	$271,624	0.26%
Miscellaneous Proceeds	$785,072	0.40%	$0	0.00%	$5,173,539	0.11%	$17,755	0.02%
Total Investment Proceeds	$196,926,074	100.00%	$19,755,189	100.00%	$4,792,730,358	100.00%	$103,321,388	100.00%
Cost of Investments Acquired (Long-Term Only):								
Bonds	$75,571,394	42.36%	$21,760,087	91.00%	$3,882,620,863	81.44%	$85,774,743	59.82%
Stocks	$99,566,888	55.81%	$2,152,598	9.00%	$732,704,111	15.37%	$52,129,389	36.35%
Mortgage Loans	$206,032	0.12%	$0	0.00%	$7,072,232	0.15%	$903,111	0.63%
Real Estate	$1,945,847	1.09%	$0	0.00%	$1,637,201	0.03%	$1,522,273	1.06%
Other Invested Assets	$0	0.00%	$0	0.00%	$140,235,538	2.94%	$3,063,152	2.14%
Miscellaneous Applications	$1,117,876	0.63%	$0	0.00%	$3,197,070	0.07%	$1,250	0.00%
Total Investments Acquired	$178,408,037	100.00%	$23,912,685	100.00%	$4,767,467,015	100.00%	$143,393,918	100.00%
Net Increase (Decrease) in Contract Loans and Premium Notes	$0		$0		$0		$0	
NET CASH FROM INVESTMENTS	$18,518,037		($4,157,496)		$25,263,343		($40,072,530)	
CASH FROM FINANCING AND MISCELLANEOUS SOURCES	Group Value		Group Value		Group Value		Group Value	
Cash Provided (Applied):								
Surplus Notes, Capital Notes	$0		$0		$0		$0	
Capital and paid in Surplus, Less Treasury Stock	$0		$0		$50,000		$28,090,407	
Borrowed Funds	$0		$0		($51,855)		($3,608,862)	
Net Deposits on Deposit-Type Contracts & Other Insurance Liabilities	$0		$0		$0		$0	
Dividends to Stockholders	$3,950,000		$0		$345,200,000		$36,261,084	
Other Cash Provided (Applied)	($14,415,626)		$63,441		($363,897,614)		($247,720,290)	
NET CASH FROM FINANCING AND MISCELLANEOUS SOURCES	($18,365,626)		$63,441		($709,099,469)		($259,499,829)	
NET CHANGE IN CASH, CASH EQUIVALENTS & SHORT-TERM INVESTMENTS	($1,714,843)		($2,513,079)		($341,216,465)		($66,783,092)	
ENDING CASH, CASH EQUIVALENTS & SHORT-TERM INVESTMENTS	$18,259,439		$4,323,857		$773,447,810		$576,278,545	

C.2 Statement of Cash Flow - By NAIC Group

	INVESTORS		LAND AMERICA		OHIO FARMERS		OLD REPUBLIC	
BEGINNING CASH, CASH EQUIVALENTS & SHORT-TERM INVESTMENTS	$5,482,490		$144,820,399		$2,783,275		$26,714,440	
CASH FROM OPERATIONS	Group Value	%	Group Value	%	Group Value	%	Group Value	%
Premiums Collected Net of Reinsurance	$69,264,294	92.72%	$2,758,196,081	90.36%	$53,904,735	96.13%	$809,954,913	96.23%
Net Investment Income	$4,577,745	6.13%	$79,070,218	2.59%	$944,875	1.69%	$31,689,032	3.76%
Miscellaneous Income	$860,546	1.15%	$215,076,977	7.05%	$1,223,361	2.18%	$80,554	0.01%
Total	$74,702,585	100.00%	$3,052,343,276	100.00%	$56,072,971	100.00%	$841,724,499	100.00%
Benefit and Loss Related Payments	$10,881,767	15.69%	$199,744,394	6.75%	$1,807,376	3.33%	$66,094,718	8.00%
Net Transfers to Separate, Segregated Accounts & Protected Cell Accounts	$0	0.00%	$0	0.00%	$0	0.00%	$0	0.00%
Commissions, Expenses Paid and Aggregate Write-Ins for Deductions	$57,507,417	82.91%	$2,734,728,365	92.36%	$51,935,711	95.67%	$748,324,794	90.59%
Dividends Paid to Policyholders	$0	0.00%	$0	0.00%	$0	0.00%	$0	0.00%
Federal and Foreign Income Taxes Paid (Recovered), Net Tax on Capital Gains (Losses)	$969,403	1.40%	$26,580,969	0.90%	$541,160	1.00%	$11,636,631	1.41%
Total	$69,358,587	100.00%	$2,961,053,728	100.00%	$54,284,247	100.00%	$826,056,143	100.00%
NET CASH FROM OPERATIONS	$5,343,998		$91,289,548		$1,788,724		$15,668,356	
CASH FROM INVESTMENTS	Group Value	%	Group Value	%	Group Value	%	Group Value	%
Proceeds from Investments Sold, Matured or Repaid:								
Bonds	$24,864,250	84.42%	$538,570,341	79.82%	$444,366	64.16%	$71,305,727	95.14%
Stocks	$4,134,634	14.04%	$132,093,972	19.58%	$248,225	35.84%	$546,076	0.73%
Mortgage Loans	$219,283	0.74%	$1,401,115	0.21%	$0	0.00%	$421,499	0.56%
Real Estate	$33,561	0.11%	$0	0.00%	$0	0.00%	$2,671,245	3.56%
Other Invested Assets	$181,104	0.61%	$777,809	0.12%	$0	0.00%	$0	0.00%
Net Gains or (Losses) on Cash, Cash Equivalents & Short-Term Investments	$0	0.00%	$0	0.00%	$0	0.00%	$0	0.00%
Miscellaneous Proceeds	$19,446	0.07%	$1,863,157	0.28%	$0	0.00%	$0	0.00%
Total Investment Proceeds	$29,452,278	100.00%	$674,706,394	100.00%	$692,591	100.00%	$74,944,547	100.00%
Cost of Investments Acquired (Long-Term Only):								
Bonds	$15,977,833	75.10%	$498,385,124	72.75%	$3,348,435	98.76%	$47,262,742	68.93%
Stocks	$4,969,804	23.36%	$162,985,127	23.79%	$12,431	0.37%	$17,679,046	25.78%
Mortgage Loans	$0	0.00%	$0	0.00%	$0	0.00%	$741,381	1.08%
Real Estate	$8,500	0.04%	$655,800	0.10%	$29,750	0.88%	$381,921	0.56%
Other Invested Assets	$319,657	1.50%	$14,942,383	2.18%	$0	0.00%	$2,500,000	3.65%
Miscellaneous Applications	$0	0.00%	$8,102,718	1.18%	$0	0.00%	$0	0.00%
Total Investments Acquired	$21,275,794	100.00%	$685,071,152	100.00%	$3,390,616	100.00%	$68,565,090	100.00%
Net Increase (Decrease) in Contract Loans and Premium Notes	$0		$0		$0		$0	
NET CASH FROM INVESTMENTS	$8,176,484		($10,364,758)		($2,698,025)		$6,379,457	
CASH FROM FINANCING AND MISCELLANEOUS SOURCES	Group Value		Group Value		Group Value		Group Value	
Cash Provided (Applied):								
Surplus Notes, Capital Notes	$0		$0		$0		$0	
Capital and paid in Surplus, Less Treasury Stock	$0		$0		$0		$0	
Borrowed Funds	($9,552)		($1,519,291)		$0		($393,249)	
Net Deposits on Deposit-Type Contracts & Other Insurance Liabilities	$0		$0		$0		$0	
Dividends to Stockholders	$10,732,722		$126,250,000		$406,115		$30,000,000	
Other Cash Provided (Applied)	$1,361,930		$12,675,103		$839,297		$11,552,258	
NET CASH FROM FINANCING AND MISCELLANEOUS SOURCES	($9,380,344)		($115,094,188)		$433,182		($18,840,991)	
NET CHANGE IN CASH, CASH EQUIVALENTS & SHORT-TERM INVESTMENTS	$4,140,138		($34,169,398)		($476,119)		$3,206,822	
ENDING CASH, CASH EQUIVALENTS & SHORT-TERM INVESTMENTS	$9,622,628		$110,651,001		$2,307,156		$29,921,262	

C.2 Statement of Cash Flow - By NAIC Group

	RELIANT HOLDING		STEWART		TRANSUNION		UNAFFILIATED COMPANIES	
BEGINNING CASH, CASH EQUIVALENTS & SHORT-TERM INVESTMENTS	$962,841		$80,845,871		$16,326,097		$173,447,568	

CASH FROM OPERATIONS

	Group Value	%	Group Value	%	Group Value	%	Group Value	%
Premiums Collected Net of Reinsurance	$13,563,512	77.54%	$1,674,068,814	94.32%	$4,710,724	84.33%	$452,346,253	93.84%
Net Investment Income	$23,567	0.13%	$34,331,448	1.93%	$834,439	14.94%	$13,309,486	2.76%
Miscellaneous Income	$3,904,714	22.32%	$66,529,649	3.75%	$41,137	0.74%	$16,378,422	3.40%
Total	$17,491,793	100.00%	$1,774,929,911	100.00%	$5,586,300	100.00%	$482,034,161	100.00%
Benefit and Loss Related Payments	$3,253,655	14.46%	$114,671,035	6.57%	$1,322,560	22.07%	$14,862,525	3.18%
Net Transfers to Separate, Segregated Accounts & Protected Cell Accounts	$0	0.00%	$0	0.00%	$0	0.00%	$60,093	0.01%
Commissions, Expenses Paid and Aggregate Write-Ins for Deductions	$19,218,454	85.44%	$1,616,055,058	92.61%	$4,926,376	82.21%	$440,027,797	94.30%
Dividends Paid to Policyholders	$0	0.00%	$0	0.00%	$0	0.00%	$0	0.00%
Federal and Foreign Income Taxes Paid (Recovered), Net Tax on Capital Gains (Losses)	$21,747	0.10%	$14,239,022	0.82%	($256,854)	(4.29)%	$11,699,592	2.51%
Total	$22,493,856	100.00%	$1,744,965,115	100.00%	$5,992,082	100.00%	$466,650,007	100.00%
NET CASH FROM OPERATIONS	($5,002,063)		$29,964,796		($405,782)		$15,384,154	

CASH FROM INVESTMENTS

	Group Value	%	Group Value	%	Group Value	%	Group Value	%
Proceeds from Investments Sold, Matured or Repaid:								
Bonds	$4,130,450	92.86%	$107,616,945	78.60%	$3,643,000	67.71%	$30,826,167	84.24%
Stocks	$0	0.00%	$27,530,607	20.11%	$1,737,688	32.29%	$3,326,106	9.09%
Mortgage Loans	$0	0.00%	$406,579	0.30%	$0	0.00%	$2,369,768	6.48%
Real Estate	$0	0.00%	$560,712	0.41%	$0	0.00%	$0	0.00%
Other Invested Assets	$4,904	0.11%	$810,407	0.59%	$0	0.00%	$19,200	0.05%
Net Gains or (Losses) on Cash, Cash Equivalents & Short-Term Investments	$0	0.00%	$0	0.00%	$0	0.00%	$812	0.00%
Miscellaneous Proceeds	$312,712	7.03%	$0	0.00%	$0	0.00%	$52,975	0.14%
Total Investment Proceeds	$4,448,066	100.00%	$136,925,250	100.00%	$5,380,688	100.00%	$36,595,028	100.00%
Cost of Investments Acquired (Long-Term Only):								
Bonds	$3,343,686	99.76%	$143,273,199	77.07%	$3,635,411	28.20%	$20,530,920	79.58%
Stocks	$0	0.00%	$40,361,567	21.71%	$9,241,041	71.68%	$2,050,643	7.95%
Mortgage Loans	$0	0.00%	$2,222,505	1.20%	$0	0.00%	$2,360,977	9.15%
Real Estate	$0	0.00%	$32,395	0.02%	$15,000	0.12%	$245,000	0.95%
Other Invested Assets	$0	0.00%	$0	0.00%	$0	0.00%	$317,000	1.23%
Miscellaneous Applications	$8,083	0.24%	$0	0.00%	$0	0.00%	$296,009	1.15%
Total Investments Acquired	$3,351,769	100.00%	$185,889,666	100.00%	$12,891,452	100.00%	$25,800,549	100.00%
Net Increase (Decrease) in Contract Loans and Premium Notes	$0		$0		$0		$0	
NET CASH FROM INVESTMENTS	$1,096,297		($48,964,416)		($7,510,764)		$10,794,479	

CASH FROM FINANCING AND MISCELLANEOUS SOURCES

	Group Value	Group Value	Group Value	Group Value
Cash Provided (Applied):				
Surplus Notes, Capital Notes	$0	$0	$0	$1,700,000
Capital and paid in Surplus, Less Treasury Stock	$3,301,233	$21,283,384	$0	$7,640,773
Borrowed Funds	$0	($4,316)	$0	$288,290
Net Deposits on Deposit-Type Contracts & Other Insurance Liabilities	$0	$0	$0	$0
Dividends to Stockholders	$0	$3,225,000	$0	$11,759,386
Other Cash Provided (Applied)	$719,842	$156,968	$1,436,425	($3,569,859)
NET CASH FROM FINANCING AND MISCELLANEOUS SOURCES	$4,021,075	$18,211,036	$1,436,425	($5,700,182)

NET CHANGE IN CASH, CASH EQUIVALENTS & SHORT-TERM INVESTMENTS	$115,309	($788,584)	($6,480,121)	$20,478,451
ENDING CASH, CASH EQUIVALENTS & SHORT-TERM INVESTMENTS	$1,078,150	$80,057,287	$9,845,976	$193,926,019

C.3 Statement of Cash Flow - By Individual Underwriter

2

C.3 Statement of Cash Flow - By Individual Underwriter

	ALAMO		ALLIANCE		ALLIANT		AMERICAN EAGLE	
BEGINNING CASH, CASH EQUIVALENTS & SHORT-TERM INVESTMENTS	$14,098,088		$3,721,143		$683,948		$1,203,155	
CASH FROM OPERATIONS	Company Value	%	Company Value	%	Company Value	%	Company Value	%
Premiums Collected Net of Reinsurance	$94,384,863	97.56%	$447	0.26%	$13,702,888	99.45%	$7,375,995	98.64%
Net Investment Income	$2,364,233	2.44%	$172,091	99.74%	$75,887	0.55%	$65,709	0.88%
Miscellaneous Income	$57	0.00%	$0	0.00%	$0	0.00%	$35,680	0.48%
Total	$96,749,153	100.00%	$172,538	100.00%	$13,778,775	100.00%	$7,477,384	100.00%
Benefit and Loss Related Payments	$4,198,333	4.36%	$67,583	35.03%	$285,183	2.08%	$48,338	0.71%
Net Transfers to Separate, Segregated Accounts & Protected Cell Accounts	$0	0.00%	$0	0.00%	$0	0.00%	$0	0.00%
Commissions, Expenses Paid and Aggregate Write-Ins for Deductions	$89,348,758	92.82%	$125,359	64.97%	$13,416,724	97.92%	$6,734,556	99.29%
Dividends Paid to Policyholders	$0	0.00%	$0	0.00%	$0	0.00%	$0	0.00%
Federal and Foreign Income Taxes Paid (Recovered), Net Tax on Capital Gains (Losses)	$2,715,385	2.82%	$1	0.00%	$0	0.00%	$0	0.00%
Total	$96,262,476	100.00%	$192,943	100.00%	$13,701,907	100.00%	$6,782,894	100.00%
NET CASH FROM OPERATIONS	$486,677		($20,405)		$76,868		$694,490	
CASH FROM INVESTMENTS	Company Value	%	Company Value	%	Company Value	%	Company Value	%
Proceeds from Investments Sold, Matured or Repaid:								
Bonds	$39,961,387	87.18%	$0	--	$425,000	100.00%	$0	--
Stocks	$5,872,505	12.81%	$0	--	$0	0.00%	$0	--
Mortgage Loans	$1,366	0.00%	$0	--	$0	0.00%	$0	--
Real Estate	$0	0.00%	$0	--	$0	0.00%	$0	--
Other Invested Assets	$0	0.00%	$0	--	$0	0.00%	$0	--
Net Gains or (Losses) on Cash, Cash Equivalents & Short-Term Investments	$0	0.00%	$0	--	$0	0.00%	$0	--
Miscellaneous Proceeds	$0	0.00%	$0	--	$0	0.00%	$0	--
Total Investment Proceeds	$45,835,258	100.00%	$0	--	$425,000	100.00%	$0	--
Cost of Investments Acquired (Long-Term Only):								
Bonds	$38,565,659	92.84%	$0	--	$1,038,188	100.00%	$0	--
Stocks	$3,000,826	7.22%	$0	--	$0	0.00%	$0	--
Mortgage Loans	$0	0.00%	$0	--	$0	0.00%	$0	--
Real Estate	$26,100	0.06%	$0	--	$0	0.00%	$0	--
Other Invested Assets	$0	0.00%	$0	--	$0	0.00%	$0	--
Miscellaneous Applications	($52,104)	(0.13)%	$0	--	$0	0.00%	$0	--
Total Investments Acquired	$41,540,481	100.00%	$0	--	$1,038,188	100.00%	$0	--
Net Increase (Decrease) in Contract Loans and Premium Notes	$0		$0		$0		$0	
NET CASH FROM INVESTMENTS	$4,294,777		$0		($613,188)		$0	
CASH FROM FINANCING AND MISCELLANEOUS SOURCES	Company Value		Company Value		Company Value		Company Value	
Cash Provided (Applied):								
Surplus Notes, Capital Notes	$0		$0		$600,000		$0	
Capital and paid in Surplus, Less Treasury Stock	$0		$0		$0		$0	
Borrowed Funds	$0		$0		$0		$185,619	
Net Deposits on Deposit-Type Contracts & Other Insurance Liabilities	$0		$0		$0		$0	
Dividends to Stockholders	$13,244,936		$0		$0		$730,408	
Other Cash Provided (Applied)	($3,893,543)		($370)		$2,483		($759,733)	
NET CASH FROM FINANCING AND MISCELLANEOUS SOURCES	($17,138,479)		($370)		$602,483		($1,304,522)	
NET CHANGE IN CASH, CASH EQUIVALENTS & SHORT-TERM INVESTMENTS	($12,357,025)		($20,775)		$66,163		($610,032)	
ENDING CASH, CASH EQUIVALENTS & SHORT-TERM INVESTMENTS	$1,741,063		$3,700,368		$750,111		$593,123	

C.3 Statement of Cash Flow - By Individual Underwriter

	AMERICAN GUARANTY		AMERICAN LAND & AIRCRAFT		AMERICAN SECURITY		ARKANSAS TIC	
BEGINNING CASH, CASH EQUIVALENTS & SHORT-TERM INVESTMENTS	$1,080,615		$816,339		$7,156,366		$4,354,233	
CASH FROM OPERATIONS	Company Value	%	Company Value	%	Company Value	%	Company Value	%
Premiums Collected Net of Reinsurance	$3,488,701	67.80%	$659,156	94.36%	$2,940,198	88.89%	$8,139,029	96.75%
Net Investment Income	$1,656,942	32.20%	$39,412	5.64%	$367,143	11.10%	$220,890	2.63%
Miscellaneous Income	$0	0.00%	$0	0.00%	$500	0.02%	$52,298	0.62%
Total	$5,145,643	100.00%	$698,568	100.00%	$3,307,841	100.00%	$8,412,217	100.00%
Benefit and Loss Related Payments	$104,491	3.00%	$0	0.00%	$0	0.00%	$131,778	1.68%
Net Transfers to Separate, Segregated Accounts & Protected Cell Accounts	$0	0.00%	$0	0.00%	$0	0.00%	$0	0.00%
Commissions, Expenses Paid and Aggregate Write-Ins for Deductions	$3,291,342	94.53%	$710,847	100.00%	$2,302,396	94.03%	$7,525,607	96.07%
Dividends Paid to Policyholders	$0	0.00%	$0	0.00%	$0	0.00%	$0	0.00%
Federal and Foreign Income Taxes Paid (Recovered), Net Tax on Capital Gains (Losses)	$85,858	2.47%	$0	0.00%	$146,222	5.97%	$175,706	2.24%
Total	$3,481,691	100.00%	$710,847	100.00%	$2,448,618	100.00%	$7,833,091	100.00%
NET CASH FROM OPERATIONS	$1,663,952		($12,279)		$859,223		$579,126	
CASH FROM INVESTMENTS	Company Value	%	Company Value	%	Company Value	%	Company Value	%
Proceeds from Investments Sold, Matured or Repaid:								
Bonds	$350,000	100.00%	$0	--	$300,000	100.00%	$0	--
Stocks	$0	0.00%	$0	--	$0	0.00%	$0	--
Mortgage Loans	$0	0.00%	$0	--	$0	0.00%	$0	--
Real Estate	$0	0.00%	$0	--	$0	0.00%	$0	--
Other Invested Assets	$0	0.00%	$0	--	$0	0.00%	$0	--
Net Gains or (Losses) on Cash, Cash Equivalents & Short-Term Investments	$0	0.00%	$0	--	$0	0.00%	$0	--
Miscellaneous Proceeds	$0	0.00%	$0	--	$0	0.00%	$0	--
Total Investment Proceeds	$350,000	100.00%	$0	--	$300,000	100.00%	$0	--
Cost of Investments Acquired (Long-Term Only):								
Bonds	$400,948	100.00%	$0	--	$0	--	$0	--
Stocks	$0	0.00%	$0	--	$0	--	$0	--
Mortgage Loans	$0	0.00%	$0	--	$0	--	$0	--
Real Estate	$0	0.00%	$0	--	$0	--	$0	--
Other Invested Assets	$0	0.00%	$0	--	$0	--	$0	--
Miscellaneous Applications	$0	0.00%	$0	--	$0	--	$0	--
Total Investments Acquired	$400,948	100.00%	$0	--	$0	--	$0	--
Net Increase (Decrease) in Contract Loans and Premium Notes	$0		$0		$0		$0	
NET CASH FROM INVESTMENTS	($50,948)		$0		$300,000		$0	
CASH FROM FINANCING AND MISCELLANEOUS SOURCES	Company Value		Company Value		Company Value		Company Value	
Cash Provided (Applied):								
Surplus Notes, Capital Notes	$0		$0		$0		$0	
Capital and paid in Surplus, Less Treasury Stock	$0		$0		$0		$0	
Borrowed Funds	$0		$0		$0		$0	
Net Deposits on Deposit-Type Contracts & Other Insurance Liabilities	$0		$0		$0		$0	
Dividends to Stockholders	$0		$0		$0		$225,000	
Other Cash Provided (Applied)	($118,398)		$0		$164,705		$0	
NET CASH FROM FINANCING AND MISCELLANEOUS SOURCES	($118,398)		$0		$164,705		($225,000)	
NET CHANGE IN CASH, CASH EQUIVALENTS & SHORT-TERM INVESTMENTS	$1,494,606		($12,279)		$1,323,928		$354,126	
ENDING CASH, CASH EQUIVALENTS & SHORT-TERM INVESTMENTS	$2,575,221		$804,060		$8,480,294		$4,708,359	

C.3 Statement of Cash Flow - By Individual Underwriter

	ARSENAL		ATTORNEYS TGF (CO)		ATTORNEYS TGF (IL)		ATTORNEYS TIF (FL)	
BEGINNING CASH, CASH EQUIVALENTS & SHORT-TERM INVESTMENTS	$573,757		$918,156		$10,717,502		$18,433,438	
CASH FROM OPERATIONS	Company Value	%	Company Value	%	Company Value	%	Company Value	%
Premiums Collected Net of Reinsurance	$1,583,908	98.07%	$9,539,694	65.82%	$10,869,475	48.95%	$367,410,227	95.10%
Net Investment Income	$25,816	1.60%	$55,911	0.39%	$1,709,187	7.70%	$8,115,939	2.10%
Miscellaneous Income	$5,315	0.33%	$4,898,980	33.80%	$9,626,250	43.35%	$10,796,183	2.79%
Total	$1,615,039	100.00%	$14,494,585	100.00%	$22,204,912	100.00%	$386,322,349	100.00%
Benefit and Loss Related Payments	$0	0.00%	$1,546,278	9.59%	$2,015,565	9.88%	$29,481,031	7.63%
Net Transfers to Separate, Segregated Accounts & Protected Cell Accounts	$0	0.00%	$0	0.00%	$0	0.00%	$0	0.00%
Commissions, Expenses Paid and Aggregate Write-Ins for Deductions	$1,610,858	97.80%	$14,239,668	88.27%	$17,209,477	84.35%	$358,471,991	92.77%
Dividends Paid to Policyholders	$0	0.00%	$0	0.00%	$0	0.00%	$0	0.00%
Federal and Foreign Income Taxes Paid (Recovered), Net Tax on Capital Gains (Losses)	$36,298	2.20%	$346,008	2.14%	$1,177,828	5.77%	($1,559,602)	(0.40)%
Total	$1,647,156	100.00%	$16,131,954	100.00%	$20,402,870	100.00%	$386,393,420	100.00%
NET CASH FROM OPERATIONS	($32,117)		($1,637,369)		$1,802,042		($71,071)	
CASH FROM INVESTMENTS	Company Value	%	Company Value	%	Company Value	%	Company Value	%
Proceeds from Investments Sold, Matured or Repaid:								
Bonds	$0	--	$1,251,862	50.97%	$0	0.00%	$83,271,808	42.87%
Stocks	$0	--	$742,747	30.24%	$1,020,636	99.02%	$109,878,961	56.57%
Mortgage Loans	$0	--	$0	0.00%	$0	0.00%	$52,651	0.03%
Real Estate	$0	--	$0	0.00%	$0	0.00%	$0	0.00%
Other Invested Assets	$0	--	$0	0.00%	$10,106	0.98%	$719,444	0.37%
Net Gains or (Losses) on Cash, Cash Equivalents & Short-Term Investments	$0	--	($6)	0.00%	$0	0.00%	$0	0.00%
Miscellaneous Proceeds	$0	--	$461,549	18.79%	$0	0.00%	$323,523	0.17%
Total Investment Proceeds	$0	--	$2,456,152	100.00%	$1,030,742	100.00%	$194,246,387	100.00%
Cost of Investments Acquired (Long-Term Only):								
Bonds	$0	--	$380,439	72.78%	$0	0.00%	$75,190,955	42.28%
Stocks	$0	--	$1,680	0.32%	$764,372	88.43%	$99,490,208	55.95%
Mortgage Loans	$0	--	$0	0.00%	$0	0.00%	$206,032	0.12%
Real Estate	$0	--	$0	0.00%	$100,000	11.57%	$1,945,847	1.09%
Other Invested Assets	$0	--	$0	0.00%	$0	0.00%	$0	0.00%
Miscellaneous Applications	$0	--	$140,634	26.90%	$0	0.00%	$988,556	0.56%
Total Investments Acquired	$0	--	$522,753	100.00%	$864,372	100.00%	$177,821,598	100.00%
Net Increase (Decrease) in Contract Loans and Premium Notes	$0		$0		$0		$0	
NET CASH FROM INVESTMENTS	$0		$1,933,399		$166,370		$16,424,789	
CASH FROM FINANCING AND MISCELLANEOUS SOURCES	Company Value		Company Value		Company Value		Company Value	
Cash Provided (Applied):								
Surplus Notes, Capital Notes	$0		$0		$0		$0	
Capital and paid in Surplus, Less Treasury Stock	$0		$0		($96,350)		$0	
Borrowed Funds	$0		$0		$0		$0	
Net Deposits on Deposit-Type Contracts & Other Insurance Liabilities	$0		$0		$0		$0	
Dividends to Stockholders	$0		$0		$0		$3,950,000	
Other Cash Provided (Applied)	$51,598		$0		$25,882		($14,435,788)	
NET CASH FROM FINANCING AND MISCELLANEOUS SOURCES	$51,598		$0		($70,468)		($18,385,788)	
NET CHANGE IN CASH, CASH EQUIVALENTS & SHORT-TERM INVESTMENTS	$19,481		$296,030		$1,897,944		($2,032,070)	
ENDING CASH, CASH EQUIVALENTS & SHORT-TERM INVESTMENTS	$593,238		$1,214,186		$12,615,446		$16,401,368	

C.3 Statement of Cash Flow - By Individual Underwriter

	BRIDGE		CENSTAR		CHICAGO T&T		CHICAGO TIC	
BEGINNING CASH, CASH EQUIVALENTS & SHORT-TERM INVESTMENTS	$7,858,767		$12,026,393		$639,958,232		$359,565,960	

CASH FROM OPERATIONS	Company Value	%	Company Value	%	Company Value	%	Company Value	%
Premiums Collected Net of Reinsurance	$19,425	21.04%	$38,770,855	97.77%	$178,675	0.05%	$1,881,996,829	81.42%
Net Investment Income	$72,886	78.96%	$686,853	1.73%	$293,387,162	86.44%	$127,341,328	5.51%
Miscellaneous Income	$0	0.00%	$196,439	0.50%	$45,859,270	13.51%	$302,084,280	13.07%
Total	$92,311	100.00%	$39,654,147	100.00%	$339,425,107	100.00%	$2,311,422,437	100.00%
Benefit and Loss Related Payments	$67,388	28.46%	$298,619	0.83%	$0	0.00%	$186,723,287	8.91%
Net Transfers to Separate, Segregated Accounts & Protected Cell Accounts	$0	0.00%	$0	0.00%	$0	0.00%	$0	0.00%
Commissions, Expenses Paid and Aggregate Write-Ins for Deductions	$213,172	90.02%	$34,205,109	94.89%	$39,764,919	89.37%	$1,884,127,845	89.87%
Dividends Paid to Policyholders	$0	0.00%	$0	0.00%	$0	0.00%	$0	0.00%
Federal and Foreign Income Taxes Paid (Recovered), Net Tax on Capital Gains (Losses)	($43,767)	(18.48)%	$1,544,999	4.29%	$4,731,692	10.63%	$25,662,551	1.22%
Total	$236,793	100.00%	$36,048,727	100.00%	$44,496,611	100.00%	$2,096,513,683	100.00%
NET CASH FROM OPERATIONS	($144,482)		$3,605,420		$294,928,496		$214,908,754	

CASH FROM INVESTMENTS	Company Value	%	Company Value	%	Company Value	%	Company Value	%
Proceeds from Investments Sold, Matured or Repaid:								
Bonds	$30,000	100.00%	$4,817,000	100.00%	$1,763,341,705	99.97%	$1,233,488,435	71.34%
Stocks	$0	0.00%	$0	0.00%	$0	0.00%	$485,986,677	28.11%
Mortgage Loans	$0	0.00%	$0	0.00%	$0	0.00%	$971,269	0.06%
Real Estate	$0	0.00%	$0	0.00%	$0	0.00%	$6,441,432	0.37%
Other Invested Assets	$0	0.00%	$0	0.00%	$0	0.00%	$2,129,683	0.12%
Net Gains or (Losses) on Cash, Cash Equivalents & Short-Term Investments	$0	0.00%	$0	0.00%	$0	0.00%	$0	0.00%
Miscellaneous Proceeds	$0	0.00%	$13	0.00%	$560,659	0.03%	$0	0.00%
Total Investment Proceeds	$30,000	100.00%	$4,817,013	100.00%	$1,763,902,364	100.00%	$1,729,017,496	100.00%
Cost of Investments Acquired (Long-Term Only):								
Bonds	$4,982	100.00%	$2,789,328	100.00%	$1,780,107,769	100.00%	$1,215,757,870	70.84%
Stocks	$0	0.00%	$0	0.00%	$50,000	0.00%	$438,804,179	25.57%
Mortgage Loans	$0	0.00%	$0	0.00%	$0	0.00%	$1,383,469	0.08%
Real Estate	$0	0.00%	$0	0.00%	$0	0.00%	$1,241,850	0.07%
Other Invested Assets	$0	0.00%	$0	0.00%	$0	0.00%	$53,337,223	3.11%
Miscellaneous Applications	$0	0.00%	$0	0.00%	$0	0.00%	$5,683,639	0.33%
Total Investments Acquired	$4,982	100.00%	$2,789,328	100.00%	$1,780,157,769	100.00%	$1,716,208,230	100.00%
Net Increase (Decrease) in Contract Loans and Premium Notes	$0		$0		$0		$0	
NET CASH FROM INVESTMENTS	$25,018		$2,027,685		($16,255,405)		$12,809,266	

CASH FROM FINANCING AND MISCELLANEOUS SOURCES	Company Value		Company Value		Company Value		Company Value	
Cash Provided (Applied):								
Surplus Notes, Capital Notes	$0		$0		$0		$0	
Capital and paid in Surplus, Less Treasury Stock	$0		$0		$50,000		$0	
Borrowed Funds	$0		$0		$0		($51,855)	
Net Deposits on Deposit-Type Contracts & Other Insurance Liabilities	$0		$0		$0		$0	
Dividends to Stockholders	$0		$0		$340,000,000		$146,000,000	
Other Cash Provided (Applied)	$0		$0		($207,954,459)		($132,210,788)	
NET CASH FROM FINANCING AND MISCELLANEOUS SOURCES	$0		$0		($547,904,459)		($278,262,643)	

NET CHANGE IN CASH, CASH EQUIVALENTS & SHORT-TERM INVESTMENTS	($119,464)		$5,633,105		($269,231,368)		($50,544,623)	
ENDING CASH, CASH EQUIVALENTS & SHORT-TERM INVESTMENTS	$7,739,303		$17,659,498		$370,726,864		$309,021,337	

2

C.3   Statement of Cash Flow - By Individual Underwriter

	CHICAGO TIC (OR)		COLUMBIAN NATIONAL		COMMERCE		COMMONWEALTH LAND	
BEGINNING CASH, CASH EQUIVALENTS & SHORT-TERM INVESTMENTS	$2,593,871		$5,044,489		$15,562,211		$43,925,579	
CASH FROM OPERATIONS	Company Value	%	Company Value	%	Company Value	%	Company Value	%
Premiums Collected Net of Reinsurance	$26,521,760	75.75%	$0	0.00%	$43,044,031	98.60%	$1,152,213,929	93.28%
Net Investment Income	$1,497,687	4.28%	$32,363	98.16%	$610,303	1.40%	$32,332,522	2.62%
Miscellaneous Income	$6,993,455	19.97%	$607	1.84%	$0	0.00%	$50,611,959	4.10%
Total	$35,012,902	100.00%	$32,970	100.00%	$43,654,334	100.00%	$1,235,158,410	100.00%
Benefit and Loss Related Payments	$533,679	1.73%	$0	0.00%	($326,705)	(0.82)%	$73,400,296	6.20%
Net Transfers to Separate, Segregated Accounts & Protected Cell Accounts	$0	0.00%	$0	0.00%	$0	0.00%	$0	0.00%
Commissions, Expenses Paid and Aggregate Write-Ins for Deductions	$29,156,144	94.75%	$110,491	20.96%	$38,760,190	97.24%	$1,078,898,979	91.11%
Dividends Paid to Policyholders	$0	0.00%	$0	0.00%	$0	0.00%	$0	0.00%
Federal and Foreign Income Taxes Paid (Recovered), Net Tax on Capital Gains (Losses)	$1,080,506	3.51%	$416,694	79.04%	$1,427,715	3.58%	$31,867,493	2.69%
Total	$30,770,329	100.00%	$527,185	100.00%	$39,861,200	100.00%	$1,184,166,768	100.00%
NET CASH FROM OPERATIONS	$4,242,573		($494,215)		$3,793,134		$50,991,642	
CASH FROM INVESTMENTS	Company Value	%	Company Value	%	Company Value	%	Company Value	%
Proceeds from Investments Sold, Matured or Repaid:								
Bonds	$10,800,729	54.60%	$159,000	100.00%	$1,502,000	100.00%	$132,918,395	68.14%
Stocks	$8,982,428	45.40%	$0	0.00%	$0	0.00%	$62,157,855	31.86%
Mortgage Loans	$0	0.00%	$0	0.00%	$0	0.00%	$0	0.00%
Real Estate	$0	0.00%	$0	0.00%	$0	0.00%	$0	0.00%
Other Invested Assets	$0	0.00%	$0	0.00%	$0	0.00%	$0	0.00%
Net Gains or (Losses) on Cash, Cash Equivalents & Short-Term Investments	$0	0.00%	$0	0.00%	$0	0.00%	$0	0.00%
Miscellaneous Proceeds	$0	0.00%	$0	0.00%	$0	0.00%	$0	0.00%
Total Investment Proceeds	$19,783,157	100.00%	$159,000	100.00%	$1,502,000	100.00%	$195,076,250	100.00%
Cost of Investments Acquired (Long-Term Only):								
Bonds	$10,738,246	55.86%	$158,283	100.00%	$1,602,545	100.00%	$101,676,041	50.83%
Stocks	$8,483,997	44.14%	$0	0.00%	$0	0.00%	$93,248,609	46.61%
Mortgage Loans	$0	0.00%	$0	0.00%	$0	0.00%	$0	0.00%
Real Estate	$0	0.00%	$0	0.00%	$0	0.00%	$0	0.00%
Other Invested Assets	$0	0.00%	$0	0.00%	$0	0.00%	$5,089,877	2.54%
Miscellaneous Applications	$0	0.00%	$0	0.00%	$0	0.00%	$27,785	0.01%
Total Investments Acquired	$19,222,243	100.00%	$158,283	100.00%	$1,602,545	100.00%	$200,042,312	100.00%
Net Increase (Decrease) in Contract Loans and Premium Notes	$0		$0		$0		$0	
NET CASH FROM INVESTMENTS	$560,914		$717		($100,545)		($4,966,062)	
CASH FROM FINANCING AND MISCELLANEOUS SOURCES	Company Value		Company Value		Company Value		Company Value	
Cash Provided (Applied):								
Surplus Notes, Capital Notes	$0		$0		$0		$0	
Capital and paid in Surplus, Less Treasury Stock	$0		$0		$0		$0	
Borrowed Funds	$0		$0		$0		$0	
Net Deposits on Deposit-Type Contracts & Other Insurance Liabilities	$0		$0		$0		$0	
Dividends to Stockholders	$5,200,000		$0		$2,400,000		$80,000,000	
Other Cash Provided (Applied)	$831,603		($1,144,412)		$2,673		$22,940,517	
NET CASH FROM FINANCING AND MISCELLANEOUS SOURCES	($4,368,397)		($1,144,412)		($2,397,327)		($57,059,483)	
NET CHANGE IN CASH, CASH EQUIVALENTS & SHORT-TERM INVESTMENTS	$435,090		($1,637,910)		$1,295,262		($11,033,903)	
ENDING CASH, CASH EQUIVALENTS & SHORT-TERM INVESTMENTS	$3,028,961		$3,406,579		$16,857,473		$32,891,676	

C.3 Statement of Cash Flow - By Individual Underwriter

	COMMONWEALTH LAND (NJ)		CONESTOGA		CT ATTORNEYS		DAKOTA HOMESTEAD	
BEGINNING CASH, CASH EQUIVALENTS & SHORT-TERM INVESTMENTS	$6,295,160		$2,766,264		$5,829,271		$637,778	

CASH FROM OPERATIONS

	Company Value	%	Company Value	%	Company Value	%	Company Value	%
Premiums Collected Net of Reinsurance	$33,559,993	89.92%	$14,309,636	97.64%	$53,236,324	93.19%	$3,892,318	92.55%
Net Investment Income	$1,971,777	5.28%	$344,855	2.35%	$2,411,019	4.22%	$129,480	3.08%
Miscellaneous Income	$1,788,493	4.79%	$809	0.01%	$1,482,140	2.59%	$183,978	4.37%
Total	$37,320,263	100.00%	$14,655,300	100.00%	$57,129,483	100.00%	$4,205,776	100.00%
Benefit and Loss Related Payments	$1,959,621	5.69%	$943,385	5.97%	$3,990,392	7.20%	$64,953	1.69%
Net Transfers to Separate, Segregated Accounts & Protected Cell Accounts	$0	0.00%	$0	0.00%	$0	0.00%	$0	0.00%
Commissions, Expenses Paid and Aggregate Write-Ins for Deductions	$31,200,589	90.61%	$14,808,681	93.73%	$51,154,255	92.28%	$3,781,291	98.44%
Dividends Paid to Policyholders	$0	0.00%	$0	0.00%	$0	0.00%	$0	0.00%
Federal and Foreign Income Taxes Paid (Recovered), Net Tax on Capital Gains (Losses)	$1,274,436	3.70%	$47,800	0.30%	$290,000	0.52%	($5,000)	(0.13%)
Total	$34,434,646	100.00%	$15,799,866	100.00%	$55,434,647	100.00%	$3,841,244	100.00%
NET CASH FROM OPERATIONS	$2,885,617		($1,144,566)		$1,694,836		$364,532	

CASH FROM INVESTMENTS

	Company Value	%	Company Value	%	Company Value	%	Company Value	%
Proceeds from Investments Sold, Matured or Repaid:								
Bonds	$3,075,745	100.00%	$575,000	96.06%	$13,522,187	87.89%	$11,198	3.91%
Stocks	$0	0.00%	$0	0.00%	$1,495,253	9.72%	$274,610	95.81%
Mortgage Loans	$0	0.00%	$23,574	3.94%	$0	0.00%	$0	0.00%
Real Estate	$0	0.00%	$0	0.00%	$0	0.00%	$0	0.00%
Other Invested Assets	$0	0.00%	$0	0.00%	$367,069	2.39%	$0	0.00%
Net Gains or (Losses) on Cash, Cash Equivalents & Short-Term Investments	$0	0.00%	$0	0.00%	$0	0.00%	$812	0.28%
Miscellaneous Proceeds	$0	0.00%	$0	0.00%	$0	0.00%	$0	0.00%
Total Investment Proceeds	$3,075,745	100.00%	$598,574	100.00%	$15,384,509	100.00%	$286,620	100.00%
Cost of Investments Acquired (Long-Term Only):								
Bonds	$4,110,921	100.00%	$475,150	70.71%	$17,652,426	89.13%	$36,856	13.66%
Stocks	$0	0.00%	$51,802	7.71%	$2,152,598	10.87%	$217,077	80.46%
Mortgage Loans	$0	0.00%	$0	0.00%	$0	0.00%	$0	0.00%
Real Estate	$0	0.00%	$145,000	21.58%	$0	0.00%	$0	0.00%
Other Invested Assets	$0	0.00%	$0	0.00%	$0	0.00%	$0	0.00%
Miscellaneous Applications	$0	0.00%	$0	0.00%	$0	0.00%	$15,874	5.88%
Total Investments Acquired	$4,110,921	100.00%	$671,952	100.00%	$19,805,024	100.00%	$269,807	100.00%
Net Increase (Decrease) in Contract Loans and Premium Notes	$0		$0		$0		$0	
NET CASH FROM INVESTMENTS	($1,035,176)		($73,378)		($4,420,515)		$16,813	

CASH FROM FINANCING AND MISCELLANEOUS SOURCES

	Company Value		Company Value		Company Value		Company Value	
Cash Provided (Applied):								
Surplus Notes, Capital Notes	$0		$0		$0		$1,100,000	
Capital and paid in Surplus, Less Treasury Stock	$0		$178,123		$0		($1,100,000)	
Borrowed Funds	$0		$0		$0		$0	
Net Deposits on Deposit-Type Contracts & Other Insurance Liabilities	$0		$0		$0		$0	
Dividends to Stockholders	$0		$0		$0		$49,766	
Other Cash Provided (Applied)	$161,318		$69,121		($42,967)		$149,824	
NET CASH FROM FINANCING AND MISCELLANEOUS SOURCES	$161,318		$247,244		($42,967)		$100,058	

NET CHANGE IN CASH, CASH EQUIVALENTS & SHORT-TERM INVESTMENTS	$2,011,759		($970,700)		($2,768,646)		$481,403	
ENDING CASH, CASH EQUIVALENTS & SHORT-TERM INVESTMENTS	$8,306,919		$1,795,564		$3,060,625		$1,119,181	

C.3 Statement of Cash Flow - By Individual Underwriter

	DREIBELBISS		EQUITY NATIONAL		FARMERS NATIONAL		FIDELITY NATIONAL	
BEGINNING CASH, CASH EQUIVALENTS & SHORT-TERM INVESTMENTS	$1,928,354		$1,882,451		$450,303		$61,790,843	

CASH FROM OPERATIONS

	Company Value	%	Company Value	%	Company Value	%	Company Value	%
Premiums Collected Net of Reinsurance	$620,383	31.39%	$236,862	10.18%	$528,581	93.61%	$1,278,365,663	89.18%
Net Investment Income	$174,215	8.81%	$230,044	9.89%	$36,094	6.39%	$44,019,177	3.07%
Miscellaneous Income	$1,182,042	59.80%	$1,859,469	79.93%	$0	0.00%	$111,006,007	7.74%
Total	$1,976,640	100.00%	$2,326,375	100.00%	$564,675	100.00%	$1,433,390,847	100.00%
Benefit and Loss Related Payments	$272,697	12.33%	$0	0.00%	$63,819	10.07%	$110,696,574	8.08%
Net Transfers to Separate, Segregated Accounts & Protected Cell Accounts	$0	0.00%	$0	0.00%	$0	0.00%	$0	0.00%
Commissions, Expenses Paid and Aggregate Write-Ins for Deductions	$1,936,643	87.56%	$2,623,191	100.00%	$570,048	89.93%	$1,222,863,282	89.31%
Dividends Paid to Policyholders	$0	0.00%	$0	0.00%	$0	0.00%	$0	0.00%
Federal and Foreign Income Taxes Paid (Recovered), Net Tax on Capital Gains (Losses)	$2,373	0.11%	$0	0.00%	$0	0.00%	$35,600,492	2.60%
Total	$2,211,713	100.00%	$2,623,191	100.00%	$633,867	100.00%	$1,369,160,348	100.00%
NET CASH FROM OPERATIONS	($235,073)		($296,816)		($69,192)		$64,230,499	

CASH FROM INVESTMENTS

	Company Value	%	Company Value	%	Company Value	%	Company Value	%
Proceeds from Investments Sold, Matured or Repaid:								
Bonds	$3,093	1.34%	$0	--	$0	--	$577,439,746	66.68%
Stocks	$227,013	98.66%	$0	--	$0	--	$241,249,890	27.86%
Mortgage Loans	$0	0.00%	$0	--	$0	--	$979,498	0.11%
Real Estate	$0	0.00%	$0	--	$0	--	$0	0.00%
Other Invested Assets	$0	0.00%	$0	--	$0	--	$42,096,306	4.86%
Net Gains or (Losses) on Cash, Cash Equivalents & Short-Term Investments	$0	0.00%	$0	--	$0	--	$0	0.00%
Miscellaneous Proceeds	$0	0.00%	$0	--	$0	--	$4,172,681	0.48%
Total Investment Proceeds	$230,106	100.00%	$0	--	$0	--	$865,938,121	100.00%
Cost of Investments Acquired (Long-Term Only):								
Bonds	$10,083	22.49%	$0	--	$0	--	$569,823,430	67.59%
Stocks	$34,758	77.51%	$0	--	$0	--	$210,122,195	24.92%
Mortgage Loans	$0	0.00%	$0	--	$0	--	$569,699	0.07%
Real Estate	$0	0.00%	$0	--	$0	--	$299,200	0.04%
Other Invested Assets	$0	0.00%	$0	--	$0	--	$62,205,946	7.38%
Miscellaneous Applications	$0	0.00%	$0	--	$0	--	$0	0.00%
Total Investments Acquired	$44,841	100.00%	$0	--	$0	--	$843,020,470	100.00%
Net Increase (Decrease) in Contract Loans and Premium Notes	$0		$0		$0		$0	
NET CASH FROM INVESTMENTS	$185,265		$0		$0		$22,917,651	

CASH FROM FINANCING AND MISCELLANEOUS SOURCES

	Company Value	Company Value	Company Value	Company Value
Cash Provided (Applied):				
Surplus Notes, Capital Notes	$0	$0	$0	$0
Capital and paid in Surplus, Less Treasury Stock	$0	$0	$459,000	$0
Borrowed Funds	$0	$0	$0	$0
Net Deposits on Deposit-Type Contracts & Other Insurance Liabilities	$0	$0	$0	$0
Dividends to Stockholders	$0	$0	$0	$79,300,000
Other Cash Provided (Applied)	$0	$0	($146,843)	($4,175,851)
NET CASH FROM FINANCING AND MISCELLANEOUS SOURCES	$0	$0	$312,157	($83,475,851)

NET CHANGE IN CASH, CASH EQUIVALENTS & SHORT-TERM INVESTMENTS	($49,808)	($296,816)	$242,965	$3,672,299
ENDING CASH, CASH EQUIVALENTS & SHORT-TERM INVESTMENTS	$1,878,546	$1,585,635	$693,268	$65,463,142

C.3 Statement of Cash Flow - By Individual Underwriter

	FIRST AMERICAN (KS)		FIRST AMERICAN (NY)		FIRST AMERICAN (OR)		FIRST AMERICAN T&T	
BEGINNING CASH, CASH EQUIVALENTS & SHORT-TERM INVESTMENTS	$9,950,302		$74,464,692		$35,707,279		$12,641,419	

CASH FROM OPERATIONS

	Company Value	%	Company Value	%	Company Value	%	Company Value	%
Premiums Collected Net of Reinsurance	$14,606,625	94.97%	$273,721,358	96.16%	$90,025,492	98.19%	$5,691,983	21.93%
Net Investment Income	$351,142	2.28%	$10,940,548	3.84%	$1,661,370	1.81%	$978,452	3.77%
Miscellaneous Income	$422,606	2.75%	$0	0.00%	$0	0.00%	$19,282,971	74.30%
Total	$15,380,373	100.00%	$284,661,906	100.00%	$91,686,862	100.00%	$25,953,406	100.00%
Benefit and Loss Related Payments	$290,960	2.10%	$9,706,888	3.82%	$2,584,659	3.07%	$158,178	0.78%
Net Transfers to Separate, Segregated Accounts & Protected Cell Accounts	$0	0.00%	$0	0.00%	$0	0.00%	$0	0.00%
Commissions, Expenses Paid and Aggregate Write-Ins for Deductions	$12,806,152	92.25%	$237,548,865	93.39%	$77,177,063	91.77%	$20,176,234	99.22%
Dividends Paid to Policyholders	$0	0.00%	$0	0.00%	$0	0.00%	$0	0.00%
Federal and Foreign Income Taxes Paid (Recovered), Net Tax on Capital Gains (Losses)	$784,582	5.65%	$7,100,000	2.79%	$4,335,000	5.15%	$0	0.00%
Total	$13,881,694	100.00%	$254,355,753	100.00%	$84,096,722	100.00%	$20,334,412	100.00%
NET CASH FROM OPERATIONS	$1,498,679		$30,306,153		$7,590,140		$5,618,994	

CASH FROM INVESTMENTS

	Company Value	%	Company Value	%	Company Value	%	Company Value	%
Proceeds from Investments Sold, Matured or Repaid:								
Bonds	$0	--	$9,460,000	89.29%	$331,869	27.05%	$0	0.00%
Stocks	$0	--	$863,371	8.15%	$802,287	65.40%	$0	0.00%
Mortgage Loans	$0	--	$0	0.00%	$92,636	7.55%	$0	0.00%
Real Estate	$0	--	$0	0.00%	$0	0.00%	$0	0.00%
Other Invested Assets	$0	--	$0	0.00%	$0	0.00%	$4,871	100.00%
Net Gains or (Losses) on Cash, Cash Equivalents & Short-Term Investments	$0	--	$271,624	2.56%	$0	0.00%	$0	0.00%
Miscellaneous Proceeds	$0	--	$0	0.00%	$0	0.00%	$0	0.00%
Total Investment Proceeds	$0	--	$10,594,995	100.00%	$1,226,792	100.00%	$4,871	100.00%
Cost of Investments Acquired (Long-Term Only):								
Bonds	$0	0.00%	$7,560,882	97.77%	$14,144,089	99.36%	$10,955,429	94.89%
Stocks	$7,432,853	100.00%	$0	0.00%	$90,949	0.64%	$0	0.00%
Mortgage Loans	$0	0.00%	$0	0.00%	$0	0.00%	$0	0.00%
Real Estate	$0	0.00%	$162,410	2.10%	$0	0.00%	$590,462	5.11%
Other Invested Assets	$0	0.00%	$10,000	0.13%	$0	0.00%	$0	0.00%
Miscellaneous Applications	$0	0.00%	$0	0.00%	$0	0.00%	$0	0.00%
Total Investments Acquired	$7,432,853	100.00%	$7,733,292	100.00%	$14,235,038	100.00%	$11,545,891	100.00%
Net Increase (Decrease) in Contract Loans and Premium Notes	$0		$0		$0		$0	
NET CASH FROM INVESTMENTS	($7,432,853)		$2,861,703		($13,008,246)		($11,541,020)	

CASH FROM FINANCING AND MISCELLANEOUS SOURCES

	Company Value	Company Value	Company Value	Company Value
Cash Provided (Applied):				
Surplus Notes, Capital Notes	$0	$0	$0	$0
Capital and paid in Surplus, Less Treasury Stock	$0	$7,875,230	$0	$0
Borrowed Funds	$0	$0	($935,975)	$0
Net Deposits on Deposit-Type Contracts & Other Insurance Liabilities	$0	$0	$0	$0
Dividends to Stockholders	$0	$1,993,663	$10,144,000	$6,000,000
Other Cash Provided (Applied)	$466,225	$12,653,776	($457,805)	$3,576,285
NET CASH FROM FINANCING AND MISCELLANEOUS SOURCES	$466,225	$18,535,343	($11,537,780)	($2,423,715)

NET CHANGE IN CASH, CASH EQUIVALENTS & SHORT-TERM INVESTMENTS	($5,467,949)	$51,703,199	($16,955,886)	($8,345,741)
ENDING CASH, CASH EQUIVALENTS & SHORT-TERM INVESTMENTS	$4,482,353	$126,167,891	$18,751,393	$4,295,678

2

C.3 Statement of Cash Flow - By Individual Underwriter

	FIRST AMERICAN TIC		FIRST AMERICAN TRANS		FOUNDERS		GENERAL T&T	
BEGINNING CASH, CASH EQUIVALENTS & SHORT-TERM INVESTMENTS	$417,958,188		$2,078,733		$850,209		$1,466,179	
CASH FROM OPERATIONS	Company Value	%	Company Value	%	Company Value	%	Company Value	%
Premiums Collected Net of Reinsurance	$3,290,629,963	84.89%	$1,592,110	94.47%	$168,403	64.04%	$2,741,270	88.21%
Net Investment Income	$204,189,246	5.27%	$92,479	5.49%	$41,264	15.69%	$269,912	8.69%
Miscellaneous Income	$381,534,700	9.84%	$800	0.05%	$53,310	20.27%	$96,495	3.11%
Total	$3,876,353,909	100.00%	$1,685,389	100.00%	$262,977	100.00%	$3,107,677	100.00%
Benefit and Loss Related Payments	$242,613,173	6.59%	$3,937	0.28%	$0	0.00%	$342,564	10.18%
Net Transfers to Separate, Segregated Accounts & Protected Cell Accounts	$0	0.00%	$0	0.00%	$0	0.00%	$0	0.00%
Commissions, Expenses Paid and Aggregate Write-Ins for Deductions	$3,341,503,367	90.74%	$1,393,310	99.72%	$308,989	100.00%	$3,188,722	94.73%
Dividends Paid to Policyholders	$0	0.00%	$0	0.00%	$0	0.00%	$0	0.00%
Federal and Foreign Income Taxes Paid (Recovered), Net Tax on Capital Gains (Losses)	$98,492,341	2.67%	$0	0.00%	$0	0.00%	($165,019)	(4.90%)
Total	$3,682,608,881	100.00%	$1,397,247	100.00%	$308,989	100.00%	$3,366,267	100.00%
NET CASH FROM OPERATIONS	$193,745,028		$288,142		($46,012)		($258,590)	
CASH FROM INVESTMENTS	Company Value	%	Company Value	%	Company Value	%	Company Value	%
Proceeds from Investments Sold, Matured or Repaid:								
Bonds	$6,549,931	12.61%	$0	--	$0	--	$2,257,389	82.04%
Stocks	$34,744,403	66.91%	$0	--	$0	--	$494,149	17.96%
Mortgage Loans	$106,294	0.20%	$0	--	$0	--	$0	0.00%
Real Estate	$7,696,640	14.82%	$0	--	$0	--	$0	0.00%
Other Invested Assets	$2,828,906	5.45%	$0	--	$0	--	$0	0.00%
Net Gains or (Losses) on Cash, Cash Equivalents & Short-Term Investments	$0	0.00%	$0	--	$0	--	$0	0.00%
Miscellaneous Proceeds	$0	0.00%	$0	--	$0	--	$0	0.00%
Total Investment Proceeds	$51,926,174	100.00%	$0	--	$0	--	$2,751,538	100.00%
Cost of Investments Acquired (Long-Term Only):								
Bonds	$22,694,645	32.38%	$0	--	$0	--	$2,005,393	71.47%
Stocks	$43,417,586	61.94%	$0	--	$0	--	$677,678	24.15%
Mortgage Loans	$163,264	0.23%	$0	--	$0	--	$80,000	2.85%
Real Estate	$769,401	1.10%	$0	--	$0	--	$0	0.00%
Other Invested Assets	$3,053,152	4.36%	$0	--	$0	--	$0	0.00%
Miscellaneous Applications	$0	0.00%	$0	--	$0	--	$42,715	1.52%
Total Investments Acquired	$70,098,048	100.00%	$0	--	$0	--	$2,805,786	100.00%
Net Increase (Decrease) in Contract Loans and Premium Notes	$0		$0		$0		$0	
NET CASH FROM INVESTMENTS	($18,171,874)		$0		$0		($54,248)	
CASH FROM FINANCING AND MISCELLANEOUS SOURCES	Company Value		Company Value		Company Value		Company Value	
Cash Provided (Applied):								
Surplus Notes, Capital Notes	$0		$0		$0		$0	
Capital and paid in Surplus, Less Treasury Stock	$0		$0		$0		($50,000)	
Borrowed Funds	$0		$0		$0		$0	
Net Deposits on Deposit-Type Contracts & Other Insurance Liabilities	$0		$0		$0		$0	
Dividends to Stockholders	$35,000,000		$0		$0		$0	
Other Cash Provided (Applied)	($262,660,448)		($288,857)		$19,635		$4,507	
NET CASH FROM FINANCING AND MISCELLANEOUS SOURCES	($297,660,448)		($288,857)		$19,635		($45,493)	
NET CHANGE IN CASH, CASH EQUIVALENTS & SHORT-TERM INVESTMENTS	($122,087,294)		($715)		($26,377)		($358,331)	
ENDING CASH, CASH EQUIVALENTS & SHORT-TERM INVESTMENTS	$295,870,894		$2,078,018		$823,832		$1,107,848	

C.3 Statement of Cash Flow - By Individual Underwriter

	GUARANTEE		GUARANTEE T&T		GUARDIAN NATIONAL		INVESTORS TIC	
BEGINNING CASH, CASH EQUIVALENTS & SHORT-TERM INVESTMENTS	$236,631		$726,210		$903,052		$5,266,386	
CASH FROM OPERATIONS	Company Value	%	Company Value	%	Company Value	%	Company Value	%
Premiums Collected Net of Reinsurance	$2,406,524	92.91%	$11,156,988	74.87%	$3,594,472	92.15%	$66,870,588	92.84%
Net Investment Income	$182,739	7.06%	($159,172)	(1.07)%	$306,371	7.85%	$4,299,709	5.97%
Miscellaneous Income	$768	0.03%	$3,903,946	26.20%	$0	0.00%	$859,616	1.19%
Total	$2,590,031	100.00%	$14,901,762	100.00%	$3,900,843	100.00%	$72,029,913	100.00%
Benefit and Loss Related Payments	$1,447,297	34.27%	$1,806,358	9.89%	($76,380)	(1.91)%	$10,727,439	16.04%
Net Transfers to Separate, Segregated Accounts & Protected Cell Accounts	$0	0.00%	$0	0.00%	$0	0.00%	$0	0.00%
Commissions, Expenses Paid and Aggregate Write-Ins for Deductions	$2,799,184	66.27%	$16,419,270	89.87%	$4,038,810	101.23%	$55,166,575	82.50%
Dividends Paid to Policyholders	$0	0.00%	$0	0.00%	$0	0.00%	$0	0.00%
Federal and Foreign Income Taxes Paid (Recovered), Net Tax on Capital Gains (Losses)	($22,874)	(0.54)%	$44,621	0.24%	$27,350	0.69%	$977,142	1.46%
Total	$4,223,607	100.00%	$18,270,249	100.00%	$3,989,780	100.00%	$66,871,156	100.00%
NET CASH FROM OPERATIONS	($1,633,576)		($3,368,487)		($88,937)		$5,158,757	
CASH FROM INVESTMENTS	Company Value	%	Company Value	%	Company Value	%	Company Value	%
Proceeds from Investments Sold, Matured or Repaid:								
Bonds	$1,025,431	100.00%	$3,105,019	90.72%	$2,074,993	75.14%	$23,814,250	84.00%
Stocks	$0	0.00%	$0	0.00%	$634,183	22.96%	$4,083,993	14.40%
Mortgage Loans	$0	0.00%	$0	0.00%	$0	0.00%	$219,283	0.77%
Real Estate	$0	0.00%	$0	0.00%	$0	0.00%	$33,561	0.12%
Other Invested Assets	$0	0.00%	$4,904	0.14%	$0	0.00%	$181,104	0.64%
Net Gains or (Losses) on Cash, Cash Equivalents & Short-Term Investments	$0	0.00%	$0	0.00%	$0	0.00%	$0	0.00%
Miscellaneous Proceeds	$0	0.00%	$312,712	9.14%	$52,469	1.90%	$19,446	0.07%
Total Investment Proceeds	$1,025,431	100.00%	$3,422,635	100.00%	$2,761,645	100.00%	$28,351,637	100.00%
Cost of Investments Acquired (Long-Term Only):								
Bonds	$999,340	99.93%	$2,344,346	99.69%	$3,014,547	99.62%	$15,324,745	74.55%
Stocks	$0	0.00%	$0	0.00%	$16,267	0.54%	$4,903,964	23.86%
Mortgage Loans	$0	0.00%	$0	0.00%	$0	0.00%	$0	0.00%
Real Estate	$0	0.00%	$0	0.00%	$0	0.00%	$8,500	0.04%
Other Invested Assets	$0	0.00%	$0	0.00%	$0	0.00%	$319,657	1.55%
Miscellaneous Applications	$681	0.07%	$7,402	0.31%	($4,617)	(0.15)%	$0	0.00%
Total Investments Acquired	$1,000,021	100.00%	$2,351,748	100.00%	$3,026,197	100.00%	$20,556,866	100.00%
Net Increase (Decrease) in Contract Loans and Premium Notes	$0		$0		$0		$0	
NET CASH FROM INVESTMENTS	$25,410		$1,070,887		($264,552)		$7,794,771	
CASH FROM FINANCING AND MISCELLANEOUS SOURCES	Company Value		Company Value		Company Value		Company Value	
Cash Provided (Applied):								
Surplus Notes, Capital Notes	$0		$0		$0		$0	
Capital and paid in Surplus, Less Treasury Stock	$1,397,290		$1,903,943		$5,000,000		$0	
Borrowed Funds	$0		$0		$0		($9,552)	
Net Deposits on Deposit-Type Contracts & Other Insurance Liabilities	$0		$0		$0		$0	
Dividends to Stockholders	$0		$0		$135,513		$10,732,722	
Other Cash Provided (Applied)	$198,910		$520,932		($103,456)		$1,345,341	
NET CASH FROM FINANCING AND MISCELLANEOUS SOURCES	$1,596,200		$2,424,875		$4,761,031		($9,396,933)	
NET CHANGE IN CASH, CASH EQUIVALENTS & SHORT-TERM INVESTMENTS	($11,966)		$127,275		$4,407,542		$3,556,595	
ENDING CASH, CASH EQUIVALENTS & SHORT-TERM INVESTMENTS	$224,665		$853,485		$5,310,594		$8,822,981	

2

C.3   Statement of Cash Flow - By Individual Underwriter

	K.E.L.		LAND CORP (CO)		LAND TIC (ST LOUIS)		LAWYERS	
BEGINNING CASH, CASH EQUIVALENTS & SHORT-TERM INVESTMENTS	$0		$1,575,129		$5,789,440		$77,797,332	

CASH FROM OPERATIONS	Company Value	%	Company Value	%	Company Value	%	Company Value	%
Premiums Collected Net of Reinsurance	$579,734	92.04%	$19,580,211	97.14%	$558,492	84.88%	$1,221,754,254	88.77%
Net Investment Income	$50,163	7.96%	$484,275	2.40%	$99,446	15.11%	$33,759,102	2.45%
Miscellaneous Income	$0	0.00%	$92,844	0.46%	$25	0.00%	$120,864,896	8.78%
Total	$629,897	100.00%	$20,157,330	100.00%	$657,963	100.00%	$1,376,378,252	100.00%
Benefit and Loss Related Payments	$0	0.00%	$226,989	1.19%	$0	0.00%	$85,456,626	6.41%
Net Transfers to Separate, Segregated Accounts & Protected Cell Accounts	$0	0.00%	$0	0.00%	$0	0.00%	$0	0.00%
Commissions, Expenses Paid and Aggregate Write-Ins for Deductions	$760,902	100.00%	$18,091,472	95.20%	$1,239,430	96.77%	$1,244,953,709	93.35%
Dividends Paid to Policyholders	$0	0.00%	$0	0.00%	$0	0.00%	$0	0.00%
Federal and Foreign Income Taxes Paid (Recovered), Net Tax on Capital Gains (Losses)	$0	0.00%	$685,000	3.60%	$41,307	3.23%	$3,243,843	0.24%
Total	$760,902	100.00%	$19,003,461	100.00%	$1,280,737	100.00%	$1,333,654,178	100.00%
NET CASH FROM OPERATIONS	($131,005)		$1,153,869		($622,774)		$42,724,074	

CASH FROM INVESTMENTS	Company Value	%	Company Value	%	Company Value	%	Company Value	%
Proceeds from Investments Sold, Matured or Repaid:								
Bonds	$0	--	$2,501,742	88.63%	$0	--	$87,675,859	55.50%
Stocks	$0	--	$321,030	11.37%	$0	--	$69,838,118	44.21%
Mortgage Loans	$0	--	$0	0.00%	$0	--	$0	0.00%
Real Estate	$0	--	$0	0.00%	$0	--	$0	0.00%
Other Invested Assets	$0	--	$0	0.00%	$0	--	$0	0.00%
Net Gains or (Losses) on Cash, Cash Equivalents & Short-Term Investments	$0	--	$0	0.00%	$0	--	$0	0.00%
Miscellaneous Proceeds	$0	--	$0	0.00%	$0	--	$459,993	0.29%
Total Investment Proceeds	$0	--	$2,822,772	100.00%	$0	--	$157,973,970	100.00%
Cost of Investments Acquired (Long-Term Only):								
Bonds	$0	--	$733,562	76.41%	$1,630,657	100.00%	$98,621,237	55.49%
Stocks	$0	--	$226,495	23.59%	$0	0.00%	$64,736,518	36.42%
Mortgage Loans	$0	--	$0	0.00%	$0	0.00%	$0	0.00%
Real Estate	$0	--	$0	0.00%	$0	0.00%	$0	0.00%
Other Invested Assets	$0	--	$0	0.00%	$0	0.00%	$8,851,606	4.98%
Miscellaneous Applications	$0	--	$0	0.00%	$0	0.00%	$5,520,689	3.11%
Total Investments Acquired	$0	--	$960,057	100.00%	$1,630,657	100.00%	$177,730,050	100.00%
Net Increase (Decrease) in Contract Loans and Premium Notes	$0		$0		$0		$0	
NET CASH FROM INVESTMENTS	$0		$1,862,715		($1,630,657)		($19,756,080)	

CASH FROM FINANCING AND MISCELLANEOUS SOURCES	Company Value	Company Value	Company Value	Company Value
Cash Provided (Applied):				
Surplus Notes, Capital Notes	$0	$0	$0	$0
Capital and paid in Surplus, Less Treasury Stock	$2,500,000	$0	$0	$0
Borrowed Funds	$0	$0	$0	($1,519,291)
Net Deposits on Deposit-Type Contracts & Other Insurance Liabilities	$0	$0	$0	$0
Dividends to Stockholders	$0	$1,791,147	$0	$40,000,000
Other Cash Provided (Applied)	$0	$150,344	$0	($8,708,061)
NET CASH FROM FINANCING AND MISCELLANEOUS SOURCES	$2,500,000	($1,640,803)	$0	($50,227,352)

	K.E.L.	LAND CORP (CO)	LAND TIC (ST LOUIS)	LAWYERS
NET CHANGE IN CASH, CASH EQUIVALENTS & SHORT-TERM INVESTMENTS	$2,368,995	$1,375,781	($2,253,431)	($27,259,358)
ENDING CASH, CASH EQUIVALENTS & SHORT-TERM INVESTMENTS	$2,368,995	$2,950,910	$3,536,009	$50,537,974

C.3 Statement of Cash Flow - By Individual Underwriter

	MANITO		MASON		MASON COUNTY		MASSACHUSETTS TIC	
BEGINNING CASH, CASH EQUIVALENTS & SHORT-TERM INVESTMENTS	$1,454,483		$712,316		$828,279		$393,179	
CASH FROM OPERATIONS	Company Value	%	Company Value	%	Company Value	%	Company Value	%
Premiums Collected Net of Reinsurance	$735,089	91.57%	$1,477,217	88.29%	$0	0.00%	($254)	(0.44)%
Net Investment Income	$67,685	8.43%	$151,166	9.04%	$31,231	100.00%	$57,813	100.44%
Miscellaneous Income	$0	0.00%	$44,670	2.67%	$0	0.00%	$0	0.00%
Total	$802,774	100.00%	$1,673,053	100.00%	$31,231	100.00%	$57,559	100.00%
Benefit and Loss Related Payments	$0	0.00%	($9,558)	(0.50)%	$0	0.00%	$0	0.00%
Net Transfers to Separate, Segregated Accounts & Protected Cell Accounts	$0	0.00%	$0	0.00%	$0	0.00%	$0	0.00%
Commissions, Expenses Paid and Aggregate Write-Ins for Deductions	$784,503	100.00%	$1,922,369	100.50%	$2,353	100.00%	$46,943	100.00%
Dividends Paid to Policyholders	$0	0.00%	$0	0.00%	$0	0.00%	$0	0.00%
Federal and Foreign Income Taxes Paid (Recovered), Net Tax on Capital Gains (Losses)	$0	0.00%	$0	0.00%	$0	0.00%	$0	0.00%
Total	$784,503	100.00%	$1,912,811	100.00%	$2,353	100.00%	$46,943	100.00%
NET CASH FROM OPERATIONS	$18,271		($239,758)		$28,878		$10,616	
CASH FROM INVESTMENTS	Company Value	%	Company Value	%	Company Value	%	Company Value	%
Proceeds from Investments Sold, Matured or Repaid:								
Bonds	$0	--	$5,012,500	99.99%	$0	--	$0	0.00%
Stocks	$0	--	$0	0.00%	$0	--	$1,330	100.00%
Mortgage Loans	$0	--	$0	0.00%	$0	--	$0	0.00%
Real Estate	$0	--	$0	0.00%	$0	--	$0	0.00%
Other Invested Assets	$0	--	$0	0.00%	$0	--	$0	0.00%
Net Gains or (Losses) on Cash, Cash Equivalents & Short-Term Investments	$0	--	$0	0.00%	$0	--	$0	0.00%
Miscellaneous Proceeds	$0	--	$506	0.01%	$0	--	$0	0.00%
Total Investment Proceeds	$0	--	$5,013,006	100.00%	$0	--	$1,330	100.00%
Cost of Investments Acquired (Long-Term Only):								
Bonds	$0	--	$3,441,394	100.00%	$0	--	$0	--
Stocks	$0	--	$0	0.00%	$0	--	$0	--
Mortgage Loans	$0	--	$0	0.00%	$0	--	$0	--
Real Estate	$0	--	$0	0.00%	$0	--	$0	--
Other Invested Assets	$0	--	$0	0.00%	$0	--	$0	--
Miscellaneous Applications	$0	--	$0	0.00%	$0	--	$0	--
Total Investments Acquired	$0	--	$3,441,394	100.00%	$0	--	$0	--
Net Increase (Decrease) in Contract Loans and Premium Notes	$0		$0		$0		$0	
NET CASH FROM INVESTMENTS	$0		$1,571,612		$0		$1,330	
CASH FROM FINANCING AND MISCELLANEOUS SOURCES	Company Value		Company Value		Company Value		Company Value	
Cash Provided (Applied):								
Surplus Notes, Capital Notes	$0		$0		$0		$0	
Capital and paid in Surplus, Less Treasury Stock	$0		$0		$0		$0	
Borrowed Funds	$0		$0		$0		$0	
Net Deposits on Deposit-Type Contracts & Other Insurance Liabilities	$0		$0		$0		$0	
Dividends to Stockholders	$0		$0		$0		$3,984	
Other Cash Provided (Applied)	($21,275)		($3,676)		$0		($88,487)	
NET CASH FROM FINANCING AND MISCELLANEOUS SOURCES	($21,275)		($3,676)		$0		($92,471)	
NET CHANGE IN CASH, CASH EQUIVALENTS & SHORT-TERM INVESTMENTS	($3,004)		$1,328,178		$28,878		($80,525)	
ENDING CASH, CASH EQUIVALENTS & SHORT-TERM INVESTMENTS	$1,451,479		$2,040,494		$857,157		$312,654	

2

C.3 Statement of Cash Flow - By Individual Underwriter

	MISSISSIPPI GUARANTY		MISSISSIPPI VALLEY		MONROE		NATIONAL	
BEGINNING CASH, CASH EQUIVALENTS & SHORT-TERM INVESTMENTS	$766,536		$1,873,492		$5,203,186		$419,812	
CASH FROM OPERATIONS	Company Value	%	Company Value	%	Company Value	%	Company Value	%
Premiums Collected Net of Reinsurance	$431,374	96.17%	$26,850,850	92.97%	$19,372,530	96.08%	$3,500,144	91.89%
Net Investment Income	$17,107	3.81%	$2,030,880	7.03%	$431,127	2.14%	$57,222	1.50%
Miscellaneous Income	$50	0.01%	$0	0.00%	$358,213	1.78%	$251,806	6.61%
Total	$448,531	100.00%	$28,881,730	100.00%	$20,161,870	100.00%	$3,809,172	100.00%
Benefit and Loss Related Payments	$0	0.00%	$1,886,967	7.46%	$306,827	1.50%	$25,839	0.63%
Net Transfers to Separate, Segregated Accounts & Protected Cell Accounts	$0	0.00%	$0	0.00%	$0	0.00%	$0	0.00%
Commissions, Expenses Paid and Aggregate Write-Ins for Deductions	$381,946	100.00%	$23,751,269	93.94%	$20,142,243	98.63%	$4,080,051	99.37%
Dividends Paid to Policyholders	$0	0.00%	$0	0.00%	$0	0.00%	$0	0.00%
Federal and Foreign Income Taxes Paid (Recovered), Net Tax on Capital Gains (Losses)	$0	0.00%	($355,913)	(1.41)%	($27,890)	(0.14)%	$0	0.00%
Total	$381,946	100.00%	$25,282,323	100.00%	$20,421,180	100.00%	$4,105,890	100.00%
NET CASH FROM OPERATIONS	$66,585		$3,599,407		($259,310)		($296,718)	
CASH FROM INVESTMENTS	Company Value	%	Company Value	%	Company Value	%	Company Value	%
Proceeds from Investments Sold, Matured or Repaid:								
Bonds	$0	--	$6,369,480	100.00%	$1,980,281	44.83%	$0	0.00%
Stocks	$0	--	$0	0.00%	$2,305,430	52.19%	$258,661	10.00%
Mortgage Loans	$0	--	$0	0.00%	$0	0.00%	$2,328,009	90.00%
Real Estate	$0	--	$0	0.00%	$0	0.00%	$0	0.00%
Other Invested Assets	$0	--	$0	0.00%	$132,000	2.99%	$0	0.00%
Net Gains or (Losses) on Cash, Cash Equivalents & Short-Term Investments	$0	--	$0	0.00%	$0	0.00%	$0	0.00%
Miscellaneous Proceeds	$0	--	$0	0.00%	$0	0.00%	$0	0.00%
Total Investment Proceeds	$0	--	$6,369,480	100.00%	$4,417,711	100.00%	$2,586,670	100.00%
Cost of Investments Acquired (Long-Term Only):								
Bonds	$0	--	$6,981,096	92.13%	$1,747,677	57.04%	$0	0.00%
Stocks	$0	--	$596,206	7.87%	$1,283,994	41.90%	$0	0.00%
Mortgage Loans	$0	--	$0	0.00%	$0	0.00%	$2,134,750	100.00%
Real Estate	$0	--	$0	0.00%	$32,395	1.06%	$0	0.00%
Other Invested Assets	$0	--	$0	0.00%	$0	0.00%	$0	0.00%
Miscellaneous Applications	$0	--	$0	0.00%	$0	0.00%	$0	0.00%
Total Investments Acquired	$0	--	$7,577,302	100.00%	$3,064,066	100.00%	$2,134,750	100.00%
Net Increase (Decrease) in Contract Loans and Premium Notes	$0		$0		$0		$0	
NET CASH FROM INVESTMENTS	$0		($1,207,822)		$1,353,645		$451,920	
CASH FROM FINANCING AND MISCELLANEOUS SOURCES	Company Value		Company Value		Company Value		Company Value	
Cash Provided (Applied):								
Surplus Notes, Capital Notes	$0		$0		$0		$0	
Capital and paid in Surplus, Less Treasury Stock	$0		$0		$0		$0	
Borrowed Funds	$0		$0		($4,316)		$102,671	
Net Deposits on Deposit-Type Contracts & Other Insurance Liabilities	$0		$0		$0		$0	
Dividends to Stockholders	$0		$900,000		$3,000,000		$0	
Other Cash Provided (Applied)	$0		$218,323		$92,561		($252,307)	
NET CASH FROM FINANCING AND MISCELLANEOUS SOURCES	$0		($681,677)		($2,911,755)		($149,636)	
NET CHANGE IN CASH, CASH EQUIVALENTS & SHORT-TERM INVESTMENTS	$66,585		$1,709,908		($1,817,420)		$5,566	
ENDING CASH, CASH EQUIVALENTS & SHORT-TERM INVESTMENTS	$833,121		$3,583,400		$3,385,766		$425,378	

C.3 Statement of Cash Flow - By Individual Underwriter

	NATIONAL ATTORNEYS		NATIONAL LAND		NATIONAL OF NY		NATIONS OF NY	
BEGINNING CASH, CASH EQUIVALENTS & SHORT-TERM INVESTMENTS	$622,688		$1,071,250		$7,196,534		$3,542,972	

CASH FROM OPERATIONS	Company Value	%	Company Value	%	Company Value	%	Company Value	%
Premiums Collected Net of Reinsurance	$733,437	51.51%	$2,479,492	85.95%	$12,041,664	93.92%	$13,552	1.44%
Net Investment Income	$86,641	6.09%	$401,102	13.90%	$778,854	6.08%	$929,329	98.56%
Miscellaneous Income	$603,657	42.40%	$4,110	0.14%	$0	0.00%	$0	0.00%
Total	$1,423,735	100.00%	$2,884,704	100.00%	$12,820,518	100.00%	$942,881	100.00%
Benefit and Loss Related Payments	$317,150	20.04%	$77,224	2.71%	$1,573,528	14.01%	$631,084	53.65%
Net Transfers to Separate, Segregated Accounts & Protected Cell Accounts	$0	0.00%	$0	0.00%	$0	0.00%	$0	0.00%
Commissions, Expenses Paid and Aggregate Write-Ins for Deductions	$1,347,650	85.16%	$2,774,106	97.29%	$10,084,391	89.77%	$586,795	49.88%
Dividends Paid to Policyholders	$0	0.00%	$0	0.00%	$0	0.00%	$0	0.00%
Federal and Foreign Income Taxes Paid (Recovered), Net Tax on Capital Gains (Losses)	($82,251)	(5.20)%	$0	0.00%	($424,161)	(3.78)%	($41,528)	(3.53)%
Total	$1,582,549	100.00%	$2,851,330	100.00%	$11,233,758	100.00%	$1,176,351	100.00%
NET CASH FROM OPERATIONS	($158,814)		$33,374		$1,586,760		($233,470)	

CASH FROM INVESTMENTS	Company Value	%	Company Value	%	Company Value	%	Company Value	%
Proceeds from Investments Sold, Matured or Repaid:								
Bonds	$150,000	67.10%	$2,110,000	100.00%	$3,020,000	100.00%	$7,489,360	99.73%
Stocks	$73,535	32.90%	$0	0.00%	$0	0.00%	$0	0.00%
Mortgage Loans	$0	0.00%	$0	0.00%	$0	0.00%	$5,545	0.07%
Real Estate	$0	0.00%	$0	0.00%	$0	0.00%	$0	0.00%
Other Invested Assets	$0	0.00%	$0	0.00%	$0	0.00%	$0	0.00%
Net Gains or (Losses) on Cash, Cash Equivalents & Short-Term Investments	$0	0.00%	$0	0.00%	$0	0.00%	$0	0.00%
Miscellaneous Proceeds	$0	0.00%	$0	0.00%	$0	0.00%	$15,037	0.20%
Total Investment Proceeds	$223,535	100.00%	$2,110,000	100.00%	$3,020,000	100.00%	$7,509,942	100.00%
Cost of Investments Acquired (Long-Term Only):								
Bonds	$0	0.00%	$1,937,816	100.00%	$3,465,320	99.32%	$8,141,714	100.00%
Stocks	$75,000	117.77%	$0	0.00%	$0	0.00%	$0	0.00%
Mortgage Loans	$0	0.00%	$0	0.00%	$0	0.00%	$0	0.00%
Real Estate	$0	0.00%	$0	0.00%	$0	0.00%	$0	0.00%
Other Invested Assets	$0	0.00%	$0	0.00%	$0	0.00%	$0	0.00%
Miscellaneous Applications	($11,314)	(17.77)%	$0	0.00%	$23,673	0.68%	$0	0.00%
Total Investments Acquired	$63,686	100.00%	$1,937,816	100.00%	$3,488,993	100.00%	$8,141,714	100.00%
Net Increase (Decrease) in Contract Loans and Premium Notes	$0		$0		$0		$0	
NET CASH FROM INVESTMENTS	$159,849		$172,184		($468,993)		($631,772)	

CASH FROM FINANCING AND MISCELLANEOUS SOURCES	Company Value		Company Value		Company Value		Company Value	
Cash Provided (Applied):								
Surplus Notes, Capital Notes	$0		$0		$0		$0	
Capital and paid in Surplus, Less Treasury Stock	$0		$0		$0		$0	
Borrowed Funds	$0		$0		$0		$0	
Net Deposits on Deposit-Type Contracts & Other Insurance Liabilities	$0		$0		$0		$0	
Dividends to Stockholders	$0		$0		$0		$0	
Other Cash Provided (Applied)	$20,162		$0		($2,803,189)		($1,249,842)	
NET CASH FROM FINANCING AND MISCELLANEOUS SOURCES	$20,162		$0		($2,803,189)		($1,249,842)	

NET CHANGE IN CASH, CASH EQUIVALENTS & SHORT-TERM INVESTMENTS	$21,197		$205,558		($1,685,422)		($2,115,084)	
ENDING CASH, CASH EQUIVALENTS & SHORT-TERM INVESTMENTS	$643,885		$1,276,808		$5,511,112		$1,427,888	

C.3 Statement of Cash Flow - By Individual Underwriter

	NEW JERSEY TIC		NORTH AMERICAN		NORTHEAST INVESTORS		OHIO BAR	
BEGINNING CASH, CASH EQUIVALENTS & SHORT-TERM INVESTMENTS	$1,007,665		$57,168,954		$216,104		$2,125,693	
CASH FROM OPERATIONS	Company Value	%	Company Value	%	Company Value	%	Company Value	%
Premiums Collected Net of Reinsurance	$17,243,680	95.01%	$108,625,327	96.55%	$2,393,706	89.56%	$13,020,588	90.31%
Net Investment Income	$374,044	2.06%	$3,550,662	3.16%	$278,036	10.40%	$1,383,608	9.60%
Miscellaneous Income	$531,506	2.93%	$333,580	0.30%	$930	0.03%	$13,010	0.09%
Total	$18,149,230	100.00%	$112,509,569	100.00%	$2,672,672	100.00%	$14,417,206	100.00%
Benefit and Loss Related Payments	$1,064,324	5.83%	$2,941,202	2.78%	$154,328	6.20%	$1,630,114	13.26%
Net Transfers to Separate, Segregated Accounts & Protected Cell Accounts	$0	0.00%	$0	0.00%	$0	0.00%	$0	0.00%
Commissions, Expenses Paid and Aggregate Write-Ins for Deductions	$17,211,864	94.24%	$98,878,424	93.49%	$2,340,842	94.11%	$10,663,603	86.74%
Dividends Paid to Policyholders	$0	0.00%	$0	0.00%	$0	0.00%	$0	0.00%
Federal and Foreign Income Taxes Paid (Recovered), Net Tax on Capital Gains (Losses)	($13,098)	(0.07)%	$3,940,910	3.73%	($7,739)	(0.31)%	$0	0.00%
Total	$18,263,090	100.00%	$105,760,536	100.00%	$2,487,431	100.00%	$12,293,717	100.00%
NET CASH FROM OPERATIONS	($113,860)		$6,749,033		$185,241		$2,123,489	
CASH FROM INVESTMENTS	Company Value	%	Company Value	%	Company Value	%	Company Value	%
Proceeds from Investments Sold, Matured or Repaid:								
Bonds	$4,370,680	100.00%	$7,600,000	99.79%	$1,050,000	95.40%	$5,838,695	100.00%
Stocks	$0	0.00%	$0	0.00%	$50,641	4.60%	$0	0.00%
Mortgage Loans	$0	0.00%	$16,287	0.21%	$0	0.00%	$0	0.00%
Real Estate	$0	0.00%	$0	0.00%	$0	0.00%	$0	0.00%
Other Invested Assets	$0	0.00%	$0	0.00%	$0	0.00%	$0	0.00%
Net Gains or (Losses) on Cash, Cash Equivalents & Short-Term Investments	$0	0.00%	$0	0.00%	$0	0.00%	$0	0.00%
Miscellaneous Proceeds	$0	0.00%	$0	0.00%	$0	0.00%	$0	0.00%
Total Investment Proceeds	$4,370,680	100.00%	$7,616,287	100.00%	$1,100,641	100.00%	$5,838,695	100.00%
Cost of Investments Acquired (Long-Term Only):								
Bonds	$4,107,661	100.00%	$208,857	100.00%	$653,088	90.84%	$7,246,025	100.00%
Stocks	$0	0.00%	$0	0.00%	$65,840	9.16%	$0	0.00%
Mortgage Loans	$0	0.00%	$0	0.00%	$0	0.00%	$0	0.00%
Real Estate	$0	0.00%	$0	0.00%	$0	0.00%	$0	0.00%
Other Invested Assets	$0	0.00%	$0	0.00%	$0	0.00%	$0	0.00%
Miscellaneous Applications	$0	0.00%	$0	0.00%	$0	0.00%	$0	0.00%
Total Investments Acquired	$4,107,661	100.00%	$208,857	100.00%	$718,928	100.00%	$7,246,025	100.00%
Net Increase (Decrease) in Contract Loans and Premium Notes	$0		$0		$0		$0	
NET CASH FROM INVESTMENTS	$263,019		$7,407,430		$381,713		($1,407,330)	
CASH FROM FINANCING AND MISCELLANEOUS SOURCES	Company Value		Company Value		Company Value		Company Value	
Cash Provided (Applied):								
Surplus Notes, Capital Notes	$0		$0		$0		$0	
Capital and paid in Surplus, Less Treasury Stock	$0		$0		$0		$0	
Borrowed Funds	$0		$0		$0		$0	
Net Deposits on Deposit-Type Contracts & Other Insurance Liabilities	$0		$0		$0		$0	
Dividends to Stockholders	$0		$0		$0		$420,000	
Other Cash Provided (Applied)	$106,408		$1,114,185		$16,589		$0	
NET CASH FROM FINANCING AND MISCELLANEOUS SOURCES	$106,408		$1,114,185		$16,589		($420,000)	
NET CHANGE IN CASH, CASH EQUIVALENTS & SHORT-TERM INVESTMENTS	$255,567		$15,270,648		$583,543		$296,159	
ENDING CASH, CASH EQUIVALENTS & SHORT-TERM INVESTMENTS	$1,263,232		$72,439,602		$799,647		$2,421,852	

C.3 Statement of Cash Flow - By Individual Underwriter

	OLD REPUBLIC GENERAL		OLD REPUBLIC NATIONAL		OLYMPIC		PACIFIC NORTHWEST	
BEGINNING CASH, CASH EQUIVALENTS & SHORT-TERM INVESTMENTS	$789,050		$22,971,283		$360,010		$8,545,340	
CASH FROM OPERATIONS	Company Value	%	Company Value	%	Company Value	%	Company Value	%
Premiums Collected Net of Reinsurance	$16,195,264	74.58%	$763,420,098	97.02%	$0	0.00%	$60,400,765	97.46%
Net Investment Income	$5,521,090	25.42%	$23,380,120	2.97%	$16,065	100.00%	$1,500,231	2.42%
Miscellaneous Income	$0	0.00%	$80,554	0.01%	$0	0.00%	$75,000	0.12%
Total	$21,716,354	100.00%	$786,880,772	100.00%	$16,065	100.00%	$61,975,996	100.00%
Benefit and Loss Related Payments	$6,403,336	52.97%	$57,699,924	7.35%	$1,345	2.70%	$3,674,785	6.17%
Net Transfers to Separate, Segregated Accounts & Protected Cell Accounts	$0	0.00%	$0	0.00%	$0	0.00%	$0	0.00%
Commissions, Expenses Paid and Aggregate Write-Ins for Deductions	$3,037,613	25.13%	$718,244,570	91.47%	$48,506	97.30%	$54,588,094	91.68%
Dividends Paid to Policyholders	$0	0.00%	$0	0.00%	$0	0.00%	$0	0.00%
Federal and Foreign Income Taxes Paid (Recovered), Net Tax on Capital Gains (Losses)	$2,646,782	21.90%	$9,259,904	1.18%	$0	0.00%	$1,281,318	2.15%
Total	$12,087,731	100.00%	$785,204,398	100.00%	$49,851	100.00%	$59,544,197	100.00%
NET CASH FROM OPERATIONS	$9,628,623		$1,676,374		($33,786)		$2,431,799	
CASH FROM INVESTMENTS	Company Value	%	Company Value	%	Company Value	%	Company Value	%
Proceeds from Investments Sold, Matured or Repaid:								
Bonds	$11,738,042	97.81%	$52,848,205	94.00%	$0	--	$7,211,262	89.80%
Stocks	$262,797	2.19%	$283,279	0.50%	$0	--	$175,135	2.18%
Mortgage Loans	$0	0.00%	$421,499	0.75%	$0	--	$643,647	8.02%
Real Estate	$0	0.00%	$2,671,245	4.75%	$0	--	$0	0.00%
Other Invested Assets	$0	0.00%	$0	0.00%	$0	--	$0	0.00%
Net Gains or (Losses) on Cash, Cash Equivalents & Short-Term Investments	$0	0.00%	$0	0.00%	$0	--	$0	0.00%
Miscellaneous Proceeds	$0	0.00%	$0	0.00%	$0	--	$0	0.00%
Total Investment Proceeds	$12,000,839	100.00%	$56,224,228	100.00%	$0	--	$8,030,044	100.00%
Cost of Investments Acquired (Long-Term Only):								
Bonds	$7,581,665	54.77%	$32,299,033	69.10%	$0	--	$8,741,674	84.75%
Stocks	$6,260,615	45.23%	$10,822,225	23.15%	$0	--	$832,882	8.07%
Mortgage Loans	$0	0.00%	$741,381	1.59%	$0	--	$739,847	7.17%
Real Estate	$0	0.00%	$381,921	0.82%	$0	--	$0	0.00%
Other Invested Assets	$0	0.00%	$2,500,000	5.35%	$0	--	$0	0.00%
Miscellaneous Applications	$0	0.00%	$0	0.00%	$0	--	$0	0.00%
Total Investments Acquired	$13,842,280	100.00%	$46,744,560	100.00%	$0	--	$10,314,403	100.00%
Net Increase (Decrease) in Contract Loans and Premium Notes	$0		$0		$0		$0	
NET CASH FROM INVESTMENTS	($1,841,441)		$9,479,668		$0		($2,284,359)	
CASH FROM FINANCING AND MISCELLANEOUS SOURCES	Company Value		Company Value		Company Value		Company Value	
Cash Provided (Applied):								
Surplus Notes, Capital Notes	$0		$0		$0		$0	
Capital and paid in Surplus, Less Treasury Stock	$0		$0		$0		$215,177	
Borrowed Funds	$0		($393,249)		$0		$0	
Net Deposits on Deposit-Type Contracts & Other Insurance Liabilities	$0		$0		$0		$0	
Dividends to Stockholders	$8,000,000		$22,000,000		$0		$490,100	
Other Cash Provided (Applied)	$677,083		$10,775,250		$0		$55,822	
NET CASH FROM FINANCING AND MISCELLANEOUS SOURCES	($7,322,917)		($11,617,999)		$0		($219,101)	
NET CHANGE IN CASH, CASH EQUIVALENTS & SHORT-TERM INVESTMENTS	$464,265		($461,957)		($33,786)		($71,661)	
ENDING CASH, CASH EQUIVALENTS & SHORT-TERM INVESTMENTS	$1,253,315		$22,509,326		$326,224		$8,473,679	

2

C.3 Statement of Cash Flow - By Individual Underwriter

	PENN ATTORNEYS		PORT LAWRENCE		PUBLIC		SEAGATE	
BEGINNING CASH, CASH EQUIVALENTS & SHORT-TERM INVESTMENTS	$3,105,051		$7,543,021		$1,007,901		$569,494	
CASH FROM OPERATIONS	Company Value	%	Company Value	%	Company Value	%	Company Value	%
Premiums Collected Net of Reinsurance	$1,926,049	79.38%	$5,626,376	70.21%	$0	0.00%	$186,090	79.08%
Net Investment Income	$500,272	20.62%	$1,084,590	13.53%	$37,590	100.00%	$24,229	10.30%
Miscellaneous Income	$0	0.00%	$1,302,771	16.26%	$0	0.00%	$25,000	10.62%
Total	$2,426,321	100.00%	$8,013,737	100.00%	$37,590	100.00%	$235,319	100.00%
Benefit and Loss Related Payments	$81,137	4.88%	$99,717	1.08%	$0	0.00%	$0	0.00%
Net Transfers to Separate, Segregated Accounts & Protected Cell Accounts	$0	0.00%	$0	0.00%	$0	0.00%	$60,093	26.06%
Commissions, Expenses Paid and Aggregate Write-Ins for Deductions	$1,202,128	72.32%	$9,118,358	98.88%	$7,247	100.00%	$170,520	73.94%
Dividends Paid to Policyholders	$0	0.00%	$0	0.00%	$0	0.00%	$0	0.00%
Federal and Foreign Income Taxes Paid (Recovered), Net Tax on Capital Gains (Losses)	$378,883	22.79%	$3,920	0.04%	$0	0.00%	$0	0.00%
Total	$1,662,148	100.00%	$9,221,995	100.00%	$7,247	100.00%	$230,613	100.00%
NET CASH FROM OPERATIONS	$764,173		($1,208,258)		$30,343		$4,706	
CASH FROM INVESTMENTS	Company Value	%	Company Value	%	Company Value	%	Company Value	%
Proceeds from Investments Sold, Matured or Repaid:								
Bonds	$2,625,529	100.00%	$3,788,361	94.94%	$0	--	$0	--
Stocks	$0	0.00%	$0	0.00%	$0	--	$0	--
Mortgage Loans	$0	0.00%	$0	0.00%	$0	--	$0	--
Real Estate	$0	0.00%	$0	0.00%	$0	--	$0	--
Other Invested Assets	$0	0.00%	$201,856	5.06%	$0	--	$0	--
Net Gains or (Losses) on Cash, Cash Equivalents & Short-Term Investments	$0	0.00%	$0	0.00%	$0	--	$0	--
Miscellaneous Proceeds	$0	0.00%	$0	0.00%	$0	--	$0	--
Total Investment Proceeds	$2,625,529	100.00%	$3,990,217	100.00%	$0	--	$0	--
Cost of Investments Acquired (Long-Term Only):								
Bonds	$2,152,565	100.00%	$2,464,713	99.95%	$0	--	$0	--
Stocks	$0	0.00%	$0	0.00%	$0	--	$0	--
Mortgage Loans	$0	0.00%	$0	0.00%	$0	--	$0	--
Real Estate	$0	0.00%	$0	0.00%	$0	--	$0	--
Other Invested Assets	$0	0.00%	$0	0.00%	$0	--	$0	--
Miscellaneous Applications	$0	0.00%	$1,250	0.05%	$0	--	$0	--
Total Investments Acquired	$2,152,565	100.00%	$2,465,963	100.00%	$0	--	$0	--
Net Increase (Decrease) in Contract Loans and Premium Notes	$0		$0		$0		$0	
NET CASH FROM INVESTMENTS	$472,964		$1,524,254		$0		$0	
CASH FROM FINANCING AND MISCELLANEOUS SOURCES	Company Value		Company Value		Company Value		Company Value	
Cash Provided (Applied):								
Surplus Notes, Capital Notes	$0		$0		$0		$0	
Capital and paid in Surplus, Less Treasury Stock	$0		$0		$0		$0	
Borrowed Funds	$0		$0		$0		$0	
Net Deposits on Deposit-Type Contracts & Other Insurance Liabilities	$0		$0		$0		$0	
Dividends to Stockholders	$845,000		$1,536,000		$0		$0	
Other Cash Provided (Applied)	$0		$0		$0		$0	
NET CASH FROM FINANCING AND MISCELLANEOUS SOURCES	($845,000)		($1,536,000)		$0		$0	
NET CHANGE IN CASH, CASH EQUIVALENTS & SHORT-TERM INVESTMENTS	$392,137		($1,220,004)		$30,343		$4,706	
ENDING CASH, CASH EQUIVALENTS & SHORT-TERM INVESTMENTS	$3,497,188		$6,323,017		$1,038,244		$574,200	

C.3 Statement of Cash Flow - By Individual Underwriter

	SECURITY TG (BALTIMORE)		SECURITY UNION		SIERRA		SOUTHERN TI CORP	
BEGINNING CASH, CASH EQUIVALENTS & SHORT-TERM INVESTMENTS	$3,753,584		$9,503,672		$504,116		$2,783,275	
CASH FROM OPERATIONS	Company Value	%	Company Value	%	Company Value	%	Company Value	%
Premiums Collected Net of Reinsurance	$22,680,696	93.97%	$64,588,904	86.26%	$1,657,224	93.72%	$53,904,735	96.13%
Net Investment Income	$507,980	2.10%	$7,999,885	10.68%	$111,004	6.28%	$944,875	1.69%
Miscellaneous Income	$946,500	3.92%	$2,292,505	3.06%	$0	0.00%	$1,223,361	2.18%
Total	$24,135,176	100.00%	$74,881,294	100.00%	$1,768,228	100.00%	$56,072,971	100.00%
Benefit and Loss Related Payments	$2,090,474	8.23%	$7,863,736	10.63%	$0	0.00%	$1,807,376	3.33%
Net Transfers to Separate, Segregated Accounts & Protected Cell Accounts	$0	0.00%	$0	0.00%	$0	0.00%	$0	0.00%
Commissions, Expenses Paid and Aggregate Write-Ins for Deductions	$23,151,345	91.11%	$66,295,901	89.61%	$1,584,148	100.00%	$51,935,711	95.67%
Dividends Paid to Policyholders	$0	0.00%	$0	0.00%	$0	0.00%	$0	0.00%
Federal and Foreign Income Taxes Paid (Recovered), Net Tax on Capital Gains (Losses)	$169,256	0.67%	($173,806)	(0.23)%	$0	0.00%	$541,160	1.00%
Total	$25,411,075	100.00%	$73,985,831	100.00%	$1,584,148	100.00%	$54,284,247	100.00%
NET CASH FROM OPERATIONS	($1,275,899)		$895,463		$184,080		$1,788,724	
CASH FROM INVESTMENTS	Company Value	%	Company Value	%	Company Value	%	Company Value	%
Proceeds from Investments Sold, Matured or Repaid:								
Bonds	$1,414,030	93.54%	$101,514,377	62.96%	$0	--	$444,366	64.16%
Stocks	$95,824	6.34%	$59,709,998	37.03%	$0	--	$248,225	35.84%
Mortgage Loans	$1,898	0.13%	$1,780	0.00%	$0	--	$0	0.00%
Real Estate	$0	0.00%	$0	0.00%	$0	--	$0	0.00%
Other Invested Assets	$0	0.00%	$0	0.00%	$0	--	$0	0.00%
Net Gains or (Losses) on Cash, Cash Equivalents & Short-Term Investments	$0	0.00%	$0	0.00%	$0	--	$0	0.00%
Miscellaneous Proceeds	$0	0.00%	$0	0.00%	$0	--	$0	0.00%
Total Investment Proceeds	$1,511,752	100.00%	$161,226,155	100.00%	$0	--	$692,591	100.00%
Cost of Investments Acquired (Long-Term Only):								
Bonds	$536,668	50.53%	$96,890,775	61.01%	$0	--	$3,348,435	98.76%
Stocks	$62,194	5.86%	$47,066,756	29.64%	$0	--	$12,431	0.37%
Mortgage Loans	$146,227	13.77%	$0	0.00%	$0	--	$0	0.00%
Real Estate	$0	0.00%	$0	0.00%	$0	--	$29,750	0.88%
Other Invested Assets	$317,000	29.85%	$20,000,000	12.59%	$0	--	$0	0.00%
Miscellaneous Applications	$0	0.00%	($5,138,163)	(3.24)%	$0	--	$0	0.00%
Total Investments Acquired	$1,062,089	100.00%	$158,819,368	100.00%	$0	--	$3,390,616	100.00%
Net Increase (Decrease) in Contract Loans and Premium Notes	$0		$0		$0		$0	
NET CASH FROM INVESTMENTS	$449,663		$2,406,787		$0		($2,698,025)	
CASH FROM FINANCING AND MISCELLANEOUS SOURCES	Company Value		Company Value		Company Value		Company Value	
Cash Provided (Applied):								
Surplus Notes, Capital Notes	$0		$0		$0		$0	
Capital and paid in Surplus, Less Treasury Stock	$0		$0		$0		$0	
Borrowed Funds	$0		$0		$0		$0	
Net Deposits on Deposit-Type Contracts & Other Insurance Liabilities	$0		$0		$0		$0	
Dividends to Stockholders	$0		$5,000,000		$0		$406,115	
Other Cash Provided (Applied)	($268,269)		$0		$0		$839,297	
NET CASH FROM FINANCING AND MISCELLANEOUS SOURCES	($268,269)		($5,000,000)		$0		$433,182	
NET CHANGE IN CASH, CASH EQUIVALENTS & SHORT-TERM INVESTMENTS	($1,094,505)		($1,697,750)		$184,080		($476,119)	
ENDING CASH, CASH EQUIVALENTS & SHORT-TERM INVESTMENTS	$2,659,079		$7,805,922		$688,196		$2,307,156	

C.3   Statement of Cash Flow - By Individual Underwriter

	STEWART (OR)		STEWART TGC		STEWART TIC		T.A. TITLE	
BEGINNING CASH, CASH EQUIVALENTS & SHORT-TERM INVESTMENTS	$1,844,662		$59,900,331		$4,751,066		$7,530,586	
CASH FROM OPERATIONS	Company Value	%	Company Value	%	Company Value	%	Company Value	%
Premiums Collected Net of Reinsurance	$10,132,953	98.42%	$1,476,229,623	94.67%	$157,714,740	87.75%	$17,063,250	96.82%
Net Investment Income	$162,326	1.58%	$33,061,319	2.12%	$5,882,593	3.27%	$559,832	3.18%
Miscellaneous Income	$0	0.00%	$49,989,455	3.21%	$16,125,573	8.97%	$0	0.00%
Total	$10,295,279	100.00%	$1,559,280,397	100.00%	$179,722,906	100.00%	$17,623,082	100.00%
Benefit and Loss Related Payments	$0	0.00%	$108,493,037	7.04%	$5,594,586	3.42%	$739,742	4.42%
Net Transfers to Separate, Segregated Accounts & Protected Cell Accounts	$0	0.00%	$0	0.00%	$0	0.00%	$0	0.00%
Commissions, Expenses Paid and Aggregate Write-Ins for Deductions	$9,799,044	100.00%	$1,422,623,435	92.36%	$153,065,264	93.54%	$15,983,597	95.58%
Dividends Paid to Policyholders	$0	0.00%	$0	0.00%	$0	0.00%	$0	0.00%
Federal and Foreign Income Taxes Paid (Recovered), Net Tax on Capital Gains (Losses)	$0	0.00%	$9,111,435	0.59%	$4,979,770	3.04%	$0	0.00%
Total	$9,799,044	100.00%	$1,540,227,907	100.00%	$163,639,620	100.00%	$16,723,339	100.00%
NET CASH FROM OPERATIONS	$496,235		$19,052,490		$16,083,286		$899,743	
CASH FROM INVESTMENTS	Company Value	%	Company Value	%	Company Value	%	Company Value	%
Proceeds from Investments Sold, Matured or Repaid:								
Bonds	$700,000	100.00%	$96,063,540	78.20%	$6,763,124	98.63%	$2,826,522	71.04%
Stocks	$0	0.00%	$25,225,177	20.53%	$0	0.00%	$107,810	2.71%
Mortgage Loans	$0	0.00%	$406,579	0.33%	$0	0.00%	$26,696	0.67%
Real Estate	$0	0.00%	$560,712	0.46%	$0	0.00%	$1,000,000	25.13%
Other Invested Assets	$0	0.00%	$584,413	0.48%	$93,994	1.37%	$0	0.00%
Net Gains or (Losses) on Cash, Cash Equivalents & Short-Term Investments	$0	0.00%	$0	0.00%	$0	0.00%	$0	0.00%
Miscellaneous Proceeds	$0	0.00%	$0	0.00%	$0	0.00%	$17,742	0.45%
Total Investment Proceeds	$700,000	100.00%	$122,840,421	100.00%	$6,857,118	100.00%	$3,978,770	100.00%
Cost of Investments Acquired (Long-Term Only):								
Bonds	$1,532,129	100.00%	$118,842,820	74.21%	$19,212,757	100.00%	$1,506,525	100.00%
Stocks	$0	0.00%	$39,077,573	24.40%	$0	0.00%	$0	0.00%
Mortgage Loans	$0	0.00%	$2,222,505	1.39%	$0	0.00%	$0	0.00%
Real Estate	$0	0.00%	$0	0.00%	$0	0.00%	$0	0.00%
Other Invested Assets	$0	0.00%	$0	0.00%	$0	0.00%	$0	0.00%
Miscellaneous Applications	$0	0.00%	$0	0.00%	$0	0.00%	$0	0.00%
Total Investments Acquired	$1,532,129	100.00%	$160,142,898	100.00%	$19,212,757	100.00%	$1,506,525	100.00%
Net Increase (Decrease) in Contract Loans and Premium Notes	$0		$0		$0		$0	
NET CASH FROM INVESTMENTS	($832,129)		($37,302,477)		($12,355,639)		$2,472,245	
CASH FROM FINANCING AND MISCELLANEOUS SOURCES	Company Value		Company Value		Company Value		Company Value	
Cash Provided (Applied):								
Surplus Notes, Capital Notes	$0		$0		$0		$0	
Capital and paid in Surplus, Less Treasury Stock	$100,000		$21,183,384		$0		$0	
Borrowed Funds	$0		$0		$0		($2,672,887)	
Net Deposits on Deposit-Type Contracts & Other Insurance Liabilities	$0		$0		$0		$0	
Dividends to Stockholders	$0		$0		$6,000,000		$767,000	
Other Cash Provided (Applied)	($69,799)		$134,576		$0		$0	
NET CASH FROM FINANCING AND MISCELLANEOUS SOURCES	$30,201		$21,317,960		($6,000,000)		($3,439,887)	
NET CHANGE IN CASH, CASH EQUIVALENTS & SHORT-TERM INVESTMENTS	($305,693)		$3,067,973		($2,272,353)		($67,899)	
ENDING CASH, CASH EQUIVALENTS & SHORT-TERM INVESTMENTS	$1,538,969		$62,968,304		$2,478,713		$7,462,687	

C.3   Statement of Cash Flow - By Individual Underwriter

	TICOR		TICOR (FL)		TITLE G&TC		TITLE GUARANTY DIV (IA)	
BEGINNING CASH, CASH EQUIVALENTS & SHORT-TERM INVESTMENTS	$18,989,367		$4,621,270		$1,117,143		$6,206,072	

CASH FROM OPERATIONS

	Company Value	%	Company Value	%	Company Value	%	Company Value	%
Premiums Collected Net of Reinsurance	$327,439,237	83.89%	$93,156,190	87.49%	$1,243,748	71.81%	$3,708,021	100.00%
Net Investment Income	$12,632,452	3.24%	$4,664,106	4.38%	$48,053	2.77%	$0	0.00%
Miscellaneous Income	$50,240,100	12.87%	$8,655,954	8.13%	$440,111	25.41%	$0	0.00%
Total	$390,311,789	100.00%	$106,476,250	100.00%	$1,731,912	100.00%	$3,708,021	100.00%
Benefit and Loss Related Payments	$28,793,806	7.75%	$21,751,372	19.43%	$1,500	0.08%	($2,440)	(0.09)%
Net Transfers to Separate, Segregated Accounts & Protected Cell Accounts	$0	0.00%	$0	0.00%	$0	0.00%	$0	0.00%
Commissions, Expenses Paid and Aggregate Write-Ins for Deductions	$338,514,095	91.13%	$95,359,808	85.20%	$1,601,900	90.71%	$2,703,729	100.09%
Dividends Paid to Policyholders	$0	0.00%	$0	0.00%	$0	0.00%	$0	0.00%
Federal and Foreign Income Taxes Paid (Recovered), Net Tax on Capital Gains (Losses)	$4,155,047	1.12%	($5,191,694)	(4.64)%	$162,547	9.20%	$0	0.00%
Total	$371,462,948	100.00%	$111,919,486	100.00%	$1,765,947	100.00%	$2,701,289	100.00%
NET CASH FROM OPERATIONS	$18,848,841		($5,443,236)		($34,035)		$1,006,732	

CASH FROM INVESTMENTS

	Company Value	%	Company Value	%	Company Value	%	Company Value	%
Proceeds from Investments Sold, Matured or Repaid:								
Bonds	$119,428,268	77.30%	$44,971,984	99.88%	$0	--	$0	--
Stocks	$34,381,712	22.25%	$0	0.00%	$0	--	$0	--
Mortgage Loans	$130,799	0.08%	$0	0.00%	$0	--	$0	--
Real Estate	$0	0.00%	$0	0.00%	$0	--	$0	--
Other Invested Assets	$179,940	0.12%	$0	0.00%	$0	--	$0	--
Net Gains or (Losses) on Cash, Cash Equivalents & Short-Term Investments	$0	0.00%	$0	0.00%	$0	--	$0	--
Miscellaneous Proceeds	$370,300	0.24%	$54,862	0.12%	$0	--	$0	--
Total Investment Proceeds	$154,491,019	100.00%	$45,026,846	100.00%	$0	--	$0	--
Cost of Investments Acquired (Long-Term Only):								
Bonds	$113,236,739	75.04%	$49,358,661	99.80%	$0	0.00%	$0	--
Stocks	$25,176,158	16.68%	$0	0.00%	$0	0.00%	$0	--
Mortgage Loans	$5,070,000	3.36%	$49,064	0.10%	$0	0.00%	$0	--
Real Estate	$21,600	0.01%	$48,451	0.10%	$0	0.00%	$0	--
Other Invested Assets	$4,692,369	3.11%	$0	0.00%	$0	0.00%	$0	--
Miscellaneous Applications	$2,703,698	1.79%	$0	0.00%	$18,352	100.00%	$0	--
Total Investments Acquired	$150,900,564	100.00%	$49,456,176	100.00%	$18,352	100.00%	$0	--
Net Increase (Decrease) in Contract Loans and Premium Notes	$0		$0		$0		$0	
NET CASH FROM INVESTMENTS	$3,590,455		($4,429,330)		($18,352)		$0	

CASH FROM FINANCING AND MISCELLANEOUS SOURCES

	Company Value	Company Value	Company Value	Company Value
Cash Provided (Applied):				
Surplus Notes, Capital Notes	$0	$0	$0	$0
Capital and paid in Surplus, Less Treasury Stock	$0	$0	$0	$0
Borrowed Funds	-$0	$0	$0	$0
Net Deposits on Deposit-Type Contracts & Other Insurance Liabilities	$0	$0	$0	$0
Dividends to Stockholders	$6,700,000	$0	$20,000	$0
Other Cash Provided (Applied)	($22,792,821)	$7,548,087	$0	($1,021,000)
NET CASH FROM FINANCING AND MISCELLANEOUS SOURCES	($29,492,821)	$7,548,087	($20,000)	($1,021,000)

NET CHANGE IN CASH, CASH EQUIVALENTS & SHORT-TERM INVESTMENTS	($7,053,525)	($2,324,479)	($72,387)	($14,268)
ENDING CASH, CASH EQUIVALENTS & SHORT-TERM INVESTMENTS	$11,935,842	$2,296,791	$1,044,756	$6,191,804

C.3 Statement of Cash Flow - By Individual Underwriter

	TITLE IC AMERICA		TITLE RESOURCES		TITLEDGE		TRANSNATION	
BEGINNING CASH, CASH EQUIVALENTS & SHORT-TERM INVESTMENTS	$922,485		$40,180,069		$0		$5,758,292	
CASH FROM OPERATIONS	Company Value	%	Company Value	%	Company Value	%	Company Value	%
Premiums Collected Net of Reinsurance	$11,864,579	94.36%	$102,403,846	98.00%	$180,389	96.77%	$277,382,786	84.78%
Net Investment Income	$709,609	5.64%	$2,090,431	2.00%	$6,030	3.23%	$7,906,646	2.42%
Miscellaneous Income	($428)	0.00%	$66	0.00%	$0	0.00%	$41,878,086	12.80%
Total	$12,573,760	100.00%	$104,494,343	100.00%	$186,419	100.00%	$327,167,518	100.00%
Benefit and Loss Related Payments	$368,685	3.04%	$3,472,442	3.35%	$0	0.00%	$30,432,026	9.23%
Net Transfers to Separate, Segregated Accounts & Protected Cell Accounts	$0	0.00%	$0	0.00%	$0	0.00%	$0	0.00%
Commissions, Expenses Paid and Aggregate Write-Ins for Deductions	$11,690,310	96.36%	$95,131,284	91.77%	$180,256	100.00%	$311,271,654	94.41%
Dividends Paid to Policyholders	$0	0.00%	$0	0.00%	$0	0.00%	$0	0.00%
Federal and Foreign Income Taxes Paid (Recovered), Net Tax on Capital Gains (Losses)	$72,640	0.60%	$5,056,633	4.88%	$0	0.00%	($12,008,378)	(3.64)%
Total	$12,131,635	100.00%	$103,660,359	100.00%	$180,256	100.00%	$329,695,302	100.00%
NET CASH FROM OPERATIONS	$442,125		$833,984		$6,163		($2,527,784)	
CASH FROM INVESTMENTS	Company Value	%	Company Value	%	Company Value	%	Company Value	%
Proceeds from Investments Sold, Matured or Repaid:								
Bonds	$1,814,264	100.00%	$515,000	98.26%	$1,515,000	100.00%	$286,464,155	99.24%
Stocks	$0	0.00%	$0	0.00%	$0	0.00%	$0	0.00%
Mortgage Loans	$0	0.00%	$0	0.00%	$0	0.00%	$0	0.00%
Real Estate	$0	0.00%	$0	0.00%	$0	0.00%	$0	0.00%
Other Invested Assets	$0	0.00%	$9,094	1.74%	$0	0.00%	$777,809	0.27%
Net Gains or (Losses) on Cash, Cash Equivalents & Short-Term Investments	$0	0.00%	$0	0.00%	$0	0.00%	$0	0.00%
Miscellaneous Proceeds	$0	0.00%	$0	0.00%	$0	0.00%	$1,403,164	0.49%
Total Investment Proceeds	$1,814,264	100.00%	$524,094	100.00%	$1,515,000	100.00%	$288,645,128	100.00%
Cost of Investments Acquired (Long-Term Only):								
Bonds	$1,633,982	93.77%	$389,961	66.10%	$2,248,200	100.00%	$267,742,823	97.02%
Stocks	$0	0.00%	$0	0.00%	$0	0.00%	$5,000,000	1.81%
Mortgage Loans	$0	0.00%	$0	0.00%	$0	0.00%	$0	0.00%
Real Estate	$0	0.00%	$0	0.00%	$0	0.00%	$0	0.00%
Other Invested Assets	$0	0.00%	$0	0.00%	$0	0.00%	$1,000,900	0.36%
Miscellaneous Applications	$108,515	6.23%	$200,012	33.90%	$0	0.00%	$2,234,728	0.81%
Total Investments Acquired	$1,742,497	100.00%	$589,973	100.00%	$2,248,200	100.00%	$275,978,451	100.00%
Net Increase (Decrease) in Contract Loans and Premium Notes	$0		$0		$0		$0	
NET CASH FROM INVESTMENTS	$71,767		($65,879)		($733,200)		$12,666,677	
CASH FROM FINANCING AND MISCELLANEOUS SOURCES	Company Value		Company Value		Company Value		Company Value	
Cash Provided (Applied):								
Surplus Notes, Capital Notes	$0		$0		$0		$0	
Capital and paid in Surplus, Less Treasury Stock	$0		$0		$750,000		$0	
Borrowed Funds	$0		$0		$0		$0	
Net Deposits on Deposit-Type Contracts & Other Insurance Liabilities	$0		$0		$0		$0	
Dividends to Stockholders	$0		$6,632,552		$0		$6,250,000	
Other Cash Provided (Applied)	$153,656		($348,816)		($22,555)		($454,975)	
NET CASH FROM FINANCING AND MISCELLANEOUS SOURCES	$153,656		($6,981,368)		$727,445		($6,704,975)	
NET CHANGE IN CASH, CASH EQUIVALENTS & SHORT-TERM INVESTMENTS	$667,548		($6,213,263)		$408		$3,433,918	
ENDING CASH, CASH EQUIVALENTS & SHORT-TERM INVESTMENTS	$1,590,033		$33,966,806		$408		$9,192,210	

2

C.3 Statement of Cash Flow - By Individual Underwriter

	TRANSUNION NATIONAL		TRANSUNION TIC		UNITED CAPITAL		UNITED GENERAL	
BEGINNING CASH, CASH EQUIVALENTS & SHORT-TERM INVESTMENTS	$6,458,485		$9,867,612		$10,121,551		$27,696,678	
CASH FROM OPERATIONS	Company Value	%	Company Value	%	Company Value	%	Company Value	%
Premiums Collected Net of Reinsurance	$3,818,686	85.52%	$892,038	79.56%	$61,420,540	96.35%	$346,591,271	97.19%
Net Investment Income	$640,899	14.35%	$193,540	17.26%	$2,390,562	3.75%	$3,761,627	1.05%
Miscellaneous Income	$5,442	0.12%	$35,695	3.18%	($66,029)	(0.10)%	$6,254,774	1.75%
Total	$4,465,027	100.00%	$1,121,273	100.00%	$63,745,073	100.00%	$356,607,672	100.00%
Benefit and Loss Related Payments	$825,147	18.77%	$497,413	31.15%	$8,127,140	12.14%	$22,034,597	6.31%
Net Transfers to Separate, Segregated Accounts & Protected Cell Accounts	$0	0.00%	$0	0.00%	$0	0.00%	$0	0.00%
Commissions, Expenses Paid and Aggregate Write-Ins for Deductions	$3,764,061	85.64%	$1,162,315	72.79%	$56,713,124	84.68%	$327,243,185	93.69%
Dividends Paid to Policyholders	$0	0.00%	$0	0.00%	$0	0.00%	$0	0.00%
Federal and Foreign Income Taxes Paid (Recovered), Net Tax on Capital Gains (Losses)	($193,838)	(4.41)%	($63,016)	(3.95)%	$2,130,935	3.18%	$0	0.00%
Total	$4,395,370	100.00%	$1,596,712	100.00%	$66,971,199	100.00%	$349,277,782	100.00%
NET CASH FROM OPERATIONS	$69,657		($475,439)		($3,226,126)		$7,329,890	
CASH FROM INVESTMENTS	Company Value	%	Company Value	%	Company Value	%	Company Value	%
Proceeds from Investments Sold, Matured or Repaid:								
Bonds	$3,643,000	100.00%	$0	0.00%	$26,621,923	94.67%	$5,897,091	95.94%
Stocks	$0	0.00%	$1,737,688	100.00%	$97,999	0.35%	$91,200	1.48%
Mortgage Loans	$0	0.00%	$0	0.00%	$1,401,115	4.98%	$0	0.00%
Real Estate	$0	0.00%	$0	0.00%	$0	0.00%	$0	0.00%
Other Invested Assets	$0	0.00%	$0	0.00%	$0	0.00%	$158,370	2.58%
Net Gains or (Losses) on Cash, Cash Equivalents & Short-Term Investments	$0	0.00%	$0	0.00%	$0	0.00%	$0	0.00%
Miscellaneous Proceeds	$0	0.00%	$0	0.00%	$0	0.00%	$0	0.00%
Total Investment Proceeds	$3,643,000	100.00%	$1,737,688	100.00%	$28,121,037	100.00%	$6,146,661	100.00%
Cost of Investments Acquired (Long-Term Only):								
Bonds	$3,635,411	95.56%	$0	0.00%	$24,600,120	96.60%	$2,493,047	100.00%
Stocks	$153,758	4.04%	$9,087,283	100.00%	$0	0.00%	$0	0.00%
Mortgage Loans	$0	0.00%	$0	0.00%	$0	0.00%	$0	0.00%
Real Estate	$15,000	0.39%	$0	0.00%	$655,800	2.58%	$0	0.00%
Other Invested Assets	$0	0.00%	$0	0.00%	$0	0.00%	$0	0.00%
Miscellaneous Applications	$0	0.00%	$0	0.00%	$211,001	0.83%	$0	0.00%
Total Investments Acquired	$3,804,169	100.00%	$9,087,283	100.00%	$25,466,921	100.00%	$2,493,047	100.00%
Net Increase (Decrease) in Contract Loans and Premium Notes	$0		$0		$0		$0	
NET CASH FROM INVESTMENTS	($161,169)		($7,349,595)		$2,654,116		$3,653,614	
CASH FROM FINANCING AND MISCELLANEOUS SOURCES	Company Value		Company Value		Company Value		Company Value	
Cash Provided (Applied):								
Surplus Notes, Capital Notes	$0		$0		$0		$0	
Capital and paid in Surplus, Less Treasury Stock	$0		$0		$0		$20,000,000	
Borrowed Funds	$0		$0		$0		$0	
Net Deposits on Deposit-Type Contracts & Other Insurance Liabilities*	$0		$0		$0		$0	
Dividends to Stockholders	$0		$0		$0		$0	
Other Cash Provided (Applied)	$499,652		$936,773		($1,417,352)		$0	
NET CASH FROM FINANCING AND MISCELLANEOUS SOURCES	$499,652		$936,773		($1,417,352)		$20,000,000	
NET CHANGE IN CASH, CASH EQUIVALENTS & SHORT-TERM INVESTMENTS	$408,140		($6,888,261)		($1,989,362)		$30,983,504	
ENDING CASH, CASH EQUIVALENTS & SHORT-TERM INVESTMENTS	$6,866,625		$2,979,351		$8,132,189		$58,680,182	

2

C.3 Statement of Cash Flow - By Individual Underwriter

	WASHINGTON TIC		WESTCOR		WESTERN NATIONAL	
BEGINNING CASH, CASH EQUIVALENTS & SHORT-TERM INVESTMENTS	$1,200,291		$1,836,878		$1,594,486	

CASH FROM OPERATIONS	Company Value	%	Company Value	%	Company Value	%
Premiums Collected Net of Reinsurance	$15,262,609	98.65%	$51,785,294	96.49%	$349,004	68.19%
Net Investment Income	$157,271	1.02%	$734,366	1.37%	$162,832	31.81%
Miscellaneous Income	$51,790	0.33%	$1,148,157	2.14%	$0	0.00%
Total	$15,471,670	100.00%	$53,667,817	100.00%	$511,836	100.00%
Benefit and Loss Related Payments	$422,819	2.72%	$484,966	0.91%	$103,224	18.54%
Net Transfers to Separate, Segregated Accounts & Protected Cell Accounts	$0	0.00%	$0	0.00%	$0	0.00%
Commissions, Expenses Paid and Aggregate Write-Ins for Deductions	$15,290,972	98.46%	$53,177,303	99.84%	$453,562	81.46%
Dividends Paid to Policyholders	$0	0.00%	$0	0.00%	$0	0.00%
Federal and Foreign Income Taxes Paid (Recovered), Net Tax on Capital Gains (Losses)	($183,796)	(1.18)%	($402,364)	(0.76)%	$0	0.00%
Total	$15,529,995	100.00%	$53,259,905	100.00%	$556,786	100.00%
NET CASH FROM OPERATIONS	($58,325)		$407,912		($44,950)	

CASH FROM INVESTMENTS	Company Value	%	Company Value	%	Company Value	%
Proceeds from Investments Sold, Matured or Repaid:						
Bonds	$1,474,222	100.00%	$625,000	100.00%	$3,951,297	100.00%
Stocks	$0	0.00%	$0	0.00%	$0	0.00%
Mortgage Loans	$0	0.00%	$0	0.00%	$0	0.00%
Real Estate	$0	0.00%	$0	0.00%	$0	0.00%
Other Invested Assets	$0	0.00%	$0	0.00%	$0	0.00%
Net Gains or (Losses) on Cash, Cash Equivalents & Short-Term Investments	$0	0.00%	$0	0.00%	$0	0.00%
Miscellaneous Proceeds	$0	0.00%	$0	0.00%	$0	0.00%
Total Investment Proceeds	$1,474,222	100.00%	$625,000	100.00%	$3,951,297	100.00%
Cost of Investments Acquired (Long-Term Only):						
Bonds	$0	--	$1,324,196	100.00%	$1,231,899	77.62%
Stocks	$0	--	$0	0.00%	$355,119	22.38%
Mortgage Loans	$0	--	$0	0.00%	$0	0.00%
Real Estate	$0	--	$0	0.00%	$0	0.00%
Other Invested Assets	$0	--	$0	0.00%	$0	0.00%
Miscellaneous Applications	$0	--	$0	0.00%	$0	0.00%
Total Investments Acquired	$0	--	$1,324,196	100.00%	$1,587,018	100.00%
Net Increase (Decrease) in Contract Loans and Premium Notes	$0		$0		$0	
NET CASH FROM INVESTMENTS	$1,474,222		($699,196)		$2,364,279	

CASH FROM FINANCING AND MISCELLANEOUS SOURCES	Company Value	Company Value	Company Value
Cash Provided (Applied):			
Surplus Notes, Capital Notes	$0	$0	$0
Capital and paid in Surplus, Less Treasury Stock	$0	$0	$0
Borrowed Funds	$0	$0	$0
Net Deposits on Deposit-Type Contracts & Other Insurance Liabilities	$0	$0	$0
Dividends to Stockholders	$0	$0	$0
Other Cash Provided (Applied)	$0	$426,303	$167,611
NET CASH FROM FINANCING AND MISCELLANEOUS SOURCES	$0	$426,303	$167,611

NET CHANGE IN CASH, CASH EQUIVALENTS & SHORT-TERM INVESTMENTS	$1,415,897	$135,019	$2,486,940
ENDING CASH, CASH EQUIVALENTS & SHORT-TERM INVESTMENTS	$2,616,188	$1,971,897	$4,081,426

Notes

Notes

2

S E C T I O N

MARKET SHARE REPORTS AND POSITION ANALYSIS

3

Overview of Schedule T Data, Market Share Reports and Position Analysis

Schedule T Data

Demotech Performance of Title Insurance Companies utilizes the data contained throughout Schedule T of the Form 9 Annual Statement to develop the Market Share reports. Schedule T presents limited data for each underwriter, but reports each jurisdiction in which an underwriter writes business. Schedule T contains Direct Premiums Written, Direct Losses Paid and Other Income data by jurisdiction. The monoline separation of Title insurance activity allows the premium and loss data from Schedule T to be used for jurisdiction-by-jurisdiction market share comparisons.

It is important to note that due to allowed exemptions and other circumstances, not all underwriters compile a Schedule T and consequently the Market Share reports are limited to only those underwriters who completed and submitted Schedule T data.

Best efforts have been made to ensure accuracy of data that does not originate in the Title underwriters' Form 9 NAIC Annual Statements. All information is presumed current as of the date of publishing. No representations or warranties are made by Demotech, Inc. as to the completeness or accuracy of the information.

Market Share Reports

Direct Premiums Written

Direct Premiums Written are premiums charged by the primary underwriter to the policyholders. Direct Premiums Written *do not* account for premiums *ceded* (paid) or *assumed* (received) through reinsurance activity. Net Premiums Written reflects these activities and is unavailable at the jurisdiction level.

According to the statutory reporting guidelines defined by the National Association of Insurance Commissioners (NAIC) in Issue Paper 57, the NAIC has designated three distribution networks in separate columns of the Schedule T, as well as in other schedules or exhibits of the Form 9 NAIC Annual Statement, as follows:

- **Direct** – Includes Direct Premiums Written at home office and branch office operations of the Title underwriter. No amounts attributable to agency operations (even wholly owned agencies) are to be included in this category.
- **Non-Affiliated Agency** – Includes Direct Premiums Written by non-affiliated agency operations. The standard for reporting as a non-affiliated agency is the affiliation standard established under the holding company laws of the state of domicile.
- **Affiliated Agency** – Includes Direct Premiums Written by affiliated agency operations, including wholly-owned agencies. The standard for reporting as an affiliated agency is the affiliation standard established under the holding company laws of the domestic state jurisdiction.

Revenues received for services performed by a Title underwriter, other than premium, are to be reported under the *Other Income* category of Schedule T and are not included in Market Share report figures.

The Market Share reports in this publication are presented in a consistent format. Direct Premiums Written are listed separately for *Direct, Non-Affiliated* and *Affiliated Agency.* Total Direct Premiums Written is the sum of the Direct Premiums Written from each of the three distribution channels. The corresponding calculation of the channel as a percentage of the total is included to facilitate relative comparisons.

Losses Paid

Direct Losses Paid are losses paid by an underwriter to settle claims. Direct Losses Paid *do not* account for reinsurance recoverable. Direct Losses Paid in the Market Share reports are limited to the Direct Losses Paid listed on Schedule T.

The ratio of Losses to Premiums is calculated, which represents Direct Losses Paid divided by Total Direct Premiums Written.

Presentation of Market Share Information

The Market Share reports are presented for analysis in five distinct series: *Industry Performance*, *Industry Composite*, *Jurisdiction*, *Organization* and *Five-Year Trend* reports.

Industry Performance

The *Industry Performance* reports present period-to-period change in Direct Premiums Written and Direct Losses Paid and are presented by NAIC Group, individual underwriter and jurisdiction.

Industry Composite

The *Industry Composite* reports present information for the entire Title insurance industry by NAIC Group, individual underwriter and jurisdiction. The jurisdiction reports are ordered by jurisdiction and by volume for comparison.

Jurisdiction

The *Jurisdiction* reports break down the premium and loss information for NAIC Group and individual underwriter by jurisdiction.

Organization

The *Organization* reports present a breakdown of premium and loss activity by jurisdiction for each NAIC Group and individual underwriter. For individual underwriters, these reports approximate the presentation of this data in Schedule T.

Five-Year Trend

The *Five-Year Trend* reports present Direct Premiums Written data for each NAIC Group, individual underwriter and jurisdiction. These reports go beyond the *Industry Performance* reports by presenting a five-year historical summarization of this information with graphic representation for enhanced interpretation.

DIRECT PREMIUMS WRITTEN COMPARISON
- BY NAIC GROUP

3

Direct Premiums Written Comparison - By NAIC Group
$ in thousands

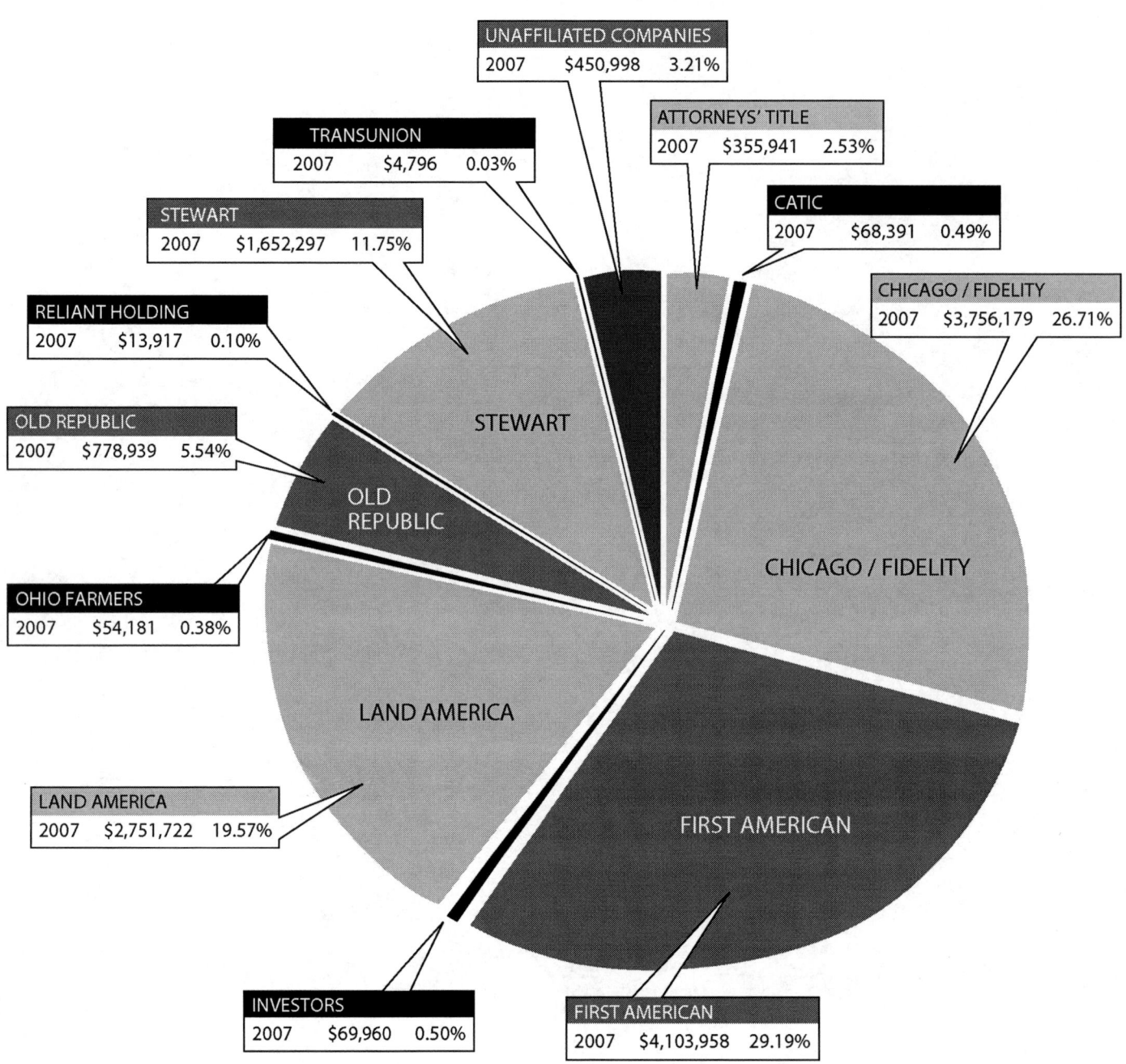

UNAFFILIATED COMPANIES
2007 $450,998   3.21%

TRANSUNION
2007 $4,796   0.03%

ATTORNEYS' TITLE
2007 $355,941   2.53%

STEWART
2007 $1,652,297   11.75%

CATIC
2007 $68,391   0.49%

RELIANT HOLDING
2007 $13,917   0.10%

CHICAGO / FIDELITY
2007 $3,756,179   26.71%

OLD REPUBLIC
2007 $778,939   5.54%

STEWART

OHIO FARMERS
2007 $54,181   0.38%

OLD
REPUBLIC

CHICAGO / FIDELITY

LAND AMERICA

LAND AMERICA
2007 $2,751,722   19.57%

FIRST AMERICAN

INVESTORS
2007 $69,960   0.50%

FIRST AMERICAN
2007 $4,103,958   29.19%

DIRECT PREMIUMS WRITTEN COMPARISON
- BY TEN LEADING JURISDICTIONS

3

Direct Premiums Written Comparison - Ten Leading Jurisdictions

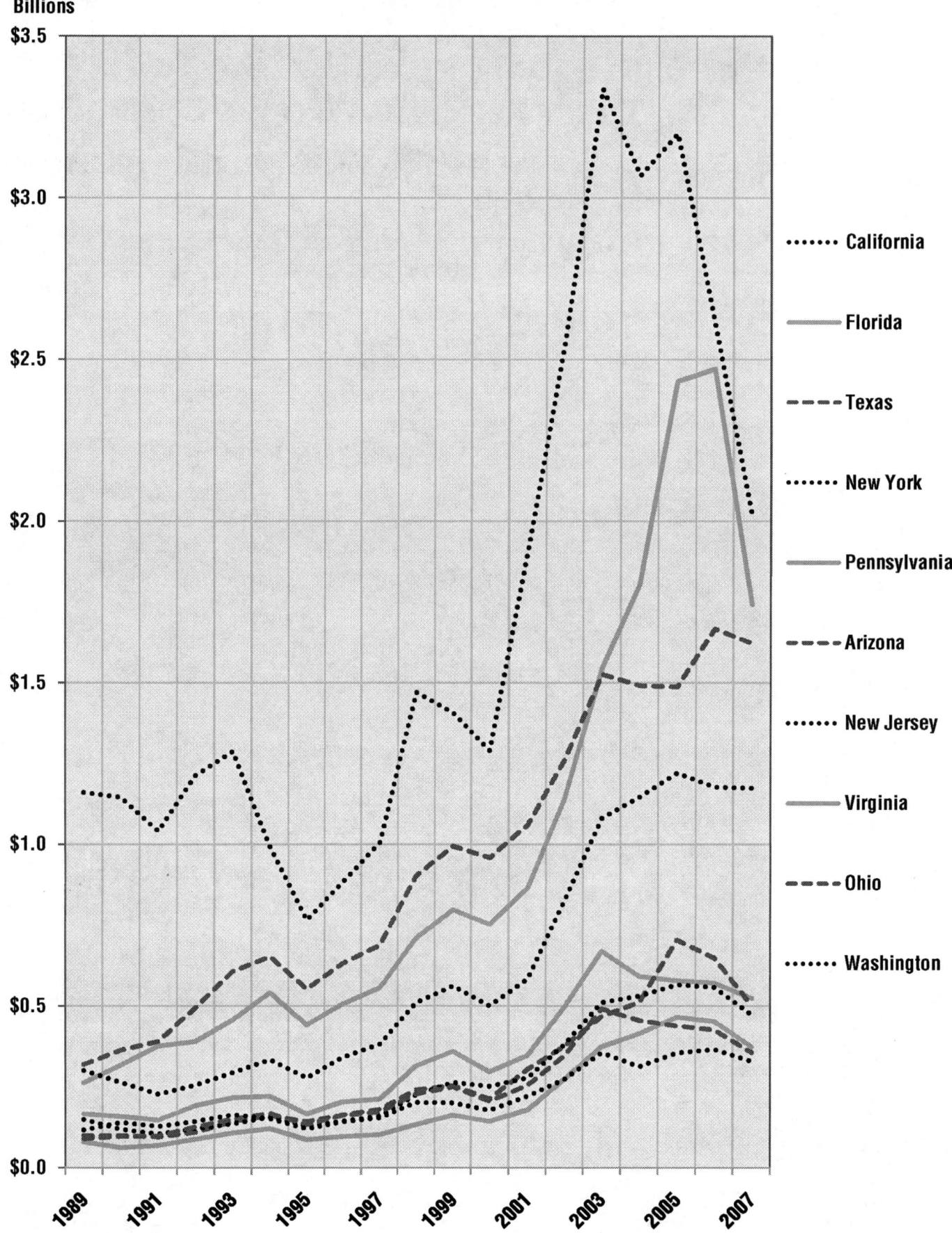

Billions

Legend:
- .... California
- ——— Florida
- – – – Texas
- .... New York
- ——— Pennsylvania
- – – – Arizona
- .... New Jersey
- ——— Virginia
- – – – Ohio
- .... Washington

A.1 INDUSTRY PERFORMANCE
- BY NAIC GROUP

3

A.1   Industry Performance - By NAIC Group

	DIRECT PREMIUMS WRITTEN			DIRECT LOSSES PAID		
	2007	2006	% CHANGE	2007	2006	% CHANGE
ATTORNEYS' TITLE						
1. NATIONAL ATTORNEYS	$831,940	$871,393	(4.53)%	$389,203	$103,813	274.91%
2. ATTORNEYS TGF (CO)	$9,268,076	$10,756,019	(13.83)%	$1,675,550	$1,676,777	(0.07)%
3. ATTORNEYS TIF (FL)	$345,841,352	$479,907,540	(27.94)%	$27,789,122	$23,939,342	16.08%
COMPOSITE	$355,941,368	$491,534,952	(27.59)%	$29,853,875	$25,719,932	16.07%
AVERAGE	$118,647,123	$163,844,984		$9,951,292	$8,573,311	
CATIC						
1. NEW JERSEY TIC	$17,131,578	$18,804,943	(8.90)%	$1,079,509	$836,204	29.10%
2. CT ATTORNEYS	$51,258,956	$57,153,475	(10.31)%	$3,455,178	$5,826,902	(40.70)%
COMPOSITE	$68,390,534	$75,958,418	(9.96)%	$4,534,687	$6,663,106	(31.94)%
AVERAGE	$34,195,267	$37,979,209		$2,267,344	$3,331,553	
CHICAGO / FIDELITY						
1. NATIONS OF NY	$0	$0	--	$494,084	$172,847	185.85%
2. TICOR	$327,197,503	$357,876,197	(8.57)%	$25,882,531	$23,297,964	11.09%
3. ALAMO	$94,218,328	$112,048,894	(15.91)%	$3,724,095	$3,087,564	20.62%
4. FIDELITY NATIONAL	$1,274,082,208	$1,519,950,497	(16.18)%	$98,953,985	$78,920,597	25.38%
5. CHICAGO TIC	$1,887,295,694	$2,277,603,877	(17.14)%	$175,879,157	$118,381,424	48.57%
6. CHICAGO TIC (OR)	$26,283,884	$33,550,465	(21.66)%	$504,698	$1,108,718	(54.48)%
7. SECURITY UNION	$63,557,688	$90,969,194	(30.13)%	$7,239,328	$5,038,241	43.69%
8. TICOR (FL)	$83,543,447	$163,672,762	(48.96)%	$18,527,889	$18,541,210	(0.07)%
COMPOSITE	$3,756,178,752	$4,555,671,886	(17.55)%	$331,205,767	$248,548,565	33.26%
AVERAGE	$469,522,344	$569,458,986		$41,400,721	$31,068,571	
FIRST AMERICAN						
1. LAND TIC (ST LOUIS)	$2,257,316	$721,764	212.75%	$0	$0	--
2. FIRST AMERICAN T&T	$6,291,430	$4,630,569	35.87%	$158,178	$195,198	(18.97)%
3. FIRST AMERICAN (KS)	$14,763,680	$14,451,423	2.16%	$290,960	$286,804	1.45%
4. FIRST AMERICAN (NY)	$239,255,687	$234,984,758	1.82%	$8,776,026	$8,573,350	2.36%
5. UNITED GENERAL	$336,602,219	$332,938,126	1.10%	$22,034,597	$10,897,186	102.20%
6. T.A. TITLE	$17,039,841	$17,261,481	(1.28)%	$739,741	$342,257	116.14%
7. PACIFIC NORTHWEST	$58,462,564	$61,222,212	(4.51)%	$1,606,744	$1,373,551	16.98%
8. OHIO BAR	$13,072,886	$15,055,518	(13.17)%	$1,630,114	$891,661	82.82%
9. FIRST AMERICAN TIC	$3,312,366,583	$3,837,650,476	(13.69)%	$242,613,173	$158,898,136	52.68%
10. CENSTAR	$39,460,038	$45,730,720	(13.71)%	$254,230	$69,285	266.93%
11. PENN ATTORNEYS	$1,777,598	$2,094,251	(15.12)%	$96,020	$156,085	(38.48)%
12. FIRST AMERICAN TRANS	$1,583,016	$1,897,970	(16.59)%	$3,937	$286,348	(98.63)%
13. FIRST AMERICAN (OR)	$55,063,867	$67,095,361	(17.93)%	$2,319,341	$2,571,839	(9.82)%
14. PORT LAWRENCE	$5,590,504	$7,055,071	(20.76)%	$99,717	$220,261	(54.73)%
15. WESTERN NATIONAL	$370,721	$792,343	(53.21)%	$103,224	$103,615	(0.38)%
16. BRIDGE	$462	$7,105	(93.50)%	$181,642	$81,700	122.33%
17. MASSACHUSETTS TIC	($254)	$1,705	(114.90)%	$0	$0	--
COMPOSITE	$4,103,958,158	$4,643,590,853	(11.62)%	$280,907,644	$184,947,276	51.89%
AVERAGE	$241,409,303	$273,152,403		$16,523,979	$10,879,252	
INVESTORS						
1. INVESTORS TIC	$67,545,872	$67,556,181	(0.02)%	$9,911,391	$5,321,289	86.26%
2. NORTHEAST INVESTORS	$2,414,626	$2,427,563	(0.53)%	$154,328	$34,924	341.90%
COMPOSITE	$69,960,498	$69,983,744	(0.03)%	$10,065,719	$5,356,213	87.93%
AVERAGE	$34,980,249	$34,991,872		$5,032,860	$2,678,107	
LAND AMERICA						
1. TITLE IC AMERICA	$11,954,127	$11,422,969	4.65%	$355,944	$1,011,953	(64.83)%
2. LAWYERS	$1,215,610,693	$1,325,370,961	(8.28)%	$80,065,025	$54,660,124	46.48%
3. COMMONWEALTH LAND	$1,152,518,329	$1,291,252,944	(10.74)%	$68,592,260	$63,119,500	8.67%
4. COMMONWEALTH LAND (NJ)	$35,387,441	$44,382,394	(20.27)%	$1,845,407	$1,637,945	12.67%
5. TRANSNATION	$274,829,875	$353,055,773	(22.16)%	$28,263,737	$22,434,106	25.99%
6. UNITED CAPITAL	$61,421,744	$124,734,083	(50.76)%	$6,674,737	$4,935,486	35.24%
COMPOSITE	$2,751,722,209	$3,150,219,124	(12.65)%	$185,797,110	$147,799,114	25.71%
AVERAGE	$458,620,368	$525,036,521		$30,966,185	$24,633,186	
OHIO FARMERS						
1. SOUTHERN TI CORP	$54,180,714	$56,060,085	(3.35)%	$1,807,377	$2,475,801	(27.00)%
COMPOSITE	$54,180,714	$56,060,085	(3.35)%	$1,807,377	$2,475,801	(27.00)%
OLD REPUBLIC						
1. MISSISSIPPI VALLEY	$25,921,894	$25,866,366	0.21%	$1,698,967	$1,790,947	(5.14)%
2. AMERICAN GUARANTY	$3,489,926	$3,488,834	0.03%	$75,291	$143,068	(47.37)%
3. OLD REPUBLIC NATIONAL	$749,527,026	$858,929,076	(12.74)%	$60,130,260	$46,505,409	29.30%
COMPOSITE	$778,938,846	$888,284,276	(12.31)%	$61,904,518	$48,439,424	27.80%
AVERAGE	$259,646,282	$296,094,759		$20,634,839	$16,146,475	

A.1 Industry Performance - By NAIC Group

	DIRECT PREMIUMS WRITTEN			DIRECT LOSSES PAID		
	2007	2006	% CHANGE	2007	2006	% CHANGE
RELIANT HOLDING						
1. GUARANTEE T&T	$11,318,905	$13,327,389	(15.07)%	$1,619,360	$1,708,519	(5.22)%
2. GUARANTEE	$2,597,595	$3,068,393	(15.34)%	$1,039,740	$1,015,487	2.39%
COMPOSITE	$13,916,500	$16,395,782	(15.12)%	$2,659,100	$2,724,006	(2.38)%
AVERAGE	$6,958,250	$8,197,891		$1,329,550	$1,362,003	
STEWART						
1. NATIONAL LAND	$2,494,729	$1,460,264	70.84%	$77,224	$133,639	(42.21)%
2. ARKANSAS TIC	$8,286,400	$7,503,726	10.43%	$131,776	$138,304	(4.72)%
3. STEWART TIC	$162,251,887	$153,902,843	5.42%	$4,872,945	$4,459,974	9.26%
4. STEWART (OR)	$10,805,501	$10,647,009	1.49%	$167,857	$86,273	94.56%
5. MONROE	$12,996,679	$13,814,675	(5.92)%	$144,923	$290,393	(50.09)%
6. STEWART TGC	$1,455,460,636	$1,770,228,416	(17.78)%	$100,536,583	$89,415,731	12.44%
7. ALLIANCE	$1,196	$1,575	(24.06)%	$67,583	$75,538	(10.53)%
COMPOSITE	$1,652,297,028	$1,957,558,508	(15.59)%	$105,998,891	$94,599,852	12.05%
AVERAGE	$236,042,433	$279,651,215		$15,142,699	$13,514,265	
TRANSUNION						
1. TRANSUNION NATIONAL	$3,913,393	$4,094,565	(4.42)%	$764,852	$2,136,929	(64.21)%
2. TRANSUNION TIC	$882,460	$5,227,050	(83.12)%	$397,148	$302,168	31.43%
COMPOSITE	$4,795,853	$9,321,615	(48.55)%	$1,162,000	$2,439,097	(52.36)%
AVERAGE	$2,397,927	$4,660,808		$581,000	$1,219,549	
UNAFFILIATED COMPANIES						
1. MASON	$1,552,282	$482,801	221.52%	$200	$0	--
2. FARMERS NATIONAL	$1,138,404	$507,308	124.40%	$63,819	$1,221	5,126.78%
3. ALLIANT	$13,990,651	$7,175,513	94.98%	$301,183	$0	--
4. NATIONAL	$3,673,916	$2,961,508	24.06%	$25,839	$7,647	237.90%
5. SEAGATE	$186,090	$155,277	19.84%	$0	$0	--
6. AMERICAN SECURITY	$2,940,198	$2,476,836	18.71%	$2,283	$48,890	(95.33)%
7. NORTH AMERICAN	$108,371,483	$94,152,959	15.10%	$2,941,203	$1,608,660	82.84%
8. AMERICAN LAND & AIRCRAFT	$659,156	$575,017	14.63%	$5,858	$5,780	1.35%
9. AMERICAN EAGLE	$3,049,169	$2,751,669	10.81%	$48,338	$33,365	44.88%
10. WESTCOR	$52,626,728	$50,067,732	5.11%	$497,466	$520,329	(4.39)%
11. K.E.L.	$583,915	$0	--	$0	$0	--
12. SIERRA	$1,966,566	$0	--	$0	$0	--
13. TITLEDGE	$181,572	$0	--	$0	$0	--
14. OLYMPIC	$0	$0	--	$16,293	$82,769	(80.32)%
15. TITLE GUARANTY DIV (IA)	$3,724,743	$3,940,490	(5.48)%	($2,440)	$3,000	(181.33)%
16. TITLE G&TC	$260,893	$276,536	(5.66)%	$1,500	$0	--
17. TITLE RESOURCES	$103,847,762	$111,033,941	(6.47)%	$3,202,064	$2,105,136	52.11%
18. FOUNDERS	$178,276	$196,515	(9.28)%	$0	$0	--
19. ATTORNEYS TGF (IL)	$10,998,778	$12,287,182	(10.49)%	$2,041,109	$2,895,206	(29.50)%
20. MANITO	$788,476	$887,535	(11.16)%	$27,274	$54,525	(49.98)%
21. GUARDIAN NATIONAL	$3,873,893	$4,553,818	(14.93)%	$283,171	$347,023	(18.40)%
22. LAND CORP (CO)	$19,602,608	$23,128,736	(15.25)%	$183,856	($218,766)	(184.04)%
23. DREIBELBISS	$632,980	$755,784	(16.25)%	$0	$21,385	(100.00)%
24. COMMERCE	$43,572,531	$55,747,567	(21.84)%	$672,349	$1,030,470	(34.75)%
25. WASHINGTON TIC	$15,624,173	$19,995,288	(21.86)%	$422,819	$316,092	33.76%
26. CONESTOGA	$13,944,371	$18,011,021	(22.58)%	$824,385	$711,960	15.79%
27. DAKOTA HOMESTEAD	$4,113,567	$5,658,289	(27.30)%	$64,953	$316,422	(79.47)%
28. SECURITY TG (BALTIMORE)	$21,925,487	$32,596,083	(32.74)%	$1,140,550	$163,532	597.45%
29. ARSENAL	$1,583,908	$2,389,734	(33.72)%	$649	$2,554	(74.59)%
30. EQUITY NATIONAL	$280,228	$449,983	(37.72)%	$0	$0	--
31. MISSISSIPPI GUARANTY	$309,646	$499,243	(37.98)%	$0	$0	--
32. GENERAL T&T	$2,777,191	$6,473,211	(57.10)%	$418,464	$617,068	(32.19)%
33. NATIONAL OF NY	$12,038,720	($442,269)	(2,822.04)%	$1,354,712	$1,787,850	(24.23)%
COMPOSITE	$450,998,361	$459,745,307	(1.90)%	$14,537,897	$12,462,118	16.66%
AVERAGE	$13,666,617	$13,931,676		$440,542	$377,640	

3

Notes

A.2 INDUSTRY PERFORMANCE
- BY INDIVIDUAL UNDERWRITER

3

A.2 Industry Performance - By Individual Underwriter

	DIRECT PREMIUMS WRITTEN			DIRECT LOSSES PAID		
	2007	2006	% CHANGE	2007	2006	% CHANGE
1. MASON	$1,552,282	$482,801	221.52%	$200	$0	--
2. LAND TIC (ST LOUIS)	$2,257,316	$721,764	212.75%	$0	$0	--
3. FARMERS NATIONAL	$1,138,404	$507,308	124.40%	$63,819	$1,221	5,126.78%
4. ALLIANT	$13,990,651	$7,175,513	94.98%	$301,183	$0	--
5. NATIONAL LAND	$2,494,729	$1,460,264	70.84%	$77,224	$133,639	(42.21)%
6. FIRST AMERICAN T&T	$6,291,430	$4,630,569	35.87%	$158,178	$195,198	(18.97)%
7. NATIONAL	$3,673,916	$2,961,508	24.06%	$25,839	$7,647	237.90%
8. SEAGATE	$186,090	$155,277	19.84%	$0	$0	--
9. AMERICAN SECURITY	$2,940,198	$2,476,836	18.71%	$2,283	$48,890	(95.33)%
10. NORTH AMERICAN	$108,371,483	$94,152,959	15.10%	$2,941,203	$1,608,660	82.84%
11. AMERICAN LAND & AIRCRAFT	$659,156	$575,017	14.63%	$5,858	$5,780	1.35%
12. AMERICAN EAGLE	$3,049,169	$2,751,669	10.81%	$48,338	$33,365	44.88%
13. ARKANSAS TIC	$8,286,400	$7,503,726	10.43%	$131,776	$138,304	(4.72)%
14. STEWART TIC	$162,251,887	$153,902,843	5.42%	$4,872,945	$4,459,974	9.26%
15. WESTCOR	$52,626,728	$50,067,732	5.11%	$497,466	$520,329	(4.39)%
16. TITLE IC AMERICA	$11,954,127	$11,422,969	4.65%	$355,944	$1,011,953	(64.83)%
17. FIRST AMERICAN (KS)	$14,763,680	$14,451,423	2.16%	$290,960	$286,804	1.45%
18. FIRST AMERICAN (NY)	$239,255,687	$234,984,758	1.82%	$8,776,026	$8,573,350	2.36%
19. STEWART (OR)	$10,805,501	$10,647,009	1.49%	$167,857	$86,273	94.56%
20. UNITED GENERAL	$336,602,219	$332,938,126	1.10%	$22,034,597	$10,897,186	102.20%
21. MISSISSIPPI VALLEY	$25,921,894	$25,866,366	0.21%	$1,698,967	$1,790,947	(5.14)%
22. AMERICAN GUARANTY	$3,489,926	$3,488,834	0.03%	$75,291	$143,068	(47.37)%
23. NATIONS OF NY	$0	$0	--	$494,084	$172,847	185.85%
24. K.E.L.	$583,915	--	--	$0	--	--
25. SIERRA	$1,966,566	--	--	$0	--	--
26. TITLEDGE	$181,572	--	--	$0	--	--
27. OLYMPIC	$0	$0	--	$16,293	$82,769	(80.32)%
28. INVESTORS TIC	$67,545,872	$67,556,181	(0.02)%	$9,911,391	$5,321,289	86.26%
29. NORTHEAST INVESTORS	$2,414,626	$2,427,563	(0.53)%	$154,328	$34,924	341.90%
30. T.A. TITLE	$17,039,841	$17,261,481	(1.28)%	$739,741	$342,257	116.14%
31. SOUTHERN TI CORP	$54,180,714	$56,060,085	(3.35)%	$1,807,377	$2,475,801	(27.00)%
32. TRANSUNION NATIONAL	$3,913,393	$4,094,565	(4.42)%	$764,852	$2,136,929	(64.21)%
33. PACIFIC NORTHWEST	$58,462,564	$61,222,212	(4.51)%	$1,606,744	$1,373,551	16.98%
34. NATIONAL ATTORNEYS	$831,940	$871,393	(4.53)%	$389,203	$103,813	274.91%
35. TITLE GUARANTY DIV (IA)	$3,724,743	$3,940,490	(5.48)%	($2,440)	$3,000	(181.33)%
36. TITLE G&TC	$260,893	$276,536	(5.66)%	$1,500	$0	--
37. MONROE	$12,996,679	$13,814,675	(5.92)%	$144,923	$290,393	(50.09)%
38. TITLE RESOURCES	$103,847,762	$111,033,941	(6.47)%	$3,202,064	$2,105,136	52.11%
39. LAWYERS	$1,215,610,693	$1,325,370,961	(8.28)%	$80,065,025	$54,660,124	46.48%
40. TICOR	$327,197,503	$357,876,197	(8.57)%	$25,882,531	$23,297,964	11.09%
41. NEW JERSEY TIC	$17,131,578	$18,804,943	(8.90)%	$1,079,509	$836,204	29.10%
42. FOUNDERS	$178,276	$196,515	(9.28)%	$0	$0	--
43. CT ATTORNEYS	$51,258,956	$57,153,475	(10.31)%	$3,455,178	$5,826,902	(40.70)%
44. ATTORNEYS TGF (IL)	$10,998,778	$12,287,182	(10.49)%	$2,041,109	$2,895,206	(29.50)%
45. COMMONWEALTH LAND	$1,152,518,329	$1,291,252,944	(10.74)%	$68,592,260	$63,119,500	8.67%
46. MANITO	$788,476	$887,535	(11.16)%	$27,274	$54,525	(49.98)%
47. OLD REPUBLIC NATIONAL	$749,527,026	$858,929,076	(12.74)%	$60,130,260	$46,505,409	29.30%
48. OHIO BAR	$13,072,886	$15,055,518	(13.17)%	$1,630,114	$891,661	82.82%
49. FIRST AMERICAN TIC	$3,312,366,583	$3,837,650,476	(13.69)%	$242,613,173	$158,898,136	52.68%
50. CENSTAR	$39,460,038	$45,730,720	(13.71)%	$254,230	$69,285	266.93%
51. ATTORNEYS TGF (CO)	$9,268,076	$10,756,019	(13.83)%	$1,675,550	$1,676,777	(0.07)%
52. GUARDIAN NATIONAL	$3,873,893	$4,553,818	(14.93)%	$283,171	$347,023	(18.40)%
53. GUARANTEE T&T	$11,318,905	$13,327,389	(15.07)%	$1,619,360	$1,708,519	(5.22)%
54. PENN ATTORNEYS	$1,777,598	$2,094,251	(15.12)%	$96,020	$156,085	(38.48)%
55. LAND CORP (CO)	$19,602,608	$23,128,736	(15.25)%	$183,856	($218,766)	(184.04)%
56. GUARANTEE	$2,597,595	$3,068,393	(15.34)%	$1,039,740	$1,015,487	2.39%
57. ALAMO	$94,218,328	$112,048,894	(15.91)%	$3,724,095	$3,087,564	20.62%
58. FIDELITY NATIONAL	$1,274,082,208	$1,519,950,497	(16.18)%	$98,953,985	$78,920,597	25.38%
59. DREIBELBISS	$632,980	$755,784	(16.25)%	$0	$21,385	(100.00)%
60. FIRST AMERICAN TRANS	$1,583,016	$1,897,970	(16.59)%	$3,937	$286,348	(98.63)%
61. CHICAGO TIC	$1,887,295,694	$2,277,603,877	(17.14)%	$175,879,157	$118,381,424	48.57%
62. STEWART TGC	$1,455,460,636	$1,770,228,416	(17.78)%	$100,536,583	$89,415,731	12.44%
63. FIRST AMERICAN (OR)	$55,063,867	$67,095,361	(17.93)%	$2,319,341	$2,571,839	(9.82)%
64. COMMONWEALTH LAND (NJ)	$35,387,441	$44,382,394	(20.27)%	$1,845,407	$1,637,945	12.67%
65. PORT LAWRENCE	$5,590,504	$7,055,071	(20.76)%	$99,717	$220,261	(54.73)%
66. CHICAGO TIC (OR)	$26,283,884	$33,550,465	(21.66)%	$504,698	$1,108,718	(54.48)%
67. COMMERCE	$43,572,531	$55,747,567	(21.84)%	$672,349	$1,030,470	(34.75)%
68. WASHINGTON TIC	$15,624,173	$19,995,288	(21.86)%	$422,819	$316,092	33.76%
69. TRANSNATION	$274,829,875	$353,055,773	(22.16)%	$28,263,737	$22,434,106	25.99%
70. CONESTOGA	$13,944,371	$18,011,021	(22.58)%	$824,385	$711,960	15.79%
71. ALLIANCE	$1,196	$1,575	(24.06)%	$67,583	$75,538	(10.53)%
72. DAKOTA HOMESTEAD	$4,113,567	$5,658,289	(27.30)%	$64,953	$316,422	(79.47)%
73. ATTORNEYS TIF (FL)	$345,841,352	$479,907,540	(27.94)%	$27,789,122	$23,939,342	16.08%
74. SECURITY UNION	$63,557,688	$90,969,194	(30.13)%	$7,239,328	$5,038,241	43.69%
75. SECURITY TG (BALTIMORE)	$21,925,487	$32,596,083	(32.74)%	$1,140,550	$163,532	597.45%
76. ARSENAL	$1,583,908	$2,389,734	(33.72)%	$649	$2,554	(74.59)%
77. EQUITY NATIONAL	$280,228	$449,983	(37.72)%	$0	$0	--
78. MISSISSIPPI GUARANTY	$309,646	$499,243	(37.98)%	$0	$0	--
79. TICOR (FL)	$83,543,447	$163,672,762	(48.96)%	$18,527,889	$18,541,210	(0.07)%
80. UNITED CAPITAL	$61,421,744	$124,734,083	(50.76)%	$6,674,737	$4,935,486	35.24%
81. WESTERN NATIONAL	$370,721	$792,343	(53.21)%	$103,224	$103,615	(0.38)%
82. GENERAL T&T	$2,777,191	$6,473,211	(57.10)%	$418,464	$617,068	(32.19)%
83. TRANSUNION TIC	$882,460	$5,227,050	(83.12)%	$397,148	$302,168	31.43%
84. BRIDGE	$462	$7,105	(93.50)%	$181,642	$81,700	122.33%
85. MASSACHUSETTS TIC	($254)	$1,705	(114.90)%	$0	$0	--
86. NATIONAL OF NY	$12,038,720	($442,269)	(2,822.04)%	$1,354,712	$1,787,850	(24.23)%
COMPOSITE	$14,061,278,821	$16,374,324,550	(14.13)%	$1,030,434,585	$782,174,504	31.74%
AVERAGE	$163,503,242	$197,281,019		$11,981,798	$9,423,789	

A.3 INDUSTRY PERFORMANCE
- BY JURISDICTION

3

A.3 Industry Performance - By Jurisdiction

	DIRECT PREMIUMS WRITTEN			DIRECT LOSSES PAID		
	2007	2006	% CHANGE	2007	2006	% CHANGE
1. NORTHERN MARIANA IS.	$779,364	$239,502	225.41%	$21,656	$133,668	(83.80)%
2. CANADA	$122,666,789	$92,785,072	32.21%	$21,008,189	$20,673,006	1.62%
3. GUAM	$5,778,664	$4,878,605	18.45%	$196,786	$134,942	45.83%
4. WYOMING	$33,370,564	$29,595,780	12.75%	$379,162	$388,490	(2.40)%
5. DELAWARE	$72,549,344	$64,772,623	12.01%	$828,373	$828,318	0.01%
6. LOUISIANA	$121,488,245	$112,870,683	7.63%	$3,425,336	$4,985,891	(31.30)%
7. MISSISSIPPI	$47,295,112	$44,769,531	5.64%	$4,404,607	$4,032,065	9.24%
8. NORTH CAROLINA	$177,655,217	$170,131,264	4.42%	$22,228,734	$16,904,789	31.49%
9. KENTUCKY	$63,852,354	$61,678,424	3.52%	$6,461,217	$7,185,738	(10.08)%
10. OKLAHOMA	$62,547,507	$60,942,048	2.63%	$1,628,648	$1,883,403	(13.53)%
11. MONTANA	$54,461,729	$54,346,389	0.21%	$1,617,807	$2,050,077	(21.09)%
12. IOWA	$7,748,191	$7,748,941	(0.01)%	$547,490	$725,704	(24.56)%
13. TENNESSEE	$162,508,747	$162,606,087	(0.06)%	$7,710,857	$8,571,606	(10.04)%
14. AGGREGATE OTHER ALIEN	$28,149,577	$28,174,035	(0.09)%	$5,232,361	$2,617,713	99.88%
15. NEW YORK	$1,174,156,762	$1,176,698,616	(0.22)%	$48,677,591	$41,442,951	17.46%
16. UTAH	$267,939,133	$268,970,130	(0.38)%	$7,945,838	$6,347,928	25.17%
17. TEXAS	$1,621,647,087	$1,646,163,239	(1.49)%	$54,963,851	$43,467,291	26.45%
18. ALABAMA	$109,581,211	$111,535,163	(1.75)%	$9,179,991	$8,103,672	13.28%
19. WEST VIRGINIA	$24,284,243	$24,884,759	(2.41)%	$1,371,144	$895,240	53.16%
20. DISTRICT OF COLUMBIA	$56,818,474	$58,270,209	(2.49)%	$5,309,954	$4,270,586	24.34%
21. MISSOURI	$75,060,727	$78,145,260	(3.95)%	$17,314,789	$12,832,650	34.93%
22. KANSAS	$43,607,234	$45,874,413	(4.94)%	$1,634,198	$2,056,826	(20.55)%
23. SOUTH CAROLINA	$139,841,966	$147,309,423	(5.07)%	$9,219,176	$9,115,518	1.14%
24. VERMONT	$14,346,936	$15,215,371	(5.71)%	$1,192,861	$1,647,398	(27.59)%
25. NEBRASKA	$38,892,717	$41,461,369	(6.20)%	$1,985,223	$1,987,336	(0.11)%
26. INDIANA	$102,314,463	$109,617,192	(6.66)%	$11,132,581	$9,638,348	15.50%
27. COLORADO	$307,841,126	$334,003,543	(7.83)%	$24,183,348	$15,056,086	60.62%
28. CONNECTICUT	$154,300,860	$167,945,236	(8.12)%	$15,596,220	$17,553,610	(11.15)%
29. PENNSYLVANIA	$524,307,342	$571,186,710	(8.21)%	$24,342,369	$16,928,940	43.79%
30. ALASKA	$32,974,232	$35,950,116	(8.28)%	$317,351	$841,275	(62.28)%
31. OREGON	$222,588,376	$246,106,910	(9.56)%	$6,055,104	$6,726,987	(9.99)%
32. WASHINGTON	$329,007,893	$366,220,342	(10.16)%	$17,353,744	$16,963,494	2.30%
33. GEORGIA	$270,808,372	$304,144,669	(10.96)%	$31,861,466	$28,416,245	12.12%
34. MASSACHUSETTS	$241,246,037	$272,450,604	(11.45)%	$23,480,231	$23,891,677	(1.72)%
35. ILLINOIS	$305,132,213	$348,922,029	(12.55)%	$33,650,588	$35,132,029	(4.22)%
36. WISCONSIN	$116,954,188	$137,008,561	(14.64)%	$7,707,448	$6,108,541	26.17%
37. NEW JERSEY	$473,431,610	$557,683,160	(15.11)%	$32,231,745	$24,936,891	29.25%
38. NEW MEXICO	$113,272,788	$133,583,787	(15.20)%	$4,808,661	$6,511,698	(26.15)%
39. IDAHO	$121,105,718	$143,074,908	(15.36)%	$3,966,432	$2,884,180	37.52%
40. MAINE	$32,679,531	$38,680,253	(15.51)%	$3,045,769	$2,955,124	3.07%
41. OHIO	$356,157,272	$426,094,176	(16.41)%	$26,121,550	$17,995,056	45.16%
42. RHODE ISLAND	$24,914,279	$29,854,174	(16.55)%	$2,599,651	$1,271,370	104.48%
43. VIRGINIA	$374,351,676	$451,704,180	(17.12)%	$25,296,343	$10,115,270	150.08%
44. NEW HAMPSHIRE	$34,566,941	$41,790,814	(17.29)%	$3,204,502	$2,595,988	23.44%
45. ARKANSAS	$48,974,940	$59,667,672	(17.92)%	$3,480,434	$2,973,705	17.04%
46. MARYLAND	$307,811,858	$376,200,541	(18.18)%	$22,826,603	$12,617,440	80.91%
47. HAWAII	$80,631,457	$100,468,654	(19.74)%	$3,461,871	$5,121,032	(32.40)%
48. PUERTO RICO	$30,370,810	$38,056,389	(20.20)%	$2,992,390	$4,389,438	(31.83)%
49. MICHIGAN	$314,793,367	$395,502,439	(20.41)%	$55,250,957	$64,755,810	(14.68)%
50. NORTH DAKOTA	$5,774,179	$7,263,892	(20.51)%	$92,252	$111,435	(17.21)%
51. SOUTH DAKOTA	$14,695,869	$18,791,033	(21.79)%	$304,664	$218,705	39.30%
52. ARIZONA	$500,894,668	$647,801,457	(22.68)%	$30,255,066	$15,724,625	92.41%
53. MINNESOTA	$119,559,447	$154,897,124	(22.81)%	$22,636,199	$12,778,995	77.14%
54. CALIFORNIA	$2,014,245,110	$2,609,938,820	(22.82)%	$227,047,873	$123,839,106	83.34%
55. U.S. VIRGIN ISLANDS	$2,359,655	$3,107,536	(24.07)%	$377,688	$201,854	87.11%
56. NEVADA	$213,523,699	$286,656,798	(25.51)%	$9,773,927	$10,134,111	(3.55)%
57. FLORIDA	$1,742,660,952	$2,449,883,896	(28.87)%	$120,493,719	$79,502,634	51.56%
COMPOSITE	$14,061,278,822	$16,374,324,551	(14.13)%	$1,030,434,585	$782,174,505	31.74%
AVERAGE	$246,689,102	$287,268,852		$18,077,800	$13,722,360	

3

B.1 INDUSTRY COMPOSITE
- DIRECT PREMIUMS WRITTEN BY JURISDICTION

3

B.1 Industry Composite - Direct Premiums Written by Jurisdiction

| | BY JURISDICTION | | | BY VOLUME | |
	DIRECT PREMIUMS WRITTEN	PERCENT OF INDUSTRY		DIRECT PREMIUMS WRITTEN	PERCENT OF INDUSTRY
1. ALABAMA	$109,581,211	0.78%	1. CALIFORNIA	$2,014,245,110	14.32%
2. ALASKA	$32,974,232	0.23%	2. FLORIDA	$1,742,660,952	12.39%
3. ARIZONA	$500,894,668	3.56%	3. TEXAS	$1,621,647,087	11.53%
4. ARKANSAS	$48,974,940	0.35%	4. NEW YORK	$1,174,156,762	8.35%
5. CALIFORNIA	$2,014,245,110	14.32%	5. PENNSYLVANIA	$524,307,342	3.73%
6. COLORADO	$307,841,126	2.19%	6. ARIZONA	$500,894,668	3.56%
7. CONNECTICUT	$154,300,860	1.10%	7. NEW JERSEY	$473,431,610	3.37%
8. DELAWARE	$72,549,344	0.52%	8. VIRGINIA	$374,351,676	2.66%
9. DISTRICT OF COLUMBIA	$56,818,474	0.40%	9. OHIO	$356,157,272	2.53%
10. FLORIDA	$1,742,660,952	12.39%	10. WASHINGTON	$329,007,893	2.34%
11. GEORGIA	$270,808,372	1.93%	11. MICHIGAN	$314,793,367	2.24%
12. HAWAII	$80,631,457	0.57%	12. COLORADO	$307,841,126	2.19%
13. IDAHO	$121,105,718	0.86%	13. MARYLAND	$307,811,858	2.19%
14. ILLINOIS	$305,132,213	2.17%	14. ILLINOIS	$305,132,213	2.17%
15. INDIANA	$102,314,463	0.73%	15. GEORGIA	$270,808,372	1.93%
16. IOWA	$7,748,191	0.06%	16. UTAH	$267,939,133	1.91%
17. KANSAS	$43,607,234	0.31%	17. MASSACHUSETTS	$241,246,037	1.72%
18. KENTUCKY	$63,852,354	0.45%	18. OREGON	$222,588,376	1.58%
19. LOUISIANA	$121,488,245	0.86%	19. NEVADA	$213,523,699	1.52%
20. MAINE	$32,679,531	0.23%	20. NORTH CAROLINA	$177,655,217	1.26%
21. MARYLAND	$307,811,858	2.19%	21. TENNESSEE	$162,508,747	1.16%
22. MASSACHUSETTS	$241,246,037	1.72%	22. CONNECTICUT	$154,300,860	1.10%
23. MICHIGAN	$314,793,367	2.24%	23. SOUTH CAROLINA	$139,841,966	0.99%
24. MINNESOTA	$119,559,447	0.85%	24. CANADA	$122,666,789	0.87%
25. MISSISSIPPI	$47,295,112	0.34%	25. LOUISIANA	$121,488,245	0.86%
26. MISSOURI	$75,060,727	0.53%	26. IDAHO	$121,105,718	0.86%
27. MONTANA	$54,461,729	0.39%	27. MINNESOTA	$119,559,447	0.85%
28. NEBRASKA	$38,892,717	0.28%	28. WISCONSIN	$116,954,188	0.83%
29. NEVADA	$213,523,699	1.52%	29. NEW MEXICO	$113,272,788	0.81%
30. NEW HAMPSHIRE	$34,566,941	0.25%	30. ALABAMA	$109,581,211	0.78%
31. NEW JERSEY	$473,431,610	3.37%	31. INDIANA	$102,314,463	0.73%
32. NEW MEXICO	$113,272,788	0.81%	32. HAWAII	$80,631,457	0.57%
33. NEW YORK	$1,174,156,762	8.35%	33. MISSOURI	$75,060,727	0.53%
34. NORTH CAROLINA	$177,655,217	1.26%	34. DELAWARE	$72,549,344	0.52%
35. NORTH DAKOTA	$5,774,179	0.04%	35. KENTUCKY	$63,852,354	0.45%
36. OHIO	$356,157,272	2.53%	36. OKLAHOMA	$62,547,507	0.44%
37. OKLAHOMA	$62,547,507	0.44%	37. DISTRICT OF COLUMBIA	$56,818,474	0.40%
38. OREGON	$222,588,376	1.58%	38. MONTANA	$54,461,729	0.39%
39. PENNSYLVANIA	$524,307,342	3.73%	39. ARKANSAS	$48,974,940	0.35%
40. RHODE ISLAND	$24,914,279	0.18%	40. MISSISSIPPI	$47,295,112	0.34%
41. SOUTH CAROLINA	$139,841,966	0.99%	41. KANSAS	$43,607,234	0.31%
42. SOUTH DAKOTA	$14,695,869	0.10%	42. NEBRASKA	$38,892,717	0.28%
43. TENNESSEE	$162,508,747	1.16%	43. NEW HAMPSHIRE	$34,566,941	0.25%
44. TEXAS	$1,621,647,087	11.53%	44. WYOMING	$33,370,564	0.24%
45. UTAH	$267,939,133	1.91%	45. ALASKA	$32,974,232	0.23%
46. VERMONT	$14,346,936	0.10%	46. MAINE	$32,679,531	0.23%
47. VIRGINIA	$374,351,676	2.66%	47. PUERTO RICO	$30,370,810	0.22%
48. WASHINGTON	$329,007,893	2.34%	48. AGGREGATE OTHER ALIEN	$28,149,577	0.20%
49. WEST VIRGINIA	$24,284,243	0.17%	49. RHODE ISLAND	$24,914,279	0.18%
50. WISCONSIN	$116,954,188	0.83%	50. WEST VIRGINIA	$24,284,243	0.17%
51. WYOMING	$33,370,564	0.24%	51. SOUTH DAKOTA	$14,695,869	0.10%
52. GUAM	$5,778,664	0.04%	52. VERMONT	$14,346,936	0.10%
53. PUERTO RICO	$30,370,810	0.22%	53. IOWA	$7,748,191	0.06%
54. U.S. VIRGIN ISLANDS	$2,359,655	0.02%	54. GUAM	$5,778,664	0.04%
55. NORTHERN MARIANA IS.	$779,364	0.00%	55. NORTH DAKOTA	$5,774,179	0.04%
56. CANADA	$122,666,789	0.87%	56. U.S. VIRGIN ISLANDS	$2,359,655	0.02%
57. AGGREGATE OTHER ALIEN	$28,149,577	0.20%	57. NORTHERN MARIANA IS.	$779,364	0.00%
COMPOSITE	$14,061,278,822	--	COMPOSITE	$14,061,278,822	--
AVERAGE	$246,689,102		AVERAGE	$246,689,102	

B.2 INDUSTRY COMPOSITE
– DIRECT LOSSES PAID BY JURISDICTION

3

B.2 Industry Composite - Direct Losses Paid by Jurisdiction

	BY JURISDICTION			BY VOLUME	
	DIRECT LOSSES PAID	PERCENT OF INDUSTRY		DIRECT LOSSES PAID	PERCENT OF INDUSTRY
1. ALABAMA	$9,179,991	0.89%	1. CALIFORNIA	$227,047,873	22.03%
2. ALASKA	$317,351	0.03%	2. FLORIDA	$120,493,719	11.69%
3. ARIZONA	$30,255,066	2.94%	3. MICHIGAN	$55,250,957	5.36%
4. ARKANSAS	$3,480,434	0.34%	4. TEXAS	$54,963,851	5.33%
5. CALIFORNIA	$227,047,873	22.03%	5. NEW YORK	$48,677,591	4.72%
6. COLORADO	$24,183,348	2.35%	6. ILLINOIS	$33,650,588	3.27%
7. CONNECTICUT	$15,596,220	1.51%	7. NEW JERSEY	$32,231,745	3.13%
8. DELAWARE	$828,373	0.08%	8. GEORGIA	$31,861,466	3.09%
9. DISTRICT OF COLUMBIA	$5,309,954	0.52%	9. ARIZONA	$30,255,066	2.94%
10. FLORIDA	$120,493,719	11.69%	10. OHIO	$26,121,550	2.54%
11. GEORGIA	$31,861,466	3.09%	11. VIRGINIA	$25,296,343	2.45%
12. HAWAII	$3,461,871	0.34%	12. PENNSYLVANIA	$24,342,369	2.36%
13. IDAHO	$3,966,432	0.38%	13. COLORADO	$24,183,348	2.35%
14. ILLINOIS	$33,650,588	3.27%	14. MASSACHUSETTS	$23,480,231	2.28%
15. INDIANA	$11,132,581	1.08%	15. MARYLAND	$22,826,603	2.22%
16. IOWA	$547,490	0.05%	16. MINNESOTA	$22,636,199	2.20%
17. KANSAS	$1,634,198	0.16%	17. NORTH CAROLINA	$22,228,734	2.16%
18. KENTUCKY	$6,461,217	0.63%	18. CANADA	$21,008,189	2.04%
19. LOUISIANA	$3,425,336	0.33%	19. WASHINGTON	$17,353,744	1.68%
20. MAINE	$3,045,769	0.30%	20. MISSOURI	$17,314,789	1.68%
21. MARYLAND	$22,826,603	2.22%	21. CONNECTICUT	$15,596,220	1.51%
22. MASSACHUSETTS	$23,480,231	2.28%	22. INDIANA	$11,132,581	1.08%
23. MICHIGAN	$55,250,957	5.36%	23. NEVADA	$9,773,927	0.95%
24. MINNESOTA	$22,636,199	2.20%	24. SOUTH CAROLINA	$9,219,176	0.89%
25. MISSISSIPPI	$4,404,607	0.43%	25. ALABAMA	$9,179,991	0.89%
26. MISSOURI	$17,314,789	1.68%	26. UTAH	$7,945,838	0.77%
27. MONTANA	$1,617,807	0.16%	27. TENNESSEE	$7,710,857	0.75%
28. NEBRASKA	$1,985,223	0.19%	28. WISCONSIN	$7,707,448	0.75%
29. NEVADA	$9,773,927	0.95%	29. KENTUCKY	$6,461,217	0.63%
30. NEW HAMPSHIRE	$3,204,502	0.31%	30. OREGON	$6,055,104	0.59%
31. NEW JERSEY	$32,231,745	3.13%	31. DISTRICT OF COLUMBIA	$5,309,954	0.52%
32. NEW MEXICO	$4,808,661	0.47%	32. AGGREGATE OTHER ALIEN	$5,232,361	0.51%
33. NEW YORK	$48,677,591	4.72%	33. NEW MEXICO	$4,808,661	0.47%
34. NORTH CAROLINA	$22,228,734	2.16%	34. MISSISSIPPI	$4,404,607	0.43%
35. NORTH DAKOTA	$92,252	0.00%	35. IDAHO	$3,966,432	0.38%
36. OHIO	$26,121,550	2.54%	36. ARKANSAS	$3,480,434	0.34%
37. OKLAHOMA	$1,628,648	0.16%	37. HAWAII	$3,461,871	0.34%
38. OREGON	$6,055,104	0.59%	38. LOUISIANA	$3,425,336	0.33%
39. PENNSYLVANIA	$24,342,369	2.36%	39. NEW HAMPSHIRE	$3,204,502	0.31%
40. RHODE ISLAND	$2,599,651	0.25%	40. MAINE	$3,045,769	0.30%
41. SOUTH CAROLINA	$9,219,176	0.89%	41. PUERTO RICO	$2,992,390	0.29%
42. SOUTH DAKOTA	$304,664	0.03%	42. RHODE ISLAND	$2,599,651	0.25%
43. TENNESSEE	$7,710,857	0.75%	43. NEBRASKA	$1,985,223	0.19%
44. TEXAS	$54,963,851	5.33%	44. KANSAS	$1,634,198	0.16%
45. UTAH	$7,945,838	0.77%	45. OKLAHOMA	$1,628,648	0.16%
46. VERMONT	$1,192,861	0.12%	46. MONTANA	$1,617,807	0.16%
47. VIRGINIA	$25,296,343	2.45%	47. WEST VIRGINIA	$1,371,144	0.13%
48. WASHINGTON	$17,353,744	1.68%	48. VERMONT	$1,192,861	0.12%
49. WEST VIRGINIA	$1,371,144	0.13%	49. DELAWARE	$828,373	0.08%
50. WISCONSIN	$7,707,448	0.75%	50. IOWA	$547,490	0.05%
51. WYOMING	$379,162	0.04%	51. WYOMING	$379,162	0.04%
52. GUAM	$196,786	0.02%	52. U.S. VIRGIN ISLANDS	$377,688	0.04%
53. PUERTO RICO	$2,992,390	0.29%	53. ALASKA	$317,351	0.03%
54. U.S. VIRGIN ISLANDS	$377,688	0.04%	54. SOUTH DAKOTA	$304,664	0.03%
55. NORTHERN MARIANA IS.	$21,656	0.00%	55. GUAM	$196,786	0.02%
56. CANADA	$21,008,189	2.04%	56. NORTH DAKOTA	$92,252	0.00%
57. AGGREGATE OTHER ALIEN	$5,232,361	0.51%	57. NORTHERN MARIANA IS.	$21,656	0.00%
COMPOSITE	$1,030,434,585	--	COMPOSITE	$1,030,434,585	--
AVERAGE	$18,077,800		AVERAGE	$18,077,800	

B.3 INDUSTRY COMPOSITE
- BY NAIC GROUP

B.3 Industry Composite - By NAIC Group

	DIRECT PREMIUMS WRITTEN							PERCENT OF GROUP	PAID LOSSES	PERCENT OF GROUP	LOSSES TO PREMIUMS
	DIRECT	% of Total	NON-AFFILIATED	% of Total	AFFILIATED	% of Total	TOTAL				
ATTORNEYS' TITLE											
1. ATTORNEYS TIF (FL)	$0	0.00%	$345,841,352	100.00%	$0	0.00%	$345,841,352	97.16%	$27,789,122	93.08%	8.04%
2. ATTORNEYS TGF (CO)	$0	0.00%	$9,268,076	100.00%	$0	0.00%	$9,268,076	2.60%	$1,675,550	5.61%	18.08%
3. NATIONAL ATTORNEYS	$831,940	100.00%	$0	0.00%	$0	0.00%	$831,940	0.23%	$389,203	1.30%	46.78%
COMPOSITE	$831,940	0.23%	$355,109,428	99.77%	$0	0.00%	$355,941,368	100.00%	$29,853,875	100.00%	8.39%
AVERAGE	$277,313		$118,369,809		$0		$118,647,123		$9,951,292		
CATIC											
1. CT ATTORNEYS	$0	0.00%	$51,258,956	100.00%	$0	0.00%	$51,258,956	74.95%	$3,455,178	76.19%	6.74%
2. NEW JERSEY TIC	$0	0.00%	$17,131,578	100.00%	$0	0.00%	$17,131,578	25.05%	$1,079,509	23.81%	6.30%
COMPOSITE	$0	0.00%	$68,390,534	100.00%	$0	0.00%	$68,390,534	100.00%	$4,534,687	100.00%	6.63%
AVERAGE	$0		$34,195,267		$0		$34,195,267		$2,267,344		
CHICAGO / FIDELITY											
1. CHICAGO TIC	$477,816,470	25.32%	$1,033,035,990	54.74%	$376,443,234	19.95%	$1,887,295,694	50.25%	$175,879,157	53.10%	9.32%
2. FIDELITY NATIONAL	$251,405,363	19.73%	$673,800,566	52.89%	$348,876,279	27.38%	$1,274,082,208	33.92%	$98,953,985	29.88%	7.77%
3. TICOR	$51,058,559	15.60%	$218,064,014	66.65%	$58,074,930	17.75%	$327,197,503	8.71%	$25,882,531	7.81%	7.91%
4. ALAMO	$0	0.00%	$42,145,575	44.73%	$52,072,753	55.27%	$94,218,328	2.51%	$3,724,095	1.12%	3.95%
5. TICOR (FL)	$0	0.00%	$83,543,447	100.00%	$0	0.00%	$83,543,447	2.22%	$18,527,889	5.59%	22.18%
6. SECURITY UNION	$11,530,727	18.14%	$36,182,556	56.93%	$15,844,405	24.93%	$63,557,688	1.69%	$7,239,328	2.19%	11.39%
7. CHICAGO TIC (OR)	$13,707,383	52.15%	$12,576,501	47.85%	$0	0.00%	$26,283,884	0.70%	$504,698	0.15%	1.92%
8. NATIONS OF NY	$0	--	$0	--	$0	--	$0	--	$494,084	0.15%	--
COMPOSITE	$805,518,502	21.45%	$2,099,348,649	55.89%	$851,311,601	22.66%	$3,756,178,752	100.00%	$331,205,767	100.00%	8.82%
AVERAGE	$100,689,813		$262,418,581		$106,413,950		$469,522,344		$41,400,721		
FIRST AMERICAN											
1. FIRST AMERICAN TIC	$622,912,926	18.81%	$1,936,771,199	58.47%	$752,682,458	22.72%	$3,312,366,583	80.71%	$242,613,173	86.37%	7.32%
2. UNITED GENERAL	$20,969,887	6.23%	$297,148,060	88.28%	$18,484,272	5.49%	$336,602,219	8.20%	$22,034,597	7.84%	6.55%
3. FIRST AMERICAN (NY)	$96,485,318	40.33%	$131,671,357	55.03%	$11,099,012	4.64%	$239,255,687	5.83%	$8,776,026	3.12%	3.67%
4. PACIFIC NORTHWEST	$0	0.00%	$16,794,834	28.73%	$41,667,730	71.27%	$58,462,564	1.42%	$1,606,744	0.57%	2.75%
5. FIRST AMERICAN (OR)	$42,031,597	76.33%	$13,032,270	23.67%	$0	0.00%	$55,063,867	1.34%	$2,319,341	0.83%	4.21%
6. CENSTAR	$0	0.00%	$39,460,038	100.00%	$0	0.00%	$39,460,038	0.96%	$254,230	0.09%	0.64%
7. T.A. TITLE	$0	0.00%	$13,742,041	80.65%	$3,297,800	19.35%	$17,039,841	0.42%	$739,741	0.26%	4.34%
8. FIRST AMERICAN (KS)	$1,550,799	10.50%	$5,813,820	39.38%	$7,399,061	50.12%	$14,763,680	0.36%	$290,960	0.10%	1.97%
9. OHIO BAR	$0	0.00%	$13,072,886	100.00%	$0	0.00%	$13,072,886	0.32%	$1,630,114	0.58%	12.47%
10. FIRST AMERICAN T&T	$6,291,430	100.00%	$0	0.00%	$0	0.00%	$6,291,430	0.15%	$158,178	0.06%	2.51%
11. PORT LAWRENCE	$2,836,725	50.74%	$2,437,031	43.59%	$316,748	5.67%	$5,590,504	0.14%	$99,717	0.04%	1.78%
12. LAND TIC (ST LOUIS)	$0	0.00%	$2,257,316	100.00%	$0	0.00%	$2,257,316	0.06%	$0	--	--
13. PENN ATTORNEYS	$1,777,598	100.00%	$0	0.00%	$0	0.00%	$1,777,598	0.04%	$96,020	0.03%	5.40%
14. FIRST AMERICAN TRANS	$108,501	6.85%	$1,474,515	93.15%	$0	0.00%	$1,583,016	0.04%	$3,937	0.00%	0.25%
15. WESTERN NATIONAL	$0	0.00%	$8,580	2.31%	$362,141	97.69%	$370,721	0.00%	$103,224	0.04%	27.84%
16. BRIDGE	$0	0.00%	$462	100.00%	$0	0.00%	$462	0.00%	$181,642	0.06%	39,316.45%
17. MASSACHUSETTS TIC	($254)	--	$0	--	$0	--	($254)	0.00%	$0	--	--
COMPOSITE	$794,964,527	19.37%	$2,473,684,409	60.28%	$835,309,222	20.35%	$4,103,958,158	100.00%	$280,907,644	100.00%	6.84%
AVERAGE	$46,762,619		$145,510,848		$49,135,837		$241,409,303		$16,523,979		
INVESTORS											
1. INVESTORS TIC	$29,790,883	44.10%	$31,463,285	46.58%	$6,291,704	9.31%	$67,545,872	96.55%	$9,911,391	98.47%	14.67%
2. NORTHEAST INVESTORS	$0	0.00%	$2,414,626	100.00%	$0	0.00%	$2,414,626	3.45%	$154,328	1.53%	6.39%
COMPOSITE	$29,790,883	42.58%	$33,877,911	48.42%	$6,291,704	8.99%	$69,960,498	100.00%	$10,065,719	100.00%	14.39%
AVERAGE	$14,895,442		$16,938,956		$3,145,852		$34,980,249		$5,032,860		
LAND AMERICA											
1. LAWYERS	$345,666,888	28.44%	$762,376,163	62.72%	$107,567,642	8.85%	$1,215,610,693	44.18%	$80,065,025	43.09%	6.59%
2. COMMONWEALTH LAND	$220,717,997	19.15%	$808,458,154	70.15%	$123,342,178	10.70%	$1,152,518,329	41.88%	$68,592,260	36.92%	5.95%
3. TRANSNATION	$69,584,981	25.32%	$124,240,351	45.21%	$81,004,543	29.47%	$274,829,875	9.99%	$28,263,737	15.21%	10.28%
4. UNITED CAPITAL	$2,264,749	3.69%	$0	0.00%	$59,156,995	96.31%	$61,421,744	2.23%	$6,674,737	3.59%	10.87%
5. COMMONWEALTH LAND (NJ)	$5,109,506	14.44%	$30,277,935	85.56%	$0	0.00%	$35,387,441	1.29%	$1,845,407	0.99%	5.21%
6. TITLE IC AMERICA	$0	0.00%	$11,954,127	100.00%	$0	0.00%	$11,954,127	0.43%	$355,944	0.19%	2.98%
COMPOSITE	$643,344,121	23.38%	$1,737,306,730	63.14%	$371,071,358	13.49%	$2,751,722,209	100.00%	$185,797,110	100.00%	6.75%
AVERAGE	$107,224,020		$289,551,122		$61,845,226		$458,620,368		$30,966,185		
OHIO FARMERS											
1. SOUTHERN TI CORP	$1,173,787	2.17%	$49,984,569	92.26%	$3,022,358	5.58%	$54,180,714	100.00%	$1,807,377	100.00%	3.34%
COMPOSITE	$1,173,787	2.17%	$49,984,569	92.26%	$3,022,358	5.58%	$54,180,714	100.00%	$1,807,377	100.00%	3.34%
OLD REPUBLIC											
1. OLD REPUBLIC NATIONAL	$14,047,794	1.87%	$604,520,309	80.65%	$130,958,923	17.47%	$749,527,026	96.22%	$60,130,260	97.13%	8.02%
2. MISSISSIPPI VALLEY	$488,573	1.88%	$25,433,321	98.12%	$0	0.00%	$25,921,894	3.33%	$1,698,967	2.74%	6.55%
3. AMERICAN GUARANTY	$26,366	0.76%	$546,233	15.65%	$2,917,327	83.59%	$3,489,926	0.45%	$75,291	0.12%	2.16%
COMPOSITE	$14,562,733	1.87%	$630,499,863	80.94%	$133,876,250	17.19%	$778,938,846	100.00%	$61,904,518	100.00%	7.95%
AVERAGE	$4,854,244		$210,166,621		$44,625,417		$259,646,282		$20,634,839		

B.3 Industry Composite - By NAIC Group

	DIRECT	% of Total	NON-AFFILIATED	% of Total	AFFILIATED	% of Total	TOTAL	PERCENT OF GROUP	PAID LOSSES	PERCENT OF GROUP	LOSSES TO PREMIUMS
RELIANT HOLDING											
1. GUARANTEE T&T	$204,520	1.81%	$2,531,709	22.37%	$8,582,676	75.83%	$11,318,905	81.33%	$1,619,360	60.90%	14.31%
2. GUARANTEE	$0	0.00%	$1,125,387	43.32%	$1,472,208	56.68%	$2,597,595	18.67%	$1,039,740	39.10%	40.03%
COMPOSITE	$204,520	1.47%	$3,657,096	26.28%	$10,054,884	72.25%	$13,916,500	100.00%	$2,659,100	100.00%	19.11%
AVERAGE	$102,260		$1,828,548		$5,027,442		$6,958,250		$1,329,550		
STEWART											
1. STEWART TGC	$157,750,939	10.84%	$796,976,776	54.76%	$500,732,921	34.40%	$1,455,460,636	88.09%	$100,536,583	94.85%	6.91%
2. STEWART TIC	$38,951,627	24.01%	$121,926,620	75.15%	$1,373,640	0.85%	$162,251,887	9.82%	$4,872,945	4.60%	3.00%
3. MONROE	$5,556,612	42.75%	$7,075,703	54.44%	$364,364	2.80%	$12,996,679	0.79%	$144,923	0.14%	1.12%
4. STEWART (OR)	$567,888	5.26%	$10,237,613	94.74%	$0	0.00%	$10,805,501	0.65%	$167,857	0.16%	1.55%
5. ARKANSAS TIC	$0	0.00%	$7,269,128	87.72%	$1,017,272	12.28%	$8,286,400	0.50%	$131,776	0.12%	1.59%
6. NATIONAL LAND	$0	0.00%	$2,494,729	100.00%	$0	0.00%	$2,494,729	0.15%	$77,224	0.07%	3.10%
7. ALLIANCE	$0	0.00%	$1,196	100.00%	$0	0.00%	$1,196	0.00%	$67,583	0.06%	5,650.75%
COMPOSITE	$202,827,066	12.28%	$945,981,765	57.25%	$503,488,197	30.47%	$1,652,297,028	100.00%	$105,998,891	100.00%	6.42%
AVERAGE	$28,975,295		$135,140,252		$71,926,885		$236,042,433		$15,142,699		
TRANSUNION											
1. TRANSUNION NATIONAL	$109,890	2.81%	$2,344,872	59.92%	$1,458,631	37.27%	$3,913,393	81.60%	$764,852	65.82%	19.54%
2. TRANSUNION TIC	$882,460	100.00%	$0	0.00%	$0	0.00%	$882,460	18.40%	$397,148	34.18%	45.00%
COMPOSITE	$992,350	20.69%	$2,344,872	48.89%	$1,458,631	30.41%	$4,795,853	100.00%	$1,162,000	100.00%	24.23%
AVERAGE	$496,175		$1,172,436		$729,316		$2,397,927		$581,000		
UNAFFILIATED COMPANIES											
1. NORTH AMERICAN	$0	0.00%	$438,203	0.40%	$107,933,280	99.60%	$108,371,483	24.03%	$2,941,203	20.23%	2.71%
2. TITLE RESOURCES	$0	0.00%	$64,857,278	62.45%	$38,990,484	37.55%	$103,847,762	23.03%	$3,202,064	22.03%	3.08%
3. WESTCOR	$288,117	0.55%	$21,121,593	40.13%	$31,217,018	59.32%	$52,626,728	11.67%	$497,466	3.42%	0.95%
4. COMMERCE	$43,152	0.10%	$1,532,096	3.52%	$41,997,283	96.38%	$43,572,531	9.66%	$672,349	4.62%	1.54%
5. SECURITY TG (BALTIMORE)	$413,935	1.89%	$20,943,251	95.52%	$568,301	2.59%	$21,925,487	4.86%	$1,140,550	7.85%	5.20%
6. LAND CORP (CO)	$0	0.00%	$0	0.00%	$19,602,608	100.00%	$19,602,608	4.35%	$183,856	1.26%	0.94%
7. WASHINGTON TIC	$172,102	1.10%	$12,559,065	80.38%	$2,893,006	18.52%	$15,624,173	3.46%	$422,819	2.91%	2.71%
8. ALLIANT	$0	0.00%	$13,990,651	100.00%	$0	0.00%	$13,990,651	3.10%	$301,183	2.07%	2.15%
9. CONESTOGA	$201,981	1.45%	$13,366,327	95.85%	$376,063	2.70%	$13,944,371	3.09%	$824,385	5.67%	5.91%
10. NATIONAL OF NY	$2,257,917	18.76%	$4,027	0.03%	$9,776,776	81.21%	$12,038,720	2.67%	$1,354,712	9.32%	11.25%
11. ATTORNEYS TGF (IL)	$10,998,778	100.00%	$0	0.00%	$0	0.00%	$10,998,778	2.44%	$2,041,109	14.04%	18.56%
12. DAKOTA HOMESTEAD	$244,546	5.94%	$3,869,021	94.06%	$0	0.00%	$4,113,567	0.91%	$64,953	0.45%	1.58%
13. GUARDIAN NATIONAL	$0	0.00%	$3,445,031	88.93%	$428,862	11.07%	$3,873,893	0.86%	$283,171	1.95%	7.31%
14. TITLE GUARANTY DIV (IA)	$3,724,743	100.00%	$0	0.00%	$0	0.00%	$3,724,743	0.83%	($2,440)	(0.02)%	(0.07)%
15. NATIONAL	$127,106	3.46%	$3,347,151	91.11%	$199,659	5.43%	$3,673,916	0.81%	$25,839	0.18%	0.70%
16. AMERICAN EAGLE	$1,906,376	62.52%	$1,142,793	37.48%	$0	0.00%	$3,049,169	0.68%	$48,338	0.33%	1.59%
17. AMERICAN SECURITY	$0	0.00%	$2,940,198	100.00%	$0	0.00%	$2,940,198	0.65%	$2,283	0.02%	0.08%
18. GENERAL T&T	$0	0.00%	$2,510,539	90.40%	$266,652	9.60%	$2,777,191	0.62%	$418,464	2.88%	15.07%
19. SIERRA	$0	0.00%	$1,966,566	100.00%	$0	0.00%	$1,966,566	0.44%	$0	--	--
20. ARSENAL	$0	0.00%	$1,583,908	100.00%	$0	0.00%	$1,583,908	0.35%	$649	0.00%	0.04%
21. MASON	$120,217	7.74%	$0	0.00%	$1,432,065	92.26%	$1,552,282	0.34%	$200	0.00%	0.01%
22. FARMERS NATIONAL	$0	0.00%	$1,138,404	100.00%	$0	0.00%	$1,138,404	0.25%	$63,819	0.44%	5.61%
23. MANITO	$0	0.00%	$97,958	12.42%	$690,518	87.58%	$788,476	0.17%	$27,274	0.19%	3.46%
24. AMERICAN LAND & AIRCRAFT	$0	0.00%	$126,906	19.25%	$532,250	80.75%	$659,156	0.15%	$5,858	0.04%	0.89%
25. DREIBELBISS	$517,581	81.77%	$115,399	18.23%	$0	0.00%	$632,980	0.14%	$0	--	--
26. K.E.L.	$0	0.00%	$8,060	1.38%	$575,855	98.62%	$583,915	0.13%	$0	--	--
27. MISSISSIPPI GUARANTY	$56,517	18.25%	$253,129	81.75%	$0	0.00%	$309,646	0.07%	$0	--	--
28. EQUITY NATIONAL	$280,228	100.00%	$0	0.00%	$0	0.00%	$280,228	0.06%	$0	--	--
29. TITLE G&TC	$260,893	100.00%	$0	0.00%	$0	0.00%	$260,893	0.06%	$1,500	0.01%	0.57%
30. SEAGATE	$186,090	100.00%	$0	0.00%	$0	0.00%	$186,090	0.04%	$0	--	--
31. TITLEDGE	$78,917	43.46%	$102,655	56.54%	$0	0.00%	$181,572	0.04%	$0	--	--
32. FOUNDERS	$178,276	100.00%	$0	0.00%	$0	0.00%	$178,276	0.04%	$0	--	--
33. OLYMPIC	$0	--	$0	--	$0	--	$0	--	$16,293	0.11%	--
COMPOSITE	$22,057,472	4.89%	$171,460,209	38.02%	$257,480,680	57.09%	$450,998,361	100.00%	$14,537,897	100.00%	3.22%
AVERAGE	$668,408		$5,195,764		$7,802,445		$13,666,617		$440,542		

3

Notes

B.4 INDUSTRY COMPOSITE
– BY INDIVIDUAL UNDERWRITER

3

B.4 Industry Composite - By Individual Underwriter

	DIRECT PREMIUMS WRITTEN							PERCENT OF INDUSTRY	PAID LOSSES	PERCENT OF INDUSTRY	LOSSES TO PREMIUMS
	DIRECT	% of Total	NON-AFFILIATED	% of Total	AFFILIATED	% of Total	TOTAL				
1. FIRST AMERICAN TIC	$622,912,926	18.81%	$1,936,771,199	58.47%	$752,682,458	22.72%	$3,312,366,583	23.56%	$242,613,173	23.54%	7.32%
2. CHICAGO TIC	$477,816,470	25.32%	$1,033,035,990	54.74%	$376,443,234	19.95%	$1,887,295,694	13.42%	$175,879,157	17.07%	9.32%
3. STEWART TGC	$157,750,939	10.84%	$796,976,776	54.76%	$500,732,921	34.40%	$1,455,460,636	10.35%	$100,536,583	9.76%	6.91%
4. FIDELITY NATIONAL	$251,405,363	19.73%	$673,800,566	52.89%	$348,876,279	27.38%	$1,274,082,208	9.06%	$98,953,985	9.60%	7.77%
5. LAWYERS	$345,666,888	28.44%	$762,376,163	62.72%	$107,567,642	8.85%	$1,215,610,693	8.65%	$80,065,025	7.77%	6.59%
6. COMMONWEALTH LAND	$220,717,997	19.15%	$808,458,154	70.15%	$123,342,178	10.70%	$1,152,518,329	8.20%	$68,592,260	6.66%	5.95%
7. OLD REPUBLIC NATIONAL	$14,047,794	1.87%	$604,520,309	80.65%	$130,958,923	17.47%	$749,527,026	5.33%	$60,130,260	5.84%	8.02%
8. ATTORNEYS TIF (FL)	$0	0.00%	$345,841,352	100.00%	$0	0.00%	$345,841,352	2.46%	$27,789,122	2.70%	8.04%
9. UNITED GENERAL	$20,969,887	6.23%	$297,148,060	88.28%	$18,484,272	5.49%	$336,602,219	2.39%	$22,034,597	2.14%	6.55%
10. TICOR	$51,058,559	15.60%	$218,064,014	66.65%	$58,074,930	17.75%	$327,197,503	2.33%	$25,882,531	2.51%	7.91%
11. TRANSNATION	$69,584,981	25.32%	$124,240,351	45.21%	$81,004,543	29.47%	$274,829,875	1.95%	$28,263,737	2.74%	10.28%
12. FIRST AMERICAN (NY)	$96,485,318	40.33%	$131,671,357	55.03%	$11,099,012	4.64%	$239,255,687	1.70%	$8,776,026	0.85%	3.67%
13. STEWART TIC	$38,951,627	24.01%	$121,926,620	75.15%	$1,373,640	0.85%	$162,251,887	1.15%	$4,872,945	0.47%	3.00%
14. NORTH AMERICAN	$0	0.00%	$438,203	0.40%	$107,933,280	99.60%	$108,371,483	0.77%	$2,941,203	0.29%	2.71%
15. TITLE RESOURCES	$0	0.00%	$64,857,278	62.45%	$38,990,484	37.55%	$103,847,762	0.74%	$3,202,064	0.31%	3.08%
16. ALAMO	$0	0.00%	$42,145,575	44.73%	$52,072,753	55.27%	$94,218,328	0.67%	$3,724,095	0.36%	3.95%
17. TICOR (FL)	$0	0.00%	$83,543,447	100.00%	$0	0.00%	$83,543,447	0.59%	$18,527,889	1.80%	22.18%
18. INVESTORS TIC	$29,790,883	44.10%	$31,463,285	46.58%	$6,291,704	9.31%	$67,545,872	0.48%	$9,911,391	0.96%	14.67%
19. SECURITY UNION	$11,530,727	18.14%	$36,182,556	56.93%	$15,844,405	24.93%	$63,557,688	0.45%	$7,239,328	0.70%	11.39%
20. UNITED CAPITAL	$2,264,749	3.69%	$0	0.00%	$59,156,995	96.31%	$61,421,744	0.44%	$6,674,737	0.65%	10.87%
21. PACIFIC NORTHWEST	$0	0.00%	$16,794,834	28.73%	$41,667,730	71.27%	$58,462,564	0.42%	$1,606,744	0.16%	2.75%
22. FIRST AMERICAN (OR)	$42,031,597	76.33%	$13,032,270	23.67%	$0	0.00%	$55,063,867	0.39%	$2,319,341	0.23%	4.21%
23. SOUTHERN TI CORP	$1,173,787	2.17%	$49,984,569	92.26%	$3,022,358	5.58%	$54,180,714	0.39%	$1,807,377	0.18%	3.34%
24. WESTCOR	$288,117	0.55%	$21,121,593	40.13%	$31,217,018	59.32%	$52,626,728	0.37%	$497,466	0.05%	0.95%
25. CT ATTORNEYS	$0	0.00%	$51,258,956	100.00%	$0	0.00%	$51,258,956	0.36%	$3,455,178	0.34%	6.74%
26. COMMERCE	$43,152	0.10%	$1,532,096	3.52%	$41,997,283	96.38%	$43,572,531	0.31%	$672,349	0.07%	1.54%
27. CENSTAR	$0	0.00%	$39,460,038	100.00%	$0	0.00%	$39,460,038	0.28%	$254,230	0.02%	0.64%
28. COMMONWEALTH LAND (NJ)	$5,109,506	14.44%	$30,277,935	85.56%	$0	0.00%	$35,387,441	0.25%	$1,845,407	0.18%	5.21%
29. CHICAGO TIC (OR)	$13,707,383	52.15%	$12,576,501	47.85%	$0	0.00%	$26,283,884	0.19%	$504,698	0.05%	1.92%
30. MISSISSIPPI VALLEY	$488,573	1.88%	$25,433,321	98.12%	$0	0.00%	$25,921,894	0.18%	$1,698,967	0.16%	6.55%
31. SECURITY TG (BALTIMORE)	$413,935	1.89%	$20,943,251	95.52%	$568,301	2.59%	$21,925,487	0.16%	$1,140,550	0.11%	5.20%
32. LAND CORP (CO)	$0	0.00%	$0	0.00%	$19,602,608	100.00%	$19,602,608	0.14%	$183,856	0.02%	0.94%
33. NEW JERSEY TIC	$0	0.00%	$17,131,578	100.00%	$0	0.00%	$17,131,578	0.12%	$1,079,509	0.10%	6.30%
34. T.A. TITLE	$0	0.00%	$13,742,041	80.65%	$3,297,800	19.35%	$17,039,841	0.12%	$739,741	0.07%	4.34%
35. WASHINGTON TIC	$172,102	1.10%	$12,559,065	80.38%	$2,893,006	18.52%	$15,624,173	0.11%	$422,819	0.04%	2.71%
36. FIRST AMERICAN (KS)	$1,550,799	10.50%	$5,813,820	39.38%	$7,399,061	50.12%	$14,763,680	0.10%	$290,960	0.03%	1.97%
37. ALLIANT	$0	0.00%	$13,990,651	100.00%	$0	0.00%	$13,990,651	0.10%	$301,183	0.03%	2.15%
38. CONESTOGA	$201,981	1.45%	$13,366,327	95.85%	$376,063	2.70%	$13,944,371	0.10%	$824,385	0.08%	5.91%
39. OHIO BAR	$0	0.00%	$13,072,886	100.00%	$0	0.00%	$13,072,886	0.09%	$1,630,114	0.16%	12.47%
40. MONROE	$5,556,612	42.75%	$7,075,703	54.44%	$364,364	2.80%	$12,996,679	0.09%	$144,923	0.01%	1.12%
41. NATIONAL OF NY	$2,257,917	18.76%	$4,027	0.03%	$9,776,776	81.21%	$12,038,720	0.09%	$1,354,712	0.13%	11.25%
42. TITLE IC AMERICA	$0	0.00%	$11,954,127	100.00%	$0	0.00%	$11,954,127	0.09%	$355,944	0.03%	2.98%
43. GUARANTEE T&T	$204,520	1.81%	$2,531,709	22.37%	$8,582,676	75.83%	$11,318,905	0.08%	$1,619,360	0.16%	14.31%
44. ATTORNEYS TGF (IL)	$10,998,778	100.00%	$0	0.00%	$0	0.00%	$10,998,778	0.08%	$2,041,109	0.20%	18.56%
45. STEWART (OR)	$567,888	5.26%	$10,237,613	94.74%	$0	0.00%	$10,805,501	0.08%	$167,857	0.02%	1.55%
46. ATTORNEYS TGF (CO)	$0	0.00%	$9,268,076	100.00%	$0	0.00%	$9,268,076	0.07%	$1,675,550	0.16%	18.08%
47. ARKANSAS TIC	$0	0.00%	$7,269,128	87.72%	$1,017,272	12.28%	$8,286,400	0.06%	$131,776	0.01%	1.59%
48. FIRST AMERICAN T&T	$6,291,430	100.00%	$0	0.00%	$0	0.00%	$6,291,430	0.04%	$158,178	0.02%	2.51%
49. PORT LAWRENCE	$2,836,725	50.74%	$2,437,031	43.59%	$316,748	5.67%	$5,590,504	0.04%	$99,717	0.00%	1.78%
50. DAKOTA HOMESTEAD	$244,546	5.94%	$3,869,021	94.06%	$0	0.00%	$4,113,567	0.03%	$64,953	0.00%	1.58%
51. TRANSUNION NATIONAL	$109,890	2.81%	$2,344,872	59.92%	$1,458,631	37.27%	$3,913,393	0.03%	$764,852	0.07%	19.54%
52. GUARDIAN NATIONAL	$0	0.00%	$3,445,031	88.93%	$428,862	11.07%	$3,873,893	0.03%	$283,171	0.03%	7.31%
53. TITLE GUARANTY DIV (IA)	$3,724,743	100.00%	$0	0.00%	$0	0.00%	$3,724,743	0.03%	($2,440)	0.00%	(0.07)%
54. NATIONAL	$127,106	3.46%	$3,347,151	91.11%	$199,659	5.43%	$3,673,916	0.03%	$25,839	0.00%	0.70%
55. AMERICAN GUARANTY	$26,366	0.76%	$546,233	15.65%	$2,917,327	83.59%	$3,489,926	0.02%	$75,291	0.00%	2.16%
56. AMERICAN EAGLE	$1,906,376	62.52%	$1,142,793	37.48%	$0	0.00%	$3,049,169	0.02%	$48,338	0.00%	1.59%
57. AMERICAN SECURITY	$0	0.00%	$2,940,198	100.00%	$0	0.00%	$2,940,198	0.02%	$2,283	0.00%	0.08%
58. GENERAL T&T	$0	0.00%	$2,510,539	90.40%	$266,652	9.60%	$2,777,191	0.02%	$418,464	0.04%	15.07%
59. GUARANTEE	$0	0.00%	$1,125,387	43.32%	$1,472,208	56.68%	$2,597,595	0.02%	$1,039,740	0.10%	40.03%
60. NATIONAL LAND	$0	0.00%	$2,494,729	100.00%	$0	0.00%	$2,494,729	0.02%	$77,224	0.00%	3.10%
61. NORTHEAST INVESTORS	$0	0.00%	$2,414,626	100.00%	$0	0.00%	$2,414,626	0.02%	$154,328	0.01%	6.39%
62. LAND TIC (ST LOUIS)	$0	0.00%	$2,257,316	100.00%	$0	0.00%	$2,257,316	0.02%	$0	--	--
63. SIERRA	$0	0.00%	$1,966,566	100.00%	$0	0.00%	$1,966,566	0.01%	$0	--	--
64. PENN ATTORNEYS	$1,777,598	100.00%	$0	0.00%	$0	0.00%	$1,777,598	0.01%	$96,020	0.00%	5.40%
65. ARSENAL	$0	0.00%	$1,583,908	100.00%	$0	0.00%	$1,583,908	0.01%	$649	0.00%	0.04%
66. FIRST AMERICAN TRANS	$108,501	6.85%	$1,474,515	93.15%	$0	0.00%	$1,583,016	0.01%	$3,937	0.00%	0.25%
67. MASON	$120,217	7.74%	$0	0.00%	$1,432,065	92.26%	$1,552,282	0.01%	$200	0.00%	0.01%
68. FARMERS NATIONAL	$0	0.00%	$1,138,404	100.00%	$0	0.00%	$1,138,404	0.00%	$63,819	0.00%	5.61%
69. TRANSUNION TIC	$882,460	100.00%	$0	0.00%	$0	0.00%	$882,460	0.00%	$397,148	0.04%	45.00%
70. NATIONAL ATTORNEYS	$831,940	100.00%	$0	0.00%	$0	0.00%	$831,940	0.00%	$389,203	0.04%	46.78%
71. MANITO	$0	0.00%	$97,958	12.42%	$690,518	87.58%	$788,476	0.00%	$27,274	0.00%	3.46%
72. AMERICAN LAND & AIRCRAFT	$0	0.00%	$126,906	19.25%	$532,250	80.75%	$659,156	0.00%	$5,858	0.00%	0.89%
73. DREIBELBISS	$517,581	81.77%	$115,399	18.23%	$0	0.00%	$632,980	0.00%	$0	--	--
74. K.E.L.	$0	0.00%	$8,060	1.38%	$575,855	98.62%	$583,915	0.00%	$0	--	--
75. WESTERN NATIONAL	$0	0.00%	$8,580	2.31%	$362,141	97.69%	$370,721	0.00%	$103,224	0.01%	27.84%
76. MISSISSIPPI GUARANTY	$56,517	18.25%	$253,129	81.75%	$0	0.00%	$309,646	0.00%	$0	--	--
77. EQUITY NATIONAL	$280,228	100.00%	$0	0.00%	$0	0.00%	$280,228	0.00%	$0	--	--
78. TITLE G&TC	$260,893	100.00%	$0	0.00%	$0	0.00%	$260,893	0.00%	$1,500	0.00%	0.57%
79. SEAGATE	$186,090	100.00%	$0	0.00%	$0	0.00%	$186,090	0.00%	$0	--	--
80. TITLEDGE	$78,917	43.46%	$102,655	56.54%	$0	0.00%	$181,572	0.00%	$0	--	--
81. FOUNDERS	$178,276	100.00%	$0	0.00%	$0	0.00%	$178,276	0.00%	$0	--	--
82. ALLIANCE	$0	0.00%	$1,196	100.00%	$0	0.00%	$1,196	0.00%	$67,583	0.00%	5,650.75%
83. BRIDGE	$0	0.00%	$462	100.00%	$0	0.00%	$462	0.00%	$181,642	0.02%	39,316.45%
84. NATIONS OF NY	$0	--	$0	--	$0	--	$0	--	$494,084	0.05%	--
85. OLYMPIC	$0	--	$0	--	$0	--	$0	--	$16,293	--	--
86. MASSACHUSETTS TIC	($254)	--	$0	--	$0	--	($254)	0.00%	$0	--	--
COMPOSITE	$2,516,267,901	17.90%	$8,571,646,035	60.96%	$2,973,364,885	21.15%	$14,061,278,821	100.00%	$1,030,434,585	100.00%	7.33%
AVERAGE	$29,258,929		$99,670,303		$34,574,010		$163,503,242		$11,981,798		

B.5 INDUSTRY COMPOSITE
- BY JURISDICTION

3

B.5 Industry Composite - By Jurisdiction

	DIRECT PREMIUMS WRITTEN							PERCENT OF INDUSTRY	PAID LOSSES	PERCENT OF INDUSTRY	LOSSES TO PREMIUMS
	DIRECT	% of Total	NON-AFFILIATED	% of Total	AFFILIATED	% of Total	TOTAL				
1. CALIFORNIA	$143,441,140	7.12%	$440,014,714	21.85%	$1,430,789,256	71.03%	$2,014,245,110	14.32%	$227,047,873	22.03%	11.27%
2. FLORIDA	$159,187,896	9.13%	$1,508,545,261	86.57%	$74,927,795	4.30%	$1,742,660,952	12.39%	$120,493,719	11.69%	6.91%
3. TEXAS	$486,805,543	30.02%	$697,292,225	43.00%	$437,549,319	26.98%	$1,621,647,087	11.53%	$54,963,851	5.33%	3.39%
4. NEW YORK	$370,822,247	31.58%	$781,297,129	66.54%	$22,037,386	1.88%	$1,174,156,762	8.35%	$48,677,591	4.72%	4.15%
5. PENNSYLVANIA	$64,391,845	12.28%	$453,567,682	86.51%	$6,347,815	1.21%	$524,307,342	3.73%	$24,342,369	2.36%	4.64%
6. ARIZONA	$165,281,287	33.00%	$188,625,166	37.66%	$146,988,215	29.35%	$500,894,668	3.56%	$30,255,066	2.94%	6.04%
7. NEW JERSEY	$68,870,922	14.55%	$388,426,766	82.04%	$16,133,922	3.41%	$473,431,610	3.37%	$32,231,745	3.13%	6.81%
8. VIRGINIA	$32,287,888	8.63%	$319,842,602	85.44%	$22,221,186	5.94%	$374,351,676	2.66%	$25,296,343	2.45%	6.76%
9. OHIO	$50,477,489	14.17%	$264,163,054	74.17%	$41,516,729	11.66%	$356,157,272	2.53%	$26,121,550	2.54%	7.33%
10. WASHINGTON	$137,318,891	41.74%	$70,750,989	21.50%	$120,938,013	36.76%	$329,007,893	2.34%	$17,353,744	1.68%	5.27%
11. MICHIGAN	$39,996,668	12.71%	$209,379,677	66.51%	$65,417,022	20.78%	$314,793,367	2.24%	$55,250,957	5.36%	17.55%
12. COLORADO	$31,470,961	10.22%	$215,393,380	69.97%	$60,976,785	19.81%	$307,841,126	2.19%	$24,183,348	2.35%	7.86%
13. MARYLAND	$29,378,563	9.54%	$265,483,630	86.25%	$12,949,665	4.21%	$307,811,858	2.19%	$22,826,603	2.22%	7.42%
14. ILLINOIS	$72,124,036	23.64%	$192,767,467	63.18%	$40,240,710	13.19%	$305,132,213	2.17%	$33,650,588	3.27%	11.03%
15. GEORGIA	$14,964,658	5.53%	$253,630,040	93.66%	$2,213,674	0.82%	$270,808,372	1.93%	$31,861,466	3.09%	11.77%
16. UTAH	$14,497,509	5.41%	$208,473,330	77.81%	$44,968,294	16.78%	$267,939,133	1.91%	$7,945,838	0.77%	2.97%
17. MASSACHUSETTS	$15,019,612	6.23%	$225,307,602	93.39%	$918,823	0.38%	$241,246,037	1.72%	$23,480,231	2.28%	9.73%
18. OREGON	$106,471,568	47.83%	$58,352,423	26.22%	$57,764,385	25.95%	$222,588,376	1.58%	$6,055,104	0.59%	2.72%
19. NEVADA	$51,471,672	24.11%	$77,593,284	36.34%	$84,458,743	39.55%	$213,523,699	1.52%	$9,773,927	0.95%	4.58%
20. NORTH CAROLINA	$55,776,828	31.40%	$107,808,460	60.68%	$14,069,929	7.92%	$177,655,217	1.26%	$22,228,734	2.16%	12.51%
21. TENNESSEE	$14,036,181	8.64%	$140,057,789	86.18%	$8,414,777	5.18%	$162,508,747	1.16%	$7,710,857	0.75%	4.74%
22. CONNECTICUT	$13,942,809	9.04%	$140,075,685	90.78%	$282,366	0.18%	$154,300,860	1.10%	$15,596,220	1.51%	10.11%
23. SOUTH CAROLINA	$3,998,023	2.86%	$134,961,706	96.51%	$882,237	0.63%	$139,841,966	0.99%	$9,219,176	0.89%	6.59%
24. CANADA	$106,838,795	87.10%	$0	0.00%	$15,827,994	12.90%	$122,666,789	0.87%	$21,008,189	2.04%	17.13%
25. LOUISIANA	$3,092,973	2.55%	$112,784,589	92.84%	$5,610,683	4.62%	$121,488,245	0.86%	$3,425,336	0.33%	2.82%
26. IDAHO	$3,283,457	2.71%	$82,370,650	68.02%	$35,451,611	29.27%	$121,105,718	0.86%	$3,966,432	0.38%	3.28%
27. MINNESOTA	$12,053,435	10.08%	$94,167,098	78.76%	$13,338,914	11.16%	$119,559,447	0.85%	$22,636,199	2.20%	18.93%
28. WISCONSIN	$18,900,532	16.16%	$90,864,513	77.69%	$7,189,143	6.15%	$116,954,188	0.83%	$7,707,448	0.75%	6.59%
29. NEW MEXICO	$38,311,591	33.82%	$52,102,875	46.00%	$22,858,322	20.18%	$113,272,788	0.81%	$4,808,661	0.47%	4.25%
30. ALABAMA	$5,363,305	4.89%	$101,805,290	92.90%	$2,412,616	2.20%	$109,581,211	0.78%	$9,179,991	0.89%	8.38%
31. INDIANA	$29,392,587	28.73%	$60,816,027	59.44%	$12,105,849	11.83%	$102,314,463	0.73%	$11,132,581	1.08%	10.88%
32. HAWAII	$12,938,164	16.05%	$38,327,039	47.53%	$29,366,254	36.42%	$80,631,457	0.57%	$3,461,871	0.34%	4.29%
33. MISSOURI	$10,539,960	14.04%	$58,465,644	77.89%	$6,055,123	8.07%	$75,060,727	0.53%	$17,314,789	1.68%	23.07%
34. DELAWARE	$41,114,664	56.67%	$30,684,588	42.29%	$750,092	1.03%	$72,549,344	0.52%	$828,373	0.08%	1.14%
35. KENTUCKY	$6,595,511	10.33%	$53,866,242	84.36%	$3,390,601	5.31%	$63,852,354	0.45%	$6,461,217	0.63%	10.12%
36. OKLAHOMA	$9,327,331	14.91%	$36,145,054	57.79%	$17,075,122	27.30%	$62,547,507	0.44%	$1,628,648	0.16%	2.60%
37. DISTRICT OF COLUMBIA	$15,797,742	27.80%	$38,982,957	68.61%	$2,037,775	3.59%	$56,818,474	0.40%	$5,309,954	0.52%	9.35%
38. MONTANA	$4,368,420	8.02%	$34,814,838	63.93%	$15,278,471	28.05%	$54,461,729	0.39%	$1,617,807	0.16%	2.97%
39. ARKANSAS	$803,611	1.64%	$44,998,226	91.88%	$3,173,103	6.48%	$48,974,940	0.35%	$3,480,434	0.34%	7.11%
40. MISSISSIPPI	$3,898,529	8.24%	$42,103,019	89.02%	$1,293,564	2.74%	$47,295,112	0.34%	$4,404,607	0.43%	9.31%
41. KANSAS	$8,644,576	19.82%	$24,064,545	55.18%	$10,898,113	24.99%	$43,607,234	0.31%	$1,634,198	0.16%	3.75%
42. NEBRASKA	$1,470,874	3.78%	$35,379,174	90.97%	$2,042,669	5.25%	$38,892,717	0.28%	$1,985,223	0.19%	5.10%
43. NEW HAMPSHIRE	$2,237,060	6.47%	$30,817,392	89.15%	$1,512,489	4.38%	$34,566,941	0.25%	$3,204,502	0.31%	9.27%
44. WYOMING	$2,190,963	6.57%	$18,584,495	55.69%	$12,595,106	37.74%	$33,370,564	0.24%	$379,162	0.04%	1.14%
45. ALASKA	$1,159,040	3.51%	$14,765,788	44.78%	$17,049,404	51.71%	$32,974,232	0.23%	$317,351	0.03%	0.96%
46. MAINE	$1,900,410	5.82%	$28,527,101	87.29%	$2,252,020	6.89%	$32,679,531	0.23%	$3,045,769	0.30%	9.32%
47. PUERTO RICO	$451,910	1.49%	$13,411,791	44.16%	$16,507,109	54.35%	$30,370,810	0.22%	$2,992,390	0.29%	9.85%
48. AGGREGATE OTHER ALIEN	$23,313,505	82.82%	$3,094,171	10.99%	$1,741,901	6.19%	$28,149,577	0.20%	$5,232,361	0.51%	18.59%
49. RHODE ISLAND	$2,443,515	9.81%	$21,285,311	85.43%	$1,185,453	4.76%	$24,914,279	0.18%	$2,599,651	0.25%	10.43%
50. WEST VIRGINIA	$1,115,268	4.59%	$23,008,948	94.75%	$160,027	0.66%	$24,284,243	0.17%	$1,371,144	0.13%	5.65%
51. SOUTH DAKOTA	$666,239	4.53%	$13,083,205	89.03%	$946,425	6.44%	$14,695,869	0.10%	$304,664	0.03%	2.07%
52. VERMONT	$718,745	5.01%	$13,612,469	94.88%	$15,722	0.11%	$14,346,936	0.10%	$1,192,861	0.12%	8.31%
53. IOWA	$4,855,046	62.66%	$2,804,026	36.19%	$89,119	1.15%	$7,748,191	0.06%	$547,490	0.05%	7.07%
54. GUAM	$0	0.00%	$5,778,664	100.00%	$0	0.00%	$5,778,664	0.04%	$196,786	0.02%	3.41%
55. NORTH DAKOTA	$379,060	6.56%	$5,248,074	90.89%	$147,045	2.55%	$5,774,179	0.04%	$92,252	0.00%	1.60%
56. U.S. VIRGIN ISLANDS	$66,847	2.83%	$2,292,808	97.17%	$0	0.00%	$2,359,655	0.02%	$377,688	0.04%	16.01%
57. NORTHERN MARIANA IS.	$0	0.00%	$779,364	100.00%	$0	0.00%	$779,364	0.00%	$21,656	0.00%	2.78%
COMPOSITE	$2,516,267,901	17.90%	$8,571,646,036	60.96%	$2,973,364,885	21.15%	$14,061,278,822	100.00%	$1,030,434,585	100.00%	7.33%
AVERAGE	$44,145,051		$150,379,755		$52,164,296		$246,689,102		$18,077,800		

3

C.1 Jurisdiction
- By NAIC Group

3

C.1   Jurisdiction - By NAIC Group

	DIRECT	% of Total	NON-AFFILIATED	% of Total	AFFILIATED	% of Total	TOTAL	PERCENT OF JURISDICTION	PAID LOSSES	PERCENT OF JURISDICTION	LOSSES TO PREMIUMS
			DIRECT PREMIUMS WRITTEN								

ALABAMA

	DIRECT	% of Total	NON-AFFILIATED	% of Total	AFFILIATED	% of Total	TOTAL	PERCENT OF JURISDICTION	PAID LOSSES	PERCENT OF JURISDICTION	LOSSES TO PREMIUMS
1. LAND AMERICA	$2,052,121	7.99%	$23,632,823	92.01%	$0	0.00%	$25,684,944	23.44%	$2,529,039	27.55%	9.85%
2. CHICAGO / FIDELITY	$1,512,400	6.25%	$21,725,384	89.71%	$979,287	4.04%	$24,217,071	22.10%	$2,085,758	22.72%	8.61%
3. FIRST AMERICAN	$1,209,050	5.05%	$22,556,764	94.28%	$159,114	0.67%	$23,924,928	21.83%	$1,496,680	16.30%	6.26%
4. STEWART	$453,681	2.52%	$16,270,053	90.51%	$1,251,794	6.96%	$17,975,528	16.40%	$1,856,083	20.22%	10.33%
5. OLD REPUBLIC	$136,053	1.00%	$13,422,826	99.00%	$0	0.00%	$13,558,879	12.37%	$790,584	8.61%	5.83%
6. OHIO FARMERS	$0	0.00%	$2,459,609	100.00%	$0	0.00%	$2,459,609	2.24%	$90,379	0.98%	3.67%
7. UNAFFILIATED COMPANIES	$0	0.00%	$967,996	100.00%	$0	0.00%	$967,996	0.88%	$191,462	2.09%	19.78%
8. INVESTORS	$0	0.00%	$493,747	100.00%	$0	0.00%	$493,747	0.45%	$49,251	0.54%	9.97%
9. TRANSUNION	$0	0.00%	$263,949	92.17%	$22,421	7.83%	$286,370	0.26%	$90,755	0.99%	31.69%
10. ATTORNEYS' TITLE	$0	0.00%	$12,139	100.00%	$0	0.00%	$12,139	0.01%	$0	--	--
COMPOSITE	**$5,363,305**	4.89%	**$101,805,290**	92.90%	**$2,412,616**	2.20%	**$109,581,211**	100.00%	**$9,179,991**	100.00%	8.38%
AVERAGE	**$536,331**		**$10,180,529**		**$241,262**		**$10,958,121**		**$917,999**		

ALASKA

	DIRECT	% of Total	NON-AFFILIATED	% of Total	AFFILIATED	% of Total	TOTAL	PERCENT OF JURISDICTION	PAID LOSSES	PERCENT OF JURISDICTION	LOSSES TO PREMIUMS
1. FIRST AMERICAN	$702,611	4.29%	$2,456,715	15.01%	$13,207,261	80.70%	$16,366,587	49.63%	$226,506	71.37%	1.38%
2. STEWART	$75,891	0.88%	$4,705,077	54.56%	$3,842,143	44.56%	$8,623,111	26.15%	($3,977)	(1.25)%	(0.05)%
3. CHICAGO / FIDELITY	$336,532	8.55%	$3,597,263	91.45%	$0	0.00%	$3,933,795	11.93%	$5,894	1.86%	0.15%
4. OLD REPUBLIC	$265	0.01%	$3,660,960	99.99%	$0	0.00%	$3,661,225	11.10%	$37,011	11.66%	1.01%
5. LAND AMERICA	$43,741	11.23%	$345,773	88.77%	$0	0.00%	$389,514	1.18%	$51,917	16.36%	13.33%
COMPOSITE	**$1,159,040**	3.51%	**$14,765,788**	44.78%	**$17,049,404**	51.71%	**$32,974,232**	100.00%	**$317,351**	100.00%	0.96%
AVERAGE	**$231,808**		**$2,953,158**		**$3,409,881**		**$6,594,846**		**$63,470**		

ARIZONA

	DIRECT	% of Total	NON-AFFILIATED	% of Total	AFFILIATED	% of Total	TOTAL	PERCENT OF JURISDICTION	PAID LOSSES	PERCENT OF JURISDICTION	LOSSES TO PREMIUMS
1. FIRST AMERICAN	$77,439,459	46.15%	$53,827,944	32.08%	$36,526,245	21.77%	$167,793,648	33.50%	$8,748,133	28.91%	5.21%
2. LAND AMERICA	$31,661,562	22.64%	$78,312,699	56.00%	$29,879,663	21.36%	$139,853,924	27.92%	$7,223,584	23.88%	5.17%
3. CHICAGO / FIDELITY	$54,934,200	40.71%	$31,611,132	23.42%	$48,406,303	35.87%	$134,951,635	26.94%	$12,633,274	41.76%	9.36%
4. UNAFFILIATED COMPANIES	$0	0.00%	$15,961,857	62.74%	$9,478,436	37.26%	$25,440,293	5.08%	$1,288,636	4.26%	5.07%
5. STEWART	$358,106	1.69%	$2,984,773	14.06%	$17,879,310	84.25%	$21,222,189	4.24%	$307,588	1.02%	1.45%
6. OLD REPUBLIC	$887,960	8.84%	$5,926,761	59.00%	$3,231,134	32.16%	$10,045,855	2.01%	$49,664	0.16%	0.49%
7. RELIANT HOLDING	$0	0.00%	$0	0.00%	$1,506,068	100.00%	$1,506,068	0.30%	$4,187	0.01%	0.28%
8. TRANSUNION	$0	0.00%	$0	0.00%	$81,056	100.00%	$81,056	0.02%	$0	--	--
COMPOSITE	**$165,281,287**	33.00%	**$188,625,166**	37.66%	**$146,988,215**	29.35%	**$500,894,668**	100.00%	**$30,255,066**	100.00%	6.04%
AVERAGE	**$20,660,161**		**$23,578,146**		**$18,373,527**		**$62,611,834**		**$3,781,883**		

ARKANSAS

	DIRECT	% of Total	NON-AFFILIATED	% of Total	AFFILIATED	% of Total	TOTAL	PERCENT OF JURISDICTION	PAID LOSSES	PERCENT OF JURISDICTION	LOSSES TO PREMIUMS
1. CHICAGO / FIDELITY	$249,914	1.66%	$14,030,566	93.46%	$731,623	4.87%	$15,012,103	30.65%	$813,494	23.37%	5.42%
2. STEWART	($1,659)	(0.01)%	$9,689,665	81.85%	$2,150,124	18.16%	$11,838,130	24.17%	$942,004	27.07%	7.96%
3. FIRST AMERICAN	$354,923	3.78%	$8,928,694	95.11%	$104,515	1.11%	$9,388,132	19.17%	$1,091,097	31.35%	11.62%
4. LAND AMERICA	$163,968	1.84%	$8,728,380	98.13%	$2,018	0.02%	$8,894,366	18.16%	$317,023	9.11%	3.56%
5. OLD REPUBLIC	$35,421	1.31%	$2,664,933	98.69%	$0	0.00%	$2,700,354	5.51%	$304,220	8.74%	11.27%
6. OHIO FARMERS	$0	0.00%	$498,173	100.00%	$0	0.00%	$498,173	1.02%	$12,239	0.35%	2.46%
7. UNAFFILIATED COMPANIES	$0	0.00%	$415,609	100.00%	$0	0.00%	$415,609	0.85%	$357	0.01%	0.09%
8. RELIANT HOLDING	$0	0.00%	$0	0.00%	$176,978	100.00%	$176,978	0.36%	$0	--	--
9. INVESTORS	$0	0.00%	$31,908	100.00%	$0	0.00%	$31,908	0.07%	$0	--	--
10. ATTORNEYS' TITLE	$0	0.00%	$10,298	100.00%	$0	0.00%	$10,298	0.02%	$0	--	--
11. TRANSUNION	$1,044	11.74%	$0	0.00%	$7,845	88.26%	$8,889	0.02%	$0	--	--
COMPOSITE	**$803,611**	1.64%	**$44,998,226**	91.88%	**$3,173,103**	6.48%	**$48,974,940**	100.00%	**$3,480,434**	100.00%	7.11%
AVERAGE	**$73,056**		**$4,090,748**		**$288,464**		**$4,452,267**		**$316,403**		

CALIFORNIA

	DIRECT	% of Total	NON-AFFILIATED	% of Total	AFFILIATED	% of Total	TOTAL	PERCENT OF JURISDICTION	PAID LOSSES	PERCENT OF JURISDICTION	LOSSES TO PREMIUMS
1. FIRST AMERICAN	$60,771,284	8.09%	$306,205,265	40.77%	$383,997,039	51.13%	$750,973,588	37.28%	$66,948,529	29.49%	8.91%
2. CHICAGO / FIDELITY	$48,250,094	7.70%	$63,827,732	10.19%	$514,418,363	82.11%	$626,496,189	31.10%	$100,649,261	44.33%	16.07%
3. LAND AMERICA	$16,434,071	5.74%	$18,167,115	6.34%	$251,872,307	87.92%	$286,473,493	14.22%	$32,438,848	14.29%	11.32%
4. STEWART	$14,241,275	8.99%	$42,096,381	26.57%	$102,120,824	64.45%	$158,458,480	7.87%	$20,135,633	8.87%	12.71%
5. UNAFFILIATED COMPANIES	$43,152	0.04%	$492,277	0.49%	$99,787,264	99.47%	$100,322,693	4.98%	$2,637,305	1.16%	2.63%
6. OLD REPUBLIC	$2,818,804	3.11%	$9,225,944	10.18%	$78,593,459	86.71%	$90,638,207	4.50%	$3,841,149	1.69%	4.24%
7. TRANSUNION	$882,460	100.00%	$0	0.00%	$0	0.00%	$882,460	0.04%	$397,148	0.17%	45.00%
COMPOSITE	**$143,441,140**	7.12%	**$440,014,714**	21.85%	**$1,430,789,256**	71.03%	**$2,014,245,110**	100.00%	**$227,047,873**	100.00%	11.27%
AVERAGE	**$20,491,591**		**$62,859,245**		**$204,398,465**		**$287,749,301**		**$32,435,410**		

COLORADO

	DIRECT	% of Total	NON-AFFILIATED	% of Total	AFFILIATED	% of Total	TOTAL	PERCENT OF JURISDICTION	PAID LOSSES	PERCENT OF JURISDICTION	LOSSES TO PREMIUMS
1. FIRST AMERICAN	$809,635	0.71%	$113,017,386	98.90%	$445,395	0.39%	$114,272,416	37.12%	$9,238,059	38.20%	8.08%
2. CHICAGO / FIDELITY	$7,931,865	18.88%	$26,352,267	62.74%	$7,721,200	18.38%	$42,005,332	13.65%	$5,689,477	23.53%	13.54%
3. UNAFFILIATED COMPANIES	$0	0.00%	$9,352,476	22.82%	$31,623,264	77.18%	$40,975,740	13.31%	$778,543	3.22%	1.90%
4. STEWART	$828,251	2.20%	$16,014,388	42.63%	$20,726,344	55.17%	$37,568,983	12.20%	$4,031,176	16.67%	10.73%
5. LAND AMERICA	$21,735,294	61.35%	$13,234,723	37.35%	$460,582	1.30%	$35,430,599	11.51%	$2,593,259	10.72%	7.32%
6. OLD REPUBLIC	$165,916	0.60%	$27,263,453	99.40%	$0	0.00%	$27,429,369	8.91%	$1,544,176	6.39%	5.63%
7. ATTORNEYS' TITLE	$0	0.00%	$6,864,905	100.00%	$0	0.00%	$6,864,905	2.23%	$270,631	1.12%	3.94%
8. OHIO FARMERS	$0	0.00%	$3,293,782	100.00%	$0	0.00%	$3,293,782	1.07%	$38,027	0.16%	1.15%
COMPOSITE	**$31,470,961**	10.22%	**$215,393,380**	69.97%	**$60,976,785**	19.81%	**$307,841,126**	100.00%	**$24,183,348**	100.00%	7.86%
AVERAGE	**$3,933,870**		**$26,924,173**		**$7,622,098**		**$38,480,141**		**$3,022,919**		

C.1 Jurisdiction - By NAIC Group

	DIRECT	% of Total	NON-AFFILIATED	% of Total	AFFILIATED	% of Total	TOTAL	PERCENT OF JURISDICTION	PAID LOSSES	PERCENT OF JURISDICTION	LOSSES TO PREMIUMS
CONNECTICUT											
1. FIRST AMERICAN	$2,905,272	5.55%	$49,257,088	94.07%	$197,810	0.38%	$52,360,170	33.93%	$4,383,027	28.10%	8.37%
2. CHICAGO / FIDELITY	$2,869,491	7.70%	$34,374,471	92.23%	$26,586	0.07%	$37,270,548	24.15%	$8,678,748	55.65%	23.29%
3. CATIC	$0	0.00%	$35,170,487	100.00%	$0	0.00%	$35,170,487	22.79%	$1,385,508	8.88%	3.94%
4. LAND AMERICA	$5,473,553	28.59%	$13,672,216	71.41%	$0	0.00%	$19,145,769	12.41%	$872,835	5.60%	4.56%
5. STEWART	$1,423,151	24.02%	$4,442,924	75.00%	$57,970	0.98%	$5,924,045	3.84%	$142,023	0.91%	2.40%
6. OLD REPUBLIC	$288,822	8.38%	$3,158,499	91.62%	$0	0.00%	$3,447,321	2.23%	$134,079	0.86%	3.89%
7. UNAFFILIATED COMPANIES	$982,520	100.00%	$0	0.00%	$0	0.00%	$982,520	0.64%	$0	--	--
COMPOSITE	$13,942,809	9.04%	$140,075,685	90.78%	$282,366	0.18%	$154,300,860	100.00%	$15,596,220	100.00%	10.11%
AVERAGE	$1,991,830		$20,010,812		$40,338		$22,042,980		$2,228,031		
DELAWARE											
1. CHICAGO / FIDELITY	$19,153,351	85.74%	$3,185,434	14.26%	$0	0.00%	$22,338,785	30.79%	$127,734	15.42%	0.57%
2. LAND AMERICA	$13,123,609	59.18%	$9,052,576	40.82%	$0	0.00%	$22,176,185	30.57%	$228,204	27.55%	1.03%
3. FIRST AMERICAN	$8,684,784	47.05%	$9,701,415	52.56%	$71,294	0.39%	$18,457,493	25.44%	$304,870	36.80%	1.65%
4. OLD REPUBLIC	$56,757	1.39%	$4,035,755	98.61%	$0	0.00%	$4,092,512	5.64%	$41,705	5.03%	1.02%
5. STEWART	$96,163	2.37%	$3,290,326	81.11%	$670,323	16.52%	$4,056,812	5.59%	$122,926	14.84%	3.03%
6. UNAFFILIATED COMPANIES	$0	0.00%	$1,419,082	100.00%	$0	0.00%	$1,419,082	1.96%	$2,934	0.35%	0.21%
7. TRANSUNION	$0	0.00%	$0	0.00%	$8,475	100.00%	$8,475	0.01%	$0	--	--
COMPOSITE	$41,114,664	56.67%	$30,684,588	42.29%	$750,092	1.03%	$72,549,344	100.00%	$828,373	100.00%	1.14%
AVERAGE	$5,873,523		$4,383,513		$107,156		$10,364,192		$118,339		
DISTRICT OF COLUMBIA											
1. FIRST AMERICAN	$9,221,625	31.65%	$19,485,540	66.87%	$430,540	1.48%	$29,137,705	51.28%	$2,278,004	42.90%	7.82%
2. LAND AMERICA	$4,605,759	34.97%	$8,550,805	64.93%	$12,513	0.10%	$13,169,077	23.18%	$1,013,092	19.08%	7.69%
3. CHICAGO / FIDELITY	$1,540,523	20.24%	$6,068,151	79.73%	$1,893	0.02%	$7,610,567	13.39%	$1,526,241	28.74%	20.05%
4. STEWART	$415,513	10.09%	$2,502,210	60.78%	$1,199,442	29.13%	$4,117,165	7.25%	$220,792	4.16%	5.36%
5. OLD REPUBLIC	$14,322	0.92%	$1,545,274	99.08%	$0	0.00%	$1,559,596	2.74%	$129,585	2.44%	8.31%
6. UNAFFILIATED COMPANIES	$0	0.00%	$672,256	65.86%	$348,462	34.14%	$1,020,718	1.80%	$108,704	2.05%	10.65%
7. OHIO FARMERS	$0	0.00%	$131,579	100.00%	$0	0.00%	$131,579	0.23%	$27,876	0.52%	21.19%
8. RELIANT HOLDING	$0	0.00%	$0	0.00%	$37,974	100.00%	$37,974	0.07%	$0	--	--
9. INVESTORS	$0	0.00%	$27,142	100.00%	$0	0.00%	$27,142	0.05%	$5,660	0.11%	20.85%
10. TRANSUNION	$0	0.00%	$0	0.00%	$6,951	100.00%	$6,951	0.01%	$0	--	--
COMPOSITE	$15,797,742	27.80%	$38,982,957	68.61%	$2,037,775	3.59%	$56,818,474	100.00%	$5,309,954	100.00%	9.35%
AVERAGE	$1,579,774		$3,898,296		$203,778		$5,681,847		$530,995		
FLORIDA											
1. CHICAGO / FIDELITY	$46,515,368	11.28%	$361,125,087	87.61%	$4,576,665	1.11%	$412,217,120	23.65%	$23,163,468	19.22%	5.62%
2. FIRST AMERICAN	$68,531,349	17.85%	$301,784,224	78.62%	$13,557,226	3.53%	$383,872,799	22.03%	$36,144,062	30.00%	9.42%
3. ATTORNEYS' TITLE	$0	0.00%	$332,905,096	100.00%	$0	0.00%	$332,905,096	19.10%	$25,507,467	21.17%	7.66%
4. LAND AMERICA	$37,630,094	14.35%	$222,834,069	84.99%	$1,726,118	0.66%	$262,190,281	15.05%	$13,859,929	11.50%	5.29%
5. STEWART	$4,775,431	2.89%	$129,810,306	78.53%	$30,708,240	18.58%	$165,293,977	9.49%	$10,596,193	8.79%	6.41%
6. OLD REPUBLIC	$1,193,556	0.89%	$133,121,159	99.11%	$0	0.00%	$134,314,715	7.71%	$10,328,952	8.57%	7.69%
7. UNAFFILIATED COMPANIES	$535,440	1.18%	$21,351,897	47.02%	$23,521,766	51.80%	$45,409,103	2.61%	$756,626	0.63%	1.67%
8. OHIO FARMERS	$0	0.00%	$3,534,245	92.24%	$297,153	7.76%	$3,831,398	0.22%	$115,101	0.10%	3.00%
9. INVESTORS	$0	0.00%	$1,428,570	100.00%	$0	0.00%	$1,428,570	0.08%	$21,190	0.02%	1.48%
10. TRANSUNION	$6,658	0.56%	$650,608	54.43%	$538,097	45.02%	$1,195,363	0.07%	$0	--	--
11. RELIANT HOLDING	$0	0.00%	$0	0.00%	$2,530	100.00%	$2,530	0.00%	$731	0.00%	28.89%
COMPOSITE	$159,187,896	9.13%	$1,508,545,261	86.57%	$74,927,795	4.30%	$1,742,660,952	100.00%	$120,493,719	100.00%	6.91%
AVERAGE	$14,471,627		$137,140,478		$6,811,618		$158,423,723		$10,953,974		
GEORGIA											
1. CHICAGO / FIDELITY	$5,397,865	5.32%	$94,771,035	93.35%	$1,357,008	1.34%	$101,525,908	37.49%	$10,887,273	34.17%	10.72%
2. FIRST AMERICAN	$3,824,348	6.28%	$56,566,106	92.83%	$546,730	0.90%	$60,937,184	22.50%	$8,502,223	26.68%	13.95%
3. LAND AMERICA	$4,190,349	8.54%	$44,839,756	91.43%	$10,131	0.02%	$49,040,236	18.11%	$5,694,549	17.87%	11.61%
4. STEWART	$1,347,309	3.96%	$32,316,217	95.56%	$152,722	0.45%	$33,816,248	12.49%	$2,086,645	6.55%	6.17%
5. OLD REPUBLIC	$195,824	0.83%	$23,403,351	99.17%	$0	0.00%	$23,599,175	8.71%	$3,476,917	10.91%	14.73%
6. OHIO FARMERS	$0	0.00%	$682,019	100.00%	$0	0.00%	$682,019	0.25%	$115,149	0.36%	16.88%
7. ATTORNEYS' TITLE	$0	0.00%	$633,526	100.00%	$0	0.00%	$633,526	0.23%	$821,978	2.58%	129.75%
8. UNAFFILIATED COMPANIES	$0	0.00%	$262,162	100.00%	$0	0.00%	$262,162	0.10%	$37,023	0.12%	14.12%
9. TRANSUNION	$0	0.00%	$66,197	31.04%	$147,083	68.96%	$213,280	0.08%	$166,651	0.52%	78.14%
10. INVESTORS	$8,963	9.09%	$89,671	90.91%	$0	0.00%	$98,634	0.04%	$73,058	0.23%	74.07%
COMPOSITE	$14,964,658	5.53%	$253,630,040	93.66%	$2,213,674	0.82%	$270,808,372	100.00%	$31,861,466	100.00%	11.77%
AVERAGE	$1,496,466		$25,363,004		$221,367		$27,080,837		$3,186,147		
HAWAII											
1. CHICAGO / FIDELITY	$11,627,661	36.91%	$19,875,110	63.09%	$0	0.00%	$31,502,771	39.07%	$1,706,729	49.30%	5.42%
2. FIRST AMERICAN	$869,885	3.00%	$7,417,798	25.56%	$20,733,026	71.44%	$29,020,709	35.99%	$475,150	13.73%	1.64%
3. OLD REPUBLIC	$105,074	1.19%	$78,373	0.89%	$8,632,417	97.92%	$8,815,864	10.93%	$532,902	15.39%	6.04%
4. LAND AMERICA	$276,230	4.50%	$5,861,334	95.49%	$811	0.01%	$6,138,375	7.61%	$687,907	19.87%	11.21%
5. STEWART	$59,314	1.15%	$5,094,424	98.85%	$0	0.00%	$5,153,738	6.39%	$59,183	1.71%	1.15%
COMPOSITE	$12,938,164	16.05%	$38,327,039	47.53%	$29,366,254	36.42%	$80,631,457	100.00%	$3,461,871	100.00%	4.29%
AVERAGE	$2,587,633		$7,665,408		$5,873,251		$16,126,291		$692,374		

C.1 Jurisdiction - By NAIC Group

	DIRECT	% of Total	NON-AFFILIATED	% of Total	AFFILIATED	% of Total	TOTAL	PERCENT OF JURISDICTION	PAID LOSSES	PERCENT OF JURISDICTION	LOSSES TO PREMIUMS
IDAHO											
1. FIRST AMERICAN	$1,753,667	4.21%	$17,646,666	42.41%	$22,209,074	53.38%	$41,609,407	34.36%	$1,167,518	29.43%	2.81%
2. LAND AMERICA	$507,677	1.52%	$25,361,682	75.97%	$7,514,013	22.51%	$33,383,372	27.57%	$942,602	23.76%	2.82%
3. CHICAGO / FIDELITY	$966,437	3.76%	$24,713,235	96.24%	$0	0.00%	$25,679,672	21.20%	$1,238,643	31.23%	4.82%
4. STEWART	$56,157	0.44%	$7,038,043	54.89%	$5,728,524	44.67%	$12,822,724	10.59%	$108,699	2.74%	0.85%
5. OLD REPUBLIC	($481)	(0.01)%	$7,611,024	100.01%	$0	0.00%	$7,610,543	6.28%	$508,970	12.83%	6.69%
COMPOSITE	$3,283,457	2.71%	$82,370,650	68.02%	$35,451,611	29.27%	$121,105,718	100.00%	$3,966,432	100.00%	3.28%
AVERAGE	$656,691		$16,474,130		$7,090,322		$24,221,144		$793,286		
ILLINOIS											
1. CHICAGO / FIDELITY	$34,088,773	25.25%	$89,507,487	66.30%	$11,412,516	8.45%	$135,008,776	44.25%	$14,690,934	43.66%	10.88%
2. FIRST AMERICAN	$18,125,789	20.13%	$53,402,348	59.30%	$18,529,294	20.57%	$90,057,431	29.51%	$6,825,875	20.28%	7.58%
3. STEWART	$1,759,049	5.53%	$24,028,734	75.54%	$6,023,601	18.94%	$31,811,384	10.43%	$2,203,377	6.55%	6.93%
4. LAND AMERICA	$7,297,051	30.96%	$16,272,429	69.04%	$1,707	0.01%	$23,571,187	7.72%	$5,894,487	17.52%	25.01%
5. UNAFFILIATED COMPANIES	$10,633,487	88.92%	$0	0.00%	$1,324,490	11.08%	$11,957,977	3.92%	$1,944,200	5.78%	16.26%
6. ATTORNEYS' TITLE	$0	0.00%	$5,356,039	100.00%	$0	0.00%	$5,356,039	1.76%	$863,901	2.57%	16.13%
7. OLD REPUBLIC	$213,689	5.38%	$3,754,970	94.62%	$0	0.00%	$3,968,659	1.30%	$626,350	1.86%	15.78%
8. INVESTORS	$6,110	0.37%	$27,192	1.64%	$1,622,461	97.99%	$1,655,763	0.54%	$19,364	0.06%	1.17%
9. RELIANT HOLDING	$0	0.00%	$418,268	25.68%	$1,210,289	74.32%	$1,628,557	0.53%	$559,736	1.66%	34.37%
10. TRANSUNION	$88	0.08%	$0	0.00%	$116,352	99.92%	$116,440	0.04%	$22,364	0.07%	19.21%
COMPOSITE	$72,124,036	23.64%	$192,767,467	63.18%	$40,240,710	13.19%	$305,132,213	100.00%	$33,650,588	100.00%	11.03%
AVERAGE	$7,212,404		$19,276,747		$4,024,071		$30,513,221		$3,365,059		
INDIANA											
1. FIRST AMERICAN	$6,024,300	19.38%	$18,563,414	59.71%	$6,502,153	20.91%	$31,089,867	30.39%	$2,525,020	22.68%	8.12%
2. CHICAGO / FIDELITY	$14,568,910	48.04%	$15,597,106	51.43%	$163,074	0.54%	$30,329,090	29.64%	$3,577,312	32.13%	11.79%
3. LAND AMERICA	$6,667,279	41.01%	$9,589,183	58.99%	$340	0.00%	$16,256,802	15.89%	$1,541,274	13.84%	9.48%
4. STEWART	$320,241	2.17%	$9,786,782	66.23%	$4,669,539	31.60%	$14,776,562	14.44%	$2,476,061	22.24%	16.76%
5. UNAFFILIATED COMPANIES	$735,000	17.66%	$3,081,264	74.04%	$345,572	8.30%	$4,161,836	4.07%	$430,526	3.87%	10.34%
6. OLD REPUBLIC	$227,177	5.62%	$3,818,019	94.38%	$0	0.00%	$4,045,196	3.95%	$125,107	1.12%	3.09%
7. ATTORNEYS' TITLE	$831,940	100.00%	$0	0.00%	$0	0.00%	$831,940	0.81%	$389,203	3.50%	46.78%
8. RELIANT HOLDING	$17,740	2.32%	$339,321	44.38%	$407,468	53.30%	$764,529	0.75%	$40,614	0.36%	5.31%
9. INVESTORS	$0	0.00%	$40,938	100.00%	$0	0.00%	$40,938	0.04%	$27,464	0.25%	67.09%
10. TRANSUNION	$0	0.00%	$0	0.00%	$17,703	100.00%	$17,703	0.02%	$0	--	--
COMPOSITE	$29,392,587	28.73%	$60,816,027	59.44%	$12,105,849	11.83%	$102,314,463	100.00%	$11,132,581	100.00%	10.88%
AVERAGE	$2,939,259		$6,081,603		$1,210,585		$10,231,446		$1,113,258		
IOWA											
1. UNAFFILIATED COMPANIES	$3,724,743	100.00%	$0	0.00%	$0	0.00%	$3,724,743	48.07%	($2,440)	(0.45)%	(0.07)%
2. LAND AMERICA	$707,687	23.26%	$2,335,100	76.74%	$55	0.00%	$3,042,842	39.27%	$170,861	31.21%	5.62%
3. CHICAGO / FIDELITY	$250,552	50.22%	$176,753	35.42%	$71,648	14.36%	$498,953	6.44%	$368,507	67.31%	73.86%
4. STEWART	$172,064	37.15%	$273,669	59.09%	$17,416	3.76%	$463,149	5.98%	$10,348	1.89%	2.23%
5. INVESTORS	$0	0.00%	$14,405	100.00%	$0	0.00%	$14,405	0.19%	$0	--	--
6. FIRST AMERICAN	$0	0.00%	$4,099	100.00%	$0	0.00%	$4,099	0.05%	$0	--	--
7. RELIANT HOLDING	$0	--	$0	--	$0	--	$0	--	$214	0.04%	--
COMPOSITE	$4,855,046	62.66%	$2,804,026	36.19%	$89,119	1.15%	$7,748,191	100.00%	$547,490	100.00%	7.07%
AVERAGE	$693,578		$400,575		$12,731		$1,106,884		$78,213		
KANSAS											
1. FIRST AMERICAN	$1,551,085	9.53%	$7,318,803	44.99%	$7,399,061	45.48%	$16,268,949	37.31%	$311,515	19.06%	1.91%
2. CHICAGO / FIDELITY	$4,495,535	40.50%	$6,604,234	59.50%	$0	0.00%	$11,099,769	25.45%	$360,235	22.04%	3.25%
3. LAND AMERICA	$2,290,414	32.69%	$4,557,101	65.04%	$158,721	2.27%	$7,006,236	16.07%	$196,892	12.05%	2.81%
4. STEWART	$301,840	5.35%	$2,620,984	46.49%	$2,715,209	48.16%	$5,638,033	12.93%	$493,020	30.17%	8.74%
5. OLD REPUBLIC	$5,702	0.17%	$2,956,623	86.57%	$452,917	13.26%	$3,415,242	7.83%	$250,881	15.35%	7.35%
6. RELIANT HOLDING	$0	0.00%	$6,800	3.80%	$172,205	96.20%	$179,005	0.41%	$21,655	1.33%	12.10%
COMPOSITE	$8,644,576	19.82%	$24,064,545	55.18%	$10,898,113	24.99%	$43,607,234	100.00%	$1,634,198	100.00%	3.75%
AVERAGE	$1,440,763		$4,010,758		$1,816,352		$7,267,872		$272,366		
KENTUCKY											
1. FIRST AMERICAN	$1,677,020	10.55%	$13,716,439	86.32%	$496,678	3.13%	$15,890,137	24.89%	$1,424,683	22.05%	8.97%
2. LAND AMERICA	$2,079,735	13.16%	$13,680,107	86.58%	$40,923	0.26%	$15,800,765	24.75%	$2,183,317	33.79%	13.82%
3. CHICAGO / FIDELITY	$2,017,719	17.55%	$8,941,164	77.77%	$537,859	4.68%	$11,496,742	18.01%	$1,085,597	16.80%	9.44%
4. STEWART	$546,525	5.69%	$7,390,922	76.94%	$1,668,069	17.37%	$9,605,516	15.04%	$730,790	11.31%	7.61%
5. OLD REPUBLIC	$268,821	3.33%	$7,797,533	96.67%	$0	0.00%	$8,066,354	12.63%	$884,380	13.69%	10.96%
6. INVESTORS	$0	0.00%	$1,927,641	75.17%	$636,760	24.83%	$2,564,401	4.02%	$130,792	2.02%	5.10%
7. UNAFFILIATED COMPANIES	$5,691	1.36%	$412,436	98.64%	$0	0.00%	$418,127	0.65%	$21,658	0.34%	5.18%
8. TRANSUNION	$0	0.00%	$0	0.00%	$10,162	100.00%	$10,162	0.02%	$0	--	--
9. RELIANT HOLDING	$0	0.00%	$0	0.00%	$150	100.00%	$150	0.00%	$0	--	--
COMPOSITE	$6,595,511	10.33%	$53,866,242	84.36%	$3,390,601	5.31%	$63,852,354	100.00%	$6,461,217	100.00%	10.12%
AVERAGE	$732,835		$5,985,138		$376,733		$7,094,706		$717,913		

C.1 Jurisdiction - By NAIC Group

	DIRECT PREMIUMS WRITTEN							PERCENT OF JURISDICTION	PAID LOSSES	PERCENT OF JURISDICTION	LOSSES TO PREMIUMS
	DIRECT	% of Total	NON-AFFILIATED	% of Total	AFFILIATED	% of Total	TOTAL				
LOUISIANA											
1. FIRST AMERICAN	$639,612	1.34%	$46,815,798	98.34%	$149,271	0.31%	$47,604,681	39.18%	($522,517)	(15.25)%	(1.10)%
2. LAND AMERICA	$1,516,763	4.77%	$30,289,197	95.20%	$9,192	0.03%	$31,815,152	26.19%	$2,221,986	64.87%	6.98%
3. CHICAGO / FIDELITY	$762,469	3.46%	$18,688,160	84.76%	$2,597,948	11.78%	$22,048,577	18.15%	$1,079,973	31.53%	4.90%
4. STEWART	$149,049	0.95%	$12,743,531	80.93%	$2,854,272	18.13%	$15,746,852	12.96%	$345,301	10.08%	2.19%
5. UNAFFILIATED COMPANIES	$0	0.00%	$2,343,439	100.00%	$0	0.00%	$2,343,439	1.93%	$136,777	3.99%	5.84%
6. OLD REPUBLIC	$25,080	1.57%	$1,572,271	98.43%	$0	0.00%	$1,597,351	1.31%	$163,816	4.78%	10.26%
7. INVESTORS	$0	0.00%	$321,368	100.00%	$0	0.00%	$321,368	0.26%	$0	--	--
8. OHIO FARMERS	$0	0.00%	$10,825	100.00%	$0	0.00%	$10,825	0.00%	$0	--	--
COMPOSITE	**$3,092,973**	2.55%	**$112,784,589**	92.84%	**$5,610,683**	4.62%	**$121,488,245**	100.00%	**$3,425,336**	100.00%	2.82%
AVERAGE	**$386,622**		**$14,098,074**		**$701,335**		**$15,186,031**		**$428,167**		
MAINE											
1. FIRST AMERICAN	$199,931	1.20%	$14,814,337	88.62%	$1,702,286	10.18%	$16,716,554	51.15%	$1,196,784	39.29%	7.16%
2. CHICAGO / FIDELITY	$252,293	3.14%	$7,775,728	96.86%	$0	0.00%	$8,028,021	24.57%	$1,159,044	38.05%	14.44%
3. LAND AMERICA	$1,373,207	27.23%	$3,669,406	72.76%	$479	0.01%	$5,043,092	15.43%	$353,748	11.61%	7.01%
4. STEWART	$26,806	1.16%	$1,750,925	76.06%	$524,213	22.77%	$2,301,944	7.04%	$310,621	10.20%	13.49%
5. OLD REPUBLIC	$48,173	8.66%	$508,379	91.34%	$0	0.00%	$556,552	1.70%	$25,572	0.84%	4.59%
6. UNAFFILIATED COMPANIES	$0	0.00%	$0	0.00%	$14,476	100.00%	$14,476	0.04%	$0	--	--
7. RELIANT HOLDING	$0	0.00%	$0	0.00%	$10,566	100.00%	$10,566	0.03%	$0	--	--
8. CATIC	$0	0.00%	$8,326	100.00%	$0	0.00%	$8,326	0.03%	$0	--	--
COMPOSITE	**$1,900,410**	5.82%	**$28,527,101**	87.29%	**$2,252,020**	6.89%	**$32,679,531**	100.00%	**$3,045,769**	100.00%	9.32%
AVERAGE	**$237,551**		**$3,565,888**		**$281,503**		**$4,084,941**		**$380,721**		
MARYLAND											
1. FIRST AMERICAN	$8,095,154	9.24%	$73,832,454	84.30%	$5,659,486	6.46%	$87,587,094	28.45%	$4,843,586	21.22%	5.53%
2. CHICAGO / FIDELITY	$8,019,717	9.93%	$72,716,160	90.00%	$61,317	0.08%	$80,797,194	26.25%	$11,178,719	48.97%	13.84%
3. LAND AMERICA	$11,529,773	16.39%	$58,594,448	83.28%	$238,067	0.34%	$70,362,288	22.86%	$2,255,712	9.88%	3.21%
4. STEWART	$1,163,121	2.90%	$36,733,767	91.49%	$2,251,554	5.61%	$40,148,442	13.04%	$2,633,944	11.54%	6.56%
5. UNAFFILIATED COMPANIES	$413,935	3.13%	$8,860,419	67.08%	$3,934,344	29.79%	$13,208,698	4.29%	$484,773	2.12%	3.67%
6. OLD REPUBLIC	$156,861	1.34%	$11,530,449	98.66%	$0	0.00%	$11,687,310	3.80%	$994,975	4.36%	8.51%
7. OHIO FARMERS	$0	0.00%	$2,039,926	73.53%	$734,177	26.47%	$2,774,103	0.90%	$79,508	0.35%	2.87%
8. INVESTORS	$0	0.00%	$1,176,007	100.00%	$0	0.00%	$1,176,007	0.38%	$355,386	1.56%	30.22%
9. TRANSUNION	$2	0.00%	$0	0.00%	$70,720	100.00%	$70,722	0.02%	$0	--	--
COMPOSITE	**$29,378,563**	9.54%	**$265,483,630**	86.25%	**$12,949,665**	4.21%	**$307,811,858**	100.00%	**$22,826,603**	100.00%	7.42%
AVERAGE	**$3,264,285**		**$29,498,181**		**$1,438,852**		**$34,201,318**		**$2,536,289**		
MASSACHUSETTS											
1. FIRST AMERICAN	$2,021,937	2.08%	$94,807,224	97.69%	$220,075	0.23%	$97,049,236	40.23%	$5,773,019	24.59%	5.95%
2. CHICAGO / FIDELITY	$3,489,440	7.31%	$44,215,123	92.66%	$14,268	0.03%	$47,718,831	19.78%	$6,991,034	29.77%	14.65%
3. LAND AMERICA	$6,276,254	15.53%	$34,120,545	84.44%	$12,402	0.03%	$40,409,201	16.75%	$5,292,281	22.54%	13.10%
4. STEWART	$2,077,606	8.23%	$22,543,803	89.32%	$617,198	2.45%	$25,238,607	10.46%	$2,474,207	10.54%	9.80%
5. OLD REPUBLIC	$297,150	1.36%	$21,526,999	98.59%	$10,220	0.05%	$21,834,369	9.05%	$1,488,095	6.34%	6.82%
6. CATIC	$0	0.00%	$8,093,908	100.00%	$0	0.00%	$8,093,908	3.36%	$1,419,832	6.05%	17.54%
7. UNAFFILIATED COMPANIES	$857,225	95.05%	$0	0.00%	$44,660	4.95%	$901,885	0.37%	$41,763	0.18%	4.63%
COMPOSITE	**$15,019,612**	6.23%	**$225,307,602**	93.39%	**$918,823**	0.38%	**$241,246,037**	100.00%	**$23,480,231**	100.00%	9.73%
AVERAGE	**$2,145,659**		**$32,186,800**		**$131,260**		**$34,463,720**		**$3,354,319**		
MICHIGAN											
1. FIRST AMERICAN	$14,317,719	11.58%	$64,821,546	52.42%	$44,511,678	36.00%	$123,650,943	39.28%	$13,151,625	23.80%	10.64%
2. CHICAGO / FIDELITY	$7,494,850	9.73%	$57,342,660	74.41%	$12,222,972	15.86%	$77,060,482	24.48%	$16,570,627	29.99%	21.50%
3. LAND AMERICA	$17,246,583	24.01%	$52,751,237	73.44%	$1,828,569	2.55%	$71,826,389	22.82%	$15,038,031	27.22%	20.94%
4. STEWART	$681,396	3.32%	$16,421,784	80.13%	$3,390,828	16.55%	$20,494,008	6.51%	$5,111,056	9.25%	24.94%
5. OLD REPUBLIC	$248,330	1.62%	$15,041,679	98.38%	$0	0.00%	$15,290,009	4.86%	$4,409,450	7.98%	28.84%
6. INVESTORS	$7,790	0.25%	$2,718,167	87.83%	$368,873	11.92%	$3,094,830	0.98%	$302,789	0.55%	9.78%
7. RELIANT HOLDING	$0	0.00%	$201,584	7.21%	$2,595,869	92.79%	$2,797,453	0.89%	$513,370	0.93%	18.35%
8. UNAFFILIATED COMPANIES	$0	0.00%	$0	0.00%	$498,233	100.00%	$498,233	0.16%	$0	--	--
9. ATTORNEYS' TITLE	$0	0.00%	$81,020	100.00%	$0	0.00%	$81,020	0.03%	$154,009	0.28%	190.09%
COMPOSITE	**$39,996,668**	12.71%	**$209,379,677**	66.51%	**$65,417,022**	20.78%	**$314,793,367**	100.00%	**$55,250,957**	100.00%	17.55%
AVERAGE	**$4,444,074**		**$23,264,409**		**$7,268,558**		**$34,977,041**		**$6,138,995**		
MINNESOTA											
1. CHICAGO / FIDELITY	$3,041,575	9.09%	$30,405,199	90.88%	$10,993	0.03%	$33,457,767	27.98%	$9,412,338	41.58%	28.13%
2. LAND AMERICA	$2,745,513	8.51%	$29,511,623	91.48%	$2,964	0.01%	$32,260,100	26.98%	$4,661,407	20.59%	14.45%
3. FIRST AMERICAN	$4,376,517	21.38%	$5,130,418	25.06%	$10,963,657	53.56%	$20,470,592	17.12%	$4,371,827	19.31%	21.36%
4. STEWART	$256,667	1.54%	$14,407,553	86.64%	$1,965,411	11.82%	$16,629,631	13.91%	$1,779,847	7.86%	10.70%
5. OLD REPUBLIC	$1,627,848	13.47%	$10,453,789	86.53%	$0	0.00%	$12,081,637	10.11%	$2,204,976	9.74%	18.25%
6. ATTORNEYS' TITLE	$0	0.00%	$3,696,692	100.00%	$0	0.00%	$3,696,692	3.09%	$188,104	0.83%	5.09%
7. INVESTORS	$0	0.00%	$482,025	100.00%	$0	0.00%	$482,025	0.40%	$17,576	0.08%	3.65%
8. UNAFFILIATED COMPANIES	$5,315	1.10%	$79,799	16.59%	$395,889	82.30%	$481,003	0.40%	$124	0.00%	0.03%
COMPOSITE	**$12,053,435**	10.08%	**$94,167,098**	78.76%	**$13,338,914**	11.16%	**$119,559,447**	100.00%	**$22,636,199**	100.00%	18.93%
AVERAGE	**$1,506,679**		**$11,770,887**		**$1,667,364**		**$14,944,931**		**$2,829,525**		

C.1 Jurisdiction - By NAIC Group

	DIRECT PREMIUMS WRITTEN							PERCENT OF	PAID	PERCENT OF	LOSSES TO
	DIRECT	% of Total	NON-AFFILIATED	% of Total	AFFILIATED	% of Total	TOTAL	JURISDICTION	LOSSES	JURISDICTION	PREMIUMS
MISSISSIPPI											
1. FIRST AMERICAN	$2,199,131	16.45%	$11,082,666	82.90%	$86,256	0.65%	$13,368,053	28.27%	$1,714,818	38.93%	12.83%
2. OLD REPUBLIC	$407,805	3.50%	$11,233,776	96.50%	$0	0.00%	$11,641,581	24.61%	$1,109,869	25.20%	9.53%
3. CHICAGO / FIDELITY	$511,387	6.76%	$6,538,102	86.43%	$515,258	6.81%	$7,564,747	15.99%	$740,727	16.82%	9.79%
4. LAND AMERICA	$564,837	8.80%	$5,851,756	91.19%	$394	0.01%	$6,416,987	13.57%	$330,107	7.49%	5.14%
5. STEWART	$158,727	4.22%	$3,079,639	81.82%	$525,456	13.96%	$3,763,822	7.96%	$319,032	7.24%	8.48%
6. UNAFFILIATED COMPANIES	$56,517	1.75%	$3,176,833	98.25%	$0	0.00%	$3,233,350	6.84%	$153,718	3.49%	4.75%
7. INVESTORS	$90	0.01%	$916,363	99.99%	$0	0.00%	$916,453	1.94%	$36,314	0.82%	3.96%
8. OHIO FARMERS	$0	0.00%	$223,884	100.00%	$0	0.00%	$223,884	0.47%	$0	--	--
9. RELIANT HOLDING	$0	0.00%	$0	0.00%	$151,012	100.00%	$151,012	0.32%	$22	0.00%	0.01%
10. TRANSUNION	$35	0.23%	$0	0.00%	$15,188	99.77%	$15,223	0.03%	$0	--	--
COMPOSITE	**$3,898,529**	8.24%	**$42,103,019**	89.02%	**$1,293,564**	2.74%	**$47,295,112**	100.00%	**$4,404,607**	100.00%	9.31%
AVERAGE	**$389,853**		**$4,210,302**		**$129,356**		**$4,729,511**		**$440,461**		
MISSOURI											
1. CHICAGO / FIDELITY	$3,573,269	17.82%	$16,396,031	81.75%	$87,569	0.44%	$20,056,869	26.72%	$3,714,095	21.45%	18.52%
2. FIRST AMERICAN	$1,449,509	7.66%	$14,961,839	79.11%	$2,501,584	13.23%	$18,912,932	25.20%	$2,882,166	16.65%	15.24%
3. LAND AMERICA	$4,484,716	27.92%	$11,567,883	72.01%	$12,184	0.08%	$16,064,783	21.40%	$6,300,989	36.39%	39.22%
4. STEWART	$264,661	2.21%	$10,057,805	83.83%	$1,676,006	13.97%	$11,998,472	15.99%	$1,517,882	8.77%	12.65%
5. OLD REPUBLIC	$69,405	1.65%	$3,084,526	73.44%	$1,046,411	24.91%	$4,200,342	5.60%	$1,823,650	10.53%	43.42%
6. UNAFFILIATED COMPANIES	$698,400	32.35%	$1,138,404	52.73%	$322,242	14.93%	$2,159,046	2.88%	$63,819	0.37%	2.96%
7. RELIANT HOLDING	$0	0.00%	$1,118,587	74.26%	$387,803	25.74%	$1,506,390	2.01%	$1,011,385	5.84%	67.14%
8. INVESTORS	$0	0.00%	$140,569	86.83%	$21,324	13.17%	$161,893	0.22%	$803	0.00%	0.50%
COMPOSITE	**$10,539,960**	14.04%	**$58,465,644**	77.89%	**$6,055,123**	8.07%	**$75,060,727**	100.00%	**$17,314,789**	100.00%	23.07%
AVERAGE	**$1,317,495**		**$7,308,206**		**$756,890**		**$9,382,591**		**$2,164,349**		
MONTANA											
1. FIRST AMERICAN	$471,301	1.98%	$13,242,153	55.66%	$10,078,993	42.36%	$23,792,447	43.69%	$761,207	47.05%	3.20%
2. CHICAGO / FIDELITY	$3,436,804	28.99%	$8,419,146	71.01%	$0	0.00%	$11,855,950	21.77%	$515,480	31.86%	4.35%
3. STEWART	$10,786	0.12%	$3,572,369	40.68%	$5,197,724	59.19%	$8,780,879	16.12%	$226,173	13.98%	2.58%
4. LAND AMERICA	$428,736	5.02%	$8,116,284	94.96%	$1,754	0.02%	$8,546,774	15.69%	$102,514	6.34%	1.20%
5. OLD REPUBLIC	$20,793	1.40%	$1,464,886	98.60%	$0	0.00%	$1,485,679	2.73%	$12,433	0.77%	0.84%
COMPOSITE	**$4,368,420**	8.02%	**$34,814,838**	63.93%	**$15,278,471**	28.05%	**$54,461,729**	100.00%	**$1,617,807**	100.00%	2.97%
AVERAGE	**$873,684**		**$6,962,968**		**$3,055,694**		**$10,892,346**		**$323,561**		
NEBRASKA											
1. OLD REPUBLIC	$33,496	0.32%	$10,356,291	99.68%	$0	0.00%	$10,389,787	26.71%	$136,282	6.86%	1.31%
2. FIRST AMERICAN	$751,155	8.17%	$6,415,603	69.79%	$2,025,866	22.04%	$9,192,624	23.64%	$214,149	10.79%	2.33%
3. CHICAGO / FIDELITY	$168,791	1.90%	$8,695,381	98.10%	$0	0.00%	$8,864,172	22.79%	$675,620	34.03%	7.62%
4. LAND AMERICA	$188,374	2.44%	$7,518,374	97.56%	$0	0.00%	$7,706,748	19.82%	$878,941	44.27%	11.40%
5. STEWART	$124,603	6.50%	$1,774,815	92.62%	$16,803	0.88%	$1,916,221	4.93%	$134,716	6.79%	7.03%
6. INVESTORS	$204,455	28.15%	$521,962	71.85%	$0	0.00%	$726,417	1.87%	($54,485)	(2.74)%	(7.50)%
7. UNAFFILIATED COMPANIES	$0	0.00%	$96,748	100.00%	$0	0.00%	$96,748	0.25%	$0	--	--
COMPOSITE	**$1,470,874**	3.78%	**$35,379,174**	90.97%	**$2,042,669**	5.25%	**$38,892,717**	100.00%	**$1,985,223**	100.00%	5.10%
AVERAGE	**$210,125**		**$5,054,168**		**$291,810**		**$5,556,102**		**$283,603**		
NEVADA											
1. CHICAGO / FIDELITY	$4,949,312	7.72%	$19,442,718	30.34%	$39,690,475	61.94%	$64,082,505	30.01%	$3,625,095	37.09%	5.66%
2. FIRST AMERICAN	$37,022,447	58.21%	$25,445,731	40.01%	$1,128,647	1.77%	$63,596,825	29.78%	$1,960,163	20.06%	3.08%
3. LAND AMERICA	$8,000,254	18.01%	$23,844,267	53.67%	$12,586,389	28.33%	$44,430,910	20.81%	$3,383,021	34.61%	7.61%
4. STEWART	$1,219,137	6.45%	$5,094,523	26.96%	$12,580,498	66.58%	$18,894,158	8.85%	$408,850	4.18%	2.16%
5. UNAFFILIATED COMPANIES	$0	0.00%	$35,531	0.24%	$14,944,771	99.76%	$14,980,302	7.02%	$361,072	3.69%	2.41%
6. OLD REPUBLIC	$280,522	3.73%	$3,730,514	49.54%	$3,519,312	46.74%	$7,530,348	3.53%	$35,726	0.37%	0.47%
7. TRANSUNION	$0	0.00%	$0	0.00%	$8,651	100.00%	$8,651	0.00%	$0	--	--
COMPOSITE	**$51,471,672**	24.11%	**$77,593,284**	36.34%	**$84,458,743**	39.55%	**$213,523,699**	100.00%	**$9,773,927**	100.00%	4.58%
AVERAGE	**$7,353,096**		**$11,084,755**		**$12,065,535**		**$30,503,386**		**$1,396,275**		
NEW HAMPSHIRE											
1. FIRST AMERICAN	$494,462	3.57%	$12,809,174	92.55%	$537,314	3.88%	$13,840,950	40.04%	$738,953	23.06%	5.34%
2. LAND AMERICA	$1,042,036	15.20%	$5,812,444	84.80%	$0	0.00%	$6,854,480	19.83%	$348,785	10.88%	5.09%
3. CHICAGO / FIDELITY	$235,672	3.67%	$6,188,280	96.33%	$0	0.00%	$6,423,952	18.58%	$1,492,578	46.58%	23.23%
4. STEWART	$198,834	4.62%	$3,133,150	72.74%	$975,175	22.64%	$4,307,159	12.46%	$369,323	11.53%	8.57%
5. OLD REPUBLIC	$266,056	9.72%	$2,471,937	90.28%	$0	0.00%	$2,737,993	7.92%	$254,458	7.94%	9.29%
6. CATIC	$0	0.00%	$402,407	100.00%	$0	0.00%	$402,407	1.16%	$405	0.01%	0.10%
COMPOSITE	**$2,237,060**	6.47%	**$30,817,392**	89.15%	**$1,512,489**	4.38%	**$34,566,941**	100.00%	**$3,204,502**	100.00%	9.27%
AVERAGE	**$372,843**		**$5,136,232**		**$252,082**		**$5,761,157**		**$534,084**		
NEW JERSEY											
1. CHICAGO / FIDELITY	$32,278,546	23.98%	$102,001,739	75.78%	$315,930	0.23%	$134,596,215	28.43%	$5,568,514	17.28%	4.14%
2. FIRST AMERICAN	$14,285,946	12.59%	$96,075,272	84.66%	$3,119,543	2.75%	$113,480,761	23.97%	$8,776,935	27.23%	7.73%
3. LAND AMERICA	$19,437,666	19.96%	$77,904,241	80.00%	$43,744	0.04%	$97,385,651	20.57%	$6,769,696	21.00%	6.95%
4. STEWART	$1,946,301	3.09%	$55,021,124	87.39%	$5,995,111	9.52%	$62,962,536	13.30%	$3,356,654	10.41%	5.33%
5. OLD REPUBLIC	$917,478	2.17%	$40,652,727	95.94%	$803,284	1.90%	$42,373,489	8.95%	$6,681,055	20.73%	15.77%
6. CATIC	$0	0.00%	$16,413,857	100.00%	$0	0.00%	$16,413,857	3.47%	$1,064,324	3.30%	6.48%
7. UNAFFILIATED COMPANIES	$4,985	0.08%	$357,806	5.75%	$5,856,310	94.17%	$6,219,101	1.31%	$13,668	0.04%	0.22%
8. OHIO FARMERS	$0	--	$0	--	$0	--	$0	--	$899	0.00%	--
COMPOSITE	**$68,870,922**	14.55%	**$388,426,766**	82.04%	**$16,133,922**	3.41%	**$473,431,610**	100.00%	**$32,231,745**	100.00%	6.81%
AVERAGE	**$8,608,865**		**$48,553,346**		**$2,016,740**		**$59,178,951**		**$4,028,968**		

C.1 Jurisdiction - By NAIC Group

	DIRECT PREMIUMS WRITTEN							PERCENT OF JURISDICTION	PAID LOSSES	PERCENT OF JURISDICTION	LOSSES TO PREMIUMS
	DIRECT	% of Total	NON-AFFILIATED	% of Total	AFFILIATED	% of Total	TOTAL				
NEW MEXICO											
1. LAND AMERICA	$9,439,200	23.63%	$20,480,907	51.27%	$10,027,706	25.10%	$39,947,813	35.27%	$1,378,538	28.67%	3.45%
2. FIRST AMERICAN	$15,171,307	47.98%	$13,913,169	44.00%	$2,534,998	8.02%	$31,619,474	27.91%	$1,754,202	36.48%	5.55%
3. CHICAGO / FIDELITY	$13,701,084	52.80%	$12,191,787	46.98%	$58,275	0.22%	$25,951,146	22.91%	$1,295,906	26.95%	4.99%
4. STEWART	$0	0.00%	$3,341,414	25.99%	$9,513,136	74.01%	$12,854,550	11.35%	$156,780	3.26%	1.22%
5. OLD REPUBLIC	$0	0.00%	$2,175,598	100.00%	$0	0.00%	$2,175,598	1.92%	$168,838	3.51%	7.76%
6. UNAFFILIATED COMPANIES	$0	0.00%	$0	0.00%	$724,207	100.00%	$724,207	0.64%	$54,397	1.13%	7.51%
COMPOSITE	$38,311,591	33.82%	$52,102,875	46.00%	$22,858,322	20.18%	$113,272,788	100.00%	$4,808,661	100.00%	4.25%
AVERAGE	$6,385,265		$8,683,813		$3,809,720		$18,878,798		$801,444		
NEW YORK											
1. CHICAGO / FIDELITY	$128,365,693	42.16%	$175,479,697	57.64%	$594,478	0.20%	$304,439,868	25.93%	$18,376,101	37.75%	6.04%
2. LAND AMERICA	$100,885,093	33.59%	$199,373,097	66.38%	$83,902	0.03%	$300,342,092	25.58%	$6,856,597	14.09%	2.28%
3. FIRST AMERICAN	$96,495,671	32.18%	$192,008,986	64.03%	$11,384,454	3.80%	$299,889,111	25.54%	$12,730,420	26.15%	4.25%
4. STEWART	$44,508,239	25.40%	$129,002,323	73.61%	$1,738,004	0.99%	$175,248,566	14.93%	$5,017,868	10.31%	2.86%
5. OLD REPUBLIC	$316,532	0.43%	$67,876,078	92.30%	$5,343,542	7.27%	$73,536,152	6.26%	$4,345,925	8.93%	5.91%
6. UNAFFILIATED COMPANIES	$251,019	1.37%	$15,142,322	82.81%	$2,893,006	15.82%	$18,286,347	1.56%	$1,196,352	2.46%	6.54%
7. INVESTORS	$0	0.00%	$2,414,626	100.00%	$0	0.00%	$2,414,626	0.21%	$154,328	0.32%	6.39%
COMPOSITE	$370,822,247	31.58%	$781,297,129	66.54%	$22,037,386	1.88%	$1,174,156,762	100.00%	$48,677,591	100.00%	4.15%
AVERAGE	$52,974,607		$111,613,876		$3,148,198		$167,736,680		$6,953,942		
NORTH CAROLINA											
1. FIRST AMERICAN	$8,810,772	15.17%	$49,092,437	84.50%	$192,851	0.33%	$58,096,060	32.70%	$3,423,809	15.40%	5.89%
2. CHICAGO / FIDELITY	$10,519,717	23.41%	$34,153,562	76.00%	$263,320	0.59%	$44,936,599	25.29%	$5,724,900	25.75%	12.74%
3. INVESTORS	$29,147,893	85.06%	$2,032,474	5.93%	$3,085,949	9.01%	$34,266,316	19.29%	$7,786,658	35.03%	22.72%
4. LAND AMERICA	$5,554,271	41.22%	$7,916,682	58.75%	$3,739	0.03%	$13,474,692	7.58%	$2,410,208	10.84%	17.89%
5. STEWART	$1,721,235	13.25%	$10,176,438	78.34%	$1,092,468	8.41%	$12,990,141	7.31%	$1,646,435	7.41%	12.67%
6. OLD REPUBLIC	$22,624	0.21%	$1,245,737	11.83%	$9,260,435	87.95%	$10,528,796	5.93%	$1,122,735	5.05%	10.66%
7. OHIO FARMERS	$106	0.00%	$2,774,562	100.00%	$0	0.00%	$2,774,668	1.56%	$3,712	0.02%	0.13%
8. ATTORNEYS' TITLE	$0	0.00%	$416,568	100.00%	$0	0.00%	$416,568	0.23%	$0	--	--
9. TRANSUNION	$210	0.12%	$0	0.00%	$171,167	99.88%	$171,377	0.10%	$110,277	0.50%	64.35%
COMPOSITE	$55,776,828	31.40%	$107,808,460	60.68%	$14,069,929	7.92%	$177,655,217	100.00%	$22,228,734	100.00%	12.51%
AVERAGE	$6,197,425		$11,978,718		$1,563,325		$19,739,469		$2,469,859		
NORTH DAKOTA											
1. FIRST AMERICAN	$277,928	17.56%	$1,157,329	73.14%	$147,045	9.29%	$1,582,302	27.40%	$21,483	23.29%	1.36%
2. CHICAGO / FIDELITY	$15,494	1.15%	$1,327,372	98.85%	$0	0.00%	$1,342,866	23.26%	$14,862	16.11%	1.11%
3. STEWART	$14,770	1.24%	$1,176,170	98.76%	$0	0.00%	$1,190,940	20.63%	$4,634	5.02%	0.39%
4. OLD REPUBLIC	$50	0.01%	$761,993	99.99%	$0	0.00%	$762,043	13.20%	$0	--	--
5. LAND AMERICA	$70,818	9.75%	$655,285	90.25%	$0	0.00%	$726,103	12.57%	$51,273	55.58%	7.06%
6. ATTORNEYS' TITLE	$0	0.00%	$169,925	100.00%	$0	0.00%	$169,925	2.94%	$0	--	--
COMPOSITE	$379,060	6.56%	$5,248,074	90.89%	$147,045	2.55%	$5,774,179	100.00%	$92,252	100.00%	1.60%
AVERAGE	$63,177		$874,679		$24,508		$962,363		$15,375		
OHIO											
1. FIRST AMERICAN	$9,673,142	7.98%	$92,664,324	76.46%	$18,854,546	15.56%	$121,192,012	34.03%	$8,338,706	31.92%	6.88%
2. CHICAGO / FIDELITY	$23,015,106	25.85%	$61,354,689	68.91%	$4,667,155	5.24%	$89,036,950	25.00%	$4,561,361	17.46%	5.12%
3. LAND AMERICA	$14,723,724	23.89%	$43,231,156	70.15%	$3,667,749	5.95%	$61,622,629	17.30%	$4,878,399	18.68%	7.92%
4. STEWART	$1,967,484	5.38%	$23,963,516	65.53%	$10,636,676	29.09%	$36,567,676	10.27%	$3,497,715	13.39%	9.57%
5. OLD REPUBLIC	$692,128	2.03%	$32,968,455	96.48%	$510,948	1.50%	$34,171,531	9.59%	$3,720,465	14.24%	10.89%
6. UNAFFILIATED COMPANIES	$186,090	1.97%	$8,280,060	87.74%	$971,072	10.29%	$9,437,222	2.65%	$914,008	3.50%	9.69%
7. RELIANT HOLDING	$186,780	10.48%	$472,033	26.48%	$1,123,621	63.04%	$1,782,434	0.50%	$204,968	0.78%	11.50%
8. OHIO FARMERS	$0	0.00%	$469,922	31.02%	$1,045,069	68.98%	$1,514,991	0.43%	($596)	0.00%	(0.04)%
9. TRANSUNION	$33,035	4.78%	$617,640	89.44%	$39,893	5.78%	$690,568	0.19%	$6,524	0.02%	0.94%
10. INVESTORS	$0	0.00%	$141,259	100.00%	$0	0.00%	$141,259	0.04%	$0	--	--
COMPOSITE	$50,477,489	14.17%	$264,163,054	74.17%	$41,516,729	11.66%	$356,157,272	100.00%	$26,121,550	100.00%	7.33%
AVERAGE	$5,047,749		$26,416,305		$4,151,673		$35,615,727		$2,612,155		
OKLAHOMA											
1. FIRST AMERICAN	$7,164,263	28.74%	$15,725,913	63.08%	$2,039,357	8.18%	$24,929,533	39.86%	$538,790	33.08%	2.16%
2. CHICAGO / FIDELITY	$107,411	0.78%	$6,369,685	46.08%	$7,345,833	53.14%	$13,822,929	22.10%	$916,606	56.28%	6.63%
3. LAND AMERICA	$82,227	1.22%	$6,581,757	97.76%	$68,824	1.02%	$6,732,808	10.76%	$121,013	7.43%	1.80%
4. UNAFFILIATED COMPANIES	$1,906,376	28.67%	$4,209,897	63.32%	$532,250	8.01%	$6,648,523	10.63%	$55,949	3.44%	0.84%
5. STEWART	$66,879	1.10%	$2,601,403	42.97%	$3,385,667	55.92%	$6,053,949	9.68%	($85,877)	(5.27)%	(1.42)%
6. OLD REPUBLIC	$175	0.00%	$656,399	17.85%	$3,019,801	82.14%	$3,676,375	5.88%	$82,167	5.05%	2.24%
7. RELIANT HOLDING	$0	0.00%	$0	0.00%	$683,390	100.00%	$683,390	1.09%	$0	--	--
COMPOSITE	$9,327,331	14.91%	$36,145,054	57.79%	$17,075,122	27.30%	$62,547,507	100.00%	$1,628,648	100.00%	2.60%
AVERAGE	$1,332,476		$5,163,579		$2,439,303		$8,935,358		$232,664		
OREGON											
1. CHICAGO / FIDELITY	$33,021,483	36.72%	$18,043,025	20.06%	$38,865,925	43.22%	$89,930,433	40.40%	$1,785,506	29.49%	1.99%
2. FIRST AMERICAN	$52,365,389	68.08%	$13,190,914	17.15%	$11,364,317	14.77%	$76,920,620	34.56%	$2,455,921	40.56%	3.19%
3. LAND AMERICA	$20,361,838	45.54%	$16,813,570	37.61%	$7,534,143	16.85%	$44,709,551	20.09%	$1,626,084	26.85%	3.64%
4. STEWART	$722,858	6.60%	$10,237,613	93.40%	$0	0.00%	$10,960,471	4.92%	$187,593	3.10%	1.71%
5. OLD REPUBLIC	$0	0.00%	$67,301	100.00%	$0	0.00%	$67,301	0.03%	$0	--	--
COMPOSITE	$106,471,568	47.83%	$58,352,423	26.22%	$57,764,385	25.95%	$222,588,376	100.00%	$6,055,104	100.00%	2.72%
AVERAGE	$21,294,314		$11,670,485		$11,552,877		$44,517,675		$1,211,021		

C.1　Jurisdiction - By NAIC Group

	DIRECT PREMIUMS WRITTEN						PERCENT OF JURISDICTION	PAID LOSSES	PERCENT OF JURISDICTION	LOSSES TO PREMIUMS
	DIRECT	% of Total	NON-AFFILIATED	% of Total	AFFILIATED	% of Total	TOTAL				

PENNSYLVANIA

	DIRECT	% of Total	NON-AFFILIATED	% of Total	AFFILIATED	% of Total	TOTAL	PERCENT OF JURISDICTION	PAID LOSSES	PERCENT OF JURISDICTION	LOSSES TO PREMIUMS
1. LAND AMERICA	$19,089,804	10.38%	$164,489,059	89.41%	$383,558	0.21%	$183,962,421	35.09%	$7,368,306	30.27%	4.01%
2. FIRST AMERICAN	$19,004,612	12.50%	$129,706,664	85.30%	$3,339,835	2.20%	$152,051,111	29.00%	$5,454,490	22.41%	3.59%
3. CHICAGO / FIDELITY	$21,441,842	21.93%	$76,196,720	77.92%	$154,953	0.16%	$97,793,515	18.65%	$5,702,855	23.43%	5.83%
4. OLD REPUBLIC	$556,153	1.31%	$41,891,870	98.69%	$0	0.00%	$42,448,023	8.10%	$3,091,682	12.70%	7.28%
5. STEWART	$4,146,574	12.18%	$29,560,885	86.86%	$326,776	0.96%	$34,034,235	6.49%	$2,221,328	9.13%	6.53%
6. UNAFFILIATED COMPANIES	$117,495	1.19%	$8,276,555	83.95%	$1,465,058	14.86%	$9,859,108	1.88%	$224,328	0.92%	2.28%
7. RELIANT HOLDING	$0	0.00%	$1,100,503	71.62%	$436,169	28.38%	$1,536,672	0.29%	$261,672	1.07%	17.03%
8. INVESTORS	$35,365	2.34%	$1,332,490	88.23%	$142,470	9.43%	$1,510,325	0.29%	$2,325	0.00%	0.15%
9. CATIC	$0	0.00%	$717,721	100.00%	$0		$717,721	0.14%	$15,185	0.06%	2.12%
10. OHIO FARMERS	$0	0.00%	$295,215	74.89%	$98,996	25.11%	$394,211	0.08%	$198	0.00%	0.05%
COMPOSITE	$64,391,845	12.28%	$453,567,682	86.51%	$6,347,815	1.21%	$524,307,342	100.00%	$24,342,369	100.00%	4.64%
AVERAGE	$6,439,185		$45,356,768		$634,782		$52,430,734		$2,434,237		

RHODE ISLAND

	DIRECT	% of Total	NON-AFFILIATED	% of Total	AFFILIATED	% of Total	TOTAL	PERCENT OF JURISDICTION	PAID LOSSES	PERCENT OF JURISDICTION	LOSSES TO PREMIUMS
1. LAND AMERICA	$1,159,452	12.11%	$8,414,989	87.89%	$0	0.00%	$9,574,441	38.43%	$353,368	13.59%	3.69%
2. CHICAGO / FIDELITY	$437,316	7.35%	$5,511,883	92.65%	$0	0.00%	$5,949,199	23.88%	$434,613	16.72%	7.31%
3. FIRST AMERICAN	$713,952	16.78%	$3,513,916	82.58%	$27,384	0.64%	$4,255,252	17.08%	$253,273	9.74%	5.95%
4. STEWART	$123,689	3.74%	$2,025,143	61.24%	$1,158,069	35.02%	$3,306,901	13.27%	$1,237,043	47.58%	37.41%
5. CATIC	$0	0.00%	$1,565,764	100.00%	$0	0.00%	$1,565,764	6.28%	$277,373	10.67%	17.71%
6. OLD REPUBLIC	$9,106	3.47%	$253,616	96.53%	$0		$262,722	1.05%	$43,981	1.69%	16.74%
COMPOSITE	$2,443,515	9.81%	$21,285,311	85.43%	$1,185,453	4.76%	$24,914,279	100.00%	$2,599,651	100.00%	10.43%
AVERAGE	$407,253		$3,547,552		$197,576		$4,152,380		$433,275		

SOUTH CAROLINA

	DIRECT	% of Total	NON-AFFILIATED	% of Total	AFFILIATED	% of Total	TOTAL	PERCENT OF JURISDICTION	PAID LOSSES	PERCENT OF JURISDICTION	LOSSES TO PREMIUMS
1. CHICAGO / FIDELITY	$1,103,928	2.17%	$49,483,392	97.21%	$316,349	0.62%	$50,903,669	36.40%	$3,090,458	33.52%	6.07%
2. LAND AMERICA	$2,043,941	7.87%	$23,932,563	92.11%	$5,156	0.02%	$25,981,660	18.58%	$2,074,256	22.50%	7.98%
3. FIRST AMERICAN	$62,556	0.25%	$24,643,744	98.38%	$344,334	1.37%	$25,050,634	17.91%	$1,552,447	16.84%	6.20%
4. STEWART	$323,342	1.84%	$17,241,337	97.93%	$41,484	0.24%	$17,606,163	12.59%	$708,085	7.68%	4.02%
5. INVESTORS	$211,897	2.80%	$7,360,564	97.18%	$1,767	0.02%	$7,574,228	5.42%	$579,164	6.28%	7.65%
6. OLD REPUBLIC	$183,541	2.80%	$6,377,095	97.20%	$0	0.00%	$6,560,636	4.69%	$401,617	4.36%	6.12%
7. UNAFFILIATED COMPANIES	$0	0.00%	$2,521,722	100.00%	$0	0.00%	$2,521,722	1.80%	$48,214	0.52%	1.91%
8. ATTORNEYS' TITLE	$0	0.00%	$1,893,029	100.00%	$0	0.00%	$1,893,029	1.35%	$359,115	3.90%	18.97%
9. TRANSUNION	$68,818	8.33%	$746,478	90.33%	$11,080	1.34%	$826,376	0.59%	$363,212	3.94%	43.95%
10. OHIO FARMERS	$0	0.00%	$761,782	100.00%	$0	0.00%	$761,782	0.54%	$8,762	0.10%	1.15%
11. RELIANT HOLDING	$0	0.00%	$0	0.00%	$162,067	100.00%	$162,067	0.12%	$33,846	0.37%	20.88%
COMPOSITE	$3,998,023	2.86%	$134,961,706	96.51%	$882,237	0.63%	$139,841,966	100.00%	$9,219,176	100.00%	6.59%
AVERAGE	$363,457		$12,269,246		$80,203		$12,712,906		$838,107		

SOUTH DAKOTA

	DIRECT	% of Total	NON-AFFILIATED	% of Total	AFFILIATED	% of Total	TOTAL	PERCENT OF JURISDICTION	PAID LOSSES	PERCENT OF JURISDICTION	LOSSES TO PREMIUMS
1. CHICAGO / FIDELITY	$111,970	3.54%	$3,049,867	96.46%	$0	0.00%	$3,161,837	21.52%	$69,984	22.97%	2.21%
2. OLD REPUBLIC	$50	0.00%	$2,859,456	100.00%	$0	0.00%	$2,859,506	19.46%	$4,632	1.52%	0.16%
3. UNAFFILIATED COMPANIES	$168,351	6.47%	$2,432,110	93.53%	$0	0.00%	$2,600,461	17.70%	$51,729	16.98%	1.99%
4. FIRST AMERICAN	$271,484	11.12%	$2,169,398	88.87%	$113	0.00%	$2,440,995	16.61%	$30,281	9.94%	1.24%
5. STEWART	$13,860	0.70%	$1,006,549	51.18%	$946,312	48.12%	$1,966,721	13.38%	$76,756	25.19%	3.90%
6. LAND AMERICA	$100,524	6.03%	$1,565,825	93.97%	$0	0.00%	$1,666,349	11.34%	$71,282	23.40%	4.28%
COMPOSITE	$666,239	4.53%	$13,083,205	89.03%	$946,425	6.44%	$14,695,869	100.00%	$304,664	100.00%	2.07%
AVERAGE	$111,040		$2,180,534		$157,738		$2,449,312		$50,777		

TENNESSEE

	DIRECT	% of Total	NON-AFFILIATED	% of Total	AFFILIATED	% of Total	TOTAL	PERCENT OF JURISDICTION	PAID LOSSES	PERCENT OF JURISDICTION	LOSSES TO PREMIUMS
1. CHICAGO / FIDELITY	$4,525,297	9.41%	$42,048,442	87.42%	$1,526,905	3.17%	$48,100,644	29.60%	$1,940,088	25.16%	4.03%
2. FIRST AMERICAN	$4,931,847	15.88%	$25,697,219	82.75%	$424,465	1.37%	$31,053,531	19.11%	$1,389,680	18.02%	4.48%
3. LAND AMERICA	$3,401,676	11.05%	$26,812,537	87.12%	$560,714	1.82%	$30,774,927	18.94%	$1,926,842	24.99%	6.26%
4. OLD REPUBLIC	$320,811	1.31%	$23,679,789	96.97%	$419,682	1.72%	$24,420,282	15.03%	$1,052,137	13.64%	4.31%
5. STEWART	$551,718	3.09%	$12,109,491	67.82%	$5,194,914	29.09%	$17,856,123	10.99%	$1,138,614	14.77%	6.38%
6. OHIO FARMERS	$0	0.00%	$7,024,297	100.00%	$0	0.00%	$7,024,297	4.32%	($71,080)	(0.92)%	(1.01)%
7. INVESTORS	$42,448	1.62%	$2,580,635	98.38%	$0	0.00%	$2,623,083	1.61%	$180,424	2.34%	6.88%
8. UNAFFILIATED COMPANIES	$262,384	71.35%	$105,379	28.65%	$0	0.00%	$367,763	0.23%	$147,452	1.91%	40.09%
9. RELIANT HOLDING	$0	0.00%	$0	0.00%	$228,810	100.00%	$228,810	0.14%	$6,700	0.09%	2.93%
10. TRANSUNION	$0	0.00%	$0	0.00%	$59,287	100.00%	$59,287	0.04%	$0	--	--
COMPOSITE	$14,036,181	8.64%	$140,057,789	86.18%	$8,414,777	5.18%	$162,508,747	100.00%	$7,710,857	100.00%	4.74%
AVERAGE	$1,403,618		$14,005,779		$841,478		$16,250,875		$771,086		

TEXAS

	DIRECT	% of Total	NON-AFFILIATED	% of Total	AFFILIATED	% of Total	TOTAL	PERCENT OF JURISDICTION	PAID LOSSES	PERCENT OF JURISDICTION	LOSSES TO PREMIUMS
1. CHICAGO / FIDELITY	$155,912,612	32.48%	$224,539,266	46.78%	$99,564,406	20.74%	$480,016,284	29.60%	$19,811,459	36.04%	4.13%
2. LAND AMERICA	$190,850,382	51.86%	$173,811,291	47.23%	$3,356,524	0.91%	$368,018,197	22.69%	$16,470,760	29.97%	4.48%
3. FIRST AMERICAN	$106,146,688	32.56%	$120,637,459	37.00%	$99,255,039	30.44%	$326,039,186	20.11%	$8,807,551	16.02%	2.70%
4. STEWART	$33,887,417	12.57%	$67,302,472	24.96%	$168,480,798	62.48%	$269,670,687	16.63%	$4,269,132	7.77%	1.58%
5. UNAFFILIATED COMPANIES	$0	0.00%	$59,358,306	51.72%	$55,406,465	48.28%	$114,764,771	7.08%	$2,273,835	4.14%	1.98%
6. OLD REPUBLIC	$8,444	0.02%	$36,987,133	76.29%	$11,486,087	23.69%	$48,481,664	2.99%	$2,631,324	4.79%	5.43%
7. OHIO FARMERS	$0	0.00%	$14,656,298	100.00%	$0	0.00%	$14,656,298	0.90%	$699,790	1.27%	4.77%
COMPOSITE	$486,805,543	30.02%	$697,292,225	43.00%	$437,549,319	26.98%	$1,621,647,087	100.00%	$54,963,851	100.00%	3.39%
AVERAGE	$69,543,649		$99,613,175		$62,507,046		$231,663,870		$7,851,979		

C.1 Jurisdiction - By NAIC Group

	DIRECT	% of Total	NON-AFFILIATED	% of Total	AFFILIATED	% of Total	TOTAL	PERCENT OF JURISDICTION	PAID LOSSES	PERCENT OF JURISDICTION	LOSSES TO PREMIUMS
UTAH											
1. FIRST AMERICAN	$11,820,677	8.89%	$88,659,604	66.67%	$32,501,673	24.44%	$132,981,954	49.63%	$2,328,609	29.31%	1.75%
2. STEWART	$761,063	1.63%	$37,616,999	80.49%	$8,358,551	17.88%	$46,736,613	17.44%	$434,934	5.47%	0.93%
3. LAND AMERICA	$212,422	0.47%	$42,497,828	94.30%	$2,355,492	5.23%	$45,065,742	16.82%	$2,656,952	33.44%	5.90%
4. CHICAGO / FIDELITY	$1,033,036	2.89%	$34,508,147	96.59%	$186,853	0.52%	$35,728,036	13.33%	$1,085,933	13.67%	3.04%
5. OLD REPUBLIC	$670,311	17.24%	$2,423,716	62.33%	$794,545	20.43%	$3,888,572	1.45%	$139,943	1.76%	3.60%
6. ATTORNEYS' TITLE	$0	0.00%	$2,403,171	100.00%	$0	0.00%	$2,403,171	0.90%	$1,299,467	16.35%	54.07%
7. RELIANT HOLDING	$0	0.00%	$0	0.00%	$761,915	100.00%	$761,915	0.28%	$0	--	--
8. UNAFFILIATED COMPANIES	$0	0.00%	$363,865	100.00%	$0	0.00%	$363,865	0.14%	$0	--	--
9. TRANSUNION	$0	0.00%	$0	0.00%	$9,265	100.00%	$9,265	0.00%	$0	--	--
COMPOSITE	**$14,497,509**	5.41%	**$208,473,330**	77.81%	**$44,968,294**	16.78%	**$267,939,133**	100.00%	**$7,945,838**	100.00%	2.97%
AVERAGE	**$1,610,834**		**$23,163,703**		**$4,996,477**		**$29,771,015**		**$882,871**		
VERMONT											
1. CATIC	$0	0.00%	$6,018,064	100.00%	$0	0.00%	$6,018,064	41.95%	$372,060	31.19%	6.18%
2. FIRST AMERICAN	$77,342	2.05%	$3,685,600	97.57%	$14,369	0.38%	$3,777,311	26.33%	$346,486	29.05%	9.17%
3. LAND AMERICA	$475,867	24.78%	$1,444,463	75.21%	$360	0.02%	$1,920,690	13.39%	$40,158	3.37%	2.09%
4. CHICAGO / FIDELITY	$86,180	6.14%	$1,318,128	93.86%	$0	0.00%	$1,404,308	9.79%	$316,805	26.56%	22.56%
5. STEWART	$73,791	6.81%	$1,008,830	93.10%	$993	0.09%	$1,083,614	7.55%	$51,364	4.31%	4.74%
6. OLD REPUBLIC	$5,565	3.89%	$137,384	96.11%	$0	0.00%	$142,949	1.00%	$65,988	5.53%	46.16%
COMPOSITE	**$718,745**	5.01%	**$13,612,469**	94.88%	**$15,722**	0.11%	**$14,346,936**	100.00%	**$1,192,861**	100.00%	8.31%
AVERAGE	**$119,791**		**$2,268,745**		**$2,620**		**$2,391,156**		**$198,810**		
VIRGINIA											
1. LAND AMERICA	$13,509,475	12.96%	$84,703,306	81.28%	$6,003,670	5.76%	$104,216,451	27.84%	$5,687,958	22.49%	5.46%
2. FIRST AMERICAN	$8,731,063	8.65%	$88,263,343	87.48%	$3,904,508	3.87%	$100,898,914	26.95%	$11,131,348	44.00%	11.03%
3. CHICAGO / FIDELITY	$7,416,294	9.90%	$66,866,899	89.29%	$604,262	0.81%	$74,887,455	20.00%	$3,378,275	13.35%	4.51%
4. STEWART	$1,150,755	1.81%	$54,963,622	86.65%	$7,315,614	11.53%	$63,429,991	16.94%	$3,209,921	12.69%	5.06%
5. OHIO FARMERS	$1,173,681	9.09%	$10,922,720	84.60%	$815,354	6.31%	$12,911,755	3.45%	$687,413	2.72%	5.32%
6. OLD REPUBLIC	$196,158	2.32%	$8,242,228	97.68%	$0	0.00%	$8,438,386	2.25%	$839,161	3.32%	9.94%
7. INVESTORS	$110,462	1.79%	$5,641,269	91.52%	$412,100	6.69%	$6,163,831	1.65%	$357,259	1.41%	5.80%
8. UNAFFILIATED COMPANIES	$0	0.00%	$239,215	7.28%	$3,048,443	92.72%	$3,287,658	0.88%	($61)	0.00%	0.00%
9. TRANSUNION	$0	0.00%	$0	0.00%	$117,235	100.00%	$117,235	0.03%	$5,069	0.02%	4.32%
COMPOSITE	**$32,287,888**	8.63%	**$319,842,602**	85.44%	**$22,221,186**	5.94%	**$374,351,676**	100.00%	**$25,296,343**	100.00%	6.76%
AVERAGE	**$3,587,543**		**$35,538,067**		**$2,469,021**		**$41,594,631**		**$2,810,705**		
WASHINGTON											
1. CHICAGO / FIDELITY	$60,052,073	53.12%	$18,783,932	16.62%	$34,207,259	30.26%	$113,043,264	34.36%	$6,204,796	35.75%	5.49%
2. FIRST AMERICAN	$55,199,257	52.60%	$21,944,425	20.91%	$27,789,415	26.48%	$104,933,097	31.89%	$5,856,351	33.75%	5.58%
3. LAND AMERICA	$21,049,911	31.56%	$19,039,723	28.55%	$26,609,862	39.90%	$66,699,496	20.27%	$3,448,794	19.87%	5.17%
4. STEWART	$528,543	1.52%	$8,761,658	25.13%	$25,579,421	73.36%	$34,869,622	10.60%	$945,546	5.45%	2.71%
5. OLD REPUBLIC	$489,107	5.17%	$2,221,251	23.47%	$6,752,056	71.36%	$9,462,414	2.88%	$898,157	5.18%	9.49%
COMPOSITE	**$137,318,891**	41.74%	**$70,750,989**	21.50%	**$120,938,013**	36.76%	**$329,007,893**	100.00%	**$17,353,744**	100.00%	5.27%
AVERAGE	**$27,463,778**		**$14,150,198**		**$24,187,603**		**$65,801,579**		**$3,470,749**		
WEST VIRGINIA											
1. FIRST AMERICAN	$102,405	1.43%	$7,004,324	97.83%	$52,716	0.74%	$7,159,445	29.48%	$235,830	17.20%	3.29%
2. LAND AMERICA	$318,917	6.67%	$4,401,886	92.07%	$60,031	1.26%	$4,780,834	19.69%	$563,724	41.11%	11.79%
3. CHICAGO / FIDELITY	$635,144	14.68%	$3,681,857	85.12%	$8,697	0.20%	$4,325,698	17.81%	$217,824	15.89%	5.04%
4. STEWART	$33,946	0.97%	$3,454,535	98.83%	$6,974	0.20%	$3,495,455	14.39%	$179,843	13.12%	5.15%
5. OLD REPUBLIC	$9,446	0.43%	$2,191,208	99.57%	$0	0.00%	$2,200,654	9.06%	$75,867	5.53%	3.45%
6. INVESTORS	$15,410	0.76%	$2,016,919	99.24%	$0	0.00%	$2,032,329	8.37%	$20,399	1.49%	1.00%
7. OHIO FARMERS	$0	0.00%	$205,731	86.68%	$31,609	13.32%	$237,340	0.98%	$0	--	--
8. UNAFFILIATED COMPANIES	$0	0.00%	$52,488	100.00%	$0	0.00%	$52,488	0.22%	$77,657	5.66%	147.95%
COMPOSITE	**$1,115,268**	4.59%	**$23,008,948**	94.75%	**$160,027**	0.66%	**$24,284,243**	100.00%	**$1,371,144**	100.00%	5.65%
AVERAGE	**$139,409**		**$2,876,119**		**$20,003**		**$3,035,530**		**$171,393**		
WISCONSIN											
1. FIRST AMERICAN	$8,174,177	20.98%	$29,099,657	74.68%	$1,692,991	4.34%	$38,966,825	33.32%	$2,154,733	27.96%	5.53%
2. CHICAGO / FIDELITY	$8,127,289	21.91%	$27,762,750	74.86%	$1,198,182	3.23%	$37,088,221	31.71%	$3,338,189	43.31%	9.00%
3. LAND AMERICA	$1,905,693	10.80%	$15,687,720	88.90%	$53,182	0.30%	$17,646,595	15.09%	$886,126	11.50%	5.02%
4. STEWART	$332,449	2.18%	$10,654,472	69.95%	$4,244,788	27.87%	$15,231,709	13.02%	$1,090,442	14.15%	7.16%
5. OLD REPUBLIC	$69,853	0.90%	$7,659,914	99.10%	$0	0.00%	$7,729,767	6.61%	$195,169	2.53%	2.52%
6. UNAFFILIATED COMPANIES	$291,071	100.00%	$0	0.00%	$0	0.00%	$291,071	0.25%	$42,789	0.56%	14.70%
COMPOSITE	**$18,900,532**	16.16%	**$90,864,513**	77.69%	**$7,189,143**	6.15%	**$116,954,188**	100.00%	**$7,707,448**	100.00%	6.59%
AVERAGE	**$3,150,089**		**$15,144,086**		**$1,198,191**		**$19,492,365**		**$1,284,575**		
WYOMING											
1. FIRST AMERICAN	$1,752,293	10.74%	$2,909,745	17.84%	$11,647,701	71.42%	$16,309,739	48.87%	$182,368	48.10%	1.12%
2. STEWART	$15,098	0.21%	$6,144,633	86.46%	$947,405	13.33%	$7,107,136	21.30%	$106,567	28.11%	1.50%
3. LAND AMERICA	$26,693	0.63%	$4,217,084	99.37%	$0	0.00%	$4,243,777	12.72%	$40,942	10.80%	0.96%
4. CHICAGO / FIDELITY	$218,603	5.67%	$3,637,464	94.33%	$0	0.00%	$3,856,067	11.56%	$19,926	5.26%	0.52%
5. OLD REPUBLIC	$0	0.00%	$1,675,569	100.00%	$0	0.00%	$1,675,569	5.02%	$29,359	7.74%	1.75%
6. UNAFFILIATED COMPANIES	$178,276	100.00%	$0	0.00%	$0	0.00%	$178,276	0.53%	$0	--	--
COMPOSITE	**$2,190,963**	6.57%	**$18,584,495**	55.69%	**$12,595,106**	37.74%	**$33,370,564**	100.00%	**$379,162**	100.00%	1.14%
AVERAGE	**$365,161**		**$3,097,416**		**$2,099,184**		**$5,561,761**		**$63,194**		

3

C.1 Jurisdiction - By NAIC Group

	DIRECT	% of Total	NON-AFFILIATED	% of Total	AFFILIATED	% of Total	TOTAL	PERCENT OF JURISDICTION	PAID LOSSES	PERCENT OF JURISDICTION	LOSSES TO PREMIUMS
			DIRECT PREMIUMS WRITTEN								
GUAM											
1. STEWART	$0	0.00%	$4,300,401	100.00%	$0	0.00%	$4,300,401	74.42%	$15,592	7.92%	0.36%
2. CHICAGO / FIDELITY	$0	0.00%	$1,478,263	100.00%	$0	0.00%	$1,478,263	25.58%	$11,326	5.76%	0.77%
3. FIRST AMERICAN	$0	--	$0	--	$0	--	$0	--	$169,868	86.32%	--
COMPOSITE	$0	0.00%	$5,778,664	100.00%	$0	0.00%	$5,778,664	100.00%	$196,786	100.00%	3.41%
AVERAGE	$0		$1,926,221		$0		$1,926,221		$65,595		
PUERTO RICO											
1. STEWART	$23,054	0.18%	$130,122	1.02%	$12,626,403	98.80%	$12,779,579	42.08%	$989,787	33.08%	7.75%
2. LAND AMERICA	$0	0.00%	$1,596,000	29.14%	$3,880,706	70.86%	$5,476,706	18.03%	$409,635	13.69%	7.48%
3. CHICAGO / FIDELITY	$428,597	7.89%	$5,001,988	92.11%	$0	0.00%	$5,430,585	17.88%	$934,771	31.24%	17.21%
4. FIRST AMERICAN	$259	0.00%	$5,363,770	100.00%	$0	0.00%	$5,364,029	17.66%	$609,815	20.38%	11.37%
5. OLD REPUBLIC	$0	0.00%	$1,074,393	100.00%	$0	0.00%	$1,074,393	3.54%	$48,382	1.62%	4.50%
6. ATTORNEYS' TITLE	$0	0.00%	$245,518	100.00%	$0	0.00%	$245,518	0.81%	$0	--	--
COMPOSITE	$451,910	1.49%	$13,411,791	44.16%	$16,507,109	54.35%	$30,370,810	100.00%	$2,992,390	100.00%	9.85%
AVERAGE	$75,318		$2,235,299		$2,751,185		$5,061,802		$498,732		
U.S. VIRGIN ISLANDS											
1. CHICAGO / FIDELITY	$66,847	6.74%	$925,496	93.26%	$0	0.00%	$992,343	42.05%	$83,037	21.99%	8.37%
2. LAND AMERICA	$0	0.00%	$644,609	100.00%	$0	0.00%	$644,609	27.32%	$36,922	9.78%	5.73%
3. STEWART	$0	0.00%	$516,458	100.00%	$0	0.00%	$516,458	21.89%	$18,555	4.91%	3.59%
4. FIRST AMERICAN	$0	0.00%	$206,245	100.00%	$0	0.00%	$206,245	8.74%	$239,174	63.33%	115.97%
COMPOSITE	$66,847	2.83%	$2,292,808	97.17%	$0	0.00%	$2,359,655	100.00%	$377,688	100.00%	16.01%
AVERAGE	$16,712		$573,202		$0		$589,914		$94,422		
NORTHERN MARIANA IS.											
1. STEWART	$0	0.00%	$779,364	100.00%	$0	0.00%	$779,364	100.00%	$21,656	100.00%	2.78%
COMPOSITE	$0	0.00%	$779,364	100.00%	$0	0.00%	$779,364	100.00%	$21,656	100.00%	2.78%
CANADA											
1. STEWART	$76,099,011	100.00%	$0	0.00%	$0	0.00%	$76,099,011	62.04%	$13,556,557	64.53%	17.81%
2. FIRST AMERICAN	$26,161,839	100.00%	$0	0.00%	$0	0.00%	$26,161,839	21.33%	$7,620,687	36.27%	29.13%
3. CHICAGO / FIDELITY	$3,857,639	19.60%	$0	0.00%	$15,827,994	80.40%	$19,685,633	16.05%	($230,821)	(1.10)%	(1.17)%
4. LAND AMERICA	$720,306	100.00%	$0	0.00%	$0	0.00%	$720,306	0.59%	$61,766	0.29%	8.57%
COMPOSITE	$106,838,795	87.10%	$0	0.00%	$15,827,994	12.90%	$122,666,789	100.00%	$21,008,189	100.00%	17.13%
AVERAGE	$26,709,699		$0		$3,956,999		$30,666,697		$5,252,047		
AGGREGATE OTHER ALIEN											
1. FIRST AMERICAN	$11,074,697	97.23%	$315,301	2.77%	$0	0.00%	$11,389,998	40.46%	$5,327,656	101.82%	46.77%
2. CHICAGO / FIDELITY	$6,396,532	89.80%	$726,300	10.20%	$0	0.00%	$7,122,832	25.30%	$108,584	2.08%	1.52%
3. LAND AMERICA	$5,586,981	93.07%	$415,817	6.93%	$0	0.00%	$6,002,798	21.32%	$370	0.00%	0.00%
4. STEWART	$255,295	7.95%	$1,215,251	37.83%	$1,741,901	54.22%	$3,212,447	11.41%	($204,249)	(3.90)%	(6.36)%
5. ATTORNEYS' TITLE	$0	0.00%	$421,502	100.00%	$0	0.00%	$421,502	1.50%	$0	--	--
COMPOSITE	$23,313,505	82.82%	$3,094,171	10.99%	$1,741,901	6.19%	$28,149,577	100.00%	$5,232,361	100.00%	18.59%
AVERAGE	$4,662,701		$618,834		$348,380		$5,629,915		$1,046,472		
INDUSTRY TOTAL											
1. FIRST AMERICAN	$794,964,527	19.37%	$2,473,684,409	60.28%	$835,309,222	20.35%	$4,103,958,158	29.19%	$280,907,644	27.26%	6.84%
2. CHICAGO / FIDELITY	$805,518,502	21.45%	$2,099,348,649	55.89%	$851,311,601	22.66%	$3,756,178,752	26.71%	$331,205,767	32.14%	8.82%
3. LAND AMERICA	$643,344,121	23.38%	$1,737,306,730	63.14%	$371,071,358	13.49%	$2,751,722,209	19.57%	$185,797,110	18.03%	6.75%
4. STEWART	$202,827,066	12.28%	$945,981,765	57.25%	$503,488,197	30.47%	$1,652,297,028	11.75%	$105,998,891	10.29%	6.42%
5. OLD REPUBLIC	$14,562,733	1.87%	$630,499,863	80.94%	$133,876,250	17.19%	$778,938,846	5.54%	$61,904,518	6.01%	7.95%
6. UNAFFILIATED COMPANIES	$22,057,472	4.89%	$171,460,209	38.02%	$257,480,680	57.09%	$450,998,361	3.21%	$14,537,897	1.41%	3.22%
7. ATTORNEYS' TITLE	$831,940	0.23%	$355,109,428	99.77%	$0	0.00%	$355,941,368	2.53%	$29,853,875	2.90%	8.39%
8. INVESTORS	$29,790,883	42.58%	$33,877,911	48.42%	$6,291,704	8.99%	$69,960,498	0.50%	$10,065,719	0.98%	14.39%
9. CATIC	$0	0.00%	$68,390,534	100.00%	$0	0.00%	$68,390,534	0.49%	$4,534,687	0.44%	6.63%
10. OHIO FARMERS	$1,173,787	2.17%	$49,984,569	92.26%	$3,022,358	5.58%	$54,180,714	0.39%	$1,807,377	0.18%	3.34%
11. RELIANT HOLDING	$204,520	1.47%	$3,657,096	26.28%	$10,054,884	72.25%	$13,916,500	0.10%	$2,659,100	0.26%	19.11%
12. TRANSUNION	$992,350	20.69%	$2,344,872	48.89%	$1,458,631	30.41%	$4,795,853	0.03%	$1,162,000	0.11%	24.23%
COMPOSITE	$2,516,267,901	17.90%	$8,571,646,035	60.96%	$2,973,364,885	21.15%	$14,061,278,821	100.00%	$1,030,434,585	100.00%	7.33%
AVERAGE	$209,688,992		$714,303,836		$247,780,407		$1,171,773,235		$85,869,549		

C.2 JURISDICTION
- BY INDIVIDUAL UNDERWRITER

3

C.2 Jurisdiction - By Individual Underwriter

	DIRECT PREMIUMS WRITTEN						PERCENT OF JURISDICTION	PAID LOSSES	PERCENT OF JURISDICTION	LOSSES TO PREMIUMS
	DIRECT	% of Total	NON-AFFILIATED	% of Total	AFFILIATED	% of Total	TOTAL			

ALABAMA

	DIRECT	% of Total	NON-AFFILIATED	% of Total	AFFILIATED	% of Total	TOTAL	PERCENT OF JURISDICTION	PAID LOSSES	PERCENT OF JURISDICTION	LOSSES TO PREMIUMS
1. FIRST AMERICAN TIC	$1,202,460	5.56%	$20,264,430	93.70%	$159,114	0.74%	$21,626,004	19.74%	$1,356,523	14.78%	6.27%
2. STEWART TGC	$453,681	2.55%	$16,081,583	90.41%	$1,251,794	7.04%	$17,787,058	16.23%	$1,856,083	20.22%	10.44%
3. LAWYERS	$1,545,089	9.71%	$14,368,473	90.29%	$0	0.00%	$15,913,562	14.52%	$1,583,899	17.25%	9.95%
4. CHICAGO TIC	$822,687	5.32%	$14,651,793	94.68%	$1	0.00%	$15,474,481	14.12%	$618,945	6.74%	4.00%
5. MISSISSIPPI VALLEY	$0	0.00%	$13,415,105	100.00%	$0	0.00%	$13,415,105	12.24%	$554,749	6.04%	4.14%
6. COMMONWEALTH LAND	$507,032	5.56%	$8,617,330	94.44%	$0	0.00%	$9,124,362	8.33%	$928,706	10.12%	10.18%
7. FIDELITY NATIONAL	$617,951	11.56%	$3,748,220	70.12%	$979,286	18.32%	$5,345,457	4.88%	$997,115	10.86%	18.65%
8. SOUTHERN TI CORP	$0	0.00%	$2,459,609	100.00%	$0	0.00%	$2,459,609	2.24%	$90,379	0.98%	3.67%
9. UNITED GENERAL	$6,590	0.29%	$2,292,334	99.71%	$0	0.00%	$2,298,924	2.10%	$140,157	1.53%	6.10%
10. TICOR (FL)	$0	0.00%	$1,962,179	100.00%	$0	0.00%	$1,962,179	1.79%	$339,464	3.70%	17.30%
11. SECURITY UNION	$4,147	0.38%	$1,074,885	99.62%	$0	0.00%	$1,079,032	0.98%	$6,394	0.07%	0.59%
12. TRANSNATION	$0	0.00%	$647,020	100.00%	$0	0.00%	$647,020	0.59%	$16,434	0.18%	2.54%
13. INVESTORS TIC	$0	0.00%	$493,747	100.00%	$0	0.00%	$493,747	0.45%	$49,251	0.54%	9.97%
14. SECURITY TG (BALTIMORE)	$0	0.00%	$490,222	100.00%	$0	0.00%	$490,222	0.45%	$191,462	2.09%	39.06%
15. CONESTOGA	$0	0.00%	$372,869	100.00%	$0	0.00%	$372,869	0.34%	$0	--	--
16. TICOR	$67,615	19.00%	$288,307	81.00%	$0	0.00%	$355,922	0.32%	$123,840	1.35%	34.79%
17. TRANSUNION NATIONAL	$0	0.00%	$263,949	92.17%	$22,421	7.83%	$286,370	0.26%	$90,755	0.99%	31.69%
18. NATIONAL LAND	$0	0.00%	$188,470	100.00%	$0	0.00%	$188,470	0.17%	$0	--	--
19. OLD REPUBLIC NATIONAL	$136,053	94.63%	$7,721	5.37%	$0	0.00%	$143,774	0.13%	$235,835	2.57%	164.03%
20. NATIONAL	$0	0.00%	$82,307	100.00%	$0	0.00%	$82,307	0.08%	$0	--	--
21. WESTCOR	$0	0.00%	$22,598	100.00%	$0	0.00%	$22,598	0.02%	$0	--	--
22. ATTORNEYS TIF (FL)	$0	0.00%	$12,139	100.00%	$0	0.00%	$12,139	0.01%	$0	--	--
COMPOSITE	$5,363,305	4.89%	$101,805,290	92.90%	$2,412,616	2.20%	$109,581,211	100.00%	$9,179,991	100.00%	8.38%
AVERAGE	$243,787		$4,627,513		$109,664		$4,980,964		$417,272		

ALASKA

	DIRECT	% of Total	NON-AFFILIATED	% of Total	AFFILIATED	% of Total	TOTAL	PERCENT OF JURISDICTION	PAID LOSSES	PERCENT OF JURISDICTION	LOSSES TO PREMIUMS
1. FIRST AMERICAN TIC	$683,603	6.32%	$2,383,589	22.04%	$7,746,859	71.64%	$10,814,051	32.80%	$213,267	67.20%	1.97%
2. STEWART TGC	$75,891	0.88%	$4,705,077	54.56%	$3,842,143	44.56%	$8,623,111	26.15%	($3,977)	(1.25)%	(0.05)%
3. PACIFIC NORTHWEST	$0	0.00%	$73,036	1.32%	$5,460,402	98.68%	$5,533,438	16.78%	$13,239	4.17%	0.24%
4. OLD REPUBLIC NATIONAL	$265	0.01%	$3,660,960	99.99%	$0	0.00%	$3,661,225	11.10%	$37,011	11.66%	1.01%
5. FIDELITY NATIONAL	$126,333	4.74%	$2,536,582	95.26%	$0	0.00%	$2,662,915	8.08%	$884	0.28%	0.03%
6. CHICAGO TIC	$189,934	15.19%	$1,060,681	84.81%	$0	0.00%	$1,250,615	3.79%	$0	--	--
7. LAWYERS	$32,559	10.36%	$281,699	89.64%	$0	0.00%	$314,258	0.95%	$50,995	16.07%	16.23%
8. COMMONWEALTH LAND	$11,182	14.86%	$64,074	85.14%	$0	0.00%	$75,256	0.23%	$0	--	--
9. TICOR	$19,276	100.00%	$0	0.00%	$0	0.00%	$19,276	0.06%	$5,010	1.58%	25.99%
10. UNITED GENERAL	$19,008	99.53%	$90	0.47%	$0	0.00%	$19,098	0.06%	$0	--	--
11. SECURITY UNION	$989	100.00%	$0	0.00%	$0	0.00%	$989	0.00%	$0	--	--
12. TRANSNATION	$0	--	$0	--	$0	--	$0	--	$922	0.29%	--
COMPOSITE	$1,159,040	3.51%	$14,765,788	44.78%	$17,049,404	51.71%	$32,974,232	100.00%	$317,351	100.00%	0.96%
AVERAGE	$96,587		$1,230,482		$1,420,784		$2,747,853		$26,446		

ARIZONA

	DIRECT	% of Total	NON-AFFILIATED	% of Total	AFFILIATED	% of Total	TOTAL	PERCENT OF JURISDICTION	PAID LOSSES	PERCENT OF JURISDICTION	LOSSES TO PREMIUMS
1. FIRST AMERICAN TIC	$77,312,374	47.97%	$47,354,992	29.38%	$36,507,960	22.65%	$161,175,326	32.18%	$8,685,505	28.71%	5.39%
2. FIDELITY NATIONAL	$27,131,108	41.15%	$25,618,258	38.86%	$13,176,808	19.99%	$65,926,174	13.16%	$5,540,234	18.31%	8.40%
3. LAWYERS	$4,075,885	7.94%	$32,407,287	63.16%	$14,830,508	28.90%	$51,313,680	10.24%	$1,970,203	6.51%	3.84%
4. TRANSNATION	$25,044,743	60.33%	$16,422,597	39.56%	$43,367	0.10%	$41,510,707	8.29%	$2,918,807	9.65%	7.03%
5. CHICAGO TIC	$27,717,915	82.19%	$5,337,847	15.83%	$669,788	1.99%	$33,725,550	6.73%	$2,054,039	6.79%	6.09%
6. COMMONWEALTH LAND	$2,540,934	7.93%	$29,482,815	92.06%	$3,153	0.01%	$32,026,902	6.39%	$1,767,674	5.84%	5.52%
7. STEWART TGC	$358,106	1.69%	$2,984,773	14.06%	$17,879,310	84.25%	$21,222,189	4.24%	$307,588	1.02%	1.45%
8. TICOR	$60,443	0.32%	$83,461	0.44%	$18,715,302	99.24%	$18,859,206	3.77%	$3,584,953	11.85%	19.01%
9. SECURITY UNION	$24,734	0.15%	$128,529	0.80%	$15,844,405	99.04%	$15,997,668	3.19%	$743,050	2.46%	4.64%
10. TITLE RESOURCES	$0	0.00%	$15,856,339	100.00%	$0	0.00%	$15,856,339	3.17%	$963,507	3.18%	6.08%
11. UNITED CAPITAL	$0	0.00%	$0	0.00%	$15,002,635	100.00%	$15,002,635	3.00%	$566,900	1.87%	3.78%
12. OLD REPUBLIC NATIONAL	$887,960	8.84%	$5,926,761	59.00%	$3,231,134	32.16%	$10,045,855	2.01%	$49,664	0.16%	0.49%
13. UNITED GENERAL	$127,085	1.92%	$6,472,952	97.80%	$18,285	0.28%	$6,618,322	1.32%	$62,628	0.21%	0.95%
14. NORTH AMERICAN	$0	0.00%	$0	0.00%	$4,679,454	100.00%	$4,679,454	0.93%	$325,129	1.07%	6.95%
15. WESTCOR	$0	0.00%	$105,518	3.22%	$3,175,196	96.78%	$3,280,714	0.65%	$0	--	--
16. COMMERCE	$0	0.00%	$0	0.00%	$1,623,786	100.00%	$1,623,786	0.32%	$0	--	--
17. GUARANTEE T&T	$0	0.00%	$0	0.00%	$1,506,068	100.00%	$1,506,068	0.30%	$4,187	0.01%	0.28%
18. TICOR (FL)	$0	0.00%	$443,037	100.00%	$0	0.00%	$443,037	0.09%	$710,998	2.35%	160.48%
19. TRANSUNION NATIONAL	$0	0.00%	$0	0.00%	$81,056	100.00%	$81,056	0.02%	$0	--	--
COMPOSITE	$165,281,287	33.00%	$188,625,166	37.66%	$146,988,215	29.35%	$500,894,668	100.00%	$30,255,066	100.00%	6.04%
AVERAGE	$8,699,015		$9,927,640		$7,736,222		$26,362,877		$1,592,372		

C.2 Jurisdiction - By Individual Underwriter

	DIRECT	% of Total	NON-AFFILIATED	% of Total	AFFILIATED	% of Total	TOTAL	PERCENT OF JURISDICTION	PAID LOSSES	PERCENT OF JURISDICTION	LOSSES TO PREMIUMS
ARKANSAS											
1. CHICAGO TIC	$182,592	2.05%	$8,740,951	97.95%	$0	0.00%	$8,923,543	18.22%	$650,758	18.70%	7.29%
2. ARKANSAS TIC	$0	0.00%	$7,269,128	87.72%	$1,017,272	12.28%	$8,286,400	16.92%	$131,776	3.79%	1.59%
3. LAWYERS	$237,311	2.88%	$8,010,608	97.10%	$2,018	0.02%	$8,249,937	16.85%	$284,438	8.17%	3.45%
4. FIRST AMERICAN TIC	$348,399	5.04%	$6,460,042	93.45%	$104,515	1.51%	$6,912,956	14.12%	$954,040	27.41%	13.80%
5. FIDELITY NATIONAL	$41,201	0.79%	$4,412,828	85.10%	$731,623	14.11%	$5,185,652	10.59%	$150,595	4.33%	2.90%
6. STEWART TGC	($1,659)	(0.05)%	$2,420,537	68.15%	$1,132,852	31.90%	$3,551,730	7.25%	$810,228	23.28%	22.81%
7. OLD REPUBLIC NATIONAL	$35,421	1.31%	$2,664,933	98.69%	$0	0.00%	$2,700,354	5.51%	$304,220	8.74%	11.27%
8. UNITED GENERAL	$6,524	0.31%	$2,115,413	99.69%	$0	0.00%	$2,121,937	4.33%	$128,189	3.68%	6.04%
9. COMMONWEALTH LAND	$4,078	0.57%	$711,872	99.43%	$0	0.00%	$715,950	1.46%	$17,874	0.51%	2.50%
10. TICOR	$25,371	3.82%	$639,479	96.18%	$0	0.00%	$664,850	1.36%	($151)	0.00%	(0.02)%
11. SOUTHERN TI CORP	$0	0.00%	$498,173	100.00%	$0	0.00%	$498,173	1.02%	$12,239	0.35%	2.46%
12. SECURITY TG (BALTIMORE)	$0	0.00%	$415,609	100.00%	$0	0.00%	$415,609	0.85%	$357	0.01%	0.09%
13. CENSTAR	$0	0.00%	$353,239	100.00%	$0	0.00%	$353,239	0.72%	$8,868	0.25%	2.51%
14. GUARANTEE T&T	$0	0.00%	$0	0.00%	$176,978	100.00%	$176,978	0.36%	$0	--	--
15. TICOR (FL)	$0	0.00%	$164,642	100.00%	$0	0.00%	$164,642	0.34%	$12,292	0.35%	7.47%
16. SECURITY UNION	$750	1.02%	$72,666	98.98%	$0	0.00%	$73,416	0.15%	$0	--	--
17. INVESTORS TIC	$0	0.00%	$31,908	100.00%	$0	0.00%	$31,908	0.07%	$0	--	--
18. ATTORNEYS TIF (FL)	$0	0.00%	$10,298	100.00%	$0	0.00%	$10,298	0.02%	$0	--	--
19. TRANSUNION NATIONAL	$1,044	11.74%	$0	0.00%	$7,845	88.26%	$8,889	0.02%	$0	--	--
20. TRANSNATION	($77,421)	--	$5,900	--	$0	--	($71,521)	(0.15)%	$14,711	0.42%	(20.57)%
COMPOSITE	**$803,611**	**1.64%**	**$44,998,226**	**91.88%**	**$3,173,103**	**6.48%**	**$48,974,940**	**100.00%**	**$3,480,434**	**100.00%**	**7.11%**
AVERAGE	**$40,181**		**$2,249,911**		**$158,655**		**$2,448,747**		**$174,022**		
CALIFORNIA											
1. FIRST AMERICAN TIC	$49,838,920	6.97%	$299,170,720	41.85%	$365,843,380	51.18%	$714,853,020	35.49%	$62,579,216	27.56%	8.75%
2. CHICAGO TIC	$33,084,828	9.52%	$22,750,947	6.55%	$291,620,278	83.93%	$347,456,053	17.25%	$66,938,187	29.48%	19.27%
3. FIDELITY NATIONAL	$3,327,542	1.25%	$40,653,438	15.24%	$222,798,085	83.51%	$266,779,065	13.24%	$27,231,599	11.99%	10.21%
4. STEWART TGC	$14,241,275	8.99%	$42,096,381	26.57%	$102,120,824	64.45%	$158,458,480	7.87%	$20,135,633	8.87%	12.71%
5. COMMONWEALTH LAND	$2,038,807	1.98%	$15,219,601	14.74%	$85,969,402	83.28%	$103,227,810	5.12%	$9,967,470	4.39%	9.66%
6. OLD REPUBLIC NATIONAL	$2,818,804	3.11%	$9,225,944	10.18%	$78,593,459	86.71%	$90,638,207	4.50%	$3,841,149	1.69%	4.24%
7. TRANSNATION	$8,051,368	11.53%	$0	0.00%	$61,762,055	88.47%	$69,813,423	3.47%	$12,568,791	5.54%	18.00%
8. LAWYERS	$4,111,967	5.91%	$2,947,514	4.23%	$62,544,126	89.86%	$69,603,607	3.46%	$4,312,713	1.90%	6.20%
9. NORTH AMERICAN	$0	0.00%	$52,268	0.09%	$58,755,709	99.91%	$58,807,977	2.92%	$2,165,215	0.95%	3.68%
10. UNITED CAPITAL	$2,231,929	5.09%	$0	0.00%	$41,596,724	94.91%	$43,828,653	2.18%	$5,589,874	2.46%	12.75%
11. UNITED GENERAL	$10,932,364	30.27%	$7,034,545	19.48%	$18,153,659	50.26%	$36,120,568	1.79%	$4,369,313	1.92%	12.10%
12. WESTCOR	$0	0.00%	$0	0.00%	$17,766,204	100.00%	$17,766,204	0.88%	$60,141	0.03%	0.34%
13. COMMERCE	$43,152	0.31%	$440,009	3.15%	$13,488,575	96.54%	$13,971,736	0.69%	$404,321	0.18%	2.89%
14. SECURITY UNION	$11,300,301	100.00%	$76	0.00%	$0	0.00%	$11,300,377	0.56%	$3,854,550	1.70%	34.11%
15. NATIONAL OF NY	$0	0.00%	$0	0.00%	$9,776,776	100.00%	$9,776,776	0.49%	$7,628	0.00%	0.08%
16. TICOR	$537,423	55.94%	$423,271	44.06%	$0	0.00%	$960,694	0.05%	$2,584,312	1.14%	269.00%
17. TRANSUNION TIC	$882,460	100.00%	$0	0.00%	$0	0.00%	$882,460	0.04%	$397,148	0.17%	45.00%
18. TICOR (FL)	$0	--	$0	--	$0	--	$0	--	$40,613	0.02%	--
COMPOSITE	**$143,441,140**	**7.12%**	**$440,014,714**	**21.85%**	**$1,430,789,256**	**71.03%**	**$2,014,245,110**	**100.00%**	**$227,047,873**	**100.00%**	**11.27%**
AVERAGE	**$7,968,952**		**$24,445,262**		**$79,488,292**		**$111,902,506**		**$12,613,771**		
COLORADO											
1. FIRST AMERICAN TIC	$780,120	0.73%	$106,190,637	98.86%	$445,395	0.41%	$107,416,152	34.89%	$7,612,745	31.48%	7.09%
2. STEWART TGC	$828,251	2.20%	$16,014,388	42.63%	$20,726,344	55.17%	$37,568,983	12.20%	$4,031,176	16.67%	10.73%
3. OLD REPUBLIC NATIONAL	$165,566	0.60%	$27,263,453	99.40%	$0	0.00%	$27,429,019	8.91%	$1,544,176	6.39%	5.63%
4. CHICAGO TIC	$1,667,959	6.69%	$15,671,488	62.85%	$7,594,479	30.46%	$24,933,926	8.10%	$4,890,162	20.22%	19.61%
5. LAND CORP (CO)	$0	0.00%	$0	0.00%	$19,602,608	100.00%	$19,602,608	6.37%	$183,856	0.76%	0.94%
6. LAWYERS	$10,093,453	64.59%	$5,444,452	34.84%	$87,986	0.56%	$15,625,891	5.08%	$1,204,623	4.98%	7.71%
7. FIDELITY NATIONAL	$6,113,393	47.21%	$6,708,847	51.81%	$126,721	0.98%	$12,948,961	4.21%	$463,230	1.92%	3.58%
8. TRANSNATION	$7,678,452	74.65%	$2,355,623	22.90%	$252,504	2.45%	$10,286,579	3.34%	$900,205	3.72%	8.75%
9. COMMONWEALTH LAND	$3,963,389	48.94%	$4,015,631	49.58%	$120,092	1.48%	$8,099,112	2.63%	$148,288	0.61%	1.83%
10. TITLE RESOURCES	$0	0.00%	$2,421,426	30.25%	$5,582,665	69.75%	$8,004,091	2.60%	$3,520	0.01%	0.04%
11. ATTORNEYS TGF (CO)	$0	0.00%	$6,864,905	100.00%	$0	0.00%	$6,864,905	2.23%	$270,631	1.12%	3.94%
12. UNITED GENERAL	$29,515	0.45%	$6,495,986	99.55%	$0	0.00%	$6,525,501	2.12%	$1,600,253	6.62%	24.52%
13. NORTH AMERICAN	$0	0.00%	$0	0.00%	$6,097,041	100.00%	$6,097,041	1.98%	$293,426	1.21%	4.81%
14. ALLIANT	$0	0.00%	$3,453,141	100.00%	$0	0.00%	$3,453,141	1.12%	$284,152	1.17%	8.23%
15. SOUTHERN TI CORP	$0	0.00%	$3,293,782	100.00%	$0	0.00%	$3,293,782	1.07%	$38,027	0.16%	1.15%
16. WESTCOR	$0	0.00%	$2,208,182	100.00%	$0	0.00%	$2,208,182	0.72%	$0	--	--
17. TICOR	$143,255	7.87%	$1,677,330	92.13%	$0	0.00%	$1,820,585	0.59%	$73,661	0.30%	4.05%
18. TITLE IC AMERICA	$0	0.00%	$1,419,017	100.00%	$0	0.00%	$1,419,017	0.46%	$340,143	1.41%	23.97%
19. DAKOTA HOMESTEAD	$0	0.00%	$1,269,727	100.00%	$0	0.00%	$1,269,727	0.41%	$13,100	0.05%	1.03%
20. TICOR (FL)	$0	0.00%	$1,267,698	100.00%	$0	0.00%	$1,267,698	0.41%	$296,919	1.23%	23.42%
21. SECURITY UNION	$7,258	0.70%	$1,026,904	99.30%	$0	0.00%	$1,034,162	0.34%	($34,495)	(0.14)%	(3.34)%
22. COMMERCE	$0	0.00%	$0	0.00%	$340,950	100.00%	$340,950	0.11%	$0	--	--
23. CENSTAR	$0	0.00%	$330,763	100.00%	$0	0.00%	$330,763	0.11%	$25,061	0.10%	7.58%
24. AMERICAN GUARANTY	$350	100.00%	$0	0.00%	$0	0.00%	$350	0.00%	$0	--	--
25. SECURITY TG (BALTIMORE)	$0	--	$0	--	$0	--	$0	--	$489	0.00%	--
COMPOSITE	**$31,470,961**	**10.22%**	**$215,393,380**	**69.97%**	**$60,976,785**	**19.81%**	**$307,841,126**	**100.00%**	**$24,183,348**	**100.00%**	**7.86%**
AVERAGE	**$1,258,838**		**$8,615,735**		**$2,439,071**		**$12,313,645**		**$967,334**		

C.2 Jurisdiction - By Individual Underwriter

	DIRECT PREMIUMS WRITTEN						PERCENT OF JURISDICTION	PAID LOSSES	PERCENT OF JURISDICTION	LOSSES TO PREMIUMS
	DIRECT	% of Total	NON-AFFILIATED	% of Total	AFFILIATED	% of Total	TOTAL				

CONNECTICUT

	DIRECT	% of Total	NON-AFFILIATED	% of Total	AFFILIATED	% of Total	TOTAL	PERCENT OF JURISDICTION	PAID LOSSES	PERCENT OF JURISDICTION	LOSSES TO PREMIUMS
1. FIRST AMERICAN TIC	$2,860,840	6.74%	$39,383,702	92.79%	$197,810	0.47%	$42,442,352	27.51%	$4,378,833	28.08%	10.32%
2. CT ATTORNEYS	$0	0.00%	$35,170,487	100.00%	$0	0.00%	$35,170,487	22.79%	$1,385,508	8.88%	3.94%
3. CHICAGO TIC	$1,025,447	7.05%	$13,523,919	92.95%	$0	0.00%	$14,549,366	9.43%	$5,295,812	33.96%	36.40%
4. FIDELITY NATIONAL	$1,750,992	12.25%	$12,516,055	87.56%	$26,586	0.19%	$14,293,633	9.26%	$2,865,392	18.37%	20.05%
5. COMMONWEALTH LAND	$2,303,515	23.35%	$7,563,452	76.65%	$0	0.00%	$9,866,967	6.39%	$513,249	3.29%	5.20%
6. UNITED GENERAL	$44,432	0.45%	$9,786,462	99.55%	$0	0.00%	$9,830,894	6.37%	$4,194	0.03%	0.04%
7. LAWYERS	$3,170,038	34.24%	$6,087,581	65.76%	$0	0.00%	$9,257,619	6.00%	$359,586	2.31%	3.88%
8. TICOR	$92,393	1.16%	$7,903,850	98.84%	$0	0.00%	$7,996,243	5.18%	$479,748	3.08%	6.00%
9. STEWART TGC	$1,423,151	24.02%	$4,442,924	75.00%	$57,970	0.98%	$5,924,045	3.84%	$142,023	0.91%	2.40%
10. OLD REPUBLIC NATIONAL	$284,552	8.26%	$3,158,499	91.74%	$0	0.00%	$3,443,051	2.23%	$134,079	0.86%	3.89%
11. NATIONAL OF NY	$982,520	100.00%	$0	0.00%	$0	0.00%	$982,520	0.64%	$0	--	--
12. TICOR (FL)	$0	0.00%	$430,647	100.00%	$0	0.00%	$430,647	0.28%	$37,796	0.24%	8.78%
13. CENSTAR	$0	0.00%	$86,924	100.00%	$0	0.00%	$86,924	0.06%	$0	--	--
14. TRANSNATION	$0	0.00%	$21,183	100.00%	$0	0.00%	$21,183	0.01%	$0	--	--
15. AMERICAN GUARANTY	$4,270	100.00%	$0	0.00%	$0	0.00%	$4,270	0.00%	$0	--	--
16. SECURITY UNION	$659	100.00%	$0	0.00%	$0	0.00%	$659	0.00%	$0	--	--
COMPOSITE	**$13,942,809**	9.04%	**$140,075,685**	90.78%	**$282,366**	0.18%	**$154,300,860**	100.00%	**$15,596,220**	100.00%	10.11%
AVERAGE	**$871,426**		**$8,754,730**		**$17,648**		**$9,643,804**		**$974,764**		

DELAWARE

	DIRECT	% of Total	NON-AFFILIATED	% of Total	AFFILIATED	% of Total	TOTAL	PERCENT OF JURISDICTION	PAID LOSSES	PERCENT OF JURISDICTION	LOSSES TO PREMIUMS
1. CHICAGO TIC	$19,063,578	92.20%	$1,611,763	7.80%	$0	0.00%	$20,675,341	28.50%	$4,548	0.55%	0.02%
2. FIRST AMERICAN TIC	$8,684,784	48.44%	$9,183,297	51.22%	$62,149	0.35%	$17,930,230	24.71%	$216,526	26.14%	1.21%
3. COMMONWEALTH LAND	$6,783,727	77.40%	$1,981,257	22.60%	$0	0.00%	$8,764,984	12.08%	$0	--	--
4. LAWYERS	$5,598,759	76.67%	$1,704,059	23.33%	$0	0.00%	$7,302,818	10.07%	($43,357)	(5.23)%	(0.59)%
5. TRANSNATION	$741,123	12.13%	$5,367,260	87.87%	$0	0.00%	$6,108,383	8.42%	$271,561	32.78%	4.45%
6. OLD REPUBLIC NATIONAL	$56,757	1.39%	$4,035,755	98.61%	$0	0.00%	$4,092,512	5.64%	$41,705	5.03%	1.02%
7. STEWART TGC	$96,163	2.37%	$3,290,326	81.11%	$670,323	16.52%	$4,056,812	5.59%	$122,926	14.84%	3.03%
8. SECURITY TG (BALTIMORE)	$0	0.00%	$1,091,559	100.00%	$0	0.00%	$1,091,559	1.50%	$2,934	0.35%	0.27%
9. FIDELITY NATIONAL	$68,465	9.06%	$687,228	90.94%	$0	0.00%	$755,693	1.04%	$49,009	5.92%	6.49%
10. TICOR	$20,946	2.90%	$701,775	97.10%	$0	0.00%	$722,721	1.00%	$35,669	4.31%	4.94%
11. UNITED GENERAL	$0	0.00%	$438,994	100.00%	$0	0.00%	$438,994	0.61%	$88,344	10.66%	20.12%
12. TICOR (FL)	$0	0.00%	$184,668	100.00%	$0	0.00%	$184,668	0.25%	$38,508	4.65%	20.85%
13. CONESTOGA	$0	0.00%	$183,053	100.00%	$0	0.00%	$183,053	0.25%	$0	--	--
14. NORTH AMERICAN	$0	0.00%	$144,470	100.00%	$0	0.00%	$144,470	0.20%	$0	--	--
15. CENSTAR	$0	0.00%	$61,996	100.00%	$0	0.00%	$61,996	0.09%	$0	--	--
16. T.A. TITLE	$0	0.00%	$17,128	65.19%	$9,145	34.81%	$26,273	0.04%	$0	--	--
17. TRANSUNION NATIONAL	$0	0.00%	$0	0.00%	$8,475	100.00%	$8,475	0.01%	$0	--	--
18. SECURITY UNION	$362	100.00%	$0	0.00%	$0	0.00%	$362	0.00%	$0	--	--
COMPOSITE	**$41,114,664**	56.67%	**$30,684,588**	42.29%	**$750,092**	1.03%	**$72,549,344**	100.00%	**$828,373**	100.00%	1.14%
AVERAGE	**$2,284,148**		**$1,704,699**		**$41,672**		**$4,030,519**		**$46,021**		

DISTRICT OF COLUMBIA

	DIRECT	% of Total	NON-AFFILIATED	% of Total	AFFILIATED	% of Total	TOTAL	PERCENT OF JURISDICTION	PAID LOSSES	PERCENT OF JURISDICTION	LOSSES TO PREMIUMS
1. FIRST AMERICAN TIC	$9,220,340	33.64%	$17,755,690	64.79%	$430,540	1.57%	$27,406,570	48.24%	$2,166,420	40.80%	7.90%
2. COMMONWEALTH LAND	$3,808,103	43.40%	$4,960,486	56.53%	$6,350	0.07%	$8,774,939	15.44%	$50,597	0.95%	0.58%
3. CHICAGO TIC	$1,253,113	25.84%	$3,597,067	74.16%	$0	0.00%	$4,850,180	8.54%	$1,117,240	21.04%	23.04%
4. LAWYERS	$797,656	18.28%	$3,559,923	81.58%	$6,163	0.14%	$4,363,742	7.68%	$962,495	18.13%	22.06%
5. STEWART TGC	$415,513	10.09%	$2,502,210	60.78%	$1,199,442	29.13%	$4,117,165	7.25%	$220,792	4.16%	5.36%
6. FIDELITY NATIONAL	$251,245	10.69%	$2,097,505	89.23%	$1,893	0.08%	$2,350,643	4.14%	$296,599	5.59%	12.62%
7. OLD REPUBLIC NATIONAL	$13,522	0.87%	$1,544,434	99.13%	$0	0.00%	$1,557,956	2.74%	$129,585	2.44%	8.32%
8. UNITED GENERAL	$1,285	0.13%	$963,469	99.87%	$0	0.00%	$964,754	1.70%	$96,374	1.81%	9.99%
9. CENSTAR	$0	0.00%	$766,381	100.00%	$0	0.00%	$766,381	1.35%	$15,210	0.29%	1.98%
10. SECURITY TG (BALTIMORE)	$0	0.00%	$434,290	98.10%	$8,399	1.90%	$442,689	0.78%	$11,532	0.22%	2.60%
11. TICOR	$36,165	9.81%	$332,556	90.19%	$0	0.00%	$368,721	0.65%	$109,095	2.05%	29.59%
12. NORTH AMERICAN	$0	0.00%	$0	0.00%	$340,063	100.00%	$340,063	0.60%	$0	--	--
13. CONESTOGA	$0	0.00%	$237,966	100.00%	$0	0.00%	$237,966	0.42%	$97,172	1.83%	40.83%
14. SOUTHERN TI CORP	$0	0.00%	$131,579	100.00%	$0	0.00%	$131,579	0.23%	$27,876	0.52%	21.19%
15. TICOR (FL)	$0	0.00%	$41,023	100.00%	$0	0.00%	$41,023	0.07%	$3,307	0.06%	8.06%
16. GUARANTEE T&T	$0	0.00%	$0	0.00%	$37,974	100.00%	$37,974	0.07%	$0	--	--
17. TRANSNATION	$0	0.00%	$30,396	100.00%	$0	0.00%	$30,396	0.05%	$0	--	--
18. INVESTORS TIC	$0	0.00%	$27,142	100.00%	$0	0.00%	$27,142	0.05%	$5,660	0.11%	20.85%
19. TRANSUNION NATIONAL	$0	0.00%	$0	0.00%	$6,951	100.00%	$6,951	0.01%	$0	--	--
20. AMERICAN GUARANTY	$800	48.78%	$840	51.22%	$0	0.00%	$1,640	0.00%	$0	--	--
COMPOSITE	**$15,797,742**	27.80%	**$38,982,957**	68.61%	**$2,037,775**	3.59%	**$56,818,474**	100.00%	**$5,309,954**	100.00%	9.35%
AVERAGE	**$789,887**		**$1,949,148**		**$101,889**		**$2,840,924**		**$265,498**		

C.2 Jurisdiction - By Individual Underwriter

	DIRECT	% of Total	NON-AFFILIATED	% of Total	AFFILIATED	% of Total	TOTAL	PERCENT OF JURISDICTION	PAID LOSSES	PERCENT OF JURISDICTION	LOSSES TO PREMIUMS
FLORIDA											
1. FIRST AMERICAN TIC	$68,410,626	20.48%	$252,144,660	75.47%	$13,557,226	4.06%	$334,112,512	19.17%	$33,439,408	27.75%	10.01%
2. ATTORNEYS TIF (FL)	$0	0.00%	$332,905,096	100.00%	$0	0.00%	$332,905,096	19.10%	$25,507,467	21.17%	7.66%
3. CHICAGO TIC	$24,511,736	12.43%	$169,574,585	85.96%	$3,187,923	1.62%	$197,274,244	11.32%	$10,529,128	8.74%	5.34%
4. STEWART TGC	$4,775,431	2.89%	$129,809,110	78.53%	$30,708,240	18.58%	$165,292,781	9.49%	$10,528,610	8.74%	6.37%
5. COMMONWEALTH LAND	$6,221,477	3.97%	$150,681,543	96.03%	$2,465	0.00%	$156,905,485	9.00%	$7,960,208	6.61%	5.07%
6. FIDELITY NATIONAL	$21,054,690	14.75%	$120,283,773	84.28%	$1,388,742	0.97%	$142,727,205	8.19%	$7,077,621	5.87%	4.96%
7. OLD REPUBLIC NATIONAL	$1,189,536	0.89%	$133,121,159	99.11%	$0	0.00%	$134,310,695	7.71%	$10,328,952	8.57%	7.69%
8. LAWYERS	$30,929,016	29.52%	$72,128,702	68.84%	$1,719,104	1.64%	$104,776,822	6.01%	$5,887,399	4.89%	5.62%
9. TICOR (FL)	$0	0.00%	$41,670,435	100.00%	$0	0.00%	$41,670,435	2.39%	$3,650,777	3.03%	8.76%
10. UNITED GENERAL	$120,723	0.37%	$32,270,302	99.63%	$0	0.00%	$32,391,025	1.86%	$2,569,858	2.13%	7.93%
11. TICOR	$889,143	2.92%	$29,596,294	97.08%	$0	0.00%	$30,485,437	1.75%	$1,865,732	1.55%	6.12%
12. WESTCOR	$288,117	1.57%	$18,097,030	98.38%	$10,653	0.06%	$18,395,800	1.06%	$178,031	0.15%	0.97%
13. CENSTAR	$0	0.00%	$17,369,262	100.00%	$0	0.00%	$17,369,262	1.00%	$134,796	0.11%	0.78%
14. NORTH AMERICAN	$0	0.00%	$241,465	1.79%	$13,261,644	98.21%	$13,503,109	0.77%	$39,427	0.03%	0.29%
15. COMMERCE	$0	0.00%	$0	0.00%	$6,789,026	100.00%	$6,789,026	0.39%	$207,947	0.17%	3.06%
16. SOUTHERN TI CORP	$0	0.00%	$3,534,245	92.24%	$297,153	7.76%	$3,831,398	0.22%	$115,101	0.10%	3.00%
17. NATIONAL	$127,106	3.82%	$3,001,315	90.18%	$199,659	6.00%	$3,328,080	0.19%	$25,839	0.02%	0.78%
18. MASON	$120,217	7.74%	$0	0.00%	$1,432,065	92.26%	$1,552,282	0.09%	$200	0.00%	0.01%
19. INVESTORS TIC	$0	0.00%	$1,428,570	100.00%	$0	0.00%	$1,428,570	0.08%	$21,190	0.02%	1.48%
20. TITLE RESOURCES	$0	0.00%	$0	0.00%	$1,252,864	100.00%	$1,252,864	0.07%	$0	--	--
21. TRANSUNION NATIONAL	$6,658	0.56%	$650,608	54.43%	$538,097	45.02%	$1,195,363	0.07%	$0	--	--
22. K.E.L.	$0	0.00%	$8,060	1.38%	$575,855	98.62%	$583,915	0.03%	$0	--	--
23. TRANSNATION	$446,781	94.57%	$23,824	5.04%	$1,826	0.39%	$472,431	0.03%	$8,581	0.00%	1.82%
24. SECURITY UNION	$59,799	100.00%	$0	0.00%	$0	0.00%	$59,799	0.00%	$19	0.00%	0.03%
25. UNITED CAPITAL	$32,820	92.34%	$0	0.00%	$2,723	7.66%	$35,543	0.00%	$3,741	0.00%	10.53%
26. NATIONAL OF NY	$0	0.00%	$4,027	100.00%	$0	0.00%	$4,027	0.00%	$305,182	0.25%	7,578.40%
27. AMERICAN GUARANTY	$4,020	100.00%	$0	0.00%	$0	0.00%	$4,020	0.00%	$0	--	--
28. GUARANTEE T&T	$0	0.00%	$0	0.00%	$2,530	100.00%	$2,530	0.00%	$731	0.00%	28.89%
29. ALLIANCE	$0	0.00%	$1,196	100.00%	$0	0.00%	$1,196	0.00%	$67,583	0.06%	5,650.75%
30. NATIONS OF NY	$0	--	$0	--	$0	--	$0	--	$40,191	0.03%	--
COMPOSITE	**$159,187,896**	**9.13%**	**$1,508,545,261**	**86.57%**	**$74,927,795**	**4.30%**	**$1,742,660,952**	**100.00%**	**$120,493,719**	**100.00%**	**6.91%**
AVERAGE	**$5,306,263**		**$50,284,842**		**$2,497,593**		**$58,088,698**		**$4,016,457**		
GEORGIA											
1. CHICAGO TIC	$2,925,671	5.69%	$48,451,197	94.31%	$0	0.00%	$51,376,868	18.97%	$5,635,683	17.69%	10.97%
2. FIRST AMERICAN TIC	$3,818,711	8.03%	$43,164,748	90.82%	$546,730	1.15%	$47,530,189	17.55%	$5,803,402	18.21%	12.21%
3. LAWYERS	$3,646,322	10.13%	$32,337,785	89.84%	$10,131	0.03%	$35,994,238	13.29%	$3,798,387	11.92%	10.55%
4. FIDELITY NATIONAL	$2,416,300	7.02%	$30,629,759	89.03%	$1,357,008	3.94%	$34,403,067	12.70%	$3,211,528	10.08%	9.34%
5. STEWART TGC	$1,347,309	3.98%	$32,316,217	95.56%	$152,722	0.45%	$33,816,248	12.49%	$2,086,645	6.55%	6.17%
6. OLD REPUBLIC NATIONAL	$194,774	0.83%	$23,403,351	99.17%	$0	0.00%	$23,598,125	8.71%	$3,476,917	10.91%	14.73%
7. COMMONWEALTH LAND	$520,418	4.17%	$11,959,823	95.83%	$0	0.00%	$12,480,241	4.61%	$1,625,050	5.10%	13.02%
8. UNITED GENERAL	$5,637	0.05%	$10,279,981	99.95%	$0	0.00%	$10,285,618	3.80%	$2,670,965	8.38%	25.97%
9. TICOR	$51,347	0.71%	$7,188,400	99.29%	$0	0.00%	$7,239,747	2.67%	$234,406	0.74%	3.24%
10. SECURITY UNION	$4,547	0.08%	$6,032,149	99.92%	$0	0.00%	$6,036,696	2.23%	$185,260	0.58%	3.07%
11. CENSTAR	$0	0.00%	$3,121,377	100.00%	$0	0.00%	$3,121,377	1.15%	$27,856	0.09%	0.89%
12. TICOR (FL)	$0	0.00%	$2,469,530	100.00%	$0	0.00%	$2,469,530	0.91%	$1,620,396	5.09%	65.62%
13. SOUTHERN TI CORP	$0	0.00%	$682,019	100.00%	$0	0.00%	$682,019	0.25%	$115,149	0.36%	16.88%
14. ATTORNEYS TIF (FL)	$0	0.00%	$633,526	100.00%	$0	0.00%	$633,526	0.23%	$821,978	2.58%	129.75%
15. TITLE IC AMERICA	$0	0.00%	$398,791	100.00%	$0	0.00%	$398,791	0.15%	$1,930	0.00%	0.48%
16. NATIONAL	$0	0.00%	$262,162	100.00%	$0	0.00%	$262,162	0.10%	$0	--	--
17. TRANSUNION NATIONAL	$0	0.00%	$66,197	31.04%	$147,083	68.96%	$213,280	0.08%	$166,651	0.52%	78.14%
18. TRANSNATION	$23,609	14.14%	$143,357	85.86%	$0	0.00%	$166,966	0.06%	$269,182	0.84%	161.22%
19. INVESTORS TIC	$8,963	9.09%	$89,671	90.91%	$0	0.00%	$98,634	0.04%	$73,058	0.23%	74.07%
20. AMERICAN GUARANTY	$1,050	100.00%	$0	0.00%	$0	0.00%	$1,050	0.00%	$0	--	--
21. NATIONAL OF NY	$0	--	$0	--	$0	--	$0	--	$37,023	0.12%	--
COMPOSITE	**$14,964,658**	**5.53%**	**$253,630,040**	**93.66%**	**$2,213,674**	**0.82%**	**$270,808,372**	**100.00%**	**$31,861,466**	**100.00%**	**11.77%**
AVERAGE	**$712,603**		**$12,077,621**		**$105,413**		**$12,895,637**		**$1,517,213**		
HAWAII											
1. FIRST AMERICAN TIC	$792,925	2.74%	$7,413,778	25.62%	$20,733,026	71.64%	$28,939,729	35.89%	$475,150	13.73%	1.64%
2. TICOR	$21,492	0.12%	$17,267,823	99.88%	$0	0.00%	$17,289,315	21.44%	$885,092	25.57%	5.12%
3. FIDELITY NATIONAL	$11,293,348	97.49%	$291,275	2.51%	$0	0.00%	$11,584,623	14.37%	$319,968	9.24%	2.76%
4. OLD REPUBLIC NATIONAL	$105,074	1.19%	$78,373	0.89%	$8,632,417	97.92%	$8,815,864	10.93%	$532,902	15.39%	6.04%
5. COMMONWEALTH LAND	$224,545	3.82%	$5,650,710	96.16%	$811	0.01%	$5,876,066	7.29%	$139,364	4.03%	2.37%
6. STEWART TGC	$59,314	1.15%	$5,094,424	98.85%	$0	0.00%	$5,153,738	6.39%	$59,183	1.71%	1.15%
7. CHICAGO TIC	$312,821	11.90%	$2,316,012	88.10%	$0	0.00%	$2,628,833	3.26%	$492,895	14.24%	18.75%
8. LAWYERS	$51,685	19.70%	$210,624	80.30%	$0	0.00%	$262,309	0.33%	$546,719	15.79%	208.43%
9. UNITED GENERAL	$76,960	95.04%	$4,020	4.96%	$0	0.00%	$80,980	0.10%	$0	--	--
10. SECURITY UNION	$0	--	$0	--	$0	--	$0	--	$8,774	0.25%	--
11. TRANSNATION	$0	--	$0	--	$0	--	$0	--	$1,824	0.05%	--
COMPOSITE	**$12,938,164**	**16.05%**	**$38,327,039**	**47.53%**	**$29,366,254**	**36.42%**	**$80,631,457**	**100.00%**	**$3,461,871**	**100.00%**	**4.29%**
AVERAGE	**$1,176,197**		**$3,484,276**		**$2,669,659**		**$7,330,132**		**$314,716**		

C.2 Jurisdiction - By Individual Underwriter

	DIRECT PREMIUMS WRITTEN						TOTAL	PERCENT OF JURISDICTION	PAID LOSSES	PERCENT OF JURISDICTION	LOSSES TO PREMIUMS
	DIRECT	% of Total	NON-AFFILIATED	% of Total	AFFILIATED	% of Total					
IDAHO											
1. FIRST AMERICAN TIC	$1,726,186	4.34%	$15,845,130	39.83%	$22,209,074	55.83%	$39,780,390	32.85%	$1,148,653	28.96%	2.89%
2. COMMONWEALTH LAND	$25,516	0.15%	$16,808,517	99.85%	$247	0.00%	$16,834,280	13.90%	$146,859	3.70%	0.87%
3. CHICAGO TIC	$347,153	2.20%	$15,465,738	97.80%	$0	0.00%	$15,812,891	13.06%	$859,155	21.66%	5.43%
4. TRANSNATION	$439,876	3.31%	$5,340,570	40.18%	$7,511,989	56.51%	$13,292,435	10.98%	$774,134	19.52%	5.82%
5. STEWART TGC	$56,157	0.44%	$7,038,043	54.89%	$5,728,524	44.67%	$12,822,724	10.59%	$108,699	2.74%	0.85%
6. OLD REPUBLIC NATIONAL	($481)	(0.01)%	$7,611,024	100.01%	$0	0.00%	$7,610,543	6.28%	$508,970	12.83%	6.69%
7. TICOR	$512,787	10.24%	$4,493,766	89.76%	$0	0.00%	$5,006,553	4.13%	$204,149	5.15%	4.08%
8. FIDELITY NATIONAL	$104,776	2.16%	$4,753,731	97.84%	$0	0.00%	$4,858,507	4.01%	$122,883	3.10%	2.53%
9. LAWYERS	$42,285	1.30%	$3,212,595	98.65%	$1,777	0.05%	$3,256,657	2.69%	$21,609	0.54%	0.66%
10. UNITED GENERAL	$27,481	1.56%	$1,735,841	98.44%	$0	0.00%	$1,763,322	1.46%	$21,154	0.53%	1.20%
11. PACIFIC NORTHWEST	$0	0.00%	$65,695	100.00%	$0	0.00%	$65,695	0.05%	($2,289)	(0.06)%	(3.48)%
12. SECURITY UNION	$1,721	100.00%	$0	0.00%	$0	0.00%	$1,721	0.00%	$52,456	1.32%	3,048.00%
COMPOSITE	**$3,283,457**	2.71%	**$82,370,650**	68.02%	**$35,451,611**	29.27%	**$121,105,718**	100.00%	**$3,966,432**	100.00%	3.28%
AVERAGE	**$273,621**		**$6,864,221**		**$2,954,301**		**$10,092,143**		**$330,536**		
ILLINOIS											
1. CHICAGO TIC	$28,585,340	29.32%	$57,607,733	59.09%	$11,301,183	11.59%	$97,494,256	31.95%	$11,383,563	33.83%	11.68%
2. FIRST AMERICAN TIC	$18,083,316	21.66%	$46,867,248	56.14%	$18,529,294	22.20%	$83,479,858	27.36%	$6,678,513	19.85%	8.00%
3. STEWART TGC	$1,759,049	5.77%	$22,681,855	74.45%	$6,023,601	19.77%	$30,464,505	9.98%	$2,182,421	6.49%	7.16%
4. TICOR	$4,540,890	18.08%	$20,575,164	81.92%	$0	0.00%	$25,116,054	8.23%	$2,146,964	6.38%	8.55%
5. LAWYERS	$6,460,593	37.46%	$10,787,203	62.54%	$522	0.00%	$17,248,318	5.65%	$4,693,921	13.95%	27.21%
6. ATTORNEYS TGF (IL)	$10,633,487	100.00%	$0	0.00%	$0	0.00%	$10,633,487	3.48%	$1,944,200	5.78%	18.28%
7. FIDELITY NATIONAL	$953,300	9.04%	$9,485,840	89.91%	$111,333	1.06%	$10,550,473	3.46%	$990,345	2.94%	9.39%
8. UNITED GENERAL	$42,473	0.76%	$5,560,713	99.24%	$0	0.00%	$5,603,186	1.84%	$146,808	0.44%	2.62%
9. COMMONWEALTH LAND	$836,834	15.41%	$4,591,878	84.59%	$0	0.00%	$5,428,712	1.78%	$992,366	2.95%	18.28%
10. ATTORNEYS TIF (FL)	$0	0.00%	$5,356,039	100.00%	$0	0.00%	$5,356,039	1.76%	$863,901	2.57%	16.13%
11. OLD REPUBLIC NATIONAL	$211,239	5.33%	$3,753,652	94.67%	$0	0.00%	$3,964,891	1.30%	$626,350	1.86%	15.80%
12. SECURITY UNION	$9,243	0.50%	$1,835,223	99.50%	$0	0.00%	$1,844,466	0.60%	$144,030	0.43%	7.81%
13. INVESTORS TIC	$6,110	0.37%	$27,192	1.64%	$1,622,461	97.99%	$1,655,763	0.54%	$19,364	0.06%	1.17%
14. GUARANTEE T&T	$0	0.00%	$418,268	25.68%	$1,210,289	74.32%	$1,628,557	0.53%	$559,736	1.66%	34.37%
15. NATIONAL LAND	$0	0.00%	$1,346,879	100.00%	$0	0.00%	$1,346,879	0.44%	$20,956	0.06%	1.56%
16. PACIFIC NORTHWEST	$0	0.00%	$974,387	100.00%	$0	0.00%	$974,387	0.32%	$554	0.00%	0.06%
17. TRANSNATION	($376)	(0.04)%	$889,489	99.91%	$1,185	0.13%	$890,298	0.29%	$206,384	0.61%	23.18%
18. COMMERCE	$0	0.00%	$0	0.00%	$868,058	100.00%	$868,058	0.28%	--	--	--
19. NORTH AMERICAN	$0	0.00%	$0	0.00%	$456,432	100.00%	$456,432	0.15%	$0	--	--
20. TRANSUNION NATIONAL	$88	0.08%	$0	0.00%	$116,352	99.92%	$116,440	0.04%	$22,364	0.07%	19.21%
21. TITLE IC AMERICA	$0	0.00%	$3,859	100.00%	$0	0.00%	$3,859	0.00%	$1,816	0.00%	47.06%
22. AMERICAN GUARANTY	$2,450	65.02%	$1,318	34.98%	$0	0.00%	$3,768	0.00%	--	--	--
23. TICOR (FL)	$0	0.00%	$3,527	100.00%	$0	0.00%	$3,527	0.00%	$26,032	0.08%	738.08%
COMPOSITE	**$72,124,036**	23.64%	**$192,767,467**	63.18%	**$40,240,710**	13.19%	**$305,132,213**	100.00%	**$33,650,588**	100.00%	11.03%
AVERAGE	**$3,135,828**		**$8,381,194**		**$1,749,596**		**$13,266,618**		**$1,463,069**		
INDIANA											
1. FIRST AMERICAN TIC	$6,010,945	20.44%	$16,897,913	57.45%	$6,502,153	22.11%	$29,411,011	28.75%	$2,291,886	20.59%	7.79%
2. CHICAGO TIC	$8,708,530	50.31%	$8,602,689	49.69%	$0	0.00%	$17,311,219	16.92%	$1,000,718	8.99%	5.78%
3. STEWART TGC	$320,241	2.17%	$9,786,782	66.23%	$4,669,539	31.60%	$14,776,562	14.44%	$2,476,061	22.24%	16.76%
4. LAWYERS	$6,330,422	57.39%	$4,698,968	42.60%	$240	0.00%	$11,029,630	10.78%	$1,123,363	10.09%	10.18%
5. TICOR	$5,451,881	55.56%	$4,360,425	44.44%	$0	0.00%	$9,812,306	9.59%	$845,604	7.60%	8.62%
6. OLD REPUBLIC NATIONAL	$226,877	5.61%	$3,818,019	94.39%	$0	0.00%	$4,044,896	3.95%	$125,107	1.12%	3.09%
7. COMMONWEALTH LAND	$245,200	6.63%	$3,452,212	93.37%	$100	0.00%	$3,697,512	3.61%	$249,215	2.24%	6.74%
8. FIDELITY NATIONAL	$407,244	15.32%	$2,087,611	78.54%	$163,074	6.14%	$2,657,929	2.60%	$1,339,807	12.04%	50.41%
9. ARSENAL	$0	0.00%	$1,583,908	100.00%	$0	0.00%	$1,583,908	1.55%	$649	0.00%	0.04%
10. CONESTOGA	$72,319	4.72%	$1,380,957	90.19%	$77,874	5.09%	$1,531,150	1.50%	$375,611	3.37%	24.53%
11. TRANSNATION	$91,657	6.02%	$1,431,293	93.98%	$0	0.00%	$1,522,950	1.49%	$167,089	1.50%	10.97%
12. NATIONAL ATTORNEYS	$831,940	100.00%	$0	0.00%	$0	0.00%	$831,940	0.81%	$389,203	3.50%	46.78%
13. CENSTAR	$0	0.00%	$797,369	100.00%	$0	0.00%	$797,369	0.78%	--	--	--
14. GUARANTEE T&T	$17,740	2.32%	$339,321	44.38%	$407,468	53.30%	$764,529	0.75%	$40,614	0.36%	5.31%
15. UNITED GENERAL	$13,355	1.78%	$737,872	98.22%	$0	0.00%	$751,227	0.73%	$111,880	1.00%	14.89%
16. DREIBELBISS	$517,581	81.77%	$115,399	18.23%	$0	0.00%	$632,980	0.62%	$0	--	--
17. TICOR (FL)	$0	0.00%	$505,294	100.00%	$0	0.00%	$505,294	0.49%	$391,001	3.51%	77.38%
18. COMMERCE	$0	0.00%	$0	0.00%	$267,698	100.00%	$267,698	0.26%	$0	--	--
19. PACIFIC NORTHWEST	$0	0.00%	$106,959	100.00%	$0	0.00%	$106,959	0.10%	$121,254	1.09%	113.36%
20. ATTORNEYS TGF (IL)	$74,220	100.00%	$0	0.00%	$0	0.00%	$74,220	0.07%	$54,120	0.49%	72.92%
21. DAKOTA HOMESTEAD	$70,880	100.00%	$0	0.00%	$0	0.00%	$70,880	0.07%	$0	--	--
22. SECURITY UNION	$1,255	2.96%	$41,087	97.04%	$0	0.00%	$42,342	0.04%	$182	0.00%	0.43%
23. INVESTORS TIC	$0	0.00%	$40,938	100.00%	$0	0.00%	$40,938	0.04%	$27,464	0.25%	67.09%
24. OHIO BAR	$0	0.00%	$23,301	100.00%	$0	0.00%	$23,301	0.02%	$0	--	--
25. TRANSUNION NATIONAL	$0	0.00%	$0	0.00%	$17,703	100.00%	$17,703	0.02%	$0	--	--
26. TITLE IC AMERICA	$0	0.00%	$6,710	100.00%	$0	0.00%	$6,710	0.00%	$1,607	0.01%	23.95%
27. GENERAL T&T	$0	0.00%	$1,000	100.00%	$0	0.00%	$1,000	0.00%	$0	--	--
28. AMERICAN GUARANTY	$300	100.00%	$0	0.00%	$0	0.00%	$300	0.00%	$0	--	--
29. NATIONAL OF NY	$0	--	$0	--	$0	--	$0	--	$146	0.00%	--
COMPOSITE	**$29,392,587**	28.73%	**$60,816,027**	59.44%	**$12,105,849**	11.83%	**$102,314,463**	100.00%	**$11,132,581**	100.00%	10.88%
AVERAGE	**$1,013,537**		**$2,097,104**		**$417,443**		**$3,528,085**		**$383,882**		

3

C.2 Jurisdiction - By Individual Underwriter

	DIRECT PREMIUMS WRITTEN							PERCENT OF JURISDICTION	PAID LOSSES	PERCENT OF JURISDICTION	LOSSES TO PREMIUMS
	DIRECT	% of Total	NON-AFFILIATED	% of Total	AFFILIATED	% of Total	TOTAL				
IOWA											
1. TITLE GUARANTY DIV (IA)	$3,724,743	100.00%	$0	0.00%	$0	0.00%	$3,724,743	48.07%	($2,440)	(0.45)%	(0.07)%
2. COMMONWEALTH LAND	$343,007	19.16%	$1,447,037	80.84%	$55	0.00%	$1,790,099	23.10%	$116,313	21.24%	6.50%
3. LAWYERS	$363,380	29.51%	$868,069	70.49%	$0	0.00%	$1,231,449	15.89%	$54,548	9.96%	4.43%
4. STEWART TGC	$172,064	37.15%	$273,669	59.09%	$17,416	3.76%	$463,149	5.98%	$10,348	1.89%	2.23%
5. CHICAGO TIC	$65,022	26.89%	$176,753	73.11%	$0	0.00%	$241,775	3.12%	$11,848	2.16%	4.90%
6. TICOR	$144,951	100.00%	$0	0.00%	$0	0.00%	$144,951	1.87%	$168,345	30.75%	116.14%
7. FIDELITY NATIONAL	$36,679	33.86%	$0	0.00%	$71,648	66.14%	$108,327	1.40%	$145,946	26.66%	134.73%
8. TRANSNATION	$1,300	6.11%	$19,994	93.89%	$0	0.00%	$21,294	0.27%	$0	--	--
9. INVESTORS TIC	$0	0.00%	$14,405	100.00%	$0	0.00%	$14,405	0.19%	$0	--	--
10. PACIFIC NORTHWEST	$0	0.00%	$4,099	100.00%	$0	0.00%	$4,099	0.05%	$0	--	--
11. SECURITY UNION	$3,900	100.00%	$0	0.00%	$0	0.00%	$3,900	0.05%	$0	--	--
12. TICOR (FL)	$0	--	$0	--	$0	--	$0	--	$42,368	7.74%	--
13. GUARANTEE T&T	$0	--	$0	--	$0	--	$0	--	$214	0.04%	--
COMPOSITE	**$4,855,046**	62.66%	**$2,804,026**	36.19%	**$89,119**	1.15%	**$7,748,191**	**100.00%**	**$547,490**	**100.00%**	**7.07%**
AVERAGE	**$373,465**		**$215,694**		**$6,855**		**$596,015**		**$42,115**		
KANSAS											
1. FIRST AMERICAN (KS)	$1,550,799	10.50%	$5,813,820	39.38%	$7,399,061	50.12%	$14,763,680	33.86%	$290,960	17.80%	1.97%
2. CHICAGO TIC	$4,201,408	52.88%	$3,743,189	47.12%	$0	0.00%	$7,944,597	18.22%	$187,930	11.50%	2.37%
3. STEWART TGC	$301,840	5.35%	$2,619,936	46.48%	$2,715,209	48.17%	$5,636,985	12.93%	$493,020	30.17%	8.75%
4. LAWYERS	$1,508,455	41.38%	$1,978,351	54.27%	$158,721	4.35%	$3,645,527	8.36%	$118,876	7.27%	3.26%
5. OLD REPUBLIC NATIONAL	$5,702	0.17%	$2,956,623	86.57%	$452,917	13.26%	$3,415,242	7.83%	$250,881	15.35%	7.35%
6. COMMONWEALTH LAND	$781,959	23.27%	$2,578,750	76.73%	$0	0.00%	$3,360,709	7.71%	$78,016	4.77%	2.32%
7. FIDELITY NATIONAL	$290,242	12.31%	$2,067,114	87.69%	$0	0.00%	$2,357,356	5.41%	$20,651	1.26%	0.88%
8. UNITED GENERAL	$286	0.02%	$1,504,983	99.98%	$0	0.00%	$1,505,269	3.45%	$20,555	1.26%	1.37%
9. TICOR	$3,456	0.64%	$534,478	99.36%	$0	0.00%	$537,934	1.23%	$35,145	2.15%	6.53%
10. SECURITY UNION	$429	0.24%	$179,165	99.76%	$0	0.00%	$179,594	0.41%	$1,078	0.07%	0.60%
11. GUARANTEE	$0	0.00%	$6,800	3.80%	$172,205	96.20%	$179,005	0.41%	$21,655	1.33%	12.10%
12. TICOR (FL)	$0	0.00%	$80,288	100.00%	$0	0.00%	$80,288	0.18%	$115,431	7.06%	143.77%
13. NATIONAL LAND	$0	0.00%	$1,048	100.00%	$0	0.00%	$1,048	0.00%	$0	--	--
COMPOSITE	**$8,644,576**	19.82%	**$24,064,545**	55.18%	**$10,898,113**	24.99%	**$43,607,234**	**100.00%**	**$1,634,198**	**100.00%**	**3.75%**
AVERAGE	**$664,967**		**$1,851,119**		**$838,316**		**$3,354,403**		**$125,708**		
KENTUCKY											
1. FIRST AMERICAN TIC	$1,676,270	11.73%	$12,115,115	84.79%	$496,678	3.48%	$14,288,063	22.38%	$1,386,718	21.46%	9.71%
2. COMMONWEALTH LAND	$1,255,853	10.19%	$11,034,281	89.50%	$38,237	0.31%	$12,328,371	19.31%	$2,079,436	32.18%	16.87%
3. CHICAGO TIC	$1,409,710	14.40%	$8,381,073	85.60%	$0	0.00%	$9,790,783	15.33%	$456,114	7.06%	4.66%
4. STEWART TGC	$546,525	5.69%	$7,390,922	76.94%	$1,668,069	17.37%	$9,605,516	15.04%	$730,790	11.31%	7.61%
5. OLD REPUBLIC NATIONAL	$268,821	3.33%	$7,797,258	96.67%	$0	0.00%	$8,066,079	12.63%	$884,380	13.69%	10.96%
6. LAWYERS	$823,817	23.81%	$2,633,706	76.11%	$2,686	0.08%	$3,460,209	5.42%	$96,871	1.50%	2.80%
7. INVESTORS TIC	$0	0.00%	$1,927,641	75.17%	$636,760	24.83%	$2,564,401	4.02%	$130,792	2.02%	5.10%
8. FIDELITY NATIONAL	$546,570	38.76%	$325,856	23.11%	$537,859	38.14%	$1,410,285	2.21%	$148,798	2.30%	10.55%
9. CENSTAR	$0	0.00%	$733,946	100.00%	$0	0.00%	$733,946	1.15%	$1,628	0.03%	0.22%
10. UNITED GENERAL	$750	0.11%	$696,269	99.89%	$0	0.00%	$697,019	1.09%	$36,337	0.56%	5.21%
11. CONESTOGA	$5,691	1.37%	$409,688	98.63%	$0	0.00%	$415,379	0.65%	$6,458	0.10%	1.55%
12. OHIO BAR	$0	0.00%	$171,109	100.00%	$0	0.00%	$171,109	0.27%	$0	--	--
13. TICOR (FL)	$0	0.00%	$160,475	100.00%	$0	0.00%	$160,475	0.25%	$312,220	4.83%	194.56%
14. TICOR	$59,039	60.69%	$38,244	39.31%	$0	0.00%	$97,283	0.15%	$161,924	2.51%	166.45%
15. SECURITY UNION	$2,400	6.33%	$35,516	93.67%	$0	0.00%	$37,916	0.06%	$0	--	--
16. TRANSNATION	$65	0.53%	$12,120	99.47%	$0	0.00%	$12,185	0.02%	$7,010	0.11%	57.53%
17. TRANSUNION NATIONAL	$0	0.00%	$0	0.00%	$10,162	100.00%	$10,162	0.02%	$0	--	--
18. SECURITY TG (BALTIMORE)	$0	0.00%	$2,748	100.00%	$0	0.00%	$2,748	0.00%	$0	--	--
19. AMERICAN GUARANTY	$0	0.00%	$275	100.00%	$0	0.00%	$275	0.00%	$0	--	--
20. GUARANTEE T&T	$0	0.00%	$0	0.00%	$150	100.00%	$150	0.00%	$0	--	--
21. NATIONAL OF NY	$0	--	$0	--	$0	--	$0	--	$15,200	0.24%	--
22. NATIONS OF NY	$0	--	$0	--	$0	--	$0	--	$6,541	0.10%	--
COMPOSITE	**$6,595,511**	10.33%	**$53,866,242**	84.36%	**$3,390,601**	5.31%	**$63,852,354**	**100.00%**	**$6,461,217**	**100.00%**	**10.12%**
AVERAGE	**$299,796**		**$2,448,466**		**$154,118**		**$2,902,380**		**$293,692**		
LOUISIANA											
1. FIRST AMERICAN TIC	$528,421	1.16%	$45,018,149	98.52%	$149,271	0.33%	$45,695,841	37.61%	($597,038)	(17.43)%	(1.31)%
2. COMMONWEALTH LAND	$143,197	0.60%	$23,825,832	99.40%	$0	0.00%	$23,969,029	19.73%	$2,021,315	59.01%	8.43%
3. STEWART TGC	$149,049	0.95%	$12,743,531	80.93%	$2,854,272	18.13%	$15,746,852	12.96%	$345,301	10.08%	2.19%
4. FIDELITY NATIONAL	$358,520	3.05%	$11,043,357	93.93%	$355,141	3.02%	$11,757,018	9.68%	$637,957	18.62%	5.43%
5. CHICAGO TIC	$379,662	3.98%	$6,927,022	72.54%	$2,242,807	23.49%	$9,549,491	7.86%	$120,211	3.51%	1.26%
6. LAWYERS	$1,373,431	17.51%	$6,463,033	82.38%	$9,192	0.12%	$7,845,656	6.46%	$200,671	5.86%	2.56%
7. SECURITY TG (BALTIMORE)	$0	0.00%	$2,343,439	100.00%	$0	0.00%	$2,343,439	1.93%	$136,777	3.99%	5.84%
8. UNITED GENERAL	$2,690	0.16%	$1,649,456	99.84%	$0	0.00%	$1,652,146	1.36%	$74,521	2.18%	4.51%
9. OLD REPUBLIC NATIONAL	$25,080	1.57%	$1,572,271	98.43%	$0	0.00%	$1,597,351	1.31%	$163,816	4.78%	10.26%
10. TICOR (FL)	$0	0.00%	$536,084	100.00%	$0	0.00%	$536,084	0.44%	$320,917	9.37%	59.86%
11. INVESTORS TIC	$0	0.00%	$321,368	100.00%	$0	0.00%	$321,368	0.26%	$0	--	--
12. FIRST AMERICAN TRANS	$108,501	42.27%	$148,193	57.73%	$0	0.00%	$256,694	0.21%	$0	--	--
13. TICOR	$23,348	11.39%	$181,697	88.61%	$0	0.00%	$205,045	0.17%	$0	--	--
14. SOUTHERN TI CORP	$0	0.00%	$10,825	100.00%	$0	0.00%	$10,825	0.00%	$0	--	--
15. SECURITY UNION	$939	100.00%	$0	0.00%	$0	0.00%	$939	0.00%	$888	0.03%	94.57%
16. TRANSNATION	$135	28.91%	$332	71.09%	$0	0.00%	$467	0.00%	$0	--	--
COMPOSITE	**$3,092,973**	2.55%	**$112,784,589**	92.84%	**$5,610,683**	4.62%	**$121,488,245**	**100.00%**	**$3,425,336**	**100.00%**	**2.82%**
AVERAGE	**$193,311**		**$7,049,037**		**$350,668**		**$7,593,015**		**$214,084**		

C.2 Jurisdiction - By Individual Underwriter

	DIRECT	% of Total	NON-AFFILIATED	% of Total	AFFILIATED	% of Total	TOTAL	PERCENT OF JURISDICTION	PAID LOSSES	PERCENT OF JURISDICTION	LOSSES TO PREMIUMS
MAINE											
1. FIRST AMERICAN TIC	$199,277	1.22%	$14,402,220	88.34%	$1,702,286	10.44%	$16,303,783	49.89%	$1,196,784	39.29%	7.34%
2. CHICAGO TIC	$99,218	2.12%	$4,578,388	97.88%	$0	0.00%	$4,677,606	14.31%	$1,019,738	33.48%	21.80%
3. LAWYERS	$1,275,834	36.29%	$2,239,055	63.69%	$479	0.01%	$3,515,368	10.76%	$197,478	6.48%	5.62%
4. TICOR	$16,308	0.59%	$2,734,744	99.41%	$0	0.00%	$2,751,052	8.42%	$70,168	2.30%	2.55%
5. STEWART TGC	$26,806	1.16%	$1,750,925	76.06%	$524,213	22.77%	$2,301,944	7.04%	$310,621	10.20%	13.49%
6. COMMONWEALTH LAND	$97,373	6.37%	$1,430,351	93.63%	$0	0.00%	$1,527,724	4.67%	$156,248	5.13%	10.23%
7. OLD REPUBLIC NATIONAL	$48,173	8.66%	$508,379	91.34%	$0	0.00%	$556,552	1.70%	$25,572	0.84%	4.59%
8. FIDELITY NATIONAL	$136,767	32.14%	$288,758	67.86%	$0	0.00%	$425,525	1.30%	$54,752	1.80%	12.87%
9. UNITED GENERAL	$654	0.16%	$412,117	99.84%	$0	0.00%	$412,771	1.26%	$0	--	--
10. TICOR (FL)	$0	0.00%	$173,838	100.00%	$0	0.00%	$173,838	0.53%	$13,000	0.43%	7.48%
11. TITLE RESOURCES	$0	0.00%	$0	0.00%	$14,476	100.00%	$14,476	0.04%	$0	--	--
12. GUARANTEE T&T	$0	0.00%	$0	0.00%	$10,566	100.00%	$10,566	0.03%	$0	--	--
13. CT ATTORNEYS	$0	0.00%	$8,326	100.00%	$0	0.00%	$8,326	0.03%	$0	--	--
14. NATIONS OF NY	$0	--	$0	--	$0	--	$0	--	$1,386	0.05%	--
15. TRANSNATION	$0	--	$0	--	$0	--	$0	--	$22	0.00%	--
COMPOSITE	**$1,900,410**	5.82%	**$28,527,101**	87.29%	**$2,252,020**	6.89%	**$32,679,531**	100.00%	**$3,045,769**	100.00%	9.32%
AVERAGE	**$126,694**		**$1,901,807**		**$150,135**		**$2,178,635**		**$203,051**		
MARYLAND											
1. FIRST AMERICAN TIC	$8,022,208	10.46%	$63,154,606	82.31%	$5,551,539	7.24%	$76,728,353	24.93%	$4,116,094	18.03%	5.36%
2. CHICAGO TIC	$7,056,050	13.79%	$44,111,055	86.21%	$0	0.00%	$51,167,105	16.62%	$7,694,950	33.71%	15.04%
3. COMMONWEALTH LAND	$6,530,007	14.74%	$37,563,497	84.78%	$212,069	0.48%	$44,305,573	14.39%	$973,641	4.27%	2.20%
4. STEWART TGC	$1,163,121	2.90%	$36,733,767	91.49%	$2,251,554	5.61%	$40,148,442	13.04%	$2,633,944	11.54%	6.56%
5. LAWYERS	$4,829,432	18.71%	$20,954,897	81.19%	$25,998	0.10%	$25,810,327	8.39%	$1,275,110	5.59%	4.94%
6. FIDELITY NATIONAL	$773,680	3.23%	$23,142,555	96.52%	$61,317	0.26%	$23,977,552	7.79%	$2,552,299	11.18%	10.64%
7. OLD REPUBLIC NATIONAL	$156,161	1.34%	$11,528,984	98.66%	$0	0.00%	$11,685,145	3.80%	$994,975	4.36%	8.51%
8. UNITED GENERAL	$72,946	0.82%	$8,774,118	99.18%	$0	0.00%	$8,847,064	2.87%	$728,884	3.19%	8.24%
9. SECURITY TG (BALTIMORE)	$413,935	5.41%	$6,689,617	87.39%	$551,239	7.20%	$7,654,791	2.49%	$375,334	1.64%	4.90%
10. TICOR (FL)	$0	0.00%	$3,443,114	100.00%	$0	0.00%	$3,443,114	1.12%	$465,084	2.04%	13.51%
11. SOUTHERN TI CORP	$0	0.00%	$2,039,926	73.53%	$734,177	26.47%	$2,774,103	0.90%	$79,508	0.35%	2.87%
12. NORTH AMERICAN	$0	0.00%	$0	0.00%	$2,532,497	100.00%	$2,532,497	0.82%	$7,125	0.03%	0.28%
13. TICOR	$189,987	8.60%	$2,019,436	91.40%	$0	0.00%	$2,209,423	0.72%	$421,405	1.85%	19.07%
14. CONESTOGA	$0	0.00%	$2,170,802	100.00%	$0	0.00%	$2,170,802	0.71%	$71,107	0.31%	3.28%
15. CENSTAR	$0	0.00%	$1,657,830	100.00%	$0	0.00%	$1,657,830	0.54%	($1,392)	0.00%	(0.08)%
16. INVESTORS TIC	$0	0.00%	$1,176,007	100.00%	$0	0.00%	$1,176,007	0.38%	$355,386	1.56%	30.22%
17. COMMERCE	$0	0.00%	$0	0.00%	$509,871	100.00%	$509,871	0.17%	$0	--	--
18. T.A. TITLE	$0	0.00%	$245,900	69.49%	$107,947	30.51%	$353,847	0.11%	$0	--	--
19. TITLE RESOURCES	$0	0.00%	$0	0.00%	$340,737	100.00%	$340,737	0.11%	$0	--	--
20. TRANSNATION	$170,334	69.13%	$76,054	30.87%	$0	0.00%	$246,388	0.08%	$6,961	0.03%	2.83%
21. TRANSUNION NATIONAL	$2	0.00%	$0	0.00%	$70,720	100.00%	$70,722	0.02%	$0	--	--
22. AMERICAN GUARANTY	$700	32.33%	$1,465	67.67%	$0	0.00%	$2,165	0.00%	$0	--	--
23. NATIONAL OF NY	$0	--	$0	--	$0	--	$0	--	$31,207	0.14%	--
24. NATIONS OF NY	$0	--	$0	--	$0	--	$0	--	$26,620	0.12%	--
25. SECURITY UNION	$0	--	$0	--	$0	--	$0	--	$18,361	0.08%	--
COMPOSITE	**$29,378,563**	9.54%	**$265,483,630**	86.25%	**$12,949,665**	4.21%	**$307,811,858**	100.00%	**$22,826,603**	100.00%	7.42%
AVERAGE	**$1,175,143**		**$10,619,345**		**$517,987**		**$12,312,474**		**$913,064**		
MASSACHUSETTS											
1. FIRST AMERICAN TIC	$1,706,933	1.91%	$87,295,614	97.84%	$220,075	0.25%	$89,222,622	36.98%	$5,856,404	24.94%	6.56%
2. STEWART TGC	$2,077,606	8.23%	$22,543,803	89.32%	$617,198	2.45%	$25,238,607	10.46%	$2,474,207	10.54%	9.80%
3. OLD REPUBLIC NATIONAL	$297,150	1.36%	$21,526,999	98.59%	$10,220	0.05%	$21,834,369	9.05%	$1,488,095	6.34%	6.82%
4. COMMONWEALTH LAND	$1,500,792	6.96%	$20,073,080	93.04%	$0	0.00%	$21,573,872	8.94%	$1,761,819	7.50%	8.17%
5. FIDELITY NATIONAL	$2,830,618	14.27%	$16,989,764	85.66%	$14,268	0.07%	$19,834,650	8.22%	$2,144,152	9.13%	10.81%
6. CHICAGO TIC	$613,287	3.10%	$19,166,204	96.90%	$0	0.00%	$19,779,491	8.20%	$2,721,268	11.59%	13.76%
7. LAWYERS	$4,775,217	25.69%	$13,797,263	74.24%	$12,402	0.07%	$18,584,882	7.70%	$3,521,190	15.00%	18.95%
8. CT ATTORNEYS	$0	0.00%	$8,093,908	100.00%	$0	0.00%	$8,093,908	3.36%	$1,419,832	6.05%	17.54%
9. TICOR	$45,535	0.60%	$7,492,537	99.40%	$0	0.00%	$7,538,072	3.12%	$1,830,567	7.80%	24.28%
10. UNITED GENERAL	$315,258	4.65%	$6,464,562	95.35%	$0	0.00%	$6,779,820	2.81%	($83,385)	(0.36)%	(1.23)%
11. CENSTAR	$0	0.00%	$1,047,048	100.00%	$0	0.00%	$1,047,048	0.43%	$0	--	--
12. NATIONAL OF NY	$576,997	100.00%	$0	0.00%	$0	0.00%	$576,997	0.24%	$41,763	0.18%	7.24%
13. TICOR (FL)	$0	0.00%	$566,618	100.00%	$0	0.00%	$566,618	0.23%	$271,567	1.16%	47.93%
14. EQUITY NATIONAL	$280,228	100.00%	$0	0.00%	$0	0.00%	$280,228	0.12%	$0	--	--
15. TRANSNATION	$245	0.10%	$250,202	99.90%	$0	0.00%	$250,447	0.10%	$9,272	0.04%	3.70%
16. TITLE RESOURCES	$0	0.00%	$0	0.00%	$44,660	100.00%	$44,660	0.02%	$0	--	--
17. SECURITY UNION	$0	--	$0	--	$0	--	$0	--	$14,017	0.06%	--
18. NATIONS OF NY	$0	--	$0	--	$0	--	$0	--	$9,463	0.04%	--
19. MASSACHUSETTS TIC	($254)	--	$0	--	$0	--	($254)	0.00%	$0	--	--
COMPOSITE	**$15,019,612**	6.23%	**$225,307,602**	93.39%	**$918,823**	0.38%	**$241,246,037**	100.00%	**$23,480,231**	100.00%	9.73%
AVERAGE	**$790,506**		**$11,858,295**		**$48,359**		**$12,697,160**		**$1,235,802**		

C.2 Jurisdiction - By Individual Underwriter

	DIRECT PREMIUMS WRITTEN							PERCENT OF JURISDICTION	PAID LOSSES	PERCENT OF JURISDICTION	LOSSES TO PREMIUMS
	DIRECT	% of Total	NON-AFFILIATED	% of Total	AFFILIATED	% of Total	TOTAL				
MICHIGAN											
1. FIRST AMERICAN TIC	$14,314,961	11.91%	$61,340,062	51.05%	$44,511,678	37.04%	$120,166,701	38.17%	$13,128,196	23.76%	10.92%
2. TRANSNATION	$8,472,063	24.83%	$24,384,023	71.47%	$1,263,113	3.70%	$34,119,199	10.84%	$4,976,684	9.01%	14.59%
3. CHICAGO TIC	$745,507	2.33%	$19,082,506	59.70%	$12,133,652	37.96%	$31,961,665	10.15%	$2,127,474	3.85%	6.66%
4. FIDELITY NATIONAL	$6,671,869	20.96%	$25,077,450	78.76%	$89,320	0.28%	$31,838,639	10.11%	$5,310,739	9.61%	16.68%
5. LAWYERS	$7,842,742	28.63%	$18,982,398	69.30%	$565,456	2.06%	$27,390,596	8.70%	$7,613,034	13.78%	27.79%
6. STEWART TGC	$681,396	3.32%	$16,421,784	80.13%	$3,390,828	16.55%	$20,494,008	6.51%	$5,111,056	9.25%	24.94%
7. OLD REPUBLIC NATIONAL	$247,680	1.62%	$15,041,679	98.38%	$0	0.00%	$15,289,359	4.86%	$4,409,450	7.98%	28.84%
8. COMMONWEALTH LAND	$931,778	9.03%	$9,384,816	90.97%	$0	0.00%	$10,316,594	3.28%	$2,448,313	4.43%	23.73%
9. TICOR	$74,331	1.20%	$6,109,445	98.80%	$0	0.00%	$6,183,776	1.96%	$4,296,994	7.78%	69.49%
10. SECURITY UNION	$3,143	0.06%	$5,204,705	99.94%	$0	0.00%	$5,207,848	1.65%	$987,696	1.79%	18.97%
11. UNITED GENERAL	$2,758	0.09%	$3,202,527	99.91%	$0	0.00%	$3,205,285	1.02%	$23,429	0.04%	0.73%
12. INVESTORS TIC	$7,790	0.25%	$2,718,167	87.83%	$368,873	11.92%	$3,094,830	0.98%	$302,789	0.55%	9.78%
13. GUARANTEE T&T	$0	0.00%	$201,584	7.21%	$2,595,869	92.79%	$2,797,453	0.89%	$513,370	0.93%	18.35%
14. TICOR (FL)	$0	0.00%	$1,868,554	100.00%	$0	0.00%	$1,868,554	0.59%	$3,847,724	6.96%	205.92%
15. COMMERCE	$0	0.00%	$0	0.00%	$498,233	100.00%	$498,233	0.16%	$0	--	--
16. CENSTAR	$0	0.00%	$278,957	100.00%	$0	0.00%	$278,957	0.09%	$0	--	--
17. ATTORNEYS TIF (FL)	$0	0.00%	$81,020	100.00%	$0	0.00%	$81,020	0.03%	$154,009	0.28%	190.09%
18. AMERICAN GUARANTY	$650	100.00%	$0	0.00%	$0	0.00%	$650	0.00%	$0	--	--
COMPOSITE	$39,996,668	12.71%	$209,379,677	66.51%	$65,417,022	20.78%	$314,793,367	100.00%	$55,250,957	100.00%	17.55%
AVERAGE	$2,222,037		$11,632,204		$3,634,279		$17,488,520		$3,069,498		
MINNESOTA											
1. COMMONWEALTH LAND	$2,207,645	10.39%	$19,042,075	89.61%	$0	0.00%	$21,249,720	17.77%	$3,476,816	15.36%	16.36%
2. CHICAGO TIC	$2,863,665	13.90%	$17,741,918	86.10%	$0	0.00%	$20,605,583	17.23%	$4,029,572	17.80%	19.56%
3. FIRST AMERICAN TIC	$4,370,766	22.89%	$3,760,335	19.69%	$10,963,657	57.42%	$19,094,758	15.97%	$3,711,295	16.40%	19.44%
4. STEWART TGC	$256,667	1.55%	$14,383,725	86.62%	$1,965,411	11.84%	$16,605,803	13.89%	$1,779,847	7.86%	10.72%
5. OLD REPUBLIC NATIONAL	$1,627,848	13.47%	$10,453,789	86.53%	$0	0.00%	$12,081,637	10.11%	$2,204,976	9.74%	18.25%
6. LAWYERS	$537,868	4.89%	$10,464,381	95.09%	$2,964	0.03%	$11,005,213	9.20%	$1,184,337	5.23%	10.76%
7. FIDELITY NATIONAL	$164,313	2.73%	$5,847,518	97.09%	$10,993	0.18%	$6,022,824	5.04%	$3,999,086	17.67%	66.40%
8. TICOR	$13,597	0.24%	$5,637,709	99.76%	$0	0.00%	$5,651,306	4.73%	$591,101	2.61%	10.46%
9. ATTORNEYS TIF (FL)	$0	0.00%	$3,696,692	100.00%	$0	0.00%	$3,696,692	3.09%	$82,652	0.37%	2.24%
10. UNITED GENERAL	$5,751	0.47%	$1,225,624	99.53%	$0	0.00%	$1,231,375	1.03%	$660,532	2.92%	53.64%
11. TICOR (FL)	$0	0.00%	$1,178,054	100.00%	$0	0.00%	$1,178,054	0.99%	$751,725	3.32%	63.81%
12. INVESTORS TIC	$0	0.00%	$482,025	100.00%	$0	0.00%	$482,025	0.40%	$17,576	0.08%	3.65%
13. COMMERCE	$0	0.00%	$0	0.00%	$358,903	100.00%	$358,903	0.30%	$0	--	--
14. DAKOTA HOMESTEAD	$5,315	6.24%	$79,799	93.76%	$0	0.00%	$85,114	0.07%	$124	0.00%	0.15%
15. LAND TIC (ST LOUIS)	$0	0.00%	$84,302	100.00%	$0	0.00%	$84,302	0.07%	$0	--	--
16. CENSTAR	$0	0.00%	$60,157	100.00%	$0	0.00%	$60,157	0.05%	$0	--	--
17. NORTH AMERICAN	$0	0.00%	$0	0.00%	$36,986	100.00%	$36,986	0.03%	$0	--	--
18. NATIONAL LAND	$0	0.00%	$23,828	100.00%	$0	0.00%	$23,828	0.02%	$0	--	--
19. TRANSNATION	$0	0.00%	$5,167	100.00%	$0	0.00%	$5,167	0.00%	$254	0.00%	4.92%
20. ATTORNEYS TGF (CO)	$0	--	$0	--	$0	--	$0	--	$105,452	0.47%	--
21. NATIONS OF NY	$0	--	$0	--	$0	--	$0	--	$40,854	0.18%	--
COMPOSITE	$12,053,435	10.08%	$94,167,098	78.76%	$13,338,914	11.16%	$119,559,447	100.00%	$22,636,199	100.00%	18.93%
AVERAGE	$573,973		$4,484,148		$635,186		$5,693,307		$1,077,914		
MISSISSIPPI											
1. FIRST AMERICAN TIC	$2,195,212	16.89%	$10,713,567	82.44%	$86,256	0.66%	$12,995,035	27.48%	$1,566,334	35.56%	12.05%
2. MISSISSIPPI VALLEY	$342,929	2.96%	$11,224,397	97.04%	$0	0.00%	$11,567,326	24.46%	$1,070,673	24.31%	9.26%
3. CHICAGO TIC	$227,211	4.56%	$4,756,036	95.44%	$0	0.00%	$4,983,247	10.54%	$275,485	6.25%	5.53%
4. LAWYERS	$526,319	10.67%	$4,407,800	89.33%	$394	0.01%	$4,934,513	10.43%	$284,583	6.46%	5.77%
5. STEWART TGC	$158,727	4.22%	$3,079,639	81.82%	$525,456	13.96%	$3,763,822	7.96%	$319,032	7.24%	8.48%
6. SECURITY TG (BALTIMORE)	$0	0.00%	$2,917,899	100.00%	$0	0.00%	$2,917,899	6.17%	$53,851	1.22%	1.85%
7. FIDELITY NATIONAL	$277,350	12.13%	$1,493,493	65.33%	$515,258	22.54%	$2,286,101	4.83%	$245,697	5.58%	10.75%
8. COMMONWEALTH LAND	$38,518	2.61%	$1,437,666	97.39%	$0	0.00%	$1,476,184	3.12%	$45,524	1.03%	3.08%
9. INVESTORS TIC	$90	0.01%	$916,363	99.99%	$0	0.00%	$916,453	1.94%	$36,314	0.82%	3.96%
10. MISSISSIPPI GUARANTY	$56,517	18.25%	$253,129	81.75%	$0	0.00%	$309,646	0.65%	$0	--	--
11. UNITED GENERAL	$3,919	1.63%	$236,459	98.37%	$0	0.00%	$240,378	0.51%	$148,484	3.37%	61.77%
12. SOUTHERN TI CORP	$0	0.00%	$223,884	100.00%	$0	0.00%	$223,884	0.47%	$0	--	--
13. TICOR	$6,826	4.43%	$147,418	95.57%	$0	0.00%	$154,244	0.33%	$27,383	0.62%	17.75%
14. GUARANTEE T&T	$0	0.00%	$0	0.00%	$151,012	100.00%	$151,012	0.32%	$22	0.00%	0.01%
15. CENSTAR	$0	0.00%	$132,640	100.00%	$0	0.00%	$132,640	0.28%	$0	--	--
16. TICOR (FL)	$0	0.00%	$88,536	100.00%	$0	0.00%	$88,536	0.19%	$192,162	4.36%	217.04%
17. OLD REPUBLIC NATIONAL	$64,501	95.90%	$2,759	4.10%	$0	0.00%	$67,260	0.14%	$39,196	0.89%	58.28%
18. SECURITY UNION	$0	0.00%	$52,619	100.00%	$0	0.00%	$52,619	0.11%	$0	--	--
19. TRANSUNION NATIONAL	$35	0.23%	$0	0.00%	$15,188	99.77%	$15,223	0.03%	$0	--	--
20. AMERICAN GUARANTY	$375	5.36%	$6,620	94.64%	$0	0.00%	$6,995	0.01%	$0	--	--
21. TRANSNATION	$0	0.00%	$6,290	100.00%	$0	0.00%	$6,290	0.01%	$0	--	--
22. WESTCOR	$0	0.00%	$4,790	100.00%	$0	0.00%	$4,790	0.01%	$0	--	--
23. CONESTOGA	$0	0.00%	$1,015	100.00%	$0	0.00%	$1,015	0.00%	$0	--	--
24. NATIONAL OF NY	$0	--	$0	--	$0	--	$0	--	$99,867	2.27%	--
COMPOSITE	$3,898,529	8.24%	$42,103,019	89.02%	$1,293,564	2.74%	$47,295,112	100.00%	$4,404,607	100.00%	9.31%
AVERAGE	$162,439		$1,754,292		$53,899		$1,970,630		$183,525		

C.2 Jurisdiction - By Individual Underwriter

	DIRECT PREMIUMS WRITTEN							PERCENT OF	PAID	PERCENT OF	LOSSES TO
	DIRECT	% of Total	NON-AFFILIATED	% of Total	AFFILIATED	% of Total	TOTAL	JURISDICTION	LOSSES	JURISDICTION	PREMIUMS

MISSOURI

	DIRECT	% of Total	NON-AFFILIATED	% of Total	AFFILIATED	% of Total	TOTAL	PERCENT OF JURISDICTION	PAID LOSSES	PERCENT OF JURISDICTION	LOSSES TO PREMIUMS
1. STEWART TGC	$264,661	2.24%	$9,879,985	83.58%	$1,676,006	14.18%	$11,820,652	15.75%	$1,517,882	8.77%	12.84%
2. CHICAGO TIC	$2,684,870	24.54%	$8,257,131	75.46%	$0	0.00%	$10,942,001	14.58%	$1,492,108	8.62%	13.64%
3. FIRST AMERICAN TIC	$1,445,495	14.81%	$5,814,380	59.56%	$2,501,584	25.63%	$9,761,459	13.00%	$2,730,179	15.77%	27.97%
4. COMMONWEALTH LAND	$3,521,706	39.97%	$5,288,425	60.03%	$0	0.00%	$8,810,131	11.74%	$4,273,771	24.68%	48.51%
5. UNITED GENERAL	$4,014	0.06%	$6,833,301	99.94%	$0	0.00%	$6,837,315	9.11%	$151,987	0.88%	2.22%
6. FIDELITY NATIONAL	$850,838	13.83%	$5,215,537	84.75%	$87,569	1.42%	$6,153,944	8.20%	$1,407,230	8.13%	22.87%
7. OLD REPUBLIC NATIONAL	$69,130	1.65%	$3,084,071	73.44%	$1,046,411	24.92%	$4,199,612	5.59%	$1,823,650	10.53%	43.42%
8. LAWYERS	$963,010	25.72%	$2,775,694	74.14%	$5,291	0.14%	$3,743,995	4.99%	$729,025	4.21%	19.47%
9. TRANSNATION	$0	0.00%	$3,503,764	99.80%	$6,893	0.20%	$3,510,657	4.68%	$1,298,193	7.50%	36.98%
10. LAND TIC (ST LOUIS)	$0	0.00%	$2,173,014	100.00%	$0	0.00%	$2,173,014	2.90%	$0	--	--
11. GUARANTEE	$0	0.00%	$1,118,587	74.26%	$387,803	25.74%	$1,506,390	2.01%	$1,011,385	5.84%	67.14%
12. TICOR (FL)	$0	0.00%	$1,250,066	100.00%	$0	0.00%	$1,250,066	1.67%	$302,086	1.74%	24.17%
13. FARMERS NATIONAL	$0	0.00%	$1,138,404	100.00%	$0	0.00%	$1,138,404	1.52%	$63,819	0.37%	5.61%
14. TICOR	$36,811	3.30%	$1,079,026	96.70%	$0	0.00%	$1,115,837	1.49%	$151,075	0.87%	13.54%
15. NATIONAL OF NY	$698,400	100.00%	$0	0.00%	$0	0.00%	$698,400	0.93%	$0	--	--
16. SECURITY UNION	$750	0.13%	$594,271	99.87%	$0	0.00%	$595,021	0.79%	$361,596	2.09%	60.77%
17. COMMERCE	$0	0.00%	$0	0.00%	$322,242	100.00%	$322,242	0.43%	$0	--	--
18. NATIONAL LAND	$0	0.00%	$177,820	100.00%	$0	0.00%	$177,820	0.24%	$0	--	--
19. INVESTORS TIC	$0	0.00%	$140,569	86.83%	$21,324	13.17%	$161,893	0.22%	$803	0.00%	0.50%
20. CENSTAR	$0	0.00%	$141,144	100.00%	$0	0.00%	$141,144	0.19%	$0	--	--
21. AMERICAN GUARANTY	$275	37.67%	$455	62.33%	$0	0.00%	$730	0.00%	$0	--	--
COMPOSITE	**$10,539,960**	14.04%	**$58,465,644**	77.89%	**$6,055,123**	8.07%	**$75,060,727**	**100.00%**	**$17,314,789**	**100.00%**	**23.07%**
AVERAGE	**$501,903**		**$2,784,078**		**$288,339**		**$3,574,320**		**$824,514**		

MONTANA

	DIRECT	% of Total	NON-AFFILIATED	% of Total	AFFILIATED	% of Total	TOTAL	PERCENT OF JURISDICTION	PAID LOSSES	PERCENT OF JURISDICTION	LOSSES TO PREMIUMS
1. FIRST AMERICAN TIC	$470,409	2.00%	$12,917,801	55.05%	$10,075,665	42.94%	$23,463,875	43.08%	$761,207	47.05%	3.24%
2. STEWART TGC	$10,786	0.12%	$3,450,887	39.85%	$5,197,724	60.02%	$8,659,397	15.90%	$226,173	13.98%	2.61%
3. CHICAGO TIC	$3,194,940	42.82%	$4,266,801	57.18%	$0	0.00%	$7,461,741	13.70%	$366,807	22.67%	4.92%
4. COMMONWEALTH LAND	$4,501	0.09%	$5,249,896	99.91%	$0	0.00%	$5,254,397	9.65%	$70,881	4.38%	1.35%
5. TICOR	$12,975	0.44%	$2,966,095	99.56%	$0	0.00%	$2,979,070	5.47%	$3,071	0.19%	0.10%
6. LAWYERS	$425,715	15.45%	$2,328,059	84.49%	$1,754	0.06%	$2,755,528	5.06%	$31,633	1.96%	1.15%
7. OLD REPUBLIC NATIONAL	$20,793	1.40%	$1,464,886	98.60%	$0	0.00%	$1,485,679	2.73%	$12,433	0.77%	0.84%
8. FIDELITY NATIONAL	$227,607	16.72%	$1,133,309	83.28%	$0	0.00%	$1,360,916	2.50%	$128,380	7.94%	9.43%
9. TRANSNATION	($1,480)	(0.28)%	$538,329	100.28%	$0	0.00%	$536,849	0.99%	$0	--	--
10. UNITED GENERAL	$892	0.27%	$324,352	98.72%	$3,328	1.01%	$328,572	0.60%	$0	--	--
11. NATIONAL LAND	$0	0.00%	$121,482	100.00%	$0	0.00%	$121,482	0.22%	$0	--	--
12. TICOR (FL)	$0	0.00%	$52,941	100.00%	$0	0.00%	$52,941	0.10%	$0	--	--
13. SECURITY UNION	$1,282	100.00%	$0	0.00%	$0	0.00%	$1,282	0.00%	$17,222	1.06%	1,343.37%
COMPOSITE	**$4,368,420**	8.02%	**$34,814,838**	63.93%	**$15,278,471**	28.05%	**$54,461,729**	**100.00%**	**$1,617,807**	**100.00%**	**2.97%**
AVERAGE	**$336,032**		**$2,678,064**		**$1,175,267**		**$4,189,364**		**$124,447**		

NEBRASKA

	DIRECT	% of Total	NON-AFFILIATED	% of Total	AFFILIATED	% of Total	TOTAL	PERCENT OF JURISDICTION	PAID LOSSES	PERCENT OF JURISDICTION	LOSSES TO PREMIUMS
1. OLD REPUBLIC NATIONAL	$33,496	0.32%	$10,356,291	99.68%	$0	0.00%	$10,389,787	26.71%	$136,282	6.86%	1.31%
2. FIRST AMERICAN TIC	$748,472	9.18%	$5,379,457	65.97%	$2,025,866	24.85%	$8,153,795	20.96%	$176,620	8.90%	2.17%
3. COMMONWEALTH LAND	$8,925	0.17%	$5,204,939	99.83%	$0	0.00%	$5,213,864	13.41%	$136,319	6.87%	2.61%
4. CHICAGO TIC	$143,604	2.89%	$4,820,708	97.11%	$0	0.00%	$4,964,312	12.76%	$201,665	10.16%	4.06%
5. LAWYERS	$179,083	7.75%	$2,131,699	92.25%	$0	0.00%	$2,310,782	5.94%	$742,086	37.38%	32.11%
6. STEWART TGC	$124,603	6.50%	$1,774,815	92.62%	$16,803	0.88%	$1,916,221	4.93%	$134,716	6.79%	7.03%
7. FIDELITY NATIONAL	$19,368	1.11%	$1,729,874	98.89%	$0	0.00%	$1,749,242	4.50%	$382,419	19.26%	21.86%
8. TICOR	$5,218	0.49%	$1,063,248	99.51%	$0	0.00%	$1,068,466	2.75%	$86,466	4.36%	8.09%
9. UNITED GENERAL	$2,683	0.26%	$1,036,146	99.74%	$0	0.00%	$1,038,829	2.67%	$37,529	1.89%	3.61%
10. INVESTORS TIC	$204,455	28.15%	$521,962	71.85%	$0	0.00%	$726,417	1.87%	($54,485)	(2.74)%	(7.50)%
11. TICOR (FL)	$0	0.00%	$704,217	100.00%	$0	0.00%	$704,217	1.81%	$5,070	0.26%	0.72%
12. SECURITY UNION	$601	0.16%	$377,334	99.84%	$0	0.00%	$377,935	0.97%	$0	--	--
13. TRANSNATION	$366	0.20%	$181,736	99.80%	$0	0.00%	$182,102	0.47%	$536	0.03%	0.29%
14. DAKOTA HOMESTEAD	$0	0.00%	$87,386	100.00%	$0	0.00%	$87,386	0.22%	$0	--	--
15. WESTCOR	$0	0.00%	$9,362	100.00%	$0	0.00%	$9,362	0.02%	$0	--	--
COMPOSITE	**$1,470,874**	3.78%	**$35,379,174**	90.97%	**$2,042,669**	5.25%	**$38,892,717**	**100.00%**	**$1,985,223**	**100.00%**	**5.10%**
AVERAGE	**$98,058**		**$2,358,612**		**$136,178**		**$2,592,848**		**$132,348**		

C.2 Jurisdiction - By Individual Underwriter

	DIRECT PREMIUMS WRITTEN						PERCENT OF JURISDICTION	PAID LOSSES	PERCENT OF JURISDICTION	LOSSES TO PREMIUMS
	DIRECT	% of Total	NON-AFFILIATED	% of Total	AFFILIATED	% of Total	TOTAL			

NEVADA

	DIRECT	% of Total	NON-AFFILIATED	% of Total	AFFILIATED	% of Total	TOTAL	PERCENT OF JURISDICTION	PAID LOSSES	PERCENT OF JURISDICTION	LOSSES TO PREMIUMS
1. FIRST AMERICAN TIC	$36,943,330	61.03%	$22,774,768	37.62%	$819,647	1.35%	$60,537,745	28.35%	$1,698,214	17.37%	2.81%
2. CHICAGO TIC	$4,291,908	12.01%	$15,081,872	42.19%	$16,372,175	45.80%	$35,745,955	16.74%	$1,711,860	17.51%	4.79%
3. COMMONWEALTH LAND	$4,056,529	18.92%	$17,342,649	80.87%	$46,387	0.22%	$21,445,565	10.04%	$1,103,281	11.29%	5.14%
4. LAWYERS	$3,886,279	19.13%	$6,442,142	31.71%	$9,985,089	49.15%	$20,313,510	9.51%	$1,762,430	18.03%	8.68%
5. STEWART TGC	$1,219,137	6.45%	$5,094,523	26.96%	$12,580,498	66.58%	$18,894,158	8.85%	$408,850	4.18%	2.16%
6. FIDELITY NATIONAL	$568,903	3.74%	$3,996,920	26.25%	$10,663,202	70.02%	$15,229,025	7.13%	$1,278,630	13.08%	8.40%
7. TICOR	$74,549	0.57%	$272,455	2.10%	$12,655,098	97.33%	$13,002,102	6.09%	$634,605	6.49%	4.88%
8. WESTCOR	$0	0.00%	$35,531	0.34%	$10,264,965	99.66%	$10,300,496	4.82%	$259,294	2.65%	2.52%
9. OLD REPUBLIC NATIONAL	$277,776	3.69%	$3,730,514	49.56%	$3,519,312	46.75%	$7,527,602	3.53%	$35,726	0.37%	0.47%
10. NORTH AMERICAN	$0	0.00%	$0	0.00%	$3,313,273	100.00%	$3,313,273	1.55%	$95,241	0.97%	2.87%
11. UNITED GENERAL	$79,117	2.59%	$2,670,963	87.31%	$309,000	10.10%	$3,059,080	1.43%	$261,949	2.68%	8.56%
12. UNITED CAPITAL	$0	0.00%	$0	0.00%	$2,554,913	100.00%	$2,554,913	1.20%	$514,222	5.26%	20.13%
13. COMMERCE	$0	0.00%	$0	0.00%	$1,366,533	100.00%	$1,366,533	0.64%	$87	0.00%	0.00%
14. TRANSNATION	$57,446	49.13%	$59,476	50.87%	$0	0.00%	$116,922	0.05%	$3,088	0.03%	2.64%
15. TICOR (FL)	$0	0.00%	$91,471	100.00%	$0	0.00%	$91,471	0.04%	$0	--	--
16. SECURITY UNION	$13,952	100.00%	$0	0.00%	$0	0.00%	$13,952	0.00%	$0	--	--
17. TRANSUNION NATIONAL	$0	0.00%	$0	0.00%	$8,651	100.00%	$8,651	0.00%	$0	--	--
18. AMERICAN GUARANTY	$2,746	100.00%	$0	0.00%	$0	0.00%	$2,746	0.00%	$0	--	--
19. NATIONAL OF NY	$0	--	$0	--	$0	--	$0	--	$6,450	0.07%	--
COMPOSITE	**$51,471,672**	24.11%	**$77,593,284**	36.34%	**$84,458,743**	39.55%	**$213,523,699**	**100.00%**	**$9,773,927**	**100.00%**	**4.58%**
AVERAGE	**$2,709,035**		**$4,083,857**		**$4,445,197**		**$11,238,089**		**$514,417**		

NEW HAMPSHIRE

	DIRECT	% of Total	NON-AFFILIATED	% of Total	AFFILIATED	% of Total	TOTAL	PERCENT OF JURISDICTION	PAID LOSSES	PERCENT OF JURISDICTION	LOSSES TO PREMIUMS
1. FIRST AMERICAN TIC	$493,382	3.72%	$12,242,719	92.23%	$537,314	4.05%	$13,273,415	38.40%	$737,003	23.00%	5.55%
2. CHICAGO TIC	$187,123	3.52%	$5,135,840	96.48%	$0	0.00%	$5,322,963	15.40%	$975,043	30.43%	18.32%
3. STEWART TGC	$198,834	4.62%	$3,133,150	72.74%	$975,175	22.64%	$4,307,159	12.46%	$369,323	11.53%	8.57%
4. COMMONWEALTH LAND	$274,092	8.38%	$2,995,187	91.62%	$0	0.00%	$3,269,279	9.46%	$207,466	6.47%	6.35%
5. OLD REPUBLIC NATIONAL	$266,056	9.72%	$2,471,937	90.28%	$0	0.00%	$2,737,993	7.92%	$254,458	7.94%	9.29%
6. LAWYERS	$767,944	30.96%	$1,712,303	69.04%	$0	0.00%	$2,480,247	7.18%	$97,751	3.05%	3.94%
7. TRANSNATION	$0	0.00%	$1,104,954	100.00%	$0	0.00%	$1,104,954	3.20%	$43,568	1.36%	3.94%
8. FIDELITY NATIONAL	$40,499	5.03%	$763,892	94.97%	$0	0.00%	$804,391	2.33%	$110,882	3.46%	13.78%
9. UNITED GENERAL	$1,080	0.19%	$566,455	99.81%	$0	0.00%	$567,535	1.64%	$1,950	0.06%	0.34%
10. CT ATTORNEYS	$0	0.00%	$402,407	100.00%	$0	0.00%	$402,407	1.16%	$405	0.01%	0.10%
11. TICOR (FL)	$0	0.00%	$212,697	100.00%	$0	0.00%	$212,697	0.62%	$190,510	5.95%	89.57%
12. TICOR	$8,050	9.59%	$75,851	90.41%	$0	0.00%	$83,901	0.24%	$216,143	6.74%	257.62%
COMPOSITE	**$2,237,060**	6.47%	**$30,817,392**	89.15%	**$1,512,489**	4.38%	**$34,566,941**	**100.00%**	**$3,204,502**	**100.00%**	**9.27%**
AVERAGE	**$186,422**		**$2,568,116**		**$126,041**		**$2,880,578**		**$267,042**		

NEW JERSEY

	DIRECT	% of Total	NON-AFFILIATED	% of Total	AFFILIATED	% of Total	TOTAL	PERCENT OF JURISDICTION	PAID LOSSES	PERCENT OF JURISDICTION	LOSSES TO PREMIUMS
1. FIRST AMERICAN TIC	$14,272,328	16.27%	$70,772,352	80.67%	$2,683,572	3.06%	$87,728,252	18.53%	$7,998,306	24.81%	9.12%
2. CHICAGO TIC	$15,975,802	22.47%	$55,116,962	77.53%	$0	0.00%	$71,092,764	15.02%	$5,479,165	17.00%	7.71%
3. STEWART TGC	$1,946,301	3.09%	$55,021,124	87.39%	$5,995,111	9.52%	$62,962,536	13.30%	$3,356,654	10.41%	5.33%
4. FIDELITY NATIONAL	$16,019,974	31.65%	$34,283,970	67.73%	$315,930	0.62%	$50,619,874	10.69%	$3,205,750	9.95%	6.33%
5. OLD REPUBLIC NATIONAL	$916,762	2.16%	$40,652,727	95.94%	$803,284	1.90%	$42,372,773	8.95%	$6,681,055	20.73%	15.77%
6. LAWYERS	$8,062,949	20.26%	$31,691,588	79.63%	$43,744	0.11%	$39,798,281	8.41%	$2,931,896	9.10%	7.37%
7. COMMONWEALTH LAND (NJ)	$5,109,506	14.44%	$30,277,935	85.56%	$0	0.00%	$35,387,441	7.47%	$1,845,407	5.73%	5.21%
8. UNITED GENERAL	$13,618	0.07%	$18,253,583	99.93%	$0	0.00%	$18,267,201	3.86%	$761,062	2.36%	4.17%
9. NEW JERSEY TIC	$0	0.00%	$16,413,857	100.00%	$0	0.00%	$16,413,857	3.47%	$1,064,324	3.30%	6.48%
10. COMMONWEALTH LAND	$6,264,390	40.81%	$9,086,783	59.19%	$0	0.00%	$15,351,173	3.24%	$1,471,330	4.56%	9.58%
11. TICOR	$272,784	2.85%	$9,307,277	97.15%	$0	0.00%	$9,580,061	2.02%	($3,519,133)	(10.92)%	(36.73)%
12. TRANSNATION	$821	0.01%	$6,847,935	99.99%	$0	0.00%	$6,848,756	1.45%	$521,063	1.62%	7.61%
13. TITLE RESOURCES	$0	0.00%	$0	0.00%	$5,516,811	100.00%	$5,516,811	1.17%	$0	--	--
14. CENSTAR	$0	0.00%	$5,150,323	100.00%	$0	0.00%	$5,150,323	1.09%	$17,567	0.05%	0.34%
15. TICOR (FL)	$0	0.00%	$3,293,530	100.00%	$0	0.00%	$3,293,530	0.70%	$56,346	0.17%	1.71%
16. T.A. TITLE	$0	0.00%	$1,899,014	81.33%	$435,971	18.67%	$2,334,985	0.49%	$0	--	--
17. NORTH AMERICAN	$0	0.00%	$0	0.00%	$339,499	100.00%	$339,499	0.07%	$0	--	--
18. CONESTOGA	$4,985	2.49%	$195,417	97.51%	$0	0.00%	$200,402	0.04%	$2,753	0.00%	1.37%
19. SECURITY TG (BALTIMORE)	$0	0.00%	$162,389	100.00%	$0	0.00%	$162,389	0.03%	$10,915	0.03%	6.72%
20. SECURITY UNION	$9,986	100.00%	$0	0.00%	$0	0.00%	$9,986	0.00%	$68,695	0.21%	687.91%
21. AMERICAN GUARANTY	$716	100.00%	$0	0.00%	$0	0.00%	$716	0.00%	$0	--	--
22. NATIONS OF NY	$0	--	$0	--	$0	--	$0	--	$277,691	0.86%	--
23. SOUTHERN TI CORP	$0	--	$0	--	$0	--	$0	--	$899	0.00%	--
COMPOSITE	**$68,870,922**	14.55%	**$388,426,766**	82.04%	**$16,133,922**	3.41%	**$473,431,610**	**100.00%**	**$32,231,745**	**100.00%**	**6.81%**
AVERAGE	**$2,994,388**		**$16,888,120**		**$701,475**		**$20,583,983**		**$1,401,380**		

3

C.2 Jurisdiction - By Individual Underwriter

	DIRECT PREMIUMS WRITTEN						TOTAL	PERCENT OF JURISDICTION	PAID LOSSES	PERCENT OF JURISDICTION	LOSSES TO PREMIUMS
	DIRECT	% of Total	NON-AFFILIATED	% of Total	AFFILIATED	% of Total					
NEW MEXICO											
1. FIRST AMERICAN TIC	$15,095,992	52.07%	$11,363,295	39.19%	$2,534,998	8.74%	$28,994,285	25.60%	$1,357,848	28.24%	4.68%
2. LAWYERS	$6,499,982	29.66%	$14,327,735	65.38%	$1,087,239	4.96%	$21,914,956	19.35%	$1,012,193	21.05%	4.62%
3. FIDELITY NATIONAL	$13,407,110	67.09%	$6,517,176	32.61%	$58,275	0.29%	$19,982,561	17.64%	$792,101	16.47%	3.96%
4. COMMONWEALTH LAND	$2,940,147	16.82%	$5,596,987	32.02%	$8,940,467	51.15%	$17,477,601	15.43%	$408,688	8.50%	2.34%
5. STEWART TGC	$0	0.00%	$3,341,414	25.99%	$9,513,136	74.01%	$12,854,550	11.35%	$156,780	3.26%	1.22%
6. CHICAGO TIC	$280,111	5.44%	$4,873,672	94.56%	$0	0.00%	$5,153,783	4.55%	$312,259	6.49%	6.06%
7. UNITED GENERAL	$75,315	2.87%	$2,549,874	97.13%	$0	0.00%	$2,625,189	2.32%	$396,354	8.24%	15.10%
8. OLD REPUBLIC NATIONAL	$0	0.00%	$2,175,598	100.00%	$0	0.00%	$2,175,598	1.92%	$168,838	3.51%	7.76%
9. COMMERCE	$0	0.00%	$0	0.00%	$724,207	100.00%	$724,207	0.64%	$0	--	--
10. TICOR	$13,863	1.96%	$693,547	98.04%	$0	0.00%	$707,410	0.62%	$187,245	3.89%	26.47%
11. TRANSNATION	($929)	(0.32)%	$291,612	100.32%	$0	0.00%	$290,683	0.26%	$990	0.02%	0.34%
12. TITLE IC AMERICA	$0	0.00%	$264,573	100.00%	$0	0.00%	$264,573	0.23%	($43,333)	(0.90)%	(16.38)%
13. SECURITY UNION	$0	0.00%	$54,921	100.00%	$0	0.00%	$54,921	0.05%	$0	--	--
14. ALAMO	$0	0.00%	$52,471	100.00%	$0	0.00%	$52,471	0.05%	$4,301	0.09%	8.20%
15. TITLE RESOURCES	$0	--	$0	--	$0	--	$0	--	$54,397	1.13%	--
COMPOSITE	$38,311,591	33.82%	$52,102,875	46.00%	$22,858,322	20.18%	$113,272,788	100.00%	$4,808,661	100.00%	4.25%
AVERAGE	$2,554,106		$3,473,525		$1,523,888		$7,551,519		$320,577		
NEW YORK											
1. FIRST AMERICAN (NY)	$96,485,318	40.33%	$131,671,357	55.03%	$11,099,012	4.64%	$239,255,687	20.38%	$8,776,026	18.03%	3.67%
2. COMMONWEALTH LAND	$56,727,723	28.45%	$142,664,825	71.55%	$0	0.00%	$199,392,548	16.98%	$5,413,757	11.12%	2.72%
3. STEWART TIC	$38,951,627	24.01%	$121,926,620	75.15%	$1,373,640	0.85%	$162,251,887	13.82%	$4,872,945	10.01%	3.00%
4. FIDELITY NATIONAL	$65,349,635	46.33%	$75,450,351	53.49%	$243,390	0.17%	$141,043,376	12.01%	$8,160,557	16.76%	5.79%
5. CHICAGO TIC	$48,938,111	44.38%	$61,336,854	55.62%	$0	0.00%	$110,274,965	9.39%	$5,227,538	10.74%	4.74%
6. LAWYERS	$44,155,351	43.74%	$56,708,272	56.18%	$83,902	0.08%	$100,947,525	8.60%	$1,442,840	2.96%	1.43%
7. OLD REPUBLIC NATIONAL	$316,532	0.43%	$67,876,078	92.30%	$5,343,542	7.27%	$73,536,152	6.26%	$4,345,925	8.93%	5.91%
8. UNITED GENERAL	$10,353	0.02%	$58,260,082	99.98%	$0	0.00%	$58,270,435	4.96%	$3,954,394	8.12%	6.79%
9. TICOR	$14,077,947	29.00%	$34,121,517	70.28%	$351,088	0.72%	$48,550,552	4.13%	$2,493,862	5.12%	5.14%
10. WASHINGTON TIC	$172,102	1.10%	$12,559,065	80.38%	$2,893,006	18.52%	$15,624,173	1.33%	$422,819	0.87%	2.71%
11. MONROE	$5,556,612	42.75%	$7,075,703	54.44%	$364,364	2.80%	$12,996,679	1.11%	$144,923	0.30%	1.12%
12. TICOR (FL)	$0	0.00%	$4,570,975	100.00%	$0	0.00%	$4,570,975	0.39%	$2,406,377	4.94%	52.64%
13. CONESTOGA	$0	0.00%	$2,480,602	100.00%	$0	0.00%	$2,480,602	0.21%	$109,306	0.22%	4.41%
14. NORTHEAST INVESTORS	$0	0.00%	$2,414,626	100.00%	$0	0.00%	$2,414,626	0.21%	$154,328	0.32%	6.39%
15. T.A. TITLE	$0	0.00%	$2,077,547	87.92%	$285,442	12.08%	$2,362,989	0.20%	$0	--	--
16. TITLEDGE	$78,917	43.46%	$102,655	56.54%	$0	0.00%	$181,572	0.02%	$0	--	--
17. TRANSNATION	$2,019	100.00%	$0	0.00%	$0	0.00%	$2,019	0.00%	$0	--	--
18. NATIONAL OF NY	$0	--	$0	--	$0	--	$0	--	$664,227	1.36%	--
19. NATIONS OF NY	$0	--	$0	--	$0	--	$0	--	$87,767	0.18%	--
COMPOSITE	$370,822,247	31.58%	$781,297,129	66.54%	$22,037,386	1.88%	$1,174,156,762	100.00%	$48,677,591	100.00%	4.15%
AVERAGE	$19,516,960		$41,120,902		$1,159,862		$61,797,724		$2,561,978		
NORTH CAROLINA											
1. INVESTORS TIC	$29,147,893	85.06%	$2,032,474	5.93%	$3,085,949	9.01%	$34,266,316	19.29%	$7,786,658	35.03%	22.72%
2. UNITED GENERAL	$7,715,440	23.91%	$24,555,193	76.09%	$0	0.00%	$32,270,633	18.16%	$350,955	1.58%	1.09%
3. CHICAGO TIC	$306,610	1.01%	$30,004,341	98.99%	$0	0.00%	$30,310,951	17.06%	$3,302,348	14.86%	10.89%
4. FIRST AMERICAN TIC	$1,095,332	4.24%	$24,537,244	95.01%	$192,851	0.75%	$25,825,427	14.54%	$3,071,533	13.82%	11.89%
5. STEWART TGC	$1,721,235	13.25%	$10,176,438	78.34%	$1,092,468	8.41%	$12,990,141	7.31%	$1,646,435	7.41%	12.67%
6. FIDELITY NATIONAL	$10,172,201	80.88%	$2,142,080	17.03%	$263,320	2.09%	$12,577,601	7.08%	$1,925,804	8.66%	15.31%
7. LAWYERS	$5,209,068	45.88%	$6,140,926	54.09%	$3,374	0.03%	$11,353,368	6.39%	$1,284,581	5.78%	11.31%
8. OLD REPUBLIC NATIONAL	$22,624	0.21%	$1,245,737	11.83%	$9,260,435	87.95%	$10,528,796	5.93%	$1,122,735	5.05%	10.66%
9. SOUTHERN TI CORP	$106	0.00%	$2,774,562	100.00%	$0	0.00%	$2,774,668	1.56%	$3,712	0.02%	0.13%
10. TRANSNATION	$120	0.01%	$1,517,212	99.99%	$0	0.00%	$1,517,332	0.85%	$37,880	0.17%	2.50%
11. TICOR (FL)	$0	0.00%	$1,394,889	100.00%	$0	0.00%	$1,394,889	0.79%	$204,655	0.92%	14.67%
12. TICOR	$39,611	6.37%	$582,020	93.63%	$0	0.00%	$621,631	0.35%	$240,144	1.08%	38.63%
13. COMMONWEALTH LAND	$345,083	57.13%	$258,544	42.81%	$365	0.06%	$603,992	0.34%	$1,087,747	4.89%	180.09%
14. ATTORNEYS TIF (FL)	$0	0.00%	$416,568	100.00%	$0	0.00%	$416,568	0.23%	$0	--	--
15. TRANSUNION NATIONAL	$210	0.12%	$0	0.00%	$171,167	99.88%	$171,377	0.10%	$110,277	0.50%	64.35%
16. SECURITY UNION	$1,295	4.11%	$30,232	95.89%	$0	0.00%	$31,527	0.02%	$51,949	0.23%	164.78%
17. BRIDGE	$0	--	$0	--	$0	--	$0	--	$1,321	0.00%	--
COMPOSITE	$55,776,828	31.40%	$107,808,460	60.68%	$14,069,929	7.92%	$177,655,217	100.00%	$22,228,734	100.00%	12.51%
AVERAGE	$3,280,990		$6,341,674		$827,643		$10,450,307		$1,307,573		
NORTH DAKOTA											
1. FIRST AMERICAN TIC	$276,946	17.86%	$1,126,434	72.65%	$147,045	9.48%	$1,550,425	26.85%	$21,483	23.29%	1.39%
2. STEWART TGC	$14,770	1.24%	$1,176,170	98.76%	$0	0.00%	$1,190,940	20.63%	$4,634	5.02%	0.39%
3. CHICAGO TIC	$2,145	0.23%	$947,504	99.77%	$0	0.00%	$949,649	16.45%	$13,312	14.43%	1.40%
4. OLD REPUBLIC NATIONAL	$50	0.01%	$761,993	99.99%	$0	0.00%	$762,043	13.20%	$0	--	--
5. COMMONWEALTH LAND	$49,187	8.95%	$500,110	91.05%	$0	0.00%	$549,297	9.51%	$48,357	52.42%	8.80%
6. FIDELITY NATIONAL	$6,514	2.62%	$242,277	97.38%	$0	0.00%	$248,791	4.31%	$1,550	1.68%	0.62%
7. LAWYERS	$21,631	12.23%	$155,175	87.77%	$0	0.00%	$176,806	3.06%	$2,916	3.16%	1.65%
8. ATTORNEYS TIF (FL)	$0	0.00%	$169,925	100.00%	$0	0.00%	$169,925	2.94%	$0	--	--
9. TICOR	$6,835	4.88%	$133,189	95.12%	$0	0.00%	$140,024	2.43%	$0	--	--
10. UNITED GENERAL	$982	3.08%	$30,895	96.92%	$0	0.00%	$31,877	0.55%	$0	--	--
11. TICOR (FL)	$0	0.00%	$4,402	100.00%	$0	0.00%	$4,402	0.08%	$0	--	--
COMPOSITE	$379,060	6.56%	$5,248,074	90.89%	$147,045	2.55%	$5,774,179	100.00%	$92,252	100.00%	1.60%
AVERAGE	$34,460		$477,098		$13,368		$524,925		$8,387		

3

C.2 Jurisdiction - By Individual Underwriter

	DIRECT	% of Total	NON-AFFILIATED	% of Total	AFFILIATED	% of Total	TOTAL	PERCENT OF JURISDICTION	PAID LOSSES	PERCENT OF JURISDICTION	LOSSES TO PREMIUMS
OHIO											
1. FIRST AMERICAN TIC	$6,830,001	6.87%	$74,063,983	74.49%	$18,536,223	18.64%	$99,430,207	27.92%	$6,086,363	23.30%	6.12%
2. CHICAGO TIC	$20,560,024	29.27%	$45,464,830	64.73%	$4,215,915	6.00%	$70,240,769	19.72%	$2,444,431	9.36%	3.48%
3. STEWART TGC	$1,967,484	5.41%	$23,777,168	65.36%	$10,636,676	29.24%	$36,381,328	10.21%	$3,441,447	13.17%	9.46%
4. LAWYERS	$12,208,600	35.38%	$19,113,853	55.39%	$3,183,624	9.23%	$34,506,077	9.69%	$2,948,018	11.29%	8.54%
5. OLD REPUBLIC NATIONAL	$691,378	2.02%	$32,967,860	96.48%	$510,948	1.50%	$34,170,186	9.59%	$3,720,465	14.24%	10.89%
6. COMMONWEALTH LAND	$1,962,441	8.70%	$20,103,779	89.16%	$481,917	2.14%	$22,548,137	6.33%	$1,855,239	7.10%	8.23%
7. OHIO BAR	$0	0.00%	$12,878,476	100.00%	$0	0.00%	$12,878,476	3.62%	$1,630,114	6.24%	12.66%
8. FIDELITY NATIONAL	$2,334,258	21.35%	$8,146,110	74.52%	$451,240	4.13%	$10,931,608	3.07%	$1,137,370	4.35%	10.40%
9. PORT LAWRENCE	$2,836,725	50.74%	$2,437,031	43.59%	$316,748	5.67%	$5,590,504	1.57%	$99,717	0.38%	1.78%
10. TRANSNATION	$552,683	12.10%	$4,013,524	87.85%	$2,208	0.05%	$4,568,415	1.28%	$75,142	0.29%	1.64%
11. GUARDIAN NATIONAL	$0	0.00%	$3,445,031	88.93%	$428,862	11.07%	$3,873,893	1.09%	$283,171	1.08%	7.31%
12. SECURITY UNION	$3,690	0.12%	$2,970,291	99.88%	$0	0.00%	$2,973,981	0.84%	$157,660	0.60%	5.30%
13. UNITED GENERAL	$6,416	0.22%	$2,942,592	99.78%	$0	0.00%	$2,949,008	0.83%	$522,512	2.00%	17.72%
14. TICOR	$117,134	4.08%	$2,755,074	95.92%	$0	0.00%	$2,872,208	0.81%	$593,227	2.27%	20.65%
15. GENERAL T&T	$0	0.00%	$2,509,539	90.40%	$266,652	9.60%	$2,776,191	0.78%	$418,464	1.60%	15.07%
16. CONESTOGA	$0	0.00%	$2,235,748	100.00%	$0	0.00%	$2,235,748	0.63%	$181,514	0.69%	8.12%
17. TICOR (FL)	$0	0.00%	$2,018,384	100.00%	$0	0.00%	$2,018,384	0.57%	$225,802	0.86%	11.19%
18. GUARANTEE T&T	$186,780	10.48%	$472,033	26.48%	$1,123,621	63.04%	$1,782,434	0.50%	$204,968	0.78%	11.50%
19. SOUTHERN TI CORP	$0	0.00%	$469,922	31.02%	$1,045,069	68.98%	$1,514,991	0.43%	($596)	(0.04)%	(0.04)%
20. TRANSUNION NATIONAL	$33,035	4.78%	$617,640	89.44%	$39,893	5.78%	$690,568	0.19%	$6,524	0.02%	0.94%
21. CENSTAR	$0	0.00%	$339,072	100.00%	$0	0.00%	$339,072	0.10%	$0	--	--
22. COMMERCE	$0	0.00%	$0	0.00%	$275,558	100.00%	$275,558	0.08%	$0	--	--
23. NATIONAL LAND	$0	0.00%	$186,348	100.00%	$0	0.00%	$186,348	0.05%	$56,268	0.22%	30.20%
24. SEAGATE	$186,090	100.00%	$0	0.00%	$0	0.00%	$186,090	0.05%	$0	--	--
25. INVESTORS TIC	$0	0.00%	$141,259	100.00%	$0	0.00%	$141,259	0.04%	$0	--	--
26. SECURITY TG (BALTIMORE)	$0	0.00%	$89,742	100.00%	$0	0.00%	$89,742	0.03%	$12,012	0.05%	13.39%
27. T.A. TITLE	$0	0.00%	$3,170	66.81%	$1,575	33.19%	$4,745	0.00%	$0	--	--
28. AMERICAN GUARANTY	$750	55.76%	$595	44.24%	$0	0.00%	$1,345	0.00%	$0	--	--
29. OLYMPIC	$0	--	$0	--	$0	--	$0	--	$16,293	0.06%	--
30. NATIONS OF NY	$0	--	$0	--	$0	--	$0	--	$2,871	0.01%	--
31. NATIONAL OF NY	$0	--	$0	--	$0	--	$0	--	$2,554	0.00%	--
COMPOSITE	**$50,477,489**	14.17%	**$264,163,054**	74.17%	**$41,516,729**	11.66%	**$356,157,272**	100.00%	**$26,121,550**	100.00%	7.33%
AVERAGE	**$1,628,306**		**$8,521,389**		**$1,339,249**		**$11,488,944**		**$842,631**		
OKLAHOMA											
1. FIRST AMERICAN TIC	$872,833	5.35%	$13,410,135	82.16%	$2,039,357	12.49%	$16,322,325	26.10%	$338,975	20.81%	2.08%
2. CHICAGO TIC	$26,599	0.34%	$1,360,037	17.15%	$6,542,605	82.51%	$7,929,241	12.68%	$391,717	24.05%	4.94%
3. FIRST AMERICAN T&T	$6,291,430	100.00%	$0	0.00%	$0	0.00%	$6,291,430	10.06%	$158,178	9.71%	2.51%
4. STEWART TGC	$66,879	1.10%	$2,601,403	42.97%	$3,385,667	55.92%	$6,053,949	9.68%	($85,877)	(5.27)%	(1.42)%
5. LAWYERS	$69,439	1.35%	$5,064,167	98.65%	$0	0.00%	$5,133,606	8.21%	$29,774	1.83%	0.58%
6. FIDELITY NATIONAL	$80,512	1.95%	$3,246,334	78.60%	$803,228	19.45%	$4,130,074	6.60%	$301,868	18.53%	7.31%
7. AMERICAN GUARANTY	$0	0.00%	$495,585	14.52%	$2,917,327	85.48%	$3,412,912	5.46%	$75,291	4.62%	2.21%
8. AMERICAN EAGLE	$1,906,376	62.52%	$1,142,793	37.48%	$0	0.00%	$3,049,169	4.87%	$48,338	2.97%	1.59%
9. AMERICAN SECURITY	$0	0.00%	$2,940,198	100.00%	$0	0.00%	$2,940,198	4.70%	$2,283	0.14%	0.08%
10. COMMONWEALTH LAND	$12,788	0.86%	$1,482,676	99.14%	$0	0.00%	$1,495,464	2.39%	$63,602	3.91%	4.25%
11. FIRST AMERICAN TRANS	$0	0.00%	$1,326,322	100.00%	$0	0.00%	$1,326,322	2.12%	$3,937	0.24%	0.30%
12. TICOR	$300	0.03%	$1,133,852	99.97%	$0	0.00%	$1,134,152	1.81%	$72,662	4.46%	6.41%
13. UNITED GENERAL	$0	0.00%	$989,456	100.00%	$0	0.00%	$989,456	1.58%	$37,700	2.31%	3.81%
14. GUARANTEE	$0	0.00%	$0	0.00%	$683,390	100.00%	$683,390	1.09%	$0	--	--
15. AMERICAN LAND & AIRCRAFT	$0	0.00%	$126,906	19.25%	$532,250	80.75%	$659,156	1.05%	$5,858	0.36%	0.89%
16. TICOR (FL)	$0	0.00%	$373,190	100.00%	$0	0.00%	$373,190	0.60%	$142,521	8.75%	38.19%
17. OLD REPUBLIC NATIONAL	$175	0.07%	$160,814	61.04%	$102,474	38.90%	$263,463	0.42%	$6,876	0.42%	2.61%
18. SECURITY UNION	$0	0.00%	$256,272	100.00%	$0	0.00%	$256,272	0.41%	$7,838	0.48%	3.06%
19. TRANSNATION	$0	0.00%	$34,914	33.66%	$68,824	66.34%	$103,738	0.17%	$27,637	1.70%	26.64%
20. TITLE RESOURCES	$0	--	$0	--	$0	--	$0	--	($530)	(0.03)%	--
COMPOSITE	**$9,327,331**	14.91%	**$36,145,054**	57.79%	**$17,075,122**	27.30%	**$62,547,507**	100.00%	**$1,628,648**	100.00%	2.60%
AVERAGE	**$466,367**		**$1,807,253**		**$853,756**		**$3,127,375**		**$81,432**		
OREGON											
1. FIRST AMERICAN (OR)	$42,031,597	79.31%	$10,964,065	20.69%	$0	0.00%	$52,995,662	23.81%	$2,319,341	38.30%	4.38%
2. FIDELITY NATIONAL	$1,085,648	3.40%	$3,180,736	9.95%	$27,690,109	86.65%	$31,956,493	14.36%	$452,632	7.48%	1.42%
3. TICOR	$17,736,886	61.34%	$2,359	0.01%	$11,175,816	38.65%	$28,915,061	12.99%	$602,183	9.95%	2.08%
4. CHICAGO TIC (OR)	$13,707,383	52.15%	$12,576,501	47.85%	$0	0.00%	$26,283,884	11.81%	$504,698	8.34%	1.92%
5. LAWYERS	$19,008,541	87.32%	$2,759,136	12.68%	$0	0.00%	$21,767,677	9.78%	$834,689	13.78%	3.83%
6. TRANSNATION	$415,787	1.98%	$13,061,398	62.17%	$7,532,379	35.85%	$21,009,564	9.44%	$757,141	12.50%	3.60%
7. PACIFIC NORTHWEST	$0	0.00%	$2,204,949	17.43%	$10,442,688	82.57%	$12,647,637	5.68%	$49,200	0.81%	0.39%
8. FIRST AMERICAN TIC	$10,164,143	91.51%	$21,900	0.20%	$921,629	8.30%	$11,107,672	4.99%	$87,380	1.44%	0.79%
9. STEWART (OR)	$567,888	5.26%	$10,237,613	94.74%	$0	0.00%	$10,805,501	4.85%	$167,857	2.77%	1.55%
10. CHICAGO TIC	$491,566	17.71%	$2,283,429	82.29%	$0	0.00%	$2,774,995	1.25%	$142,013	2.35%	5.12%
11. COMMONWEALTH LAND	$937,510	48.52%	$993,036	51.39%	$1,764	0.09%	$1,932,310	0.87%	$34,254	0.57%	1.77%
12. UNITED GENERAL	$169,649	100.00%	$0	0.00%	$0	0.00%	$169,649	0.08%	$0	--	--
13. STEWART TGC	$154,970	100.00%	$0	0.00%	$0	0.00%	$154,970	0.07%	$19,736	0.33%	12.74%
14. OLD REPUBLIC NATIONAL	$0	0.00%	$67,301	100.00%	$0	0.00%	$67,301	0.03%	$0	--	--
15. SECURITY UNION	$0	--	$0	--	$0	--	$0	--	$83,980	1.39%	--
COMPOSITE	**$106,471,568**	47.83%	**$58,352,423**	26.22%	**$57,764,385**	25.95%	**$222,588,376**	100.00%	**$6,055,104**	100.00%	2.72%
AVERAGE	**$7,098,105**		**$3,890,162**		**$3,850,959**		**$14,839,225**		**$403,674**		

C.2 Jurisdiction - By Individual Underwriter

	DIRECT PREMIUMS WRITTEN							PERCENT OF JURISDICTION	PAID LOSSES	PERCENT OF JURISDICTION	LOSSES TO PREMIUMS
	DIRECT	% of Total	NON-AFFILIATED	% of Total	AFFILIATED	% of Total	TOTAL				

PENNSYLVANIA

	DIRECT	% of Total	NON-AFFILIATED	% of Total	AFFILIATED	% of Total	TOTAL	% JURISDICTION	PAID LOSSES	% LOSSES JURISDICTION	LOSSES TO PREMIUMS
1. FIRST AMERICAN TIC	$16,970,290	14.47%	$99,431,006	84.78%	$882,115	0.75%	$117,283,411	22.37%	$3,671,579	15.08%	3.13%
2. LAWYERS	$8,378,894	8.91%	$85,411,192	90.81%	$267,431	0.28%	$94,057,517	17.94%	$4,720,283	19.39%	5.02%
3. COMMONWEALTH LAND	$10,706,572	12.07%	$77,907,313	87.80%	$116,127	0.13%	$88,730,012	16.92%	$2,621,211	10.77%	2.95%
4. CHICAGO TIC	$16,407,906	37.97%	$26,803,885	62.03%	$0	0.00%	$43,211,791	8.24%	$2,343,310	9.63%	5.42%
5. OLD REPUBLIC NATIONAL	$555,244	1.31%	$41,891,870	98.69%	$0	0.00%	$42,447,114	8.10%	$3,091,682	12.70%	7.28%
6. FIDELITY NATIONAL	$4,781,547	11.72%	$35,864,596	87.90%	$154,953	0.38%	$40,801,096	7.78%	$2,348,958	9.65%	5.76%
7. STEWART TGC	$4,146,574	12.18%	$29,560,885	86.86%	$326,776	0.96%	$34,034,235	6.49%	$2,221,328	9.13%	6.53%
8. UNITED GENERAL	$256,724	1.56%	$16,151,439	98.44%	$0	0.00%	$16,408,163	3.13%	$922,514	3.79%	5.62%
9. T.A. TITLE	$0	0.00%	$9,499,282	79.45%	$2,457,720	20.55%	$11,957,002	2.28%	$739,741	3.04%	6.19%
10. TICOR	$249,815	2.88%	$8,414,216	97.12%	$0	0.00%	$8,664,031	1.65%	$789,667	3.24%	9.11%
11. TICOR (FL)	$0	0.00%	$5,114,023	100.00%	$0	0.00%	$5,114,023	0.98%	$220,920	0.91%	4.32%
12. SECURITY TG (BALTIMORE)	$0	0.00%	$4,832,823	99.82%	$8,663	0.18%	$4,841,486	0.92%	$216,590	0.89%	4.47%
13. CENSTAR	$0	0.00%	$4,624,937	100.00%	$0	0.00%	$4,624,937	0.88%	$24,636	0.10%	0.53%
14. CONESTOGA	$117,495	3.12%	$3,345,774	88.95%	$298,189	7.93%	$3,761,458	0.72%	($19,536)	(0.08)%	(0.52)%
15. PENN ATTORNEYS	$1,777,598	100.00%	$0	0.00%	$0	0.00%	$1,777,598	0.34%	$96,020	0.39%	5.40%
16. GUARANTEE T&T	$0	0.00%	$1,100,503	71.62%	$436,169	28.38%	$1,536,672	0.29%	$261,672	1.07%	17.03%
17. INVESTORS TIC	$35,365	2.34%	$1,332,490	88.23%	$142,470	9.43%	$1,510,325	0.29%	$2,325	0.00%	0.15%
18. TRANSNATION	$4,338	0.37%	$1,170,554	99.63%	$0	0.00%	$1,174,892	0.22%	$26,812	0.11%	2.28%
19. MANITO	$0	0.00%	$97,958	12.42%	$690,518	87.58%	$788,476	0.15%	$27,274	0.11%	3.46%
20. NEW JERSEY TIC	$0	0.00%	$717,721	100.00%	$0	0.00%	$717,721	0.14%	$15,185	0.06%	2.12%
21. TITLE RESOURCES	$0	0.00%	$0	0.00%	$467,688	100.00%	$467,688	0.09%	$0	--	--
22. SOUTHERN TI CORP	$0	0.00%	$295,215	74.89%	$98,996	25.11%	$394,211	0.08%	$198	0.00%	0.05%
23. SECURITY UNION	$2,574	100.00%	$0	0.00%	$0	0.00%	$2,574	0.00%	$0	--	--
24. AMERICAN GUARANTY	$909	100.00%	$0	0.00%	$0	0.00%	$909	0.00%	$0	--	--
COMPOSITE	**$64,391,845**	12.28%	**$453,567,682**	86.51%	**$6,347,815**	1.21%	**$524,307,342**	**100.00%**	**$24,342,369**	**100.00%**	**4.64%**
AVERAGE	**$2,682,994**		**$18,898,653**		**$264,492**		**$21,846,139**		**$1,014,265**		

RHODE ISLAND

	DIRECT	% of Total	NON-AFFILIATED	% of Total	AFFILIATED	% of Total	TOTAL	% JURISDICTION	PAID LOSSES	% LOSSES JURISDICTION	LOSSES TO PREMIUMS
1. COMMONWEALTH LAND	$590,897	7.28%	$7,529,990	92.72%	$0	0.00%	$8,120,887	32.60%	$311,546	11.98%	3.84%
2. CHICAGO TIC	$91,983	2.57%	$3,483,802	97.43%	$0	0.00%	$3,575,785	14.35%	$273,864	10.53%	7.66%
3. STEWART TGC	$123,689	3.74%	$2,025,143	61.24%	$1,158,069	35.02%	$3,306,901	13.27%	$1,237,043	47.58%	37.41%
4. UNITED GENERAL	$426,746	13.70%	$2,688,608	86.30%	$0	0.00%	$3,115,354	12.50%	$2,317	0.09%	0.07%
5. FIDELITY NATIONAL	$334,325	15.48%	$1,825,085	84.52%	$0	0.00%	$2,159,410	8.67%	$144,094	5.54%	6.67%
6. CT ATTORNEYS	$0	0.00%	$1,565,764	100.00%	$0	0.00%	$1,565,764	6.28%	$277,373	10.67%	17.71%
7. LAWYERS	$568,555	39.47%	$871,861	60.53%	$0	0.00%	$1,440,416	5.78%	$41,822	1.61%	2.90%
8. FIRST AMERICAN TIC	$287,206	25.20%	$825,308	72.40%	$27,384	2.40%	$1,139,898	4.58%	$250,956	9.65%	22.02%
9. OLD REPUBLIC NATIONAL	$9,106	3.47%	$253,616	96.53%	$0	0.00%	$262,722	1.05%	$43,981	1.69%	16.74%
10. TICOR (FL)	$0	0.00%	$113,092	100.00%	$0	0.00%	$113,092	0.45%	$9,517	0.37%	8.42%
11. TICOR	$11,008	10.91%	$89,904	89.09%	$0	0.00%	$100,912	0.41%	$7,138	0.27%	7.07%
12. TRANSNATION	$0	0.00%	$13,138	100.00%	$0	0.00%	$13,138	0.05%	$0	--	--
COMPOSITE	**$2,443,515**	9.81%	**$21,285,311**	85.43%	**$1,185,453**	4.76%	**$24,914,279**	**100.00%**	**$2,599,651**	**100.00%**	**10.43%**
AVERAGE	**$203,626**		**$1,773,776**		**$98,788**		**$2,076,190**		**$216,638**		

SOUTH CAROLINA

	DIRECT	% of Total	NON-AFFILIATED	% of Total	AFFILIATED	% of Total	TOTAL	% JURISDICTION	PAID LOSSES	% LOSSES JURISDICTION	LOSSES TO PREMIUMS
1. CHICAGO TIC	$587,785	1.48%	$39,082,136	98.52%	$0	0.00%	$39,669,921	28.37%	$2,338,894	25.37%	5.90%
2. FIRST AMERICAN TIC	$60,923	0.25%	$23,571,207	98.31%	$344,334	1.44%	$23,976,464	17.15%	$1,286,853	13.96%	5.37%
3. LAWYERS	$1,896,686	8.00%	$21,811,108	91.98%	$5,156	0.02%	$23,712,950	16.96%	$1,638,715	17.78%	6.91%
4. STEWART TGC	$323,342	1.84%	$17,241,337	97.93%	$41,484	0.24%	$17,606,163	12.59%	$708,085	7.68%	4.02%
5. FIDELITY NATIONAL	$327,189	3.16%	$9,706,204	93.78%	$316,349	3.06%	$10,349,742	7.40%	$632,672	6.86%	6.11%
6. INVESTORS TIC	$211,897	2.80%	$7,360,564	97.18%	$1,767	0.02%	$7,574,228	5.42%	$579,164	6.28%	7.65%
7. OLD REPUBLIC NATIONAL	$183,241	2.80%	$6,352,912	97.20%	$0	0.00%	$6,536,153	4.67%	$401,617	4.36%	6.14%
8. COMMONWEALTH LAND	$147,255	6.72%	$2,043,426	93.28%	$0	0.00%	$2,190,681	1.57%	$436,344	4.73%	19.92%
9. ATTORNEYS TIF (FL)	$0	0.00%	$1,893,029	100.00%	$0	0.00%	$1,893,029	1.35%	$359,115	3.90%	18.97%
10. SECURITY TG (BALTIMORE)	$0	0.00%	$1,429,635	100.00%	$0	0.00%	$1,429,635	1.02%	$48,214	0.52%	3.37%
11. COMMERCE	$0	0.00%	$1,092,087	100.00%	$0	0.00%	$1,092,087	0.78%	$0	--	--
12. UNITED GENERAL	$1,633	0.17%	$954,208	99.83%	$0	0.00%	$955,841	0.68%	$85,273	0.92%	8.92%
13. TRANSUNION NATIONAL	$68,818	8.33%	$746,478	90.33%	$11,080	1.34%	$826,376	0.59%	$363,212	3.94%	43.95%
14. SOUTHERN TI CORP	$0	0.00%	$761,782	100.00%	$0	0.00%	$761,782	0.54%	$8,762	0.10%	1.15%
15. TICOR (FL)	$0	0.00%	$522,993	100.00%	$0	0.00%	$522,993	0.37%	$85,133	0.92%	16.28%
16. TICOR	$183,892	51.66%	$172,059	48.34%	$0	0.00%	$355,951	0.25%	$33,759	0.37%	9.48%
17. GUARANTEE T&T	$0	0.00%	$0	0.00%	$162,067	100.00%	$162,067	0.12%	$33,846	0.37%	20.88%
18. CENSTAR	$0	0.00%	$117,867	100.00%	$0	0.00%	$117,867	0.08%	$0	--	--
19. TRANSNATION	$0	0.00%	$45,008	100.00%	$0	0.00%	$45,008	0.03%	$0	--	--
20. TITLE IC AMERICA	$0	0.00%	$33,021	100.00%	$0	0.00%	$33,021	0.02%	($803)	0.00%	(2.43)%
21. AMERICAN GUARANTY	$300	1.23%	$24,183	98.77%	$0	0.00%	$24,483	0.02%	$0	--	--
22. SECURITY UNION	$5,062	100.00%	$0	0.00%	$0	0.00%	$5,062	0.00%	$0	--	--
23. BRIDGE	$0	0.00%	$462	100.00%	$0	0.00%	$462	0.00%	$180,321	1.96%	39,030.52%
COMPOSITE	**$3,998,023**	2.86%	**$134,961,706**	96.51%	**$882,237**	0.63%	**$139,841,966**	**100.00%**	**$9,219,176**	**100.00%**	**6.59%**
AVERAGE	**$173,827**		**$5,867,900**		**$38,358**		**$6,080,085**		**$400,834**		

C.2 Jurisdiction - By Individual Underwriter

	DIRECT PREMIUMS WRITTEN							PERCENT OF JURISDICTION	PAID LOSSES	PERCENT OF JURISDICTION	LOSSES TO PREMIUMS
	DIRECT	% of Total	NON-AFFILIATED	% of Total	AFFILIATED	% of Total	TOTAL				

SOUTH DAKOTA

	DIRECT	% of Total	NON-AFFILIATED	% of Total	AFFILIATED	% of Total	TOTAL	PERCENT OF JURISDICTION	PAID LOSSES	PERCENT OF JURISDICTION	LOSSES TO PREMIUMS
1. OLD REPUBLIC NATIONAL	$50	0.00%	$2,859,456	100.00%	$0	0.00%	$2,859,506	19.46%	$4,632	1.52%	0.16%
2. DAKOTA HOMESTEAD	$168,351	6.47%	$2,432,110	93.53%	$0	0.00%	$2,600,461	17.70%	$51,729	16.98%	1.99%
3. FIRST AMERICAN TIC	$270,786	11.10%	$2,169,308	88.90%	$113	0.00%	$2,440,207	16.60%	$30,281	9.94%	1.24%
4. CHICAGO TIC	$25,112	1.19%	$2,082,505	98.81%	$0	0.00%	$2,107,617	14.34%	$57,480	18.87%	2.73%
5. STEWART TGC	$13,860	0.70%	$1,006,549	51.18%	$946,312	48.12%	$1,966,721	13.38%	$76,756	25.19%	3.90%
6. COMMONWEALTH LAND	$75,216	4.60%	$1,561,625	95.40%	$0	0.00%	$1,636,841	11.14%	$69,623	22.85%	4.25%
7. SECURITY UNION	$0	0.00%	$828,139	100.00%	$0	0.00%	$828,139	5.64%	$0	--	--
8. TICOR	$57,718	29.31%	$139,223	70.69%	$0	0.00%	$196,941	1.34%	$12,504	4.10%	6.35%
9. LAWYERS	$25,308	85.77%	$4,200	14.23%	$0	0.00%	$29,508	0.20%	$1,659	0.54%	5.62%
10. FIDELITY NATIONAL	$29,140	100.00%	$0	0.00%	$0	0.00%	$29,140	0.20%	$0	--	--
11. UNITED GENERAL	$698	88.58%	$90	11.42%	$0	0.00%	$788	0.00%	$0	--	--
COMPOSITE	**$666,239**	4.53%	**$13,083,205**	89.03%	**$946,425**	6.44%	**$14,695,869**	**100.00%**	**$304,664**	**100.00%**	**2.07%**
AVERAGE	**$60,567**		**$1,189,382**		**$86,039**		**$1,335,988**		**$27,697**		

TENNESSEE

	DIRECT	% of Total	NON-AFFILIATED	% of Total	AFFILIATED	% of Total	TOTAL	PERCENT OF JURISDICTION	PAID LOSSES	PERCENT OF JURISDICTION	LOSSES TO PREMIUMS
1. CHICAGO TIC	$3,259,611	10.90%	$26,633,518	89.10%	$0	0.00%	$29,893,129	18.39%	$643,091	8.34%	2.15%
2. FIRST AMERICAN TIC	$4,926,978	17.68%	$22,518,584	80.80%	$424,465	1.52%	$27,870,027	17.15%	$1,249,213	16.20%	4.48%
3. LAWYERS	$3,264,278	13.60%	$20,173,665	84.06%	$560,714	2.34%	$23,998,657	14.77%	$1,032,836	13.39%	4.30%
4. OLD REPUBLIC NATIONAL	$175,167	0.75%	$22,884,046	97.47%	$419,682	1.79%	$23,478,895	14.45%	$978,592	12.69%	4.17%
5. STEWART TGC	$551,718	3.09%	$12,109,491	67.82%	$5,194,914	29.09%	$17,856,123	10.99%	$1,138,614	14.77%	6.38%
6. FIDELITY NATIONAL	$1,187,178	9.73%	$9,490,497	77.76%	$1,526,905	12.51%	$12,204,580	7.51%	$515,284	6.68%	4.22%
7. SOUTHERN TI CORP	$0	0.00%	$7,024,297	100.00%	$0	0.00%	$7,024,297	4.32%	($71,080)	(0.92)%	(1.01)%
8. COMMONWEALTH LAND	$137,398	2.15%	$6,253,092	97.85%	$0	0.00%	$6,390,490	3.93%	$787,623	10.21%	12.32%
9. INVESTORS TIC	$42,448	1.62%	$2,580,635	98.38%	$0	0.00%	$2,623,083	1.61%	$180,424	2.34%	6.88%
10. SECURITY UNION	$1,254	0.05%	$2,382,441	99.95%	$0	0.00%	$2,383,695	1.47%	$93,937	1.22%	3.94%
11. TICOR	$77,254	3.25%	$2,299,581	96.75%	$0	0.00%	$2,376,835	1.46%	$290,971	3.77%	12.24%
12. UNITED GENERAL	$4,869	0.21%	$2,314,967	99.79%	$0	0.00%	$2,319,836	1.43%	$140,467	1.82%	6.06%
13. TICOR (FL)	$0	0.00%	$1,242,405	100.00%	$0	0.00%	$1,242,405	0.76%	$396,805	5.15%	31.94%
14. MISSISSIPPI VALLEY	$145,644	15.50%	$793,819	84.50%	$0	0.00%	$939,463	0.58%	$73,545	0.95%	7.83%
15. CENSTAR	$0	0.00%	$863,668	100.00%	$0	0.00%	$863,668	0.53%	$0	--	--
16. TRANSNATION	$0	0.00%	$385,780	100.00%	$0	0.00%	$385,780	0.24%	$105,243	1.36%	27.28%
17. TITLE G&TC	$260,893	100.00%	$0	0.00%	$0	0.00%	$260,893	0.16%	$1,500	0.02%	0.57%
18. GUARANTEE	$0	0.00%	$0	0.00%	$228,810	100.00%	$228,810	0.14%	$6,700	0.09%	2.93%
19. CONESTOGA	$1,491	1.30%	$113,221	98.70%	$0	0.00%	$114,712	0.07%	$0	--	--
20. TRANSUNION NATIONAL	$0	0.00%	$0	0.00%	$59,287	100.00%	$59,287	0.04%	$0	--	--
21. AMERICAN GUARANTY	$0	0.00%	$1,924	100.00%	$0	0.00%	$1,924	0.00%	$0	--	--
22. NATIONAL	$0	0.00%	$1,367	100.00%	$0	0.00%	$1,367	0.00%	$0	--	--
23. NATIONAL OF NY	$0	--	$0	--	$0	--	$0	--	$143,465	1.86%	--
24. TITLE IC AMERICA	$0	--	$0	--	$0	--	$0	--	$1,140	0.01%	--
25. SECURITY TG (BALTIMORE)	$0	--	($9,209)	--	$0	--	($9,209)	0.00%	$2,487	0.03%	(27.01)%
COMPOSITE	**$14,036,181**	8.64%	**$140,057,789**	86.18%	**$8,414,777**	5.18%	**$162,508,747**	**100.00%**	**$7,710,857**	**100.00%**	**4.74%**
AVERAGE	**$561,447**		**$5,602,312**		**$336,591**		**$6,500,350**		**$308,434**		

TEXAS

	DIRECT	% of Total	NON-AFFILIATED	% of Total	AFFILIATED	% of Total	TOTAL	PERCENT OF JURISDICTION	PAID LOSSES	PERCENT OF JURISDICTION	LOSSES TO PREMIUMS
1. FIRST AMERICAN TIC	$106,146,688	35.96%	$89,771,897	30.41%	$99,255,039	33.63%	$295,173,624	18.20%	$8,675,667	15.78%	2.94%
2. STEWART TGC	$33,887,417	12.59%	$66,853,618	24.83%	$168,480,798	62.58%	$269,221,833	16.60%	$4,269,132	7.77%	1.59%
3. LAWYERS	$110,469,357	48.98%	$111,711,900	49.53%	$3,356,524	1.49%	$225,537,781	13.91%	$9,840,364	17.90%	4.36%
4. CHICAGO TIC	$115,031,241	56.64%	$87,495,654	43.08%	$560,361	0.28%	$203,087,256	12.52%	$9,147,849	16.64%	4.50%
5. FIDELITY NATIONAL	$36,403,051	24.32%	$66,319,966	44.32%	$46,931,292	31.36%	$149,654,309	9.23%	$5,592,548	10.17%	3.74%
6. COMMONWEALTH LAND	$80,381,025	61.68%	$49,944,637	38.32%	$0	0.00%	$130,325,662	8.04%	$6,519,952	11.86%	5.00%
7. ALAMO	$0	0.00%	$42,093,104	44.70%	$52,072,753	55.30%	$94,165,857	5.81%	$3,719,794	6.77%	3.95%
8. TITLE RESOURCES	$0	0.00%	$46,579,513	64.57%	$25,562,327	35.43%	$72,141,840	4.45%	$2,181,170	3.97%	3.02%
9. OLD REPUBLIC NATIONAL	$8,444	0.02%	$36,987,133	76.29%	$11,486,087	23.69%	$48,481,664	2.99%	$2,631,324	4.79%	5.43%
10. UNITED GENERAL	$0	0.00%	$27,349,669	100.00%	$0	0.00%	$27,349,669	1.69%	$131,884	0.24%	0.48%
11. TICOR	$4,477,907	16.71%	$22,325,177	83.29%	$0	0.00%	$26,803,084	1.65%	$1,171,779	2.13%	4.37%
12. NORTH AMERICAN	$0	0.00%	$0	0.00%	$17,070,426	100.00%	$17,070,426	1.05%	$15,640	0.03%	0.09%
13. SOUTHERN TI CORP	$0	0.00%	$14,656,298	100.00%	$0	0.00%	$14,656,298	0.90%	$699,790	1.27%	4.77%
14. COMMERCE	$0	0.00%	$0	0.00%	$12,773,712	100.00%	$12,773,712	0.79%	$59,994	0.11%	0.47%
15. ALLIANT	$0	0.00%	$10,537,510	100.00%	$0	0.00%	$10,537,510	0.65%	$17,031	0.03%	0.16%
16. TITLE IC AMERICA	$0	0.00%	$9,828,156	100.00%	$0	0.00%	$9,828,156	0.61%	$53,444	0.10%	0.54%
17. SECURITY UNION	$413	0.01%	$5,221,026	99.99%	$0	0.00%	$5,221,439	0.32%	$123,412	0.22%	2.36%
18. PACIFIC NORTHWEST	$0	0.00%	$3,515,893	100.00%	$0	0.00%	$3,515,893	0.22%	$0	--	--
19. TRANSNATION	$0	0.00%	$2,326,598	100.00%	$0	0.00%	$2,326,598	0.14%	$57,000	0.10%	2.45%
20. SIERRA	$0	0.00%	$1,966,566	100.00%	$0	0.00%	$1,966,566	0.12%	$0	--	--
21. TICOR (FL)	$0	0.00%	$1,084,339	100.00%	$0	0.00%	$1,084,339	0.07%	$56,077	0.10%	5.17%
22. NATIONAL LAND	$0	0.00%	$448,854	100.00%	$0	0.00%	$448,854	0.03%	$0	--	--
23. WESTCOR	$0	0.00%	$274,717	100.00%	$0	0.00%	$274,717	0.02%	$0	--	--
COMPOSITE	**$486,805,543**	30.02%	**$697,292,225**	43.00%	**$437,549,319**	26.98%	**$1,621,647,087**	**100.00%**	**$54,963,851**	**100.00%**	**3.39%**
AVERAGE	**$21,165,458**		**$30,317,053**		**$19,023,883**		**$70,506,395**		**$2,389,733**		

C.2 Jurisdiction - By Individual Underwriter

	DIRECT	% of Total	NON-AFFILIATED	% of Total	AFFILIATED	% of Total	TOTAL	PERCENT OF JURISDICTION	PAID LOSSES	PERCENT OF JURISDICTION	LOSSES TO PREMIUMS
UTAH											
1. FIRST AMERICAN TIC	$11,736,485	9.37%	$81,385,669	64.97%	$32,139,532	25.66%	$125,261,686	46.75%	$2,159,045	27.17%	1.72%
2. STEWART TGC	$761,063	1.63%	$37,616,999	80.49%	$8,358,551	17.88%	$46,736,613	17.44%	$434,934	5.47%	0.93%
3. FIDELITY NATIONAL	$595,825	2.78%	$20,622,079	96.34%	$186,853	0.87%	$21,404,757	7.99%	$890,467	11.21%	4.16%
4. LAWYERS	$182,862	0.92%	$19,629,036	99.08%	$239	0.00%	$19,812,137	7.39%	$1,935,213	24.36%	9.77%
5. TRANSNATION	$0	0.00%	$12,801,335	100.00%	$0	0.00%	$12,801,335	4.78%	$73,513	0.93%	0.57%
6. COMMONWEALTH LAND	$29,560	0.24%	$10,067,457	80.85%	$2,355,253	18.91%	$12,452,270	4.65%	$648,226	8.16%	5.21%
7. CHICAGO TIC	$380,001	3.49%	$10,521,945	96.51%	$0	0.00%	$10,901,946	4.07%	$185,650	2.34%	1.70%
8. UNITED GENERAL	$84,192	1.22%	$6,825,534	98.78%	$0	0.00%	$6,909,726	2.58%	$66,340	0.83%	0.96%
9. OLD REPUBLIC NATIONAL	$665,306	17.13%	$2,423,716	62.41%	$794,545	20.46%	$3,883,567	1.45%	$139,943	1.76%	3.60%
10. SECURITY UNION	$22,140	0.77%	$2,871,506	99.23%	$0	0.00%	$2,893,646	1.08%	$9,816	0.12%	0.34%
11. ATTORNEYS TGF (CO)	$0	0.00%	$2,403,171	100.00%	$0	0.00%	$2,403,171	0.90%	$1,299,467	16.35%	54.07%
12. GUARANTEE T&T	$0	0.00%	$0	0.00%	$761,915	100.00%	$761,915	0.28%	$0	--	--
13. PACIFIC NORTHWEST	$0	0.00%	$439,821	100.00%	$0	0.00%	$439,821	0.16%	$0	--	--
14. WESTERN NATIONAL	$0	0.00%	$8,580	2.31%	$362,141	97.69%	$370,721	0.14%	$103,224	1.30%	27.84%
15. WESTCOR	$0	0.00%	$363,865	100.00%	$0	0.00%	$363,865	0.14%	$0	--	--
16. TICOR	$35,070	12.02%	$256,807	87.98%	$0	0.00%	$291,877	0.11%	$0	--	--
17. TICOR (FL)	$0	0.00%	$235,810	100.00%	$0	0.00%	$235,810	0.09%	$0	--	--
18. TRANSUNION NATIONAL	$0	0.00%	$0	0.00%	$9,265	100.00%	$9,265	0.00%	$0	--	--
19. AMERICAN GUARANTY	$5,005	100.00%	$0	0.00%	$0	0.00%	$5,005	0.00%	$0	--	--
COMPOSITE	**$14,497,509**	5.41%	**$208,473,330**	77.81%	**$44,968,294**	16.78%	**$267,939,133**	100.00%	**$7,945,838**	100.00%	2.97%
AVERAGE	**$763,027**		**$10,972,281**		**$2,366,752**		**$14,102,060**		**$418,202**		
VERMONT											
1. CT ATTORNEYS	$0	0.00%	$6,018,064	100.00%	$0	0.00%	$6,018,064	41.95%	$372,060	31.19%	6.18%
2. FIRST AMERICAN TIC	$76,370	2.08%	$3,585,787	97.53%	$14,369	0.39%	$3,676,526	25.63%	$346,486	29.05%	9.42%
3. LAWYERS	$467,547	30.21%	$1,079,976	69.77%	$360	0.02%	$1,547,883	10.79%	$16,842	1.41%	1.09%
4. CHICAGO TIC	$79,236	7.03%	$1,048,472	92.97%	$0	0.00%	$1,127,708	7.86%	$29,851	2.50%	2.65%
5. STEWART TGC	$73,791	6.81%	$1,008,830	93.10%	$993	0.09%	$1,083,614	7.55%	$51,364	4.31%	4.74%
6. COMMONWEALTH LAND	$8,320	2.23%	$364,487	97.77%	$0	0.00%	$372,807	2.60%	$23,316	1.95%	6.25%
7. OLD REPUBLIC NATIONAL	$5,565	3.89%	$137,384	96.11%	$0	0.00%	$142,949	1.00%	$65,988	5.53%	46.16%
8. FIDELITY NATIONAL	$2,859	2.06%	$136,042	97.94%	$0	0.00%	$138,901	0.97%	$258,209	21.65%	185.89%
9. TICOR (FL)	$0	0.00%	$107,951	100.00%	$0	0.00%	$107,951	0.75%	$13,154	1.10%	12.19%
10. UNITED GENERAL	$972	0.96%	$99,813	99.04%	$0	0.00%	$100,785	0.70%	$0	--	--
11. TICOR	$3,898	13.19%	$25,663	86.81%	$0	0.00%	$29,561	0.21%	$15,591	1.31%	52.74%
12. SECURITY UNION	$187	100.00%	$0	0.00%	$0	0.00%	$187	0.00%	$0	--	--
COMPOSITE	**$718,745**	5.01%	**$13,612,469**	94.88%	**$15,722**	0.11%	**$14,346,936**	100.00%	**$1,192,861**	100.00%	8.31%
AVERAGE	**$59,895**		**$1,134,372**		**$1,310**		**$1,195,578**		**$99,405**		
VIRGINIA											
1. FIRST AMERICAN TIC	$8,697,911	9.74%	$76,684,740	85.89%	$3,904,508	4.37%	$89,287,159	23.85%	$10,550,560	41.71%	11.82%
2. STEWART TGC	$1,150,755	1.81%	$54,963,622	86.65%	$7,315,614	11.53%	$63,429,991	16.94%	$3,209,921	12.69%	5.06%
3. LAWYERS	$8,163,211	13.68%	$50,572,153	84.73%	$950,989	1.59%	$59,686,353	15.94%	$4,180,112	16.52%	7.00%
4. CHICAGO TIC	$6,113,809	14.56%	$35,869,518	85.44%	$0	0.00%	$41,983,327	11.21%	$1,489,596	5.89%	3.55%
5. COMMONWEALTH LAND	$5,239,951	15.01%	$24,721,866	70.83%	$4,939,573	14.15%	$34,901,390	9.32%	$1,398,678	5.53%	4.01%
6. FIDELITY NATIONAL	$1,178,444	4.19%	$26,330,018	93.66%	$604,262	2.15%	$28,112,724	7.51%	$1,641,866	6.49%	5.84%
7. SOUTHERN TI CORP	$1,173,681	9.09%	$10,922,720	84.60%	$815,354	6.31%	$12,911,755	3.45%	$687,413	2.72%	5.32%
8. UNITED GENERAL	$33,152	0.32%	$10,326,541	99.68%	$0	0.00%	$10,359,693	2.77%	$580,788	2.30%	5.61%
9. TRANSNATION	$106,313	1.10%	$9,409,287	97.72%	$113,108	1.17%	$9,628,708	2.57%	$109,168	0.43%	1.13%
10. OLD REPUBLIC NATIONAL	$195,458	2.32%	$8,230,779	97.68%	$0	0.00%	$8,426,237	2.25%	$839,161	3.32%	9.96%
11. INVESTORS TIC	$110,462	1.79%	$5,641,269	91.52%	$412,100	6.69%	$6,163,831	1.65%	$357,259	1.41%	5.80%
12. TICOR (FL)	$0	0.00%	$3,053,509	100.00%	$0	0.00%	$3,053,509	0.82%	$168,616	0.67%	5.52%
13. COMMERCE	$0	0.00%	$0	0.00%	$1,789,931	100.00%	$1,789,931	0.48%	$0	--	--
14. TICOR	$105,405	6.98%	$1,405,183	93.02%	$0	0.00%	$1,510,588	0.40%	$77,497	0.31%	5.13%
15. CENSTAR	$0	0.00%	$1,252,062	100.00%	$0	0.00%	$1,252,062	0.33%	$0	--	--
16. NORTH AMERICAN	$0	0.00%	$0	0.00%	$1,050,256	100.00%	$1,050,256	0.28%	$0	--	--
17. CONESTOGA	$0	0.00%	$239,215	100.00%	$0	0.00%	$239,215	0.06%	$0	--	--
18. SECURITY UNION	$18,636	8.20%	$208,671	91.80%	$0	0.00%	$227,307	0.06%	$0	--	--
19. TITLE RESOURCES	$0	0.00%	$0	0.00%	$208,256	100.00%	$208,256	0.06%	$0	--	--
20. TRANSUNION NATIONAL	$0	0.00%	$0	0.00%	$117,235	100.00%	$117,235	0.03%	$5,069	0.02%	4.32%
21. AMERICAN GUARANTY	$700	5.76%	$11,449	94.24%	$0	0.00%	$12,149	0.00%	$0	--	--
22. NATIONS OF NY	$0	--	$0	--	$0	--	$0	--	$700	0.00%	--
23. SECURITY TG (BALTIMORE)	$0	--	$0	--	$0	--	$0	--	($61)	0.00%	--
COMPOSITE	**$32,287,888**	8.63%	**$319,842,602**	85.44%	**$22,221,186**	5.94%	**$374,351,676**	100.00%	**$25,296,343**	100.00%	6.76%
AVERAGE	**$1,403,821**		**$13,906,200**		**$966,139**		**$16,276,160**		**$1,099,841**		

C.2 Jurisdiction - By Individual Underwriter

	DIRECT PREMIUMS WRITTEN							PERCENT OF JURISDICTION	PAID LOSSES	PERCENT OF JURISDICTION	LOSSES TO PREMIUMS
	DIRECT	% of Total	NON-AFFILIATED	% of Total	AFFILIATED	% of Total	TOTAL				

WASHINGTON
1. CHICAGO TIC	$58,298,376	74.38%	$15,905,442	20.29%	$4,174,073	5.33%	$78,377,891	23.82%	$4,452,553	25.66%	5.68%
2. FIRST AMERICAN TIC	$54,989,908	79.23%	$12,389,270	17.85%	$2,024,775	2.92%	$69,403,953	21.09%	$4,430,647	25.53%	6.38%
3. PACIFIC NORTHWEST	$0	0.00%	$9,409,995	26.75%	$25,764,640	73.25%	$35,174,635	10.69%	$1,424,786	8.21%	4.05%
4. STEWART TGC	$528,543	1.52%	$8,761,658	25.13%	$25,579,421	73.36%	$34,869,622	10.60%	$945,646	5.45%	2.71%
5. TRANSNATION	$17,361,980	62.73%	$7,927,716	28.64%	$2,388,805	8.63%	$27,678,501	8.41%	$1,951,097	11.24%	7.05%
6. COMMONWEALTH LAND	$1,007,454	3.99%	$7,496,831	29.73%	$16,715,966	66.28%	$25,220,251	7.67%	$1,225,757	7.06%	4.86%
7. FIDELITY NATIONAL	$1,622,013	8.73%	$928,297	4.99%	$16,039,053	86.28%	$18,589,363	5.65%	$1,020,724	5.88%	5.49%
8. TICOR	$110,405	0.70%	$1,627,028	10.34%	$13,994,133	88.96%	$15,731,566	4.78%	$357,184	2.06%	2.27%
9. LAWYERS	$2,680,477	19.42%	$3,615,176	26.20%	$7,505,091	54.38%	$13,800,744	4.19%	$271,940	1.57%	1.97%
10. OLD REPUBLIC NATIONAL	$489,107	5.17%	$2,221,251	23.47%	$6,752,056	71.36%	$9,462,414	2.88%	$898,157	5.18%	9.49%
11. UNITED GENERAL	$209,349	59.05%	$145,160	40.95%	$0	0.00%	$354,509	0.11%	$918	0.00%	0.26%
12. SECURITY UNION	$21,279	6.18%	$323,165	93.82%	$0	0.00%	$344,444	0.10%	$148,777	0.86%	43.19%
13. TICOR (FL)	$0	--	$0	--	$0	--	$0	--	$225,558	1.30%	--
COMPOSITE	$137,318,891	41.74%	$70,750,989	21.50%	$120,938,013	36.76%	$329,007,893	100.00%	$17,353,744	100.00%	5.27%
AVERAGE	$10,562,992		$5,442,384		$9,302,924		$25,308,299		$1,334,903		

WEST VIRGINIA
1. FIRST AMERICAN TIC	$101,422	1.45%	$6,824,423	97.79%	$52,716	0.76%	$6,978,561	28.74%	$235,830	17.20%	3.38%
2. LAWYERS	$253,183	7.04%	$3,341,681	92.86%	$3,744	0.10%	$3,598,608	14.82%	$377,610	27.54%	10.49%
3. STEWART TGC	$33,946	0.97%	$3,454,535	98.83%	$6,974	0.20%	$3,495,455	14.39%	$179,843	13.12%	5.15%
4. CHICAGO TIC	$492,668	20.48%	$1,912,565	79.52%	$0	0.00%	$2,405,233	9.90%	($20,414)	(1.49)%	(0.85)%
5. OLD REPUBLIC NATIONAL	$9,446	0.43%	$2,190,058	99.57%	$0	0.00%	$2,199,504	9.06%	$75,867	5.53%	3.45%
6. INVESTORS TIC	$15,410	0.76%	$2,016,919	99.24%	$0	0.00%	$2,032,329	8.37%	$20,399	1.49%	1.00%
7. FIDELITY NATIONAL	$99,096	5.84%	$1,590,089	93.65%	$8,697	0.51%	$1,697,882	6.99%	$59,730	4.36%	3.52%
8. COMMONWEALTH LAND	$65,163	5.90%	$1,039,251	94.10%	$0	0.00%	$1,104,414	4.55%	$186,114	13.57%	16.85%
9. SOUTHERN TI CORP	$0	0.00%	$205,731	86.68%	$31,609	13.32%	$237,340	0.98%	$0	--	--
10. TICOR	$43,680	28.82%	$107,872	71.18%	$0	0.00%	$151,552	0.62%	$4,428	0.32%	2.92%
11. UNITED GENERAL	$983	0.88%	$110,334	99.12%	$0	0.00%	$111,317	0.46%	$0	--	--
12. TRANSNATION	$571	0.73%	$20,954	26.93%	$56,287	72.34%	$77,812	0.32%	$0	--	--
13. TICOR (FL)	$0	0.00%	$71,331	100.00%	$0	0.00%	$71,331	0.29%	$174,080	12.70%	244.05%
14. CENSTAR	$0	0.00%	$69,567	100.00%	$0	0.00%	$69,567	0.29%	$0	--	--
15. SECURITY TG (BALTIMORE)	$0	0.00%	$52,488	100.00%	$0	0.00%	$52,488	0.22%	$77,657	5.66%	147.95%
16. AMERICAN GUARANTY	$0	0.00%	$1,150	100.00%	$0	0.00%	$1,150	0.00%	$0	--	--
17. SECURITY UNION	($300)	--	$0	--	$0	--	($300)	0.00%	$0	--	--
COMPOSITE	$1,115,268	4.59%	$23,008,948	94.75%	$160,027	0.66%	$24,284,243	100.00%	$1,371,144	100.00%	5.65%
AVERAGE	$65,604		$1,353,468		$9,413		$1,428,485		$80,656		

WISCONSIN
1. FIRST AMERICAN TIC	$8,167,878	22.70%	$26,115,472	72.59%	$1,692,991	4.71%	$35,976,341	30.76%	$2,146,503	27.85%	5.97%
2. CHICAGO TIC	$7,761,876	32.86%	$15,859,841	67.14%	$0	0.00%	$23,621,717	20.20%	$2,318,641	30.08%	9.82%
3. STEWART TGC	$332,449	2.18%	$10,654,472	69.95%	$4,244,788	27.87%	$15,231,709	13.02%	$1,090,442	14.15%	7.16%
4. LAWYERS	$1,832,428	22.43%	$6,284,714	76.92%	$53,182	0.65%	$8,170,324	6.99%	$468,272	6.08%	5.73%
5. COMMONWEALTH LAND	$72,273	0.91%	$7,850,573	99.09%	$0	0.00%	$7,922,846	6.77%	$361,016	4.68%	4.56%
6. OLD REPUBLIC NATIONAL	$69,853	0.90%	$7,659,540	99.10%	$0	0.00%	$7,729,393	6.61%	$195,169	2.53%	2.53%
7. TICOR	$231,305	3.55%	$5,108,099	78.31%	$1,183,493	18.14%	$6,522,897	5.58%	$568,021	7.37%	8.71%
8. SECURITY UNION	$1,350	0.03%	$4,380,763	99.97%	$0	0.00%	$4,382,113	3.75%	$131,856	1.71%	3.01%
9. FIRST AMERICAN (OR)	$0	0.00%	$2,068,205	100.00%	$0	0.00%	$2,068,205	1.77%	$0	--	--
10. FIDELITY NATIONAL	$132,758	7.51%	$1,621,056	91.66%	$14,689	0.83%	$1,768,503	1.51%	$175,310	2.27%	9.91%
11. TRANSNATION	$992	0.06%	$1,552,433	99.94%	$0	0.00%	$1,553,425	1.33%	$56,838	0.74%	3.66%
12. UNITED GENERAL	$6,299	0.77%	$812,471	99.23%	$0	0.00%	$818,770	0.70%	$8,230	0.11%	1.01%
13. TICOR (FL)	$0	0.00%	$792,991	100.00%	$0	0.00%	$792,991	0.68%	$144,361	1.87%	18.20%
14. ATTORNEYS TGF (IL)	$291,071	100.00%	$0	0.00%	$0	0.00%	$291,071	0.25%	$42,789	0.56%	14.70%
15. CENSTAR	$0	0.00%	$103,509	100.00%	$0	0.00%	$103,509	0.09%	$0	--	--
16. AMERICAN GUARANTY	$0	0.00%	$374	100.00%	$0	0.00%	$374	0.00%	$0	--	--
COMPOSITE	$18,900,532	16.16%	$90,864,513	77.69%	$7,189,143	6.15%	$116,954,188	100.00%	$7,707,448	100.00%	6.59%
AVERAGE	$1,181,283		$5,679,032		$449,321		$7,309,637		$481,716		

WYOMING
1. FIRST AMERICAN TIC	$1,746,026	10.71%	$2,908,500	17.84%	$11,647,701	71.45%	$16,302,227	48.85%	$182,368	48.10%	1.12%
2. STEWART TGC	$15,098	0.21%	$6,144,633	86.46%	$947,405	13.33%	$7,107,136	21.30%	$106,567	28.11%	1.50%
3. CHICAGO TIC	$150,234	4.29%	$3,352,080	95.71%	$0	0.00%	$3,502,314	10.50%	$7,382	1.95%	0.21%
4. LAWYERS	$26,171	0.90%	$2,885,900	99.10%	$0	0.00%	$2,912,071	8.73%	$0	--	--
5. OLD REPUBLIC NATIONAL	$0	0.00%	$1,675,569	100.00%	$0	0.00%	$1,675,569	5.02%	$29,359	7.74%	1.75%
6. COMMONWEALTH LAND	$522	0.04%	$1,331,184	99.96%	$0	0.00%	$1,331,706	3.99%	$40,942	10.80%	3.07%
7. FIDELITY NATIONAL	$47,935	14.38%	$285,384	85.62%	$0	0.00%	$333,319	1.00%	$12,544	3.31%	3.76%
8. FOUNDERS	$178,276	100.00%	$0	0.00%	$0	0.00%	$178,276	0.53%	$0	--	--
9. TICOR	$20,434	100.00%	$0	0.00%	$0	0.00%	$20,434	0.06%	$0	--	--
10. UNITED GENERAL	$6,267	83.43%	$1,245	16.57%	$0	0.00%	$7,512	0.02%	$0	--	--
COMPOSITE	$2,190,963	6.57%	$18,584,495	55.69%	$12,595,106	37.74%	$33,370,564	100.00%	$379,162	100.00%	1.14%
AVERAGE	$219,096		$1,858,450		$1,259,511		$3,337,056		$37,916		

GUAM
1. STEWART TGC	$0	0.00%	$4,300,401	100.00%	$0	0.00%	$4,300,401	74.42%	$15,592	7.92%	0.36%
2. TICOR	$0	0.00%	$1,478,263	100.00%	$0	0.00%	$1,478,263	25.58%	$11,326	5.76%	0.77%
3. FIRST AMERICAN TIC	$0	--	$0	--	$0	--	$0	--	$169,868	86.32%	--
COMPOSITE	$0	0.00%	$5,778,664	100.00%	$0	0.00%	$5,778,664	100.00%	$196,786	100.00%	3.41%
AVERAGE	$0		$1,926,221		$0		$1,926,221		$65,595		

C.2 Jurisdiction - By Individual Underwriter

	DIRECT PREMIUMS WRITTEN							PERCENT OF JURISDICTION	PAID LOSSES	PERCENT OF JURISDICTION	LOSSES TO PREMIUMS
	DIRECT	% of Total	NON-AFFILIATED	% of Total	AFFILIATED	% of Total	TOTAL				
PUERTO RICO											
1. STEWART TGC	$23,054	0.18%	$130,122	1.02%	$12,626,403	98.80%	$12,779,579	42.08%	$989,787	33.08%	7.75%
2. FIRST AMERICAN TIC	$259	0.00%	$5,363,770	100.00%	$0	0.00%	$5,364,029	17.66%	$609,815	20.38%	11.37%
3. CHICAGO TIC	$65,014	1.28%	$5,001,988	98.72%	$0	0.00%	$5,067,002	16.68%	$600,154	20.06%	11.84%
4. COMMONWEALTH LAND	$0	0.00%	$0	0.00%	$3,391,378	100.00%	$3,391,378	11.17%	$122,359	4.09%	3.61%
5. LAWYERS	$0	0.00%	$1,596,000	76.53%	$489,328	23.47%	$2,085,328	6.87%	$287,276	9.60%	13.78%
6. OLD REPUBLIC NATIONAL	$0	0.00%	$1,074,393	100.00%	$0	0.00%	$1,074,393	3.54%	$48,382	1.62%	4.50%
7. FIDELITY NATIONAL	$363,583	100.00%	$0	0.00%	$0	0.00%	$363,583	1.20%	$334,617	11.18%	92.03%
8. ATTORNEYS TIF (FL)	$0	0.00%	$245,518	100.00%	$0	0.00%	$245,518	0.81%	$0	--	--
COMPOSITE	$451,910	1.49%	$13,411,791	44.16%	$16,507,109	54.35%	$30,370,810	100.00%	$2,992,390	100.00%	9.85%
AVERAGE	$56,489		$1,676,474		$2,063,389		$3,796,351		$374,049		
U.S. VIRGIN ISLANDS											
1. CHICAGO TIC	$66,847	8.98%	$677,804	91.02%	$0	0.00%	$744,651	31.56%	$66,388	17.58%	8.92%
2. LAWYERS	$0	0.00%	$644,609	100.00%	$0	0.00%	$644,609	27.32%	$36,422	9.64%	5.65%
3. STEWART TGC	$0	0.00%	$516,458	100.00%	$0	0.00%	$516,458	21.89%	$18,555	4.91%	3.59%
4. FIDELITY NATIONAL	$0	0.00%	$245,872	100.00%	$0	0.00%	$245,872	10.42%	$16,319	4.32%	6.64%
5. FIRST AMERICAN TIC	$0	0.00%	$206,245	100.00%	$0	0.00%	$206,245	8.74%	$239,174	63.33%	115.97%
6. TICOR	$0	0.00%	$1,820	100.00%	$0	0.00%	$1,820	0.08%	$0	--	--
7. COMMONWEALTH LAND	$0	--	$0	--	$0	--	$0	--	$500	0.13%	--
8. SECURITY UNION	$0	--	$0	--	$0	--	$0	--	$330	0.09%	--
COMPOSITE	$66,847	2.83%	$2,292,808	97.17%	$0	0.00%	$2,359,655	100.00%	$377,688	100.00%	16.01%
AVERAGE	$8,356		$286,601		$0		$294,957		$47,211		
NORTHERN MARIANA IS.											
1. STEWART TGC	$0	0.00%	$779,364	100.00%	$0	0.00%	$779,364	100.00%	$21,656	100.00%	2.78%
COMPOSITE	$0	0.00%	$779,364	100.00%	$0	0.00%	$779,364	100.00%	$21,656	100.00%	2.78%
CANADA											
1. STEWART TGC	$76,099,011	100.00%	$0	0.00%	$0	0.00%	$76,099,011	62.04%	$13,556,557	64.53%	17.81%
2. FIRST AMERICAN TIC	$26,161,839	100.00%	$0	0.00%	$0	0.00%	$26,161,839	21.33%	$7,620,687	36.27%	29.13%
3. CHICAGO TIC	$3,857,639	19.60%	$0	0.00%	$15,827,994	80.40%	$19,685,633	16.05%	($230,821)	(1.10)%	(1.17)%
4. LAWYERS	$720,306	100.00%	$0	0.00%	$0	0.00%	$720,306	0.59%	$61,766	0.29%	8.57%
COMPOSITE	$106,838,795	87.10%	$0	0.00%	$15,827,994	12.90%	$122,666,789	100.00%	$21,008,189	100.00%	17.13%
AVERAGE	$26,709,699		$0		$3,956,999		$30,666,697		$5,252,047		
AGGREGATE OTHER ALIEN											
1. FIRST AMERICAN TIC	$11,074,697	97.23%	$315,301	2.77%	$0	0.00%	$11,389,998	40.46%	$5,327,656	101.82%	46.77%
2. FIDELITY NATIONAL	$6,392,857	100.00%	$0	0.00%	$0	0.00%	$6,392,857	22.71%	$108,584	2.08%	1.70%
3. LAWYERS	$4,300,498	91.18%	$415,817	8.82%	$0	0.00%	$4,716,315	16.75%	$370	0.00%	0.00%
4. STEWART TGC	$255,295	7.95%	$1,215,251	37.83%	$1,741,901	54.22%	$3,212,447	11.41%	($204,249)	(3.90)%	(6.36)%
5. COMMONWEALTH LAND	$1,286,483	100.00%	$0	0.00%	$0	0.00%	$1,286,483	4.57%	$0	--	--
6. CHICAGO TIC	$3,675	0.50%	$726,300	99.50%	$0	0.00%	$729,975	2.59%	$0	--	--
7. ATTORNEYS TIF (FL)	$0	0.00%	$421,502	100.00%	$0	0.00%	$421,502	1.50%	$0	--	--
COMPOSITE	$23,313,505	82.82%	$3,094,171	10.99%	$1,741,901	6.19%	$28,149,577	100.00%	$5,232,361	100.00%	18.59%
AVERAGE	$3,330,501		$442,024		$248,843		$4,021,368		$747,480		

See pg. 154, *B.4 Industry Composite Report - By Individual Underwriter* for summary of Industry Total Market Share by Individual Underwriter.

D.1 ORGANIZATION
- NAIC GROUP BY JURISDICTION

3

D.1 Organization - NAIC Group by Jurisdiction

	DIRECT PREMIUMS WRITTEN							PERCENT OF GROUP	PAID LOSSES	PERCENT OF GROUP	LOSSES TO PREMIUMS
	DIRECT	% of Total	NON-AFFILIATED	% of Total	AFFILIATED	% of Total	TOTAL				

ATTORNEYS' TITLE

	DIRECT	% of Total	NON-AFFILIATED	% of Total	AFFILIATED	% of Total	TOTAL	PERCENT OF GROUP	PAID LOSSES	PERCENT OF GROUP	LOSSES TO PREMIUMS
1. FLORIDA	$0	0.00%	$332,905,096	100.00%	$0	0.00%	$332,905,096	93.53%	$25,507,467	85.44%	7.66%
2. COLORADO	$0	0.00%	$6,864,905	100.00%	$0	0.00%	$6,864,905	1.93%	$270,631	0.91%	3.94%
3. ILLINOIS	$0	0.00%	$5,356,039	100.00%	$0	0.00%	$5,356,039	1.50%	$863,901	2.89%	16.13%
4. MINNESOTA	$0	0.00%	$3,696,692	100.00%	$0	0.00%	$3,696,692	1.04%	$188,104	0.63%	5.09%
5. UTAH	$0	0.00%	$2,403,171	100.00%	$0	0.00%	$2,403,171	0.68%	$1,299,467	4.35%	54.07%
6. SOUTH CAROLINA	$0	0.00%	$1,893,029	100.00%	$0	0.00%	$1,893,029	0.53%	$359,115	1.20%	18.97%
7. INDIANA	$831,940	100.00%	$0	0.00%	$0	0.00%	$831,940	0.23%	$389,203	1.30%	46.78%
8. GEORGIA	$0	0.00%	$633,526	100.00%	$0	0.00%	$633,526	0.18%	$821,978	2.75%	129.75%
9. AGGREGATE OTHER ALIEN	$0	0.00%	$421,502	100.00%	$0	0.00%	$421,502	0.12%	$0	--	--
10. NORTH CAROLINA	$0	0.00%	$416,568	100.00%	$0	0.00%	$416,568	0.12%	$0	--	--
11. PUERTO RICO	$0	0.00%	$245,518	100.00%	$0	0.00%	$245,518	0.07%	$0	--	--
12. NORTH DAKOTA	$0	0.00%	$169,925	100.00%	$0	0.00%	$169,925	0.05%	$0	--	--
13. MICHIGAN	$0	0.00%	$81,020	100.00%	$0	0.00%	$81,020	0.02%	$154,009	0.52%	190.09%
14. ALABAMA	$0	0.00%	$12,139	100.00%	$0	0.00%	$12,139	0.00%	$0	--	--
15. ARKANSAS	$0	0.00%	$10,298	100.00%	$0	0.00%	$10,298	0.00%	$0	--	--
COMPOSITE	**$831,940**	0.23%	**$355,109,428**	99.77%	**$0**	0.00%	**$355,941,368**	100.00%	**$29,853,875**	100.00%	8.39%
AVERAGE	**$55,463**		**$23,673,962**		**$0**		**$23,729,425**		**$1,990,258**		

CATIC

	DIRECT	% of Total	NON-AFFILIATED	% of Total	AFFILIATED	% of Total	TOTAL	PERCENT OF GROUP	PAID LOSSES	PERCENT OF GROUP	LOSSES TO PREMIUMS
1. CONNECTICUT	$0	0.00%	$35,170,487	100.00%	$0	0.00%	$35,170,487	51.43%	$1,385,508	30.55%	3.94%
2. NEW JERSEY	$0	0.00%	$16,413,857	100.00%	$0	0.00%	$16,413,857	24.00%	$1,064,324	23.47%	6.48%
3. MASSACHUSETTS	$0	0.00%	$8,093,908	100.00%	$0	0.00%	$8,093,908	11.83%	$1,419,832	31.31%	17.54%
4. VERMONT	$0	0.00%	$6,018,064	100.00%	$0	0.00%	$6,018,064	8.80%	$372,060	8.20%	6.18%
5. RHODE ISLAND	$0	0.00%	$1,565,764	100.00%	$0	0.00%	$1,565,764	2.29%	$277,373	6.12%	17.71%
6. PENNSYLVANIA	$0	0.00%	$717,721	100.00%	$0	0.00%	$717,721	1.05%	$15,185	0.33%	2.12%
7. NEW HAMPSHIRE	$0	0.00%	$402,407	100.00%	$0	0.00%	$402,407	0.59%	$405	0.00%	0.10%
8. MAINE	$0	0.00%	$8,326	100.00%	$0	0.00%	$8,326	0.01%	$0	--	--
COMPOSITE	**$0**	0.00%	**$68,390,534**	100.00%	**$0**	0.00%	**$68,390,534**	100.00%	**$4,534,687**	100.00%	6.63%
AVERAGE	**$0**		**$8,548,817**		**$0**		**$8,548,817**		**$566,836**		

D.1   Organization - NAIC Group by Jurisdiction

	DIRECT PREMIUMS WRITTEN							PERCENT OF GROUP	PAID LOSSES	PERCENT OF GROUP	LOSSES TO PREMIUMS
	DIRECT	% of Total	NON-AFFILIATED	% of Total	AFFILIATED	% of Total	TOTAL				

CHICAGO / FIDELITY

		DIRECT	% of Total	NON-AFFILIATED	% of Total	AFFILIATED	% of Total	TOTAL	PERCENT OF GROUP	PAID LOSSES	PERCENT OF GROUP	LOSSES TO PREMIUMS
1.	CALIFORNIA	$48,250,094	7.70%	$63,827,732	10.19%	$514,418,363	82.11%	$626,496,189	16.68%	$100,649,261	30.39%	16.07%
2.	TEXAS	$155,912,612	32.48%	$224,539,266	46.78%	$99,564,406	20.74%	$480,016,284	12.78%	$19,811,459	5.98%	4.13%
3.	FLORIDA	$46,515,368	11.28%	$361,125,087	87.61%	$4,576,665	1.11%	$412,217,120	10.97%	$23,163,468	6.99%	5.62%
4.	NEW YORK	$128,365,693	42.16%	$175,479,697	57.64%	$594,478	0.20%	$304,439,868	8.11%	$18,376,101	5.55%	6.04%
5.	ILLINOIS	$34,088,773	25.25%	$89,507,487	66.30%	$11,412,516	8.45%	$135,008,776	3.59%	$14,690,934	4.44%	10.88%
6.	ARIZONA	$54,934,200	40.71%	$31,611,132	23.42%	$48,406,303	35.87%	$134,951,635	3.59%	$12,633,274	3.81%	9.36%
7.	NEW JERSEY	$32,278,546	23.98%	$102,001,739	75.78%	$315,930	0.23%	$134,596,215	3.58%	$5,568,514	1.68%	4.14%
8.	WASHINGTON	$60,052,073	53.12%	$18,783,932	16.62%	$34,207,259	30.26%	$113,043,264	3.01%	$6,204,796	1.87%	5.49%
9.	GEORGIA	$5,397,865	5.32%	$94,771,035	93.35%	$1,357,008	1.34%	$101,525,908	2.70%	$10,887,273	3.29%	10.72%
10.	PENNSYLVANIA	$21,441,842	21.93%	$76,196,720	77.92%	$154,953	0.16%	$97,793,515	2.60%	$5,702,855	1.72%	5.83%
11.	OREGON	$33,021,483	36.72%	$18,043,025	20.06%	$38,865,925	43.22%	$89,930,433	2.39%	$1,785,506	0.54%	1.99%
12.	OHIO	$23,015,106	25.85%	$61,354,689	68.91%	$4,667,155	5.24%	$89,036,950	2.37%	$4,561,361	1.38%	5.12%
13.	MARYLAND	$8,019,717	9.93%	$72,716,160	90.00%	$61,317	0.08%	$80,797,194	2.15%	$11,178,719	3.38%	13.84%
14.	MICHIGAN	$7,494,850	9.73%	$57,342,660	74.41%	$12,222,972	15.86%	$77,060,482	2.05%	$16,570,627	5.00%	21.50%
15.	VIRGINIA	$7,416,294	9.90%	$66,866,899	89.29%	$604,262	0.81%	$74,887,455	1.99%	$3,378,275	1.02%	4.51%
16.	NEVADA	$4,949,312	7.72%	$19,442,718	30.34%	$39,690,475	61.94%	$64,082,505	1.71%	$3,625,095	1.09%	5.66%
17.	SOUTH CAROLINA	$1,103,928	2.17%	$49,483,392	97.21%	$316,349	0.62%	$50,903,669	1.36%	$3,090,458	0.93%	6.07%
18.	TENNESSEE	$4,525,297	9.41%	$42,048,442	87.42%	$1,526,905	3.17%	$48,100,644	1.28%	$1,940,088	0.59%	4.03%
19.	MASSACHUSETTS	$3,489,440	7.31%	$44,215,123	92.66%	$14,268	0.03%	$47,718,831	1.27%	$6,991,034	2.11%	14.65%
20.	NORTH CAROLINA	$10,519,717	23.41%	$34,153,562	76.00%	$263,320	0.59%	$44,936,599	1.20%	$5,724,900	1.73%	12.74%
21.	COLORADO	$7,931,865	18.88%	$26,352,267	62.74%	$7,721,200	18.38%	$42,005,332	1.12%	$5,689,477	1.72%	13.54%
22.	CONNECTICUT	$2,869,491	7.70%	$34,374,471	92.23%	$26,586	0.07%	$37,270,548	0.99%	$8,678,748	2.62%	23.29%
23.	WISCONSIN	$8,127,289	21.91%	$27,762,750	74.86%	$1,198,182	3.23%	$37,088,221	0.99%	$3,338,189	1.01%	9.00%
24.	UTAH	$1,033,036	2.89%	$34,508,147	96.59%	$186,853	0.52%	$35,728,036	0.95%	$1,085,933	0.33%	3.04%
25.	MINNESOTA	$3,041,575	9.09%	$30,405,199	90.88%	$10,993	0.03%	$33,457,767	0.89%	$9,412,338	2.84%	28.13%
26.	HAWAII	$11,627,661	36.91%	$19,875,110	63.09%	$0	0.00%	$31,502,771	0.84%	$1,706,729	0.52%	5.42%
27.	INDIANA	$14,568,910	48.04%	$15,597,106	51.43%	$163,074	0.54%	$30,329,090	0.81%	$3,577,312	1.08%	11.79%
28.	NEW MEXICO	$13,701,084	52.80%	$12,191,787	46.98%	$58,275	0.22%	$25,951,146	0.69%	$1,295,906	0.39%	4.99%
29.	IDAHO	$966,437	3.76%	$24,713,235	96.24%	$0	0.00%	$25,679,672	0.68%	$1,238,643	0.37%	4.82%
30.	ALABAMA	$1,512,400	6.25%	$21,725,384	89.71%	$979,287	4.04%	$24,217,071	0.64%	$2,085,758	0.63%	8.61%
31.	DELAWARE	$19,153,351	85.74%	$3,185,434	14.26%	$0	0.00%	$22,338,785	0.59%	$127,734	0.04%	0.57%
32.	LOUISIANA	$762,469	3.46%	$18,688,160	84.76%	$2,597,948	11.78%	$22,048,577	0.59%	$1,079,973	0.33%	4.90%
33.	MISSOURI	$3,573,269	17.82%	$16,396,031	81.75%	$87,569	0.44%	$20,056,869	0.53%	$3,714,095	1.12%	18.52%
34.	CANADA	$3,857,639	19.60%	$0	0.00%	$15,827,994	80.40%	$19,685,633	0.52%	($230,821)	(0.07)%	(1.17)%
35.	ARKANSAS	$249,914	1.66%	$14,030,566	93.46%	$731,623	4.87%	$15,012,103	0.40%	$813,494	0.25%	5.42%
36.	OKLAHOMA	$107,411	0.78%	$6,369,685	46.08%	$7,345,833	53.14%	$13,822,929	0.37%	$916,606	0.28%	6.63%
37.	MONTANA	$3,436,804	28.99%	$8,419,146	71.01%	$0	0.00%	$11,855,950	0.32%	$515,480	0.16%	4.35%
38.	KENTUCKY	$2,017,719	17.55%	$8,941,164	77.77%	$537,859	4.68%	$11,496,742	0.31%	$1,085,597	0.33%	9.44%
39.	KANSAS	$4,495,535	40.50%	$6,604,234	59.50%	$0	0.00%	$11,099,769	0.30%	$360,235	0.11%	3.25%
40.	NEBRASKA	$168,791	1.90%	$8,695,381	98.10%	$0	0.00%	$8,864,172	0.24%	$675,620	0.20%	7.62%
41.	MAINE	$252,293	3.14%	$7,775,728	96.86%	$0	0.00%	$8,028,021	0.21%	$1,159,044	0.35%	14.44%
42.	DISTRICT OF COLUMBIA	$1,540,523	20.24%	$6,068,151	79.73%	$1,893	0.02%	$7,610,567	0.20%	$1,526,241	0.46%	20.05%
43.	MISSISSIPPI	$511,387	6.76%	$6,538,102	86.43%	$515,258	6.81%	$7,564,747	0.20%	$740,727	0.22%	9.79%
44.	AGGREGATE OTHER ALIEN	$6,396,532	89.80%	$726,300	10.20%	$0	0.00%	$7,122,832	0.19%	$108,584	0.03%	1.52%
45.	NEW HAMPSHIRE	$235,672	3.67%	$6,188,280	96.33%	$0	0.00%	$6,423,952	0.17%	$1,492,578	0.45%	23.23%
46.	RHODE ISLAND	$437,316	7.35%	$5,511,883	92.65%	$0	0.00%	$5,949,199	0.16%	$434,613	0.13%	7.31%
47.	PUERTO RICO	$428,597	7.89%	$5,001,988	92.11%	$0	0.00%	$5,430,585	0.14%	$934,771	0.28%	17.21%
48.	WEST VIRGINIA	$635,144	14.68%	$3,681,857	85.12%	$8,697	0.20%	$4,325,698	0.12%	$217,824	0.07%	5.04%
49.	ALASKA	$336,532	8.55%	$3,597,263	91.45%	$0	0.00%	$3,933,795	0.10%	$5,894	0.00%	0.15%
50.	WYOMING	$218,603	5.67%	$3,637,464	94.33%	$0	0.00%	$3,856,067	0.10%	$19,950	0.00%	0.52%
51.	SOUTH DAKOTA	$111,970	3.54%	$3,049,867	96.46%	$0	0.00%	$3,161,837	0.08%	$69,984	0.02%	2.21%
52.	GUAM	$0	0.00%	$1,478,263	100.00%	$0	0.00%	$1,478,263	0.04%	$11,326	0.00%	0.77%
53.	VERMONT	$86,180	6.14%	$1,318,128	93.86%	$0	0.00%	$1,404,308	0.04%	$316,805	0.10%	22.56%
54.	NORTH DAKOTA	$15,494	1.15%	$1,327,372	98.85%	$0	0.00%	$1,342,866	0.04%	$14,862	0.00%	1.11%
55.	U.S. VIRGIN ISLANDS	$66,847	6.74%	$925,496	93.26%	$0	0.00%	$992,343	0.03%	$83,037	0.03%	8.37%
56.	IOWA	$250,552	50.22%	$176,753	35.42%	$71,648	14.36%	$498,953	0.01%	$368,507	0.11%	73.86%
	COMPOSITE	**$805,518,502**	21.45%	**$2,099,348,649**	55.89%	**$851,311,601**	22.66%	**$3,756,178,752**	100.00%	**$331,205,767**	100.00%	8.82%
	AVERAGE	**$14,384,259**		**$37,488,369**		**$15,201,993**		**$67,074,621**		**$5,914,389**		

D.1 Organization - NAIC Group by Jurisdiction

	DIRECT	% of Total	DIRECT PREMIUMS WRITTEN NON-AFFILIATED	% of Total	AFFILIATED	% of Total	TOTAL	PERCENT OF GROUP	PAID LOSSES	PERCENT OF GROUP	LOSSES TO PREMIUMS
FIRST AMERICAN											
1. CALIFORNIA	$60,771,284	8.09%	$306,205,265	40.77%	$383,997,039	51.13%	$750,973,588	18.30%	$66,948,529	23.83%	8.91%
2. FLORIDA	$68,531,349	17.85%	$301,784,224	78.62%	$13,557,226	3.53%	$383,872,799	9.35%	$36,144,062	12.87%	9.42%
3. TEXAS	$106,146,688	32.56%	$120,637,459	37.00%	$99,255,039	30.44%	$326,039,186	7.94%	$8,807,551	3.14%	2.70%
4. NEW YORK	$96,495,671	32.18%	$192,008,986	64.03%	$11,384,454	3.80%	$299,889,111	7.31%	$12,730,420	4.53%	4.25%
5. ARIZONA	$77,439,459	46.15%	$53,827,944	32.08%	$36,526,245	21.77%	$167,793,648	4.09%	$8,748,133	3.11%	5.21%
6. PENNSYLVANIA	$19,004,612	12.50%	$129,706,664	85.30%	$3,339,835	2.20%	$152,051,111	3.70%	$5,454,490	1.94%	3.59%
7. UTAH	$11,820,677	8.89%	$88,659,604	66.67%	$32,501,673	24.44%	$132,981,954	3.24%	$2,328,609	0.83%	1.75%
8. MICHIGAN	$14,317,719	11.58%	$64,821,546	52.42%	$44,511,678	36.00%	$123,650,943	3.01%	$13,151,625	4.68%	10.64%
9. OHIO	$9,673,142	7.98%	$92,664,324	76.46%	$18,854,546	15.56%	$121,192,012	2.95%	$8,338,706	2.97%	6.88%
10. COLORADO	$809,635	0.71%	$113,017,386	98.90%	$445,395	0.39%	$114,272,416	2.78%	$9,238,059	3.29%	8.08%
11. NEW JERSEY	$14,285,946	12.59%	$96,075,272	84.66%	$3,119,543	2.75%	$113,480,761	2.77%	$8,776,935	3.12%	7.73%
12. WASHINGTON	$55,199,257	52.60%	$21,944,425	20.91%	$27,789,415	26.48%	$104,933,097	2.56%	$5,856,351	2.08%	5.58%
13. VIRGINIA	$8,731,063	8.65%	$88,263,343	87.48%	$3,904,508	3.87%	$100,898,914	2.46%	$11,131,348	3.96%	11.03%
14. MASSACHUSETTS	$2,021,937	2.08%	$94,807,224	97.69%	$220,075	0.23%	$97,049,236	2.36%	$5,773,019	2.06%	5.95%
15. ILLINOIS	$18,125,789	20.13%	$53,402,348	59.30%	$18,529,294	20.57%	$90,057,431	2.19%	$6,825,875	2.43%	7.58%
16. MARYLAND	$8,095,154	9.24%	$73,832,454	84.30%	$5,659,486	6.46%	$87,587,094	2.13%	$4,843,586	1.72%	5.53%
17. OREGON	$52,365,389	68.08%	$13,190,914	17.15%	$11,364,317	14.77%	$76,920,620	1.87%	$2,455,921	0.87%	3.19%
18. NEVADA	$37,022,447	58.21%	$25,445,731	40.01%	$1,128,647	1.77%	$63,596,825	1.55%	$1,960,163	0.70%	3.08%
19. GEORGIA	$3,824,348	6.28%	$56,566,106	92.83%	$546,730	0.90%	$60,937,184	1.48%	$8,502,223	3.03%	13.95%
20. NORTH CAROLINA	$8,810,772	15.17%	$49,092,437	84.50%	$192,851	0.33%	$58,096,060	1.42%	$3,423,809	1.22%	5.89%
21. CONNECTICUT	$2,905,272	5.55%	$49,257,088	94.07%	$197,810	0.38%	$52,360,170	1.28%	$4,383,027	1.56%	8.37%
22. LOUISIANA	$639,612	1.34%	$46,815,798	98.34%	$149,271	0.31%	$47,604,681	1.16%	($522,517)	(0.19)%	(1.10)%
23. IDAHO	$1,753,667	4.21%	$17,646,666	42.41%	$22,209,074	53.38%	$41,609,407	1.01%	$1,167,518	0.42%	2.81%
24. WISCONSIN	$8,174,177	20.98%	$29,099,657	74.68%	$1,692,991	4.34%	$38,966,825	0.95%	$2,154,733	0.77%	5.53%
25. NEW MEXICO	$15,171,307	47.98%	$13,913,169	44.00%	$2,534,998	8.02%	$31,619,474	0.77%	$1,754,202	0.62%	5.55%
26. INDIANA	$6,024,300	19.38%	$18,563,414	59.71%	$6,502,153	20.91%	$31,089,867	0.76%	$2,525,020	0.90%	8.12%
27. TENNESSEE	$4,931,847	15.88%	$25,697,219	82.75%	$424,465	1.37%	$31,053,531	0.76%	$1,389,680	0.49%	4.48%
28. DISTRICT OF COLUMBIA	$9,221,625	31.65%	$19,485,540	66.87%	$430,540	1.48%	$29,137,705	0.71%	$2,278,004	0.81%	7.82%
29. HAWAII	$869,885	3.00%	$7,417,798	25.56%	$20,733,026	71.44%	$29,020,709	0.71%	$475,150	0.17%	1.64%
30. CANADA	$26,161,839	100.00%	$0	0.00%	$0	0.00%	$26,161,839	0.64%	$7,620,687	2.71%	29.13%
31. SOUTH CAROLINA	$62,556	0.25%	$24,643,744	98.38%	$344,334	1.37%	$25,050,634	0.61%	$1,552,447	0.55%	6.20%
32. OKLAHOMA	$7,164,263	28.74%	$15,725,913	63.08%	$2,039,357	8.18%	$24,929,533	0.61%	$538,790	0.19%	2.16%
33. ALABAMA	$1,209,050	5.05%	$22,556,764	94.28%	$159,114	0.67%	$23,924,928	0.58%	$1,496,680	0.53%	6.26%
34. MONTANA	$471,301	1.98%	$13,242,153	55.66%	$10,078,993	42.36%	$23,792,447	0.58%	$761,207	0.27%	3.20%
35. MINNESOTA	$4,376,517	21.38%	$5,130,418	25.06%	$10,963,657	53.56%	$20,470,592	0.50%	$4,371,827	1.56%	21.36%
36. MISSOURI	$1,449,509	7.66%	$14,961,839	79.11%	$2,501,584	13.23%	$18,912,932	0.46%	$2,882,166	1.03%	15.24%
37. DELAWARE	$8,684,784	47.05%	$9,701,415	52.56%	$71,294	0.39%	$18,457,493	0.45%	$304,870	0.11%	1.65%
38. MAINE	$199,931	1.20%	$14,814,337	88.62%	$1,702,286	10.18%	$16,716,554	0.41%	$1,196,784	0.43%	7.16%
39. ALASKA	$702,611	4.29%	$2,456,715	15.01%	$13,207,261	80.70%	$16,366,587	0.40%	$226,506	0.08%	1.38%
40. WYOMING	$1,752,293	10.74%	$2,909,745	17.84%	$11,647,701	71.42%	$16,309,739	0.40%	$182,368	0.06%	1.12%
41. KANSAS	$1,551,085	9.53%	$7,318,803	44.99%	$7,399,061	45.48%	$16,268,949	0.40%	$311,515	0.11%	1.91%
42. KENTUCKY	$1,677,020	10.55%	$13,716,439	86.32%	$496,678	3.13%	$15,890,137	0.39%	$1,424,683	0.51%	8.97%
43. NEW HAMPSHIRE	$494,462	3.57%	$12,809,174	92.55%	$537,314	3.88%	$13,840,950	0.34%	$738,953	0.26%	5.34%
44. MISSISSIPPI	$2,199,131	16.45%	$11,082,666	82.90%	$86,256	0.65%	$13,368,053	0.33%	$1,714,818	0.61%	12.83%
45. AGGREGATE OTHER ALIEN	$11,074,697	97.23%	$315,301	2.77%	$0	0.00%	$11,389,998	0.28%	$5,327,656	1.90%	46.77%
46. ARKANSAS	$354,923	3.78%	$8,928,694	95.11%	$104,515	1.11%	$9,388,132	0.23%	$1,091,097	0.39%	11.62%
47. NEBRASKA	$751,155	8.17%	$6,415,603	69.79%	$2,025,866	22.04%	$9,192,624	0.22%	$214,149	0.08%	2.33%
48. WEST VIRGINIA	$102,405	1.43%	$7,004,324	97.83%	$52,716	0.74%	$7,159,445	0.17%	$235,830	0.08%	3.29%
49. PUERTO RICO	$259	0.00%	$5,363,770	100.00%	$0	0.00%	$5,364,029	0.13%	$609,815	0.22%	11.37%
50. RHODE ISLAND	$713,952	16.78%	$3,513,916	82.58%	$27,384	0.64%	$4,255,252	0.10%	$253,273	0.09%	5.95%
51. VERMONT	$77,342	2.05%	$3,685,600	97.57%	$14,369	0.38%	$3,777,311	0.09%	$346,486	0.12%	9.17%
52. SOUTH DAKOTA	$271,484	11.12%	$2,169,398	88.87%	$113	0.00%	$2,440,995	0.06%	$30,281	0.01%	1.24%
53. NORTH DAKOTA	$277,928	17.56%	$1,157,329	73.14%	$147,045	9.29%	$1,582,302	0.04%	$21,483	0.00%	1.36%
54. U.S. VIRGIN ISLANDS	$0	0.00%	$206,245	100.00%	$0	0.00%	$206,245	0.00%	$239,174	0.09%	115.97%
55. IOWA	$0	0.00%	$4,099	100.00%	$0	0.00%	$4,099	0.00%	$0	--	--
56. GUAM	$0	--	$0	--	$0	--	$0	--	$169,868	0.06%	--
COMPOSITE	**$794,964,527**	19.37%	**$2,473,684,409**	60.28%	**$835,309,222**	20.35%	**$4,103,958,158**	100.00%	**$280,907,644**	100.00%	6.84%
AVERAGE	**$14,195,795**		**$44,172,936**		**$14,916,236**		**$73,284,967**		**$5,016,208**		

D.1 Organization - NAIC Group by Jurisdiction

	DIRECT PREMIUMS WRITTEN							PERCENT OF GROUP	PAID LOSSES	PERCENT OF GROUP	LOSSES TO PREMIUMS
	DIRECT	% of Total	NON-AFFILIATED	% of Total	AFFILIATED	% of Total	TOTAL				

INVESTORS

	DIRECT	% of Total	NON-AFFILIATED	% of Total	AFFILIATED	% of Total	TOTAL	PERCENT OF GROUP	PAID LOSSES	PERCENT OF GROUP	LOSSES TO PREMIUMS
1. NORTH CAROLINA	$29,147,893	85.06%	$2,032,474	5.93%	$3,085,949	9.01%	$34,266,316	48.98%	$7,786,658	77.36%	22.72%
2. SOUTH CAROLINA	$211,897	2.80%	$7,360,564	97.18%	$1,767	0.02%	$7,574,228	10.83%	$579,164	5.75%	7.65%
3. VIRGINIA	$110,462	1.79%	$5,641,269	91.52%	$412,100	6.69%	$6,163,831	8.81%	$357,259	3.55%	5.80%
4. MICHIGAN	$7,790	0.25%	$2,718,167	87.83%	$368,873	11.92%	$3,094,830	4.42%	$302,789	3.01%	9.78%
5. TENNESSEE	$42,448	1.62%	$2,580,635	98.38%	$0	0.00%	$2,623,083	3.75%	$180,424	1.79%	6.88%
6. KENTUCKY	$0	0.00%	$1,927,641	75.17%	$636,760	24.83%	$2,564,401	3.67%	$130,792	1.30%	5.10%
7. NEW YORK	$0	0.00%	$2,414,626	100.00%	$0	0.00%	$2,414,626	3.45%	$154,328	1.53%	6.39%
8. WEST VIRGINIA	$15,410	0.76%	$2,016,919	99.24%	$0	0.00%	$2,032,329	2.90%	$20,399	0.20%	1.00%
9. ILLINOIS	$6,110	0.37%	$27,192	1.64%	$1,622,461	97.99%	$1,655,763	2.37%	$19,364	0.19%	1.17%
10. PENNSYLVANIA	$35,365	2.34%	$1,332,490	88.23%	$142,470	9.43%	$1,510,325	2.16%	$2,325	0.02%	0.15%
11. FLORIDA	$0	0.00%	$1,428,570	100.00%	$0	0.00%	$1,428,570	2.04%	$21,190	0.21%	1.48%
12. MARYLAND	$0	0.00%	$1,176,007	100.00%	$0	0.00%	$1,176,007	1.68%	$355,386	3.53%	30.22%
13. MISSISSIPPI	$90	0.01%	$916,363	99.99%	$0	0.00%	$916,453	1.31%	$36,314	0.36%	3.96%
14. NEBRASKA	$204,455	28.15%	$521,962	71.85%	$0	0.00%	$726,417	1.04%	($54,485)	(0.54)%	(7.50)%
15. ALABAMA	$0	0.00%	$493,747	100.00%	$0	0.00%	$493,747	0.71%	$49,251	0.49%	9.97%
16. MINNESOTA	$0	0.00%	$482,025	100.00%	$0	0.00%	$482,025	0.69%	$17,576	0.17%	3.65%
17. LOUISIANA	$0	0.00%	$321,368	100.00%	$0	0.00%	$321,368	0.46%	$0	--	--
18. MISSOURI	$0	0.00%	$140,569	86.83%	$21,324	13.17%	$161,893	0.23%	$803	0.00%	0.50%
19. OHIO	$0	0.00%	$141,259	100.00%	$0	0.00%	$141,259	0.20%	$0	--	--
20. GEORGIA	$8,963	9.09%	$89,671	90.91%	$0	0.00%	$98,634	0.14%	$73,058	0.73%	74.07%
21. INDIANA	$0	0.00%	$40,938	100.00%	$0	0.00%	$40,938	0.06%	$27,464	0.27%	67.09%
22. ARKANSAS	$0	0.00%	$31,908	100.00%	$0	0.00%	$31,908	0.05%	$0	--	--
23. DISTRICT OF COLUMBIA	$0	0.00%	$27,142	100.00%	$0	0.00%	$27,142	0.04%	$5,660	0.06%	20.85%
24. IOWA	$0	0.00%	$14,405	100.00%	$0	0.00%	$14,405	0.02%	$0	--	--
COMPOSITE	$29,790,883	42.58%	$33,877,911	48.42%	$6,291,704	8.99%	$69,960,498	100.00%	$10,065,719	100.00%	14.39%
AVERAGE	$1,241,287		$1,411,580		$262,154		$2,915,021		$419,405		

D.1 Organization - NAIC Group by Jurisdiction

	DIRECT PREMIUMS WRITTEN							PERCENT OF GROUP	PAID LOSSES	PERCENT OF GROUP	LOSSES TO PREMIUMS
	DIRECT	% of Total	NON-AFFILIATED	% of Total	AFFILIATED	% of Total	TOTAL				

LAND AMERICA

	DIRECT	% of Total	NON-AFFILIATED	% of Total	AFFILIATED	% of Total	TOTAL	PERCENT OF GROUP	PAID LOSSES	PERCENT OF GROUP	LOSSES TO PREMIUMS
1. TEXAS	$190,850,382	51.86%	$173,811,291	47.23%	$3,356,524	0.91%	$368,018,197	13.37%	$16,470,760	8.86%	4.48%
2. NEW YORK	$100,885,093	33.59%	$199,373,097	66.38%	$83,902	0.03%	$300,342,092	10.91%	$6,856,597	3.69%	2.28%
3. CALIFORNIA	$16,434,071	5.74%	$18,167,115	6.34%	$251,872,307	87.92%	$286,473,493	10.41%	$32,438,848	17.46%	11.32%
4. FLORIDA	$37,630,094	14.35%	$222,834,069	84.99%	$1,726,118	0.66%	$262,190,281	9.53%	$13,859,929	7.46%	5.29%
5. PENNSYLVANIA	$19,089,804	10.38%	$164,489,059	89.41%	$383,558	0.21%	$183,962,421	6.69%	$7,368,306	3.97%	4.01%
6. ARIZONA	$31,661,562	22.64%	$78,312,699	56.00%	$29,879,663	21.36%	$139,853,924	5.08%	$7,223,584	3.89%	5.17%
7. VIRGINIA	$13,509,475	12.96%	$84,703,306	81.28%	$6,003,670	5.76%	$104,216,451	3.79%	$5,687,958	3.06%	5.46%
8. NEW JERSEY	$19,437,666	19.96%	$77,904,241	80.00%	$43,744	0.04%	$97,385,651	3.54%	$6,769,696	3.64%	6.95%
9. MICHIGAN	$17,246,583	24.01%	$52,751,237	73.44%	$1,828,569	2.55%	$71,826,389	2.61%	$15,038,031	8.09%	20.94%
10. MARYLAND	$11,529,773	16.39%	$58,594,448	83.28%	$238,067	0.34%	$70,362,288	2.56%	$2,255,712	1.21%	3.21%
11. WASHINGTON	$21,049,911	31.56%	$19,039,723	28.55%	$26,609,862	39.90%	$66,699,496	2.42%	$3,448,794	1.86%	5.17%
12. OHIO	$14,723,724	23.89%	$43,231,156	70.15%	$3,667,749	5.95%	$61,622,629	2.24%	$4,878,399	2.63%	7.92%
13. GEORGIA	$4,190,349	8.54%	$44,839,756	91.43%	$10,131	0.02%	$49,040,236	1.78%	$5,694,549	3.06%	11.61%
14. UTAH	$212,422	0.47%	$42,497,828	94.30%	$2,355,492	5.23%	$45,065,742	1.64%	$2,656,952	1.43%	5.90%
15. OREGON	$20,361,838	45.54%	$16,813,570	37.61%	$7,534,143	16.85%	$44,709,551	1.62%	$1,626,084	0.88%	3.64%
16. NEVADA	$8,000,254	18.01%	$23,844,267	53.67%	$12,586,389	28.33%	$44,430,910	1.61%	$3,383,021	1.82%	7.61%
17. MASSACHUSETTS	$6,276,254	15.53%	$34,120,545	84.44%	$12,402	0.03%	$40,409,201	1.47%	$5,292,281	2.85%	13.10%
18. NEW MEXICO	$9,439,200	23.63%	$20,480,907	51.27%	$10,027,706	25.10%	$39,947,813	1.45%	$1,378,538	0.74%	3.45%
19. COLORADO	$21,735,294	61.35%	$13,234,723	37.35%	$460,582	1.30%	$35,430,599	1.29%	$2,593,259	1.40%	7.32%
20. IDAHO	$507,677	1.52%	$25,361,682	75.97%	$7,514,013	22.51%	$33,383,372	1.21%	$942,602	0.51%	2.82%
21. MINNESOTA	$2,745,513	8.51%	$29,511,623	91.48%	$2,964	0.01%	$32,260,100	1.17%	$4,661,407	2.51%	14.45%
22. LOUISIANA	$1,516,763	4.77%	$30,289,197	95.20%	$9,192	0.03%	$31,815,152	1.16%	$2,221,986	1.20%	6.98%
23. TENNESSEE	$3,401,676	11.05%	$26,812,537	87.12%	$560,714	1.82%	$30,774,927	1.12%	$1,926,842	1.04%	6.26%
24. SOUTH CAROLINA	$2,043,941	7.87%	$23,932,563	92.11%	$5,156	0.02%	$25,981,660	0.94%	$2,074,256	1.12%	7.98%
25. ALABAMA	$2,052,121	7.99%	$23,632,823	92.01%	$0	0.00%	$25,684,944	0.93%	$2,529,039	1.36%	9.85%
26. ILLINOIS	$7,297,051	30.96%	$16,272,429	69.04%	$1,707	0.01%	$23,571,187	0.86%	$5,894,487	3.17%	25.01%
27. DELAWARE	$13,123,609	59.18%	$9,052,576	40.82%	$0	0.00%	$22,176,185	0.81%	$228,204	0.12%	1.03%
28. CONNECTICUT	$5,473,553	28.59%	$13,672,216	71.41%	$0	0.00%	$19,145,769	0.70%	$872,835	0.47%	4.56%
29. WISCONSIN	$1,905,693	10.80%	$15,687,720	88.90%	$53,182	0.30%	$17,646,595	0.64%	$886,126	0.48%	5.02%
30. INDIANA	$6,667,279	41.01%	$9,589,183	58.99%	$340	0.00%	$16,256,802	0.59%	$1,541,274	0.83%	9.48%
31. MISSOURI	$4,484,716	27.92%	$11,567,883	72.01%	$12,184	0.08%	$16,064,783	0.58%	$6,300,989	3.39%	39.22%
32. KENTUCKY	$2,079,735	13.16%	$13,680,107	86.58%	$40,923	0.26%	$15,800,765	0.57%	$2,183,317	1.18%	13.82%
33. NORTH CAROLINA	$5,554,271	41.22%	$7,916,682	58.75%	$3,739	0.03%	$13,474,692	0.49%	$2,410,208	1.30%	17.89%
34. DISTRICT OF COLUMBIA	$4,605,759	34.97%	$8,550,805	64.93%	$12,513	0.10%	$13,169,077	0.48%	$1,013,092	0.55%	7.69%
35. RHODE ISLAND	$1,159,452	12.11%	$8,414,989	87.89%	$0	0.00%	$9,574,441	0.35%	$353,368	0.19%	3.69%
36. ARKANSAS	$163,968	1.84%	$8,728,380	98.13%	$2,018	0.02%	$8,894,366	0.32%	$317,023	0.17%	3.56%
37. MONTANA	$428,736	5.02%	$8,116,284	94.96%	$1,754	0.02%	$8,546,774	0.31%	$102,514	0.06%	1.20%
38. NEBRASKA	$188,374	2.44%	$7,518,374	97.56%	$0	0.00%	$7,706,748	0.28%	$878,941	0.47%	11.40%
39. KANSAS	$2,290,414	32.69%	$4,557,101	65.04%	$158,721	2.27%	$7,006,236	0.25%	$196,892	0.11%	2.81%
40. NEW HAMPSHIRE	$1,042,036	15.20%	$5,812,444	84.80%	$0	0.00%	$6,854,480	0.25%	$348,785	0.19%	5.09%
41. OKLAHOMA	$82,227	1.22%	$6,581,757	97.76%	$68,824	1.02%	$6,732,808	0.24%	$121,013	0.07%	1.80%
42. MISSISSIPPI	$564,837	8.80%	$5,851,756	91.19%	$394	0.01%	$6,416,987	0.23%	$330,107	0.18%	5.14%
43. HAWAII	$276,230	4.50%	$5,861,334	95.49%	$811	0.01%	$6,138,375	0.22%	$687,907	0.37%	11.21%
44. AGGREGATE OTHER ALIEN	$5,586,981	93.07%	$415,817	6.93%	$0	0.00%	$6,002,798	0.22%	$370	0.00%	0.00%
45. PUERTO RICO	$0	0.00%	$1,596,000	29.14%	$3,880,706	70.86%	$5,476,706	0.20%	$409,635	0.22%	7.48%
46. MAINE	$1,373,207	27.23%	$3,669,406	72.76%	$479	0.01%	$5,043,092	0.18%	$353,748	0.19%	7.01%
47. WEST VIRGINIA	$318,917	6.67%	$4,401,886	92.07%	$60,031	1.26%	$4,780,834	0.17%	$563,724	0.30%	11.79%
48. WYOMING	$26,693	0.63%	$4,217,084	99.37%	$0	0.00%	$4,243,777	0.15%	$40,942	0.02%	0.96%
49. IOWA	$707,687	23.26%	$2,335,100	76.74%	$55	0.00%	$3,042,842	0.11%	$170,861	0.09%	5.62%
50. VERMONT	$475,867	24.78%	$1,444,463	75.21%	$360	0.02%	$1,920,690	0.07%	$40,158	0.02%	2.09%
51. SOUTH DAKOTA	$100,524	6.03%	$1,565,825	93.97%	$0	0.00%	$1,666,349	0.06%	$71,282	0.04%	4.28%
52. NORTH DAKOTA	$70,818	9.75%	$655,285	90.25%	$0	0.00%	$726,103	0.03%	$51,273	0.03%	7.06%
53. CANADA	$720,306	100.00%	$0	0.00%	$0	0.00%	$720,306	0.03%	$61,766	0.03%	8.57%
54. U.S. VIRGIN ISLANDS	$0	0.00%	$644,609	100.00%	$0	0.00%	$644,609	0.02%	$36,922	0.02%	5.73%
55. ALASKA	$43,741	11.23%	$345,773	88.77%	$0	0.00%	$389,514	0.01%	$51,917	0.03%	13.33%
COMPOSITE	**$643,344,121**	23.38%	**$1,737,306,730**	63.14%	**$371,071,358**	13.49%	**$2,751,722,209**	100.00%	**$185,797,110**	100.00%	**6.75%**
AVERAGE	**$11,697,166**		**$31,587,395**		**$6,746,752**		**$50,031,313**		**$3,378,129**		

OHIO FARMERS

	DIRECT	% of Total	NON-AFFILIATED	% of Total	AFFILIATED	% of Total	TOTAL	PERCENT OF GROUP	PAID LOSSES	PERCENT OF GROUP	LOSSES TO PREMIUMS
1. TEXAS	$0	0.00%	$14,656,298	100.00%	$0	0.00%	$14,656,298	27.05%	$699,790	38.72%	4.77%
2. VIRGINIA	$1,173,681	9.09%	$10,922,720	84.60%	$815,354	6.31%	$12,911,755	23.83%	$687,413	38.03%	5.32%
3. TENNESSEE	$0	0.00%	$7,024,297	100.00%	$0	0.00%	$7,024,297	12.96%	($71,080)	(3.93)%	(1.01)%
4. FLORIDA	$0	0.00%	$3,534,245	92.24%	$297,153	7.76%	$3,831,398	7.07%	$115,101	6.37%	3.00%
5. COLORADO	$0	0.00%	$3,293,782	100.00%	$0	0.00%	$3,293,782	6.08%	$38,027	2.10%	1.15%
6. NORTH CAROLINA	$106	0.00%	$2,774,562	100.00%	$0	0.00%	$2,774,668	5.12%	$3,712	0.21%	0.13%
7. MARYLAND	$0	0.00%	$2,039,926	73.53%	$734,177	26.47%	$2,774,103	5.12%	$79,508	4.40%	2.87%
8. ALABAMA	$0	0.00%	$2,459,609	100.00%	$0	0.00%	$2,459,609	4.54%	$90,379	5.00%	3.67%
9. OHIO	$0	0.00%	$469,922	31.02%	$1,045,069	68.98%	$1,514,991	2.80%	($596)	(0.03)%	(0.04)%
10. SOUTH CAROLINA	$0	0.00%	$761,782	100.00%	$0	0.00%	$761,782	1.41%	$8,762	0.48%	1.15%
11. GEORGIA	$0	0.00%	$682,019	100.00%	$0	0.00%	$682,019	1.26%	$115,149	6.37%	16.88%
12. ARKANSAS	$0	0.00%	$498,173	100.00%	$0	0.00%	$498,173	0.92%	$12,239	0.68%	2.46%
13. PENNSYLVANIA	$0	0.00%	$295,215	74.89%	$98,996	25.11%	$394,211	0.73%	$198	0.01%	0.05%
14. WEST VIRGINIA	$0	0.00%	$205,731	86.68%	$31,609	13.32%	$237,340	0.44%	$0	--	--
15. MISSISSIPPI	$0	0.00%	$223,884	100.00%	$0	0.00%	$223,884	0.41%	$0	--	--
16. DISTRICT OF COLUMBIA	$0	0.00%	$131,579	100.00%	$0	0.00%	$131,579	0.24%	$27,876	1.54%	21.19%
17. LOUISIANA	$0	0.00%	$10,825	100.00%	$0	0.00%	$10,825	0.02%	$0	--	--
18. NEW JERSEY	$0	--	$0	--	$0	--	$0	--	$899	0.05%	--
COMPOSITE	**$1,173,787**	2.17%	**$49,984,569**	92.26%	**$3,022,358**	5.58%	**$54,180,714**	100.00%	**$1,807,377**	100.00%	**3.34%**
AVERAGE	**$65,210**		**$2,776,921**		**$167,909**		**$3,010,040**		**$100,410**		

D.1   Organization - NAIC Group by Jurisdiction

	DIRECT PREMIUMS WRITTEN							PERCENT OF GROUP	PAID LOSSES	PERCENT OF GROUP	LOSSES TO PREMIUMS
	DIRECT	% of Total	NON-AFFILIATED	% of Total	AFFILIATED	% of Total	TOTAL				

OLD REPUBLIC

		DIRECT	% of Total	NON-AFFILIATED	% of Total	AFFILIATED	% of Total	TOTAL	PERCENT OF GROUP	PAID LOSSES	PERCENT OF GROUP	LOSSES TO PREMIUMS
1.	FLORIDA	$1,193,556	0.89%	$133,121,159	99.11%	$0	0.00%	$134,314,715	17.24%	$10,328,952	16.69%	7.69%
2.	CALIFORNIA	$2,818,804	3.11%	$9,225,944	10.18%	$78,593,459	86.71%	$90,638,207	11.64%	$3,841,149	6.20%	4.24%
3.	NEW YORK	$316,532	0.43%	$67,876,078	92.30%	$5,343,542	7.27%	$73,536,152	9.44%	$4,345,925	7.02%	5.91%
4.	TEXAS	$8,444	0.02%	$36,987,133	76.29%	$11,486,087	23.69%	$48,481,664	6.22%	$2,631,324	4.25%	5.43%
5.	PENNSYLVANIA	$556,153	1.31%	$41,891,870	98.69%	$0	0.00%	$42,448,023	5.45%	$3,091,682	4.99%	7.28%
6.	NEW JERSEY	$917,478	2.17%	$40,652,727	95.94%	$803,284	1.90%	$42,373,489	5.44%	$6,681,055	10.79%	15.77%
7.	OHIO	$692,128	2.03%	$32,968,455	96.48%	$510,948	1.50%	$34,171,531	4.39%	$3,720,465	6.01%	10.89%
8.	COLORADO	$165,916	0.60%	$27,263,453	99.40%	$0	0.00%	$27,429,369	3.52%	$1,544,176	2.49%	5.63%
9.	TENNESSEE	$320,811	1.31%	$23,679,789	96.97%	$419,682	1.72%	$24,420,282	3.14%	$1,052,137	1.70%	4.31%
10.	GEORGIA	$195,824	0.83%	$23,403,351	99.17%	$0	0.00%	$23,599,175	3.03%	$3,476,917	5.62%	14.73%
11.	MASSACHUSETTS	$297,150	1.36%	$21,526,999	98.59%	$10,220	0.05%	$21,834,369	2.80%	$1,488,095	2.40%	6.82%
12.	MICHIGAN	$248,330	1.62%	$15,041,679	98.38%	$0	0.00%	$15,290,009	1.96%	$4,409,450	7.12%	28.84%
13.	ALABAMA	$136,053	1.00%	$13,422,826	99.00%	$0	0.00%	$13,558,879	1.74%	$790,584	1.28%	5.83%
14.	MINNESOTA	$1,627,848	13.47%	$10,453,789	86.53%	$0	0.00%	$12,081,637	1.55%	$2,204,976	3.56%	18.25%
15.	MARYLAND	$156,861	1.34%	$11,530,449	98.66%	$0	0.00%	$11,687,310	1.50%	$994,975	1.61%	8.51%
16.	MISSISSIPPI	$407,805	3.50%	$11,233,776	96.50%	$0	0.00%	$11,641,581	1.49%	$1,109,869	1.79%	9.53%
17.	NORTH CAROLINA	$22,624	0.21%	$1,245,737	11.83%	$9,260,435	87.95%	$10,528,796	1.35%	$1,122,735	1.81%	10.66%
18.	NEBRASKA	$33,496	0.32%	$10,356,291	99.68%	$0	0.00%	$10,389,787	1.33%	$136,282	0.22%	1.31%
19.	ARIZONA	$887,960	8.84%	$5,926,761	59.00%	$3,231,134	32.16%	$10,045,855	1.29%	$49,664	0.08%	0.49%
20.	WASHINGTON	$489,107	5.17%	$2,221,251	23.47%	$6,752,056	71.36%	$9,462,414	1.21%	$898,157	1.45%	9.49%
21.	HAWAII	$105,074	1.19%	$78,373	0.89%	$8,632,417	97.92%	$8,815,864	1.13%	$532,902	0.86%	6.04%
22.	VIRGINIA	$196,158	2.32%	$8,242,228	97.68%	$0	0.00%	$8,438,386	1.08%	$839,161	1.36%	9.94%
23.	KENTUCKY	$268,821	3.33%	$7,797,533	96.67%	$0	0.00%	$8,066,354	1.04%	$884,380	1.43%	10.96%
24.	WISCONSIN	$69,853	0.90%	$7,659,914	99.10%	$0	0.00%	$7,729,767	0.99%	$195,169	0.32%	2.52%
25.	IDAHO	($481)	(0.01)%	$7,611,024	100.01%	$0	0.00%	$7,610,543	0.98%	$508,970	0.82%	6.69%
26.	NEVADA	$280,522	3.73%	$3,730,514	49.54%	$3,519,312	46.74%	$7,530,348	0.97%	$35,726	0.06%	0.47%
27.	SOUTH CAROLINA	$183,541	2.80%	$6,377,095	97.20%	$0	0.00%	$6,560,636	0.84%	$401,617	0.65%	6.12%
28.	MISSOURI	$69,405	1.65%	$3,084,526	73.44%	$1,046,411	24.91%	$4,200,342	0.54%	$1,823,650	2.95%	43.42%
29.	DELAWARE	$56,757	1.39%	$4,035,755	98.61%	$0	0.00%	$4,092,512	0.53%	$41,705	0.07%	1.02%
30.	INDIANA	$227,177	5.62%	$3,818,019	94.38%	$0	0.00%	$4,045,196	0.52%	$125,107	0.20%	3.09%
31.	ILLINOIS	$213,689	5.38%	$3,754,970	94.62%	$0	0.00%	$3,968,659	0.51%	$626,350	1.01%	15.78%
32.	UTAH	$670,311	17.24%	$2,423,716	62.33%	$794,545	20.43%	$3,888,572	0.50%	$139,943	0.23%	3.60%
33.	OKLAHOMA	$175	0.00%	$656,399	17.85%	$3,019,801	82.14%	$3,676,375	0.47%	$82,167	0.13%	2.24%
34.	ALASKA	$265	0.01%	$3,660,960	99.99%	$0	0.00%	$3,661,225	0.47%	$37,011	0.06%	1.01%
35.	CONNECTICUT	$288,822	8.38%	$3,158,499	91.62%	$0	0.00%	$3,447,321	0.44%	$134,079	0.22%	3.89%
36.	KANSAS	$5,702	0.17%	$2,956,623	86.57%	$452,917	13.26%	$3,415,242	0.44%	$250,881	0.41%	7.35%
37.	SOUTH DAKOTA	$50	0.00%	$2,859,456	100.00%	$0	0.00%	$2,859,506	0.37%	$4,632	0.00%	0.16%
38.	NEW HAMPSHIRE	$266,056	9.72%	$2,471,937	90.28%	$0	0.00%	$2,737,993	0.35%	$254,458	0.41%	9.29%
39.	ARKANSAS	$35,421	1.31%	$2,664,933	98.69%	$0	0.00%	$2,700,354	0.35%	$304,220	0.49%	11.27%
40.	WEST VIRGINIA	$9,446	0.43%	$2,191,208	99.57%	$0	0.00%	$2,200,654	0.28%	$75,867	0.12%	3.45%
41.	NEW MEXICO	$0	0.00%	$2,175,598	100.00%	$0	0.00%	$2,175,598	0.28%	$168,838	0.27%	7.76%
42.	WYOMING	$0	0.00%	$1,675,569	100.00%	$0	0.00%	$1,675,569	0.22%	$29,359	0.05%	1.75%
43.	LOUISIANA	$25,080	1.57%	$1,572,271	98.43%	$0	0.00%	$1,597,351	0.21%	$163,816	0.26%	10.26%
44.	DISTRICT OF COLUMBIA	$14,322	0.92%	$1,545,274	99.08%	$0	0.00%	$1,559,596	0.20%	$129,585	0.21%	8.31%
45.	MONTANA	$20,793	1.40%	$1,464,886	98.60%	$0	0.00%	$1,485,679	0.19%	$12,433	0.02%	0.84%
46.	PUERTO RICO	$0	0.00%	$1,074,393	100.00%	$0	0.00%	$1,074,393	0.14%	$48,382	0.08%	4.50%
47.	NORTH DAKOTA	$50	0.01%	$761,993	99.99%	$0	0.00%	$762,043	0.10%	$0	--	--
48.	MAINE	$48,173	8.66%	$508,379	91.34%	$0	0.00%	$556,552	0.07%	$25,572	0.04%	4.59%
49.	RHODE ISLAND	$9,106	3.47%	$253,616	96.53%	$0	0.00%	$262,722	0.03%	$43,981	0.07%	16.74%
50.	VERMONT	$5,565	3.89%	$137,384	96.11%	$0	0.00%	$142,949	0.02%	$65,988	0.11%	46.16%
51.	OREGON	$0	0.00%	$67,301	100.00%	$0	0.00%	$67,301	0.00%	$0	--	--
	COMPOSITE	$14,562,733	1.87%	$630,499,863	80.94%	$133,876,250	17.19%	$778,938,846	100.00%	$61,904,518	100.00%	7.95%
	AVERAGE	$285,544		$12,362,742		$2,625,025		$15,273,311		$1,213,814		

RELIANT HOLDING

		DIRECT	% of Total	NON-AFFILIATED	% of Total	AFFILIATED	% of Total	TOTAL	PERCENT OF GROUP	PAID LOSSES	PERCENT OF GROUP	LOSSES TO PREMIUMS
1.	MICHIGAN	$0	0.00%	$201,584	7.21%	$2,595,869	92.79%	$2,797,453	20.10%	$513,370	19.31%	18.35%
2.	OHIO	$186,780	10.48%	$472,033	26.48%	$1,123,621	63.04%	$1,782,434	12.81%	$204,968	7.71%	11.50%
3.	ILLINOIS	$0	0.00%	$418,268	25.68%	$1,210,289	74.32%	$1,628,557	11.70%	$559,736	21.05%	34.37%
4.	PENNSYLVANIA	$0	0.00%	$1,100,503	71.62%	$436,169	28.38%	$1,536,672	11.04%	$261,672	9.84%	17.03%
5.	MISSOURI	$0	0.00%	$1,118,587	74.26%	$387,803	25.74%	$1,506,390	10.82%	$1,011,385	38.03%	67.14%
6.	ARIZONA	$0	0.00%	$0	0.00%	$1,506,068	100.00%	$1,506,068	10.82%	$4,187	0.16%	0.28%
7.	INDIANA	$17,740	2.32%	$339,321	44.38%	$407,468	53.30%	$764,529	5.49%	$40,614	1.53%	5.31%
8.	UTAH	$0	0.00%	$0	0.00%	$761,915	100.00%	$761,915	5.47%	$0	--	--
9.	OKLAHOMA	$0	0.00%	$0	0.00%	$683,390	100.00%	$683,390	4.91%	$0	--	--
10.	TENNESSEE	$0	0.00%	$0	0.00%	$228,810	100.00%	$228,810	1.64%	$6,700	0.25%	2.93%
11.	KANSAS	$0	0.00%	$6,800	3.80%	$172,205	96.20%	$179,005	1.29%	$21,655	0.81%	12.10%
12.	ARKANSAS	$0	0.00%	$0	0.00%	$176,978	100.00%	$176,978	1.27%	$0	--	--
13.	SOUTH CAROLINA	$0	0.00%	$0	0.00%	$162,067	100.00%	$162,067	1.16%	$33,846	1.27%	20.88%
14.	MISSISSIPPI	$0	0.00%	$0	0.00%	$151,012	100.00%	$151,012	1.09%	$22	0.00%	0.01%
15.	DISTRICT OF COLUMBIA	$0	0.00%	$0	0.00%	$37,974	100.00%	$37,974	0.27%	$0	--	--
16.	MAINE	$0	0.00%	$0	0.00%	$10,566	100.00%	$10,566	0.08%	$0	--	--
17.	FLORIDA	$0	0.00%	$0	0.00%	$2,530	100.00%	$2,530	0.02%	$731	0.03%	28.89%
18.	KENTUCKY	$0	0.00%	$0	0.00%	$150	100.00%	$150	0.00%	$0	--	--
19.	IOWA	$0	--	$0	--	$0	--	$0	--	$214	0.00%	--
	COMPOSITE	$204,520	1.47%	$3,657,096	26.28%	$10,054,884	72.25%	$13,916,500	100.00%	$2,659,100	100.00%	19.11%
	AVERAGE	$10,764		$192,479		$529,204		$732,447		$139,953		

D.1 Organization - NAIC Group by Jurisdiction

	DIRECT PREMIUMS WRITTEN							PERCENT OF GROUP	PAID LOSSES	PERCENT OF GROUP	LOSSES TO PREMIUMS
	DIRECT	% of Total	NON-AFFILIATED	% of Total	AFFILIATED	% of Total	TOTAL				

STEWART

		DIRECT	% of Total	NON-AFFILIATED	% of Total	AFFILIATED	% of Total	TOTAL	PERCENT OF GROUP	PAID LOSSES	PERCENT OF GROUP	LOSSES TO PREMIUMS
1.	TEXAS	$33,887,417	12.57%	$67,302,472	24.96%	$168,480,798	62.48%	$269,670,687	16.32%	$4,269,132	4.03%	1.58%
2.	NEW YORK	$44,508,239	25.40%	$129,002,323	73.61%	$1,738,004	0.99%	$175,248,566	10.61%	$5,017,868	4.73%	2.86%
3.	FLORIDA	$4,775,431	2.89%	$129,810,306	78.53%	$30,708,240	18.58%	$165,293,977	10.00%	$10,596,193	10.00%	6.41%
4.	CALIFORNIA	$14,241,275	8.99%	$42,096,381	26.57%	$102,120,824	64.45%	$158,458,480	9.59%	$20,135,633	19.00%	12.71%
5.	CANADA	$76,099,011	100.00%	$0	0.00%	$0	0.00%	$76,099,011	4.61%	$13,556,557	12.79%	17.81%
6.	VIRGINIA	$1,150,755	1.81%	$54,963,622	86.65%	$7,315,614	11.53%	$63,429,991	3.84%	$3,209,921	3.03%	5.06%
7.	NEW JERSEY	$1,946,301	3.09%	$55,021,124	87.39%	$5,995,111	9.52%	$62,962,536	3.81%	$3,356,654	3.17%	5.33%
8.	UTAH	$761,063	1.63%	$37,616,999	80.49%	$8,358,551	17.88%	$46,736,613	2.83%	$434,934	0.41%	0.93%
9.	MARYLAND	$1,163,121	2.90%	$36,733,767	91.49%	$2,251,554	5.61%	$40,148,442	2.43%	$2,633,944	2.48%	6.56%
10.	COLORADO	$828,251	2.20%	$16,014,388	42.63%	$20,726,344	55.17%	$37,568,983	2.27%	$4,031,176	3.80%	10.73%
11.	OHIO	$1,967,484	5.38%	$23,963,516	65.53%	$10,636,676	29.09%	$36,567,676	2.21%	$3,497,715	3.30%	9.57%
12.	WASHINGTON	$528,543	1.52%	$8,761,658	25.13%	$25,579,421	73.36%	$34,869,622	2.11%	$945,646	0.89%	2.71%
13.	PENNSYLVANIA	$4,146,574	12.18%	$29,560,885	86.86%	$326,776	0.96%	$34,034,235	2.06%	$2,221,328	2.10%	6.53%
14.	GEORGIA	$1,347,309	3.98%	$32,316,217	95.56%	$152,722	0.45%	$33,816,248	2.05%	$2,086,645	1.97%	6.17%
15.	ILLINOIS	$1,759,049	5.53%	$24,028,734	75.54%	$6,023,601	18.94%	$31,811,384	1.93%	$2,203,377	2.08%	6.93%
16.	MASSACHUSETTS	$2,077,606	8.23%	$22,543,803	89.32%	$617,198	2.45%	$25,238,607	1.53%	$2,474,207	2.33%	9.80%
17.	ARIZONA	$358,106	1.69%	$2,984,773	14.06%	$17,879,310	84.25%	$21,222,189	1.28%	$307,588	0.29%	1.45%
18.	MICHIGAN	$681,396	3.32%	$16,421,784	80.13%	$3,390,828	16.55%	$20,494,008	1.24%	$5,111,056	4.82%	24.94%
19.	NEVADA	$1,219,137	6.45%	$5,094,523	26.96%	$12,580,498	66.58%	$18,894,158	1.14%	$408,850	0.39%	2.16%
20.	ALABAMA	$453,681	2.52%	$16,270,053	90.51%	$1,251,794	6.96%	$17,975,528	1.09%	$1,856,083	1.75%	10.33%
21.	TENNESSEE	$551,718	3.09%	$12,109,491	67.82%	$5,194,914	29.09%	$17,856,123	1.08%	$1,138,614	1.07%	6.38%
22.	SOUTH CAROLINA	$323,342	1.84%	$17,241,337	97.93%	$41,484	0.24%	$17,606,163	1.07%	$708,085	0.67%	4.02%
23.	MINNESOTA	$256,667	1.54%	$14,407,553	86.64%	$1,965,411	11.82%	$16,629,631	1.01%	$1,779,847	1.68%	10.70%
24.	LOUISIANA	$149,049	0.95%	$12,743,531	80.93%	$2,854,272	18.13%	$15,746,852	0.95%	$345,301	0.33%	2.19%
25.	WISCONSIN	$332,449	2.18%	$10,654,472	69.95%	$4,244,788	27.87%	$15,231,709	0.92%	$1,090,442	1.03%	7.16%
26.	INDIANA	$320,241	2.17%	$9,786,782	66.23%	$4,669,539	31.60%	$14,776,562	0.89%	$2,476,061	2.34%	16.76%
27.	NORTH CAROLINA	$1,721,235	13.25%	$10,176,438	78.34%	$1,092,468	8.41%	$12,990,141	0.79%	$1,646,435	1.55%	12.67%
28.	NEW MEXICO	$0	0.00%	$3,341,414	25.99%	$9,513,136	74.01%	$12,854,550	0.78%	$156,780	0.15%	1.22%
29.	IDAHO	$56,157	0.44%	$7,038,043	54.89%	$5,728,524	44.67%	$12,822,724	0.78%	$108,699	0.10%	0.85%
30.	PUERTO RICO	$23,054	0.18%	$130,122	1.02%	$12,626,403	98.80%	$12,779,579	0.77%	$989,787	0.93%	7.75%
31.	MISSOURI	$264,661	2.21%	$10,057,805	83.83%	$1,676,006	13.97%	$11,998,472	0.73%	$1,517,882	1.43%	12.65%
32.	ARKANSAS	($1,659)	(0.01)%	$9,689,665	81.85%	$2,150,124	18.16%	$11,838,130	0.72%	$942,004	0.89%	7.96%
33.	OREGON	$722,858	6.60%	$10,237,613	93.40%	$0	0.00%	$10,960,471	0.66%	$187,593	0.18%	1.71%
34.	KENTUCKY	$546,525	5.69%	$7,390,922	76.94%	$1,668,069	17.37%	$9,605,516	0.58%	$730,790	0.69%	7.61%
35.	MONTANA	$10,786	0.12%	$3,572,369	40.68%	$5,197,724	59.19%	$8,780,879	0.53%	$226,173	0.21%	2.58%
36.	ALASKA	$75,891	0.88%	$4,705,077	54.56%	$3,842,143	44.56%	$8,623,111	0.52%	($3,977)	0.00%	(0.05)%
37.	WYOMING	$15,098	0.21%	$6,144,633	86.46%	$947,405	13.33%	$7,107,136	0.43%	$106,567	0.10%	1.50%
38.	OKLAHOMA	$66,879	1.10%	$2,601,403	42.97%	$3,385,667	55.92%	$6,053,949	0.37%	($85,877)	(0.08)%	(1.42)%
39.	CONNECTICUT	$1,423,151	24.02%	$4,442,924	75.00%	$57,970	0.98%	$5,924,045	0.36%	$142,023	0.13%	2.40%
40.	KANSAS	$301,840	5.35%	$2,620,984	46.49%	$2,715,209	48.16%	$5,638,033	0.34%	$493,020	0.47%	8.74%
41.	HAWAII	$59,314	1.15%	$5,094,424	98.85%	$0	0.00%	$5,153,738	0.31%	$59,183	0.06%	1.15%
42.	NEW HAMPSHIRE	$198,834	4.62%	$3,133,150	72.74%	$975,175	22.64%	$4,307,159	0.26%	$369,323	0.35%	8.57%
43.	GUAM	$0	0.00%	$4,300,401	100.00%	$0	0.00%	$4,300,401	0.26%	$15,592	0.01%	0.36%
44.	DISTRICT OF COLUMBIA	$415,513	10.09%	$2,502,210	60.78%	$1,199,442	29.13%	$4,117,165	0.25%	$220,792	0.21%	5.36%
45.	DELAWARE	$96,163	2.37%	$3,290,326	81.11%	$670,323	16.52%	$4,056,812	0.25%	$122,926	0.12%	3.03%
46.	MISSISSIPPI	$158,727	4.22%	$3,079,639	81.82%	$525,456	13.96%	$3,763,822	0.23%	$319,032	0.30%	8.48%
47.	WEST VIRGINIA	$33,946	0.97%	$3,454,535	98.83%	$6,974	0.20%	$3,495,455	0.21%	$179,843	0.17%	5.15%
48.	RHODE ISLAND	$123,689	3.74%	$2,025,143	61.24%	$1,158,069	35.02%	$3,306,901	0.20%	$1,237,043	1.17%	37.41%
49.	AGGREGATE OTHER ALIEN	$255,295	7.95%	$1,215,251	37.83%	$1,741,901	54.22%	$3,212,447	0.19%	($204,249)	(0.19)%	(6.36)%
50.	MAINE	$26,806	1.16%	$1,750,925	76.06%	$524,213	22.77%	$2,301,944	0.14%	$310,621	0.29%	13.49%
51.	SOUTH DAKOTA	$13,860	0.70%	$1,006,549	51.18%	$946,312	48.12%	$1,966,721	0.12%	$76,756	0.07%	3.90%
52.	NEBRASKA	$124,603	6.50%	$1,774,815	92.62%	$16,803	0.88%	$1,916,221	0.12%	$134,716	0.13%	7.03%
53.	NORTH DAKOTA	$14,770	1.24%	$1,176,170	98.76%	$0	0.00%	$1,190,940	0.07%	$4,634	0.00%	0.39%
54.	VERMONT	$73,791	6.81%	$1,008,830	93.10%	$993	0.09%	$1,083,614	0.07%	$51,364	0.05%	4.74%
55.	NORTHERN MARIANA IS.	$0	0.00%	$779,364	100.00%	$0	0.00%	$779,364	0.05%	$21,656	0.02%	2.78%
56.	U.S. VIRGIN ISLANDS	$0	0.00%	$516,458	100.00%	$0	0.00%	$516,458	0.03%	$18,555	0.02%	3.59%
57.	IOWA	$172,064	37.15%	$273,669	59.09%	$17,416	3.76%	$463,149	0.03%	$10,348	0.00%	2.23%
	COMPOSITE	$202,827,066	12.28%	$945,981,765	57.25%	$503,488,197	30.47%	$1,652,297,028	100.00%	$105,998,891	100.00%	6.42%
	AVERAGE	$3,558,370		$16,596,171		$8,833,126		$28,987,667		$1,859,630		

3

D.1 Organization - NAIC Group by Jurisdiction

	DIRECT PREMIUMS WRITTEN							PERCENT OF GROUP	PAID LOSSES	PERCENT OF GROUP	LOSSES TO PREMIUMS
	DIRECT	% of Total	NON-AFFILIATED	% of Total	AFFILIATED	% of Total	TOTAL				

TRANSUNION

	DIRECT	% of Total	NON-AFFILIATED	% of Total	AFFILIATED	% of Total	TOTAL	PERCENT OF GROUP	PAID LOSSES	PERCENT OF GROUP	LOSSES TO PREMIUMS
1. FLORIDA	$6,658	0.56%	$650,608	54.43%	$538,097	45.02%	$1,195,363	24.92%	$0	--	--
2. CALIFORNIA	$882,460	100.00%	$0	0.00%	$0	0.00%	$882,460	18.40%	$397,148	34.18%	45.00%
3. SOUTH CAROLINA	$68,818	8.33%	$746,478	90.33%	$11,080	1.34%	$826,376	17.23%	$363,212	31.26%	43.95%
4. OHIO	$33,035	4.78%	$617,640	89.44%	$39,893	5.78%	$690,568	14.40%	$6,524	0.56%	0.94%
5. ALABAMA	$0	0.00%	$263,949	92.17%	$22,421	7.83%	$286,370	5.97%	$90,755	7.81%	31.69%
6. GEORGIA	$0	0.00%	$66,197	31.04%	$147,083	68.96%	$213,280	4.45%	$166,651	14.34%	78.14%
7. NORTH CAROLINA	$210	0.12%	$0	0.00%	$171,167	99.88%	$171,377	3.57%	$110,277	9.49%	64.35%
8. VIRGINIA	$0	0.00%	$0	0.00%	$117,235	100.00%	$117,235	2.44%	$5,069	0.44%	4.32%
9. ILLINOIS	$88	0.08%	$0	0.00%	$116,352	99.92%	$116,440	2.43%	$22,364	1.92%	19.21%
10. ARIZONA	$0	0.00%	$0	0.00%	$81,056	100.00%	$81,056	1.69%	$0	--	--
11. MARYLAND	$2	0.00%	$0	0.00%	$70,720	100.00%	$70,722	1.47%	$0	--	--
12. TENNESSEE	$0	0.00%	$0	0.00%	$59,287	100.00%	$59,287	1.24%	$0	--	--
13. INDIANA	$0	0.00%	$0	0.00%	$17,703	100.00%	$17,703	0.37%	$0	--	--
14. MISSISSIPPI	$35	0.23%	$0	0.00%	$15,188	99.77%	$15,223	0.32%	$0	--	--
15. KENTUCKY	$0	0.00%	$0	0.00%	$10,162	100.00%	$10,162	0.21%	$0	--	--
16. UTAH	$0	0.00%	$0	0.00%	$9,265	100.00%	$9,265	0.19%	$0	--	--
17. ARKANSAS	$1,044	11.74%	$0	0.00%	$7,845	88.26%	$8,889	0.19%	$0	--	--
18. NEVADA	$0	0.00%	$0	0.00%	$8,651	100.00%	$8,651	0.18%	$0	--	--
19. DELAWARE	$0	0.00%	$0	0.00%	$8,475	100.00%	$8,475	0.18%	$0	--	--
20. DISTRICT OF COLUMBIA	$0	0.00%	$0	0.00%	$6,951	100.00%	$6,951	0.14%	$0	--	--
COMPOSITE	$992,350	20.69%	$2,344,872	48.89%	$1,458,631	30.41%	$4,795,853	100.00%	$1,162,000	100.00%	24.23%
AVERAGE	$49,618		$117,244		$72,932		$239,793		$58,100		

UNAFFILIATED COMPANIES

	DIRECT	% of Total	NON-AFFILIATED	% of Total	AFFILIATED	% of Total	TOTAL	PERCENT OF GROUP	PAID LOSSES	PERCENT OF GROUP	LOSSES TO PREMIUMS
1. TEXAS	$0	0.00%	$59,358,306	51.72%	$55,406,465	48.28%	$114,764,771	25.45%	$2,273,835	15.64%	1.98%
2. CALIFORNIA	$43,152	0.04%	$492,277	0.49%	$99,787,264	99.47%	$100,322,693	22.24%	$2,637,305	18.14%	2.63%
3. FLORIDA	$535,440	1.18%	$21,351,897	47.02%	$23,521,766	51.80%	$45,409,103	10.07%	$756,626	5.20%	1.67%
4. COLORADO	$0	0.00%	$9,352,476	22.82%	$31,623,264	77.18%	$40,975,740	9.09%	$778,543	5.36%	1.90%
5. ARIZONA	$0	0.00%	$15,961,857	62.74%	$9,478,436	37.26%	$25,440,293	5.64%	$1,288,636	8.86%	5.07%
6. NEW YORK	$251,019	1.37%	$15,142,322	82.81%	$2,893,006	15.82%	$18,286,347	4.05%	$1,196,352	8.23%	6.54%
7. NEVADA	$0	0.00%	$35,531	0.24%	$14,944,771	99.76%	$14,980,302	3.32%	$361,072	2.48%	2.41%
8. MARYLAND	$413,935	3.13%	$8,860,419	67.08%	$3,934,344	29.79%	$13,208,698	2.93%	$484,773	3.33%	3.67%
9. ILLINOIS	$10,633,487	88.92%	$0	0.00%	$1,324,490	11.08%	$11,957,977	2.65%	$1,944,200	13.37%	16.26%
10. PENNSYLVANIA	$117,495	1.19%	$8,276,555	83.95%	$1,465,058	14.86%	$9,859,108	2.19%	$224,328	1.54%	2.28%
11. OHIO	$186,090	1.97%	$8,280,060	87.74%	$971,072	10.29%	$9,437,222	2.09%	$914,008	6.29%	9.69%
12. OKLAHOMA	$1,906,376	28.67%	$4,209,897	63.32%	$532,250	8.01%	$6,648,523	1.47%	$55,949	0.38%	0.84%
13. NEW JERSEY	$4,985	0.08%	$357,806	5.75%	$5,856,310	94.17%	$6,219,101	1.38%	$13,668	0.09%	0.22%
14. INDIANA	$735,000	17.66%	$3,081,264	74.04%	$345,572	8.30%	$4,161,836	0.92%	$430,526	2.96%	10.34%
15. IOWA	$3,724,743	100.00%	$0	0.00%	$0	0.00%	$3,724,743	0.83%	($2,440)	(0.02)%	(0.07)%
16. VIRGINIA	$0	0.00%	$239,215	7.28%	$3,048,443	92.72%	$3,287,658	0.73%	($61)	0.00%	0.00%
17. MISSISSIPPI	$56,517	1.75%	$3,176,833	98.25%	$0	0.00%	$3,233,350	0.72%	$153,718	1.06%	4.75%
18. SOUTH DAKOTA	$168,351	6.47%	$2,432,110	93.53%	$0	0.00%	$2,600,461	0.58%	$51,729	0.36%	1.99%
19. SOUTH CAROLINA	$0	0.00%	$2,521,722	100.00%	$0	0.00%	$2,521,722	0.56%	$48,214	0.33%	1.91%
20. LOUISIANA	$0	0.00%	$2,343,439	100.00%	$0	0.00%	$2,343,439	0.52%	$136,777	0.94%	5.84%
21. MISSOURI	$698,400	32.35%	$1,138,404	52.73%	$322,242	14.93%	$2,159,046	0.48%	$63,819	0.44%	2.96%
22. DELAWARE	$0	0.00%	$1,419,082	100.00%	$0	0.00%	$1,419,082	0.31%	$2,934	0.02%	0.21%
23. DISTRICT OF COLUMBIA	$0	0.00%	$672,256	65.86%	$348,462	34.14%	$1,020,718	0.23%	$108,704	0.75%	10.65%
24. CONNECTICUT	$982,520	100.00%	$0	0.00%	$0	0.00%	$982,520	0.22%	$0	--	--
25. ALABAMA	$0	0.00%	$967,996	100.00%	$0	0.00%	$967,996	0.21%	$191,462	1.32%	19.78%
26. MASSACHUSETTS	$857,225	95.05%	$0	0.00%	$44,660	4.95%	$901,885	0.20%	$41,763	0.29%	4.63%
27. NEW MEXICO	$0	0.00%	$0	0.00%	$724,207	100.00%	$724,207	0.16%	$54,397	0.37%	7.51%
28. MICHIGAN	$0	0.00%	$0	0.00%	$498,233	100.00%	$498,233	0.11%	$0	--	--
29. MINNESOTA	$5,315	1.10%	$79,799	16.59%	$395,889	82.30%	$481,003	0.11%	$124	0.00%	0.03%
30. KENTUCKY	$5,691	1.36%	$412,436	98.64%	$0	0.00%	$418,127	0.09%	$21,658	0.15%	5.18%
31. ARKANSAS	$0	0.00%	$415,609	100.00%	$0	0.00%	$415,609	0.09%	$357	0.00%	0.09%
32. TENNESSEE	$262,384	71.35%	$105,379	28.65%	$0	0.00%	$367,763	0.08%	$147,452	1.01%	40.09%
33. UTAH	$0	0.00%	$363,865	100.00%	$0	0.00%	$363,865	0.08%	$0	--	--
34. WISCONSIN	$291,071	100.00%	$0	0.00%	$0	0.00%	$291,071	0.06%	$42,789	0.29%	14.70%
35. GEORGIA	$0	0.00%	$262,162	100.00%	$0	0.00%	$262,162	0.06%	$37,023	0.25%	14.12%
36. WYOMING	$178,276	100.00%	$0	0.00%	$0	0.00%	$178,276	0.04%	$0	--	--
37. NEBRASKA	$0	0.00%	$96,748	100.00%	$0	0.00%	$96,748	0.02%	$0	--	--
38. WEST VIRGINIA	$0	0.00%	$52,488	100.00%	$0	0.00%	$52,488	0.01%	$77,657	0.53%	147.95%
39. MAINE	$0	0.00%	$0	0.00%	$14,476	100.00%	$14,476	0.00%	$0	--	--
COMPOSITE	$22,057,472	4.89%	$171,460,210	38.02%	$257,480,680	57.09%	$450,998,362	100.00%	$14,537,897	100.00%	3.22%
AVERAGE	$565,576		$4,396,416		$6,602,069		$11,564,061		$372,767		

3

Notes

D.2 ORGANIZATION
- INDIVIDUAL UNDERWRITER BY JURISDICTION

3

D.2 Organization - Individual Underwriter by Jurisdiction

	DIRECT	% of Total	NON-AFFILIATED	% of Total	AFFILIATED	% of Total	TOTAL	PERCENT OF UNDERWRITER	PAID LOSSES	PERCENT OF UNDERWRITER	LOSSES TO PREMIUMS
ALAMO											
1. TEXAS	$0	0.00%	$42,093,104	44.70%	$52,072,753	55.30%	$94,165,857	99.94%	$3,719,794	99.88%	3.95%
2. NEW MEXICO	$0	0.00%	$52,471	100.00%	$0	0.00%	$52,471	0.06%	$4,301	0.12%	8.20%
COMPOSITE	$0	0.00%	$42,145,575	44.73%	$52,072,753	55.27%	$94,218,328	100.00%	$3,724,095	100.00%	3.95%
AVERAGE	$0		$21,072,788		$26,036,377		$47,109,164		$1,862,048		
ALLIANCE											
1. FLORIDA	$0	0.00%	$1,196	100.00%	$0	0.00%	$1,196	100.00%	$67,583	100.00%	5,650.75%
COMPOSITE	$0	0.00%	$1,196	100.00%	$0	0.00%	$1,196	100.00%	$67,583	100.00%	5,650.75%
ALLIANT											
1. TEXAS	$0	0.00%	$10,537,510	100.00%	$0	0.00%	$10,537,510	75.32%	$17,031	5.65%	0.16%
2. COLORADO	$0	0.00%	$3,453,141	100.00%	$0	0.00%	$3,453,141	24.68%	$284,152	94.35%	8.23%
COMPOSITE	$0	0.00%	$13,990,651	100.00%	$0	0.00%	$13,990,651	100.00%	$301,183	100.00%	2.15%
AVERAGE	$0		$6,995,326		$0		$6,995,326		$150,592		
AMERICAN EAGLE											
1. OKLAHOMA	$1,906,376	62.52%	$1,142,793	37.48%	$0	0.00%	$3,049,169	100.00%	$48,338	100.00%	1.59%
COMPOSITE	$1,906,376	62.52%	$1,142,793	37.48%	$0	0.00%	$3,049,169	100.00%	$48,338	100.00%	1.59%
AMERICAN GUARANTY											
1. OKLAHOMA	$0	0.00%	$495,585	14.52%	$2,917,327	85.48%	$3,412,912	97.79%	$75,291	100.00%	2.21%
2. SOUTH CAROLINA	$300	1.23%	$24,183	98.77%	$0	0.00%	$24,483	0.70%	$0	--	--
3. VIRGINIA	$700	5.76%	$11,449	94.24%	$0	0.00%	$12,149	0.35%	$0	--	--
4. MISSISSIPPI	$375	5.36%	$6,620	94.64%	$0	0.00%	$6,995	0.20%	$0	--	--
5. UTAH	$5,005	100.00%	$0	0.00%	$0	0.00%	$5,005	0.14%	$0	--	--
6. CONNECTICUT	$4,270	100.00%	$0	0.00%	$0	0.00%	$4,270	0.12%	$0	--	--
7. FLORIDA	$4,020	100.00%	$0	0.00%	$0	0.00%	$4,020	0.12%	$0	--	--
8. ILLINOIS	$2,450	65.02%	$1,318	34.98%	$0	0.00%	$3,768	0.11%	$0	--	--
9. NEVADA	$2,746	100.00%	$0	0.00%	$0	0.00%	$2,746	0.08%	$0	--	--
10. MARYLAND	$700	32.33%	$1,465	67.67%	$0	0.00%	$2,165	0.06%	$0	--	--
11. TENNESSEE	$0	0.00%	$1,924	100.00%	$0	0.00%	$1,924	0.06%	$0	--	--
12. DISTRICT OF COLUMBIA	$800	48.78%	$840	51.22%	$0	0.00%	$1,640	0.05%	$0	--	--
13. OHIO	$750	55.76%	$595	44.24%	$0	0.00%	$1,345	0.04%	$0	--	--
14. WEST VIRGINIA	$0	0.00%	$1,150	100.00%	$0	0.00%	$1,150	0.03%	$0	--	--
15. GEORGIA	$1,050	100.00%	$0	0.00%	$0	0.00%	$1,050	0.03%	$0	--	--
16. PENNSYLVANIA	$909	100.00%	$0	0.00%	$0	0.00%	$909	0.03%	$0	--	--
17. MISSOURI	$275	37.67%	$455	62.33%	$0	0.00%	$730	0.02%	$0	--	--
18. NEW JERSEY	$716	100.00%	$0	0.00%	$0	0.00%	$716	0.02%	$0	--	--
19. MICHIGAN	$650	100.00%	$0	0.00%	$0	0.00%	$650	0.02%	$0	--	--
20. WISCONSIN	$0	0.00%	$374	100.00%	$0	0.00%	$374	0.01%	$0	--	--
21. COLORADO	$350	100.00%	$0	0.00%	$0	0.00%	$350	0.01%	$0	--	--
22. INDIANA	$300	100.00%	$0	0.00%	$0	0.00%	$300	0.00%	$0	--	--
23. KENTUCKY	$0	0.00%	$275	100.00%	$0	0.00%	$275	0.00%	$0	--	--
COMPOSITE	$26,366	0.76%	$546,233	15.65%	$2,917,327	83.59%	$3,489,926	100.00%	$75,291	100.00%	2.16%
AVERAGE	$1,146		$23,749		$126,840		$151,736		$3,274		
AMERICAN LAND & AIRCRAFT											
1. OKLAHOMA	$0	0.00%	$126,906	19.25%	$532,250	80.75%	$659,156	100.00%	$5,858	100.00%	0.89%
COMPOSITE	$0	0.00%	$126,906	19.25%	$532,250	80.75%	$659,156	100.00%	$5,858	100.00%	0.89%
AMERICAN SECURITY											
1. OKLAHOMA	$0	0.00%	$2,940,198	100.00%	$0	0.00%	$2,940,198	100.00%	$2,283	100.00%	0.08%
COMPOSITE	$0	0.00%	$2,940,198	100.00%	$0	0.00%	$2,940,198	100.00%	$2,283	100.00%	0.08%
ARKANSAS TIC											
1. ARKANSAS	$0	0.00%	$7,269,128	87.72%	$1,017,272	12.28%	$8,286,400	100.00%	$131,776	100.00%	1.59%
COMPOSITE	$0	0.00%	$7,269,128	87.72%	$1,017,272	12.28%	$8,286,400	100.00%	$131,776	100.00%	1.59%
ARSENAL											
1. INDIANA	$0	0.00%	$1,583,908	100.00%	$0	0.00%	$1,583,908	100.00%	$649	100.00%	0.04%
COMPOSITE	$0	0.00%	$1,583,908	100.00%	$0	0.00%	$1,583,908	100.00%	$649	100.00%	0.04%
ATTORNEYS TGF (CO)											
1. COLORADO	$0	0.00%	$6,864,905	100.00%	$0	0.00%	$6,864,905	74.07%	$270,631	16.15%	3.94%
2. UTAH	$0	0.00%	$2,403,171	100.00%	$0	0.00%	$2,403,171	25.93%	$1,299,467	77.55%	54.07%
3. MINNESOTA	$0	--	$0	--	$0	--	$0	--	$105,452	6.29%	
COMPOSITE	$0	0.00%	$9,268,076	100.00%	$0	0.00%	$9,268,076	100.00%	$1,675,550	100.00%	18.08%
AVERAGE	$0		$3,089,359		$0		$3,089,359		$558,517		

D.2 Organization - Individual Underwriter by Jurisdiction

	DIRECT PREMIUMS WRITTEN							PERCENT OF	PAID	PERCENT OF	LOSSES TO
	DIRECT	% of Total	NON-AFFILIATED	% of Total	AFFILIATED	% of Total	TOTAL	UNDERWRITER	LOSSES	UNDERWRITER	PREMIUMS

ATTORNEYS TGF (IL)

	DIRECT	% of Total	NON-AFFILIATED	% of Total	AFFILIATED	% of Total	TOTAL	PERCENT OF UNDERWRITER	PAID LOSSES	PERCENT OF UNDERWRITER	LOSSES TO PREMIUMS
1. ILLINOIS	$10,633,487	100.00%	$0	0.00%	$0	0.00%	$10,633,487	96.68%	$1,944,200	95.25%	18.28%
2. WISCONSIN	$291,071	100.00%	$0	0.00%	$0	0.00%	$291,071	2.65%	$42,789	2.10%	14.70%
3. INDIANA	$74,220	100.00%	$0	0.00%	$0	0.00%	$74,220	0.67%	$54,120	2.65%	72.92%
COMPOSITE	**$10,998,778**	100.00%	**$0**	0.00%	**$0**	0.00%	**$10,998,778**	100.00%	**$2,041,109**	100.00%	**18.56%**
AVERAGE	**$3,666,259**		**$0**		**$0**		**$3,666,259**		**$680,370**		

ATTORNEYS TIF (FL)

	DIRECT	% of Total	NON-AFFILIATED	% of Total	AFFILIATED	% of Total	TOTAL	PERCENT OF UNDERWRITER	PAID LOSSES	PERCENT OF UNDERWRITER	LOSSES TO PREMIUMS
1. FLORIDA	$0	0.00%	$332,905,096	100.00%	$0	0.00%	$332,905,096	96.26%	$25,507,467	91.79%	7.66%
2. ILLINOIS	$0	0.00%	$5,356,039	100.00%	$0	0.00%	$5,356,039	1.55%	$863,901	3.11%	16.13%
3. MINNESOTA	$0	0.00%	$3,696,692	100.00%	$0	0.00%	$3,696,692	1.07%	$82,652	0.30%	2.24%
4. SOUTH CAROLINA	$0	0.00%	$1,893,029	100.00%	$0	0.00%	$1,893,029	0.55%	$359,115	1.29%	18.97%
5. GEORGIA	$0	0.00%	$633,526	100.00%	$0	0.00%	$633,526	0.18%	$821,978	2.96%	129.75%
6. AGGREGATE OTHER ALIEN	$0	0.00%	$421,502	100.00%	$0	0.00%	$421,502	0.12%	$0	--	--
7. NORTH CAROLINA	$0	0.00%	$416,568	100.00%	$0	0.00%	$416,568	0.12%	$0	--	--
8. PUERTO RICO	$0	0.00%	$245,518	100.00%	$0	0.00%	$245,518	0.07%	$0	--	--
9. NORTH DAKOTA	$0	0.00%	$169,925	100.00%	$0	0.00%	$169,925	0.05%	$0	--	--
10. MICHIGAN	$0	0.00%	$81,020	100.00%	$0	0.00%	$81,020	0.02%	$154,009	0.55%	190.09%
11. ALABAMA	$0	0.00%	$12,139	100.00%	$0	0.00%	$12,139	0.00%	$0	--	--
12. ARKANSAS	$0	0.00%	$10,298	100.00%	$0	0.00%	$10,298	0.00%	$0	--	--
COMPOSITE	**$0**	0.00%	**$345,841,352**	100.00%	**$0**	0.00%	**$345,841,352**	100.00%	**$27,789,122**	100.00%	**8.04%**
AVERAGE	**$0**		**$28,820,113**		**$0**		**$28,820,113**		**$2,315,760**		

BRIDGE

	DIRECT	% of Total	NON-AFFILIATED	% of Total	AFFILIATED	% of Total	TOTAL	PERCENT OF UNDERWRITER	PAID LOSSES	PERCENT OF UNDERWRITER	LOSSES TO PREMIUMS
1. SOUTH CAROLINA	$0	0.00%	$462	100.00%	$0	0.00%	$462	100.00%	$180,321	99.27%	39,030.52%
2. NORTH CAROLINA	$0	--	$0	--	$0	--	$0	--	$1,321	0.73%	--
COMPOSITE	**$0**	0.00%	**$462**	100.00%	**$0**	0.00%	**$462**	100.00%	**$181,642**	100.00%	**39,316.45%**
AVERAGE	**$0**		**$231**		**$0**		**$231**		**$90,821**		

CENSTAR

	DIRECT	% of Total	NON-AFFILIATED	% of Total	AFFILIATED	% of Total	TOTAL	PERCENT OF UNDERWRITER	PAID LOSSES	PERCENT OF UNDERWRITER	LOSSES TO PREMIUMS
1. FLORIDA	$0	0.00%	$17,369,262	100.00%	$0	0.00%	$17,369,262	44.02%	$134,796	53.02%	0.78%
2. NEW JERSEY	$0	0.00%	$5,150,323	100.00%	$0	0.00%	$5,150,323	13.05%	$17,567	6.91%	0.34%
3. PENNSYLVANIA	$0	0.00%	$4,624,937	100.00%	$0	0.00%	$4,624,937	11.72%	$24,636	9.69%	0.53%
4. GEORGIA	$0	0.00%	$3,121,377	100.00%	$0	0.00%	$3,121,377	7.91%	$27,856	10.96%	0.89%
5. MARYLAND	$0	0.00%	$1,657,830	100.00%	$0	0.00%	$1,657,830	4.20%	($1,392)	(0.55)%	(0.08)%
6. VIRGINIA	$0	0.00%	$1,252,062	100.00%	$0	0.00%	$1,252,062	3.17%	$0	--	--
7. MASSACHUSETTS	$0	0.00%	$1,047,048	100.00%	$0	0.00%	$1,047,048	2.65%	$0	--	--
8. TENNESSEE	$0	0.00%	$863,668	100.00%	$0	0.00%	$863,668	2.19%	$0	--	--
9. INDIANA	$0	0.00%	$797,369	100.00%	$0	0.00%	$797,369	2.02%	$0	--	--
10. DISTRICT OF COLUMBIA	$0	0.00%	$766,381	100.00%	$0	0.00%	$766,381	1.94%	$15,210	5.98%	1.98%
11. KENTUCKY	$0	0.00%	$733,946	100.00%	$0	0.00%	$733,946	1.86%	$1,628	0.64%	0.22%
12. ARKANSAS	$0	0.00%	$353,239	100.00%	$0	0.00%	$353,239	0.90%	$8,868	3.49%	2.51%
13. OHIO	$0	0.00%	$339,072	100.00%	$0	0.00%	$339,072	0.86%	$0	--	--
14. COLORADO	$0	0.00%	$330,763	100.00%	$0	0.00%	$330,763	0.84%	$25,061	9.86%	7.58%
15. MICHIGAN	$0	0.00%	$278,957	100.00%	$0	0.00%	$278,957	0.71%	$0	--	--
16. MISSOURI	$0	0.00%	$141,144	100.00%	$0	0.00%	$141,144	0.36%	$0	--	--
17. MISSISSIPPI	$0	0.00%	$132,640	100.00%	$0	0.00%	$132,640	0.34%	$0	--	--
18. SOUTH CAROLINA	$0	0.00%	$117,867	100.00%	$0	0.00%	$117,867	0.30%	$0	--	--
19. WISCONSIN	$0	0.00%	$103,509	100.00%	$0	0.00%	$103,509	0.26%	$0	--	--
20. CONNECTICUT	$0	0.00%	$86,924	100.00%	$0	0.00%	$86,924	0.22%	$0	--	--
21. WEST VIRGINIA	$0	0.00%	$69,567	100.00%	$0	0.00%	$69,567	0.18%	$0	--	--
22. DELAWARE	$0	0.00%	$61,996	100.00%	$0	0.00%	$61,996	0.16%	$0	--	--
23. MINNESOTA	$0	0.00%	$60,157	100.00%	$0	0.00%	$60,157	0.15%	$0	--	--
COMPOSITE	**$0**	0.00%	**$39,460,038**	100.00%	**$0**	0.00%	**$39,460,038**	100.00%	**$254,230**	100.00%	**0.64%**
AVERAGE	**$0**		**$1,715,654**		**$0**		**$1,715,654**		**$11,053**		

3

D.2 Organization - Individual Underwriter by Jurisdiction

	DIRECT	% of Total	NON-AFFILIATED	% of Total	AFFILIATED	% of Total	TOTAL	PERCENT OF UNDERWRITER	PAID LOSSES	PERCENT OF UNDERWRITER	LOSSES TO PREMIUMS
CHICAGO TIC											
1. CALIFORNIA	$33,084,828	9.52%	$22,750,947	6.55%	$291,620,278	83.93%	$347,456,053	18.41%	$66,938,187	38.06%	19.27%
2. TEXAS	$115,031,241	56.64%	$87,495,654	43.08%	$560,361	0.28%	$203,087,256	10.76%	$9,147,849	5.20%	4.50%
3. FLORIDA	$24,511,736	12.43%	$169,574,585	85.96%	$3,187,923	1.62%	$197,274,244	10.45%	$10,529,128	5.99%	5.34%
4. NEW YORK	$48,938,111	44.38%	$61,336,854	55.62%	$0	0.00%	$110,274,965	5.84%	$5,227,538	2.97%	4.74%
5. ILLINOIS	$28,585,340	29.32%	$57,607,733	59.09%	$11,301,183	11.59%	$97,494,256	5.17%	$11,383,563	6.47%	11.68%
6. WASHINGTON	$58,298,376	74.38%	$15,905,442	20.29%	$4,174,073	5.33%	$78,377,891	4.15%	$4,452,553	2.53%	5.68%
7. NEW JERSEY	$15,975,802	22.47%	$55,116,962	77.53%	$0	0.00%	$71,092,764	3.77%	$5,479,165	3.12%	7.71%
8. OHIO	$20,560,024	29.27%	$45,464,830	64.73%	$4,215,915	6.00%	$70,240,769	3.72%	$2,444,431	1.39%	3.48%
9. GEORGIA	$2,925,671	5.69%	$48,451,197	94.31%	$0	0.00%	$51,376,868	2.72%	$5,635,683	3.20%	10.97%
10. MARYLAND	$7,056,050	13.79%	$44,111,055	86.21%	$0	0.00%	$51,167,105	2.71%	$7,694,950	4.38%	15.04%
11. PENNSYLVANIA	$16,407,906	37.97%	$26,803,885	62.03%	$0	0.00%	$43,211,791	2.29%	$2,343,310	1.33%	5.42%
12. VIRGINIA	$6,113,809	14.56%	$35,869,518	85.44%	$0	0.00%	$41,983,327	2.22%	$1,489,596	0.85%	3.55%
13. SOUTH CAROLINA	$587,785	1.48%	$39,082,136	98.52%	$0	0.00%	$39,669,921	2.10%	$2,338,894	1.33%	5.90%
14. NEVADA	$4,291,908	12.01%	$15,081,872	42.19%	$16,372,175	45.80%	$35,745,955	1.89%	$1,711,860	0.97%	4.79%
15. ARIZONA	$27,717,915	82.19%	$5,337,847	15.83%	$669,788	1.99%	$33,725,550	1.79%	$2,054,039	1.17%	6.09%
16. MICHIGAN	$745,507	2.33%	$19,082,506	59.70%	$12,133,652	37.96%	$31,961,665	1.69%	$2,127,474	1.21%	6.66%
17. NORTH CAROLINA	$306,610	1.01%	$30,004,341	98.99%	$0	0.00%	$30,310,951	1.61%	$3,302,348	1.88%	10.89%
18. TENNESSEE	$3,259,611	10.90%	$26,633,518	89.10%	$0	0.00%	$29,893,129	1.58%	$643,091	0.37%	2.15%
19. COLORADO	$1,667,959	6.69%	$15,671,488	62.85%	$7,594,479	30.46%	$24,933,926	1.32%	$4,890,162	2.78%	19.61%
20. WISCONSIN	$7,761,876	32.86%	$15,859,841	67.14%	$0	0.00%	$23,621,717	1.25%	$2,318,641	1.32%	9.82%
21. DELAWARE	$19,063,578	92.20%	$1,611,763	7.80%	$0	0.00%	$20,675,341	1.10%	$4,548	0.00%	0.02%
22. MINNESOTA	$2,863,665	13.90%	$17,741,918	86.10%	$0	0.00%	$20,605,583	1.09%	$4,029,572	2.29%	19.56%
23. MASSACHUSETTS	$613,287	3.10%	$19,166,204	96.90%	$0	0.00%	$19,779,491	1.05%	$2,721,268	1.55%	13.76%
24. CANADA	$3,857,639	19.60%	$0	0.00%	$15,827,994	80.40%	$19,685,633	1.04%	($230,821)	(0.13)%	(1.17)%
25. INDIANA	$8,708,530	50.31%	$8,602,689	49.69%	$0	0.00%	$17,311,219	0.92%	$1,000,718	0.57%	5.78%
26. IDAHO	$347,153	2.20%	$15,465,738	97.80%	$0	0.00%	$15,812,891	0.84%	$859,155	0.49%	5.43%
27. ALABAMA	$822,687	5.32%	$14,651,793	94.68%	$1	0.00%	$15,474,481	0.82%	$618,945	0.35%	4.00%
28. CONNECTICUT	$1,025,447	7.05%	$13,523,919	92.95%	$0	0.00%	$14,549,366	0.77%	$5,295,812	3.01%	36.40%
29. MISSOURI	$2,684,870	24.54%	$8,257,131	75.46%	$0	0.00%	$10,942,001	0.58%	$1,492,108	0.85%	13.64%
30. UTAH	$380,001	3.49%	$10,521,945	96.51%	$0	0.00%	$10,901,946	0.58%	$185,650	0.11%	1.70%
31. KENTUCKY	$1,409,710	14.40%	$8,381,073	85.60%	$0	0.00%	$9,790,783	0.52%	$456,114	0.26%	4.66%
32. LOUISIANA	$379,662	3.98%	$6,927,022	72.54%	$2,242,807	23.49%	$9,549,491	0.51%	$120,211	0.07%	1.26%
33. ARKANSAS	$182,592	2.05%	$8,740,951	97.95%	$0	0.00%	$8,923,543	0.47%	$650,758	0.37%	7.29%
34. KANSAS	$4,201,408	52.88%	$3,743,189	47.12%	$0	0.00%	$7,944,597	0.42%	$187,930	0.11%	2.37%
35. OKLAHOMA	$26,599	0.34%	$1,360,037	17.15%	$6,542,605	82.51%	$7,929,241	0.42%	$391,717	0.22%	4.94%
36. MONTANA	$3,194,940	42.82%	$4,266,801	57.18%	$0	0.00%	$7,461,741	0.40%	$366,807	0.21%	4.92%
37. NEW HAMPSHIRE	$187,123	3.52%	$5,135,840	96.48%	$0	0.00%	$5,322,963	0.28%	$975,043	0.55%	18.32%
38. NEW MEXICO	$280,111	5.44%	$4,873,672	94.56%	$0	0.00%	$5,153,783	0.27%	$312,259	0.18%	6.06%
39. PUERTO RICO	$65,014	1.28%	$5,001,988	98.72%	$0	0.00%	$5,067,002	0.27%	$600,154	0.34%	11.84%
40. MISSISSIPPI	$227,211	4.56%	$4,756,036	95.44%	$0	0.00%	$4,983,247	0.26%	$275,485	0.16%	5.53%
41. NEBRASKA	$143,604	2.89%	$4,820,708	97.11%	$0	0.00%	$4,964,312	0.26%	$201,665	0.11%	4.06%
42. DISTRICT OF COLUMBIA	$1,253,113	25.84%	$3,597,067	74.16%	$0	0.00%	$4,850,180	0.26%	$1,117,240	0.64%	23.04%
43. MAINE	$99,218	2.12%	$4,578,388	97.88%	$0	0.00%	$4,677,606	0.25%	$1,019,738	0.58%	21.80%
44. RHODE ISLAND	$91,983	2.57%	$3,483,802	97.43%	$0	0.00%	$3,575,785	0.19%	$273,864	0.16%	7.66%
45. WYOMING	$150,234	4.29%	$3,352,080	95.71%	$0	0.00%	$3,502,314	0.19%	$7,382	0.00%	0.21%
46. OREGON	$491,566	17.71%	$2,283,429	82.29%	$0	0.00%	$2,774,995	0.15%	$142,013	0.08%	5.12%
47. HAWAII	$312,821	11.90%	$2,316,012	88.10%	$0	0.00%	$2,628,833	0.14%	$492,895	0.28%	18.75%
48. WEST VIRGINIA	$492,668	20.48%	$1,912,565	79.52%	$0	0.00%	$2,405,233	0.13%	($20,414)	(0.01)%	(0.85)%
49. SOUTH DAKOTA	$25,112	1.19%	$2,082,505	98.81%	$0	0.00%	$2,107,617	0.11%	$57,480	0.03%	2.73%
50. ALASKA	$189,934	15.19%	$1,060,681	84.81%	$0	0.00%	$1,250,615	0.07%	$0	--	--
51. VERMONT	$79,236	7.03%	$1,048,472	92.97%	$0	0.00%	$1,127,708	0.06%	$29,851	0.02%	2.65%
52. NORTH DAKOTA	$2,145	0.23%	$947,504	99.77%	$0	0.00%	$949,649	0.05%	$13,312	0.00%	1.40%
53. U.S. VIRGIN ISLANDS	$66,847	8.98%	$677,804	91.02%	$0	0.00%	$744,651	0.04%	$66,388	0.04%	8.92%
54. AGGREGATE OTHER ALIEN	$3,675	0.50%	$726,300	99.50%	$0	0.00%	$729,975	0.04%	$0	--	--
55. IOWA	$65,022	26.89%	$176,753	73.11%	$0	0.00%	$241,775	0.01%	$11,848	0.00%	4.90%
COMPOSITE	**$477,816,470**	**25.32%**	**$1,033,035,990**	**54.74%**	**$376,443,234**	**19.95%**	**$1,887,295,694**	**100.00%**	**$175,879,157**	**100.00%**	**9.32%**
AVERAGE	**$8,687,572**		**$18,782,473**		**$6,844,422**		**$34,314,467**		**$3,197,803**		
CHICAGO TIC (OR)											
1. OREGON	$13,707,383	52.15%	$12,576,501	47.85%	$0	0.00%	$26,283,884	100.00%	$504,698	100.00%	1.92%
COMPOSITE	**$13,707,383**	**52.15%**	**$12,576,501**	**47.85%**	**$0**	**0.00%**	**$26,283,884**	**100.00%**	**$504,698**	**100.00%**	**1.92%**

D.2 Organization - Individual Underwriter by Jurisdiction

	DIRECT PREMIUMS WRITTEN							PERCENT OF UNDERWRITER	PAID LOSSES	PERCENT OF UNDERWRITER	LOSSES TO PREMIUMS
	DIRECT	% of Total	NON-AFFILIATED	% of Total	AFFILIATED	% of Total	TOTAL				

COMMERCE

	DIRECT	% of Total	NON-AFFILIATED	% of Total	AFFILIATED	% of Total	TOTAL	PERCENT OF UNDERWRITER	PAID LOSSES	PERCENT OF UNDERWRITER	LOSSES TO PREMIUMS
1. CALIFORNIA	$43,152	0.31%	$440,009	3.15%	$13,488,575	96.54%	$13,971,736	32.07%	$404,321	60.14%	2.89%
2. TEXAS	$0	0.00%	$0	0.00%	$12,773,712	100.00%	$12,773,712	29.32%	$59,994	8.92%	0.47%
3. FLORIDA	$0	0.00%	$0	0.00%	$6,789,026	100.00%	$6,789,026	15.58%	$207,947	30.93%	3.06%
4. VIRGINIA	$0	0.00%	$0	0.00%	$1,789,931	100.00%	$1,789,931	4.11%	$0	--	--
5. ARIZONA	$0	0.00%	$0	0.00%	$1,623,786	100.00%	$1,623,786	3.73%	$0	--	--
6. NEVADA	$0	0.00%	$0	0.00%	$1,366,533	100.00%	$1,366,533	3.14%	$87	0.01%	0.00%
7. SOUTH CAROLINA	$0	0.00%	$1,092,087	100.00%	$0	0.00%	$1,092,087	2.51%	$0	--	--
8. ILLINOIS	$0	0.00%	$0	0.00%	$868,058	100.00%	$868,058	1.99%	$0	--	--
9. NEW MEXICO	$0	0.00%	$0	0.00%	$724,207	100.00%	$724,207	1.66%	$0	--	--
10. MARYLAND	$0	0.00%	$0	0.00%	$509,871	100.00%	$509,871	1.17%	$0	--	--
11. MICHIGAN	$0	0.00%	$0	0.00%	$498,233	100.00%	$498,233	1.14%	$0	--	--
12. MINNESOTA	$0	0.00%	$0	0.00%	$358,903	100.00%	$358,903	0.82%	$0	--	--
13. COLORADO	$0	0.00%	$0	0.00%	$340,950	100.00%	$340,950	0.78%	$0	--	--
14. MISSOURI	$0	0.00%	$0	0.00%	$322,242	100.00%	$322,242	0.74%	$0	--	--
15. OHIO	$0	0.00%	$0	0.00%	$275,558	100.00%	$275,558	0.63%	$0	--	--
16. INDIANA	$0	0.00%	$0	0.00%	$267,698	100.00%	$267,698	0.61%	$0	--	--
COMPOSITE	**$43,152**	0.10%	**$1,532,096**	3.52%	**$41,997,283**	96.38%	**$43,572,531**	**100.00%**	**$672,349**	**100.00%**	**1.54%**
AVERAGE	**$2,697**		**$95,756**		**$2,624,830**		**$2,723,283**		**$42,022**		

COMMONWEALTH LAND

	DIRECT	% of Total	NON-AFFILIATED	% of Total	AFFILIATED	% of Total	TOTAL	PERCENT OF UNDERWRITER	PAID LOSSES	PERCENT OF UNDERWRITER	LOSSES TO PREMIUMS
1. NEW YORK	$56,727,723	28.45%	$142,664,825	71.55%	$0	0.00%	$199,392,548	17.30%	$5,413,757	7.89%	2.72%
2. FLORIDA	$6,221,477	3.97%	$150,681,543	96.03%	$2,465	0.00%	$156,905,485	13.61%	$7,960,208	11.61%	5.07%
3. TEXAS	$80,381,025	61.68%	$49,944,637	38.32%	$0	0.00%	$130,325,662	11.31%	$6,519,952	9.51%	5.00%
4. CALIFORNIA	$2,038,807	1.98%	$15,219,601	14.74%	$85,969,402	83.28%	$103,227,810	8.96%	$9,967,470	14.53%	9.66%
5. PENNSYLVANIA	$10,706,572	12.07%	$77,907,313	87.80%	$116,127	0.13%	$88,730,012	7.70%	$2,621,211	3.82%	2.95%
6. MARYLAND	$6,530,007	14.74%	$37,563,497	84.78%	$212,069	0.48%	$44,305,573	3.84%	$973,641	1.42%	2.20%
7. VIRGINIA	$5,239,951	15.01%	$24,721,866	70.83%	$4,939,573	14.15%	$34,901,390	3.03%	$1,398,678	2.04%	4.01%
8. ARIZONA	$2,540,934	7.93%	$29,482,815	92.06%	$3,153	0.01%	$32,026,902	2.78%	$1,767,674	2.58%	5.52%
9. WASHINGTON	$1,007,454	3.99%	$7,496,831	29.73%	$16,715,966	66.28%	$25,220,251	2.19%	$1,225,757	1.79%	4.86%
10. LOUISIANA	$143,197	0.60%	$23,825,832	99.40%	$0	0.00%	$23,969,029	2.08%	$2,021,315	2.95%	8.43%
11. OHIO	$1,962,441	8.70%	$20,103,779	89.16%	$481,917	2.14%	$22,548,137	1.96%	$1,855,239	2.70%	8.23%
12. MASSACHUSETTS	$1,500,792	6.96%	$20,073,080	93.04%	$0	0.00%	$21,573,872	1.87%	$1,761,819	2.57%	8.17%
13. NEVADA	$4,056,529	18.92%	$17,342,649	80.87%	$46,387	0.22%	$21,445,565	1.86%	$1,103,281	1.61%	5.14%
14. MINNESOTA	$2,207,645	10.39%	$19,042,075	89.61%	$0	0.00%	$21,249,720	1.84%	$3,476,816	5.07%	16.36%
15. NEW MEXICO	$2,940,147	16.82%	$5,596,987	32.02%	$8,940,467	51.15%	$17,477,601	1.52%	$408,688	0.60%	2.34%
16. IDAHO	$25,516	0.15%	$16,808,517	99.85%	$247	0.00%	$16,834,280	1.46%	$146,859	0.21%	0.87%
17. NEW JERSEY	$6,264,390	40.81%	$9,086,783	59.19%	$0	0.00%	$15,351,173	1.33%	$1,471,330	2.15%	9.58%
18. GEORGIA	$520,418	4.17%	$11,959,823	95.83%	$0	0.00%	$12,480,241	1.08%	$1,625,050	2.37%	13.02%
19. UTAH	$29,560	0.24%	$10,067,457	80.85%	$2,355,253	18.91%	$12,452,270	1.08%	$648,226	0.95%	5.21%
20. KENTUCKY	$1,255,853	10.19%	$11,034,281	89.50%	$38,237	0.31%	$12,328,371	1.07%	$2,079,436	3.03%	16.87%
21. MICHIGAN	$931,778	9.03%	$9,384,816	90.97%	$0	0.00%	$10,316,594	0.90%	$2,448,313	3.57%	23.73%
22. CONNECTICUT	$2,303,515	23.35%	$7,563,452	76.65%	$0	0.00%	$9,866,967	0.86%	$513,249	0.75%	5.20%
23. ALABAMA	$507,032	5.56%	$8,617,330	94.44%	$0	0.00%	$9,124,362	0.79%	$928,706	1.35%	10.18%
24. MISSOURI	$3,521,706	39.97%	$5,288,425	60.03%	$0	0.00%	$8,810,131	0.76%	$4,273,771	6.23%	48.51%
25. DISTRICT OF COLUMBIA	$3,808,103	43.40%	$4,960,486	56.53%	$6,350	0.07%	$8,774,939	0.76%	$50,597	0.07%	0.58%
26. DELAWARE	$6,783,727	77.40%	$1,981,257	22.60%	$0	0.00%	$8,764,984	0.76%	$0	--	--
27. RHODE ISLAND	$590,897	7.28%	$7,529,990	92.72%	$0	0.00%	$8,120,887	0.70%	$311,546	0.45%	3.84%
28. COLORADO	$3,963,389	48.94%	$4,015,631	49.58%	$120,092	1.48%	$8,099,112	0.70%	$148,288	0.22%	1.83%
29. WISCONSIN	$72,273	0.91%	$7,850,573	99.09%	$0	0.00%	$7,922,846	0.69%	$361,016	0.53%	4.56%
30. TENNESSEE	$137,398	2.15%	$6,253,092	97.85%	$0	0.00%	$6,390,490	0.55%	$787,623	1.15%	12.32%
31. HAWAII	$224,545	3.82%	$5,650,710	96.16%	$811	0.01%	$5,876,066	0.51%	$139,364	0.20%	2.37%
32. ILLINOIS	$836,834	15.41%	$4,591,878	84.59%	$0	0.00%	$5,428,712	0.47%	$992,366	1.45%	18.28%
33. MONTANA	$4,501	0.09%	$5,249,896	99.91%	$0	0.00%	$5,254,397	0.46%	$70,881	0.10%	1.35%
34. NEBRASKA	$8,925	0.17%	$5,204,939	99.83%	$0	0.00%	$5,213,864	0.45%	$136,319	0.20%	2.61%
35. INDIANA	$245,200	6.63%	$3,452,212	93.37%	$100	0.00%	$3,697,512	0.32%	$249,215	0.36%	6.74%
36. PUERTO RICO	$0	0.00%	$0	0.00%	$3,391,378	100.00%	$3,391,378	0.29%	$122,359	0.18%	3.61%
37. KANSAS	$781,959	23.27%	$2,578,750	76.73%	$0	0.00%	$3,360,709	0.29%	$78,016	0.11%	2.32%
38. NEW HAMPSHIRE	$274,092	8.38%	$2,995,187	91.62%	$0	0.00%	$3,269,279	0.28%	$207,466	0.30%	6.35%
39. SOUTH CAROLINA	$147,255	6.72%	$2,043,426	93.28%	$0	0.00%	$2,190,681	0.19%	$436,344	0.64%	19.92%
40. OREGON	$937,510	48.52%	$993,036	51.39%	$1,764	0.09%	$1,932,310	0.17%	$34,254	0.05%	1.77%
41. IOWA	$343,007	19.16%	$1,447,037	80.84%	$55	0.00%	$1,790,099	0.16%	$116,313	0.17%	6.50%
42. SOUTH DAKOTA	$75,216	4.60%	$1,561,625	95.40%	$0	0.00%	$1,636,841	0.14%	$69,623	0.10%	4.25%
43. MAINE	$97,373	6.37%	$1,430,351	93.63%	$0	0.00%	$1,527,724	0.13%	$156,248	0.23%	10.23%
44. OKLAHOMA	$12,788	0.86%	$1,482,676	99.14%	$0	0.00%	$1,495,464	0.13%	$63,602	0.09%	4.25%
45. MISSISSIPPI	$38,518	2.61%	$1,437,666	97.39%	$0	0.00%	$1,476,184	0.13%	$45,524	0.07%	3.08%
46. WYOMING	$522	0.04%	$1,331,184	99.96%	$0	0.00%	$1,331,706	0.12%	$40,942	0.06%	3.07%
47. AGGREGATE OTHER ALIEN	$1,286,483	100.00%	$0	0.00%	$0	0.00%	$1,286,483	0.11%	$0	--	--
48. WEST VIRGINIA	$65,163	5.90%	$1,039,251	94.10%	$0	0.00%	$1,104,414	0.10%	$186,114	0.27%	16.85%
49. ARKANSAS	$4,078	0.57%	$711,872	99.43%	$0	0.00%	$715,950	0.06%	$17,874	0.03%	2.50%
50. NORTH CAROLINA	$345,083	57.13%	$258,544	42.81%	$365	0.06%	$603,992	0.05%	$1,087,747	1.59%	180.09%
51. NORTH DAKOTA	$49,187	8.95%	$500,110	91.05%	$0	0.00%	$549,297	0.05%	$48,357	0.07%	8.80%
52. VERMONT	$8,320	2.23%	$364,487	97.77%	$0	0.00%	$372,807	0.03%	$23,316	0.03%	6.25%
53. ALASKA	$11,182	14.86%	$64,074	85.14%	$0	0.00%	$75,256	0.00%	$0	--	--
54. U.S. VIRGIN ISLANDS	$0	--	$0	--	$0	--	$0	--	$500	0.00%	--
COMPOSITE	**$220,717,997**	19.15%	**$808,458,154**	70.15%	**$123,342,178**	10.70%	**$1,152,518,329**	**100.00%**	**$68,592,260**	**100.00%**	**5.95%**
AVERAGE	**$4,087,370**		**$14,971,447**		**$2,284,114**		**$21,342,932**		**$1,270,227**		

D.2 Organization - Individual Underwriter by Jurisdiction

	DIRECT	% of Total	NON-AFFILIATED	% of Total	AFFILIATED	% of Total	TOTAL	PERCENT OF UNDERWRITER	PAID LOSSES	PERCENT OF UNDERWRITER	LOSSES TO PREMIUMS
COMMONWEALTH LAND (NJ)											
1. NEW JERSEY	$5,109,506	14.44%	$30,277,935	85.56%	$0	0.00%	$35,387,441	100.00%	$1,845,407	100.00%	5.21%
COMPOSITE	$5,109,506	14.44%	$30,277,935	85.56%	$0	0.00%	$35,387,441	100.00%	$1,845,407	100.00%	5.21%
CONESTOGA											
1. PENNSYLVANIA	$117,495	3.12%	$3,345,774	88.95%	$298,189	7.93%	$3,761,458	26.97%	($19,536)	(2.37)%	(0.52)%
2. NEW YORK	$0	0.00%	$2,480,602	100.00%	$0	0.00%	$2,480,602	17.79%	$109,306	13.26%	4.41%
3. OHIO	$0	0.00%	$2,235,748	100.00%	$0	0.00%	$2,235,748	16.03%	$181,514	22.02%	8.12%
4. MARYLAND	$0	0.00%	$2,170,802	100.00%	$0	0.00%	$2,170,802	15.57%	$71,107	8.63%	3.28%
5. INDIANA	$72,319	4.72%	$1,380,957	90.19%	$77,874	5.09%	$1,531,150	10.98%	$375,611	45.56%	24.53%
6. KENTUCKY	$5,691	1.37%	$409,688	98.63%	$0	0.00%	$415,379	2.98%	$6,458	0.78%	1.55%
7. ALABAMA	$0	0.00%	$372,869	100.00%	$0	0.00%	$372,869	2.67%	$0	--	--
8. VIRGINIA	$0	0.00%	$239,215	100.00%	$0	0.00%	$239,215	1.72%	$0	--	--
9. DISTRICT OF COLUMBIA	$0	0.00%	$237,966	100.00%	$0	0.00%	$237,966	1.71%	$97,172	11.79%	40.83%
10. NEW JERSEY	$4,985	2.49%	$195,417	97.51%	$0	0.00%	$200,402	1.44%	$2,753	0.33%	1.37%
11. DELAWARE	$0	0.00%	$183,053	100.00%	$0	0.00%	$183,053	1.31%	$0	--	--
12. TENNESSEE	$1,491	1.30%	$113,221	98.70%	$0	0.00%	$114,712	0.82%	$0	--	--
13. MISSISSIPPI	$0	0.00%	$1,015	100.00%	$0	0.00%	$1,015	0.00%	$0	--	--
COMPOSITE	$201,981	1.45%	$13,366,327	95.85%	$376,063	2.70%	$13,944,371	100.00%	$824,385	100.00%	5.91%
AVERAGE	$15,537		$1,028,179		$28,928		$1,072,644		$63,414		
CT ATTORNEYS											
1. CONNECTICUT	$0	0.00%	$35,170,487	100.00%	$0	0.00%	$35,170,487	68.61%	$1,385,508	40.10%	3.94%
2. MASSACHUSETTS	$0	0.00%	$8,093,908	100.00%	$0	0.00%	$8,093,908	15.79%	$1,419,832	41.09%	17.54%
3. VERMONT	$0	0.00%	$6,018,064	100.00%	$0	0.00%	$6,018,064	11.74%	$372,060	10.77%	6.18%
4. RHODE ISLAND	$0	0.00%	$1,565,764	100.00%	$0	0.00%	$1,565,764	3.05%	$277,373	8.03%	17.71%
5. NEW HAMPSHIRE	$0	0.00%	$402,407	100.00%	$0	0.00%	$402,407	0.79%	$405	0.01%	0.10%
6. MAINE	$0	0.00%	$8,326	100.00%	$0	0.00%	$8,326	0.02%	$0	--	--
COMPOSITE	$0	0.00%	$51,258,956	100.00%	$0	0.00%	$51,258,956	100.00%	$3,455,178	100.00%	6.74%
AVERAGE	$0		$8,543,159		$0		$8,543,159		$575,863		
DAKOTA HOMESTEAD											
1. SOUTH DAKOTA	$168,351	6.47%	$2,432,110	93.53%	$0	0.00%	$2,600,461	63.22%	$51,729	79.64%	1.99%
2. COLORADO	$0	0.00%	$1,269,727	100.00%	$0	0.00%	$1,269,727	30.87%	$13,100	20.17%	1.03%
3. NEBRASKA	$0	0.00%	$87,386	100.00%	$0	0.00%	$87,386	2.12%	$0	--	--
4. MINNESOTA	$5,315	6.24%	$79,799	93.76%	$0	0.00%	$85,114	2.07%	$124	0.19%	0.15%
5. INDIANA	$70,880	100.00%	$0	0.00%	$0	0.00%	$70,880	1.72%	$0	--	--
COMPOSITE	$244,546	5.94%	$3,869,022	94.06%	$0	0.00%	$4,113,568	100.00%	$64,953	100.00%	1.58%
AVERAGE	$48,909		$773,804		$0		$822,714		$12,991		
DREIBELBISS											
1. INDIANA	$517,581	81.77%	$115,399	18.23%	$0	0.00%	$632,980	100.00%	$0	--	--
COMPOSITE	$517,581	81.77%	$115,399	18.23%	$0	0.00%	$632,980	100.00%	$0	--	0.00%
EQUITY NATIONAL											
1. MASSACHUSETTS	$280,228	100.00%	$0	0.00%	$0	0.00%	$280,228	100.00%	$0	--	--
COMPOSITE	$280,228	100.00%	$0	0.00%	$0	0.00%	$280,228	100.00%	$0	--	0.00%
FARMERS NATIONAL											
1. MISSOURI	$0	0.00%	$1,138,404	100.00%	$0	0.00%	$1,138,404	100.00%	$63,819	100.00%	5.61%
COMPOSITE	$0	0.00%	$1,138,404	100.00%	$0	0.00%	$1,138,404	100.00%	$63,819	100.00%	5.61%

D.2 Organization - Individual Underwriter by Jurisdiction

	DIRECT PREMIUMS WRITTEN							PERCENT OF UNDERWRITER	PAID LOSSES	PERCENT OF UNDERWRITER	LOSSES TO PREMIUMS
	DIRECT	% of Total	NON-AFFILIATED	% of Total	AFFILIATED	% of Total	TOTAL				

FIDELITY NATIONAL

	DIRECT	% of Total	NON-AFFILIATED	% of Total	AFFILIATED	% of Total	TOTAL	PERCENT OF UNDERWRITER	PAID LOSSES	PERCENT OF UNDERWRITER	LOSSES TO PREMIUMS
1. CALIFORNIA	$3,327,542	1.25%	$40,653,438	15.24%	$222,798,085	83.51%	$266,779,065	20.94%	$27,231,599	27.52%	10.21%
2. TEXAS	$36,403,051	24.32%	$66,319,966	44.32%	$46,931,292	31.36%	$149,654,309	11.75%	$5,592,548	5.65%	3.74%
3. FLORIDA	$21,054,690	14.75%	$120,283,773	84.28%	$1,388,742	0.97%	$142,727,205	11.20%	$7,077,621	7.15%	4.96%
4. NEW YORK	$65,349,635	46.33%	$75,450,351	53.49%	$243,390	0.17%	$141,043,376	11.07%	$8,160,557	8.25%	5.79%
5. ARIZONA	$27,131,108	41.15%	$25,618,258	38.86%	$13,176,808	19.99%	$65,926,174	5.17%	$5,540,234	5.60%	8.40%
6. NEW JERSEY	$16,019,974	31.65%	$34,283,970	67.73%	$315,930	0.62%	$50,619,874	3.97%	$3,205,750	3.24%	6.33%
7. PENNSYLVANIA	$4,781,547	11.72%	$35,864,596	87.90%	$154,953	0.38%	$40,801,096	3.20%	$2,348,958	2.37%	5.76%
8. GEORGIA	$2,416,300	7.02%	$30,629,759	89.03%	$1,357,008	3.94%	$34,403,067	2.70%	$3,211,528	3.25%	9.34%
9. OREGON	$1,085,648	3.40%	$3,180,736	9.95%	$27,690,109	86.65%	$31,956,493	2.51%	$452,632	0.46%	1.42%
10. MICHIGAN	$6,671,869	20.96%	$25,077,450	78.76%	$89,320	0.28%	$31,838,639	2.50%	$5,310,739	5.37%	16.68%
11. VIRGINIA	$1,178,444	4.19%	$26,330,018	93.66%	$604,262	2.15%	$28,112,724	2.21%	$1,641,866	1.66%	5.84%
12. MARYLAND	$773,680	3.23%	$23,142,555	96.52%	$61,317	0.26%	$23,977,552	1.88%	$2,552,299	2.58%	10.64%
13. UTAH	$595,825	2.78%	$20,622,079	96.34%	$186,853	0.87%	$21,404,757	1.68%	$890,467	0.90%	4.16%
14. NEW MEXICO	$13,407,110	67.09%	$6,517,176	32.61%	$58,275	0.29%	$19,982,561	1.57%	$792,101	0.80%	3.96%
15. MASSACHUSETTS	$2,830,618	14.27%	$16,989,764	85.66%	$14,268	0.07%	$19,834,650	1.56%	$2,144,152	2.17%	10.81%
16. WASHINGTON	$1,622,013	8.73%	$928,297	4.99%	$16,039,053	86.28%	$18,589,363	1.46%	$1,020,724	1.03%	5.49%
17. NEVADA	$568,903	3.74%	$3,996,920	26.25%	$10,663,202	70.02%	$15,229,025	1.20%	$1,278,630	1.29%	8.40%
18. CONNECTICUT	$1,750,992	12.25%	$12,516,055	87.56%	$26,586	0.19%	$14,293,633	1.12%	$2,865,392	2.90%	20.05%
19. COLORADO	$6,113,393	47.21%	$6,708,847	51.81%	$126,721	0.98%	$12,948,961	1.02%	$463,230	0.47%	3.58%
20. NORTH CAROLINA	$10,172,201	80.88%	$2,142,080	17.03%	$263,320	2.09%	$12,577,601	0.99%	$1,925,804	1.95%	15.31%
21. TENNESSEE	$1,187,178	9.73%	$9,490,497	77.76%	$1,526,905	12.51%	$12,204,580	0.96%	$515,284	0.52%	4.22%
22. LOUISIANA	$358,520	3.05%	$11,043,357	93.93%	$355,141	3.02%	$11,757,018	0.92%	$637,957	0.64%	5.43%
23. HAWAII	$11,293,348	97.49%	$291,275	2.51%	$0	0.00%	$11,584,623	0.91%	$319,968	0.32%	2.76%
24. OHIO	$2,334,258	21.35%	$8,146,110	74.52%	$451,240	4.13%	$10,931,608	0.86%	$1,137,370	1.15%	10.40%
25. ILLINOIS	$953,300	9.04%	$9,485,840	89.91%	$111,333	1.06%	$10,550,473	0.83%	$990,345	1.00%	9.39%
26. SOUTH CAROLINA	$327,189	3.16%	$9,706,204	93.78%	$316,349	3.06%	$10,349,742	0.81%	$632,672	0.64%	6.11%
27. AGGREGATE OTHER ALIEN	$6,392,857	100.00%	$0	0.00%	$0	0.00%	$6,392,857	0.50%	$108,584	0.11%	1.70%
28. MISSOURI	$850,838	13.83%	$5,215,537	84.75%	$87,569	1.42%	$6,153,944	0.48%	$1,407,230	1.42%	22.87%
29. MINNESOTA	$164,313	2.73%	$5,847,518	97.09%	$10,993	0.18%	$6,022,824	0.47%	$3,999,086	4.04%	66.40%
30. ALABAMA	$617,951	11.56%	$3,748,220	70.12%	$979,286	18.32%	$5,345,457	0.42%	$997,115	1.01%	18.65%
31. ARKANSAS	$41,201	0.79%	$4,412,828	85.10%	$731,623	14.11%	$5,185,652	0.41%	$150,595	0.15%	2.90%
32. IDAHO	$104,776	2.16%	$4,753,731	97.84%	$0	0.00%	$4,858,507	0.38%	$122,883	0.12%	2.53%
33. OKLAHOMA	$80,512	1.95%	$3,246,334	78.60%	$803,228	19.45%	$4,130,074	0.32%	$301,868	0.31%	7.31%
34. ALASKA	$126,333	4.74%	$2,536,582	95.26%	$0	0.00%	$2,662,915	0.21%	$884	0.00%	0.03%
35. INDIANA	$407,244	15.32%	$2,087,611	78.54%	$163,074	6.14%	$2,657,929	0.21%	$1,339,807	1.35%	50.41%
36. KANSAS	$290,242	12.31%	$2,067,114	87.69%	$0	0.00%	$2,357,356	0.19%	$20,651	0.02%	0.88%
37. DISTRICT OF COLUMBIA	$251,245	10.69%	$2,097,505	89.23%	$1,893	0.08%	$2,350,643	0.18%	$296,599	0.30%	12.62%
38. MISSISSIPPI	$277,350	12.13%	$1,493,493	65.33%	$515,258	22.54%	$2,286,101	0.18%	$245,697	0.25%	10.75%
39. RHODE ISLAND	$334,325	15.48%	$1,825,085	84.52%	$0	0.00%	$2,159,410	0.17%	$144,094	0.15%	6.67%
40. WISCONSIN	$132,758	7.51%	$1,621,056	91.66%	$14,689	0.83%	$1,768,503	0.14%	$175,310	0.18%	9.91%
41. NEBRASKA	$19,368	1.11%	$1,729,874	98.89%	$0	0.00%	$1,749,242	0.14%	$382,419	0.39%	21.86%
42. WEST VIRGINIA	$99,096	5.84%	$1,590,089	93.65%	$8,697	0.51%	$1,697,882	0.13%	$59,730	0.06%	3.52%
43. KENTUCKY	$546,570	38.76%	$325,856	23.11%	$537,859	38.14%	$1,410,285	0.11%	$148,798	0.15%	10.55%
44. MONTANA	$227,607	16.72%	$1,133,309	83.28%	$0	0.00%	$1,360,916	0.11%	$128,380	0.13%	9.43%
45. NEW HAMPSHIRE	$40,499	5.03%	$763,892	94.97%	$0	0.00%	$804,391	0.06%	$110,882	0.11%	13.78%
46. DELAWARE	$68,465	9.06%	$687,228	90.94%	$0	0.00%	$755,693	0.06%	$49,009	0.05%	6.49%
47. MAINE	$136,767	32.14%	$288,758	67.86%	$0	0.00%	$425,525	0.03%	$54,752	0.06%	12.87%
48. PUERTO RICO	$363,583	100.00%	$0	0.00%	$0	0.00%	$363,583	0.03%	$334,617	0.34%	92.03%
49. WYOMING	$47,935	14.38%	$285,384	85.62%	$0	0.00%	$333,319	0.03%	$12,544	0.01%	3.76%
50. NORTH DAKOTA	$6,514	2.62%	$242,277	97.38%	$0	0.00%	$248,791	0.02%	$1,550	0.00%	0.62%
51. U.S. VIRGIN ISLANDS	$0	0.00%	$245,872	100.00%	$0	0.00%	$245,872	0.02%	$16,319	0.02%	6.64%
52. VERMONT	$2,859	2.06%	$136,042	97.94%	$0	0.00%	$138,901	0.01%	$258,209	0.26%	185.89%
53. IOWA	$36,679	33.86%	$0	0.00%	$71,648	66.14%	$108,327	0.00%	$145,946	0.15%	134.73%
54. SOUTH DAKOTA	$29,140	100.00%	$0	0.00%	$0	0.00%	$29,140	0.00%	$0	--	--
COMPOSITE	**$251,405,363**	19.73%	**$673,800,566**	52.89%	**$348,876,279**	27.38%	**$1,274,082,208**	**100.00%**	**$98,953,985**	**100.00%**	**7.77%**
AVERAGE	**$4,655,655**		**$12,477,788**		**$6,460,672**		**$23,594,115**		**$1,832,481**		

FIRST AMERICAN (KS)

	DIRECT	% of Total	NON-AFFILIATED	% of Total	AFFILIATED	% of Total	TOTAL	PERCENT OF UNDERWRITER	PAID LOSSES	PERCENT OF UNDERWRITER	LOSSES TO PREMIUMS
1. KANSAS	$1,550,799	10.50%	$5,813,820	39.38%	$7,399,061	50.12%	$14,763,680	100.00%	$290,960	100.00%	1.97%
COMPOSITE	**$1,550,799**	10.50%	**$5,813,820**	39.38%	**$7,399,061**	50.12%	**$14,763,680**	**100.00%**	**$290,960**	**100.00%**	**1.97%**

FIRST AMERICAN (NY)

	DIRECT	% of Total	NON-AFFILIATED	% of Total	AFFILIATED	% of Total	TOTAL	PERCENT OF UNDERWRITER	PAID LOSSES	PERCENT OF UNDERWRITER	LOSSES TO PREMIUMS
1. NEW YORK	$96,485,318	40.33%	$131,671,357	55.03%	$11,099,012	4.64%	$239,255,687	100.00%	$8,776,026	100.00%	3.67%
COMPOSITE	**$96,485,318**	40.33%	**$131,671,357**	55.03%	**$11,099,012**	4.64%	**$239,255,687**	**100.00%**	**$8,776,026**	**100.00%**	**3.67%**

FIRST AMERICAN (OR)

	DIRECT	% of Total	NON-AFFILIATED	% of Total	AFFILIATED	% of Total	TOTAL	PERCENT OF UNDERWRITER	PAID LOSSES	PERCENT OF UNDERWRITER	LOSSES TO PREMIUMS
1. OREGON	$42,031,597	79.31%	$10,964,065	20.69%	$0	0.00%	$52,995,662	96.24%	$2,319,341	100.00%	4.38%
2. WISCONSIN	$0	0.00%	$2,068,205	100.00%	$0	0.00%	$2,068,205	3.76%	$0	--	--
COMPOSITE	**$42,031,597**	76.33%	**$13,032,270**	23.67%	**$0**	0.00%	**$55,063,867**	**100.00%**	**$2,319,341**	**100.00%**	**4.21%**
AVERAGE	**$21,015,799**		**$6,516,135**		**$0**		**$27,531,934**		**$1,159,671**		

FIRST AMERICAN T&T

	DIRECT	% of Total	NON-AFFILIATED	% of Total	AFFILIATED	% of Total	TOTAL	PERCENT OF UNDERWRITER	PAID LOSSES	PERCENT OF UNDERWRITER	LOSSES TO PREMIUMS
1. OKLAHOMA	$6,291,430	100.00%	$0	0.00%	$0	0.00%	$6,291,430	100.00%	$158,178	100.00%	2.51%
COMPOSITE	**$6,291,430**	100.00%	**$0**	0.00%	**$0**	0.00%	**$6,291,430**	**100.00%**	**$158,178**	**100.00%**	**2.51%**

D.2 Organization - Individual Underwriter by Jurisdiction

	DIRECT	% of Total	NON-AFFILIATED	% of Total	AFFILIATED	% of Total	TOTAL	PERCENT OF UNDERWRITER	PAID LOSSES	PERCENT OF UNDERWRITER	LOSSES TO PREMIUMS
FIRST AMERICAN TIC											
1. CALIFORNIA	$49,838,920	6.97%	$299,170,720	41.85%	$365,843,380	51.18%	$714,853,020	21.58%	$62,579,216	25.79%	8.75%
2. FLORIDA	$68,410,626	20.48%	$252,144,660	75.47%	$13,557,226	4.06%	$334,112,512	10.09%	$33,439,408	13.78%	10.01%
3. TEXAS	$106,146,688	35.96%	$89,771,897	30.41%	$99,255,039	33.63%	$295,173,624	8.91%	$8,675,667	3.58%	2.94%
4. ARIZONA	$77,312,374	47.97%	$47,354,992	29.38%	$36,507,960	22.65%	$161,175,326	4.87%	$8,685,505	3.58%	5.39%
5. UTAH	$11,736,485	9.37%	$81,385,669	64.97%	$32,139,532	25.66%	$125,261,686	3.78%	$2,159,045	0.89%	1.72%
6. MICHIGAN	$14,314,961	11.91%	$61,340,062	51.05%	$44,511,678	37.04%	$120,166,701	3.63%	$13,128,196	5.41%	10.92%
7. PENNSYLVANIA	$16,970,290	14.47%	$99,431,006	84.78%	$882,115	0.75%	$117,283,411	3.54%	$3,671,579	1.51%	3.13%
8. COLORADO	$780,120	0.73%	$106,190,637	98.86%	$445,395	0.41%	$107,416,152	3.24%	$7,612,745	3.14%	7.09%
9. OHIO	$6,830,001	6.87%	$74,063,983	74.49%	$18,536,223	18.64%	$99,430,207	3.00%	$6,086,363	2.51%	6.12%
10. VIRGINIA	$8,697,911	9.74%	$76,684,740	85.89%	$3,904,508	4.37%	$89,287,159	2.70%	$10,550,560	4.35%	11.82%
11. MASSACHUSETTS	$1,706,933	1.91%	$87,295,614	97.84%	$220,075	0.25%	$89,222,622	2.69%	$5,856,404	2.41%	6.56%
12. NEW JERSEY	$14,272,328	16.27%	$70,772,352	80.67%	$2,683,572	3.06%	$87,728,252	2.65%	$7,998,306	3.30%	9.12%
13. ILLINOIS	$18,083,316	21.66%	$46,867,248	56.14%	$18,529,294	22.20%	$83,479,858	2.52%	$6,678,513	2.75%	8.00%
14. MARYLAND	$8,022,208	10.46%	$63,154,606	82.31%	$5,551,539	7.24%	$76,728,353	2.32%	$4,116,094	1.70%	5.36%
15. WASHINGTON	$54,989,908	79.23%	$12,389,270	17.85%	$2,024,775	2.92%	$69,403,953	2.10%	$4,430,647	1.83%	6.38%
16. NEVADA	$36,943,330	61.03%	$22,774,768	37.62%	$819,647	1.35%	$60,537,745	1.83%	$1,698,214	0.70%	2.81%
17. GEORGIA	$3,818,711	8.03%	$43,164,748	90.82%	$546,730	1.15%	$47,530,189	1.43%	$5,803,402	2.39%	12.21%
18. LOUISIANA	$528,421	1.16%	$45,018,149	98.52%	$149,271	0.33%	$45,695,841	1.38%	($597,038)	(0.25)%	(1.31)%
19. CONNECTICUT	$2,860,840	6.74%	$39,383,702	92.79%	$197,810	0.47%	$42,442,352	1.28%	$4,378,833	1.80%	10.32%
20. IDAHO	$1,726,186	4.34%	$15,845,130	39.83%	$22,209,074	55.83%	$39,780,390	1.20%	$1,148,653	0.47%	2.89%
21. WISCONSIN	$8,167,878	22.70%	$26,115,472	72.59%	$1,692,991	4.71%	$35,976,341	1.09%	$2,146,503	0.88%	5.97%
22. INDIANA	$6,010,945	20.44%	$16,897,913	57.45%	$6,502,153	22.11%	$29,411,011	0.89%	$2,291,886	0.94%	7.79%
23. NEW MEXICO	$15,095,992	52.07%	$11,363,295	39.19%	$2,534,998	8.74%	$28,994,285	0.88%	$1,357,848	0.56%	4.68%
24. HAWAII	$792,925	2.74%	$7,413,778	25.62%	$20,733,026	71.64%	$28,939,729	0.87%	$475,150	0.20%	1.64%
25. TENNESSEE	$4,926,978	17.68%	$22,518,584	80.80%	$424,465	1.52%	$27,870,027	0.84%	$1,249,213	0.51%	4.48%
26. DISTRICT OF COLUMBIA	$9,220,340	33.64%	$17,755,690	64.79%	$430,540	1.57%	$27,406,570	0.83%	$2,166,420	0.89%	7.90%
27. CANADA	$26,161,839	100.00%	$0	0.00%	$0	0.00%	$26,161,839	0.79%	$7,620,687	3.14%	29.13%
28. NORTH CAROLINA	$1,095,332	4.24%	$24,537,244	95.01%	$192,851	0.75%	$25,825,427	0.78%	$3,071,533	1.27%	11.89%
29. SOUTH CAROLINA	$60,923	0.25%	$23,571,207	98.31%	$344,334	1.44%	$23,976,464	0.72%	$1,286,853	0.53%	5.37%
30. MONTANA	$470,409	2.00%	$12,917,801	55.05%	$10,075,665	42.94%	$23,463,875	0.71%	$761,207	0.31%	3.24%
31. ALABAMA	$1,202,460	5.56%	$20,264,430	93.70%	$159,114	0.74%	$21,626,004	0.65%	$1,356,523	0.56%	6.27%
32. MINNESOTA	$4,370,766	22.89%	$3,760,335	19.69%	$10,963,657	57.42%	$19,094,758	0.58%	$3,711,295	1.53%	19.44%
33. DELAWARE	$8,684,784	48.44%	$9,183,297	51.22%	$62,149	0.35%	$17,930,230	0.54%	$216,526	0.09%	1.21%
34. OKLAHOMA	$872,833	5.35%	$13,410,135	82.16%	$2,039,357	12.49%	$16,322,325	0.49%	$338,975	0.14%	2.08%
35. MAINE	$199,277	1.22%	$14,402,220	88.34%	$1,702,286	10.44%	$16,303,783	0.49%	$1,196,784	0.49%	7.34%
36. WYOMING	$1,746,026	10.71%	$2,908,500	17.84%	$11,647,701	71.45%	$16,302,227	0.49%	$182,368	0.08%	1.12%
37. KENTUCKY	$1,676,270	11.73%	$12,115,115	84.79%	$496,678	3.48%	$14,288,063	0.43%	$1,386,718	0.57%	9.71%
38. NEW HAMPSHIRE	$493,382	3.72%	$12,242,719	92.23%	$537,314	4.05%	$13,273,415	0.40%	$737,003	0.30%	5.55%
39. MISSISSIPPI	$2,195,212	16.89%	$10,713,567	82.44%	$86,256	0.66%	$12,995,035	0.39%	$1,566,334	0.65%	12.05%
40. AGGREGATE OTHER ALIEN	$11,074,697	97.23%	$315,301	2.77%	$0	0.00%	$11,389,998	0.34%	$5,327,656	2.20%	46.77%
41. OREGON	$10,164,143	91.51%	$21,900	0.20%	$921,629	8.30%	$11,107,672	0.34%	$87,380	0.04%	0.79%
42. ALASKA	$683,603	6.32%	$2,383,589	22.04%	$7,746,859	71.64%	$10,814,051	0.33%	$213,267	0.09%	1.97%
43. MISSOURI	$1,445,495	14.81%	$5,814,380	59.56%	$2,501,584	25.63%	$9,761,459	0.29%	$2,730,179	1.13%	27.97%
44. NEBRASKA	$748,472	9.18%	$5,379,457	65.97%	$2,025,866	24.85%	$8,153,795	0.25%	$176,620	0.07%	2.17%
45. WEST VIRGINIA	$101,422	1.45%	$6,824,423	97.79%	$52,716	0.76%	$6,978,561	0.21%	$235,830	0.10%	3.38%
46. ARKANSAS	$348,399	5.04%	$6,460,042	93.45%	$104,515	1.51%	$6,912,956	0.21%	$954,040	0.39%	13.80%
47. PUERTO RICO	$259	0.00%	$5,363,770	100.00%	$0	0.00%	$5,364,029	0.16%	$609,815	0.25%	11.37%
48. VERMONT	$76,370	2.08%	$3,585,787	97.53%	$14,369	0.39%	$3,676,526	0.11%	$346,486	0.14%	9.42%
49. SOUTH DAKOTA	$270,786	11.10%	$2,169,308	88.90%	$113	0.00%	$2,440,207	0.07%	$30,281	0.01%	1.24%
50. NORTH DAKOTA	$276,946	17.86%	$1,126,434	72.65%	$147,045	9.48%	$1,550,425	0.05%	$21,483	0.00%	1.39%
51. RHODE ISLAND	$287,206	25.20%	$825,308	72.40%	$27,384	2.40%	$1,139,898	0.03%	$250,956	0.10%	22.02%
52. U.S. VIRGIN ISLANDS	$0	0.00%	$206,245	100.00%	$0	0.00%	$206,245	0.00%	$239,174	0.10%	115.97%
53. GUAM	$0	--	$0	--	$0	--	$0	--	$169,868	0.07%	--
COMPOSITE	**$622,912,926**	18.81%	**$1,936,771,199**	58.47%	**$752,682,458**	22.72%	**$3,312,366,583**	**100.00%**	**$242,613,173**	**100.00%**	**7.32%**
AVERAGE	**$11,753,074**		**$36,542,853**		**$14,201,556**		**$62,497,483**		**$4,577,607**		
FIRST AMERICAN TRANS											
1. OKLAHOMA	$0	0.00%	$1,326,322	100.00%	$0	0.00%	$1,326,322	83.78%	$3,937	100.00%	0.30%
2. LOUISIANA	$108,501	42.27%	$148,193	57.73%	$0	0.00%	$256,694	16.22%	$0	--	--
COMPOSITE	**$108,501**	6.85%	**$1,474,515**	93.15%	**$0**	0.00%	**$1,583,016**	**100.00%**	**$3,937**	**100.00%**	**0.25%**
AVERAGE	**$54,251**		**$737,258**		**$0**		**$791,508**		**$1,969**		
FOUNDERS											
1. WYOMING	$178,276	100.00%	$0	0.00%	$0	0.00%	$178,276	100.00%	$0	--	--
COMPOSITE	**$178,276**	100.00%	**$0**	0.00%	**$0**	0.00%	**$178,276**	**100.00%**	**$0**	--	**0.00%**
GENERAL T&T											
1. OHIO	$0	0.00%	$2,509,539	90.40%	$266,652	9.60%	$2,776,191	99.96%	$418,464	100.00%	15.07%
2. INDIANA	$0	0.00%	$1,000	100.00%	$0	0.00%	$1,000	0.04%	$0	--	--
COMPOSITE	**$0**	0.00%	**$2,510,539**	90.40%	**$266,652**	9.60%	**$2,777,191**	**100.00%**	**$418,464**	**100.00%**	**15.07%**
AVERAGE	**$0**		**$1,255,270**		**$133,326**		**$1,388,596**		**$209,232**		

D.2 Organization - Individual Underwriter by Jurisdiction

	DIRECT PREMIUMS WRITTEN							PERCENT OF UNDERWRITER	PAID LOSSES	PERCENT OF UNDERWRITER	LOSSES TO PREMIUMS
	DIRECT	% of Total	NON-AFFILIATED	% of Total	AFFILIATED	% of Total	TOTAL				
GUARANTEE											
1. MISSOURI	$0	0.00%	$1,118,587	74.26%	$387,803	25.74%	$1,506,390	57.99%	$1,011,385	97.27%	67.14%
2. OKLAHOMA	$0	0.00%	$0	0.00%	$683,390	100.00%	$683,390	26.31%	$0	--	--
3. TENNESSEE	$0	0.00%	$0	0.00%	$228,810	100.00%	$228,810	8.81%	$6,700	0.64%	2.93%
4. KANSAS	$0	0.00%	$6,800	3.80%	$172,205	96.20%	$179,005	6.89%	$21,655	2.08%	12.10%
COMPOSITE	$0	0.00%	$1,125,387	43.32%	$1,472,208	56.68%	$2,597,595	100.00%	$1,039,740	100.00%	40.03%
AVERAGE	$0		$281,347		$368,052		$649,399		$259,935		
GUARANTEE T&T											
1. MICHIGAN	$0	0.00%	$201,584	7.21%	$2,595,869	92.79%	$2,797,453	24.71%	$513,370	31.70%	18.35%
2. OHIO	$186,780	10.48%	$472,033	26.48%	$1,123,621	63.04%	$1,782,434	15.75%	$204,968	12.66%	11.50%
3. ILLINOIS	$0	0.00%	$418,268	25.68%	$1,210,289	74.32%	$1,628,557	14.39%	$559,736	34.57%	34.37%
4. PENNSYLVANIA	$0	0.00%	$1,100,503	71.62%	$436,169	28.38%	$1,536,672	13.58%	$261,672	16.16%	17.03%
5. ARIZONA	$0	0.00%	$0	0.00%	$1,506,068	100.00%	$1,506,068	13.31%	$4,187	0.26%	0.28%
6. INDIANA	$17,740	2.32%	$339,321	44.38%	$407,468	53.30%	$764,529	6.75%	$40,614	2.51%	5.31%
7. UTAH	$0	0.00%	$0	0.00%	$761,915	100.00%	$761,915	6.73%	$0	--	--
8. ARKANSAS	$0	0.00%	$0	0.00%	$176,978	100.00%	$176,978	1.56%	$0	--	--
9. SOUTH CAROLINA	$0	0.00%	$0	0.00%	$162,067	100.00%	$162,067	1.43%	$33,846	2.09%	20.88%
10. MISSISSIPPI	$0	0.00%	$0	0.00%	$151,012	100.00%	$151,012	1.33%	$22	0.00%	0.01%
11. DISTRICT OF COLUMBIA	$0	0.00%	$0	0.00%	$37,974	100.00%	$37,974	0.34%	$0	--	--
12. MAINE	$0	0.00%	$0	0.00%	$10,566	100.00%	$10,566	0.09%	$0	--	--
13. FLORIDA	$0	0.00%	$0	0.00%	$2,530	100.00%	$2,530	0.02%	$731	0.05%	28.89%
14. KENTUCKY	$0	0.00%	$0	0.00%	$150	100.00%	$150	0.00%	$0	--	--
15. IOWA	$0	--	$0	--	$0	--	$0	--	$214	0.01%	--
COMPOSITE	$204,520	1.81%	$2,531,709	22.37%	$8,582,676	75.83%	$11,318,905	100.00%	$1,619,360	100.00%	14.31%
AVERAGE	$13,635		$168,781		$572,178		$754,594		$107,957		
GUARDIAN NATIONAL											
1. OHIO	$0	0.00%	$3,445,031	88.93%	$428,862	11.07%	$3,873,893	100.00%	$283,171	100.00%	7.31%
COMPOSITE	$0	0.00%	$3,445,031	88.93%	$428,862	11.07%	$3,873,893	100.00%	$283,171	100.00%	7.31%
INVESTORS TIC											
1. NORTH CAROLINA	$29,147,893	85.06%	$2,032,474	5.93%	$3,085,949	9.01%	$34,266,316	50.73%	$7,786,658	78.56%	22.72%
2. SOUTH CAROLINA	$211,897	2.80%	$7,360,564	97.18%	$1,767	0.02%	$7,574,228	11.21%	$579,164	5.84%	7.65%
3. VIRGINIA	$110,462	1.79%	$5,641,269	91.52%	$412,100	6.69%	$6,163,831	9.13%	$357,259	3.60%	5.80%
4. MICHIGAN	$7,790	0.25%	$2,718,167	87.83%	$368,873	11.92%	$3,094,830	4.58%	$302,789	3.05%	9.78%
5. TENNESSEE	$42,448	1.62%	$2,580,635	98.38%	$0	0.00%	$2,623,083	3.88%	$180,424	1.82%	6.88%
6. KENTUCKY	$0	0.00%	$1,927,641	75.17%	$636,760	24.83%	$2,564,401	3.80%	$130,792	1.32%	5.10%
7. WEST VIRGINIA	$15,410	0.76%	$2,016,919	99.24%	$0	0.00%	$2,032,329	3.01%	$20,399	0.21%	1.00%
8. ILLINOIS	$6,110	0.37%	$27,192	1.64%	$1,622,461	97.99%	$1,655,763	2.45%	$19,364	0.20%	1.17%
9. PENNSYLVANIA	$35,365	2.34%	$1,332,490	88.23%	$142,470	9.43%	$1,510,325	2.24%	$2,325	0.02%	0.15%
10. FLORIDA	$0	0.00%	$1,428,570	100.00%	$0	0.00%	$1,428,570	2.11%	$21,190	0.21%	1.48%
11. MARYLAND	$0	0.00%	$1,176,007	100.00%	$0	0.00%	$1,176,007	1.74%	$355,386	3.59%	30.22%
12. MISSISSIPPI	$90	0.01%	$916,363	99.99%	$0	0.00%	$916,453	1.36%	$36,314	0.37%	3.96%
13. NEBRASKA	$204,455	28.15%	$521,962	71.85%	$0	0.00%	$726,417	1.08%	($54,485)	(0.55)%	(7.50)%
14. ALABAMA	$0	0.00%	$493,747	100.00%	$0	0.00%	$493,747	0.73%	$49,251	0.50%	9.97%
15. MINNESOTA	$0	0.00%	$482,025	100.00%	$0	0.00%	$482,025	0.71%	$17,576	0.18%	3.65%
16. LOUISIANA	$0	0.00%	$321,368	100.00%	$0	0.00%	$321,368	0.48%	$0	--	--
17. MISSOURI	$0	0.00%	$140,569	86.83%	$21,324	13.17%	$161,893	0.24%	$803	0.00%	0.50%
18. OHIO	$0	0.00%	$141,259	100.00%	$0	0.00%	$141,259	0.21%	$0	--	--
19. GEORGIA	$8,963	9.09%	$89,671	90.91%	$0	0.00%	$98,634	0.15%	$73,058	0.74%	74.07%
20. INDIANA	$0	0.00%	$40,938	100.00%	$0	0.00%	$40,938	0.06%	$27,464	0.28%	67.09%
21. ARKANSAS	$0	0.00%	$31,908	100.00%	$0	0.00%	$31,908	0.05%	$0	--	--
22. DISTRICT OF COLUMBIA	$0	0.00%	$27,142	100.00%	$0	0.00%	$27,142	0.04%	$5,660	0.06%	20.85%
23. IOWA	$0	0.00%	$14,405	100.00%	$0	0.00%	$14,405	0.02%	$0	--	--
COMPOSITE	$29,790,883	44.10%	$31,463,285	46.58%	$6,291,704	9.31%	$67,545,872	100.00%	$9,911,391	100.00%	14.67%
AVERAGE	$1,295,256		$1,367,969		$273,552		$2,936,777		$430,930		
K.E.L.											
1. FLORIDA	$0	0.00%	$8,060	1.38%	$575,855	98.62%	$583,915	100.00%	$0	--	--
COMPOSITE	$0	0.00%	$8,060	1.38%	$575,855	98.62%	$583,915	100.00%	$0	--	0.00%
LAND CORP (CO)											
1. COLORADO	$0	0.00%	$0	0.00%	$19,602,608	100.00%	$19,602,608	100.00%	$183,856	100.00%	0.94%
COMPOSITE	$0	0.00%	$0	0.00%	$19,602,608	100.00%	$19,602,608	100.00%	$183,856	100.00%	0.94%
LAND TIC (ST LOUIS)											
1. MISSOURI	$0	0.00%	$2,173,014	100.00%	$0	0.00%	$2,173,014	96.27%	$0	--	--
2. MINNESOTA	$0	0.00%	$84,302	100.00%	$0	0.00%	$84,302	3.73%	$0	--	--
COMPOSITE	$0	0.00%	$2,257,316	100.00%	$0	0.00%	$2,257,316	100.00%	$0	--	0.00%
AVERAGE	$0		$1,128,658		$0		$1,128,658		$0		

D.2 Organization - Individual Underwriter by Jurisdiction

	DIRECT PREMIUMS WRITTEN							PERCENT OF	PAID	PERCENT OF	LOSSES TO
	DIRECT	% of Total	NON-AFFILIATED	% of Total	AFFILIATED	% of Total	TOTAL	UNDERWRITER	LOSSES	UNDERWRITER	PREMIUMS

LAWYERS

	DIRECT	% of Total	NON-AFFILIATED	% of Total	AFFILIATED	% of Total	TOTAL	PERCENT OF UNDERWRITER	PAID LOSSES	PERCENT OF UNDERWRITER	LOSSES TO PREMIUMS
1. TEXAS	$110,469,357	48.98%	$111,711,900	49.53%	$3,356,524	1.49%	$225,537,781	18.55%	$9,840,364	12.29%	4.36%
2. FLORIDA	$30,929,016	29.52%	$72,128,702	68.84%	$1,719,104	1.64%	$104,776,822	8.62%	$5,887,399	7.35%	5.62%
3. NEW YORK	$44,155,351	43.74%	$56,708,272	56.18%	$83,902	0.08%	$100,947,525	8.30%	$1,442,840	1.80%	1.43%
4. PENNSYLVANIA	$8,378,894	8.91%	$85,411,192	90.81%	$267,431	0.28%	$94,057,517	7.74%	$4,720,283	5.90%	5.02%
5. CALIFORNIA	$4,111,967	5.91%	$2,947,514	4.23%	$62,544,126	89.86%	$69,603,607	5.73%	$4,312,713	5.39%	6.20%
6. VIRGINIA	$8,163,211	13.68%	$50,572,153	84.73%	$950,989	1.59%	$59,686,353	4.91%	$4,180,112	5.22%	7.00%
7. ARIZONA	$4,075,885	7.94%	$32,407,287	63.16%	$14,830,508	28.90%	$51,313,680	4.22%	$1,970,203	2.46%	3.84%
8. NEW JERSEY	$8,062,949	20.26%	$31,691,588	79.63%	$43,744	0.11%	$39,798,281	3.27%	$2,931,896	3.66%	7.37%
9. GEORGIA	$3,646,322	10.13%	$32,337,785	89.84%	$10,131	0.03%	$35,994,238	2.96%	$3,798,387	4.74%	10.55%
10. OHIO	$12,208,600	35.38%	$19,113,853	55.39%	$3,183,624	9.23%	$34,506,077	2.84%	$2,948,018	3.68%	8.54%
11. MICHIGAN	$7,842,742	28.63%	$18,982,398	69.30%	$565,456	2.06%	$27,390,596	2.25%	$7,613,034	9.51%	27.79%
12. MARYLAND	$4,829,432	18.71%	$20,954,897	81.19%	$25,998	0.10%	$25,810,327	2.12%	$1,275,110	1.59%	4.94%
13. TENNESSEE	$3,264,278	13.60%	$20,173,665	84.06%	$560,714	2.34%	$23,998,657	1.97%	$1,032,836	1.29%	4.30%
14. SOUTH CAROLINA	$1,896,686	8.00%	$21,811,108	91.98%	$5,156	0.02%	$23,712,950	1.95%	$1,638,715	2.05%	6.91%
15. NEW MEXICO	$6,499,982	29.66%	$14,327,735	65.38%	$1,087,239	4.96%	$21,914,956	1.80%	$1,012,193	1.26%	4.62%
16. OREGON	$19,008,541	87.32%	$2,759,136	12.68%	$0	0.00%	$21,767,677	1.79%	$834,689	1.04%	3.83%
17. NEVADA	$3,886,279	19.13%	$6,442,142	31.71%	$9,985,089	49.15%	$20,313,510	1.67%	$1,762,430	2.20%	8.68%
18. UTAH	$182,862	0.92%	$19,629,036	99.08%	$239	0.00%	$19,812,137	1.63%	$1,935,213	2.42%	9.77%
19. MASSACHUSETTS	$4,775,217	25.69%	$13,797,263	74.24%	$12,402	0.07%	$18,584,882	1.53%	$3,521,190	4.40%	18.95%
20. ILLINOIS	$6,460,593	37.46%	$10,787,203	62.54%	$522	0.00%	$17,248,318	1.42%	$4,693,921	5.86%	27.21%
21. ALABAMA	$1,545,089	9.71%	$14,368,473	90.29%	$0	0.00%	$15,913,562	1.31%	$1,583,899	1.98%	9.95%
22. COLORADO	$10,093,453	64.59%	$5,444,452	34.84%	$87,986	0.56%	$15,625,891	1.29%	$1,204,623	1.50%	7.71%
23. WASHINGTON	$2,680,477	19.42%	$3,615,176	26.20%	$7,505,091	54.38%	$13,800,744	1.14%	$271,940	0.34%	1.97%
24. NORTH CAROLINA	$5,209,068	45.88%	$6,140,926	54.09%	$3,374	0.03%	$11,353,368	0.93%	$1,284,581	1.60%	11.31%
25. INDIANA	$6,330,422	57.39%	$4,698,968	42.60%	$240	0.00%	$11,029,630	0.91%	$1,123,363	1.40%	10.18%
26. MINNESOTA	$537,868	4.89%	$10,464,381	95.09%	$2,964	0.03%	$11,005,213	0.91%	$1,184,337	1.48%	10.76%
27. CONNECTICUT	$3,170,038	34.24%	$6,087,581	65.76%	$0	0.00%	$9,257,619	0.76%	$359,586	0.45%	3.88%
28. ARKANSAS	$237,311	2.88%	$8,010,608	97.10%	$2,018	0.02%	$8,249,937	0.68%	$284,438	0.36%	3.45%
29. WISCONSIN	$1,832,428	22.43%	$6,284,714	76.92%	$53,182	0.65%	$8,170,324	0.67%	$468,272	0.58%	5.73%
30. LOUISIANA	$1,373,431	17.51%	$6,463,033	82.38%	$9,192	0.12%	$7,845,656	0.65%	$200,671	0.25%	2.56%
31. DELAWARE	$5,598,759	76.67%	$1,704,059	23.33%	$0	0.00%	$7,302,818	0.60%	($43,357)	(0.05)%	(0.59)%
32. OKLAHOMA	$69,439	1.35%	$5,064,167	98.65%	$0	0.00%	$5,133,606	0.42%	$29,774	0.04%	0.58%
33. MISSISSIPPI	$526,319	10.67%	$4,407,800	89.33%	$394	0.01%	$4,934,513	0.41%	$284,583	0.36%	5.77%
34. AGGREGATE OTHER ALIEN	$4,300,498	91.18%	$415,817	8.82%	$0	0.00%	$4,716,315	0.39%	$370	0.00%	0.00%
35. DISTRICT OF COLUMBIA	$797,656	18.28%	$3,559,923	81.58%	$6,163	0.14%	$4,363,742	0.36%	$962,495	1.20%	22.06%
36. MISSOURI	$963,010	25.72%	$2,775,694	74.14%	$5,291	0.14%	$3,743,995	0.31%	$729,025	0.91%	19.47%
37. KANSAS	$1,508,455	41.38%	$1,978,351	54.27%	$158,721	4.35%	$3,645,527	0.30%	$118,876	0.15%	3.26%
38. WEST VIRGINIA	$253,183	7.04%	$3,341,681	92.86%	$3,744	0.10%	$3,598,608	0.30%	$377,610	0.47%	10.49%
39. MAINE	$1,275,834	36.29%	$2,239,055	63.69%	$479	0.01%	$3,515,368	0.29%	$197,478	0.25%	5.62%
40. KENTUCKY	$823,817	23.81%	$2,633,706	76.11%	$2,686	0.08%	$3,460,209	0.28%	$96,871	0.12%	2.80%
41. IDAHO	$42,285	1.30%	$3,212,595	98.65%	$1,777	0.05%	$3,256,657	0.27%	$21,609	0.03%	0.66%
42. WYOMING	$26,171	0.90%	$2,885,900	99.10%	$0	0.00%	$2,912,071	0.24%	$0	--	--
43. MONTANA	$425,715	15.45%	$2,328,059	84.49%	$1,754	0.06%	$2,755,528	0.23%	$31,633	0.04%	1.15%
44. NEW HAMPSHIRE	$767,944	30.96%	$1,712,303	69.04%	$0	0.00%	$2,480,247	0.20%	$97,751	0.12%	3.94%
45. NEBRASKA	$179,083	7.75%	$2,131,699	92.25%	$0	0.00%	$2,310,782	0.19%	$742,086	0.93%	32.11%
46. PUERTO RICO	$0	0.00%	$1,596,000	76.53%	$489,328	23.47%	$2,085,328	0.17%	$287,276	0.36%	13.78%
47. VERMONT	$467,547	30.21%	$1,079,976	69.77%	$360	0.02%	$1,547,883	0.13%	$16,842	0.02%	1.09%
48. RHODE ISLAND	$568,555	39.47%	$871,861	60.53%	$0	0.00%	$1,440,416	0.12%	$41,822	0.05%	2.90%
49. IOWA	$363,380	29.51%	$868,069	70.49%	$0	0.00%	$1,231,449	0.10%	$54,548	0.07%	4.43%
50. CANADA	$720,306	100.00%	$0	0.00%	$0	0.00%	$720,306	0.06%	$61,766	0.08%	8.57%
51. U.S. VIRGIN ISLANDS	$0	0.00%	$644,609	100.00%	$0	0.00%	$644,609	0.05%	$36,422	0.05%	5.65%
52. ALASKA	$32,559	10.36%	$281,699	89.64%	$0	0.00%	$314,258	0.03%	$50,995	0.06%	16.23%
53. HAWAII	$51,685	19.70%	$210,624	80.30%	$0	0.00%	$262,309	0.02%	$546,719	0.68%	208.43%
54. NORTH DAKOTA	$21,631	12.23%	$155,175	87.77%	$0	0.00%	$176,806	0.01%	$2,916	0.00%	1.65%
55. SOUTH DAKOTA	$25,308	85.77%	$4,200	14.23%	$0	0.00%	$29,508	0.00%	$1,659	0.00%	5.62%
COMPOSITE	$345,666,888	28.44%	$762,376,163	62.72%	$107,567,642	8.85%	$1,215,610,693	100.00%	$80,065,025	100.00%	6.59%
AVERAGE	$6,284,853		$13,861,385		$1,955,775		$22,102,013		$1,455,728		

MANITO

	DIRECT	% of Total	NON-AFFILIATED	% of Total	AFFILIATED	% of Total	TOTAL	PERCENT OF UNDERWRITER	PAID LOSSES	PERCENT OF UNDERWRITER	LOSSES TO PREMIUMS
1. PENNSYLVANIA	$0	0.00%	$97,958	12.42%	$690,518	87.58%	$788,476	100.00%	$27,274	100.00%	3.46%
COMPOSITE	$0	0.00%	$97,958	12.42%	$690,518	87.58%	$788,476	100.00%	$27,274	100.00%	3.46%

MASON

	DIRECT	% of Total	NON-AFFILIATED	% of Total	AFFILIATED	% of Total	TOTAL	PERCENT OF UNDERWRITER	PAID LOSSES	PERCENT OF UNDERWRITER	LOSSES TO PREMIUMS
1. FLORIDA	$120,217	7.74%	$0	0.00%	$1,432,065	92.26%	$1,552,282	100.00%	$200	100.00%	0.01%
COMPOSITE	$120,217	7.74%	$0	0.00%	$1,432,065	92.26%	$1,552,282	100.00%	$200	100.00%	0.01%

MASSACHUSETTS TIC

	DIRECT	% of Total	NON-AFFILIATED	% of Total	AFFILIATED	% of Total	TOTAL	PERCENT OF UNDERWRITER	PAID LOSSES	PERCENT OF UNDERWRITER	LOSSES TO PREMIUMS
1. MASSACHUSETTS	($254)	--	$0	--	$0	--	($254)	--	$0	--	--
COMPOSITE	($254)	--	$0	--	$0	--	($254)	--	$0	--	--

MISSISSIPPI GUARANTY

	DIRECT	% of Total	NON-AFFILIATED	% of Total	AFFILIATED	% of Total	TOTAL	PERCENT OF UNDERWRITER	PAID LOSSES	PERCENT OF UNDERWRITER	LOSSES TO PREMIUMS
1. MISSISSIPPI	$56,517	18.25%	$253,129	81.75%	$0	0.00%	$309,646	100.00%	$0	--	--
COMPOSITE	$56,517	18.25%	$253,129	81.75%	$0	0.00%	$309,646	100.00%	$0	--	0.00%

D.2 Organization - Individual Underwriter by Jurisdiction

	DIRECT PREMIUMS WRITTEN						TOTAL	PERCENT OF UNDERWRITER	PAID LOSSES	PERCENT OF UNDERWRITER	LOSSES TO PREMIUMS
	DIRECT	% of Total	NON-AFFILIATED	% of Total	AFFILIATED	% of Total					
MISSISSIPPI VALLEY											
1. ALABAMA	$0	0.00%	$13,415,105	100.00%	$0	0.00%	$13,415,105	51.75%	$554,749	32.65%	4.14%
2. MISSISSIPPI	$342,929	2.96%	$11,224,397	97.04%	$0	0.00%	$11,567,326	44.62%	$1,070,673	63.02%	9.26%
3. TENNESSEE	$145,644	15.50%	$793,819	84.50%	$0	0.00%	$939,463	3.62%	$73,545	4.33%	7.83%
COMPOSITE	$488,573	1.88%	$25,433,321	98.12%	$0	0.00%	$25,921,894	100.00%	$1,698,967	100.00%	6.55%
AVERAGE	$162,858		$8,477,774		$0		$8,640,631		$566,322		
MONROE											
1. NEW YORK	$5,556,612	42.75%	$7,075,703	54.44%	$364,364	2.80%	$12,996,679	100.00%	$144,923	100.00%	1.12%
COMPOSITE	$5,556,612	42.75%	$7,075,703	54.44%	$364,364	2.80%	$12,996,679	100.00%	$144,923	100.00%	1.12%
NATIONAL											
1. FLORIDA	$127,106	3.82%	$3,001,315	90.18%	$199,659	6.00%	$3,328,080	90.59%	$25,839	100.00%	0.78%
2. GEORGIA	$0	0.00%	$262,162	100.00%	$0	0.00%	$262,162	7.14%	$0	--	--
3. ALABAMA	$0	0.00%	$82,307	100.00%	$0	0.00%	$82,307	2.24%	$0	--	--
4. TENNESSEE	$0	0.00%	$1,367	100.00%	$0	0.00%	$1,367	0.04%	$0	--	--
COMPOSITE	$127,106	3.46%	$3,347,151	91.11%	$199,659	5.43%	$3,673,916	100.00%	$25,839	100.00%	0.70%
AVERAGE	$31,777		$836,788		$49,915		$918,479		$6,460		
NATIONAL ATTORNEYS											
1. INDIANA	$831,940	100.00%	$0	0.00%	$0	0.00%	$831,940	100.00%	$389,203	100.00%	46.78%
COMPOSITE	$831,940	100.00%	$0	0.00%	$0	0.00%	$831,940	100.00%	$389,203	100.00%	46.78%
NATIONAL LAND											
1. ILLINOIS	$0	0.00%	$1,346,879	100.00%	$0	0.00%	$1,346,879	53.99%	$20,956	27.14%	1.56%
2. TEXAS	$0	0.00%	$448,854	100.00%	$0	0.00%	$448,854	17.99%	$0	--	--
3. ALABAMA	$0	0.00%	$188,470	100.00%	$0	0.00%	$188,470	7.55%	$0	--	--
4. OHIO	$0	0.00%	$186,348	100.00%	$0	0.00%	$186,348	7.47%	$56,268	72.86%	30.20%
5. MISSOURI	$0	0.00%	$177,820	100.00%	$0	0.00%	$177,820	7.13%	$0	--	--
6. MONTANA	$0	0.00%	$121,482	100.00%	$0	0.00%	$121,482	4.87%	$0	--	--
7. MINNESOTA	$0	0.00%	$23,828	100.00%	$0	0.00%	$23,828	0.96%	$0	--	--
8. KANSAS	$0	0.00%	$1,048	100.00%	$0	0.00%	$1,048	0.04%	$0	--	--
COMPOSITE	$0	0.00%	$2,494,729	100.00%	$0	0.00%	$2,494,729	100.00%	$77,224	100.00%	3.10%
AVERAGE	$0		$311,841		$0		$311,841		$9,653		
NATIONAL OF NY											
1. CALIFORNIA	$0	0.00%	$0	0.00%	$9,776,776	100.00%	$9,776,776	81.21%	$7,628	0.56%	0.08%
2. CONNECTICUT	$982,520	100.00%	$0	0.00%	$0	0.00%	$982,520	8.16%	$0	--	--
3. MISSOURI	$698,400	100.00%	$0	0.00%	$0	0.00%	$698,400	5.80%	$0	--	--
4. MASSACHUSETTS	$576,997	100.00%	$0	0.00%	$0	0.00%	$576,997	4.79%	$41,763	3.08%	7.24%
5. FLORIDA	$0	0.00%	$4,027	100.00%	$0	0.00%	$4,027	0.03%	$305,182	22.53%	7,578.40%
6. NEW YORK	$0	--	$0	--	$0	--	$0	--	$664,227	49.03%	--
7. TENNESSEE	$0	--	$0	--	$0	--	$0	--	$143,465	10.59%	--
8. MISSISSIPPI	$0	--	$0	--	$0	--	$0	--	$99,867	7.37%	--
9. GEORGIA	$0	--	$0	--	$0	--	$0	--	$37,023	2.73%	--
10. MARYLAND	$0	--	$0	--	$0	--	$0	--	$31,207	2.30%	--
11. KENTUCKY	$0	--	$0	--	$0	--	$0	--	$15,200	1.12%	--
12. NEVADA	$0	--	$0	--	$0	--	$0	--	$6,450	0.48%	--
13. OHIO	$0	--	$0	--	$0	--	$0	--	$2,554	0.19%	--
14. INDIANA	$0	--	$0	--	$0	--	$0	--	$146	0.01%	--
COMPOSITE	$2,257,917	18.76%	$4,027	0.03%	$9,776,776	81.21%	$12,038,720	100.00%	$1,354,712	100.00%	11.25%
AVERAGE	$161,280		$288		$698,341		$859,909		$96,765		
NATIONS OF NY											
1. NEW JERSEY	$0	--	$0	--	$0	--	$0	--	$277,691	56.20%	--
2. NEW YORK	$0	--	$0	--	$0	--	$0	--	$87,767	17.76%	--
3. MINNESOTA	$0	--	$0	--	$0	--	$0	--	$40,854	8.27%	--
4. FLORIDA	$0	--	$0	--	$0	--	$0	--	$40,191	8.13%	--
5. MARYLAND	$0	--	$0	--	$0	--	$0	--	$26,620	5.39%	--
6. MASSACHUSETTS	$0	--	$0	--	$0	--	$0	--	$9,463	1.92%	--
7. KENTUCKY	$0	--	$0	--	$0	--	$0	--	$6,541	1.32%	--
8. OHIO	$0	--	$0	--	$0	--	$0	--	$2,871	0.58%	--
9. MAINE	$0	--	$0	--	$0	--	$0	--	$1,386	0.28%	--
10. VIRGINIA	$0	--	$0	--	$0	--	$0	--	$700	0.14%	--
COMPOSITE	$0	--	$0	--	$0	--	$0	--	$494,084	100.00%	--
AVERAGE	$0		$0		$0		$0		$49,408		
NEW JERSEY TIC											
1. NEW JERSEY	$0	0.00%	$16,413,857	100.00%	$0	0.00%	$16,413,857	95.81%	$1,064,324	98.59%	6.48%
2. PENNSYLVANIA	$0	0.00%	$717,721	100.00%	$0	0.00%	$717,721	4.19%	$15,185	1.41%	2.12%
COMPOSITE	$0	0.00%	$17,131,578	100.00%	$0	0.00%	$17,131,578	100.00%	$1,079,509	100.00%	6.30%
AVERAGE	$0		$8,565,789		$0		$8,565,789		$539,755		

Market Share Reports and Position Analysis - Organization

D.2 Organization - Individual Underwriter by Jurisdiction

	DIRECT	% of Total	NON-AFFILIATED	% of Total	AFFILIATED	% of Total	TOTAL	PERCENT OF UNDERWRITER	PAID LOSSES	PERCENT OF UNDERWRITER	LOSSES TO PREMIUMS
NORTH AMERICAN											
1. CALIFORNIA	$0	0.00%	$52,268	0.09%	$58,755,709	99.91%	$58,807,977	54.27%	$2,165,215	73.62%	3.68%
2. TEXAS	$0	0.00%	$0	0.00%	$17,070,426	100.00%	$17,070,426	15.75%	$15,640	0.53%	0.09%
3. FLORIDA	$0	0.00%	$241,465	1.79%	$13,261,644	98.21%	$13,503,109	12.46%	$39,427	1.34%	0.29%
4. COLORADO	$0	0.00%	$0	0.00%	$6,097,041	100.00%	$6,097,041	5.63%	$293,426	9.98%	4.81%
5. ARIZONA	$0	0.00%	$0	0.00%	$4,679,454	100.00%	$4,679,454	4.32%	$325,129	11.05%	6.95%
6. NEVADA	$0	0.00%	$0	0.00%	$3,313,273	100.00%	$3,313,273	3.06%	$95,241	3.24%	2.87%
7. MARYLAND	$0	0.00%	$0	0.00%	$2,532,497	100.00%	$2,532,497	2.34%	$7,125	0.24%	0.28%
8. VIRGINIA	$0	0.00%	$0	0.00%	$1,050,256	100.00%	$1,050,256	0.97%	$0	--	--
9. ILLINOIS	$0	0.00%	$0	0.00%	$456,432	100.00%	$456,432	0.42%	$0	--	--
10. DISTRICT OF COLUMBIA	$0	0.00%	$0	0.00%	$340,063	100.00%	$340,063	0.31%	$0	--	--
11. NEW JERSEY	$0	0.00%	$0	0.00%	$339,499	100.00%	$339,499	0.31%	$0	--	--
12. DELAWARE	$0	0.00%	$144,470	100.00%	$0	0.00%	$144,470	0.13%	$0	--	--
13. MINNESOTA	$0	0.00%	$0	0.00%	$36,986	100.00%	$36,986	0.03%	$0	--	--
COMPOSITE	$0	0.00%	$438,203	0.40%	$107,933,280	99.60%	$108,371,483	100.00%	$2,941,203	100.00%	2.71%
AVERAGE	$0		$33,708		$8,302,560		$8,336,268		$226,246		
NORTHEAST INVESTORS											
1. NEW YORK	$0	0.00%	$2,414,626	100.00%	$0	0.00%	$2,414,626	100.00%	$154,328	100.00%	6.39%
COMPOSITE	$0	0.00%	$2,414,626	100.00%	$0	0.00%	$2,414,626	100.00%	$154,328	100.00%	6.39%
OHIO BAR											
1. OHIO	$0	0.00%	$12,878,476	100.00%	$0	0.00%	$12,878,476	98.51%	$1,630,114	100.00%	12.66%
2. KENTUCKY	$0	0.00%	$171,109	100.00%	$0	0.00%	$171,109	1.31%	$0	--	--
3. INDIANA	$0	0.00%	$23,301	100.00%	$0	0.00%	$23,301	0.18%	$0	--	--
COMPOSITE	$0	0.00%	$13,072,886	100.00%	$0	0.00%	$13,072,886	100.00%	$1,630,114	100.00%	12.47%
AVERAGE	$0		$4,357,629		$0		$4,357,629		$543,371		

D.2 Organization - Individual Underwriter by Jurisdiction

	DIRECT PREMIUMS WRITTEN							PERCENT OF UNDERWRITER	PAID LOSSES	PERCENT OF UNDERWRITER	LOSSES TO PREMIUMS
	DIRECT	% of Total	NON-AFFILIATED	% of Total	AFFILIATED	% of Total	TOTAL				
OLD REPUBLIC NATIONAL											
1. FLORIDA	$1,189,536	0.89%	$133,121,159	99.11%	$0	0.00%	$134,310,695	17.92%	$10,328,952	17.18%	7.69%
2. CALIFORNIA	$2,818,804	3.11%	$9,225,944	10.18%	$78,593,459	86.71%	$90,638,207	12.09%	$3,841,149	6.39%	4.24%
3. NEW YORK	$316,532	0.43%	$67,876,078	92.30%	$5,343,542	7.27%	$73,536,152	9.81%	$4,345,925	7.23%	5.91%
4. TEXAS	$8,444	0.02%	$36,987,133	76.29%	$11,486,087	23.69%	$48,481,664	6.47%	$2,631,324	4.38%	5.43%
5. PENNSYLVANIA	$555,244	1.31%	$41,891,870	98.69%	$0	0.00%	$42,447,114	5.66%	$3,091,682	5.14%	7.28%
6. NEW JERSEY	$916,762	2.16%	$40,652,727	95.94%	$803,284	1.90%	$42,372,773	5.65%	$6,681,055	11.11%	15.77%
7. OHIO	$691,378	2.02%	$32,967,860	96.48%	$510,948	1.50%	$34,170,186	4.56%	$3,720,465	6.19%	10.89%
8. COLORADO	$165,566	0.60%	$27,263,453	99.40%	$0	0.00%	$27,429,019	3.66%	$1,544,176	2.57%	5.63%
9. GEORGIA	$194,774	0.83%	$23,403,351	99.17%	$0	0.00%	$23,598,125	3.15%	$3,476,917	5.78%	14.73%
10. TENNESSEE	$175,167	0.75%	$22,884,046	97.47%	$419,682	1.79%	$23,478,895	3.13%	$978,592	1.63%	4.17%
11. MASSACHUSETTS	$297,150	1.36%	$21,526,999	98.59%	$10,220	0.05%	$21,834,369	2.91%	$1,488,095	2.47%	6.82%
12. MICHIGAN	$247,680	1.62%	$15,041,679	98.38%	$0	0.00%	$15,289,359	2.04%	$4,409,450	7.33%	28.84%
13. MINNESOTA	$1,627,848	13.47%	$10,453,789	86.53%	$0	0.00%	$12,081,637	1.61%	$2,204,976	3.67%	18.25%
14. MARYLAND	$156,161	1.34%	$11,528,984	98.66%	$0	0.00%	$11,685,145	1.56%	$994,975	1.65%	8.51%
15. NORTH CAROLINA	$22,624	0.21%	$1,245,737	11.83%	$9,260,435	87.95%	$10,528,796	1.40%	$1,122,735	1.87%	10.66%
16. NEBRASKA	$33,496	0.32%	$10,356,291	99.68%	$0	0.00%	$10,389,787	1.39%	$136,282	0.23%	1.31%
17. ARIZONA	$887,960	8.84%	$5,926,761	59.00%	$3,231,134	32.16%	$10,045,855	1.34%	$49,664	0.08%	0.49%
18. WASHINGTON	$489,107	5.17%	$2,221,251	23.47%	$6,752,056	71.36%	$9,462,414	1.26%	$898,157	1.49%	9.49%
19. HAWAII	$105,074	1.19%	$78,373	0.89%	$8,632,417	97.92%	$8,815,864	1.18%	$532,902	0.89%	6.04%
20. VIRGINIA	$195,458	2.32%	$8,230,779	97.68%	$0	0.00%	$8,426,237	1.12%	$839,161	1.40%	9.96%
21. KENTUCKY	$268,821	3.33%	$7,797,258	96.67%	$0	0.00%	$8,066,079	1.08%	$884,380	1.47%	10.96%
22. WISCONSIN	$69,853	0.90%	$7,659,540	99.10%	$0	0.00%	$7,729,393	1.03%	$195,169	0.32%	2.53%
23. IDAHO	($481)	(0.01)%	$7,611,024	100.01%	$0	0.00%	$7,610,543	1.02%	$508,970	0.85%	6.69%
24. NEVADA	$277,776	3.69%	$3,730,514	49.56%	$3,519,312	46.75%	$7,527,602	1.00%	$35,726	0.06%	0.47%
25. SOUTH CAROLINA	$183,241	2.80%	$6,352,912	97.20%	$0	0.00%	$6,536,153	0.87%	$401,617	0.67%	6.14%
26. MISSOURI	$69,130	1.65%	$3,084,071	73.44%	$1,046,411	24.92%	$4,199,612	0.56%	$1,823,650	3.03%	43.42%
27. DELAWARE	$56,757	1.39%	$4,035,755	98.61%	$0	0.00%	$4,092,512	0.55%	$41,705	0.07%	1.02%
28. INDIANA	$226,877	5.61%	$3,818,019	94.39%	$0	0.00%	$4,044,896	0.54%	$125,107	0.21%	3.09%
29. ILLINOIS	$211,239	5.33%	$3,753,652	94.67%	$0	0.00%	$3,964,891	0.53%	$626,350	1.04%	15.80%
30. UTAH	$665,306	17.13%	$2,423,716	62.41%	$794,545	20.46%	$3,883,567	0.52%	$139,943	0.23%	3.60%
31. ALASKA	$265	0.01%	$3,660,960	99.99%	$0	0.00%	$3,661,225	0.49%	$37,011	0.06%	1.01%
32. CONNECTICUT	$284,552	8.26%	$3,158,499	91.74%	$0	0.00%	$3,443,051	0.46%	$134,079	0.22%	3.89%
33. KANSAS	$5,702	0.17%	$2,956,623	86.57%	$452,917	13.26%	$3,415,242	0.46%	$250,881	0.42%	7.35%
34. SOUTH DAKOTA	$50	0.00%	$2,859,456	100.00%	$0	0.00%	$2,859,506	0.38%	$4,632	0.00%	0.16%
35. NEW HAMPSHIRE	$266,056	9.72%	$2,471,937	90.28%	$0	0.00%	$2,737,993	0.37%	$254,458	0.42%	9.29%
36. ARKANSAS	$35,421	1.31%	$2,664,933	98.69%	$0	0.00%	$2,700,354	0.36%	$304,220	0.51%	11.27%
37. WEST VIRGINIA	$9,446	0.43%	$2,190,058	99.57%	$0	0.00%	$2,199,504	0.29%	$75,867	0.13%	3.45%
38. NEW MEXICO	$0	0.00%	$2,175,598	100.00%	$0	0.00%	$2,175,598	0.29%	$168,838	0.28%	7.76%
39. WYOMING	$0	0.00%	$1,675,569	100.00%	$0	0.00%	$1,675,569	0.22%	$29,359	0.05%	1.75%
40. LOUISIANA	$25,080	1.57%	$1,572,271	98.43%	$0	0.00%	$1,597,351	0.21%	$163,816	0.27%	10.26%
41. DISTRICT OF COLUMBIA	$13,522	0.87%	$1,544,434	99.13%	$0	0.00%	$1,557,956	0.21%	$129,585	0.22%	8.32%
42. MONTANA	$20,793	1.40%	$1,464,886	98.60%	$0	0.00%	$1,485,679	0.20%	$12,433	0.02%	0.84%
43. PUERTO RICO	$0	0.00%	$1,074,393	100.00%	$0	0.00%	$1,074,393	0.14%	$48,382	0.08%	4.50%
44. NORTH DAKOTA	$50	0.01%	$761,993	99.99%	$0	0.00%	$762,043	0.10%	$0	--	--
45. MAINE	$48,173	8.66%	$508,379	91.34%	$0	0.00%	$556,552	0.07%	$25,572	0.04%	4.59%
46. OKLAHOMA	$175	0.07%	$160,814	61.04%	$102,474	38.90%	$263,463	0.04%	$6,876	0.01%	2.61%
47. RHODE ISLAND	$9,106	3.47%	$253,616	96.53%	$0	0.00%	$262,722	0.04%	$43,981	0.07%	16.74%
48. ALABAMA	$136,053	94.63%	$7,721	5.37%	$0	0.00%	$143,774	0.02%	$235,835	0.39%	164.03%
49. VERMONT	$5,565	3.89%	$137,384	96.11%	$0	0.00%	$142,949	0.02%	$65,988	0.11%	46.16%
50. OREGON	$0	0.00%	$67,301	100.00%	$0	0.00%	$67,301	0.00%	$0	--	--
51. MISSISSIPPI	$64,501	95.90%	$2,759	4.10%	$0	0.00%	$67,260	0.00%	$39,196	0.07%	58.28%
COMPOSITE	**$14,047,794**	1.87%	**$604,520,309**	80.65%	**$130,958,923**	17.47%	**$749,527,026**	100.00%	**$60,130,260**	100.00%	8.02%
AVERAGE	**$275,447**		**$11,853,339**		**$2,567,822**		**$14,696,608**		**$1,179,025**		
OLYMPIC											
1. OHIO	$0	--	$0	--	$0	--	$0	--	$16,293	100.00%	--
COMPOSITE	**$0**	--	**$0**	--	**$0**	--	**$0**	--	**$16,293**	100.00%	--
PACIFIC NORTHWEST											
1. WASHINGTON	$0	0.00%	$9,409,995	26.75%	$25,764,640	73.25%	$35,174,635	60.17%	$1,424,786	88.68%	4.05%
2. OREGON	$0	0.00%	$2,204,949	17.43%	$10,442,688	82.57%	$12,647,637	21.63%	$49,200	3.06%	0.39%
3. ALASKA	$0	0.00%	$73,036	1.32%	$5,460,402	98.68%	$5,533,438	9.46%	$13,239	0.82%	0.24%
4. TEXAS	$0	0.00%	$3,515,893	100.00%	$0	0.00%	$3,515,893	6.01%	$0	--	--
5. ILLINOIS	$0	0.00%	$974,387	100.00%	$0	0.00%	$974,387	1.67%	$554	0.03%	0.06%
6. UTAH	$0	0.00%	$439,821	100.00%	$0	0.00%	$439,821	0.75%	$0	--	--
7. INDIANA	$0	0.00%	$106,959	100.00%	$0	0.00%	$106,959	0.18%	$121,254	7.55%	113.36%
8. IDAHO	$0	0.00%	$65,695	100.00%	$0	0.00%	$65,695	0.11%	($2,289)	(0.14)%	(3.48)%
9. IOWA	$0	0.00%	$4,099	100.00%	$0	0.00%	$4,099	0.00%	$0	--	--
COMPOSITE	**$0**	0.00%	**$16,794,834**	28.73%	**$41,667,730**	71.27%	**$58,462,564**	100.00%	**$1,606,744**	100.00%	2.75%
AVERAGE	**$0**		**$1,866,093**		**$4,629,748**		**$6,495,840**		**$178,527**		
PENN ATTORNEYS											
1. PENNSYLVANIA	$1,777,598	100.00%	$0	0.00%	$0	0.00%	$1,777,598	100.00%	$96,020	100.00%	5.40%
COMPOSITE	**$1,777,598**	100.00%	**$0**	0.00%	**$0**	0.00%	**$1,777,598**	100.00%	**$96,020**	100.00%	5.40%

D.2 Organization - Individual Underwriter by Jurisdiction

	DIRECT	% of Total	NON-AFFILIATED	% of Total	AFFILIATED	% of Total	TOTAL	PERCENT OF UNDERWRITER	PAID LOSSES	PERCENT OF UNDERWRITER	LOSSES TO PREMIUMS
PORT LAWRENCE											
1. OHIO	$2,836,725	50.74%	$2,437,031	43.59%	$316,748	5.67%	$5,590,504	100.00%	$99,717	100.00%	1.78%
COMPOSITE	$2,836,725	50.74%	$2,437,031	43.59%	$316,748	5.67%	$5,590,504	100.00%	$99,717	100.00%	1.78%
SEAGATE											
1. OHIO	$186,090	100.00%	$0	0.00%	$0	0.00%	$186,090	100.00%	$0	--	--
COMPOSITE	$186,090	100.00%	$0	0.00%	$0	0.00%	$186,090	100.00%	$0	--	0.00%
SECURITY TG (BALTIMORE)											
1. MARYLAND	$413,935	5.41%	$6,689,617	87.39%	$551,239	7.20%	$7,654,791	34.91%	$375,334	32.91%	4.90%
2. PENNSYLVANIA	$0	0.00%	$4,832,823	99.82%	$8,663	0.18%	$4,841,486	22.08%	$216,590	18.99%	4.47%
3. MISSISSIPPI	$0	0.00%	$2,917,899	100.00%	$0	0.00%	$2,917,899	13.31%	$53,851	4.72%	1.85%
4. LOUISIANA	$0	0.00%	$2,343,439	100.00%	$0	0.00%	$2,343,439	10.69%	$136,777	11.99%	5.84%
5. SOUTH CAROLINA	$0	0.00%	$1,429,635	100.00%	$0	0.00%	$1,429,635	6.52%	$48,214	4.23%	3.37%
6. DELAWARE	$0	0.00%	$1,091,559	100.00%	$0	0.00%	$1,091,559	4.98%	$2,934	0.26%	0.27%
7. ALABAMA	$0	0.00%	$490,222	100.00%	$0	0.00%	$490,222	2.24%	$191,462	16.79%	39.06%
8. DISTRICT OF COLUMBIA	$0	0.00%	$434,290	98.10%	$8,399	1.90%	$442,689	2.02%	$11,532	1.01%	2.60%
9. ARKANSAS	$0	0.00%	$415,609	100.00%	$0	0.00%	$415,609	1.90%	$357	0.03%	0.09%
10. NEW JERSEY	$0	0.00%	$162,389	100.00%	$0	0.00%	$162,389	0.74%	$10,915	0.96%	6.72%
11. OHIO	$0	0.00%	$89,742	100.00%	$0	0.00%	$89,742	0.41%	$12,012	1.05%	13.39%
12. WEST VIRGINIA	$0	0.00%	$52,488	100.00%	$0	0.00%	$52,488	0.24%	$77,657	6.81%	147.95%
13. KENTUCKY	$0	0.00%	$2,748	100.00%	$0	0.00%	$2,748	0.01%	$0	--	--
14. COLORADO	$0	--	$0	--	$0	--	$0	--	$489	0.04%	--
15. VIRGINIA	$0	--	$0	--	$0	--	$0	--	($61)	0.00%	--
16. TENNESSEE	$0	--	($9,209)	--	$0	--	($9,209)	(0.04)%	$2,487	0.22%	(27.01)%
COMPOSITE	$413,935	1.89%	$20,943,251	95.52%	$568,301	2.59%	$21,925,487	100.00%	$1,140,550	100.00%	5.20%
AVERAGE	$25,871		$1,308,953		$35,519		$1,370,343		$71,284		
SECURITY UNION											
1. ARIZONA	$24,734	0.15%	$128,529	0.80%	$15,844,405	99.04%	$15,997,668	25.17%	$743,050	10.26%	4.64%
2. CALIFORNIA	$11,300,301	100.00%	$76	0.00%	$0	0.00%	$11,300,377	17.78%	$3,854,550	53.24%	34.11%
3. GEORGIA	$4,547	0.08%	$6,032,149	99.92%	$0	0.00%	$6,036,696	9.50%	$185,260	2.56%	3.07%
4. TEXAS	$413	0.01%	$5,221,026	99.99%	$0	0.00%	$5,221,439	8.22%	$123,412	1.70%	2.36%
5. MICHIGAN	$3,143	0.06%	$5,204,705	99.94%	$0	0.00%	$5,207,848	8.19%	$987,696	13.64%	18.97%
6. WISCONSIN	$1,350	0.03%	$4,380,763	99.97%	$0	0.00%	$4,382,113	6.89%	$131,856	1.82%	3.01%
7. OHIO	$3,690	0.12%	$2,970,291	99.88%	$0	0.00%	$2,973,981	4.68%	$157,660	2.18%	5.30%
8. UTAH	$22,140	0.77%	$2,871,506	99.23%	$0	0.00%	$2,893,646	4.55%	$9,816	0.14%	0.34%
9. TENNESSEE	$1,254	0.05%	$2,382,441	99.95%	$0	0.00%	$2,383,695	3.75%	$93,937	1.30%	3.94%
10. ILLINOIS	$9,243	0.50%	$1,835,223	99.50%	$0	0.00%	$1,844,466	2.90%	$144,030	1.99%	7.81%
11. ALABAMA	$4,147	0.38%	$1,074,885	99.62%	$0	0.00%	$1,079,032	1.70%	$6,394	0.09%	0.59%
12. COLORADO	$7,258	0.70%	$1,026,904	99.30%	$0	0.00%	$1,034,162	1.63%	($34,495)	(0.48)%	(3.34)%
13. SOUTH DAKOTA	$0	0.00%	$828,139	100.00%	$0	0.00%	$828,139	1.30%	$0	--	--
14. MISSOURI	$750	0.13%	$594,271	99.87%	$0	0.00%	$595,021	0.94%	$361,596	4.99%	60.77%
15. NEBRASKA	$601	0.16%	$377,334	99.84%	$0	0.00%	$377,935	0.59%	$0	--	--
16. WASHINGTON	$21,279	6.18%	$323,165	93.82%	$0	0.00%	$344,444	0.54%	$148,777	2.06%	43.19%
17. OKLAHOMA	$0	0.00%	$256,272	100.00%	$0	0.00%	$256,272	0.40%	$7,838	0.11%	3.06%
18. VIRGINIA	$18,636	8.20%	$208,671	91.80%	$0	0.00%	$227,307	0.36%	$0	--	--
19. KANSAS	$429	0.24%	$179,165	99.76%	$0	0.00%	$179,594	0.28%	$1,078	0.01%	0.60%
20. ARKANSAS	$750	1.02%	$72,666	98.98%	$0	0.00%	$73,416	0.12%	$0	--	--
21. FLORIDA	$59,799	100.00%	$0	0.00%	$0	0.00%	$59,799	0.09%	$19	0.00%	0.03%
22. NEW MEXICO	$0	0.00%	$54,921	100.00%	$0	0.00%	$54,921	0.09%	$0	--	--
23. MISSISSIPPI	$0	0.00%	$52,619	100.00%	$0	0.00%	$52,619	0.08%	$0	--	--
24. INDIANA	$1,255	2.96%	$41,087	97.04%	$0	0.00%	$42,342	0.07%	$182	0.00%	0.43%
25. KENTUCKY	$2,400	6.33%	$35,516	93.67%	$0	0.00%	$37,916	0.06%	$0	--	--
26. NORTH CAROLINA	$1,295	4.11%	$30,232	95.89%	$0	0.00%	$31,527	0.05%	$51,949	0.72%	164.78%
27. NEVADA	$13,952	100.00%	$0	0.00%	$0	0.00%	$13,952	0.02%	$0	--	--
28. NEW JERSEY	$9,986	100.00%	$0	0.00%	$0	0.00%	$9,986	0.02%	$68,695	0.95%	687.91%
29. SOUTH CAROLINA	$5,062	100.00%	$0	0.00%	$0	0.00%	$5,062	0.00%	$0	--	--
30. IOWA	$3,900	100.00%	$0	0.00%	$0	0.00%	$3,900	0.00%	$0	--	--
31. PENNSYLVANIA	$2,574	100.00%	$0	0.00%	$0	0.00%	$2,574	0.00%	$0	--	--
32. IDAHO	$1,721	100.00%	$0	0.00%	$0	0.00%	$1,721	0.00%	$52,456	0.72%	3,048.00%
33. MONTANA	$1,282	100.00%	$0	0.00%	$0	0.00%	$1,282	0.00%	$17,222	0.24%	1,343.37%
34. ALASKA	$989	100.00%	$0	0.00%	$0	0.00%	$989	0.00%	$0	--	--
35. LOUISIANA	$939	100.00%	$0	0.00%	$0	0.00%	$939	0.00%	$888	0.01%	94.57%
36. CONNECTICUT	$659	100.00%	$0	0.00%	$0	0.00%	$659	0.00%	$0	--	--
37. DELAWARE	$362	100.00%	$0	0.00%	$0	0.00%	$362	0.00%	$0	--	--
38. VERMONT	$187	100.00%	$0	0.00%	$0	0.00%	$187	0.00%	$0	--	--
39. OREGON	$0	--	$0	--	$0	--	$0	--	$83,980	1.16%	--
40. MARYLAND	$0	--	$0	--	$0	--	$0	--	$18,361	0.25%	--
41. MASSACHUSETTS	$0	--	$0	--	$0	--	$0	--	$14,017	0.19%	--
42. HAWAII	$0	--	$0	--	$0	--	$0	--	$8,774	0.12%	--
43. U.S. VIRGIN ISLANDS	$0	--	$0	--	$0	--	$0	--	$330	0.00%	--
44. WEST VIRGINIA	($300)	--	$0	--	$0	--	($300)	0.00%	$0	--	--
COMPOSITE	$11,530,727	18.14%	$36,182,556	56.93%	$15,844,405	24.93%	$63,557,688	100.00%	$7,239,328	100.00%	11.39%
AVERAGE	$262,062		$822,331		$360,100		$1,444,493		$164,530		

D.2 Organization - Individual Underwriter by Jurisdiction

	DIRECT PREMIUMS WRITTEN							PERCENT OF	PAID	PERCENT OF	LOSSES TO
	DIRECT	% of Total	NON-AFFILIATED	% of Total	AFFILIATED	% of Total	TOTAL	UNDERWRITER	LOSSES	UNDERWRITER	PREMIUMS

SIERRA

	DIRECT	% of Total	NON-AFFILIATED	% of Total	AFFILIATED	% of Total	TOTAL	PERCENT OF UNDERWRITER	PAID LOSSES	PERCENT OF UNDERWRITER	LOSSES TO PREMIUMS
1. TEXAS	$0	0.00%	$1,966,566	100.00%	$0	0.00%	$1,966,566	100.00%	$0	--	--
COMPOSITE	$0	0.00%	$1,966,566	100.00%	$0	0.00%	$1,966,566	100.00%	$0	--	0.00%

SOUTHERN TI CORP

	DIRECT	% of Total	NON-AFFILIATED	% of Total	AFFILIATED	% of Total	TOTAL	PERCENT OF UNDERWRITER	PAID LOSSES	PERCENT OF UNDERWRITER	LOSSES TO PREMIUMS
1. TEXAS	$0	0.00%	$14,656,298	100.00%	$0	0.00%	$14,656,298	27.05%	$699,790	38.72%	4.77%
2. VIRGINIA	$1,173,681	9.09%	$10,922,720	84.60%	$815,354	6.31%	$12,911,755	23.83%	$687,413	38.03%	5.32%
3. TENNESSEE	$0	0.00%	$7,024,297	100.00%	$0	0.00%	$7,024,297	12.96%	($71,080)	(3.93)%	(1.01)%
4. FLORIDA	$0	0.00%	$3,534,245	92.24%	$297,153	7.76%	$3,831,398	7.07%	$115,101	6.37%	3.00%
5. COLORADO	$0	0.00%	$3,293,782	100.00%	$0	0.00%	$3,293,782	6.08%	$38,027	2.10%	1.15%
6. NORTH CAROLINA	$106	0.00%	$2,774,562	100.00%	$0	0.00%	$2,774,668	5.12%	$3,712	0.21%	0.13%
7. MARYLAND	$0	0.00%	$2,039,926	73.53%	$734,177	26.47%	$2,774,103	5.12%	$79,508	4.40%	2.87%
8. ALABAMA	$0	0.00%	$2,459,609	100.00%	$0	0.00%	$2,459,609	4.54%	$90,379	5.00%	3.67%
9. OHIO	$0	0.00%	$469,922	31.02%	$1,045,069	68.98%	$1,514,991	2.80%	($596)	(0.03)%	(0.04)%
10. SOUTH CAROLINA	$0	0.00%	$761,782	100.00%	$0	0.00%	$761,782	1.41%	$8,762	0.48%	1.15%
11. GEORGIA	$0	0.00%	$682,019	100.00%	$0	0.00%	$682,019	1.26%	$115,149	6.37%	16.88%
12. ARKANSAS	$0	0.00%	$498,173	100.00%	$0	0.00%	$498,173	0.92%	$12,239	0.68%	2.46%
13. PENNSYLVANIA	$0	0.00%	$295,215	74.89%	$98,996	25.11%	$394,211	0.73%	$198	0.01%	0.05%
14. WEST VIRGINIA	$0	0.00%	$205,731	86.68%	$31,609	13.32%	$237,340	0.44%	$0	--	--
15. MISSISSIPPI	$0	0.00%	$223,884	100.00%	$0	0.00%	$223,884	0.41%	$0	--	--
16. DISTRICT OF COLUMBIA	$0	0.00%	$131,579	100.00%	$0	0.00%	$131,579	0.24%	$27,876	1.54%	21.19%
17. LOUISIANA	$0	0.00%	$10,825	100.00%	$0	0.00%	$10,825	0.02%	$0	--	--
18. NEW JERSEY	$0	--	$0	--	$0	--	$0	--	$899	0.05%	--
COMPOSITE	$1,173,787	2.17%	$49,984,569	92.26%	$3,022,358	5.58%	$54,180,714	100.00%	$1,807,377	100.00%	3.34%
AVERAGE	$65,210		$2,776,921		$167,909		$3,010,040		$100,410		

STEWART (OR)

	DIRECT	% of Total	NON-AFFILIATED	% of Total	AFFILIATED	% of Total	TOTAL	PERCENT OF UNDERWRITER	PAID LOSSES	PERCENT OF UNDERWRITER	LOSSES TO PREMIUMS
1. OREGON	$567,888	5.26%	$10,237,613	94.74%	$0	0.00%	$10,805,501	100.00%	$167,857	100.00%	1.55%
COMPOSITE	$567,888	5.26%	$10,237,613	94.74%	$0	0.00%	$10,805,501	100.00%	$167,857	100.00%	1.55%

3

D.2 Organization - Individual Underwriter by Jurisdiction

	DIRECT PREMIUMS WRITTEN							PERCENT OF UNDERWRITER	PAID LOSSES	PERCENT OF UNDERWRITER	LOSSES TO PREMIUMS
	DIRECT	% of Total	NON-AFFILIATED	% of Total	AFFILIATED	% of Total	TOTAL				
STEWART TGC											
1. TEXAS	$33,887,417	12.59%	$66,853,618	24.83%	$168,480,798	62.58%	$269,221,833	18.50%	$4,269,132	4.25%	1.59%
2. FLORIDA	$4,775,431	2.89%	$129,809,110	78.53%	$30,708,240	18.58%	$165,292,781	11.36%	$10,528,610	10.47%	6.37%
3. CALIFORNIA	$14,241,275	8.99%	$42,096,381	26.57%	$102,120,824	64.45%	$158,458,480	10.89%	$20,135,633	20.03%	12.71%
4. CANADA	$76,099,011	100.00%	$0	0.00%	$0	0.00%	$76,099,011	5.23%	$13,556,557	13.48%	17.81%
5. VIRGINIA	$1,150,755	1.81%	$54,963,622	86.65%	$7,315,614	11.53%	$63,429,991	4.36%	$3,209,921	3.19%	5.06%
6. NEW JERSEY	$1,946,301	3.09%	$55,021,124	87.39%	$5,995,111	9.52%	$62,962,536	4.33%	$3,356,654	3.34%	5.33%
7. UTAH	$761,063	1.63%	$37,616,999	80.49%	$8,358,551	17.88%	$46,736,613	3.21%	$434,934	0.43%	0.93%
8. MARYLAND	$1,163,121	2.90%	$36,733,767	91.49%	$2,251,554	5.61%	$40,148,442	2.76%	$2,633,944	2.62%	6.56%
9. COLORADO	$828,251	2.20%	$16,014,388	42.63%	$20,726,344	55.17%	$37,568,983	2.58%	$4,031,176	4.01%	10.73%
10. OHIO	$1,967,484	5.41%	$23,777,168	65.36%	$10,636,676	29.24%	$36,381,328	2.50%	$3,441,447	3.42%	9.46%
11. WASHINGTON	$528,543	1.52%	$8,761,658	25.13%	$25,579,421	73.36%	$34,869,622	2.40%	$945,646	0.94%	2.71%
12. PENNSYLVANIA	$4,146,574	12.18%	$29,560,885	86.86%	$326,776	0.96%	$34,034,235	2.34%	$2,221,328	2.21%	6.53%
13. GEORGIA	$1,347,309	3.98%	$32,316,217	95.56%	$152,722	0.45%	$33,816,248	2.32%	$2,086,645	2.08%	6.17%
14. ILLINOIS	$1,759,049	5.77%	$22,681,855	74.45%	$6,023,601	19.77%	$30,464,505	2.09%	$2,182,421	2.17%	7.16%
15. MASSACHUSETTS	$2,077,606	8.23%	$22,543,803	89.32%	$617,198	2.45%	$25,238,607	1.73%	$2,474,207	2.46%	9.80%
16. ARIZONA	$358,106	1.69%	$2,984,773	14.06%	$17,879,310	84.25%	$21,222,189	1.46%	$307,588	0.31%	1.45%
17. MICHIGAN	$681,396	3.32%	$16,421,784	80.13%	$3,390,828	16.55%	$20,494,008	1.41%	$5,111,056	5.08%	24.94%
18. NEVADA	$1,219,137	6.45%	$5,094,523	26.96%	$12,580,498	66.58%	$18,894,158	1.30%	$408,850	0.41%	2.16%
19. TENNESSEE	$551,718	3.09%	$12,109,491	67.82%	$5,194,914	29.09%	$17,856,123	1.23%	$1,138,614	1.13%	6.38%
20. ALABAMA	$453,681	2.55%	$16,081,583	90.41%	$1,251,794	7.04%	$17,787,058	1.22%	$1,856,083	1.85%	10.44%
21. SOUTH CAROLINA	$323,342	1.84%	$17,241,337	97.93%	$41,484	0.24%	$17,606,163	1.21%	$708,085	0.70%	4.02%
22. MINNESOTA	$256,667	1.55%	$14,383,725	86.62%	$1,965,411	11.84%	$16,605,803	1.14%	$1,779,847	1.77%	10.72%
23. LOUISIANA	$149,049	0.95%	$12,743,531	80.93%	$2,854,272	18.13%	$15,746,852	1.08%	$345,301	0.34%	2.19%
24. WISCONSIN	$332,449	2.18%	$10,654,472	69.95%	$4,244,788	27.87%	$15,231,709	1.05%	$1,090,442	1.08%	7.16%
25. INDIANA	$320,241	2.17%	$9,786,782	66.23%	$4,669,539	31.60%	$14,776,562	1.02%	$2,476,061	2.46%	16.76%
26. NORTH CAROLINA	$1,721,235	13.25%	$10,176,438	78.34%	$1,092,468	8.41%	$12,990,141	0.89%	$1,646,435	1.64%	12.67%
27. NEW MEXICO	$0	0.00%	$3,341,414	25.99%	$9,513,136	74.01%	$12,854,550	0.88%	$156,780	0.16%	1.22%
28. IDAHO	$56,157	0.44%	$7,038,043	54.89%	$5,728,524	44.67%	$12,822,724	0.88%	$108,699	0.11%	0.85%
29. PUERTO RICO	$23,054	0.18%	$130,122	1.02%	$12,626,403	98.80%	$12,779,579	0.88%	$989,787	0.98%	7.75%
30. MISSOURI	$264,661	2.24%	$9,879,985	83.58%	$1,676,006	14.18%	$11,820,652	0.81%	$1,517,882	1.51%	12.84%
31. KENTUCKY	$546,525	5.69%	$7,390,922	76.94%	$1,668,069	17.37%	$9,605,516	0.66%	$730,790	0.73%	7.61%
32. MONTANA	$10,786	0.12%	$3,450,887	39.85%	$5,197,724	60.02%	$8,659,397	0.59%	$226,173	0.22%	2.61%
33. ALASKA	$75,891	0.88%	$4,705,077	54.56%	$3,842,143	44.56%	$8,623,111	0.59%	($3,977)	0.00%	(0.05)%
34. WYOMING	$15,098	0.21%	$6,144,633	86.46%	$947,405	13.33%	$7,107,136	0.49%	$106,567	0.11%	1.50%
35. OKLAHOMA	$66,879	1.10%	$2,601,403	42.97%	$3,385,667	55.92%	$6,053,949	0.42%	($85,877)	(0.09)%	(1.42)%
36. CONNECTICUT	$1,423,151	24.02%	$4,442,924	75.00%	$57,970	0.98%	$5,924,045	0.41%	$142,023	0.14%	2.40%
37. KANSAS	$301,840	5.35%	$2,619,936	46.48%	$2,715,209	48.17%	$5,636,985	0.39%	$493,020	0.49%	8.75%
38. HAWAII	$59,314	1.15%	$5,094,424	98.85%	$0	0.00%	$5,153,738	0.35%	$59,183	0.06%	1.15%
39. NEW HAMPSHIRE	$198,834	4.62%	$3,133,150	72.74%	$975,175	22.64%	$4,307,159	0.30%	$369,323	0.37%	8.57%
40. GUAM	$0	0.00%	$4,300,401	100.00%	$0	0.00%	$4,300,401	0.30%	$15,592	0.02%	0.36%
41. DISTRICT OF COLUMBIA	$415,513	10.09%	$2,502,210	60.78%	$1,199,442	29.13%	$4,117,165	0.28%	$220,792	0.22%	5.36%
42. DELAWARE	$96,163	2.37%	$3,290,326	81.11%	$670,323	16.52%	$4,056,812	0.28%	$122,926	0.12%	3.03%
43. MISSISSIPPI	$158,727	4.22%	$3,079,639	81.82%	$525,456	13.96%	$3,763,822	0.26%	$319,032	0.32%	8.48%
44. ARKANSAS	($1,659)	(0.05)%	$2,420,537	68.15%	$1,132,852	31.90%	$3,551,730	0.24%	$810,228	0.81%	22.81%
45. WEST VIRGINIA	$33,946	0.97%	$3,454,535	98.83%	$6,974	0.20%	$3,495,455	0.24%	$179,843	0.18%	5.15%
46. RHODE ISLAND	$123,689	3.74%	$2,025,143	61.24%	$1,158,069	35.02%	$3,306,901	0.23%	$1,237,043	1.23%	37.41%
47. AGGREGATE OTHER ALIEN	$255,295	7.95%	$1,215,251	37.83%	$1,741,901	54.22%	$3,212,447	0.22%	($204,249)	(0.20)%	(6.36)%
48. MAINE	$26,806	1.16%	$1,750,925	76.06%	$524,213	22.77%	$2,301,944	0.16%	$310,621	0.31%	13.49%
49. SOUTH DAKOTA	$13,860	0.70%	$1,006,549	51.18%	$946,312	48.12%	$1,966,721	0.14%	$76,756	0.08%	3.90%
50. NEBRASKA	$124,603	6.50%	$1,774,815	92.62%	$16,803	0.88%	$1,916,221	0.13%	$134,716	0.13%	7.03%
51. NORTH DAKOTA	$14,770	1.24%	$1,176,170	98.76%	$0	0.00%	$1,190,940	0.08%	$4,634	0.00%	0.39%
52. VERMONT	$73,791	6.81%	$1,008,830	93.10%	$993	0.09%	$1,083,614	0.07%	$51,364	0.05%	4.74%
53. NORTHERN MARIANA IS.	$0	0.00%	$779,364	100.00%	$0	0.00%	$779,364	0.05%	$21,656	0.02%	2.78%
54. U.S. VIRGIN ISLANDS	$0	0.00%	$516,458	100.00%	$0	0.00%	$516,458	0.04%	$18,555	0.02%	3.59%
55. IOWA	$172,064	37.15%	$273,669	59.09%	$17,416	3.76%	$463,149	0.03%	$10,348	0.01%	2.23%
56. OREGON	$154,970	100.00%	$0	0.00%	$0	0.00%	$154,970	0.01%	$19,736	0.02%	12.74%
COMPOSITE	**$157,750,939**	10.84%	**$796,976,776**	54.76%	**$500,732,921**	34.40%	**$1,455,460,636**	100.00%	**$100,536,583**	100.00%	6.91%
AVERAGE	**$2,816,981**		**$14,231,728**		**$8,941,659**		**$25,990,369**		**$1,795,296**		
STEWART TIC											
1. NEW YORK	$38,951,627	24.01%	$121,926,620	75.15%	$1,373,640	0.85%	$162,251,887	100.00%	$4,872,945	100.00%	3.00%
COMPOSITE	**$38,951,627**	24.01%	**$121,926,620**	75.15%	**$1,373,640**	0.85%	**$162,251,887**	100.00%	**$4,872,945**	100.00%	3.00%
T.A. TITLE											
1. PENNSYLVANIA	$0	0.00%	$9,499,282	79.45%	$2,457,720	20.55%	$11,957,002	70.17%	$739,741	100.00%	6.19%
2. NEW YORK	$0	0.00%	$2,077,547	87.92%	$285,442	12.08%	$2,362,989	13.87%	$0	--	--
3. NEW JERSEY	$0	0.00%	$1,899,014	81.33%	$435,971	18.67%	$2,334,985	13.70%	$0	--	--
4. MARYLAND	$0	0.00%	$245,900	69.49%	$107,947	30.51%	$353,847	2.08%	$0	--	--
5. DELAWARE	$0	0.00%	$17,128	65.19%	$9,145	34.81%	$26,273	0.15%	$0	--	--
6. OHIO	$0	0.00%	$3,170	66.81%	$1,575	33.19%	$4,745	0.03%	$0	--	--
COMPOSITE	**$0**	0.00%	**$13,742,041**	80.65%	**$3,297,800**	19.35%	**$17,039,841**	100.00%	**$739,741**	100.00%	4.34%
AVERAGE	**$0**		**$2,290,340**		**$549,633**		**$2,839,974**		**$123,290**		

D.2 Organization - Individual Underwriter by Jurisdiction

	DIRECT PREMIUMS WRITTEN							PERCENT OF UNDERWRITER	PAID LOSSES	PERCENT OF UNDERWRITER	LOSSES TO PREMIUMS
	DIRECT	% of Total	NON-AFFILIATED	% of Total	AFFILIATED	% of Total	TOTAL				

TICOR

	DIRECT	% of Total	NON-AFFILIATED	% of Total	AFFILIATED	% of Total	TOTAL	PERCENT OF UNDERWRITER	PAID LOSSES	PERCENT OF UNDERWRITER	LOSSES TO PREMIUMS
1. NEW YORK	$14,077,947	29.00%	$34,121,517	70.28%	$351,088	0.72%	$48,550,552	14.84%	$2,493,862	9.64%	5.14%
2. FLORIDA	$889,143	2.92%	$29,596,294	97.08%	$0	0.00%	$30,485,437	9.32%	$1,865,732	7.21%	6.12%
3. OREGON	$17,736,886	61.34%	$2,359	0.01%	$11,175,816	38.65%	$28,915,061	8.84%	$602,183	2.33%	2.08%
4. TEXAS	$4,477,907	16.71%	$22,325,177	83.29%	$0	0.00%	$26,803,084	8.19%	$1,171,779	4.53%	4.37%
5. ILLINOIS	$4,540,890	18.08%	$20,575,164	81.92%	$0	0.00%	$25,116,054	7.68%	$2,146,964	8.30%	8.55%
6. ARIZONA	$60,443	0.32%	$83,461	0.44%	$18,715,302	99.24%	$18,859,206	5.76%	$3,584,953	13.85%	19.01%
7. HAWAII	$21,492	0.12%	$17,267,823	99.88%	$0	0.00%	$17,289,315	5.28%	$885,092	3.42%	5.12%
8. WASHINGTON	$110,405	0.70%	$1,627,028	10.34%	$13,994,133	88.96%	$15,731,566	4.81%	$357,184	1.38%	2.27%
9. NEVADA	$74,549	0.57%	$272,455	2.10%	$12,655,098	97.33%	$13,002,102	3.97%	$634,605	2.45%	4.88%
10. INDIANA	$5,451,881	55.56%	$4,360,425	44.44%	$0	0.00%	$9,812,306	3.00%	$845,604	3.27%	8.62%
11. NEW JERSEY	$272,784	2.85%	$9,307,277	97.15%	$0	0.00%	$9,580,061	2.93%	($3,519,133)	(13.60)%	(36.73)%
12. PENNSYLVANIA	$249,815	2.88%	$8,414,216	97.12%	$0	0.00%	$8,664,031	2.65%	$789,667	3.05%	9.11%
13. CONNECTICUT	$92,393	1.16%	$7,903,850	98.84%	$0	0.00%	$7,996,243	2.44%	$479,748	1.85%	6.00%
14. MASSACHUSETTS	$45,535	0.60%	$7,492,537	99.40%	$0	0.00%	$7,538,072	2.30%	$1,830,567	7.07%	24.28%
15. GEORGIA	$51,347	0.71%	$7,188,400	99.29%	$0	0.00%	$7,239,747	2.21%	$234,406	0.91%	3.24%
16. WISCONSIN	$231,305	3.55%	$5,108,099	78.31%	$1,183,493	18.14%	$6,522,897	1.99%	$568,021	2.19%	8.71%
17. MICHIGAN	$74,331	1.20%	$6,109,445	98.80%	$0	0.00%	$6,183,776	1.89%	$4,296,994	16.60%	69.49%
18. MINNESOTA	$13,597	0.24%	$5,637,709	99.76%	$0	0.00%	$5,651,306	1.73%	$591,101	2.28%	10.46%
19. IDAHO	$512,787	10.24%	$4,493,766	89.76%	$0	0.00%	$5,006,553	1.53%	$204,149	0.79%	4.08%
20. MONTANA	$12,975	0.44%	$2,966,095	99.56%	$0	0.00%	$2,979,070	0.91%	$3,071	0.01%	0.10%
21. OHIO	$117,134	4.08%	$2,755,074	95.92%	$0	0.00%	$2,872,208	0.88%	$593,227	2.29%	20.65%
22. MAINE	$16,308	0.59%	$2,734,744	99.41%	$0	0.00%	$2,751,052	0.84%	$70,168	0.27%	2.55%
23. TENNESSEE	$77,254	3.25%	$2,299,581	96.75%	$0	0.00%	$2,376,835	0.73%	$290,971	1.12%	12.24%
24. MARYLAND	$189,987	8.60%	$2,019,436	91.40%	$0	0.00%	$2,209,423	0.68%	$421,405	1.63%	19.07%
25. COLORADO	$143,255	7.87%	$1,677,330	92.13%	$0	0.00%	$1,820,585	0.56%	$73,661	0.28%	4.05%
26. VIRGINIA	$105,405	6.98%	$1,405,183	93.02%	$0	0.00%	$1,510,588	0.46%	$77,497	0.30%	5.13%
27. GUAM	$0	0.00%	$1,478,263	100.00%	$0	0.00%	$1,478,263	0.45%	$11,326	0.04%	0.77%
28. OKLAHOMA	$300	0.03%	$1,133,852	99.97%	$0	0.00%	$1,134,152	0.35%	$72,662	0.28%	6.41%
29. MISSOURI	$36,811	3.30%	$1,079,026	96.70%	$0	0.00%	$1,115,837	0.34%	$151,075	0.58%	13.54%
30. NEBRASKA	$5,218	0.49%	$1,063,248	99.51%	$0	0.00%	$1,068,466	0.33%	$86,466	0.33%	8.09%
31. CALIFORNIA	$537,423	55.94%	$423,271	44.06%	$0	0.00%	$960,694	0.29%	$2,584,312	9.98%	269.00%
32. DELAWARE	$20,946	2.90%	$701,775	97.10%	$0	0.00%	$722,721	0.22%	$35,669	0.14%	4.94%
33. NEW MEXICO	$13,863	1.96%	$693,547	98.04%	$0	0.00%	$707,410	0.22%	$187,245	0.72%	26.47%
34. ARKANSAS	$25,371	3.82%	$639,479	96.18%	$0	0.00%	$664,850	0.20%	($151)	0.00%	(0.02)%
35. NORTH CAROLINA	$39,611	6.37%	$582,020	93.63%	$0	0.00%	$621,631	0.19%	$240,144	0.93%	38.63%
36. KANSAS	$3,456	0.64%	$534,478	99.36%	$0	0.00%	$537,934	0.16%	$35,145	0.14%	6.53%
37. DISTRICT OF COLUMBIA	$36,165	9.81%	$332,556	90.19%	$0	0.00%	$368,721	0.11%	$109,095	0.42%	29.59%
38. SOUTH CAROLINA	$183,892	51.66%	$172,059	48.34%	$0	0.00%	$355,951	0.11%	$33,759	0.13%	9.48%
39. ALABAMA	$67,615	19.00%	$288,307	81.00%	$0	0.00%	$355,922	0.11%	$123,840	0.48%	34.79%
40. UTAH	$35,070	12.02%	$256,807	87.98%	$0	0.00%	$291,877	0.09%	$0	--	--
41. LOUISIANA	$23,348	11.39%	$181,697	88.61%	$0	0.00%	$205,045	0.06%	$0	--	--
42. SOUTH DAKOTA	$57,718	29.31%	$139,223	70.69%	$0	0.00%	$196,941	0.06%	$12,504	0.05%	6.35%
43. MISSISSIPPI	$6,826	4.43%	$147,418	95.57%	$0	0.00%	$154,244	0.05%	$27,383	0.11%	17.75%
44. WEST VIRGINIA	$43,680	28.82%	$107,872	71.18%	$0	0.00%	$151,552	0.05%	$4,428	0.02%	2.92%
45. IOWA	$144,951	100.00%	$0	0.00%	$0	0.00%	$144,951	0.04%	$168,345	0.65%	116.14%
46. NORTH DAKOTA	$6,835	4.88%	$133,189	95.12%	$0	0.00%	$140,024	0.04%	$0	--	--
47. RHODE ISLAND	$11,008	10.91%	$89,904	89.09%	$0	0.00%	$100,912	0.03%	$7,138	0.03%	7.07%
48. KENTUCKY	$59,039	60.69%	$38,244	39.31%	$0	0.00%	$97,283	0.03%	$161,924	0.63%	166.45%
49. NEW HAMPSHIRE	$8,050	9.59%	$75,851	90.41%	$0	0.00%	$83,901	0.03%	$216,143	0.84%	257.62%
50. VERMONT	$3,898	13.19%	$25,663	86.81%	$0	0.00%	$29,561	0.00%	$15,591	0.06%	52.74%
51. WYOMING	$20,434	100.00%	$0	0.00%	$0	0.00%	$20,434	0.00%	$0	--	--
52. ALASKA	$19,276	100.00%	$0	0.00%	$0	0.00%	$19,276	0.00%	$5,010	0.02%	25.99%
53. U.S. VIRGIN ISLANDS	$0	0.00%	$1,820	100.00%	$0	0.00%	$1,820	0.00%	$0	--	--
COMPOSITE	$51,058,559	15.60%	$218,064,014	66.65%	$58,074,930	17.75%	$327,197,503	100.00%	$25,882,531	100.00%	7.91%
AVERAGE	$963,369		$4,114,415		$1,095,753		$6,173,538		$488,350		

D.2 Organization - Individual Underwriter by Jurisdiction

	DIRECT	% of Total	DIRECT PREMIUMS WRITTEN NON-AFFILIATED	% of Total	AFFILIATED	% of Total	TOTAL	PERCENT OF UNDERWRITER	PAID LOSSES	PERCENT OF UNDERWRITER	LOSSES TO PREMIUMS
TICOR (FL)											
1. FLORIDA	$0	0.00%	$41,670,435	100.00%	$0	0.00%	$41,670,435	49.88%	$3,650,777	19.70%	8.76%
2. PENNSYLVANIA	$0	0.00%	$5,114,023	100.00%	$0	0.00%	$5,114,023	6.12%	$220,920	1.19%	4.32%
3. NEW YORK	$0	0.00%	$4,570,975	100.00%	$0	0.00%	$4,570,975	5.47%	$2,406,377	12.99%	52.64%
4. MARYLAND	$0	0.00%	$3,443,114	100.00%	$0	0.00%	$3,443,114	4.12%	$465,084	2.51%	13.51%
5. NEW JERSEY	$0	0.00%	$3,293,530	100.00%	$0	0.00%	$3,293,530	3.94%	$56,346	0.30%	1.71%
6. VIRGINIA	$0	0.00%	$3,053,509	100.00%	$0	0.00%	$3,053,509	3.65%	$168,616	0.91%	5.52%
7. GEORGIA	$0	0.00%	$2,469,530	100.00%	$0	0.00%	$2,469,530	2.96%	$1,620,396	8.75%	65.62%
8. OHIO	$0	0.00%	$2,018,384	100.00%	$0	0.00%	$2,018,384	2.42%	$225,802	1.22%	11.19%
9. ALABAMA	$0	0.00%	$1,962,179	100.00%	$0	0.00%	$1,962,179	2.35%	$339,464	1.83%	17.30%
10. MICHIGAN	$0	0.00%	$1,868,554	100.00%	$0	0.00%	$1,868,554	2.24%	$3,847,724	20.77%	205.92%
11. NORTH CAROLINA	$0	0.00%	$1,394,889	100.00%	$0	0.00%	$1,394,889	1.67%	$204,655	1.10%	14.67%
12. COLORADO	$0	0.00%	$1,267,698	100.00%	$0	0.00%	$1,267,698	1.52%	$296,919	1.60%	23.42%
13. MISSOURI	$0	0.00%	$1,250,066	100.00%	$0	0.00%	$1,250,066	1.50%	$302,086	1.63%	24.17%
14. TENNESSEE	$0	0.00%	$1,242,405	100.00%	$0	0.00%	$1,242,405	1.49%	$396,805	2.14%	31.94%
15. MINNESOTA	$0	0.00%	$1,178,054	100.00%	$0	0.00%	$1,178,054	1.41%	$751,725	4.06%	63.81%
16. TEXAS	$0	0.00%	$1,084,339	100.00%	$0	0.00%	$1,084,339	1.30%	$56,077	0.30%	5.17%
17. WISCONSIN	$0	0.00%	$792,991	100.00%	$0	0.00%	$792,991	0.95%	$144,361	0.78%	18.20%
18. NEBRASKA	$0	0.00%	$704,217	100.00%	$0	0.00%	$704,217	0.84%	$5,070	0.03%	0.72%
19. MASSACHUSETTS	$0	0.00%	$566,618	100.00%	$0	0.00%	$566,618	0.68%	$271,567	1.47%	47.93%
20. LOUISIANA	$0	0.00%	$536,084	100.00%	$0	0.00%	$536,084	0.64%	$320,917	1.73%	59.86%
21. SOUTH CAROLINA	$0	0.00%	$522,993	100.00%	$0	0.00%	$522,993	0.63%	$85,133	0.46%	16.28%
22. INDIANA	$0	0.00%	$505,294	100.00%	$0	0.00%	$505,294	0.60%	$391,001	2.11%	77.38%
23. ARIZONA	$0	0.00%	$443,037	100.00%	$0	0.00%	$443,037	0.53%	$710,998	3.84%	160.48%
24. CONNECTICUT	$0	0.00%	$430,647	100.00%	$0	0.00%	$430,647	0.52%	$37,796	0.20%	8.78%
25. OKLAHOMA	$0	0.00%	$373,190	100.00%	$0	0.00%	$373,190	0.45%	$142,521	0.77%	38.19%
26. UTAH	$0	0.00%	$235,810	100.00%	$0	0.00%	$235,810	0.28%	$0	--	--
27. NEW HAMPSHIRE	$0	0.00%	$212,697	100.00%	$0	0.00%	$212,697	0.25%	$190,510	1.03%	89.57%
28. DELAWARE	$0	0.00%	$184,668	100.00%	$0	0.00%	$184,668	0.22%	$38,508	0.21%	20.85%
29. MAINE	$0	0.00%	$173,838	100.00%	$0	0.00%	$173,838	0.21%	$13,000	0.07%	7.48%
30. ARKANSAS	$0	0.00%	$164,642	100.00%	$0	0.00%	$164,642	0.20%	$12,292	0.07%	7.47%
31. KENTUCKY	$0	0.00%	$160,475	100.00%	$0	0.00%	$160,475	0.19%	$312,220	1.69%	194.56%
32. RHODE ISLAND	$0	0.00%	$113,092	100.00%	$0	0.00%	$113,092	0.14%	$9,517	0.05%	8.42%
33. VERMONT	$0	0.00%	$107,951	100.00%	$0	0.00%	$107,951	0.13%	$13,154	0.07%	12.19%
34. NEVADA	$0	0.00%	$91,471	100.00%	$0	0.00%	$91,471	0.11%	$0	--	--
35. MISSISSIPPI	$0	0.00%	$88,536	100.00%	$0	0.00%	$88,536	0.11%	$192,162	1.04%	217.04%
36. KANSAS	$0	0.00%	$80,288	100.00%	$0	0.00%	$80,288	0.10%	$115,431	0.62%	143.77%
37. WEST VIRGINIA	$0	0.00%	$71,331	100.00%	$0	0.00%	$71,331	0.09%	$174,080	0.94%	244.05%
38. MONTANA	$0	0.00%	$52,941	100.00%	$0	0.00%	$52,941	0.06%	$0	--	--
39. DISTRICT OF COLUMBIA	$0	0.00%	$41,023	100.00%	$0	0.00%	$41,023	0.05%	$3,307	0.02%	8.06%
40. NORTH DAKOTA	$0	0.00%	$4,402	100.00%	$0	0.00%	$4,402	0.00%	$0	--	--
41. ILLINOIS	$0	0.00%	$3,527	100.00%	$0	0.00%	$3,527	0.00%	$26,032	0.14%	738.08%
42. WASHINGTON	$0	--	$0	--	$0	--	$0	--	$225,558	1.22%	--
43. IOWA	$0	--	$0	--	$0	--	$0	--	$42,368	0.23%	--
44. CALIFORNIA	$0	--	$0	--	$0	--	$0	--	$40,613	0.22%	--
COMPOSITE	$0	0.00%	$83,543,447	100.00%	$0	0.00%	$83,543,447	100.00%	$18,527,889	100.00%	22.18%
AVERAGE	$0		$1,898,715		$0		$1,898,715		$421,088		
TITLE G&TC											
1. TENNESSEE	$260,893	100.00%	$0	0.00%	$0	0.00%	$260,893	100.00%	$1,500	100.00%	0.57%
COMPOSITE	$260,893	100.00%	$0	0.00%	$0	0.00%	$260,893	100.00%	$1,500	100.00%	0.57%
TITLE GUARANTY DIV (IA)											
1. IOWA	$3,724,743	100.00%	$0	0.00%	$0	0.00%	$3,724,743	100.00%	($2,440)	100.00%	(0.07)%
COMPOSITE	$3,724,743	100.00%	$0	0.00%	$0	0.00%	$3,724,743	100.00%	($2,440)	--	(0.07)%
TITLE IC AMERICA											
1. TEXAS	$0	0.00%	$9,828,156	100.00%	$0	0.00%	$9,828,156	82.22%	$53,444	15.01%	0.54%
2. COLORADO	$0	0.00%	$1,419,017	100.00%	$0	0.00%	$1,419,017	11.87%	$340,143	95.56%	23.97%
3. GEORGIA	$0	0.00%	$398,791	100.00%	$0	0.00%	$398,791	3.34%	$1,930	0.54%	0.48%
4. NEW MEXICO	$0	0.00%	$264,573	100.00%	$0	0.00%	$264,573	2.21%	($43,333)	(12.17)%	(16.38)%
5. SOUTH CAROLINA	$0	0.00%	$33,021	100.00%	$0	0.00%	$33,021	0.28%	($803)	(0.23)%	(2.43)%
6. INDIANA	$0	0.00%	$6,710	100.00%	$0	0.00%	$6,710	0.06%	$1,607	0.45%	23.95%
7. ILLINOIS	$0	0.00%	$3,859	100.00%	$0	0.00%	$3,859	0.03%	$1,816	0.51%	47.06%
8. TENNESSEE	$0	--	$0	--	$0	--	$0	--	$1,140	0.32%	--
COMPOSITE	$0	0.00%	$11,954,127	100.00%	$0	0.00%	$11,954,127	100.00%	$355,944	100.00%	2.98%
AVERAGE	$0		$1,494,266		$0		$1,494,266		$44,493		

D.2 Organization - Individual Underwriter by Jurisdiction

	DIRECT PREMIUMS WRITTEN						PERCENT OF UNDERWRITER	PAID LOSSES	PERCENT OF UNDERWRITER	LOSSES TO PREMIUMS
	DIRECT	% of Total	NON-AFFILIATED	% of Total	AFFILIATED	% of Total	TOTAL			

TITLE RESOURCES

	DIRECT	%	NON-AFFILIATED	%	AFFILIATED	%	TOTAL	PCT UW	PAID LOSSES	PCT UW	L/P
1. TEXAS	$0	0.00%	$46,579,513	64.57%	$25,562,327	35.43%	$72,141,840	69.47%	$2,181,170	68.12%	3.02%
2. ARIZONA	$0	0.00%	$15,856,339	100.00%	$0	0.00%	$15,856,339	15.27%	$963,507	30.09%	6.08%
3. COLORADO	$0	0.00%	$2,421,426	30.25%	$5,582,665	69.75%	$8,004,091	7.71%	$3,520	0.11%	0.04%
4. NEW JERSEY	$0	0.00%	$0	0.00%	$5,516,811	100.00%	$5,516,811	5.31%	$0	--	--
5. FLORIDA	$0	0.00%	$0	0.00%	$1,252,864	100.00%	$1,252,864	1.21%	$0	--	--
6. PENNSYLVANIA	$0	0.00%	$0	0.00%	$467,688	100.00%	$467,688	0.45%	$0	--	--
7. MARYLAND	$0	0.00%	$0	0.00%	$340,737	100.00%	$340,737	0.33%	$0	--	--
8. VIRGINIA	$0	0.00%	$0	0.00%	$208,256	100.00%	$208,256	0.20%	$0	--	--
9. MASSACHUSETTS	$0	0.00%	$0	0.00%	$44,660	100.00%	$44,660	0.04%	$0	--	--
10. MAINE	$0	0.00%	$0	0.00%	$14,476	100.00%	$14,476	0.01%	$0	--	--
11. NEW MEXICO	$0	--	$0	--	$0	--	$0	--	$54,397	1.70%	--
12. OKLAHOMA	$0	--	$0	--	$0	--	$0	--	($530)	(0.02)%	--
COMPOSITE	$0	0.00%	$64,857,278	62.45%	$38,990,484	37.55%	$103,847,762	100.00%	$3,202,064	100.00%	3.08%
AVERAGE	$0		$5,404,773		$3,249,207		$8,653,980		$266,839		

TITLEDGE

	DIRECT	%	NON-AFFILIATED	%	AFFILIATED	%	TOTAL	PCT UW	PAID LOSSES	PCT UW	L/P
1. NEW YORK	$78,917	43.46%	$102,655	56.54%	$0	0.00%	$181,572	100.00%	$0	--	--
COMPOSITE	$78,917	43.46%	$102,655	56.54%	$0	0.00%	$181,572	100.00%	$0	--	0.00%

TRANSNATION

	DIRECT	%	NON-AFFILIATED	%	AFFILIATED	%	TOTAL	PCT UW	PAID LOSSES	PCT UW	L/P
1. CALIFORNIA	$8,051,368	11.53%	$0	0.00%	$61,762,055	88.47%	$69,813,423	25.40%	$12,568,791	44.47%	18.00%
2. ARIZONA	$25,044,743	60.33%	$16,422,597	39.56%	$43,367	0.10%	$41,510,707	15.10%	$2,918,807	10.33%	7.03%
3. MICHIGAN	$8,472,063	24.83%	$24,384,023	71.47%	$1,263,113	3.70%	$34,119,199	12.41%	$4,976,684	17.61%	14.59%
4. WASHINGTON	$17,361,980	62.73%	$7,927,716	28.64%	$2,388,805	8.63%	$27,678,501	10.07%	$1,951,097	6.90%	7.05%
5. OREGON	$415,787	1.98%	$13,061,398	62.17%	$7,532,379	35.85%	$21,009,564	7.64%	$757,141	2.68%	3.60%
6. IDAHO	$439,876	3.31%	$5,340,570	40.18%	$7,511,989	56.51%	$13,292,435	4.84%	$774,134	2.74%	5.82%
7. UTAH	$0	0.00%	$12,801,335	100.00%	$0	0.00%	$12,801,335	4.66%	$73,513	0.26%	0.57%
8. COLORADO	$7,678,452	74.65%	$2,355,623	22.90%	$252,504	2.45%	$10,286,579	3.74%	$900,205	3.19%	8.75%
9. VIRGINIA	$106,313	1.10%	$9,409,287	97.72%	$113,108	1.17%	$9,628,708	3.50%	$109,168	0.39%	1.13%
10. NEW JERSEY	$821	0.01%	$6,847,935	99.99%	$0	0.00%	$6,848,756	2.49%	$521,063	1.84%	7.61%
11. DELAWARE	$741,123	12.13%	$5,367,260	87.87%	$0	0.00%	$6,108,383	2.22%	$271,561	0.96%	4.45%
12. OHIO	$552,683	12.10%	$4,013,524	87.85%	$2,208	0.05%	$4,568,415	1.66%	$75,142	0.27%	1.64%
13. MISSOURI	$0	0.00%	$3,503,764	99.80%	$6,893	0.20%	$3,510,657	1.28%	$1,298,193	4.59%	36.98%
14. TEXAS	$0	0.00%	$2,326,598	100.00%	$0	0.00%	$2,326,598	0.85%	$57,000	0.20%	2.45%
15. WISCONSIN	$992	0.06%	$1,552,433	99.94%	$0	0.00%	$1,553,425	0.57%	$56,838	0.20%	3.66%
16. INDIANA	$91,657	6.02%	$1,431,293	93.98%	$0	0.00%	$1,522,950	0.55%	$167,089	0.59%	10.97%
17. NORTH CAROLINA	$120	0.01%	$1,517,212	99.99%	$0	0.00%	$1,517,332	0.55%	$37,880	0.13%	2.50%
18. PENNSYLVANIA	$4,338	0.37%	$1,170,554	99.63%	$0	0.00%	$1,174,892	0.43%	$26,812	0.09%	2.28%
19. NEW HAMPSHIRE	$0	0.00%	$1,104,954	100.00%	$0	0.00%	$1,104,954	0.40%	$43,568	0.15%	3.94%
20. ILLINOIS	($376)	(0.04)%	$889,489	99.91%	$1,185	0.13%	$890,298	0.32%	$206,384	0.73%	23.18%
21. ALABAMA	$0	0.00%	$647,020	100.00%	$0	0.00%	$647,020	0.24%	$16,434	0.06%	2.54%
22. MONTANA	($1,480)	(0.28)%	$538,329	100.28%	$0	0.00%	$536,849	0.20%	$0	--	--
23. FLORIDA	$446,781	94.57%	$23,824	5.04%	$1,826	0.39%	$472,431	0.17%	$8,581	0.03%	1.82%
24. TENNESSEE	$0	0.00%	$385,780	100.00%	$0	0.00%	$385,780	0.14%	$105,243	0.37%	27.28%
25. NEW MEXICO	($929)	(0.32)%	$291,612	100.32%	$0	0.00%	$290,683	0.11%	$990	0.00%	0.34%
26. MASSACHUSETTS	$245	0.10%	$250,202	99.90%	$0	0.00%	$250,447	0.09%	$9,272	0.03%	3.70%
27. MARYLAND	$170,334	69.13%	$76,054	30.87%	$0	0.00%	$246,388	0.09%	$6,961	0.02%	2.83%
28. NEBRASKA	$366	0.20%	$181,736	99.80%	$0	0.00%	$182,102	0.07%	$536	0.00%	0.29%
29. GEORGIA	$23,609	14.14%	$143,357	85.86%	$0	0.00%	$166,966	0.06%	$269,182	0.95%	161.22%
30. NEVADA	$57,446	49.13%	$59,476	50.87%	$0	0.00%	$116,922	0.04%	$3,088	0.01%	2.64%
31. OKLAHOMA	$0	0.00%	$34,914	33.66%	$68,824	66.34%	$103,738	0.04%	$27,637	0.10%	26.64%
32. WEST VIRGINIA	$571	0.73%	$20,954	26.93%	$56,287	72.34%	$77,812	0.03%	$0	--	--
33. SOUTH CAROLINA	$0	0.00%	$45,008	100.00%	$0	0.00%	$45,008	0.02%	$0	--	--
34. DISTRICT OF COLUMBIA	$0	0.00%	$30,396	100.00%	$0	0.00%	$30,396	0.01%	$0	--	--
35. IOWA	$1,300	6.11%	$19,994	93.89%	$0	0.00%	$21,294	0.00%	$0	--	--
36. CONNECTICUT	$0	0.00%	$21,183	100.00%	$0	0.00%	$21,183	0.00%	$0	--	--
37. RHODE ISLAND	$0	0.00%	$13,138	100.00%	$0	0.00%	$13,138	0.00%	$0	--	--
38. KENTUCKY	$65	0.53%	$12,120	99.47%	$0	0.00%	$12,185	0.00%	$7,010	0.02%	57.53%
39. MISSISSIPPI	$0	0.00%	$6,290	100.00%	$0	0.00%	$6,290	0.00%	$0	--	--
40. MINNESOTA	$0	0.00%	$5,167	100.00%	$0	0.00%	$5,167	0.00%	$254	0.00%	4.92%
41. NEW YORK	$2,019	100.00%	$0	0.00%	$0	0.00%	$2,019	0.00%	$0	--	--
42. LOUISIANA	$135	28.91%	$332	71.09%	$0	0.00%	$467	0.00%	$0	--	--
43. HAWAII	$0	--	$0	--	$0	--	$0	--	$1,824	0.00%	--
44. ALASKA	$0	--	$0	--	$0	--	$0	--	$922	0.00%	--
45. MAINE	$0	--	$0	--	$0	--	$0	--	$22	0.00%	--
46. ARKANSAS	($77,421)	--	$5,900	--	$0	--	($71,521)	(0.03)%	$14,711	0.05%	(20.57)%
COMPOSITE	$69,584,981	25.32%	$124,240,351	45.21%	$81,004,543	29.47%	$274,829,875	100.00%	$28,263,737	100.00%	10.28%
AVERAGE	$1,512,717		$2,700,877		$1,760,968		$5,974,563		$614,429		

D.2 Organization - Individual Underwriter by Jurisdiction

	DIRECT PREMIUMS WRITTEN										
	DIRECT	% of Total	NON-AFFILIATED	% of Total	AFFILIATED	% of Total	TOTAL	PERCENT OF UNDERWRITER	PAID LOSSES	PERCENT OF UNDERWRITER	LOSSES TO PREMIUMS

TRANSUNION NATIONAL

	DIRECT	% of Total	NON-AFFILIATED	% of Total	AFFILIATED	% of Total	TOTAL	PERCENT OF UNDERWRITER	PAID LOSSES	PERCENT OF UNDERWRITER	LOSSES TO PREMIUMS
1. FLORIDA	$6,658	0.56%	$650,608	54.43%	$538,097	45.02%	$1,195,363	30.55%	$0	--	--
2. SOUTH CAROLINA	$68,818	8.33%	$746,478	90.33%	$11,080	1.34%	$826,376	21.12%	$363,212	47.49%	43.95%
3. OHIO	$33,035	4.78%	$617,640	89.44%	$39,893	5.78%	$690,568	17.65%	$6,524	0.85%	0.94%
4. ALABAMA	$0	0.00%	$263,949	92.17%	$22,421	7.83%	$286,370	7.32%	$90,755	11.87%	31.69%
5. GEORGIA	$0	0.00%	$66,197	31.04%	$147,083	68.96%	$213,280	5.45%	$166,651	21.79%	78.14%
6. NORTH CAROLINA	$210	0.12%	$0	0.00%	$171,167	99.88%	$171,377	4.38%	$110,277	14.42%	64.35%
7. VIRGINIA	$0	0.00%	$0	0.00%	$117,235	100.00%	$117,235	3.00%	$5,069	0.66%	4.32%
8. ILLINOIS	$88	0.08%	$0	0.00%	$116,352	99.92%	$116,440	2.98%	$22,364	2.92%	19.21%
9. ARIZONA	$0	0.00%	$0	0.00%	$81,056	100.00%	$81,056	2.07%	$0	--	--
10. MARYLAND	$2	0.00%	$0	0.00%	$70,720	100.00%	$70,722	1.81%	$0	--	--
11. TENNESSEE	$0	0.00%	$0	0.00%	$59,287	100.00%	$59,287	1.51%	$0	--	--
12. INDIANA	$0	0.00%	$0	0.00%	$17,703	100.00%	$17,703	0.45%	$0	--	--
13. MISSISSIPPI	$35	0.23%	$0	0.00%	$15,188	99.77%	$15,223	0.39%	$0	--	--
14. KENTUCKY	$0	0.00%	$0	0.00%	$10,162	100.00%	$10,162	0.26%	$0	--	--
15. UTAH	$0	0.00%	$0	0.00%	$9,265	100.00%	$9,265	0.24%	$0	--	--
16. ARKANSAS	$1,044	11.74%	$0	0.00%	$7,845	88.26%	$8,889	0.23%	$0	--	--
17. NEVADA	$0	0.00%	$0	0.00%	$8,651	100.00%	$8,651	0.22%	$0	--	--
18. DELAWARE	$0	0.00%	$0	0.00%	$8,475	100.00%	$8,475	0.22%	$0	--	--
19. DISTRICT OF COLUMBIA	$0	0.00%	$0	0.00%	$6,951	100.00%	$6,951	0.18%	$0	--	--
COMPOSITE	$109,890	2.81%	$2,344,872	59.92%	$1,458,631	37.27%	$3,913,393	100.00%	$764,852	100.00%	19.54%
AVERAGE	$5,784		$123,414		$76,770		$205,968		$40,255		

TRANSUNION TIC

	DIRECT	% of Total	NON-AFFILIATED	% of Total	AFFILIATED	% of Total	TOTAL	PERCENT OF UNDERWRITER	PAID LOSSES	PERCENT OF UNDERWRITER	LOSSES TO PREMIUMS
1. CALIFORNIA	$882,460	100.00%	$0	0.00%	$0	0.00%	$882,460	100.00%	$397,148	100.00%	45.00%
COMPOSITE	$882,460	100.00%	$0	0.00%	$0	0.00%	$882,460	100.00%	$397,148	100.00%	45.00%

UNITED CAPITAL

	DIRECT	% of Total	NON-AFFILIATED	% of Total	AFFILIATED	% of Total	TOTAL	PERCENT OF UNDERWRITER	PAID LOSSES	PERCENT OF UNDERWRITER	LOSSES TO PREMIUMS
1. CALIFORNIA	$2,231,929	5.09%	$0	0.00%	$41,596,724	94.91%	$43,828,653	71.36%	$5,589,874	83.75%	12.75%
2. ARIZONA	$0	0.00%	$0	0.00%	$15,002,635	100.00%	$15,002,635	24.43%	$566,900	8.49%	3.78%
3. NEVADA	$0	0.00%	$0	0.00%	$2,554,913	100.00%	$2,554,913	4.16%	$514,222	7.70%	20.13%
4. FLORIDA	$32,820	92.34%	$0	0.00%	$2,723	7.66%	$35,543	0.06%	$3,741	0.06%	10.53%
COMPOSITE	$2,264,749	3.69%	$0	0.00%	$59,156,995	96.31%	$61,421,744	100.00%	$6,674,737	100.00%	10.87%
AVERAGE	$566,187		$0		$14,789,249		$15,355,436		$1,668,684		

3

D.2 Organization - Individual Underwriter by Jurisdiction

	DIRECT	% of Total	NON-AFFILIATED	% of Total	AFFILIATED	% of Total	TOTAL	PERCENT OF UNDERWRITER	PAID LOSSES	PERCENT OF UNDERWRITER	LOSSES TO PREMIUMS
UNITED GENERAL											
1. NEW YORK	$10,353	0.02%	$58,260,082	99.98%	$0	0.00%	$58,270,435	17.31%	$3,954,394	17.95%	6.79%
2. CALIFORNIA	$10,932,364	30.27%	$7,034,545	19.48%	$18,153,659	50.26%	$36,120,568	10.73%	$4,369,313	19.83%	12.10%
3. FLORIDA	$120,723	0.37%	$32,270,302	99.63%	$0	0.00%	$32,391,025	9.62%	$2,569,858	11.66%	7.93%
4. NORTH CAROLINA	$7,715,440	23.91%	$24,555,193	76.09%	$0	0.00%	$32,270,633	9.59%	$350,955	1.59%	1.09%
5. TEXAS	$0	0.00%	$27,349,669	100.00%	$0	0.00%	$27,349,669	8.13%	$131,884	0.60%	0.48%
6. NEW JERSEY	$13,618	0.07%	$18,253,583	99.93%	$0	0.00%	$18,267,201	5.43%	$761,062	3.45%	4.17%
7. PENNSYLVANIA	$256,724	1.56%	$16,151,439	98.44%	$0	0.00%	$16,408,163	4.87%	$922,514	4.19%	5.62%
8. VIRGINIA	$33,152	0.32%	$10,326,541	99.68%	$0	0.00%	$10,359,693	3.08%	$580,788	2.64%	5.61%
9. GEORGIA	$5,637	0.05%	$10,279,981	99.95%	$0	0.00%	$10,285,618	3.06%	$2,670,965	12.12%	25.97%
10. CONNECTICUT	$44,432	0.45%	$9,786,462	99.55%	$0	0.00%	$9,830,894	2.92%	$4,194	0.02%	0.04%
11. MARYLAND	$72,946	0.82%	$8,774,118	99.18%	$0	0.00%	$8,847,064	2.63%	$728,884	3.31%	8.24%
12. UTAH	$84,192	1.22%	$6,825,534	98.78%	$0	0.00%	$6,909,726	2.05%	$66,340	0.30%	0.96%
13. MISSOURI	$4,014	0.06%	$6,833,301	99.94%	$0	0.00%	$6,837,315	2.03%	$151,987	0.69%	2.22%
14. MASSACHUSETTS	$315,258	4.65%	$6,464,562	95.35%	$0	0.00%	$6,779,820	2.01%	($83,385)	(0.38)%	(1.23)%
15. ARIZONA	$127,085	1.92%	$6,472,952	97.80%	$18,285	0.28%	$6,618,322	1.97%	$62,628	0.28%	0.95%
16. COLORADO	$29,515	0.45%	$6,495,986	99.55%	$0	0.00%	$6,525,501	1.94%	$1,600,253	7.26%	24.52%
17. ILLINOIS	$42,473	0.76%	$5,560,713	99.24%	$0	0.00%	$5,603,186	1.66%	$146,808	0.67%	2.62%
18. MICHIGAN	$2,758	0.09%	$3,202,527	99.91%	$0	0.00%	$3,205,285	0.95%	$23,429	0.11%	0.73%
19. RHODE ISLAND	$426,746	13.70%	$2,688,608	86.30%	$0	0.00%	$3,115,354	0.93%	$2,317	0.01%	0.07%
20. NEVADA	$79,117	2.59%	$2,670,963	87.31%	$309,000	10.10%	$3,059,080	0.91%	$261,949	1.19%	8.56%
21. OHIO	$6,416	0.22%	$2,942,592	99.78%	$0	0.00%	$2,949,008	0.88%	$522,512	2.37%	17.72%
22. NEW MEXICO	$75,315	2.87%	$2,549,874	97.13%	$0	0.00%	$2,625,189	0.78%	$396,354	1.80%	15.10%
23. TENNESSEE	$4,869	0.21%	$2,314,967	99.79%	$0	0.00%	$2,319,836	0.69%	$140,467	0.64%	6.06%
24. ALABAMA	$6,590	0.29%	$2,292,334	99.71%	$0	0.00%	$2,298,924	0.68%	$140,157	0.64%	6.10%
25. ARKANSAS	$6,524	0.31%	$2,115,413	99.69%	$0	0.00%	$2,121,937	0.63%	$128,189	0.58%	6.04%
26. IDAHO	$27,481	1.56%	$1,735,841	98.44%	$0	0.00%	$1,763,322	0.52%	$21,154	0.10%	1.20%
27. LOUISIANA	$2,690	0.16%	$1,649,456	99.84%	$0	0.00%	$1,652,146	0.49%	$74,521	0.34%	4.51%
28. KANSAS	$286	0.02%	$1,504,983	99.98%	$0	0.00%	$1,505,269	0.45%	$20,555	0.09%	1.37%
29. MINNESOTA	$5,751	0.47%	$1,225,624	99.53%	$0	0.00%	$1,231,375	0.37%	$660,532	3.00%	53.64%
30. NEBRASKA	$2,683	0.26%	$1,036,146	99.74%	$0	0.00%	$1,038,829	0.31%	$37,529	0.17%	3.61%
31. OKLAHOMA	$0	0.00%	$989,456	100.00%	$0	0.00%	$989,456	0.29%	$37,700	0.17%	3.81%
32. DISTRICT OF COLUMBIA	$1,285	0.13%	$963,469	99.87%	$0	0.00%	$964,754	0.29%	$96,374	0.44%	9.99%
33. SOUTH CAROLINA	$1,633	0.17%	$954,208	99.83%	$0	0.00%	$955,841	0.28%	$85,273	0.39%	8.92%
34. WISCONSIN	$6,299	0.77%	$812,471	99.23%	$0	0.00%	$818,770	0.24%	$8,230	0.04%	1.01%
35. INDIANA	$13,355	1.78%	$737,872	98.22%	$0	0.00%	$751,227	0.22%	$111,880	0.51%	14.89%
36. KENTUCKY	$750	0.11%	$696,269	99.89%	$0	0.00%	$697,019	0.21%	$36,337	0.16%	5.21%
37. NEW HAMPSHIRE	$1,080	0.19%	$566,455	99.81%	$0	0.00%	$567,535	0.17%	$1,950	0.01%	0.34%
38. DELAWARE	$0	0.00%	$438,994	100.00%	$0	0.00%	$438,994	0.13%	$88,344	0.40%	20.12%
39. MAINE	$654	0.16%	$412,117	99.84%	$0	0.00%	$412,771	0.12%	$0	--	--
40. WASHINGTON	$209,349	59.05%	$145,160	40.95%	$0	0.00%	$354,509	0.11%	$918	0.00%	0.26%
41. MONTANA	$892	0.27%	$324,352	98.72%	$3,328	1.01%	$328,572	0.10%	$0	--	--
42. MISSISSIPPI	$3,919	1.63%	$236,459	98.37%	$0	0.00%	$240,378	0.07%	$148,484	0.67%	61.77%
43. OREGON	$169,649	100.00%	$0	0.00%	$0	0.00%	$169,649	0.05%	$0	--	--
44. WEST VIRGINIA	$983	0.88%	$110,334	99.12%	$0	0.00%	$111,317	0.03%	$0	--	--
45. VERMONT	$972	0.96%	$99,813	99.04%	$0	0.00%	$100,785	0.03%	$0	--	--
46. HAWAII	$76,960	95.04%	$4,020	4.96%	$0	0.00%	$80,980	0.02%	$0	--	--
47. NORTH DAKOTA	$982	3.08%	$30,895	96.92%	$0	0.00%	$31,877	0.00%	$0	--	--
48. ALASKA	$19,008	99.53%	$90	0.47%	$0	0.00%	$19,098	0.00%	$0	--	--
49. WYOMING	$6,267	83.43%	$1,245	16.57%	$0	0.00%	$7,512	0.00%	$0	--	--
50. SOUTH DAKOTA	$698	88.58%	$90	11.42%	$0	0.00%	$788	0.00%	$0	--	--
COMPOSITE	**$20,969,887**	6.23%	**$297,148,060**	88.28%	**$18,484,272**	5.49%	**$336,602,219**	**100.00%**	**$22,034,597**	**100.00%**	**6.55%**
AVERAGE	**$419,398**		**$5,942,961**		**$369,685**		**$6,732,044**		**$440,692**		
WASHINGTON TIC											
1. NEW YORK	$172,102	1.10%	$12,559,065	80.38%	$2,893,006	18.52%	$15,624,173	100.00%	$422,819	100.00%	2.71%
COMPOSITE	**$172,102**	1.10%	**$12,559,065**	80.38%	**$2,893,006**	18.52%	**$15,624,173**	**100.00%**	**$422,819**	**100.00%**	**2.71%**
WESTCOR											
1. FLORIDA	$288,117	1.57%	$18,097,030	98.38%	$10,653	0.06%	$18,395,800	34.96%	$178,031	35.79%	0.97%
2. CALIFORNIA	$0	0.00%	$0	0.00%	$17,766,204	100.00%	$17,766,204	33.76%	$60,141	12.09%	0.34%
3. NEVADA	$0	0.00%	$35,531	0.34%	$10,264,965	99.66%	$10,300,496	19.57%	$259,294	52.12%	2.52%
4. ARIZONA	$0	0.00%	$105,518	3.22%	$3,175,196	96.78%	$3,280,714	6.23%	$0	--	--
5. COLORADO	$0	0.00%	$2,208,182	100.00%	$0	0.00%	$2,208,182	4.20%	$0	--	--
6. UTAH	$0	0.00%	$363,865	100.00%	$0	0.00%	$363,865	0.69%	$0	--	--
7. TEXAS	$0	0.00%	$274,717	100.00%	$0	0.00%	$274,717	0.52%	$0	--	--
8. ALABAMA	$0	0.00%	$22,598	100.00%	$0	0.00%	$22,598	0.04%	$0	--	--
9. NEBRASKA	$0	0.00%	$9,362	100.00%	$0	0.00%	$9,362	0.02%	$0	--	--
10. MISSISSIPPI	$0	0.00%	$4,790	100.00%	$0	0.00%	$4,790	0.00%	$0	--	--
COMPOSITE	**$288,117**	0.55%	**$21,121,593**	40.13%	**$31,217,018**	59.32%	**$52,626,728**	**100.00%**	**$497,466**	**100.00%**	**0.95%**
AVERAGE	**$28,812**		**$2,112,159**		**$3,121,702**		**$5,262,673**		**$49,747**		
WESTERN NATIONAL											
1. UTAH	$0	0.00%	$8,580	2.31%	$362,141	97.69%	$370,721	100.00%	$103,224	100.00%	27.84%
COMPOSITE	**$0**	0.00%	**$8,580**	2.31%	**$362,141**	97.69%	**$370,721**	**100.00%**	**$103,224**	**100.00%**	**27.84%**

Notes

E.1 FIVE-YEAR TREND
- DIRECT PREMIUMS WRITTEN BY NAIC GROUP

3

E.1 Five-Year Trend - Direct Premiums Written by NAIC Group

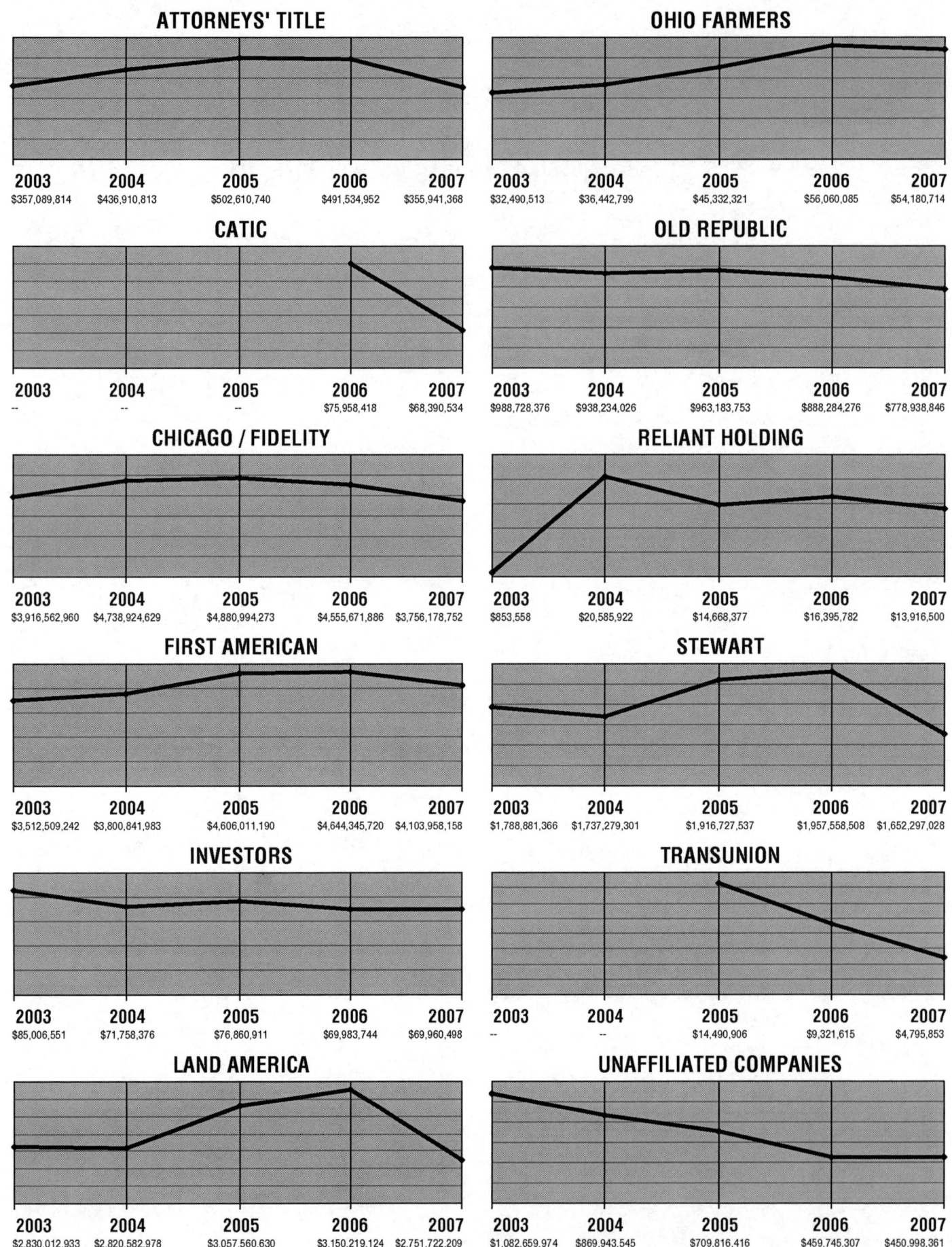

ATTORNEYS' TITLE

2003	2004	2005	2006	2007
$357,089,814	$436,910,813	$502,610,740	$491,534,952	$355,941,368

OHIO FARMERS

2003	2004	2005	2006	2007
$32,490,513	$36,442,799	$45,332,321	$56,060,085	$54,180,714

CATIC

2003	2004	2005	2006	2007
--	--	--	$75,958,418	$68,390,534

OLD REPUBLIC

2003	2004	2005	2006	2007
$988,728,376	$938,234,026	$963,183,753	$888,284,276	$778,938,846

CHICAGO / FIDELITY

2003	2004	2005	2006	2007
$3,916,562,960	$4,738,924,629	$4,880,994,273	$4,555,671,886	$3,756,178,752

RELIANT HOLDING

2003	2004	2005	2006	2007
$853,558	$20,585,922	$14,668,377	$16,395,782	$13,916,500

FIRST AMERICAN

2003	2004	2005	2006	2007
$3,512,509,242	$3,800,841,983	$4,606,011,190	$4,644,345,720	$4,103,958,158

STEWART

2003	2004	2005	2006	2007
$1,788,881,366	$1,737,279,301	$1,916,727,537	$1,957,558,508	$1,652,297,028

INVESTORS

2003	2004	2005	2006	2007
$85,006,551	$71,758,376	$76,860,911	$69,983,744	$69,960,498

TRANSUNION

2003	2004	2005	2006	2007
--	--	$14,490,906	$9,321,615	$4,795,853

LAND AMERICA

2003	2004	2005	2006	2007
$2,830,012,933	$2,820,582,978	$3,057,560,630	$3,150,219,124	$2,751,722,209

UNAFFILIATED COMPANIES

2003	2004	2005	2006	2007
$1,082,659,974	$869,943,545	$709,816,416	$459,745,307	$450,998,361

E.2 FIVE-YEAR TREND
- DIRECT PREMIUMS WRITTEN BY INDIVIDUAL UNDERWRITER

3

E.2 Five-Year Trend - Direct Premiums Written by Individual Underwriter

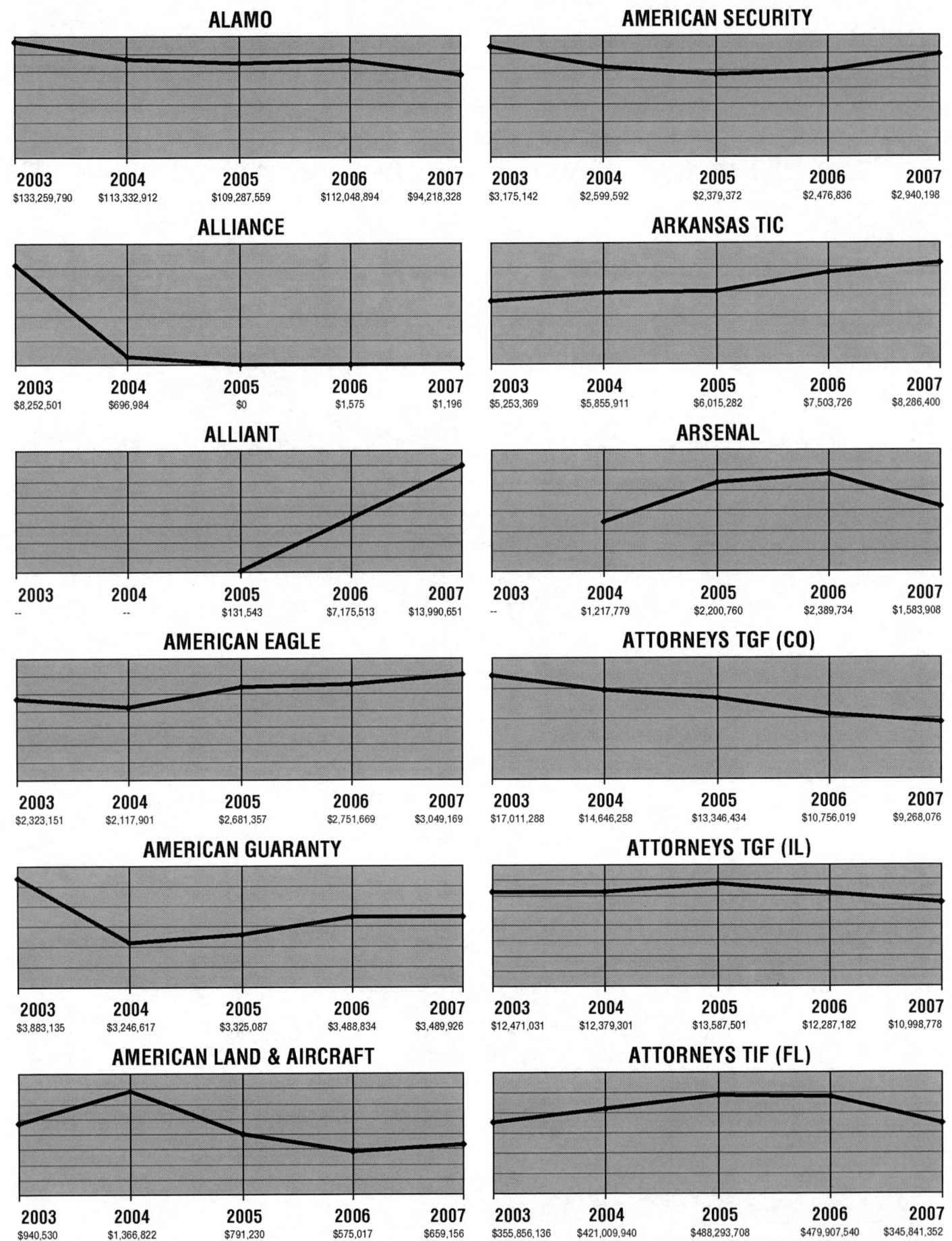

ALAMO

2003	2004	2005	2006	2007
$133,259,790	$113,332,912	$109,287,559	$112,048,894	$94,218,328

AMERICAN SECURITY

2003	2004	2005	2006	2007
$3,175,142	$2,599,592	$2,379,372	$2,476,836	$2,940,198

ALLIANCE

2003	2004	2005	2006	2007
$8,252,501	$696,984	$0	$1,575	$1,196

ARKANSAS TIC

2003	2004	2005	2006	2007
$5,253,369	$5,855,911	$6,015,282	$7,503,726	$8,286,400

ALLIANT

2003	2004	2005	2006	2007
--	--	$131,543	$7,175,513	$13,990,651

ARSENAL

2003	2004	2005	2006	2007
--	$1,217,779	$2,200,760	$2,389,734	$1,583,908

AMERICAN EAGLE

2003	2004	2005	2006	2007
$2,323,151	$2,117,901	$2,681,357	$2,751,669	$3,049,169

ATTORNEYS TGF (CO)

2003	2004	2005	2006	2007
$17,011,288	$14,646,258	$13,346,434	$10,756,019	$9,268,076

AMERICAN GUARANTY

2003	2004	2005	2006	2007
$3,883,135	$3,246,617	$3,325,087	$3,488,834	$3,489,926

ATTORNEYS TGF (IL)

2003	2004	2005	2006	2007
$12,471,031	$12,379,301	$13,587,501	$12,287,182	$10,998,778

AMERICAN LAND & AIRCRAFT

2003	2004	2005	2006	2007
$940,530	$1,366,822	$791,230	$575,017	$659,156

ATTORNEYS TIF (FL)

2003	2004	2005	2006	2007
$355,856,136	$421,009,940	$488,293,708	$479,907,540	$345,841,352

E.2 Five-Year Trend - Direct Premiums Written by Individual Underwriter

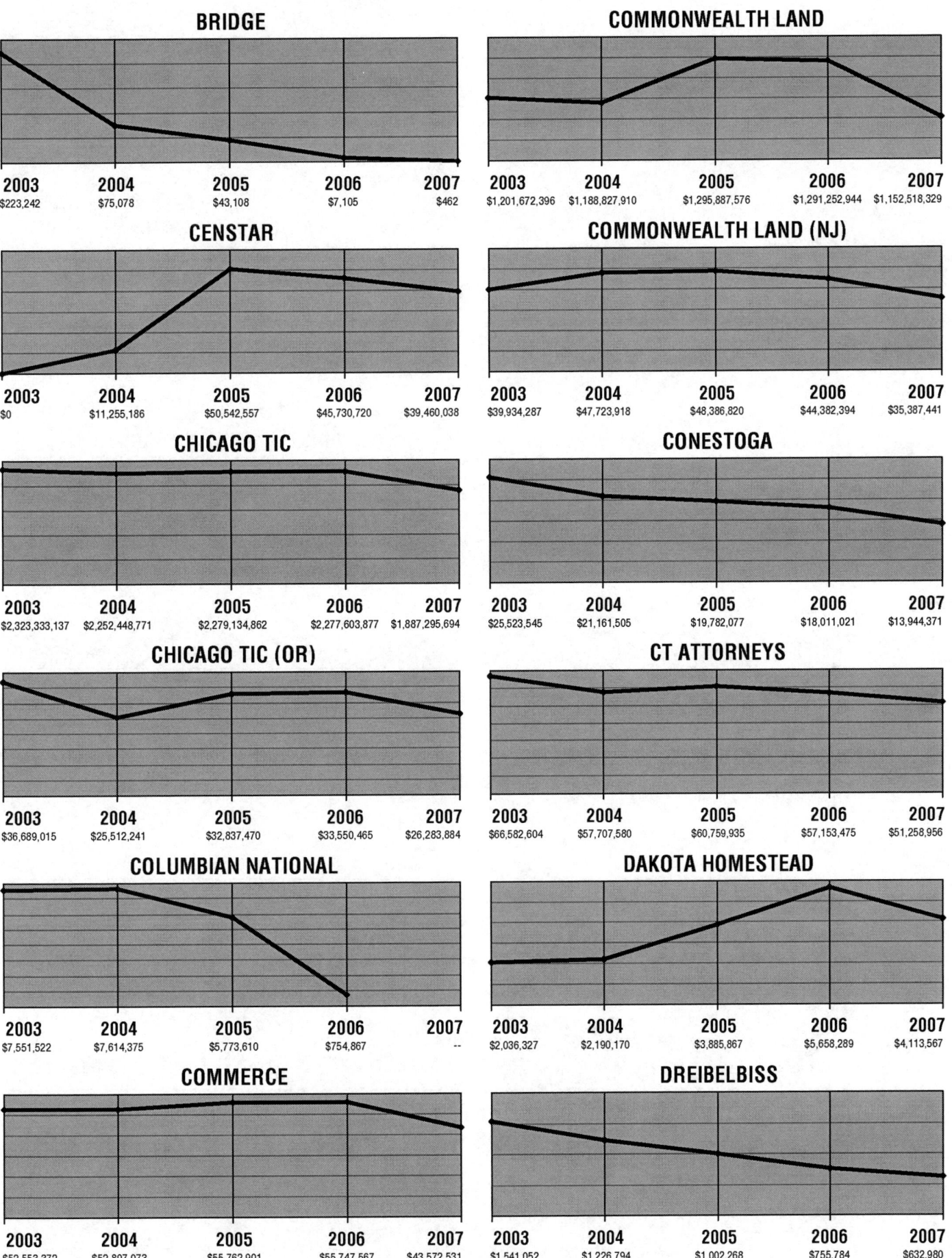

BRIDGE

2003	2004	2005	2006	2007
$223,242	$75,078	$43,108	$7,105	$462

COMMONWEALTH LAND

2003	2004	2005	2006	2007
$1,201,672,396	$1,188,827,910	$1,295,887,576	$1,291,252,944	$1,152,518,329

CENSTAR

2003	2004	2005	2006	2007
$0	$11,255,186	$50,542,557	$45,730,720	$39,460,038

COMMONWEALTH LAND (NJ)

2003	2004	2005	2006	2007
$39,934,287	$47,723,918	$48,386,820	$44,382,394	$35,387,441

CHICAGO TIC

2003	2004	2005	2006	2007
$2,323,333,137	$2,252,448,771	$2,279,134,862	$2,277,603,877	$1,887,295,694

CONESTOGA

2003	2004	2005	2006	2007
$25,523,545	$21,161,505	$19,782,077	$18,011,021	$13,944,371

CHICAGO TIC (OR)

2003	2004	2005	2006	2007
$36,689,015	$25,512,241	$32,837,470	$33,550,465	$26,283,884

CT ATTORNEYS

2003	2004	2005	2006	2007
$66,582,604	$57,707,580	$60,759,935	$57,153,475	$51,258,956

COLUMBIAN NATIONAL

2003	2004	2005	2006	2007
$7,551,522	$7,614,375	$5,773,610	$754,867	--

DAKOTA HOMESTEAD

2003	2004	2005	2006	2007
$2,036,327	$2,190,170	$3,885,867	$5,658,289	$4,113,567

COMMERCE

2003	2004	2005	2006	2007
$52,553,372	$52,897,073	$55,762,901	$55,747,567	$43,572,531

DREIBELBISS

2003	2004	2005	2006	2007
$1,541,052	$1,226,794	$1,002,268	$755,784	$632,980

E.2 Five-Year Trend - Direct Premiums Written by Individual Underwriter

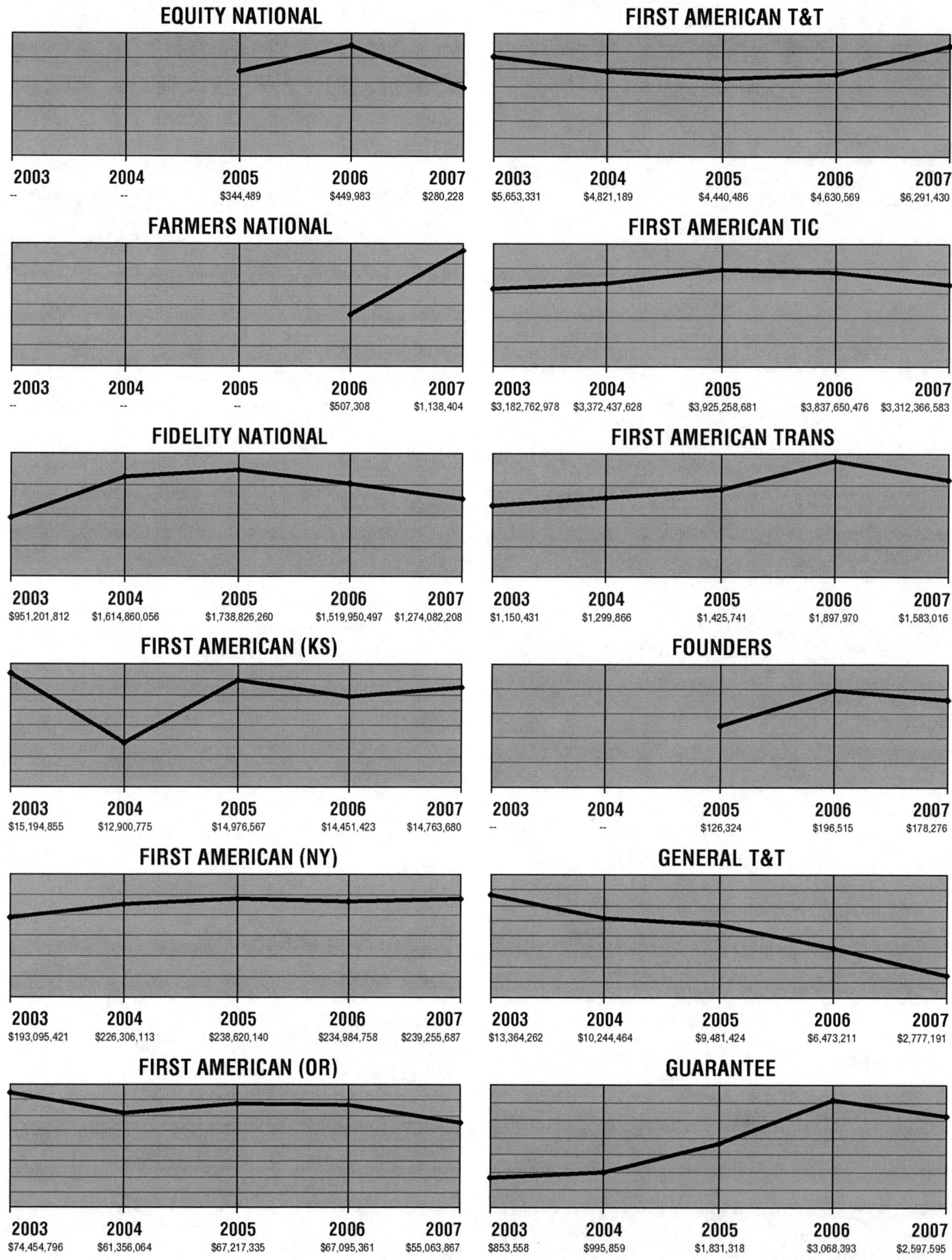

EQUITY NATIONAL

2003	2004	2005	2006	2007
--	--	$344,489	$449,983	$280,228

FIRST AMERICAN T&T

2003	2004	2005	2006	2007
$5,653,331	$4,821,189	$4,440,486	$4,630,569	$6,291,430

FARMERS NATIONAL

2003	2004	2005	2006	2007
--	--	--	$507,308	$1,138,404

FIRST AMERICAN TIC

2003	2004	2005	2006	2007
$3,182,762,978	$3,372,437,628	$3,925,258,681	$3,837,650,476	$3,312,366,583

FIDELITY NATIONAL

2003	2004	2005	2006	2007
$951,201,812	$1,614,860,056	$1,738,826,260	$1,519,950,497	$1,274,082,208

FIRST AMERICAN TRANS

2003	2004	2005	2006	2007
$1,150,431	$1,299,866	$1,425,741	$1,897,970	$1,583,016

FIRST AMERICAN (KS)

2003	2004	2005	2006	2007
$15,194,855	$12,900,775	$14,976,567	$14,451,423	$14,763,680

FOUNDERS

2003	2004	2005	2006	2007
--	--	$126,324	$196,515	$178,276

FIRST AMERICAN (NY)

2003	2004	2005	2006	2007
$193,095,421	$226,306,113	$238,620,140	$234,984,758	$239,255,687

GENERAL T&T

2003	2004	2005	2006	2007
$13,364,262	$10,244,464	$9,481,424	$6,473,211	$2,777,191

FIRST AMERICAN (OR)

2003	2004	2005	2006	2007
$74,454,796	$61,356,064	$67,217,335	$67,095,361	$55,063,867

GUARANTEE

2003	2004	2005	2006	2007
$853,558	$995,859	$1,831,318	$3,068,393	$2,597,595

E.2   Five-Year Trend - Direct Premiums Written by Individual Underwriter

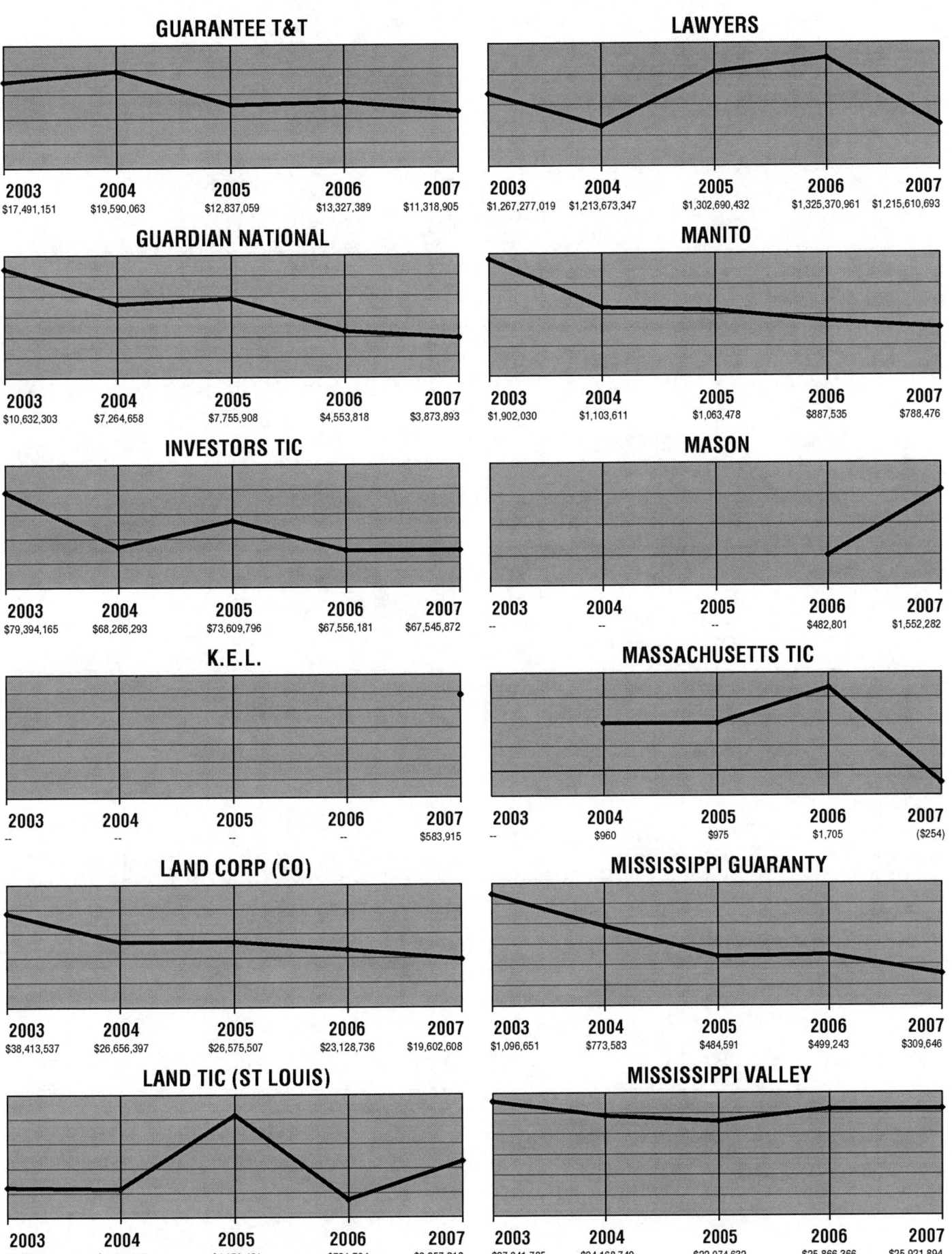

GUARANTEE T&T

2003	2004	2005	2006	2007
$17,491,151	$19,590,063	$12,837,059	$13,327,389	$11,318,905

LAWYERS

2003	2004	2005	2006	2007
$1,267,277,019	$1,213,673,347	$1,302,690,432	$1,325,370,961	$1,215,610,693

GUARDIAN NATIONAL

2003	2004	2005	2006	2007
$10,632,303	$7,264,658	$7,755,908	$4,553,818	$3,873,893

MANITO

2003	2004	2005	2006	2007
$1,902,030	$1,103,611	$1,063,478	$887,535	$788,476

INVESTORS TIC

2003	2004	2005	2006	2007
$79,394,165	$68,266,293	$73,609,796	$67,556,181	$67,545,872

MASON

2003	2004	2005	2006	2007
--	--	--	$482,801	$1,552,282

K.E.L.

2003	2004	2005	2006	2007
--	--	--	--	$583,915

MASSACHUSETTS TIC

2003	2004	2005	2006	2007
--	$960	$975	$1,705	($254)

LAND CORP (CO)

2003	2004	2005	2006	2007
$38,413,537	$26,656,397	$26,575,507	$23,128,736	$19,602,608

MISSISSIPPI GUARANTY

2003	2004	2005	2006	2007
$1,096,651	$773,583	$484,591	$499,243	$309,646

LAND TIC (ST LOUIS)

2003	2004	2005	2006	2007
$1,228,514	$1,173,808	$4,150,421	$721,764	$2,257,316

MISSISSIPPI VALLEY

2003	2004	2005	2006	2007
$27,841,785	$24,168,749	$22,974,632	$25,866,366	$25,921,894

3

E.2   Five-Year Trend - Direct Premiums Written by Individual Underwriter

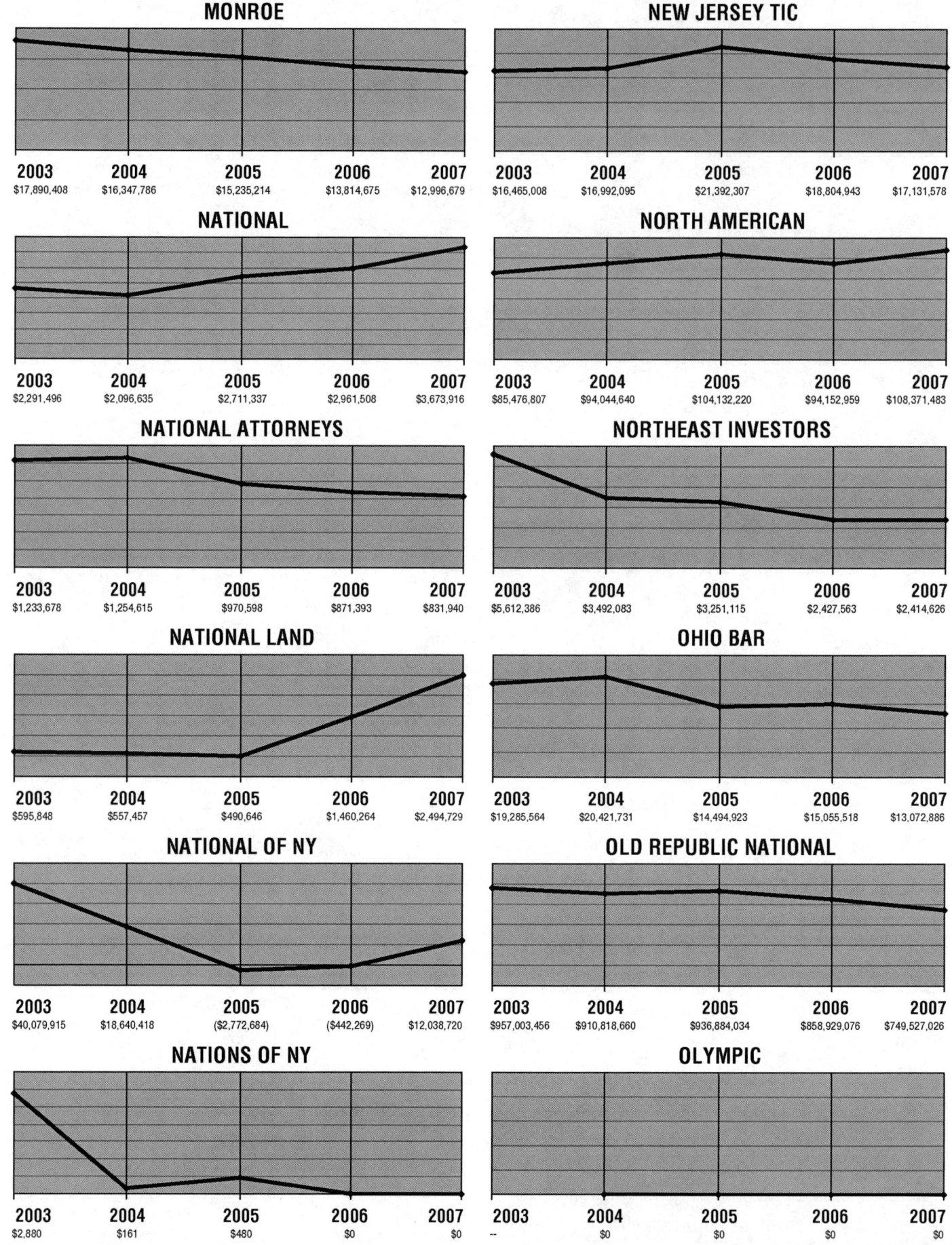

MONROE

2003	2004	2005	2006	2007
$17,890,408	$16,347,786	$15,235,214	$13,814,675	$12,996,679

NEW JERSEY TIC

2003	2004	2005	2006	2007
$16,465,008	$16,992,095	$21,392,307	$18,804,943	$17,131,578

NATIONAL

2003	2004	2005	2006	2007
$2,291,496	$2,096,635	$2,711,337	$2,961,508	$3,673,916

NORTH AMERICAN

2003	2004	2005	2006	2007
$85,476,807	$94,044,640	$104,132,220	$94,152,959	$108,371,483

NATIONAL ATTORNEYS

2003	2004	2005	2006	2007
$1,233,678	$1,254,615	$970,598	$871,393	$831,940

NORTHEAST INVESTORS

2003	2004	2005	2006	2007
$5,612,386	$3,492,083	$3,251,115	$2,427,563	$2,414,626

NATIONAL LAND

2003	2004	2005	2006	2007
$595,848	$557,457	$490,646	$1,460,264	$2,494,729

OHIO BAR

2003	2004	2005	2006	2007
$19,285,564	$20,421,731	$14,494,923	$15,055,518	$13,072,886

NATIONAL OF NY

2003	2004	2005	2006	2007
$40,079,915	$18,640,418	($2,772,684)	($442,269)	$12,038,720

OLD REPUBLIC NATIONAL

2003	2004	2005	2006	2007
$957,003,456	$910,818,660	$936,884,034	$858,929,076	$749,527,026

NATIONS OF NY

2003	2004	2005	2006	2007
$2,880	$161	$480	$0	$0

OLYMPIC

2003	2004	2005	2006	2007
--	$0	$0	$0	$0

E.2 Five-Year Trend - Direct Premiums Written by Individual Underwriter

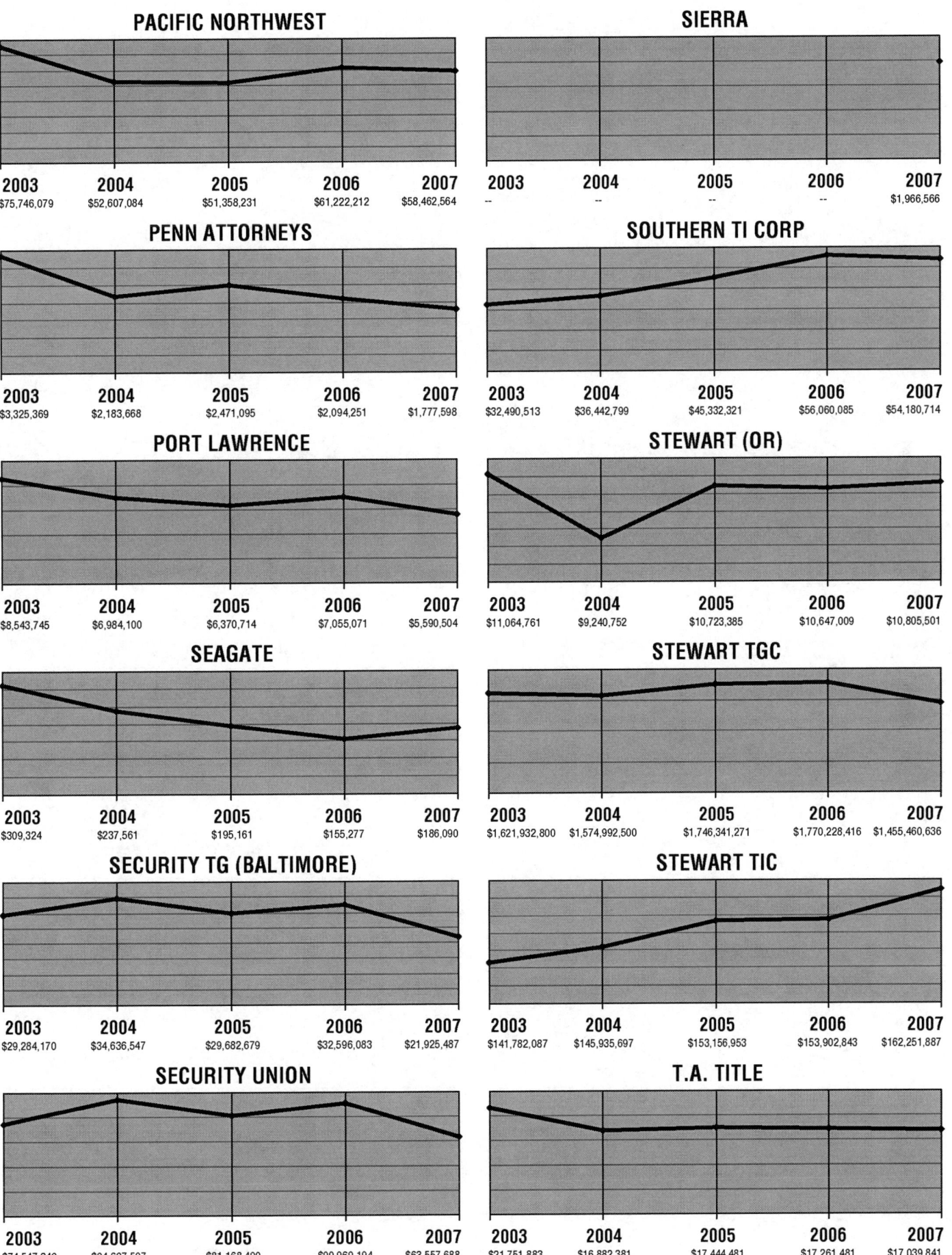

PACIFIC NORTHWEST

2003	2004	2005	2006	2007
$75,746,079	$52,607,084	$51,358,231	$61,222,212	$58,462,564

SIERRA

2003	2004	2005	2006	2007
--	--	--	--	$1,966,566

PENN ATTORNEYS

2003	2004	2005	2006	2007
$3,325,369	$2,183,668	$2,471,095	$2,094,251	$1,777,598

SOUTHERN TI CORP

2003	2004	2005	2006	2007
$32,490,513	$36,442,799	$45,332,321	$56,060,085	$54,180,714

PORT LAWRENCE

2003	2004	2005	2006	2007
$8,543,745	$6,984,100	$6,370,714	$7,055,071	$5,590,504

STEWART (OR)

2003	2004	2005	2006	2007
$11,064,761	$9,240,752	$10,723,385	$10,647,009	$10,805,501

SEAGATE

2003	2004	2005	2006	2007
$309,324	$237,561	$195,161	$155,277	$186,090

STEWART TGC

2003	2004	2005	2006	2007
$1,621,932,800	$1,574,992,500	$1,746,341,271	$1,770,228,416	$1,455,460,636

SECURITY TG (BALTIMORE)

2003	2004	2005	2006	2007
$29,284,170	$34,636,547	$29,682,679	$32,596,083	$21,925,487

STEWART TIC

2003	2004	2005	2006	2007
$141,782,087	$145,935,697	$153,156,953	$153,902,843	$162,251,887

SECURITY UNION

2003	2004	2005	2006	2007
$74,547,249	$94,697,507	$81,168,490	$90,969,194	$63,557,688

T.A. TITLE

2003	2004	2005	2006	2007
$21,751,883	$16,882,381	$17,444,481	$17,261,481	$17,039,841

3

E.2 Five-Year Trend - Direct Premiums Written by Individual Underwriter

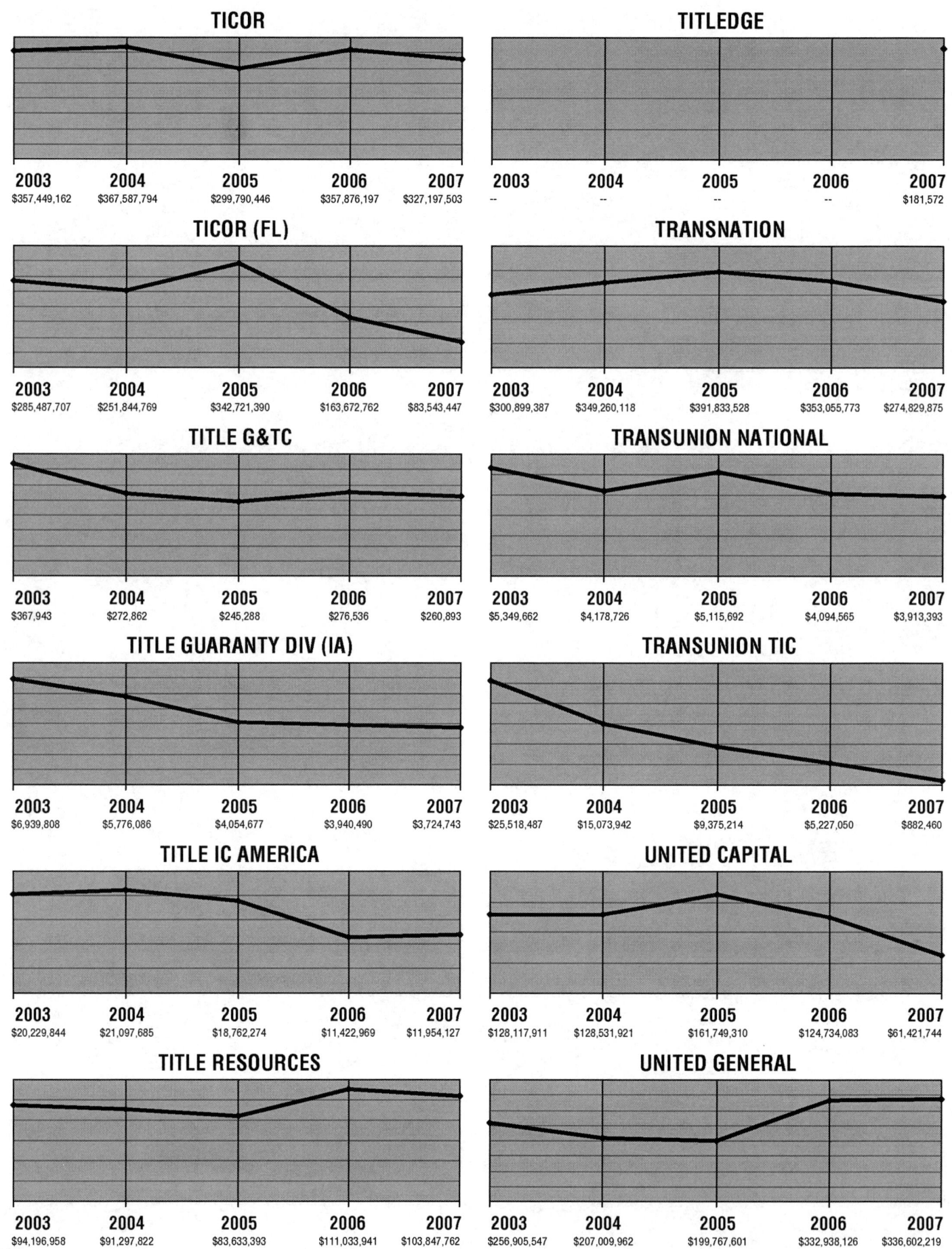

TICOR

2003	2004	2005	2006	2007
$357,449,162	$367,587,794	$299,790,446	$357,876,197	$327,197,503

TITLEDGE

2003	2004	2005	2006	2007
--	--	--	--	$181,572

TICOR (FL)

2003	2004	2005	2006	2007
$285,487,707	$251,844,769	$342,721,390	$163,672,762	$83,543,447

TRANSNATION

2003	2004	2005	2006	2007
$300,899,387	$349,260,118	$391,833,528	$353,055,773	$274,829,875

TITLE G&TC

2003	2004	2005	2006	2007
$367,943	$272,862	$245,288	$276,536	$260,893

TRANSUNION NATIONAL

2003	2004	2005	2006	2007
$5,349,662	$4,178,726	$5,115,692	$4,094,565	$3,913,393

TITLE GUARANTY DIV (IA)

2003	2004	2005	2006	2007
$6,939,808	$5,776,086	$4,054,677	$3,940,490	$3,724,743

TRANSUNION TIC

2003	2004	2005	2006	2007
$25,518,487	$15,073,942	$9,375,214	$5,227,050	$882,460

TITLE IC AMERICA

2003	2004	2005	2006	2007
$20,229,844	$21,097,685	$18,762,274	$11,422,969	$11,954,127

UNITED CAPITAL

2003	2004	2005	2006	2007
$128,117,911	$128,531,921	$161,749,310	$124,734,083	$61,421,744

TITLE RESOURCES

2003	2004	2005	2006	2007
$94,196,958	$91,297,822	$83,633,393	$111,033,941	$103,847,762

UNITED GENERAL

2003	2004	2005	2006	2007
$256,905,547	$207,009,962	$199,767,601	$332,938,126	$336,602,219

E.2   Five-Year Trend - Direct Premiums Written by Individual Underwriter

WASHINGTON TIC

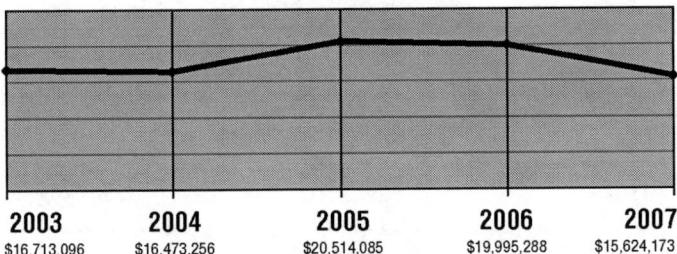

2003	2004	2005	2006	2007
$16,713,096	$16,473,256	$20,514,085	$19,995,288	$15,624,173

WESTCOR

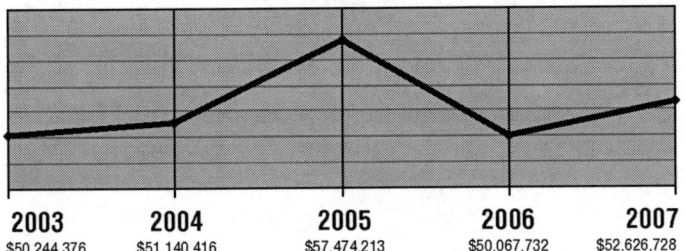

2003	2004	2005	2006	2007
$50,244,376	$51,140,416	$57,474,213	$50,067,732	$52,626,728

WESTERN NATIONAL

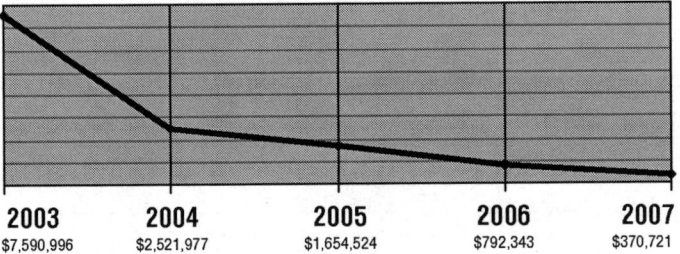

2003	2004	2005	2006	2007
$7,590,996	$2,521,977	$1,654,524	$792,343	$370,721

3

Notes

E.3 FIVE-YEAR TREND
- DIRECT PREMIUMS WRITTEN BY JURISDICTION

3

E.3 Five-Year Trend - Direct Premiums Written by Jurisdiction

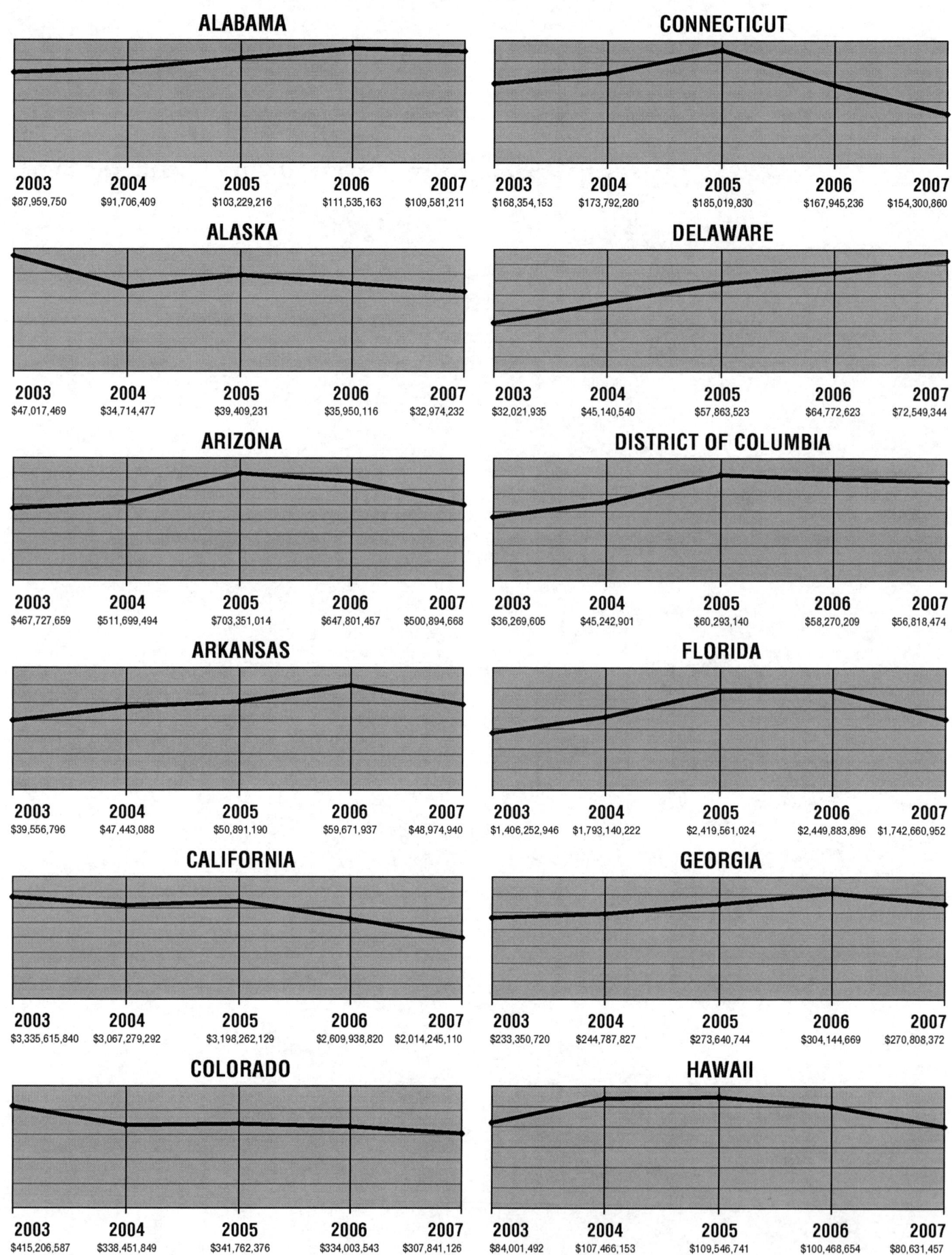

ALABAMA

2003	2004	2005	2006	2007
$87,959,750	$91,706,409	$103,229,216	$111,535,163	$109,581,211

ALASKA

2003	2004	2005	2006	2007
$47,017,469	$34,714,477	$39,409,231	$35,950,116	$32,974,232

ARIZONA

2003	2004	2005	2006	2007
$467,727,659	$511,699,494	$703,351,014	$647,801,457	$500,894,668

ARKANSAS

2003	2004	2005	2006	2007
$39,556,796	$47,443,088	$50,891,190	$59,671,937	$48,974,940

CALIFORNIA

2003	2004	2005	2006	2007
$3,335,615,840	$3,067,279,292	$3,198,262,129	$2,609,938,820	$2,014,245,110

COLORADO

2003	2004	2005	2006	2007
$415,206,587	$338,451,849	$341,762,376	$334,003,543	$307,841,126

CONNECTICUT

2003	2004	2005	2006	2007
$168,354,153	$173,792,280	$185,019,830	$167,945,236	$154,300,860

DELAWARE

2003	2004	2005	2006	2007
$32,021,935	$45,140,540	$57,863,523	$64,772,623	$72,549,344

DISTRICT OF COLUMBIA

2003	2004	2005	2006	2007
$36,269,605	$45,242,901	$60,293,140	$58,270,209	$56,818,474

FLORIDA

2003	2004	2005	2006	2007
$1,406,252,946	$1,793,140,222	$2,419,561,024	$2,449,883,896	$1,742,660,952

GEORGIA

2003	2004	2005	2006	2007
$233,350,720	$244,787,827	$273,640,744	$304,144,669	$270,808,372

HAWAII

2003	2004	2005	2006	2007
$84,001,492	$107,466,153	$109,546,741	$100,468,654	$80,631,457

3

E.3 Five-Year Trend - Direct Premiums Written by Jurisdiction

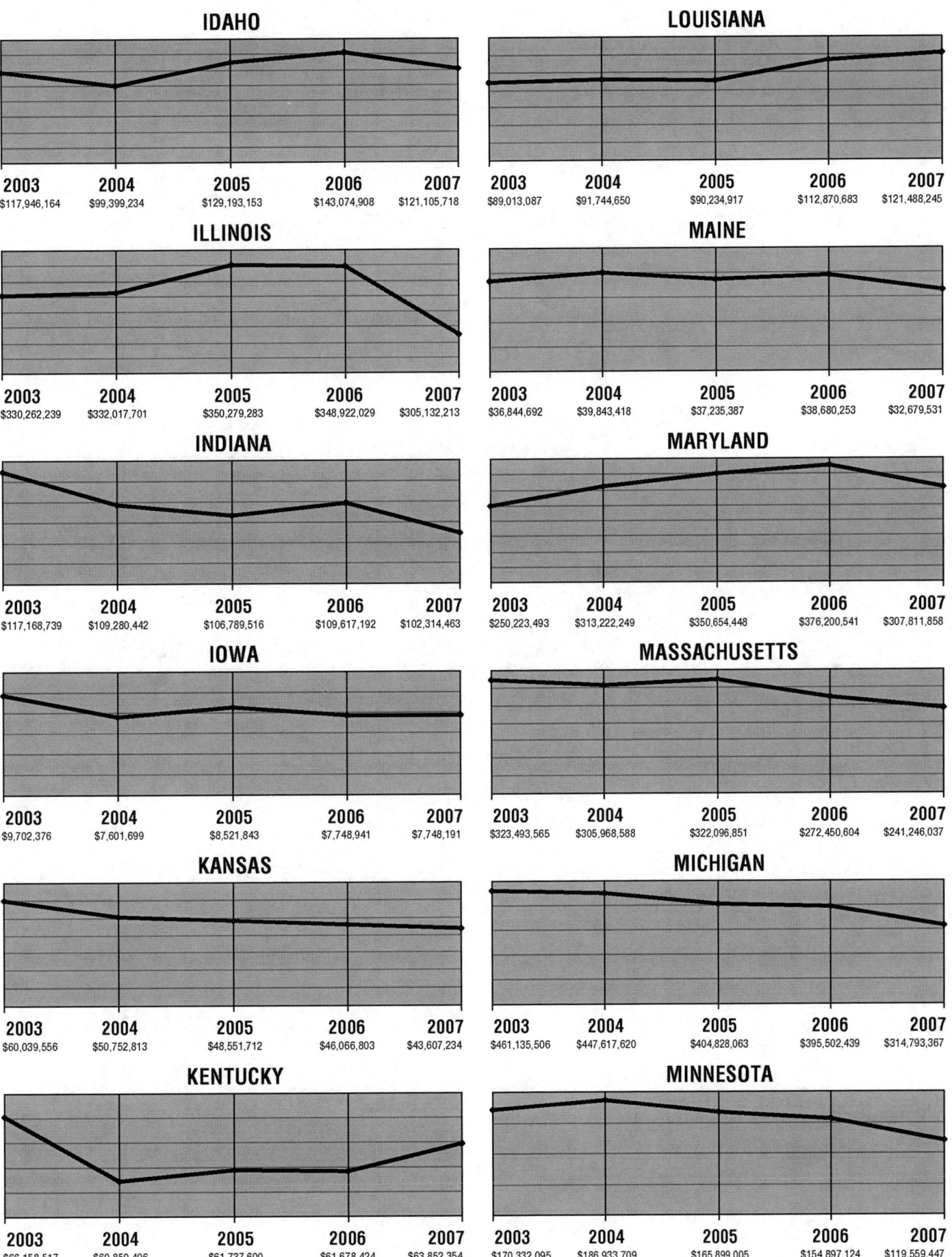

IDAHO

2003	2004	2005	2006	2007
$117,946,164	$99,399,234	$129,193,153	$143,074,908	$121,105,718

LOUISIANA

2003	2004	2005	2006	2007
$89,013,087	$91,744,650	$90,234,917	$112,870,683	$121,488,245

ILLINOIS

2003	2004	2005	2006	2007
$330,262,239	$332,017,701	$350,279,283	$348,922,029	$305,132,213

MAINE

2003	2004	2005	2006	2007
$36,844,692	$39,843,418	$37,235,387	$38,680,253	$32,679,531

INDIANA

2003	2004	2005	2006	2007
$117,168,739	$109,280,442	$106,789,516	$109,617,192	$102,314,463

MARYLAND

2003	2004	2005	2006	2007
$250,223,493	$313,222,249	$350,654,448	$376,200,541	$307,811,858

IOWA

2003	2004	2005	2006	2007
$9,702,376	$7,601,699	$8,521,843	$7,748,941	$7,748,191

MASSACHUSETTS

2003	2004	2005	2006	2007
$323,493,565	$305,968,588	$322,096,851	$272,450,604	$241,246,037

KANSAS

2003	2004	2005	2006	2007
$60,039,556	$50,752,813	$48,551,712	$46,066,803	$43,607,234

MICHIGAN

2003	2004	2005	2006	2007
$461,135,506	$447,617,620	$404,828,063	$395,502,439	$314,793,367

KENTUCKY

2003	2004	2005	2006	2007
$66,158,517	$60,850,406	$61,737,600	$61,678,424	$63,852,354

MINNESOTA

2003	2004	2005	2006	2007
$170,332,095	$186,933,709	$165,899,005	$154,897,124	$119,559,447

3

E.3 Five-Year Trend - Direct Premiums Written by Jurisdiction

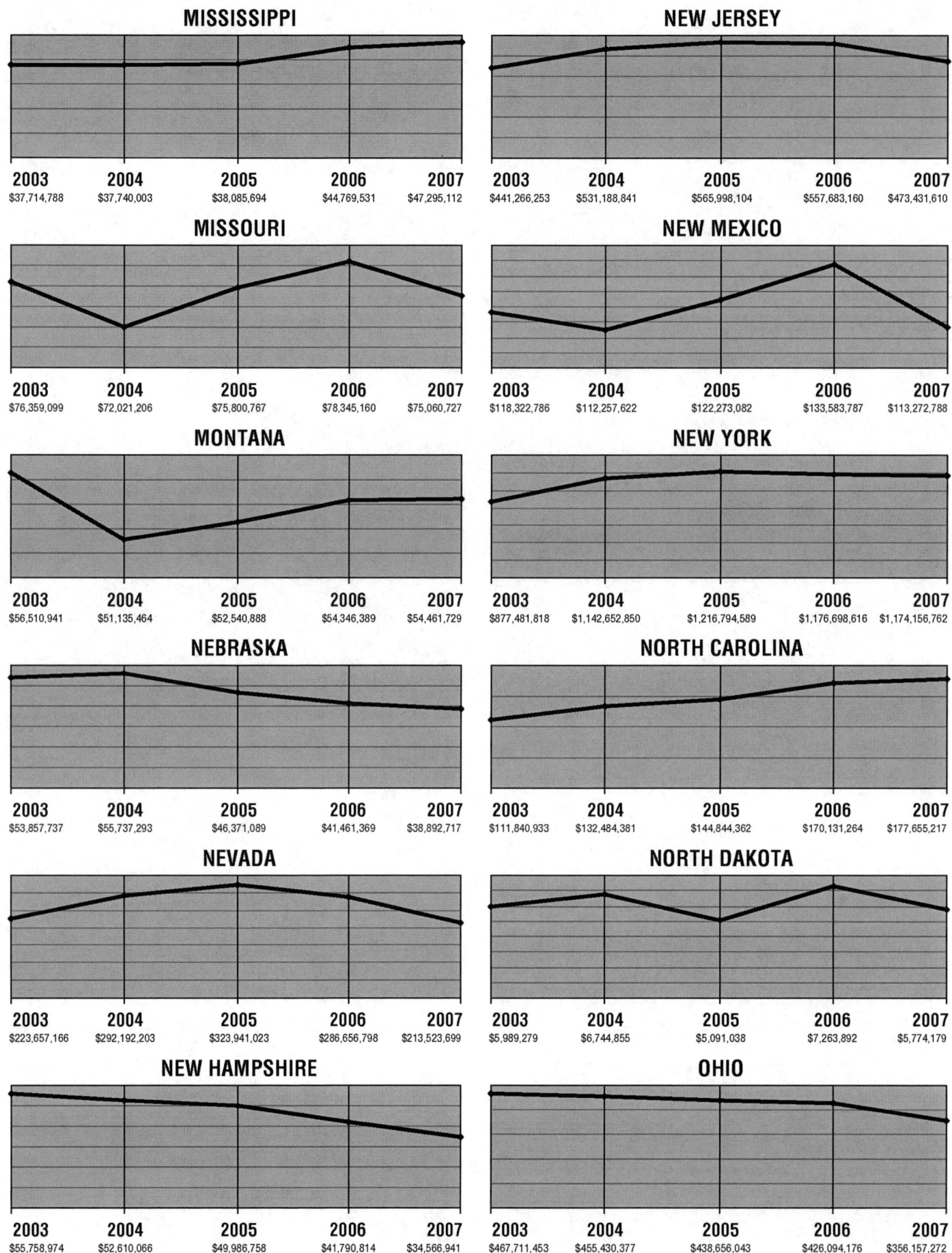

MISSISSIPPI

2003	2004	2005	2006	2007
$37,714,788	$37,740,003	$38,085,694	$44,769,531	$47,295,112

MISSOURI

2003	2004	2005	2006	2007
$76,359,099	$72,021,206	$75,800,767	$78,345,160	$75,060,727

MONTANA

2003	2004	2005	2006	2007
$56,510,941	$51,135,464	$52,540,888	$54,346,389	$54,461,729

NEBRASKA

2003	2004	2005	2006	2007
$53,857,737	$55,737,293	$46,371,089	$41,461,369	$38,892,717

NEVADA

2003	2004	2005	2006	2007
$223,657,166	$292,192,203	$323,941,023	$286,656,798	$213,523,699

NEW HAMPSHIRE

2003	2004	2005	2006	2007
$55,758,974	$52,610,066	$49,986,758	$41,790,814	$34,566,941

NEW JERSEY

2003	2004	2005	2006	2007
$441,266,253	$531,188,841	$565,998,104	$557,683,160	$473,431,610

NEW MEXICO

2003	2004	2005	2006	2007
$118,322,786	$112,257,622	$122,273,082	$133,583,787	$113,272,788

NEW YORK

2003	2004	2005	2006	2007
$877,481,818	$1,142,652,850	$1,216,794,589	$1,176,698,616	$1,174,156,762

NORTH CAROLINA

2003	2004	2005	2006	2007
$111,840,933	$132,484,381	$144,844,362	$170,131,264	$177,655,217

NORTH DAKOTA

2003	2004	2005	2006	2007
$5,989,279	$6,744,855	$5,091,038	$7,263,892	$5,774,179

OHIO

2003	2004	2005	2006	2007
$467,711,453	$455,430,377	$438,656,043	$426,094,176	$356,157,272

E.3 Five-Year Trend - Direct Premiums Written by Jurisdiction

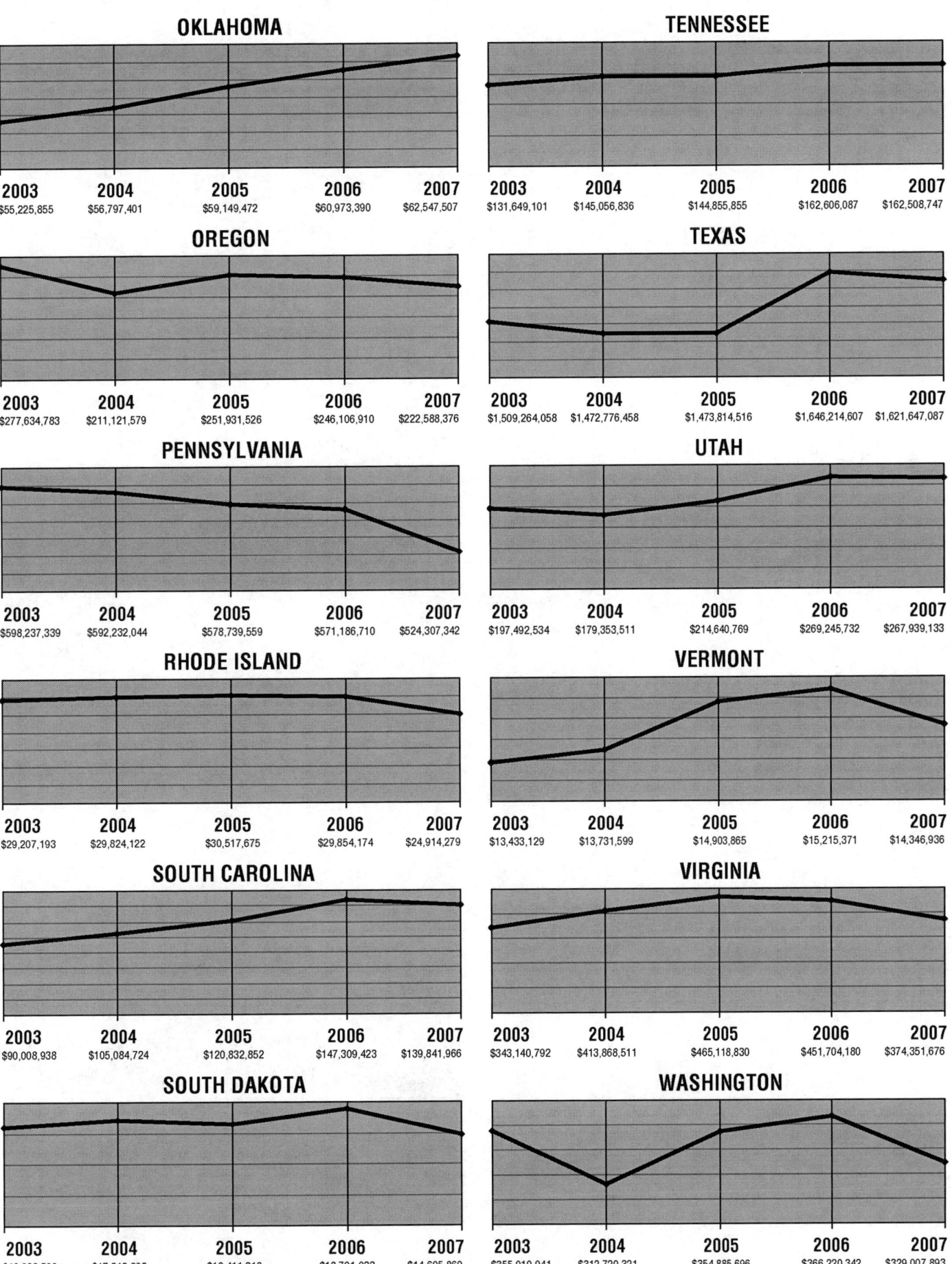

OKLAHOMA

2003	2004	2005	2006	2007
$55,225,855	$56,797,401	$59,149,472	$60,973,390	$62,547,507

TENNESSEE

2003	2004	2005	2006	2007
$131,649,101	$145,056,836	$144,855,855	$162,606,087	$162,508,747

OREGON

2003	2004	2005	2006	2007
$277,634,783	$211,121,579	$251,931,526	$246,106,910	$222,588,376

TEXAS

2003	2004	2005	2006	2007
$1,509,264,058	$1,472,776,458	$1,473,814,516	$1,646,214,607	$1,621,647,087

PENNSYLVANIA

2003	2004	2005	2006	2007
$598,237,339	$592,232,044	$578,739,559	$571,186,710	$524,307,342

UTAH

2003	2004	2005	2006	2007
$197,492,534	$179,353,511	$214,640,769	$269,245,732	$267,939,133

RHODE ISLAND

2003	2004	2005	2006	2007
$29,207,193	$29,824,122	$30,517,675	$29,854,174	$24,914,279

VERMONT

2003	2004	2005	2006	2007
$13,433,129	$13,731,599	$14,903,865	$15,215,371	$14,346,936

SOUTH CAROLINA

2003	2004	2005	2006	2007
$90,008,938	$105,084,724	$120,832,852	$147,309,423	$139,841,966

VIRGINIA

2003	2004	2005	2006	2007
$343,140,792	$413,868,511	$465,118,830	$451,704,180	$374,351,676

SOUTH DAKOTA

2003	2004	2005	2006	2007
$16,068,509	$17,212,698	$16,411,316	$18,791,033	$14,695,869

WASHINGTON

2003	2004	2005	2006	2007
$355,919,941	$312,720,321	$354,885,696	$366,220,342	$329,007,893

3

E.3 Five-Year Trend - Direct Premiums Written by Jurisdiction

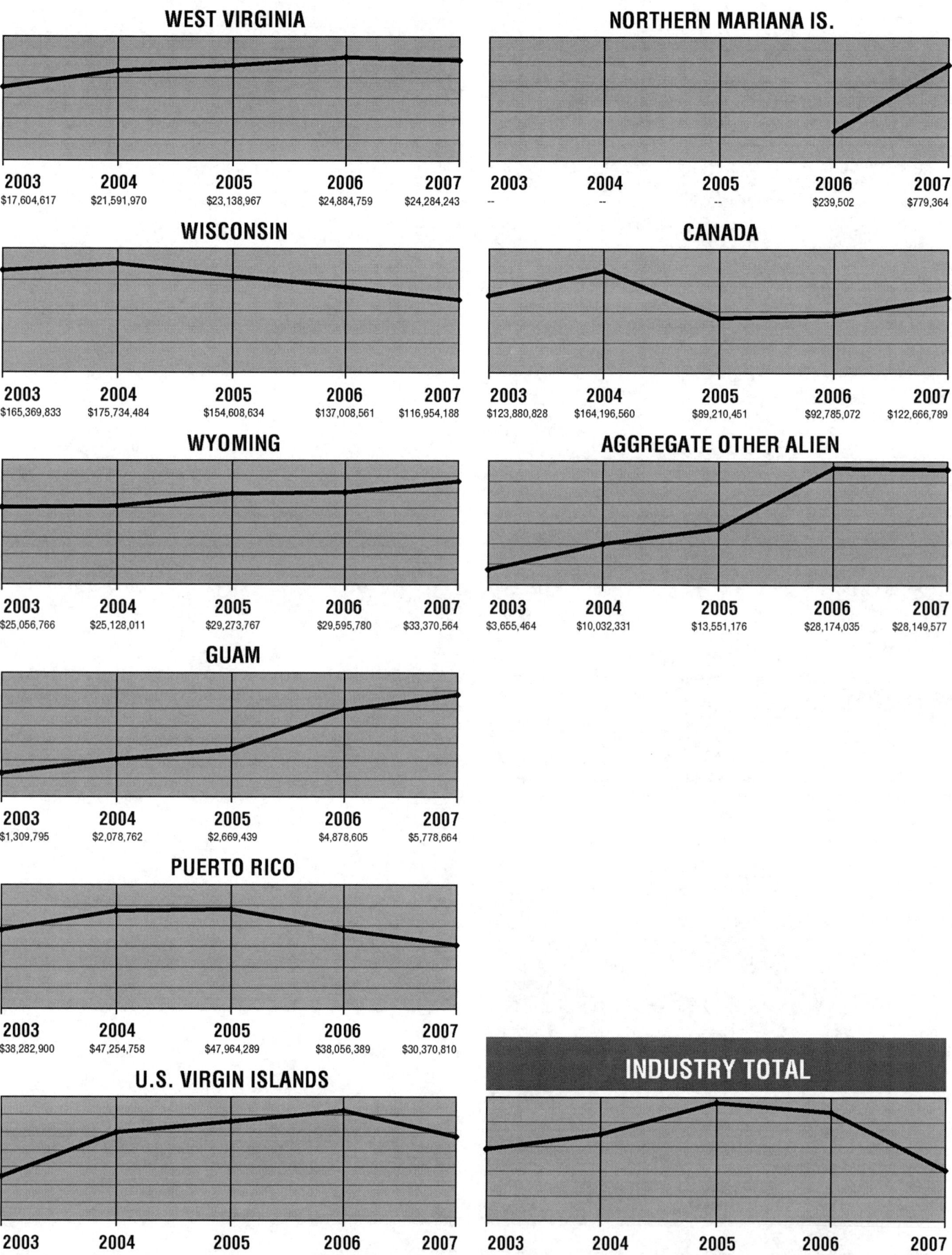

WEST VIRGINIA

2003	2004	2005	2006	2007
$17,604,617	$21,591,970	$23,138,967	$24,884,759	$24,284,243

WISCONSIN

2003	2004	2005	2006	2007
$165,369,833	$175,734,484	$154,608,634	$137,008,561	$116,954,188

WYOMING

2003	2004	2005	2006	2007
$25,056,766	$25,128,011	$29,273,767	$29,595,780	$33,370,564

GUAM

2003	2004	2005	2006	2007
$1,309,795	$2,078,762	$2,669,439	$4,878,605	$5,778,664

PUERTO RICO

2003	2004	2005	2006	2007
$38,282,900	$47,254,758	$47,964,289	$38,056,389	$30,370,810

U.S. VIRGIN ISLANDS

2003	2004	2005	2006	2007
$1,232,898	$2,489,411	$2,803,026	$3,107,536	$2,359,655

NORTHERN MARIANA IS.

2003	2004	2005	2006	2007
--	--	--	$239,502	$779,364

CANADA

2003	2004	2005	2006	2007
$123,880,828	$164,196,560	$89,210,451	$92,785,072	$122,666,789

AGGREGATE OTHER ALIEN

2003	2004	2005	2006	2007
$3,655,464	$10,032,331	$13,551,176	$28,174,035	$28,149,577

INDUSTRY TOTAL

2003	2004	2005	2006	2007
$14,905,801,481	$15,486,578,314	$16,788,257,054	$16,375,079,417	$14,061,278,821

Notes

3

Notes

S E C T I O N

FINANCIAL STABILITY RATINGS® (FSRs) AND
COMMERCIAL REAL ESTATE RECOMMENDATIONS (CRERs)

4

4

Description of Financial Stability Ratings® (FSRs)

Our Philosophy

Our philosophy is that Financial Stability Ratings® (FSRs) should be based on a quantitative model and should be independent of size. Small, well-managed underwriters can be more financially stable than larger, highly leveraged competitors. Demotech's review reflects financial analysis and critical ratios while also considering operational indicators of success, such as business and marketing plans and operational efficiencies. Committed to this unique philosophy, Demotech serves the insurance industry by proactively satisfying the evolving uses and demands for ratings.

Financial Stability Ratings® - An Adaptive Solution

While Financial Stability Ratings® have adapted to meet market demands, our chief tenets of securing accreditation and facilitating activities for rated organizations have remained since Financial Stability Ratings® were introduced.

Since 1992, Demotech has reviewed the financial stability of Title underwriters and published independent opinions of underwriter financial strength.

In 1994, when Fannie Mae promulgated Title underwriter guidelines, Demotech had already developed a proven approach with an impressive track record and was named as an approved Title underwriter rating service.

Our Approach – The Financial Stability Analysis Model

A Financial Stability Rating® is based on several financial variables. Demotech combines a review of critical balance sheet and income statement items with strategic ratios weighted by using regression and multivariate analysis. These proprietary calculations comprise our Financial Stability Analysis Model.

Our Financial Stability Analysis Model was the first risk-based capital or dynamic financial analysis model universally applied to the insurance industry. Its components, as well as selected operational indicators, complete our review and are combined to produce our opinion, summarized as a Financial Stability Rating®.

Why a Financial Stability Rating® is Important to Your Organization

Financial Stability Ratings® are an assessment of an underwriter's on-going financial stability. Based on a predominantly quantitative analysis, a Financial Stability Rating® provides an impartial perspective on financial strength. Financial Stability Ratings® streamline the administrative process by addressing concerns related to the financial stability of an underwriter while simultaneously enhancing the image of well-rated underwriters.

Since their introduction in 1992, Financial Stability Ratings® have been an integral part of the Title insurance industry. We review and rate more Title underwriters than any other service.

4

Financial Stability Rating® Definitions

The following Financial Stability Ratings® represent our opinion of financial stability regardless of general economic conditions or the phase of the underwriting cycle.

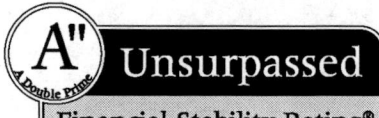

In our opinion, underwriters earning an *FSR of A''* (A Double Prime) have an *Unsurpassed* ability to maintain liquidity of invested assets, quality reinsurance, acceptable financial leverage and realistic pricing while simultaneously establishing loss and loss adjustment expense reserves at reasonable levels.

In our opinion, underwriters earning an *FSR of A'* (A Prime) have an *Unsurpassed* ability to maintain liquidity of invested assets, quality reinsurance, acceptable financial leverage and realistic pricing while simultaneously establishing loss and loss adjustment expense reserves at reasonable levels.

The distinction between an underwriter earning an FSR of A'' and one earning an FSR of A' may be related to the magnitude of policyholders' surplus, market share, national presence or other objective factors.

In our opinion, underwriters earning an *FSR of A* have an *Exceptional* ability to maintain liquidity of invested assets, quality reinsurance, acceptable financial leverage and realistic pricing while simultaneously establishing loss and loss adjustment expense reserves at reasonable levels.

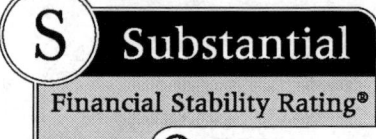

In our opinion, underwriters earning an *FSR of S* have a *Substantial* ability to maintain liquidity of invested assets, quality reinsurance, acceptable financial leverage and realistic pricing while simultaneously establishing loss and loss adjustment expense reserves at reasonable levels.

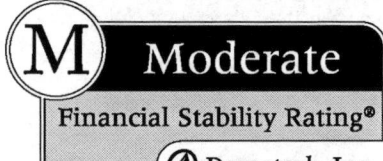

In our opinion, underwriters earning an *FSR of M* have a *Moderate* ability to maintain liquidity of invested assets, quality reinsurance, acceptable financial leverage and realistic pricing while simultaneously establishing loss and loss adjustment expense reserves.

Underwriters receiving an *FSR of L* are *Licensed* by state regulatory authorities. In our opinion, their ability to withstand general economic downturns or deterioration in the underwriting cycle is limited.

Description of Commercial Real Estate Recommendations (CRERs)

Reinsurance Considerations

Most Title underwriters purchase reinsurance to limit the maximum exposure from a single transaction to a predetermined maximum. There are two basic types of reinsurance, *Facultative* and *Treaty*. *Facultative Reinsurance* involves the reinsurer's evaluation of a specific risk as submitted by the Title underwriter. *Treaty Reinsurance* involves, more or less, automatic coverage under predefined and mutually acceptable circumstances and conditions expressed in the contract between a Title underwriter and a reinsurer.

Commercial Transactions

The initial reaction to a commercial transaction might be that "this is one area where only the larger Title underwriters are acceptable." The reality is that, through reinsurance, many underwriters successfully enter the commercial real estate marketplace by gaining access to the expertise and financial strength of larger Title underwriters.

Costs associated with the reinsurance of commercial transactions can be a substantial percentage of the Title insurance premium. Due to the commission schedule associated with Title insurance, commercial business is often written on a direct basis. Title underwriters that utilize agency production sources often require the producing agent to participate in the cost of reinsurance.

In some circumstances, larger Title underwriters prefer to have regional Title underwriters "lead the transaction." This situation might occur when the profit margin in the reinsurance component of the transaction is attractive, while the margin associated with the primary transaction, policy issuance, pre-closing meetings, closing and related efforts is not equally as attractive. This situation is most likely to occur on regional commercial transactions.

Large real estate transactions, regardless of the originating Title underwriter, are reviewed by the closing processor, general counsel and experienced upper management of the Title underwriters that participate in the reinsurance associated with the transaction. Through reinsurance to regional underwriters, larger underwriters are involved in commercial transactions. This process protects commercial lenders.

Commercial Real Estate Recommendations

Highly Recommended – In our opinion, Title underwriters receiving a Commercial Real Estate Recommendation of *Highly Recommended* for Commercial Real Estate Transactions have substantial financial resources as well as significant in-house capacity and expertise.

Strongly Recommended – In our opinion, Title underwriters receiving a Commercial Real Estate Recommendation of *Strongly Recommended* for Commercial Real Estate Transactions have adequate financial resources of their own and significant in-house capacity and expertise, or they have access to the necessary resources because of their placement of reinsurance coverage.

Recommended – In our opinion, Title underwriters receiving a Commercial Real Estate Recommendation of *Recommended* for Commercial Real Estate Transactions have sufficient financial resources of their own and sufficient in-house capacity and expertise, or they have access to the necessary resources because of their placement of reinsurance coverage.

4

Summary of Financial Stability Ratings® (FSRs) and Commercial Real Estate Recommendation (CRERs)

A" (A Double Prime) - Unsurpassed

COMPANY	FINANCIAL STABILITY RATING®	COMMERCIAL REAL ESTATE RECOMMENDATION
American Guaranty Title Insurance Company	A"	Highly Recommended
Arkansas Title Insurance Company	A"	Highly Recommended
Attorneys' Title Insurance Fund, Inc. (FL)	A"	Highly Recommended
Censtar Title Insurance Company	A"	Highly Recommended
Chicago Title and Trust Company	A"	Highly Recommended
Chicago Title Insurance Company	A"	Highly Recommended
Commonwealth Land Title Insurance Company	A"	Highly Recommended
Commonwealth Land Title Insurance Company of New Jersey	A"	Highly Recommended
First American Title Insurance Company	A"	Highly Recommended
First American Title Insurance Company of New York	A"	Highly Recommended
Investors Title Insurance Company	A"	Highly Recommended
Mississippi Valley Title Insurance Company	A"	Highly Recommended
National Land Title Insurance Company	A"	Highly Recommended
Northeast Investors Title Insurance Company	A"	Highly Recommended
Old Republic General Title Insurance Corporation	A"	Highly Recommended
Old Republic National Title Insurance Company	A"	Highly Recommended
Pacific Northwest Title Insurance Company, Inc.	A"	Highly Recommended
Stewart Title Guaranty Company	A"	Highly Recommended
Stewart Title Insurance Company	A"	Highly Recommended

A' (A Prime) - Unsurpassed

COMPANY	FINANCIAL STABILITY RATING®	COMMERCIAL REAL ESTATE RECOMMENDATION
Alamo Title Insurance	A'	Highly Recommended
Alliance Title of America, Inc.	A'	Strongly Recommended
American Security Title Insurance Company	A'	Recommended
Attorneys' Title Guaranty Fund, Inc. (IL)	A'	Highly Recommended
Bridge Title Insurance Company	A'	Highly Recommended
Chicago Title Insurance Company of Oregon	A'	Highly Recommended
Columbian National Title Insurance Company	A'	Recommended
Conestoga Title Insurance Co.	A'	Strongly Recommended
Connecticut Attorneys Title Insurance Company	A'	Strongly Recommended
Fidelity National Title Insurance Company	A'	Highly Recommended
First American Title & Trust Company	A'	Highly Recommended
First American Title Insurance Company of Oregon	A'	Highly Recommended
Guardian National Title Insurance Company	A'	Recommended
Land Title Insurance Company (St. Louis)	A'	Highly Recommended
Land Title Insurance Corporation	A'	Recommended
Lawyers Title Insurance Corporation	A'	Highly Recommended
Monroe Title Insurance Corporation	A'	Strongly Recommended
New Jersey Title Insurance Company	A'	Strongly Recommended
North American Title Insurance Company	A'	Strongly Recommended
Penn Attorneys Title Insurance Company	A'	Strongly Recommended
Security Title Guarantee Corporation of Baltimore (The)	A'	Strongly Recommended
Security Union Title Insurance Company	A'	Highly Recommended
Southern Title Insurance Corporation	A'	Strongly Recommended
Ticor Title Insurance Company	A'	Highly Recommended
Title Guaranty Division of the Iowa Finance Authority	A'	Not Applicable
Title Resources Guaranty Company	A'	Recommended
TransUnion National Title Insurance Company	A'	Strongly Recommended
United Capital Title Insurance Company	A'	Highly Recommended
United General Title Insurance Company	A'	Strongly Recommended
Westcor Land Title Insurance Company	A'	Recommended

Important: Financial Stability Ratings® must be verified by visiting **www.demotech.com**

Summary of Financial Stability Ratings® (FSRs) and Commercial Real Estate Recommendation (CRERs)

A - Exceptional

COMPANY	2008 FINANCIAL STABILITY RATING®	COMMERCIAL REAL ESTATE RECOMMENDATION
Alliant National Title Insurance Company	A	Not Applicable
American Eagle Title Insurance Company	A	Not Applicable
Bankers Guarantee Title & Trust Company (The)	A	Not Applicable
Commerce Title Insurance Company	A	Recommended
Dakota Homestead Title Insurance Company	A	Recommended
Dreibelbiss Title Company, Inc.	A	Recommended
Farmers National Title Insurance Company	A	Not Applicable
First American Title Insurance Company of Kansas, Inc.	A	Highly Recommended
First American Transportation Title Insurance Company	A	Not Applicable
General Title & Trust Company	A	Recommended
Manito Title Insurance Company	A	Recommended
Mason County Title Insurance Company	A	Not Applicable
Mason Title Insurance Company	A	Not Applicable
Massachusetts Title Insurance Company	A	Not Applicable
Mortgage Guarantee & Title Company	A	Strongly Recommended
National Attorneys' Title Assurance Fund, Inc.	A	Recommended
National Title Insurance Company	A	Recommended
National Title Insurance of New York, Inc.	A	Recommended
Nations Title Insurance of New York, Inc.	A	Strongly Recommended
Ohio Bar Title Insurance Company	A	Not Applicable
Pilgrim Title Insurance Company	A	Not Applicable
Port Lawrence Title & Trust Company	A	Strongly Recommended
Public Title Insurance Company	A	Not Applicable
Sierra Title Insurance Guaranty Company	A	Not Applicable
T.A. Title Insurance Company	A	Recommended
Ticor Title Insurance Company of Florida	A	Highly Recommended
Title Insurance Company of America	A	Highly Recommended
Transnation Title Insurance Company	A	Highly Recommended
TransUnion Title Insurance Company	A	Recommended
Western National Title Insurance Company	A	Strongly Recommended

S - Substantial

COMPANY	2008 FINANCIAL STABILITY RATING®	COMMERCIAL REAL ESTATE RECOMMENDATION
American Land and Aircraft Title Company	S	Recommended
Arsenal Insurance Corporation	S	Not Applicable
Attorneys' Title Guaranty Fund, Inc. (CO)	S	Recommended
Equity National Title Insurance Company	S	Not Applicable
Founders Title Insurance	S	Not Applicable
K.E.L. Title Insurance Group	S	Not Applicable
Mississippi Guaranty Title Insurance Company	S	Not Applicable
Seagate Title & Abstract Company, Inc.	S	Not Applicable
Title Guaranty and Trust Company of Chattanooga	S	Not Applicable
Titledge Insurance Company of New York	S	Not Applicable
Washington Title Insurance Company	S	Recommended

Not Rated

COMPANY	2008 FINANCIAL STABILITY RATING®	COMMERCIAL REAL ESTATE RECOMMENDATION
First American Title Insurance Company of Louisiana	Not Rated	Not Applicable
Guarantee Title and Trust Company	Not Rated	Not Applicable
Guarantee Title Insurance Company	Not Rated	Not Applicable
Olympic Title Insurance Company	Not Rated	Not Applicable
Stewart Title Insurance Company of Oregon	Not Rated	Not Applicable

Important: Financial Stability Ratings® must be verified by visiting **www.demotech.com**

Notes

S E C T I O N

FINANCIAL RATIOS AND ANALYSIS

5

Limitations of Statutory Accounting and Ratio Analysis

Statutory Accounting Disclaimer

Title underwriters are required to use an accounting system unique to the insurance industry when filing annual and quarterly financial reports with state regulators and the National Association of Insurance Commissioners (NAIC). This system is based on Statutory Accounting Principles (SAP). To ensure that insurers have sufficient capital and surplus to cover insured losses, SAP accounting is more conservative than Generally Accepted Accounting Principles (GAAP), as defined by the Financial Accounting Standards Board (FASB).

The two systems differ principally in matters relating to the timing of expenses, tax accounting, the treatment of capital gains and accounting for surplus. SAP is based on the liquidation perspective, with the focus of financial accounting and reporting on the liquidation values of an underwriter's assets and liabilities. GAAP accounting focuses on a business as a going concern. When compared to GAAP, SAP appears to understate assets and overstate liabilities. Simply put, SAP recognizes liabilities earlier or at a higher value and recognizes assets later or at a lower value.

SAP accounting is defined by state law according to uniform codes established by the NAIC. Underwriters reporting to the Securities and Exchange Commission must maintain and submit financial reports that meet GAAP standards in addition to the preparation of the SAP statements.

SOME DISTINCTIONS BETWEEN GAAP AND SAP

	GAAP	SAP
Sales Cost	Accounted for over the period in which the premium is earned, i.e., the policy period.	Accounted for immediately on the sale of a policy.
Unearned Income	Taxes on unearned income can be deferred until the income is earned.	Some taxes must be paid on a portion of unearned premium.
Reinsurance Recoverables	Net worth may include reinsurance payments that may not be recovered.	Net worth cannot include potentially unrecoverable reinsurance payments.
Nonadmitted Assets	Certain assets, e.g., furniture and equipment, can be included in net worth.	Such assets cannot be included in net worth.
Taxes on Unrealized Capital Gains	Deferred taxes on unrealized capital gains cannot be included in net worth.	Those anticipated taxes need not be deducted from net worth.
Bonds	Insurers must carry certain bonds at fair market value.	Most bonds can be carried at their amortized value.
Surplus Notes	Surplus notes, a highly subordinated form of debt, must be carried as liabilities.	Surplus notes can be included as part of policyholders' surplus.

Source: Insurance Information Institute

Limitations of Ratio Analysis

There are limitations in the ratio calculations presented within this publication, including but not limited to:

1. The source of the ratio calculations is statutory financial data, as entered into the Form 9 Annual Statements. Therefore, the same factors that cause financial statements themselves to have shortcomings will affect the ratios computed from them. For instance, null and zero values are treated the same and certain unique circumstances may produce abnormal ratio results.

2. The reports and analysis in this publication rely on both the summary and supporting schedules within the Form 9 Annual Statements. The figures presented in the ratio calculations presented in *Section 5 - Financial Ratios and Analysis* may differ slightly from figures presented in *Section 2 - Statutory Financial Statements* and other sections of the publication.

   > Differences between results in *Section 2* and *Section 5* are due to discrepancies between summary and supporting Form 9 Annual Statement schedules, reported underwriter data. These data discrepancies are inherent to the reported underwriter data and fall within the accepted error tolerances associated with Form 9 cross-checks and detail reporting. In some instances, the discrepancy in the underwriter statement and supporting schedules causes minor deviations in the *Composite* totals reported between sections.

   > In general, the reports presented in *Section 2* extract figures from the supporting schedules, recalculating net and aggregate figures and the ratios presented in *Section 5* pull directly from the main financial reports.

3. Changes in ratios may correlate with each other.

4. When comparing ratios between periods for the same underwriter, one should recognize conditions may have changed between the periods being compared (for example, different geographic markets served, changes in economic conditions, pricing, accounting practices, corporate acquisitions, etc.).

5. When comparing ratios of a particular underwriter with those of another underwriter, one should recognize differences between underwriters (for example, differences in the methods of operation, types of financing, states of operation, etc.).

6. Financial ratios alone may not provide direct market indicators. However, the ratios may indicate relative benchmarks and areas that should be more thoroughly analyzed.

7. For percentage calculations within the ratio analysis, *Composite* refers to the weighted average results for the industry.

8. Where appropriate, ratios that present composite values are net of *Consolidated Eliminations*. While best efforts were extended, the necessary information to discern the full historical *Consolidated Eliminations* was not available; therefore, *Consolidated Eliminations* are limited to 2005 to present.

   The following reports reflect *Consolidated Eliminations* in their *Composite* calculations:

   a. A.8 Net Investment Gain (Loss)
   b. A.9 Yield on Invested Assets
   c. A.11 Net Income Before Taxes to Net Admitted Assets
   d. A.12 Return on Policyholders' Surplus (PHS)
   e. B.1 Key Operating Position Results and Ratios
   f. B.2 Net Liquid Assets
   g. B.3 Total Liabilities to Net Liquid Assets
   h. B.5 Net Premiums Written (NPW) to Net Liquid Assets
   i. B.6 Policyholders' Surplus (PHS)
   j. B.7 Net Premiums Written (NPW) to Policyholders' Surplus (PHS)
   k. B.8 Implied Equity (Deficit) in the Statutory Premium Reserve (SPR) — **New!**
   l. C.1 Key Losses & Ability to Meet Losses Results and Ratios
   m. C.3 Losses & Loss Adjustment Expenses (LAE) Incurred to Net Operating and Investment Gain (Loss)
   n. C.4 Losses & Loss Adjustment Expenses (LAE) Incurred to Net Operating and Investment Gain (Loss) & Known Claims Reserve
   o. C.5 Losses & Loss Adjustment Expenses (LAE) Incurred to Policyholders' Surplus (PHS) and Reserves
   p. C.6 Losses & Loss Adjustment Expenses (LAE) Incurred to Net Liquid Assets
   q. C.9 Loss Reserves to Policyholders' Surplus (PHS)
   r. C.11 Loss Reserve Development to Policyholders Surplus (PHS) — **New!**

Notes

5

MEASUREMENTS OF
OPERATING RESULTS

5

Measurements of Operating Results

A.1 Key Operating Results and Ratios

This report presents key operating results and ratios for each Title underwriter. Included in this analysis are *A.2 - Total Operating Income, A.3 - Loss Ratio, A.4 - Adjusted Loss Ratio, A.5 - Operating Expense Ratio, A.6 - Combined Ratio* as well as *A.7 - Operating Profit Margin.*

This report is sorted in alphabetical order by Title underwriter.

A.2 Total Operating Income

This report presents *Total Operating Income*, the aggregate revenue from title insurance and related income activities, including Title Insurance Premiums Earned, Escrow and Settlement Services as well as Other Title Fees and Service Charges, along with Aggregate Write-Ins for Other Operating Income. *Total Operating Income* excludes Investment and Other Income.

To ensure reasonableness of results, if prior year *Total Operating Income* is less than or equal to $0, then the percentage change is not presented.

This report is sorted in descending order by *Total Operating Income*.

This report presents five years of analysis.

A.3 Loss Ratio

This report presents the *Loss Ratio*, a summary of a Title underwriter's underlying loss experience on its book of business. The *Loss Ratio* considers *C.2 - Losses and Loss Adjustment Expenses (LAE) Incurred*, net of reinsurance recoveries. Unless otherwise noted, all future references to the *Loss Ratio* include both incurred Losses *and* Loss Adjustment Expenses.

A.2 - Total Operating Income includes revenue from title insurance and related income activities. Thus, the *Loss Ratio* contains all income, losses and loss settlement costs associated with title activities in one summary measure.

This report is sorted in ascending order by the current year ratio results.

This report presents five years of analysis.

A.4 Adjusted Loss Ratio

This report presents *C.2 - Losses and Loss Adjustment Expenses (LAE) Incurred* compared to *Net Operating Income* (Total Operating Income less Amounts Retained by Agents). Traditional Property and Casualty reporting and the Loss Ratio calculation fail to recognize the loss containment activities associated with title underwriting. Agents perform a large portion of these underwriting activities, which are reflected as a component of Amounts Retained by Agents. Excluding Agent Retention from Total Operating Income recognizes the key role of agent underwriting in loss containment and mitigation and is intended to present a Loss Ratio that more accurately reflects costs associated with title losses and loss adjustment expenses.

This report is sorted in ascending order by the current year ratio results.

This report presents five years of analysis.

A.5 Operating Expense Ratio

This report presents *Operating Expense*, including Amounts Retained by Agents, as a percentage of *A.2 - Total Operating Income*. Losses and Loss Adjustment Expenses (LAE) Incurred are not included in the *Operating Expenses* incurred for the calculation of this ratio.

This ratio indicates the extent to which the Title underwriter's operating expenses consume revenue, leaving a balance for losses, loss adjustment expenses and potential profit.

To ensure reasonableness of results, if *A.2 - Total Operating Income* is less than or equal to $0, then the *Operating Expense Ratio* is not presented.

This report is sorted in ascending order by the current year ratio results.

This report presents five years of analysis.

A.6 Combined Ratio

This report presents the combination of *A.3 - Loss Ratio* and the *A.5 - Operating Expense Ratio*.

The *Combined Ratio* is a benchmark for determining underwriting profitability for each Title underwriter. A *Combined Ratio* less than 100% indicates an underwriting profit (gain), while a *Combined Ratio* exceeding 100% indicates an underwriting loss.

These ratios are sorted in ascending order by ratio.

This report presents five years of analysis.

A.7 Operating Profit Margin

This report presents *Operating Profit Margin* (*Operating Profit* before Losses and Loss Adjustment Expenses (LAE)) as a percentage of *Net Operating Income* (Total Operating Income less Amounts Retained by Agents).

Operating Profit Margin reveals if the Title underwriter earns a profit from its Net Operating Revenue after agent retention and operating expenses but before losses are considered.

To ensure reasonableness of results, if *Operating Profit* is $0 or if *Net Operating Income* is less than or equal to $0, then the *Operating Profit Margin* is not presented.

This report is sorted in descending order by the current year ratio results.

This report presents five years of analysis.

A.8 Net Investment Gain (Loss)

This report presents the main components of *Net Investment Gain (Loss)*. Displaying the *Net Investment Income Earned* and the *Realized Gain (Loss)* separately reveals the contribution of each component to *Net Investment Gain (Loss)* for the respective period.

To ensure reasonableness of results, if prior year *Net Investment Income Earned*, *Realized Gain (Loss)* or *Net Investment Gain (Loss)* is less than or equal to $0, then the percentage change is not presented.

This report is sorted in alphabetical order by Title underwriter.

This report reflects *Consolidated Eliminations* in the *Composite* calculation.

A.9 Yield on Invested Assets

This report presents *A.8 - Net Investment Gain (Loss)*, which includes Realized Gains (Losses), as a percentage of the average beginning and ending *Invested Assets*.

Yield on Invested Assets measures comparative performance of investments and can be influenced by interest rates, movement of the stock and bond markets, performance of affiliates as well as the timing and the amount of funds available for investment.

This report is sorted in descending order by the current year ratio results.

This report presents five years of analysis.

This report reflects *Consolidated Eliminations* in the *Composite* calculation.

A.10 Net Operating Gain (Loss) to Total Operating Income

This report presents overall profitability from all title insurance and related income activities, including Losses and Loss Adjustment Expenses (LAE) Incurred, before consideration of Investment and Other Income.

To ensure reasonableness of results, if *Net Operating Gain (Loss)* is $0 or if *A.2 - Total Operating Income* is less than or equal to $0, then the ratio is not presented.

This report is sorted in descending order by the current year ratio results.

This report presents five years of analysis.

A.11 Net Income Before Taxes to Net Admitted Assets

This report presents *Net Income Before Taxes* as a percent of the average beginning and ending *Net Admitted Assets*.

This report is sorted in descending order by the current year ratio results.

This report presents five years of analysis.

This report reflects *Consolidated Eliminations* in the *Composite* calculation.

A.12 Return on Policyholders' Surplus (PHS)

This report presents *Net Income* as a percentage of the average beginning and ending *Policyholders' Surplus (PHS)*.

Return on Policyholders' Surplus measures a Title underwriter's efficiency in utilizing its surplus on a total return basis. Total return is calculated as the overall after-tax profitability from underwriting and investment activity, including Unrealized Capital Gains (Loss).

This report is sorted in descending order by the current year ratio results.

This report presents five years of analysis.

This report reflects *Consolidated Eliminations* in the *Composite* calculation.

A.1 Key Operating Results and Ratios

COMPANY	A.2 TOTAL OPERATING INCOME	A.3 LOSS RATIO	A.4 ADJUSTED LOSS RATIO	A.5 OPERATING EXPENSE RATIO	A.6 COMBINED RATIO	A.7 OPERATING PROFIT MARGIN
1. ALAMO	$94,868,348	4.79%	30.75%	94.06%	98.84%	38.18%
2. ALLIANCE	$54,338	122.53%	124.45%	215.95%	338.48%	(117.77)%
3. ALLIANT	$13,587,506	7.17%	57.63%	99.01%	106.18%	7.98%
4. AMERICAN EAGLE	$7,538,338	0.41%	0.47%	95.53%	95.93%	5.09%
5. AMERICAN GUARANTY	$3,338,958	3.82%	24.34%	98.90%	102.72%	7.00%
6. AMERICAN LAND & AIRCRAFT	$594,713	0.99%	4.29%	107.89%	108.87%	(34.37)%
7. AMERICAN SECURITY	$2,940,698	0.08%	0.27%	78.22%	78.29%	76.80%
8. ARKANSAS TIC	$8,079,115	1.93%	9.09%	93.44%	95.37%	30.89%
9. ARSENAL	$1,589,223	0.04%	0.19%	101.36%	101.40%	(6.44)%
10. ATTORNEYS TGF (CO)	$13,791,525	2.59%	8.42%	100.50%	103.09%	(1.62)%
11. ATTORNEYS TGF (IL)	$20,161,742	8.98%	8.98%	100.04%	109.02%	(0.04)%
12. ATTORNEYS TIF (FL)	$360,555,798	12.28%	37.10%	98.67%	110.95%	4.01%
13. BRIDGE	$19,541	923.21%	939.85%	557.31%	1,480.52%	(465.55)%
14. CENSTAR	$37,915,111	0.94%	5.83%	89.23%	90.17%	66.75%
15. CHICAGO T&T	$46,037,947	0.00%	0.00%	82.60%	82.60%	17.40%
16. CHICAGO TIC	$2,108,437,310	9.21%	19.67%	88.91%	98.12%	23.69%
17. CHICAGO TIC (OR)	$33,259,216	1.97%	2.98%	85.18%	87.15%	22.44%
18. COLUMBIAN NATIONAL	$0	--	--	--	--	--
19. COMMERCE	$42,512,147	1.07%	7.82%	90.33%	91.40%	70.43%
20. COMMONWEALTH LAND	$1,214,894,310	6.58%	17.60%	89.19%	95.77%	28.91%
21. COMMONWEALTH LAND (NJ)	$35,399,052	5.37%	19.93%	88.11%	93.48%	44.16%
22. CONESTOGA	$14,176,902	7.00%	26.47%	102.60%	109.60%	(9.83)%
23. CT ATTORNEYS	$54,095,917	7.55%	19.90%	94.30%	101.85%	15.02%
24. DAKOTA HOMESTEAD	$4,034,545	6.24%	23.29%	94.78%	101.03%	19.47%
25. DREIBELBISS	$1,763,918	12.29%	12.89%	109.62%	121.90%	(10.09)%
26. EQUITY NATIONAL	$2,068,352	0.00%	0.00%	107.96%	107.96%	(7.96)%
27. FARMERS NATIONAL	$803,193	8.57%	20.06%	136.86%	145.43%	(86.28)%
28. FIDELITY NATIONAL	$1,369,360,612	7.74%	20.04%	89.17%	96.91%	28.04%
29. FIRST AMERICAN (KS)	$14,338,022	5.28%	24.20%	88.96%	94.23%	50.64%
30. FIRST AMERICAN (NY)	$271,881,908	3.67%	6.62%	92.37%	96.04%	13.76%
31. FIRST AMERICAN (OR)	$88,512,105	3.30%	3.81%	88.50%	91.80%	13.27%
32. FIRST AMERICAN T&T	$25,404,401	0.86%	0.90%	80.49%	81.35%	20.50%
33. FIRST AMERICAN TIC	$3,630,841,157	10.32%	27.09%	92.09%	102.40%	20.78%
34. FIRST AMERICAN TRANS	$1,432,315	(1.12)%	(2.31)%	96.50%	95.38%	7.20%
35. FOUNDERS	$221,713	0.00%	0.00%	139.36%	139.36%	(39.36)%
36. GENERAL T&T	$2,780,740	16.45%	68.51%	114.30%	130.75%	(59.52)%
37. GUARANTEE	$2,262,039	38.61%	94.50%	88.83%	127.44%	27.33%
38. GUARANTEE T&T	$14,997,723	10.50%	26.63%	98.03%	108.53%	4.99%
39. GUARDIAN NATIONAL	$3,594,472	(2.12)%	(16.24)%	112.36%	110.24%	(94.47)%
40. INVESTORS TIC	$66,853,213	13.43%	22.24%	82.92%	96.34%	28.29%
41. K.E.L.	$554,387	0.00%	0.00%	140.21%	140.21%	(153.07)%
42. LAND CORP (CO)	$19,814,055	1.37%	10.62%	91.12%	92.50%	68.61%
43. LAND TIC (ST LOUIS)	$2,248,990	0.00%	0.00%	131.15%	131.15%	(63.25)%
44. LAWYERS	$1,324,909,286	6.75%	14.32%	94.84%	101.59%	10.94%
45. MANITO	$740,110	5.31%	42.63%	106.00%	111.31%	(48.13)%
46. MASON	$1,519,252	0.80%	2.36%	126.86%	127.66%	(78.95)%
47. MASON COUNTY	$0	--	--	--	--	--
48. MASSACHUSETTS TIC	($254)	0.00%	0.00%	--	--	--
49. MISSISSIPPI GUARANTY	$298,973	0.00%	0.00%	144.66%	144.66%	(113.43)%
50. MISSISSIPPI VALLEY	$25,410,166	13.56%	45.95%	93.48%	107.04%	22.09%
51. MONROE	$19,801,051	2.92%	4.22%	99.75%	102.67%	0.36%
52. NATIONAL	$3,704,331	(0.24)%	(0.73)%	108.80%	108.55%	(26.35)%
53. NATIONAL ATTORNEYS	$1,337,094	19.98%	19.98%	100.79%	120.77%	(0.79)%
54. NATIONAL LAND	$2,502,043	2.70%	15.80%	126.76%	129.46%	(156.62)%
55. NATIONAL OF NY	$11,194,386	9.49%	42.17%	92.82%	102.31%	31.90%
56. NATIONS OF NY	$895,124	52.66%	52.66%	33.27%	85.93%	66.73%
57. NEW JERSEY TIC	$17,330,838	7.02%	55.46%	99.95%	106.97%	0.39%
58. NORTH AMERICAN	$109,101,307	2.22%	16.37%	90.01%	92.23%	73.59%
59. NORTHEAST INVESTORS	$2,403,559	6.21%	31.92%	96.01%	102.22%	20.50%
60. OHIO BAR	$12,974,760	11.14%	51.15%	89.18%	100.32%	49.67%
61. OLD REPUBLIC GENERAL	$15,384,796	55.96%	55.96%	19.71%	75.67%	80.29%
62. OLD REPUBLIC NATIONAL	$770,478,042	7.32%	32.01%	92.57%	99.89%	32.48%
63. OLYMPIC	$0	--	--	--	--	--
64. PACIFIC NORTHWEST	$60,167,709	2.89%	23.36%	90.88%	93.77%	73.78%
65. PENN ATTORNEYS	$1,823,123	2.47%	2.47%	64.35%	66.81%	35.65%
66. PORT LAWRENCE	$6,785,918	0.52%	0.73%	98.45%	98.96%	2.19%
67. PUBLIC	$0	--	--	--	--	--
68. SEAGATE	$190,389	0.00%	0.00%	92.19%	92.19%	18.88%
69. SECURITY TG (BALTIMORE)	$23,148,068	7.10%	27.47%	99.49%	106.59%	1.98%
70. SECURITY UNION	$66,621,757	15.09%	43.11%	93.55%	108.64%	18.42%
71. SIERRA	$1,923,075	0.00%	0.00%	96.84%	96.84%	24.19%
72. SOUTHERN TI CORP	$53,404,248	7.00%	32.35%	97.11%	104.11%	13.37%
73. STEWART (OR)	$9,836,516	0.00%	0.00%	99.63%	99.63%	5.96%
74. STEWART TGC	$1,499,604,706	8.79%	32.98%	94.45%	103.24%	20.81%
75. STEWART TIC	$172,582,288	3.17%	8.13%	89.72%	92.89%	26.37%
76. T.A. TITLE	$16,852,621	3.23%	24.79%	95.55%	98.78%	34.17%
77. TICOR	$377,091,400	8.46%	20.46%	86.98%	95.44%	31.48%
78. TICOR (FL)	$93,604,625	26.54%	83.91%	99.64%	126.18%	1.14%
79. TITLE G&TC	$1,683,746	0.09%	0.09%	94.37%	94.46%	5.63%
80. TITLE GUARANTY DIV (IA)	$3,648,197	0.00%	0.00%	67.40%	67.40%	31.98%
81. TITLE IC AMERICA	$11,614,194	1.83%	14.35%	100.13%	101.96%	(1.03)%
82. TITLE RESOURCES	$103,117,424	2.64%	20.30%	92.01%	94.65%	61.44%
83. TITLEDGE	$174,297	0.00%	0.00%	110.41%	110.41%	(88.35)%
84. TRANSNATION	$299,589,827	12.04%	29.82%	104.55%	116.59%	(11.27)%
85. TRANSUNION NATIONAL	$3,636,583	31.80%	118.51%	102.36%	134.15%	(8.79)%
86. TRANSUNION TIC	$1,553,321	5.19%	5.19%	99.87%	105.06%	0.13%
87. UNITED CAPITAL	$61,768,602	13.71%	95.10%	92.04%	105.75%	55.21%
88. UNITED GENERAL	$329,196,284	8.28%	33.67%	98.99%	107.27%	4.09%
89. WASHINGTON TIC	$15,187,593	2.86%	20.69%	99.38%	102.24%	4.50%
90. WESTCOR	$51,967,673	1.76%	10.60%	100.74%	102.50%	(4.50)%
91. WESTERN NATIONAL	$453,266	(14.51)%	(59.37)%	91.17%	76.66%	36.14%
COMPOSITE	$15,224,827,929	8.52%	22.48%	92.06%	100.58%	20.94%
AVERAGE	$167,305,801					

A.2 Total Operating Income

COMPANY	2007	2006	2006 TO 2007	2005	2005 TO 2006	2004	2004 TO 2005	2003	2003 TO 2004
1. FIRST AMERICAN TIC	$3,630,841,157	$4,082,969,405	(11.07)%	$4,135,996,641	(1.28)%	$3,563,471,945	16.07%	$3,355,339,438	6.20%
2. CHICAGO TIC	$2,108,437,310	$2,483,370,566	(15.10)%	$2,437,205,743	1.89%	$2,431,922,228	0.22%	$2,514,325,968	(3.28)%
3. STEWART TGC	$1,499,604,706	$1,806,052,051	(16.97)%	$1,785,825,953	1.13%	$1,583,128,809	12.80%	$1,598,756,616	(0.98)%
4. FIDELITY NATIONAL	$1,369,360,612	$1,613,531,904	(15.13)%	$1,809,266,803	(10.82)%	$1,650,116,357	9.64%	$968,372,992	70.40%
5. LAWYERS	$1,324,909,286	$1,431,032,126	(7.42)%	$1,408,656,251	1.59%	$1,295,699,123	8.72%	$1,370,687,475	(5.47)%
6. COMMONWEALTH LAND	$1,214,894,310	$1,428,406,919	(14.95)%	$1,322,272,629	8.03%	$1,213,457,235	8.97%	$1,223,401,140	(0.81)%
7. OLD REPUBLIC NATIONAL	$770,478,042	$874,686,901	(11.91)%	$940,720,587	(7.02)%	$910,718,350	3.29%	$932,483,375	(2.33)%
8. TICOR	$377,091,400	$407,903,943	(7.55)%	$350,271,886	16.45%	$408,588,602	(14.27)%	$403,672,808	1.22%
9. ATTORNEYS TIF (FL)	$360,555,798	$503,448,142	(28.38)%	$514,432,116	(2.14)%	$453,366,366	13.47%	$398,089,203	13.89%
10. UNITED GENERAL	$329,196,284	$322,733,812	2.00%	$201,120,726	60.47%	$205,249,870	(2.01)%	$252,221,901	(18.62)%
11. TRANSNATION	$299,589,827	$390,359,114	(23.25)%	$450,069,050	(13.27)%	$393,598,616	14.35%	$358,997,917	9.64%
12. FIRST AMERICAN (NY)	$271,881,908	$261,510,076	3.97%	$264,202,901	(1.02)%	$243,450,789	8.52%	$204,623,291	18.98%
13. STEWART TIC	$172,582,288	$159,418,256	8.26%	$157,305,092	1.34%	$150,228,820	4.71%	$143,746,098	4.51%
14. NORTH AMERICAN	$109,101,307	$93,013,381	17.30%	$102,206,060	(8.99)%	$92,149,506	10.91%	$84,413,725	9.16%
15. TITLE RESOURCES	$103,117,424	$110,332,778	(6.54)%	$83,953,400	31.42%	$89,765,095	(6.47)%	$92,114,347	(2.55)%
16. ALAMO	$94,868,348	$113,246,418	(16.23)%	$111,991,566	1.12%	$114,190,904	(1.93)%	$132,090,713	(13.55)%
17. TICOR (FL)	$93,604,625	$176,403,032	(46.94)%	$343,267,937	(48.61)%	$258,893,436	32.59%	$287,951,542	(10.09)%
18. FIRST AMERICAN (OR)	$88,512,105	$99,398,127	(10.95)%	$103,943,574	(4.37)%	$93,790,629	10.83%	$106,600,825	(12.02)%
19. INVESTORS TIC	$66,853,213	$66,499,974	0.53%	$71,383,500	(6.84)%	$65,979,496	8.19%	$75,526,589	(12.64)%
20. SECURITY UNION	$66,621,757	$94,202,126	(29.28)%	$84,173,767	11.91%	$123,212,331	(31.68)%	$106,210,958	16.01%
21. UNITED CAPITAL	$61,768,602	$121,741,880	(49.26)%	$157,501,983	(22.70)%	$123,966,915	27.05%	$122,951,137	0.83%
22. PACIFIC NORTHWEST	$60,167,709	$62,284,469	(3.40)%	$50,744,995	22.74%	$52,155,625	(2.70)%	$71,247,691	(26.80)%
23. CT ATTORNEYS	$54,095,917	$59,697,758	(9.38)%	$63,019,407	(5.27)%	$59,156,407	6.53%	$68,764,182	(13.97)%
24. SOUTHERN TI CORP	$53,404,248	$55,480,631	(3.74)%	$46,119,513	20.30%	$37,575,572	22.74%	$35,538,251	5.76%
25. WESTCOR	$51,967,673	$49,399,961	5.20%	$56,134,768	(12.00)%	$48,954,110	14.67%	$48,128,787	1.71%
26. CHICAGO T&T	$46,037,947	$51,424,868	(10.48)%	$54,122,292	(4.98)%	$49,218,883	9.96%	$56,624,662	(13.08)%
27. COMMERCE	$42,512,147	$53,515,285	(20.56)%	$52,487,263	1.96%	$48,851,948	7.44%	$50,007,918	(2.31)%
28. CENSTAR	$37,915,111	$43,871,413	(13.58)%	$48,807,591	(10.11)%	$10,906,753	347.59%	$0	--
29. COMMONWEALTH LAND (NJ)	$35,399,052	$44,478,752	(20.41)%	$48,781,425	(8.82)%	$48,283,965	1.03%	$41,784,035	15.56%
30. CHICAGO TIC (OR)	$33,259,216	$40,928,459	(18.74)%	$41,002,723	(0.18)%	$33,140,588	23.72%	$45,381,030	(26.97)%
31. MISSISSIPPI VALLEY	$25,410,166	$25,269,645	0.56%	$22,323,176	13.20%	$23,209,102	(3.82)%	$26,800,427	(13.40)%
32. FIRST AMERICAN T&T	$25,404,401	$15,699,775	61.81%	$17,119,159	(8.29)%	$17,296,471	(1.03)%	$20,315,555	(14.86)%
33. SECURITY TG (BALTIMORE)	$23,148,068	$32,686,605	(29.18)%	$30,042,914	8.80%	$34,445,988	(12.78)%	$29,148,158	18.18%
34. ATTORNEYS TGF (IL)	$20,161,742	$22,066,768	(8.63)%	$24,355,884	(9.40)%	$22,096,825	10.22%	$22,391,114	(1.31)%
35. LAND CORP (CO)	$19,814,055	$23,223,556	(14.68)%	$26,560,357	(12.56)%	$26,648,173	(0.33)%	$37,475,638	(28.89)%
36. MONROE	$19,801,051	$20,099,690	(1.49)%	$21,515,780	(6.58)%	$22,963,927	(6.31)%	$25,574,415	(10.21)%
37. NEW JERSEY TIC	$17,330,838	$18,917,459	(8.39)%	$21,536,729	(12.16)%	$17,114,479	25.84%	$17,235,613	(0.70)%
38. T.A. TITLE	$16,852,621	$17,319,910	(2.70)%	$17,655,414	(1.90)%	$17,135,246	3.04%	$22,087,974	(22.42)%
39. OLD REPUBLIC GENERAL	$15,384,796	$16,604,599	(7.35)%	$19,314,438	(14.03)%	$20,741,070	(6.88)%	$21,568,978	(3.84)%
40. WASHINGTON TIC	$15,187,593	$19,069,403	(20.36)%	$19,734,092	(3.37)%	$15,810,790	24.81%	$16,056,910	(1.53)%
41. GUARANTEE T&T	$14,997,723	$15,889,031	(5.61)%	$13,925,762	14.10%	$20,802,726	(33.06)%	$19,829,231	4.91%
42. FIRST AMERICAN (KS)	$14,338,022	$13,907,507	3.10%	$14,517,770	(4.20)%	$12,347,453	17.58%	$14,890,748	(17.08)%
43. CONESTOGA	$14,176,902	$17,567,681	(19.30)%	$19,334,786	(9.14)%	$20,732,994	(6.74)%	$24,930,008	(16.84)%
44. ATTORNEYS TGF (CO)	$13,791,525	$15,316,318	(9.96)%	$17,776,452	(13.84)%	$21,663,158	(17.94)%	$23,404,226	(7.44)%
45. ALLIANT	$13,587,506	$6,906,479	96.74%	$125,932	5,384.29%				
46. OHIO BAR	$12,974,760	$14,714,375	(11.82)%	$14,155,061	3.95%	$19,390,569	(27.00)%	$18,302,909	5.94%
47. TITLE IC AMERICA	$11,614,194	$11,555,707	0.51%	$18,795,879	(38.52)%	$21,012,364	(10.55)%	$20,200,360	4.02%
48. NATIONAL OF NY	$11,194,386	($63,373)	--	($2,274,788)	--	$23,106,009	(109.85)%	$48,113,243	(51.98)%
49. STEWART (OR)	$9,836,516	$9,698,609	1.42%	$9,697,656	0.01%	$8,412,144	15.28%	$10,035,229	(16.17)%
50. ARKANSAS TIC	$8,079,115	$7,323,364	10.32%	$5,963,589	22.80%	$5,713,149	4.38%	$5,182,966	10.23%
51. AMERICAN EAGLE	$7,538,338	$6,673,822	12.95%	$7,028,820	(5.05)%	$5,233,147	34.31%	$6,556,565	(20.18)%
52. PORT LAWRENCE	$6,785,918	$8,983,868	(24.47)%	$8,604,701	4.41%	$9,441,767	(8.87)%	$12,177,020	(22.46)%
53. DAKOTA HOMESTEAD	$4,034,545	$5,355,340	(24.66)%	$3,714,545	44.17%	$2,084,457	78.20%	$2,131,965	(2.23)%
54. NATIONAL	$3,704,331	$3,080,900	20.24%	$2,825,148	9.05%	$2,369,521	19.23%	$2,654,796	(10.75)%
55. TITLE GUARANTY DIV (IA)	$3,648,197	$3,792,182	(3.80)%	$3,861,826	(1.80)%	$5,412,697	(28.65)%	$6,385,054	(15.23)%
56. TRANSUNION NATIONAL	$3,636,583	$3,754,051	(3.13)%	$4,639,111	(19.08)%	$3,848,569	20.54%	$4,898,134	(21.43)%
57. GUARDIAN NATIONAL	$3,594,472	$4,197,443	(14.37)%	$7,039,280	(40.37)%	$6,606,693	6.55%	$10,506,975	(37.12)%
58. AMERICAN GUARANTY	$3,338,958	$3,324,885	0.42%	$3,162,510	5.13%	$8,130,778	(61.10)%	$10,381,949	(21.68)%
59. AMERICAN SECURITY	$2,940,698	$2,476,836	18.73%	$2,379,672	4.08%	$2,599,592	(8.46)%	$3,175,142	(18.13)%
60. GENERAL T&T	$2,780,740	$6,071,178	(54.20)%	$8,761,005	(30.70)%	$9,395,469	(6.75)%	$12,132,491	(22.56)%
61. NATIONAL LAND	$2,502,043	$1,534,302	63.07%	$622,476	146.48%	$650,776	(4.35)%	$696,878	(6.62)%
62. NORTHEAST INVESTORS	$2,403,559	$2,423,968	(0.84)%	$3,220,000	(24.72)%	$3,445,451	(6.54)%	$5,510,714	(37.48)%
63. GUARANTEE	$2,262,039	$2,672,297	(15.35)%	$1,543,910	73.09%	$830,184	85.97%	$697,040	19.10%
64. LAND TIC (ST LOUIS)	$2,248,990	$742,352	202.95%	$4,171,011	(82.20)%	$1,194,396	249.22%	$1,275,480	(6.36)%
65. EQUITY NATIONAL	$2,068,352	$9,228,601	(77.59)%	$3,467,268	166.16%	--	--	--	--
66. SIERRA	$1,923,075	$0	--						
67. PENN ATTORNEYS	$1,823,123	$2,162,548	(15.70)%	$2,546,301	(15.07)%	$2,351,246	8.30%	$3,250,203	(27.66)%
68. DREIBELBISS	$1,763,918	$2,100,046	(16.00)%	$2,605,639	(19.41)%	$3,017,946	(13.66)%	$4,424,942	(31.80)%
69. TITLE G&TC	$1,683,746	$1,751,997	(3.90)%	$1,388,670	26.16%	$1,201,857	15.54%	$1,355,916	(11.36)%
70. ARSENAL	$1,589,223	$2,396,143	(33.68)%	$2,152,938	11.30%	$1,217,779	76.79%	--	--
71. TRANSUNION TIC	$1,553,321	$6,133,397	(74.67)%	$9,791,349	(37.36)%	$15,132,279	(35.29)%	$25,693,803	(41.11)%
72. MASON	$1,519,252	$458,293	231.50%						
73. FIRST AMERICAN TRANS	$1,432,315	$1,832,970	(21.86)%	$1,406,038	30.36%	$1,309,099	7.41%	$1,105,791	18.39%
74. NATIONAL ATTORNEYS	$1,337,094	$1,347,627	(0.78)%	$1,320,379	2.06%	$1,483,846	(11.02)%	$1,434,721	3.42%
75. NATIONS OF NY	$895,124	$970,997	(7.81)%	$971,571	(0.06)%	$976,622	(0.52)%	$1,136,548	(14.07)%
76. FARMERS NATIONAL	$803,193	$337,679	137.86%	--	--	--	--	--	--
77. MANITO	$740,110	$833,485	(11.20)%	$1,010,952	(17.55)%	$1,037,052	(2.52)%	$1,796,472	(42.27)%
78. AMERICAN LAND & AIRCRAFT	$594,713	$520,775	14.20%	$708,324	(26.48)%	$1,233,701	(42.59)%	$865,946	42.47%
79. K.E.L.	$554,387	--	--	--	--	--	--	--	--
80. WESTERN NATIONAL	$453,266	$858,990	(47.23)%	$1,784,114	(51.85)%	$2,450,565	(27.20)%	$7,445,158	(67.09)%
81. MISSISSIPPI GUARANTY	$298,973	$536,886	(44.31)%	$547,502	(1.94)%	$770,768	(28.97)%	$1,196,027	(35.56)%
82. FOUNDERS	$221,713	$237,688	(6.72)%	$139,882	69.92%	--	--	--	--
83. SEAGATE	$190,389	$140,506	35.50%	$175,645	(20.01)%	$213,805	(17.85)%	$278,392	(23.20)%
84. TITLEDGE	$174,297	--	--	--	--	--	--	--	--
85. ALLIANCE	$54,338	$70,829	(23.28)%	$123,684	(42.73)%	$735,385	(83.18)%	$7,919,495	(90.71)%
86. BRIDGE	$19,541	$27,008	(27.65)%	$60,527	(55.38)%	$97,293	(37.79)%	$233,756	(58.38)%
87. COLUMBIAN NATIONAL	$0	$637,556	(100.00)%	$5,393,964	(88.18)%	$7,189,206	(24.97)%	$7,159,453	0.42%
88. MASON COUNTY	$0	$0	--	$0	--	$0	--	$0	--
89. OLYMPIC	$0	$0	--	$0	--	$0	--	$0	--
90. PUBLIC	$0	$0	--	--	--	--	--	--	--
91. MASSACHUSETTS TIC	($254)	$1,705	(114.90)%	$975	74.87%	$960	1.56%	$0	--
COMPOSITE	$15,224,827,929	$17,512,784,745	(13.06)%	$17,726,333,921	(1.20)%	$16,325,494,816	8.58%	$15,718,065,142	3.86%
AVERAGE	$167,305,801	$196,772,862	(14.98)%	$208,545,105	(5.64)%	$199,091,400	4.75%	$194,050,187	2.60%

5

A.3 Loss Ratio

COMPANY	2007 C.2 - L&LAE INCURRED	2007 A.2 - TOTAL OPERATING INCOME	2007 LOSS RATIO	2006 LOSS RATIO	2005 LOSS RATIO	2004 LOSS RATIO	2003 LOSS RATIO
1. OLYMPIC	$26,670	$0	--	--	--	--	--
2. MASON COUNTY	$0	$0	--	--	--	--	--
3. PUBLIC	$0	$0	--	--	--	--	--
4. COLUMBIAN NATIONAL	$0	$0	--	0.00%	11.87%	29.35%	4.25%
5. WESTERN NATIONAL	($65,757)	$453,266	(14.51)%	27.72%	(1.26)%	0.99%	1.62%
6. GUARDIAN NATIONAL	($76,380)	$3,594,472	(2.12)%	8.55%	0.54%	3.16%	2.58%
7. FIRST AMERICAN TRANS	($16,063)	$1,432,315	(1.12)%	12.36%	2.61%	5.81%	1.10%
8. NATIONAL	($9,014)	$3,704,331	(0.24)%	1.62%	0.00%	0.00%	0.08%
9. CHICAGO T&T	$0	$46,037,947	0.00%	0.00%	0.00%	0.00%	0.00%
10. STEWART (OR)	$0	$9,836,516	0.00%	0.00%	0.00%	0.00%	0.00%
11. TITLE GUARANTY DIV (IA)	$0	$3,648,197	0.00%	4.75%	6.97%	2.49%	1.18%
12. LAND TIC (ST LOUIS)	$0	$2,248,990	0.00%	0.00%	0.00%	0.00%	0.00%
13. EQUITY NATIONAL	$0	$2,068,352	0.00%	0.00%	0.00%	--	--
14. SIERRA	$0	$1,923,075	0.00%	--	--	--	--
15. K.E.L.	$0	$554,387	0.00%	--	--	--	--
16. MISSISSIPPI GUARANTY	$0	$298,973	0.00%	0.00%	0.00%	0.00%	0.00%
17. FOUNDERS	$0	$221,713	0.00%	0.00%	0.00%	--	--
18. SEAGATE	$0	$190,389	0.00%	0.00%	0.00%	0.00%	0.00%
19. TITLEDGE	$0	$174,297	0.00%	--	--	--	--
20. MASSACHUSETTS TIC	$0	($254)	0.00%	0.00%	0.00%	0.00%	--
21. ARSENAL	$649	$1,589,223	0.04%	0.11%	0.22%	0.00%	--
22. AMERICAN SECURITY	$2,283	$2,940,698	0.08%	1.97%	0.00%	0.00%	0.17%
23. TITLE G&TC	$1,500	$1,683,746	0.09%	0.00%	0.11%	0.19%	0.55%
24. AMERICAN EAGLE	$30,838	$7,538,338	0.41%	0.54%	1.43%	1.25%	2.53%
25. PORT LAWRENCE	$35,011	$6,785,918	0.52%	(1.79)%	1.04%	0.42%	1.12%
26. MASON	$12,200	$1,519,252	0.80%	0.00%	--	--	--
27. FIRST AMERICAN T&T	$218,147	$25,404,401	0.86%	1.18%	2.08%	2.25%	1.70%
28. CENSTAR	$356,768	$37,915,111	0.94%	0.24%	0.12%	0.00%	--
29. AMERICAN LAND & AIRCRAFT	$5,858	$594,713	0.99%	1.11%	0.00%	0.00%	0.00%
30. COMMERCE	$456,599	$42,512,147	1.07%	2.13%	1.13%	1.41%	0.98%
31. LAND CORP (CO)	$272,282	$19,814,055	1.37%	(0.96)%	0.99%	(1.08)%	2.50%
32. WESTCOR	$912,036	$51,967,673	1.76%	0.24%	2.01%	1.30%	1.59%
33. TITLE IC AMERICA	$211,989	$11,614,194	1.83%	9.47%	5.14%	1.34%	1.94%
34. ARKANSAS TIC	$155,822	$8,079,115	1.93%	3.56%	0.79%	8.60%	4.20%
35. CHICAGO TIC (OR)	$655,119	$33,259,216	1.97%	0.74%	3.03%	3.95%	1.80%
36. NORTH AMERICAN	$2,424,736	$109,101,307	2.22%	2.65%	2.29%	2.40%	3.30%
37. PENN ATTORNEYS	$44,947	$1,823,123	2.47%	4.65%	8.84%	(3.65)%	0.83%
38. ATTORNEYS TGF (CO)	$357,311	$13,791,525	2.59%	2.71%	5.93%	6.35%	1.06%
39. TITLE RESOURCES	$2,723,053	$103,117,424	2.64%	2.84%	1.94%	2.04%	1.61%
40. NATIONAL LAND	$67,550	$2,502,043	2.70%	4.47%	24.72%	6.35%	28.26%
41. WASHINGTON TIC	$433,920	$15,187,593	2.86%	2.20%	0.48%	1.97%	0.83%
42. PACIFIC NORTHWEST	$1,737,205	$60,167,709	2.89%	1.98%	1.91%	2.14%	2.02%
43. MONROE	$577,627	$19,801,051	2.92%	1.90%	2.64%	2.03%	0.58%
44. STEWART TIC	$5,470,985	$172,582,288	3.17%	3.92%	2.15%	2.80%	3.44%
45. T.A. TITLE	$544,743	$16,852,621	3.23%	2.50%	0.87%	3.38%	0.80%
46. FIRST AMERICAN (OR)	$2,919,785	$88,512,105	3.30%	2.28%	2.96%	1.18%	1.58%
47. FIRST AMERICAN (NY)	$9,991,046	$271,881,908	3.67%	3.36%	2.42%	2.96%	4.01%
48. AMERICAN GUARANTY	$127,491	$3,338,958	3.82%	2.39%	5.14%	1.70%	0.98%
49. ALAMO	$4,542,653	$94,868,348	4.79%	2.22%	2.72%	2.49%	1.96%
50. TRANSUNION TIC	$80,643	$1,553,321	5.19%	7.86%	9.35%	3.26%	0.98%
51. FIRST AMERICAN (KS)	$756,653	$14,338,022	5.28%	3.61%	6.57%	4.98%	4.69%
52. MANITO	$39,324	$740,110	5.31%	1.74%	0.49%	(7.35)%	2.78%
53. COMMONWEALTH LAND (NJ)	$1,900,138	$35,399,052	5.37%	6.07%	2.76%	3.80%	1.46%
54. NORTHEAST INVESTORS	$149,328	$2,403,559	6.21%	1.26%	2.13%	(0.24)%	0.18%
55. DAKOTA HOMESTEAD	$251,953	$4,034,545	6.24%	3.46%	7.56%	(1.72)%	2.48%
56. COMMONWEALTH LAND	$79,989,583	$1,214,894,310	6.58%	5.76%	4.55%	4.41%	3.78%
57. LAWYERS	$89,456,441	$1,324,909,286	6.75%	4.96%	5.00%	4.07%	3.79%
58. CONESTOGA	$991,906	$14,176,902	7.00%	2.05%	5.31%	9.62%	2.10%
59. SOUTHERN TI CORP	$3,737,322	$53,404,248	7.00%	4.07%	2.02%	2.61%	2.59%
60. NEW JERSEY TIC	$1,216,094	$17,330,838	7.02%	4.21%	2.77%	5.63%	4.20%
61. SECURITY TG (BALTIMORE)	$1,643,655	$23,148,068	7.10%	1.52%	7.40%	1.53%	2.83%
62. ALLIANT	$974,113	$13,587,506	7.17%	0.31%	0.00%	--	--
63. OLD REPUBLIC NATIONAL	$56,386,474	$770,478,042	7.32%	6.58%	5.70%	4.08%	3.46%
64. CT ATTORNEYS	$4,086,369	$54,095,917	7.55%	10.20%	3.80%	3.42%	2.01%
65. FIDELITY NATIONAL	$105,973,212	$1,369,360,612	7.74%	4.40%	6.95%	6.34%	5.58%
66. UNITED GENERAL	$27,244,717	$329,196,284	8.28%	3.07%	5.59%	3.87%	3.12%
67. TICOR	$31,901,301	$377,091,400	8.46%	6.08%	6.26%	5.98%	7.56%
68. FARMERS NATIONAL	$68,819	$803,193	8.57%	0.36%	--	--	--
69. STEWART TGC	$131,848,241	$1,499,604,706	8.79%	5.56%	4.76%	4.26%	3.04%
70. ATTORNEYS TGF (IL)	$1,811,083	$20,161,742	8.98%	11.04%	11.10%	14.49%	13.19%
71. CHICAGO TIC	$194,183,381	$2,108,437,310	9.21%	4.33%	6.86%	4.37%	3.91%
72. NATIONAL OF NY	$1,062,613	$11,194,386	9.49%	(1,986.69)%	(85.00)%	22.26%	4.28%
73. FIRST AMERICAN TIC	$374,613,626	$3,630,841,157	10.32%	4.72%	4.36%	3.57%	3.90%
74. GUARANTEE T&T	$1,575,079	$14,997,723	10.50%	10.51%	9.65%	7.81%	6.30%
75. OHIO BAR	$1,445,381	$12,974,760	11.14%	2.96%	(7.28)%	(0.39)%	15.04%
76. TRANSNATION	$36,073,083	$299,589,827	12.04%	7.11%	4.44%	4.24%	5.18%
77. ATTORNEYS TIF (FL)	$44,278,625	$360,555,798	12.28%	5.25%	4.69%	2.55%	4.64%
78. DREIBELBISS	$216,747	$1,763,918	12.29%	2.76%	(5.97)%	1.64%	1.02%
79. INVESTORS TIC	$8,975,058	$66,853,213	13.43%	10.97%	8.24%	10.68%	7.38%
80. MISSISSIPPI VALLEY	$3,445,735	$25,410,166	13.56%	4.58%	10.62%	(0.95)%	7.96%
81. UNITED CAPITAL	$8,465,810	$61,768,602	13.71%	5.57%	1.58%	1.00%	0.32%
82. SECURITY UNION	$10,051,219	$66,621,757	15.09%	6.51%	7.92%	5.00%	3.76%
83. GENERAL T&T	$457,564	$2,780,740	16.45%	10.01%	2.20%	1.20%	1.25%
84. NATIONAL ATTORNEYS	$267,150	$1,337,094	19.98%	9.08%	1.92%	5.09%	10.15%
85. TICOR (FL)	$24,844,213	$93,604,625	26.54%	9.93%	8.02%	7.66%	4.19%
86. TRANSUNION NATIONAL	$1,156,259	$3,636,583	31.80%	25.77%	43.86%	11.71%	6.77%
87. GUARANTEE	$873,275	$2,262,039	38.61%	48.30%	9.33%	1.75%	23.59%
88. NATIONS OF NY	$471,332	$895,124	52.66%	26.07%	10.28%	66.19%	117.12%
89. OLD REPUBLIC GENERAL	$8,609,260	$15,384,796	55.96%	25.13%	20.47%	20.73%	40.15%
90. ALLIANCE	$66,580	$54,338	122.53%	86.08%	(102.58)%	41.80%	7.92%
91. BRIDGE	$180,404	$19,541	923.21%	323.77%	104.48%	177.05%	0.64%
COMPOSITE	$1,296,969,372	$15,224,827,929	8.52%	4.97%	5.16%	4.28%	3.93%
AVERAGE	$14,252,411	$167,305,801	8.52%				

COMPANY INDEX
Companies listed alphabetically, with ratio index for reference.

5

A.4 Adjusted Loss Ratio

COMPANY	2007 C.2 - L&LAE INCURRED	2007 NET OPERATING INCOME	2007 ADJUSTED LOSS RATIO	2006 ADJUSTED LOSS RATIO	2005 ADJUSTED LOSS RATIO	2004 ADJUSTED LOSS RATIO	2003 ADJUSTED LOSS RATIO
1. OLYMPIC	$26,670	$0	--	--	--	--	--
2. MASON COUNTY	$0	$0	--	--	--	--	--
3. PUBLIC	$0	$0	--	--	--	--	--
4. COLUMBIAN NATIONAL	$0	$0	--	0.00%	46.04%	118.58%	15.14%
5. WESTERN NATIONAL	($65,757)	$110,757	(59.37)%	184.94%	(8.79)%	19.78%	27.54%
6. GUARDIAN NATIONAL	($76,380)	$470,359	(16.24)%	75.11%	5.69%	31.59%	16.27%
7. FIRST AMERICAN TRANS	($16,063)	$695,907	(2.31)%	20.45%	4.65%	11.02%	2.20%
8. NATIONAL	($9,014)	$1,236,697	(0.73)%	4.39%	0.00%	0.00%	0.17%
9. CHICAGO T&T	$0	$46,037,947	0.00%	0.00%	0.00%	0.00%	0.00%
10. TITLE GUARANTY DIV (IA)	$0	$3,648,197	0.00%	4.75%	6.97%	2.49%	1.18%
11. EQUITY NATIONAL	$0	$2,068,352	0.00%	0.00%	0.00%	--	--
12. LAND TIC (ST LOUIS)	$0	$1,107,567	0.00%	0.00%	0.00%	0.00%	0.00%
13. STEWART (OR)	$0	$615,430	0.00%	0.00%	0.00%	0.00%	0.00%
14. SIERRA	$0	$251,380	0.00%	--	--	--	--
15. FOUNDERS	$0	$221,713	0.00%	0.00%	0.00%	--	--
16. K.E.L.	$0	$145,647	0.00%	--	--	--	--
17. MISSISSIPPI GUARANTY	$0	$117,696	0.00%	0.00%	0.00%	0.00%	0.00%
18. SEAGATE	$0	$78,735	0.00%	0.00%	0.00%	0.00%	0.00%
19. TITLEDGE	$0	$20,542	0.00%	--	--	--	--
20. MASSACHUSETTS TIC	$0	($254)	0.00%	0.00%	0.00%	0.00%	--
21. TITLE G&TC	$1,500	$1,683,746	0.09%	0.00%	0.11%	0.19%	0.55%
22. ARSENAL	$649	$335,910	0.19%	0.53%	1.24%	0.00%	--
23. AMERICAN SECURITY	$2,283	$834,100	0.27%	5.44%	0.00%	0.00%	0.46%
24. AMERICAN EAGLE	$30,838	$6,622,068	0.47%	0.61%	1.57%	1.36%	2.63%
25. PORT LAWRENCE	$35,011	$4,817,268	0.73%	(2.79)%	1.36%	0.53%	1.31%
26. FIRST AMERICAN T&T	$218,147	$24,177,001	0.90%	1.25%	2.19%	2.37%	1.79%
27. MASON	$12,200	$516,819	2.36%	0.00%	--	--	--
28. PENN ATTORNEYS	$44,947	$1,823,123	2.47%	4.65%	8.84%	(3.65)%	0.83%
29. CHICAGO TIC (OR)	$655,119	$21,971,311	2.98%	1.22%	4.78%	5.90%	2.99%
30. FIRST AMERICAN (OR)	$2,919,785	$76,723,081	3.81%	2.51%	3.25%	1.34%	1.97%
31. MONROE	$577,627	$13,680,455	4.22%	2.83%	3.99%	2.98%	0.81%
32. AMERICAN LAND & AIRCRAFT	$5,858	$136,495	4.29%	4.72%	0.00%	0.00%	0.00%
33. TRANSUNION TIC	$80,643	$1,553,321	5.19%	33.39%	55.59%	27.86%	7.85%
34. CENSTAR	$356,768	$6,116,752	5.83%	1.48%	0.62%	0.00%	--
35. FIRST AMERICAN (NY)	$9,991,046	$150,822,195	6.62%	6.74%	5.00%	7.24%	10.10%
36. COMMERCE	$456,599	$5,837,840	7.82%	16.62%	10.28%	15.44%	8.63%
37. STEWART TIC	$5,470,985	$67,294,473	8.13%	11.56%	6.16%	8.31%	13.60%
38. ATTORNEYS TGF (CO)	$357,311	$4,242,365	8.42%	9.69%	23.18%	21.56%	3.92%
39. ATTORNEYS TGF (IL)	$1,811,083	$20,161,742	8.98%	11.04%	11.10%	14.49%	13.19%
40. ARKANSAS TIC	$155,822	$1,714,847	9.09%	15.83%	3.10%	32.88%	14.93%
41. WESTCOR	$912,036	$8,604,094	10.60%	1.38%	17.40%	20.66%	24.74%
42. LAND CORP (CO)	$272,282	$2,563,760	10.62%	(7.73)%	9.21%	(9.50)%	25.54%
43. DREIBELBISS	$216,747	$1,681,196	12.89%	2.93%	(6.42)%	1.84%	1.07%
44. LAWYERS	$89,456,441	$624,640,813	14.32%	11.06%	11.29%	9.90%	8.96%
45. TITLE IC AMERICA	$211,989	$1,476,906	14.35%	56.85%	32.86%	8.88%	12.71%
46. NATIONAL LAND	$67,550	$427,473	15.80%	18.12%	66.41%	18.75%	71.18%
47. NORTH AMERICAN	$2,424,736	$14,811,942	16.37%	31.73%	27.27%	28.99%	36.52%
48. COMMONWEALTH LAND	$79,989,583	$454,485,229	17.60%	14.46%	13.48%	13.64%	11.60%
49. CHICAGO TIC	$194,183,381	$987,304,028	19.67%	10.47%	18.04%	11.23%	9.15%
50. CT ATTORNEYS	$4,086,369	$20,531,254	19.90%	27.28%	10.14%	9.24%	5.20%
51. COMMONWEALTH LAND (NJ)	$1,900,138	$9,532,417	19.93%	21.83%	7.95%	9.52%	3.45%
52. NATIONAL ATTORNEYS	$267,150	$1,337,094	19.98%	9.08%	1.92%	5.09%	10.15%
53. FIDELITY NATIONAL	$105,973,212	$528,798,574	20.04%	12.13%	20.78%	22.16%	23.62%
54. FARMERS NATIONAL	$68,819	$343,096	20.06%	1.07%	--	--	--
55. TITLE RESOURCES	$2,723,053	$13,412,928	20.30%	21.46%	13.71%	16.49%	13.15%
56. TICOR	$31,901,301	$155,953,152	20.46%	15.19%	15.67%	18.07%	19.69%
57. WASHINGTON TIC	$433,920	$2,096,977	20.69%	18.57%	3.71%	14.67%	6.13%
58. INVESTORS TIC	$8,975,058	$40,363,951	22.24%	17.48%	13.50%	17.84%	13.70%
59. DAKOTA HOMESTEAD	$251,953	$1,081,612	23.29%	18.81%	39.15%	(7.25)%	8.35%
60. PACIFIC NORTHWEST	$1,737,205	$7,437,407	23.36%	17.08%	21.46%	23.29%	48.11%
61. FIRST AMERICAN (KS)	$756,653	$3,126,928	24.20%	20.12%	37.42%	26.89%	21.30%
62. AMERICAN GUARANTY	$127,491	$523,709	24.34%	16.43%	36.28%	1.76%	1.02%
63. T.A. TITLE	$544,743	$2,197,253	24.79%	13.24%	4.00%	14.42%	3.03%
64. CONESTOGA	$991,906	$3,747,887	26.47%	8.62%	21.32%	37.76%	7.98%
65. GUARANTEE T&T	$1,575,079	$5,914,509	26.63%	31.55%	34.53%	28.80%	17.36%
66. FIRST AMERICAN TIC	$374,613,626	$1,382,720,921	27.09%	13.70%	13.27%	10.81%	11.85%
67. SECURITY TG (BALTIMORE)	$1,643,655	$5,982,732	27.47%	7.16%	35.45%	7.16%	13.16%
68. TRANSNATION	$36,073,083	$120,964,166	29.82%	17.37%	9.91%	10.23%	9.21%
69. ALAMO	$4,542,653	$14,772,702	30.75%	14.03%	15.89%	15.94%	13.74%
70. NORTHEAST INVESTORS	$149,328	$467,861	31.92%	6.45%	11.09%	(1.25)%	0.97%
71. OLD REPUBLIC NATIONAL	$56,386,474	$176,149,542	32.01%	28.79%	26.99%	20.05%	18.42%
72. SOUTHERN TI CORP	$3,737,322	$11,552,387	32.35%	18.29%	7.88%	8.89%	7.35%
73. STEWART TGC	$131,848,241	$399,836,214	32.98%	23.80%	21.95%	23.25%	18.43%
74. UNITED GENERAL	$27,244,717	$80,914,366	33.67%	13.87%	25.24%	24.75%	25.03%
75. ATTORNEYS TIF (FL)	$44,278,625	$119,351,849	37.10%	15.63%	13.86%	7.31%	12.42%
76. NATIONAL OF NY	$1,062,613	$2,519,566	42.17%	311.90%	(844.48)%	54.56%	12.19%
77. MANITO	$39,324	$92,235	42.63%	13.93%	3.70%	(58.90)%	20.19%
78. SECURITY UNION	$10,051,219	$23,315,421	43.11%	17.35%	18.10%	9.58%	7.37%
79. MISSISSIPPI VALLEY	$3,445,735	$7,498,395	45.95%	15.25%	36.36%	(3.43)%	27.03%
80. OHIO BAR	$1,445,381	$2,825,658	51.15%	15.66%	(37.03)%	(2.18)%	82.44%
81. NATIONS OF NY	$471,332	$895,124	52.66%	26.07%	10.28%	66.23%	117.36%
82. NEW JERSEY TIC	$1,216,094	$2,192,862	55.46%	32.20%	20.03%	38.32%	28.30%
83. OLD REPUBLIC GENERAL	$8,609,260	$15,384,796	55.96%	25.13%	20.47%	20.73%	40.15%
84. ALLIANT	$974,113	$1,690,289	57.63%	2.66%	0.00%	--	--
85. GENERAL T&T	$457,564	$667,906	68.51%	60.19%	14.11%	8.29%	9.23%
86. TICOR (FL)	$24,844,213	$29,607,675	83.91%	32.73%	28.99%	17.71%	15.99%
87. GUARANTEE	$873,275	$924,136	94.50%	130.77%	27.07%	2.55%	32.77%
88. UNITED CAPITAL	$8,465,810	$8,902,051	95.10%	42.72%	13.27%	11.95%	4.26%
89. TRANSUNION NATIONAL	$1,156,259	$975,686	118.51%	103.68%	201.09%	48.20%	27.97%
90. ALLIANCE	$66,580	$53,500	124.45%	87.45%	(102.58)%	124.14%	29.27%
91. BRIDGE	$180,404	$19,195	939.85%	396.84%	214.08%	388.26%	2.25%
COMPOSITE	$1,296,969,372	$5,770,563,008	22.48%	14.06%	15.41%	13.17%	11.98%
AVERAGE	$14,252,411	$63,412,780	22.47%				

5

A.5 Operating Expense Ratio

COMPANY	2007 OPERATING EXPENSE	A.2 - TOTAL OPERATING INCOME	2007 OPERATING EXPENSE RATIO	2006 OPERATING EXPENSE RATIO	2005 OPERATING EXPENSE RATIO	2004 OPERATING EXPENSE RATIO	2003 OPERATING EXPENSE RATIO
1. COLUMBIAN NATIONAL	$139,316	$0	--	162.05%	96.83%	92.50%	90.62%
2. OLYMPIC	$19,633	$0	--	--	--	--	--
3. MASON COUNTY	$7,538	$0	--	--	--	--	--
4. PUBLIC	$7,247	$0	--	--	--	--	--
5. MASSACHUSETTS TIC	$47,343	($254)	--	1,447.45%	2,588.72%	2,576.04%	--
6. OLD REPUBLIC GENERAL	$3,032,226	$15,384,796	19.71%	21.31%	17.73%	15.86%	13.85%
7. NATIONS OF NY	$297,817	$895,124	33.27%	36.35%	43.57%	76.41%	91.81%
8. PENN ATTORNEYS	$1,173,159	$1,823,123	64.35%	69.73%	62.77%	64.79%	52.42%
9. TITLE GUARANTY DIV (IA)	$2,481,484	$3,648,197	68.02%	54.88%	46.97%	30.86%	24.65%
10. AMERICAN SECURITY	$2,300,113	$2,940,698	78.22%	71.01%	73.17%	65.57%	71.59%
11. FIRST AMERICAN T&T	$20,447,786	$25,404,401	80.49%	79.27%	78.55%	76.36%	69.91%
12. CHICAGO T&T	$38,026,337	$46,037,947	82.60%	93.90%	90.14%	46.37%	82.81%
13. INVESTORS TIC	$55,433,642	$66,853,213	82.92%	79.67%	76.29%	75.74%	77.07%
14. CHICAGO TIC (OR)	$28,329,828	$33,259,216	85.18%	83.01%	79.38%	78.06%	82.79%
15. TICOR	$327,993,550	$377,091,400	86.98%	87.33%	89.14%	90.56%	86.13%
16. COMMONWEALTH LAND (NJ)	$31,189,583	$35,399,052	88.11%	86.02%	82.03%	78.90%	76.17%
17. FIRST AMERICAN (OR)	$78,334,284	$88,512,105	88.50%	82.30%	81.22%	85.51%	79.19%
18. GUARANTEE	$2,009,451	$2,262,039	88.83%	92.57%	111.55%	88.26%	92.86%
19. CHICAGO TIC	$1,874,565,198	$2,108,437,310	88.91%	88.02%	87.63%	86.58%	83.43%
20. FIRST AMERICAN (KS)	$12,754,452	$14,338,022	88.96%	91.40%	91.95%	84.58%	87.27%
21. FIDELITY NATIONAL	$1,221,068,915	$1,369,360,612	89.17%	90.23%	89.95%	90.44%	89.63%
22. OHIO BAR	$11,571,122	$12,974,760	89.18%	89.61%	90.06%	91.11%	91.42%
23. COMMONWEALTH LAND	$1,083,516,820	$1,214,894,310	89.19%	85.16%	90.47%	91.17%	90.00%
24. CENSTAR	$33,881,989	$37,915,111	89.23%	90.53%	87.85%	87.30%	--
25. STEWART TIC	$154,836,415	$172,582,288	89.72%	93.10%	89.75%	92.35%	92.65%
26. NORTH AMERICAN	$98,201,775	$109,101,307	90.01%	94.73%	93.42%	93.38%	93.10%
27. COMMERCE	$38,400,755	$42,512,147	90.33%	91.29%	92.44%	93.69%	93.71%
28. PACIFIC NORTHWEST	$54,680,163	$60,167,709	90.88%	92.38%	95.42%	95.37%	98.51%
29. LAND CORP (CO)	$18,055,061	$19,814,055	91.12%	91.16%	91.38%	90.22%	91.41%
30. WESTERN NATIONAL	$413,236	$453,266	91.17%	106.54%	94.01%	101.94%	96.23%
31. TITLE RESOURCES	$94,876,281	$103,117,424	92.01%	91.15%	91.16%	92.08%	92.07%
32. UNITED CAPITAL	$56,853,636	$61,768,602	92.04%	91.67%	95.08%	95.23%	94.62%
33. FIRST AMERICAN TIC	$3,343,519,077	$3,630,841,157	92.09%	92.13%	91.78%	93.30%	91.55%
34. SEAGATE	$175,520	$190,389	92.19%	111.58%	105.63%	97.64%	90.47%
35. FIRST AMERICAN (NY)	$251,130,486	$271,881,908	92.37%	94.17%	96.14%	95.78%	94.77%
36. OLD REPUBLIC NATIONAL	$713,256,104	$770,478,042	92.57%	91.59%	91.77%	92.40%	93.51%
37. NATIONAL OF NY	$10,390,746	$11,194,386	92.82%	--	--	88.47%	89.02%
38. ARKANSAS TIC	$7,549,382	$8,079,115	93.44%	91.18%	92.74%	90.32%	87.92%
39. MISSISSIPPI VALLEY	$23,753,787	$25,410,166	93.48%	92.57%	94.25%	94.49%	90.10%
40. SECURITY UNION	$62,327,142	$66,621,757	93.55%	89.88%	88.35%	86.91%	91.70%
41. ALAMO	$89,228,814	$94,868,348	94.06%	92.68%	92.53%	93.61%	96.35%
42. CT ATTORNEYS	$51,011,296	$54,095,917	94.30%	95.12%	92.63%	91.02%	86.45%
43. TITLE G&TC	$1,589,008	$1,683,746	94.37%	86.73%	90.48%	86.75%	88.18%
44. STEWART TGC	$1,416,388,898	$1,499,604,706	94.45%	92.81%	91.97%	94.42%	94.80%
45. DAKOTA HOMESTEAD	$3,823,957	$4,034,545	94.78%	96.07%	99.16%	94.73%	84.59%
46. LAWYERS	$1,256,547,871	$1,324,909,286	94.84%	92.66%	92.91%	93.39%	90.60%
47. AMERICAN EAGLE	$7,201,062	$7,538,338	95.53%	96.24%	92.95%	93.00%	72.84%
48. T.A. TITLE	$16,101,842	$16,852,621	95.55%	93.49%	90.90%	92.56%	86.96%
49. NORTHEAST INVESTORS	$2,307,627	$2,403,559	96.01%	100.54%	96.00%	92.90%	93.10%
50. FIRST AMERICAN TRANS	$1,382,233	$1,432,315	96.50%	74.36%	87.79%	74.98%	98.43%
51. SIERRA	$1,862,277	$1,923,075	96.84%	--	--	--	--
52. SOUTHERN TI CORP	$51,859,442	$53,404,248	97.11%	96.28%	94.28%	93.63%	90.93%
53. GUARANTEE T&T	$14,702,319	$14,997,723	98.03%	97.19%	98.38%	95.03%	93.76%
54. PORT LAWRENCE	$6,680,601	$6,785,918	98.45%	100.42%	91.06%	85.65%	75.99%
55. ATTORNEYS TIF (FL)	$355,763,865	$360,555,798	98.67%	89.36%	87.36%	87.86%	86.90%
56. AMERICAN GUARANTY	$3,302,317	$3,338,958	98.90%	96.36%	93.21%	84.16%	72.12%
57. UNITED GENERAL	$325,885,020	$329,196,284	98.99%	101.77%	98.22%	95.01%	94.70%
58. ALLIANT	$13,452,669	$13,587,506	99.01%	103.98%	325.48%	--	--
59. WASHINGTON TIC	$15,093,282	$15,187,593	99.38%	100.53%	98.13%	98.79%	98.97%
60. SECURITY TG (BALTIMORE)	$23,029,482	$23,148,068	99.49%	95.94%	96.67%	94.35%	95.46%
61. STEWART (OR)	$9,799,809	$9,836,516	99.63%	101.17%	101.76%	101.12%	101.16%
62. TICOR (FL)	$93,268,161	$93,604,625	99.64%	93.79%	89.48%	90.37%	89.08%
63. MONROE	$19,752,264	$19,801,051	99.75%	101.01%	95.58%	94.33%	90.18%
64. TRANSUNION TIC	$1,551,230	$1,553,321	99.87%	95.79%	92.75%	98.07%	96.65%
65. NEW JERSEY TIC	$17,322,234	$17,330,838	99.95%	97.35%	96.82%	95.87%	95.51%
66. ATTORNEYS TGF (IL)	$20,168,882	$20,161,742	100.04%	86.75%	82.70%	92.54%	84.70%
67. TITLE IC AMERICA	$11,629,474	$11,614,194	100.13%	96.09%	91.29%	100.31%	93.41%
68. ATTORNEYS TGF (CO)	$13,860,124	$13,791,525	100.50%	101.56%	98.75%	90.76%	97.79%
69. WESTCOR	$52,354,461	$51,967,673	100.74%	99.12%	98.58%	97.34%	96.44%
70. NATIONAL ATTORNEYS	$1,347,650	$1,337,094	100.79%	95.40%	96.70%	83.06%	80.91%
71. ARSENAL	$1,610,858	$1,589,223	101.36%	93.91%	90.82%	92.89%	--
72. TRANSUNION NATIONAL	$3,722,389	$3,636,583	102.36%	115.79%	105.99%	110.75%	93.31%
73. CONESTOGA	$14,545,453	$14,176,902	102.60%	100.60%	99.01%	96.35%	89.20%
74. TRANSNATION	$313,225,196	$299,589,827	104.55%	98.20%	91.50%	89.35%	87.16%
75. MANITO	$784,503	$740,110	106.00%	102.93%	99.26%	101.46%	92.85%
76. AMERICAN LAND & AIRCRAFT	$641,622	$594,713	107.89%	102.58%	103.53%	101.09%	100.65%
77. EQUITY NATIONAL	$2,233,086	$2,068,352	107.96%	104.36%	101.25%	--	--
78. NATIONAL	$4,030,224	$3,704,331	108.80%	111.06%	114.06%	113.97%	104.41%
79. DREIBELBISS	$1,933,548	$1,763,918	109.62%	107.39%	105.35%	100.01%	92.93%
80. TITLEDGE	$192,445	$174,297	110.41%	--	--	--	--
81. GUARDIAN NATIONAL	$4,038,810	$3,594,472	112.36%	101.19%	99.07%	98.77%	88.79%
82. GENERAL T&T	$3,178,262	$2,780,740	114.30%	99.10%	94.75%	96.09%	95.50%
83. NATIONAL LAND	$3,171,572	$2,502,043	126.76%	112.59%	90.11%	108.39%	80.26%
84. MASON	$1,927,284	$1,519,252	126.86%	167.80%	--	--	--
85. LAND TIC (ST LOUIS)	$2,949,475	$2,248,990	131.15%	84.62%	95.93%	63.13%	75.95%
86. FARMERS NATIONAL	$1,099,230	$803,193	136.86%	214.02%	--	--	--
87. FOUNDERS	$308,989	$221,713	139.36%	139.29%	153.99%	--	--
88. K.E.L.	$777,331	$554,387	140.21%	--	--	--	--
89. MISSISSIPPI GUARANTY	$432,481	$298,973	144.66%	97.02%	112.48%	112.21%	91.26%
90. ALLIANCE	$117,344	$54,338	215.95%	477.28%	95.82%	90.80%	84.46%
91. BRIDGE	$108,904	$19,541	557.31%	207.88%	130.51%	141.05%	122.65%
COMPOSITE	$14,016,295,576	$15,224,827,929	92.06%	90.97%	90.75%	91.11%	89.74%
AVERAGE	$154,025,226	$167,305,801	92.06%				

5

A.6 Combined Ratio

COMPANY	2007 A.3 - LOSS RATIO	2007 A.5 - OPERATING EXPENSE RATIO	2007 COMBINED RATIO	2006 COMBINED RATIO	2005 COMBINED RATIO	2004 COMBINED RATIO	2003 COMBINED RATIO
1. MASON COUNTY	--	--	--	--	--	--	--
2. OLYMPIC	--	--	--	--	--	--	--
3. PUBLIC	--	--	--	--	--	--	--
4. COLUMBIAN NATIONAL	--	--	--	162.05%	108.70%	121.85%	94.87%
5. MASSACHUSETTS TIC	0.00%	--	--	1,447.45%	2,588.72%	2,576.04%	--
6. PENN ATTORNEYS	2.47%	64.35%	66.81%	74.39%	71.61%	61.14%	53.25%
7. TITLE GUARANTY DIV (IA)	0.00%	68.02%	68.02%	59.62%	53.94%	33.35%	25.83%
8. OLD REPUBLIC GENERAL	55.96%	19.71%	75.67%	46.43%	38.20%	36.58%	54.00%
9. WESTERN NATIONAL	(14.51)%	91.17%	76.66%	134.26%	92.75%	102.93%	97.84%
10. AMERICAN SECURITY	0.08%	78.22%	78.29%	72.98%	73.17%	65.57%	71.76%
11. FIRST AMERICAN T&T	0.86%	80.49%	81.35%	80.46%	80.63%	78.61%	71.60%
12. CHICAGO T&T	0.00%	82.60%	82.60%	93.90%	90.14%	46.37%	82.81%
13. NATIONS OF NY	52.66%	33.27%	85.93%	62.43%	53.84%	142.60%	208.93%
14. CHICAGO TIC (OR)	1.97%	85.18%	87.15%	83.75%	82.41%	82.01%	84.59%
15. CENSTAR	0.94%	89.23%	90.17%	90.77%	87.97%	87.30%	--
16. COMMERCE	1.07%	90.33%	91.40%	93.43%	93.57%	95.10%	94.69%
17. FIRST AMERICAN (OR)	3.30%	88.50%	91.80%	84.58%	84.18%	86.69%	80.76%
18. SEAGATE	0.00%	92.19%	92.19%	111.58%	105.63%	97.64%	90.47%
19. NORTH AMERICAN	2.22%	90.01%	92.23%	97.37%	95.71%	95.78%	96.40%
20. LAND CORP (CO)	1.37%	91.12%	92.50%	90.20%	92.37%	89.14%	93.92%
21. STEWART TIC	3.17%	89.72%	92.89%	97.02%	91.90%	95.15%	96.09%
22. COMMONWEALTH LAND (NJ)	5.37%	88.11%	93.48%	92.09%	84.80%	82.69%	77.63%
23. PACIFIC NORTHWEST	2.89%	90.88%	93.77%	94.36%	97.33%	97.52%	100.53%
24. FIRST AMERICAN (KS)	5.28%	88.96%	94.23%	95.01%	98.52%	89.56%	91.96%
25. TITLE G&TC	0.09%	94.37%	94.46%	86.73%	90.58%	86.94%	88.73%
26. TITLE RESOURCES	2.64%	92.01%	94.65%	93.99%	93.10%	94.12%	93.69%
27. ARKANSAS TIC	1.93%	93.44%	95.37%	94.74%	93.54%	98.92%	92.12%
28. FIRST AMERICAN TRANS	(1.12)%	96.50%	95.38%	86.72%	90.40%	80.79%	99.53%
29. TICOR	8.46%	86.98%	95.44%	93.41%	95.40%	96.54%	93.70%
30. COMMONWEALTH LAND	6.58%	89.19%	95.77%	90.92%	95.02%	95.58%	93.78%
31. AMERICAN EAGLE	0.41%	95.53%	95.93%	96.79%	94.38%	94.25%	75.38%
32. FIRST AMERICAN (NY)	3.67%	92.37%	96.04%	97.53%	98.57%	98.74%	98.77%
33. INVESTORS TIC	13.43%	82.92%	96.34%	90.64%	84.53%	86.42%	84.46%
34. SIERRA	0.00%	96.84%	96.84%	--	--	--	--
35. FIDELITY NATIONAL	7.74%	89.17%	96.91%	94.63%	96.90%	96.78%	95.21%
36. CHICAGO TIC	9.21%	88.91%	98.12%	92.35%	94.49%	90.95%	87.34%
37. T.A. TITLE	3.23%	95.55%	98.78%	95.99%	91.77%	95.94%	87.77%
38. ALAMO	4.79%	94.06%	98.84%	94.90%	95.25%	96.10%	98.31%
39. PORT LAWRENCE	0.52%	98.45%	98.96%	98.62%	92.10%	86.07%	77.11%
40. STEWART (OR)	0.00%	99.63%	99.63%	101.17%	101.76%	101.12%	101.16%
41. OLD REPUBLIC NATIONAL	7.32%	92.57%	99.89%	98.16%	97.47%	96.48%	96.97%
42. OHIO BAR	11.14%	89.18%	100.32%	92.57%	82.78%	90.72%	106.46%
43. DAKOTA HOMESTEAD	6.24%	94.78%	101.03%	99.53%	106.72%	93.01%	87.08%
44. ARSENAL	0.04%	101.36%	101.40%	94.02%	91.04%	92.89%	--
45. LAWYERS	6.75%	94.84%	101.59%	97.62%	97.91%	97.46%	94.39%
46. CT ATTORNEYS	7.55%	94.30%	101.85%	105.32%	96.43%	94.44%	88.46%
47. TITLE IC AMERICA	1.83%	100.13%	101.96%	105.56%	96.42%	101.65%	95.35%
48. NORTHEAST INVESTORS	6.21%	96.01%	102.22%	101.80%	98.13%	92.67%	93.28%
49. WASHINGTON TIC	2.86%	99.38%	102.24%	102.73%	98.61%	100.76%	99.81%
50. NATIONAL OF NY	9.49%	92.82%	102.31%	--	--	110.73%	93.30%
51. FIRST AMERICAN TIC	10.32%	92.09%	102.40%	96.86%	96.14%	96.87%	95.45%
52. WESTCOR	1.76%	100.74%	102.50%	99.36%	100.59%	98.64%	98.03%
53. MONROE	2.92%	99.75%	102.67%	102.91%	98.23%	96.35%	90.76%
54. AMERICAN GUARANTY	3.82%	98.90%	102.72%	98.74%	98.35%	85.86%	73.11%
55. ATTORNEYS TGF (CO)	2.59%	100.50%	103.09%	104.27%	104.69%	97.11%	98.85%
56. STEWART TGC	8.79%	94.45%	103.24%	98.37%	96.73%	98.68%	97.85%
57. SOUTHERN TI CORP	7.00%	97.11%	104.11%	100.35%	96.30%	96.24%	93.52%
58. TRANSUNION TIC	5.19%	99.87%	105.06%	103.65%	102.09%	101.33%	97.63%
59. UNITED CAPITAL	13.71%	92.04%	105.75%	97.24%	96.66%	96.22%	94.95%
60. ALLIANT	7.17%	99.01%	106.18%	104.29%	325.48%	--	--
61. SECURITY TG (BALTIMORE)	7.10%	99.49%	106.59%	97.47%	104.07%	95.88%	98.29%
62. NEW JERSEY TIC	7.02%	99.95%	106.97%	101.56%	99.59%	101.50%	99.71%
63. MISSISSIPPI VALLEY	13.56%	93.48%	107.04%	97.16%	104.87%	93.54%	98.06%
64. UNITED GENERAL	8.28%	98.99%	107.27%	104.83%	103.80%	98.88%	97.82%
65. EQUITY NATIONAL	0.00%	107.96%	107.96%	104.36%	101.25%	--	--
66. GUARANTEE T&T	10.50%	98.03%	108.53%	107.69%	108.03%	102.84%	100.06%
67. NATIONAL	(0.24)%	108.80%	108.55%	112.68%	114.06%	113.97%	104.49%
68. SECURITY UNION	15.09%	93.55%	108.64%	96.39%	96.27%	91.91%	95.47%
69. AMERICAN LAND & AIRCRAFT	0.99%	107.89%	108.87%	103.69%	103.53%	101.09%	100.65%
70. ATTORNEYS TGF (IL)	8.98%	100.04%	109.02%	97.79%	93.80%	107.03%	97.89%
71. CONESTOGA	7.00%	102.60%	109.60%	102.65%	104.32%	105.96%	91.30%
72. GUARDIAN NATIONAL	(2.12)%	112.36%	110.24%	109.74%	99.61%	101.93%	91.37%
73. TITLEDGE	0.00%	110.41%	110.41%	--	--	--	--
74. ATTORNEYS TIF (FL)	12.28%	98.67%	110.95%	94.60%	92.05%	90.41%	91.54%
75. MANITO	5.31%	106.00%	111.31%	104.67%	99.76%	94.11%	95.64%
76. TRANSNATION	12.04%	104.55%	116.59%	105.31%	95.94%	93.58%	92.34%
77. NATIONAL ATTORNEYS	19.98%	100.79%	120.77%	104.48%	98.62%	88.16%	91.06%
78. DREIBELBISS	12.29%	109.62%	121.90%	110.15%	99.38%	101.65%	93.95%
79. TICOR (FL)	26.54%	99.64%	126.18%	103.72%	97.50%	98.03%	93.27%
80. GUARANTEE	38.61%	88.83%	127.44%	140.88%	120.87%	90.01%	116.45%
81. MASON	0.80%	126.86%	127.66%	167.80%	--	--	--
82. NATIONAL LAND	2.70%	126.76%	129.46%	117.06%	114.83%	114.73%	108.51%
83. GENERAL T&T	16.45%	114.30%	130.75%	109.10%	96.95%	97.29%	96.75%
84. LAND TIC (ST LOUIS)	0.00%	131.15%	131.15%	84.62%	95.93%	63.13%	75.95%
85. TRANSUNION NATIONAL	31.80%	102.36%	134.15%	141.55%	149.85%	122.46%	100.08%
86. FOUNDERS	0.00%	139.36%	139.36%	139.29%	153.99%	--	--
87. K.E.L.	0.00%	140.21%	140.21%	--	--	--	--
88. MISSISSIPPI GUARANTY	0.00%	144.66%	144.66%	97.02%	112.48%	112.21%	91.26%
89. FARMERS NATIONAL	8.57%	136.86%	145.43%	214.38%	--	--	--
90. ALLIANCE	122.53%	215.95%	338.48%	563.37%	(6.77)%	132.60%	92.38%
91. BRIDGE	923.21%	557.31%	1,480.52%	531.65%	234.99%	318.10%	123.29%
COMPOSITE	8.52%	92.06%	100.58%	95.94%	95.92%	95.39%	93.67%

5

A.7 Operating Profit Margin

COMPANY	2007 OPERATING PROFIT	2007 NET OPERATING INCOME	2007 OPERATING PROFIT MARGIN	2006 OPERATING PROFIT MARGIN	2005 OPERATING PROFIT MARGIN	2004 OPERATING PROFIT MARGIN	2003 OPERATING PROFIT MARGIN
1. OLD REPUBLIC GENERAL	$12,352,570	$15,384,796	80.29%	78.69%	82.27%	84.14%	86.15%
2. AMERICAN SECURITY	$640,585	$834,100	76.80%	79.89%	70.05%	75.67%	75.80%
3. PACIFIC NORTHWEST	$5,487,546	$7,437,407	73.78%	65.85%	51.50%	50.28%	35.53%
4. NORTH AMERICAN	$10,899,532	$14,811,942	73.59%	63.24%	78.20%	79.89%	76.37%
5. COMMERCE	$4,111,392	$5,837,840	70.43%	67.80%	69.01%	69.04%	55.43%
6. LAND CORP (CO)	$1,758,994	$2,563,760	68.61%	71.56%	80.41%	86.25%	87.64%
7. CENSTAR	$4,083,122	$6,116,752	66.75%	59.44%	64.27%	60.30%	--
8. NATIONS OF NY	$597,307	$895,124	66.73%	63.65%	56.45%	23.61%	8.21%
9. TITLE RESOURCES	$8,241,143	$13,412,928	61.44%	66.89%	62.44%	63.90%	64.64%
10. UNITED CAPITAL	$4,914,966	$8,902,051	55.21%	63.86%	41.38%	57.20%	70.85%
11. FIRST AMERICAN (KS)	$1,583,570	$3,126,928	50.64%	47.92%	45.85%	83.26%	57.86%
12. OHIO BAR	$1,403,638	$2,825,658	49.67%	54.92%	50.52%	50.28%	47.01%
13. COMMONWEALTH LAND (NJ)	$4,209,469	$9,532,417	44.16%	50.23%	51.71%	52.93%	56.31%
14. ALAMO	$5,639,534	$14,772,702	38.18%	46.20%	43.67%	40.87%	25.59%
15. WESTERN NATIONAL	$40,030	$110,757	36.14%	(43.62)%	41.83%	(38.86)%	64.23%
16. PENN ATTORNEYS	$649,964	$1,823,123	35.65%	30.27%	37.23%	35.21%	47.58%
17. T.A. TITLE	$750,779	$2,197,253	34.17%	34.45%	41.78%	31.75%	49.29%
18. OLD REPUBLIC NATIONAL	$57,221,938	$176,149,542	32.48%	36.83%	39.00%	37.34%	34.55%
19. TITLE GUARANTY DIV (IA)	$1,166,713	$3,648,197	31.98%	45.12%	53.03%	69.14%	75.35%
20. NATIONAL OF NY	$803,640	$2,519,566	31.90%	29.84%	--	28.26%	31.27%
21. TICOR	$49,097,850	$155,953,152	31.48%	31.66%	27.17%	28.51%	36.09%
22. ARKANSAS TIC	$529,733	$1,714,847	30.89%	39.20%	28.29%	37.01%	42.91%
23. COMMONWEALTH LAND	$131,377,490	$454,485,229	28.91%	37.24%	28.24%	27.29%	30.67%
24. INVESTORS TIC	$11,419,571	$40,363,951	28.29%	32.39%	38.87%	40.52%	42.54%
25. FIDELITY NATIONAL	$148,291,697	$528,798,574	28.04%	26.96%	30.04%	33.43%	43.88%
26. GUARANTEE	$252,588	$924,136	27.33%	20.11%	(33.51)%	17.07%	9.92%
27. STEWART TIC	$17,745,873	$67,294,473	26.37%	20.37%	29.38%	22.70%	29.03%
28. SIERRA	$60,798	$251,380	24.19%	--	--	--	--
29. CHICAGO TIC	$233,872,112	$987,304,028	23.69%	28.97%	32.51%	34.49%	38.74%
30. CHICAGO TIC (OR)	$4,929,388	$21,971,311	22.44%	28.05%	32.60%	32.77%	28.61%
31. MISSISSIPPI VALLEY	$1,656,379	$7,498,395	22.09%	24.71%	19.70%	19.81%	33.60%
32. STEWART TGC	$83,215,808	$399,836,214	20.81%	30.80%	37.04%	30.44%	31.47%
33. FIRST AMERICAN TIC	$287,322,080	$1,382,720,921	20.78%	22.82%	25.03%	20.28%	25.69%
34. FIRST AMERICAN T&T	$4,956,615	$24,177,001	20.50%	21.84%	22.58%	24.89%	31.68%
35. NORTHEAST INVESTORS	$95,932	$467,861	20.50%	(2.75)%	20.82%	37.51%	37.24%
36. DAKOTA HOMESTEAD	$210,588	$1,081,612	19.47%	21.37%	4.36%	22.27%	51.82%
37. SEAGATE	$14,869	$78,735	18.88%	(34.37)%	(16.89)%	7.09%	28.58%
38. SECURITY UNION	$4,294,615	$23,315,421	18.42%	26.97%	26.63%	25.11%	16.24%
39. CHICAGO T&T	$8,011,610	$46,037,947	17.40%	6.10%	9.86%	53.63%	17.19%
40. CT ATTORNEYS	$3,084,621	$20,531,254	15.02%	13.04%	19.69%	24.27%	35.04%
41. FIRST AMERICAN (NY)	$20,751,422	$150,822,195	13.76%	11.70%	7.95%	10.31%	13.20%
42. SOUTHERN TI CORP	$1,544,806	$11,552,387	13.37%	16.73%	22.29%	21.68%	25.77%
43. FIRST AMERICAN (OR)	$10,177,821	$76,723,081	13.27%	19.51%	20.60%	16.38%	25.92%
44. LAWYERS	$68,361,415	$624,640,813	10.94%	16.37%	16.00%	16.08%	22.23%
45. ALLIANT	$134,837	$1,690,289	7.98%	(34.14)%	(2,013.24)%	--	--
46. FIRST AMERICAN TRANS	$50,082	$695,907	7.20%	42.40%	21.76%	47.48%	3.14%
47. AMERICAN GUARANTY	$36,641	$523,709	7.00%	25.08%	47.94%	16.41%	28.81%
48. STEWART (OR)	$36,707	$615,430	5.96%	(96.68)%	(366.25)%	(99.09)%	(150.70)%
49. TITLE G&TC	$94,738	$1,683,746	5.63%	13.27%	9.52%	13.25%	11.82%
50. AMERICAN EAGLE	$337,276	$6,622,068	5.09%	4.21%	7.71%	7.63%	28.21%
51. GUARANTEE T&T	$295,404	$5,914,509	4.99%	8.45%	5.80%	18.33%	17.20%
52. WASHINGTON TIC	$94,311	$2,096,977	4.50%	(4.49)%	14.55%	9.03%	7.57%
53. UNITED GENERAL	$3,311,264	$80,914,366	4.09%	(8.00)%	8.06%	31.94%	42.53%
54. ATTORNEYS TIF (FL)	$4,791,933	$119,351,849	4.01%	31.71%	37.37%	34.84%	35.09%
55. PORT LAWRENCE	$105,317	$4,817,268	2.19%	(0.65)%	11.69%	18.11%	28.21%
56. SECURITY TG (BALTIMORE)	$118,586	$5,982,732	1.98%	19.10%	15.97%	26.40%	21.12%
57. TICOR (FL)	$336,464	$29,607,675	1.14%	20.48%	38.03%	22.26%	41.71%
58. NEW JERSEY TIC	$8,604	$2,192,862	0.39%	20.27%	22.97%	28.10%	30.27%
59. MONROE	$48,787	$13,680,455	0.36%	(1.51)%	6.66%	8.34%	13.82%
60. TRANSUNION TIC	$2,091	$1,553,321	0.13%	17.89%	43.13%	16.50%	26.85%
61. ATTORNEYS TGF (IL)	($7,140)	$20,161,742	(0.04)%	13.25%	17.30%	7.46%	15.30%
62. NATIONAL ATTORNEYS	($10,556)	$1,337,094	(0.79)%	4.60%	3.30%	16.94%	19.09%
63. TITLE IC AMERICA	($15,280)	$1,476,906	(1.03)%	23.46%	55.74%	(2.05)%	43.13%
64. ATTORNEYS TGF (CO)	($68,599)	$4,242,365	(1.62)%	(5.58)%	4.87%	31.39%	8.15%
65. WESTCOR	($386,788)	$8,604,094	(4.50)%	5.01%	12.31%	42.37%	55.51%
66. ARSENAL	($21,635)	$335,910	(6.44)%	30.29%	51.02%	36.36%	--
67. EQUITY NATIONAL	($164,734)	$2,068,352	(7.96)%	(4.36)%	(1.25)%	--	--
68. TRANSUNION NATIONAL	($85,806)	$975,686	(8.79)%	(63.53)%	(27.45)%	(44.27)%	27.62%
69. CONESTOGA	($368,551)	$3,747,887	(9.83)%	(2.51)%	3.97%	14.35%	41.14%
70. DREIBELBISS	($169,630)	$1,681,196	(10.09)%	(7.85)%	(5.75)%	(0.01)%	7.38%
71. TRANSNATION	($13,635,369)	$120,964,166	(11.27)%	4.39%	18.98%	25.71%	22.82%
72. NATIONAL	($325,893)	$1,236,697	(26.35)%	(29.90)%	(37.81)%	(33.45)%	(9.96)%
73. AMERICAN LAND & AIRCRAFT	($46,909)	$136,495	(34.37)%	(10.96)%	(16.63)%	(4.82)%	(2.63)%
74. FOUNDERS	($87,276)	$221,713	(39.36)%	(39.29)%	(53.99)%	--	--
75. MANITO	($44,393)	$92,235	(48.13)%	(23.40)%	5.53%	(11.73)%	51.84%
76. GENERAL T&T	($397,522)	$667,906	(59.52)%	5.44%	33.70%	27.10%	33.21%
77. LAND TIC (ST LOUIS)	($700,485)	$1,107,567	(63.25)%	27.88%	45.13%	68.48%	47.53%
78. MASON	($408,032)	$516,819	(78.95)%	(258.20)%	--	--	--
79. FARMERS NATIONAL	($296,037)	$343,096	(86.28)%	(337.49)%	--	--	--
80. TITLEDGE	($18,148)	$20,542	(88.35)%	--	--	--	--
81. GUARDIAN NATIONAL	($444,338)	$470,359	(94.47)%	(10.50)%	9.77%	12.30%	70.67%
82. MISSISSIPPI GUARANTY	($133,508)	$117,696	(113.43)%	5.69%	(28.12)%	(34.92)%	20.75%
83. ALLIANCE	($63,006)	$53,500	(117.77)%	(383.25)%	4.18%	27.33%	57.45%
84. K.E.L.	($222,947)	$145,647	(153.07)%	--	--	--	--
85. NATIONAL LAND	($669,529)	$427,473	(156.62)%	(51.07)%	26.57%	(24.78)%	49.73%
86. BRIDGE	($89,363)	$19,195	(465.55)%	(132.23)%	(62.50)%	(90.02)%	(79.35)%
87. PUBLIC	($7,247)	$0	--	--	--	--	--
88. MASON COUNTY	($7,538)	$0	--	--	--	--	--
89. OLYMPIC	($19,633)	$0	--	--	--	--	--
90. MASSACHUSETTS TIC	($47,597)	($254)	--	(1,347.45)%	(2,488.72)%	(2,476.04)%	--
91. COLUMBIAN NATIONAL	($139,316)	$0	--	(335.53)%	12.31%	30.31%	33.42%
COMPOSITE	$1,208,532,353	$5,770,563,008	20.94%	25.54%	27.59%	27.36%	31.27%
AVERAGE	$13,280,575	$63,412,780	20.94%				

5

A.8 Net Investment Gain (Loss)

COMPANY	NET INVESTMENT INCOME EARNED			REALIZED GAIN (LOSS)			NET INVESTMENT GAIN (LOSS)		
	2007	2006	2006 TO 2007	2007	2006	2006 TO 2007	2007	2006	2006 TO 2007
1. ALAMO	$1,958,503	$16,895,821	(88.41)%	$920,620	($1,006,275)	--	$2,879,123	$15,889,546	(81.88)%
2. ALLIANCE	$172,226	$166,971	3.15%	$0	($1,150)	--	$172,226	$165,821	3.86%
3. ALLIANT	$116,880	$85,737	36.32%	$944	($832)	--	$117,824	$84,905	38.77%
4. AMERICAN EAGLE	$65,709	$70,066	(6.22)%	$0	$0	--	$65,709	$70,066	(6.22)%
5. AMERICAN GUARANTY	$1,553,637	$619,019	150.98%	$0	$380	(100.00)%	$1,553,637	$619,399	150.83%
6. AMERICAN LAND & AIRCRAFT	$40,829	$25,211	61.95%	$0	$0	--	$40,829	$25,211	61.95%
7. AMERICAN SECURITY	$367,143	$294,287	24.76%	$0	$0	--	$367,143	$294,287	24.76%
8. ARKANSAS TIC	$220,890	$146,892	50.38%	$0	$0	--	$220,890	$146,892	50.38%
9. ARSENAL	$25,816	$21,210	21.72%	$0	$0	--	$25,816	$21,210	21.72%
10. ATTORNEYS TGF (CO)	$45,252	$125,445	(63.93)%	$85,805	$117,823	(27.17)%	$131,057	$243,268	(46.13)%
11. ATTORNEYS TGF (IL)	$1,656,985	$1,980,334	(16.33)%	$194,964	$80	243,605.00%	$1,851,949	$1,980,414	(6.49)%
12. ATTORNEYS TIF (FL)	$7,300,683	$6,412,871	13.84%	$10,177,378	$5,374,995	89.35%	$17,478,061	$11,787,866	48.27%
13. BRIDGE	$85,682	$57,429	49.20%	$0	$0	--	$85,682	$57,429	49.20%
14. CENSTAR	$679,761	$583,066	16.58%	($1,362)	($2,675)	--	$678,399	$580,391	16.89%
15. CHICAGO T&T	$290,461,654	$351,982,067	(17.48)%	$27,093	$9,780	177.02%	$290,488,747	$351,991,847	(17.47)%
16. CHICAGO TIC	$115,113,277	$132,129,816	(12.88)%	$7,212,799	$510,834	1,311.97%	$122,326,076	$132,640,650	(7.78)%
17. CHICAGO TIC (OR)	$1,152,795	$1,545,640	(25.42)%	($1,358)	($19,229)	--	$1,151,437	$1,526,411	(24.57)%
18. COLUMBIAN NATIONAL	$38,289	$158,968	(75.91)%	$0	$14,337	(100.00)%	$38,289	$173,305	(77.91)%
19. COMMERCE	$626,185	$511,364	22.45%	$0	$0	--	$626,185	$511,364	22.45%
20. COMMONWEALTH LAND	$29,461,702	$37,159,908	(20.72)%	$3,028,893	$2,441,195	24.07%	$32,490,595	$39,601,103	(17.96)%
21. COMMONWEALTH LAND (NJ)	$1,825,496	$1,872,240	(2.50)%	$5,457	($50,240)	--	$1,830,953	$1,822,000	0.49%
22. CONESTOGA	$337,732	$323,823	4.30%	$0	$0	--	$337,732	$323,823	4.30%
23. CT ATTORNEYS	$2,404,707	$2,164,795	11.08%	$29,473	$487,379	(93.95)%	$2,434,180	$2,652,174	(8.22)%
24. DAKOTA HOMESTEAD	$79,714	$118,384	(32.66)%	$18,355	$22,066	(16.82)%	$98,069	$140,451	(30.18)%
25. DREIBELBISS	$163,001	$212,795	(23.40)%	$4,653	$24,945	(81.35)%	$167,654	$237,740	(29.48)%
26. EQUITY NATIONAL	$230,044	$600,730	(61.71)%	$0	$0	--	$230,044	$600,730	(61.71)%
27. FARMERS NATIONAL	$41,556	$36,720	13.17%	$0	$0	--	$41,556	$36,720	13.17%
28. FIDELITY NATIONAL	$36,388,258	$46,889,960	(22.40)%	$3,043,736	$4,073,215	(25.27)%	$39,431,994	$50,963,175	(22.63)%
29. FIRST AMERICAN (KS)	$351,141	$331,436	5.95%	$0	$0	--	$351,141	$331,436	5.95%
30. FIRST AMERICAN (NY)	$10,940,548	$9,984,961	9.57%	$271,625	$75,432	260.09%	$11,212,173	$10,060,393	11.45%
31. FIRST AMERICAN (OR)	$1,590,147	$1,574,581	0.99%	$168,650	$487,499	(65.41)%	$1,758,797	$2,062,080	(14.71)%
32. FIRST AMERICAN T&T	$1,107,891	$3,333,514	(66.77)%	$0	($2,842)	--	$1,107,891	$3,330,672	(66.74)%
33. FIRST AMERICAN TIC	$195,715,802	$138,508,373	41.30%	($56,889,509)	$477,533	(12,013.21)%	$138,826,293	$138,985,906	(0.11)%
34. FIRST AMERICAN TRANS	$92,479	$81,173	13.93%	$0	$0	--	$92,479	$81,173	13.93%
35. FOUNDERS	$41,264	$33,914	21.67%	$0	$0	--	$41,264	$33,914	21.67%
36. GENERAL T&T	$267,819	$248,183	7.91%	$60,573	$29,116	108.04%	$328,392	$277,299	18.43%
37. GUARANTEE	$98,999	$71,026	39.38%	$0	$2,820	(100.00)%	$98,999	$73,846	34.06%
38. GUARANTEE T&T	($2,528)	$203,721	(101.24)%	$1,760	$611,429	(99.71)%	($768)	$815,150	(100.09)%
39. GUARDIAN NATIONAL	$306,371	$191,239	60.20%	$210,417	$103,698	102.91%	$516,788	$294,937	75.22%
40. INVESTORS TIC	$4,009,684	$3,790,968	5.77%	$344,666	$363,892	(5.28)%	$4,354,350	$4,154,860	4.80%
41. K.E.L.	$55,398	--	--	$0	--	--	$55,398	--	--
42. LAND CORP (CO)	$436,317	$433,937	0.55%	$31,740	$73,639	(56.90)%	$468,057	$507,576	(7.79)%
43. LAND TIC (ST LOUIS)	$243,373	$282,641	(13.89)%	$0	$0	--	$243,373	$282,641	(13.89)%
44. LAWYERS	$22,168,287	$34,239,197	(35.25)%	$6,258,207	($3,391,158)	--	$28,426,494	$30,848,039	(7.85)%
45. MANITO	$67,685	$54,575	24.02%	$0	$0	--	$67,685	$54,575	24.02%
46. MASON	$160,175	$108,406	47.75%	$18,849	($648)	--	$179,024	$107,758	66.14%
47. MASON COUNTY	$31,231	$30,578	2.14%	$0	$0	--	$31,231	$30,578	2.14%
48. MASSACHUSETTS TIC	$57,813	$53,816	7.43%	$1,180	$27	4,270.37%	$58,993	$53,843	9.56%
49. MISSISSIPPI GUARANTY	$17,107	$11,674	46.54%	$0	$0	--	$17,107	$11,674	46.54%
50. MISSISSIPPI VALLEY	$1,900,667	$1,768,813	7.45%	$10,925	($15,392)	--	$1,911,592	$1,753,421	9.02%
51. MONROE	$503,477	$641,915	(21.57)%	$327,125	$304,355	7.48%	$830,602	$946,270	(12.22)%
52. NATIONAL	$57,222	$48,405	18.22%	$104,776	$26,631	293.44%	$161,998	$75,036	115.89%
53. NATIONAL ATTORNEYS	$86,641	$52,962	63.59%	$6,065	$12,479	(51.40)%	$92,706	$65,441	41.66%
54. NATIONAL LAND	$396,943	$249,228	59.27%	$0	$0	--	$396,943	$249,228	59.27%
55. NATIONAL OF NY	$620,283	$567,831	9.24%	$0	($710)	--	$620,283	$567,121	9.37%
56. NATIONS OF NY	$725,966	$655,842	10.69%	($1,938)	$348	(656.90)%	$724,028	$656,190	10.34%
57. NEW JERSEY TIC	$374,044	$478,432	(21.82)%	$25,114	$25,348	(0.92)%	$399,158	$503,780	(20.77)%
58. NORTH AMERICAN	$3,642,852	$1,536,845	137.03%	$0	$0	--	$3,642,852	$1,536,845	137.03%
59. NORTHEAST INVESTORS	$237,760	$222,615	6.80%	($5,920)	($193)	--	$231,840	$222,422	4.23%
60. OHIO BAR	$1,242,982	$993,664	25.09%	$2,136	$0	--	$1,245,118	$993,664	25.31%
61. OLD REPUBLIC GENERAL	$5,016,179	$4,895,722	2.46%	$35,514	$9,699	266.16%	$5,051,693	$4,905,421	2.98%
62. OLD REPUBLIC NATIONAL	$20,519,650	$20,627,301	(0.52)%	$641,585	$30,259	2,020.31%	$21,161,235	$20,657,560	2.44%
63. OLYMPIC	$10,677	$10,777	(0.93)%	$5,388	$1,352	298.52%	$16,065	$12,129	32.45%
64. PACIFIC NORTHWEST	$1,489,812	$1,210,323	23.09%	($59,411)	($33,292)	--	$1,430,401	$1,177,031	21.53%
65. PENN ATTORNEYS	$459,407	$411,456	11.65%	$0	$0	--	$459,407	$411,456	11.65%
66. PORT LAWRENCE	$1,071,905	$1,457,228	(26.44)%	($176,554)	$2,354	(7,600.17)%	$895,351	$1,459,582	(38.66)%
67. PUBLIC	$35,090	$17,752	97.67%	$0	$0	--	$35,090	$17,752	97.67%
68. SEAGATE	$24,229	$22,298	8.66%	$0	$0	--	$24,229	$22,298	8.66%
69. SECURITY TG (BALTIMORE)	$493,989	$475,889	3.80%	($33,925)	($73,791)	--	$460,064	$402,098	14.42%
70. SECURITY UNION	$7,368,227	$7,650,952	(3.70)%	$868,864	$343,308	153.09%	$8,237,091	$7,994,260	3.04%
71. SIERRA	$140,652	$72,664	93.56%	$0	$0	--	$140,652	$72,664	93.56%
72. SOUTHERN TI CORP	$913,640	$766,178	19.25%	$8,609	$19,624	(56.13)%	$922,249	$785,802	17.36%
73. STEWART (OR)	$175,981	$133,573	31.75%	$0	$0	--	$175,981	$133,573	31.75%
74. STEWART TGC	$28,137,696	$20,853,478	34.93%	$3,445,843	$2,267,570	51.96%	$31,583,539	$23,121,048	36.60%
75. STEWART TIC	$5,574,578	$2,208,994	152.36%	$8,233	($236,502)	--	$5,582,811	$1,972,492	183.03%
76. T.A. TITLE	$516,884	$626,062	(17.44)%	$475,814	$162,155	193.43%	$992,698	$788,217	25.94%
77. TICOR	$10,885,620	$26,511,072	(58.94)%	($5,044,091)	$1,396,262	(461.26)%	$5,841,529	$27,907,334	(79.07)%
78. TICOR (FL)	$4,039,640	$4,772,056	(15.35)%	$84,093	$269,170	(68.76)%	$4,123,733	$5,041,226	(18.20)%
79. TITLE G&TC	$38,802	$18,997	104.25%	$0	$0	--	$38,802	$18,997	104.25%
80. TITLE GUARANTY DIV (IA)	$0	$0	--	$0	$0	--	$0	$0	--
81. TITLE IC AMERICA	$638,482	$626,911	1.85%	$1,835	$86,468	(97.88)%	$640,317	$713,379	(10.24)%
82. TITLE RESOURCES	$1,697,987	$1,398,860	21.38%	$0	$319,023	(100.00)%	$1,697,987	$1,717,883	(1.16)%
83. TITLEDGE	$28,862	--	--	$0	--	--	$28,862	--	--
84. TRANSNATION	$6,656,185	$9,379,014	(29.03)%	$494,234	($1,363,058)	--	$7,150,419	$8,015,956	(10.80)%
85. TRANSUNION NATIONAL	$650,881	$403,157	61.45%	$0	$0	--	$650,881	$403,157	61.45%
86. TRANSUNION TIC	$304,066	$143,142	112.42%	$10,850	($1,448)	--	$314,916	$141,694	122.25%
87. UNITED CAPITAL	$2,332,794	$2,011,901	15.95%	($108,525)	$358,528	(130.27)%	$2,224,269	$2,370,429	(6.17)%
88. UNITED GENERAL	$3,724,034	$1,773,074	110.03%	($818,526)	($54,349)	--	$2,905,508	$1,718,725	69.05%
89. WASHINGTON TIC	$142,825	$108,842	31.22%	$1,299	$0	--	$144,124	$108,842	32.42%
90. WESTCOR	$725,026	$665,553	8.94%	($867,387)	$0	--	($142,361)	$665,553	(121.39)%
91. WESTERN NATIONAL	$120,546	$157,518	(23.47)%	$0	$307	(100.00)%	$120,546	$157,825	(23.62)%
COMPOSITE	$566,010,993	$608,091,869	(6.92)%	($25,332,367)	$14,683,570	(272.52)%	$540,678,626	$622,775,440	(13.18)%
AVERAGE	$9,275,765	$10,262,773	(9.62)%	($278,378)	$164,984	(268.73)%	$8,997,387	$10,427,757	(13.72)%

All content © 2008 Demotech, Inc. - www.demotech.com

5

A.9 Yield on Invested Assets

COMPANY	2007 A.8 - NET INVESTMENT GAIN (LOSS)	2007 AVERAGE INVESTED ASSETS	2007 YIELD ON INVESTED ASSETS	2006 YIELD ON INVESTED ASSETS	2005 YIELD ON INVESTED ASSETS	2004 YIELD ON INVESTED ASSETS	2003 YIELD ON INVESTED ASSETS
1. CHICAGO T&T	$290,488,747	$1,613,685,326	18.00%	19.06%	14.85%	38.60%	7.62%
2. EQUITY NATIONAL	$230,044	$1,734,043	13.27%	31.65%	14.23%	--	--
3. AMERICAN GUARANTY	$1,553,637	$13,235,056	11.74%	5.11%	16.33%	16.85%	3.07%
4. SECURITY UNION	$8,237,091	$73,728,778	11.17%	9.43%	12.63%	26.06%	11.12%
5. FIRST AMERICAN TIC	$138,826,293	$1,387,372,490	10.01%	8.76%	11.22%	6.13%	13.88%
6. T.A. TITLE	$992,698	$11,601,876	8.56%	6.54%	1.92%	1.27%	2.03%
7. CHICAGO TIC	$122,326,076	$1,494,384,287	8.19%	8.92%	10.06%	11.50%	16.08%
8. STEWART TIC	$5,582,811	$70,281,473	7.94%	2.82%	3.86%	5.56%	6.95%
9. TITLEDGE	$28,862	$376,491	7.67%	--	--	--	--
10. ATTORNEYS TGF (IL)	$1,851,949	$24,552,073	7.54%	9.06%	7.58%	3.64%	5.68%
11. GUARDIAN NATIONAL	$516,788	$7,079,083	7.30%	6.27%	3.88%	4.08%	(3.11)%
12. FIRST AMERICAN T&T	$1,107,891	$15,711,459	7.05%	21.61%	1.18%	0.67%	3.52%
13. FIRST AMERICAN (NY)	$11,212,173	$168,592,644	6.65%	7.05%	2.79%	2.46%	3.30%
14. MASON	$179,024	$2,705,400	6.62%	7.65%	--	--	--
15. ATTORNEYS TIF (FL)	$17,478,061	$270,689,403	6.46%	4.53%	2.77%	4.68%	2.70%
16. NATIONAL ATTORNEYS	$92,706	$1,516,945	6.11%	4.25%	3.67%	0.56%	1.50%
17. DREIBELBISS	$167,654	$2,809,277	5.97%	8.29%	6.50%	5.54%	7.16%
18. LAWYERS	$28,426,494	$484,516,176	5.87%	5.90%	6.51%	4.67%	6.19%
19. NATIONAL LAND	$396,943	$6,807,357	5.83%	4.48%	3.43%	3.25%	2.64%
20. ALAMO	$2,879,123	$52,574,288	5.48%	24.81%	2.55%	2.92%	5.87%
21. SIERRA	$140,652	$2,607,645	5.39%	5.80%	--	--	--
22. PACIFIC NORTHWEST	$1,430,401	$26,625,947	5.37%	4.84%	3.38%	1.62%	1.61%
23. AMERICAN LAND & AIRCRAFT	$40,829	$810,200	5.04%	3.18%	2.99%	1.57%	2.11%
24. GUARANTEE	$98,999	$1,973,872	5.02%	3.39%	2.74%	2.32%	4.55%
25. AMERICAN EAGLE	$65,709	$1,317,013	4.99%	4.40%	4.76%	1.25%	2.09%
26. SOUTHERN TI CORP	$922,249	$18,541,842	4.97%	4.78%	4.06%	4.05%	4.93%
27. GENERAL T&T	$328,392	$6,616,845	4.96%	4.19%	4.16%	3.76%	4.18%
28. FOUNDERS	$41,264	$837,021	4.93%	3.95%	2.58%	--	--
29. WASHINGTON TIC	$144,124	$2,942,790	4.90%	3.51%	2.01%	0.83%	1.16%
30. ARKANSAS TIC	$220,890	$4,531,296	4.87%	3.52%	1.87%	1.06%	1.52%
31. TRANSNATION	$7,150,419	$147,157,742	4.86%	4.81%	5.06%	3.90%	4.13%
32. OHIO BAR	$1,245,118	$25,675,092	4.85%	4.08%	3.66%	3.48%	3.08%
33. COMMONWEALTH LAND	$32,490,595	$681,198,189	4.77%	5.77%	6.08%	4.72%	6.14%
34. FIDELITY NATIONAL	$39,431,994	$826,853,566	4.77%	6.00%	13.56%	5.27%	8.77%
35. NEW JERSEY TIC	$399,158	$8,382,101	4.76%	6.17%	5.77%	6.78%	9.66%
36. NORTH AMERICAN	$3,642,852	$76,773,046	4.75%	3.59%	1.86%	1.24%	1.58%
37. OLD REPUBLIC GENERAL	$5,051,693	$106,856,897	4.73%	4.79%	4.86%	5.90%	5.16%
38. TITLE IC AMERICA	$640,317	$13,627,778	4.70%	5.61%	4.65%	4.91%	5.92%
39. OLYMPIC	$16,065	$343,117	4.68%	3.52%	1.07%	0.00%	(45.65)%
40. K.E.L.	$55,398	$1,184,498	4.68%	--	--	--	--
41. MANITO	$67,685	$1,452,981	4.66%	3.73%	1.98%	1.89%	1.70%
42. ALLIANCE	$172,226	$3,710,756	4.64%	4.35%	2.70%	1.16%	1.11%
43. AMERICAN SECURITY	$367,143	$7,968,330	4.61%	4.13%	2.63%	1.57%	2.05%
44. OLD REPUBLIC NATIONAL	$21,161,235	$460,048,906	4.60%	4.43%	4.39%	5.29%	4.33%
45. COMMONWEALTH LAND (NJ)	$1,830,953	$39,877,080	4.59%	4.76%	3.87%	3.34%	3.85%
46. PENN ATTORNEYS	$459,407	$10,006,157	4.59%	4.27%	3.88%	2.69%	3.45%
47. CONESTOGA	$337,732	$7,430,372	4.55%	4.16%	3.54%	3.72%	2.87%
48. PORT LAWRENCE	$895,351	$19,881,243	4.50%	6.17%	5.11%	1.57%	0.88%
49. UNITED CAPITAL	$2,224,269	$49,592,285	4.49%	4.99%	3.89%	3.71%	4.74%
50. INVESTORS TIC	$4,354,350	$97,313,432	4.47%	4.39%	3.78%	3.43%	4.39%
51. MISSISSIPPI VALLEY	$1,911,592	$42,777,916	4.47%	4.32%	4.45%	4.42%	5.06%
52. FIRST AMERICAN TRANS	$92,479	$2,078,375	4.45%	4.69%	1.42%	0.55%	1.27%
53. LAND TIC (ST LOUIS)	$243,373	$5,478,614	4.44%	3.93%	3.20%	2.88%	3.06%
54. ARSENAL	$25,816	$583,498	4.42%	3.69%	3.52%	1.56%	--
55. TITLE RESOURCES	$1,697,987	$38,961,556	4.36%	4.27%	2.67%	1.49%	1.40%
56. CHICAGO TIC (OR)	$1,151,437	$26,654,840	4.32%	5.68%	5.28%	3.11%	15.29%
57. TRANSUNION NATIONAL	$650,881	$15,121,485	4.30%	3.37%	2.96%	3.65%	2.87%
58. CT ATTORNEYS	$2,434,180	$56,753,402	4.29%	4.72%	6.02%	3.01%	5.87%
59. SEAGATE	$24,229	$571,847	4.24%	3.71%	1.19%	0.88%	1.20%
60. FARMERS NATIONAL	$41,556	$991,786	4.19%	8.44%	--	--	--
61. MONROE	$830,602	$20,167,356	4.12%	4.51%	3.46%	2.96%	2.00%
62. TICOR (FL)	$4,123,733	$102,810,723	4.01%	4.58%	4.22%	5.28%	3.70%
63. NORTHEAST INVESTORS	$231,840	$5,835,858	3.97%	3.94%	3.33%	2.92%	3.77%
64. UNITED GENERAL	$2,905,508	$74,205,792	3.92%	3.08%	3.02%	2.07%	2.26%
65. ALLIANT	$117,824	$3,046,431	3.87%	3.35%	2.29%	--	--
66. MASON COUNTY	$31,231	$815,996	3.83%	3.88%	2.09%	0.85%	0.85%
67. NATIONAL OF NY	$620,283	$16,375,633	3.79%	3.26%	2.57%	1.59%	2.73%
68. SECURITY TG (BALTIMORE)	$460,064	$12,521,298	3.67%	3.04%	1.92%	2.05%	1.64%
69. LAND CORP (CO)	$468,057	$12,779,944	3.66%	3.91%	3.46%	3.54%	3.18%
70. STEWART (OR)	$175,981	$4,827,339	3.65%	3.08%	2.31%	2.44%	2.87%
71. FIRST AMERICAN (OR)	$1,758,797	$48,782,281	3.61%	3.88%	3.02%	1.57%	1.76%
72. NATIONAL	$161,998	$4,687,421	3.46%	1.74%	11.13%	4.16%	3.07%
73. PUBLIC	$35,090	$1,023,073	3.43%	3.52%	--	--	--
74. NATIONS OF NY	$724,028	$21,223,610	3.41%	3.20%	2.92%	2.59%	3.54%
75. STEWART TGC	$31,583,539	$994,165,608	3.18%	2.39%	2.32%	2.72%	3.10%
76. ATTORNEYS TGF (CO)	$131,057	$4,202,365	3.12%	4.55%	0.94%	2.40%	2.03%
77. TRANSUNION TIC	$314,916	$10,204,354	3.09%	1.66%	(46.00)%	0.77%	0.64%
78. FIRST AMERICAN (KS)	$351,141	$11,392,565	3.08%	3.23%	2.21%	1.04%	0.49%
79. COMMERCE	$626,185	$20,477,604	3.06%	2.84%	1.96%	1.11%	1.17%
80. DAKOTA HOMESTEAD	$98,069	$3,334,760	2.94%	4.42%	3.59%	3.75%	0.46%
81. TITLE G&TC	$38,802	$1,326,628	2.92%	1.53%	3.23%	3.09%	3.44%
82. WESTERN NATIONAL	$120,546	$4,576,363	2.63%	3.44%	3.49%	2.76%	1.50%
83. TICOR	$5,841,529	$222,947,328	2.62%	11.56%	8.78%	5.61%	11.32%
84. CENSTAR	$678,399	$26,902,572	2.52%	2.52%	2.62%	3.01%	3.06%
85. MASSACHUSETTS TIC	$58,993	$2,461,790	2.40%	2.57%	2.54%	2.60%	2.42%
86. MISSISSIPPI GUARANTY	$17,107	$799,829	2.14%	1.58%	1.00%	0.52%	1.04%
87. BRIDGE	$85,682	$8,170,758	1.05%	0.70%	0.25%	47.94%	0.21%
88. COLUMBIAN NATIONAL	$38,289	$4,384,318	0.87%	2.40%	1.10%	1.66%	1.59%
89. TITLE GUARANTY DIV (IA)	$0	$6,198,938	0.00%	0.00%	0.00%	0.00%	0.00%
90. GUARANTEE T&T	($768)	$6,084,972	(0.01)%	11.47%	14.18%	7.21%	9.37%
91. WESTCOR	($142,361)	$21,024,106	(0.68)%	3.06%	4.68%	4.94%	1.82%
COMPOSITE	$540,678,626	$10,223,822,933	5.29%	5.85%	6.26%	11.56%	8.44%
AVERAGE	$8,997,387	$112,349,703	8.01%				

5

A.10 Net Operating Gain (Loss) to Total Operating Income

COMPANY	2007 NET OPERATING GAIN (LOSS)	2007 A.2 - TOTAL OPERATING INCOME	2007 OPERATING GAIN TO REVENUE	2006 OPERATING GAIN TO REVENUE	2005 OPERATING GAIN TO REVENUE	2004 OPERATING GAIN TO REVENUE	2003 OPERATING GAIN TO REVENUE
1. PENN ATTORNEYS	$605,017	$1,823,123	33.18%	25.61%	28.38%	38.85%	46.75%
2. TITLE GUARANTY DIV (IA)	$1,166,713	$3,648,197	31.98%	40.37%	46.06%	66.64%	74.16%
3. OLD REPUBLIC GENERAL	$3,743,310	$15,384,796	24.33%	53.56%	61.79%	63.41%	46.00%
4. WESTERN NATIONAL	$105,787	$453,266	23.33%	(34.25)%	7.25%	(2.93)%	2.15%
5. AMERICAN SECURITY	$638,302	$2,940,698	21.70%	27.01%	26.82%	34.42%	28.24%
6. FIRST AMERICAN T&T	$4,738,468	$25,404,401	18.65%	19.54%	19.36%	21.38%	28.39%
7. CHICAGO T&T	$8,011,610	$46,037,947	17.40%	6.09%	9.85%	53.62%	17.19%
8. NATIONS OF NY	$125,975	$895,124	14.07%	37.57%	46.15%	(42.59)%	(108.92)%
9. CHICAGO TIC (OR)	$4,274,269	$33,259,216	12.85%	16.25%	17.59%	17.99%	15.41%
10. CENSTAR	$3,726,354	$37,915,111	9.82%	9.23%	12.03%	12.69%	--
11. COMMERCE	$3,654,793	$42,512,147	8.59%	6.57%	6.42%	4.90%	5.31%
12. FIRST AMERICAN (OR)	$7,258,036	$88,512,105	8.20%	15.41%	15.82%	13.30%	19.23%
13. SEAGATE	$14,869	$190,389	7.80%	(11.58)%	(5.62)%	2.36%	9.52%
14. NORTH AMERICAN	$8,474,796	$109,101,307	7.76%	2.62%	4.28%	4.21%	3.59%
15. LAND CORP (CO)	$1,486,712	$19,814,055	7.50%	9.80%	7.62%	10.85%	6.08%
16. STEWART TIC	$12,274,888	$172,582,288	7.11%	2.98%	8.10%	4.85%	3.90%
17. COMMONWEALTH LAND (NJ)	$2,309,331	$35,399,052	6.52%	7.90%	15.20%	17.30%	22.37%
18. PACIFIC NORTHWEST	$3,750,341	$60,167,709	6.23%	5.64%	2.67%	2.48%	(0.52)%
19. FIRST AMERICAN (KS)	$826,917	$14,338,022	5.76%	4.98%	1.48%	10.43%	8.04%
20. TITLE G&TC	$93,238	$1,683,746	5.53%	13.26%	9.41%	13.05%	11.26%
21. TITLE RESOURCES	$5,518,090	$103,117,424	5.35%	6.01%	6.90%	5.87%	6.31%
22. ARKANSAS TIC	$373,911	$8,079,115	4.62%	5.25%	6.46%	1.08%	7.87%
23. FIRST AMERICAN TRANS	$66,145	$1,432,315	4.61%	13.27%	9.60%	19.21%	0.46%
24. TICOR	$17,196,549	$377,091,404	4.56%	6.59%	4.59%	3.45%	6.30%
25. COMMONWEALTH LAND	$51,387,907	$1,214,894,310	4.22%	9.07%	4.98%	4.41%	6.21%
26. AMERICAN EAGLE	$306,438	$7,538,338	4.06%	3.21%	5.62%	5.75%	24.62%
27. FIRST AMERICAN (NY)	$10,760,376	$271,881,908	3.95%	2.47%	1.43%	1.25%	1.22%
28. INVESTORS TIC	$2,444,513	$66,853,213	3.65%	9.35%	15.47%	13.57%	15.54%
29. SIERRA	$60,798	$1,923,075	3.16%	--	--	--	--
30. FIDELITY NATIONAL	$42,318,485	$1,369,360,612	3.09%	5.37%	3.09%	3.22%	4.78%
31. CHICAGO TIC	$39,688,731	$2,108,437,310	1.88%	7.64%	5.50%	9.04%	12.65%
32. T.A. TITLE	$206,036	$16,852,621	1.22%	4.00%	8.23%	4.06%	12.23%
33. ALAMO	$1,096,881	$94,868,348	1.15%	5.09%	4.75%	3.89%	1.68%
34. PORT LAWRENCE	$70,306	$6,785,918	1.03%	1.37%	7.90%	13.93%	22.89%
35. STEWART (OR)	$36,707	$9,836,516	0.37%	(1.16)%	(1.76)%	(1.12)%	(1.15)%
36. OLD REPUBLIC NATIONAL	$835,464	$770,478,042	0.10%	1.83%	2.53%	3.51%	3.02%
37. OHIO BAR	($41,743)	$12,974,760	(0.32)%	7.42%	17.21%	9.27%	(6.46)%
38. DAKOTA HOMESTEAD	($41,365)	$4,034,545	(1.02)%	0.47%	(6.72)%	6.99%	12.92%
39. ARSENAL	($22,284)	$1,589,223	(1.40)%	5.98%	8.96%	7.10%	--
40. LAWYERS	($21,095,061)	$1,324,909,286	(1.59)%	2.37%	2.08%	2.54%	5.61%
41. CT ATTORNEYS	($1,001,748)	$54,095,917	(1.85)%	(5.32)%	3.57%	5.55%	11.53%
42. TITLE IC AMERICA	($227,269)	$11,614,194	(1.95)%	(5.56)%	3.57%	(1.64)%	4.64%
43. NORTHEAST INVESTORS	($53,396)	$2,403,559	(2.22)%	(1.79)%	1.86%	7.33%	6.71%
44. WASHINGTON TIC	($339,609)	$15,187,593	(2.23)%	(2.73)%	1.39%	(0.75)%	0.19%
45. NATIONAL OF NY	($258,973)	$11,194,386	(2.31)%	--	--	(10.73)%	6.69%
46. FIRST AMERICAN TIC	($87,291,546)	$3,630,841,157	(2.40)%	3.14%	3.86%	3.12%	4.55%
47. WESTCOR	($1,298,824)	$51,967,673	(2.49)%	0.63%	(0.58)%	1.36%	1.97%
48. MONROE	($528,840)	$19,801,051	(2.67)%	(2.91)%	1.77%	3.64%	9.24%
49. AMERICAN GUARANTY	($90,850)	$3,338,958	(2.72)%	1.25%	1.65%	14.13%	26.89%
50. ATTORNEYS TGF (CO)	($425,910)	$13,791,525	(3.08)%	(4.27)%	(4.68)%	2.89%	1.14%
51. STEWART TGC	($48,632,433)	$1,499,604,706	(3.24)%	1.63%	3.27%	1.31%	2.15%
52. SOUTHERN TI CORP	($2,192,516)	$53,404,248	(4.10)%	(0.34)%	3.69%	3.75%	6.48%
53. TRANSUNION TIC	($78,552)	$1,553,321	(5.05)%	(3.64)%	(2.09)%	(1.32)%	2.36%
54. UNITED CAPITAL	($3,550,844)	$61,768,602	(5.74)%	2.75%	3.34%	3.77%	5.05%
55. ALLIANT	($839,276)	$13,587,506	(6.17)%	(4.29)%	(225.47)%	--	--
56. SECURITY TG (BALTIMORE)	($1,525,069)	$23,148,068	(6.58)%	2.53%	(4.06)%	4.11%	1.71%
57. NEW JERSEY TIC	($1,207,490)	$17,330,838	(6.96)%	(1.55)%	0.40%	(1.50)%	0.29%
58. MISSISSIPPI VALLEY	($1,789,356)	$25,410,166	(7.04)%	2.84%	(4.86)%	6.46%	1.93%
59. UNITED GENERAL	($23,933,453)	$329,196,284	(7.27)%	(4.83)%	(3.80)%	1.12%	2.18%
60. EQUITY NATIONAL	($164,734)	$2,068,352	(7.96)%	(4.36)%	(1.24)%	--	--
61. GUARANTEE T&T	($1,279,675)	$14,997,723	(8.53)%	(7.69)%	(8.03)%	(2.84)%	(0.05)%
62. NATIONAL	($316,879)	$3,704,331	(8.55)%	(12.68)%	(14.05)%	(13.96)%	(4.48)%
63. SECURITY UNION	($5,756,604)	$66,621,757	(8.64)%	3.60%	3.73%	8.09%	4.53%
64. AMERICAN LAND & AIRCRAFT	($52,767)	$594,713	(8.87)%	(3.68)%	(3.52)%	(1.09)%	(0.65)%
65. ATTORNEYS TGF (IL)	($1,818,223)	$20,161,742	(9.01)%	2.20%	6.19%	(7.03)%	2.10%
66. CONESTOGA	($1,360,457)	$14,176,902	(9.59)%	(2.65)%	(4.32)%	(5.96)%	8.70%
67. GUARDIAN NATIONAL	($367,958)	$3,594,472	(10.23)%	(9.74)%	0.39%	(1.92)%	8.62%
68. TITLEDGE	($18,168)	$174,297	(10.41)%	--	--	--	--
69. ATTORNEYS TIF (FL)	($39,486,692)	$360,555,798	(10.95)%	5.39%	7.94%	9.59%	8.46%
70. MANITO	($83,717)	$740,110	(11.31)%	(4.66)%	0.24%	5.88%	4.36%
71. TRANSNATION	($49,708,452)	$299,589,827	(16.59)%	(5.31)%	4.06%	6.41%	7.65%
72. NATIONAL ATTORNEYS	($277,706)	$1,337,094	(20.76)%	(4.48)%	1.38%	11.84%	8.93%
73. DREIBELBISS	($386,377)	$1,763,918	(21.90)%	(10.14)%	0.62%	(1.64)%	6.05%
74. TICOR (FL)	($24,507,749)	$93,604,625	(26.18)%	(3.71)%	2.50%	1.96%	6.73%
75. GUARANTEE	($620,687)	$2,262,039	(27.43)%	(40.87)%	(20.87)%	9.98%	(16.44)%
76. MASON	($420,232)	$1,519,252	(27.66)%	(67.79)%	--	--	--
77. NATIONAL LAND	($737,079)	$2,502,043	(29.45)%	(17.05)%	(14.83)%	(14.73)%	(8.51)%
78. GENERAL T&T	($855,086)	$2,780,740	(30.75)%	(9.10)%	3.04%	2.71%	3.24%
79. LAND TIC (ST LOUIS)	($700,485)	$2,248,990	(31.14)%	15.37%	4.07%	36.87%	24.05%
80. TRANSUNION NATIONAL	($1,242,065)	$3,636,583	(34.15)%	(41.55)%	(49.84)%	(22.45)%	(0.08)%
81. FOUNDERS	($87,236)	$221,713	(39.36)%	(39.29)%	(53.98)%	--	--
82. K.E.L.	($222,944)	$554,387	(40.21)%	--	--	--	--
83. MISSISSIPPI GUARANTY	($133,508)	$298,973	(44.65)%	2.97%	(12.47)%	(12.21)%	8.74%
84. FARMERS NATIONAL	($364,856)	$803,193	(45.42)%	(114.38)%	--	--	--
85. ALLIANCE	($129,586)	$54,338	(238.48)%	(463.36)%	106.76%	(32.59)%	7.62%
86. BRIDGE	($269,767)	$19,541	(1,380.51)%	(431.65)%	(134.98)%	(218.10)%	(23.29)%
87. PUBLIC	($7,247)	$0	--	--	--	--	--
88. MASON COUNTY	($7,538)	$0	--	--	--	--	--
89. OLYMPIC	($46,303)	$0	--	--	--	--	--
90. MASSACHUSETTS TIC	($47,597)	($254)	--	(1,347.44)%	(2,488.71)%	(2,476.04)%	--
91. COLUMBIAN NATIONAL	($139,316)	$0	--	(62.04)%	(8.69)%	(21.84)%	5.13%
COMPOSITE	($88,437,019)	$15,224,827,929	(0.58)%	4.06%	4.08%	4.61%	6.33%
AVERAGE	($971,835)	$167,305,801	(0.58)%				

5

A.11 Net Income Before Taxes to Net Admitted Assets

COMPANY	2007 NET INCOME BEFORE TAXES	2007 AVERAGE NET ADMITTED ASSETS	2007 RETURN ON ASSETS	2006 RETURN ON ASSETS	2005 RETURN ON ASSETS	2004 RETURN ON ASSETS	2003 RETURN ON ASSETS
1. FIRST AMERICAN T&T	$5,861,607	$17,847,426	32.84%	38.01%	21.78%	29.38%	53.49%
2. STEWART TIC	$17,857,699	$76,108,196	23.46%	8.79%	22.05%	18.81%	19.02%
3. COMMERCE	$4,280,978	$21,975,771	19.48%	20.00%	20.74%	14.86%	17.33%
4. AMERICAN EAGLE	$407,827	$2,131,510	19.13%	15.24%	22.68%	15.87%	87.13%
5. CHICAGO TIC (OR)	$5,425,706	$28,392,054	19.10%	27.84%	28.71%	22.28%	38.66%
6. CHICAGO T&T	$298,500,357	$1,619,502,883	18.43%	18.94%	14.74%	39.53%	8.14%
7. PACIFIC NORTHWEST	$5,180,742	$29,804,126	17.38%	16.90%	8.20%	6.78%	(0.49)%
8. TITLE RESOURCES	$7,216,143	$42,591,511	16.94%	19.29%	17.20%	16.50%	21.04%
9. CENSTAR	$4,404,753	$27,998,813	15.73%	18.43%	30.62%	11.57%	2.75%
10. NORTH AMERICAN	$12,451,228	$79,281,484	15.70%	9.24%	12.77%	11.82%	11.06%
11. FIRST AMERICAN (OR)	$9,016,833	$65,306,210	13.80%	24.78%	25.68%	21.52%	44.45%
12. LAND CORP (CO)	$1,983,084	$14,672,488	13.51%	18.85%	16.25%	20.77%	18.33%
13. ARKANSAS TIC	$594,801	$4,792,199	12.41%	12.20%	11.54%	2.65%	13.21%
14. AMERICAN SECURITY	$1,005,445	$8,170,210	12.30%	13.13%	12.10%	16.75%	18.58%
15. FIRST AMERICAN (NY)	$21,972,549	$183,969,054	11.94%	10.47%	5.27%	4.77%	5.46%
16. COMMONWEALTH LAND	$83,878,502	$762,560,949	10.99%	21.87%	14.45%	12.43%	17.99%
17. AMERICAN GUARANTY	$1,462,787	$13,588,552	10.76%	5.26%	15.98%	27.35%	41.70%
18. PENN ATTORNEYS	$1,064,424	$10,271,956	10.36%	9.65%	11.35%	13.26%	24.72%
19. COMMONWEALTH LAND (NJ)	$4,140,284	$40,742,957	10.16%	13.03%	21.42%	25.64%	31.78%
20. FIRST AMERICAN (KS)	$1,178,058	$11,712,673	10.05%	9.56%	4.24%	16.63%	19.17%
21. CHICAGO TIC	$162,014,807	$1,628,419,106	9.94%	20.02%	18.41%	27.07%	41.79%
22. T.A. TITLE	$1,198,734	$12,485,122	9.60%	12.02%	14.79%	7.94%	25.04%
23. TICOR	$23,033,194	$248,089,415	9.28%	20.60%	13.77%	10.30%	20.66%
24. FIDELITY NATIONAL	$81,391,063	$880,987,594	9.23%	15.10%	19.06%	11.78%	19.84%
25. TITLE G&TC	$132,040	$1,467,956	8.99%	18.39%	13.16%	15.30%	19.46%
26. OLD REPUBLIC GENERAL	$8,795,003	$116,069,374	7.57%	11.92%	14.88%	17.72%	15.27%
27. FIRST AMERICAN TRANS	$158,624	$2,182,282	7.26%	18.44%	11.98%	24.74%	1.74%
28. SIERRA	$201,450	$2,786,324	7.22%	(0.49)%	--	--	--
29. ALAMO	$3,976,004	$56,342,539	7.05%	31.81%	9.72%	8.93%	8.59%
30. INVESTORS TIC	$6,798,863	$107,383,984	6.33%	9.91%	14.87%	13.32%	19.46%
31. SEAGATE	$39,098	$685,649	5.70%	0.86%	(0.34)%	1.59%	5.48%
32. WESTERN NATIONAL	$226,333	$4,714,162	4.80%	(2.89)%	6.21%	1.21%	4.98%
33. OHIO BAR	$1,203,375	$26,527,788	4.53%	8.15%	13.83%	12.02%	(3.20)%
34. OLD REPUBLIC NATIONAL	$21,996,699	$491,381,306	4.47%	7.38%	9.14%	12.14%	11.02%
35. STEWART (OR)	$212,688	$5,017,395	4.23%	0.45%	(2.05)%	(0.36)%	(1.24)%
36. PORT LAWRENCE	$965,657	$22,898,686	4.21%	6.14%	7.40%	7.84%	17.19%
37. NATIONS OF NY	$850,003	$21,738,928	3.91%	4.74%	4.85%	0.34%	(2.53)%
38. EQUITY NATIONAL	$65,310	$1,844,832	3.54%	9.87%	9.71%	--	--
39. NORTHEAST INVESTORS	$178,444	$6,032,136	2.95%	3.07%	4.37%	8.40%	12.56%
40. TITLE IC AMERICA	$413,048	$14,299,388	2.88%	0.52%	9.27%	1.74%	12.52%
41. MASON COUNTY	$23,693	$842,718	2.81%	2.78%	(1.42)%	(2.22)%	(1.10)%
42. TITLEDGE	$10,714	$391,642	2.73%	--	--	--	--
43. PUBLIC	$27,843	$1,024,323	2.71%	2.05%	--	--	--
44. FIRST AMERICAN TIC	$51,534,747	$1,982,989,280	2.59%	12.69%	16.93%	11.09%	20.66%
45. SECURITY UNION	$2,480,487	$95,571,543	2.59%	10.54%	12.56%	29.37%	13.72%
46. TITLE GUARANTY DIV (IA)	$145,713	$6,206,040	2.34%	(4.08)%	(1.45)%	(18.54)%	68.25%
47. CT ATTORNEYS	$1,357,042	$59,764,865	2.27%	(0.88)%	9.38%	8.94%	36.53%
48. TRANSUNION TIC	$236,364	$10,516,641	2.24%	(0.90)%	(40.85)%	(2.00)%	5.58%
49. NATIONAL OF NY	$361,310	$16,608,510	2.17%	(3.18)%	(15.95)%	(13.78)%	25.16%
50. GUARDIAN NATIONAL	$148,830	$7,389,739	2.01%	(2.30)%	4.28%	0.76%	25.75%
51. DAKOTA HOMESTEAD	$56,704	$3,344,082	1.69%	5.15%	(4.42)%	8.86%	13.28%
52. MONROE	$301,762	$22,135,697	1.36%	1.58%	4.92%	6.53%	13.27%
53. ALLIANCE	$42,640	$3,718,244	1.14%	(4.25)%	6.00%	(4.49)%	15.81%
54. LAWYERS	$7,331,468	$655,249,293	1.11%	9.24%	9.12%	8.54%	17.44%
55. ARSENAL	$3,532	$584,704	0.60%	28.52%	26.50%	17.11%	--
56. MASSACHUSETTS TIC	$11,396	$2,466,171	0.46%	1.46%	1.15%	1.06%	0.51%
57. MISSISSIPPI VALLEY	$122,236	$44,412,699	0.27%	5.86%	1.61%	8.11%	6.25%
58. ATTORNEYS TGF (IL)	$33,726	$27,240,720	0.12%	10.21%	13.37%	(7.29)%	6.90%
59. MANITO	($16,032)	$1,478,058	(1.08)%	1.04%	2.11%	5.72%	6.51%
60. STEWART TGC	($13,534,192)	$1,060,949,733	(1.27)%	5.61%	8.55%	5.31%	8.01%
61. AMERICAN LAND & AIRCRAFT	($11,938)	$816,368	(1.46)%	4.80%	(0.19)%	(0.14)%	1.35%
62. BRIDGE	($184,085)	$8,262,243	(2.22)%	(0.70)%	(0.77)%	34.94%	(0.44)%
63. COLUMBIAN NATIONAL	($100,419)	$4,472,863	(2.24)%	(2.52)%	(3.91)%	(14.45)%	5.25%
64. UNITED CAPITAL	($1,326,575)	$52,197,497	(2.54)%	11.58%	16.63%	18.60%	33.15%
65. NATIONAL	($154,881)	$5,170,776	(2.99)%	(6.82)%	1.34%	(3.51)%	0.31%
66. TRANSUNION NATIONAL	($591,184)	$15,330,177	(3.85)%	(9.25)%	(21.21)%	(6.05)%	2.73%
67. WASHINGTON TIC	($195,485)	$3,961,983	(4.93)%	(10.06)%	8.53%	(3.06)%	2.28%
68. NATIONAL LAND	($340,136)	$6,874,163	(4.94)%	(0.22)%	1.31%	1.09%	1.32%
69. FOUNDERS	($46,012)	$849,321	(5.41)%	(6.82)%	(5.93)%	--	--
70. ATTORNEYS TGF (CO)	($294,853)	$5,449,520	(5.41)%	(6.08)%	(10.48)%	10.00%	5.10%
71. SOUTHERN TI CORP	($1,270,267)	$22,279,629	(5.70)%	2.91%	12.32%	11.75%	20.64%
72. WESTCOR	($1,441,185)	$24,687,419	(5.83)%	3.94%	2.72%	8.14%	8.08%
73. ATTORNEYS TIF (FL)	($22,008,631)	$326,309,622	(6.74)%	12.44%	17.19%	22.53%	20.35%
74. SECURITY TG (BALTIMORE)	($1,063,284)	$14,721,309	(7.22)%	8.13%	(6.45)%	11.85%	5.63%
75. DREIBELBISS	($218,723)	$2,987,679	(7.32)%	0.80%	5.71%	3.45%	15.06%
76. GENERAL T&T	($526,694)	$6,921,585	(7.60)%	(4.02)%	8.38%	8.65%	13.98%
77. LAND TIC (ST LOUIS)	($457,112)	$5,563,446	(8.21)%	5.03%	4.99%	10.66%	8.84%
78. NEW JERSEY TIC	($808,332)	$9,809,502	(8.24)%	1.80%	5.87%	2.62%	8.94%
79. OLYMPIC	($30,238)	$361,467	(8.36)%	(2.23)%	(28.44)%	(31.87)%	(75.43)%
80. MASON	($241,208)	$2,748,147	(8.77)%	(14.28)%	--	--	--
81. NATIONAL ATTORNEYS	($185,000)	$1,975,720	(9.36)%	0.24%	3.69%	9.44%	8.47%
82. CONESTOGA	($1,021,916)	$8,732,472	(11.70)%	(1.55)%	(6.50)%	(11.14)%	32.06%
83. MISSISSIPPI GUARANTY	($116,401)	$954,404	(12.19)%	2.91%	(6.88)%	(9.91)%	12.95%
84. K.E.L.	($167,546)	$1,189,206	(14.08)%	--	--	--	--
85. GUARANTEE T&T	($1,280,443)	$8,481,085	(15.09)%	(4.40)%	0.98%	0.75%	8.80%
86. TICOR (FL)	($19,501,690)	$120,255,360	(16.21)%	(1.14)%	10.35%	9.40%	24.04%
87. GUARANTEE	($520,920)	$2,815,255	(18.50)%	(37.04)%	(10.79)%	5.79%	3.23%
88. UNITED GENERAL	($21,027,945)	$104,817,572	(20.06)%	(17.83)%	(9.47)%	5.34%	11.95%
89. ALLIANT	($721,452)	$3,423,802	(21.07)%	(7.87)%	(21.44)%	--	--
90. TRANSNATION	($42,558,033)	$167,539,136	(25.40)%	(6.90)%	13.90%	17.57%	20.09%
91. FARMERS NATIONAL	($313,133)	$1,090,125	(28.72)%	(71.76)%	--	--	--
COMPOSITE	$455,604,907	$10,573,623,948	4.31%	11.12%	11.99%	17.54%	18.82%
AVERAGE	$8,062,511	$128,095,695	1.80%				

5

A.12 Return on Policyholders' Surplus (PHS)

COMPANY	NET INCOME (2007)	AVERAGE PHS (2007)	RETURN ON PHS 2007	RETURN ON PHS 2006	RETURN ON PHS 2005	RETURN ON PHS 2004	RETURN ON PHS 2003
1. CHICAGO TIC	$129,246,669	$351,974,953	36.72%	57.42%	44.16%	53.40%	85.55%
2. CHICAGO T&T	$289,913,524	$792,657,651	36.57%	38.22%	30.59%	82.93%	18.33%
3. STEWART TIC	$11,724,163	$32,674,000	35.88%	11.47%	38.99%	28.60%	32.71%
4. COMMERCE	$2,801,840	$8,688,998	32.24%	33.82%	34.95%	16.23%	20.01%
5. FIRST AMERICAN T&T	$4,095,920	$13,815,690	29.64%	39.29%	26.40%	41.34%	68.07%
6. CHICAGO TIC (OR)	$3,913,228	$13,777,300	28.40%	38.14%	42.72%	35.80%	54.64%
7. TICOR	$16,674,345	$60,292,716	27.65%	68.14%	42.16%	27.12%	43.81%
8. PACIFIC NORTHWEST	$3,443,317	$13,597,795	25.32%	27.92%	10.26%	14.89%	(0.07)%
9. FIDELITY NATIONAL	$58,097,256	$255,835,858	22.70%	34.66%	54.23%	23.86%	41.79%
10. COMMONWEALTH LAND	$62,784,680	$283,933,143	22.11%	69.10%	38.89%	32.36%	41.42%
11. TITLE GUARANTY DIV (IA)	$145,713	$666,849	21.85%	(34.51)%	(9.73)%	(78.46)%	253.45%
12. FIRST AMERICAN (OR)	$5,978,208	$32,525,974	18.37%	31.37%	36.42%	32.76%	64.62%
13. NORTH AMERICAN	$8,278,766	$46,736,255	17.71%	14.60%	17.97%	18.20%	21.22%
14. TITLE RESOURCES	$4,648,063	$26,720,016	17.39%	19.56%	17.45%	17.31%	22.53%
15. ARKANSAS TIC	$371,309	$2,323,550	15.98%	15.76%	15.67%	2.14%	21.45%
16. AMERICAN EAGLE	$150,735	$1,036,440	14.54%	8.71%	14.68%	12.32%	73.12%
17. FIRST AMERICAN (NY)	$13,447,842	$98,765,724	13.61%	13.68%	4.84%	4.50%	3.67%
18. LAND CORP (CO)	$1,358,724	$10,054,782	13.51%	19.24%	17.39%	21.77%	18.41%
19. CENSTAR	$3,233,018	$24,339,594	13.28%	13.61%	21.96%	8.15%	2.75%
20. OLD REPUBLIC GENERAL	$6,211,326	$47,715,367	13.01%	19.77%	24.11%	29.44%	26.28%
21. OLD REPUBLIC NATIONAL	$14,681,746	$117,597,854	12.48%	20.59%	27.02%	33.93%	31.82%
22. AMERICAN GUARANTY	$1,294,920	$10,859,917	11.92%	4.17%	18.59%	31.14%	41.23%
23. FIRST AMERICAN (KS)	$633,868	$5,563,232	11.39%	11.24%	9.24%	14.97%	21.22%
24. T.A. TITLE	$779,522	$7,089,077	10.99%	13.78%	17.71%	8.95%	46.45%
25. AMERICAN SECURITY	$859,223	$7,994,210	10.74%	12.33%	12.21%	16.79%	18.48%
26. ALAMO	$3,298,904	$31,682,751	10.41%	53.40%	13.64%	11.95%	11.21%
27. OHIO BAR	$847,075	$8,609,752	9.83%	18.44%	35.92%	40.82%	(17.82)%
28. INVESTORS TIC	$5,126,419	$52,376,909	9.78%	13.67%	19.16%	18.06%	25.41%
29. TITLE G&TC	$82,871	$880,543	9.41%	20.42%	20.42%	30.30%	46.18%
30. COMMONWEALTH LAND (NJ)	$2,974,997	$31,681,095	9.39%	11.90%	18.69%	21.46%	26.63%
31. PENN ATTORNEYS	$691,887	$8,401,457	8.23%	7.81%	9.57%	12.14%	20.88%
32. SEAGATE	$39,098	$487,508	8.01%	1.34%	(0.58)%	2.68%	8.99%
33. TRANSUNION TIC	$299,380	$3,759,084	7.96%	(11.17)%	(183.43)%	(6.79)%	8.05%
34. NATIONS OF NY	$865,565	$12,205,086	7.09%	8.06%	9.79%	2.15%	(1.08)%
35. FIRST AMERICAN TRANS	$81,360	$1,211,780	6.71%	17.66%	11.06%	25.23%	1.44%
36. SECURITY UNION	$3,611,410	$56,684,226	6.37%	14.94%	17.73%	42.75%	19.46%
37. WESTERN NATIONAL	$192,113	$3,270,290	5.87%	(1.40)%	6.22%	1.16%	4.00%
38. SIERRA	$140,486	$2,590,633	5.42%	(0.49)%	--	--	--
39. STEWART (OR)	$127,290	$2,740,686	4.64%	0.49%	(3.54)%	(0.75)%	(2.11)%
40. PORT LAWRENCE	$600,137	$15,020,838	3.99%	5.41%	9.55%	9.30%	18.59%
41. MONROE	$446,971	$12,728,296	3.51%	3.82%	7.40%	10.38%	19.11%
42. TITLE IC AMERICA	$348,515	$10,405,907	3.34%	1.81%	9.12%	2.49%	12.46%
43. NORTHEAST INVESTORS	$180,394	$5,423,048	3.32%	3.37%	3.88%	6.73%	9.65%
44. GUARDIAN NATIONAL	$121,480	$4,286,226	2.83%	(2.86)%	6.74%	(1.20)%	40.16%
45. PUBLIC	$27,843	$1,024,323	2.71%	2.05%	--	--	--
46. DAKOTA HOMESTEAD	$56,704	$2,176,411	2.60%	7.55%	(5.65)%	8.70%	13.29%
47. MASON COUNTY	$20,291	$811,703	2.49%	2.88%	(1.49)%	(2.34)%	(1.15)%
48. TITLEDGE	$9,125	$376,543	2.42%	--	--	--	--
49. MISSISSIPPI VALLEY	$234,270	$9,920,492	2.36%	17.77%	6.14%	23.34%	19.02%
50. EQUITY NATIONAL	$31,699	$1,415,646	2.23%	8.64%	5.08%	--	--
51. FIRST AMERICAN TIC	$12,082,433	$590,119,439	2.04%	23.00%	30.36%	17.48%	32.89%
52. CT ATTORNEYS	$843,665	$41,492,403	2.03%	(0.58)%	9.15%	9.35%	34.89%
53. NATIONAL OF NY	$146,151	$7,712,764	1.89%	(3.46)%	(27.95)%	(24.22)%	37.39%
54. ALLIANCE	$36,169	$3,046,623	1.18%	(3.47)%	6.20%	(6.47)%	18.08%
55. LAWYERS	$1,971,396	$173,643,820	1.13%	25.21%	16.31%	13.81%	25.31%
56. MASSACHUSETTS TIC	$20,060	$2,301,928	0.87%	1.42%	1.47%	1.45%	1.01%
57. MANITO	($16,032)	$1,264,706	(1.26)%	1.05%	2.19%	6.39%	4.64%
58. STEWART TGC	($6,458,657)	$512,204,857	(1.26)%	7.40%	12.45%	6.71%	10.42%
59. BRIDGE	($117,171)	$8,052,326	(1.45)%	(0.57)%	(0.37)%	37.07%	(0.35)%
60. ATTORNEYS TGF (IL)	($130,643)	$8,665,038	(1.50)%	24.14%	35.38%	(21.62)%	17.50%
61. AMERICAN LAND & AIRCRAFT	($11,938)	$749,423	(1.59)%	5.28%	(0.21)%	(0.16)%	(0.51)%
62. COLUMBIAN NATIONAL	($68,307)	$3,631,029	(1.88)%	5.14%	15.44%	(33.43)%	5.18%
63. DREIBELBISS	($93,990)	$2,598,576	(3.61)%	0.42%	2.00%	3.64%	15.68%
64. ATTORNEYS TIF (FL)	($5,840,823)	$154,245,242	(3.78)%	18.06%	24.24%	31.73%	33.98%
65. TRANSUNION NATIONAL	($397,346)	$10,268,277	(3.86)%	(9.77)%	(26.61)%	(6.72)%	3.68%
66. UNITED CAPITAL	($942,258)	$23,757,908	(3.96)%	16.55%	23.36%	22.47%	40.23%
67. ATTORNEYS TGF (CO)	($77,762)	$1,535,102	(5.06)%	(16.97)%	(28.12)%	28.63%	12.31%
68. NATIONAL	($154,881)	$2,976,783	(5.20)%	(11.04)%	2.13%	(5.46)%	0.51%
69. FOUNDERS	($46,012)	$818,120	(5.62)%	(7.00)%	(6.06)%	--	--
70. NATIONAL ATTORNEYS	($102,749)	$1,640,959	(6.26)%	0.44%	2.82%	8.15%	7.07%
71. NATIONAL LAND	($340,136)	$5,365,227	(6.33)%	(0.29)%	2.01%	2.06%	2.19%
72. ARSENAL	($32,766)	$499,208	(6.56)%	23.76%	27.58%	17.33%	--
73. NEW JERSEY TIC	($405,519)	$5,025,065	(8.06)%	3.32%	10.65%	4.53%	15.15%
74. OLYMPIC	($30,238)	$351,270	(8.60)%	(2.29)%	(31.39)%	(34.12)%	(74.33)%
75. MASON	($241,208)	$2,671,550	(9.02)%	(14.51)%	--	--	--
76. LAND TIC (ST LOUIS)	($554,284)	$4,923,768	(11.25)%	4.36%	5.15%	6.87%	6.74%
77. SOUTHERN TI CORP	($1,020,999)	$8,188,186	(12.46)%	1.52%	16.23%	11.89%	21.79%
78. WASHINGTON TIC	($110,400)	$839,451	(13.15)%	(34.40)%	23.96%	(8.30)%	4.74%
79. K.E.L.	($167,546)	$1,166,227	(14.36)%	--	--	--	--
80. WESTCOR	($1,471,180)	$9,967,920	(14.75)%	4.55%	4.61%	10.39%	8.95%
81. SECURITY TG (BALTIMORE)	($628,284)	$4,126,268	(15.22)%	17.02%	(12.64)%	25.31%	12.45%
82. CONESTOGA	($641,202)	$3,769,065	(17.01)%	(5.63)%	(12.19)%	(14.70)%	39.84%
83. GENERAL T&T	($331,251)	$1,794,870	(18.45)%	(8.31)%	23.31%	5.17%	13.76%
84. ALLIANT	($721,452)	$2,435,796	(29.61)%	(8.71)%	(21.97)%	--	--
85. MISSISSIPPI GUARANTY	($116,401)	$358,302	(32.48)%	7.84%	(19.14)%	(20.94)%	24.43%
86. GUARANTEE	($520,920)	$1,464,009	(35.58)%	(54.54)%	(14.17)%	4.63%	2.60%
87. TICOR (FL)	($10,924,392)	$27,722,232	(39.40)%	7.91%	38.00%	14.74%	42.34%
88. FARMERS NATIONAL	($313,133)	$784,033	(39.93)%	(86.87)%	--	--	--
89. UNITED GENERAL	($15,142,796)	$25,951,064	(58.35)%	(43.12)%	(19.35)%	7.07%	21.02%
90. TRANSNATION	($29,527,216)	$42,585,600	(69.33)%	(9.69)%	20.37%	30.66%	30.39%
91. GUARANTEE T&T	($1,280,443)	$1,776,357	(72.08)%	(16.10)%	3.47%	0.55%	12.02%
COMPOSITE	$323,260,155	$3,166,814,653	10.21%	38.08%	32.16%	33.99%	32.42%
AVERAGE	$6,608,173	$46,702,186	14.14%				

5

5

MEASUREMENTS OF
OPERATING POSITION/SITUATION

5

Measurements of Operating Position/Situation

B.1 Key Operating Position Results and Ratios

This report presents key operating position results and ratios for each Title underwriter. Included in this report are *B.2 - Net Liquid Assets, B.3 - Total Liabilities to Net Liquid Assets, B.4 - Net Premiums Written (NPW), B.5 - Net Premiums Written to Net Liquid Assets, B.6 - Policyholders' Surplus (PHS)* as well as *B.7 - Net Premiums Written (NPW) to Policyholders' Surplus (PHS)*.

This report is sorted in alphabetical order by Title underwriter.

This report reflects *Consolidation Eliminations* in the *Composite* calculation.

B.2 Net Liquid Assets

This report presents the *Net Liquid Assets*, the sum of Cash and Invested Assets less Investments in Mortgage Loans on Real Estate, less Real Estate (Schedule A), less Total Liabilities.

To ensure reasonableness of results, if prior year *Net Liquid Assets* is less than or equal to $0, then the percentage change is not presented.

This report is sorted in descending order by *Net Liquid Assets*.

This report presents five years of analysis.

This report reflects *Consolidation Eliminations* in the *Composite* calculation.

B.3 Total Liabilities to Net Liquid Assets

This report presents *Total Liabilities* as a percentage of *B.2 - Net Liquid Assets*.

This is a comparative presentation of the Title underwriter's ability to meet extraordinary claims. A value less than 100% is considered favorable because it indicates that the Title underwriter has more than $1 of *Net Liquid Assets* for each $1 of *Total Liabilities*.

To ensure reasonableness of results, if *B.2 - Net Liquid Assets* is less than or equal to $0, then the ratio is not presented.

This report is sorted in ascending order by the current year ratio results.

This report presents five years of analysis.

This report reflects *Consolidation Eliminations* in the *Composite* calculation.

B.4 Net Premiums Written (NPW)

This report presents *Net Premiums Written (NPW)*, a Title underwriter's Gross Premiums Written (direct plus assumed business) less ceded reinsurance premiums.

To ensure reasonableness of results, if prior year *Net Premiums Written* is less than or equal to $0, then the percentage change is not presented.

This report is sorted in descending order by *Net Premiums Written*.

This report presents five years of analysis.

B.5 Net Premiums Written (NPW) to Net Liquid Assets

This report presents *B.4 - Net Premiums Written (NPW)* as a percentage of *B.2 - Net Liquid Assets*.

This analysis demonstrates the support underlying the level of premiums a Title underwriter writes.

To ensure reasonableness of results, if *B.2 - Net Liquid Assets* or *B.4 - Net Premiums Written (NPW)* is less than or equal to $0, then the ratio is not presented.

This report is sorted in ascending order by the current year ratio results.

This report presents five years of analysis.

This report reflects *Consolidation Eliminations* in the *Composite* calculation.

B.6 Policyholders' Surplus (PHS)

This report presents *Policyholders' Surplus (PHS)*. With Statutory Accounting Principles (SAP), *Policyholders' Surplus* is substituted for Owners' Equity to reflect the priority given policyholders' claims over any owners' claims and is a general measure of statutory net worth.

This report is sorted in descending order by *Policyholders' Surplus*.

This report presents five years of analysis.

This report reflects *Consolidation Eliminations* in the *Composite* calculation.

B.7   Net Premiums Written (NPW) to Policyholders' Surplus (PHS)

This report presents *B.4 - Net Premiums Written (NPW)* as a percentage of *B.6 - Policyholders' Surplus (PHS)*.

This analysis evaluates the comparative degree to which Policyholders' Surplus is exposed to potential losses and provides an indication of the insurer's ability to sustain adverse development (when losses exceed originally estimated amounts, depleting Policyholders' Surplus).

To ensure reasonableness of results, if *B.4 - Net Premiums Written (NPW)* is less than or equal to $0, then the ratio is not presented.

This report is sorted in ascending order by the current year ratio results.

This report presents five years of analysis.

This report reflects *Consolidation Eliminations* in the *Composite* calculation.

B.8   Implied Equity (Deficit) in the Statutory Premium Reserve (SPR) – New!

This report presents the *Implied Equity (Deficit) in the Statutory Premium Reserve (SPR)* carried on the balance sheet of the Title underwriter.

If the actuarial estimate of the *Total Schedule P Reserves* at year end (Known Claims Reserve, Net Incurred But Not Reported Reserve and Unallocated Loss Adjustment Expense Reserve less discount for time value of money, if allowed) is less than the total of the Known Claims Reserve, Statutory Premium Reserve and the Aggregate of Other Reserves Required by Law, the implication is that there is equity in the Statutory Premium Reserve. Conversely, if a net recognized Supplemental Reserve is established, the implication is that the Statutory Premium Reserve may not be sufficient.

This report is sorted in alphabetical order by Title underwriter.

This report reflects *Consolidation Eliminations* in the *Composite* calculation.

This report is a new analysis introduced in the 2008 publication.

B.9   Agency Premium and Retention

This report measures the percentage of *Direct Premiums Written* (before reinsurance) that comes from *Agency Operations* and the *Amounts Retained by Agents* as a percentage of agency derived premiums. *Agency Operations* include both Affiliated and Non-Affiliated activity.

This analysis illustrates the importance of *Agency Operations* to the generation of *Total Direct Premiums Written*, as well as the relative reliance on agents by each Title underwriter.

This report is sorted in descending order by the current year ratio results.

B.1 Key Operating Position/Situation Results and Ratios

COMPANY	B.2 NET LIQUID ASSETS	B.3 LIABILITIES TO NET LIQUID ASSETS	B.4 NET PREMIUMS WRITTEN	B.5 NPW TO NET LIQUID ASSETS	B.6 PHS	B.7 NPW TO PHS
1. ALAMO	$21,757,762	101.89%	$94,165,105	432.79%	$26,226,592	359.04%
2. ALLIANCE	$3,100,706	19.34%	$447	0.01%	$3,107,663	0.01%
3. ALLIANT	$1,871,402	81.02%	$13,883,261	741.86%	$2,354,553	589.63%
4. AMERICAN EAGLE	($387,008)	--	$2,995,458	--	$716,768	417.91%
5. AMERICAN GUARANTY	$10,532,088	26.36%	$3,489,926	33.14%	$11,507,581	30.33%
6. AMERICAN LAND & AIRCRAFT	$739,228	8.77%	$593,864	80.34%	$742,516	79.98%
7. AMERICAN SECURITY	$8,304,294	2.12%	$2,940,198	35.41%	$8,504,479	34.57%
8. ARKANSAS TIC	$2,107,597	123.40%	$8,213,976	389.73%	$2,388,523	343.89%
9. ARSENAL	$483,654	22.66%	$1,583,908	327.49%	$484,161	327.14%
10. ATTORNEYS TGF (CO)	($889,008)	--	$8,740,480	--	$1,776,152	492.10%
11. ATTORNEYS TGF (IL)	$4,975,119	399.68%	$10,652,985	214.13%	$9,754,476	109.21%
12. ATTORNEYS TIF (FL)	$81,702,918	213.55%	$345,668,134	423.08%	$149,827,744	230.71%
13. BRIDGE	$7,884,405	2.72%	$462	0.01%	$7,993,676	0.01%
14. CENSTAR	$24,279,008	18.21%	$38,247,288	157.53%	$25,141,601	152.13%
15. CHICAGO T&T	$659,204,334	109.58%	$178,675	0.03%	$664,634,623	0.03%
16. CHICAGO TIC	$102,515,127	1,271.69%	$1,884,525,225	1,838.29%	$274,482,538	686.57%
17. CHICAGO TIC (OR)	$12,022,950	119.76%	$26,222,954	218.11%	$13,566,887	193.29%
18. COLUMBIAN NATIONAL	$3,538,522	2.99%	$0	0.00%	$3,538,522	0.00%
19. COMMERCE	$7,703,478	175.00%	$42,908,676	557.00%	$8,811,912	486.94%
20. COMMONWEALTH LAND	$167,717,570	292.84%	$1,154,117,346	688.13%	$254,092,477	454.21%
21. COMMONWEALTH LAND (NJ)	$32,314,821	27.91%	$33,700,593	104.29%	$33,132,445	101.71%
22. CONESTOGA	$608,695	778.92%	$13,755,596	2,259.85%	$3,483,884	394.84%
23. CT ATTORNEYS	$38,818,515	48.48%	$51,216,178	131.94%	$41,839,283	122.41%
24. DAKOTA HOMESTEAD	$2,259,937	57.67%	$3,892,318	172.23%	$2,266,306	171.75%
25. DREIBELBISS	$2,169,435	14.31%	$581,876	26.82%	$2,650,439	21.95%
26. EQUITY NATIONAL	$1,437,919	10.27%	$236,862	16.47%	$1,438,140	16.47%
27. FARMERS NATIONAL	$693,686	60.49%	$927,258	133.67%	$817,207	113.47%
28. FIDELITY NATIONAL	$180,914,080	344.42%	$1,269,698,976	701.82%	$237,682,104	534.20%
29. FIRST AMERICAN (KS)	$5,605,495	120.77%	$14,513,623	258.92%	$5,833,793	248.79%
30. FIRST AMERICAN (NY)	$96,487,286	99.36%	$238,030,662	246.70%	$107,386,170	221.66%
31. FIRST AMERICAN (OR)	$10,651,631	300.05%	$61,020,845	572.88%	$32,041,274	190.44%
32. FIRST AMERICAN T&T	$12,921,642	28.10%	$6,291,430	48.69%	$16,413,088	38.33%
33. FIRST AMERICAN TIC	($305,977,294)	--	$3,301,702,288	--	$426,527,243	774.09%
34. FIRST AMERICAN TRANS	$1,089,431	90.74%	$1,583,015	145.31%	$1,254,245	126.21%
35. FOUNDERS	$787,772	4.58%	$176,004	22.34%	$800,122	22.00%
36. GENERAL T&T	$869,491	595.81%	$2,676,371	307.81%	$1,595,193	167.78%
37. GUARANTEE	$562,561	248.30%	$2,436,121	433.04%	$1,228,016	198.38%
38. GUARANTEE T&T	($1,283,505)	--	$11,281,699	--	$1,219,340	925.23%
39. GUARDIAN NATIONAL	$6,433,613	46.81%	$3,729,355	57.97%	$6,798,513	54.86%
40. INVESTORS TIC	$39,221,709	141.71%	$67,316,207	171.63%	$50,102,762	134.36%
41. K.E.L.	$2,323,038	1.98%	$583,915	25.14%	$2,332,454	25.03%
42. LAND CORP (CO)	$7,957,008	57.64%	$19,580,211	246.08%	$9,842,596	198.93%
43. LAND TIC (ST LOUIS)	$4,908,115	5.29%	$2,247,316	45.79%	$4,984,385	45.09%
44. LAWYERS	($27,391,668)	--	$1,216,983,337	--	$129,286,409	941.31%
45. MANITO	$1,234,710	17.56%	$735,089	59.54%	$1,256,691	58.49%
46. MASON	$2,484,176	4.39%	$1,519,982	61.19%	$2,546,042	59.70%
47. MASON COUNTY	$796,804	4.33%	$0	0.00%	$822,687	0.00%
48. MASSACHUSETTS TIC	$2,456,787	4.81%	($254)	(0.01)%	$2,465,550	--
49. MISSISSIPPI GUARANTY	$247,812	236.19%	$289,499	116.82%	$300,100	96.47%
50. MISSISSIPPI VALLEY	$8,098,652	444.46%	$25,388,544	313.49%	$9,683,618	262.18%
51. MONROE	$8,217,098	113.22%	$12,949,458	157.59%	$11,498,871	112.62%
52. NATIONAL	$2,170,559	106.06%	$3,500,144	161.26%	$3,050,235	114.75%
53. NATIONAL ATTORNEYS	$1,117,976	31.68%	$733,437	65.60%	$1,566,898	46.81%
54. NATIONAL LAND	$5,158,724	33.51%	$2,485,692	48.18%	$5,233,777	47.49%
55. NATIONAL OF NY	$6,480,320	142.22%	$12,041,204	185.81%	$6,713,364	179.36%
56. NATIONS OF NY	$12,211,638	66.92%	$19,007	0.16%	$12,627,192	0.15%
57. NEW JERSEY TIC	$3,307,074	154.34%	$17,120,677	517.70%	$4,846,327	353.27%
58. NORTH AMERICAN	$48,443,220	66.38%	$108,367,683	223.70%	$50,899,292	212.91%
59. NORTHEAST INVESTORS	$5,340,719	11.29%	$2,422,930	45.37%	$5,540,475	43.73%
60. OHIO BAR	$8,529,819	210.49%	$13,072,886	153.26%	$9,026,842	144.82%
61. OLD REPUBLIC GENERAL	$37,923,626	182.34%	$14,067,656	37.09%	$46,185,038	30.46%
62. OLD REPUBLIC NATIONAL	$77,086,077	477.91%	$739,319,536	959.08%	$116,001,825	637.33%
63. OLYMPIC	$305,841	6.66%	$0	0.00%	$336,151	0.00%
64. PACIFIC NORTHWEST	$9,952,203	156.24%	$58,302,403	585.82%	$15,156,843	384.66%
65. PENN ATTORNEYS	$8,121,465	22.59%	$1,725,400	21.24%	$8,351,671	20.66%
66. PORT LAWRENCE	$10,512,518	73.77%	$5,590,504	53.18%	$14,673,740	38.10%
67. PUBLIC	$1,038,244	0.00%	$0	0.00%	$1,038,244	0.00%
68. SEAGATE	$378,209	51.82%	$186,090	49.20%	$474,557	39.21%
69. SECURITY TG (BALTIMORE)	$1,064,266	961.08%	$21,800,759	2,048.43%	$3,764,091	579.18%
70. SECURITY UNION	$26,923,488	138.99%	$63,649,182	236.41%	$46,565,183	136.69%
71. SIERRA	$2,319,791	16.87%	$1,966,565	84.77%	$2,657,562	74.00%
72. SOUTHERN TI CORP	$3,719,413	421.33%	$53,821,007	1,447.03%	$7,715,606	697.56%
73. STEWART (OR)	$2,656,810	91.62%	$10,134,011	381.44%	$2,873,991	352.61%
74. STEWART TGC	$443,778,009	127.57%	$1,464,681,077	330.05%	$515,901,015	283.91%
75. STEWART TIC	$28,627,079	157.98%	$159,077,298	555.69%	$34,515,499	460.89%
76. T.A. TITLE	$5,002,074	111.72%	$16,990,956	339.68%	$6,503,339	261.27%
77. TICOR	$37,617,379	452.74%	$326,626,510	868.29%	$67,686,913	482.55%
78. TICOR (FL)	$7,367,657	1,293.30%	$83,321,498	1,130.91%	$25,586,476	325.65%
79. TITLE G&TC	$623,579	86.76%	$260,893	41.84%	$907,607	28.75%
80. TITLE GUARANTY DIV (IA)	$726,128	752.72%	$3,686,225	507.65%	$739,705	498.34%
81. TITLE IC AMERICA	$10,980,291	34.13%	$11,896,936	108.35%	$11,666,575	101.97%
82. TITLE RESOURCES	$21,429,502	66.95%	$103,629,865	483.59%	$25,711,604	403.05%
83. TITLEDGE	$722,784	4.18%	$181,572	25.12%	$753,085	24.11%
84. TRANSNATION	$2,081,320	6,594.03%	$276,607,560	13,290.01%	$22,334,782	1,238.46%
85. TRANSUNION NATIONAL	$9,849,369	56.11%	$3,760,507	38.18%	$10,048,532	37.42%
86. TRANSUNION TIC	$3,552,891	193.88%	$882,460	24.84%	$3,880,844	22.74%
87. UNITED CAPITAL	$18,108,877	156.96%	$61,421,744	339.18%	$22,767,542	269.78%
88. UNITED GENERAL	($3,247,002)	--	$342,976,132	--	$27,974,272	1,226.04%
89. WASHINGTON TIC	($152,428)	--	$15,328,218	--	$876,497	1,748.80%
90. WESTCOR	$5,311,186	289.96%	$51,972,327	978.54%	$8,662,482	599.97%
91. WESTERN NATIONAL	$3,256,315	42.43%	$370,721	11.38%	$3,358,552	11.04%
COMPOSITE	$1,131,664,181	656.85%	$14,058,172,014	1,242.26%	$2,778,616,712	505.94%
AVERAGE	$23,378,067		$154,485,407		$41,476,447	

5

B.2 Net Liquid Assets

COMPANY	2007	2006	2006 TO 2007	2005	2005 TO 2006	2004	2004 TO 2005	2003	2003 TO 2004
1. CHICAGO T&T	$659,204,334	$914,475,854	(27.91)%	$848,940,879	7.72%	$647,684,373	31.07%	$731,421,361	(11.45)%
2. STEWART TGC	$443,778,009	$442,401,074	0.31%	$430,462,512	2.77%	$366,530,513	17.44%	$320,299,675	14.43%
3. FIDELITY NATIONAL	$180,914,080	$218,126,592	(17.06)%	$221,376,832	(1.47)%	$137,607,219	60.88%	$121,830,462	12.95%
4. COMMONWEALTH LAND	$167,717,570	$236,674,699	(29.14)%	$97,234,132	143.41%	$61,807,880	57.32%	$69,239,626	(10.73)%
5. CHICAGO TIC	$102,515,127	$290,265,773	(64.68)%	$254,344,883	14.12%	$347,049,625	(26.71)%	$353,431,825	(1.81)%
6. FIRST AMERICAN (NY)	$96,487,286	$70,291,341	37.27%	$61,136,344	14.97%	$52,339,452	16.81%	$58,437,207	(10.43)%
7. ATTORNEYS TIF (FL)	$81,702,918	$92,360,323	(11.54)%	$77,113,778	19.77%	$56,476,063	36.54%	$38,574,814	46.41%
8. OLD REPUBLIC NATIONAL	$77,086,077	$79,799,254	(3.40)%	$77,566,806	2.88%	$73,131,692	6.06%	$52,204,781	40.09%
9. NORTH AMERICAN	$48,443,220	$18,792,297	157.78%	$15,888,971	18.27%	$12,888,153	23.28%	$9,880,169	30.44%
10. INVESTORS TIC	$39,221,709	$44,210,972	(11.29)%	$39,453,881	12.06%	$35,779,647	10.27%	$30,859,679	15.94%
11. CT ATTORNEYS	$38,818,515	$38,143,363	1.77%	$37,509,830	1.69%	$34,502,743	8.72%	$28,031,929	23.08%
12. OLD REPUBLIC GENERAL	$37,923,626	$38,810,728	(2.29)%	$30,125,966	28.83%	$29,342,413	2.67%	$20,644,916	42.13%
13. TICOR	$37,617,379	$28,849,629	30.39%	$49,219,626	(41.39)%	$39,541,733	24.48%	$58,367,625	(32.25)%
14. COMMONWEALTH LAND (NJ)	$32,314,821	$29,315,614	10.23%	$28,140,134	4.18%	$30,343,728	(7.26)%	$25,886,528	17.22%
15. STEWART TIC	$28,627,079	$25,067,475	14.20%	$32,458,031	(22.77)%	$13,903,038	133.46%	$12,747,318	9.07%
16. SECURITY UNION	$26,923,488	$42,323,502	(36.39)%	$40,928,644	3.41%	$44,033,005	(7.05)%	$44,479,327	(1.00)%
17. CENSTAR	$24,279,008	$22,207,697	9.33%	$18,433,954	20.47%	$15,651,622	17.78%	$14,893,103	5.09%
18. ALAMO	$21,757,762	$33,917,941	(35.85)%	$30,043,445	12.90%	$30,262,071	(0.72)%	$31,387,113	(3.58)%
19. TITLE RESOURCES	$21,429,502	$24,527,911	(12.63)%	$24,909,832	(1.53)%	$21,536,167	15.67%	$17,430,858	23.55%
20. UNITED CAPITAL	$18,108,877	$22,270,721	(18.69)%	$18,859,999	18.08%	$13,508,876	39.61%	$12,212,349	10.62%
21. FIRST AMERICAN T&T	$12,921,642	$9,846,744	31.23%	$8,260,665	19.20%	$5,829,893	41.69%	$3,956,685	47.34%
22. NATIONS OF NY	$12,211,638	$11,136,942	9.65%	$8,232,020	35.29%	$7,668,258	7.35%	$7,418,435	3.37%
23. CHICAGO TIC (OR)	$12,022,950	$12,057,222	(0.28)%	$10,453,961	15.34%	$8,660,463	20.71%	$12,088,484	(28.36)%
24. TITLE IC AMERICA	$10,980,291	$8,488,301	29.36%	$9,075,698	(6.47)%	$7,850,955	15.60%	$7,030,657	11.67%
25. FIRST AMERICAN (OR)	$10,651,631	$12,475,340	(14.62)%	$9,035,321	38.07%	$10,545,642	(14.32)%	$13,503,805	(21.91)%
26. AMERICAN GUARANTY	$10,532,088	$9,117,243	15.52%	$8,490,401	7.38%	$7,033,159	20.72%	$4,057,868	73.32%
27. PORT LAWRENCE	$10,512,518	$13,099,356	(19.75)%	$11,694,192	12.02%	$10,630,139	10.01%	$9,350,701	13.68%
28. PACIFIC NORTHWEST	$9,952,203	$6,586,751	51.09%	$3,622,100	81.85%	$3,462,150	4.62%	$934,899	270.32%
29. TRANSUNION NATIONAL	$9,849,369	$10,254,799	(3.95)%	$3,889,607	163.65%	$5,542,094	(29.82)%	$5,303,547	4.50%
30. OHIO BAR	$8,529,819	$6,984,291	22.13%	$5,796,703	20.49%	$4,482,724	29.31%	$2,864,794	56.48%
31. AMERICAN SECURITY	$8,304,294	$7,280,366	14.06%	$6,629,861	9.81%	$5,982,152	10.83%	$5,208,571	14.85%
32. MONROE	$8,217,098	$10,539,036	(22.03)%	$9,726,333	8.36%	$8,756,141	11.08%	$7,758,431	12.86%
33. PENN ATTORNEYS	$8,121,465	$8,149,851	(0.35)%	$7,379,784	10.43%	$6,548,153	12.70%	$5,546,091	18.07%
34. MISSISSIPPI VALLEY	$8,098,652	$8,472,766	(4.42)%	$7,789,563	8.77%	$8,178,274	(4.75)%	$6,525,000	25.34%
35. LAND CORP (CO)	$7,957,008	$8,367,466	(4.91)%	$7,597,286	10.14%	$8,932,602	(14.95)%	$8,369,724	6.73%
36. BRIDGE	$7,884,405	$8,037,275	(1.90)%	$8,028,246	0.11%	$4,544,198	76.67%	$8,051,535	(43.56)%
37. COMMERCE	$7,703,478	$6,678,184	15.35%	$4,213,926	58.48%	$6,801,614	(38.05)%	$8,227,440	(17.33)%
38. TICOR (FL)	$7,367,657	$11,417,549	(35.47)%	$13,408,502	(14.85)%	$23,314,071	(42.49)%	$37,798,233	(38.32)%
39. NATIONAL OF NY	$6,480,320	$8,479,452	(23.58)%	$5,851,481	44.91%	$2,919,796	100.41%	$5,361,047	(45.54)%
40. GUARDIAN NATIONAL	$6,433,613	$1,517,526	323.95%	$1,833,645	(17.24)%	$1,742,624	5.22%	$1,806,436	(3.53)%
41. FIRST AMERICAN (KS)	$5,605,495	$4,880,757	14.85%	$3,870,753	26.09%	$3,418,710	13.22%	$3,451,099	(0.94)%
42. NORTHEAST INVESTORS	$5,340,719	$5,112,820	4.46%	$4,965,595	2.96%	$3,833,612	29.53%	$3,625,208	5.75%
43. WESTCOR	$5,311,186	$7,298,025	(27.22)%	$9,517,404	(23.32)%	$5,785,262	64.51%	$5,808,195	(0.39)%
44. NATIONAL LAND	$5,158,724	$5,438,119	(5.14)%	$2,899,645	87.54%	$2,807,369	3.29%	$2,750,997	2.05%
45. T.A. TITLE	$5,002,074	$6,821,698	(26.67)%	$5,790,429	17.81%	$3,750,789	54.38%	$2,116,857	77.19%
46. ATTORNEYS TGF (IL)	$4,975,119	$4,761,487	4.49%	$2,618,111	81.87%	$310,026	744.48%	($585,549)	--
47. LAND TIC (ST LOUIS)	$4,908,115	$4,769,757	2.90%	$3,759,671	26.87%	$4,448,160	(15.48)%	$4,186,635	6.25%
48. SOUTHERN TI CORP	$3,719,413	$4,649,675	(20.01)%	$4,009,107	15.98%	$3,211,849	24.82%	$2,946,135	9.02%
49. TRANSUNION TIC	$3,552,891	$3,340,704	6.35%	$1,349,427	147.56%	($1,327,415)	--	($1,382,029)	--
50. COLUMBIAN NATIONAL	$3,462,022	$4,074,407	(15.03)%	$2,031,464	100.57%	$3,690,701	(44.96)%	$5,303,957	(30.42)%
51. NEW JERSEY TIC	$3,307,074	$3,863,015	(14.39)%	$3,571,747	8.15%	$3,277,265	8.99%	$3,591,018	(8.74)%
52. WESTERN NATIONAL	$3,256,315	$3,008,667	8.23%	$3,151,057	(4.52)%	$3,010,962	4.65%	$2,926,182	2.90%
53. ALLIANCE	$3,100,706	$2,977,562	4.14%	$2,994,812	(0.58)%	$2,331,130	28.47%	$2,399,696	(2.86)%
54. STEWART (OR)	$2,656,810	$2,444,451	8.69%	$2,307,992	5.91%	$1,877,047	22.96%	$1,699,618	10.44%
55. MASON	$2,484,176	$2,773,429	(10.43)%	--	--	--	--	--	--
56. MASSACHUSETTS TIC	$2,456,787	$2,138,306	14.89%	$1,655,888	29.13%	$1,516,445	9.20%	$1,293,100	17.27%
57. K.E.L.	$2,323,038	--	--	--	--	--	--	--	--
58. SIERRA	$2,319,791	$2,504,117	(7.36)%	--	--	--	--	--	--
59. DAKOTA HOMESTEAD	$2,259,937	$2,074,236	8.95%	$2,236,159	(7.24)%	$2,505,374	(10.75)%	$2,215,810	13.07%
60. NATIONAL	$2,170,559	$2,182,796	(0.56)%	$2,245,840	(2.81)%	$1,997,920	12.41%	$2,129,389	(6.17)%
61. DREIBELBISS	$2,169,435	$2,075,432	4.53%	$1,937,596	7.11%	$1,653,456	17.18%	$1,649,788	0.22%
62. ARKANSAS TIC	$2,107,597	$2,017,699	4.46%	$1,775,013	13.67%	$1,436,840	23.54%	$1,606,966	(10.59)%
63. TRANSNATION	$2,081,320	$40,171,923	(94.82)%	$66,334,826	(39.44)%	$43,935,795	50.98%	$54,426,476	(19.27)%
64. ALLIANT	$1,871,402	$2,245,445	(16.66)%	$2,301,381	(2.43)%	--	--	--	--
65. EQUITY NATIONAL	$1,437,919	$1,171,795	22.71%	$1,267,901	(7.58)%	--	--	--	--
66. MANITO	$1,234,710	$1,244,550	(0.79)%	$1,218,602	2.13%	$1,227,812	(0.75)%	$1,323,751	(7.25)%
67. NATIONAL ATTORNEYS	$1,117,976	$1,246,391	(10.30)%	$1,189,426	4.79%	$1,148,934	3.52%	$1,138,622	0.91%
68. FIRST AMERICAN TRANS	$1,089,431	$956,371	13.92%	$802,921	19.10%	$688,631	16.60%	$571,547	20.49%
69. SECURITY TG (BALTIMORE)	$1,064,266	$2,643,919	(59.75)%	$2,406,963	9.84%	$3,557,501	(32.34)%	$3,461,629	2.77%
70. PUBLIC	$1,038,244	$1,007,901	3.01%	--	--	--	--	--	--
71. GENERAL T&T	$869,491	$1,375,061	(36.77)%	$1,391,059	(1.15)%	$993,439	40.02%	$744,557	33.43%
72. MASON COUNTY	$796,804	$773,157	3.06%	$745,776	3.67%	$784,576	(4.95)%	$799,765	(1.90)%
73. FOUNDERS	$787,772	$823,867	(4.38)%	$851,045	(3.19)%	--	--	--	--
74. AMERICAN LAND & AIRCRAFT	$739,228	$747,281	(1.08)%	$693,903	7.69%	$709,941	(2.26)%	$705,507	0.63%
75. TITLE GUARANTY DIV (IA)	$726,128	$593,366	22.37%	$775,326	(23.47)%	$804,621	(3.64)%	$1,811,363	(55.58)%
76. TITLEDGE	$722,784	--	--	--	--	--	--	--	--
77. FARMERS NATIONAL	$693,686	$700,981	(1.04)%	--	--	--	--	--	--
78. TITLE G&TC	$623,579	$603,128	3.39%	$466,832	29.20%	$349,973	33.39%	$182,506	91.76%
79. CONESTOGA	$608,695	$1,166,437	(47.82)%	$1,308,808	(10.88)%	$1,030,976	26.95%	$2,515,502	(59.02)%
80. GUARANTEE	$562,561	$882,692	(36.27)%	$1,660,513	(46.84)%	$1,678,729	(1.09)%	$1,551,979	8.17%
81. ARSENAL	$483,654	$512,348	(5.60)%	$509,955	0.47%	$1,053,991	(51.62)%	--	--
82. SEAGATE	$378,209	$369,204	2.44%	$342,099	7.92%	$358,176	(4.49)%	$332,397	7.76%
83. OLYMPIC	$305,841	$360,000	(15.04)%	$309,744	16.23%	$317,965	(2.59)%	$395,935	(19.69)%
84. MISSISSIPPI GUARANTY	$247,812	$159,640	55.23%	$128,289	24.44%	$176,545	(27.33)%	$336,515	(47.54)%
85. WASHINGTON TIC	($152,428)	($207,056)	--	($33,670)	--	($229,530)	--	$819,608	(128.00)%
86. AMERICAN EAGLE	($387,008)	$830,893	(146.58)%	$1,124,119	(26.08)%	$898,154	25.16%	$1,013,990	(11.42)%
87. ATTORNEYS TGF (CO)	($889,000)	($1,409,877)	--	($622,003)	--	$608,497	(202.30)%	$1,022,903	(40.51)%
88. GUARANTEE T&T	($1,283,505)	($386,018)	--	$623,421	(161.92)%	$1,328,778	(53.08)%	$1,965,068	(32.38)%
89. UNITED GENERAL	($3,247,002)	($5,996,654)	--	$3,372,570	(277.81)%	$11,282,334	(70.11)%	$12,027,840	(6.20)%
90. LAWYERS	($27,391,668)	$32,985,456	(183.04)%	$34,793,059	(5.20)%	$34,508,464	0.82%	$81,984,784	(57.91)%
91. FIRST AMERICAN TIC	($305,977,294)	($14,737,113)	--	$288,157,862	(105.11)%	$219,030,254	31.56%	$229,923,772	(4.74)%
COMPOSITE	$2,127,404,108	$3,041,861,413	(30.06)%	$3,059,966,211	(0.59)%	$2,589,125,173	18.19%	$2,660,212,136	(2.67)%
AVERAGE	$23,378,067	$34,178,218	(31.60)%	$35,999,602	(5.06)%	$31,574,697	14.01%	$32,842,125	(3.86)%

5

B.3 Total Liabilities to Net Liquid Assets

	2007			2006	2005	2004	2003
COMPANY	TOTAL LIABILITIES	B.2 - NET LIQUID ASSETS	RATIO	RATIO	RATIO	RATIO	RATIO
1. WASHINGTON TIC	$3,068,563	($152,428)	--	--	--	--	216.86%
2. AMERICAN EAGLE	$1,406,603	($387,008)	--	94.30%	39.84%	55.52%	40.65%
3. ATTORNEYS TGF (CO)	$3,029,311	($889,008)	--	--	--	723.19%	554.06%
4. GUARANTEE T&T	$6,705,610	($1,283,505)	--	--	1,007.38%	501.57%	289.39%
5. UNITED GENERAL	$91,127,118	($3,247,002)	--	--	1,381.52%	366.43%	313.90%
6. LAWYERS	$485,289,739	($27,391,668)	--	1,448.88%	1,384.78%	1,195.95%	440.14%
7. FIRST AMERICAN TIC	$1,446,753,312	($305,977,294)	--	--	431.04%	492.94%	378.57%
8. PUBLIC	$0	$1,038,244	0.00%	0.00%	--	--	--
9. K.E.L.	$45,957	$2,323,038	1.98%	--	--	--	--
10. AMERICAN SECURITY	$176,000	$8,304,294	2.12%	2.42%	2.65%	2.94%	3.38%
11. BRIDGE	$214,292	$7,884,405	2.72%	2.56%	2.69%	6.80%	3.18%
12. COLUMBIAN NATIONAL	$103,487	$3,462,022	2.99%	27.71%	355.64%	143.62%	81.76%
13. TITLEDGE	$30,198	$722,784	4.18%	--	--	--	--
14. MASON COUNTY	$34,470	$796,804	4.33%	3.56%	4.01%	6.02%	4.51%
15. MASON	$109,123	$2,484,176	4.39%	1.59%	--	--	--
16. FOUNDERS	$36,060	$787,772	4.58%	3.20%	2.11%	--	--
17. MASSACHUSETTS TIC	$118,272	$2,456,787	4.81%	9.83%	11.41%	10.88%	11.34%
18. LAND TIC (ST LOUIS)	$259,672	$4,908,115	5.29%	21.38%	128.80%	12.16%	7.80%
19. OLYMPIC	$20,383	$305,841	6.66%	0.00%	6.47%	15.62%	1.26%
20. AMERICAN LAND & AIRCRAFT	$64,832	$739,228	8.77%	9.24%	11.22%	11.81%	9.27%
21. EQUITY NATIONAL	$147,716	$1,437,919	10.27%	60.65%	50.95%	--	--
22. NORTHEAST INVESTORS	$602,766	$5,340,719	11.29%	12.04%	12.00%	15.29%	17.15%
23. DREIBELBISS	$310,454	$2,169,435	14.31%	22.54%	33.02%	45.27%	66.62%
24. SIERRA	$391,381	$2,319,791	16.87%	0.00%	--	--	--
25. MANITO	$216,769	$1,234,710	17.56%	16.87%	20.81%	22.51%	23.16%
26. CENSTAR	$4,420,438	$24,279,008	18.21%	13.05%	14.17%	6.05%	0.09%
27. ALLIANCE	$599,662	$3,100,706	19.34%	24.97%	30.28%	69.65%	68.02%
28. PENN ATTORNEYS	$1,834,746	$8,121,465	22.59%	23.39%	25.12%	36.00%	32.53%
29. ARSENAL	$109,584	$483,654	22.66%	11.99%	12.63%	1.30%	--
30. AMERICAN GUARANTY	$2,776,365	$10,532,088	26.36%	29.40%	29.32%	38.20%	66.82%
31. COMMONWEALTH LAND (NJ)	$9,019,669	$32,314,821	27.91%	31.06%	35.01%	25.35%	29.27%
32. FIRST AMERICAN T&T	$3,631,434	$12,921,642	28.10%	45.01%	100.31%	126.19%	167.26%
33. NATIONAL ATTORNEYS	$354,221	$1,117,976	31.68%	25.30%	27.60%	32.34%	36.39%
34. NATIONAL LAND	$1,728,455	$5,158,724	33.51%	23.71%	51.28%	57.46%	63.74%
35. TITLE IC AMERICA	$3,747,365	$10,980,291	34.13%	47.59%	42.05%	57.87%	59.32%
36. WESTERN NATIONAL	$1,381,751	$3,256,315	42.43%	50.06%	47.55%	55.38%	60.42%
37. GUARDIAN NATIONAL	$3,011,373	$6,433,613	46.81%	210.58%	156.24%	139.74%	97.62%
38. CT ATTORNEYS	$18,819,571	$38,818,515	48.48%	46.47%	50.51%	54.93%	61.67%
39. SEAGATE	$195,991	$378,209	51.82%	54.25%	85.36%	76.05%	79.61%
40. TRANSUNION NATIONAL	$5,526,969	$9,849,369	56.11%	44.83%	132.66%	63.68%	59.65%
41. LAND CORP (CO)	$4,586,526	$7,957,008	57.64%	55.56%	70.82%	61.50%	71.58%
42. DAKOTA HOMESTEAD	$1,303,382	$2,259,937	57.67%	49.75%	45.23%	17.52%	23.43%
43. FARMERS NATIONAL	$419,582	$693,686	60.49%	24.16%	--	--	--
44. NORTH AMERICAN	$32,158,738	$48,443,220	66.38%	129.27%	168.00%	173.43%	214.83%
45. NATIONS OF NY	$8,172,302	$12,211,638	66.92%	97.83%	131.21%	143.67%	153.79%
46. TITLE RESOURCES	$14,347,303	$21,429,502	66.95%	70.92%	53.32%	61.56%	71.81%
47. PORT LAWRENCE	$7,755,221	$10,512,518	73.77%	61.08%	120.43%	90.94%	77.86%
48. ALLIANT	$1,516,163	$1,871,402	81.02%	20.48%	2.49%	--	--
49. TITLE G&TC	$541,044	$623,579	86.76%	105.08%	110.03%	159.87%	359.90%
50. FIRST AMERICAN TRANS	$988,586	$1,089,431	90.74%	117.37%	72.68%	67.51%	61.36%
51. STEWART (OR)	$2,434,138	$2,656,810	91.62%	86.70%	78.05%	88.45%	86.00%
52. FIRST AMERICAN (NY)	$95,872,922	$96,487,286	99.36%	106.04%	129.56%	123.11%	83.74%
53. ALAMO	$22,169,518	$21,757,762	101.89%	80.05%	122.74%	121.16%	101.58%
54. NATIONAL	$2,302,030	$2,170,559	106.06%	95.56%	64.68%	93.53%	64.24%
55. CHICAGO T&T	$722,383,376	$659,204,334	109.58%	101.84%	117.61%	128.78%	106.57%
56. T.A. TITLE	$5,588,179	$5,002,074	111.72%	76.28%	87.53%	129.55%	305.38%
57. MONROE	$9,303,550	$8,217,098	113.22%	90.25%	97.85%	117.02%	141.69%
58. CHICAGO TIC (OR)	$14,398,196	$12,022,950	119.76%	123.01%	157.04%	201.13%	125.99%
59. FIRST AMERICAN (KS)	$6,769,891	$5,605,495	120.77%	113.28%	160.88%	155.27%	93.16%
60. ARKANSAS TIC	$2,600,762	$2,107,597	123.40%	115.80%	124.47%	151.15%	126.51%
61. STEWART TGC	$566,123,531	$443,778,009	127.57%	120.11%	122.77%	131.53%	130.22%
62. SECURITY UNION	$37,420,423	$26,923,488	138.99%	95.35%	111.48%	106.67%	116.55%
63. INVESTORS TIC	$55,581,895	$39,221,709	141.71%	123.12%	126.18%	128.81%	138.83%
64. NATIONAL OF NY	$9,216,496	$6,480,320	142.22%	101.13%	203.54%	350.12%	194.98%
65. NEW JERSEY TIC	$5,104,286	$3,307,074	154.34%	115.57%	119.29%	111.24%	90.14%
66. PACIFIC NORTHWEST	$15,548,948	$9,952,203	156.24%	256.02%	485.89%	494.11%	1,731.20%
67. UNITED CAPITAL	$28,424,123	$18,108,877	156.96%	127.77%	128.43%	136.38%	107.29%
68. STEWART TIC	$45,225,366	$28,627,079	157.98%	166.12%	126.09%	276.32%	263.96%
69. COMMERCE	$13,480,750	$7,703,478	175.00%	196.05%	279.99%	109.59%	90.18%
70. OLD REPUBLIC GENERAL	$69,148,885	$37,923,626	182.34%	174.07%	225.16%	220.72%	293.08%
71. TRANSUNION TIC	$6,888,204	$3,552,891	193.88%	198.37%	426.24%	--	--
72. OHIO BAR	$17,954,477	$8,529,819	210.49%	256.03%	310.39%	383.35%	571.76%
73. ATTORNEYS TIF (FL)	$174,477,082	$81,702,918	213.55%	183.68%	206.89%	244.39%	329.85%
74. MISSISSIPPI GUARANTY	$585,309	$247,812	236.19%	380.17%	455.68%	312.54%	121.34%
75. GUARANTEE	$1,396,825	$562,561	248.30%	125.26%	39.63%	34.65%	48.66%
76. WESTCOR	$15,400,201	$5,311,186	289.96%	192.36%	132.62%	207.94%	159.73%
77. COMMONWEALTH LAND	$491,145,534	$167,717,570	292.84%	196.94%	587.18%	794.86%	651.59%
78. FIRST AMERICAN (OR)	$31,960,107	$10,651,631	300.05%	269.33%	465.13%	305.58%	219.06%
79. FIDELITY NATIONAL	$623,107,279	$180,914,080	344.42%	287.54%	283.90%	383.71%	244.77%
80. ATTORNEYS TGF (IL)	$19,884,504	$4,975,119	399.68%	362.64%	644.05%	4,800.80%	--
81. SOUTHERN TI CORP	$15,670,916	$3,719,413	421.33%	269.09%	282.40%	314.09%	233.68%
82. MISSISSIPPI VALLEY	$35,995,416	$8,098,652	444.46%	389.35%	409.64%	372.25%	447.42%
83. TICOR	$170,308,285	$37,617,379	452.74%	711.57%	403.69%	540.95%	310.23%
84. OLD REPUBLIC NATIONAL	$368,402,069	$77,086,077	477.91%	475.15%	489.18%	457.80%	631.26%
85. GENERAL T&T	$5,180,548	$869,491	595.81%	368.92%	341.38%	421.61%	421.78%
86. TITLE GUARANTY DIV (IA)	$5,465,676	$726,128	752.72%	945.91%	655.04%	624.70%	228.93%
87. CONESTOGA	$4,741,242	$608,695	778.92%	444.57%	383.65%	445.58%	158.82%
88. SECURITY TG (BALTIMORE)	$10,228,415	$1,064,266	961.08%	414.60%	432.62%	281.37%	256.65%
89. CHICAGO TIC	$1,303,675,705	$102,515,127	1,271.69%	430.37%	454.93%	247.47%	232.86%
90. TICOR (FL)	$95,285,888	$7,367,657	1,293.30%	786.34%	774.63%	326.03%	180.41%
91. TRANSNATION	$137,242,911	$2,081,320	6,594.03%	280.45%	168.58%	270.87%	174.70%
COMPOSITE	$7,433,302,387	$2,127,404,108	349.41%	242.36%	240.78%	243.20%	205.60%
AVERAGE	$81,684,642	$23,378,067	349.41%				

5

B.4 Net Premiums Written (NPW)

COMPANY	2007	2006	2006 TO 2007	2005	2005 TO 2006	2004	2004 TO 2005	2003	2003 TO 2004
1. FIRST AMERICAN TIC	$3,301,702,288	$3,844,052,530	(14.11)%	$3,933,318,530	(2.27)%	$3,371,011,877	16.68%	$3,183,729,430	5.88%
2. CHICAGO TIC	$1,884,525,225	$2,277,093,376	(17.24)%	$2,278,341,896	(0.05)%	$2,250,195,423	1.25%	$2,322,757,685	(3.12)%
3. STEWART TGC	$1,464,681,077	$1,777,800,347	(17.61)%	$1,750,622,613	1.55%	$1,577,302,638	10.99%	$1,623,466,407	(2.84)%
4. FIDELITY NATIONAL	$1,269,698,976	$1,520,825,523	(16.51)%	$1,737,640,475	(12.48)%	$1,612,229,533	7.78%	$950,367,083	69.64%
5. LAWYERS	$1,216,983,337	$1,327,658,111	(8.34)%	$1,306,785,825	1.60%	$1,211,733,563	7.84%	$1,265,950,641	(4.28)%
6. COMMONWEALTH LAND	$1,154,117,346	$1,293,972,459	(10.81)%	$1,296,929,186	(0.23)%	$1,190,239,524	8.96%	$1,203,820,388	(1.13)%
7. OLD REPUBLIC NATIONAL	$739,319,536	$848,098,867	(12.83)%	$918,999,345	(7.71)%	$889,883,016	3.27%	$933,679,259	(4.69)%
8. ATTORNEYS TIF (FL)	$345,668,134	$478,618,547	(27.78)%	$488,196,601	(1.96)%	$420,711,546	16.04%	$356,519,441	18.01%
9. UNITED GENERAL	$342,976,132	$332,785,598	3.06%	$199,303,461	66.97%	$206,253,535	(3.37)%	$256,186,966	(19.49)%
10. TICOR	$326,626,510	$357,839,930	(8.72)%	$300,086,190	19.25%	$367,695,784	(18.39)%	$357,622,484	2.82%
11. TRANSNATION	$276,607,560	$354,501,120	(21.97)%	$392,845,496	(9.76)%	$349,242,002	12.49%	$301,275,326	15.92%
12. FIRST AMERICAN (NY)	$238,030,662	$234,380,871	1.56%	$238,131,742	(1.58)%	$226,574,240	5.10%	$193,167,654	17.29%
13. STEWART TIC	$159,077,298	$151,617,120	4.92%	$151,745,446	(0.08)%	$145,456,059	4.32%	$141,947,995	2.47%
14. NORTH AMERICAN	$108,367,683	$94,152,314	15.10%	$104,131,105	(9.58)%	$94,044,640	10.73%	$85,459,878	10.05%
15. TITLE RESOURCES	$103,629,865	$110,819,354	(6.49)%	$83,489,399	32.73%	$91,173,758	(8.43)%	$94,116,676	(3.13)%
16. ALAMO	$94,165,105	$112,080,497	(15.98)%	$109,236,256	2.60%	$113,343,880	(3.62)%	$133,284,546	(14.96)%
17. TICOR (FL)	$83,321,498	$163,692,117	(49.10)%	$342,642,790	(52.23)%	$251,329,006	36.33%	$284,994,216	(11.81)%
18. INVESTORS TIC	$67,316,207	$67,118,384	0.29%	$73,311,708	(8.45)%	$67,969,575	7.86%	$78,956,866	(13.92)%
19. SECURITY UNION	$63,649,182	$91,076,117	(30.11)%	$81,231,926	12.12%	$94,691,997	(14.21)%	$74,663,324	26.83%
20. UNITED CAPITAL	$61,421,744	$124,329,406	(50.60)%	$161,684,310	(23.10)%	$128,189,921	26.13%	$127,827,911	0.28%
21. FIRST AMERICAN (OR)	$61,020,845	$66,849,712	(8.72)%	$66,730,865	0.18%	$60,853,169	9.66%	$73,905,919	(17.66)%
22. PACIFIC NORTHWEST	$58,302,403	$61,087,472	(4.56)%	$51,242,251	19.21%	$52,813,832	(2.98)%	$75,630,972	(30.17)%
23. SOUTHERN TI CORP	$53,821,007	$55,463,098	(2.96)%	$44,969,115	23.34%	$36,183,987	24.28%	$32,290,125	12.06%
24. WESTCOR	$51,972,327	$49,528,207	4.93%	$56,864,121	(12.90)%	$50,627,144	12.32%	$49,750,147	1.76%
25. CT ATTORNEYS	$51,216,178	$57,129,846	(10.35)%	$60,720,967	(5.91)%	$57,684,657	5.26%	$66,525,295	(13.29)%
26. COMMERCE	$42,908,676	$54,635,598	(21.46)%	$53,803,803	1.55%	$50,223,571	7.13%	$49,544,751	1.37%
27. CENSTAR	$38,247,288	$44,344,708	(13.75)%	$48,811,033	(9.15)%	$10,861,253	349.41%	$0	--
28. COMMONWEALTH LAND (NJ)	$33,700,593	$42,483,050	(20.67)%	$46,259,141	(8.16)%	$45,578,030	1.49%	$38,227,711	19.23%
29. CHICAGO TIC (OR)	$26,222,954	$33,521,972	(21.77)%	$32,814,252	2.16%	$25,484,065	28.76%	$36,654,817	(30.48)%
30. MISSISSIPPI VALLEY	$25,388,544	$25,373,994	0.06%	$22,551,374	12.52%	$23,805,086	(5.27)%	$27,525,027	(13.51)%
31. SECURITY TG (BALTIMORE)	$21,800,759	$32,453,743	(32.83)%	$29,524,990	9.92%	$34,563,116	(14.58)%	$29,197,197	18.38%
32. LAND CORP (CO)	$19,580,211	$23,002,589	(14.88)%	$26,418,124	(12.93)%	$26,515,999	(0.37)%	$38,260,193	(30.70)%
33. NEW JERSEY TIC	$17,120,677	$18,794,682	(8.91)%	$21,383,500	(12.11)%	$16,992,095	25.84%	$16,465,008	3.20%
34. T.A. TITLE	$16,990,956	$17,218,436	(1.32)%	$17,416,339	(1.14)%	$16,816,405	3.57%	$21,680,859	(22.44)%
35. WASHINGTON TIC	$15,328,218	$19,309,288	(20.62)%	$19,975,201	(3.33)%	$16,026,808	24.64%	$16,347,480	(1.96)%
36. FIRST AMERICAN (KS)	$14,513,623	$14,055,287	3.26%	$14,722,174	(4.53)%	$12,533,917	17.46%	$15,068,074	(16.82)%
37. OLD REPUBLIC GENERAL	$14,067,656	$16,084,347	(12.54)%	$22,930,833	(29.86)%	$24,619,182	(6.86)%	$26,594,657	(7.43)%
38. ALLIANT	$13,883,261	$7,128,829	94.75%	$130,821	5,349.30%	--	--	--	--
39. CONESTOGA	$13,755,596	$17,772,601	(22.60)%	$19,588,006	(9.27)%	$20,919,674	(6.37)%	$25,112,977	(16.70)%
40. OHIO BAR	$13,072,886	$15,055,518	(13.17)%	$14,494,923	3.87%	$20,421,731	(29.02)%	$19,285,564	5.89%
41. MONROE	$12,949,458	$13,667,733	(5.26)%	$15,130,598	(9.67)%	$16,241,791	(6.84)%	$17,792,079	(8.71)%
42. NATIONAL OF NY	$12,041,204	($441,840)	--	($2,775,921)	--	$18,614,752	(114.91)%	$39,982,106	(53.44)%
43. TITLE IC AMERICA	$11,896,936	$11,382,965	4.52%	$18,729,587	(39.22)%	$20,972,036	(10.69)%	$20,327,971	3.17%
44. GUARANTEE T&T	$11,281,699	$13,301,811	(15.19)%	$12,814,784	3.80%	$19,572,919	(34.53)%	$17,473,575	12.01%
45. ATTORNEYS TGF (IL)	$10,652,985	$11,861,022	(10.18)%	$13,194,273	(10.10)%	$11,979,284	10.14%	$12,179,189	(1.64)%
46. STEWART (OR)	$10,134,011	$10,007,793	1.26%	$10,079,978	(0.72)%	$8,686,295	16.04%	$10,400,868	(16.48)%
47. ATTORNEYS TGF (CO)	$8,740,480	$10,130,230	(13.72)%	$12,487,772	(18.88)%	$13,736,043	(9.09)%	$16,037,726	(14.35)%
48. ARKANSAS TIC	$8,213,976	$7,448,764	10.27%	$5,995,405	24.24%	$5,816,880	3.07%	$5,239,713	11.02%
49. FIRST AMERICAN T&T	$6,291,430	$4,630,569	35.87%	$4,440,486	4.28%	$4,820,189	(7.88)%	$5,653,331	(14.74)%
50. PORT LAWRENCE	$5,590,504	$7,055,071	(20.76)%	$6,370,714	10.74%	$6,984,100	(8.78)%	$8,543,745	(18.25)%
51. DAKOTA HOMESTEAD	$3,892,318	$5,473,746	(28.89)%	$3,782,955	44.69%	$2,101,243	80.03%	$1,953,614	7.56%
52. TRANSUNION NATIONAL	$3,760,507	$3,909,584	(3.81)%	$4,917,612	(20.50)%	$4,057,254	21.21%	$5,230,484	(22.43)%
53. GUARDIAN NATIONAL	$3,729,355	$4,376,056	(14.78)%	$7,489,564	(41.57)%	$7,212,670	3.84%	$10,250,829	(29.64)%
54. TITLE GUARANTY DIV (IA)	$3,686,225	$3,940,490	(6.45)%	$3,987,820	(1.19)%	$5,711,184	(30.18)%	$6,881,599	(17.01)%
55. NATIONAL	$3,500,144	$2,872,610	21.85%	$2,629,361	9.25%	$2,036,670	29.10%	$2,236,141	(8.92)%
56. AMERICAN GUARANTY	$3,489,926	$3,488,834	0.03%	$3,325,087	4.92%	$3,246,617	2.42%	$3,883,135	(16.39)%
57. AMERICAN EAGLE	$2,995,458	$2,709,921	10.54%	$2,648,383	2.32%	$2,033,929	30.21%	$2,255,520	(9.82)%
58. AMERICAN SECURITY	$2,940,198	$2,476,836	18.71%	$2,379,672	4.08%	$2,599,592	(8.46)%	$3,175,142	(18.13)%
59. GENERAL T&T	$2,676,371	$6,264,388	(57.28)%	$9,256,810	(32.33)%	$9,726,952	(4.83)%	$12,852,967	(24.32)%
60. NATIONAL LAND	$2,485,692	$1,442,071	72.37%	$486,496	196.42%	$540,282	(9.96)%	$572,947	(5.70)%
61. GUARANTEE	$2,436,121	$2,908,650	(16.25)%	$1,717,635	69.34%	$901,639	90.50%	$788,697	14.32%
62. NORTHEAST INVESTORS	$2,422,930	$2,445,938	(0.94)%	$3,254,046	(24.83)%	$3,500,125	(7.03)%	$5,617,687	(37.69)%
63. LAND TIC (ST LOUIS)	$2,247,316	$711,764	215.74%	$4,140,421	(82.81)%	$1,163,808	255.76%	$1,218,515	(4.49)%
64. SIERRA	$1,966,565	$0	--	--	--	--	--	--	--
65. PENN ATTORNEYS	$1,725,400	$2,040,456	(15.44)%	$2,405,557	(15.18)%	$2,214,712	8.62%	$3,053,751	(27.48)%
66. ARSENAL	$1,583,908	$2,389,734	(33.72)%	$2,200,760	8.59%	$1,217,779	80.72%	--	--
67. FIRST AMERICAN TRANS	$1,583,015	$1,897,970	(16.59)%	$1,425,741	33.12%	$1,299,866	9.68%	$1,150,431	12.99%
68. MASON	$1,519,982	$475,326	219.78%	--	--	--	--	--	--
69. FARMERS NATIONAL	$927,258	$365,819	153.47%						
70. TRANSUNION TIC	$882,460	$5,227,050	(83.12)%	$9,375,214	(44.25)%	$15,073,942	(37.81)%	$25,518,487	(40.93)%
71. MANITO	$735,089	$829,425	(11.37)%	$999,195	(16.99)%	$1,041,431	(4.06)%	$1,805,154	(42.31)%
72. NATIONAL ATTORNEYS	$733,437	$792,061	(7.40)%	$834,630	(5.10)%	$1,096,055	(23.85)%	$1,077,584	1.71%
73. AMERICAN LAND & AIRCRAFT	$593,864	$518,084	14.63%	$712,890	(27.33)%	$1,236,016	(42.32)%	$880,996	40.30%
74. K.E.L.	$583,915	--	--	--	--	--	--	--	--
75. DREIBELBISS	$581,876	$729,834	(20.27)%	$966,937	(24.52)%	$1,202,054	(19.56)%	$1,479,125	(18.73)%
76. WESTERN NATIONAL	$370,721	$789,978	(53.07)%	$1,652,362	(52.19)%	$2,521,300	(34.46)%	$7,584,142	(66.76)%
77. MISSISSIPPI GUARANTY	$289,499	$483,380	(40.11)%	$461,978	4.63%	$731,781	(36.87)%	$1,059,223	(30.91)%
78. TITLE G&TC	$260,893	$276,536	(5.66)%	$245,288	12.74%	$272,862	(10.11)%	$367,943	(25.84)%
79. EQUITY NATIONAL	$236,862	$371,527	(36.25)%	$344,489	7.85%	--	--	--	--
80. SEAGATE	$186,090	$155,277	19.84%	$195,161	(20.44)%	$237,561	(17.85)%	$309,324	(23.20)%
81. TITLEDGE	$181,572	--	--	--	--	--	--	--	--
82. CHICAGO T&T	$178,675	$25,139	610.75%	$6,342	296.39%	$26,119	(75.72)%	$92,190	(71.67)%
83. FOUNDERS	$176,004	$195,752	(10.09)%	$124,059	57.79%	--	--	--	--
84. NATIONS OF NY	$19,007	$2,350	708.81%	$3,385	(30.58)%	$6,522	(48.10)%	$6,250	4.35%
85. BRIDGE	$462	$7,105	(93.50)%	$43,109	(83.52)%	$75,047	(42.56)%	$222,725	(66.31)%
86. ALLIANCE	$447	$770	(41.95)%	$28,040	(97.25)%	$636,090	(95.59)%	$7,954,160	(92.00)%
87. COLUMBIAN NATIONAL	$0	$637,556	(100.00)%	$5,452,158	(88.31)%	$7,453,054	(26.85)%	$7,421,397	0.43%
88. MASON COUNTY	$0	$0	--	$0	--	$0	--	$0	--
89. OLYMPIC	$0	$0	--	$0	--	$0	--	$0	--
90. PUBLIC	$0	$0	--	$0	--	$0	--	$0	--
91. MASSACHUSETTS TIC	($254)	$1,705	(114.90)%	$975	74.87%	$960	1.56%	$0	--
COMPOSITE	$14,058,172,014	$16,384,083,405	(14.20)%	$16,793,987,941	(2.44)%	$15,471,394,643	8.55%	$14,898,391,411	3.85%
AVERAGE	$154,485,407	$184,090,825	(16.08)%	$197,576,329	(6.83)%	$188,675,544	4.72%	$183,930,758	2.58%

5

All content © 2008 Demotech, Inc. - www.demotech.com

B.5 Net Premiums Written (NPW) to Net Liquid Assets

COMPANY	B.4 - NPW	B.2 - NET LIQUID ASSETS	NPW TO NET LIQUID ASSETS 2007	NPW TO NET LIQUID ASSETS 2006	NPW TO NET LIQUID ASSETS 2005	NPW TO NET LIQUID ASSETS 2004	NPW TO NET LIQUID ASSETS 2003
1. COLUMBIAN NATIONAL	$0	$3,462,022	--	15.65%	268.39%	201.94%	139.92%
2. MASSACHUSETTS TIC	($254)	$2,456,787	--	0.08%	0.06%	0.06%	--
3. PUBLIC	$0	$1,038,244	--	--	--	--	--
4. MASON COUNTY	$0	$796,804	--	--	--	--	--
5. OLYMPIC	$0	$305,841	--	--	--	--	--
6. WASHINGTON TIC	$15,328,218	($152,428)	--	--	--	--	1,994.55%
7. AMERICAN EAGLE	$2,995,458	($387,008)	--	326.15%	235.60%	226.46%	222.44%
8. ATTORNEYS TGF (CO)	$8,740,480	($889,008)	--	--	--	2,257.37%	1,567.86%
9. GUARANTEE T&T	$11,281,699	($1,283,505)	--	--	2,055.56%	1,473.00%	889.21%
10. UNITED GENERAL	$342,976,132	($3,247,002)	--	--	5,909.54%	1,828.11%	2,129.95%
11. LAWYERS	$1,216,983,337	($27,391,668)	--	4,024.98%	3,755.88%	3,511.41%	1,544.13%
12. FIRST AMERICAN TIC	$3,301,702,288	($305,977,294)	--	--	1,364.99%	1,539.06%	1,384.69%
13. BRIDGE	$462	$7,884,405	0.01%	0.09%	0.54%	1.65%	2.77%
14. ALLIANCE	$447	$3,100,706	0.01%	0.03%	0.94%	27.29%	331.47%
15. CHICAGO T&T	$178,675	$659,204,334	0.03%	0.00%	0.00%	0.00%	0.01%
16. NATIONS OF NY	$19,007	$12,211,638	0.16%	0.02%	0.04%	0.09%	0.08%
17. WESTERN NATIONAL	$370,721	$3,256,315	11.38%	26.26%	52.44%	83.74%	259.18%
18. EQUITY NATIONAL	$236,862	$1,437,919	16.47%	31.71%	27.17%	--	--
19. PENN ATTORNEYS	$1,725,400	$8,121,465	21.24%	25.04%	32.60%	33.82%	55.06%
20. FOUNDERS	$176,004	$787,772	22.34%	23.76%	14.58%	--	--
21. TRANSUNION TIC	$882,460	$3,552,891	24.84%	156.47%	694.76%	--	--
22. TITLEDGE	$181,572	$722,784	25.12%	--	--	--	--
23. K.E.L.	$583,915	$2,323,038	25.14%		--	--	--
24. DREIBELBISS	$581,876	$2,169,435	26.82%	35.17%	49.90%	72.70%	89.66%
25. AMERICAN GUARANTY	$3,489,926	$10,532,088	33.14%	38.27%	39.16%	46.16%	95.69%
26. AMERICAN SECURITY	$2,940,198	$8,304,294	35.41%	34.02%	35.89%	43.46%	60.96%
27. OLD REPUBLIC GENERAL	$14,067,656	$37,923,626	37.09%	41.44%	76.12%	83.90%	128.82%
28. TRANSUNION NATIONAL	$3,760,507	$9,849,369	38.18%	38.12%	126.43%	73.21%	98.62%
29. TITLE G&TC	$260,893	$623,579	41.84%	45.85%	52.54%	77.97%	201.61%
30. NORTHEAST INVESTORS	$2,422,930	$5,340,719	45.37%	47.84%	65.53%	91.30%	154.96%
31. LAND TIC (ST LOUIS)	$2,247,316	$4,908,115	45.79%	14.92%	110.13%	26.16%	29.10%
32. NATIONAL LAND	$2,485,692	$5,158,724	48.18%	26.52%	16.78%	19.25%	20.83%
33. FIRST AMERICAN T&T	$6,291,430	$12,921,642	48.69%	47.03%	53.75%	82.68%	142.88%
34. SEAGATE	$186,090	$378,209	49.20%	42.06%	57.05%	66.33%	93.06%
35. PORT LAWRENCE	$5,590,504	$10,512,518	53.18%	53.86%	54.48%	65.70%	91.37%
36. GUARDIAN NATIONAL	$3,729,355	$6,433,613	57.97%	288.37%	408.45%	413.90%	567.46%
37. MANITO	$735,089	$1,234,710	59.54%	66.64%	82.00%	84.82%	136.37%
38. MASON	$1,519,982	$2,484,176	61.19%	17.14%	--	--	--
39. NATIONAL ATTORNEYS	$733,437	$1,117,976	65.60%	63.55%	70.17%	95.40%	94.64%
40. AMERICAN LAND & AIRCRAFT	$593,864	$739,228	80.34%	69.33%	102.74%	174.10%	124.87%
41. SIERRA	$1,966,565	$2,319,791	84.77%	--	--	--	--
42. COMMONWEALTH LAND (NJ)	$33,700,593	$32,314,821	104.29%	144.92%	164.39%	150.21%	147.67%
43. TITLE IC AMERICA	$11,896,936	$10,980,291	108.35%	134.10%	206.37%	267.13%	289.13%
44. MISSISSIPPI GUARANTY	$289,499	$247,812	116.82%	302.79%	360.11%	414.50%	314.76%
45. CT ATTORNEYS	$51,216,178	$38,818,515	131.94%	149.78%	161.88%	167.19%	237.32%
46. FARMERS NATIONAL	$927,258	$693,686	133.67%	52.19%	--	--	--
47. FIRST AMERICAN TRANS	$1,583,015	$1,089,431	145.31%	198.47%	177.57%	188.76%	201.28%
48. OHIO BAR	$13,072,886	$8,529,819	153.26%	215.56%	250.05%	455.57%	673.19%
49. CENSTAR	$38,247,288	$24,279,008	157.53%	199.68%	264.79%	69.39%	--
50. MONROE	$12,949,458	$8,217,098	157.59%	129.69%	155.56%	185.49%	229.33%
51. NATIONAL	$3,500,144	$2,170,559	161.26%	131.60%	117.08%	101.94%	105.01%
52. INVESTORS TIC	$67,316,207	$39,221,709	171.63%	151.81%	185.82%	189.97%	255.86%
53. DAKOTA HOMESTEAD	$3,892,318	$2,259,937	172.23%	263.89%	169.17%	83.87%	88.17%
54. NATIONAL OF NY	$12,041,204	$6,480,320	185.81%	--	--	637.54%	745.79%
55. ATTORNEYS TGF (IL)	$10,652,965	$4,975,119	214.13%	249.10%	503.96%	3,863.96%	--
56. CHICAGO TIC (OR)	$26,222,954	$12,022,950	218.11%	278.02%	313.89%	294.26%	303.22%
57. NORTH AMERICAN	$108,367,683	$48,443,220	223.70%	501.02%	655.37%	729.70%	864.96%
58. SECURITY UNION	$63,649,182	$26,923,488	236.41%	215.19%	198.47%	215.05%	167.86%
59. LAND CORP (CO)	$19,580,211	$7,957,008	246.08%	274.91%	347.73%	296.85%	457.13%
60. FIRST AMERICAN (NY)	$238,030,662	$96,487,286	246.70%	333.44%	389.51%	432.89%	330.56%
61. FIRST AMERICAN (KS)	$14,513,623	$5,605,495	258.92%	287.97%	380.34%	366.63%	436.62%
62. GENERAL T&T	$2,676,371	$869,491	307.81%	455.57%	665.45%	979.12%	1,726.26%
63. MISSISSIPPI VALLEY	$25,388,544	$8,098,652	313.49%	299.48%	289.51%	291.08%	421.84%
64. ARSENAL	$1,583,908	$483,654	327.49%	466.43%	431.56%	115.54%	--
65. STEWART TGC	$1,464,681,077	$443,778,009	330.05%	401.85%	406.68%	430.33%	506.86%
66. UNITED CAPITAL	$61,421,744	$18,108,877	339.18%	558.26%	857.29%	948.93%	1,046.71%
67. T.A. TITLE	$16,990,956	$5,002,074	339.68%	252.41%	300.78%	448.34%	1,024.20%
68. STEWART (OR)	$10,134,011	$2,656,810	381.44%	409.41%	436.74%	462.76%	611.95%
69. ARKANSAS TIC	$8,213,976	$2,107,597	389.73%	369.17%	337.77%	404.84%	326.06%
70. ATTORNEYS TIF (FL)	$345,668,134	$81,702,918	423.08%	518.21%	633.09%	744.94%	924.23%
71. ALAMO	$94,165,105	$21,757,762	432.79%	330.45%	363.59%	374.54%	424.65%
72. GUARANTEE	$2,436,121	$562,561	433.04%	329.52%	103.44%	53.71%	50.82%
73. TITLE RESOURCES	$103,629,865	$21,429,502	483.59%	451.81%	335.17%	423.35%	539.94%
74. TITLE GUARANTY DIV (IA)	$3,686,225	$726,128	507.65%	664.09%	514.34%	709.80%	379.91%
75. NEW JERSEY TIC	$17,120,677	$3,307,074	517.70%	486.53%	598.68%	518.48%	458.51%
76. STEWART TIC	$159,077,298	$28,627,079	555.69%	604.84%	467.51%	1,046.22%	1,113.55%
77. COMMERCE	$42,908,676	$7,703,478	557.00%	818.12%	1,276.81%	738.41%	602.19%
78. FIRST AMERICAN (OR)	$61,020,845	$10,651,631	572.88%	535.85%	738.56%	577.05%	547.30%
79. PACIFIC NORTHWEST	$58,302,403	$9,952,203	585.82%	927.43%	1,414.71%	1,525.46%	8,089.75%
80. COMMONWEALTH LAND	$1,154,117,346	$167,717,570	688.13%	546.73%	1,333.82%	1,925.71%	1,738.63%
81. FIDELITY NATIONAL	$1,269,698,976	$180,914,080	701.82%	697.22%	784.92%	1,171.62%	780.07%
82. ALLIANT	$13,883,261	$1,871,402	741.86%	317.48%	5.68%	--	--
83. TICOR	$326,626,510	$37,617,379	868.29%	1,240.36%	609.69%	929.89%	612.71%
84. OLD REPUBLIC NATIONAL	$739,319,536	$77,086,077	959.08%	1,062.79%	1,184.78%	1,216.82%	1,788.49%
85. WESTCOR	$51,972,327	$5,311,186	978.54%	678.65%	597.48%	875.11%	856.55%
86. TICOR (FL)	$83,321,498	$7,367,657	1,130.91%	1,433.69%	2,555.41%	1,078.01%	753.99%
87. SOUTHERN TI CORP	$53,821,007	$3,719,413	1,447.03%	1,192.84%	1,121.67%	1,126.58%	1,096.02%
88. CHICAGO TIC	$1,884,525,225	$102,515,127	1,838.29%	784.49%	895.77%	648.38%	657.20%
89. SECURITY TG (BALTIMORE)	$21,800,759	$1,064,266	2,048.43%	1,227.49%	1,226.65%	971.56%	843.45%
90. CONESTOGA	$13,755,596	$608,695	2,259.85%	1,523.67%	1,496.63%	2,029.11%	998.33%
91. TRANSNATION	$276,607,560	$2,081,320	13,290.01%	882.46%	592.22%	794.89%	553.55%
COMPOSITE	$14,058,172,014	$2,127,404,108	660.81%	538.62%	548.83%	597.55%	560.05%
AVERAGE	$154,485,407	$23,378,067	660.81%				

B.6 Policyholders' Surplus (PHS)

COMPANY	2007	2006	2006 TO 2007	2005	2005 TO 2006	2004	2004 TO 2005	2003	2003 TO 2004
1. CHICAGO T&T	$664,634,623	$920,680,679	(27.81)%	$899,158,228	2.39%	$692,187,601	29.90%	$749,820,799	(7.69)%
2. STEWART TGC	$515,901,015	$508,508,698	1.45%	$488,193,002	4.16%	$417,905,733	16.82%	$374,795,833	11.50%
3. FIRST AMERICAN TIC	$426,527,243	$753,711,631	(43.41)%	$877,882,145	(14.14)%	$746,045,466	17.67%	$746,580,611	(0.07)%
4. CHICAGO TIC	$274,482,538	$429,467,367	(36.09)%	$385,826,750	11.31%	$492,205,285	(21.61)%	$499,157,557	(1.39)%
5. COMMONWEALTH LAND	$254,092,477	$313,773,809	(19.02)%	$198,389,869	58.16%	$165,628,246	19.78%	$169,499,867	(2.28)%
6. FIDELITY NATIONAL	$237,682,104	$273,989,612	(13.25)%	$293,247,411	(6.57)%	$219,703,840	33.47%	$159,931,431	37.37%
7. ATTORNEYS TIF (FL)	$149,827,744	$158,662,740	(5.57)%	$138,624,439	14.46%	$112,735,937	22.96%	$86,630,555	30.13%
8. LAWYERS	$129,286,409	$218,001,231	(40.69)%	$225,800,152	(3.45)%	$237,640,169	(4.98)%	$264,950,129	(10.31)%
9. OLD REPUBLIC NATIONAL	$116,001,825	$119,193,883	(2.68)%	$116,093,295	2.67%	$113,986,814	1.85%	$99,831,819	14.18%
10. FIRST AMERICAN (NY)	$107,386,170	$90,145,277	19.13%	$71,550,958	25.99%	$64,600,811	10.76%	$66,220,290	(2.45)%
11. TICOR	$67,686,913	$52,898,518	27.96%	$74,944,826	(29.42)%	$66,081,191	13.41%	$81,962,678	(19.38)%
12. NORTH AMERICAN	$50,899,292	$21,271,401	139.29%	$18,433,712	15.39%	$15,925,842	15.75%	$13,240,915	20.28%
13. INVESTORS TIC	$50,102,762	$54,651,055	(8.32)%	$50,473,518	8.28%	$45,928,373	9.90%	$40,047,557	14.68%
14. SECURITY UNION	$46,565,183	$66,803,268	(30.30)%	$63,223,090	5.66%	$73,297,924	(13.75)%	$63,996,280	14.53%
15. OLD REPUBLIC GENERAL	$46,185,038	$49,245,695	(6.22)%	$46,856,877	5.10%	$43,725,265	7.16%	$37,940,513	15.25%
16. CT ATTORNEYS	$41,839,283	$41,145,521	1.69%	$41,983,532	(2.00)%	$38,723,447	8.42%	$33,595,575	15.26%
17. STEWART TIC	$34,515,499	$30,832,501	11.95%	$39,670,535	(22.28)%	$18,527,571	114.12%	$15,992,483	15.85%
18. COMMONWEALTH LAND (NJ)	$33,132,445	$30,229,744	9.60%	$32,705,775	(7.57)%	$32,742,877	(0.11)%	$26,506,357	23.53%
19. FIRST AMERICAN (OR)	$32,041,274	$33,010,673	(2.94)%	$31,649,740	4.30%	$34,283,486	(7.68)%	$26,535,249	29.20%
20. UNITED GENERAL	$27,974,272	$23,409,480	19.50%	$18,036,634	29.79%	$22,784,914	(20.84)%	$24,239,623	(6.00)%
21. ALAMO	$26,226,592	$37,138,910	(29.38)%	$34,999,574	6.11%	$35,956,697	(2.66)%	$37,740,841	(4.73)%
22. TITLE RESOURCES	$25,711,604	$27,728,428	(7.27)%	$28,184,662	(1.62)%	$23,940,622	17.73%	$20,019,439	19.59%
23. TICOR (FL)	$25,586,476	$29,857,989	(14.31)%	$40,660,194	(26.57)%	$34,342,887	18.39%	$42,384,436	(18.97)%
24. CENSTAR	$25,141,601	$23,537,586	6.81%	$21,179,144	11.14%	$16,182,314	30.88%	$14,993,801	7.93%
25. UNITED CAPITAL	$22,767,542	$24,748,274	(8.00)%	$21,439,006	15.44%	$16,753,113	27.97%	$13,433,150	24.71%
26. TRANSNATION	$22,334,782	$62,836,418	(64.46)%	$81,661,373	(23.05)%	$75,561,924	8.07%	$67,803,740	11.44%
27. FIRST AMERICAN T&T	$16,413,088	$11,218,295	46.31%	$9,794,427	14.54%	$7,070,697	38.52%	$4,669,761	51.41%
28. PACIFIC NORTHWEST	$15,156,843	$12,038,746	25.90%	$8,969,305	34.22%	$7,876,586	13.87%	$6,509,045	21.01%
29. PORT LAWRENCE	$14,673,740	$15,367,935	(4.52)%	$14,051,729	9.37%	$12,686,659	10.76%	$11,354,805	11.73%
30. CHICAGO TIC (OR)	$13,566,887	$13,987,712	(3.01)%	$13,508,979	3.54%	$12,629,354	6.96%	$15,685,698	(19.48)%
31. NATIONS OF NY	$12,627,192	$11,782,979	7.16%	$9,545,295	23.44%	$9,861,881	(3.21)%	$9,611,025	2.61%
32. TITLE IC AMERICA	$11,666,575	$9,145,238	27.57%	$9,956,366	(8.15)%	$8,866,626	12.29%	$9,162,818	(3.23)%
33. AMERICAN GUARANTY	$11,507,581	$10,212,253	12.68%	$9,740,005	4.85%	$8,529,799	14.19%	$5,603,387	52.23%
34. MONROE	$11,498,871	$13,957,721	(17.62)%	$12,651,821	10.32%	$11,759,030	7.59%	$10,862,080	8.26%
35. TRANSUNION NATIONAL	$10,048,532	$10,488,021	(4.19)%	$4,764,263	120.14%	$5,814,113	(18.06)%	$5,473,127	6.23%
36. LAND CORP (CO)	$9,842,596	$10,266,967	(4.13)%	$9,525,559	7.78%	$10,813,213	(11.91)%	$10,458,871	3.39%
37. ATTORNEYS TGF (IL)	$9,754,476	$7,575,600	28.76%	$6,600,025	14.78%	$5,160,923	27.88%	$5,653,366	(8.71)%
38. MISSISSIPPI VALLEY	$9,683,618	$10,157,366	(4.66)%	$9,301,479	9.20%	$9,540,886	(2.51)%	$8,280,543	15.22%
39. OHIO BAR	$9,026,842	$8,192,661	10.18%	$7,128,481	14.93%	$4,954,876	43.87%	$3,251,469	52.39%
40. COMMERCE	$8,811,912	$8,566,084	2.87%	$6,810,356	25.78%	$9,395,147	(27.51)%	$10,237,281	(8.23)%
41. WESTCOR	$8,662,482	$11,273,355	(23.16)%	$11,857,738	(4.93)%	$7,909,361	49.92%	$7,142,861	10.73%
42. AMERICAN SECURITY	$8,504,479	$7,483,940	13.64%	$6,831,914	9.54%	$6,178,766	10.57%	$5,233,035	18.07%
43. PENN ATTORNEYS	$8,351,671	$8,451,243	(1.18)%	$7,782,327	8.60%	$6,939,386	12.15%	$5,970,130	16.24%
44. BRIDGE	$7,993,676	$8,110,974	(1.45)%	$8,155,215	(0.54)%	$8,200,040	(0.55)%	$8,076,412	1.53%
45. SOUTHERN TI CORP	$7,715,606	$8,660,765	(10.91)%	$8,160,238	6.13%	$7,663,688	6.48%	$7,507,489	2.08%
46. GUARDIAN NATIONAL	$6,798,513	$1,773,938	283.24%	$2,065,171	(14.12)%	$1,954,893	5.64%	$1,912,908	2.19%
47. NATIONAL OF NY	$6,713,364	$8,712,163	(22.94)%	$6,638,703	31.23%	$5,324,992	24.67%	$6,655,691	(19.99)%
48. T.A. TITLE	$6,503,339	$7,674,814	(15.26)%	$6,716,076	14.28%	$5,698,526	17.86%	$5,092,483	11.90%
49. FIRST AMERICAN (KS)	$5,833,793	$5,292,676	10.22%	$4,395,656	20.41%	$4,009,118	9.64%	$3,928,348	2.06%
50. NORTHEAST INVESTORS	$5,540,475	$5,305,620	4.43%	$5,116,156	3.70%	$4,050,048	26.32%	$3,764,937	7.57%
51. NATIONAL LAND	$5,233,777	$5,496,677	(4.78)%	$2,946,228	86.57%	$2,871,776	2.59%	$2,786,170	3.07%
52. LAND TIC (ST LOUIS)	$4,984,985	$4,863,151	2.49%	$5,026,652	(3.25)%	$5,107,282	(1.58)%	$4,844,228	5.43%
53. NEW JERSEY TIC	$4,846,327	$5,253,800	(7.76)%	$5,043,068	4.18%	$4,689,020	7.55%	$4,759,445	(1.48)%
54. TRANSUNION TIC	$3,880,844	$3,637,326	6.69%	$2,081,061	74.78%	$1,019,205	104.18%	$3,874,019	(73.69)%
55. SECURITY TG (BALTIMORE)	$3,764,091	$4,488,445	(16.14)%	$4,423,104	1.48%	$5,100,947	(13.29)%	$4,422,746	15.33%
56. COLUMBIAN NATIONAL	$3,538,522	$4,224,274	(16.23)%	$2,222,890	90.04%	$4,034,045	(44.90)%	$5,912,839	(31.77)%
57. CONESTOGA	$3,483,884	$4,054,246	(14.07)%	$4,010,182	1.10%	$4,069,958	(1.45)%	$4,636,848	(12.24)%
58. WESTERN NATIONAL	$3,358,552	$3,182,028	5.55%	$3,227,101	(1.40)%	$3,051,179	5.77%	$2,978,957	2.42%
59. ALLIANCE	$3,107,663	$2,985,582	4.09%	$3,003,220	(0.59)%	$2,397,177	25.28%	$2,730,895	(12.22)%
60. NATIONAL	$3,050,235	$2,903,330	5.06%	$2,816,671	3.08%	$2,767,651	1.77%	$3,033,574	(8.77)%
61. STEWART (OR)	$2,873,991	$2,607,381	10.23%	$2,500,409	4.28%	$2,045,225	22.26%	$1,832,328	11.62%
62. SIERRA	$2,657,562	$2,523,704	5.30%	--	--	--	--	--	--
63. DREIBELBISS	$2,650,439	$2,546,712	4.07%	$2,489,971	2.28%	$2,341,634	6.33%	$2,272,641	3.04%
64. MASON	$2,546,042	$2,797,057	(8.97)%	--	--	--	--	--	--
65. MASSACHUSETTS TIC	$2,465,550	$2,138,307	15.30%	$1,668,911	28.13%	$1,526,652	9.32%	$1,305,087	16.98%
66. ARKANSAS TIC	$2,388,523	$2,258,571	5.75%	$1,909,169	18.30%	$1,616,427	18.11%	$1,739,812	(7.09)%
67. ALLIANT	$2,354,553	$2,517,038	(6.46)%	$2,338,360	7.64%	--	--	--	--
68. K.E.L.	$2,332,454	--	--	--	--	--	--	--	--
69. DAKOTA HOMESTEAD	$2,266,306	$2,086,515	8.62%	$2,299,216	(9.25)%	$2,510,934	(8.43)%	$2,217,611	13.23%
70. ATTORNEYS TGF (CO)	$1,776,152	$1,294,052	37.26%	$2,257,689	(42.68)%	$3,050,646	(25.99)%	$2,534,102	20.38%
71. GENERAL T&T	$1,595,193	$1,994,547	(20.02)%	$1,857,179	7.40%	$1,521,525	22.06%	$1,232,839	23.42%
72. NATIONAL ATTORNEYS	$1,566,898	$1,715,019	(8.64)%	$1,675,933	2.33%	$1,619,789	3.47%	$1,499,333	8.03%
73. EQUITY NATIONAL	$1,438,140	$1,393,151	3.23%	$1,267,901	9.88%	--	--	--	--
74. MANITO	$1,256,691	$1,272,722	(1.26)%	$1,259,415	1.06%	$1,232,128	2.21%	$1,349,637	(8.71)%
75. FIRST AMERICAN TRANS	$1,254,245	$999,317	25.51%	$813,732	22.81%	$690,451	17.86%	$572,868	20.53%
76. GUARANTEE	$1,228,016	$1,900,452	(35.37)%	$1,834,232	3.59%	$1,722,916	6.46%	$1,629,519	5.73%
77. GUARANTEE T&T	$1,219,340	$2,508,374	(51.39)%	$2,603,115	(3.64)%	$2,503,935	3.96%	$2,864,606	(12.59)%
78. PUBLIC	$1,038,244	$1,010,401	2.76%	--	--	--	--	--	--
79. TITLE G&TC	$907,607	$853,479	6.34%	$732,665	16.49%	$712,113	2.89%	$529,898	34.39%
80. WASHINGTON TIC	$876,497	$802,405	9.23%	$935,232	(14.20)%	$848,468	10.23%	$1,034,769	(18.00)%
81. MASON COUNTY	$822,687	$800,718	2.74%	$775,672	3.23%	$784,576	(1.13)%	$799,765	(1.90)%
82. FARMERS NATIONAL	$817,207	$804,466	1.58%	--	--	--	--	--	--
83. FOUNDERS	$800,122	$836,118	(4.31)%	$862,907	(3.10)%	--	--	--	--
84. TITLEDGE	$753,085	--	--	--	--	--	--	--	--
85. AMERICAN LAND & AIRCRAFT	$742,516	$756,330	(1.83)%	$709,631	6.58%	$712,697	(0.43)%	$711,689	0.14%
86. TITLE GUARANTY DIV (IA)	$739,705	$593,992	24.53%	$841,774	(29.44)%	$927,909	(9.28)%	$2,109,582	(56.01)%
87. AMERICAN EAGLE	$716,768	$1,356,111	(47.15)%	$1,663,755	(18.49)%	$1,496,232	11.20%	$1,607,390	(6.92)%
88. ARSENAL	$484,161	$514,254	(5.85)%	$513,559	0.14%	$1,094,835	(53.09)%	--	--
89. SEAGATE	$474,557	$500,459	(5.18)%	$395,804	26.44%	$398,146	(0.59)%	$387,592	2.72%
90. OLYMPIC	$336,151	$366,389	(8.25)%	$324,316	12.97%	$346,651	(6.44)%	$428,996	(19.19)%
91. MISSISSIPPI GUARANTY	$300,100	$416,502	(27.95)%	$288,834	44.20%	$349,982	(17.47)%	$512,220	(31.67)%
COMPOSITE	$2,778,616,712	$3,534,001,754	(21.37)%	$3,472,361,515	1.78%	$4,105,448,178	(15.42)%	$4,019,101,103	2.15%
AVERAGE	$41,476,447	$52,858,769	(21.53)%	$54,241,827	(2.55)%	$50,066,441	8.34%	$49,618,532	0.90%

5

B.7   Net Premiums Written (NPW) to Policyholders' Surplus (PHS)

COMPANY	2007 B.4 - NPW	2007 B.6 - PHS	2007 NPW TO PHS	2006 NPW TO PHS	2005 NPW TO PHS	2004 NPW TO PHS	2003 NPW TO PHS
1. MASSACHUSETTS TIC	($254)	$2,465,550	--	0.08%	0.06%	0.06%	0.00%
2. COLUMBIAN NATIONAL	$0	$3,538,522	0.00%	15.09%	245.27%	184.75%	125.51%
3. PUBLIC	$0	$1,038,244	0.00%	0.00%	--	--	--
4. MASON COUNTY	$0	$822,687	0.00%	0.00%	0.00%	0.00%	0.00%
5. OLYMPIC	$0	$336,151	0.00%	0.00%	0.00%	0.00%	0.00%
6. BRIDGE	$462	$7,993,676	0.01%	0.09%	0.53%	0.92%	2.76%
7. ALLIANCE	$447	$3,107,663	0.01%	0.03%	0.93%	26.53%	291.27%
8. CHICAGO T&T	$178,675	$664,634,623	0.03%	0.00%	0.00%	0.00%	0.01%
9. NATIONS OF NY	$19,007	$12,627,192	0.15%	0.02%	0.04%	0.07%	0.07%
10. WESTERN NATIONAL	$370,721	$3,358,552	11.04%	24.83%	51.20%	82.63%	254.59%
11. EQUITY NATIONAL	$236,862	$1,438,140	16.47%	26.67%	27.17%	--	--
12. PENN ATTORNEYS	$1,725,400	$8,351,671	20.66%	24.14%	30.91%	31.92%	51.15%
13. DREIBELBISS	$581,876	$2,650,439	21.95%	28.66%	38.83%	51.33%	65.08%
14. FOUNDERS	$176,004	$800,122	22.00%	23.41%	14.38%	--	--
15. TRANSUNION TIC	$882,460	$3,880,844	22.74%	143.71%	450.50%	1,478.99%	658.71%
16. TITLEDGE	$181,572	$753,085	24.11%	--	--	--	--
17. K.E.L.	$583,915	$2,332,454	25.03%	--	--	--	--
18. TITLE G&TC	$260,893	$907,607	28.75%	32.40%	33.48%	38.32%	69.44%
19. AMERICAN GUARANTY	$3,489,926	$11,507,581	30.33%	34.16%	34.14%	38.06%	69.30%
20. OLD REPUBLIC GENERAL	$14,067,656	$46,185,038	30.46%	32.66%	48.94%	56.30%	70.10%
21. AMERICAN SECURITY	$2,940,198	$8,504,479	34.57%	33.10%	34.83%	42.07%	60.67%
22. TRANSUNION NATIONAL	$3,760,507	$10,048,532	37.42%	37.28%	103.22%	69.78%	95.57%
23. PORT LAWRENCE	$5,590,504	$14,673,740	38.10%	45.91%	45.34%	55.05%	75.24%
24. FIRST AMERICAN T&T	$6,291,430	$16,413,088	38.33%	41.28%	45.34%	68.17%	121.06%
25. SEAGATE	$186,090	$474,557	39.21%	31.03%	49.31%	59.67%	79.81%
26. NORTHEAST INVESTORS	$2,422,930	$5,540,475	43.73%	46.10%	63.60%	86.42%	149.21%
27. LAND TIC (ST LOUIS)	$2,247,316	$4,984,385	45.09%	14.64%	82.37%	22.79%	25.15%
28. NATIONAL ATTORNEYS	$733,437	$1,566,898	46.81%	46.18%	49.80%	67.67%	71.87%
29. NATIONAL LAND	$2,485,692	$5,233,777	47.49%	26.24%	16.51%	18.81%	20.56%
30. GUARDIAN NATIONAL	$3,729,355	$6,798,513	54.86%	246.69%	362.66%	368.95%	535.88%
31. MANITO	$735,089	$1,256,691	58.49%	65.17%	79.34%	84.52%	133.75%
32. MASON	$1,519,982	$2,546,042	59.70%	16.99%	--	--	--
33. SIERRA	$1,966,565	$2,657,562	74.00%	0.00%	--	--	--
34. AMERICAN LAND & AIRCRAFT	$593,864	$742,516	79.98%	68.50%	100.46%	173.43%	123.79%
35. MISSISSIPPI GUARANTY	$289,499	$300,100	96.47%	116.06%	159.95%	209.09%	206.79%
36. COMMONWEALTH LAND (NJ)	$33,700,593	$33,132,445	101.71%	140.53%	141.44%	139.20%	144.22%
37. TITLE IC AMERICA	$11,896,936	$11,666,575	101.97%	124.47%	188.12%	236.53%	221.85%
38. ATTORNEYS TGF (IL)	$10,652,985	$9,754,476	109.21%	156.57%	199.91%	232.12%	215.43%
39. MONROE	$12,949,458	$11,498,871	112.62%	97.92%	119.59%	138.12%	163.80%
40. FARMERS NATIONAL	$927,258	$817,207	113.47%	45.47%	--	--	--
41. NATIONAL	$3,500,144	$3,050,235	114.75%	98.94%	93.35%	73.59%	73.71%
42. CT ATTORNEYS	$51,216,178	$41,839,283	122.41%	138.85%	144.63%	148.97%	198.02%
43. FIRST AMERICAN TRANS	$1,583,015	$1,254,245	126.21%	189.93%	175.21%	188.26%	200.82%
44. INVESTORS TIC	$67,316,207	$50,102,762	134.36%	122.81%	145.25%	147.99%	197.16%
45. SECURITY UNION	$63,649,182	$46,565,183	136.69%	136.33%	128.48%	129.19%	116.67%
46. OHIO BAR	$13,072,886	$9,026,842	144.82%	183.77%	203.34%	412.15%	593.13%
47. CENSTAR	$38,247,288	$25,141,601	152.13%	188.40%	230.47%	67.12%	0.00%
48. GENERAL T&T	$2,676,371	$1,595,193	167.78%	314.08%	498.43%	639.29%	1,042.55%
49. DAKOTA HOMESTEAD	$3,892,318	$2,266,306	171.75%	262.34%	164.53%	83.68%	88.10%
50. NATIONAL OF NY	$12,041,204	$6,713,364	179.36%	--	--	349.57%	600.72%
51. FIRST AMERICAN (OR)	$61,020,845	$32,041,274	190.44%	202.51%	210.84%	177.50%	278.52%
52. CHICAGO TIC (OR)	$26,222,954	$13,566,887	193.29%	239.65%	242.91%	201.78%	233.68%
53. GUARANTEE	$2,436,121	$1,228,016	198.38%	153.09%	93.64%	52.33%	48.40%
54. LAND CORP (CO)	$19,580,211	$9,842,596	198.93%	224.04%	277.34%	245.22%	365.82%
55. NORTH AMERICAN	$108,367,683	$50,899,292	212.91%	442.62%	564.89%	590.52%	645.42%
56. FIRST AMERICAN (NY)	$238,030,662	$107,386,170	221.66%	260.00%	332.81%	350.73%	291.70%
57. ATTORNEYS TIF (FL)	$345,668,134	$149,827,744	230.71%	301.66%	352.17%	373.18%	411.54%
58. FIRST AMERICAN (KS)	$14,513,623	$5,833,793	248.79%	265.56%	334.93%	312.64%	383.57%
59. T.A. TITLE	$16,990,956	$6,503,339	261.27%	224.35%	259.32%	295.10%	425.74%
60. MISSISSIPPI VALLEY	$25,388,544	$9,683,618	262.18%	249.81%	242.45%	249.51%	332.41%
61. UNITED CAPITAL	$61,421,744	$22,767,542	269.78%	502.38%	754.16%	765.17%	951.59%
62. STEWART TGC	$1,464,681,077	$515,901,015	283.91%	349.61%	358.59%	377.43%	433.16%
63. TICOR (FL)	$83,321,498	$25,586,476	325.65%	548.24%	842.70%	731.82%	672.40%
64. ARSENAL	$1,583,908	$484,161	327.14%	464.70%	428.53%	111.23%	--
65. ARKANSAS TIC	$8,213,976	$2,388,523	343.89%	329.80%	314.03%	359.86%	301.17%
66. STEWART (OR)	$10,134,011	$2,873,991	352.61%	383.83%	403.13%	424.71%	567.63%
67. NEW JERSEY TIC	$17,120,677	$4,846,327	353.27%	357.74%	424.02%	362.38%	345.94%
68. ALAMO	$94,165,105	$26,226,592	359.04%	301.79%	312.11%	315.22%	353.16%
69. PACIFIC NORTHWEST	$58,302,403	$15,156,843	384.66%	507.42%	571.31%	670.52%	1,161.94%
70. CONESTOGA	$13,755,596	$3,483,884	394.84%	438.37%	488.46%	514.11%	541.60%
71. TITLE RESOURCES	$103,629,865	$25,711,604	403.05%	399.66%	296.22%	380.83%	470.13%
72. AMERICAN EAGLE	$2,995,458	$716,768	417.91%	199.83%	159.18%	135.94%	140.32%
73. COMMONWEALTH LAND	$1,154,117,346	$254,092,477	454.21%	412.39%	653.73%	718.62%	710.22%
74. STEWART TIC	$159,077,298	$34,515,499	460.89%	491.74%	382.51%	785.08%	887.59%
75. TICOR	$326,626,510	$67,686,913	482.55%	676.46%	400.41%	556.43%	436.32%
76. COMMERCE	$42,908,676	$8,811,912	486.94%	637.81%	790.03%	534.57%	483.96%
77. ATTORNEYS TGF (CO)	$8,740,480	$1,776,152	492.10%	782.83%	553.12%	450.27%	632.88%
78. TITLE GUARANTY DIV (IA)	$3,686,225	$739,705	498.34%	663.39%	473.74%	615.49%	326.21%
79. FIDELITY NATIONAL	$1,269,698,976	$237,682,104	534.20%	555.07%	592.55%	733.82%	594.23%
80. SECURITY TG (BALTIMORE)	$21,800,759	$3,764,091	579.18%	723.05%	667.52%	677.58%	660.16%
81. ALLIANT	$13,883,261	$2,354,553	589.63%	283.22%	5.59%	--	--
82. WESTCOR	$51,972,327	$8,662,482	599.97%	439.34%	479.55%	640.09%	696.50%
83. OLD REPUBLIC NATIONAL	$739,391,536	$116,001,825	637.33%	711.53%	791.60%	780.69%	935.25%
84. CHICAGO TIC	$1,884,525,225	$274,482,538	686.57%	530.21%	590.51%	457.17%	465.34%
85. SOUTHERN TI CORP	$53,821,007	$7,715,606	697.56%	640.39%	551.08%	472.15%	430.11%
86. FIRST AMERICAN TIC	$3,301,702,288	$426,527,243	774.09%	510.02%	448.05%	451.85%	426.44%
87. GUARANTEE T&T	$11,281,699	$1,219,340	925.23%	530.30%	492.29%	781.69%	609.98%
88. LAWYERS	$1,216,983,337	$129,286,409	941.31%	609.01%	578.74%	509.90%	477.81%
89. UNITED GENERAL	$342,976,132	$27,974,272	1,226.04%	1,421.58%	1,104.99%	905.22%	1,056.89%
90. TRANSNATION	$276,607,560	$22,334,782	1,238.46%	564.17%	481.07%	462.19%	444.33%
91. WASHINGTON TIC	$15,328,218	$876,497	1,748.80%	2,406.43%	2,135.86%	1,888.91%	1,579.82%
COMPOSITE	$14,058,172,014	$2,778,616,712	505.94%	463.61%	483.65%	376.85%	370.69%
AVERAGE	$154,485,407	$41,476,447	372.47%				

5

B.8 Implied Equity (Deficit) in the Statutory Premium Reserve (SPR) - New!

COMPANY	TOTAL SCH P RESERVES	2007					2006	
		CARRIED RESERVES	IMPLIED SUPPLEMENTAL RESERVES	CARRIED SUPPLEMENTAL RESERVES	IMPLIED EQUITY IN SPR	IMPLIED EQUITY TO PHS	IMPLIED EQUITY IN SPR	IMPLIED EQUITY TO PHS
1. ALAMO	$13,275,953	$19,920,273	($6,644,320)	$0	$6,644,320	25.33%	$10,374,505	27.93%
2. ALLIANCE	$577,774	$336,727	$241,047	$241,047	$0	0.00%	$0	0.00%
3. ALLIANT	$1,267,330	$1,267,325	$5	$50,000	$49,995	2.12%	$227,240	9.02%
4. AMERICAN EAGLE	$424,000	$424,000	$0	$0	$0	0.00%	$0	0.00%
5. AMERICAN GUARANTY	$1,014,491	$2,633,828	($1,619,337)	$0	$1,619,337	14.07%	$1,244,756	12.18%
6. AMERICAN LAND & AIRCRAFT	$0	$47,015	($47,015)	$0	$47,015	6.33%	$47,864	6.32%
7. AMERICAN SECURITY	$176,000	$176,000	$176,000	$176,000	$0	0.00%	$0	0.00%
8. ARKANSAS TIC	$1,312,110	$2,409,720	($1,097,610)	$0	$1,097,610	45.95%	$807,451	35.75%
9. ARSENAL	$0	$50,000	($50,000)	$0	$50,000	10.32%	$50,000	9.72%
10. ATTORNEYS TGF (CO)	$2,631,645	$2,269,134	$362,511	$362,511	$0	0.00%	$0	0.00%
11. ATTORNEYS TGF (IL)	$11,981,000	$10,088,605	$1,892,395	$1,892,395	$0	0.00%	$0	0.00%
12. ATTORNEYS TIF (FL)	$162,730,000	$162,731,000	($1,000)	$0	$1,000	0.00%	$0	0.00%
13. BRIDGE	$127,466	$170,157	($42,691)	$0	$42,691	0.53%	$61,770	0.76%
14. CENSTAR	$3,715,851	$1,460,289	$2,255,562	$2,255,562	$0	0.00%	$0	0.00%
15. CHICAGO T&T	$0	$0	$0	$0	$0	0.00%	$0	0.00%
16. CHICAGO TIC	$667,791,848	$956,722,235	($288,930,387)	$0	$288,930,387	105.26%	$293,061,196	68.23%
17. CHICAGO TIC (OR)	$5,641,242	$11,132,992	($5,491,750)	$0	$5,491,750	40.47%	$5,516,557	39.43%
18. COLUMBIAN NATIONAL	$0	$0	$0	$0	$0	0.00%	$0	0.00%
19. COMMERCE	$6,372,000	$11,462,480	($5,090,480)	$0	$5,090,480	57.76%	$5,589,950	65.25%
20. COMMONWEALTH LAND	$348,086,875	$425,495,974	($77,409,099)	$0	$77,409,099	30.46%	$96,263,459	30.67%
21. COMMONWEALTH LAND (NJ)	$7,590,364	$8,504,925	($914,561)	$0	$914,561	2.76%	$2,012,464	6.65%
22. CONESTOGA	$4,084,350	$4,387,261	($302,911)	$0	$302,911	8.69%	$493,226	12.16%
23. CT ATTORNEYS	$16,546,851	$16,590,467	($43,616)	$0	$43,616	0.10%	$249,070	0.60%
24. DAKOTA HOMESTEAD	$712,000	$1,162,622	($450,622)	$0	$450,622	19.88%	$583,871	27.98%
25. DREIBELBISS	$202,300	$72,000	$130,300	$130,300	$0	0.00%	$0	0.00%
26. EQUITY NATIONAL	$0	$111,701	($111,701)	$0	$111,701	7.76%	$83,722	6.00%
27. FARMERS NATIONAL	$53,000	$157,975	($104,975)	$0	$104,975	12.84%	$28,140	3.49%
28. FIDELITY NATIONAL	$451,889,693	$526,224,289	($74,334,596)	$0	$74,334,596	31.27%	$114,380,437	41.74%
29. FIRST AMERICAN (KS)	$3,105,303	$5,395,341	($2,290,038)	$0	$2,290,038	39.25%	$2,341,830	44.24%
30. FIRST AMERICAN (NY)	$53,214,601	$56,267,722	($3,053,121)	$0	$3,053,121	2.84%	$6,569,898	7.28%
31. FIRST AMERICAN (OR)	$10,631,640	$22,204,555	($11,572,915)	$0	$11,572,915	36.11%	$11,476,388	34.76%
32. FIRST AMERICAN T&T	$1,324,172	$1,324,172	$0	$0	$0	0.00%	$0	0.00%
33. FIRST AMERICAN TIC	$1,091,921,390	$988,052,703	$103,868,687	$103,885,000	$16,313	0.00%	$114,687,482	15.21%
34. FIRST AMERICAN TRANS	$277,000	$475,908	($198,908)	$0	$198,908	15.85%	$82,408	8.24%
35. FOUNDERS	$0	$25,068	($25,068)	$0	$25,068	3.13%	$0	0.00%
36. GENERAL T&T	$305,000	$4,974,075	($4,669,075)	$0	$4,669,075	292.69%	$4,532,849	227.26%
37. GUARANTEE	$1,078,699	$1,280,392	($201,693)	$0	$201,693	16.42%	$2,611	0.13%
38. GUARANTEE T&T	$3,745,748	$6,544,229	($2,798,481)	$0	$2,798,481	229.50%	$2,610,559	104.07%
39. GUARDIAN NATIONAL	$1,264,053	$2,851,787	($1,587,734)	$0	$1,587,734	23.35%	$1,403,351	79.10%
40. INVESTORS TIC	$36,475,000	$43,262,724	($6,787,724)	$0	$6,787,724	13.54%	$6,848,353	12.53%
41. K.E.L.	$27,719	$29,528	($1,809)	$0	$1,809	0.07%	--	--
42. LAND CORP (CO)	$4,119,000	$4,119,000	$0	$0	$0	0.00%	$0	0.00%
43. LAND TIC (ST LOUIS)	$0	$47,952	($47,952)	$0	$47,952	0.96%	$49,601	1.01%
44. LAWYERS	$368,871,828	$410,526,660	($41,654,832)	$0	$41,654,832	32.21%	$64,405,391	29.54%
45. MANITO	$162,050	$193,783	($31,733)	$0	$31,733	2.52%	$36,754	2.88%
46. MASON	$66,542	$74,433	($7,891)	$0	$7,891	0.30%	$0	0.00%
47. MASON COUNTY	$0	$0	$0	$0	$0	0.00%	$0	0.00%
48. MASSACHUSETTS TIC	$0	$100,000	($100,000)	$0	$100,000	4.05%	$100,000	4.67%
49. MISSISSIPPI GUARANTY	$0	$556,777	($556,777)	$0	$556,777	185.53%	$527,290	126.59%
50. MISSISSIPPI VALLEY	$16,317,623	$34,974,661	($18,657,038)	$0	$18,657,038	192.66%	$17,742,144	174.67%
51. MONROE	$2,164,300	$6,842,394	($4,678,094)	$0	$4,678,094	40.68%	$4,794,742	34.35%
52. NATIONAL	$200,500	$425,627	($225,127)	$0	$225,127	7.38%	$187,508	6.45%
53. NATIONAL ATTORNEYS	$200,000	$50,000	$150,000	$150,000	$0	0.00%	$0	0.00%
54. NATIONAL LAND	$314,167	$1,208,860	($894,693)	$0	$894,693	17.09%	$869,934	15.82%
55. NATIONAL OF NY	$5,716,736	$6,718,427	($1,001,691)	$0	$1,001,691	14.92%	$834,872	9.58%
56. NATIONS OF NY	$3,840,872	$4,702,399	($861,527)	$0	$861,527	6.82%	$2,663,644	22.60%
57. NEW JERSEY TIC	$4,127,000	$4,710,480	($583,480)	$0	$583,480	12.03%	$865,136	16.46%
58. NORTH AMERICAN	$25,122,953	$29,139,032	($4,016,079)	$0	$4,016,079	7.89%	$4,098,724	19.26%
59. NORTHEAST INVESTORS	$500,000	$542,982	($42,982)	$0	$42,982	0.77%	$37,681	0.71%
60. OHIO BAR	$3,890,817	$15,277,012	($11,386,195)	$0	$11,386,195	126.13%	$11,872,059	144.91%
61. OLD REPUBLIC GENERAL	$22,811,599	$68,415,226	($45,603,627)	$0	$45,603,627	98.74%	$36,599,742	74.32%
62. OLD REPUBLIC NATIONAL	$240,561,224	$323,288,788	($82,727,564)	$0	$82,727,564	71.31%	$93,754,703	78.65%
63. OLYMPIC	$10,377	$10,377	$0	$0	$0	0.00%	$0	0.00%
64. PACIFIC NORTHWEST	$8,639,765	$12,754,954	($4,115,189)	$0	$4,115,189	27.15%	$6,610,701	54.91%
65. PENN ATTORNEYS	$787,062	$1,171,707	($384,645)	$0	$384,645	4.60%	$403,762	4.77%
66. PORT LAWRENCE	$1,465,542	$5,650,020	($4,184,478)	$0	$4,184,478	28.51%	$4,182,003	27.21%
67. PUBLIC	$0	$0	$0	$0	$0	0.00%	$0	0.00%
68. SEAGATE	$0	$192,675	($192,675)	$0	$192,675	40.60%	$196,974	39.35%
69. SECURITY TG (BALTIMORE)	$8,684,699	$10,107,172	($1,422,473)	$0	$1,422,473	37.79%	$1,301,157	28.98%
70. SECURITY UNION	$32,388,553	$32,390,155	($1,602)	$0	$1,602	0.00%	$173,673	0.25%
71. SIERRA	$50,118	$43,490	$6,628	$6,628	$0	0.00%	$0	0.00%
72. SOUTHERN TI CORP	$10,239,516	$14,276,208	($4,036,692)	$0	$4,036,692	52.31%	$3,368,370	38.89%
73. STEWART (OR)	$0	$2,274,776	($2,274,776)	$0	$2,274,776	79.15%	$1,977,281	75.83%
74. STEWART TGC	$430,270,109	$519,864,058	($89,593,949)	$0	$89,593,949	17.36%	$129,796,825	25.52%
75. STEWART TIC	$36,837,870	$36,838,465	($595)	$0	$595	0.00%	$12	0.00%
76. T.A. TITLE	$3,699,537	$4,877,495	($1,177,958)	$0	$1,177,958	18.11%	$1,540,425	20.07%
77. TICOR	$117,657,002	$135,148,093	($17,491,091)	$0	$17,491,091	25.84%	$19,574,998	37.00%
78. TICOR (FL)	$76,086,592	$82,107,499	($6,020,907)	$0	$6,020,907	23.53%	$7,709,270	25.81%
79. TITLE G&TC	$0	$346,463	($346,463)	$0	$346,463	38.17%	$346,803	40.63%
80. TITLE GUARANTY DIV (IA)	$340,218	$5,009,535	($4,669,317)	$0	$4,669,317	631.24%	$0	0.00%
81. TITLE IC AMERICA	$3,137,407	$3,372,565	($235,158)	$0	$235,158	2.01%	$0	0.00%
82. TITLE RESOURCES	$9,593,000	$13,462,175	($3,869,175)	$0	$3,869,175	15.04%	$4,698,761	16.94%
83. TITLEDGE	$13,315	$7,275	$6,040	$6,040	$0	0.00%	--	--
84. TRANSNATION	$124,551,751	$114,949,851	$9,601,900	$9,601,900	$0	0.00%	$1	0.00%
85. TRANSUNION NATIONAL	$4,205,340	$4,303,549	($98,209)	$0	$98,209	0.97%	$93,843	0.89%
86. TRANSUNION TIC	$1,287,252	$3,369,219	($2,081,967)	$0	$2,081,967	53.64%	$1,479,133	40.66%
87. UNITED CAPITAL	$22,766,058	$28,210,811	($5,444,753)	$0	$5,444,753	23.91%	$8,666,918	35.02%
88. UNITED GENERAL	$56,624,853	$75,893,792	($19,268,939)	$0	$19,268,939	68.88%	$12,393,276	52.94%
89. WASHINGTON TIC	$2,284,409	$2,054,031	$230,378	$230,378	$0	0.00%	$504	0.06%
90. WESTCOR	$6,068,126	$14,086,904	($8,018,778)	$0	$8,018,778	92.56%	$7,286,966	64.63%
91. WESTERN NATIONAL	$848,000	$1,212,000	($364,000)	$0	$364,000	10.83%	$332,000	10.43%
COMPOSITE	$4,569,098,150	$5,334,421,005	($765,322,855)	$118,987,761	$884,310,616	31.83%	$1,133,204,988	32.07%
AVERAGE	$50,209,870	$58,620,011	($8,410,141)	$1,307,558	$9,717,699	23.42%	$12,732,640	24.08%

All content © 2008 Demotech, Inc. - www.demotech.com

5

B.9 Agency Premium and Retention

| COMPANY | DIRECT PREMIUMS WRITTEN | | | AGENT % OF PREMIUMS | RETAINED BY AGENTS | NET RETENTION % |
	DIRECT	AGENCY OPERATIONS	TOTAL			
1. TITLEDGE	$78,917	$102,655	$181,572	56.54%	$153,755	149.78%
2. ATTORNEYS TGF (CO)	$0	$9,268,076	$9,268,076	100.00%	$9,549,160	103.03%
3. WESTERN NATIONAL	$0	$370,721	$370,721	100.00%	$342,509	92.39%
4. FIRST AMERICAN (OR)	$42,031,597	$13,032,270	$55,063,867	23.67%	$11,789,024	90.46%
5. PACIFIC NORTHWEST	$0	$58,462,564	$58,462,564	100.00%	$52,730,302	90.19%
6. STEWART (OR)	$567,888	$10,237,613	$10,805,501	94.74%	$9,221,086	90.07%
7. CHICAGO TIC (OR)	$13,707,383	$12,576,501	$26,283,884	47.85%	$11,287,905	89.75%
8. UNITED CAPITAL	$2,264,749	$59,156,995	$61,421,744	96.31%	$52,866,551	89.37%
9. NATIONAL OF NY	$2,257,917	$9,780,803	$12,038,720	81.24%	$8,674,820	88.69%
10. NEW JERSEY TIC	$0	$17,124,472	$17,124,472	100.00%	$15,137,976	88.40%
11. LAND CORP (CO)	$0	$19,602,608	$19,602,608	100.00%	$17,250,295	88.00%
12. TRANSNATION	$69,584,981	$205,244,894	$274,829,875	74.68%	$178,625,661	87.03%
13. NORTH AMERICAN	$0	$108,371,483	$108,371,483	100.00%	$94,289,365	87.01%
14. TITLE RESOURCES	$0	$103,847,762	$103,847,762	100.00%	$89,704,496	86.38%
15. T.A. TITLE	$0	$17,039,841	$17,039,841	100.00%	$14,655,368	86.01%
16. COMMONWEALTH LAND (NJ)	$5,109,506	$30,277,935	$35,387,441	85.56%	$25,866,635	85.43%
17. STEWART TIC	$38,951,627	$123,300,260	$162,251,887	75.99%	$105,287,815	85.39%
18. ALLIANT	$0	$13,990,651	$13,990,651	100.00%	$11,897,217	85.04%
19. ALAMO	$0	$94,218,328	$94,218,328	100.00%	$80,095,646	85.01%
20. SIERRA	$0	$1,966,565	$1,966,565	100.00%	$1,671,695	85.01%
21. FIRST AMERICAN (KS)	$1,550,799	$13,212,881	$14,763,680	89.50%	$11,211,094	84.85%
22. TITLE IC AMERICA	$0	$11,954,125	$11,954,125	100.00%	$10,137,288	84.80%
23. FIRST AMERICAN (NY)	$96,485,318	$142,770,369	$239,255,687	59.67%	$121,059,713	84.79%
24. STEWART TGC	$157,750,939	$1,297,709,697	$1,455,460,636	89.16%	$1,099,768,492	84.75%
25. WASHINGTON TIC	$172,102	$15,452,071	$15,624,173	98.90%	$13,090,616	84.72%
26. COMMERCE	$43,152	$43,529,379	$43,572,531	99.90%	$36,674,307	84.25%
27. FIRST AMERICAN TIC	$622,912,926	$2,689,453,657	$3,312,366,583	81.19%	$2,248,120,236	83.59%
28. SECURITY UNION	$11,530,727	$52,026,961	$63,557,688	81.86%	$43,306,336	83.24%
29. NATIONAL LAND	$0	$2,494,729	$2,494,729	100.00%	$2,074,570	83.16%
30. WESTCOR	$288,117	$52,338,611	$52,626,728	99.45%	$43,363,579	82.85%
31. MONROE	$5,556,612	$7,440,067	$12,996,679	57.25%	$6,120,596	82.27%
32. FIDELITY NATIONAL	$251,405,363	$1,022,676,845	$1,274,082,208	80.27%	$840,562,038	82.19%
33. MANITO	$0	$788,476	$788,476	100.00%	$647,875	82.17%
34. GUARANTEE T&T	$204,520	$11,114,386	$11,318,906	98.19%	$9,083,214	81.72%
35. COMMONWEALTH LAND	$220,717,997	$931,800,332	$1,152,518,329	80.85%	$760,409,081	81.61%
36. AMERICAN GUARANTY	$26,366	$3,463,560	$3,489,926	99.24%	$2,815,249	81.28%
37. OLD REPUBLIC NATIONAL	$14,047,794	$735,479,232	$749,527,026	98.13%	$594,328,500	80.81%
38. GUARDIAN NATIONAL	$0	$3,873,893	$3,873,893	100.00%	$3,124,113	80.65%
39. CENSTAR	$0	$39,460,039	$39,460,039	100.00%	$31,798,359	80.58%
40. LAWYERS	$345,666,888	$869,943,802	$1,215,610,690	71.56%	$700,268,473	80.50%
41. AMERICAN EAGLE	$1,906,376	$1,142,793	$3,049,169	37.48%	$916,270	80.18%
42. NORTHEAST INVESTORS	$0	$2,414,626	$2,414,626	100.00%	$1,935,698	80.17%
43. TICOR	$51,058,558	$276,138,942	$327,197,500	84.40%	$221,138,248	80.08%
44. SECURITY TG (BALTIMORE)	$413,934	$21,511,552	$21,925,486	98.11%	$17,165,336	79.80%
45. CHICAGO TIC	$477,816,470	$1,409,479,222	$1,887,295,692	74.68%	$1,121,133,282	79.54%
46. ARSENAL	$0	$1,583,908	$1,583,908	100.00%	$1,253,313	79.13%
47. SOUTHERN TI CORP	$1,173,787	$53,006,927	$54,180,714	97.83%	$41,851,861	78.96%
48. UNITED GENERAL	$20,969,887	$315,632,332	$336,602,219	93.77%	$248,281,918	78.66%
49. OHIO BAR	$0	$13,072,886	$13,072,886	100.00%	$10,149,102	77.63%
50. ARKANSAS TIC	$0	$8,286,400	$8,286,400	100.00%	$6,364,268	76.80%
51. TICOR (FL)	$0	$83,543,448	$83,543,448	100.00%	$63,996,950	76.60%
52. DAKOTA HOMESTEAD	$244,546	$3,869,021	$4,113,567	94.06%	$2,952,933	76.32%
53. GENERAL T&T	$0	$2,777,191	$2,777,191	100.00%	$2,112,834	76.08%
54. CONESTOGA	$201,980	$13,742,390	$13,944,370	98.55%	$10,429,015	75.89%
55. BRIDGE	$0	$462	$462	100.00%	$346	74.89%
56. DREIBELBISS	$517,581	$115,399	$632,980	18.23%	$82,722	71.68%
57. AMERICAN SECURITY	$0	$2,940,198	$2,940,198	100.00%	$2,106,598	71.65%
58. MISSISSIPPI GUARANTY	$56,517	$253,129	$309,646	81.75%	$181,277	71.61%
59. PORT LAWRENCE	$2,836,725	$2,753,779	$5,590,504	49.26%	$1,968,650	71.49%
60. MISSISSIPPI VALLEY	$488,573	$25,433,321	$25,921,894	98.12%	$17,911,771	70.43%
61. INVESTORS TIC	$29,790,883	$37,754,989	$67,545,872	55.90%	$26,489,262	70.16%
62. ALLIANCE	$0	$1,196	$1,196	100.00%	$838	70.07%
63. K.E.L.	$0	$583,915	$583,915	100.00%	$408,740	70.00%
64. MASON	$120,217	$1,432,065	$1,552,282	92.26%	$1,002,433	70.00%
65. TRANSUNION NATIONAL	$109,890	$3,803,503	$3,913,393	97.19%	$2,660,897	69.96%
66. ATTORNEYS TIF (FL)	$0	$345,841,353	$345,841,353	100.00%	$241,203,949	69.74%
67. NATIONAL	$127,106	$3,546,810	$3,673,916	96.54%	$2,467,634	69.57%
68. AMERICAN LAND & AIRCRAFT	$0	$659,156	$659,156	100.00%	$458,218	69.52%
69. CT ATTORNEYS	$0	$51,258,956	$51,258,956	100.00%	$33,564,663	65.48%
70. GUARANTEE	$0	$2,597,594	$2,597,594	100.00%	$1,337,903	51.51%
71. LAND TIC (ST LOUIS)	$0	$2,257,316	$2,257,316	100.00%	$1,141,423	50.57%
72. FIRST AMERICAN TRANS	$108,501	$1,474,514	$1,583,015	93.15%	$736,408	49.94%
73. FARMERS NATIONAL	$0	$1,138,404	$1,138,404	100.00%	$460,097	40.42%
74. FIRST AMERICAN T&T	$6,291,430	$0	$6,291,430	0.00%	$1,227,400	--
75. SEAGATE	$186,090	$0	$186,090	0.00%	$111,654	--
76. ATTORNEYS TGF (IL)	$10,998,779	$0	$10,998,779	0.00%	$0	--
77. TITLE GUARANTY DIV (IA)	$3,724,743	$0	$3,724,743	0.00%	$0	--
78. PENN ATTORNEYS	$1,777,598	$0	$1,777,598	0.00%	$0	--
79. TRANSUNION TIC	$882,460	$0	$882,460	0.00%	$0	--
80. NATIONAL ATTORNEYS	$831,940	$0	$831,940	0.00%	$0	--
81. EQUITY NATIONAL	$280,228	$0	$280,228	0.00%	$0	--
82. TITLE G&TC	$260,893	$0	$260,893	0.00%	$0	--
83. FOUNDERS	$178,276	$0	$178,276	0.00%	$0	--
84. MASSACHUSETTS TIC	($254)	$0	($254)	0.00%	$0	--
85. CHICAGO T&T	$0	$0	$0	--	$0	--
86. COLUMBIAN NATIONAL	$0	$0	$0	--	$0	--
87. MASON COUNTY	$0	$0	$0	--	$0	--
88. NATIONS OF NY	$0	$0	$0	--	$0	--
89. OLD REPUBLIC GENERAL	$0	$0	$0	--	$0	--
90. OLYMPIC	$0	$0	$0	--	$0	--
91. PUBLIC	$0	$0	$0	--	$0	--
COMPOSITE	$2,516,267,899	$11,545,003,806	$14,061,271,705	82.10%	$9,454,264,921	81.89%
AVERAGE	$27,651,296	$126,868,174	$154,519,469	82.10%	$103,893,021	81.89%

5

MEASUREMENTS OF
LOSSES AND ABILITY TO MEET LOSSES

5

Measurements of Losses and Ability to Meet Losses

C.1 Key Losses and Ability to Meet Losses Results and Ratios

This report presents key losses and ability to meet losses results and ratios for each Title underwriter. Included in this report are *C.2 - Losses and Loss Adjustment Expenses (LAE) Incurred, C.3 - Losses and Loss Adjustment Expenses Incurred to Net Operating and Investment Gain (Loss), C.4 - Losses and Loss Adjustment Expenses Incurred to Net Operating and Investment Gain (Loss) and Known Claims Reserve, C.5 - Losses and Loss Adjustment Expenses Incurred to Policyholders' Surplus (PHS) and Reserves, C.6 - Losses and Loss Adjustment Expenses Incurred to Net Liquid Assets* as well as *C.9 - Reserves to Policyholders' Surplus.*

This report is sorted in alphabetical order by Title underwriter.

This report reflects *Consolidation Eliminations* in the *Composite* calculation.

C.2 Losses & Loss Adjustment Expenses (LAE) Incurred

This report presents *Losses and Loss Adjustment Expenses (LAE)* Incurred for the past five years, calculating the changes from year to year. Losses Incurred for a specific period are the total amounts paid by the Title underwriter for losses that have occurred, plus changes in the reserves for payment expected to be made in the future for reported losses. Loss Adjustment Expenses are the costs paid by the Title underwriter in adjusting and settling losses.

To ensure reasonableness of results, if prior year *Losses and Loss Adjustment Expenses (LAE) Incurred* is less than or equal to $0, then the percentage change is not presented.

This report is sorted in descending order by *Losses and Loss Adjustment Expenses (LAE) Incurred* for the current year.

This report presents five years of analysis.

C.3 Losses & Loss Adjustment Expenses (LAE) Incurred to Net Operating and Investment Gain (Loss)

This report presents *C.2 - Losses and Loss Adjustment Expenses (LAE) Incurred* as a percentage of the applicable year's *Operating Gain (Loss)* (before Losses and Loss Adjustment Expenses Incurred and Taxes) and Net Investment Gain (Loss).

This report is sorted in descending order by the current year ratio results.

This report presents five years of analysis.

This report reflects *Consolidation Eliminations* in the *Composite* calculation.

C.4 Losses & Loss Adjustment Expenses (LAE) Incurred to Net Operating and Investment Gain (Loss) and Known Claims Reserve

This report presents *C.2 - Losses and Loss Adjustment Expenses (LAE) Incurred* as a percentage of the applicable year's *Operating Gain (Loss)* (before Losses and Loss Adjustment Expenses Incurred and Taxes) plus Net Investment Gain (Loss) and Known Claims Reserve (KCR).

This report is sorted in descending order by the current year ratio results.

This report presents five years of analysis.

This report reflects *Consolidation Eliminations* in the *Composite* calculation.

C.5 Losses & Loss Adjustment Expenses (LAE) Incurred to Policyholders' Surplus (PHS) and Reserves

This report presents *C.2 - Losses and Loss Adjustment Expenses (LAE) Incurred* as a percentage of the sum of *Policyholders' Surplus (PHS) and Reserves.*

This report is sorted in descending order by the current year ratio results.

This report presents five years of analysis.

This report reflects *Consolidation Eliminations* in the *Composite* calculation.

C.6 Losses & Loss Adjustment Expenses (LAE) Incurred to Net Liquid Assets

This report presents *C.2 - Losses and Loss Adjustment Expenses (LAE) Incurred* as a percentage of *B.2 - Net Liquid Assets.*

To ensure reasonableness of results, if *B.2 - Net Liquid Assets* is less than or equal to $0, then the ratio is not presented.

This report is sorted in ascending order by the current year ratio results.

This report presents five years of analysis.

This report reflects *Consolidation Eliminations* in the *Composite* calculation.

C.7 Composite of Losses & Loss Adjustment Expenses (LAE) Incurred

This report presents *C.2 - Losses and Loss Adjustment Expenses (LAE) Incurred* for the current year for each of the three distribution channels – *Direct, Non-Affiliated Agencies* and *Affiliated Agencies Operations*.

This report is sorted in descending order by Losses and Loss Adjustment Expenses (LAE) Incurred.

C.8 Direct and Agency Loss Ratios

This report presents *Losses and Loss Adjustment Expenses (LAE) Incurred* for each of the three distribution channels, *Direct, Non-Affiliated Agencies* and *Affiliated Agencies Operations,* as a percentage of the respective *Direct Premiums Written* for each channel.

This report is sorted in alphabetical order by Title underwriter.

C.9 Reserves to Policyholders' Surplus (PHS)

This report presents *Known Claims Reserve, Statutory Premium Reserve (SPR)* and other required reserves to *B.6 - Policyholders' Surplus (PHS).* With Statutory Accounting Principles (SAP), Policyholders' Surplus is substituted for Owners' Equity to reflect the priority given policyholders' claims over any owners' claims and is a general measure of statutory net worth.

This report is sorted in descending order by the current year ratio results.

This report presents five years of analysis.

This report reflects *Consolidation Eliminations* in the *Composite* calculation.

C.10 Loss Reserve Development

This report presents the redundancy or deficiency of Losses and Loss Adjustment Expenses (LAE) Incurred relative to the first and second most recent calendar years for all prior policy years. A similar measure is included as a component of Schedule P reporting for traditional Property and Casualty companies.

The *One Year Development* is determined by comparing the Losses and Loss Adjustment Expenses (LAE) Incurred for each respective policy year, valued at the end of the current calendar year, to that same policy year's Losses and Loss Adjustment Expenses (LAE) Incurred, valued at the end of the preceding calendar year.

The *Two Year Development* is computed using the same mechanics. However, for the *Two Year Development*, the current calendar year values are compared to the values of the second preceding calendar year.

If the cumulative result is negative, this indicates that the Losses and Loss Adjustment Expenses (LAE) Incurred have decreased as of the end of the current calendar year compared to the respective first or second most recent calendar year. A cumulative negative result indicates favorable development of reserves, as the more recent estimate of Losses and Loss Adjustment Expenses (LAE) Incurred has declined. If the cumulative result is positive, this indicates that the Losses and Loss Adjustment Expenses (LAE) Incurred have increased as of the end of the current calendar year compared to the respective first or second most recent calendar year.

This report presents five years of analysis.

This report is sorted in alphabetical order by Title underwriter.

C.11 Loss Reserve Development to Policyholders' Surplus (PHS) – New!

This report presents the relationship of *C.10 - Loss Reserve Development* to the respective year's *B.6 - Policyholder' Surplus (PHS).*

The *One Year Loss Reserve Development to Policyholders' Surplus* ratio measures the development of Losses and Loss Adjustment Expenses (LAE) Incurred compared to Losses and Loss Adjustment Expenses (LAE) Incurred reported one year prior. The ratio is calculated by dividing the *One Year Loss Reserve Development* by the prior year *Policyholders' Surplus.*

The *Two Year Loss Reserve Development to Policyholders' Surplus* ratio measures the development of Losses and Loss Adjustment Expenses (LAE) Incurred compared to Losses and Loss Adjustment Expenses (LAE) Incurred reported two years prior. The ratio is calculated by dividing the *Two Year Loss Reserve Development* by the second prior year Policyholders' Surplus.

This report is sorted in alphabetical order by Title underwriter.

This report reflects *Consolidation Eliminations* in the *Composite* calculation.

This report is a new analysis introduced in the 2008 publication.

5

C.1 Key Losses and Ability to Meet Losses Results and Ratios

COMPANY	C.2 L&LAE INCURRED	C.3 L&LAE TO OPERATING GAIN	C.4 L&LAE TO OPER INVEST GAIN & KCR	C.5 L&LAE TO PHS & RESERVES	C.6 L&LAE TO NET LIQUID ASSETS	C.9 RESERVES TO PHS
1. ALAMO	$4,542,653	53.33%	43.37%	9.84%	20.87%	75.95%
2. ALLIANCE	$66,579	60.96%	41.09%	1.81%	2.14%	18.59%
3. ALLIANT	$974,113	385.54%	102.86%	26.90%	52.05%	53.82%
4. AMERICAN EAGLE	$30,838	7.65%	7.50%	2.70%	--	59.15%
5. AMERICAN GUARANTY	$127,491	8.02%	7.66%	0.90%	1.21%	22.89%
6. AMERICAN LAND & AIRCRAFT	$5,858	(96.35)%	(96.34)%	0.74%	0.79%	6.33%
7. AMERICAN SECURITY	$2,283	0.23%	0.22%	0.03%	0.02%	2.07%
8. ARKANSAS TIC	$155,822	20.76%	14.60%	3.25%	7.39%	100.89%
9. ARSENAL	$649	15.52%	15.52%	0.12%	0.13%	10.33%
10. ATTORNEYS TGF (CO)	$357,311	572.08%	71.93%	8.11%	--	148.17%
11. ATTORNEYS TGF (IL)	$1,811,083	98.17%	45.62%	8.33%	36.40%	122.83%
12. ATTORNEYS TIF (FL)	$44,278,625	198.83%	68.98%	14.17%	54.19%	108.61%
13. BRIDGE	$180,404	(4,900.95)%	3,770.19%	2.21%	2.28%	2.13%
14. CENSTAR	$356,768	7.49%	7.34%	1.24%	1.46%	14.78%
15. CHICAGO T&T	$0	0.00%	0.00%	0.00%	0.00%	0.00%
16. CHICAGO TIC	$194,183,378	54.52%	39.85%	15.77%	189.41%	348.55%
17. CHICAGO TIC (OR)	$655,119	10.77%	9.97%	2.65%	5.44%	82.06%
18. COLUMBIAN NATIONAL	$0	0.00%	0.00%	0.00%	0.00%	0.00%
19. COMMERCE	$456,599	9.64%	9.21%	2.25%	5.92%	130.07%
20. COMMONWEALTH LAND	$79,989,583	48.81%	35.11%	11.77%	47.69%	167.46%
21. COMMONWEALTH LAND (NJ)	$1,900,137	31.46%	24.29%	4.56%	5.88%	25.67%
22. CONESTOGA	$991,906	(3,218.49)%	328.95%	12.60%	162.95%	125.93%
23. CT ATTORNEYS	$4,086,369	74.04%	59.38%	6.99%	10.52%	39.65%
24. DAKOTA HOMESTEAD	$251,953	81.63%	39.02%	7.35%	11.14%	51.30%
25. DREIBELBISS	$216,747	(10,968.98)%	1,082.43%	7.60%	9.99%	7.63%
26. EQUITY NATIONAL	$0	0.00%	0.00%	0.00%	0.00%	7.77%
27. FARMERS NATIONAL	$68,819	(27.04)%	(27.58)%	7.06%	9.92%	19.33%
28. FIDELITY NATIONAL	$105,973,214	56.45%	36.66%	13.87%	58.57%	221.40%
29. FIRST AMERICAN (KS)	$756,653	39.11%	34.51%	6.74%	13.49%	92.48%
30. FIRST AMERICAN (NY)	$9,991,046	31.26%	23.99%	6.10%	10.35%	52.40%
31. FIRST AMERICAN (OR)	$2,919,785	24.46%	20.35%	5.38%	27.41%	69.30%
32. FIRST AMERICAN T&T	$217,877	3.59%	3.57%	1.23%	1.68%	8.07%
33. FIRST AMERICAN TIC	$374,613,626	87.91%	66.10%	24.67%	--	256.01%
34. FIRST AMERICAN TRANS	($16,063)	(11.27)%	(10.88)%	(0.93)%	(1.47)%	37.94%
35. FOUNDERS	$0	0.00%	0.00%	0.00%	0.00%	3.13%
36. GENERAL T&T	$457,564	(661.89)%	397.98%	6.84%	52.62%	319.40%
37. GUARANTEE	$873,275	248.38%	179.95%	34.81%	155.23%	104.27%
38. GUARANTEE T&T	$1,575,074	534.59%	357.66%	20.29%	--	536.70%
39. GUARDIAN NATIONAL	($76,380)	(105.42)%	(19.09)%	(0.79)%	(1.18)%	41.95%
40. INVESTORS TIC	$8,975,058	56.90%	45.56%	9.61%	22.88%	86.35%
41. K.E.L.	$0	0.00%	0.00%	0.00%	0.00%	1.27%
42. LAND CORP (CO)	$272,282	12.23%	11.39%	1.95%	3.42%	41.84%
43. LAND TIC (ST LOUIS)	$0	0.00%	0.00%	0.00%	0.00%	0.96%
44. LAWYERS	$89,456,439	92.43%	51.84%	16.57%	--	317.53%
45. MANITO	$39,324	168.83%	111.26%	2.71%	3.18%	15.42%
46. MASON	$12,200	(5.33)%	(5.62)%	0.47%	0.49%	2.92%
47. MASON COUNTY	$0	0.00%	0.00%	0.00%	0.00%	3.15%
48. MASSACHUSETTS TIC	$0	0.00%	0.00%	0.00%	0.00%	4.06%
49. MISSISSIPPI GUARANTY	$0	0.00%	0.00%	0.00%	0.00%	185.53%
50. MISSISSIPPI VALLEY	$3,445,735	96.57%	46.33%	7.72%	42.54%	361.17%
51. MONROE	$577,628	65.69%	34.34%	3.15%	7.02%	59.50%
52. NATIONAL	($9,014)	5.50%	5.76%	(0.26)%	(0.41)%	13.95%
53. NATIONAL ATTORNEYS	$267,150	325.20%	325.19%	15.12%	23.89%	12.76%
54. NATIONAL LAND	$67,550	(24.78)%	(37.23)%	1.05%	1.30%	23.10%
55. NATIONAL OF NY	$1,062,612	74.63%	25.19%	7.91%	16.39%	100.08%
56. NATIONS OF NY	$471,333	35.67%	26.28%	2.72%	3.85%	37.24%
57. NEW JERSEY TIC	$1,216,094	298.24%	162.69%	12.72%	36.77%	97.21%
58. NORTH AMERICAN	$2,424,736	16.67%	15.92%	3.03%	5.00%	57.25%
59. NORTHEAST INVESTORS	$149,328	45.56%	45.14%	2.45%	2.79%	9.80%
60. OHIO BAR	$1,445,381	54.57%	45.74%	5.95%	16.94%	169.24%
61. OLD REPUBLIC GENERAL	$8,609,260	49.47%	34.06%	7.51%	22.70%	148.13%
62. OLD REPUBLIC NATIONAL	$56,386,474	71.94%	40.36%	12.84%	73.14%	278.69%
63. OLYMPIC	$26,670	(747.48)%	391.68%	7.70%	8.72%	3.09%
64. PACIFIC NORTHWEST	$1,737,205	25.11%	22.99%	6.22%	17.45%	84.15%
65. PENN ATTORNEYS	$44,947	4.05%	3.49%	0.47%	0.55%	14.03%
66. PORT LAWRENCE	$35,011	3.50%	3.38%	0.17%	0.33%	38.50%
67. PUBLIC	$0	0.00%	0.00%	0.00%	0.00%	0.00%
68. SEAGATE	$0	0.00%	0.00%	0.00%	0.00%	40.60%
69. SECURITY TG (BALTIMORE)	$1,643,655	284.05%	76.77%	11.85%	154.44%	268.52%
70. SECURITY UNION	$10,051,219	80.21%	44.91%	12.73%	37.33%	69.56%
71. SIERRA	$0	0.00%	0.00%	0.00%	0.00%	1.89%
72. SOUTHERN TI CORP	$3,737,323	151.49%	65.09%	16.99%	100.48%	185.03%
73. STEWART (OR)	$0	0.00%	0.00%	0.00%	0.00%	79.15%
74. STEWART TGC	$131,848,241	114.85%	63.92%	12.73%	29.71%	100.77%
75. STEWART TIC	$5,470,985	23.45%	16.59%	7.67%	19.11%	106.73%
76. T.A. TITLE	$544,743	31.24%	28.52%	4.79%	10.89%	75.00%
77. TICOR	$31,901,304	58.07%	41.48%	15.73%	84.80%	199.67%
78. TICOR (FL)	$24,844,212	557.02%	109.91%	23.07%	337.20%	320.90%
79. TITLE G&TC	$1,500	1.12%	1.12%	0.12%	0.24%	38.17%
80. TITLE GUARANTY DIV (IA)	$0	0.00%	0.00%	0.00%	0.00%	677.23%
81. TITLE IC AMERICA	$211,989	33.92%	22.28%	1.41%	1.93%	28.91%
82. TITLE RESOURCES	$2,723,051	27.40%	26.30%	6.95%	12.70%	52.36%
83. TITLEDGE	$0	0.00%	0.00%	0.00%	0.00%	1.77%
84. TRANSNATION	$36,073,084	(556.26)%	287.74%	24.56%	1,733.18%	557.66%
85. TRANSUNION NATIONAL	$1,156,258	204.62%	85.43%	8.06%	11.73%	42.83%
86. TRANSUNION TIC	$80,642	25.44%	17.33%	1.11%	2.26%	86.82%
87. UNITED CAPITAL	$8,465,810	118.58%	74.76%	16.61%	46.74%	123.91%
88. UNITED GENERAL	$27,244,717	438.25%	139.75%	26.23%	--	271.30%
89. WASHINGTON TIC	$433,920	181.99%	112.45%	13.73%	--	260.63%
90. WESTCOR	$912,036	(172.36)%	1,403.60%	4.01%	17.17%	162.62%
91. WESTERN NATIONAL	($65,757)	(40.95)%	(31.47)%	(1.44)%	(2.01)%	36.11%
COMPOSITE	$1,296,969,093	63.98%	44.96%	14.05%	60.96%	144.49%
AVERAGE	$14,252,408					

5

C.2 Losses & Loss Adjustment Expenses (LAE) Incurred

COMPANY	2007	2006	2006 TO 2007	2005	2005 TO 2006	2004	2004 TO 2005	2003	2003 TO 2004
1. FIRST AMERICAN TIC	$374,613,626	$192,854,101	94.25%	$180,248,538	6.99%	$127,139,570	41.77%	$130,870,833	(2.85)%
2. CHICAGO TIC	$194,183,378	$107,527,159	80.59%	$167,190,159	(35.69)%	$106,252,029	57.35%	$98,416,011	7.96%
3. STEWART TGC	$131,848,241	$100,418,956	31.30%	$84,928,763	18.24%	$67,501,892	25.82%	$48,666,944	38.70%
4. FIDELITY NATIONAL	$105,973,214	$70,996,930	49.26%	$125,732,838	(43.53)%	$104,630,443	20.17%	$54,061,863	93.54%
5. LAWYERS	$89,456,439	$70,983,361	26.02%	$70,426,915	0.79%	$52,740,278	33.54%	$51,920,094	1.58%
6. COMMONWEALTH LAND	$79,989,583	$82,299,590	(2.81)%	$60,175,186	36.77%	$53,505,975	12.46%	$46,271,131	15.64%
7. OLD REPUBLIC NATIONAL	$56,386,474	$57,530,621	(1.99)%	$53,580,746	7.37%	$37,170,243	44.15%	$32,231,915	15.32%
8. ATTORNEYS TIF (FL)	$44,278,625	$26,406,495	67.68%	$24,111,467	9.52%	$11,553,283	108.70%	$18,458,829	(37.41)%
9. TRANSNATION	$36,073,084	$27,772,309	29.89%	$19,962,170	39.12%	$16,684,016	19.65%	$18,590,449	(10.26)%
10. TICOR	$31,901,304	$24,811,891	28.57%	$21,924,524	13.17%	$24,439,311	(10.29)%	$30,536,889	(19.97)%
11. UNITED GENERAL	$27,244,717	$9,893,569	175.38%	$11,232,645	(11.92)%	$7,940,787	41.46%	$7,873,989	0.85%
12. TICOR (FL)	$24,844,212	$17,517,897	41.82%	$27,533,876	(36.38)%	$19,842,615	38.76%	$12,055,119	64.60%
13. SECURITY UNION	$10,051,219	$6,131,491	63.93%	$6,666,041	(8.02)%	$6,154,978	8.30%	$3,997,848	53.96%
14. FIRST AMERICAN (NY)	$9,991,046	$8,782,858	13.76%	$6,403,781	37.15%	$7,213,198	(11.22)%	$8,197,511	(12.01)%
15. INVESTORS TIC	$8,975,058	$7,296,317	23.01%	$5,879,958	24.09%	$7,046,750	(16.56)%	$5,575,526	26.39%
16. OLD REPUBLIC GENERAL	$8,609,260	$4,172,415	106.34%	$3,953,818	5.53%	$4,298,924	(8.03)%	$8,660,383	(50.36)%
17. UNITED CAPITAL	$8,465,810	$6,781,471	24.84%	$2,483,037	173.11%	$1,236,143	100.87%	$397,535	210.95%
18. STEWART TIC	$5,470,985	$6,246,430	(12.41)%	$3,383,259	84.63%	$4,208,768	(19.61)%	$4,946,289	(14.91)%
19. ALAMO	$4,542,653	$2,516,764	80.50%	$3,044,471	(17.33)%	$2,847,088	6.93%	$2,588,332	10.00%
20. CT ATTORNEYS	$4,086,369	$6,089,256	(32.89)%	$2,392,336	154.53%	$2,021,630	18.34%	$1,381,403	46.35%
21. SOUTHERN TI CORP	$3,737,323	$2,258,236	65.50%	$932,711	142.12%	$981,449	(4.97)%	$919,380	6.75%
22. MISSISSIPPI VALLEY	$3,445,735	$1,158,089	197.54%	$2,369,656	(51.13)%	($221,338)	--	$2,134,324	(110.37)%
23. FIRST AMERICAN (OR)	$2,919,785	$2,267,456	28.77%	$3,078,073	(26.34)%	$1,108,151	177.77%	$1,682,638	(34.14)%
24. TITLE RESOURCES	$2,723,051	$3,132,170	(13.06)%	$1,629,920	92.17%	$1,834,604	(11.16)%	$1,485,848	23.47%
25. NORTH AMERICAN	$2,424,736	$2,460,306	(1.45)%	$2,344,914	4.92%	$2,214,660	5.88%	$2,783,104	(20.42)%
26. COMMONWEALTH LAND (NJ)	$1,900,137	$2,701,856	(29.67)%	$1,347,468	100.51%	$1,832,692	(26.48)%	$610,298	200.29%
27. ATTORNEYS TGF (IL)	$1,811,083	$2,436,947	(25.68)%	$2,703,257	(9.85)%	$3,202,020	(15.58)%	$2,954,384	8.38%
28. PACIFIC NORTHWEST	$1,737,205	$1,230,336	41.20%	$968,643	27.02%	$1,118,070	(13.36)%	$1,436,250	(22.15)%
29. SECURITY TG (BALTIMORE)	$1,643,655	$497,117	230.64%	$2,224,136	(77.65)%	$527,724	321.46%	$823,586	(35.92)%
30. GUARANTEE T&T	$1,575,074	$1,669,784	(5.67)%	$1,344,000	24.24%	$1,625,500	(17.32)%	$1,250,000	30.04%
31. OHIO BAR	$1,445,381	$436,133	231.41%	($1,030,903)	--	($74,713)	--	$2,752,682	(102.71)%
32. NEW JERSEY TIC	$1,216,094	$796,204	52.74%	$594,934	33.83%	$962,936	(38.22)%	$723,880	33.02%
33. TRANSUNION NATIONAL	$1,156,258	$967,267	19.54%	$2,034,743	(52.46)%	$450,486	351.68%	$331,757	35.79%
34. NATIONAL OF NY	$1,062,612	$1,259,023	(15.60)%	$1,933,564	(34.89)%	$5,143,113	(62.40)%	$2,058,293	149.87%
35. CONESTOGA	$991,906	$360,889	174.85%	$1,026,790	(64.85)%	$1,993,640	(48.50)%	$522,341	281.67%
36. ALLIANT	$974,113	$21,400	4,451.93%	$0	--	--	--	--	--
37. WESTCOR	$912,036	$119,471	663.38%	$1,130,059	(89.43)%	$635,130	77.93%	$763,550	(16.82)%
38. GUARANTEE	$873,275	$1,290,776	(32.34)%	$143,993	796.42%	$14,539	890.39%	$164,425	(91.16)%
39. FIRST AMERICAN (KS)	$756,653	$502,115	50.69%	$954,020	(47.37)%	$614,993	55.13%	$697,761	(11.86)%
40. CHICAGO TIC (OR)	$655,119	$301,247	117.47%	$1,240,874	(75.72)%	$1,308,003	(5.13)%	$815,927	60.31%
41. MONROE	$577,628	$382,017	51.20%	$568,914	(32.85)%	$465,115	22.32%	$147,466	215.40%
42. T.A. TITLE	$544,743	$433,256	25.73%	$153,983	181.37%	$579,310	(73.42)%	$177,215	226.90%
43. NATIONS OF NY	$471,333	$253,181	86.16%	$99,845	153.57%	$646,431	(84.55)%	$1,331,133	(51.44)%
44. GENERAL T&T	$457,564	$607,568	(24.69)%	$192,444	215.71%	$112,382	71.24%	$151,772	(25.95)%
45. COMMERCE	$456,599	$1,142,106	(60.02)%	$590,939	93.27%	$689,433	(14.29)%	$489,809	40.76%
46. WASHINGTON TIC	$433,920	$419,448	3.45%	$94,056	345.96%	$310,751	(69.73)%	$133,636	132.54%
47. ATTORNEYS TGF (CO)	$357,311	$415,284	(13.96)%	$1,054,350	(60.61)%	$1,374,836	(23.31)%	$248,721	452.76%
48. CENSTAR	$356,768	$103,319	245.31%	$57,745	78.92%	$0	--	$0	--
49. LAND CORP (CO)	$272,282	($221,916)	--	$262,060	(184.68)%	($287,093)	--	$937,919	(130.61)%
50. NATIONAL ATTORNEYS	$267,150	$122,406	118.25%	$25,341	383.04%	$75,556	(66.46)%	$145,645	(48.12)%
51. DAKOTA HOMESTEAD	$251,953	$185,422	35.88%	$281,000	(34.01)%	($35,775)	--	$52,949	(167.57)%
52. FIRST AMERICAN T&T	$217,877	$186,018	17.13%	$356,375	(47.80)%	$389,614	(8.53)%	$344,535	13.08%
53. DREIBELBISS	$216,747	$57,985	273.80%	($155,490)	--	$49,589	(413.56)%	$45,331	9.39%
54. TITLE IC AMERICA	$211,989	$1,094,709	(80.64)%	$965,423	13.39%	$281,042	243.52%	$392,478	(28.39)%
55. BRIDGE	$180,404	$87,445	106.31%	$63,240	38.27%	$172,261	(63.29)%	$1,500	11,384.07%
56. ARKANSAS TIC	$155,822	$260,867	(40.27)%	$47,349	450.95%	$489,154	(90.32)%	$217,807	124.58%
57. NORTHEAST INVESTORS	$149,328	$30,554	388.73%	$68,670	(55.51)%	($8,131)	--	$9,902	(182.11)%
58. AMERICAN GUARANTY	$127,491	$79,314	60.74%	$162,480	(51.19)%	$138,280	17.50%	$102,040	35.52%
59. TRANSUNION TIC	$80,642	$482,011	(83.27)%	$915,166	(47.33)%	$493,183	85.56%	$251,208	96.32%
60. FARMERS NATIONAL	$68,819	$1,221	5,536.28%	--	--	--	--	--	--
61. NATIONAL LAND	$67,550	$68,523	(1.42)%	$153,886	(55.47)%	$41,300	272.61%	$196,278	(78.96)%
62. ALLIANCE	$66,579	$60,972	9.20%	($126,878)	--	$307,399	(141.27)%	$627,115	(50.98)%
63. PENN ATTORNEYS	$44,947	$100,627	(55.33)%	$225,148	(55.31)%	($85,824)	--	$27,000	(417.87)%
64. MANITO	$39,324	$14,525	170.73%	$4,967	192.43%	($76,217)	--	$50,000	(252.43)%
65. PORT LAWRENCE	$35,011	($161,059)	--	$89,482	(279.99)%	$39,836	124.63%	$136,284	(70.77)%
66. AMERICAN EAGLE	$30,838	$36,365	(15.20)%	$100,744	(63.90)%	$65,233	54.44%	$165,958	(60.69)%
67. OLYMPIC	$26,670	$2,687	892.56%	$84,424	(96.82)%	$88,136	(4.21)%	$6,838	1,188.91%
68. MASON	$12,200	$0	--	--	--	--	--	--	--
69. AMERICAN LAND & AIRCRAFT	$5,858	$5,780	1.35%	$0	--	$0	--	$0	--
70. AMERICAN SECURITY	$2,283	$48,890	(95.33)%	$0	--	$0	--	$5,500	(100.00)%
71. TITLE G&TC	$1,500	$0	--	$1,460	(100.00)%	$2,314	(36.91)%	$7,500	(69.15)%
72. ARSENAL	$649	$2,554	(74.59)%	$4,788	(46.66)%	$0	--	--	--
73. TITLE GUARANTY DIV (IA)	$0	$180,000	(100.00)%	$269,005	(33.09)%	$135,000	99.26%	$75,365	79.13%
74. COLUMBIAN NATIONAL	$0	$0	--	$640,124	(100.00)%	$2,109,905	(69.66)%	$304,352	593.24%
75. MASON COUNTY	$0	$0	--	$0	--	$6,000	(100.00)%	$0	--
76. CHICAGO T&T	$0	$0	--	$0	--	$0	--	$0	--
77. LAND TIC (ST LOUIS)	$0	$0	--	$0	--	$0	--	$0	--
78. MASSACHUSETTS TIC	$0	$0	--	$0	--	$0	--	$0	--
79. MISSISSIPPI GUARANTY	$0	$0	--	$0	--	$0	--	$0	--
80. SEAGATE	$0	$0	--	$0	--	$0	--	$0	--
81. STEWART (OR)	$0	$0	--	$0	--	$0	--	$0	--
82. EQUITY NATIONAL	$0	$0	--	$0	--	--	--	--	--
83. FOUNDERS	$0	$0	--	--	--	--	--	--	--
84. PUBLIC	$0	$0	--	--	--	--	--	--	--
85. SIERRA	$0	$0	--	--	--	--	--	--	--
86. K.E.L.	$0	--	--	--	--	--	--	--	--
87. TITLEDGE	$0	--	--	--	--	--	--	--	--
88. NATIONAL	($9,014)	$50,000	(118.03)%	$0	--	$0	--	$2,015	(100.00)%
89. FIRST AMERICAN TRANS	($16,063)	$226,633	(107.09)%	$36,703	517.48%	$76,026	(51.72)%	$12,212	522.55%
90. WESTERN NATIONAL	($65,757)	$238,100	(127.62)%	($22,456)	--	$24,242	(192.63)%	$120,469	(79.88)%
91. GUARDIAN NATIONAL	($76,380)	$358,739	(121.29)%	$38,345	835.56%	$208,641	(81.62)%	$271,102	(23.04)%
COMPOSITE	$1,296,969,093	$870,252,256	49.03%	$915,529,012	(4.95)%	$698,577,509	31.06%	$617,798,395	13.08%
AVERAGE	$14,252,408	$9,778,115	45.76%	$10,770,930	(9.22)%	$8,519,238	26.43%	$7,627,141	11.70%

COMPANY INDEX

5

C.3 Losses & Loss Adjustment Expenses (LAE) Incurred to Net Operating and Investment Gain (Loss)

COMPANY	2007 C.2 - L&LAE INCURRED	2007 OPERATING GAIN (LOSS)	2007 L&LAE TO OPERATING GAIN	2006 L&LAE TO OPERATING GAIN	2005 L&LAE TO OPERATING GAIN	2004 L&LAE TO OPERATING GAIN	2003 L&LAE TO OPERATING GAIN
1. ATTORNEYS TGF (CO)	$357,311	$62,458	572.08%	9,666.76%	379.10%	63.71%	38.79%
2. TICOR (FL)	$24,844,212	$4,460,196	557.02%	109.48%	67.60%	65.64%	34.61%
3. GUARANTEE T&T	$1,575,074	$294,631	534.59%	132.28%	99.11%	99.39%	65.74%
4. UNITED GENERAL	$27,244,717	$6,216,772	438.25%	(248.26)%	218.73%	70.22%	54.73%
5. ALLIANT	$974,113	$252,661	385.54%	(11.25)%	0.00%	--	--
6. NATIONAL ATTORNEYS	$267,150	$82,150	325.20%	96.06%	25.51%	29.07%	49.44%
7. NEW JERSEY TIC	$1,216,094	$407,762	298.24%	79.23%	53.44%	81.79%	51.97%
8. SECURITY TG (BALTIMORE)	$1,643,655	$578,650	284.05%	28.77%	177.13%	23.87%	54.61%
9. GUARANTEE	$873,275	$351,587	248.38%	473.99%	(125.34)%	9.67%	108.92%
10. TRANSUNION NATIONAL	$1,156,258	$565,074	204.62%	(510.27)%	(21,531.67)%	(480.12)%	59.33%
11. ATTORNEYS TIF (FL)	$44,278,625	$22,269,994	198.83%	40.39%	33.82%	18.08%	32.90%
12. WASHINGTON TIC	$433,920	$238,435	181.99%	5,720.01%	22.02%	146.16%	69.27%
13. MANITO	$39,324	$23,292	168.83%	48.13%	13.47%	(528.33)%	32.25%
14. SOUTHERN TI CORP	$3,737,323	$2,467,056	151.49%	79.19%	28.90%	34.20%	25.16%
15. UNITED CAPITAL	$8,465,810	$7,139,235	118.58%	54.22%	26.98%	17.71%	5.25%
16. STEWART TGC	$131,848,241	$114,799,347	114.85%	65.62%	51.69%	61.35%	46.79%
17. ATTORNEYS TGF (IL)	$1,811,083	$1,844,809	98.17%	49.68%	48.15%	143.09%	69.26%
18. MISSISSIPPI VALLEY	$3,445,735	$3,567,911	96.57%	31.90%	78.34%	(7.58)%	49.17%
19. LAWYERS	$89,456,439	$96,787,907	92.43%	52.24%	53.21%	49.17%	32.96%
20. FIRST AMERICAN TIC	$374,613,626	$426,148,373	87.91%	41.91%	35.05%	39.96%	29.82%
21. DAKOTA HOMESTEAD	$251,953	$308,657	81.63%	52.80%	197.21%	(16.53)%	15.65%
22. SECURITY UNION	$10,051,219	$12,531,706	80.21%	34.99%	31.65%	15.07%	21.15%
23. NATIONAL OF NY	$1,062,612	$1,423,922	74.63%	183.11%	(246.05)%	177.78%	36.44%
24. CT ATTORNEYS	$4,086,369	$5,518,801	74.04%	109.44%	30.08%	29.76%	12.94%
25. OLD REPUBLIC NATIONAL	$56,386,474	$78,383,173	71.94%	61.04%	55.39%	41.07%	42.26%
26. MONROE	$577,628	$879,390	65.69%	51.45%	34.33%	24.50%	5.11%
27. ALLIANCE	$66,579	$109,219	60.96%	(60.13)%	(114.12)%	269.83%	49.34%
28. TICOR	$31,901,304	$54,939,382	58.07%	31.17%	36.50%	46.62%	37.58%
29. INVESTORS TIC	$8,975,058	$15,773,921	56.90%	41.28%	29.13%	37.69%	27.55%
30. FIDELITY NATIONAL	$105,973,214	$187,723,693	56.45%	34.02%	44.13%	53.73%	41.30%
31. OHIO BAR	$1,445,381	$2,648,756	54.57%	17.29%	(46.03)%	(3.07)%	128.46%
32. CHICAGO TIC	$194,183,378	$356,198,185	54.52%	25.00%	38.55%	23.03%	16.88%
33. ALAMO	$4,542,653	$8,518,657	53.33%	10.41%	30.22%	30.93%	30.50%
34. OLD REPUBLIC GENERAL	$8,609,260	$17,404,263	49.47%	23.22%	19.22%	18.99%	38.48%
35. COMMONWEALTH LAND	$79,989,583	$163,868,085	48.81%	32.71%	36.87%	40.37%	30.00%
36. NORTHEAST INVESTORS	$149,328	$327,772	45.56%	14.59%	23.26%	(2.19)%	1.87%
37. FIRST AMERICAN (KS)	$756,653	$1,934,711	39.11%	32.87%	69.28%	31.00%	36.25%
38. NATIONS OF NY	$471,333	$1,321,336	35.67%	19.87%	9.07%	89.92%	169.17%
39. TITLE IC AMERICA	$211,989	$625,037	33.92%	93.96%	43.37%	54.60%	20.29%
40. COMMONWEALTH LAND (NJ)	$1,900,137	$6,040,421	31.46%	33.60%	13.16%	16.10%	5.45%
41. FIRST AMERICAN (NY)	$9,991,046	$31,963,595	31.26%	34.70%	46.46%	55.29%	58.70%
42. T.A. TITLE	$544,743	$1,743,477	31.24%	22.62%	8.52%	41.58%	5.79%
43. TITLE RESOURCES	$2,723,051	$9,939,128	27.40%	27.28%	19.41%	24.17%	19.34%
44. TRANSUNION TIC	$80,642	$317,006	25.44%	120.50%	(44.29)%	146.11%	27.35%
45. PACIFIC NORTHWEST	$1,737,205	$6,917,947	25.11%	20.78%	31.42%	40.79%	107.69%
46. FIRST AMERICAN (OR)	$2,919,785	$11,936,618	24.46%	11.54%	14.60%	7.74%	7.36%
47. STEWART TIC	$5,470,985	$23,328,684	23.45%	48.14%	18.24%	29.56%	36.71%
48. ARKANSAS TIC	$155,822	$750,623	20.76%	32.90%	9.40%	83.00%	32.18%
49. NORTH AMERICAN	$2,424,736	$14,542,384	16.67%	38.20%	31.47%	33.98%	44.37%
50. ARSENAL	$649	$4,181	15.52%	1.53%	2.11%	0.00%	--
51. LAND CORP (CO)	$272,282	$2,227,051	12.23%	(8.66)%	9.49%	(9.22)%	25.94%
52. CHICAGO TIC (OR)	$655,119	$6,080,825	10.77%	3.55%	12.59%	16.15%	7.01%
53. COMMERCE	$456,599	$4,737,577	9.64%	22.09%	13.85%	21.19%	14.75%
54. AMERICAN GUARANTY	$127,491	$1,590,278	8.02%	10.71%	7.98%	4.92%	3.30%
55. AMERICAN EAGLE	$30,838	$402,985	7.65%	11.34%	17.78%	16.99%	9.18%
56. CENSTAR	$356,768	$4,761,521	7.49%	2.18%	0.90%	0.00%	0.00%
57. NATIONAL	($9,014)	($163,895)	5.50%	(18.81)%	0.00%	0.00%	11.75%
58. PENN ATTORNEYS	$44,947	$1,109,371	4.05%	9.44%	17.32%	(8.20)%	1.52%
59. FIRST AMERICAN T&T	$217,877	$6,064,236	3.59%	2.82%	9.26%	9.35%	5.31%
60. PORT LAWRENCE	$35,011	$1,000,668	3.50%	(11.32)%	4.57%	2.42%	4.46%
61. TITLE G&TC	$1,500	$133,540	1.12%	0.00%	0.87%	1.21%	4.07%
62. AMERICAN SECURITY	$2,283	$1,007,728	0.23%	4.83%	0.00%	0.00%	0.54%
63. CHICAGO T&T	$0	$298,500,357	0.00%	0.00%	0.00%	0.00%	0.00%
64. TITLE GUARANTY DIV (IA)	$0	$1,166,713	0.00%	10.52%	13.14%	3.61%	1.57%
65. STEWART (OR)	$0	$212,688	0.00%	0.00%	0.00%	0.00%	0.00%
66. SIERRA	$0	$201,450	0.00%	0.00%	--	--	--
67. EQUITY NATIONAL	$0	$65,310	0.00%	0.00%	0.00%	--	--
68. SEAGATE	$0	$39,090	0.00%	0.00%	0.00%	0.00%	0.00%
69. PUBLIC	$0	$27,843	0.00%	0.00%	--	--	--
70. MASON COUNTY	$0	$23,693	0.00%	0.00%	0.00%	(47.65)%	0.00%
71. MASSACHUSETTS TIC	$0	$11,396	0.00%	0.00%	0.00%	0.00%	0.00%
72. TITLEDGE	$0	$10,714	0.00%	--	--	--	--
73. FOUNDERS	$0	($46,012)	0.00%	0.00%	0.00%	--	--
74. COLUMBIAN NATIONAL	$0	($101,027)	0.00%	0.00%	235.84%	304.20%	37.10%
75. MISSISSIPPI GUARANTY	$0	($116,401)	0.00%	0.00%	0.00%	0.00%	0.00%
76. K.E.L.	$0	($167,546)	0.00%	--	--	--	--
77. LAND TIC (ST LOUIS)	$0	($457,112)	0.00%	0.00%	0.00%	0.00%	0.00%
78. MASON	$12,200	($229,008)	(5.33)%	0.00%	--	--	--
79. FIRST AMERICAN TRANS	($16,063)	$142,561	(11.27)%	41.12%	19.35%	22.81%	39.66%
80. NATIONAL LAND	$67,550	($272,586)	(24.78)%	122.26%	72.41%	45.61%	76.45%
81. FARMERS NATIONAL	$68,819	($254,481)	(27.04)%	(0.35)%	--	--	--
82. WESTERN NATIONAL	($65,757)	$160,576	(40.95)%	234.20%	(8.33)%	29.60%	34.64%
83. AMERICAN LAND & AIRCRAFT	$5,858	($6,080)	(96.35)%	49.05%	0.00%	0.00%	0.00%
84. GUARDIAN NATIONAL	($76,380)	$72,450	(105.42)%	146.55%	16.11%	87.16%	25.07%
85. WESTCOR	$912,036	($529,149)	(172.36)%	10.86%	65.13%	30.03%	39.17%
86. TRANSNATION	$36,073,084	($6,484,949)	(556.26)%	184.63%	42.52%	34.69%	35.49%
87. GENERAL T&T	$457,564	($69,130)	(661.89)%	182.87%	27.16%	20.48%	21.71%
88. OLYMPIC	$26,670	($3,568)	(747.48)%	(51.27)%	(403.73)%	(196.69)%	(1.29)%
89. CONESTOGA	$991,906	($30,819)	(3,218.49)%	165.02%	227.39%	193.57%	18.18%
90. BRIDGE	$180,404	($3,681)	(4,900.95)%	309.07%	(3,342.49)%	5.53%	(4.26)%
91. DREIBELBISS	$216,747	($1,976)	(10,968.98)%	70.16%	(359.15)%	30.65%	8.78%
COMPOSITE	$1,296,969,093	$1,749,210,700	74.15%	39.48%	40.58%	28.29%	27.35%
AVERAGE	$14,252,408	$22,277,959	63.98%				

5

C.4 Losses & Loss Adjustment Expenses (LAE) Incurred to Net Operating and Investment Gain & Known Claims Reserve

COMPANY	2007 C.2 - L&LAE INCURRED	2007 OPERATING GAIN (LOSS) & KCR	2007 L&LAE TO OPER INVEST GAIN & KCR	2006 L&LAE TO OPER INVEST GAIN & KCR	2005 L&LAE TO OPER INVEST GAIN & KCR	2004 L&LAE TO OPER INVEST GAIN & KCR	2003 L&LAE TO OPER INVEST GAIN & KCR
1. BRIDGE	$180,404	$4,785	3,770.20%	230.14%	3,059.51%	5.42%	(4.26)%
2. WESTCOR	$912,036	$64,978	1,403.61%	8.45%	58.60%	18.93%	26.02%
3. DREIBELBISS	$216,747	$20,024	1,082.44%	36.11%	(183.70)%	11.45%	5.46%
4. GENERAL T&T	$457,564	$114,970	397.99%	127.31%	22.30%	16.25%	17.62%
5. OLYMPIC	$26,670	$6,809	391.69%	(51.27)%	(1,067.17)%	(463.65)%	(1.30)%
6. GUARANTEE T&T	$1,575,074	$440,379	357.66%	114.97%	90.24%	73.25%	56.18%
7. CONESTOGA	$991,906	$301,531	328.96%	71.81%	81.40%	103.86%	15.81%
8. NATIONAL ATTORNEYS	$267,150	$82,150	325.20%	96.06%	25.51%	24.78%	42.89%
9. TRANSNATION	$36,073,084	$12,536,365	287.75%	97.71%	35.15%	27.54%	28.96%
10. GUARANTEE	$873,275	$485,286	179.95%	225.47%	(159.99)%	7.91%	54.81%
11. NEW JERSEY TIC	$1,216,094	$747,456	162.70%	65.91%	40.15%	62.22%	41.16%
12. UNITED GENERAL	$27,244,717	$19,494,625	139.76%	199.66%	70.17%	38.76%	37.52%
13. WASHINGTON TIC	$433,920	$385,844	112.46%	292.01%	20.44%	103.54%	39.00%
14. MANITO	$39,324	$35,342	111.27%	48.13%	6.46%	(118.30)%	19.60%
15. TICOR (FL)	$24,844,212	$22,603,924	109.91%	56.41%	46.20%	48.34%	29.22%
16. ALLIANT	$974,113	$946,991	102.86%	(12.68)%	0.00%	--	--
17. TRANSUNION NATIONAL	$1,156,258	$1,353,414	85.43%	361.37%	121.38%	206.48%	43.21%
18. SECURITY TG (BALTIMORE)	$1,643,655	$2,140,973	76.77%	15.15%	78.02%	16.73%	36.29%
19. UNITED CAPITAL	$8,465,810	$11,322,643	74.77%	41.45%	22.14%	15.13%	4.62%
20. ATTORNEYS TGF (CO)	$357,311	$496,694	71.94%	25.44%	40.89%	36.74%	7.94%
21. ATTORNEYS TIF (FL)	$44,278,625	$64,184,680	68.99%	28.54%	24.66%	13.79%	22.64%
22. FIRST AMERICAN TIC	$374,613,626	$566,665,763	66.11%	34.16%	30.18%	32.23%	26.21%
23. SOUTHERN TI CORP	$3,737,323	$5,741,572	65.09%	53.82%	19.47%	22.50%	18.77%
24. STEWART TGC	$131,848,241	$206,255,456	63.92%	45.41%	37.39%	42.31%	33.43%
25. CT ATTORNEYS	$4,086,369	$6,880,652	59.39%	92.79%	26.62%	27.59%	12.37%
26. LAWYERS	$89,456,439	$172,561,368	51.84%	34.19%	36.57%	32.89%	24.18%
27. MISSISSIPPI VALLEY	$3,445,735	$7,436,058	46.34%	19.50%	38.58%	(3.88)%	26.76%
28. OHIO BAR	$1,445,381	$3,159,573	45.75%	13.55%	(31.55)%	(1.93)%	59.27%
29. ATTORNEYS TGF (IL)	$1,811,083	$3,969,803	45.62%	33.18%	31.37%	57.55%	43.32%
30. INVESTORS TIC	$8,975,058	$19,697,971	45.56%	31.25%	23.92%	30.69%	23.14%
31. NORTHEAST INVESTORS	$149,328	$330,772	45.15%	14.05%	22.32%	(2.19)%	1.84%
32. SECURITY UNION	$10,051,219	$22,379,259	44.91%	24.35%	23.69%	13.22%	16.37%
33. ALAMO	$4,542,653	$10,472,610	43.38%	9.76%	23.76%	24.61%	24.55%
34. TICOR	$31,901,304	$76,900,384	41.48%	25.20%	27.58%	29.09%	27.28%
35. ALLIANCE	$66,579	$161,993	41.10%	(128.02)%	(76.52)%	69.26%	39.01%
36. OLD REPUBLIC NATIONAL	$56,386,474	$139,699,104	40.36%	36.67%	36.21%	29.55%	30.13%
37. CHICAGO TIC	$194,183,378	$487,208,034	39.86%	19.42%	28.87%	19.36%	14.60%
38. DAKOTA HOMESTEAD	$251,953	$645,657	39.02%	37.00%	66.35%	(16.53)%	13.64%
39. FIDELITY NATIONAL	$105,973,214	$289,059,757	36.66%	22.56%	30.73%	34.87%	29.28%
40. COMMONWEALTH LAND	$79,989,583	$227,822,612	35.11%	26.64%	29.12%	31.87%	24.26%
41. FIRST AMERICAN (KS)	$756,653	$2,192,014	34.52%	29.12%	56.31%	28.43%	31.05%
42. MONROE	$577,628	$1,681,690	34.35%	29.98%	25.44%	19.63%	4.71%
43. OLD REPUBLIC GENERAL	$8,609,260	$25,270,990	34.07%	17.65%	15.22%	15.14%	31.10%
44. T.A. TITLE	$544,743	$1,910,014	28.52%	19.03%	7.23%	32.89%	5.19%
45. TITLE RESOURCES	$2,723,051	$10,352,834	26.30%	24.74%	18.51%	23.33%	18.01%
46. NATIONS OF NY	$471,333	$1,793,208	26.28%	13.28%	5.50%	30.26%	51.93%
47. NATIONAL OF NY	$1,062,612	$4,217,658	25.19%	31.54%	58.63%	69.80%	27.06%
48. COMMONWEALTH LAND (NJ)	$1,900,137	$7,819,849	24.30%	27.35%	12.05%	15.09%	5.04%
49. FIRST AMERICAN (NY)	$9,991,046	$41,633,196	24.00%	25.32%	26.72%	30.62%	35.14%
50. PACIFIC NORTHWEST	$1,737,205	$7,554,551	23.00%	18.35%	24.15%	29.62%	59.54%
51. TITLE IC AMERICA	$211,989	$951,442	22.28%	66.42%	35.79%	32.15%	16.83%
52. FIRST AMERICAN (OR)	$2,919,785	$14,341,722	20.36%	10.44%	13.01%	7.06%	6.73%
53. TRANSUNION TIC	$80,642	$465,258	17.33%	49.89%	(58.16)%	56.38%	23.05%
54. STEWART TIC	$5,470,985	$32,972,554	16.59%	27.46%	12.41%	17.97%	21.54%
55. NORTH AMERICAN	$2,424,736	$15,230,000	15.92%	30.47%	27.51%	29.77%	36.73%
56. ARSENAL	$649	$4,181	15.52%	1.53%	2.11%	0.00%	--
57. ARKANSAS TIC	$155,822	$1,066,733	14.61%	24.05%	7.03%	52.02%	21.22%
58. LAND CORP (CO)	$272,282	$2,389,619	11.39%	(8.28)%	8.95%	(8.49)%	22.52%
59. CHICAGO TIC (OR)	$655,119	$6,565,067	9.98%	3.41%	11.20%	13.70%	6.45%
60. COMMERCE	$456,599	$4,953,565	9.22%	21.38%	13.28%	20.46%	14.03%
61. AMERICAN GUARANTY	$127,491	$1,664,278	7.66%	10.02%	7.46%	4.80%	3.26%
62. AMERICAN EAGLE	$30,838	$410,985	7.50%	10.50%	17.10%	16.20%	9.03%
63. CENSTAR	$356,768	$4,854,597	7.35%	2.17%	0.90%	0.00%	0.00%
64. NATIONAL	($9,014)	($156,395)	5.76%	(22.38)%	0.00%	0.00%	11.75%
65. FIRST AMERICAN T&T	$217,877	$6,102,787	3.57%	2.80%	8.93%	9.25%	5.29%
66. PENN ATTORNEYS	$44,947	$1,286,433	3.49%	7.78%	14.22%	(6.47)%	1.34%
67. PORT LAWRENCE	$35,011	$1,035,210	3.38%	(10.59)%	3.67%	1.95%	3.84%
68. TITLE G&TC	$1,500	$133,540	1.12%	0.00%	0.87%	1.21%	4.07%
69. AMERICAN SECURITY	$2,283	$1,007,728	0.23%	4.83%	0.00%	0.00%	0.54%
70. CHICAGO T&T	$0	$298,500,357	0.00%	0.00%	0.00%	0.00%	0.00%
71. TITLE GUARANTY DIV (IA)	$0	$1,506,931	0.00%	8.78%	12.18%	3.54%	1.57%
72. STEWART (OR)	$0	$212,688	0.00%	0.00%	0.00%	0.00%	0.00%
73. SIERRA	$0	$201,450	0.00%	0.00%	--	--	--
74. EQUITY NATIONAL	$0	$65,310	0.00%	0.00%	0.00%	--	--
75. SEAGATE	$0	$39,098	0.00%	0.00%	0.00%	0.00%	0.00%
76. PUBLIC	$0	$27,843	0.00%	0.00%	--	--	--
77. MASON COUNTY	$0	$23,693	0.00%	0.00%	0.00%	(91.01)%	0.00%
78. MASSACHUSETTS TIC	$0	$11,396	0.00%	0.00%	0.00%	0.00%	0.00%
79. TITLEDGE	$0	$10,714	0.00%	--	--	--	--
80. FOUNDERS	$0	($46,012)	0.00%	0.00%	0.00%	--	--
81. COLUMBIAN NATIONAL	$0	($101,027)	0.00%	0.00%	235.84%	115.97%	25.82%
82. MISSISSIPPI GUARANTY	$0	($116,401)	0.00%	0.00%	0.00%	0.00%	0.00%
83. K.E.L.	$0	($167,546)	0.00%	--	--	--	--
84. LAND TIC (ST LOUIS)	$0	($457,112)	0.00%	0.00%	0.00%	0.00%	0.00%
85. MASON	$12,200	($217,008)	(5.62)%	0.00%	--	--	--
86. FIRST AMERICAN TRANS	($16,063)	$147,561	(10.89)%	39.33%	13.38%	18.63%	34.12%
87. GUARDIAN NATIONAL	($76,380)	$400,003	(19.09)%	40.37%	4.98%	25.52%	16.28%
88. FARMERS NATIONAL	$68,819	($249,481)	(27.58)%	(0.35)%	--	--	--
89. WESTERN NATIONAL	($65,757)	$208,930	(31.47)%	74.64%	(6.37)%	8.08%	17.67%
90. NATIONAL LAND	$67,550	($181,419)	(37.23)%	49.68%	40.66%	14.43%	40.80%
91. AMERICAN LAND & AIRCRAFT	$5,858	($6,080)	(96.35)%	49.05%	0.00%	0.00%	0.00%
COMPOSITE	$1,296,969,093	$2,606,253,858	49.76%	29.45%	30.65%	22.77%	22.22%
AVERAGE	$14,252,408	$31,696,016	44.97%				

5

C.5 Losses & Loss Adjustment Expenses (LAE) Incurred to Policyholders' Surplus (PHS) and Reserves

COMPANY	2007 C.2 - L&LAE INCURRED	2007 PHS & RESERVES	2007 L&LAE TO PHS & RESERVES	2006 L&LAE TO PHS & RESERVES	2005 L&LAE TO PHS & RESERVES	2004 L&LAE TO PHS & RESERVES	2003 L&LAE TO PHS & RESERVES
1. GUARANTEE	$873,275	$2,508,408	34.81%	43.42%	6.01%	0.69%	8.01%
2. ALLIANT	$974,113	$3,621,878	26.90%	0.77%	0.00%	--	--
3. UNITED GENERAL	$27,244,717	$103,868,064	26.23%	12.88%	19.82%	13.52%	13.99%
4. FIRST AMERICAN TIC	$374,613,626	$1,518,464,946	24.67%	11.67%	10.81%	8.94%	9.94%
5. TRANSNATION	$36,073,084	$146,886,532	24.56%	17.15%	12.29%	10.25%	12.92%
6. TICOR (FL)	$24,844,212	$107,693,975	23.07%	15.73%	21.52%	19.83%	12.49%
7. GUARANTEE T&T	$1,575,074	$7,763,569	20.29%	18.74%	15.58%	19.01%	15.80%
8. SOUTHERN TI CORP	$3,737,323	$21,991,814	16.99%	11.66%	5.38%	6.35%	6.72%
9. UNITED CAPITAL	$8,465,810	$50,978,353	16.61%	12.78%	5.52%	3.63%	1.52%
10. LAWYERS	$89,456,439	$539,813,069	16.57%	11.69%	12.18%	9.49%	9.18%
11. CHICAGO TIC	$194,183,378	$1,231,204,774	15.77%	8.27%	13.79%	8.90%	8.65%
12. TICOR	$31,901,304	$202,835,006	15.73%	13.40%	10.66%	11.77%	14.10%
13. NATIONAL ATTORNEYS	$267,150	$1,766,898	15.12%	6.56%	1.39%	4.16%	8.60%
14. ATTORNEYS TIF (FL)	$44,278,625	$312,558,174	14.17%	8.50%	8.67%	5.00%	9.61%
15. FIDELITY NATIONAL	$105,973,214	$763,906,393	13.87%	8.95%	15.68%	15.78%	14.24%
16. WASHINGTON TIC	$433,920	$3,160,906	13.73%	13.67%	3.12%	11.82%	5.23%
17. OLD REPUBLIC NATIONAL	$56,386,474	$439,290,613	12.84%	12.76%	12.35%	9.12%	8.47%
18. SECURITY NATIONAL	$10,051,219	$78,955,338	12.73%	6.28%	7.18%	6.07%	4.40%
19. STEWART TGC	$131,848,241	$1,035,765,073	12.73%	10.11%	8.97%	7.95%	6.49%
20. NEW JERSEY TIC	$1,216,094	$9,557,501	12.72%	8.37%	6.56%	11.79%	9.22%
21. CONESTOGA	$991,906	$7,871,146	12.60%	4.22%	11.96%	24.25%	6.66%
22. SECURITY TG (BALTIMORE)	$1,643,655	$13,871,263	11.85%	3.30%	15.52%	3.78%	6.73%
23. COMMONWEALTH LAND	$79,989,583	$679,588,451	11.77%	11.08%	8.73%	8.75%	7.97%
24. ALAMO	$4,542,653	$46,146,865	9.84%	4.38%	5.30%	4.77%	4.27%
25. INVESTORS TIC	$8,975,058	$93,365,486	9.61%	7.45%	6.50%	8.51%	7.56%
26. ATTORNEYS TGF (IL)	$1,811,083	$21,735,476	8.33%	12.21%	14.82%	20.83%	20.93%
27. ATTORNEYS TGF (CO)	$357,311	$4,407,797	8.11%	7.75%	15.18%	19.81%	3.41%
28. TRANSUNION NATIONAL	$1,156,258	$14,352,081	8.06%	6.75%	21.03%	4.97%	3.95%
29. NATIONAL OF NY	$1,062,612	$13,431,791	7.91%	8.34%	13.64%	37.39%	16.59%
30. MISSISSIPPI VALLEY	$3,445,793	$44,658,279	7.72%	2.74%	5.86%	(0.57)%	5.82%
31. OLYMPIC	$26,670	$346,528	7.70%	0.73%	25.03%	23.66%	1.58%
32. STEWART TIC	$5,470,985	$71,353,964	7.67%	9.58%	4.83%	9.07%	11.94%
33. DREIBELBISS	$216,747	$2,852,739	7.60%	2.07%	(5.73)%	1.72%	1.59%
34. OLD REPUBLIC GENERAL	$8,609,260	$114,600,264	7.51%	3.57%	3.45%	3.97%	8.82%
35. DAKOTA HOMESTEAD	$251,953	$3,428,928	7.35%	6.14%	8.86%	(1.22)%	2.00%
36. FARMERS NATIONAL	$68,819	$975,182	7.06%	0.15%	--	--	--
37. CT ATTORNEYS	$4,086,369	$58,429,750	6.99%	10.73%	4.22%	3.92%	3.07%
38. TITLE RESOURCES	$2,723,051	$39,173,485	6.95%	7.56%	4.01%	5.00%	4.69%
39. GENERAL T&T	$457,564	$6,690,168	6.84%	8.70%	2.98%	2.08%	3.54%
40. FIRST AMERICAN (KS)	$756,653	$11,229,133	6.74%	5.01%	11.09%	8.35%	10.42%
41. PACIFIC NORTHWEST	$1,737,205	$27,911,796	6.22%	4.60%	3.89%	4.78%	6.69%
42. FIRST AMERICAN (NY)	$9,991,046	$163,653,892	6.10%	6.22%	5.39%	6.73%	7.94%
43. OHIO BAR	$1,445,381	$24,303,854	5.95%	1.85%	(4.59)%	(0.37)%	14.73%
44. FIRST AMERICAN (OR)	$2,919,785	$54,245,829	5.38%	4.22%	5.98%	2.16%	3.91%
45. T.A. TITLE	$544,743	$11,380,834	4.79%	3.46%	1.36%	5.75%	1.92%
46. COMMONWEALTH LAND (NJ)	$1,900,137	$41,637,370	4.56%	6.98%	3.37%	4.65%	1.86%
47. WESTCOR	$912,036	$22,749,387	4.01%	0.50%	4.88%	3.43%	5.07%
48. ARKANSAS TIC	$155,822	$4,798,243	3.25%	5.85%	1.24%	13.68%	6.09%
49. MONROE	$577,628	$18,341,265	3.15%	1.87%	2.98%	2.60%	0.89%
50. NORTH AMERICAN	$2,424,736	$80,038,724	3.03%	5.59%	5.96%	6.38%	9.15%
51. NATIONS OF NY	$471,333	$17,329,591	2.72%	1.44%	0.61%	3.53%	6.86%
52. MANITO	$39,324	$1,450,473	2.71%	1.00%	0.33%	(5.13)%	3.03%
53. AMERICAN EAGLE	$30,838	$1,140,768	2.70%	2.03%	4.95%	3.49%	8.65%
54. CHICAGO TIC (OR)	$655,119	$24,699,879	2.65%	1.20%	5.01%	5.60%	3.16%
55. NORTHEAST INVESTORS	$149,328	$6,083,457	2.45%	0.52%	1.22%	(0.18)%	0.24%
56. COMMERCE	$456,599	$20,273,380	2.25%	5.83%	3.53%	4.57%	3.35%
57. BRIDGE	$180,404	$8,163,833	2.21%	1.05%	0.76%	2.03%	0.02%
58. LAND CORP (CO)	$272,282	$13,961,164	1.95%	(1.53)%	1.82%	(1.82)%	6.01%
59. ALLIANCE	$66,579	$3,685,437	1.81%	1.65%	(3.31)%	7.73%	14.70%
60. TITLE IC AMERICA	$211,989	$15,039,140	1.41%	8.59%	7.22%	2.16%	3.04%
61. CENSTAR	$356,768	$28,857,452	1.24%	0.41%	0.27%	0.00%	0.00%
62. FIRST AMERICAN T&T	$217,877	$17,737,260	1.23%	1.50%	3.26%	4.89%	6.33%
63. TRANSUNION TIC	$80,642	$7,250,063	1.11%	5.98%	13.26%	7.98%	2.89%
64. NATIONAL LAND	$67,550	$6,442,637	1.05%	1.02%	3.51%	0.93%	4.36%
65. AMERICAN GUARANTY	$127,491	$14,141,409	0.90%	0.63%	1.34%	1.29%	1.35%
66. AMERICAN LAND & AIRCRAFT	$5,858	$789,531	0.74%	0.72%	0.00%	0.00%	0.00%
67. PENN ATTORNEYS	$44,947	$9,523,378	0.47%	1.04%	2.49%	(1.06)%	0.38%
68. MASON	$12,200	$2,620,475	0.47%	0.00%	--	--	--
69. PORT LAWRENCE	$35,011	$20,323,760	0.17%	(0.77)%	0.46%	0.22%	0.84%
70. ARSENAL	$649	$534,161	0.12%	0.45%	0.85%	0.00%	--
71. TITLE G&TC	$1,500	$1,254,070	0.12%	0.00%	0.14%	0.22%	0.86%
72. AMERICAN SECURITY	$2,283	$8,680,479	0.03%	0.64%	0.00%	0.00%	0.10%
73. CHICAGO T&T	$0	$664,634,623	0.00%	0.00%	0.00%	0.00%	0.00%
74. TITLE GUARANTY DIV (IA)	$0	$5,749,240	0.00%	3.27%	4.93%	2.54%	1.22%
75. STEWART (OR)	$0	$5,148,767	0.00%	0.00%	0.00%	0.00%	0.00%
76. LAND TIC (ST LOUIS)	$0	$5,032,337	0.00%	0.00%	0.00%	0.00%	0.00%
77. COLUMBIAN NATIONAL	$0	$3,538,522	0.00%	0.00%	28.80%	23.17%	3.08%
78. SIERRA	$0	$2,707,680	0.00%	0.00%	--	--	--
79. MASSACHUSETTS TIC	$0	$2,565,550	0.00%	0.00%	0.00%	0.00%	0.00%
80. K.E.L.	$0	$2,361,982	0.00%	--	--	--	--
81. EQUITY NATIONAL	$0	$1,549,841	0.00%	0.00%	0.00%	--	--
82. PUBLIC	$0	$1,038,244	0.00%	0.00%	--	--	--
83. MISSISSIPPI GUARANTY	$0	$856,877	0.00%	0.00%	0.00%	0.00%	0.00%
84. MASON COUNTY	$0	$848,570	0.00%	0.00%	0.00%	0.73%	0.00%
85. FOUNDERS	$0	$825,190	0.00%	0.00%	0.00%	--	--
86. TITLEDGE	$0	$766,400	0.00%	--	--	--	--
87. SEAGATE	$0	$667,232	0.00%	0.00%	0.00%	0.00%	0.00%
88. NATIONAL	($9,014)	$3,475,862	(0.26)%	1.51%	0.00%	0.00%	0.06%
89. GUARDIAN NATIONAL	($76,380)	$9,650,300	(0.79)%	7.46%	0.80%	4.86%	7.42%
90. FIRST AMERICAN TRANS	($16,063)	$1,730,153	(0.93)%	16.87%	3.18%	7.81%	1.55%
91. WESTERN NATIONAL	($65,757)	$4,571,195	(1.44)%	5.12%	(0.49)%	0.51%	2.57%
COMPOSITE	$1,296,969,093	$8,232,121,689	15.75%	10.16%	11.08%	8.32%	8.02%
AVERAGE	$14,252,408	$101,405,073	14.05%				

5

C.6 Losses & Loss Adjustment Expenses (LAE) Incurred to Net Liquid Assets

COMPANY	2007 C.2 - L&LAE INCURRED	2007 B.2 - NET LIQUID ASSETS	2007 L&LAE TO NET LIQUID ASSETS	2006 L&LAE TO NET LIQUID ASSETS	2005 L&LAE TO NET LIQUID ASSETS	2004 L&LAE TO NET LIQUID ASSETS	2003 L&LAE TO NET LIQUID ASSETS
1. WASHINGTON TIC	$433,920	($152,428)	--	--	--	--	16.30%
2. AMERICAN EAGLE	$30,838	($387,008)	--	4.38%	8.96%	7.26%	16.37%
3. ATTORNEYS TGF (CO)	$357,311	($889,008)	--	--	225.94%	24.32%	
4. GUARANTEE T&T	$1,575,074	($1,283,505)	--	--	215.58%	122.33%	63.61%
5. UNITED GENERAL	$27,244,717	($3,247,002)	--	--	333.06%	70.38%	65.46%
6. LAWYERS	$89,456,439	($27,391,668)	--	215.20%	202.42%	152.83%	63.33%
7. FIRST AMERICAN TIC	$374,613,626	($305,977,294)	--	--	62.55%	58.05%	56.92%
8. WESTERN NATIONAL	($65,757)	$3,256,315	(2.02)%	7.91%	(0.71)%	0.81%	4.12%
9. FIRST AMERICAN TRANS	($16,063)	$1,089,431	(1.47)%	23.70%	4.57%	11.04%	2.14%
10. GUARDIAN NATIONAL	($76,380)	$6,433,613	(1.19)%	23.64%	2.09%	11.97%	15.01%
11. NATIONAL	($9,014)	$2,170,559	(0.42)%	2.29%	0.00%	0.00%	0.09%
12. CHICAGO T&T	$0	$659,204,334	0.00%	0.00%	0.00%	0.00%	0.00%
13. LAND TIC (ST LOUIS)	$0	$4,908,115	0.00%	0.00%	0.00%	0.00%	0.00%
14. COLUMBIAN NATIONAL	$0	$3,462,022	0.00%	0.00%	31.51%	57.17%	5.74%
15. STEWART (OR)	$0	$2,656,810	0.00%	0.00%	0.00%	0.00%	0.00%
16. MASSACHUSETTS TIC	$0	$2,456,787	0.00%	0.00%	0.00%	0.00%	0.00%
17. K.E.L.	$0	$2,323,038	0.00%	--	--	--	--
18. SIERRA	$0	$2,319,791	0.00%	0.00%	--	--	--
19. EQUITY NATIONAL	$0	$1,437,919	0.00%	0.00%	0.00%	--	--
20. PUBLIC	$0	$1,038,244	0.00%	0.00%	--	--	--
21. MASON COUNTY	$0	$796,804	0.00%	0.00%	0.00%	0.76%	0.00%
22. FOUNDERS	$0	$787,772	0.00%	0.00%	0.00%	--	--
23. TITLE GUARANTY DIV (IA)	$0	$726,128	0.00%	30.34%	34.70%	16.78%	4.16%
24. TITLEDGE	$0	$722,784	0.00%	--	--	--	--
25. SEAGATE	$0	$378,209	0.00%	0.00%	0.00%	0.00%	0.00%
26. MISSISSIPPI GUARANTY	$0	$247,812	0.00%	0.00%	0.00%	0.00%	0.00%
27. AMERICAN SECURITY	$2,283	$8,304,294	0.03%	0.67%	0.00%	0.00%	0.11%
28. ARSENAL	$649	$483,654	0.13%	0.50%	0.94%	0.00%	
29. TITLE G&TC	$1,500	$623,579	0.24%	0.00%	0.31%	0.66%	4.11%
30. PORT LAWRENCE	$35,011	$10,512,518	0.33%	(1.23)%	0.77%	0.37%	1.46%
31. MASON	$12,200	$2,484,176	0.49%	0.00%	--	--	--
32. PENN ATTORNEYS	$44,947	$8,121,465	0.55%	1.23%	3.05%	(1.31)%	0.49%
33. AMERICAN LAND & AIRCRAFT	$5,858	$739,228	0.79%	0.77%	0.00%	0.00%	0.00%
34. AMERICAN GUARANTY	$127,491	$10,532,088	1.21%	0.87%	1.91%	1.97%	2.51%
35. NATIONAL LAND	$67,550	$5,158,724	1.31%	1.26%	5.31%	1.47%	7.13%
36. CENSTAR	$356,768	$24,279,008	1.47%	0.47%	0.31%	0.00%	0.00%
37. FIRST AMERICAN T&T	$217,877	$12,921,642	1.69%	1.89%	4.31%	6.68%	8.71%
38. TITLE IC AMERICA	$211,989	$10,980,291	1.93%	12.90%	10.64%	3.58%	5.58%
39. ALLIANCE	$66,579	$3,100,706	2.15%	2.05%	(4.24)%	13.19%	26.13%
40. TRANSUNION TIC	$80,642	$3,552,891	2.27%	14.43%	67.82%	--	--
41. BRIDGE	$180,404	$7,884,405	2.29%	1.09%	0.79%	3.79%	0.02%
42. NORTHEAST INVESTORS	$149,328	$5,340,719	2.80%	0.60%	1.38%	(0.21)%	0.27%
43. MANITO	$39,324	$1,234,710	3.18%	1.17%	0.41%	(6.21)%	3.78%
44. LAND CORP (CO)	$272,282	$7,957,008	3.42%	(2.65)%	3.45%	(3.21)%	11.21%
45. NATIONS OF NY	$471,333	$12,211,638	3.86%	2.27%	1.21%	8.43%	17.94%
46. NORTH AMERICAN	$2,424,736	$48,443,220	5.01%	13.09%	14.76%	17.18%	28.17%
47. CHICAGO TIC (OR)	$655,119	$12,022,950	5.45%	2.50%	11.87%	15.10%	6.75%
48. COMMONWEALTH LAND (NJ)	$1,900,137	$32,314,821	5.88%	9.22%	4.79%	6.04%	2.36%
49. COMMERCE	$456,599	$7,703,478	5.93%	17.10%	14.02%	10.14%	5.95%
50. MONROE	$577,628	$8,217,098	7.03%	3.62%	5.85%	5.31%	1.90%
51. ARKANSAS TIC	$155,822	$2,107,597	7.39%	12.93%	2.67%	34.04%	13.55%
52. OLYMPIC	$26,670	$305,841	8.72%	0.75%	27.26%	27.72%	1.73%
53. FARMERS NATIONAL	$68,819	$693,686	9.92%	0.17%	--	--	--
54. DREIBELBISS	$216,747	$2,169,435	9.99%	2.79%	(8.02)%	3.00%	2.75%
55. FIRST AMERICAN (NY)	$9,991,046	$96,487,286	10.35%	12.49%	10.47%	13.78%	14.03%
56. CT ATTORNEYS	$4,086,369	$38,818,515	10.53%	15.96%	6.38%	5.86%	4.93%
57. T.A. TITLE	$544,743	$5,002,074	10.89%	6.35%	2.66%	15.45%	8.37%
58. DAKOTA HOMESTEAD	$251,953	$2,259,937	11.15%	8.94%	12.57%	(1.43)%	2.39%
59. TRANSUNION NATIONAL	$1,156,258	$9,849,369	11.74%	9.43%	52.31%	8.13%	6.26%
60. TITLE RESOURCES	$2,723,051	$21,429,502	12.71%	12.77%	6.54%	8.52%	8.52%
61. FIRST AMERICAN (KS)	$756,653	$5,605,495	13.50%	10.29%	24.65%	17.99%	20.22%
62. NATIONAL OF NY	$1,062,612	$6,480,320	16.40%	14.85%	33.04%	176.15%	38.39%
63. OHIO BAR	$1,445,381	$8,529,819	16.95%	6.24%	(17.78)%	(1.67)%	96.09%
64. WESTCOR	$912,036	$5,311,186	17.17%	1.64%	11.87%	10.98%	13.15%
65. PACIFIC NORTHWEST	$1,737,205	$9,952,203	17.46%	18.68%	26.74%	32.29%	153.63%
66. STEWART TIC	$5,470,985	$28,627,079	19.11%	24.92%	10.42%	30.27%	38.80%
67. ALAMO	$4,542,653	$21,757,762	20.88%	7.42%	10.13%	9.41%	8.25%
68. OLD REPUBLIC GENERAL	$8,609,260	$37,923,626	22.70%	10.75%	13.12%	14.65%	41.95%
69. INVESTORS TIC	$8,975,058	$39,221,709	22.88%	16.50%	14.90%	19.69%	18.07%
70. NATIONAL ATTORNEYS	$267,150	$1,117,976	23.90%	9.82%	2.13%	6.58%	12.79%
71. FIRST AMERICAN (OR)	$2,919,785	$10,651,631	27.41%	18.18%	34.07%	10.51%	12.46%
72. STEWART TGC	$131,848,241	$443,778,009	29.71%	22.70%	19.73%	18.42%	15.19%
73. ATTORNEYS TGF (IL)	$1,811,083	$4,975,119	36.40%	51.18%	103.25%	1,032.82%	--
74. NEW JERSEY TIC	$1,216,094	$3,307,074	36.77%	20.61%	16.66%	29.38%	20.16%
75. SECURITY UNION	$10,051,219	$26,923,488	37.33%	14.49%	16.29%	13.98%	8.99%
76. MISSISSIPPI VALLEY	$3,445,735	$8,098,652	42.55%	13.67%	30.42%	(2.71)%	32.71%
77. UNITED CAPITAL	$8,465,810	$18,108,877	46.75%	30.45%	13.17%	9.15%	3.26%
78. COMMONWEALTH LAND	$79,989,583	$167,717,570	47.69%	34.77%	61.89%	86.57%	66.83%
79. ALLIANT	$974,113	$1,871,402	52.05%	0.95%	0.00%	--	--
80. GENERAL T&T	$457,564	$869,491	52.62%	44.18%	13.83%	11.31%	20.38%
81. ATTORNEYS TIF (FL)	$44,278,625	$81,702,918	54.19%	28.59%	31.27%	20.46%	47.85%
82. FIDELITY NATIONAL	$105,973,214	$180,914,080	58.58%	32.55%	56.80%	76.04%	44.37%
83. OLD REPUBLIC NATIONAL	$56,386,474	$77,086,077	73.15%	72.09%	69.08%	50.83%	61.74%
84. TICOR	$31,901,304	$37,617,379	84.80%	86.00%	44.54%	61.81%	52.32%
85. SOUTHERN TI CORP	$3,737,323	$3,719,413	100.48%	48.57%	23.26%	30.56%	31.21%
86. SECURITY TG (BALTIMORE)	$1,643,655	$1,064,266	154.44%	18.80%	92.40%	14.83%	23.79%
87. GUARANTEE	$873,275	$562,561	155.23%	146.23%	8.67%	0.87%	10.59%
88. CONESTOGA	$991,906	$608,695	162.96%	30.94%	78.45%	193.37%	20.76%
89. CHICAGO TIC	$194,183,378	$102,515,127	189.42%	37.04%	65.73%	30.62%	27.85%
90. TICOR (FL)	$24,844,212	$7,367,657	337.21%	153.43%	205.35%	85.11%	31.89%
91. TRANSNATION	$36,073,084	$2,081,320	1,733.18%	69.13%	30.09%	37.97%	34.16%
COMPOSITE	$1,296,969,093	$1,131,664,181	114.61%	46.50%	47.64%	26.98%	23.22%
AVERAGE	$14,252,408	$23,378,067	60.96%				

5

C.7 Composite of Losses & Loss Adjustment Expenses (LAE) Incurred

	COMPANY	DIRECT OPERATIONS		NON-AFFILIATED OPERATIONS		AFFILIATED OPERATIONS		C.2 - L&LAE INCURRED
1.	FIRST AMERICAN TIC	$83,223,223	22.22%	$221,153,902	59.04%	$70,236,501	18.75%	$374,613,626
2.	CHICAGO TIC	$114,016,898	58.72%	$77,138,667	39.72%	$3,027,813	1.56%	$194,183,378
3.	STEWART TGC	$32,516,708	24.66%	$78,461,680	59.51%	$20,869,853	15.83%	$131,848,241
4.	FIDELITY NATIONAL	$16,952,424	16.00%	$53,690,682	50.66%	$35,330,108	33.34%	$105,973,214
5.	LAWYERS	$20,651,853	23.09%	$60,624,870	67.77%	$8,179,716	9.14%	$89,456,439
6.	COMMONWEALTH LAND	$19,511,239	24.39%	$60,285,391	75.37%	$192,953	0.24%	$79,989,583
7.	OLD REPUBLIC NATIONAL	$2,702,904	4.79%	$51,306,924	90.99%	$2,376,646	4.21%	$56,386,474
8.	ATTORNEYS TIF (FL)	$0	0.00%	$44,278,625	100.00%	$0	0.00%	$44,278,625
9.	TRANSNATION	$14,317,146	39.69%	$12,652,030	35.07%	$9,103,908	25.24%	$36,073,084
10.	TICOR	$10,184,090	31.92%	$20,582,354	64.52%	$1,134,860	3.56%	$31,901,304
11.	UNITED GENERAL	$1,388,675	5.10%	$24,761,096	90.88%	$1,094,946	4.02%	$27,244,717
12.	TICOR (FL)	$329,429	1.33%	$24,514,783	98.67%	$0	0.00%	$24,844,212
13.	SECURITY UNION	$4,987,809	49.62%	$5,063,513	50.38%	($103)	0.00%	$10,051,219
14.	FIRST AMERICAN (NY)	$2,933,200	29.36%	$7,055,793	70.62%	$2,053	0.02%	$9,991,046
15.	INVESTORS TIC	$7,237,616	80.64%	$1,684,413	18.77%	$53,029	0.59%	$8,975,058
16.	OLD REPUBLIC GENERAL	$0	0.00%	$3,410,996	39.62%	$5,198,264	60.38%	$8,609,260
17.	UNITED CAPITAL	$0	0.00%	$0	0.00%	$8,465,810	100.00%	$8,465,810
18.	STEWART TIC	($6,910)	(0.13)%	$5,477,895	100.13%	$0	0.00%	$5,470,985
19.	ALAMO	$0	0.00%	$3,099,742	68.24%	$1,442,911	31.76%	$4,542,653
20.	CT ATTORNEYS	$0	0.00%	$4,086,369	100.00%	$0	0.00%	$4,086,369
21.	SOUTHERN TI CORP	$21,545	0.58%	$3,689,804	98.73%	$25,974	0.69%	$3,737,323
22.	MISSISSIPPI VALLEY	$304,285	8.83%	$3,141,450	91.17%	$0	0.00%	$3,445,735
23.	FIRST AMERICAN (OR)	$1,475,918	50.55%	$1,443,867	49.45%	$0	0.00%	$2,919,785
24.	TITLE RESOURCES	$0	0.00%	$1,989,236	73.05%	$733,815	26.95%	$2,723,051
25.	NORTH AMERICAN	$0	0.00%	$0	0.00%	$2,424,736	100.00%	$2,424,736
26.	COMMONWEALTH LAND (NJ)	$383,394	20.18%	$1,516,743	79.82%	$0	0.00%	$1,900,137
27.	ATTORNEYS TGF (IL)	$1,811,083	100.00%	$0	0.00%	$0	0.00%	$1,811,083
28.	PACIFIC NORTHWEST	$277,652	15.98%	$919,196	52.91%	$540,357	31.10%	$1,737,205
29.	SECURITY TG (BALTIMORE)	$7,125	0.43%	$1,636,530	99.57%	$0	0.00%	$1,643,655
30.	GUARANTEE T&T	$249,694	15.85%	$740,941	47.04%	$584,439	37.11%	$1,575,074
31.	OHIO BAR	$0	0.00%	$1,445,381	100.00%	$0	0.00%	$1,445,381
32.	NEW JERSEY TIC	$0	0.00%	$1,216,094	100.00%	$0	0.00%	$1,216,094
33.	TRANSUNION NATIONAL	$0	0.00%	$739,060	63.92%	$417,198	36.08%	$1,156,258
34.	NATIONAL OF NY	$111,590	10.50%	$1,226,413	115.41%	($275,391)	(25.92)%	$1,062,612
35.	CONESTOGA	$12,755	1.29%	$957,461	96.53%	$21,690	2.19%	$991,906
36.	ALLIANT	$0	0.00%	$974,113	100.00%	$0	0.00%	$974,113
37.	WESTCOR	$156,272	17.13%	$208,299	22.84%	$547,465	60.03%	$912,036
38.	GUARANTEE	$0	0.00%	$873,275	100.00%	$0	0.00%	$873,275
39.	FIRST AMERICAN (KS)	$128,072	16.93%	$128,605	17.00%	$499,976	66.08%	$756,653
40.	CHICAGO TIC (OR)	$415,182	63.38%	$239,937	36.62%	$0	0.00%	$655,119
41.	MONROE	$474,023	82.06%	$94,191	16.31%	$9,414	1.63%	$577,628
42.	T.A. TITLE	$0	0.00%	$544,743	100.00%	$0	0.00%	$544,743
43.	NATIONS OF NY	$3,052	0.65%	$468,281	99.35%	$0	0.00%	$471,333
44.	GENERAL T&T	$0	0.00%	$345,028	75.41%	$112,536	24.59%	$457,564
45.	COMMERCE	$0	0.00%	$0	0.00%	$456,599	100.00%	$456,599
46.	WASHINGTON TIC	$22,599	5.21%	$394,142	90.83%	$17,179	3.96%	$433,920
47.	ATTORNEYS TGF (CO)	$0	0.00%	$357,311	100.00%	$0	0.00%	$357,311
48.	CENSTAR	$0	0.00%	$356,768	100.00%	$0	0.00%	$356,768
49.	LAND CORP (CO)	$0	0.00%	$0	0.00%	$272,282	100.00%	$272,282
50.	NATIONAL ATTORNEYS	$267,150	100.00%	$0	0.00%	$0	0.00%	$267,150
51.	DAKOTA HOMESTEAD	$0	0.00%	$251,953	100.00%	$0	0.00%	$251,953
52.	FIRST AMERICAN T&T	$217,877	100.00%	$0	0.00%	$0	0.00%	$217,877
53.	DREIBELBISS	$216,747	100.00%	$0	0.00%	$0	0.00%	$216,747
54.	TITLE IC AMERICA	$0	0.00%	$211,989	100.00%	$0	0.00%	$211,989
55.	BRIDGE	$0	0.00%	$180,404	100.00%	$0	0.00%	$180,404
56.	ARKANSAS TIC	$0	0.00%	$190,251	122.10%	($34,429)	(22.10)%	$155,822
57.	NORTHEAST INVESTORS	$0	0.00%	$149,328	100.00%	$0	0.00%	$149,328
58.	AMERICAN GUARANTY	$87,168	68.37%	$0	0.00%	$40,323	31.63%	$127,491
59.	TRANSUNION TIC	$96,031	119.08%	$0	0.00%	($15,389)	(19.08)%	$80,642
60.	FARMERS NATIONAL	$0	0.00%	$68,819	100.00%	$0	0.00%	$68,819
61.	NATIONAL LAND	$0	0.00%	$67,550	100.00%	$0	0.00%	$67,550
62.	ALLIANCE	$0	0.00%	$66,579	100.00%	$0	0.00%	$66,579
63.	PENN ATTORNEYS	$44,947	100.00%	$0	0.00%	$0	0.00%	$44,947
64.	MANITO	$0	0.00%	$39,324	100.00%	$0	0.00%	$39,324
65.	PORT LAWRENCE	$35,011	100.00%	$0	0.00%	$0	0.00%	$35,011
66.	AMERICAN EAGLE	$30,838	100.00%	$0	0.00%	$0	0.00%	$30,838
67.	OLYMPIC	$26,670	100.00%	$0	0.00%	$0	0.00%	$26,670
68.	MASON	$200	1.64%	$0	0.00%	$12,000	98.36%	$12,200
69.	AMERICAN LAND & AIRCRAFT	$5,858	100.00%	$0	0.00%	$0	0.00%	$5,858
70.	AMERICAN SECURITY	$0	0.00%	$2,283	100.00%	$0	0.00%	$2,283
71.	TITLE G&TC	$1,500	100.00%	$0	0.00%	$0	0.00%	$1,500
72.	ARSENAL	$0	0.00%	$649	100.00%	$0	0.00%	$649
73.	CHICAGO T&T	$0	--	$0	--	$0	--	$0
74.	COLUMBIAN NATIONAL	$0	--	$0	--	$0	--	$0
75.	EQUITY NATIONAL	$0	--	$0	--	$0	--	$0
76.	FOUNDERS	$0	--	$0	--	$0	--	$0
77.	K.E.L.	$0	--	$0	--	$0	--	$0
78.	LAND TIC (ST LOUIS)	$0	--	$0	--	$0	--	$0
79.	MASON COUNTY	$0	--	$0	--	$0	--	$0
80.	MASSACHUSETTS TIC	$0	--	$0	--	$0	--	$0
81.	MISSISSIPPI GUARANTY	$0	--	$0	--	$0	--	$0
82.	PUBLIC	$0	--	$0	--	$0	--	$0
83.	SEAGATE	$0	--	$0	--	$0	--	$0
84.	SIERRA	$0	--	$0	--	$0	--	$0
85.	STEWART (OR)	$0	--	$0	--	$0	--	$0
86.	TITLE GUARANTY DIV (IA)	$0	--	$0	--	$0	--	$0
87.	TITLEDGE	$0		$0		$0		$0
88.	NATIONAL	$0	0.00%	($9,014)	100.00%	$0	0.00%	($9,014)
89.	FIRST AMERICAN TRANS	$0	0.00%	($16,063)	100.00%	$0	0.00%	($16,063)
90.	WESTERN NATIONAL	$0	0.00%	$0	0.00%	($65,757)	100.00%	($65,757)
91.	GUARDIAN NATIONAL	$0	0.00%	($80,356)	105.21%	$3,976	(5.21)%	($76,380)
	COMPOSITE	$337,830,542	26.04%	$786,100,290	60.61%	$173,038,261	13.34%	$1,296,969,093
	AVERAGE	$3,712,424	26.04%	$8,638,465	60.61%	$1,901,519	13.34%	$14,252,408

5

C.8 Direct and Agency Loss Ratios

COMPANY	DIRECT PREMIUMS WRITTEN			LOSSES & LAE INCURRED			DIRECT AND AGENCY LOSS RATIO		
	DIRECT OPERATIONS	NON-AFFILIATED OPERATIONS	AFFILIATED OPERATIONS	DIRECT OPERATIONS	NON-AFFILIATED OPERATIONS	AFFILIATED OPERATIONS	DIRECT OPERATIONS	NON-AFFILIATED OPERATIONS	AFFILIATED OPERATIONS
1. ALAMO	$0	$42,145,575	$52,072,753	$0	$3,099,742	$1,442,911	--	7.35%	2.77%
2. ALLIANCE	$0	$1,196	$0	$0	$66,579	$0	--	5,566.81%	--
3. ALLIANT	$0	$13,990,651	$0	$0	$974,113	$0	--	6.96%	--
4. AMERICAN EAGLE	$1,906,376	$1,142,793	$0	$30,838	$0	$0	1.62%	0.00%	--
5. AMERICAN GUARANTY	$26,366	$546,233	$2,917,327	$87,168	$0	$40,323	330.61%	0.00%	1.38%
6. AMERICAN LAND & AIRCRAFT	$0	$126,906	$532,250	$5,858	$0	$0	--	0.00%	0.00%
7. AMERICAN SECURITY	$0	$2,940,198	$0	$0	$2,283	$0	--	0.08%	--
8. ARKANSAS TIC	$0	$7,269,128	$1,017,272	$0	$190,251	($34,429)	--	2.62%	(3.38)%
9. ARSENAL	$0	$1,583,908	$0	$0	$649	$0	--	0.04%	--
10. ATTORNEYS TGF (CO)	$0	$9,268,076	$0	$0	$357,311	$0	--	3.86%	--
11. ATTORNEYS TGF (IL)	$10,998,779	$0	$0	$1,811,083	$0	$0	16.47%	--	--
12. ATTORNEYS TIF (FL)	$0	$345,841,353	$0	$0	$44,278,625	$0	--	12.80%	--
13. BRIDGE	$0	$462	$0	$0	$180,404	$0	--	39,048.48%	--
14. CENSTAR	$0	$39,460,039	$0	$0	$356,768	$0	--	0.90%	--
15. CHICAGO T&T	$0	$0	$0	$0	$0	$0	--	--	--
16. CHICAGO TIC	$477,816,470	$1,033,035,988	$376,443,234	$114,016,898	$77,138,667	$3,027,813	23.86%	7.47%	0.80%
17. CHICAGO TIC (OR)	$13,707,383	$12,576,501	$0	$415,182	$239,937	$0	3.03%	1.91%	--
18. COLUMBIAN NATIONAL	$0	$0	$0	$0	$0	$0	--	--	--
19. COMMERCE	$43,152	$1,532,096	$41,997,283	$0	$0	$456,599	0.00%	0.00%	1.09%
20. COMMONWEALTH LAND	$220,717,997	$808,458,154	$123,342,178	$19,511,239	$60,285,391	$192,953	8.84%	7.46%	0.16%
21. COMMONWEALTH LAND (NJ)	$5,109,506	$30,277,935	$0	$383,394	$1,516,743	$0	7.50%	5.01%	--
22. CONESTOGA	$201,980	$13,366,327	$376,063	$12,755	$957,461	$21,690	6.31%	7.16%	5.77%
23. CT ATTORNEYS	$0	$51,258,956	$0	$0	$4,086,369	$0	--	7.97%	--
24. DAKOTA HOMESTEAD	$244,546	$3,869,021	$0	$0	$251,953	$0	0.00%	6.51%	--
25. DREIBELBISS	$517,581	$115,399	$0	$216,747	$0	$0	41.88%	0.00%	--
26. EQUITY NATIONAL	$280,228	$0	$0	$0	$0	$0	0.00%	--	--
27. FARMERS NATIONAL	$0	$1,138,404	$0	$0	$68,819	$0	--	6.05%	--
28. FIDELITY NATIONAL	$251,405,363	$673,800,566	$348,876,279	$16,952,424	$53,690,682	$35,330,108	6.74%	7.97%	10.13%
29. FIRST AMERICAN (KS)	$1,550,799	$5,813,820	$7,399,061	$128,072	$128,605	$499,976	8.26%	2.21%	6.76%
30. FIRST AMERICAN (NY)	$96,485,318	$131,671,357	$11,099,012	$2,933,200	$7,055,793	$2,053	3.04%	5.36%	0.02%
31. FIRST AMERICAN (OR)	$42,031,597	$13,032,270	$0	$1,475,918	$1,443,867	$0	3.51%	11.08%	--
32. FIRST AMERICAN T&T	$6,291,430	$0	$0	$217,877	$0	$0	3.46%	--	--
33. FIRST AMERICAN TIC	$622,912,926	$1,936,771,199	$752,682,458	$83,223,223	$221,153,902	$70,236,501	13.36%	11.42%	9.33%
34. FIRST AMERICAN TRANS	$108,501	$1,474,514	$0	$0	($16,063)	$0	0.00%	(1.09)%	--
35. FOUNDERS	$178,276	$0	$0	$0	$0	$0	0.00%	--	--
36. GENERAL T&T	$0	$2,510,539	$266,652	$0	$345,028	$112,536	--	13.74%	42.20%
37. GUARANTEE	$0	$1,125,386	$1,472,208	$0	$873,275	$0	--	77.60%	0.00%
38. GUARANTEE T&T	$204,520	$2,531,710	$8,582,676	$249,694	$740,941	$584,439	122.09%	29.27%	6.81%
39. GUARDIAN NATIONAL	$0	$3,445,031	$428,862	$0	($80,356)	$3,976	--	(2.33)%	0.93%
40. INVESTORS TIC	$29,790,883	$31,463,285	$6,291,704	$7,237,616	$1,684,413	$53,029	24.29%	5.35%	0.84%
41. K.E.L.	$0	$8,460	$575,455	$0	$0	$0	--	0.00%	0.00%
42. LAND CORP (CO)	$0	$0	$19,602,608	$0	$0	$272,282	--	--	1.39%
43. LAND TIC (ST LOUIS)	$0	$2,257,316	$0	$0	$0	$0	--	0.00%	--
44. LAWYERS	$345,666,888	$762,376,163	$107,567,639	$20,651,853	$60,624,870	$8,179,716	5.97%	7.95%	7.60%
45. MANITO	$0	$97,958	$690,518	$0	$39,324	$0	--	40.14%	0.00%
46. MASON	$120,217	$0	$1,432,065	$200	$0	$12,000	0.17%	--	0.84%
47. MASON COUNTY	$0	$0	$0	$0	$0	$0	--	--	--
48. MASSACHUSETTS TIC	($254)	$0	$0	$0	$0	$0	0.00%	--	--
49. MISSISSIPPI GUARANTY	$56,517	$253,129	$0	$0	$0	$0	0.00%	0.00%	--
50. MISSISSIPPI VALLEY	$488,573	$25,433,321	$0	$304,285	$3,141,450	$0	62.28%	12.35%	--
51. MONROE	$5,556,612	$7,075,703	$364,364	$474,023	$94,191	$9,414	8.53%	1.33%	2.58%
52. NATIONAL	$127,106	$3,347,151	$199,659	$0	($9,014)	$0	0.00%	(0.27)%	0.00%
53. NATIONAL ATTORNEYS	$831,940	$0	$0	$267,150	$0	$0	32.11%	--	--
54. NATIONAL LAND	$0	$2,494,729	$0	$0	$67,550	$0	--	2.71%	--
55. NATIONAL OF NY	$2,257,917	$4,027	$9,776,776	$111,590	$1,226,413	($275,391)	4.94%	30,454.76%	(2.82)%
56. NATIONS OF NY	$0	$0	$0	$3,052	$468,281	$0	--	--	--
57. NEW JERSEY TIC	$0	$17,124,472	$0	$0	$1,216,094	$0	--	7.10%	--
58. NORTH AMERICAN	$0	$438,203	$107,933,280	$0	$0	$2,424,736	--	0.00%	2.25%
59. NORTHEAST INVESTORS	$0	$2,414,626	$0	$0	$149,328	$0	--	6.18%	--
60. OHIO BAR	$0	$13,072,886	$0	$0	$1,445,381	$0	--	11.06%	--
61. OLD REPUBLIC GENERAL	$0	$0	$0	$0	$3,410,996	$5,198,264	--	--	--
62. OLD REPUBLIC NATIONAL	$14,047,794	$604,520,309	$130,958,923	$2,702,904	$51,306,924	$2,376,646	19.24%	8.49%	1.81%
63. OLYMPIC	$0	$0	$0	$26,670	$0	$0	--	--	--
64. PACIFIC NORTHWEST	$0	$16,794,834	$41,667,730	$277,652	$919,196	$540,357	--	5.47%	1.30%
65. PENN ATTORNEYS	$1,777,598	$0	$0	$44,947	$0	$0	2.53%	--	--
66. PORT LAWRENCE	$2,836,725	$2,437,031	$316,748	$35,011	$0	$0	1.23%	0.00%	0.00%
67. PUBLIC	$0	$0	$0	$0	$0	$0	--	--	--
68. SEAGATE	$186,090	$0	$0	$0	$0	$0	0.00%	--	--
69. SECURITY TG (BALTIMORE)	$413,934	$20,943,251	$568,301	$7,125	$1,636,530	$0	1.72%	7.81%	0.00%
70. SECURITY UNION	$11,530,727	$36,182,556	$15,844,405	$4,987,809	$5,063,513	($103)	43.26%	13.99%	0.00%
71. SIERRA	$0	$1,966,565	$0	$0	$0	$0	--	0.00%	--
72. SOUTHERN TI CORP	$1,173,787	$49,984,569	$3,022,358	$21,545	$3,689,804	$25,974	1.84%	7.38%	0.86%
73. STEWART (OR)	$567,888	$10,237,613	$0	$0	$0	$0	0.00%	0.00%	--
74. STEWART TGC	$157,750,939	$796,976,776	$500,732,921	$32,516,708	$78,461,680	$20,869,853	20.61%	9.84%	4.17%
75. STEWART TIC	$38,951,627	$121,926,620	$1,373,640	($6,910)	$5,477,895	$0	(0.02)%	4.49%	0.00%
76. T.A. TITLE	$0	$13,742,041	$3,297,800	$0	$544,743	$0	--	3.96%	--
77. TICOR	$51,058,558	$218,064,012	$58,074,930	$10,184,090	$20,582,354	$1,134,860	19.95%	9.44%	1.95%
78. TICOR (FL)	$0	$83,543,448	$0	$329,429	$24,514,783	$0	--	29.34%	--
79. TITLE G&TC	$260,893	$0	$0	$1,500	$0	$0	0.57%	--	--
80. TITLE GUARANTY DIV (IA)	$3,724,743	$0	$0	$0	$0	$0	0.00%	--	--
81. TITLE IC AMERICA	$0	$11,954,125	$0	$0	$211,989	$0	--	1.77%	--
82. TITLE RESOURCES	$0	$64,857,278	$38,990,484	$0	$1,989,236	$733,815	--	3.07%	1.88%
83. TITLEDGE	$78,917	$102,655	$0	$0	$0	$0	0.00%	0.00%	--
84. TRANSNATION	$69,584,981	$124,240,351	$81,004,543	$14,317,146	$12,652,030	$9,103,908	20.58%	10.18%	11.24%
85. TRANSUNION NATIONAL	$109,890	$2,344,872	$1,458,631	$0	$739,060	$417,198	0.00%	31.52%	28.60%
86. TRANSUNION TIC	$882,460	$0	$0	$96,031	$0	($15,389)	10.88%	--	--
87. UNITED CAPITAL	$2,264,749	$0	$59,156,995	$0	$0	$8,465,810	0.00%	--	14.31%
88. UNITED GENERAL	$20,969,887	$297,148,060	$18,484,272	$1,388,675	$24,761,096	$1,094,946	6.62%	8.33%	5.92%
89. WASHINGTON TIC	$172,102	$12,559,065	$2,893,006	$22,599	$394,142	$17,179	13.13%	3.14%	0.59%
90. WESTCOR	$288,117	$21,121,593	$31,217,018	$156,272	$208,299	$547,465	54.24%	0.99%	1.75%
91. WESTERN NATIONAL	$0	$8,580	$362,141	$0	$0	($65,757)	--	0.00%	(18.16)%
COMPOSITE	$2,516,267,899	$8,571,639,324	$2,973,364,482	$337,830,542	$786,100,290	$173,038,261	13.43%	9.17%	5.82%
AVERAGE	$27,651,296	$94,193,839	$32,674,335	$3,712,424	$8,638,465	$1,901,519	13.43%	9.17%	5.82%

All content © 2008 Demotech, Inc. - www.demotech.com

C.9 Reserves to Policyholders' Surplus (PHS)

COMPANY	KNOWN CLAIMS RESERVE	STATUTORY PREMIUM RESERVE (SPR)	AGGREGATE OTHER RESERVE	SUPPLEMENTAL RESERVE	B.6 - PHS	RESERVES TO PHS
1. TITLE GUARANTY DIV (IA)	$340,218	$3,669,317	$1,000,000	$0	$739,705	677.23%
2. TRANSNATION	$19,021,314	$95,928,536	$0	$9,601,900	$22,334,782	557.66%
3. GUARANTEE T&T	$145,748	$6,398,481	$0	$0	$1,219,340	536.70%
4. MISSISSIPPI VALLEY	$3,868,087	$31,106,574	$0	$0	$9,683,618	361.17%
5. CHICAGO TIC	$131,009,849	$825,712,387	$0	$0	$274,482,538	348.55%
6. TICOR (FL)	$18,143,728	$63,963,771	$0	$0	$25,586,476	320.90%
7. GENERAL T&T	$184,100	$4,789,975	$120,900	$0	$1,595,193	319.40%
8. LAWYERS	$75,773,461	$334,753,199	$0	$0	$129,286,409	317.53%
9. OLD REPUBLIC NATIONAL	$61,315,931	$261,902,857	$70,000	$0	$116,001,825	278.69%
10. UNITED GENERAL	$13,277,853	$62,615,939	$0	$0	$27,974,272	271.30%
11. SECURITY TG (BALTIMORE)	$1,562,323	$8,544,849	$0	$0	$3,764,091	268.52%
12. WASHINGTON TIC	$147,409	$1,906,622	$0	$230,378	$876,497	260.63%
13. FIRST AMERICAN TIC	$140,517,390	$847,535,313	$0	$103,885,000	$426,527,243	256.01%
14. FIDELITY NATIONAL	$101,336,064	$424,888,225	$0	$0	$237,682,104	221.40%
15. TICOR	$21,961,002	$113,187,091	$0	$0	$67,686,913	199.67%
16. MISSISSIPPI GUARANTY	$0	$506,777	$50,000	$0	$300,100	185.53%
17. SOUTHERN TI CORP	$3,274,516	$11,001,692	$0	$0	$7,715,606	185.03%
18. OHIO BAR	$510,817	$14,766,195	$0	$0	$9,026,842	169.24%
19. COMMONWEALTH LAND	$63,954,527	$361,541,447	$0	$0	$254,092,477	167.46%
20. WESTCOR	$594,127	$13,492,778	$0	$0	$8,662,482	162.62%
21. ATTORNEYS TGF (CO)	$434,236	$1,834,898	$0	$362,511	$1,776,152	148.17%
22. OLD REPUBLIC GENERAL	$7,866,727	$60,548,499	$0	$0	$46,185,038	148.13%
23. COMMERCE	$215,988	$11,245,480	$0	$0	$8,811,912	130.07%
24. CONESTOGA	$332,350	$4,054,912	$0	$0	$3,483,884	125.93%
25. UNITED CAPITAL	$4,183,408	$24,027,403	$0	$0	$22,767,542	123.91%
26. ATTORNEYS TGF (IL)	$2,124,994	$7,963,611	$0	$1,892,395	$9,754,476	122.83%
27. ATTORNEYS TIF (FL)	$41,914,686	$120,815,744	$0	$0	$149,827,744	108.61%
28. STEWART TIC	$9,643,870	$27,194,595	$0	$0	$34,515,499	106.73%
29. GUARANTEE	$133,699	$946,693	$200,000	$0	$1,228,016	104.27%
30. ARKANSAS TIC	$316,110	$2,093,610	$0	$0	$2,388,523	100.89%
31. STEWART TGC	$91,456,109	$428,407,949	$0	$0	$515,901,015	100.77%
32. NATIONAL OF NY	$2,793,736	$3,924,691	$0	$0	$6,713,364	100.08%
33. NEW JERSEY TIC	$339,694	$4,371,480	$0	$0	$4,846,327	97.21%
34. FIRST AMERICAN (KS)	$257,303	$5,138,037	$0	$0	$5,833,793	92.48%
35. TRANSUNION TIC	$148,252	$3,220,967	$0	$0	$3,880,844	86.82%
36. INVESTORS TIC	$3,924,050	$39,338,674	$0	$0	$50,102,762	86.35%
37. PACIFIC NORTHWEST	$636,604	$12,118,349	$0	$0	$15,156,843	84.15%
38. CHICAGO TIC (OR)	$484,242	$10,648,750	$0	$0	$13,566,887	82.06%
39. STEWART (OR)	$0	$2,274,776	$0	$0	$2,873,991	79.15%
40. ALAMO	$1,953,953	$17,966,320	$0	$0	$26,226,592	75.95%
41. T.A. TITLE	$166,537	$4,710,958	$0	$0	$6,503,339	75.00%
42. SECURITY UNION	$9,847,553	$22,542,602	$0	$0	$46,565,183	69.56%
43. FIRST AMERICAN (OR)	$2,405,104	$19,799,451	$0	$0	$32,041,274	69.30%
44. MONROE	$802,300	$6,040,094	$0	$0	$11,498,871	59.50%
45. AMERICAN EAGLE	$8,000	$416,000	$0	$0	$716,768	59.15%
46. NORTH AMERICAN	$687,616	$28,451,816	$0	$0	$50,899,292	57.25%
47. ALLIANT	$694,330	$522,995	$0	$50,000	$2,354,553	53.82%
48. FIRST AMERICAN (NY)	$9,669,601	$46,598,121	$0	$0	$107,386,170	52.40%
49. TITLE RESOURCES	$413,706	$13,035,201	$12,974	$0	$25,711,604	52.36%
50. DAKOTA HOMESTEAD	$337,000	$825,622	$0	$0	$2,266,306	51.30%
51. TRANSUNION NATIONAL	$788,340	$3,515,209	$0	$0	$10,048,532	42.83%
52. GUARDIAN NATIONAL	$327,553	$2,524,234	$0	$0	$6,798,513	41.95%
53. LAND CORP (CO)	$162,568	$3,956,000	$0	$0	$9,842,596	41.84%
54. SEAGATE	$0	$192,675	$0	$0	$474,557	40.60%
55. CT ATTORNEYS	$1,361,851	$15,228,616	$0	$0	$41,839,283	39.65%
56. PORT LAWRENCE	$34,542	$5,615,498	$0	$0	$14,673,740	38.50%
57. TITLE G&TC	$0	$246,463	$100,000	$0	$907,607	38.17%
58. FIRST AMERICAN TRANS	$5,000	$470,908	$0	$0	$1,254,245	37.94%
59. NATIONS OF NY	$471,872	$4,230,527	$0	$0	$12,627,192	37.24%
60. WESTERN NATIONAL	$48,354	$1,164,289	$0	$0	$3,358,552	36.11%
61. TITLE IC AMERICA	$326,405	$3,046,160	$0	$0	$11,666,575	28.91%
62. COMMONWEALTH LAND (NJ)	$1,779,428	$6,725,497	$0	$0	$33,132,445	25.67%
63. NATIONAL LAND	$91,167	$1,117,693	$0	$0	$5,233,777	23.10%
64. AMERICAN GUARANTY	$74,000	$2,559,828	$0	$0	$11,507,581	22.89%
65. FARMERS NATIONAL	$5,000	$152,975	$0	$0	$817,207	19.33%
66. ALLIANCE	$52,774	$283,953	$0	$241,047	$3,107,663	18.59%
67. MANITO	$12,050	$181,732	$0	$0	$1,256,691	15.42%
68. CENSTAR	$93,076	$1,367,213	$0	$2,255,562	$25,141,601	14.78%
69. PENN ATTORNEYS	$177,062	$994,645	$0	$0	$8,351,671	14.03%
70. NATIONAL	$7,500	$418,127	$0	$0	$3,050,235	13.95%
71. NATIONAL ATTORNEYS	$0	$50,000	$0	$150,000	$1,566,898	12.76%
72. ARSENAL	$0	$50,000	$0	$0	$484,161	10.33%
73. NORTHEAST INVESTORS	$3,000	$539,982	$0	$0	$5,540,475	9.80%
74. FIRST AMERICAN T&T	$38,551	$1,285,621	$0	$0	$16,413,088	8.07%
75. EQUITY NATIONAL	$0	$111,701	$0	$0	$1,438,140	7.77%
76. DREIBELBISS	$22,000	$50,000	$0	$130,300	$2,650,439	7.63%
77. AMERICAN LAND & AIRCRAFT	$0	$47,015	$0	$0	$742,516	6.33%
78. MASSACHUSETTS TIC	$0	$100,000	$0	$0	$2,465,550	4.06%
79. MASON COUNTY	$0	$883	$25,000	$0	$822,687	3.15%
80. FOUNDERS	$0	$25,068	$0	$0	$800,122	3.13%
81. OLYMPIC	$10,377	$0	$0	$0	$336,151	3.09%
82. MASON	$12,000	$62,433	$0	$0	$2,546,042	2.92%
83. BRIDGE	$8,466	$161,691	$0	$0	$7,993,676	2.13%
84. AMERICAN SECURITY	$0	$0	$0	$176,000	$8,504,479	2.07%
85. SIERRA	$0	$43,490	$0	$6,628	$2,657,562	1.89%
86. TITLEDGE	$0	$7,275	$0	$6,040	$753,085	1.77%
87. K.E.L.	$0	$29,528	$0	$0	$2,332,454	1.27%
88. LAND TIC (ST LOUIS)	$0	$47,952	$0	$0	$4,984,385	0.96%
89. CHICAGO T&T	$0	$0	$0	$0	$664,634,623	0.00%
90. COLUMBIAN NATIONAL	$0	$0	$0	$0	$3,538,522	0.00%
91. PUBLIC	$0	$0	$0	$0	$1,038,244	0.00%
COMPOSITE	$857,043,158	$4,475,895,184	$1,578,874	$118,987,761	$2,778,616,712	196.27%
AVERAGE	$9,418,057	$49,185,661	$17,350	$1,307,558	$41,476,447	144.49%

5

C.10 Loss Reserve Development

(000's Omitted) COMPANY	2007 ONE YEAR DEVELOPMENT	2007 TWO YEAR DEVELOPMENT	2006 ONE YEAR DEVELOPMENT	2006 TWO YEAR DEVELOPMENT	2005 ONE YEAR DEVELOPMENT	2005 TWO YEAR DEVELOPMENT	2004 ONE YEAR DEVELOPMENT	2004 TWO YEAR DEVELOPMENT	2003 ONE YEAR DEVELOPMENT	2003 TWO YEAR DEVELOPMENT
1. ALAMO	$4,216	$4,543	$1,164	$2,056	$847	$110	($1,078)	($787)	$2,775	$4,161
2. ALLIANCE	($25)	($72)	($47)	($627)	($581)	($420)	$124	$603	$931	$1,364
3. ALLIANT	$429	$3	$0	$0	$0	$0	--	--	--	--
4. AMERICAN EAGLE	($30)	$31	$4	$6	($6)	$0	($23)	($136)	$57	$112
5. AMERICAN GUARANTY	($290)	($370)	($93)	$109	$222	$301	$114	$68	$129	$191
6. AMERICAN LAND & AIRCRAFT	--	--								
7. AMERICAN SECURITY	($41)	($72)	($39)	($70)	($37)	($63)	($30)	($65)	$13	$24
8. ARKANSAS TIC	($343)	($101)	$153	($64)	($95)	$276	($121)	$2	$288	$503
9. ARSENAL	$0	$0	$2	$2	--	--	--	--	--	--
10. ATTORNEYS TGF (CO)	$104	$1,085	$863	$1,373	$402	$497	$13	$223	$957	$4,366
11. ATTORNEYS TGF (IL)	($1,562)	($926)	($140)	$1,385	$836	$2,084	$169	$1,170	$3,729	$5,790
12. ATTORNEYS TIF (FL)	$4,005	($11,096)	($7,442)	($13,129)	($6,021)	($14,573)	($8,988)	($11,551)	$26,830	$48,969
13. BRIDGE	$156	$243	$1	($17)	($16)	$105	$163	$99	($58)	($90)
14. CENSTAR	$128	($25)	$10	$3	$0	$0	--	--	--	--
15. CHICAGO T&T	$0	$0	$0	$0	$0	$0	$0	$0	$0	$0
16. CHICAGO TIC	$117,129	$101,868	$8,016	$24,969	$16,033	$165	($7,686)	($29,349)	$91,685	$188,168
17. CHICAGO TIC (OR)	($500)	($961)	($606)	($265)	($135)	($1,161)	($616)	($654)	$1,218	$3,070
18. COLUMBIAN NATIONAL	$0	($4,650)	($4,650)	($5,807)	($1,264)	($1,269)	$248	($284)	$57	$329
19. COMMERCE	($706)	$71	$656	$581	$515	$520	$166	($1,783)	($1,666)	$259
20. COMMONWEALTH LAND	($2,706)	$9,331	$11,987	$8,582	($3,758)	($11,354)	$6,876	$5,871	$73,976	$110,902
21. COMMONWEALTH LAND (NJ)	$1,524	$1,261	($357)	($820)	($328)	$140	$667	$485	$1,396	$2,185
22. CONESTOGA	$239	($219)	($454)	($250)	$191	$1,025	$863	$882	$1,106	$1,962
23. CT ATTORNEYS	$2,502	$6,909	$4,955	$5,179	$465	($812)	($708)	($1,018)	($6,276)	($3,697)
24. DAKOTA HOMESTEAD	$27	$122	$108	$45	$34	($15)	($45)	($36)	$33	$68
25. DREIBELBISS	$115	$150	$32	($180)	($255)	($230)	$6	$43	$79	$265
26. EQUITY NATIONAL	$0	$0	$0	$0	$0	$0	--	--	--	--
27. FARMERS NATIONAL	$46	$0	$0	$0	--	--	--	--	--	--
28. FIDELITY NATIONAL	$49,373	$51,770	$5,094	$48,239	$46,873	$46,066	$11,795	$33,148	$53,328	$67,858
29. FIRST AMERICAN (KS)	$243	$75	($165)	$276	$274	$652	$224	$515	$697	$1,053
30. FIRST AMERICAN (NY)	$8,390	$11,893	$5,160	$6,618	$3,441	$4,722	$2,817	($3,734)	($3,262)	$873
31. FIRST AMERICAN (OR)	$608	($40)	($354)	($1,285)	($958)	($767)	($126)	($769)	$1,696	$3,349
32. FIRST AMERICAN T&T	($23)	($217)	($632)	($695)	$8	$99	$113	($55)	$430	$481
33. FIRST AMERICAN TIC	$221,278	$209,846	$34,093	$116,328	$77,828	$64,539	$21,689	$30,305	$156,878	$247,543
34. FIRST AMERICAN TRANS	($20)	$36	$190	$48	($162)	($64)	$67	($12)	$21	$77
35. FOUNDERS	$0	$0	$0	$0	--	--	--	--	--	--
36. GENERAL T&T	$357	$454	$158	$272	$193	$256	$63	$29	$46	($97)
37. GUARANTEE	$1,619	$2,835	$1,581	$1,085	$118	$81	$7	$135	$181	$231
38. GUARANTEE T&T	$3,343	$4,786	$2,192	$2,534	$787	$1,233	$1,104	$1,582	$1,526	$1,579
39. GUARDIAN NATIONAL	($343)	($120)	$189	$224	($73)	$33	$142	$450	$510	$664
40. INVESTORS TIC	$1,529	($3,541)	($1,562)	($1,843)	($1,598)	($330)	$623	($1,329)	$8,803	$14,382
41. K.E.L.	$0	$0	--	--	--	--	--	--	--	--
42. LAND CORP (CO)	($747)	($2,384)	($1,888)	($2,826)	($1,139)	($2,572)	($1,704)	($1,660)	$1,633	$3,077
43. LAND TIC (ST LOUIS)	$0	$0	$0	$0	$0	$0	--	--	$0	($3,684)
44. LAWYERS	$34,782	$19,697	($6,871)	$179,802	$181,695	$140,940	($9,373)	$16,286	$96,625	$168,817
45. MANITO	$5	($5)	($12)	($38)	($28)	($72)	($46)	($7)	$61	$45
46. MASON	$0	$0	$0	$0	--	--	--	--	--	--
47. MASON COUNTY	--	--	--	--	--	--	--	--	--	--
48. MASSACHUSETTS TIC	$0	$0	$0	$0	$0	$0	--	--	--	--
49. MISSISSIPPI GUARANTY	$0	$0	$0	$0	$0	$0	--	--	--	--
50. MISSISSIPPI VALLEY	$370	($326)	$59	($1,654)	($1,525)	($1,524)	$1	$250	$3,064	$5,968
51. MONROE	$140	$179	$142	$546	$366	$607	$237	$185	$94	$331
52. NATIONAL	($46)	($58)	($28)	($14)	$1	($31)	($26)	($34)	$20	$30
53. NATIONAL ATTORNEYS	$101	$195	($10,693)	($10,744)	($125)	($68)	($132)	$31	$69	$57
54. NATIONAL LAND	($105)	($85)	$6	($82)	($82)	($170)	($96)	($147)	($4)	($258)
55. NATIONAL OF NY	$1,124	$1,780	$786	$1,261	$233	$3,478	$3,249	$560	$2,927	$3,723
56. NATIONS OF NY	$1,112	$884	($228)	($1,283)	($1,055)	($1,691)	($636)	$558	$1,208	$6,573
57. NEW JERSEY TIC	$606	$1,160	$695	$915	$431	$1,692	$1,415	$1,418	$999	$2,102
58. NORTH AMERICAN	($4,182)	($4,299)	($5,111)	($4,882)	($2,226)	($3,324)	($2,559)	($2,273)	$3,716	$6,164
59. NORTHEAST INVESTORS	$76	($104)	($40)	($103)	($86)	($111)	($39)	($123)	$86	$184
60. OHIO BAR	$1,351	$1,357	($40)	($229)	($11,924)	($12,029)	$30	$2,511	$2,752	$4,610
61. OLD REPUBLIC GENERAL	($9,222)	($14,532)	($4,144)	($9,917)	($5,977)	($8,489)	($6,273)	($4,847)	$8,070	$12,713
62. OLD REPUBLIC NATIONAL	($3,962)	$4,379	$11,733	$1,535	($547)	($2,728)	($2,159)	$2,787	$59,582	$91,043
63. OLYMPIC	$0	($54)	($54)	($109)	($109)	($2)	--	--	($339)	$2
64. PACIFIC NORTHWEST	($199)	$425	$707	$2,552	$1,823	$1,521	($116)	$176	$1,843	$3,769
65. PENN ATTORNEYS	($6)	($78)	($92)	($41)	$10	($509)	($278)	($371)	$27	$431
66. PORT LAWRENCE	($66)	($425)	($403)	$294	$702	$535	$5	$129	$171	$558
67. PUBLIC	$0	$0	$0	$0	--	--	--	--	--	--
68. SEAGATE	$0	$0	$0	$0	$0	$0	--	--	$0	$0
69. SECURITY TG (BALTIMORE)	($762)	($2,070)	($1,552)	($885)	$218	($507)	($807)	($482)	$1,534	$2,812
70. SECURITY UNION	$2,521	$2,425	$1,289	($1,142)	($2,154)	($1,930)	($262)	($1,780)	$3,335	$25,774
71. SIERRA	$0	$0	--	--	--	--	--	--	--	--
72. SOUTHERN TI CORP	$1,744	$563	$1,313	$309	$128	$795	$1,416	$2,067	$1,469	$2,346
73. STEWART (OR)	$10	($155)	($82)	($54)	($16)	($94)	($80)	($56)	$221	$510
74. STEWART TGC	$63,312	$64,161	$20,254	$33,359	$20,471	$28,386	$8,930	$8,027	$65,295	$146,805
75. STEWART TIC	($381)	($246)	$1,206	($1,140)	($2,769)	($2,828)	($123)	$984	$6,821	$14,163
76. T.A. TITLE	$445	($518)	($883)	($458)	$211	($25)	($138)	($358)	$310	$2,619
77. TICOR	($3,162)	$9,103	$16,862	$6,908	($3,796)	$3,823	$5,092	$26,230	$41,302	$59,097
78. TICOR (FL)	$9,792	$15,887	$6,893	$27,506	$22,222	$29,540	$15,232	$21,564	$19,921	$31,486
79. TITLE G&TC	--	--	--	--	--	--	--	--	($77)	($138)
80. TITLE GUARANTY DIV (IA)	--	--	--	--	--	--	--	--	--	--
81. TITLE IC AMERICA	($670)	$532	$1,043	($858)	($1,226)	($1,379)	$560	$1,449	$1,337	$1,568
82. TITLE RESOURCES	$1,000	$1,389	$455	$83	($387)	$37	$316	$180	$2,166	$3,927
83. TITLEDGE	$0	$0	--	--	--	--	--	--	--	--
84. TRANSNATION	$24,296	$25,631	$11,879	$5,863	($739)	($946)	$5,890	$11,765	$27,242	$45,566
85. TRANSUNION NATIONAL	$536	$1,345	$871	$1,721	$1,306	$1,407	($192)	$146	$948	$1,322
86. TRANSUNION TIC	($910)	($791)	($141)	$17	$482	($866)	($663)	($874)	$401	$1,329
87. UNITED CAPITAL	$5,905	$6,820	$3,907	($812)	($617)	($2,405)	($758)	($1,065)	$4,602	$7,355
88. UNITED GENERAL	$14,726	$3,371	($19,919)	($11,101)	$3,368	($1,857)	($2,475)	$4,513	$18,045	$26,502
89. WASHINGTON TIC	$97	$5	($142)	($300)	($296)	($203)	($2)	($28)	$484	$997
90. WESTCOR	($388)	($585)	($209)	($1,015)	($1,005)	($1,485)	($549)	($1,153)	$701	$3,100
91. WESTERN NATIONAL	($178)	($80)	($1,547)	($1,600)	($1,600)	($1,720)	($225)	($247)	$213	$328
COMPOSITE	$549,836	$519,395	$86,095	$406,347	$327,963	$254,937	$41,293	$110,297	$854,426	$1,522,790
AVERAGE	$6,248	$5,902	$978	$4,618	$3,858	$2,999	$566	$1,511	$10,816	$19,276

5

C.11 Loss Reserve Development to Policyholders' Surplus (PHS) - New!

(000's Omitted)

COMPANY	2007 B.6 - PHS	2006 PHS	ONE YEAR DEVELOPMENT	ONE YEAR DEV TO PHS	2005 PHS	TWO YEAR DEVELOPMENT	TWO YEAR DEV TO PHS
1. ALAMO	$26,227	$37,139	$4,216	11	$35,000	$4,543	13
2. ALLIANCE	$3,108	$2,986	($25)	(1)	$3,003	($72)	(2)
3. ALLIANT	$2,355	$2,517	$429	17	$2,338	$3	0
4. AMERICAN EAGLE	$717	$1,356	($30)	(2)	$1,664	$31	2
5. AMERICAN GUARANTY	$11,508	$10,212	($290)	(3)	$9,740	($370)	(4)
6. AMERICAN LAND & AIRCRAFT	$743	$756	--	--	$710	--	--
7. AMERICAN SECURITY	$8,504	$7,484	($41)	(1)	$6,832	($72)	(1)
8. ARKANSAS TIC	$2,389	$2,259	($343)	(15)	$1,909	($101)	(5)
9. ARSENAL	$484	$514	$0	0	$514	$0	0
10. ATTORNEYS TGF (CO)	$1,776	$1,294	$104	8	$2,325	$1,085	47
11. ATTORNEYS TGF (IL)	$9,754	$7,576	($1,562)	(21)	$6,600	($926)	(14)
12. ATTORNEYS TIF (FL)	$149,828	$158,663	$4,005	3	$138,624	($11,096)	(8)
13. BRIDGE	$7,994	$8,111	$156	2	$8,155	$243	3
14. CENSTAR	$25,142	$23,538	$128	1	$21,179	($25)	0
15. CHICAGO T&T	$664,635	$920,681	$0	0	$899,158	$0	0
16. CHICAGO TIC	$274,483	$429,467	$117,129	27	$385,827	$101,868	26
17. CHICAGO TIC (OR)	$13,567	$13,988	($500)	(4)	$13,509	($961)	(7)
18. COLUMBIAN NATIONAL	$3,539	$3,724	$0	0	$3,915	($4,650)	(119)
19. COMMERCE	$8,812	$8,566	($706)	(8)	$6,810	$71	1
20. COMMONWEALTH LAND	$254,092	$313,774	($2,706)	(1)	$196,727	$9,331	5
21. COMMONWEALTH LAND (NJ)	$33,132	$30,230	$1,524	5	$32,706	$1,261	4
22. CONESTOGA	$3,484	$4,054	$239	6	$4,010	($219)	(5)
23. CT ATTORNEYS	$41,839	$41,146	$2,502	6	$41,984	$6,909	16
24. DAKOTA HOMESTEAD	$2,266	$2,087	$27	1	$2,299	$122	5
25. DREIBELBISS	$2,650	$2,547	$115	5	$2,490	$150	6
26. EQUITY NATIONAL	$1,438	$1,393	$0	0	$1,268	$0	0
27. FARMERS NATIONAL	$817	$751	$46	6	$0	$0	0
28. FIDELITY NATIONAL	$237,682	$273,990	$49,373	18	$293,247	$51,770	18
29. FIRST AMERICAN (KS)	$5,834	$5,293	$243	5	$4,396	$75	2
30. FIRST AMERICAN (NY)	$107,386	$90,145	$8,390	9	$71,551	$11,893	17
31. FIRST AMERICAN (OR)	$32,041	$33,011	$608	2	$31,650	($40)	0
32. FIRST AMERICAN T&T	$16,413	$11,218	($23)	0	$9,794	($217)	(2)
33. FIRST AMERICAN TIC	$426,527	$753,712	$221,278	29	$877,882	$209,846	24
34. FIRST AMERICAN TRANS	$1,254	$1,169	($20)	(2)	$814	$36	4
35. FOUNDERS	$800	$836	$0	0	$863	$0	0
36. GENERAL T&T	$1,595	$1,995	$357	18	$1,857	$454	24
37. GUARANTEE	$1,228	$1,700	$1,619	95	$1,834	$2,835	155
38. GUARANTEE T&T	$1,219	$2,333	$3,343	143	$2,508	$4,786	191
39. GUARDIAN NATIONAL	$6,799	$1,774	($343)	(19)	$2,065	($120)	(6)
40. INVESTORS TIC	$50,103	$54,651	$1,529	3	$50,474	($3,541)	(7)
41. K.E.L.	$2,332	$0	$0	0	--	$0	--
42. LAND CORP (CO)	$9,843	$10,267	($747)	(7)	$9,526	($2,384)	(25)
43. LAND TIC (ST LOUIS)	$4,984	$4,863	$0	0	$5,027	$0	0
44. LAWYERS	$129,286	$218,001	$34,782	16	$225,800	$19,697	9
45. MANITO	$1,257	$1,273	$5	0	$1,259	($5)	0
46. MASON	$2,546	$2,797	$0	0	$0	$0	0
47. MASON COUNTY	$823	$801	--	--	$776	--	--
48. MASSACHUSETTS TIC	$2,466	$2,138	$0	0	$1,669	$0	0
49. MISSISSIPPI GUARANTY	$300	$417	$0	0	$289	$0	0
50. MISSISSIPPI VALLEY	$9,684	$10,157	$370	4	$9,301	($326)	(4)
51. MONROE	$11,499	$13,958	$140	1	$12,652	$179	1
52. NATIONAL	$3,050	$2,903	($46)	(2)	$2,817	($58)	(2)
53. NATIONAL ATTORNEYS	$1,567	$1,715	$101	6	$1,676	$195	12
54. NATIONAL LAND	$5,234	$5,497	($105)	(2)	$2,946	($85)	(3)
55. NATIONAL OF NY	$6,713	$8,712	$1,124	13	$6,639	$1,780	27
56. NATIONS OF NY	$12,627	$11,783	$1,112	9	$9,545	$884	9
57. NEW JERSEY TIC	$4,846	$5,204	$606	12	$5,043	$1,160	23
58. NORTH AMERICAN	$50,899	$42,573	($4,182)	(10)	$18,434	($4,299)	(23)
59. NORTHEAST INVESTORS	$5,540	$5,306	$76	1	$5,116	($104)	(2)
60. OHIO BAR	$9,027	$8,193	$1,351	16	$7,128	$1,357	19
61. OLD REPUBLIC GENERAL	$46,185	$49,246	($9,222)	(19)	$46,857	($14,532)	(31)
62. OLD REPUBLIC NATIONAL	$116,002	$119,194	($3,962)	(3)	$116,093	$4,379	4
63. OLYMPIC	$336	$366	$0	0	$324	($54)	(17)
64. PACIFIC NORTHWEST	$15,157	$12,039	($199)	(2)	$8,969	$425	5
65. PENN ATTORNEYS	$8,352	$8,451	($6)	0	$7,782	($78)	(1)
66. PORT LAWRENCE	$14,674	$15,368	($66)	0	$14,052	($425)	(3)
67. PUBLIC	$1,038	$1,010	$0	0	$0	$0	0
68. SEAGATE	$475	$500	$0	0	$396	$0	0
69. SECURITY TG (BALTIMORE)	$3,764	$4,488	($762)	(17)	$4,423	($2,070)	(47)
70. SECURITY UNION	$46,565	$66,803	$2,521	4	$63,223	$2,425	4
71. SIERRA	$2,658	$2,524	$0	0	--	$0	--
72. SOUTHERN TI CORP	$7,716	$8,661	$1,744	20	$8,160	$563	7
73. STEWART (OR)	$2,874	$2,607	$10	0	$2,500	($155)	(6)
74. STEWART TGC	$515,901	$508,509	$63,312	12	$488,193	$64,161	13
75. STEWART TIC	$34,515	$30,833	($381)	(1)	$39,671	($246)	(1)
76. T.A. TITLE	$6,503	$7,675	$445	6	$6,716	($518)	(8)
77. TICOR	$67,687	$52,899	($3,162)	(6)	$74,945	$9,103	12
78. TICOR (FL)	$25,586	$29,858	$9,792	33	$40,660	$15,887	39
79. TITLE G&TC	$908	$853	--	--	$733	--	--
80. TITLE GUARANTY DIV (IA)	$740	$594	--	--	$842	--	--
81. TITLE IC AMERICA	$11,667	$9,145	($670)	(7)	$9,956	$532	5
82. TITLE RESOURCES	$25,712	$27,728	$1,000	4	$28,185	$1,389	5
83. TITLEDGE	$753	$0	$0	0	$0	$0	--
84. TRANSNATION	$22,335	$62,836	$24,296	39	$81,661	$25,631	31
85. TRANSUNION NATIONAL	$10,049	$10,488	$536	5	$4,764	$1,345	28
86. TRANSUNION TIC	$3,881	$3,637	($910)	(25)	$1,770	($791)	(45)
87. UNITED CAPITAL	$22,768	$24,748	$5,905	24	$21,439	$6,820	32
88. UNITED GENERAL	$27,974	$23,928	$14,726	62	$18,037	$3,371	19
89. WASHINGTON TIC	$876	$802	$97	12	$935	$5	1
90. WESTCOR	$8,662	$11,293	($388)	(3)	$11,749	($585)	(5)
91. WESTERN NATIONAL	$3,359	$3,182	($178)	(6)	$3,227	($80)	(2)
COMPOSITE	$2,778,619	$3,555,948	$549,836	15	$3,508,532	$519,395	15
AVERAGE	$41,476	$51,928	$6,320	12	$49,435	$5,970	12

5

Notes

Notes

5

S E C T I O N

DASHBOARDS

6

6

A.1 UNDERWRITER DASHBOARDS

6

Alamo Title Insurance

601 Riverside Ave.
Jacksonville, FL 32204

(904) 854-8100

WEBSITE:	STATE OF DOMICILE:
www.fnf.com	Texas

PRESIDENT:	ESTABLISHED:	JURISDICTION LICENSE(S):
Raymond Randall Quirk	10/1/1922	2

A' A Prime · **Unsurpassed** · Financial Stability Rating® · Demotech, Inc.

NAIC Number: **50598**

ALAMO

NAIC Group: **CHICAGO / FIDELITY**

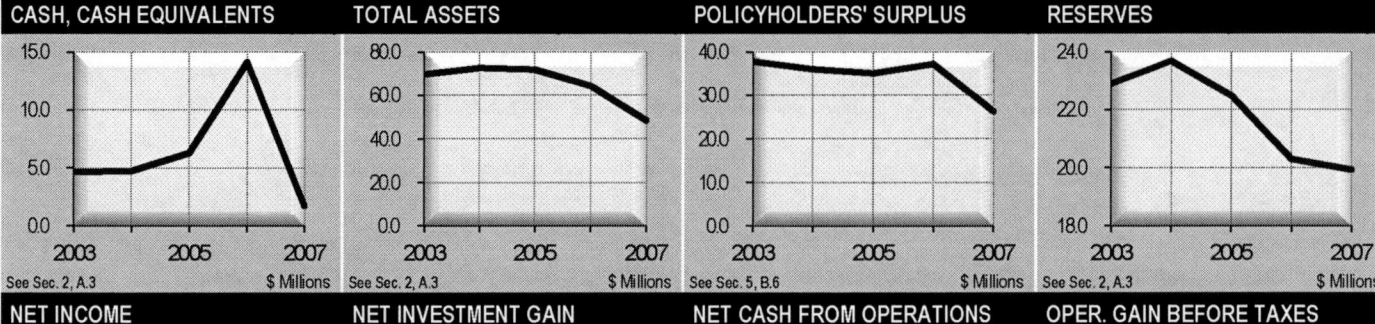

CASH, CASH EQUIVALENTS — See Sec. 2, A.3 — $ Millions
TOTAL ASSETS — See Sec. 2, A.3 — $ Millions
POLICYHOLDERS' SURPLUS — See Sec. 5, B.6 — $ Millions
RESERVES — See Sec. 2, A.3 — $ Millions

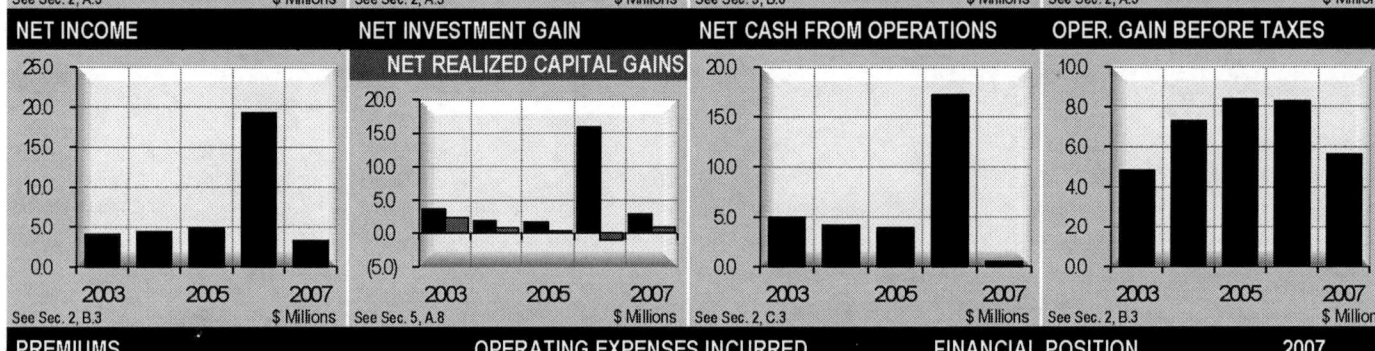

NET INCOME — See Sec. 2, B.3 — $ Millions
NET INVESTMENT GAIN / NET REALIZED CAPITAL GAINS — See Sec. 5, A.8 — $ Millions
NET CASH FROM OPERATIONS — See Sec. 2, C.3 — $ Millions
OPER. GAIN BEFORE TAXES — See Sec. 2, B.3 — $ Millions

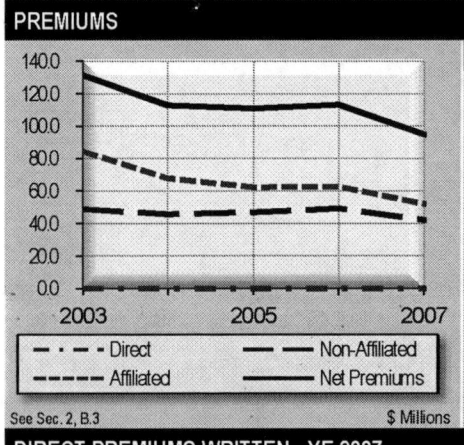

PREMIUMS
- · - Direct
- — Non-Affiliated
- --- Affiliated
- — Net Premiums

See Sec. 2, B.3 — $ Millions

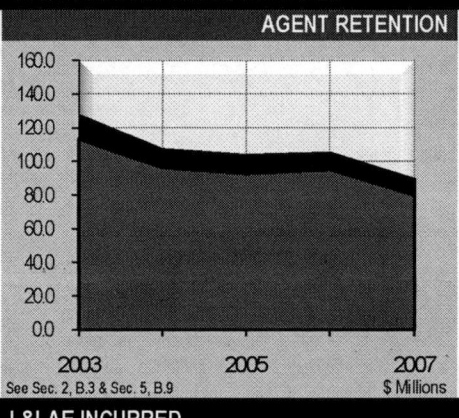

OPERATING EXPENSES INCURRED / AGENT RETENTION — See Sec. 2, B.3 & Sec. 5, B.9 — $ Millions

FINANCIAL POSITION	2007
Cash, Cash Equivalents & Short-Term Investments	$1,741,063
Total Assets	$48,396,113
Policyholders' Surplus	$26,226,592
Reserves	$19,920,273
OPERATING RESULTS	
Net Income	$3,298,907
Net Investment Gain	$2,879,123
Net Realized Capital Gains	$920,620
Net Cash from Operations	$486,677
Oper. Gain Before Taxes	$5,639,537

DIRECT PREMIUMS WRITTEN - YE 2007

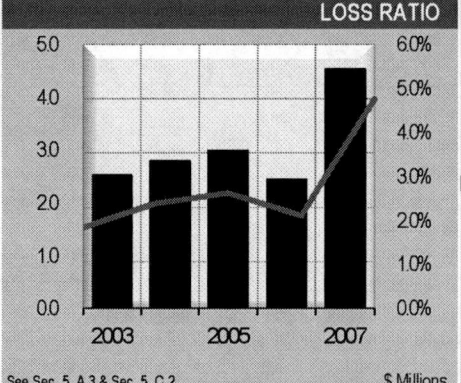

□ Direct ■ Non-Affiliated ■ Affiliated

See Sec. 3, B.4

L&LAE INCURRED / LOSS RATIO — See Sec. 5, A.3 & Sec. 5, C.2 — $ Millions

UNDERWRITING RESULTS	
Direct	$0
Non-Affiliated	$42,145,575
Affiliated	$52,072,753
Direct Premiums Written	$94,218,328
Net Premiums Earned	$94,868,291
Operating Expenses Incurred	$89,228,814
Agent Retention	$80,095,646
L&LAE Incurred	$4,542,653
Loss Ratio	4.79%

Alliance Title of America, Inc.

3401 W Cypress St, 2nd Fl.
Tampa, FL 33607

(813) 876-0619

WEBSITE:	STATE OF DOMICILE:
www.stewart.com	Florida

PRESIDENT:	ESTABLISHED:	JURISDICTION LICENSE(S):
Harold Eugene Hickman	8/14/1996	1

A' Unsurpassed
A Prime
Financial Stability Rating®
Demotech, Inc.

NAIC Number: **50035**

ALLIANCE

NAIC Group: **STEWART**

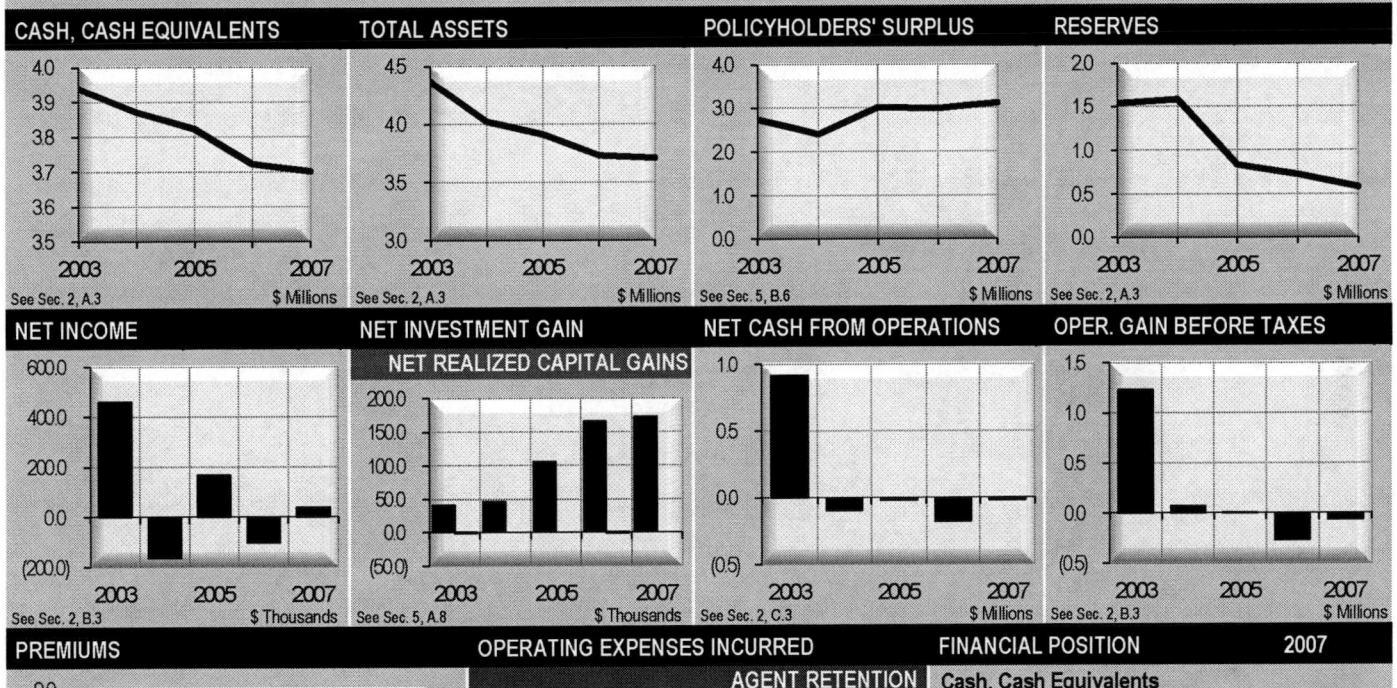

CASH, CASH EQUIVALENTS — See Sec. 2, A.3 — $ Millions
TOTAL ASSETS — See Sec. 2, A.3 — $ Millions
POLICYHOLDERS' SURPLUS — See Sec. 5, B.6 — $ Millions
RESERVES — See Sec. 2, A.3 — $ Millions

NET INCOME — See Sec. 2, B.3 — $ Thousands
NET INVESTMENT GAIN / NET REALIZED CAPITAL GAINS — See Sec. 5, A.8 — $ Thousands
NET CASH FROM OPERATIONS — See Sec. 2, C.3 — $ Millions
OPER. GAIN BEFORE TAXES — See Sec. 2, B.3 — $ Millions

PREMIUMS — See Sec. 2, B.3 — $ Millions
Legend: Direct; Affiliated; Non-Affiliated; Net Premiums

OPERATING EXPENSES INCURRED / AGENT RETENTION — See Sec. 2, B.3 & Sec. 5, B.9 — $ Millions

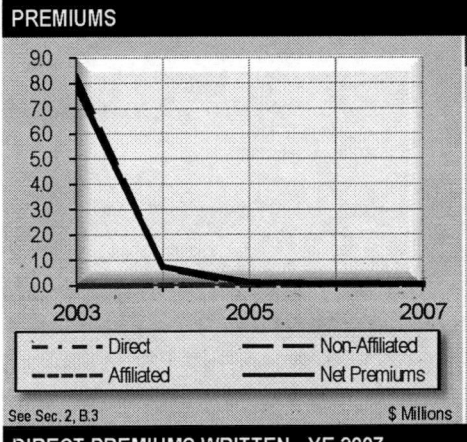

DIRECT PREMIUMS WRITTEN - YE 2007 — See Sec. 3, B.4
Legend: Direct; Non-Affiliated; Affiliated

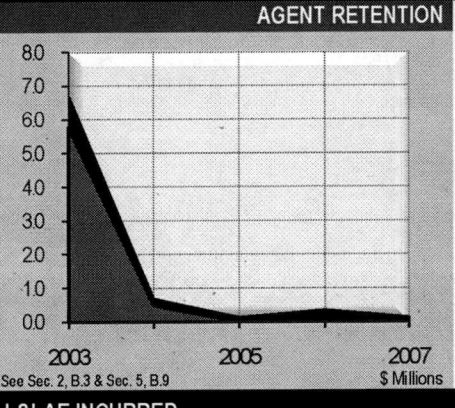

L&LAE INCURRED / LOSS RATIO — See Sec. 5, A.3 & Sec. 5, C.2 — $ Thousands

FINANCIAL POSITION	2007
Cash, Cash Equivalents & Short-Term Investments	$3,700,368
Total Assets	$3,707,325
Policyholders' Surplus	$3,107,663
Reserves	$577,774
OPERATING RESULTS	
Net Income	$36,170
Net Investment Gain	$172,226
Net Realized Capital Gains	$0
Net Cash from Operations	($20,405)
Oper. Gain Before Taxes	($63,006)
UNDERWRITING RESULTS	
Direct	$0
Non-Affiliated	$1,196
Affiliated	$0
Direct Premiums Written	$1,196
Net Premiums Earned	$54,338
Operating Expenses Incurred	$117,344
Agent Retention	$838
L&LAE Incurred	$66,579
Loss Ratio	122.53%

6

Alliant National Title Insurance Company

2101 Ken Pratt Blvd.
Ste. 102
Longmont, CO 80501

(303) 682-9800

Formerly Agents Title Insurance Company, Inc.

WEBSITE:	STATE OF DOMICILE:
www.alliantnational.com	Colorado

CHIEF EXECUTIVE OFFICER:	ESTABLISHED:	JURISDICTION LICENSE(S):
Robert J. Grubb	7/27/2005	2

A Exceptional
Financial Stability Rating®
Demotech, Inc.

NAIC Number:
12309

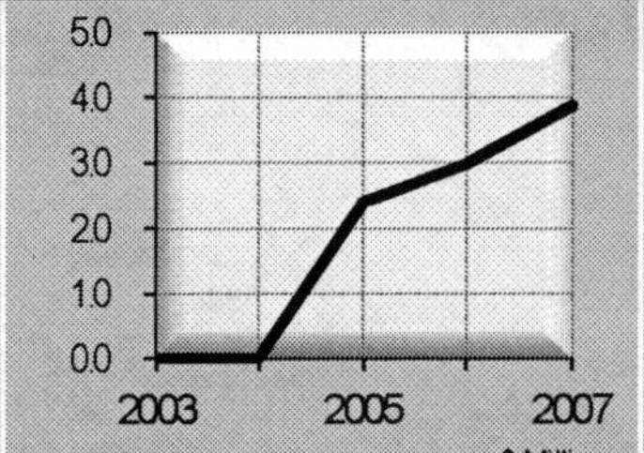

ALLIANT

NAIC Group:
UNAFFILIATED

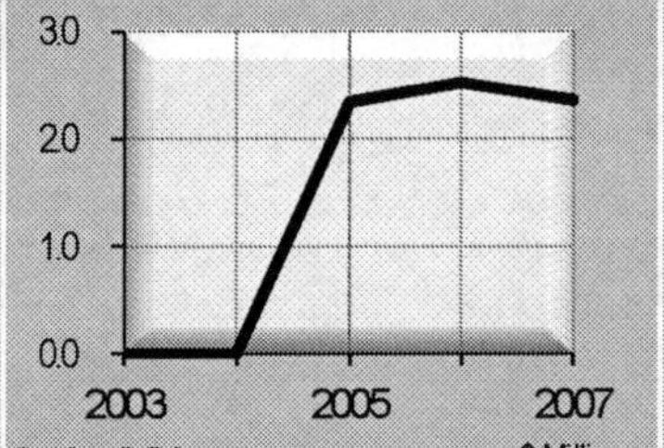

CASH, CASH EQUIVALENTS	TOTAL ASSETS	POLICYHOLDERS' SURPLUS	RESERVES

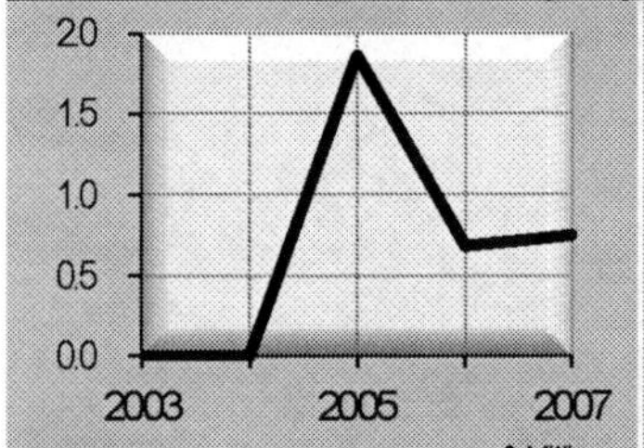

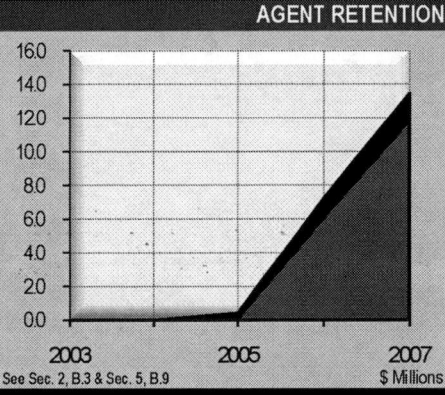

See Sec. 2, A.3 — $ Millions | See Sec. 2, A.3 — $ Millions | See Sec. 5, B.6 — $ Millions | See Sec. 2, A.3 — $ Millions

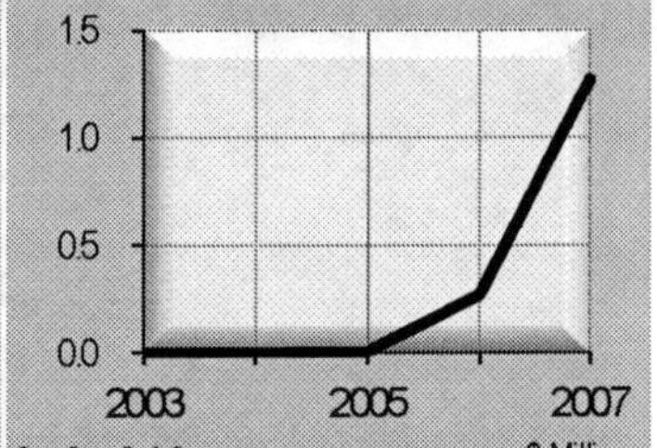

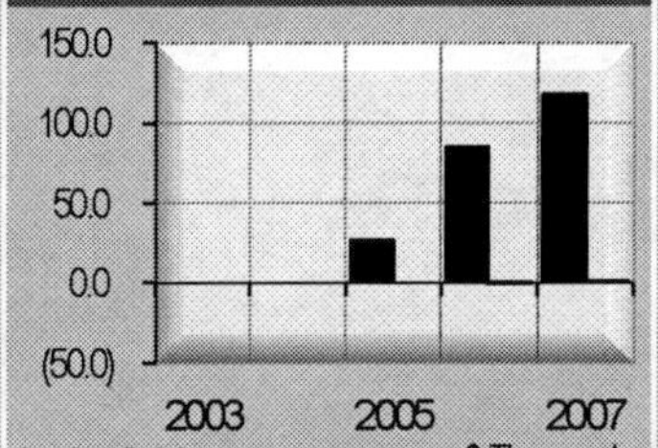

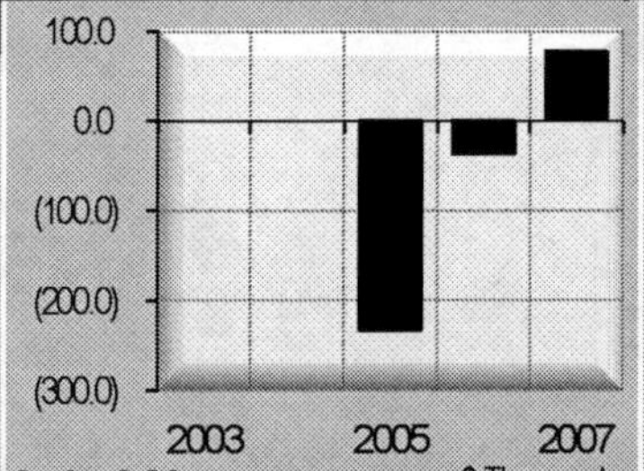

NET INCOME	NET INVESTMENT GAIN / NET REALIZED CAPITAL GAINS	NET CASH FROM OPERATIONS	OPER. GAIN BEFORE TAXES

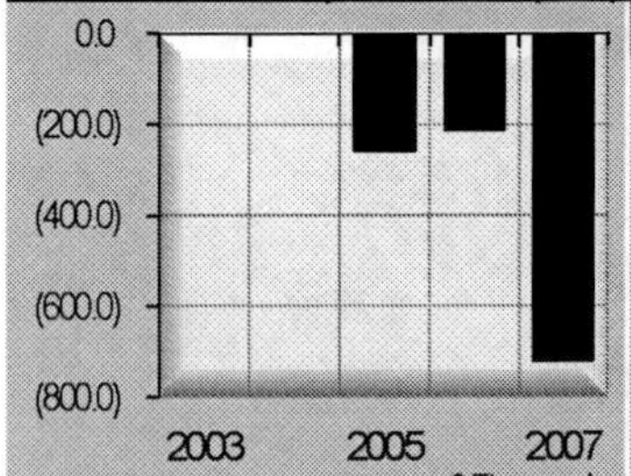

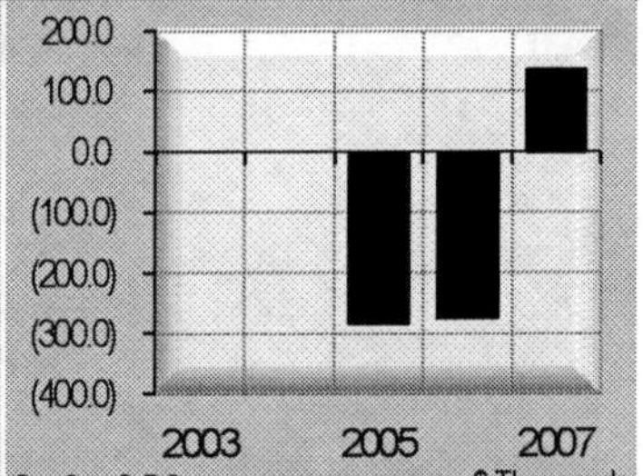

See Sec. 2, B.3 — $ Thousands | See Sec. 5, A.8 — $ Thousands | See Sec. 2, C.3 — $ Thousands | See Sec. 2, B.3 — $ Thousands

PREMIUMS	OPERATING EXPENSES INCURRED — AGENT RETENTION

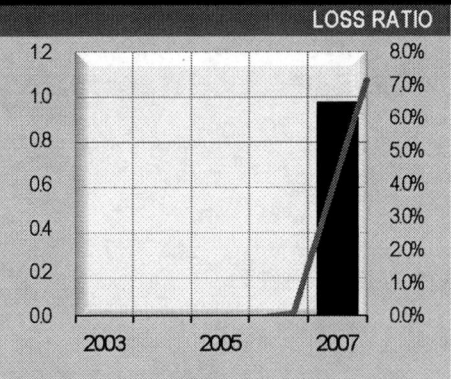

Legend: — · — · Direct   — — Non-Affiliated   ----- Affiliated   —— Net Premiums

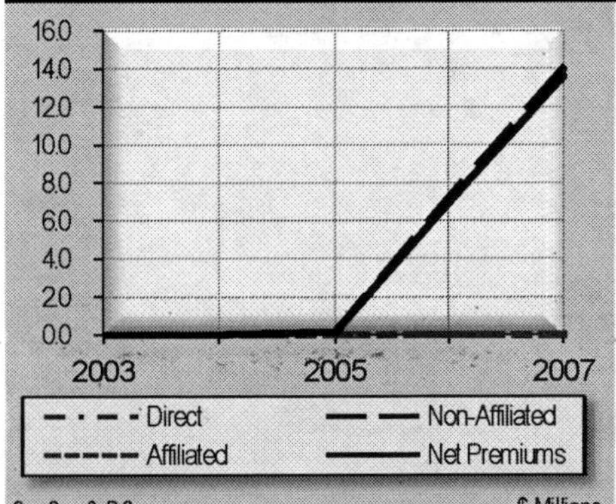

See Sec. 2, B.3 — $ Millions | See Sec. 2, B.3 & Sec. 5, B.9 — $ Millions

DIRECT PREMIUMS WRITTEN - YE 2007

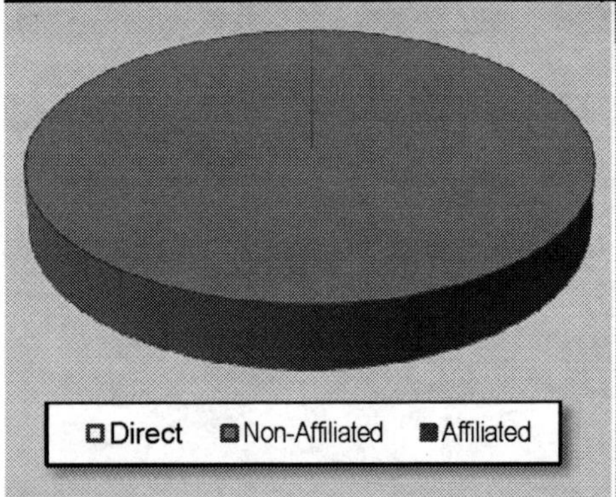

Legend: □ Direct   ▨ Non-Affiliated   ■ Affiliated

See Sec. 3, B.4

L&LAE INCURRED — LOSS RATIO

See Sec. 5, A.3 & Sec. 5, C.2 — $ Millions

FINANCIAL POSITION	2007
Cash, Cash Equivalents & Short-Term Investments	$750,111
Total Assets	$3,870,716
Policyholders' Surplus	$2,354,553
Reserves	$1,267,325
OPERATING RESULTS	
Net Income	($721,452)
Net Investment Gain	$117,824
Net Realized Capital Gains	$944
Net Cash from Operations	$76,868
Oper. Gain Before Taxes	$134,837
UNDERWRITING RESULTS	
Direct	$0
Non-Affiliated	$13,990,651
Affiliated	$0
Direct Premiums Written	$13,990,651
Net Premiums Earned	$13,587,506
Operating Expenses Incurred	$13,452,669
Agent Retention	$11,897,217
L&LAE Incurred	$974,113
Loss Ratio	7.17%

6

American Eagle Title Insurance Company

1141 N Robinson, Ste. 100
Oklahoma City, OK 73103

(405) 232-6700

WEBSITE:	STATE OF DOMICILE:
www.ameagletitle.com	Oklahoma

PRESIDENT:	ESTABLISHED:	JURISDICTION LICENSE(S):
Eric Ronald Offen	10/14/1994	1

A Exceptional
Financial Stability Rating®
Demotech, Inc.

NAIC Number:
50001

AMERICAN EAGLE

NAIC Group:
UNAFFILIATED

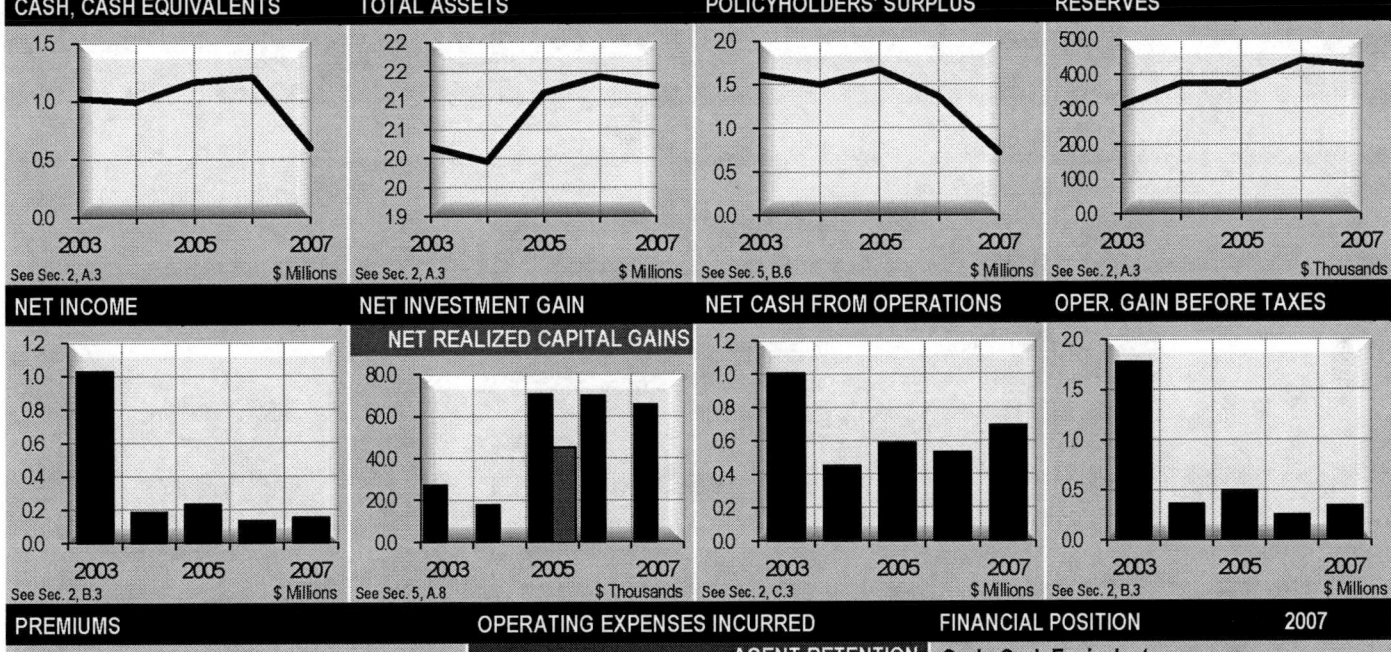

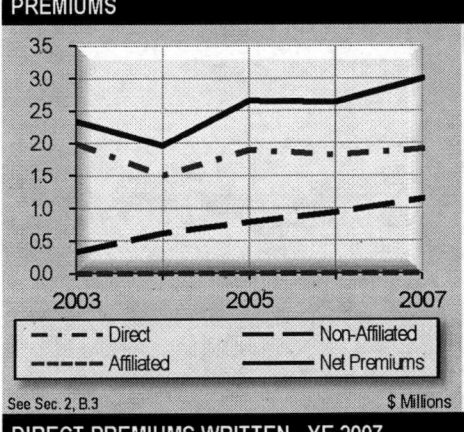

DIRECT PREMIUMS WRITTEN - YE 2007

□ Direct ■ Non-Affiliated ■ Affiliated

See Sec. 3, B.4

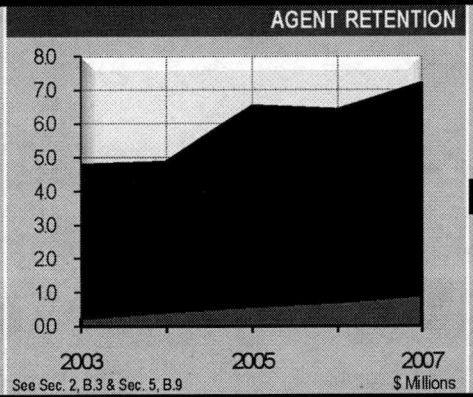

FINANCIAL POSITION	2007
Cash, Cash Equivalents & Short-Term Investments	$593,123
Total Assets	$2,123,371
Policyholders' Surplus	$716,768
Reserves	$424,000
OPERATING RESULTS	
Net Income	$150,735
Net Investment Gain	$65,709
Net Realized Capital Gains	$0
Net Cash from Operations	$694,490
Oper. Gain Before Taxes	$337,276
UNDERWRITING RESULTS	
Direct	$1,906,376
Non-Affiliated	$1,142,793
Affiliated	$0
Direct Premiums Written	$3,049,169
Net Premiums Earned	$2,992,458
Operating Expenses Incurred	$7,201,062
Agent Retention	$916,270
L&LAE Incurred	$30,838
Loss Ratio	0.41%

6

American Guaranty Title Insurance Company

4040 N Tulsa
Oklahoma City, OK 73112

(405) 942-4848

WEBSITE:	STATE OF DOMICILE:
www.oldrepublictitle.com	Oklahoma

PRESIDENT & CEO:	ESTABLISHED:	JURISDICTION LICENSE(S):
Rande Keith Yeager	7/2/1979	47

A″ Unsurpassed Financial Stability Rating®
Demotech, Inc.

NAIC Number: **51411**

AMERICAN GUARANTY

NAIC Group: **OLD REPUBLIC**

CASH, CASH EQUIVALENTS
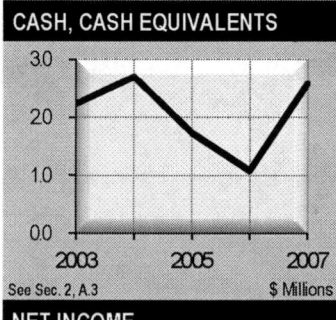
See Sec. 2, A.3 — $ Millions

TOTAL ASSETS
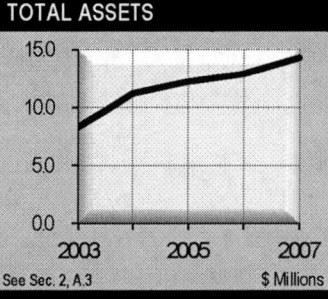
See Sec. 2, A.3 — $ Millions

POLICYHOLDERS' SURPLUS
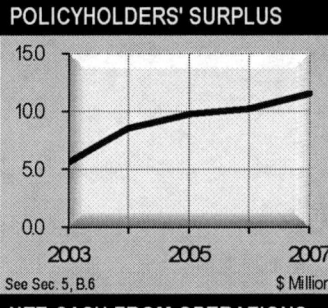
See Sec. 5, B.6 — $ Millions

RESERVES
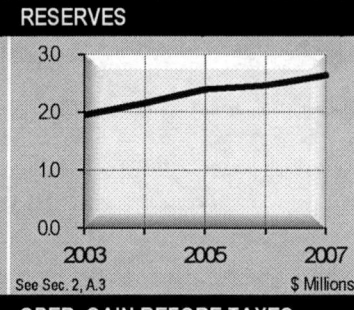
See Sec. 2, A.3 — $ Millions

NET INCOME
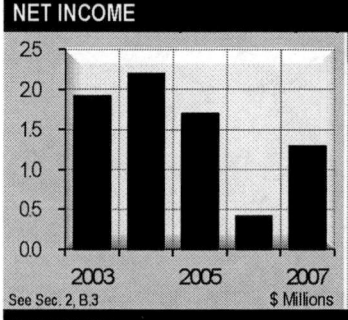
See Sec. 2, B.3 — $ Millions

NET INVESTMENT GAIN
NET REALIZED CAPITAL GAINS
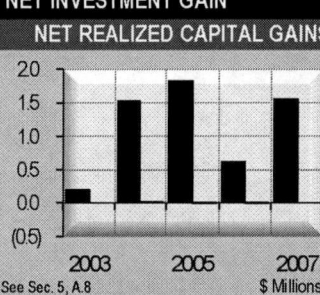
See Sec. 5, A.8 — $ Millions

NET CASH FROM OPERATIONS
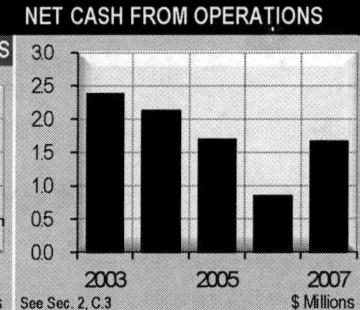
See Sec. 2, C.3 — $ Millions

OPER. GAIN BEFORE TAXES
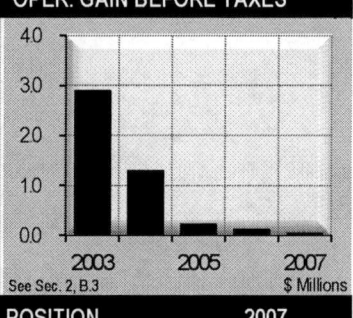
See Sec. 2, B.3 — $ Millions

PREMIUMS

Legend:
- – · – Direct
- – – Non-Affiliated
- ----- Affiliated
- —— Net Premiums

See Sec. 2, B.3 — $ Millions

OPERATING EXPENSES INCURRED
AGENT RETENTION
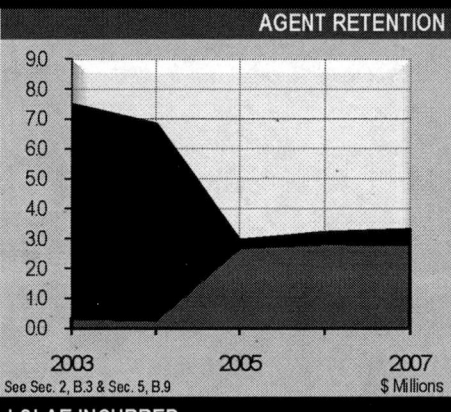
See Sec. 2, B.3 & Sec. 5, B.9 — $ Millions

DIRECT PREMIUMS WRITTEN - YE 2007

Legend:
- □ Direct
- ▨ Non-Affiliated
- ■ Affiliated

See Sec. 3, B.4

L&LAE INCURRED
LOSS RATIO

See Sec. 5, A.3 & Sec. 5, C.2 — $ Thousands

FINANCIAL POSITION 2007

Cash, Cash Equivalents & Short-Term Investments	$2,575,221
Total Assets	$14,283,946
Policyholders' Surplus	$11,507,581
Reserves	$2,633,828

OPERATING RESULTS

Net Income	$1,294,920
Net Investment Gain	$1,553,637
Net Realized Capital Gains	$0
Net Cash from Operations	$1,663,952
Oper. Gain Before Taxes	$36,641

UNDERWRITING RESULTS

Direct	$26,366
Non-Affiliated	$546,233
Affiliated	$2,917,327
Direct Premiums Written	$3,489,926
Net Premiums Earned	$3,338,923
Operating Expenses Incurred	$3,302,317
Agent Retention	$2,815,249
L&LAE Incurred	$127,491
Loss Ratio	3.82%

American Land and Aircraft Title Company

Six NE 63rd St., Ste. 100
Oklahoma City, OK 73105

(405) 359-9472

WEBSITE:	STATE OF DOMICILE:
www.alatc.com	Oklahoma

PRESIDENT:	ESTABLISHED:	JURISDICTION LICENSE(S):
Larry Dwain Witt	6/24/1998	1

S Substantial
Financial Stability Rating®
⚭ Demotech, Inc.

NAIC Number:
11450

AMERICAN LAND & AIRCRAFT

NAIC Group:
UNAFFILIATED

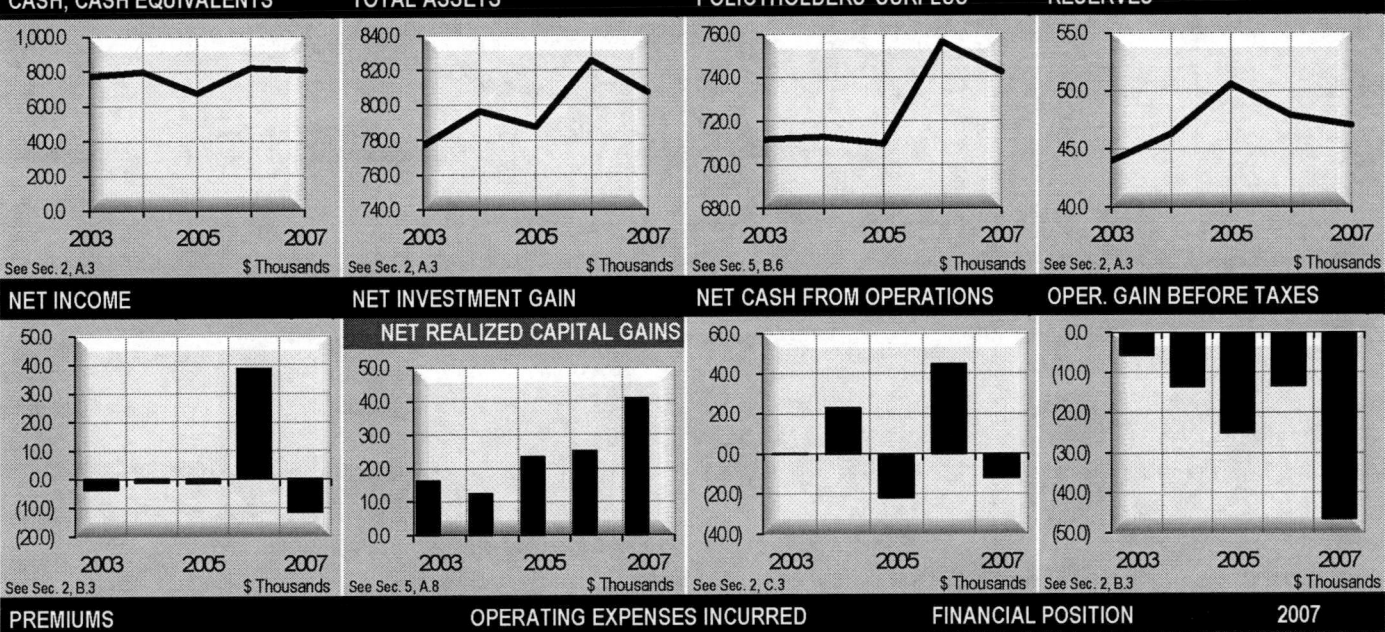

CASH, CASH EQUIVALENTS — See Sec. 2, A.3 — $ Thousands
TOTAL ASSETS — See Sec. 2, A.3 — $ Thousands
POLICYHOLDERS' SURPLUS — See Sec. 5, B.6 — $ Thousands
RESERVES — See Sec. 2, A.3 — $ Thousands

NET INCOME — See Sec. 2, B.3 — $ Thousands
NET INVESTMENT GAIN / NET REALIZED CAPITAL GAINS — See Sec. 5, A.8 — $ Thousands
NET CASH FROM OPERATIONS — See Sec. 2, C.3 — $ Thousands
OPER. GAIN BEFORE TAXES — See Sec. 2, B.3 — $ Thousands

PREMIUMS
- · - Direct
- - - - Affiliated
- - - Non-Affiliated
— Net Premiums
See Sec. 2, B.3 — $ Millions

OPERATING EXPENSES INCURRED / AGENT RETENTION — See Sec. 2, B.3 & Sec. 5, B.9 — $ Millions

FINANCIAL POSITION	2007
Cash, Cash Equivalents & Short-Term Investments	$804,060
Total Assets	$807,348
Policyholders' Surplus	$742,516
Reserves	$47,015
OPERATING RESULTS	
Net Income	($11,584)
Net Investment Gain	$40,829
Net Realized Capital Gains	$0
Net Cash from Operations	($12,279)
Oper. Gain Before Taxes	($46,555)

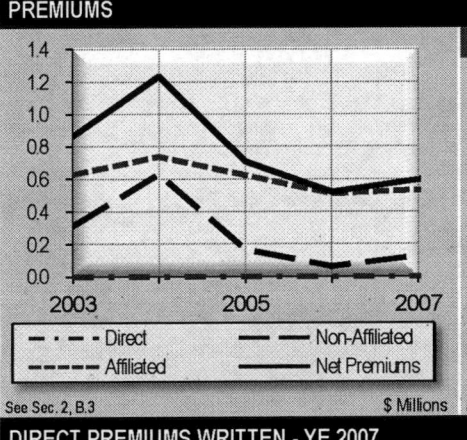

DIRECT PREMIUMS WRITTEN - YE 2007
☐ Direct ■ Non-Affiliated ■ Affiliated
See Sec. 3, B.4

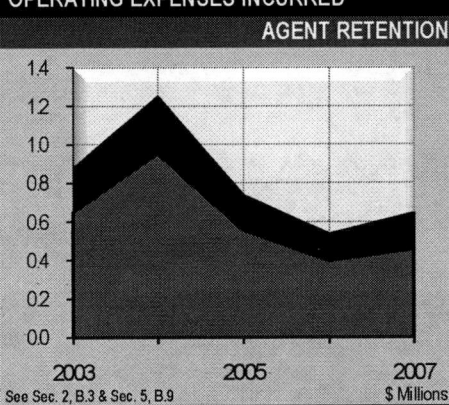

L&LAE INCURRED / LOSS RATIO — See Sec. 5, A.3 & Sec. 5, C.2 — $ Thousands

UNDERWRITING RESULTS	
Direct	$0
Non-Affiliated	$126,906
Affiliated	$532,250
Direct Premiums Written	$659,156
Net Premiums Earned	$594,713
Operating Expenses Incurred	$641,622
Agent Retention	$458,218
L&LAE Incurred	$5,858
Loss Ratio	0.99%

6

American Security Title Insurance Company

1000 W 15th St
Edmond, OK 73013

(405) 348-1248

WEBSITE:	STATE OF DOMICILE:	
–	Oklahoma	
PRESIDENT:	**ESTABLISHED:**	**JURISDICTION LICENSE(S):**
Steve Dale Raimes	6/28/1978	1

A' Unsurpassed
Financial Stability Rating®
Demotech, Inc.

NAIC Number:
51365

AMERICAN SECURITY

NAIC Group:
UNAFFILIATED

CASH, CASH EQUIVALENTS

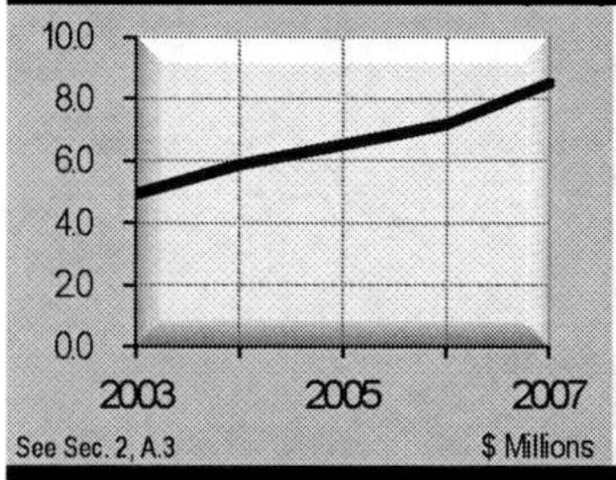
10.0
8.0
6.0
4.0
2.0
0.0
2003
2005
2007

See Sec. 2, A.3 $ Millions

TOTAL ASSETS

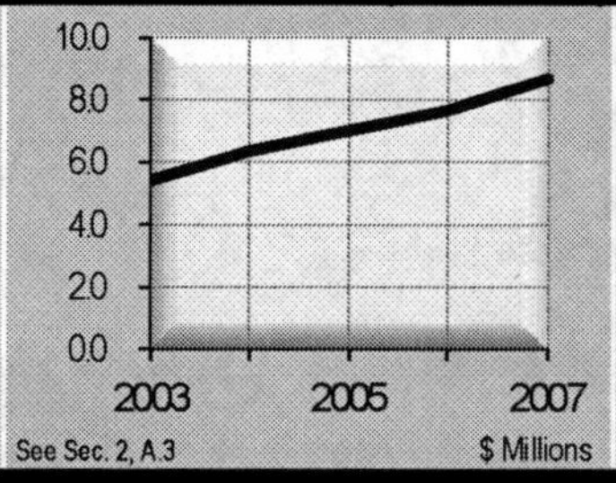
10.0
8.0
6.0
4.0
2.0
0.0
2003
2005
2007

See Sec. 2, A.3 $ Millions

POLICYHOLDERS' SURPLUS

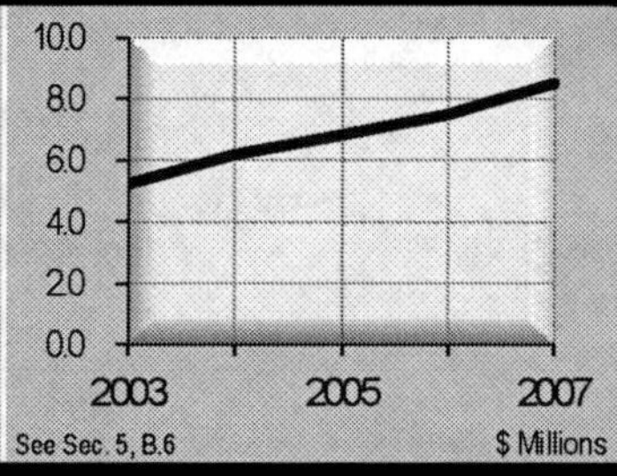
10.0
8.0
6.0
4.0
2.0
0.0
2003
2005
2007

See Sec. 5, B.6 $ Millions

RESERVES

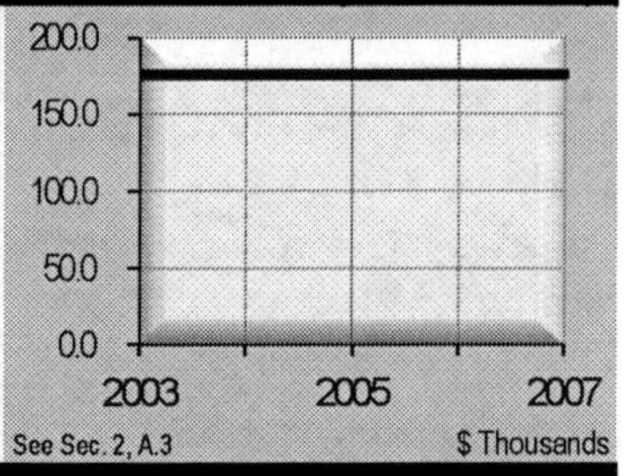
200.0
150.0
100.0
50.0
0.0
2003
2005
2007

See Sec. 2, A.3 $ Thousands

NET INCOME

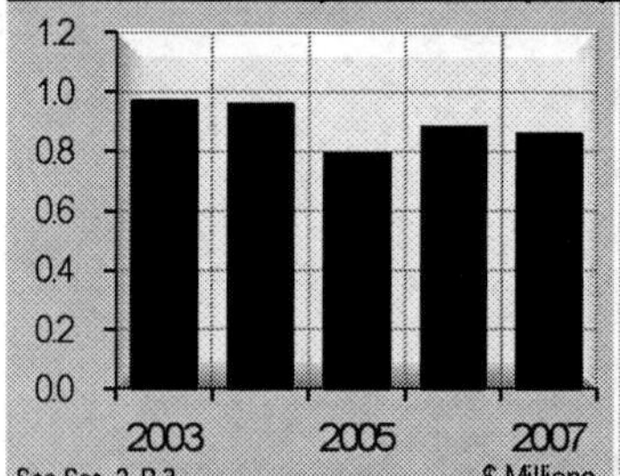
1.2
1.0
0.8
0.6
0.4
0.2
0.0
2003
2005
2007

See Sec. 2, B.3 $ Millions

NET INVESTMENT GAIN

NET REALIZED CAPITAL GAINS

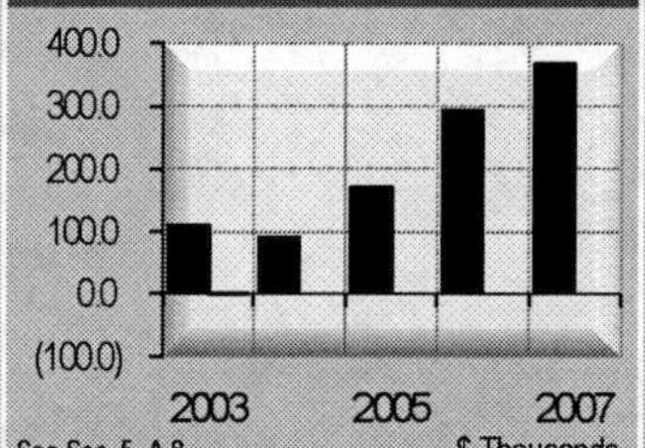
400.0
300.0
200.0
100.0
0.0
(100.0)
2003
2005
2007

See Sec. 5, A.8 $ Thousands

NET CASH FROM OPERATIONS

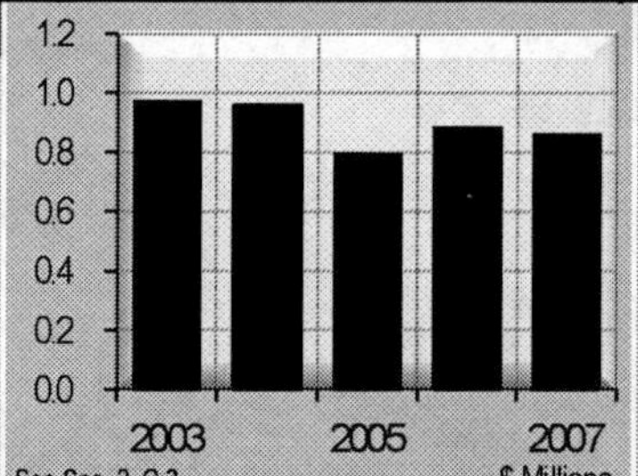
1.2
1.0
0.8
0.6
0.4
0.2
0.0
2003
2005
2007

See Sec. 2, C.3 $ Millions

OPER. GAIN BEFORE TAXES

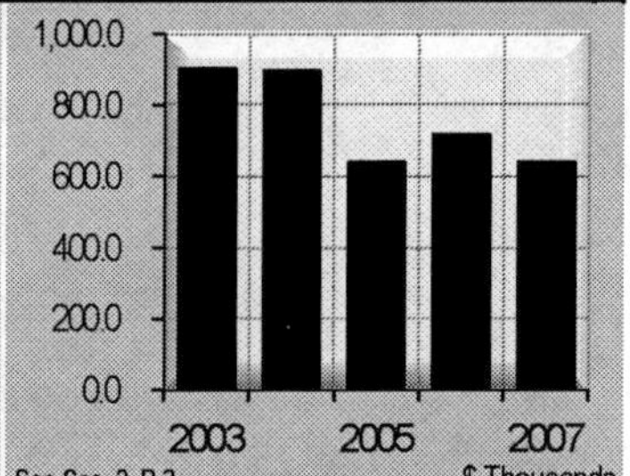
1,000.0
800.0
600.0
400.0
200.0
0.0
2003
2005
2007

See Sec. 2, B.3 $ Thousands

PREMIUMS

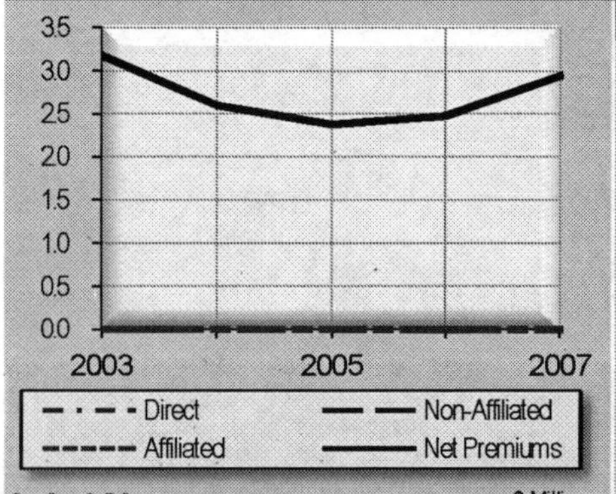
3.5
3.0
2.5
2.0
1.5
1.0
0.5
0.0
2003
2005
2007
Direct
Non-Affiliated
Affiliated
Net Premiums

See Sec. 2, B.3 $ Millions

OPERATING EXPENSES INCURRED

AGENT RETENTION

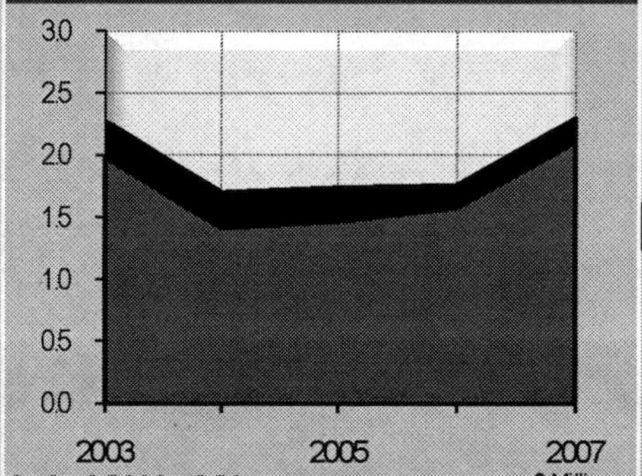
3.0
2.5
2.0
1.5
1.0
0.5
0.0
2003
2005
2007

See Sec. 2, B.3 & Sec. 5, B.9 $ Millions

FINANCIAL POSITION	2007
Cash, Cash Equivalents & Short-Term Investments	$8,480,294
Total Assets	$8,680,479
Policyholders' Surplus	$8,504,479
Reserves	$176,000
OPERATING RESULTS	
Net Income	$859,223
Net Investment Gain	$367,143
Net Realized Capital Gains	$0
Net Cash from Operations	$859,223
Oper. Gain Before Taxes	$640,585

DIRECT PREMIUMS WRITTEN - YE 2007

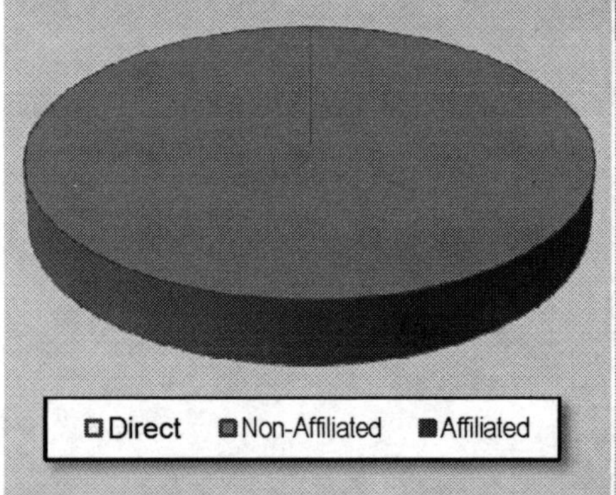
Direct
Non-Affiliated
Affiliated

See Sec. 3, B.4

L&LAE INCURRED

LOSS RATIO

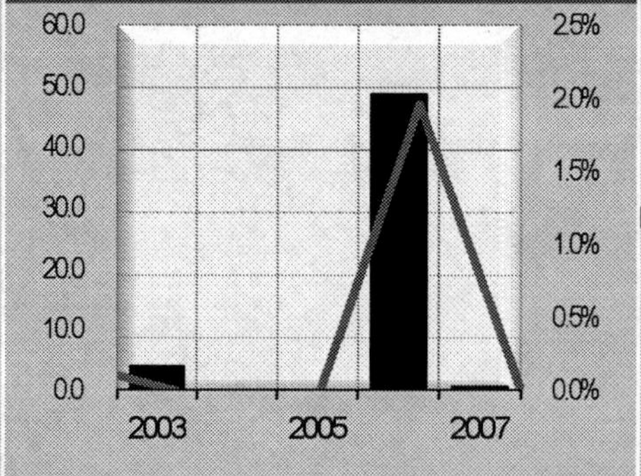
60.0
50.0
40.0
30.0
20.0
10.0
0.0
2003
2005
2007
2.5%
2.0%
1.5%
1.0%
0.5%
0.0%

See Sec. 5, A.3 & Sec. 5, C.2 $ Thousands

UNDERWRITING RESULTS	
Direct	$0
Non-Affiliated	$2,940,198
Affiliated	$0
Direct Premiums Written	**$2,940,198**
Net Premiums Earned	$2,940,198
Operating Expenses Incurred	$2,300,113
Agent Retention	$2,106,598
L&LAE Incurred	$2,283
Loss Ratio	0.08%

Arkansas Title Insurance Company

17300 Chenal Pkwy.
Little Rock, AR 72223

(501) 228-8200

WEBSITE:	STATE OF DOMICILE:
www.arkansastitle.com	Arkansas

CHIEF EXECUTIVE OFFICER:	ESTABLISHED:	JURISDICTION LICENSE(S):
Don A. Eilbott	5/3/1982	1

A" **Unsurpassed**
Financial Stability Rating®
Demotech, Inc.

NAIC Number:
50725

ARKANSAS TIC

NAIC Group:
STEWART

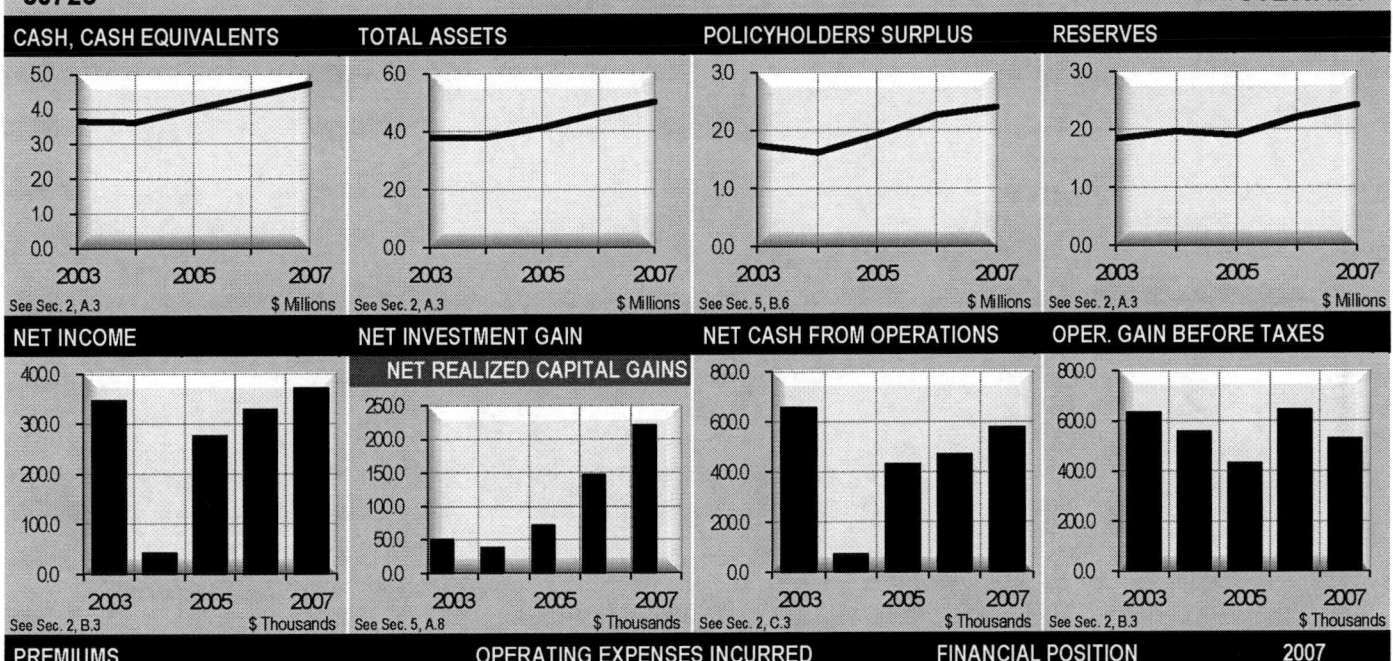

CASH, CASH EQUIVALENTS — See Sec. 2, A.3 — $ Millions
TOTAL ASSETS — See Sec. 2, A.3 — $ Millions
POLICYHOLDERS' SURPLUS — See Sec. 5, B.6 — $ Millions
RESERVES — See Sec. 2, A.3 — $ Millions

NET INCOME — See Sec. 2, B.3 — $ Thousands
NET INVESTMENT GAIN / NET REALIZED CAPITAL GAINS — See Sec. 5, A.8 — $ Thousands
NET CASH FROM OPERATIONS — See Sec. 2, C.3 — $ Thousands
OPER. GAIN BEFORE TAXES — See Sec. 2, B.3 — $ Thousands

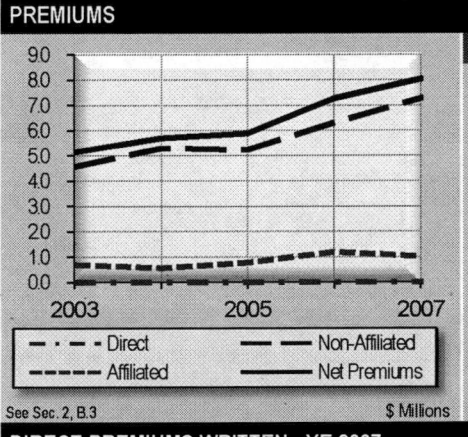

PREMIUMS — See Sec. 2, B.3 — $ Millions
- - - Direct
—— Non-Affiliated
----- Affiliated
—— Net Premiums

OPERATING EXPENSES INCURRED / AGENT RETENTION — See Sec. 2, B.3 & Sec. 5, B.9 — $ Millions

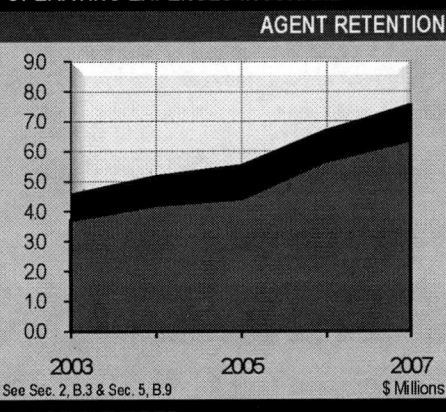

DIRECT PREMIUMS WRITTEN - YE 2007 — See Sec. 3, B.4
□ Direct ■ Non-Affiliated ■ Affiliated

L&LAE INCURRED / LOSS RATIO — See Sec. 5, A.3 & Sec. 5, C.2 — $ Thousands

FINANCIAL POSITION	2007
Cash, Cash Equivalents & Short-Term Investments	$4,708,359
Total Assets	$4,989,285
Policyholders' Surplus	$2,388,523
Reserves	$2,409,720
OPERATING RESULTS	
Net Income	$371,309
Net Investment Gain	$220,890
Net Realized Capital Gains	$0
Net Cash from Operations	$579,126
Oper. Gain Before Taxes	$529,733
UNDERWRITING RESULTS	
Direct	$0
Non-Affiliated	$7,269,128
Affiliated	$1,017,272
Direct Premiums Written	$8,286,400
Net Premiums Earned	$8,026,817
Operating Expenses Incurred	$7,549,382
Agent Retention	$6,364,268
L&LAE Incurred	$155,822
Loss Ratio	1.93%

6

Arsenal Insurance Corporation

11711 N Pennsylvania St.
Ste. 110
Carmel, IN 46032

(317) 571-3319

WEBSITE:	STATE OF DOMICILE:
www.arsenalins.com	Indiana

PRESIDENT:	ESTABLISHED:	JURISDICTION LICENSE(S):
Andrew R. Drake	8/15/2003	1

S Substantial
Financial Stability Rating®
Demotech, Inc.

NAIC Number: **11865**

ARSENAL

NAIC Group: **UNAFFILIATED**

CASH, CASH EQUIVALENTS
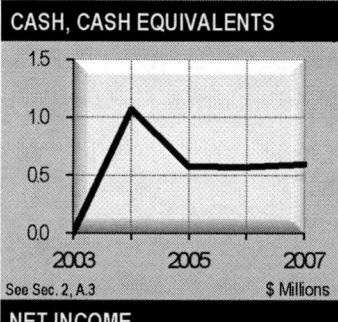
See Sec. 2, A.3 — $ Millions

TOTAL ASSETS
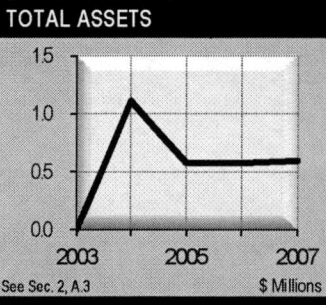
See Sec. 2, A.3 — $ Millions

POLICYHOLDERS' SURPLUS
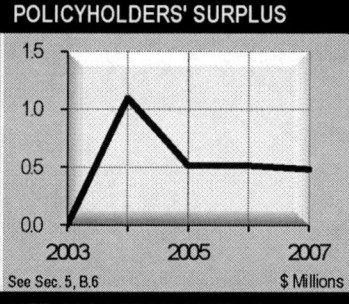
See Sec. 5, B.6 — $ Millions

RESERVES
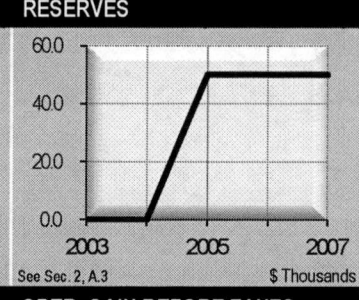
See Sec. 2, A.3 — $ Thousands

NET INCOME
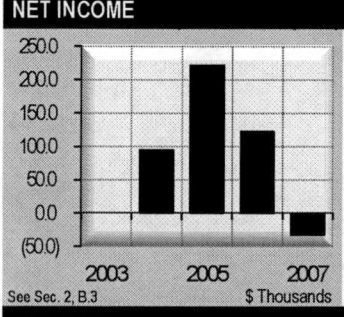
See Sec. 2, B.3 — $ Thousands

NET INVESTMENT GAIN / NET REALIZED CAPITAL GAINS
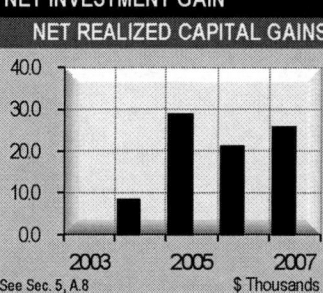
See Sec. 5, A.8 — $ Thousands

NET CASH FROM OPERATIONS
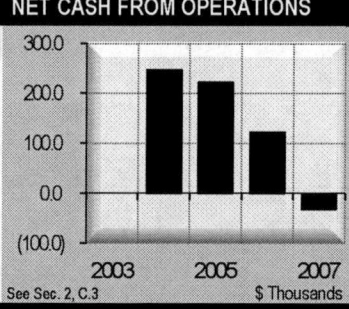
See Sec. 2, C.3 — $ Thousands

OPER. GAIN BEFORE TAXES
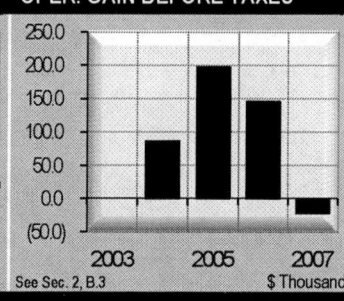
See Sec. 2, B.3 — $ Thousands

PREMIUMS
See Sec. 2, B.3 — $ Millions

- – · – Direct
- – – Non-Affiliated
- ----- Affiliated
- —— Net Premiums

OPERATING EXPENSES INCURRED / AGENT RETENTION
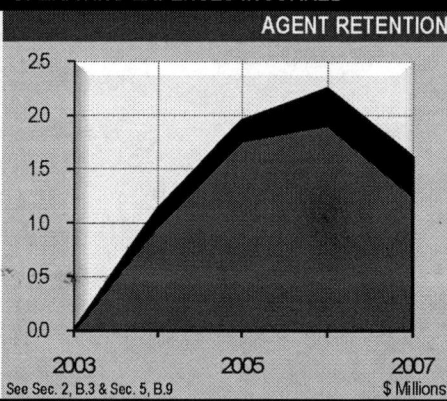
See Sec. 2, B.3 & Sec. 5, B.9 — $ Millions

DIRECT PREMIUMS WRITTEN - YE 2007
See Sec. 3, B.4

☐ Direct ▨ Non-Affiliated ■ Affiliated

L&LAE INCURRED / LOSS RATIO
See Sec. 5, A.3 & Sec. 5, C.2 — $ Thousands

FINANCIAL POSITION 2007

Cash, Cash Equivalents & Short-Term Investments	$593,238
Total Assets	$593,745
Policyholders' Surplus	$484,161
Reserves	$50,000

OPERATING RESULTS

Net Income	($32,766)
Net Investment Gain	$25,816
Net Realized Capital Gains	$0
Net Cash from Operations	($32,117)
Oper. Gain Before Taxes	($21,635)

UNDERWRITING RESULTS

Direct	$0
Non-Affiliated	$1,583,908
Affiliated	$0
Direct Premiums Written	$1,583,908
Net Premiums Earned	$1,583,908
Operating Expenses Incurred	$1,610,858
Agent Retention	$1,253,313
L&LAE Incurred	$649
Loss Ratio	0.04%

6

Attorneys' Title Guaranty Fund, Inc. (CO)

999 18th St., Ste. 1101
Denver, CO 80202

(303) 292-3055

WEBSITE:	STATE OF DOMICILE:
www.atgf.net	Colorado

PRESIDENT:	ESTABLISHED:	JURISDICTION LICENSE(S):
Christopher J. Condie	10/11/1960	2

S Substantial
Financial Stability Rating®
⬦ Demotech, Inc.

NAIC Number:
51560

ATTORNEYS TGF (CO)

NAIC Group:
ATTORNEYS' TITLE

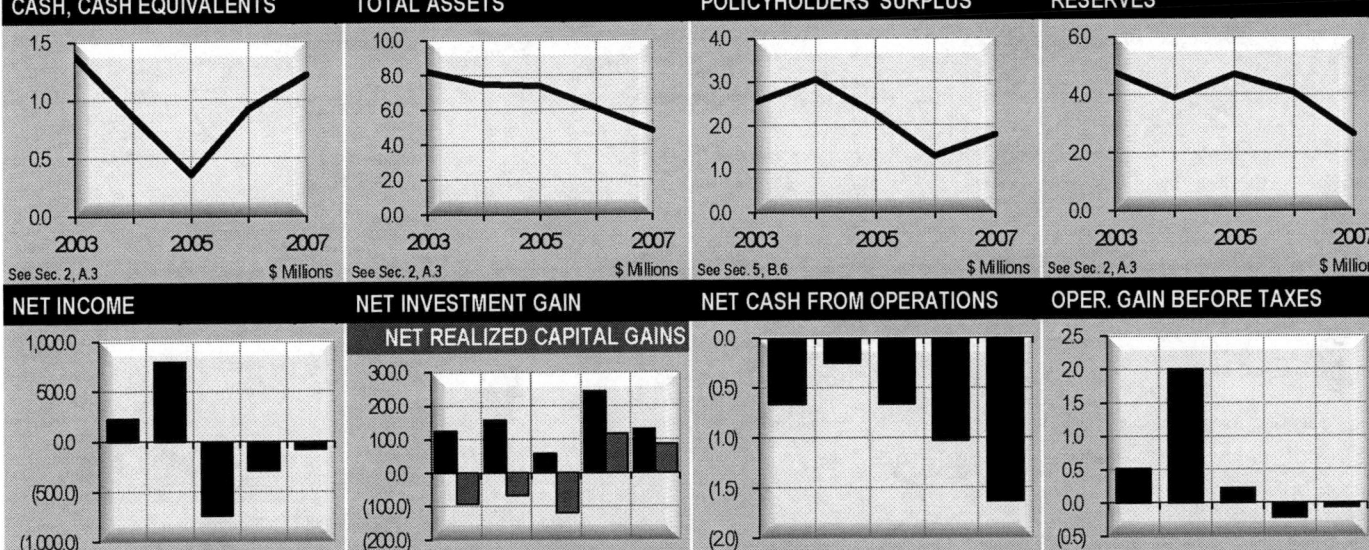

CASH, CASH EQUIVALENTS — See Sec. 2, A.3 — $ Millions
TOTAL ASSETS — See Sec. 2, A.3 — $ Millions
POLICYHOLDERS' SURPLUS — See Sec. 5, B.6 — $ Millions
RESERVES — See Sec. 2, A.3 — $ Millions

NET INCOME — See Sec. 2, B.3 — $ Thousands
NET INVESTMENT GAIN / NET REALIZED CAPITAL GAINS — See Sec. 5, A.8 — $ Thousands
NET CASH FROM OPERATIONS — See Sec. 2, C.3 — $ Millions
OPER. GAIN BEFORE TAXES — See Sec. 2, B.3 — $ Millions

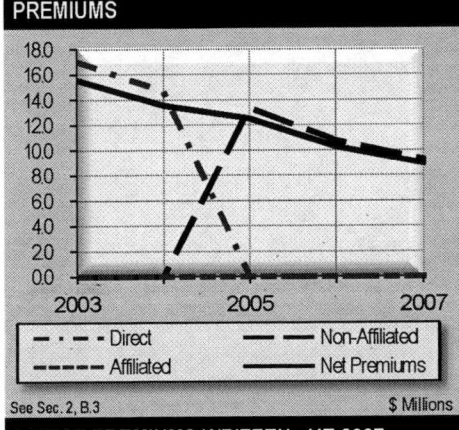

PREMIUMS
- – · – Direct
- – – – Affiliated
- – – Non-Affiliated
- —— Net Premiums

See Sec. 2, B.3 — $ Millions

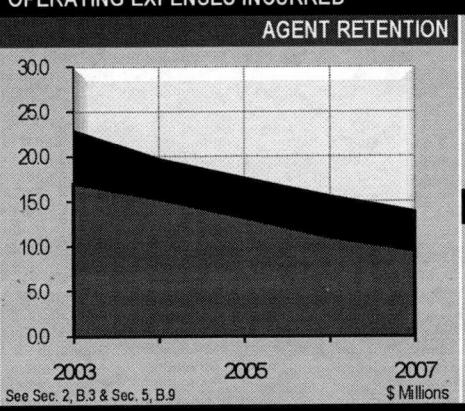

OPERATING EXPENSES INCURRED / AGENT RETENTION
See Sec. 2, B.3 & Sec. 5, B.9 — $ Millions

FINANCIAL POSITION	2007
Cash, Cash Equivalents & Short-Term Investments	$1,214,186
Total Assets	$4,805,463
Policyholders' Surplus	$1,776,152
Reserves	$2,631,645
OPERATING RESULTS	
Net Income	($77,762)
Net Investment Gain	$131,057
Net Realized Capital Gains	$85,805
Net Cash from Operations	($1,637,369)
Oper. Gain Before Taxes	($68,599)

DIRECT PREMIUMS WRITTEN - YE 2007
□ Direct ■ Non-Affiliated ■ Affiliated
See Sec. 3, B.4

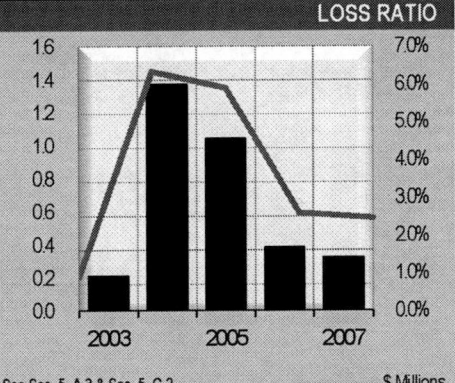

L&LAE INCURRED / LOSS RATIO
See Sec. 5, A.3 & Sec. 5, C.2 — $ Millions

UNDERWRITING RESULTS	
Direct	$0
Non-Affiliated	$9,268,076
Affiliated	$0
Direct Premiums Written	$9,268,076
Net Premiums Earned	$8,935,625
Operating Expenses Incurred	$13,860,124
Agent Retention	$9,549,160
L&LAE Incurred	$357,311
Loss Ratio	2.59%

6

Attorneys' Title Guaranty Fund, Inc. (IL)

2408 Windsor Pl.
Champaign, IL 61820

(217) 359-2000

WEBSITE:	STATE OF DOMICILE:
www.atgf.com	Illinois

PRESIDENT:	ESTABLISHED:	JURISDICTION LICENSE(S):
Peter J. Birnbaum	8/5/1987	3

A' Unsurpassed
Financial Stability Rating®
Demotech, Inc.

NAIC Number: **50004**

ATTORNEYS TGF (IL)

NAIC Group: **UNAFFILIATED**

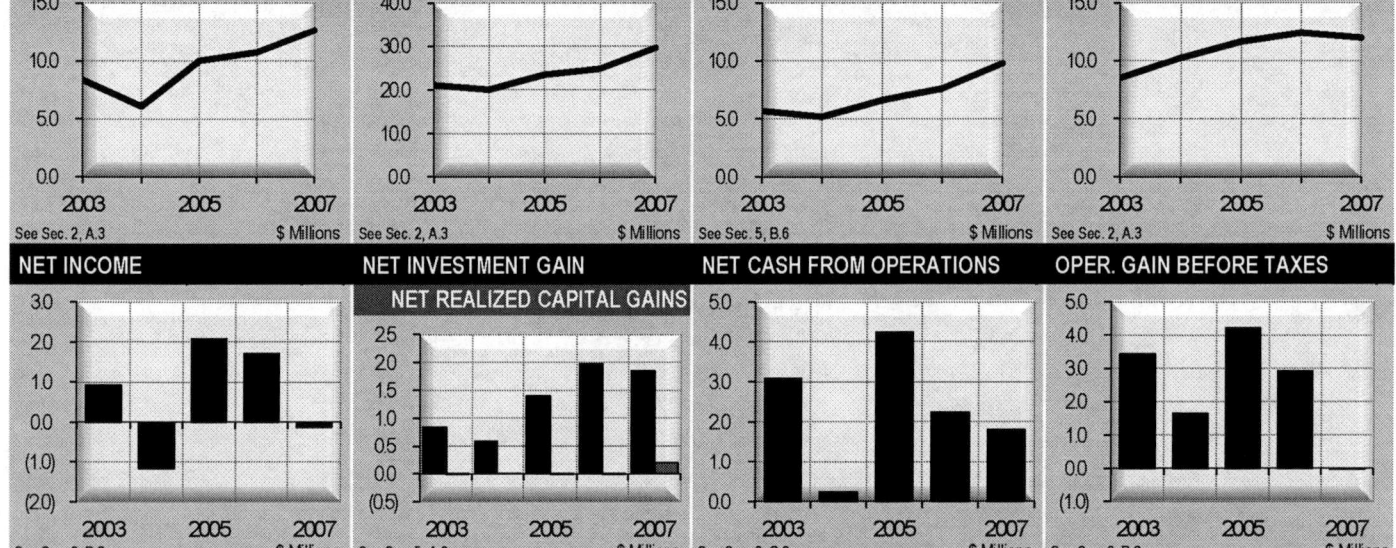

CASH, CASH EQUIVALENTS — See Sec. 2, A.3 — $ Millions

TOTAL ASSETS — See Sec. 2, A.3 — $ Millions

POLICYHOLDERS' SURPLUS — See Sec. 5, B.6 — $ Millions

RESERVES — See Sec. 2, A.3 — $ Millions

NET INCOME — See Sec. 2, B.3 — $ Millions

NET INVESTMENT GAIN / NET REALIZED CAPITAL GAINS — See Sec. 5, A.8 — $ Millions

NET CASH FROM OPERATIONS — See Sec. 2, C.3 — $ Millions

OPER. GAIN BEFORE TAXES — See Sec. 2, B.3 — $ Millions

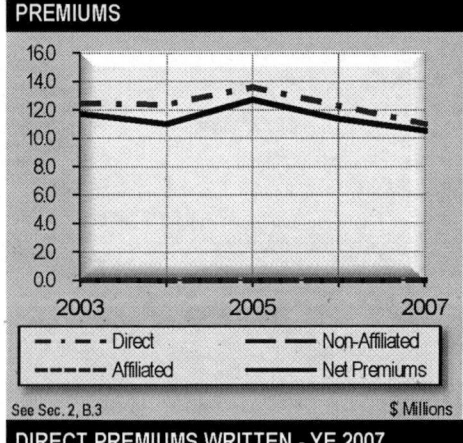

PREMIUMS — See Sec. 2, B.3 — $ Millions

- – · – Direct
- – – Non-Affiliated
- - - - Affiliated
- —— Net Premiums

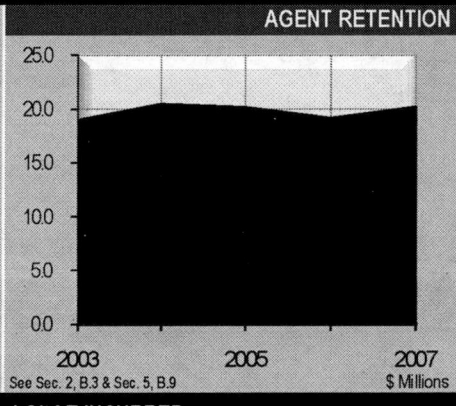

OPERATING EXPENSES INCURRED / AGENT RETENTION — See Sec. 2, B.3 & Sec. 5, B.9 — $ Millions

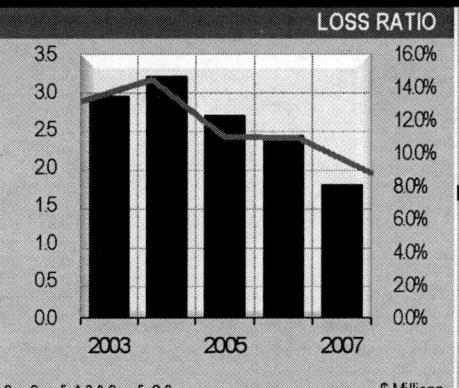

DIRECT PREMIUMS WRITTEN - YE 2007 — See Sec. 3, B.4

☐ Direct ■ Non-Affiliated ■ Affiliated

L&LAE INCURRED / LOSS RATIO — See Sec. 5, A.3 & Sec. 5, C.2 — $ Millions

FINANCIAL POSITION 2007

Cash, Cash Equivalents & Short-Term Investments	$12,615,446
Total Assets	$29,638,980
Policyholders' Surplus	$9,754,476
Reserves	$11,981,000

OPERATING RESULTS

Net Income	($130,643)
Net Investment Gain	$1,851,949
Net Realized Capital Gains	$194,964
Net Cash from Operations	$1,802,042
Oper. Gain Before Taxes	($7,140)

UNDERWRITING RESULTS

Direct	$10,998,779
Non-Affiliated	$0
Affiliated	$0
Direct Premiums Written	**$10,998,779**
Net Premiums Earned	$10,535,492
Operating Expenses Incurred	$20,168,882
Agent Retention	$0
L&LAE Incurred	$1,811,083
Loss Ratio	8.98%

Attorneys' Title Insurance Fund, Inc. (FL)

6545 Corporate Centre Blvd.
Orlando, FL 32822

(407) 240-3863
Doing Business in Illinois as The Florida Fund

WEBSITE:	STATE OF DOMICILE:
www.thefund.com	Florida

PRESIDENT:	ESTABLISHED:	JURISDICTION LICENSE(S):
Charles James Kovaleski	11/21/1985	13

A" Unsurpassed
Financial Stability Rating®
Demotech, Inc.

NAIC Number:
50687

ATTORNEYS TIF (FL)

NAIC Group:
ATTORNEYS' TITLE

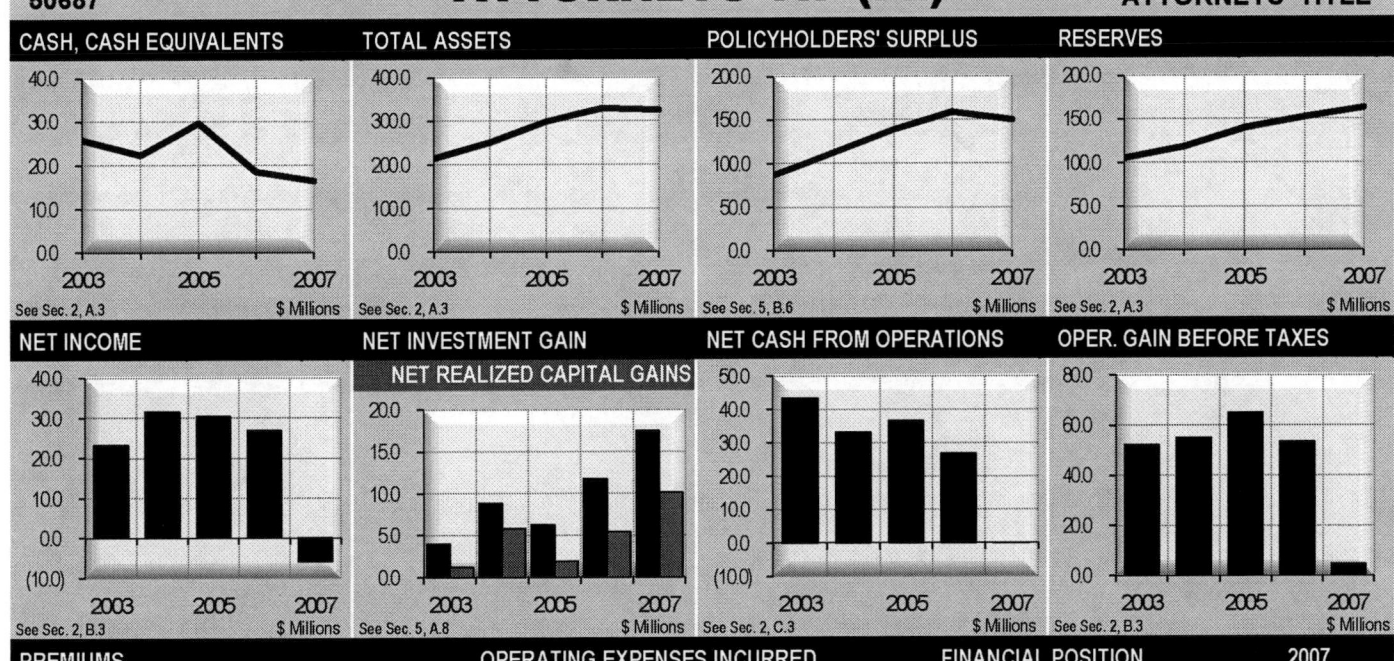

CASH, CASH EQUIVALENTS	See Sec. 2, A.3 — $ Millions	
TOTAL ASSETS	See Sec. 2, A.3 — $ Millions	
POLICYHOLDERS' SURPLUS	See Sec. 5, B.6 — $ Millions	
RESERVES	See Sec. 2, A.3 — $ Millions	
NET INCOME	See Sec. 2, B.3 — $ Millions	
NET INVESTMENT GAIN / NET REALIZED CAPITAL GAINS	See Sec. 5, A.8 — $ Millions	
NET CASH FROM OPERATIONS	See Sec. 2, C.3 — $ Millions	
OPER. GAIN BEFORE TAXES	See Sec. 2, B.3 — $ Millions	

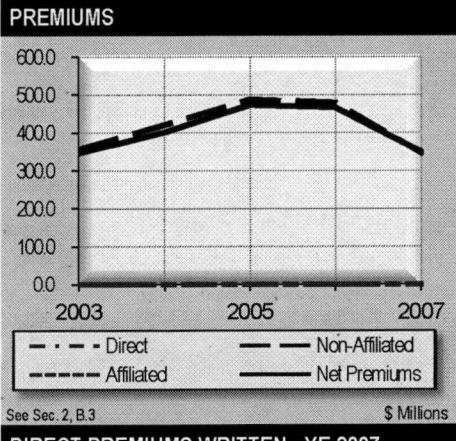

PREMIUMS

- · - Direct
- - - - Affiliated
- —— Non-Affiliated
- —— Net Premiums

See Sec. 2, B.3 — $ Millions

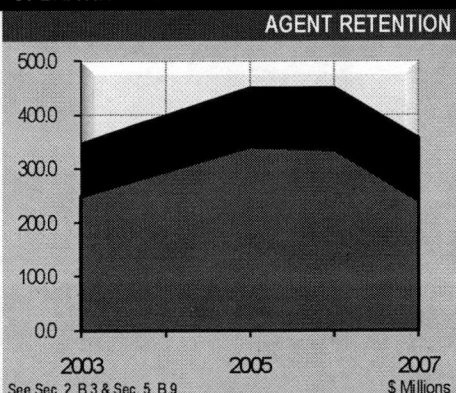

OPERATING EXPENSES INCURRED

AGENT RETENTION

See Sec. 2, B.3 & Sec. 5, B.9 — $ Millions

DIRECT PREMIUMS WRITTEN - YE 2007

□ Direct   ■ Non-Affiliated   ■ Affiliated

See Sec. 3, B.4

L&LAE INCURRED

LOSS RATIO

See Sec. 5, A.3 & Sec. 5, C.2 — $ Millions

FINANCIAL POSITION — 2007

Cash, Cash Equivalents & Short-Term Investments	$16,401,367
Total Assets	$324,304,826
Policyholders' Surplus	$149,827,744
Reserves	$162,730,430

OPERATING RESULTS

Net Income	($5,840,823)
Net Investment Gain	$17,478,061
Net Realized Capital Gains	$10,177,378
Net Cash from Operations	($71,071)
Oper. Gain Before Taxes	$4,791,933

UNDERWRITING RESULTS

Direct	$0
Non-Affiliated	$345,841,353
Affiliated	$0
Direct Premiums Written	$345,841,353
Net Premiums Earned	$349,759,615
Operating Expenses Incurred	$355,763,865
Agent Retention	$241,203,949
L&LAE Incurred	$44,278,625
Loss Ratio	12.28%

6

Bridge Title Insurance Company

7777 Washington Ave. S
Edina, MN 55439

(800) 854-3643

Formerly First American Title Insurance Company of North Carolina

WEBSITE:	STATE OF DOMICILE:
www.firstam.com	California

PRESIDENT:	ESTABLISHED:	JURISDICTION LICENSE(S):
Melville Roma Bois	11/21/1962	8

A' A Prime **Unsurpassed**
Financial Stability Rating®
Demotech, Inc.

NAIC Number:
50008

BRIDGE

NAIC Group:
FIRST AMERICAN

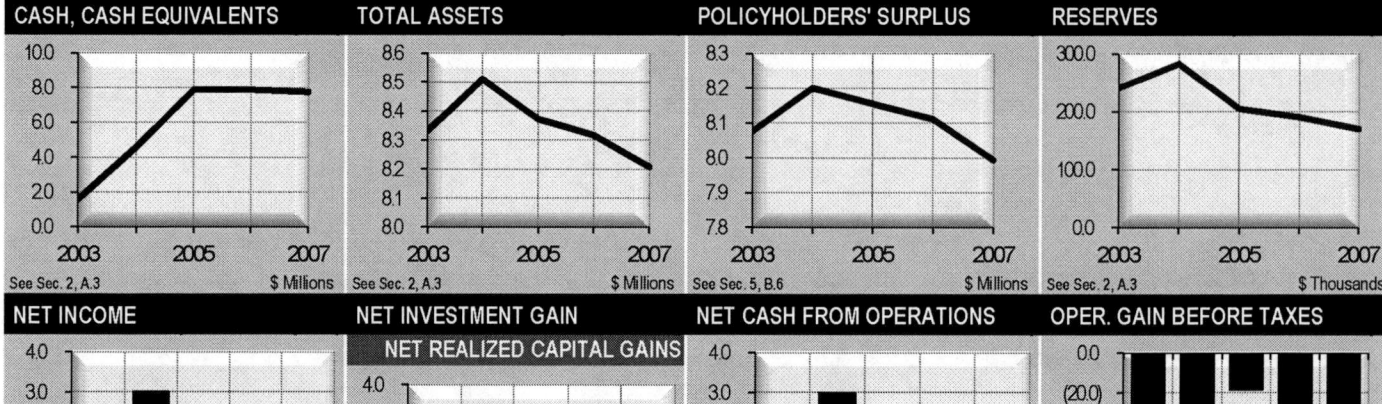

CASH, CASH EQUIVALENTS — See Sec. 2, A.3 — $ Millions
TOTAL ASSETS — See Sec. 2, A.3 — $ Millions
POLICYHOLDERS' SURPLUS — See Sec. 5, B.6 — $ Millions
RESERVES — See Sec. 2, A.3 — $ Thousands

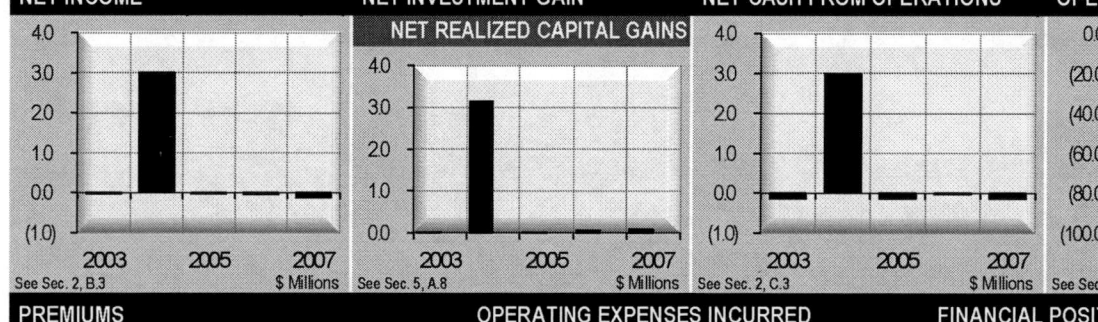

NET INCOME — See Sec. 2, B.3 — $ Millions
NET INVESTMENT GAIN / NET REALIZED CAPITAL GAINS — See Sec. 5, A.8 — $ Millions
NET CASH FROM OPERATIONS — See Sec. 2, C.3 — $ Millions
OPER. GAIN BEFORE TAXES — See Sec. 2, B.3 — $ Thousands

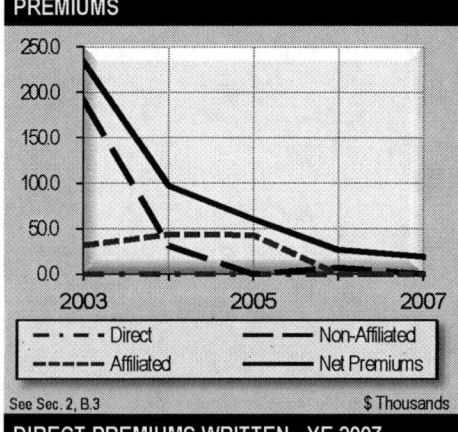

PREMIUMS
- – · – Direct
- – – Non-Affiliated
- - - - Affiliated
- —— Net Premiums

See Sec. 2, B.3 — $ Thousands

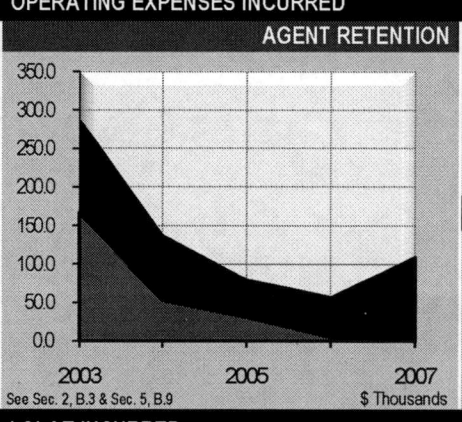

OPERATING EXPENSES INCURRED / AGENT RETENTION
See Sec. 2, B.3 & Sec. 5, B.9 — $ Thousands

FINANCIAL POSITION	2007
Cash, Cash Equivalents & Short-Term Investments	$7,739,303
Total Assets	$8,207,968
Policyholders' Surplus	$7,993,676
Reserves	$170,157
OPERATING RESULTS	
Net Income	($117,171)
Net Investment Gain	$85,682
Net Realized Capital Gains	$0
Net Cash from Operations	($144,482)
Oper. Gain Before Taxes	($89,363)

DIRECT PREMIUMS WRITTEN - YE 2007
☐ Direct ▨ Non-Affiliated ■ Affiliated
See Sec. 3, B.4

L&LAE INCURRED / LOSS RATIO
See Sec. 5, A.3 & Sec. 5, C.2 — $ Thousands

UNDERWRITING RESULTS	
Direct	$0
Non-Affiliated	$462
Affiliated	$0
Direct Premiums Written	$462
Net Premiums Earned	$19,541
Operating Expenses Incurred	$108,904
Agent Retention	$346
L&LAE Incurred	$180,404
Loss Ratio	923.21%

6

Censtar Title Insurance Company

7777 Washington Ave. S
Edina, MN 55439

(877) 774-0360

Formerly First American Title Insurance Company of Texas

WEBSITE:	STATE OF DOMICILE:
www.firstam.com	Texas

PRESIDENT:	ESTABLISHED:	JURISDICTION LICENSE(S):
Melville Roma Bois	8/28/1928	37

A" Unsurpassed
Financial Stability Rating®
Demotech, Inc.

NAIC Number:
50636

CENSTAR

NAIC Group:
FIRST AMERICAN

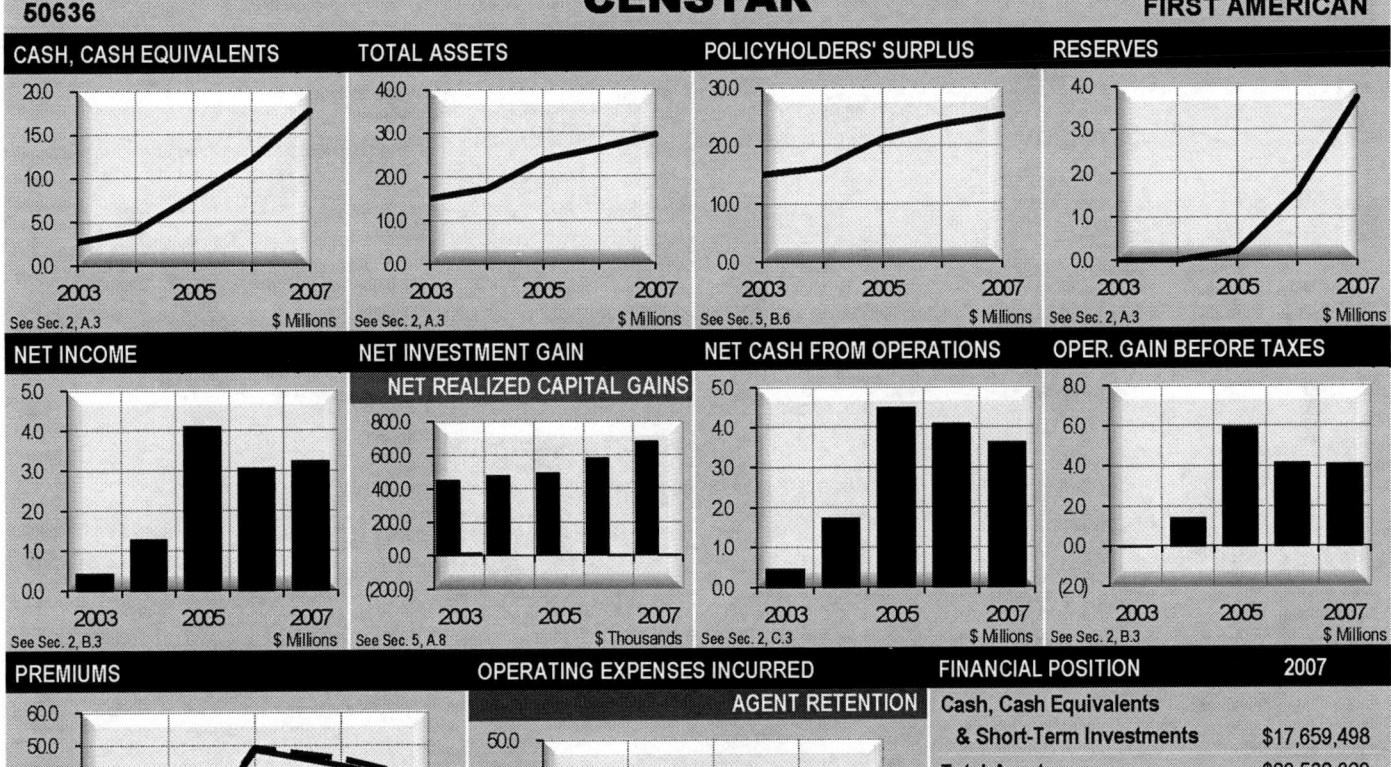

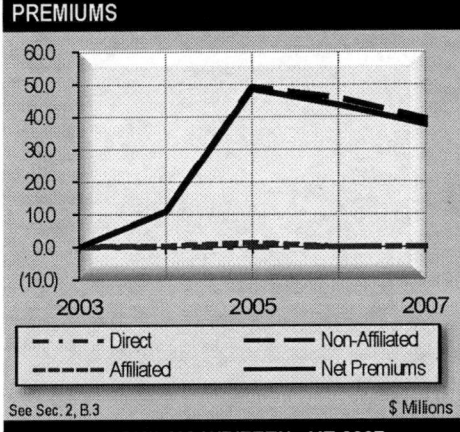

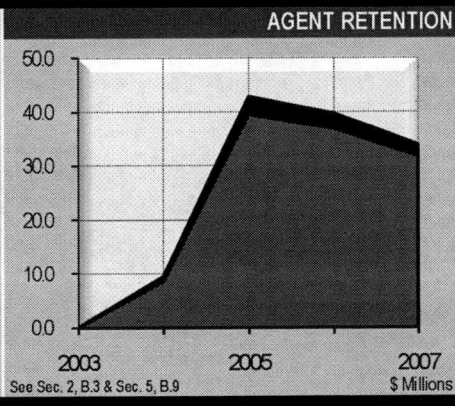

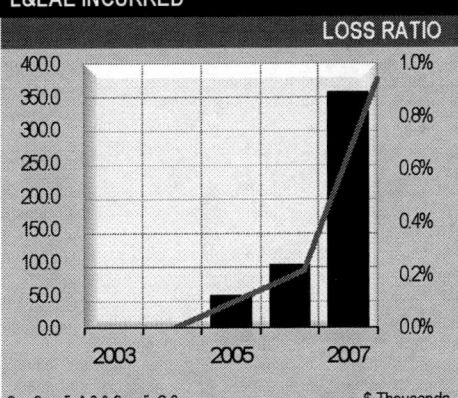

FINANCIAL POSITION	2007
Cash, Cash Equivalents & Short-Term Investments	$17,659,498
Total Assets	$29,562,039
Policyholders' Surplus	$25,141,601
Reserves	$3,715,851
OPERATING RESULTS	
Net Income	$3,233,018
Net Investment Gain	$678,399
Net Realized Capital Gains	($1,362)
Net Cash from Operations	$3,605,420
Oper. Gain Before Taxes	$4,083,122
UNDERWRITING RESULTS	
Direct	$0
Non-Affiliated	$39,460,039
Affiliated	$0
Direct Premiums Written	$39,460,039
Net Premiums Earned	$37,718,672
Operating Expenses Incurred	$33,831,989
Agent Retention	$31,798,359
L&LAE Incurred	$356,768
Loss Ratio	0.94%

6

Chicago Title and Trust Company

171 N Clark St, 8th Fl.
Chicago, IL 60601

(312) 223-2000

WEBSITE:	STATE OF DOMICILE:
www.fnf.com	Illinois

CHAIRMAN, PRESIDENT & CEO:	ESTABLISHED:	JURISDICTION LICENSE(S):
Raymond Randall Quirk	7/31/1912	1

A" Unsurpassed
A Double Prime
Financial Stability Rating®
Demotech, Inc.

NAIC Number:

CHICAGO T&T

NAIC Group:
CHICAGO / FIDELITY

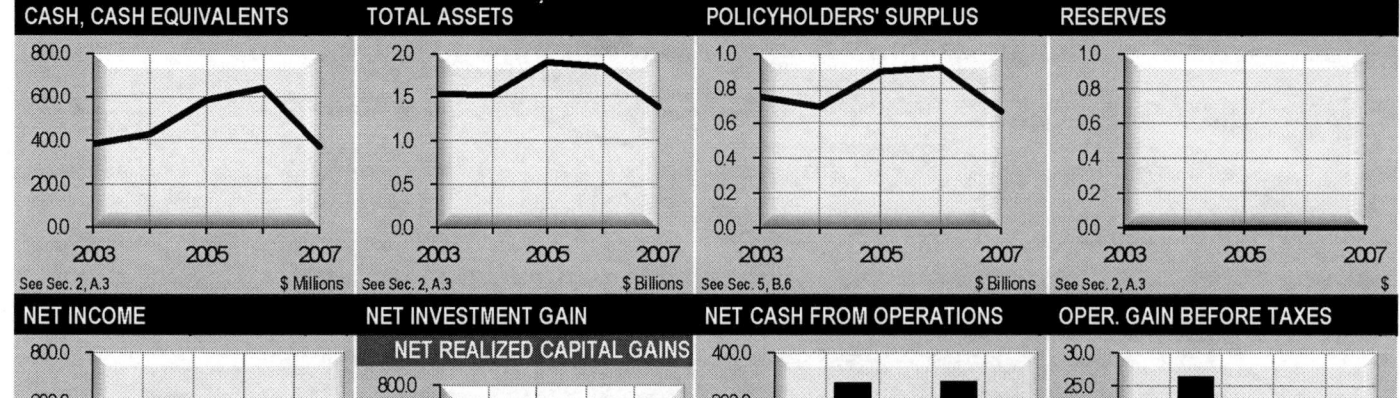

CASH, CASH EQUIVALENTS — See Sec. 2, A.3 — $ Millions
TOTAL ASSETS — See Sec. 2, A.3 — $ Billions
POLICYHOLDERS' SURPLUS — See Sec. 5, B.6 — $ Billions
RESERVES — See Sec. 2, A.3 — $

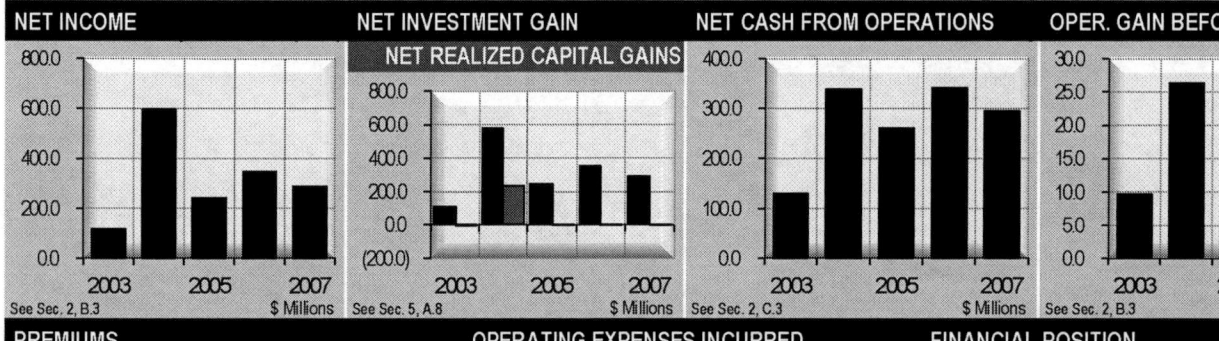

NET INCOME — See Sec. 2, B.3 — $ Millions
NET INVESTMENT GAIN / NET REALIZED CAPITAL GAINS — See Sec. 5, A.8 — $ Millions
NET CASH FROM OPERATIONS — See Sec. 2, C.3 — $ Millions
OPER. GAIN BEFORE TAXES — See Sec. 2, B.3 — $ Millions

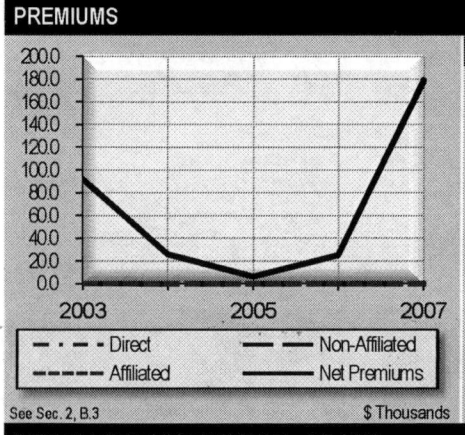

PREMIUMS
- – · – Direct
- ----- Affiliated
- – – Non-Affiliated
- —— Net Premiums

See Sec. 2, B.3 — $ Thousands

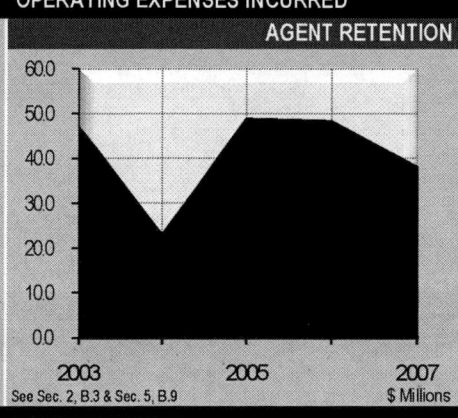

OPERATING EXPENSES INCURRED
AGENT RETENTION
See Sec. 2, B.3 & Sec. 5, B.9 — $ Millions

FINANCIAL POSITION	2007
Cash, Cash Equivalents & Short-Term Investments	$370,726,862
Total Assets	$1,387,017,999
Policyholders' Surplus	$664,634,623
Reserves	$0
OPERATING RESULTS	
Net Income	$289,913,524
Net Investment Gain	$290,488,747
Net Realized Capital Gains	$27,093
Net Cash from Operations	$294,928,496
Oper. Gain Before Taxes	$8,011,610

DIRECT PREMIUMS WRITTEN - YE 2007

□ Direct ■ Non-Affiliated ■ Affiliated

See Sec. 3, B.4

L&LAE INCURRED
LOSS RATIO
See Sec. 5, A.3 & Sec. 5, C.2 — $

UNDERWRITING RESULTS	
Direct	$0
Non-Affiliated	$0
Affiliated	$0
Direct Premiums Written	$0
Net Premiums Earned	$178,675
Operating Expenses Incurred	$38,026,337
Agent Retention	$0
L&LAE Incurred	$0
Loss Ratio	0.00%

Chicago Title Insurance Company

601 Riverside Ave.
Jacksonville, FL 32204

(904) 854-8100

WEBSITE:	STATE OF DOMICILE:
www.fnf.com	Nebraska

CHAIRMAN, PRESIDENT & CEO:	ESTABLISHED:	JURISDICTION LICENSE(S):
Raymond Randall Quirk	8/30/1961	53

A" Unsurpassed
Financial Stability Rating®
Demotech, Inc.

NAIC Number:
50229

CHICAGO TIC

NAIC Group:
CHICAGO / FIDELITY

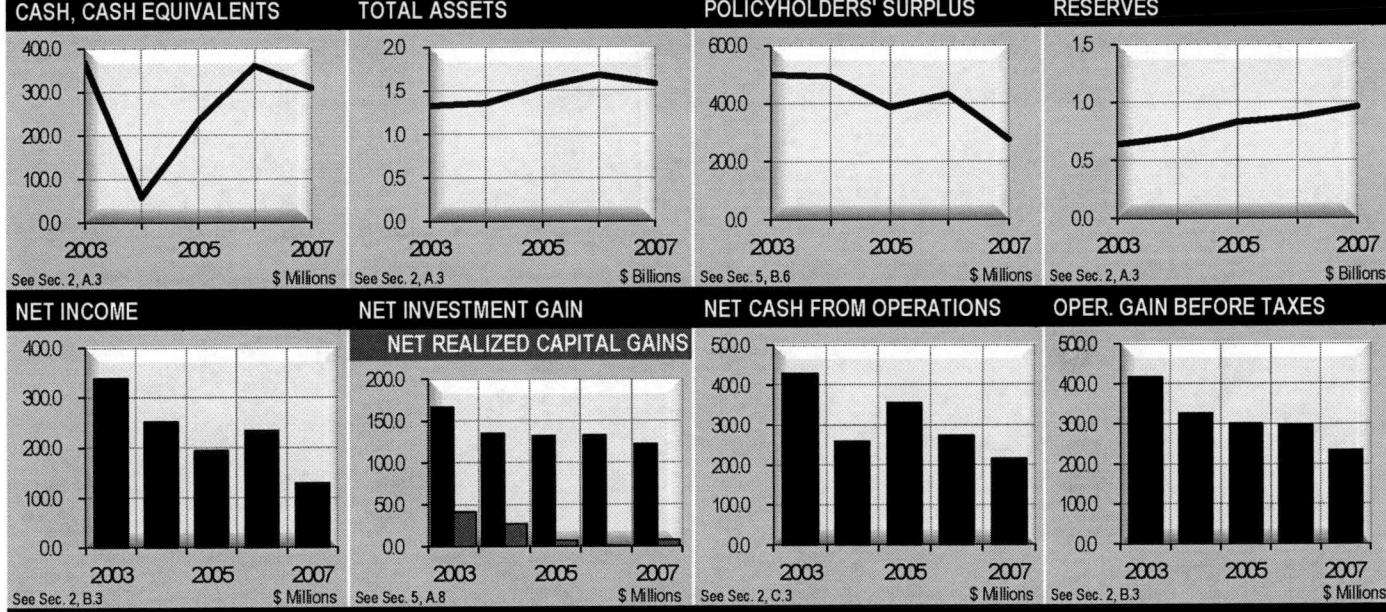

CASH, CASH EQUIVALENTS — See Sec. 2, A.3 — $ Millions
TOTAL ASSETS — See Sec. 2, A.3 — $ Billions
POLICYHOLDERS' SURPLUS — See Sec. 5, B.6 — $ Millions
RESERVES — See Sec. 2, A.3 — $ Billions

NET INCOME — See Sec. 2, B.3 — $ Millions
NET INVESTMENT GAIN / NET REALIZED CAPITAL GAINS — See Sec. 5, A.8 — $ Millions
NET CASH FROM OPERATIONS — See Sec. 2, C.3 — $ Millions
OPER. GAIN BEFORE TAXES — See Sec. 2, B.3 — $ Millions

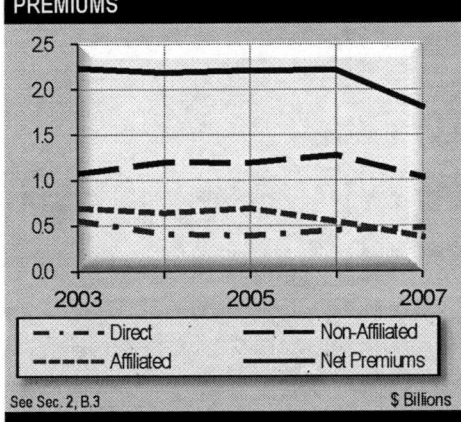

PREMIUMS
- · - · Direct
- - - Non-Affiliated
- - - - Affiliated
- —— Net Premiums

See Sec. 2, B.3 — $ Billions

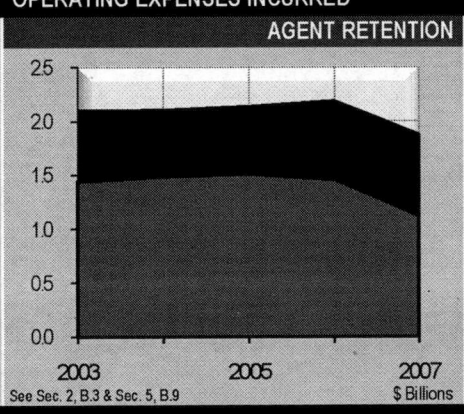

OPERATING EXPENSES INCURRED / AGENT RETENTION
See Sec. 2, B.3 & Sec. 5, B.9 — $ Billions

DIRECT PREMIUMS WRITTEN - YE 2007
□ Direct ▨ Non-Affiliated ▪ Affiliated
See Sec. 3, B.4

L&LAE INCURRED / LOSS RATIO
See Sec. 5, A.3 & Sec. 5, C.2 — $ Millions

FINANCIAL POSITION	2007
Cash, Cash Equivalents & Short-Term Investments	$309,021,337
Total Assets	$1,578,158,243
Policyholders' Surplus	$274,482,538
Reserves	$956,722,236
OPERATING RESULTS	
Net Income	$129,246,681
Net Investment Gain	$122,326,076
Net Realized Capital Gains	$7,212,799
Net Cash from Operations	$214,908,754
Oper. Gain Before Taxes	$233,872,121
UNDERWRITING RESULTS	
Direct	$477,816,470
Non-Affiliated	$1,033,035,988
Affiliated	$376,443,234
Direct Premiums Written	$1,887,295,692
Net Premiums Earned	$1,806,353,030
Operating Expenses Incurred	$1,874,565,198
Agent Retention	$1,121,133,282
L&LAE Incurred	$194,183,378
Loss Ratio	9.21%

6

Chicago Title Insurance Company of Oregon

601 Riverside Ave.
Jacksonville, FL 32204

(904) 854-8100

WEBSITE:	STATE OF DOMICILE:
www.fnf.com	Oregon

PRESIDENT:	ESTABLISHED:	JURISDICTION LICENSE(S):
Bradley Jack London	5/1/1970	2

A' Unsurpassed
Financial Stability Rating®
Demotech, Inc.

NAIC Number:
50490

CHICAGO TIC (OR)

NAIC Group:
CHICAGO / FIDELITY

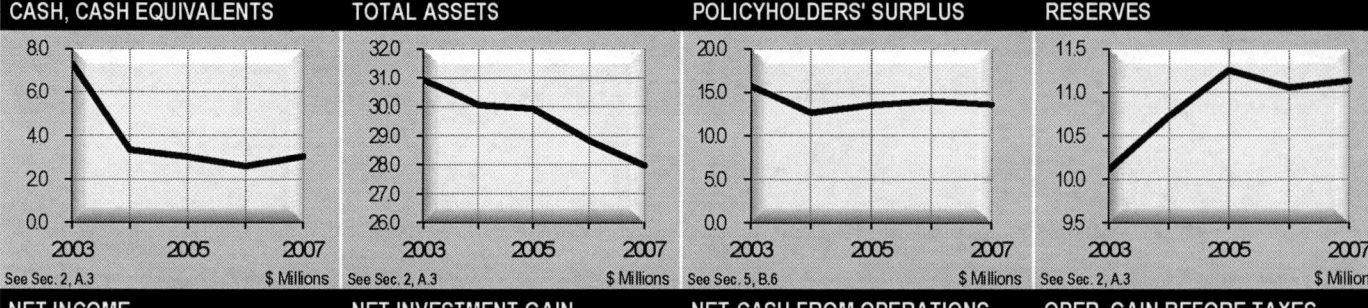

CASH, CASH EQUIVALENTS — See Sec. 2, A.3 — $ Millions
TOTAL ASSETS — See Sec. 2, A.3 — $ Millions
POLICYHOLDERS' SURPLUS — See Sec. 5, B.6 — $ Millions
RESERVES — See Sec. 2, A.3 — $ Millions

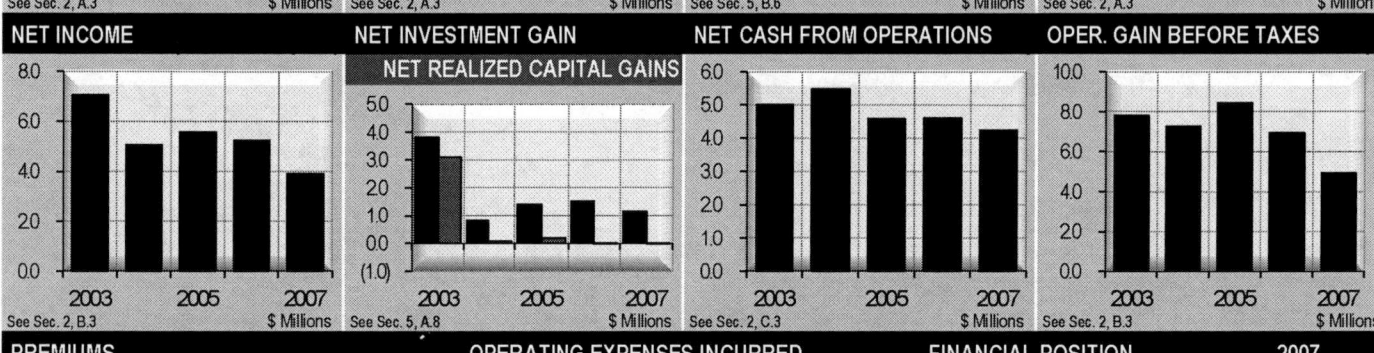

NET INCOME — See Sec. 2, B.3 — $ Millions
NET INVESTMENT GAIN / NET REALIZED CAPITAL GAINS — See Sec. 5, A.8 — $ Millions
NET CASH FROM OPERATIONS — See Sec. 2, C.3 — $ Millions
OPER. GAIN BEFORE TAXES — See Sec. 2, B.3 — $ Millions

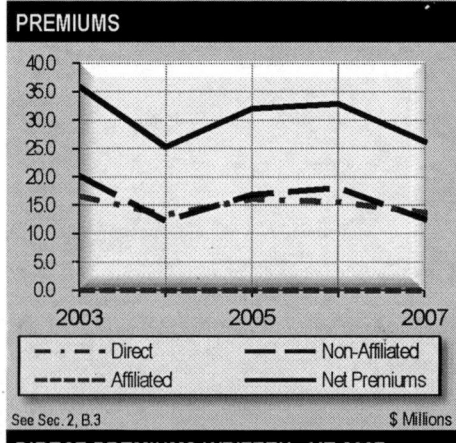

PREMIUMS
- Direct
- Affiliated
- Non-Affiliated
- Net Premiums

See Sec. 2, B.3 — $ Millions

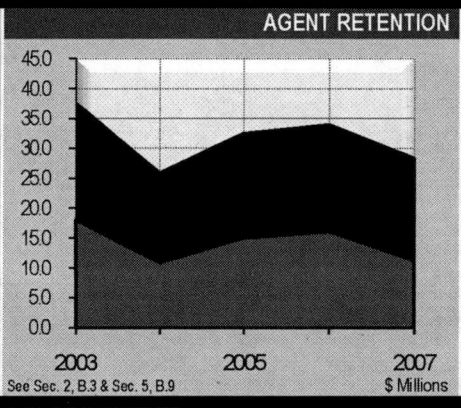

OPERATING EXPENSES INCURRED / AGENT RETENTION
See Sec. 2, B.3 & Sec. 5, B.9 — $ Millions

FINANCIAL POSITION	2007
Cash, Cash Equivalents & Short-Term Investments	$3,028,961
Total Assets	$27,965,083
Policyholders' Surplus	$13,566,887
Reserves	$11,132,992
OPERATING RESULTS	
Net Income	$3,913,229
Net Investment Gain	$1,151,437
Net Realized Capital Gains	($1,358)
Net Cash from Operations	$4,242,573
Oper. Gain Before Taxes	$4,929,389

DIRECT PREMIUMS WRITTEN - YE 2007
- Direct
- Non-Affiliated
- Affiliated

See Sec. 3, B.4

L&LAE INCURRED / LOSS RATIO
See Sec. 5, A.3 & Sec. 5, C.2 — $ Millions

UNDERWRITING RESULTS	
Direct	$13,707,383
Non-Affiliated	$12,576,501
Affiliated	$0
Direct Premiums Written	$26,283,884
Net Premiums Earned	$26,265,761
Operating Expenses Incurred	$28,329,828
Agent Retention	$11,287,905
L&LAE Incurred	$655,119
Loss Ratio	1.97%

Columbian National Title Insurance Company

2921 SW Wanamaker Dr.
Ste. 100
Topeka, KS 66614
(785) 232-4365

WEBSITE:	STATE OF DOMICILE:
www.columbiantitle.com	Kansas

PRESIDENT:	ESTABLISHED:	JURISDICTION LICENSE(S):
John Wallace Dozier, Jr.	6/9/1978	12

A' Unsurpassed
Financial Stability Rating®
Demotech, Inc.

NAIC Number:
51373

COLUMBIAN NATIONAL

NAIC Group:
FIRST AMERICAN

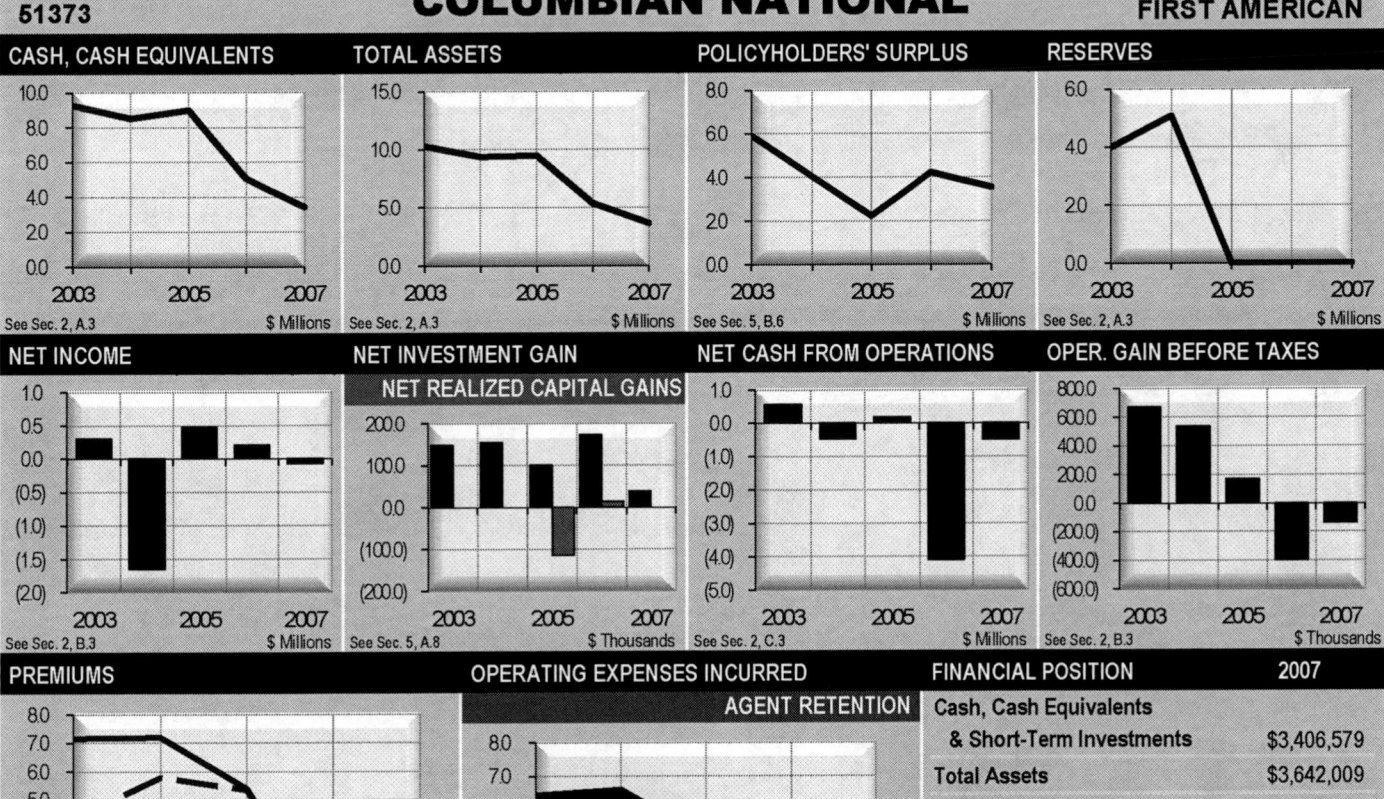

CASH, CASH EQUIVALENTS — See Sec. 2, A.3 — $ Millions

TOTAL ASSETS — See Sec. 2, A.3 — $ Millions

POLICYHOLDERS' SURPLUS — See Sec. 5, B.6 — $ Millions

RESERVES — See Sec. 2, A.3 — $ Millions

NET INCOME — See Sec. 2, B.3 — $ Millions

NET INVESTMENT GAIN / NET REALIZED CAPITAL GAINS — See Sec. 5, A.8 — $ Thousands

NET CASH FROM OPERATIONS — See Sec. 2, C.3 — $ Millions

OPER. GAIN BEFORE TAXES — See Sec. 2, B.3 — $ Thousands

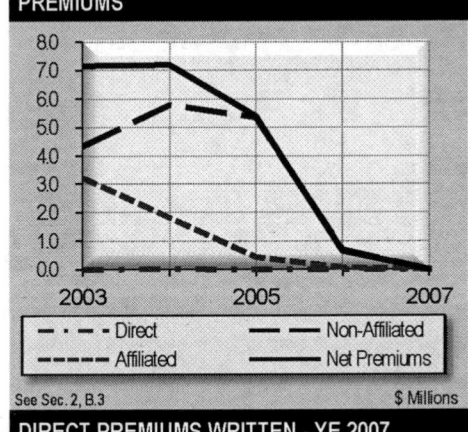

PREMIUMS — See Sec. 2, B.3 — $ Millions
- · - Direct
- - - Non-Affiliated
- - - - Affiliated
- —— Net Premiums

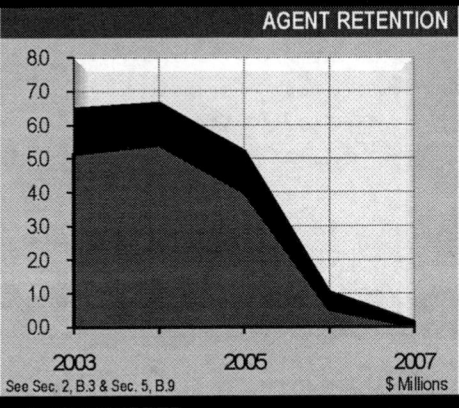

OPERATING EXPENSES INCURRED / AGENT RETENTION — See Sec. 2, B.3 & Sec. 5, B.9 — $ Millions

DIRECT PREMIUMS WRITTEN - YE 2007 — See Sec. 3, B.4
☐ Direct ◼ Non-Affiliated ◼ Affiliated

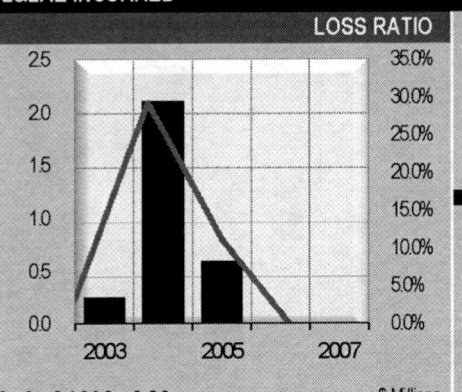

L&LAE INCURRED / LOSS RATIO — See Sec. 5, A.3 & Sec. 5, C.2 — $ Millions

FINANCIAL POSITION	2007
Cash, Cash Equivalents & Short-Term Investments	$3,406,579
Total Assets	$3,642,009
Policyholders' Surplus	$3,538,522
Reserves	$0
OPERATING RESULTS	
Net Income	($68,307)
Net Investment Gain	$38,289
Net Realized Capital Gains	$0
Net Cash from Operations	($494,215)
Oper. Gain Before Taxes	($139,316)
UNDERWRITING RESULTS	
Direct	$0
Non-Affiliated	$0
Affiliated	$0
Direct Premiums Written	$0
Net Premiums Earned	$0
Operating Expenses Incurred	$139,316
Agent Retention	$0
L&LAE Incurred	$0
Loss Ratio	--

6

Commerce Title Insurance Company

2828 N Harwood, 11th Fl.
Dallas, TX 75201

(214) 758-7204

Formerly Benefit Land Title Insurance Company

WEBSITE:	STATE OF DOMICILE:
www.commercetitleinsco.com	California

CHAIRMAN, PRESIDENT & CEO:	ESTABLISHED:	JURISDICTION LICENSE(S):
Timothy Michael Bartosh	8/19/1993	22

A Exceptional
Financial Stability Rating®
Demotech, Inc.

NAIC Number:
50026

COMMERCE

NAIC Group:
UNAFFILIATED

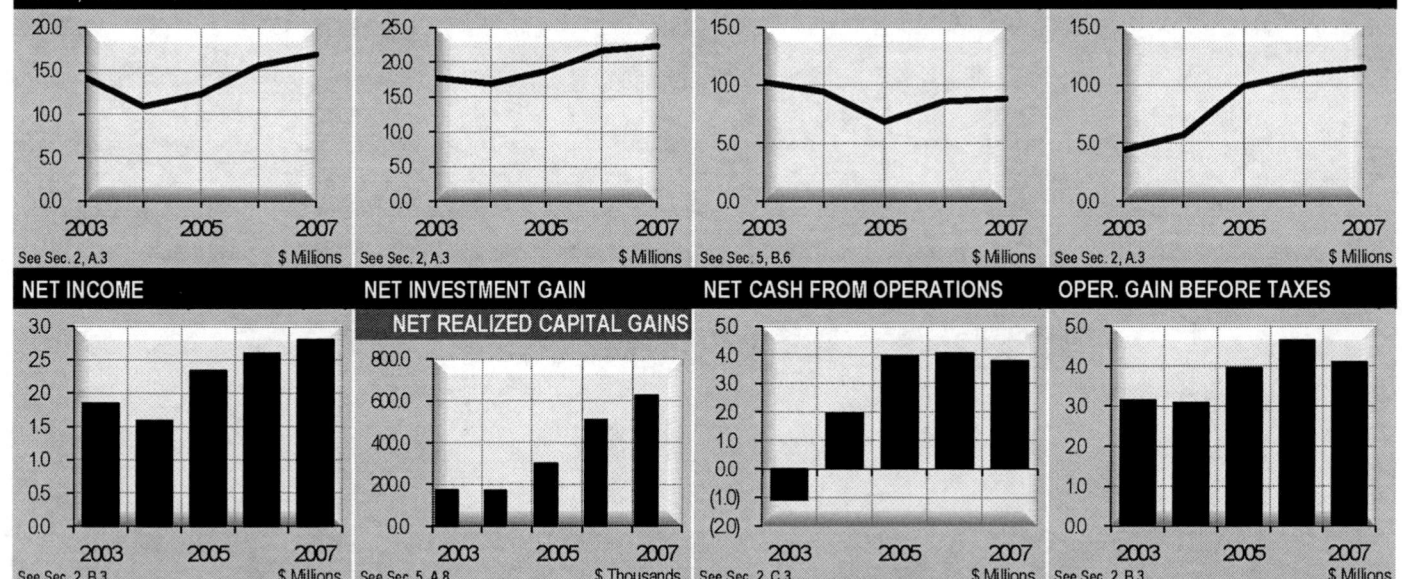

CASH, CASH EQUIVALENTS — See Sec. 2, A.3 — $ Millions
TOTAL ASSETS — See Sec. 2, A.3 — $ Millions
POLICYHOLDERS' SURPLUS — See Sec. 5, B.6 — $ Millions
RESERVES — See Sec. 2, A.3 — $ Millions

NET INCOME — See Sec. 2, B.3 — $ Millions
NET INVESTMENT GAIN / NET REALIZED CAPITAL GAINS — See Sec. 5, A.8 — $ Thousands
NET CASH FROM OPERATIONS — See Sec. 2, C.3 — $ Millions
OPER. GAIN BEFORE TAXES — See Sec. 2, B.3 — $ Millions

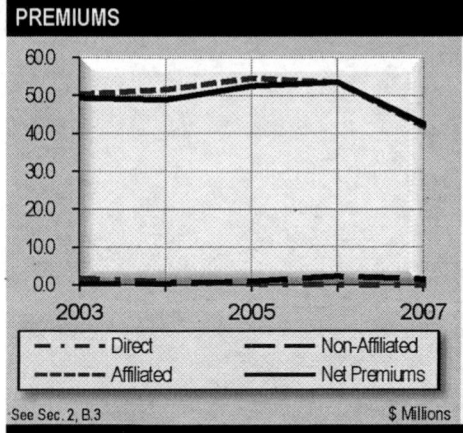

PREMIUMS — See Sec. 2, B.3 — $ Millions
- - · - Direct
- - - - Affiliated
——— Non-Affiliated
——— Net Premiums

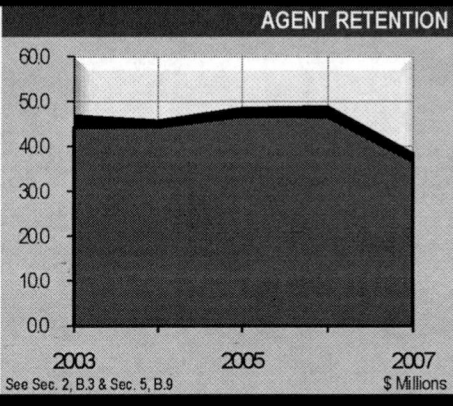

OPERATING EXPENSES INCURRED / AGENT RETENTION — See Sec. 2, B.3 & Sec. 5, B.9 — $ Millions

DIRECT PREMIUMS WRITTEN - YE 2007 — See Sec. 3, B.4
☐ Direct ☐ Non-Affiliated ■ Affiliated

L&LAE INCURRED / LOSS RATIO — See Sec. 5, A.3 & Sec. 5, C.2 — $ Millions

FINANCIAL POSITION	2007
Cash, Cash Equivalents & Short-Term Investments	$16,857,473
Total Assets	$22,292,662
Policyholders' Surplus	$8,811,912
Reserves	$11,461,468
OPERATING RESULTS	
Net Income	$2,799,730
Net Investment Gain	$626,185
Net Realized Capital Gains	$0
Net Cash from Operations	$3,793,134
Oper. Gain Before Taxes	$4,109,282
UNDERWRITING RESULTS	
Direct	$43,152
Non-Affiliated	$1,532,096
Affiliated	$41,997,283
Direct Premiums Written	$43,572,531
Net Premiums Earned	$42,512,147
Operating Expenses Incurred	$38,400,755
Agent Retention	$36,674,307
L&LAE Incurred	$456,599
Loss Ratio	1.07%

6

Commonwealth Land Title Insurance Company

5600 Cox Rd.
Glen Allen, VA 23060

(804) 267-8000

Formerly Commonwealth Land Title Insurance Company Of Philadelphia (1929)

WEBSITE:	STATE OF DOMICILE:
www.landam.com	Nebraska

PRESIDENT & CEO:	ESTABLISHED:	JURISDICTION LICENSE(S):
Theodore Lindy Chandler, Jr.	3/31/1944	53

A" Unsurpassed
A Double Prime
Financial Stability Rating®
Demotech, Inc.

NAIC Number:
50083

COMMONWEALTH LAND

NAIC Group:
LAND AMERICA

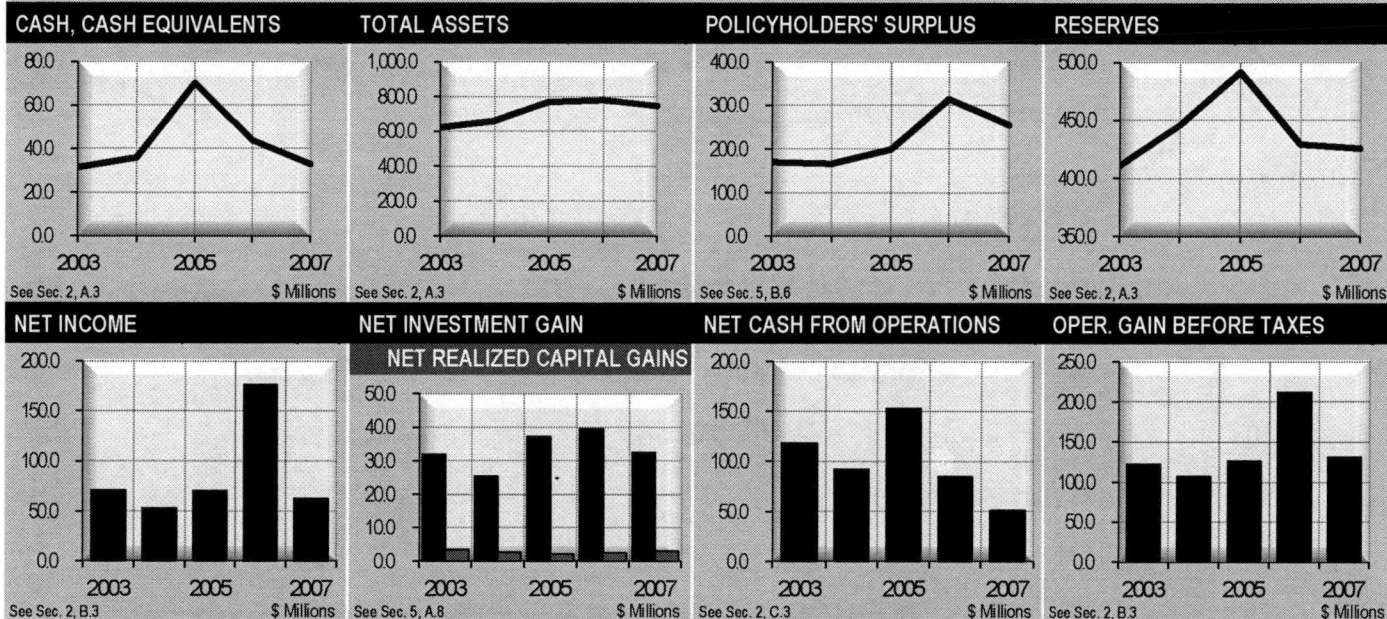

FINANCIAL POSITION	2007
Cash, Cash Equivalents & Short-Term Investments	$32,891,679
Total Assets	$745,238,011
Policyholders' Surplus	$254,092,477
Reserves	$425,495,974
OPERATING RESULTS	
Net Income	$62,784,680
Net Investment Gain	$32,490,595
Net Realized Capital Gains	$3,028,893
Net Cash from Operations	$50,991,642
Oper. Gain Before Taxes	$131,377,490
UNDERWRITING RESULTS	
Direct	$220,717,997
Non-Affiliated	$808,458,154
Affiliated	$123,342,178
Direct Premiums Written	**$1,152,518,329**
Net Premiums Earned	$1,164,353,355
Operating Expenses Incurred	$1,083,516,820
Agent Retention	$760,409,081
L&LAE Incurred	$79,989,583
Loss Ratio	6.58%

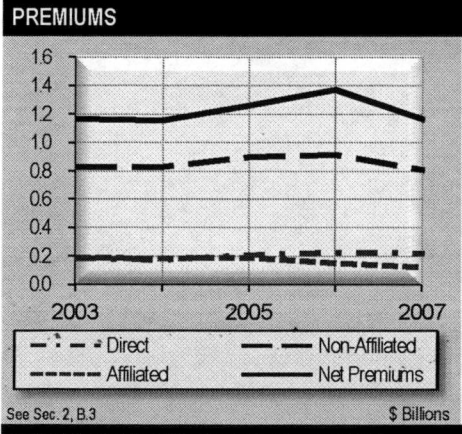

See Sec. 3, B.4

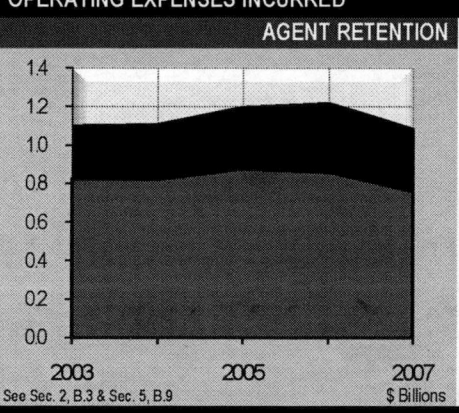

See Sec. 5, A.3 & Sec. 5, C.2 — $ Millions

6

Commonwealth Land Title Insurance Company of New Jersey

5600 Cox Rd.
Glen Allen, VA 23060

(804) 267-8000

Formerly Continental Title Insurance Company

WEBSITE:	STATE OF DOMICILE:
www.landam.com	New Jersey

PRESIDENT & CEO:	ESTABLISHED:	JURISDICTION LICENSE(S):
Theodore Lindy Chandler, Jr.	3/6/1888	5

A'' Unsurpassed
Financial Stability Rating®
Demotech, Inc.

NAIC Number:
51195

COMMONWEALTH LAND (NJ)

NAIC Group:
LAND AMERICA

CASH, CASH EQUIVALENTS
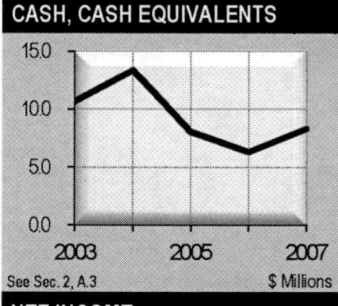
See Sec. 2, A.3 — $ Millions

TOTAL ASSETS
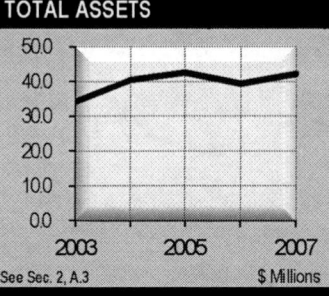
See Sec. 2, A.3 — $ Millions

POLICYHOLDERS' SURPLUS
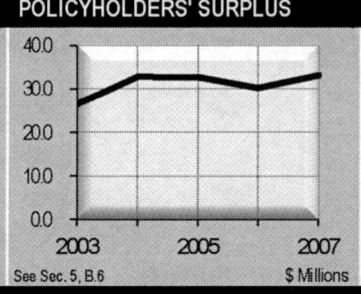
See Sec. 5, B.6 — $ Millions

RESERVES
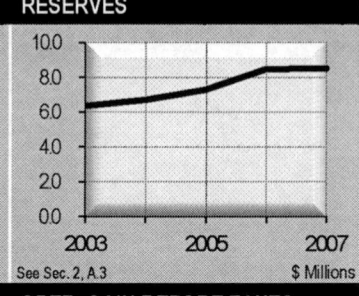
See Sec. 2, A.3 — $ Millions

NET INCOME
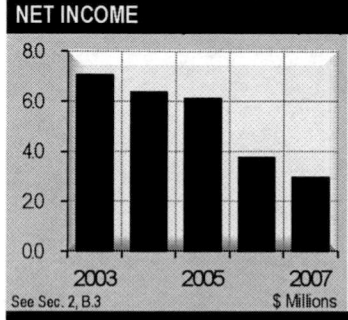
See Sec. 2, B.3 — $ Millions

NET INVESTMENT GAIN
NET REALIZED CAPITAL GAINS
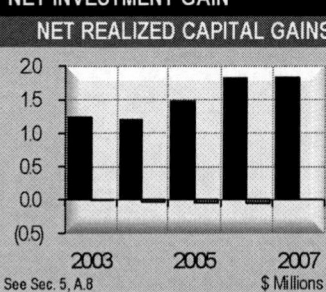
See Sec. 5, A.8 — $ Millions

NET CASH FROM OPERATIONS
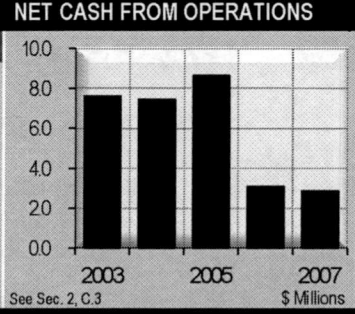
See Sec. 2, C.3 — $ Millions

OPER. GAIN BEFORE TAXES
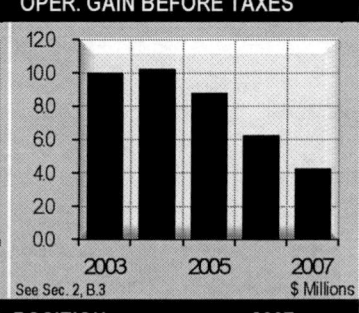
See Sec. 2, B.3 — $ Millions

PREMIUMS

Direct · — · —
Affiliated - - - -
Non-Affiliated — — —
Net Premiums ———

See Sec. 2, B.3 — $ Millions

OPERATING EXPENSES INCURRED
AGENT RETENTION

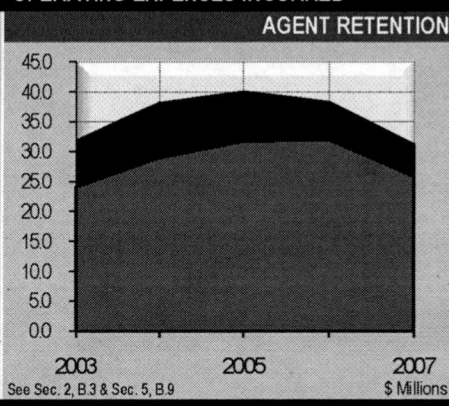

See Sec. 2, B.3 & Sec. 5, B.9 — $ Millions

FINANCIAL POSITION — 2007

Cash, Cash Equivalents & Short-Term Investments	$8,306,919
Total Assets	$42,152,114
Policyholders' Surplus	$33,132,445
Reserves	$8,504,925

OPERATING RESULTS

Net Income	$2,974,998
Net Investment Gain	$1,830,953
Net Realized Capital Gains	$5,457
Net Cash from Operations	$2,885,617
Oper. Gain Before Taxes	$4,209,469

DIRECT PREMIUMS WRITTEN - YE 2007

□ Direct   ■ Non-Affiliated   ■ Affiliated

See Sec. 3, B.4

L&LAE INCURRED
LOSS RATIO

See Sec. 5, A.3 & Sec. 5, C.2 — $ Millions

UNDERWRITING RESULTS

Direct	$5,109,506
Non-Affiliated	$30,277,935
Affiliated	$0
Direct Premiums Written	$35,387,441
Net Premiums Earned	$33,610,559
Operating Expenses Incurred	$31,189,583
Agent Retention	$25,866,635
L&LAE Incurred	$1,900,137
Loss Ratio	5.37%

6

Conestoga Title Insurance Co.

123 E King St.
Lancaster, PA 17602

(717) 299-4805

WEBSITE:	STATE OF DOMICILE:
www.contitle.com	Pennsylvania

PRESIDENT & CEO:	ESTABLISHED:	JURISDICTION LICENSE(S):
Sam Ferguson Musser	10/11/1973	15

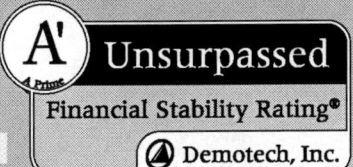

A' Unsurpassed
Financial Stability Rating®
Demotech, Inc.

NAIC Number:		NAIC Group:
51209	**CONESTOGA**	**UNAFFILIATED**

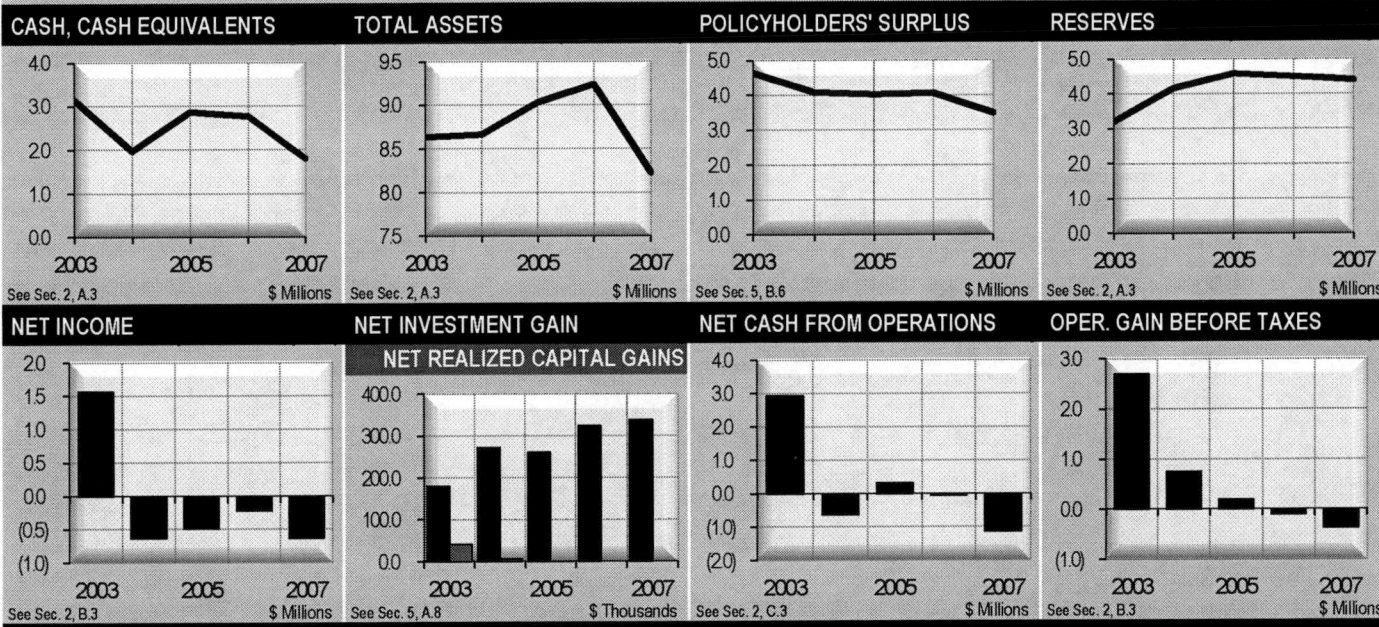

CASH, CASH EQUIVALENTS — See Sec. 2, A.3 — $ Millions
TOTAL ASSETS — See Sec. 2, A.3 — $ Millions
POLICYHOLDERS' SURPLUS — See Sec. 5, B.6 — $ Millions
RESERVES — See Sec. 2, A.3 — $ Millions

NET INCOME — See Sec. 2, B.3 — $ Millions
NET INVESTMENT GAIN / NET REALIZED CAPITAL GAINS — See Sec. 5, A.8 — $ Thousands
NET CASH FROM OPERATIONS — See Sec. 2, C.3 — $ Millions
OPER. GAIN BEFORE TAXES — See Sec. 2, B.3 — $ Millions

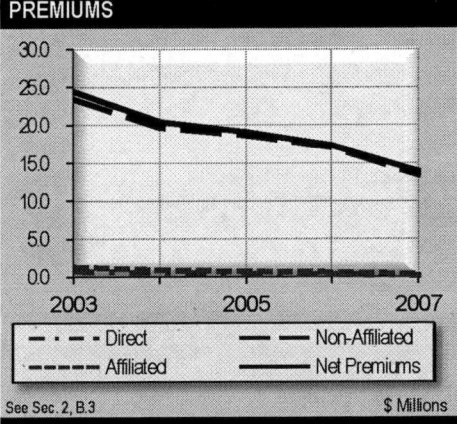

PREMIUMS — See Sec. 2, B.3 — $ Millions
- - - Direct
----- Affiliated
—— Non-Affiliated
—— Net Premiums

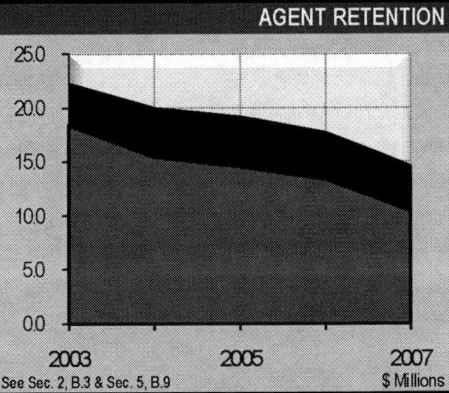

OPERATING EXPENSES INCURRED / AGENT RETENTION — See Sec. 2, B.3 & Sec. 5, B.9 — $ Millions

DIRECT PREMIUMS WRITTEN - YE 2007 — See Sec. 3, B.4
☐ Direct ■ Non-Affiliated ■ Affiliated

L&LAE INCURRED / LOSS RATIO — See Sec. 5, A.3 & Sec. 5, C.2 — $ Millions

FINANCIAL POSITION	2007
Cash, Cash Equivalents & Short-Term Investments	$1,795,564
Total Assets	$8,225,126
Policyholders' Surplus	$3,483,884
Reserves	$4,387,262

OPERATING RESULTS	
Net Income	($641,202)
Net Investment Gain	$337,732
Net Realized Capital Gains	$0
Net Cash from Operations	($1,144,566)
Oper. Gain Before Taxes	($368,551)

UNDERWRITING RESULTS	
Direct	$201,980
Non-Affiliated	$13,366,327
Affiliated	$376,063
Direct Premiums Written	$13,944,370
Net Premiums Earned	$13,907,911
Operating Expenses Incurred	$14,545,453
Agent Retention	$10,429,015
L&LAE Incurred	$991,906
Loss Ratio	7.00%

6

Connecticut Attorneys Title Insurance Company

101 Corporate Pl.
Rocky Hill, CT 06067

(860) 257-0606

WEBSITE:	STATE OF DOMICILE:
www.caticaccess.com	Connecticut

PRESIDENT & CEO:	ESTABLISHED:	JURISDICTION LICENSE(S):
Richard Joseph Patterson	6/26/2001	7

A' Unsurpassed
A Prime Financial Stability Rating®
Demotech, Inc.

NAIC Number:
51268

CT ATTORNEYS

NAIC Group:
CATIC

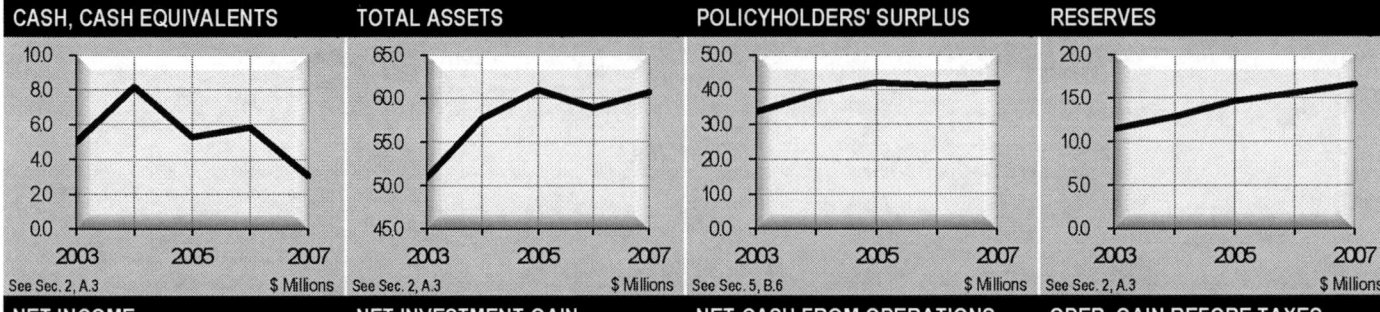

CASH, CASH EQUIVALENTS — See Sec. 2, A.3 — $ Millions
TOTAL ASSETS — See Sec. 2, A.3 — $ Millions
POLICYHOLDERS' SURPLUS — See Sec. 5, B.6 — $ Millions
RESERVES — See Sec. 2, A.3 — $ Millions

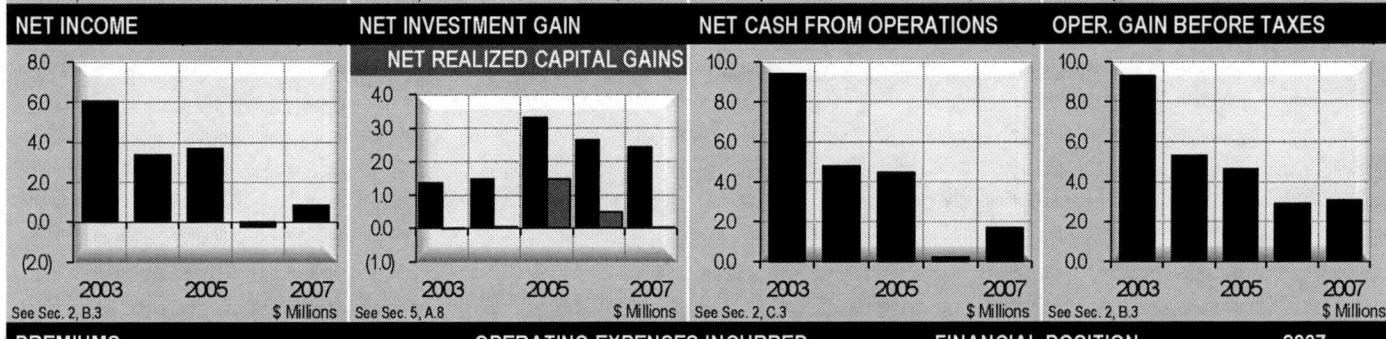

NET INCOME — See Sec. 2, B.3 — $ Millions
NET INVESTMENT GAIN / NET REALIZED CAPITAL GAINS — See Sec. 5, A.8 — $ Millions
NET CASH FROM OPERATIONS — See Sec. 2, C.3 — $ Millions
OPER. GAIN BEFORE TAXES — See Sec. 2, B.3 — $ Millions

PREMIUMS

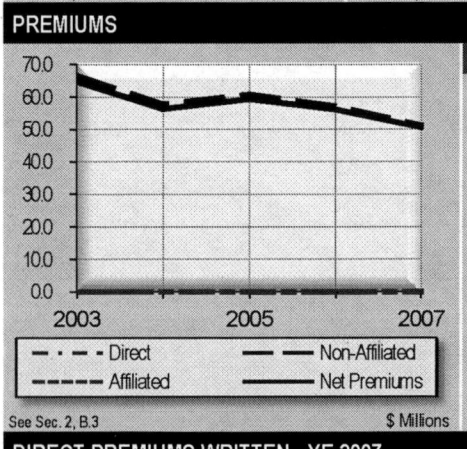

Direct — Non-Affiliated
Affiliated — Net Premiums

See Sec. 2, B.3 — $ Millions

OPERATING EXPENSES INCURRED
AGENT RETENTION

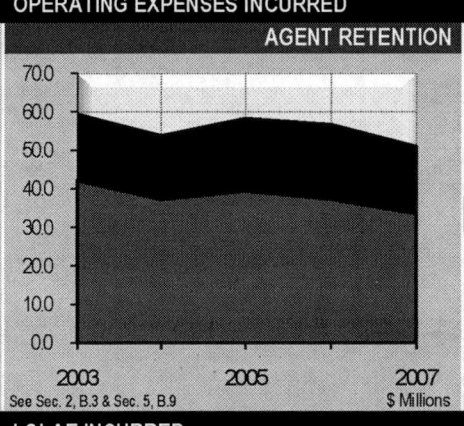

See Sec. 2, B.3 & Sec. 5, B.9 — $ Millions

DIRECT PREMIUMS WRITTEN - YE 2007

☐ Direct ■ Non-Affiliated ■ Affiliated

See Sec. 3, B.4

L&LAE INCURRED
LOSS RATIO

See Sec. 5, A.3 & Sec. 5, C.2 — $ Millions

FINANCIAL POSITION	2007
Cash, Cash Equivalents & Short-Term Investments	$3,060,625
Total Assets	$60,658,854
Policyholders' Surplus	$41,839,283
Reserves	$16,590,467
OPERATING RESULTS	
Net Income	$843,665
Net Investment Gain	$2,434,180
Net Realized Capital Gains	$29,473
Net Cash from Operations	$1,694,836
Oper. Gain Before Taxes	$3,084,621
UNDERWRITING RESULTS	
Direct	$0
Non-Affiliated	$51,258,956
Affiliated	$0
Direct Premiums Written	**$51,258,956**
Net Premiums Earned	$50,593,631
Operating Expenses Incurred	$51,011,296
Agent Retention	$33,564,663
L&LAE Incurred	$4,086,369
Loss Ratio	7.55%

6

Dakota Homestead Title Insurance Company

315 S Phillips Ave.
Sioux Falls, SD 57104

(605) 336-0388

WEBSITE:	STATE OF DOMICILE:
www.dakotahomestead.com	South Dakota

PRESIDENT:	ESTABLISHED:	JURISDICTION LICENSE(S):
Chad L. Hansen	3/1/1993	11

A **Exceptional**
Financial Stability Rating®
Demotech, Inc.

NAIC Number:
50020

DAKOTA HOMESTEAD

NAIC Group:
UNAFFILIATED

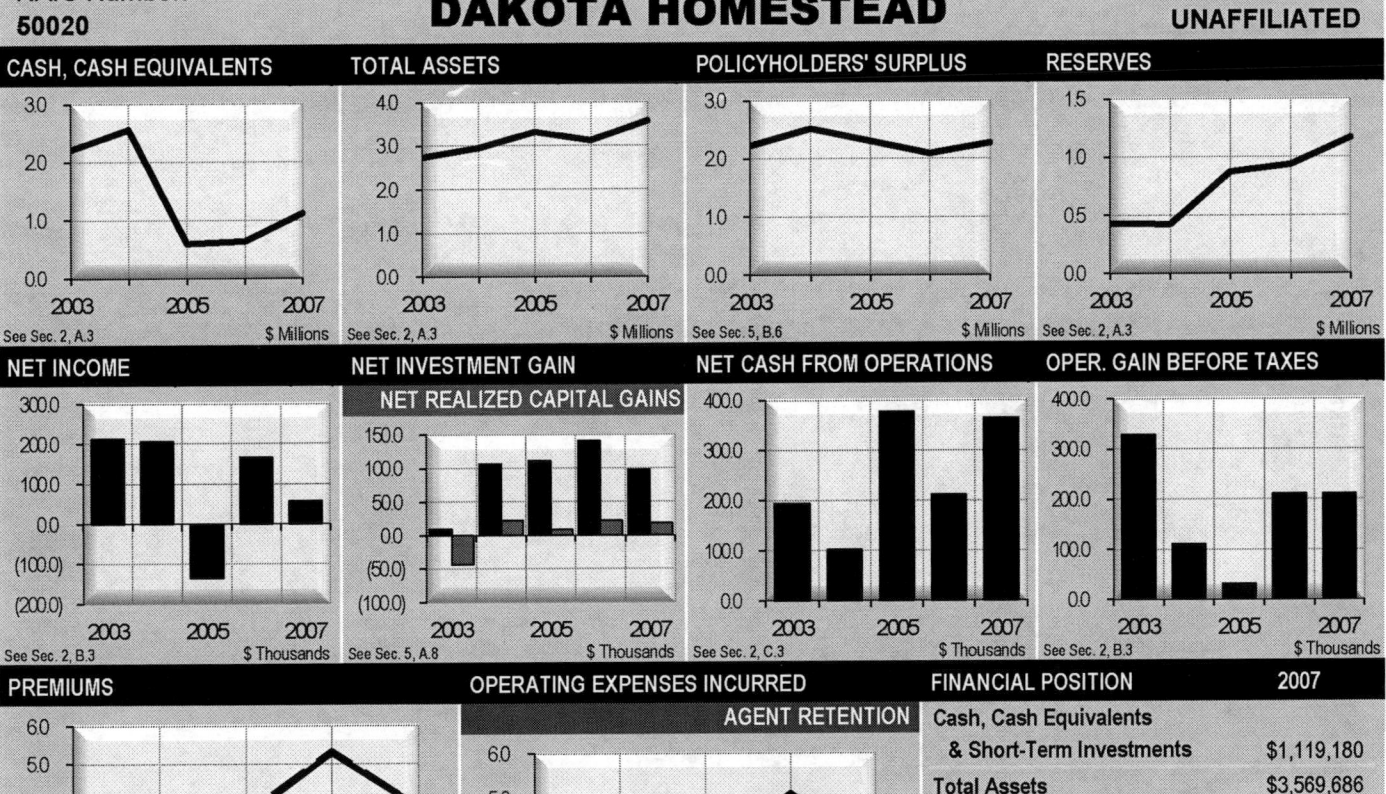

FINANCIAL POSITION	2007
Cash, Cash Equivalents & Short-Term Investments	$1,119,180
Total Assets	$3,569,686
Policyholders' Surplus	$2,266,306
Reserves	$1,162,622
OPERATING RESULTS	
Net Income	$56,704
Net Investment Gain	$98,069
Net Realized Capital Gains	$18,355
Net Cash from Operations	$364,532
Oper. Gain Before Taxes	$210,588

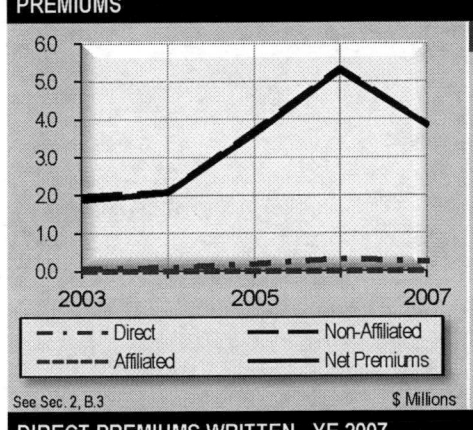

DIRECT PREMIUMS WRITTEN - YE 2007

□ Direct ■ Non-Affiliated ■ Affiliated

See Sec. 3, B.4

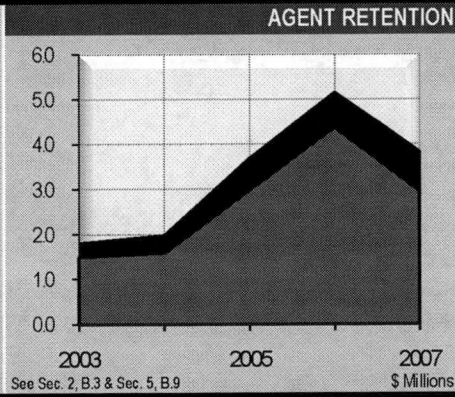

See Sec. 5, A.3 & Sec. 5, C.2 $ Thousands

UNDERWRITING RESULTS	
Direct	$244,546
Non-Affiliated	$3,869,021
Affiliated	$0
Direct Premiums Written	$4,113,567
Net Premiums Earned	$3,850,567
Operating Expenses Incurred	$3,823,957
Agent Retention	$2,952,933
L&LAE Incurred	$251,953
Loss Ratio	6.24%

6

Dreibelbiss Title Company, Inc.

127 W Wayne St.
Fort Wayne, IN 46802-2503

(260) 422-8500

WEBSITE:	STATE OF DOMICILE:
www.titlesbycd.com	Indiana

PRESIDENT:	ESTABLISHED:	JURISDICTION LICENSE(S):
Darice L. Kabisch	8/1/1916	1

A Exceptional
Financial Stability Rating®
⬥ Demotech, Inc.

NAIC Number:
51381

DREIBELBISS

NAIC Group:
UNAFFILIATED

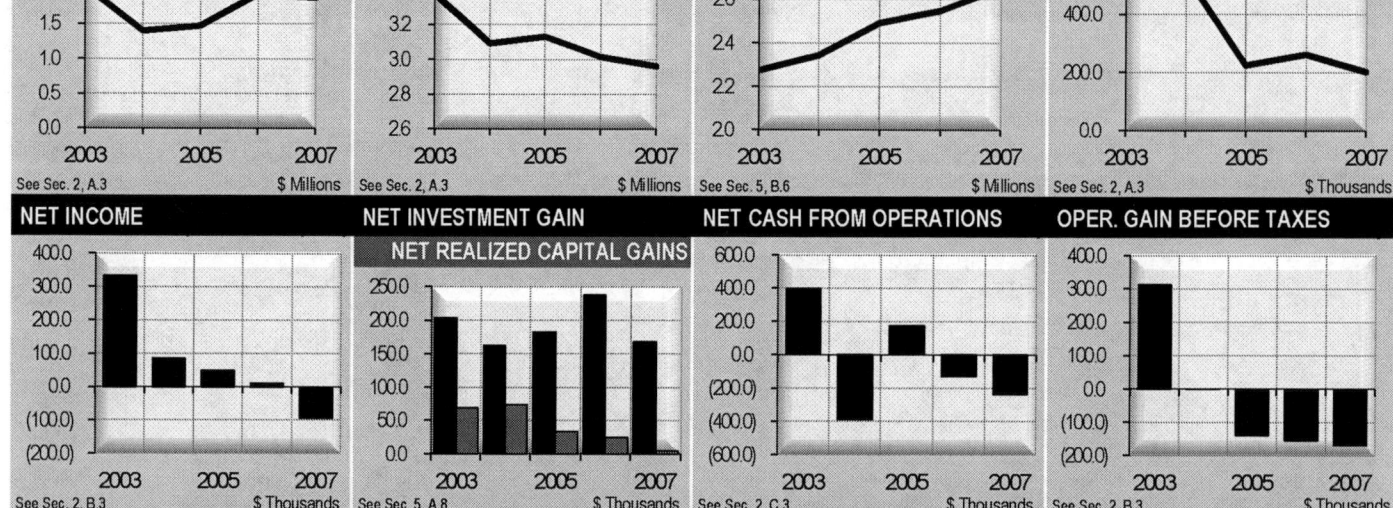

CASH, CASH EQUIVALENTS — See Sec. 2, A.3 — $ Millions
TOTAL ASSETS — See Sec. 2, A.3 — $ Millions
POLICYHOLDERS' SURPLUS — See Sec. 5, B.6 — $ Millions
RESERVES — See Sec. 2, A.3 — $ Thousands

NET INCOME — See Sec. 2, B.3 — $ Thousands
NET INVESTMENT GAIN / NET REALIZED CAPITAL GAINS — See Sec. 5, A.8 — $ Thousands
NET CASH FROM OPERATIONS — See Sec. 2, C.3 — $ Thousands
OPER. GAIN BEFORE TAXES — See Sec. 2, B.3 — $ Thousands

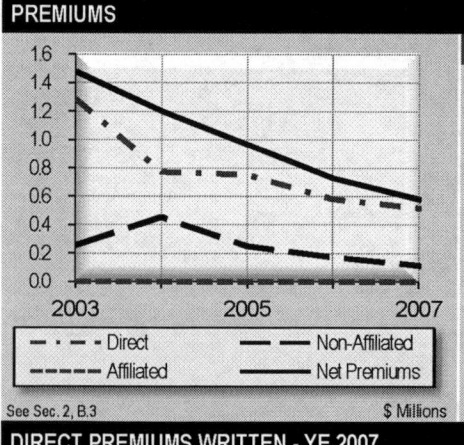

PREMIUMS
- – - – Direct
- – – Non-Affiliated
- - - - Affiliated
- —— Net Premiums
See Sec. 2, B.3 — $ Millions

DIRECT PREMIUMS WRITTEN - YE 2007
□ Direct ▨ Non-Affiliated ■ Affiliated
See Sec. 3, B.4

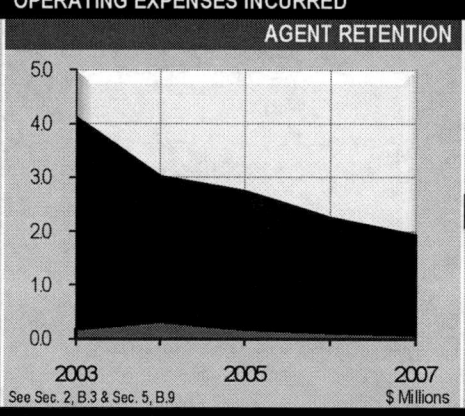

OPERATING EXPENSES INCURRED / AGENT RETENTION
See Sec. 2, B.3 & Sec. 5, B.9 — $ Millions

L&LAE INCURRED / LOSS RATIO
See Sec. 5, A.3 & Sec. 5, C.2 — $ Thousands

FINANCIAL POSITION	2007
Cash, Cash Equivalents & Short-Term Investments	$1,878,546
Total Assets	$2,960,893
Policyholders' Surplus	$2,650,439
Reserves	$202,300
OPERATING RESULTS	
Net Income	($93,990)
Net Investment Gain	$167,654
Net Realized Capital Gains	$4,653
Net Cash from Operations	($235,073)
Oper. Gain Before Taxes	($169,630)

UNDERWRITING RESULTS	
Direct	$517,581
Non-Affiliated	$115,399
Affiliated	$0
Direct Premiums Written	$632,980
Net Premiums Earned	$581,876
Operating Expenses Incurred	$1,933,548
Agent Retention	$82,722
L&LAE Incurred	$216,747
Loss Ratio	12.29%

Disclaimer: The information presented was compiled from Form 9 statements prepared and submitted by underwriters in accordance with Statutory Accounting Principles. No representations or warranties are made by Demotech, Inc. as to the completeness or accuracy of the information. Financial Stability Ratings® must be verified by visiting www.demotech.com.

© Demotech, Inc. *Demotech Performance of Title Insurance Companies*, its contents and material cannot be reproduced or copied, in part or in its entirety, without the express written permission of Demotech, Inc.

Equity National Title Insurance Company

401 Wampanoag Trl., Ste. 300
East Providence, RI 02228

(401) 434-5500

WEBSITE:	STATE OF DOMICILE:
www.equitynational.com	Massachusetts

PRESIDENT:	ESTABLISHED:	JURISDICTION LICENSE(S):
James K. O'Donnell	12/16/2004	1

S Substantial
Financial Stability Rating®
Demotech, Inc.

NAIC Number:
12234

EQUITY NATIONAL

NAIC Group:
UNAFFILIATED

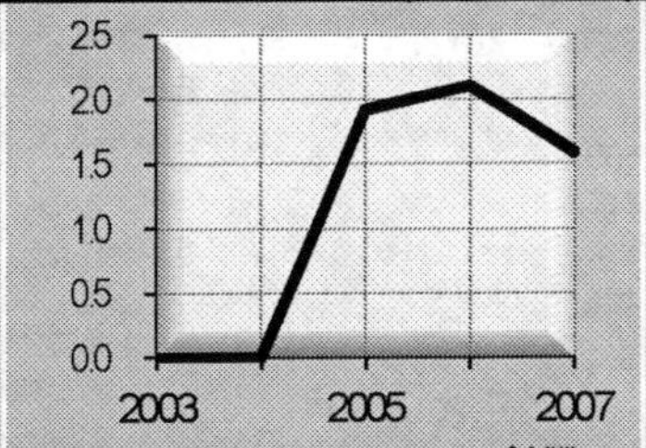

CASH, CASH EQUIVALENTS
(graph, 2003–2007, $ Millions) See Sec. 2, A.3

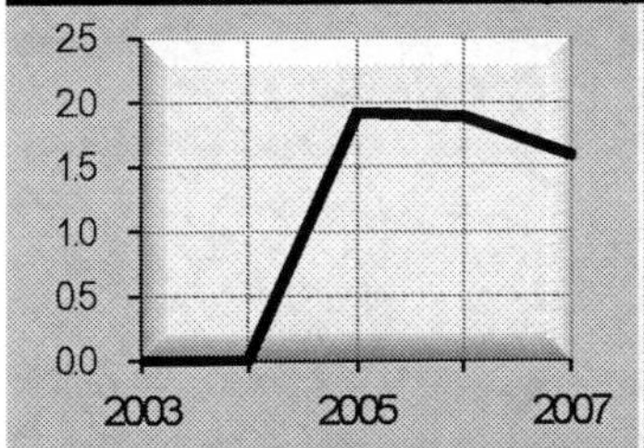

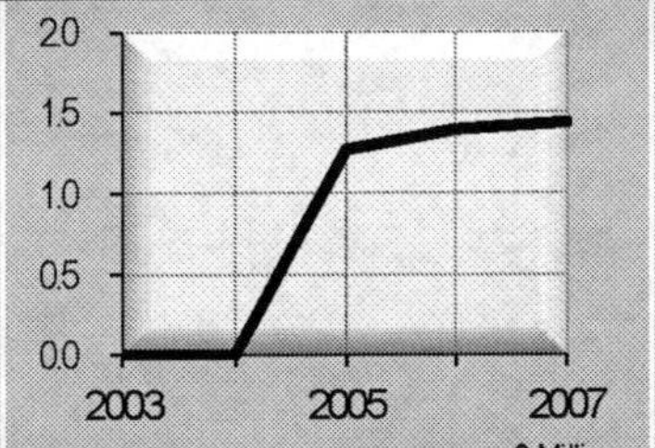

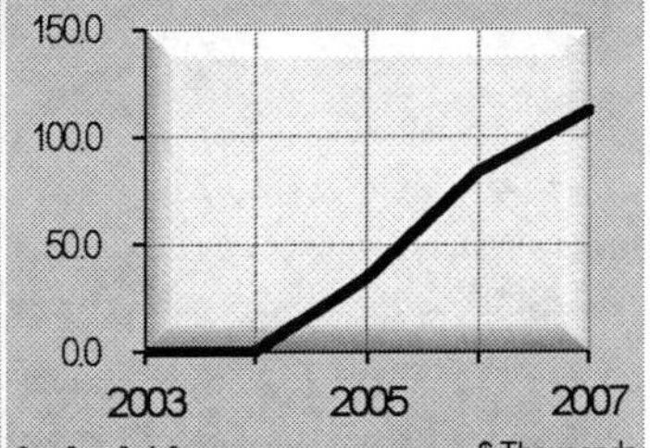

TOTAL ASSETS
(graph, 2003–2007, $ Millions) See Sec. 2, A.3

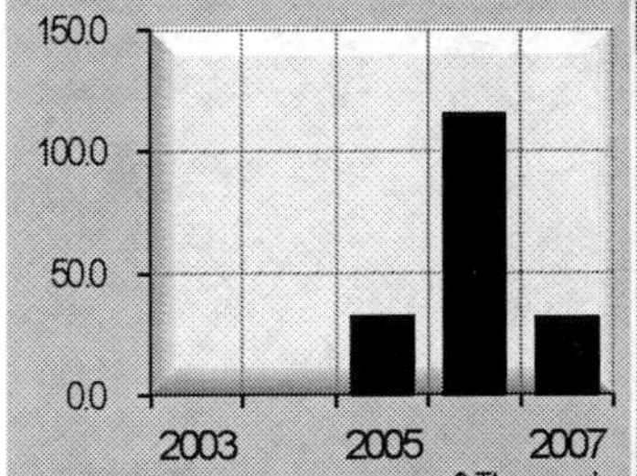

POLICYHOLDERS' SURPLUS
(graph, 2003–2007, $ Millions) See Sec. 5, B.6

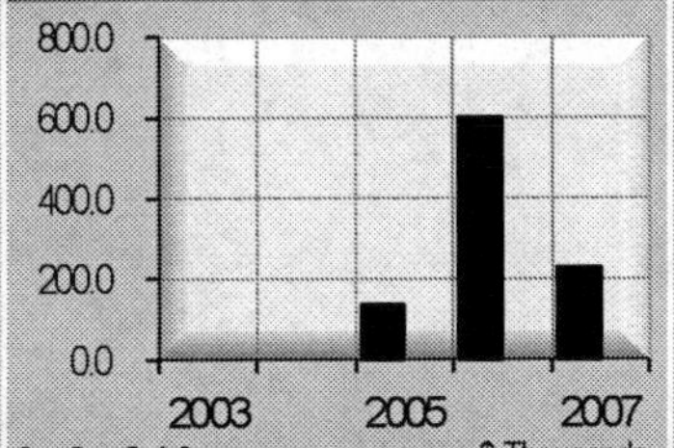

RESERVES
(graph, 2003–2007, $ Thousands) See Sec. 2, A.3

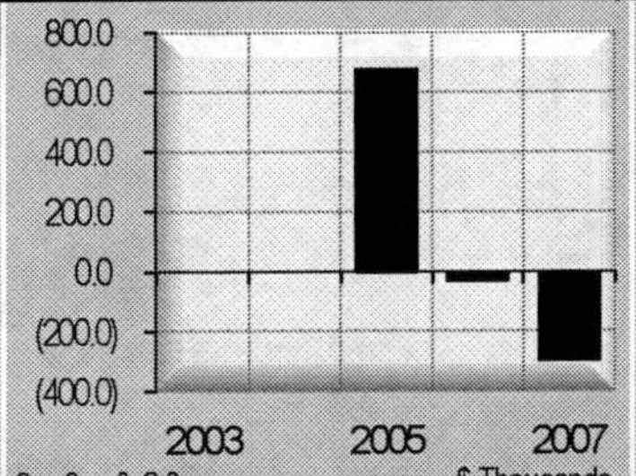

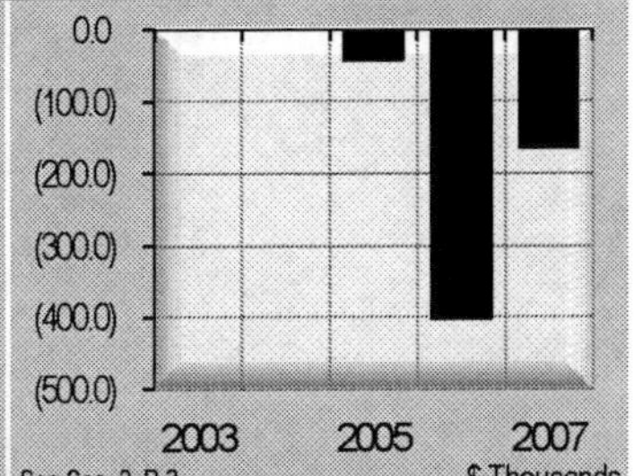

NET INCOME
(graph, 2003–2007, $ Thousands) See Sec. 2, B.3

NET INVESTMENT GAIN / NET REALIZED CAPITAL GAINS
(graph, 2003–2007, $ Thousands) See Sec. 5, A.8

NET CASH FROM OPERATIONS
(graph, 2003–2007, $ Thousands) See Sec. 2, C.3

OPER. GAIN BEFORE TAXES
(graph, 2003–2007, $ Thousands) See Sec. 2, B.3

PREMIUMS
(graph, 2003–2007, $ Thousands)
- – · – Direct
- – – Non-Affiliated
- – – – Affiliated
- —— Net Premiums

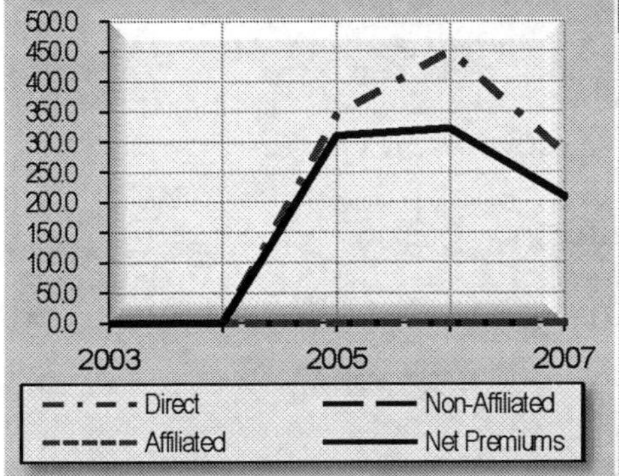

See Sec. 2, B.3

OPERATING EXPENSES INCURRED / AGENT RETENTION
(graph, 2003–2007, $ Millions) See Sec. 2, B.3 & Sec. 5, B.9

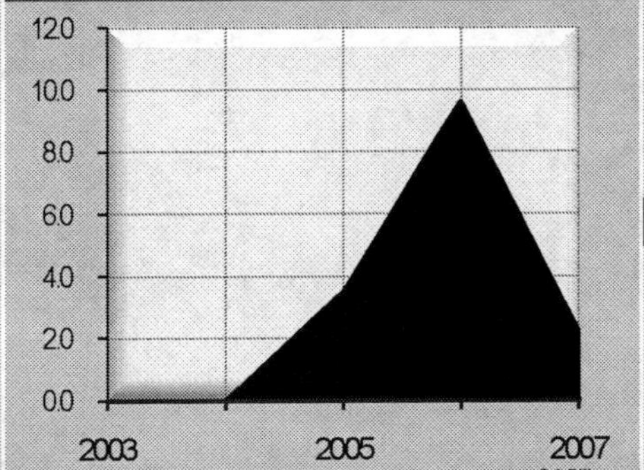

DIRECT PREMIUMS WRITTEN - YE 2007
(pie chart)
☐ Direct ▪ Non-Affiliated ▪ Affiliated

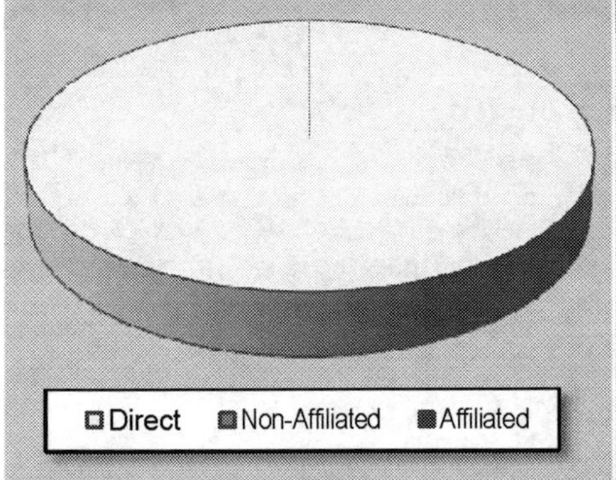

See Sec. 3, B.4

L&LAE INCURRED / LOSS RATIO
(graph, 2003–2007) See Sec. 5, A.3 & Sec. 5, C.2

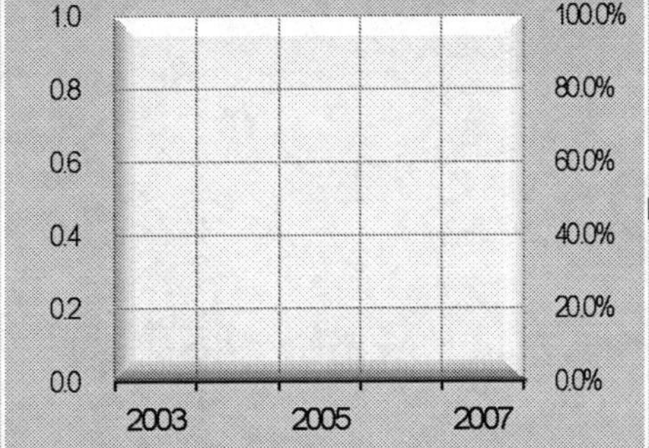

FINANCIAL POSITION	2007
Cash, Cash Equivalents & Short-Term Investments	$1,585,635
Total Assets	$1,585,856
Policyholders' Surplus	$1,438,140
Reserves	$111,701
OPERATING RESULTS	
Net Income	$31,699
Net Investment Gain	$230,044
Net Realized Capital Gains	$0
Net Cash from Operations	($296,816)
Oper. Gain Before Taxes	($164,734)
UNDERWRITING RESULTS	
Direct	$280,228
Non-Affiliated	$0
Affiliated	$0
Direct Premiums Written	$280,228
Net Premiums Earned	$208,883
Operating Expenses Incurred	$2,233,086
Agent Retention	$0
L&LAE Incurred	$0
Loss Ratio	0.00%

6

Farmers National Title Insurance Company

1207 W Broadway, Ste. C
Columbia, MO 65203

(573) 442-3351

WEBSITE:	STATE OF DOMICILE:
www.farmerstitle.com	Missouri

		JURISDICTION
PRESIDENT & CEO:	ESTABLISHED:	LICENSE(S):
David A. Townsend	10/26/2005	1

A Exceptional
Financial Stability Rating®
Demotech, Inc.

NAIC Number:
12522

FARMERS NATIONAL

NAIC Group:
UNAFFILIATED

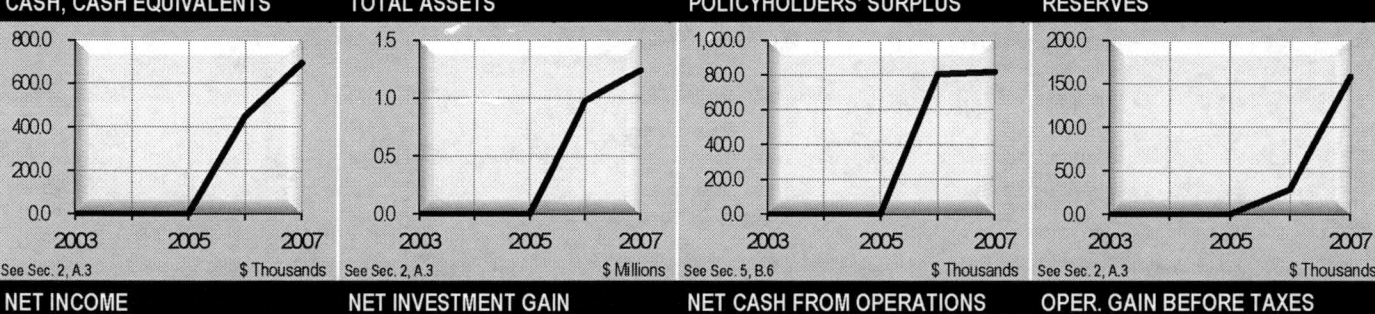

CASH, CASH EQUIVALENTS — See Sec. 2, A.3 — $ Thousands
TOTAL ASSETS — See Sec. 2, A.3 — $ Millions
POLICYHOLDERS' SURPLUS — See Sec. 5, B.6 — $ Thousands
RESERVES — See Sec. 2, A.3 — $ Thousands

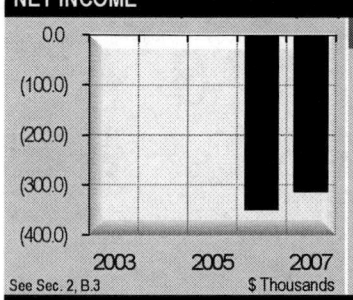
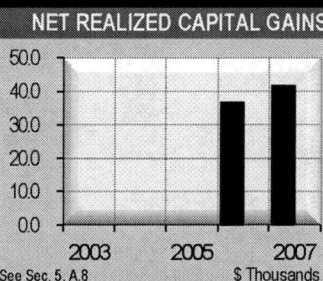
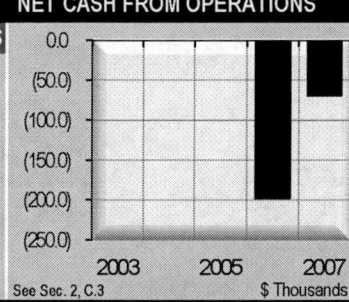

NET INCOME — See Sec. 2, B.3 — $ Thousands
NET INVESTMENT GAIN / NET REALIZED CAPITAL GAINS — See Sec. 5, A.8 — $ Thousands
NET CASH FROM OPERATIONS — See Sec. 2, C.3 — $ Thousands
OPER. GAIN BEFORE TAXES — See Sec. 2, B.3 — $ Thousands

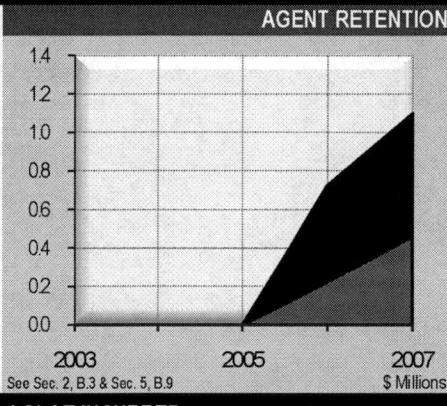

PREMIUMS — See Sec. 2, B.3 — $ Millions
- – · – Direct
- – – Non-Affiliated
- ----- Affiliated
- —— Net Premiums

OPERATING EXPENSES INCURRED / AGENT RETENTION — See Sec. 2, B.3 & Sec. 5, B.9 — $ Millions

FINANCIAL POSITION	2007
Cash, Cash Equivalents & Short-Term Investments	$693,268
Total Assets	$1,236,789
Policyholders' Surplus	$817,207
Reserves	$157,975
OPERATING RESULTS	
Net Income	($313,133)
Net Investment Gain	$41,556
Net Realized Capital Gains	$0
Net Cash from Operations	($69,192)
Oper. Gain Before Taxes	($296,037)

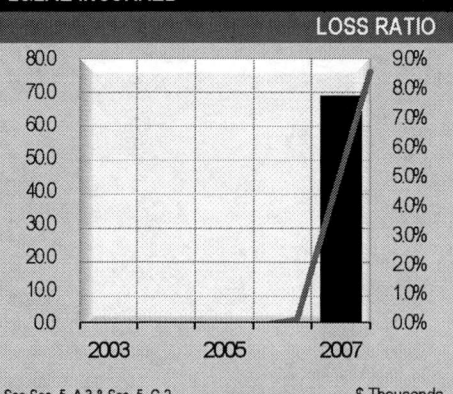

DIRECT PREMIUMS WRITTEN - YE 2007 — See Sec. 3, B.4
- ☐ Direct
- ▨ Non-Affiliated
- ▮ Affiliated

L&LAE INCURRED / LOSS RATIO — See Sec. 5, A.3 & Sec. 5, C.2 — $ Thousands

UNDERWRITING RESULTS	
Direct	$0
Non-Affiliated	$1,138,404
Affiliated	$0
Direct Premiums Written	$1,138,404
Net Premiums Earned	$802,423
Operating Expenses Incurred	$1,099,230
Agent Retention	$460,097
L&LAE Incurred	$68,819
Loss Ratio	8.57%

Fidelity National Title Insurance Company

601 Riverside Ave.
Jacksonville, FL 32204

(904) 854-8100

WEBSITE:	STATE OF DOMICILE:
www.fnf.com	California

PRESIDENT & CEO:	ESTABLISHED:	JURISDICTION LICENSE(S):
Raymond Randall Quirk	10/6/1981	50

A' Unsurpassed
Financial Stability Rating®
Demotech, Inc.

NAIC Number:
51586

FIDELITY NATIONAL

NAIC Group:
CHICAGO / FIDELITY

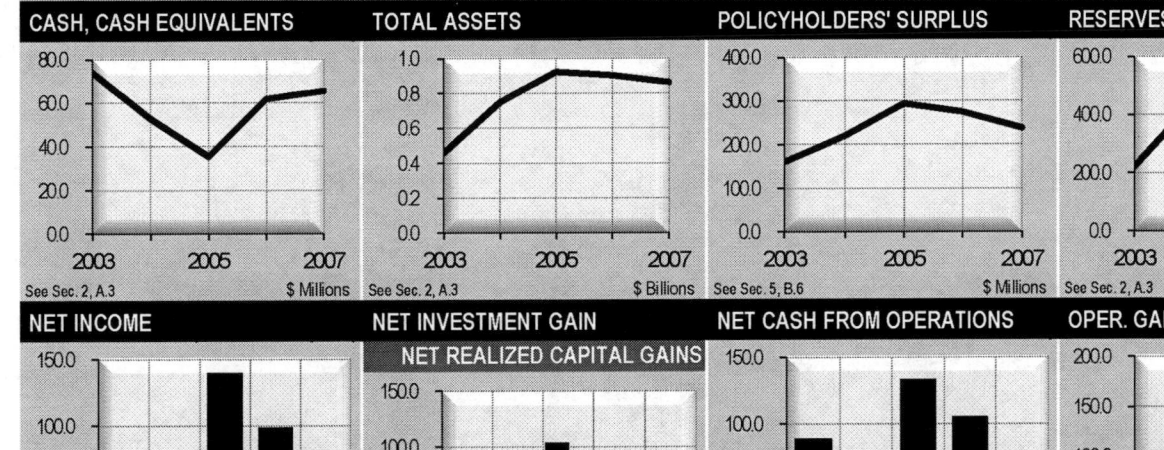

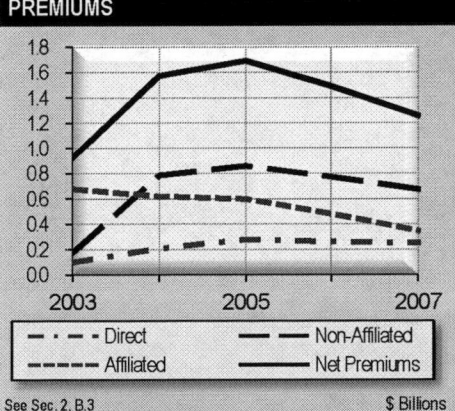

DIRECT PREMIUMS WRITTEN - YE 2007

Direct / Non-Affiliated / Affiliated

See Sec. 3, B.4

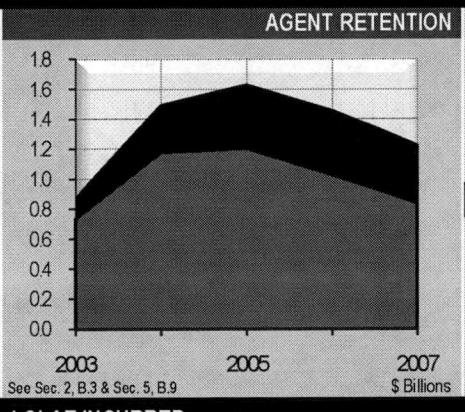

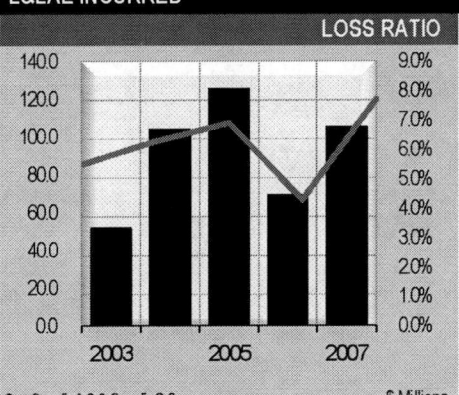

FINANCIAL POSITION	2007
Cash, Cash Equivalents & Short-Term Investments	$65,463,142
Total Assets	$860,789,383
Policyholders' Surplus	$237,682,104
Reserves	$526,224,289
OPERATING RESULTS	
Net Income	$58,097,258
Net Investment Gain	$39,431,994
Net Realized Capital Gains	$3,043,736
Net Cash from Operations	$64,230,499
Oper. Gain Before Taxes	$148,291,701
UNDERWRITING RESULTS	
Direct	$251,405,363
Non-Affiliated	$673,800,566
Affiliated	$348,876,279
Direct Premiums Written	**$1,274,082,208**
Net Premiums Earned	$1,257,995,188
Operating Expenses Incurred	$1,221,068,915
Agent Retention	$840,562,038
L&LAE Incurred	$105,973,214
Loss Ratio	7.74%

6

First American Title & Trust Company

133 NW 8th St.
Oklahoma City, OK 73102

(405) 236-2861

Formerly Southwest Title & Trust

WEBSITE:	STATE OF DOMICILE:
www.firstam.com	Oklahoma

PRESIDENT:	ESTABLISHED:	JURISDICTION LICENSE(S):
Monica Amis Wittrock	9/1/1960	1

A' Unsurpassed
Financial Stability Rating®
Demotech, Inc.

NAIC Number:
50037

FIRST AMERICAN T&T

NAIC Group:
FIRST AMERICAN

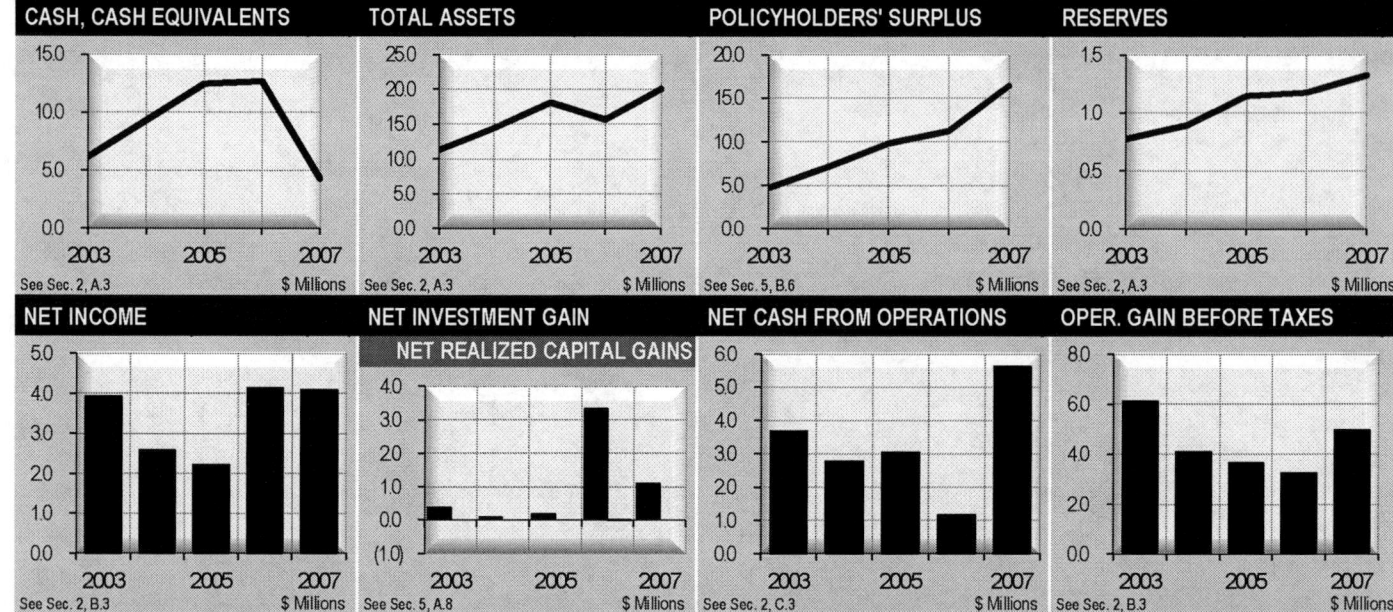

CASH, CASH EQUIVALENTS — See Sec. 2, A.3 — $ Millions

TOTAL ASSETS — See Sec. 2, A.3 — $ Millions

POLICYHOLDERS' SURPLUS — See Sec. 5, B.6 — $ Millions

RESERVES — See Sec. 2, A.3 — $ Millions

NET INCOME — See Sec. 2, B.3 — $ Millions

NET INVESTMENT GAIN / NET REALIZED CAPITAL GAINS — See Sec. 5, A.8 — $ Millions

NET CASH FROM OPERATIONS — See Sec. 2, C.3 — $ Millions

OPER. GAIN BEFORE TAXES — See Sec. 2, B.3 — $ Millions

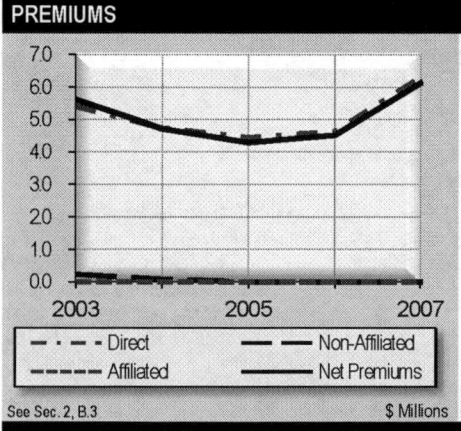

PREMIUMS

- — · — Direct
- — — Non-Affiliated
- – – – – Affiliated
- ——— Net Premiums

See Sec. 2, B.3 — $ Millions

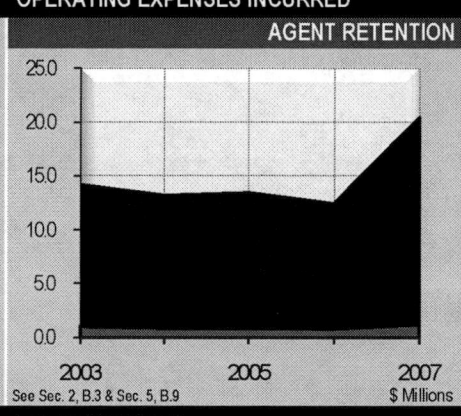

OPERATING EXPENSES INCURRED / AGENT RETENTION

See Sec. 2, B.3 & Sec. 5, B.9 — $ Millions

DIRECT PREMIUMS WRITTEN - YE 2007

☐ Direct   ■ Non-Affiliated   ■ Affiliated

See Sec. 3, B.4

L&LAE INCURRED / LOSS RATIO

See Sec. 5, A.3 & Sec. 5, C.2 — $ Thousands

FINANCIAL POSITION	2007
Cash, Cash Equivalents & Short-Term Investments	$4,292,578
Total Assets	$20,044,522
Policyholders' Surplus	$16,413,088
Reserves	$1,324,172
OPERATING RESULTS	
Net Income	$4,096,190
Net Investment Gain	$1,107,891
Net Realized Capital Gains	$0
Net Cash from Operations	$5,618,994
Oper. Gain Before Taxes	$4,956,615
UNDERWRITING RESULTS	
Direct	$6,291,430
Non-Affiliated	$0
Affiliated	$0
Direct Premiums Written	$6,291,430
Net Premiums Earned	$6,121,430
Operating Expenses Incurred	$20,447,786
Agent Retention	$1,227,400
L&LAE Incurred	$217,877
Loss Ratio	0.86%

First American Title Insurance Company

1 First American Way
Santa Ana, CA 92707

(714) 800-3000

WEBSITE:	STATE OF DOMICILE:
www.firstam.com	California

VICE CHAIRMAN:	ESTABLISHED:	JURISDICTION LICENSE(S):
Gary Lewis Kermott	9/24/1968	52

A" Unsurpassed
Financial Stability Rating®
Demotech, Inc.

NAIC Number:
50814

FIRST AMERICAN TIC

NAIC Group:
FIRST AMERICAN

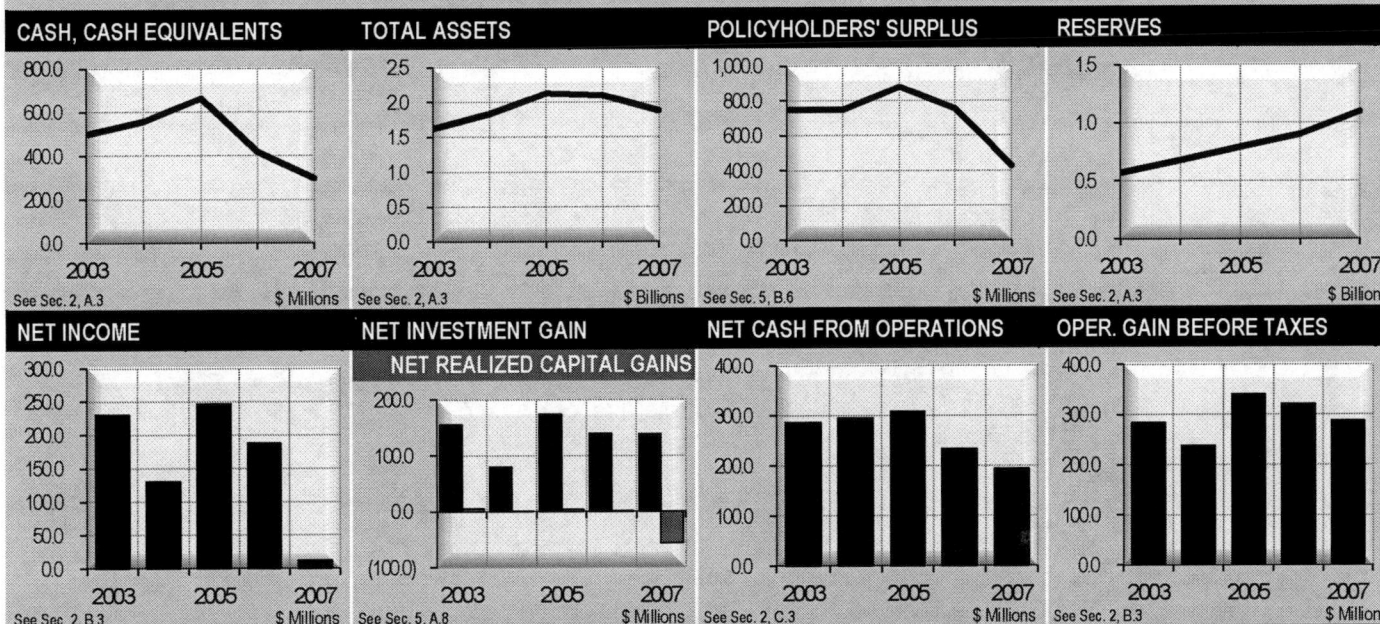

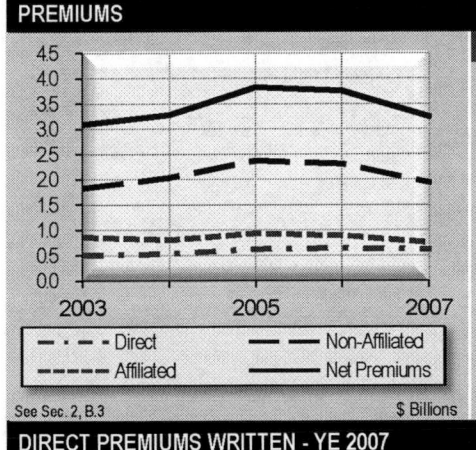

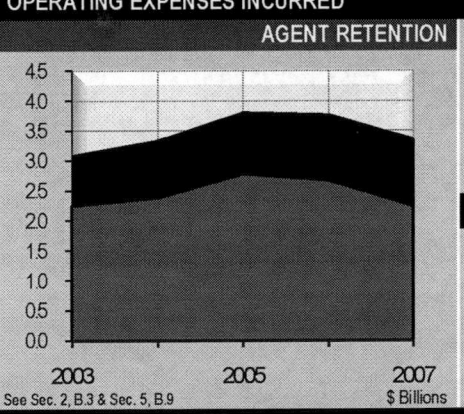

FINANCIAL POSITION	2007
Cash, Cash Equivalents & Short-Term Investments	$295,870,894
Total Assets	$1,873,280,555
Policyholders' Surplus	$426,527,243
Reserves	$1,091,937,703
OPERATING RESULTS	
Net Income	$12,082,432
Net Investment Gain	$138,826,293
Net Realized Capital Gains	($56,889,509)
Net Cash from Operations	$193,745,028
Oper. Gain Before Taxes	$287,322,079

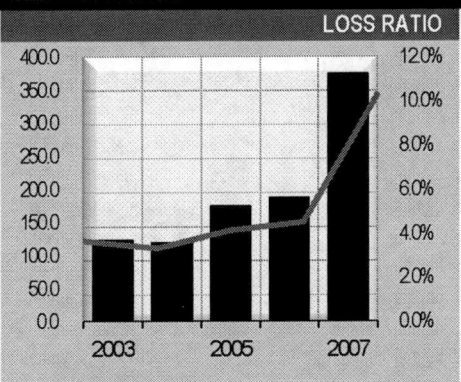

See Sec. 3, B.4

See Sec. 5, A.3 & Sec. 5, C.2 $ Millions

UNDERWRITING RESULTS	
Direct	$622,912,926
Non-Affiliated	$1,936,771,199
Affiliated	$752,682,458
Direct Premiums Written	$3,312,366,583
Net Premiums Earned	$3,249,306,457
Operating Expenses Incurred	$3,343,519,077
Agent Retention	$2,248,120,236
L&LAE Incurred	$374,613,626
Loss Ratio	10.32%

6

First American Title Insurance Company of Kansas, Inc.

1653 Larkin Williams Rd.
Fenton, MO 63026

(314) 821-5515

WEBSITE:	STATE OF DOMICILE:
www.firstam.com	Kansas

PRESIDENT:	ESTABLISHED:	JURISDICTION LICENSE(S):
Craig Lane Burns	5/22/1998	1

A **Exceptional**
Financial Stability Rating®
Demotech, Inc.

NAIC Number:
50043

FIRST AMERICAN (KS)

NAIC Group:
FIRST AMERICAN

CASH, CASH EQUIVALENTS	TOTAL ASSETS	POLICYHOLDERS' SURPLUS	RESERVES

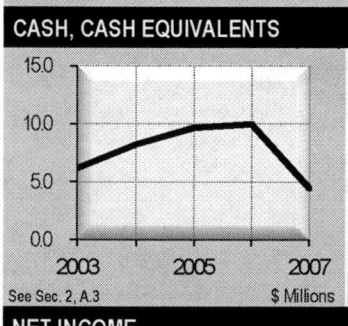 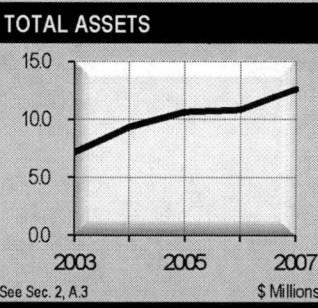 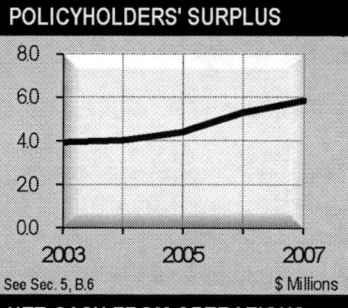 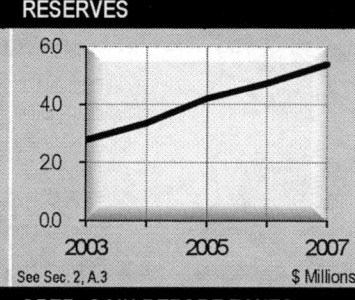

See Sec. 2, A.3 — $ Millions | See Sec. 2, A.3 — $ Millions | See Sec. 5, B.6 — $ Millions | See Sec. 2, A.3 — $ Millions

NET INCOME	NET INVESTMENT GAIN / NET REALIZED CAPITAL GAINS	NET CASH FROM OPERATIONS	OPER. GAIN BEFORE TAXES

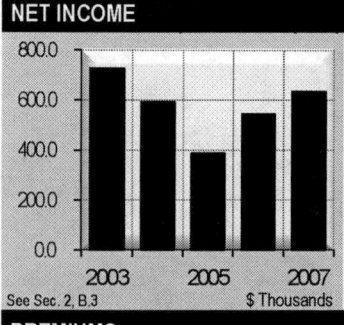 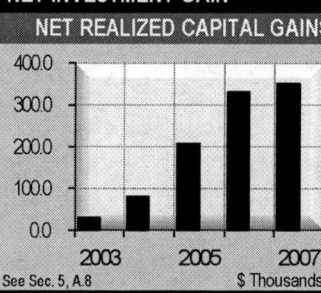 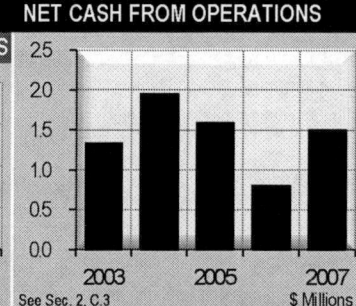 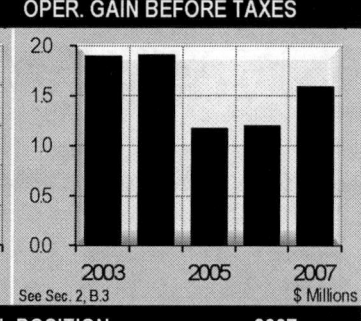

See Sec. 2, B.3 — $ Thousands | See Sec. 5, A.8 — $ Thousands | See Sec. 2, C.3 — $ Millions | See Sec. 2, B.3 — $ Millions

PREMIUMS	OPERATING EXPENSES INCURRED / AGENT RETENTION

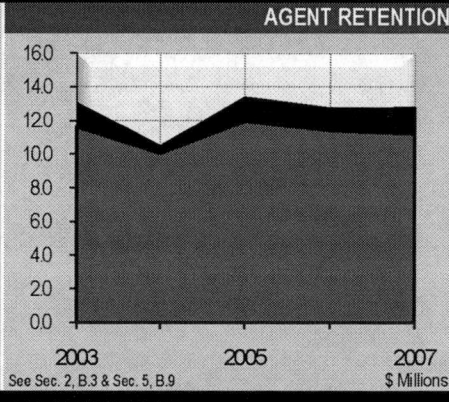

- · - Direct — Non-Affiliated
- - - - Affiliated — Net Premiums

See Sec. 2, B.3 — $ Millions | See Sec. 2, B.3 & Sec. 5, B.9 — $ Millions

FINANCIAL POSITION	2007
Cash, Cash Equivalents & Short-Term Investments	$4,482,353
Total Assets	$12,603,683
Policyholders' Surplus	$5,833,793
Reserves	$5,395,340
OPERATING RESULTS	
Net Income	$633,868
Net Investment Gain	$351,141
Net Realized Capital Gains	$0
Net Cash from Operations	$1,498,679
Oper. Gain Before Taxes	$1,583,570

DIRECT PREMIUMS WRITTEN - YE 2007	L&LAE INCURRED / LOSS RATIO

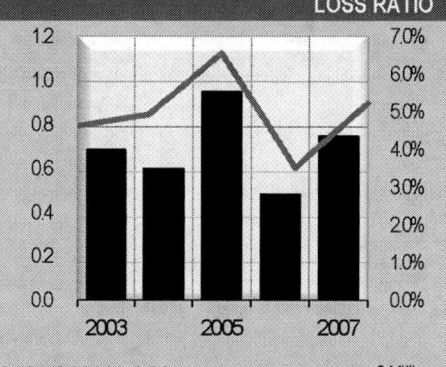

☐ Direct ■ Non-Affiliated ■ Affiliated

See Sec. 3, B.4 | See Sec. 5, A.3 & Sec. 5, C.2 — $ Millions

UNDERWRITING RESULTS	
Direct	$1,550,799
Non-Affiliated	$5,813,820
Affiliated	$7,399,061
Direct Premiums Written	**$14,763,680**
Net Premiums Earned	$13,915,416
Operating Expenses Incurred	$12,754,452
Agent Retention	$11,211,094
L&LAE Incurred	$756,653
Loss Ratio	5.28%

First American Title Insurance Company of New York

633 Third Ave.
New York, NY 10017

(212) 922-9700

WEBSITE:
www.firstamny.com

PRESIDENT:
James M. Orphanides

STATE OF DOMICILE:
New York

ESTABLISHED:
9/14/1967

JURISDICTION LICENSE(S):
4

A" Unsurpassed
Financial Stability Rating®
Demotech, Inc.

NAIC Number:
51039

FIRST AMERICAN (NY)

NAIC Group:
FIRST AMERICAN

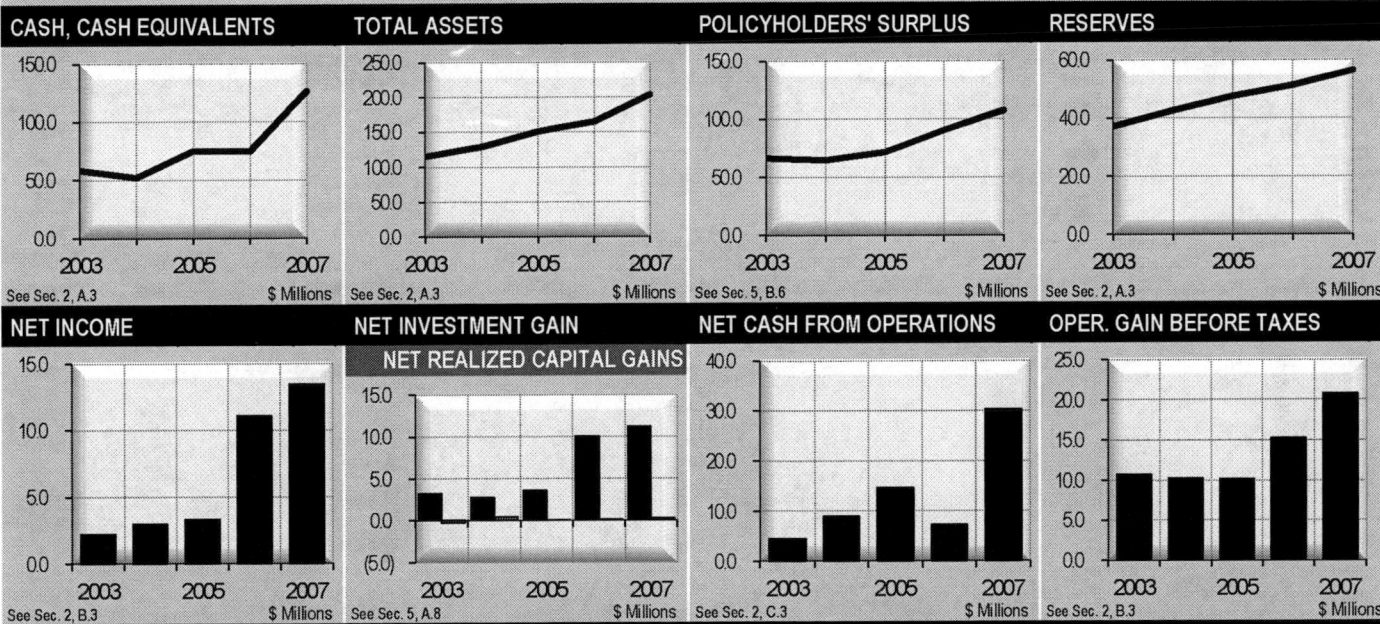

CASH, CASH EQUIVALENTS — See Sec. 2, A.3 — $ Millions

TOTAL ASSETS — See Sec. 2, A.3 — $ Millions

POLICYHOLDERS' SURPLUS — See Sec. 5, B.6 — $ Millions

RESERVES — See Sec. 2, A.3 — $ Millions

NET INCOME — See Sec. 2, B.3 — $ Millions

NET INVESTMENT GAIN / NET REALIZED CAPITAL GAINS — See Sec. 5, A.8 — $ Millions

NET CASH FROM OPERATIONS — See Sec. 2, C.3 — $ Millions

OPER. GAIN BEFORE TAXES — See Sec. 2, B.3 — $ Millions

PREMIUMS — See Sec. 2, B.3 — $ Millions
- · - Direct
- — — Non-Affiliated
- - - - Affiliated
- —— Net Premiums

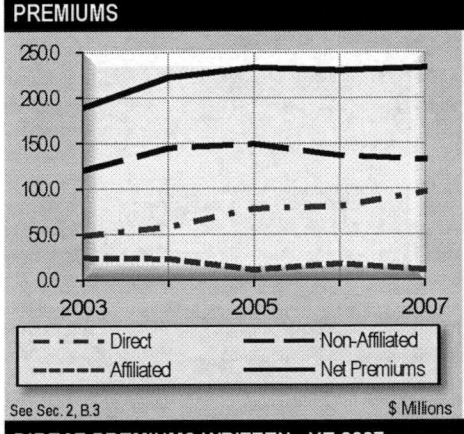

OPERATING EXPENSES INCURRED / AGENT RETENTION — See Sec. 2, B.3 & Sec. 5, B.9 — $ Millions

DIRECT PREMIUMS WRITTEN - YE 2007 — See Sec. 3, B.4
- ☐ Direct
- ▨ Non-Affiliated
- ■ Affiliated

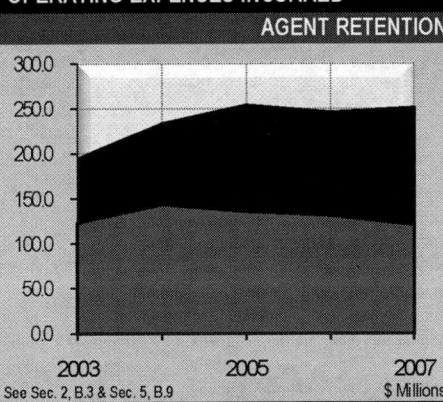

L&LAE INCURRED / LOSS RATIO — See Sec. 5, A.3 & Sec. 5, C.2 — $ Millions

FINANCIAL POSITION	2007
Cash, Cash Equivalents & Short-Term Investments	$126,167,891
Total Assets	$203,259,092
Policyholders' Surplus	$107,386,170
Reserves	$56,267,722
OPERATING RESULTS	
Net Income	$13,447,842
Net Investment Gain	$11,212,173
Net Realized Capital Gains	$271,625
Net Cash from Operations	$30,306,153
Oper. Gain Before Taxes	$20,751,422
UNDERWRITING RESULTS	
Direct	$96,485,318
Non-Affiliated	$131,671,357
Affiliated	$11,099,012
Direct Premiums Written	$239,255,687
Net Premiums Earned	$233,124,439
Operating Expenses Incurred	$251,130,486
Agent Retention	$121,059,713
L&LAE Incurred	$9,991,046
Loss Ratio	3.67%

6

First American Title Insurance Company of Oregon

222 SW Columbia St., 4th Fl.
Portland, OR 97201

(503) 222-3651

Also Known As Title Insurance Company Of Oregon

WEBSITE:	STATE OF DOMICILE:
www.firstam.com	Oregon

PRESIDENT:	ESTABLISHED:	JURISDICTION LICENSE(S):
Steven Ernest Brown	10/16/1937	3

A' A Prime **Unsurpassed**
Financial Stability Rating®
🔶 Demotech, Inc.

NAIC Number:
50504

FIRST AMERICAN (OR)

NAIC Group:
FIRST AMERICAN

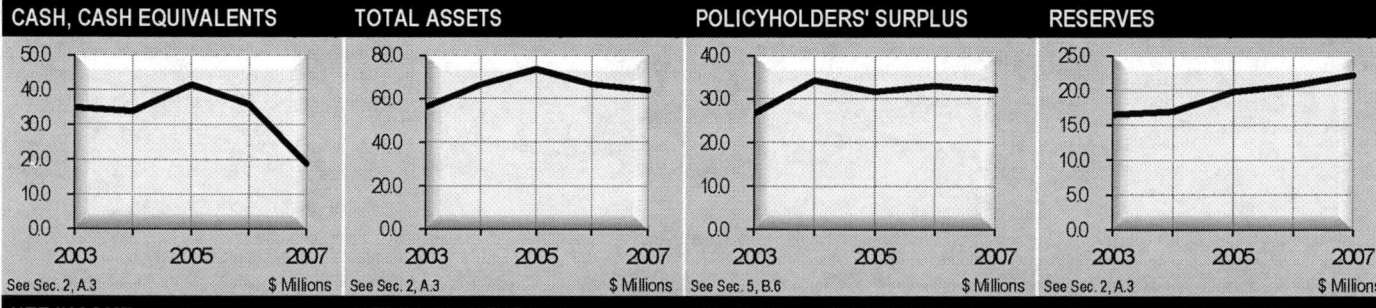

CASH, CASH EQUIVALENTS — See Sec. 2, A.3 — $ Millions
TOTAL ASSETS — See Sec. 2, A.3 — $ Millions
POLICYHOLDERS' SURPLUS — See Sec. 5, B.6 — $ Millions
RESERVES — See Sec. 2, A.3 — $ Millions

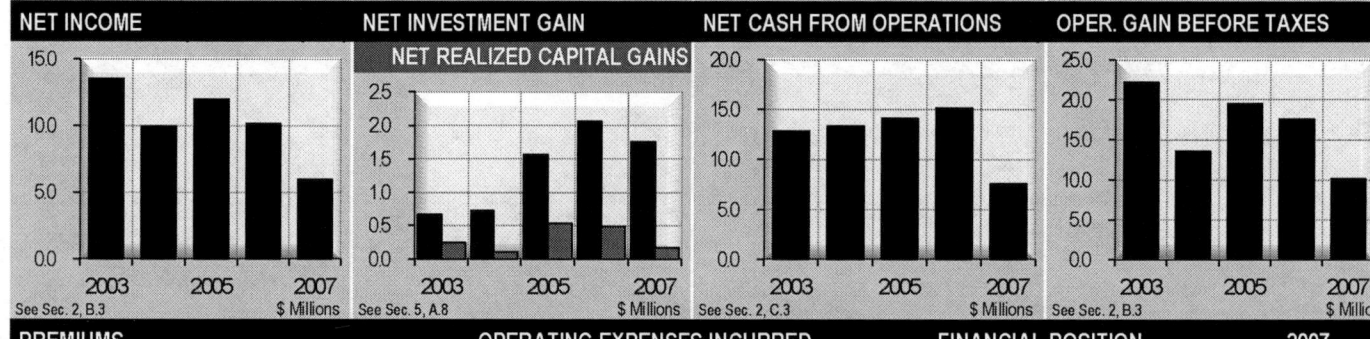

NET INCOME — See Sec. 2, B.3 — $ Millions
NET INVESTMENT GAIN / NET REALIZED CAPITAL GAINS — See Sec. 5, A.8 — $ Millions
NET CASH FROM OPERATIONS — See Sec. 2, C.3 — $ Millions
OPER. GAIN BEFORE TAXES — See Sec. 2, B.3 — $ Millions

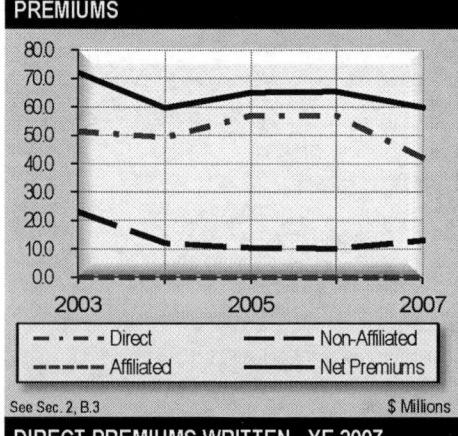

PREMIUMS
- – · – Direct
- – – – Non-Affiliated
- – – – – Affiliated
- ——— Net Premiums

See Sec. 2, B.3 — $ Millions

OPERATING EXPENSES INCURRED / AGENT RETENTION — See Sec. 2, B.3 & Sec. 5, B.9 — $ Millions

FINANCIAL POSITION	2007
Cash, Cash Equivalents & Short-Term Investments	$18,751,393
Total Assets	$64,001,382
Policyholders' Surplus	$32,041,274
Reserves	$22,204,555
OPERATING RESULTS	
Net Income	$5,978,208
Net Investment Gain	$1,758,797
Net Realized Capital Gains	$168,650
Net Cash from Operations	$7,590,140
Oper. Gain Before Taxes	$10,177,821

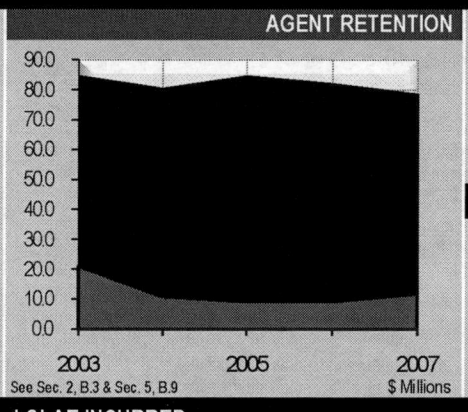

DIRECT PREMIUMS WRITTEN - YE 2007
☐ Direct ▨ Non-Affiliated ■ Affiliated
See Sec. 3, B.4

L&LAE INCURRED / LOSS RATIO — See Sec. 5, A.3 & Sec. 5, C.2 — $ Millions

UNDERWRITING RESULTS	
Direct	$42,031,597
Non-Affiliated	$13,032,270
Affiliated	$0
Direct Premiums Written	$55,063,867
Net Premiums Earned	$59,893,994
Operating Expenses Incurred	$78,334,284
Agent Retention	$11,789,024
L&LAE Incurred	$2,919,785
Loss Ratio	3.30%

First American Transportation Title Insurance Company

510 Bienville St
New Orleans, LA 70130

(504) 588-9252

Formerly Louisiana First Title Insurance Company

WEBSITE:	STATE OF DOMICILE:
www.firstam.com	Louisiana

PRESIDENT:	ESTABLISHED:	JURISDICTION LICENSE(S):
John Newton Casbon	8/13/1980	2

A Exceptional
Financial Stability Rating®
Demotech, Inc.

NAIC Number:
51527

FIRST AMERICAN TRANS

NAIC Group:
FIRST AMERICAN

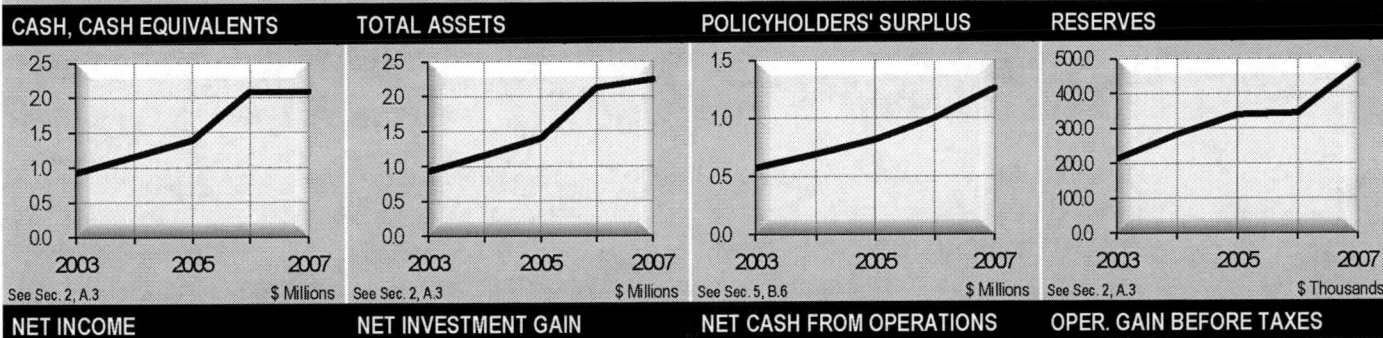

CASH, CASH EQUIVALENTS — See Sec. 2, A.3 — $ Millions
TOTAL ASSETS — See Sec. 2, A.3 — $ Millions
POLICYHOLDERS' SURPLUS — See Sec. 5, B.6 — $ Millions
RESERVES — See Sec. 2, A.3 — $ Thousands

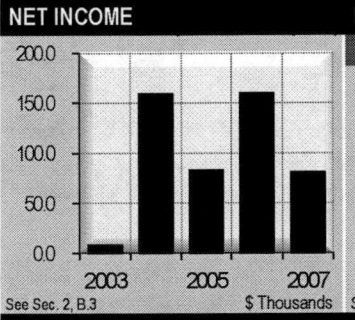

NET INCOME — See Sec. 2, B.3 — $ Thousands

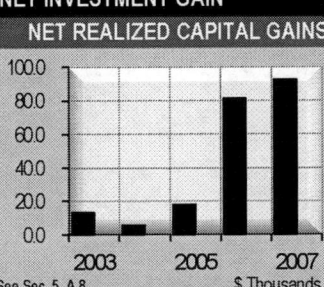

NET INVESTMENT GAIN / NET REALIZED CAPITAL GAINS — See Sec. 5, A.8 — $ Thousands

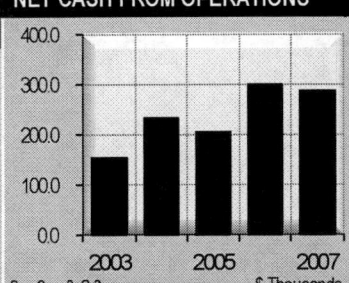

NET CASH FROM OPERATIONS — See Sec. 2, C.3 — $ Thousands

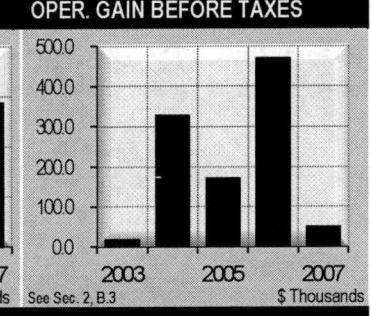

OPER. GAIN BEFORE TAXES — See Sec. 2, B.3 — $ Thousands

PREMIUMS

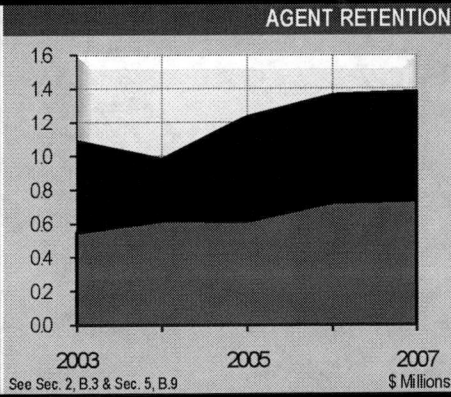

- - Direct
----- Affiliated
-- Non-Affiliated
— Net Premiums

See Sec. 2, B.3 — $ Millions

OPERATING EXPENSES INCURRED / AGENT RETENTION

See Sec. 2, B.3 & Sec. 5, B.9 — $ Millions

DIRECT PREMIUMS WRITTEN - YE 2007

□ Direct ▨ Non-Affiliated ■ Affiliated

See Sec. 3, B.4

L&LAE INCURRED / LOSS RATIO

See Sec. 5, A.3 & Sec. 5, C.2 — $ Thousands

FINANCIAL POSITION	2007
Cash, Cash Equivalents & Short-Term Investments	$2,078,017
Total Assets	$2,242,831
Policyholders' Surplus	$1,254,245
Reserves	$475,908
OPERATING RESULTS	
Net Income	$81,360
Net Investment Gain	$92,479
Net Realized Capital Gains	$0
Net Cash from Operations	$288,142
Oper. Gain Before Taxes	$50,082
UNDERWRITING RESULTS	
Direct	$108,501
Non-Affiliated	$1,474,514
Affiliated	$0
Direct Premiums Written	$1,583,015
Net Premiums Earned	$1,431,515
Operating Expenses Incurred	$1,382,233
Agent Retention	$736,408
L&LAE Incurred	($16,063)
Loss Ratio	(1.12)%

6

Founders Title Insurance

1814 Warren Ave.
Cheyenne, WY 82001

(307) 632-4414

WEBSITE:	STATE OF DOMICILE:
–	Wyoming

PRESIDENT:	ESTABLISHED:	JURISDICTION LICENSE(S):
Ted O. Simola	12/31/2003	1

S Substantial
Financial Stability Rating®
Demotech, Inc.

NAIC Number:
11974

FOUNDERS

NAIC Group:
UNAFFILIATED

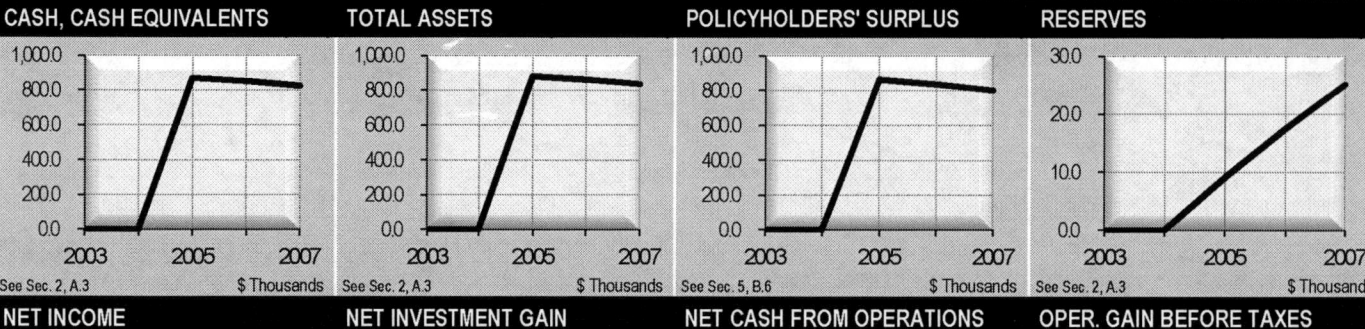

CASH, CASH EQUIVALENTS — See Sec. 2, A.3 — $ Thousands
TOTAL ASSETS — See Sec. 2, A.3 — $ Thousands
POLICYHOLDERS' SURPLUS — See Sec. 5, B.6 — $ Thousands
RESERVES — See Sec. 2, A.3 — $ Thousands

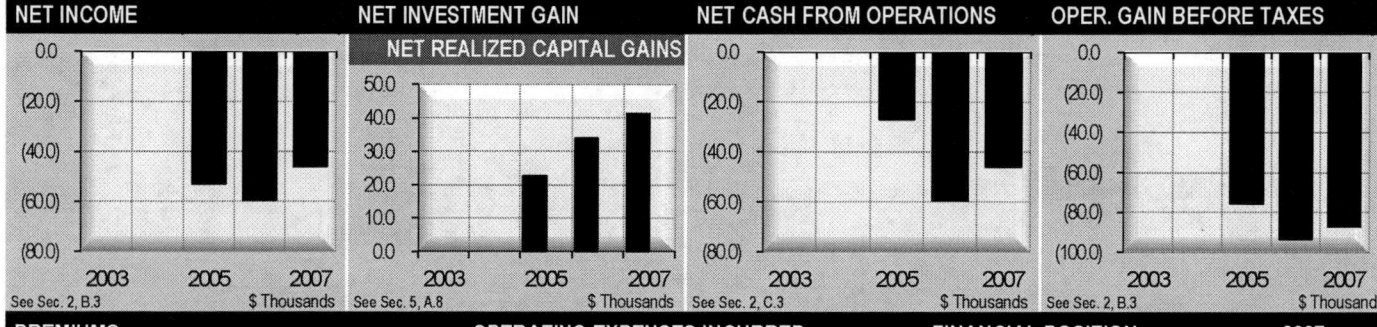

NET INCOME — See Sec. 2, B.3 — $ Thousands
NET INVESTMENT GAIN / NET REALIZED CAPITAL GAINS — See Sec. 5, A.8 — $ Thousands
NET CASH FROM OPERATIONS — See Sec. 2, C.3 — $ Thousands
OPER. GAIN BEFORE TAXES — See Sec. 2, B.3 — $ Thousands

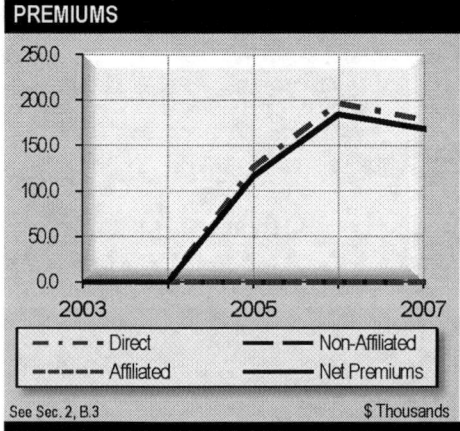

PREMIUMS
- – · – Direct
- - - - - Affiliated
- — — Non-Affiliated
- ——— Net Premiums

See Sec. 2, B.3 — $ Thousands

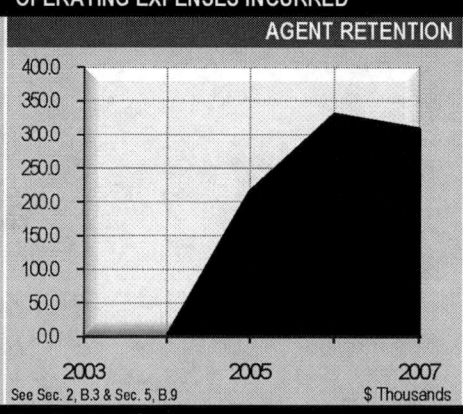

OPERATING EXPENSES INCURRED / AGENT RETENTION
See Sec. 2, B.3 & Sec. 5, B.9 — $ Thousands

FINANCIAL POSITION	2007
Cash, Cash Equivalents & Short-Term Investments	$823,832
Total Assets	$836,182
Policyholders' Surplus	$800,122
Reserves	$25,068
OPERATING RESULTS	
Net Income	($46,012)
Net Investment Gain	$41,264
Net Realized Capital Gains	$0
Net Cash from Operations	($46,012)
Oper. Gain Before Taxes	($87,276)

DIRECT PREMIUMS WRITTEN - YE 2007
- ☐ Direct
- ▩ Non-Affiliated
- ■ Affiliated

See Sec. 3, B.4

L&LAE INCURRED / LOSS RATIO
See Sec. 5, A.3 & Sec. 5, C.2 — $

UNDERWRITING RESULTS	
Direct	$178,276
Non-Affiliated	$0
Affiliated	$0
Direct Premiums Written	$178,276
Net Premiums Earned	$168,403
Operating Expenses Incurred	$308,989
Agent Retention	$0
L&LAE Incurred	$0
Loss Ratio	0.00%

General Title & Trust Company

24262 Broadway Ave.
Cleveland, OH 44146

(440) 232-5511

WEBSITE:	STATE OF DOMICILE:
www.generaltitleandtrust.com	Ohio

PRESIDENT:	ESTABLISHED:	JURISDICTION LICENSE(S):
Louis S. Frank	3/25/1925	2

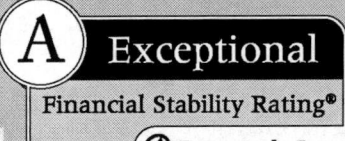

A Exceptional
Financial Stability Rating®
Demotech, Inc.

NAIC Number:
50172

GENERAL T&T

NAIC Group:
UNAFFILIATED

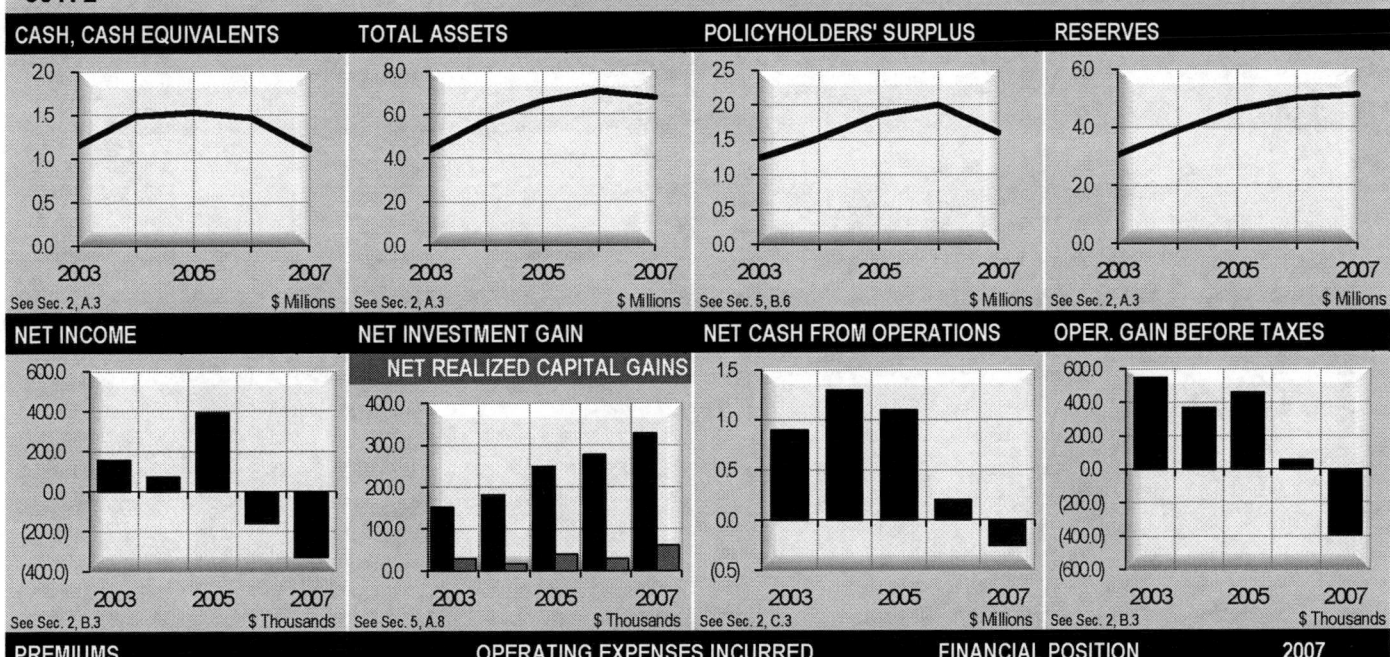

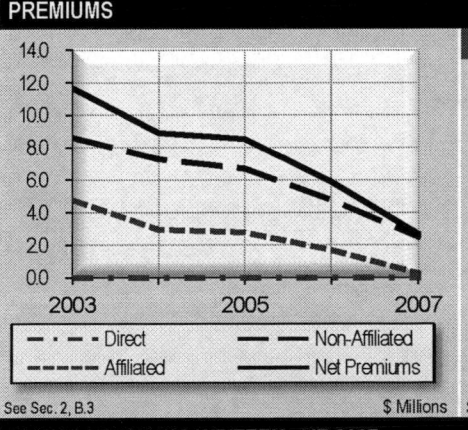

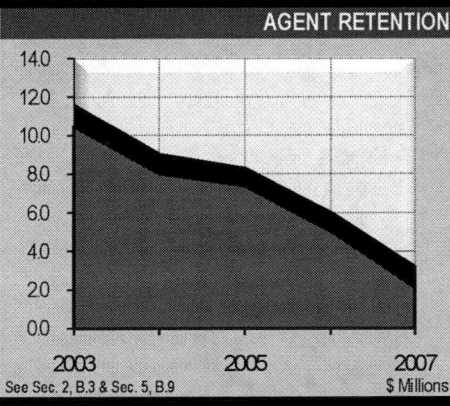

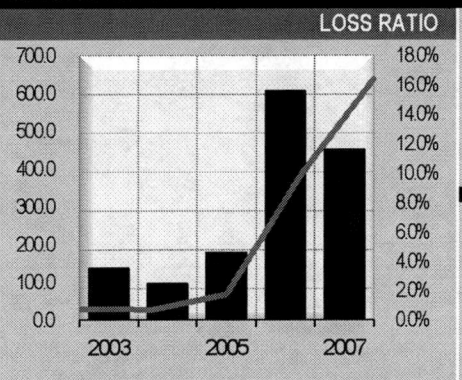

FINANCIAL POSITION	2007
Cash, Cash Equivalents & Short-Term Investments	$1,107,848
Total Assets	$6,775,741
Policyholders' Surplus	$1,595,193
Reserves	$5,094,975
OPERATING RESULTS	
Net Income	($331,252)
Net Investment Gain	$328,392
Net Realized Capital Gains	$60,573
Net Cash from Operations	($258,590)
Oper. Gain Before Taxes	($397,523)
UNDERWRITING RESULTS	
Direct	$0
Non-Affiliated	$2,510,539
Affiliated	$266,652
Direct Premiums Written	**$2,777,191**
Net Premiums Earned	$2,684,245
Operating Expenses Incurred	$3,178,262
Agent Retention	$2,112,834
L&LAE Incurred	$457,564
Loss Ratio	16.45%

6

Disclaimer: The information presented was compiled from Form 9 statements prepared and submitted by underwriters in accordance with Statutory Accounting Principles. No representations or warranties are made by Demotech, Inc. as to the completeness or accuracy of the information. Financial Stability Ratings® must be verified by visiting www.demotech.com.
©Demotech, Inc. Demotech Performance of Title Insurance Companies, its contents and material cannot be reproduced or copied, in part or in its entirety, without the express written permission of Demotech, Inc.

Guarantee Title and Trust Company

8230 Montgomery Rd., Ste. 200
Cincinnati, OH 45236

(513) 794-4020

WEBSITE:	STATE OF DOMICILE:
www.gtitle.com	Ohio

PRESIDENT:	ESTABLISHED:	JURISDICTION LICENSE(S):
Hiram Edward Blomquist	4/29/1899	14

NR Not Rated
Financial Stability Rating®
Demotech, Inc.

NAIC Number:
50180

GUARANTEE T&T

NAIC Group:
RELIANT HOLDING

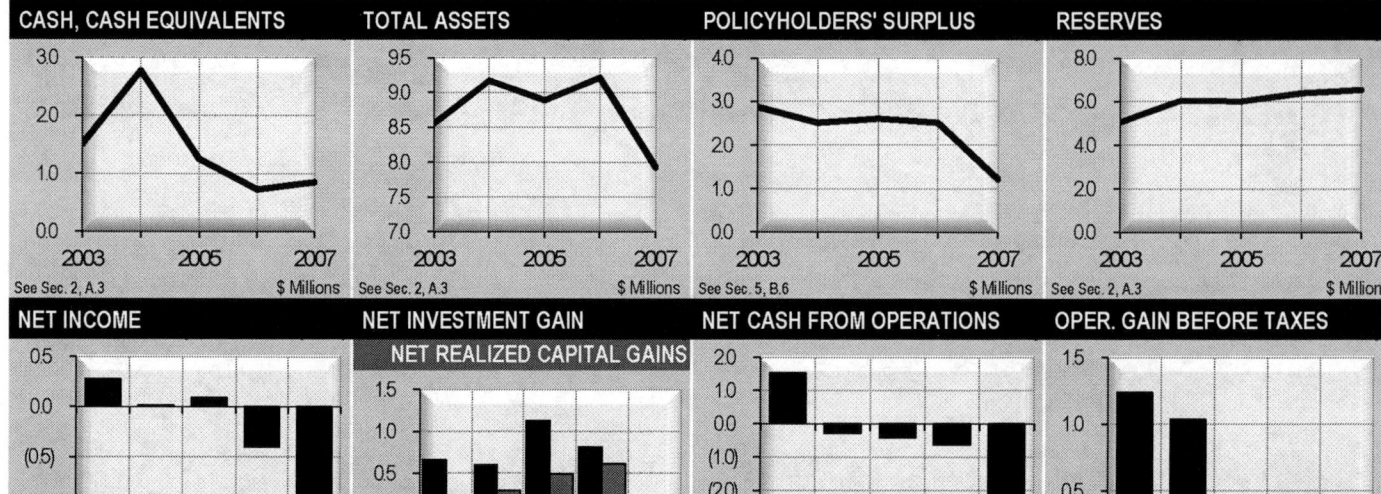

CASH, CASH EQUIVALENTS — See Sec. 2, A.3 — $ Millions
TOTAL ASSETS — See Sec. 2, A.3 — $ Millions
POLICYHOLDERS' SURPLUS — See Sec. 5, B.6 — $ Millions
RESERVES — See Sec. 2, A.3 — $ Millions

NET INCOME — See Sec. 2, B.3 — $ Millions
NET INVESTMENT GAIN / NET REALIZED CAPITAL GAINS — See Sec. 5, A.8 — $ Millions
NET CASH FROM OPERATIONS — See Sec. 2, C.3 — $ Millions
OPER. GAIN BEFORE TAXES — See Sec. 2, B.3 — $ Millions

FINANCIAL POSITION	2007
Cash, Cash Equivalents & Short-Term Investments	$853,485
Total Assets	$7,924,950
Policyholders' Surplus	$1,219,340
Reserves	$6,544,229
OPERATING RESULTS	
Net Income	($1,269,818)
Net Investment Gain	($768)
Net Realized Capital Gains	$1,760
Net Cash from Operations	($3,368,487)
Oper. Gain Before Taxes	$306,024

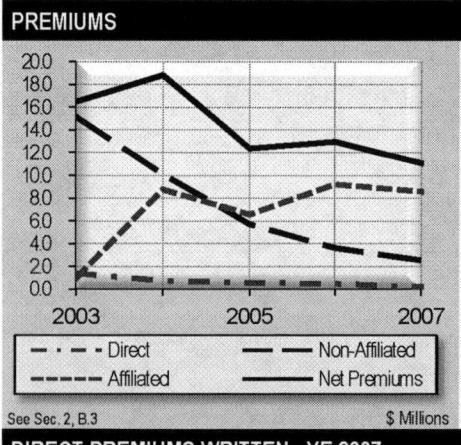

PREMIUMS
— · — Direct
- - - Non-Affiliated
- - - - Affiliated
—— Net Premiums
See Sec. 2, B.3 — $ Millions

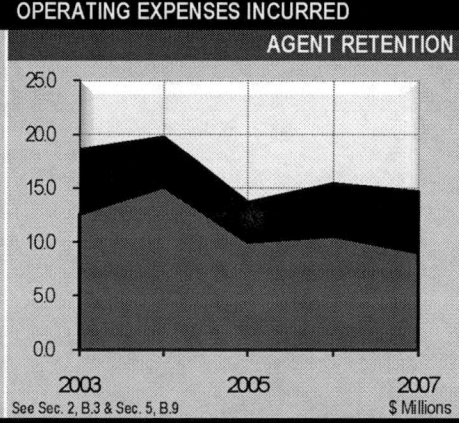

OPERATING EXPENSES INCURRED / AGENT RETENTION — See Sec. 2, B.3 & Sec. 5, B.9 — $ Millions

UNDERWRITING RESULTS	
Direct	$204,520
Non-Affiliated	$2,531,710
Affiliated	$8,582,676
Direct Premiums Written	$11,318,906
Net Premiums Earned	$11,093,777
Operating Expenses Incurred	$14,702,319
Agent Retention	$9,083,214
L&LAE Incurred	$1,575,074
Loss Ratio	10.50%

DIRECT PREMIUMS WRITTEN - YE 2007
☐ Direct ■ Non-Affiliated ■ Affiliated
See Sec. 3, B.4

L&LAE INCURRED / LOSS RATIO
See Sec. 5, A.3 & Sec. 5, C.2 — $ Millions

Guarantee Title Insurance Company

2 City Place Dr., Ste. 70
St. Louis, MO 63141

(314) 995-3940

Formerly The Bar Plan Title Insurance Company

WEBSITE:	STATE OF DOMICILE:
www.gtitle.com	Missouri

PRESIDENT:	ESTABLISHED:	JURISDICTION LICENSE(S):
Hiram Edward Blomquist	3/21/1995	4

NR **Not Rated**
Financial Stability Rating®
Demotech, Inc.

NAIC Number:
50034

GUARANTEE

NAIC Group:
RELIANT HOLDING

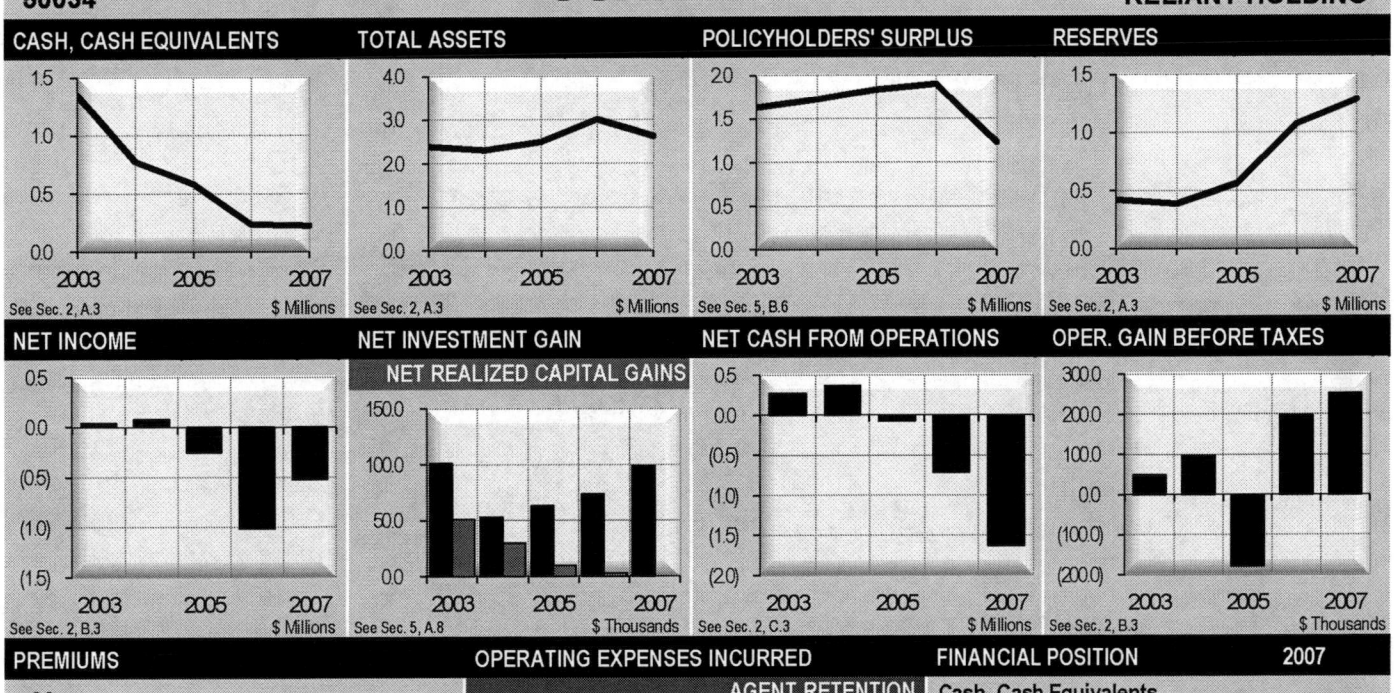

CASH, CASH EQUIVALENTS — See Sec. 2, A.3 — $ Millions
TOTAL ASSETS — See Sec. 2, A.3 — $ Millions
POLICYHOLDERS' SURPLUS — See Sec. 5, B.6 — $ Millions
RESERVES — See Sec. 2, A.3 — $ Millions

NET INCOME — See Sec. 2, B.3 — $ Millions
NET INVESTMENT GAIN / NET REALIZED CAPITAL GAINS — See Sec. 5, A.8 — $ Thousands
NET CASH FROM OPERATIONS — See Sec. 2, C.3 — $ Millions
OPER. GAIN BEFORE TAXES — See Sec. 2, B.3 — $ Thousands

PREMIUMS — See Sec. 2, B.3 — $ Millions
- · - · Direct
- - - - Affiliated
- —— Non-Affiliated
- —— Net Premiums

FINANCIAL POSITION	2007
Cash, Cash Equivalents & Short-Term Investments	$224,665
Total Assets	$2,624,841
Policyholders' Surplus	$1,228,016
Reserves	$1,280,392

OPERATING RESULTS	
Net Income	($520,922)
Net Investment Gain	$98,999
Net Realized Capital Gains	$0
Net Cash from Operations	($1,633,576)
Oper. Gain Before Taxes	$252,586

OPERATING EXPENSES INCURRED / AGENT RETENTION — See Sec. 2, B.3 & Sec. 5, B.9 — $ Millions

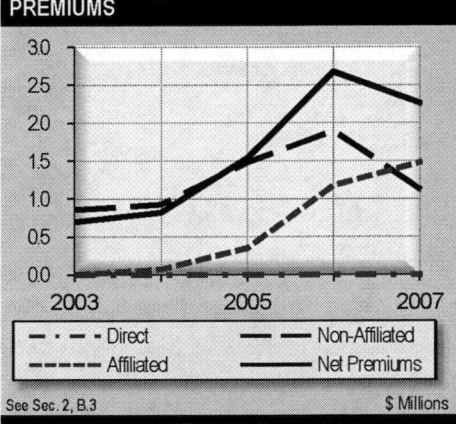

DIRECT PREMIUMS WRITTEN - YE 2007 — See Sec. 3, B.4
- ☐ Direct
- ▨ Non-Affiliated
- ■ Affiliated

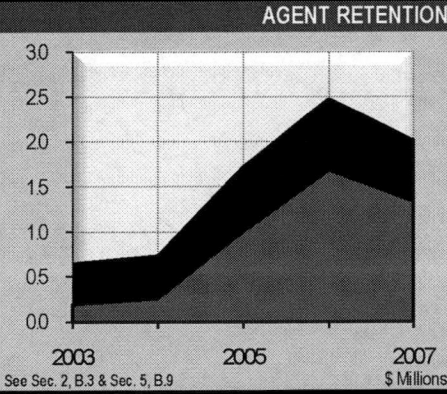

L&LAE INCURRED / LOSS RATIO — See Sec. 5, A.3 & Sec. 5, C.2 — $ Millions

UNDERWRITING RESULTS	
Direct	$0
Non-Affiliated	$1,125,386
Affiliated	$1,472,208
Direct Premiums Written	$2,597,594
Net Premiums Earned	$2,262,039
Operating Expenses Incurred	$2,009,451
Agent Retention	$1,337,903
L&LAE Incurred	$873,275
Loss Ratio	38.61%

6

Guardian National Title Insurance Company

4600 Rockside Rd., Ste. 104
Independence, OH 44131

(800) 362-2305

WEBSITE:	STATE OF DOMICILE:
www.gtinsurance.com	Ohio

PRESIDENT:	ESTABLISHED:	JURISDICTION LICENSE(S):
Michael F. Waiwood	4/7/1978	15

A' Prime **Unsurpassed**
Financial Stability Rating®
Demotech, Inc.

NAIC Number:
51632

GUARDIAN NATIONAL

NAIC Group:
UNAFFILIATED

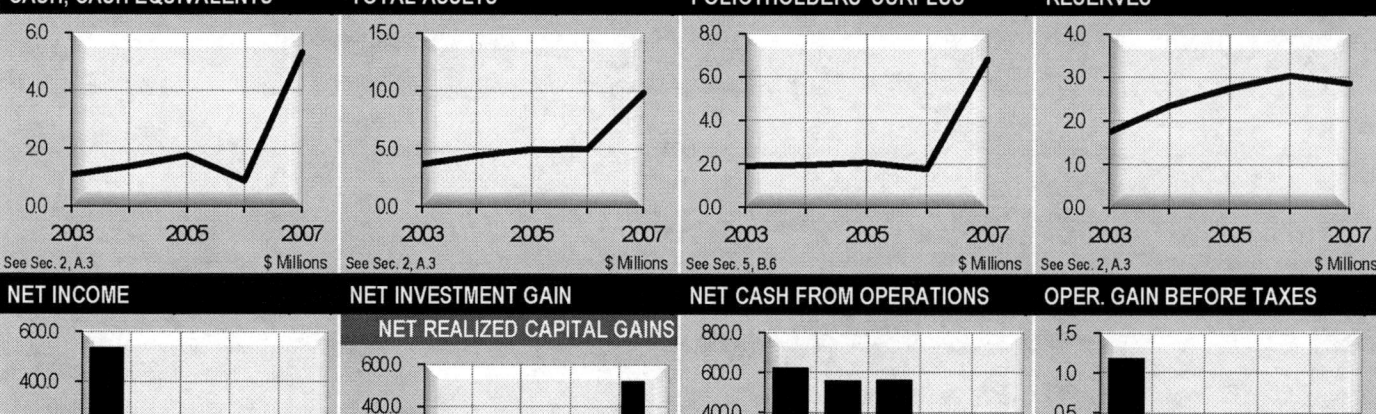

CASH, CASH EQUIVALENTS — See Sec. 2, A.3 — $ Millions
TOTAL ASSETS — See Sec. 2, A.3 — $ Millions
POLICYHOLDERS' SURPLUS — See Sec. 5, B.6 — $ Millions
RESERVES — See Sec. 2, A.3 — $ Millions

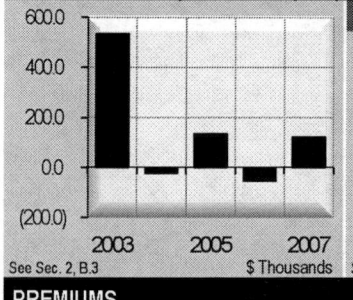

NET INCOME — See Sec. 2, B.3 — $ Thousands

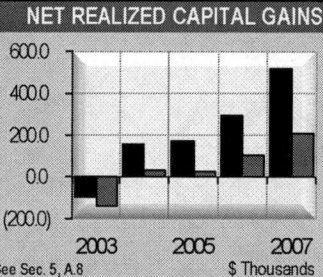

NET INVESTMENT GAIN / NET REALIZED CAPITAL GAINS — See Sec. 5, A.8 — $ Thousands

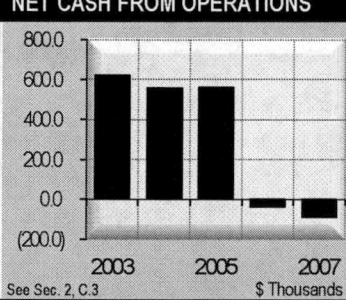

NET CASH FROM OPERATIONS — See Sec. 2, C.3 — $ Thousands

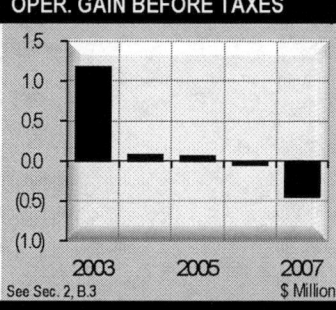

OPER. GAIN BEFORE TAXES — See Sec. 2, B.3 — $ Millions

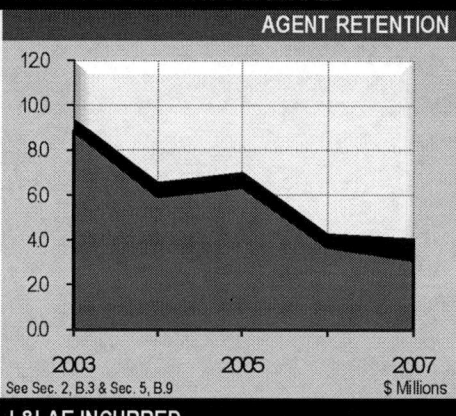

PREMIUMS — See Sec. 2, B.3 — $ Millions

- - · - Direct
- - - - Affiliated
—— Non-Affiliated
—— Net Premiums

OPERATING EXPENSES INCURRED / AGENT RETENTION — See Sec. 2, B.3 & Sec. 5, B.9 — $ Millions

FINANCIAL POSITION	2007
Cash, Cash Equivalents & Short-Term Investments	$5,310,594
Total Assets	$9,809,886
Policyholders' Surplus	$6,798,513
Reserves	$2,851,787
OPERATING RESULTS	
Net Income	$121,480
Net Investment Gain	$516,788
Net Realized Capital Gains	$210,417
Net Cash from Operations	($88,937)
Oper. Gain Before Taxes	($444,338)

DIRECT PREMIUMS WRITTEN - YE 2007 — See Sec. 3, B.4

☐ Direct ◼ Non-Affiliated ◼ Affiliated

L&LAE INCURRED / LOSS RATIO — See Sec. 5, A.3 & Sec. 5, C.2 — $ Thousands

UNDERWRITING RESULTS	
Direct	$0
Non-Affiliated	$3,445,031
Affiliated	$428,862
Direct Premiums Written	**$3,873,893**
Net Premiums Earned	$3,594,472
Operating Expenses Incurred	$4,038,810
Agent Retention	$3,124,113
L&LAE Incurred	($76,380)
Loss Ratio	(2.12)%

6

Investors Title Insurance Company

121 N Columbia St.
Chapel Hill, NC 27514

(919) 968-2200

WEBSITE:	STATE OF DOMICILE:
www.invtitle.com	North Carolina

PRESIDENT & COO:	ESTABLISHED:	JURISDICTION LICENSE(S):
William Morris Fine	1/28/1972	45

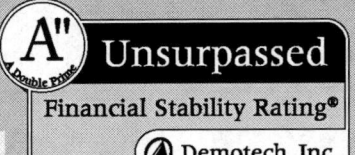

A" Unsurpassed
Financial Stability Rating®
Demotech, Inc.

NAIC Number: **50369**

INVESTORS TIC

NAIC Group: **INVESTORS**

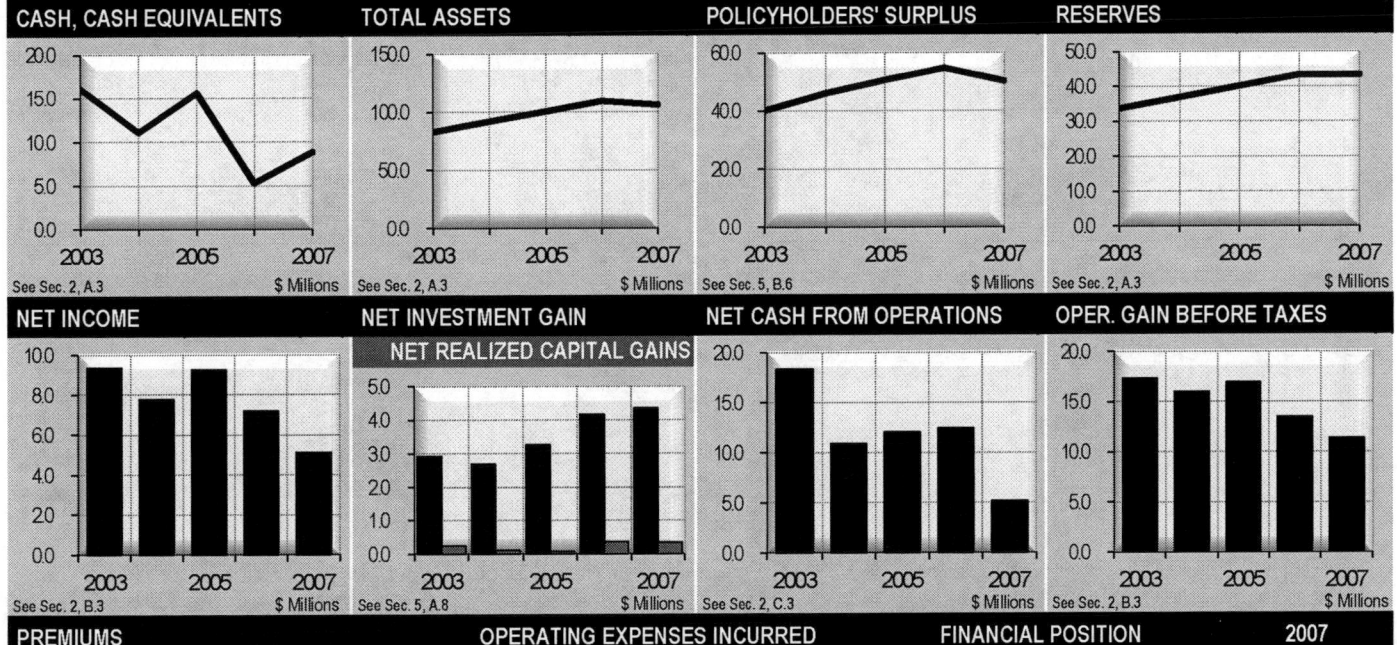

CASH, CASH EQUIVALENTS — See Sec. 2, A.3 — $ Millions

TOTAL ASSETS — See Sec. 2, A.3 — $ Millions

POLICYHOLDERS' SURPLUS — See Sec. 5, B.6 — $ Millions

RESERVES — See Sec. 2, A.3 — $ Millions

NET INCOME — See Sec. 2, B.3 — $ Millions

NET INVESTMENT GAIN / NET REALIZED CAPITAL GAINS — See Sec. 5, A.8 — $ Millions

NET CASH FROM OPERATIONS — See Sec. 2, C.3 — $ Millions

OPER. GAIN BEFORE TAXES — See Sec. 2, B.3 — $ Millions

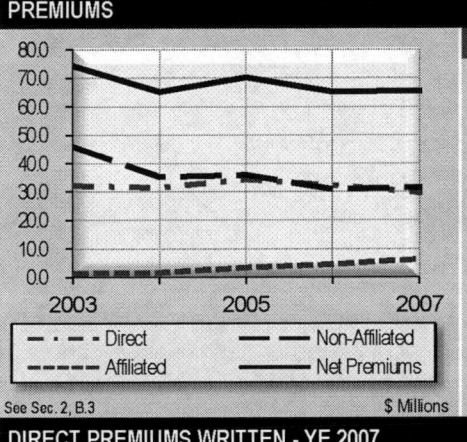

PREMIUMS — See Sec. 2, B.3 — $ Millions

- Direct
- Affiliated
- Non-Affiliated
- Net Premiums

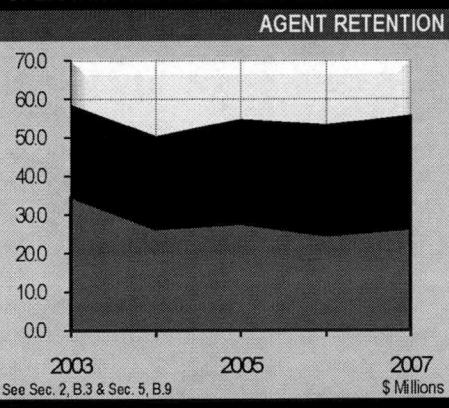

OPERATING EXPENSES INCURRED / AGENT RETENTION — See Sec. 2, B.3 & Sec. 5, B.9 — $ Millions

FINANCIAL POSITION	2007
Cash, Cash Equivalents & Short-Term Investments	$8,822,981
Total Assets	$105,684,657
Policyholders' Surplus	$50,102,762
Reserves	$43,262,724
OPERATING RESULTS	
Net Income	$5,126,419
Net Investment Gain	$4,354,350
Net Realized Capital Gains	$344,666
Net Cash from Operations	$5,158,757
Oper. Gain Before Taxes	$11,419,571

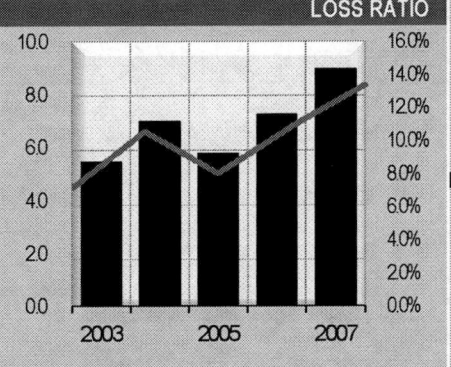

DIRECT PREMIUMS WRITTEN - YE 2007 — See Sec. 3, B.4

- ☐ Direct
- ▨ Non-Affiliated
- ■ Affiliated

L&LAE INCURRED / LOSS RATIO — See Sec. 5, A.3 & Sec. 5, C.2 — $ Millions

UNDERWRITING RESULTS	
Direct	$29,790,883
Non-Affiliated	$31,463,285
Affiliated	$6,291,704
Direct Premiums Written	**$67,545,872**
Net Premiums Earned	$65,565,455
Operating Expenses Incurred	$55,433,642
Agent Retention	$26,489,262
L&LAE Incurred	$8,975,058
Loss Ratio	13.43%

6

K.E.L. Title Insurance Group

151 Wymore Rd., Ste. 2100
Altamonte Springs, FL 32714

(407) 513-1900

WEBSITE: www.keltitle.com	**STATE OF DOMICILE:** Florida
PRESIDENT: Sheryl Campbell Hughes	**ESTABLISHED:** 4/24/2007 — **JURISDICTION LICENSE(S):** 1

S Substantial
Financial Stability Rating®
Demotech, Inc.

NAIC Number:
12953

K.E.L.

NAIC Group:
UNAFFILIATED

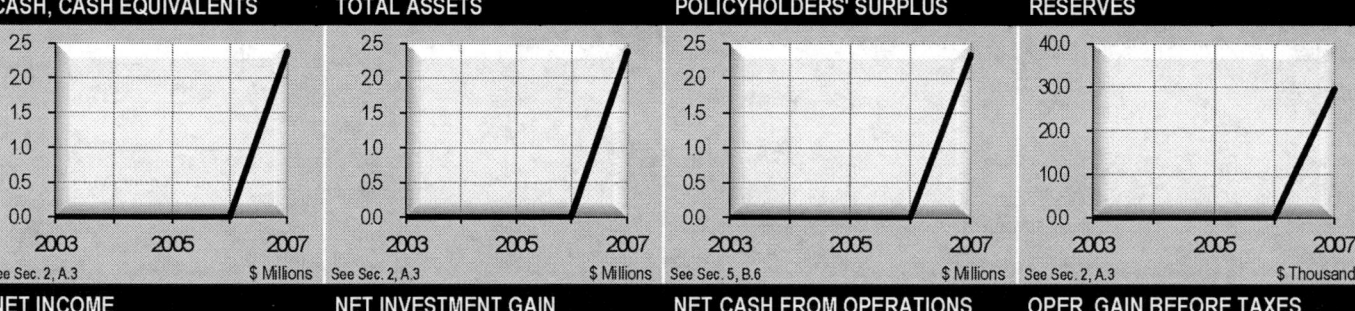

CASH, CASH EQUIVALENTS — See Sec. 2, A.3 — $ Millions
TOTAL ASSETS — See Sec. 2, A.3 — $ Millions
POLICYHOLDERS' SURPLUS — See Sec. 5, B.6 — $ Millions
RESERVES — See Sec. 2, A.3 — $ Thousands

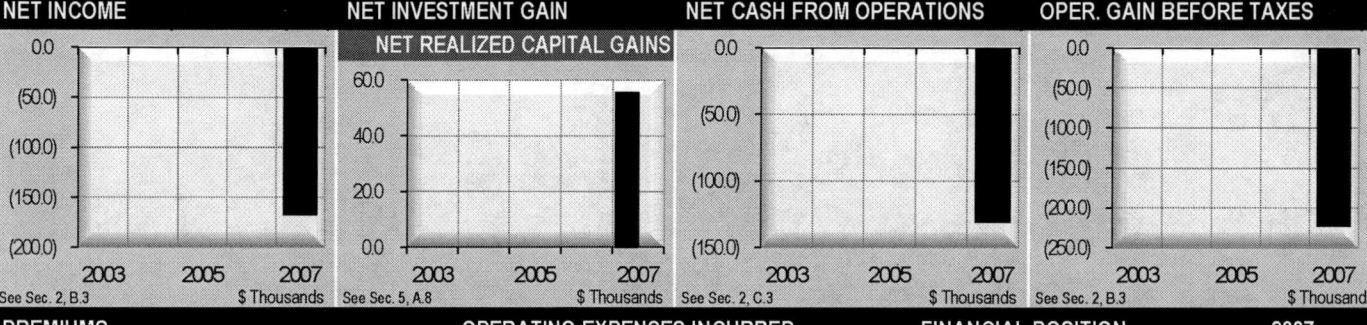

NET INCOME — See Sec. 2, B.3 — $ Thousands
NET INVESTMENT GAIN / NET REALIZED CAPITAL GAINS — See Sec. 5, A.8 — $ Thousands
NET CASH FROM OPERATIONS — See Sec. 2, C.3 — $ Thousands
OPER. GAIN BEFORE TAXES — See Sec. 2, B.3 — $ Thousands

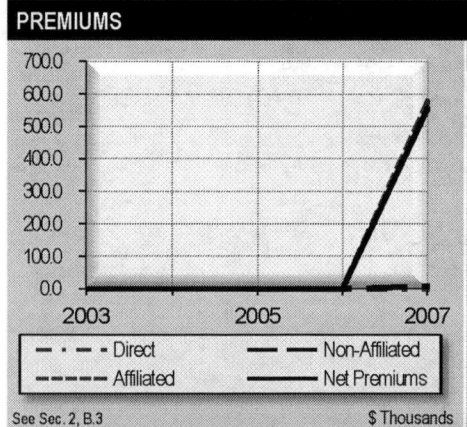

PREMIUMS
- · – · – Direct
- – – – Affiliated
- – – Non-Affiliated
- —— Net Premiums

See Sec. 2, B.3 — $ Thousands

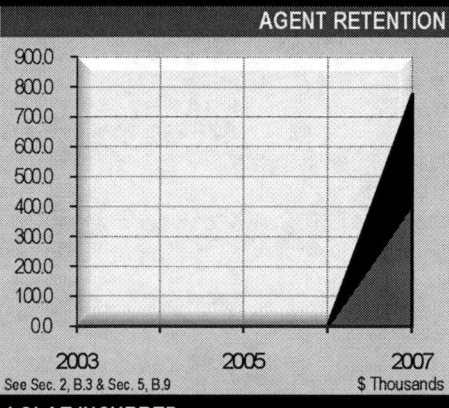

OPERATING EXPENSES INCURRED / AGENT RETENTION
See Sec. 2, B.3 & Sec. 5, B.9 — $ Thousands

FINANCIAL POSITION	2007
Cash, Cash Equivalents & Short-Term Investments	$2,368,995
Total Assets	$2,378,411
Policyholders' Surplus	$2,332,454
Reserves	$29,528
OPERATING RESULTS	
Net Income	($167,546)
Net Investment Gain	$55,398
Net Realized Capital Gains	$0
Net Cash from Operations	($131,005)
Oper. Gain Before Taxes	($222,944)

DIRECT PREMIUMS WRITTEN - YE 2007

- ☐ Direct
- ■ Non-Affiliated
- ■ Affiliated

See Sec. 3, B.4

L&LAE INCURRED / LOSS RATIO
See Sec. 5, A.3 & Sec. 5, C.2 — $

UNDERWRITING RESULTS	
Direct	$0
Non-Affiliated	$8,460
Affiliated	$575,455
Direct Premiums Written	$583,915
Net Premiums Earned	$554,387
Operating Expenses Incurred	$777,331
Agent Retention	$408,740
L&LAE Incurred	$0
Loss Ratio	0.00%

6

Land Title Insurance Company (St. Louis)

1653 Larkin Williams Rd.
Ste. 100
Fenton, MO 63026

(314) 821-5515

WEBSITE:	STATE OF DOMICILE:
www.firstam.com	Missouri

PRESIDENT:	ESTABLISHED:	JURISDICTION LICENSE(S):
Robert Glen Meckfessel	12/31/1901	2

A' A Prime
Unsurpassed
Financial Stability Rating®
Demotech, Inc.

NAIC Number:
50237

LAND TIC (ST LOUIS)

NAIC Group:
FIRST AMERICAN

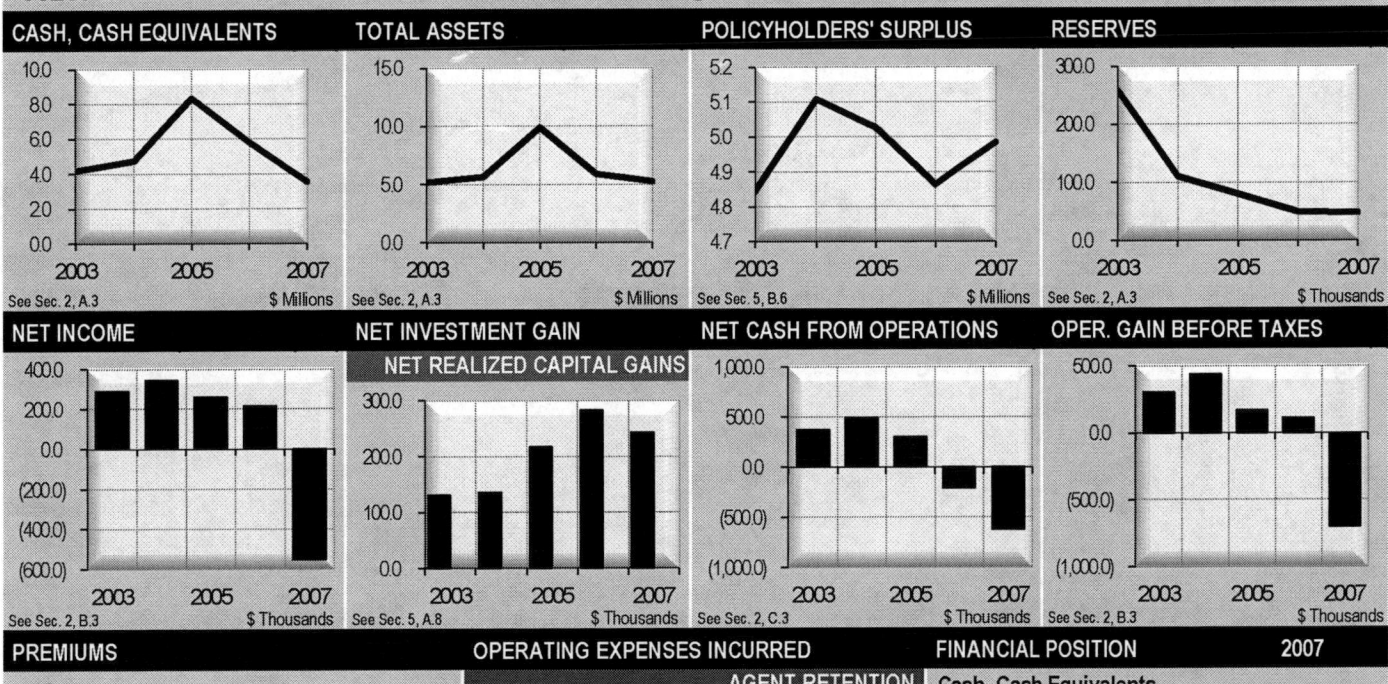

CASH, CASH EQUIVALENTS — See Sec. 2, A.3 — $ Millions
TOTAL ASSETS — See Sec. 2, A.3 — $ Millions
POLICYHOLDERS' SURPLUS — See Sec. 5, B.6 — $ Millions
RESERVES — See Sec. 2, A.3 — $ Thousands

NET INCOME — See Sec. 2, B.3 — $ Thousands
NET INVESTMENT GAIN / NET REALIZED CAPITAL GAINS — See Sec. 5, A.8 — $ Thousands
NET CASH FROM OPERATIONS — See Sec. 2, C.3 — $ Thousands
OPER. GAIN BEFORE TAXES — See Sec. 2, B.3 — $ Thousands

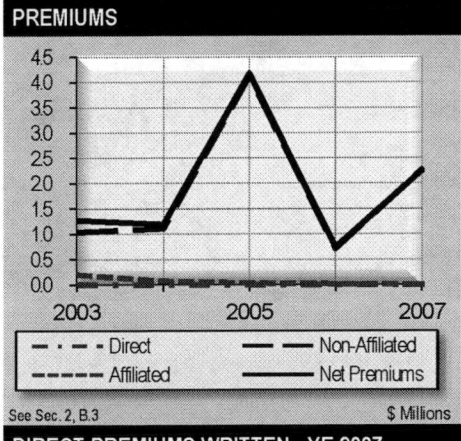

PREMIUMS

- · - Direct
----- Affiliated
— Non-Affiliated
— Net Premiums

See Sec. 2, B.3 — $ Millions

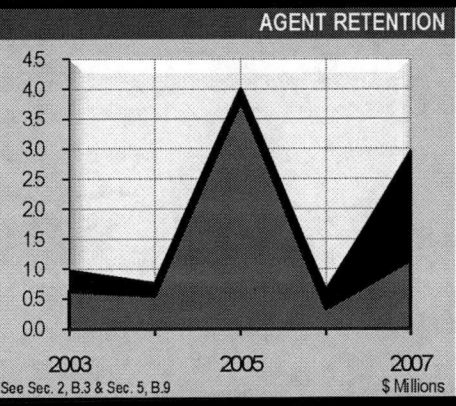

OPERATING EXPENSES INCURRED / AGENT RETENTION
See Sec. 2, B.3 & Sec. 5, B.9 — $ Millions

DIRECT PREMIUMS WRITTEN - YE 2007

☐ Direct ▩ Non-Affiliated ▪ Affiliated

See Sec. 3, B.4

L&LAE INCURRED / LOSS RATIO

See Sec. 5, A.3 & Sec. 5, C.2 — $

FINANCIAL POSITION	2007
Cash, Cash Equivalents & Short-Term Investments	$3,536,009
Total Assets	$5,244,057
Policyholders' Surplus	$4,984,385
Reserves	$47,952

OPERATING RESULTS	
Net Income	($554,284)
Net Investment Gain	$243,373
Net Realized Capital Gains	$0
Net Cash from Operations	($622,774)
Oper. Gain Before Taxes	($700,485)

UNDERWRITING RESULTS	
Direct	$0
Non-Affiliated	$2,257,316
Affiliated	$0
Direct Premiums Written	$2,257,316
Net Premiums Earned	$2,248,965
Operating Expenses Incurred	$2,949,475
Agent Retention	$1,141,423
L&LAE Incurred	$0
Loss Ratio	0.00%

6

Land Title Insurance Corporation

3033 E First Ave., Ste. 708
Denver, CO 80206

(303) 331-6296

WEBSITE:	STATE OF DOMICILE:
–	Colorado

PRESIDENT:	ESTABLISHED:	JURISDICTION LICENSE(S):
John Evans Freyer	6/30/1994	2

A' Unsurpassed Financial Stability Rating®
Demotech, Inc.

NAIC Number: **50002**

LAND CORP (CO)

NAIC Group: **UNAFFILIATED**

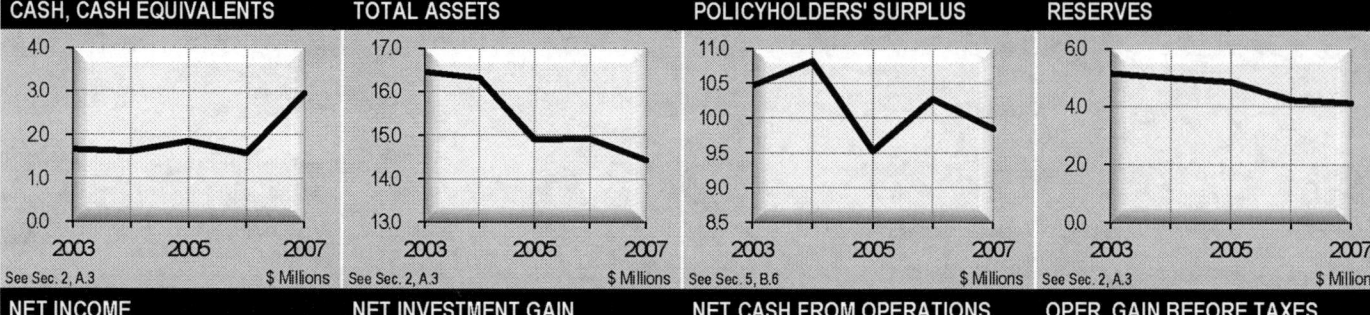

CASH, CASH EQUIVALENTS — See Sec. 2, A.3 — $ Millions
TOTAL ASSETS — See Sec. 2, A.3 — $ Millions
POLICYHOLDERS' SURPLUS — See Sec. 5, B.6 — $ Millions
RESERVES — See Sec. 2, A.3 — $ Millions

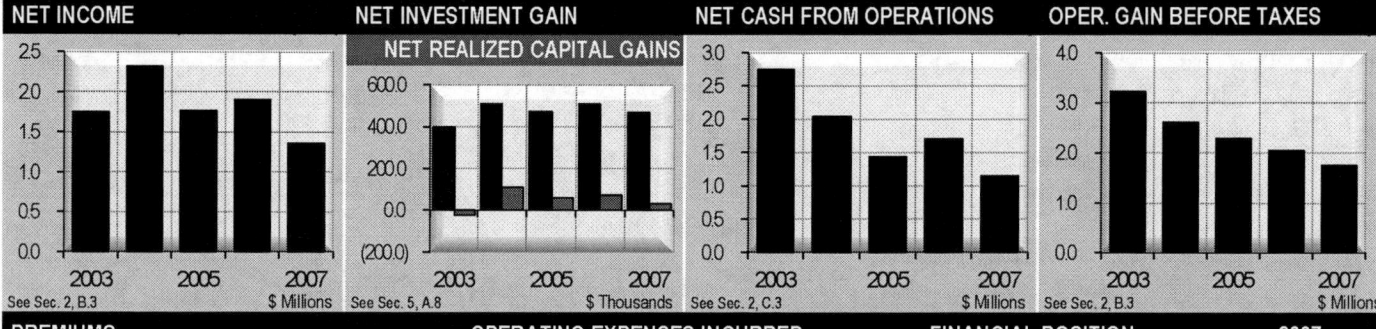

NET INCOME — See Sec. 2, B.3 — $ Millions
NET INVESTMENT GAIN / NET REALIZED CAPITAL GAINS — See Sec. 5, A.8 — $ Thousands
NET CASH FROM OPERATIONS — See Sec. 2, C.3 — $ Millions
OPER. GAIN BEFORE TAXES — See Sec. 2, B.3 — $ Millions

FINANCIAL POSITION	2007
Cash, Cash Equivalents & Short-Term Investments	$2,950,910
Total Assets	$14,429,122
Policyholders' Surplus	$9,842,596
Reserves	$4,118,568
OPERATING RESULTS	
Net Income	$1,358,724
Net Investment Gain	$468,057
Net Realized Capital Gains	$31,740
Net Cash from Operations	$1,153,869
Oper. Gain Before Taxes	$1,758,994

PREMIUMS — See Sec. 2, B.3 — $ Millions
Direct — Non-Affiliated — Affiliated — Net Premiums

OPERATING EXPENSES INCURRED / AGENT RETENTION — See Sec. 2, B.3 & Sec. 5, B.9 — $ Millions

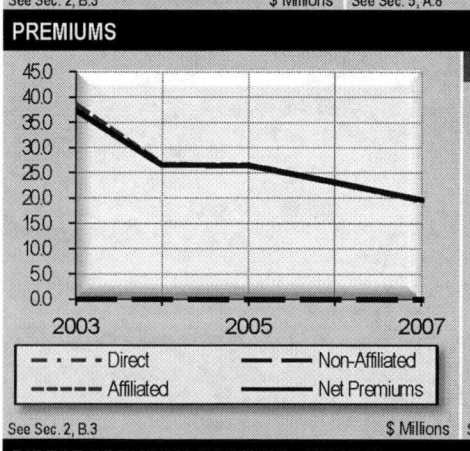

DIRECT PREMIUMS WRITTEN - YE 2007 — See Sec. 3, B.4
□ Direct ■ Non-Affiliated ■ Affiliated

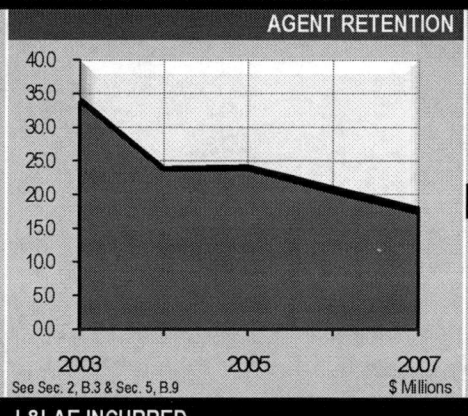

L&LAE INCURRED / LOSS RATIO — See Sec. 5, A.3 & Sec. 5, C.2 — $ Millions

UNDERWRITING RESULTS	
Direct	$0
Non-Affiliated	$0
Affiliated	$19,602,608
Direct Premiums Written	$19,602,608
Net Premiums Earned	$19,721,211
Operating Expenses Incurred	$18,055,061
Agent Retention	$17,250,295
L&LAE Incurred	$272,282
Loss Ratio	1.37%

Lawyers Title Insurance Corporation

5600 Cox Rd.
Glen Allen, VA 23060

(804) 267-8000

Merged with Land Title Insurance Company (NAIC # 50822)

WEBSITE:	STATE OF DOMICILE:
www.landam.com	Nebraska

PRESIDENT & CEO:	ESTABLISHED:	JURISDICTION LICENSE(S):
Theodore Lindy Chandler, Jr.	4/9/1925	53

A' Unsurpassed
A Prime
Financial Stability Rating®
Demotech, Inc.

NAIC Number:
50024

LAWYERS

NAIC Group:
LAND AMERICA

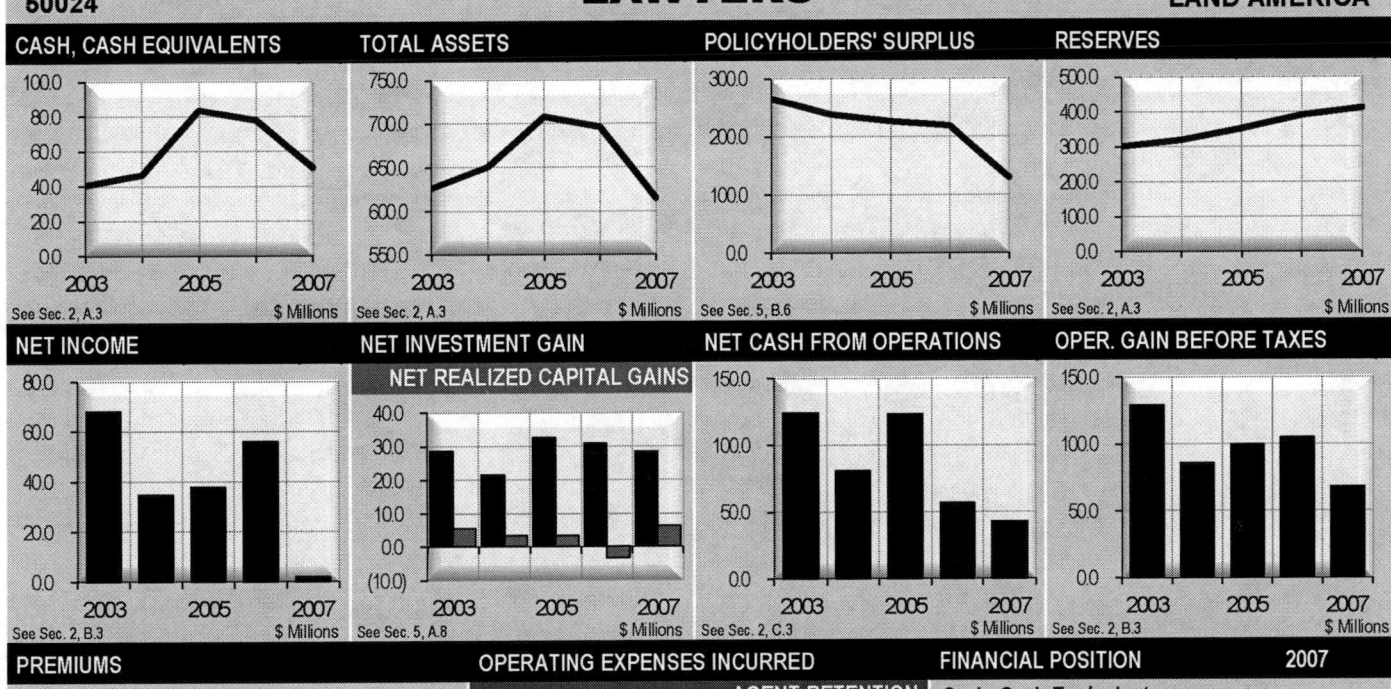

CASH, CASH EQUIVALENTS — See Sec. 2, A.3 — $ Millions

TOTAL ASSETS — See Sec. 2, A.3 — $ Millions

POLICYHOLDERS' SURPLUS — See Sec. 5, B.6 — $ Millions

RESERVES — See Sec. 2, A.3 — $ Millions

NET INCOME — See Sec. 2, B.3 — $ Millions

NET INVESTMENT GAIN / NET REALIZED CAPITAL GAINS — See Sec. 5, A.8 — $ Millions

NET CASH FROM OPERATIONS — See Sec. 2, C.3 — $ Millions

OPER. GAIN BEFORE TAXES — See Sec. 2, B.3 — $ Millions

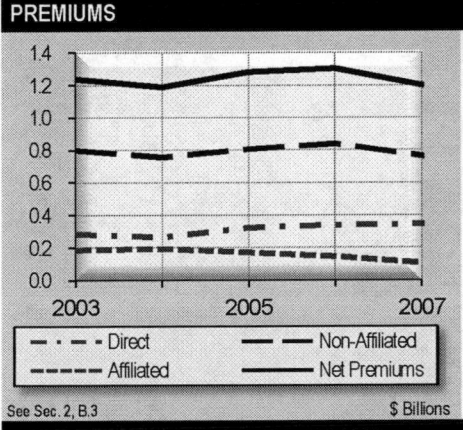

PREMIUMS — See Sec. 2, B.3 — $ Billions
- · - Direct
- - - - Non-Affiliated
- - - - Affiliated
—— Net Premiums

OPERATING EXPENSES INCURRED / AGENT RETENTION — See Sec. 2, B.3 & Sec. 5, B.9 — $ Billions

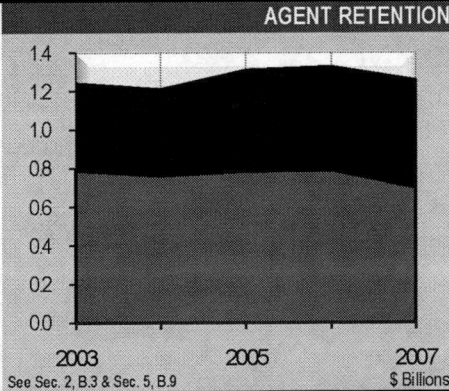

DIRECT PREMIUMS WRITTEN - YE 2007 — See Sec. 3, B.4
☐ Direct ▦ Non-Affiliated ▪ Affiliated

L&LAE INCURRED / LOSS RATIO — See Sec. 5, A.3 & Sec. 5, C.2 — $ Millions

FINANCIAL POSITION	2007
Cash, Cash Equivalents & Short-Term Investments	$50,537,974
Total Assets	$614,576,148
Policyholders' Surplus	$129,286,409
Reserves	$410,526,660
OPERATING RESULTS	
Net Income	$1,971,393
Net Investment Gain	$28,426,494
Net Realized Capital Gains	$6,258,207
Net Cash from Operations	$42,724,074
Oper. Gain Before Taxes	$68,361,410
UNDERWRITING RESULTS	
Direct	$345,666,888
Non-Affiliated	$762,376,163
Affiliated	$107,567,639
Direct Premiums Written	$1,215,610,690
Net Premiums Earned	$1,199,933,194
Operating Expenses Incurred	$1,256,547,871
Agent Retention	$700,268,473
L&LAE Incurred	$89,456,439
Loss Ratio	6.75%

6

Manito Title Insurance Company

100 W Market St.
West Chester, PA 19382

(610) 436-4767

WEBSITE:	STATE OF DOMICILE:
www.manitotitle.com	Pennsylvania

PRESIDENT:	ESTABLISHED:	JURISDICTION LICENSE(S):
Bruce Alan West	11/12/1979	1

A Exceptional
Financial Stability Rating®
Demotech, Inc.

NAIC Number:
51446

MANITO

NAIC Group:
UNAFFILIATED

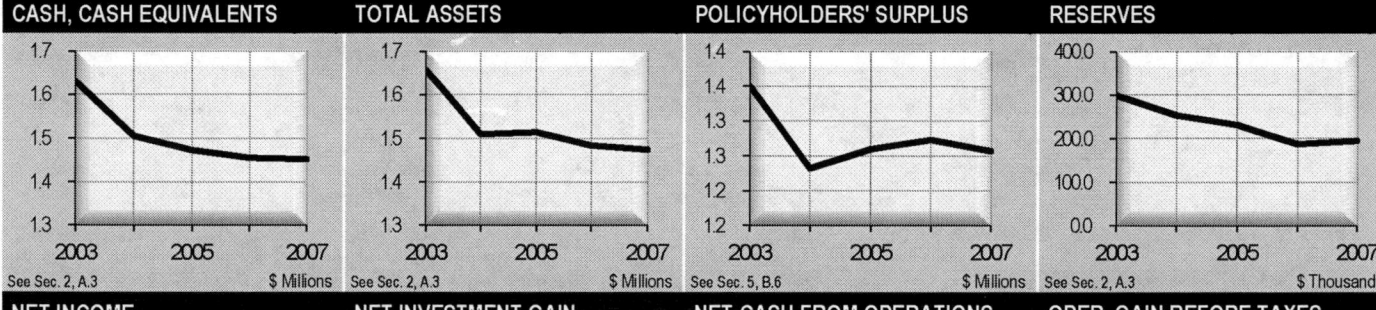

CASH, CASH EQUIVALENTS — See Sec. 2, A.3 — $ Millions
TOTAL ASSETS — See Sec. 2, A.3 — $ Millions
POLICYHOLDERS' SURPLUS — See Sec. 5, B.6 — $ Millions
RESERVES — See Sec. 2, A.3 — $ Thousands

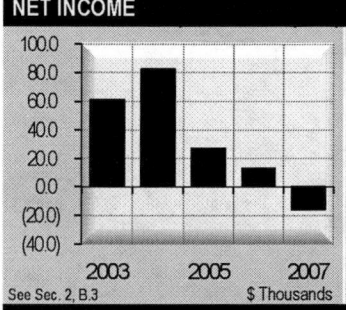
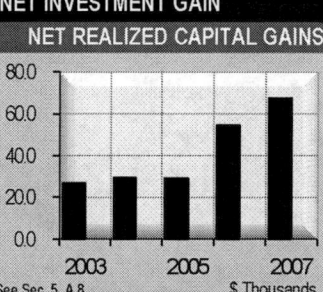
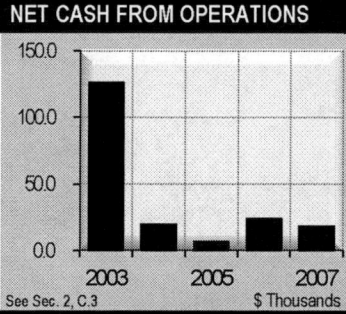
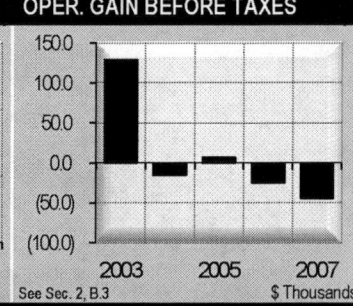

NET INCOME — See Sec. 2, B.3 — $ Thousands
NET INVESTMENT GAIN / NET REALIZED CAPITAL GAINS — See Sec. 5, A.8 — $ Thousands
NET CASH FROM OPERATIONS — See Sec. 2, C.3 — $ Thousands
OPER. GAIN BEFORE TAXES — See Sec. 2, B.3 — $ Thousands

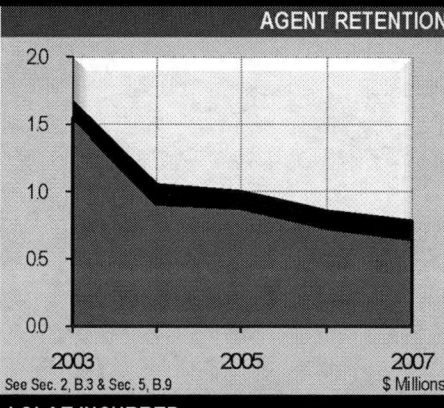

PREMIUMS
- · - · - Direct
- - - - Affiliated
- - - Non-Affiliated
- —— Net Premiums

See Sec. 2, B.3 — $ Millions

OPERATING EXPENSES INCURRED / AGENT RETENTION
See Sec. 2, B.3 & Sec. 5, B.9 — $ Millions

DIRECT PREMIUMS WRITTEN - YE 2007
□ Direct ▨ Non-Affiliated ■ Affiliated
See Sec. 3, B.4

L&LAE INCURRED / LOSS RATIO
See Sec. 5, A.3 & Sec. 5, C.2 — $ Thousands

FINANCIAL POSITION	2007
Cash, Cash Equivalents & Short-Term Investments	$1,451,479
Total Assets	$1,473,460
Policyholders' Surplus	$1,256,691
Reserves	$193,782

OPERATING RESULTS	
Net Income	($16,032)
Net Investment Gain	$67,685
Net Realized Capital Gains	$0
Net Cash from Operations	$18,271
Oper. Gain Before Taxes	($44,393)

UNDERWRITING RESULTS	
Direct	$0
Non-Affiliated	$97,958
Affiliated	$690,518
Direct Premiums Written	$788,476
Net Premiums Earned	$740,110
Operating Expenses Incurred	$784,503
Agent Retention	$647,875
L&LAE Incurred	$39,324
Loss Ratio	5.31%

Mason County Title Insurance Company

130 W Railroad
Shelton, WA 98584

(360) 701-6090

WEBSITE: www.masoncountytitle.com

PRESIDENT: Phil C. Bayley

STATE OF DOMICILE: Washington

ESTABLISHED: 9/7/1909

JURISDICTION LICENSE(S): 1

A Exceptional
Financial Stability Rating®
Demotech, Inc.

NAIC Number:
50962

MASON COUNTY

NAIC Group:
UNAFFILIATED

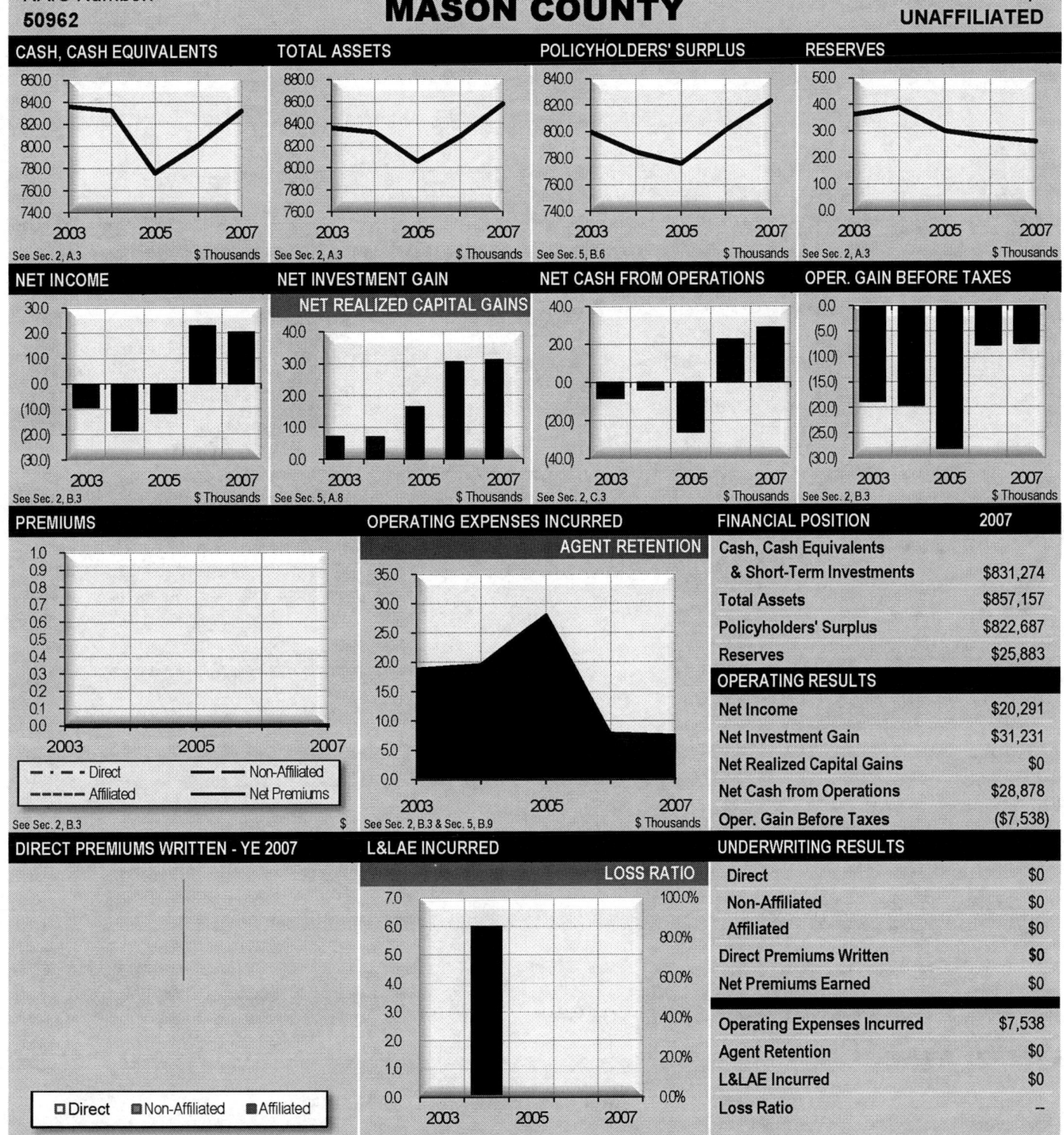

FINANCIAL POSITION	2007
Cash, Cash Equivalents & Short-Term Investments	$831,274
Total Assets	$857,157
Policyholders' Surplus	$822,687
Reserves	$25,883
OPERATING RESULTS	
Net Income	$20,291
Net Investment Gain	$31,231
Net Realized Capital Gains	$0
Net Cash from Operations	$28,878
Oper. Gain Before Taxes	($7,538)
UNDERWRITING RESULTS	
Direct	$0
Non-Affiliated	$0
Affiliated	$0
Direct Premiums Written	$0
Net Premiums Earned	$0
Operating Expenses Incurred	$7,538
Agent Retention	$0
L&LAE Incurred	$0
Loss Ratio	--

6

Mason Title Insurance Company

27544 Cashford Cir., Ste. 101
Wesley Chapel, FL 33544

(813) 286-2604

WEBSITE:	STATE OF DOMICILE:
www.masontitle.com	Florida

CHIEF EXECUTIVE OFFICER:	ESTABLISHED:	JURISDICTION LICENSE(S):
John R. Baumgart	2/21/2006	1

A Exceptional
Financial Stability Rating®
Demotech, Inc.

NAIC Number:
12550

MASON

NAIC Group:
UNAFFILIATED

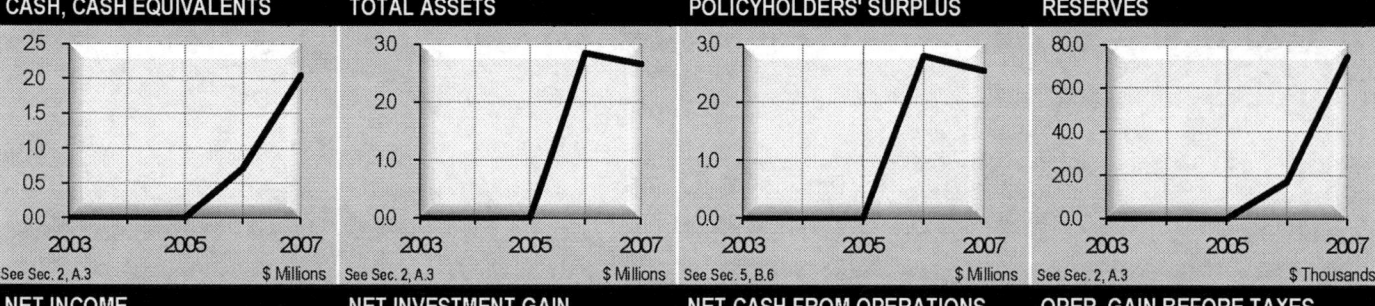

CASH, CASH EQUIVALENTS — See Sec. 2, A.3 — $ Millions
TOTAL ASSETS — See Sec. 2, A.3 — $ Millions
POLICYHOLDERS' SURPLUS — See Sec. 5, B.6 — $ Millions
RESERVES — See Sec. 2, A.3 — $ Thousands

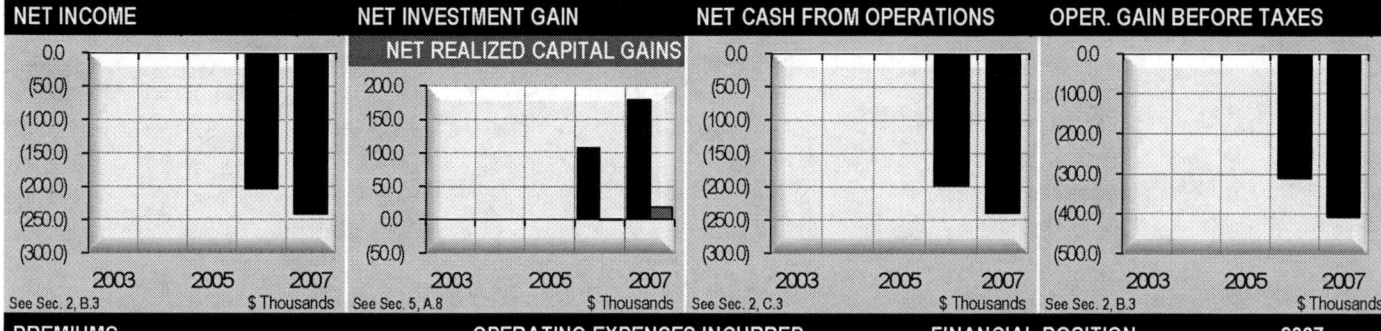

NET INCOME — See Sec. 2, B.3 — $ Thousands
NET INVESTMENT GAIN / NET REALIZED CAPITAL GAINS — See Sec. 5, A.8 — $ Thousands
NET CASH FROM OPERATIONS — See Sec. 2, C.3 — $ Thousands
OPER. GAIN BEFORE TAXES — See Sec. 2, B.3 — $ Thousands

PREMIUMS

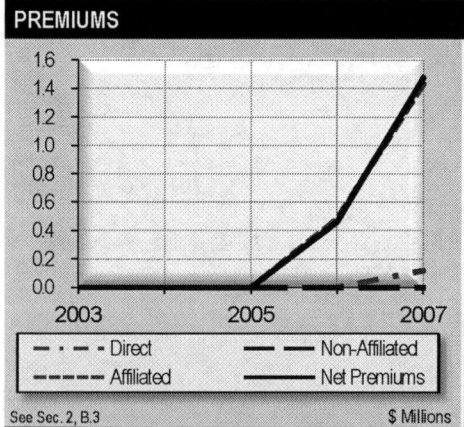

- – · – Direct
- – – Non-Affiliated
- ----- Affiliated
- —— Net Premiums

See Sec. 2, B.3 — $ Millions

OPERATING EXPENSES INCURRED / AGENT RETENTION

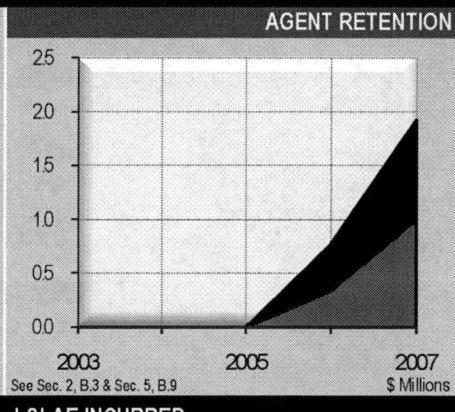

See Sec. 2, B.3 & Sec. 5, B.9 — $ Millions

FINANCIAL POSITION	2007
Cash, Cash Equivalents & Short-Term Investments	$2,040,494
Total Assets	$2,655,165
Policyholders' Surplus	$2,546,042
Reserves	$74,433
OPERATING RESULTS	
Net Income	($241,208)
Net Investment Gain	$179,024
Net Realized Capital Gains	$18,849
Net Cash from Operations	($239,758)
Oper. Gain Before Taxes	($408,032)

DIRECT PREMIUMS WRITTEN - YE 2007

See Sec. 3, B.4

- □ Direct
- ▨ Non-Affiliated
- ■ Affiliated

L&LAE INCURRED / LOSS RATIO

See Sec. 5, A.3 & Sec. 5, C.2 — $ Thousands

UNDERWRITING RESULTS	
Direct	$120,217
Non-Affiliated	$0
Affiliated	$1,432,065
Direct Premiums Written	$1,552,282
Net Premiums Earned	$1,474,582
Operating Expenses Incurred	$1,927,284
Agent Retention	$1,002,433
L&LAE Incurred	$12,200
Loss Ratio	0.80%

6

Massachusetts Title Insurance Company

101 Huntington Ave.
Boston, MA 02199

(617) 345-0088

WEBSITE:	STATE OF DOMICILE:
www.firstamne.com	Massachusetts

PRESIDENT:	ESTABLISHED:	JURISDICTION LICENSE(S):
Joseph J. Attura	1/1/1885	1

A Exceptional
Financial Stability Rating®
Demotech, Inc.

NAIC Number:
50989

MASSACHUSETTS TIC

NAIC Group:
FIRST AMERICAN

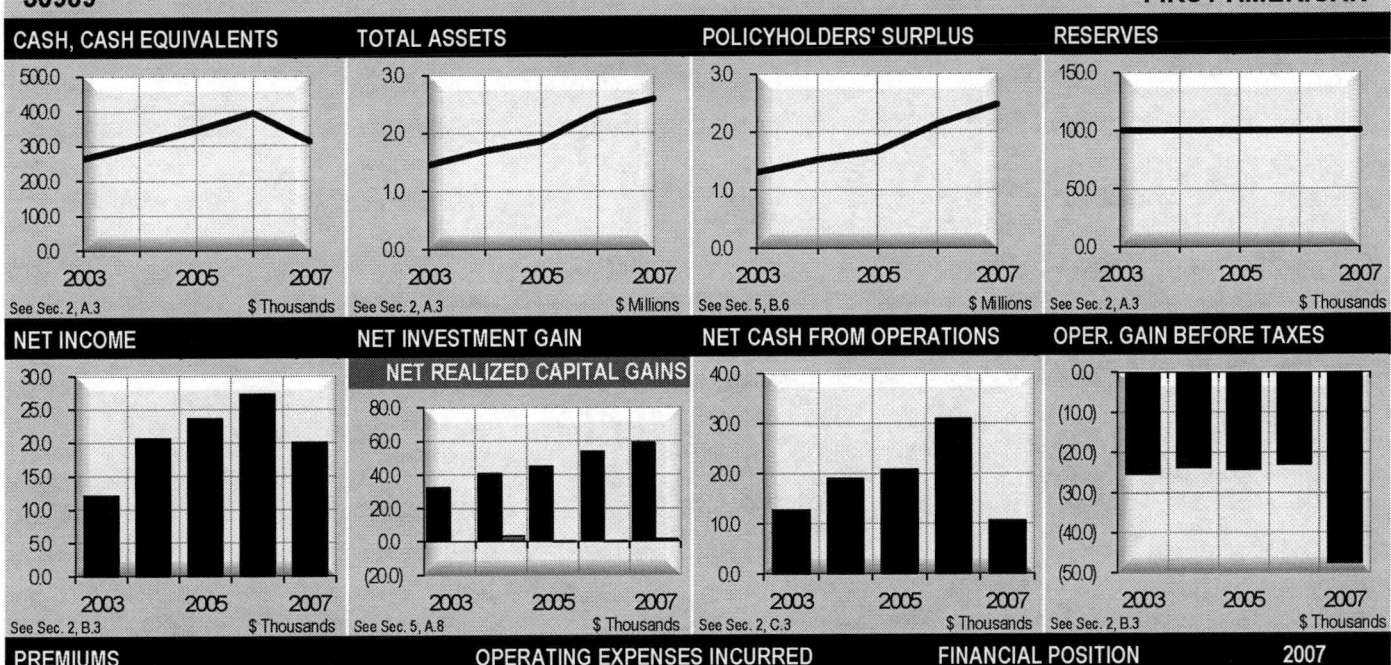

FINANCIAL POSITION — 2007

Cash, Cash Equivalents & Short-Term Investments	$312,654
Total Assets	$2,583,822
Policyholders' Surplus	$2,465,550
Reserves	$100,000

OPERATING RESULTS

Net Income	$20,060
Net Investment Gain	$58,993
Net Realized Capital Gains	$1,180
Net Cash from Operations	$10,616
Oper. Gain Before Taxes	($47,597)

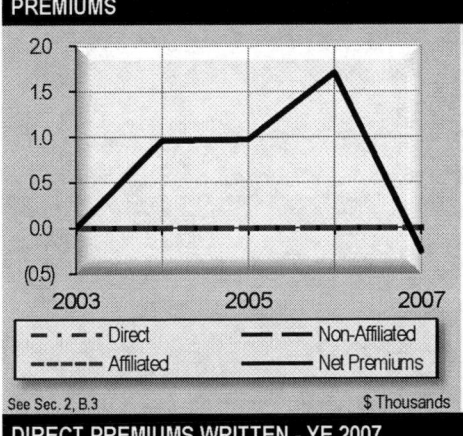

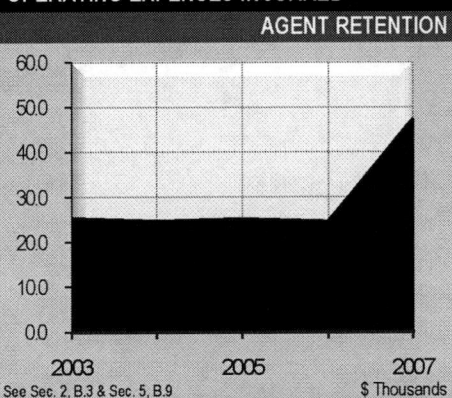

UNDERWRITING RESULTS

Direct	($254)
Non-Affiliated	$0
Affiliated	$0
Direct Premiums Written	($254)
Net Premiums Earned	($254)
Operating Expenses Incurred	$47,343
Agent Retention	$0
L&LAE Incurred	$0
Loss Ratio	0.00%

6

Mississippi Guaranty Title Insurance Company

1755 Lelia Dr., Ste. 102
Jackson, MS 39216

(601) 362-2010

WEBSITE:	STATE OF DOMICILE:
–	Mississippi

PRESIDENT:	ESTABLISHED:	JURISDICTION LICENSE(S):
Rowan Hurt Taylor, Jr.	7/2/1996	1

S Substantial
Financial Stability Rating®
Demotech, Inc.

NAIC Number:
50030

MISSISSIPPI GUARANTY

NAIC Group:
UNAFFILIATED

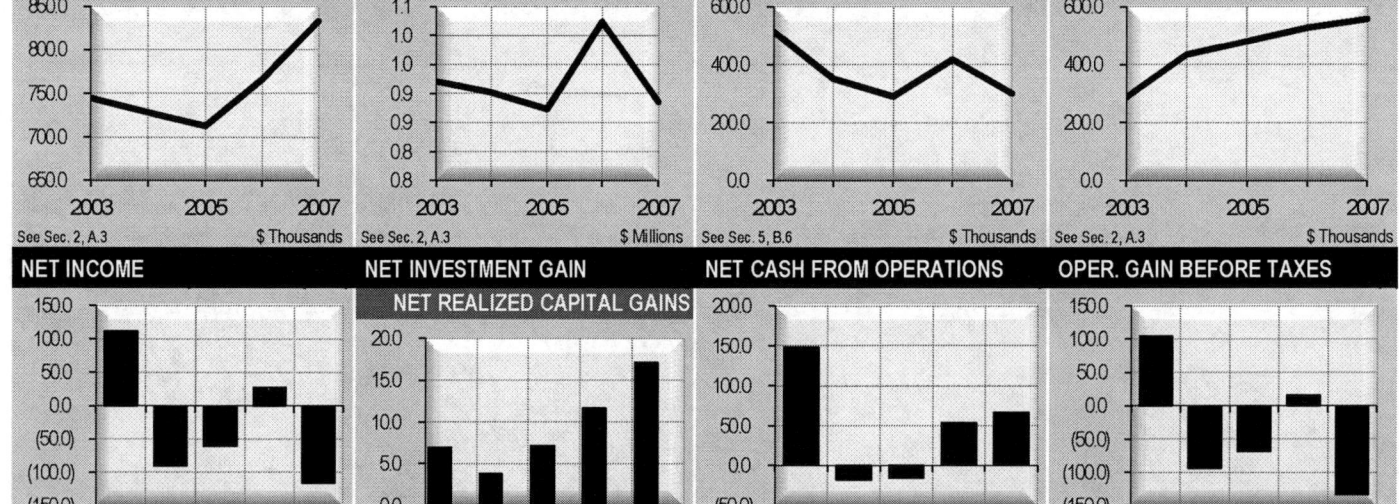

CASH, CASH EQUIVALENTS — See Sec. 2, A.3 — $ Thousands
TOTAL ASSETS — See Sec. 2, A.3 — $ Millions
POLICYHOLDERS' SURPLUS — See Sec. 5, B.6 — $ Thousands
RESERVES — See Sec. 2, A.3 — $ Thousands

NET INCOME — See Sec. 2, B.3 — $ Thousands
NET INVESTMENT GAIN / NET REALIZED CAPITAL GAINS — See Sec. 5, A.8 — $ Thousands
NET CASH FROM OPERATIONS — See Sec. 2, C.3 — $ Thousands
OPER. GAIN BEFORE TAXES — See Sec. 2, B.3 — $ Thousands

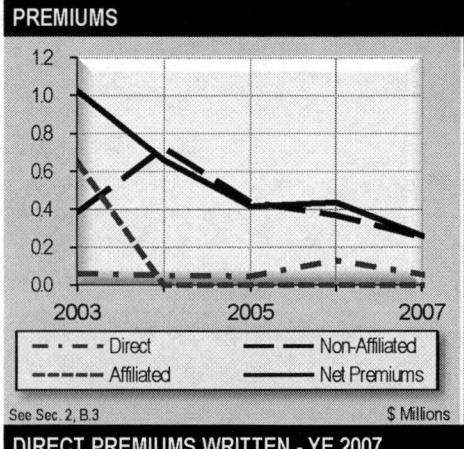

PREMIUMS

- · - Direct
- - - Affiliated
—— Non-Affiliated
—— Net Premiums

See Sec. 2, B.3 — $ Millions

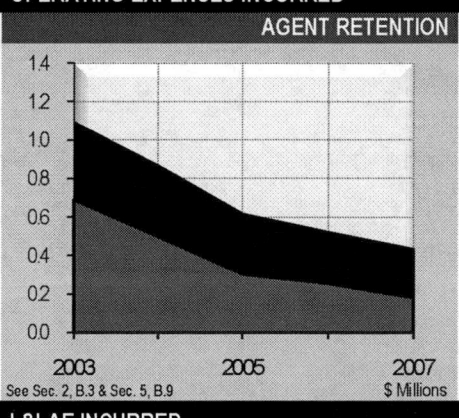

OPERATING EXPENSES INCURRED / AGENT RETENTION
See Sec. 2, B.3 & Sec. 5, B.9 — $ Millions

FINANCIAL POSITION	2007
Cash, Cash Equivalents & Short-Term Investments	$833,121
Total Assets	$885,409
Policyholders' Surplus	$300,100
Reserves	$556,777
OPERATING RESULTS	
Net Income	($116,402)
Net Investment Gain	$17,107
Net Realized Capital Gains	$0
Net Cash from Operations	$66,585
Oper. Gain Before Taxes	($133,509)
UNDERWRITING RESULTS	
Direct	$56,517
Non-Affiliated	$253,129
Affiliated	$0
Direct Premiums Written	$309,646
Net Premiums Earned	$260,012
Operating Expenses Incurred	$432,481
Agent Retention	$181,277
L&LAE Incurred	$0
Loss Ratio	0.00%

DIRECT PREMIUMS WRITTEN - YE 2007

☐ Direct ■ Non-Affiliated ■ Affiliated

See Sec. 3, B.4

L&LAE INCURRED / LOSS RATIO
See Sec. 5, A.3 & Sec. 5, C.2 — $

Mississippi Valley Title Insurance Company

315 Tombigbee St.
Jackson, MS 39201

(601) 969-0222

WEBSITE:	STATE OF DOMICILE:
www.mvt.com	Mississippi

CHAIRMAN:	ESTABLISHED:	JURISDICTION LICENSE(S):
James Michael Sellari	5/30/1941	3

A" Unsurpassed
Financial Stability Rating®
Demotech, Inc.

NAIC Number:
51004

MISSISSIPPI VALLEY

NAIC Group:
OLD REPUBLIC

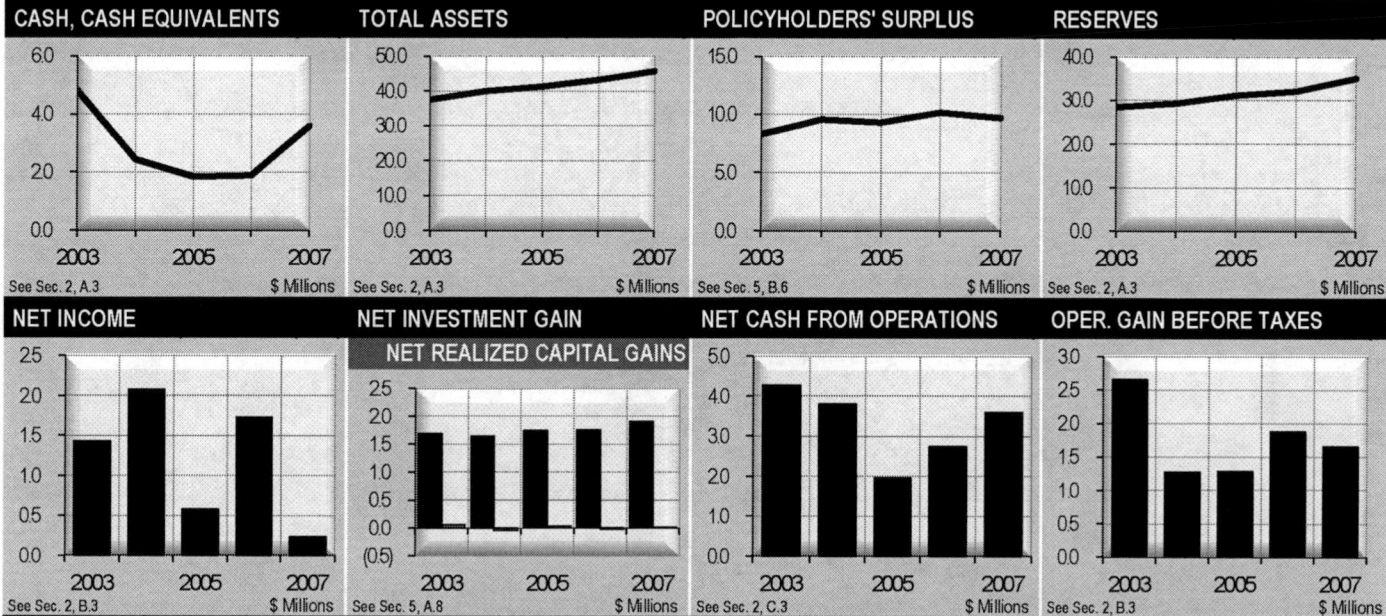

CASH, CASH EQUIVALENTS — See Sec. 2, A.3 — $ Millions
TOTAL ASSETS — See Sec. 2, A.3 — $ Millions
POLICYHOLDERS' SURPLUS — See Sec. 5, B.6 — $ Millions
RESERVES — See Sec. 2, A.3 — $ Millions

NET INCOME — See Sec. 2, B.3 — $ Millions
NET INVESTMENT GAIN / NET REALIZED CAPITAL GAINS — See Sec. 5, A.8 — $ Millions
NET CASH FROM OPERATIONS — See Sec. 2, C.3 — $ Millions
OPER. GAIN BEFORE TAXES — See Sec. 2, B.3 — $ Millions

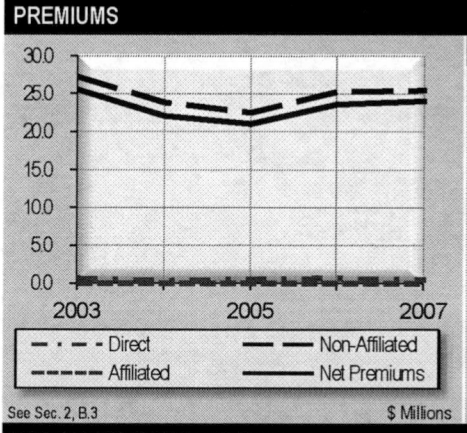

PREMIUMS
- – · – Direct
- – – Non-Affiliated
- ----- Affiliated
- —— Net Premiums

See Sec. 2, B.3 — $ Millions

OPERATING EXPENSES INCURRED / AGENT RETENTION — See Sec. 2, B.3 & Sec. 5, B.9 — $ Millions

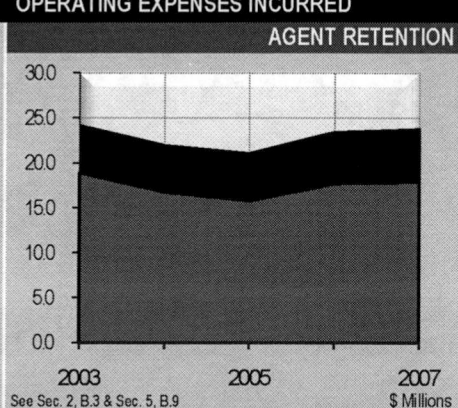

DIRECT PREMIUMS WRITTEN - YE 2007
□ Direct ▨ Non-Affiliated ▪ Affiliated
See Sec. 3, B.4

L&LAE INCURRED / LOSS RATIO — See Sec. 5, A.3 & Sec. 5, C.2 — $ Millions

FINANCIAL POSITION	2007
Cash, Cash Equivalents & Short-Term Investments	$3,583,400
Total Assets	$45,679,034
Policyholders' Surplus	$9,683,618
Reserves	$34,974,661
OPERATING RESULTS	
Net Income	$234,270
Net Investment Gain	$1,911,592
Net Realized Capital Gains	$10,925
Net Cash from Operations	$3,599,407
Oper. Gain Before Taxes	$1,656,379
UNDERWRITING RESULTS	
Direct	$488,573
Non-Affiliated	$25,433,321
Affiliated	$0
Direct Premiums Written	$25,921,894
Net Premiums Earned	$24,055,698
Operating Expenses Incurred	$23,753,787
Agent Retention	$17,911,771
L&LAE Incurred	$3,445,735
Loss Ratio	13.56%

6

Monroe Title Insurance Corporation

47 W Main St.
Rochester, NY 14614-1499

(585) 232-2070

WEBSITE:	STATE OF DOMICILE:
www.monroetitle.com	New York

PRESIDENT:	ESTABLISHED:	JURISDICTION LICENSE(S):
Thomas A. Podsiadlo	10/1/1922	1

A' A Prime **Unsurpassed**
Financial Stability Rating®
Demotech, Inc.

NAIC Number:
51063

MONROE

NAIC Group:
STEWART

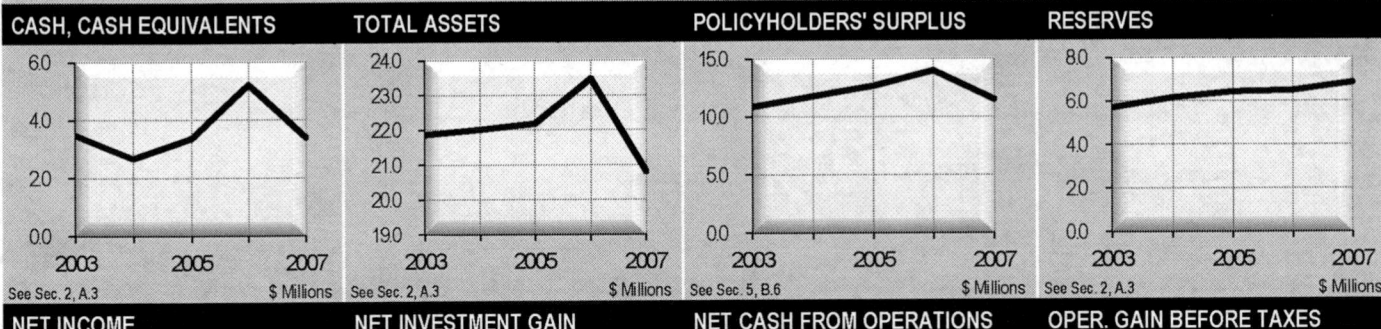

CASH, CASH EQUIVALENTS — See Sec. 2, A.3 — $ Millions
TOTAL ASSETS — See Sec. 2, A.3 — $ Millions
POLICYHOLDERS' SURPLUS — See Sec. 5, B.6 — $ Millions
RESERVES — See Sec. 2, A.3 — $ Millions

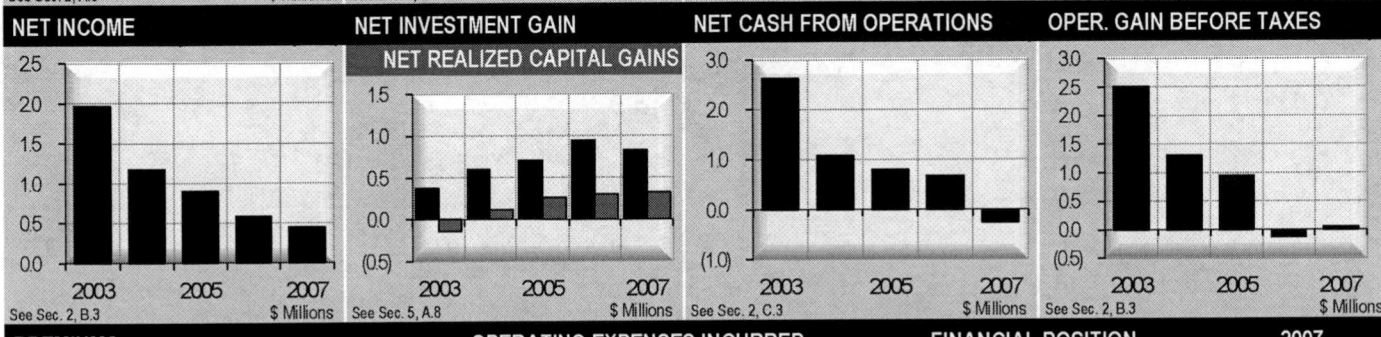

NET INCOME — See Sec. 2, B.3 — $ Millions
NET INVESTMENT GAIN / NET REALIZED CAPITAL GAINS — See Sec. 5, A.8 — $ Millions
NET CASH FROM OPERATIONS — See Sec. 2, C.3 — $ Millions
OPER. GAIN BEFORE TAXES — See Sec. 2, B.3 — $ Millions

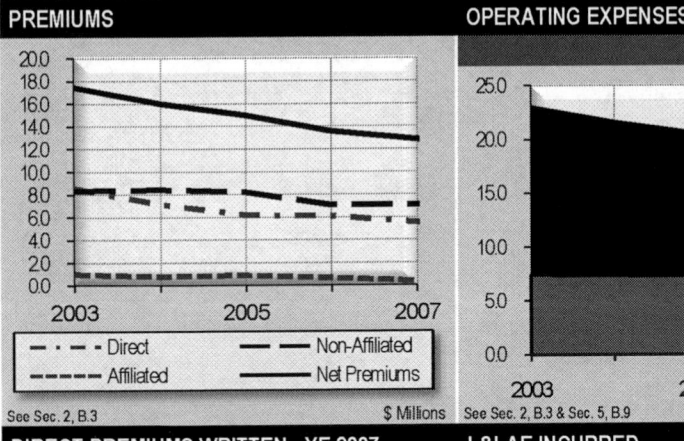

PREMIUMS — See Sec. 2, B.3 — $ Millions
- · - Direct
- - - - Affiliated
- — Non-Affiliated
- — Net Premiums

DIRECT PREMIUMS WRITTEN - YE 2007 — See Sec. 3, B.4
□ Direct ■ Non-Affiliated ■ Affiliated

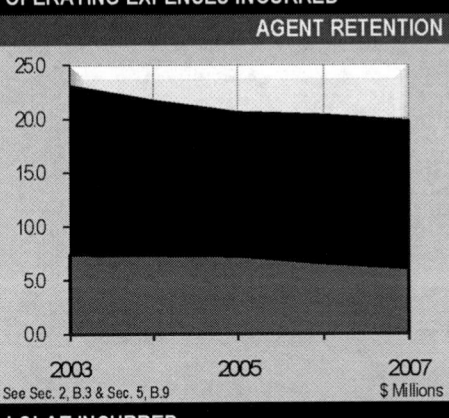

OPERATING EXPENSES INCURRED / AGENT RETENTION — See Sec. 2, B.3 & Sec. 5, B.9 — $ Millions

L&LAE INCURRED / LOSS RATIO — See Sec. 5, A.3 & Sec. 5, C.2 — $ Thousands

FINANCIAL POSITION	2007
Cash, Cash Equivalents & Short-Term Investments	$3,385,766
Total Assets	$20,802,421
Policyholders' Surplus	$11,498,871
Reserves	$6,842,394

OPERATING RESULTS	
Net Income	$446,972
Net Investment Gain	$830,602
Net Realized Capital Gains	$327,125
Net Cash from Operations	($259,310)
Oper. Gain Before Taxes	$48,789

UNDERWRITING RESULTS	
Direct	$5,556,612
Non-Affiliated	$7,075,703
Affiliated	$364,364
Direct Premiums Written	$12,996,679
Net Premiums Earned	$12,853,104
Operating Expenses Incurred	$19,752,264
Agent Retention	$6,120,596
L&LAE Incurred	$577,628
Loss Ratio	2.92%

National Attorneys' Title Assurance Fund, Inc.

306 W Pike St.
Vevay, IN 47043

(812) 427-9062

WEBSITE:	STATE OF DOMICILE:
www.nataf.net	Indiana
PRESIDENT:	ESTABLISHED:	JURISDICTION LICENSE(S):
Ronald J. Hocker	5/2/1958	1

A Exceptional
Financial Stability Rating®
Demotech, Inc.

NAIC Number:
50938

NATIONAL ATTORNEYS

NAIC Group:
ATTORNEYS' TITLE

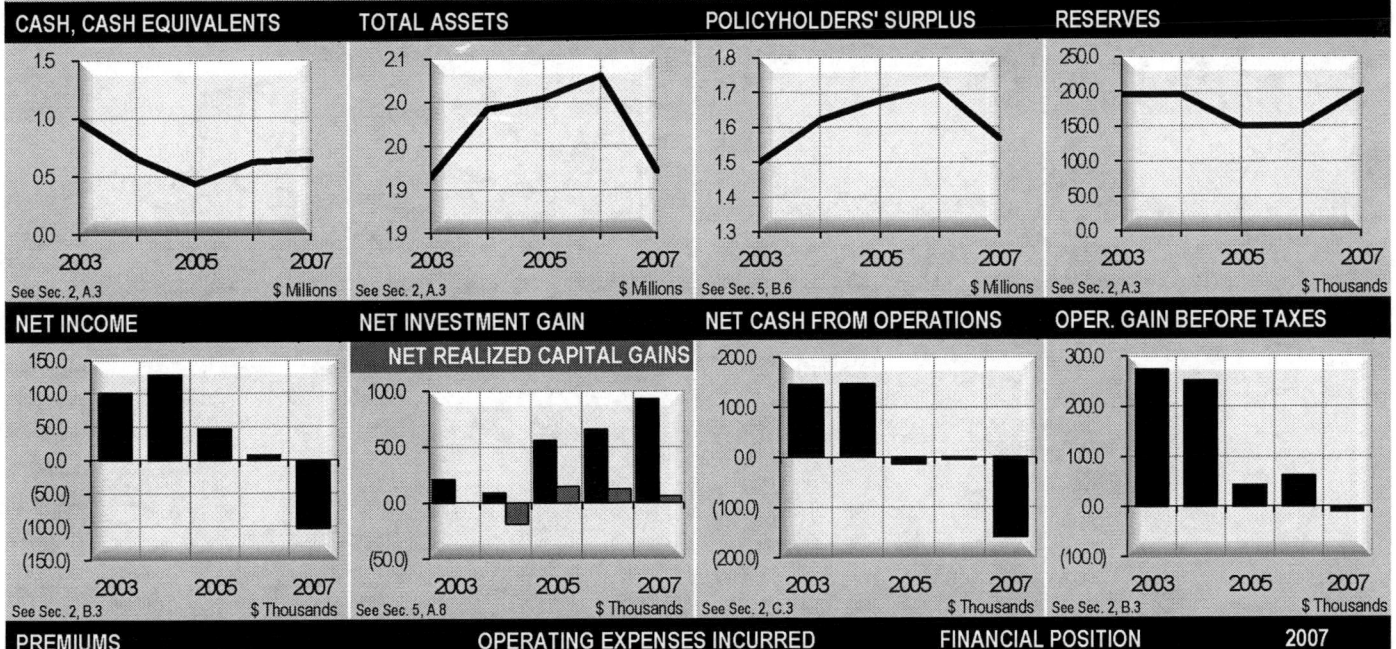

CASH, CASH EQUIVALENTS	TOTAL ASSETS	POLICYHOLDERS' SURPLUS	RESERVES
See Sec. 2, A.3 $ Millions	See Sec. 2, A.3 $ Millions	See Sec. 5, B.6 $ Millions	See Sec. 2, A.3 $ Thousands

NET INCOME	NET INVESTMENT GAIN / NET REALIZED CAPITAL GAINS	NET CASH FROM OPERATIONS	OPER. GAIN BEFORE TAXES
See Sec. 2, B.3 $ Thousands	See Sec. 5, A.8 $ Thousands	See Sec. 2, C.3 $ Thousands	See Sec. 2, B.3 $ Thousands

PREMIUMS	OPERATING EXPENSES INCURRED / AGENT RETENTION	FINANCIAL POSITION	2007

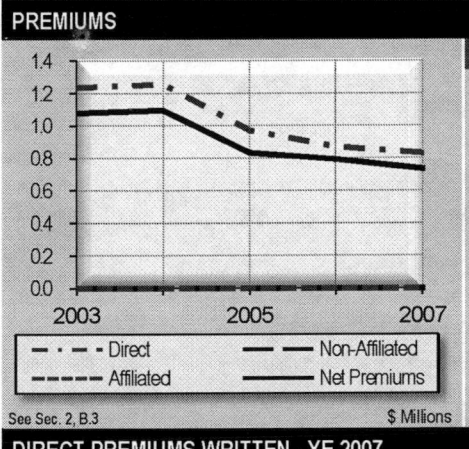

- – · – · Direct
- – – – Non-Affiliated
- – – – – Affiliated
- —— Net Premiums

See Sec. 2, B.3 $ Millions
See Sec. 2, B.3 & Sec. 5, B.9 $ Millions

FINANCIAL POSITION	2007
Cash, Cash Equivalents & Short-Term Investments	$643,886
Total Assets	$1,921,120
Policyholders' Surplus	$1,566,898
Reserves	$200,000
OPERATING RESULTS	
Net Income	($102,748)
Net Investment Gain	$92,706
Net Realized Capital Gains	$6,065
Net Cash from Operations	($158,814)
Oper. Gain Before Taxes	($10,555)

DIRECT PREMIUMS WRITTEN - YE 2007	L&LAE INCURRED / LOSS RATIO	UNDERWRITING RESULTS	

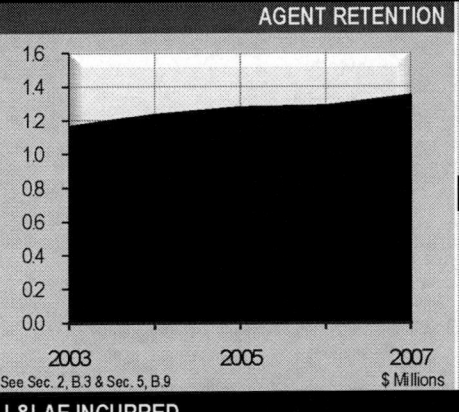

□ Direct ■ Non-Affiliated ■ Affiliated

See Sec. 3, B.4
See Sec. 5, A.3 & Sec. 5, C.2 $ Thousands

UNDERWRITING RESULTS	
Direct	$831,940
Non-Affiliated	$0
Affiliated	$0
Direct Premiums Written	$831,940
Net Premiums Earned	$733,437
Operating Expenses Incurred	$1,347,650
Agent Retention	$0
L&LAE Incurred	$267,150
Loss Ratio	19.98%

6

National Land Title Insurance Company

2800 W Higgins Road, Ste. 835
Hoffman Estates, IL 60169

(800) 533-6584

WEBSITE:	STATE OF DOMICILE:
www.nltic.com	Illinois

CHAIRMAN:	ESTABLISHED:	JURISDICTION LICENSE(S):
Thomas J. Sagehorn	11/28/1970	13

A" Unsurpassed
Financial Stability Rating®
Demotech, Inc.

NAIC Number:
50156

NATIONAL LAND

NAIC Group:
STEWART

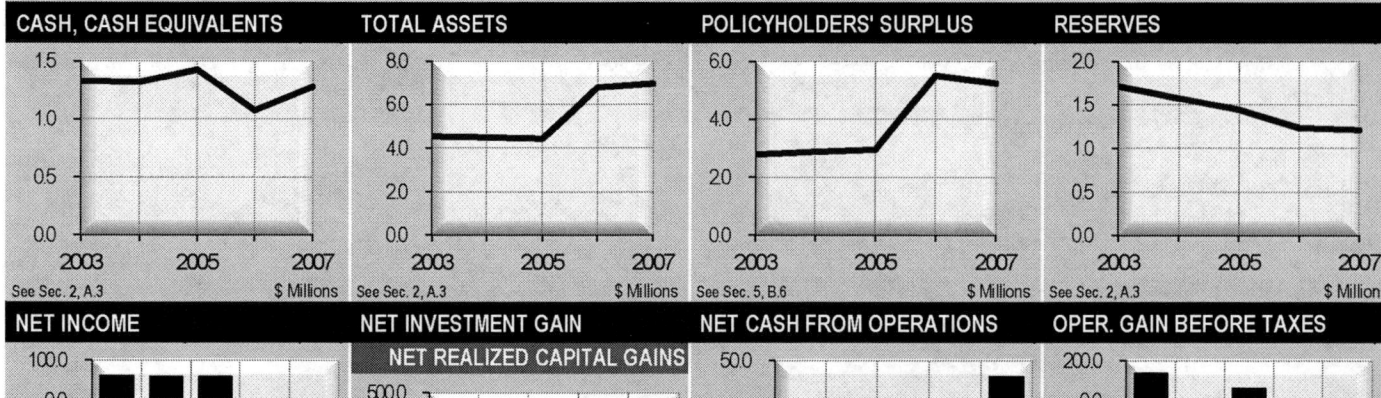

CASH, CASH EQUIVALENTS — See Sec. 2, A.3 — $ Millions
TOTAL ASSETS — See Sec. 2, A.3 — $ Millions
POLICYHOLDERS' SURPLUS — See Sec. 5, B.6 — $ Millions
RESERVES — See Sec. 2, A.3 — $ Millions

NET INCOME — See Sec. 2, B.3 — $ Thousands
NET INVESTMENT GAIN / NET REALIZED CAPITAL GAINS — See Sec. 5, A.8 — $ Thousands
NET CASH FROM OPERATIONS — See Sec. 2, C.3 — $ Thousands
OPER. GAIN BEFORE TAXES — See Sec. 2, B.3 — $ Thousands

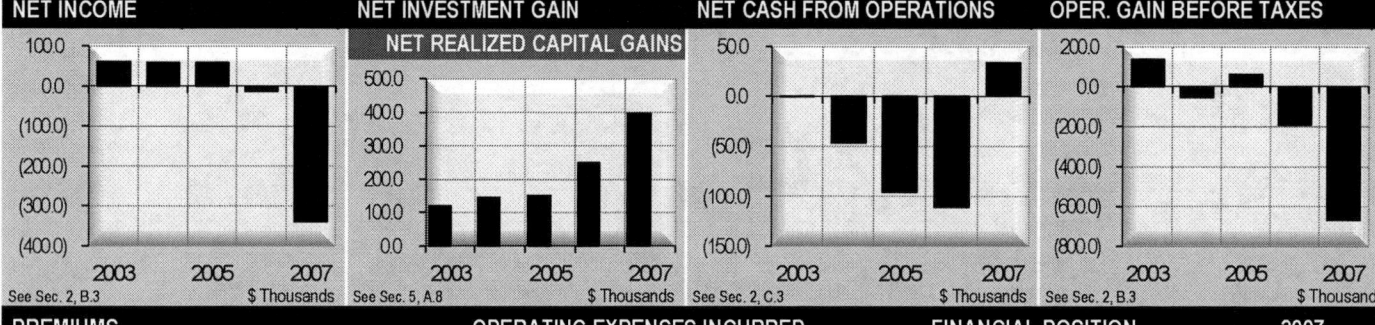

PREMIUMS — See Sec. 2, B.3 — $ Millions
- · - Direct
- - - Affiliated
—— Non-Affiliated
—— Net Premiums

OPERATING EXPENSES INCURRED / AGENT RETENTION — See Sec. 2, B.3 & Sec. 5, B.9 — $ Millions

FINANCIAL POSITION	2007
Cash, Cash Equivalents & Short-Term Investments	$1,276,808
Total Assets	$6,962,232
Policyholders' Surplus	$5,233,777
Reserves	$1,208,860
OPERATING RESULTS	
Net Income	($340,136)
Net Investment Gain	$396,943
Net Realized Capital Gains	$0
Net Cash from Operations	$33,374
Oper. Gain Before Taxes	($669,529)

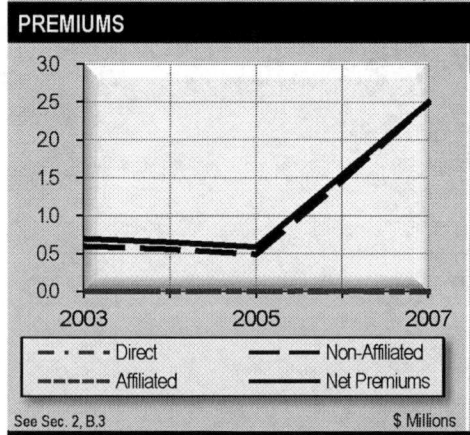

DIRECT PREMIUMS WRITTEN - YE 2007 — See Sec. 3, B.4
□ Direct ▨ Non-Affiliated ■ Affiliated

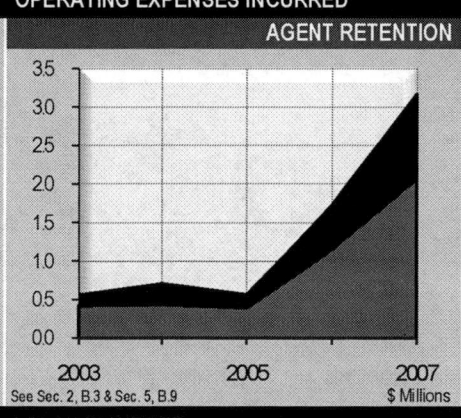

L&LAE INCURRED / LOSS RATIO — See Sec. 5, A.3 & Sec. 5, C.2 — $ Thousands

UNDERWRITING RESULTS	
Direct	$0
Non-Affiliated	$2,494,729
Affiliated	$0
Direct Premiums Written	$2,494,729
Net Premiums Earned	$2,497,933
Operating Expenses Incurred	$3,171,572
Agent Retention	$2,074,570
L&LAE Incurred	$67,550
Loss Ratio	2.70%

National Title Insurance Company

151 SW 27th Ave.
Miami, FL 33135

(305) 642-6220

WEBSITE:	STATE OF DOMICILE:
www.nationaltitleinsurance.com	Florida

PRESIDENT:	ESTABLISHED:	JURISDICTION LICENSE(S):
William L. Randol Jr.	7/31/1936	7

A Exceptional
Financial Stability Rating®
Demotech, Inc.

NAIC Number:
50695

NATIONAL

NAIC Group:
UNAFFILIATED

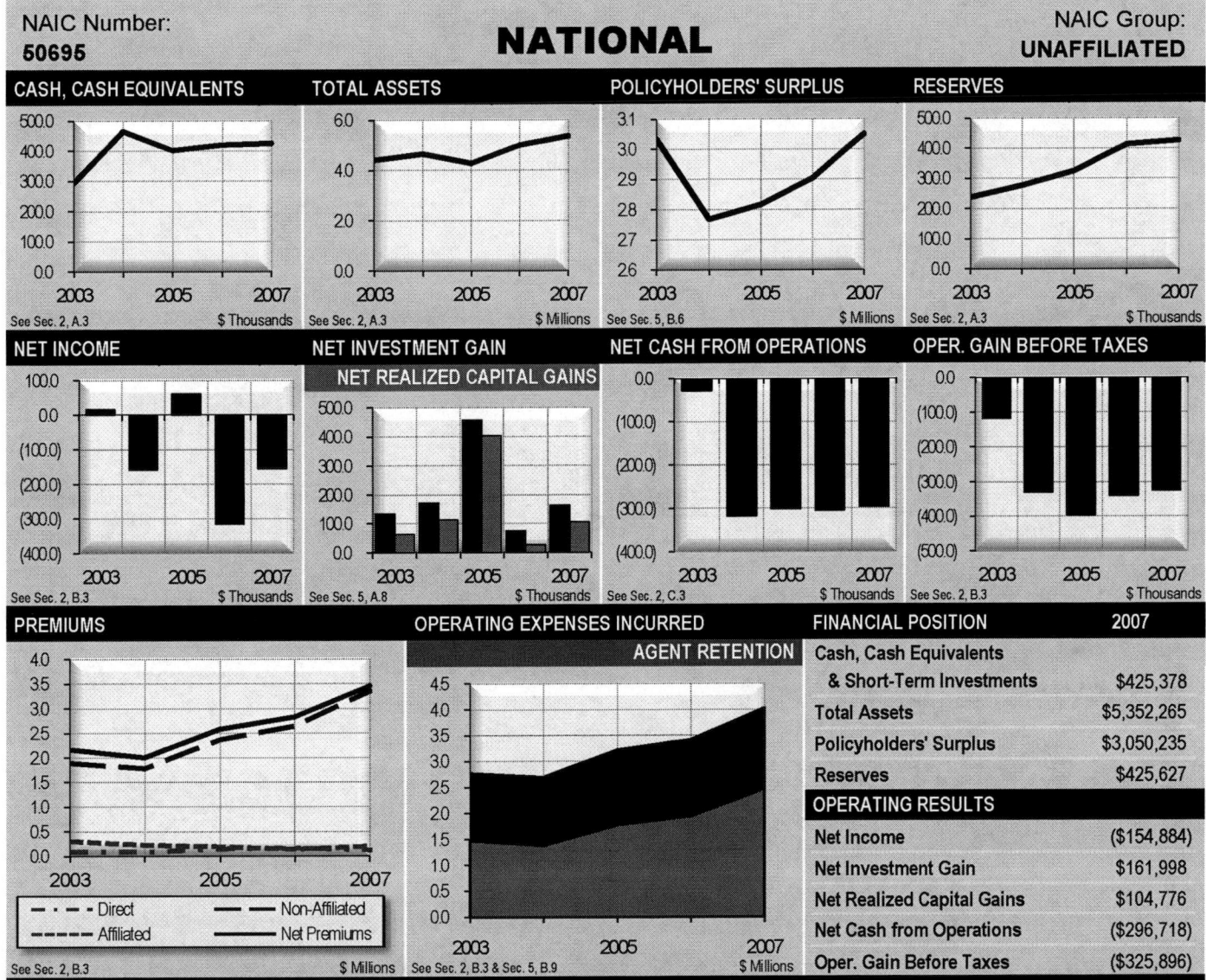

FINANCIAL POSITION	2007
Cash, Cash Equivalents & Short-Term Investments	$425,378
Total Assets	$5,352,265
Policyholders' Surplus	$3,050,235
Reserves	$425,627

OPERATING RESULTS	
Net Income	($154,884)
Net Investment Gain	$161,998
Net Realized Capital Gains	$104,776
Net Cash from Operations	($296,718)
Oper. Gain Before Taxes	($325,896)

UNDERWRITING RESULTS	
Direct	$127,106
Non-Affiliated	$3,347,151
Affiliated	$199,659
Direct Premiums Written	$3,673,916
Net Premiums Earned	$3,452,525
Operating Expenses Incurred	$4,030,224
Agent Retention	$2,467,634
L&LAE Incurred	($9,014)
Loss Ratio	(0.24)%

6

National Title Insurance of New York, Inc.

601 Riverside Ave.
Jacksonville, FL 32204

(904) 854-8100

WEBSITE:	STATE OF DOMICILE:
www.nationaltitleins.com	New York

PRESIDENT:	ESTABLISHED:	JURISDICTION LICENSE(S):
Eric David Swenson	3/14/1929	39

A Exceptional
Financial Stability Rating®
Demotech, Inc.

NAIC Number:
51020

NATIONAL OF NY

NAIC Group:
UNAFFILIATED

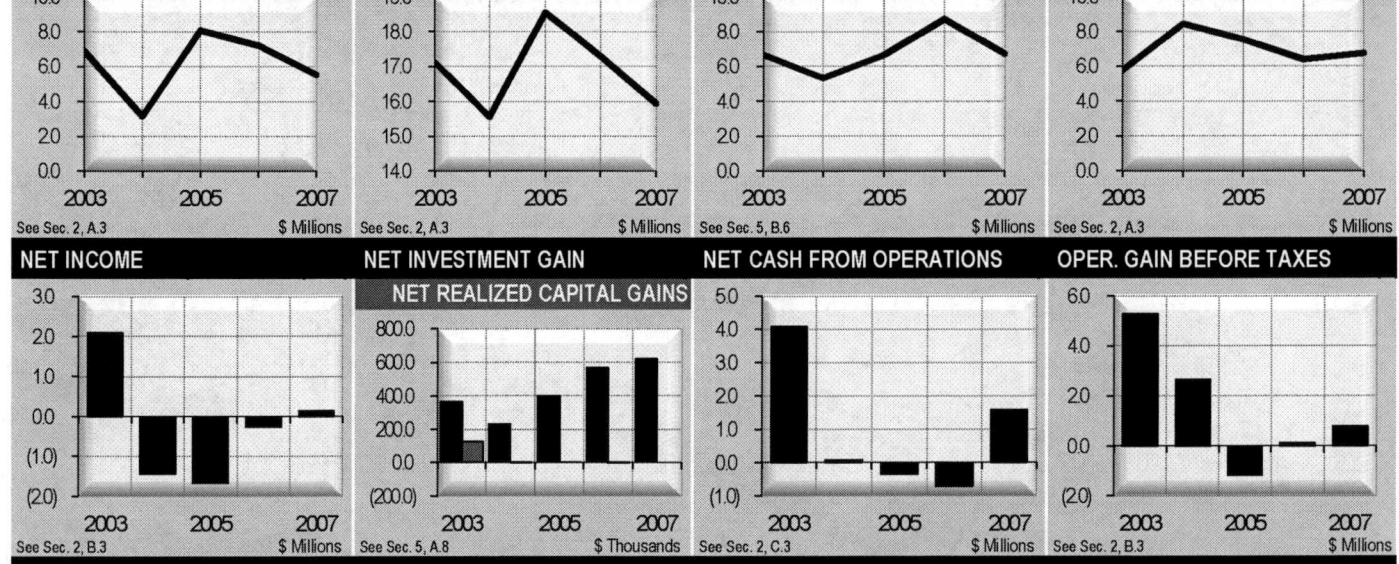

CASH, CASH EQUIVALENTS — See Sec. 2, A.3 — $ Millions
TOTAL ASSETS — See Sec. 2, A.3 — $ Millions
POLICYHOLDERS' SURPLUS — See Sec. 5, B.6 — $ Millions
RESERVES — See Sec. 2, A.3 — $ Millions

NET INCOME — See Sec. 2, B.3 — $ Millions
NET INVESTMENT GAIN / NET REALIZED CAPITAL GAINS — See Sec. 5, A.8 — $ Thousands
NET CASH FROM OPERATIONS — See Sec. 2, C.3 — $ Millions
OPER. GAIN BEFORE TAXES — See Sec. 2, B.3 — $ Millions

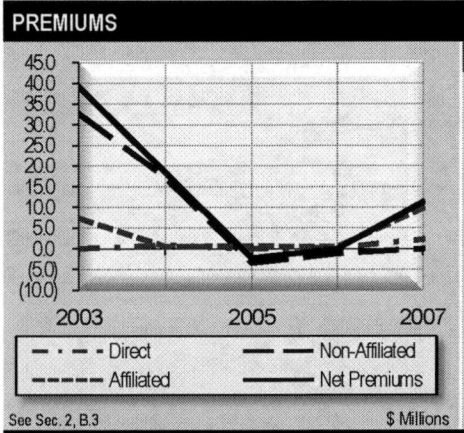

PREMIUMS
- – · – Direct
- – – Non-Affiliated
- – – – Affiliated
- —— Net Premiums

See Sec. 2, B.3 — $ Millions

DIRECT PREMIUMS WRITTEN - YE 2007
☐ Direct ▨ Non-Affiliated ■ Affiliated
See Sec. 3, B.4

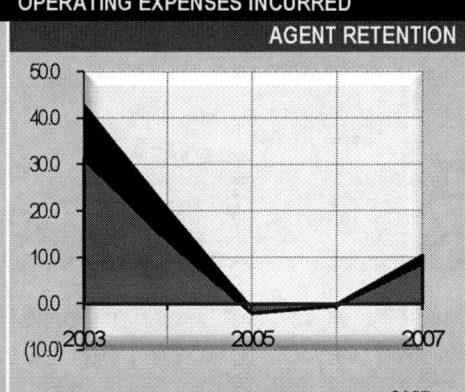

OPERATING EXPENSES INCURRED / AGENT RETENTION
See Sec. 2, B.3 & Sec. 5, B.9 — $ Millions

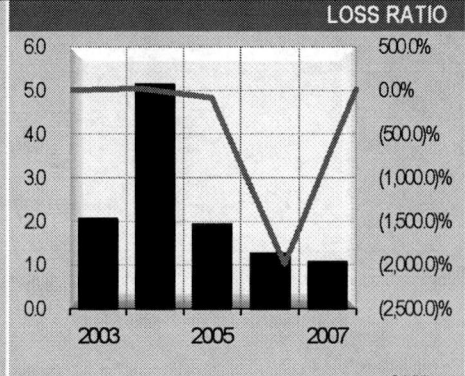

L&LAE INCURRED / LOSS RATIO
See Sec. 5, A.3 & Sec. 5, C.2 — $ Millions

FINANCIAL POSITION	2007
Cash, Cash Equivalents & Short-Term Investments	$5,511,112
Total Assets	$15,929,860
Policyholders' Surplus	$6,713,364
Reserves	$6,718,427
OPERATING RESULTS	
Net Income	$146,157
Net Investment Gain	$620,283
Net Realized Capital Gains	$0
Net Cash from Operations	$1,586,760
Oper. Gain Before Taxes	$803,639
UNDERWRITING RESULTS	
Direct	$2,257,917
Non-Affiliated	$4,027
Affiliated	$9,776,776
Direct Premiums Written	**$12,038,720**
Net Premiums Earned	**$11,194,386**
Operating Expenses Incurred	$10,390,746
Agent Retention	$8,674,820
L&LAE Incurred	$1,062,612
Loss Ratio	9.49%

6

Nations Title Insurance of New York, Inc.

601 Riverside Ave.
Jacksonville, FL 32204

(904) 854-8100

WEBSITE:	STATE OF DOMICILE:
www.fnf.com	New York

PRESIDENT:	ESTABLISHED:	JURISDICTION LICENSE(S):
Raymond Randall Quirk	11/15/1927	23

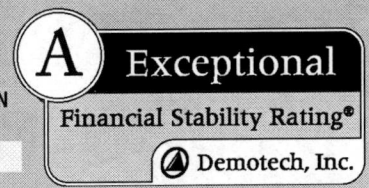

A Exceptional
Financial Stability Rating®
Demotech, Inc.

NAIC Number:
51101

NATIONS OF NY

NAIC Group:
CHICAGO / FIDELITY

CASH, CASH EQUIVALENTS
See Sec. 2, A.3 — $ Millions

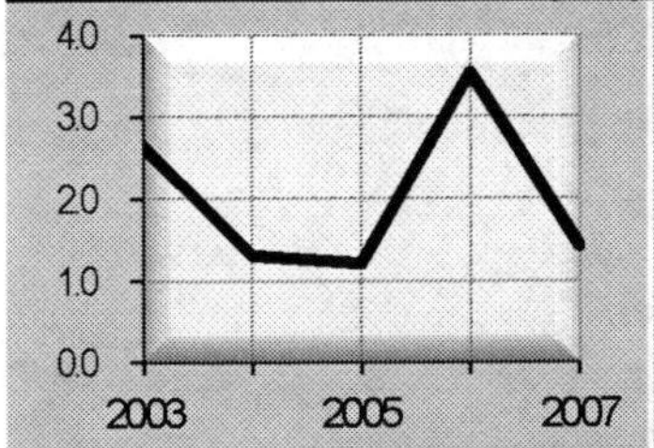

TOTAL ASSETS
See Sec. 2, A.3 — $ Millions

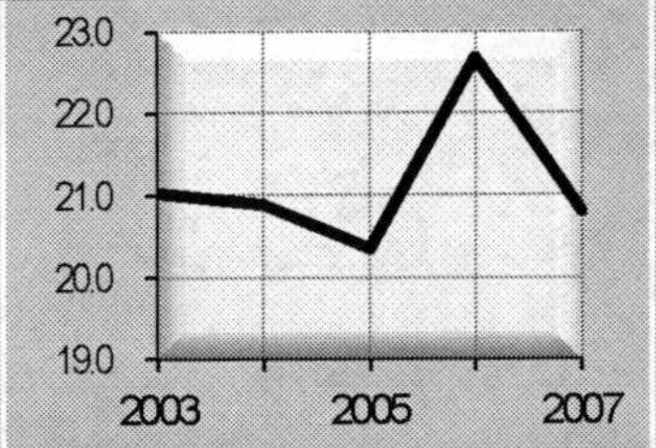

POLICYHOLDERS' SURPLUS
See Sec. 5, B.6 — $ Millions

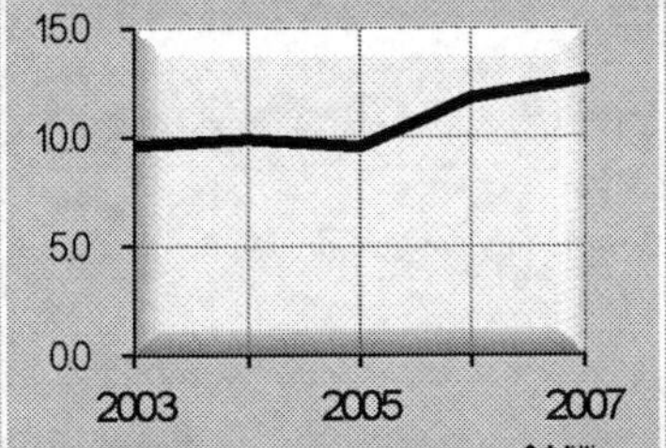

RESERVES
See Sec. 2, A.3 — $ Millions

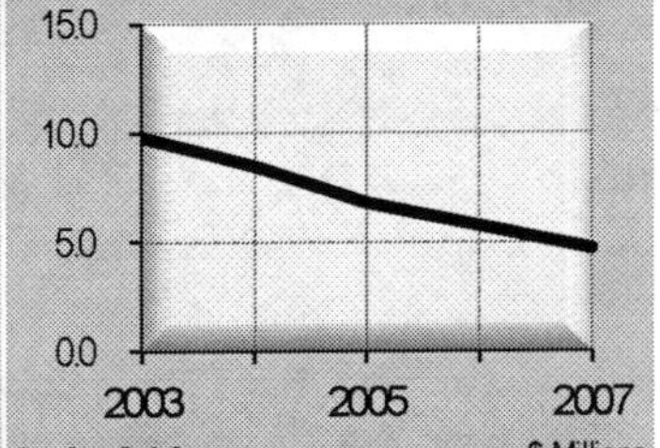

NET INCOME
See Sec. 2, B.3 — $ Millions

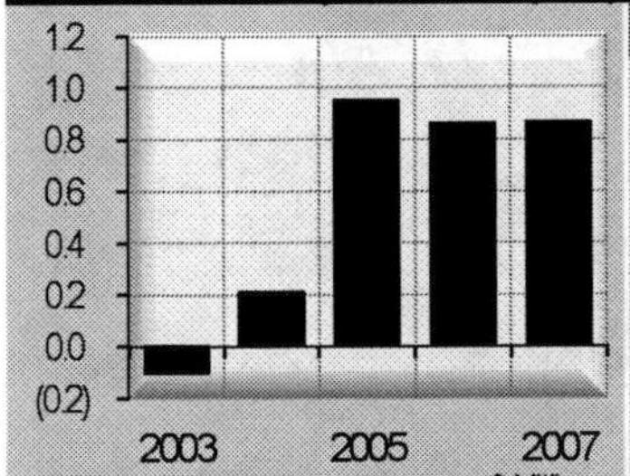

NET INVESTMENT GAIN
NET REALIZED CAPITAL GAINS
See Sec. 5, A.8 — $ Thousands

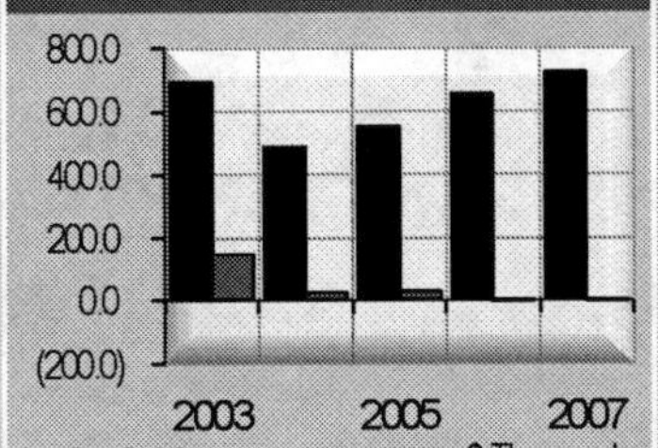

NET CASH FROM OPERATIONS
See Sec. 2, C.3 — $ Millions

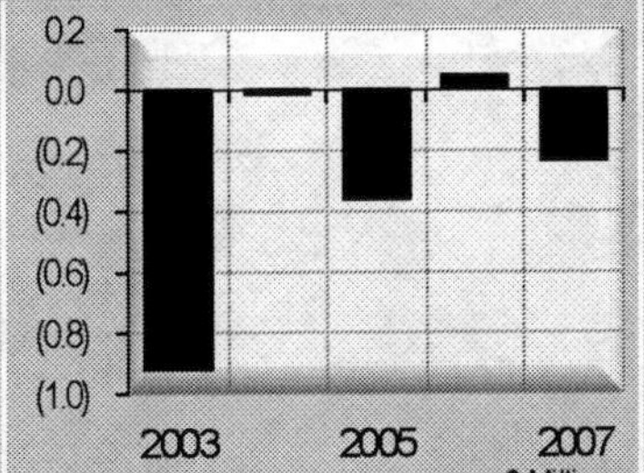

OPER. GAIN BEFORE TAXES
See Sec. 2, B.3 — $ Thousands

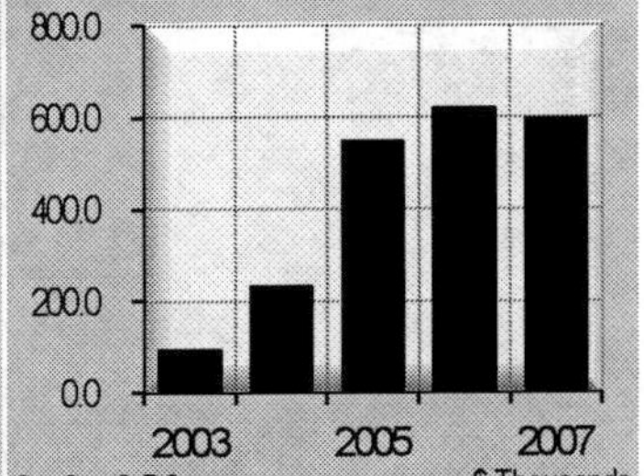

PREMIUMS
See Sec. 2, B.3 — $ Millions

- -- Direct
- ----- Affiliated
- --- Non-Affiliated
- —— Net Premiums

OPERATING EXPENSES INCURRED
AGENT RETENTION
See Sec. 2, B.3 & Sec. 5, B.9 — $ Millions

DIRECT PREMIUMS WRITTEN - YE 2007
See Sec. 3, B.4

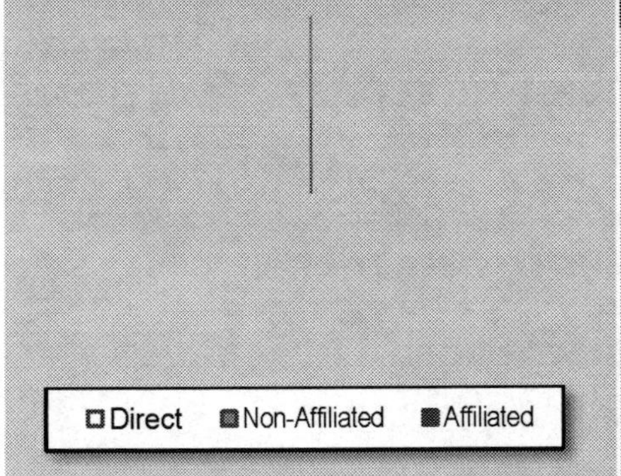

☐ Direct ☐ Non-Affiliated ☐ Affiliated

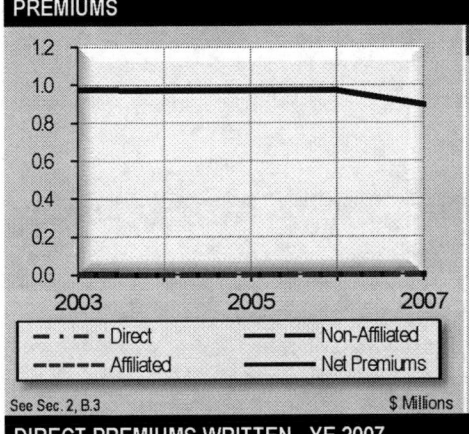

L&LAE INCURRED
LOSS RATIO
See Sec. 5, A.3 & Sec. 5, C.2 — $ Millions

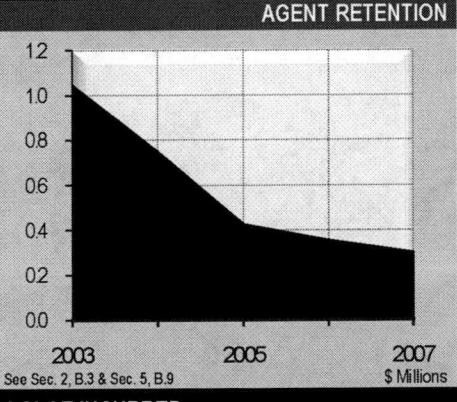

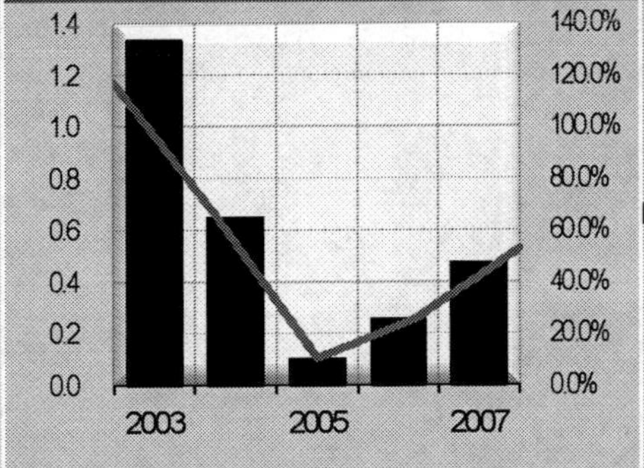

FINANCIAL POSITION	2007
Cash, Cash Equivalents & Short-Term Investments	$1,427,890
Total Assets	$20,799,494
Policyholders' Surplus	$12,627,192
Reserves	$4,702,399
OPERATING RESULTS	
Net Income	$865,566
Net Investment Gain	$724,028
Net Realized Capital Gains	($1,938)
Net Cash from Operations	($233,470)
Oper. Gain Before Taxes	$597,309
UNDERWRITING RESULTS	
Direct	$0
Non-Affiliated	$0
Affiliated	$0
Direct Premiums Written	$0
Net Premiums Earned	$895,124
Operating Expenses Incurred	$297,817
Agent Retention	$0
L&LAE Incurred	$471,333
Loss Ratio	52.66%

6

New Jersey Title Insurance Company

400 Lanidex Plz.
Parsippany, NJ 07054

(973) 952-0110

WEBSITE:	STATE OF DOMICILE:
www.njtic.com	New Jersey

PRESIDENT:	ESTABLISHED:	JURISDICTION LICENSE(S):
Carl Robert Samson	6/9/1937	3

A' Unsurpassed
Financial Stability Rating®
Demotech, Inc.

NAIC Number:
51187

NEW JERSEY TIC

NAIC Group:
CATIC

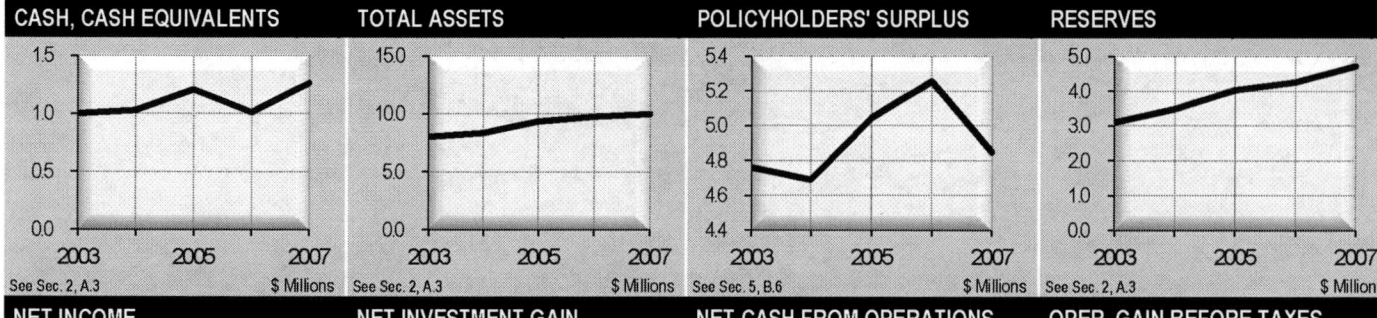

CASH, CASH EQUIVALENTS — See Sec. 2, A.3 — $ Millions
TOTAL ASSETS — See Sec. 2, A.3 — $ Millions
POLICYHOLDERS' SURPLUS — See Sec. 5, B.6 — $ Millions
RESERVES — See Sec. 2, A.3 — $ Millions

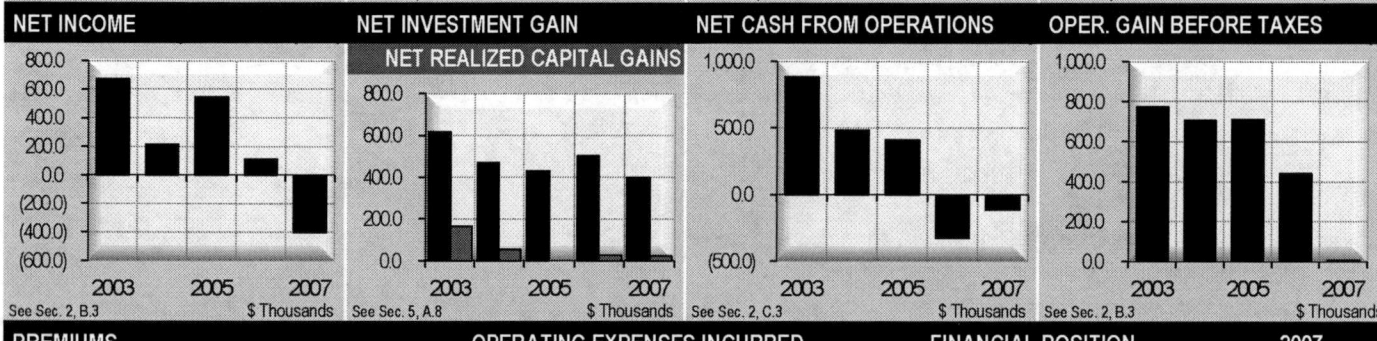

NET INCOME — See Sec. 2, B.3 — $ Thousands
NET INVESTMENT GAIN / NET REALIZED CAPITAL GAINS — See Sec. 5, A.8 — $ Thousands
NET CASH FROM OPERATIONS — See Sec. 2, C.3 — $ Thousands
OPER. GAIN BEFORE TAXES — See Sec. 2, B.3 — $ Thousands

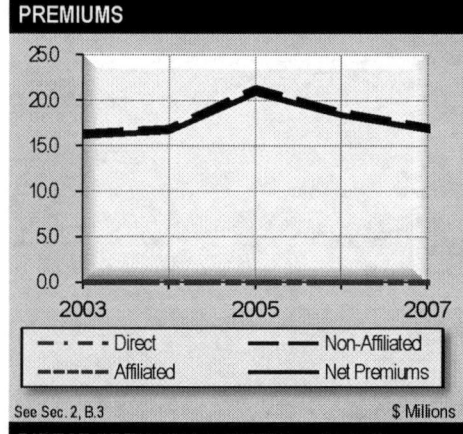

PREMIUMS
- · - · - Direct
- - - - Affiliated
- —— Non-Affiliated
- —— Net Premiums

See Sec. 2, B.3 — $ Millions

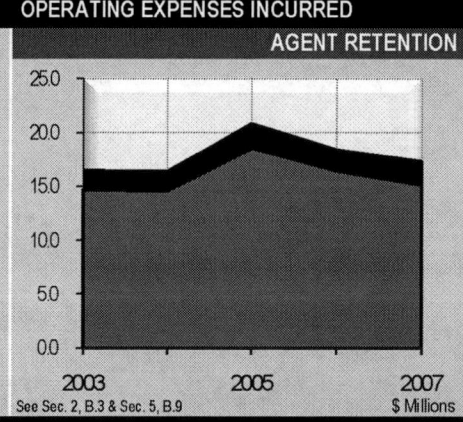

OPERATING EXPENSES INCURRED / AGENT RETENTION
See Sec. 2, B.3 & Sec. 5, B.9 — $ Millions

FINANCIAL POSITION	2007
Cash, Cash Equivalents & Short-Term Investments	$1,263,232
Total Assets	$9,950,613
Policyholders' Surplus	$4,846,327
Reserves	$4,711,174
OPERATING RESULTS	
Net Income	($405,519)
Net Investment Gain	$399,158
Net Realized Capital Gains	$25,114
Net Cash from Operations	($113,860)
Oper. Gain Before Taxes	$8,604

DIRECT PREMIUMS WRITTEN - YE 2007
See Sec. 3, B.4

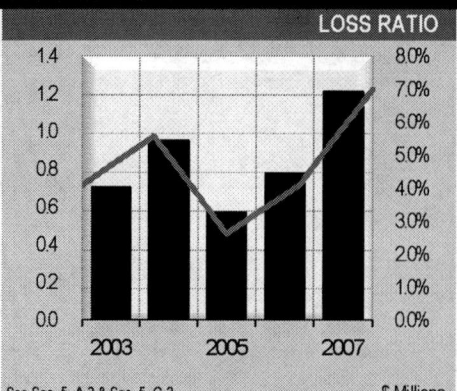

- □ Direct
- ▨ Non-Affiliated
- ■ Affiliated

L&LAE INCURRED / LOSS RATIO
See Sec. 5, A.3 & Sec. 5, C.2 — $ Millions

UNDERWRITING RESULTS	
Direct	$0
Non-Affiliated	$17,124,472
Affiliated	$0
Direct Premiums Written	**$17,124,472**
Net Premiums Earned	$16,799,332
Operating Expenses Incurred	$17,322,234
Agent Retention	$15,137,976
L&LAE Incurred	$1,216,094
Loss Ratio	7.02%

North American Title Insurance Company

1855 Gateway Blvd., Ste. 600
Concord, CA 94520

(925) 935-5599

Merged with North American Title Insurance Corporation (NAIC # 50000)

WEBSITE:	STATE OF DOMICILE:
www.nat.com	California

PRESIDENT:	ESTABLISHED:	JURISDICTION LICENSE(S):
Emilio Fernandez	9/18/1958	19

A' Unsurpassed
A Prime
Financial Stability Rating®
Demotech, Inc.

NAIC Number:
50130

NORTH AMERICAN

NAIC Group:
UNAFFILIATED

CASH, CASH EQUIVALENTS
See Sec. 2, A.3 — $ Millions

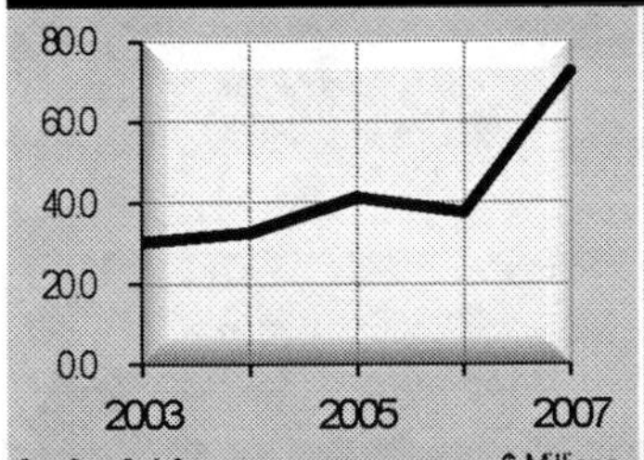

TOTAL ASSETS
See Sec. 2, A.3 — $ Millions

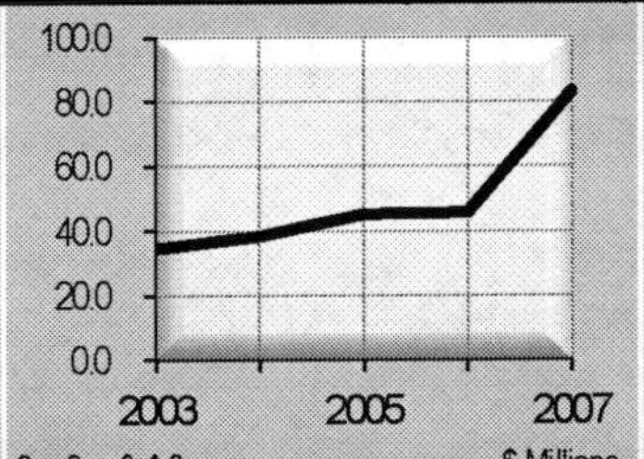

POLICYHOLDERS' SURPLUS
See Sec. 5, B.6 — $ Millions

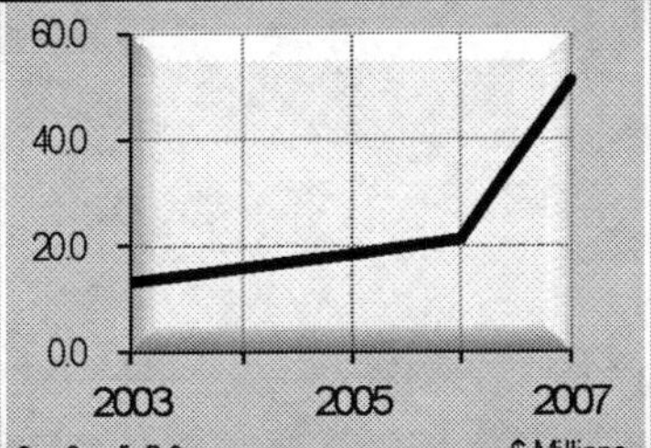

RESERVES
See Sec. 2, A.3 — $ Millions

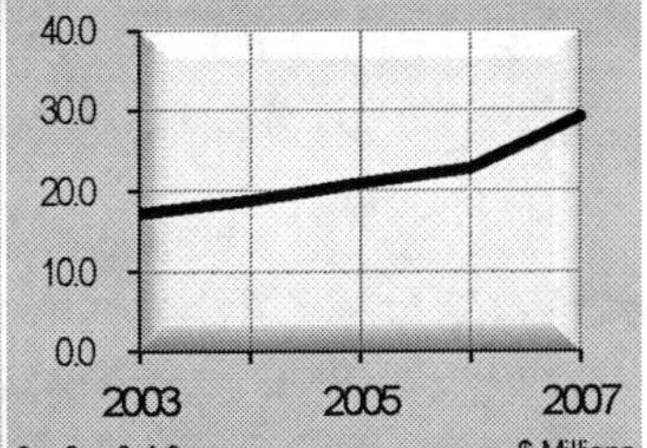

NET INCOME
See Sec. 2, B.3 — $ Millions

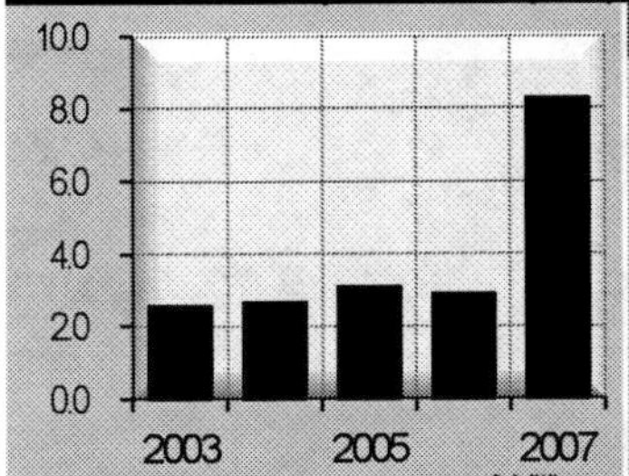

NET INVESTMENT GAIN
NET REALIZED CAPITAL GAINS
See Sec. 5, A.8 — $ Millions

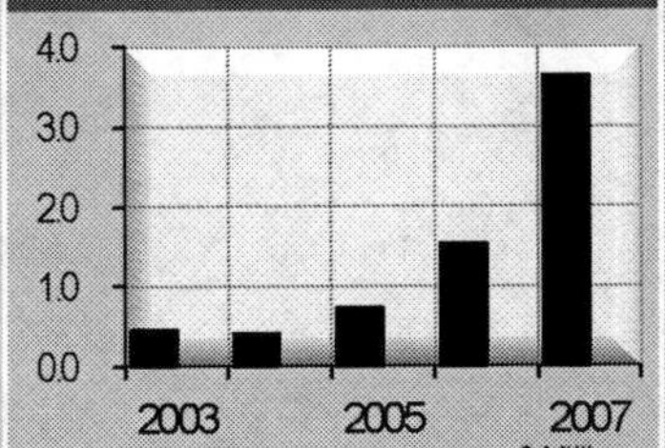

NET CASH FROM OPERATIONS
See Sec. 2, C.3 — $ Millions

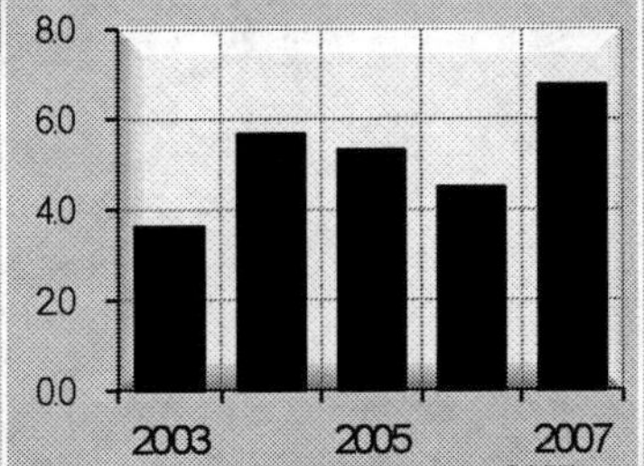

OPER. GAIN BEFORE TAXES
See Sec. 2, B.3 — $ Millions

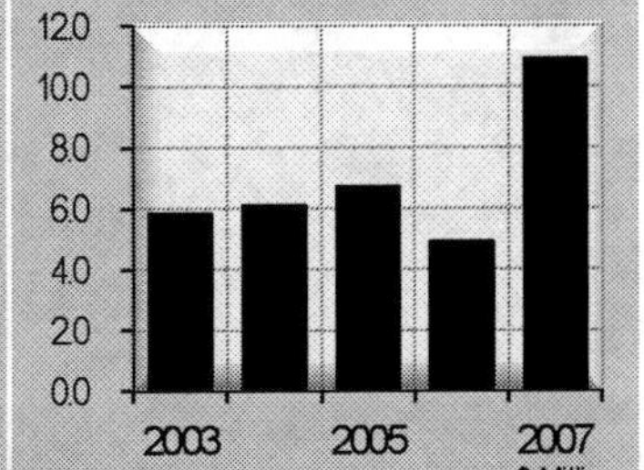

PREMIUMS

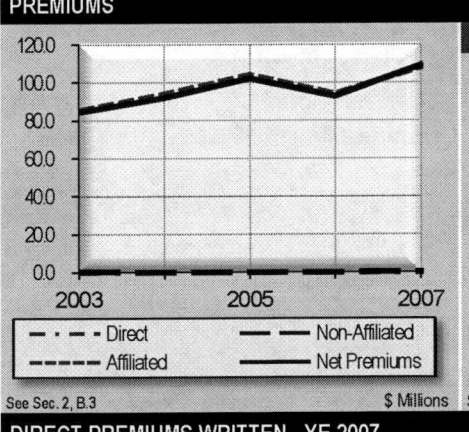

- — · — Direct
- - - - - Affiliated
- — — Non-Affiliated
- —— Net Premiums

See Sec. 2, B.3 — $ Millions

OPERATING EXPENSES INCURRED
AGENT RETENTION

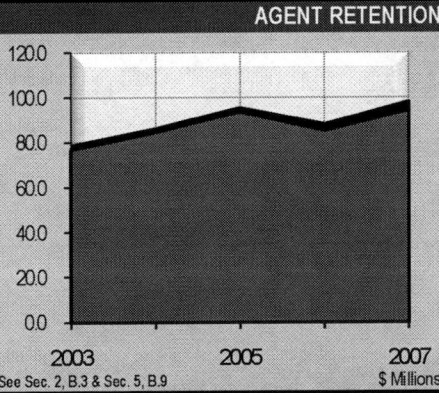

See Sec. 2, B.3 & Sec. 5, B.9 — $ Millions

FINANCIAL POSITION — 2007

Cash, Cash Equivalents & Short-Term Investments	$72,439,602
Total Assets	$83,058,030
Policyholders' Surplus	$50,899,292
Reserves	$29,139,432

OPERATING RESULTS

Net Income	$8,278,591
Net Investment Gain	$3,642,852
Net Realized Capital Gains	$0
Net Cash from Operations	$6,749,033
Oper. Gain Before Taxes	$10,899,357

DIRECT PREMIUMS WRITTEN - YE 2007

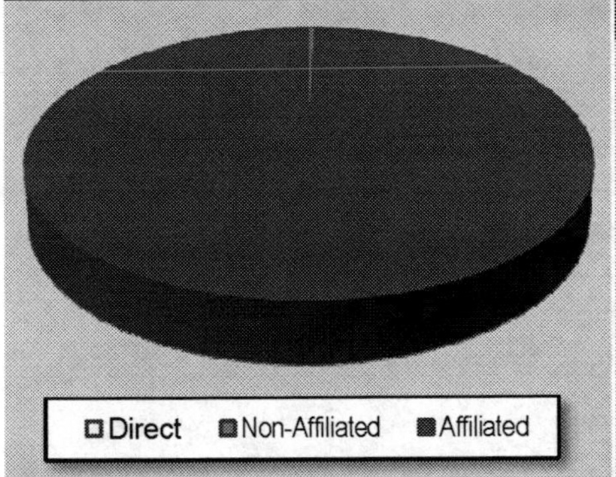

☐ Direct ▪ Non-Affiliated ▪ Affiliated

See Sec. 3, B.4

L&LAE INCURRED
LOSS RATIO
See Sec. 5, A.3 & Sec. 5, C.2 — $ Millions

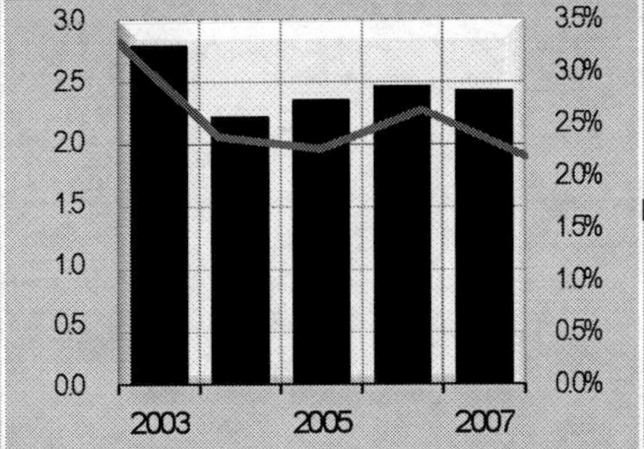

UNDERWRITING RESULTS

Direct	$0
Non-Affiliated	$438,203
Affiliated	$107,933,280
Direct Premiums Written	$108,371,483
Net Premiums Earned	$109,101,307
Operating Expenses Incurred	$98,201,775
Agent Retention	$94,289,365
L&LAE Incurred	$2,424,736
Loss Ratio	2.22%

6

Northeast Investors Title Insurance Company

121 N Columbia St.
Chapel Hill, NC 27514

(919) 968-2200

WEBSITE:	STATE OF DOMICILE:
www.invtitle.com	South Carolina

PRESIDENT & COO:	ESTABLISHED:	JURISDICTION LICENSE(S):
William Morris Fine	2/23/1973	20

A" Unsurpassed
Financial Stability Rating®
Demotech, Inc.

NAIC Number: **50377**

NORTHEAST INVESTORS

NAIC Group: **INVESTORS**

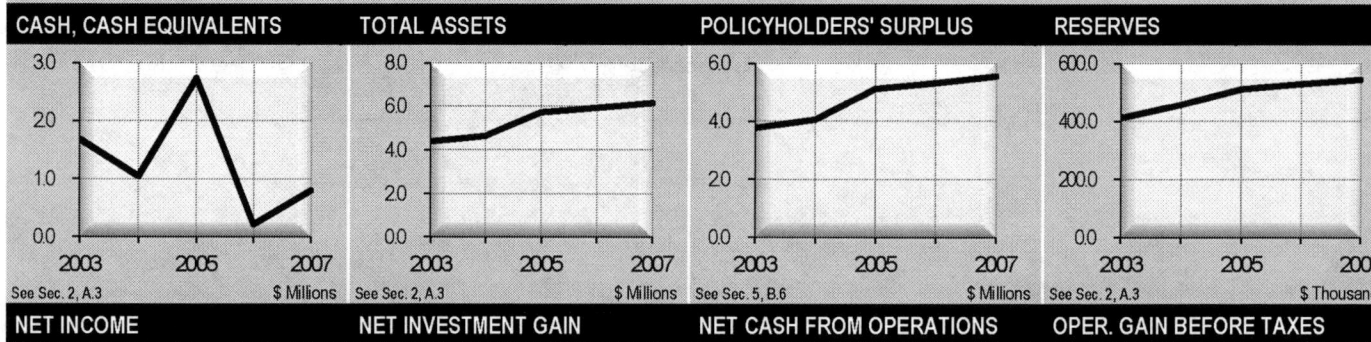

CASH, CASH EQUIVALENTS — See Sec. 2, A.3 — $ Millions
TOTAL ASSETS — See Sec. 2, A.3 — $ Millions
POLICYHOLDERS' SURPLUS — See Sec. 5, B.6 — $ Millions
RESERVES — See Sec. 2, A.3 — $ Thousands

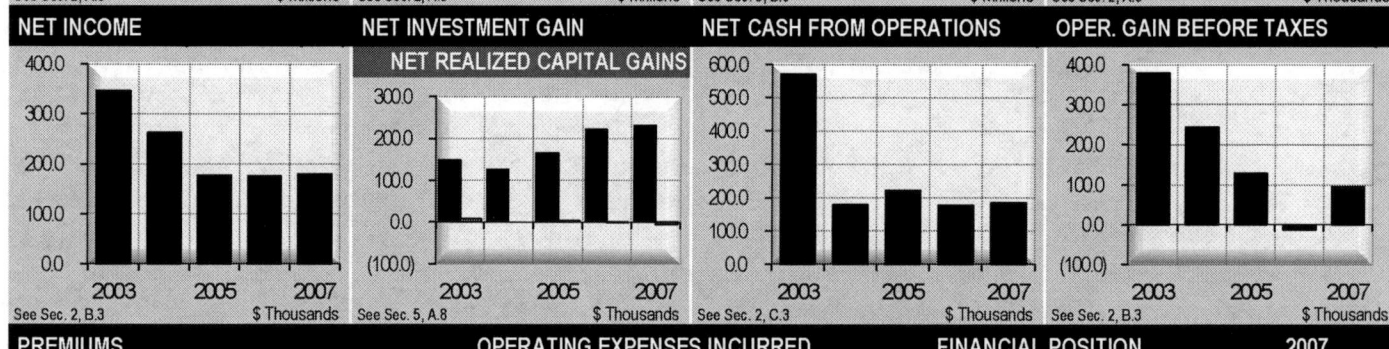

NET INCOME — See Sec. 2, B.3 — $ Thousands
NET INVESTMENT GAIN / NET REALIZED CAPITAL GAINS — See Sec. 5, A.8 — $ Thousands
NET CASH FROM OPERATIONS — See Sec. 2, C.3 — $ Thousands
OPER. GAIN BEFORE TAXES — See Sec. 2, B.3 — $ Thousands

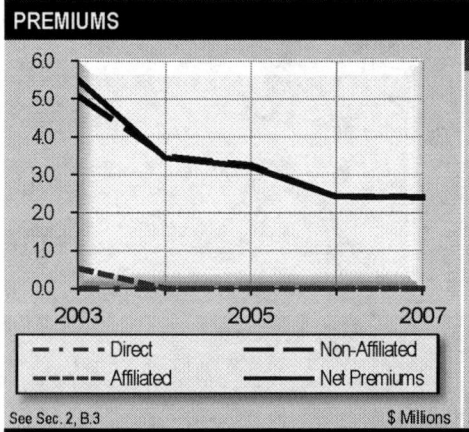

PREMIUMS
- - · - Direct
—— Non-Affiliated
----- Affiliated
—— Net Premiums
See Sec. 2, B.3 — $ Millions

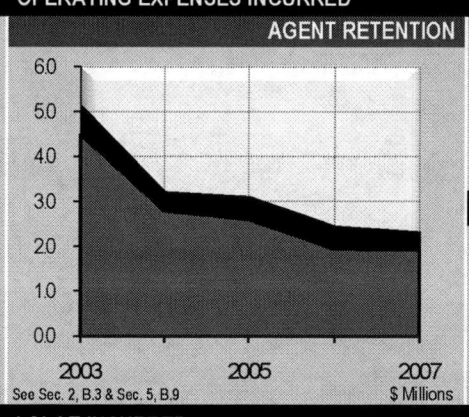

OPERATING EXPENSES INCURRED / AGENT RETENTION
See Sec. 2, B.3 & Sec. 5, B.9 — $ Millions

FINANCIAL POSITION	2007
Cash, Cash Equivalents & Short-Term Investments	$799,647
Total Assets	$6,143,241
Policyholders' Surplus	$5,540,475
Reserves	$542,982
OPERATING RESULTS	
Net Income	$180,394
Net Investment Gain	$231,840
Net Realized Capital Gains	($5,920)
Net Cash from Operations	$185,241
Oper. Gain Before Taxes	$95,932

DIRECT PREMIUMS WRITTEN - YE 2007

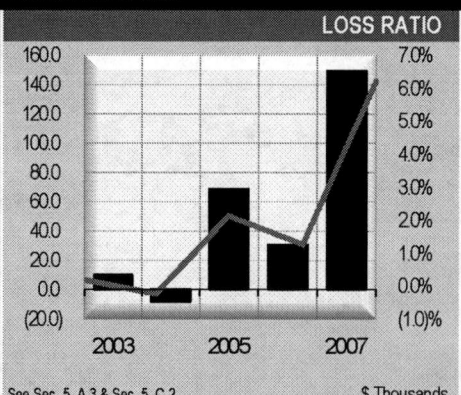

☐ Direct ▨ Non-Affiliated ▪ Affiliated
See Sec. 3, B.4

L&LAE INCURRED / LOSS RATIO
See Sec. 5, A.3 & Sec. 5, C.2 — $ Thousands

UNDERWRITING RESULTS	
Direct	$0
Non-Affiliated	$2,414,626
Affiliated	$0
Direct Premiums Written	**$2,414,626**
Net Premiums Earned	$2,402,629
Operating Expenses Incurred	$2,307,627
Agent Retention	$1,935,698
L&LAE Incurred	$149,328
Loss Ratio	6.21%

Ohio Bar Title Insurance Company

341 S Third St, Ste. 100
Columbus, OH 43215

(800) 628-4853

WEBSITE:	STATE OF DOMICILE:
www.ohiobartitle.com	Ohio

PRESIDENT:	ESTABLISHED:	JURISDICTION LICENSE(S):
Samuel John Halkias	7/27/1953	4

A Exceptional
Financial Stability Rating®
Demotech, Inc.

NAIC Number:
51330

OHIO BAR

NAIC Group:
FIRST AMERICAN

CASH, CASH EQUIVALENTS
See Sec. 2, A.3 — $ Millions

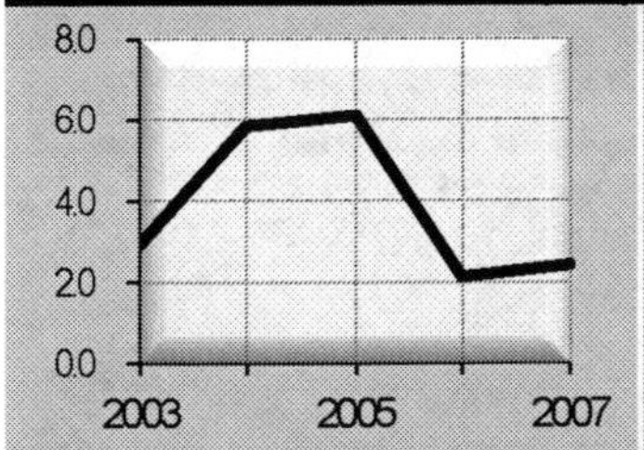

TOTAL ASSETS
See Sec. 2, A.3 — $ Millions

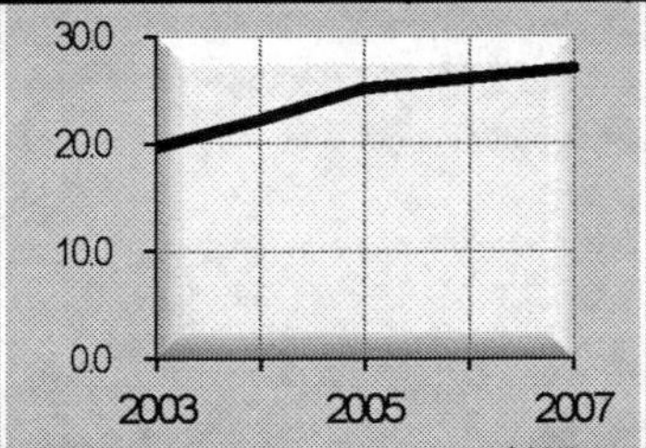

POLICYHOLDERS' SURPLUS
See Sec. 5, B.6 — $ Millions

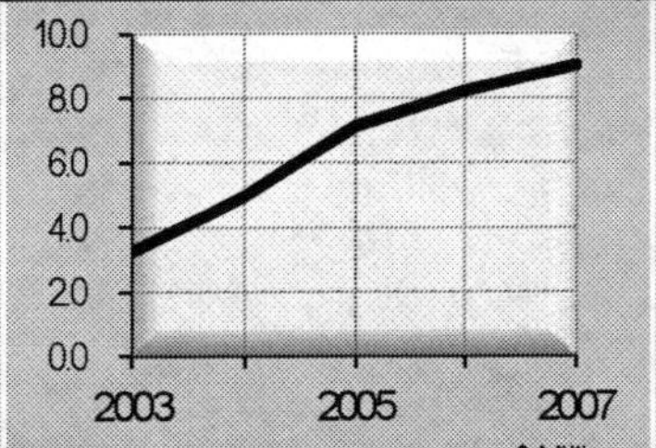

RESERVES
See Sec. 2, A.3 — $ Millions

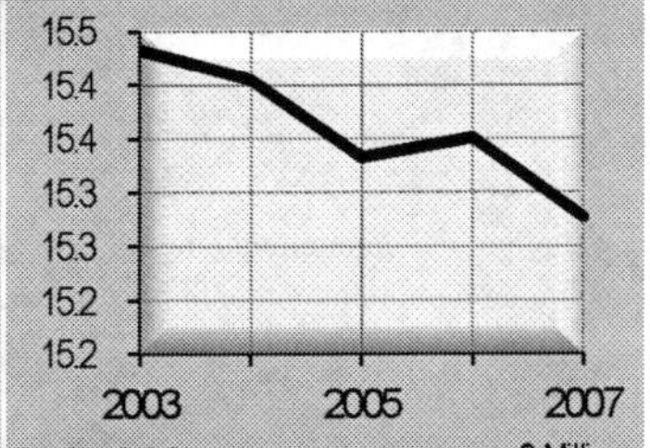

NET INCOME
See Sec. 2, B.3 — $ Millions

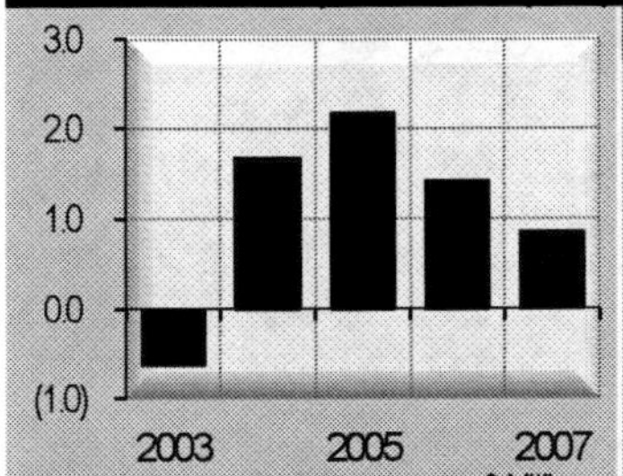

NET INVESTMENT GAIN
NET REALIZED CAPITAL GAINS
See Sec. 5, A.8 — $ Millions

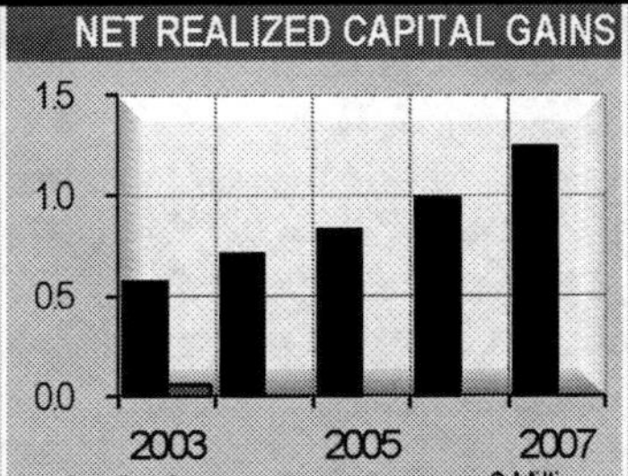

NET CASH FROM OPERATIONS
See Sec. 2, C.3 — $ Millions

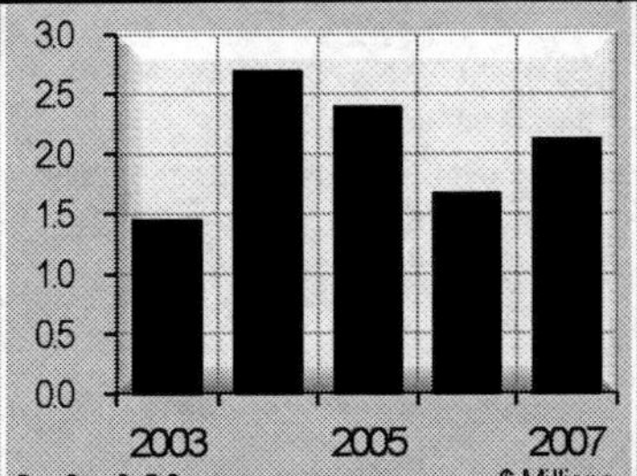

OPER. GAIN BEFORE TAXES
See Sec. 2, B.3 — $ Millions

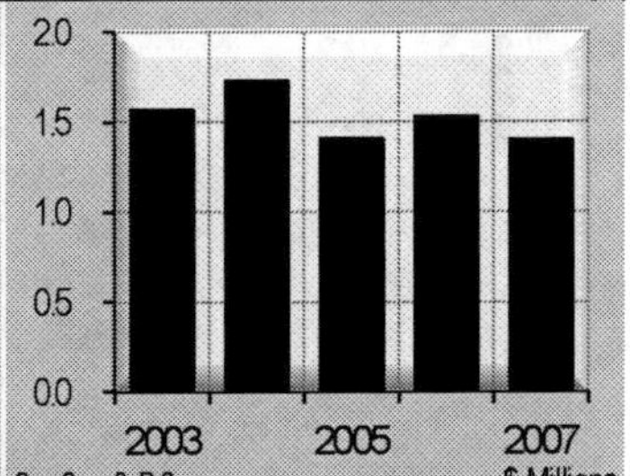

PREMIUMS
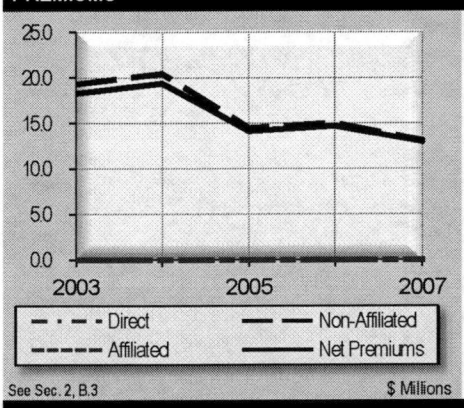

- — · — Direct
- ----- Affiliated
- — — Non-Affiliated
- —— Net Premiums

See Sec. 2, B.3 — $ Millions

OPERATING EXPENSES INCURRED
AGENT RETENTION
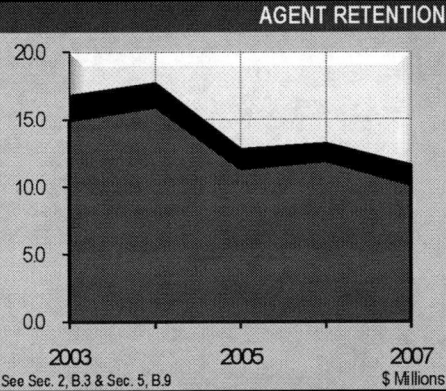
See Sec. 2, B.3 & Sec. 5, B.9 — $ Millions

FINANCIAL POSITION	2007
Cash, Cash Equivalents & Short-Term Investments	$2,421,852
Total Assets	$26,981,319
Policyholders' Surplus	$9,026,842
Reserves	$15,277,012
OPERATING RESULTS	
Net Income	$847,075
Net Investment Gain	$1,245,118
Net Realized Capital Gains	$2,136
Net Cash from Operations	$2,123,489
Oper. Gain Before Taxes	$1,403,638

DIRECT PREMIUMS WRITTEN - YE 2007

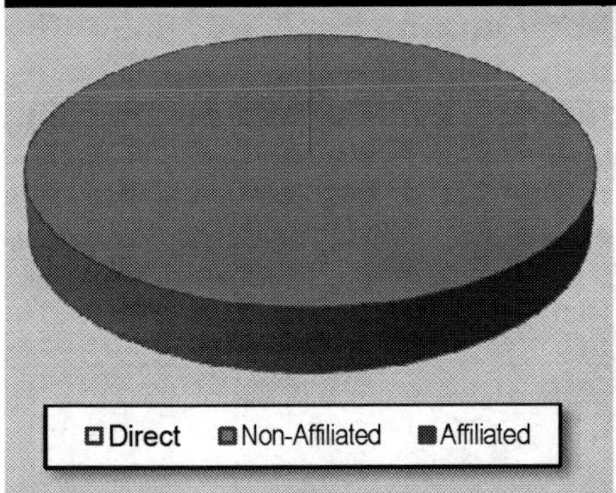

- □ Direct
- ■ Non-Affiliated
- ■ Affiliated

See Sec. 3, B.4

L&LAE INCURRED
LOSS RATIO
See Sec. 5, A.3 & Sec. 5, C.2 — $ Millions

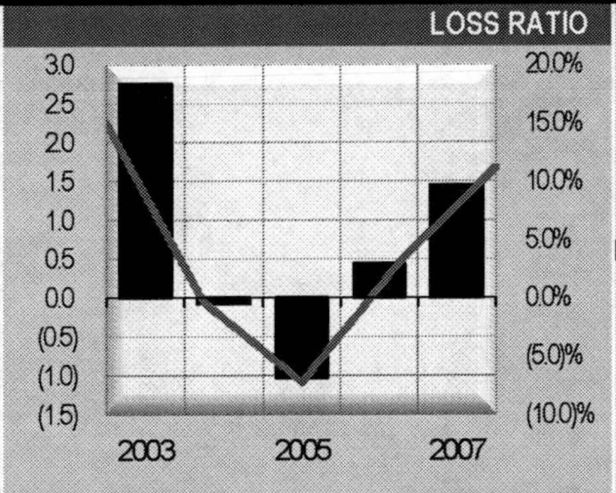

UNDERWRITING RESULTS	
Direct	$0
Non-Affiliated	$13,072,886
Affiliated	$0
Direct Premiums Written	$13,072,886
Net Premiums Earned	$12,961,750
Operating Expenses Incurred	$11,571,122
Agent Retention	$10,149,102
L&LAE Incurred	$1,445,381
Loss Ratio	11.14%

6

Old Republic General Title Insurance Corporation

400 Second Ave. S
Minneapolis, MN 55401-2499

(612) 371-1111

WEBSITE:	STATE OF DOMICILE:	
www.oldrepublictitle.com	Ohio	
PRESIDENT & COO:	ESTABLISHED:	JURISDICTION LICENSE(S):
Rande Keith Yeager	8/3/1994	2

A" Unsurpassed
Financial Stability Rating®
Demotech, Inc.

NAIC Number:
50005

OLD REPUBLIC GENERAL

NAIC Group:
OLD REPUBLIC

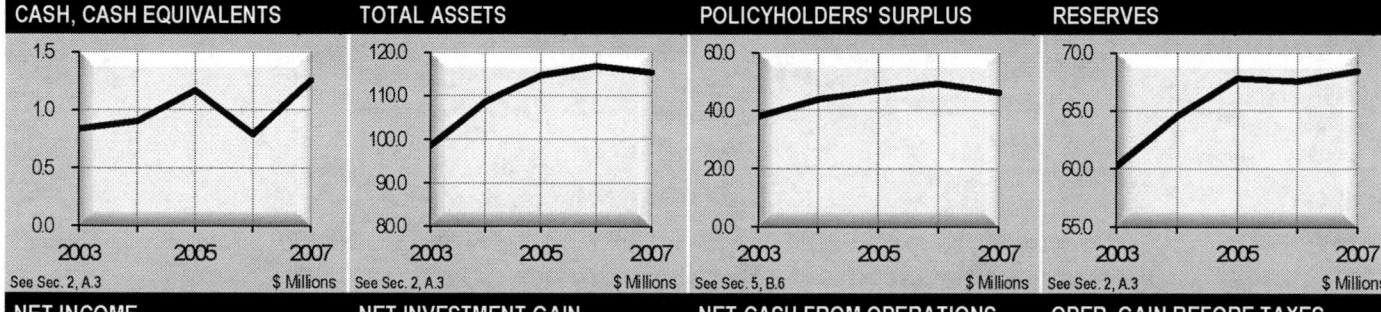

CASH, CASH EQUIVALENTS — See Sec. 2, A.3 — $ Millions
TOTAL ASSETS — See Sec. 2, A.3 — $ Millions
POLICYHOLDERS' SURPLUS — See Sec. 5, B.6 — $ Millions
RESERVES — See Sec. 2, A.3 — $ Millions

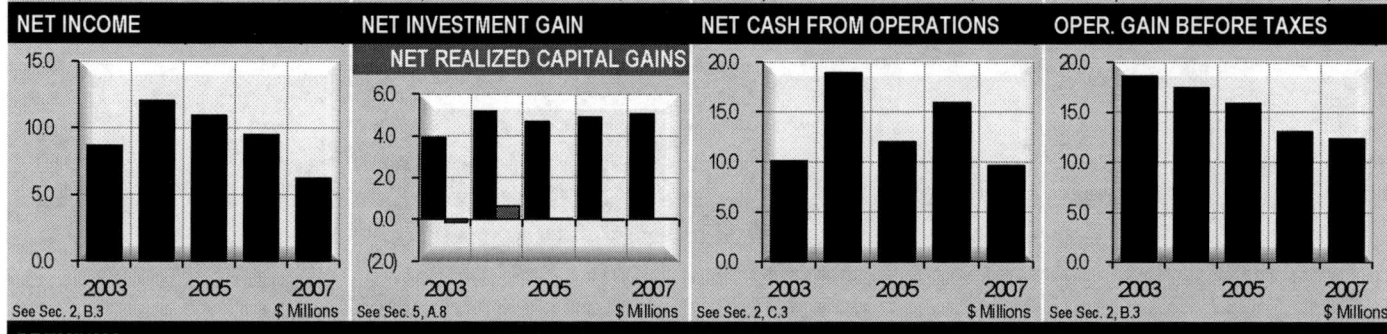

NET INCOME — See Sec. 2, B.3 — $ Millions
NET INVESTMENT GAIN / NET REALIZED CAPITAL GAINS — See Sec. 5, A.8 — $ Millions
NET CASH FROM OPERATIONS — See Sec. 2, C.3 — $ Millions
OPER. GAIN BEFORE TAXES — See Sec. 2, B.3 — $ Millions

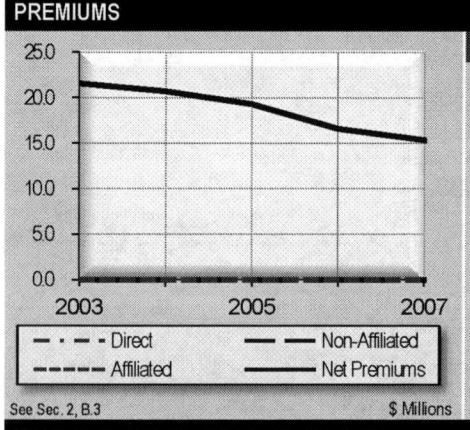

PREMIUMS

- – · – Direct
- – – – Non-Affiliated
- – – – – Affiliated
- ——— Net Premiums

See Sec. 2, B.3 — $ Millions

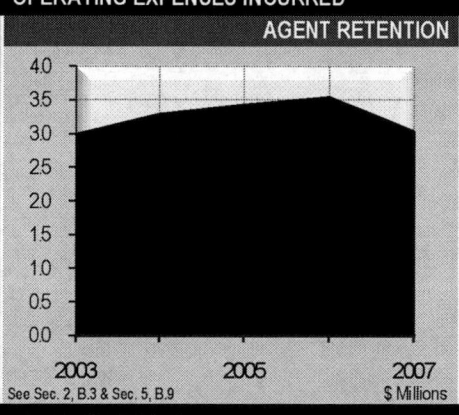

OPERATING EXPENSES INCURRED / AGENT RETENTION
See Sec. 2, B.3 & Sec. 5, B.9 — $ Millions

FINANCIAL POSITION	2007
Cash, Cash Equivalents & Short-Term Investments	$1,253,315
Total Assets	$115,333,923
Policyholders' Surplus	$46,185,038
Reserves	$68,415,226
OPERATING RESULTS	
Net Income	$6,211,326
Net Investment Gain	$5,051,693
Net Realized Capital Gains	$35,514
Net Cash from Operations	$9,628,623
Oper. Gain Before Taxes	$12,352,570

DIRECT PREMIUMS WRITTEN - YE 2007
See Sec. 3, B.4

- □ Direct
- ▨ Non-Affiliated
- ■ Affiliated

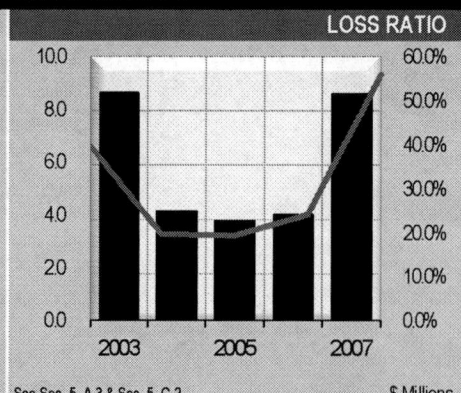

L&LAE INCURRED / LOSS RATIO
See Sec. 5, A.3 & Sec. 5, C.2 — $ Millions

UNDERWRITING RESULTS	
Direct	$0
Non-Affiliated	$0
Affiliated	$0
Direct Premiums Written	$0
Net Premiums Earned	$15,384,796
Operating Expenses Incurred	$3,032,226
Agent Retention	$0
L&LAE Incurred	$8,609,260
Loss Ratio	55.96%

6

Old Republic National Title Insurance Company

400 Second Ave. S
Minneapolis, MN 55401-2499

(612) 371-1111

WEBSITE:	STATE OF DOMICILE:
www.oldrepublictitle.com	Minnesota

PRESIDENT & CEO:	ESTABLISHED:	JURISDICTION LICENSE(S):
Rande Keith Yeager	8/20/1907	52

A" Unsurpassed
A Double Prime
Financial Stability Rating®
🔵 Demotech, Inc.

NAIC Number:
50520

OLD REPUBLIC NATIONAL

NAIC Group:
OLD REPUBLIC

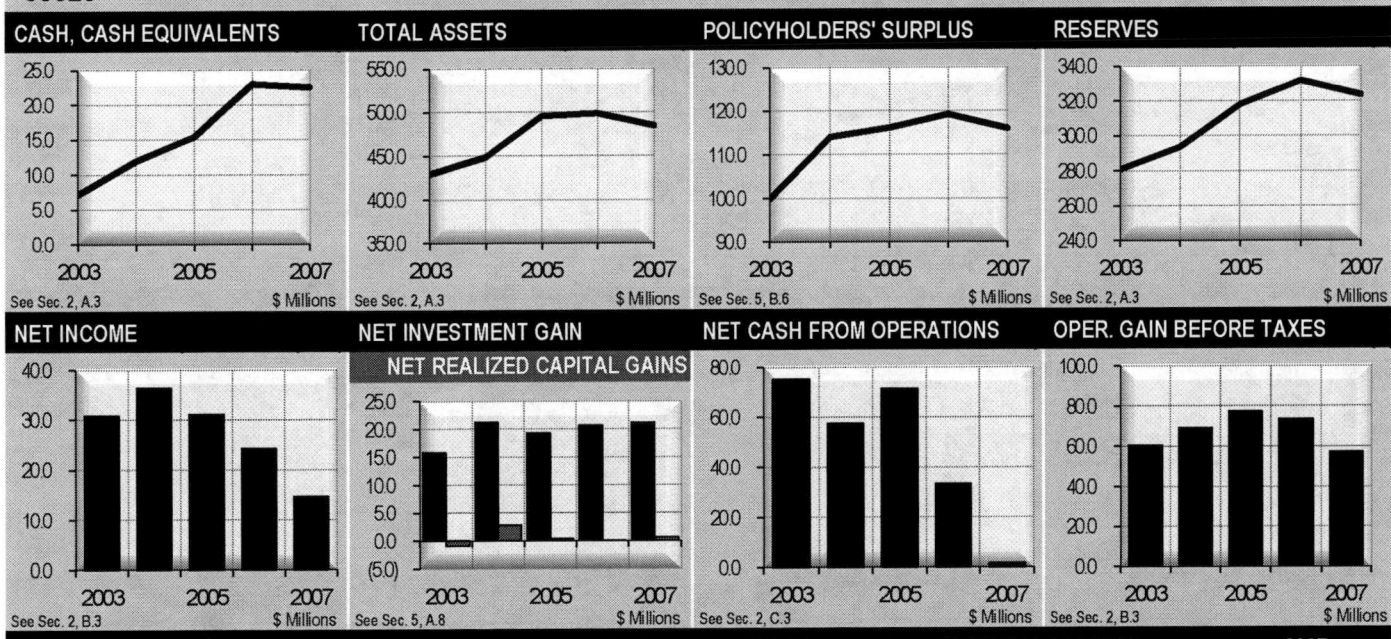

CASH, CASH EQUIVALENTS — See Sec. 2, A.3 — $ Millions
TOTAL ASSETS — See Sec. 2, A.3 — $ Millions
POLICYHOLDERS' SURPLUS — See Sec. 5, B.6 — $ Millions
RESERVES — See Sec. 2, A.3 — $ Millions

NET INCOME — See Sec. 2, B.3 — $ Millions
NET INVESTMENT GAIN / NET REALIZED CAPITAL GAINS — See Sec. 5, A.8 — $ Millions
NET CASH FROM OPERATIONS — See Sec. 2, C.3 — $ Millions
OPER. GAIN BEFORE TAXES — See Sec. 2, B.3 — $ Millions

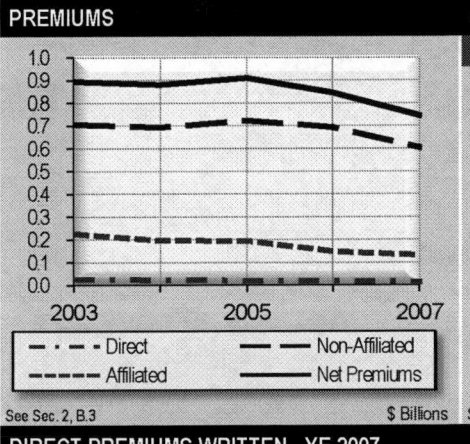

PREMIUMS — See Sec. 2, B.3 — $ Billions
- · - Direct
- - - - Affiliated
- —— Non-Affiliated
- —— Net Premiums

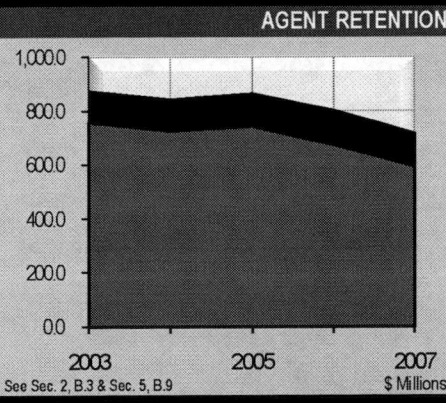

OPERATING EXPENSES INCURRED / AGENT RETENTION — See Sec. 2, B.3 & Sec. 5, B.9 — $ Millions

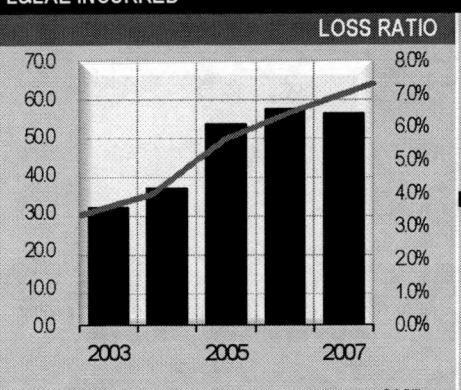

DIRECT PREMIUMS WRITTEN - YE 2007 — See Sec. 3, B.4
- ☐ Direct
- ■ Non-Affiliated
- ■ Affiliated

L&LAE INCURRED / LOSS RATIO — See Sec. 5, A.3 & Sec. 5, C.2 — $ Millions

FINANCIAL POSITION	2007
Cash, Cash Equivalents & Short-Term Investments	$22,509,326
Total Assets	$484,403,894
Policyholders' Surplus	$116,001,825
Reserves	$323,288,788
OPERATING RESULTS	
Net Income	$14,681,746
Net Investment Gain	$21,161,235
Net Realized Capital Gains	$641,585
Net Cash from Operations	$1,676,374
Oper. Gain Before Taxes	$57,221,938
UNDERWRITING RESULTS	
Direct	$14,047,794
Non-Affiliated	$604,520,309
Affiliated	$130,958,923
Direct Premiums Written	**$749,527,026**
Net Premiums Earned	$746,309,406
Operating Expenses Incurred	$713,256,104
Agent Retention	$594,328,500
L&LAE Incurred	$56,386,474
Loss Ratio	7.32%

6

Olympic Title Insurance Company

555 S Front St., Ste. 400
Columbus, OH 43215

(614) 583-2414
Currently not writing business

WEBSITE:	STATE OF DOMICILE:
–	Ohio

PRESIDENT:	ESTABLISHED:	JURISDICTION LICENSE(S):
William J. Mosimann, Jr.	11/29/1984	1

NR Not Rated
Financial Stability Rating®
Demotech, Inc.

NAIC Number:
50440

OLYMPIC

NAIC Group:
UNAFFILIATED

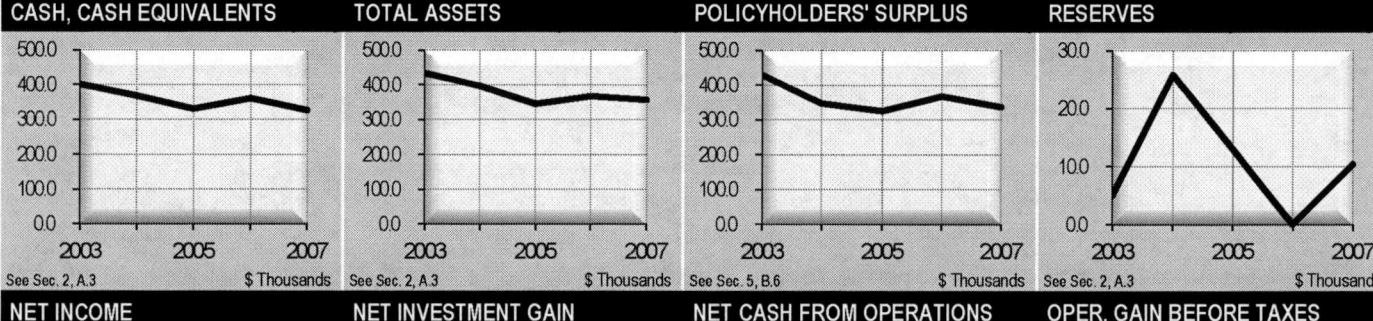

CASH, CASH EQUIVALENTS — See Sec. 2, A.3 — $ Thousands
TOTAL ASSETS — See Sec. 2, A.3 — $ Thousands
POLICYHOLDERS' SURPLUS — See Sec. 5, B.6 — $ Thousands
RESERVES — See Sec. 2, A.3 — $ Thousands

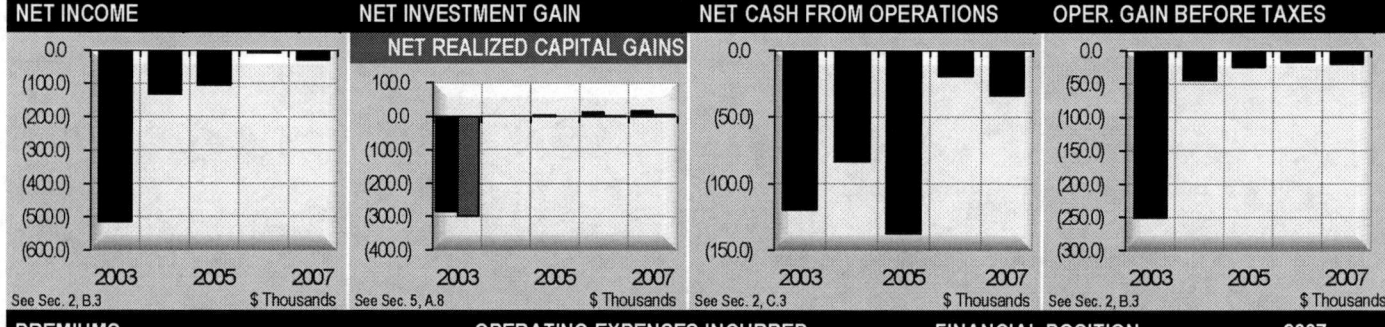

NET INCOME — See Sec. 2, B.3 — $ Thousands
NET INVESTMENT GAIN / NET REALIZED CAPITAL GAINS — See Sec. 5, A.8 — $ Thousands
NET CASH FROM OPERATIONS — See Sec. 2, C.3 — $ Thousands
OPER. GAIN BEFORE TAXES — See Sec. 2, B.3 — $ Thousands

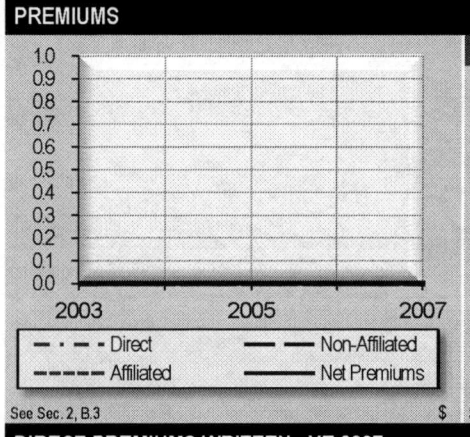

PREMIUMS
- - · - Direct
-------- Affiliated
——— Non-Affiliated
——— Net Premiums
See Sec. 2, B.3 — $

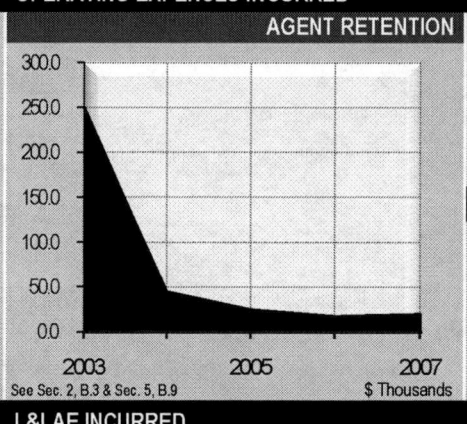

OPERATING EXPENSES INCURRED / AGENT RETENTION — See Sec. 2, B.3 & Sec. 5, B.9 — $ Thousands

FINANCIAL POSITION	2007
Cash, Cash Equivalents & Short-Term Investments	$326,224
Total Assets	$356,534
Policyholders' Surplus	$336,151
Reserves	$10,377
OPERATING RESULTS	
Net Income	($30,237)
Net Investment Gain	$16,065
Net Realized Capital Gains	$5,388
Net Cash from Operations	($33,786)
Oper. Gain Before Taxes	($19,632)

DIRECT PREMIUMS WRITTEN - YE 2007
☐ Direct ▨ Non-Affiliated ■ Affiliated
See Sec. 3, B.4

L&LAE INCURRED / LOSS RATIO — See Sec. 5, A.3 & Sec. 5, C.2 — $ Thousands

UNDERWRITING RESULTS	
Direct	$0
Non-Affiliated	$0
Affiliated	$0
Direct Premiums Written	$0
Net Premiums Earned	$0
Operating Expenses Incurred	$19,633
Agent Retention	$0
L&LAE Incurred	$26,670
Loss Ratio	--

Pacific Northwest Title Insurance Company, Inc.

215 Columbia St.
Seattle, WA 98104-1511

(206) 622-1040

WEBSITE: www.pnwt.com
PRESIDENT: Raymond Lloyd Davis

STATE OF DOMICILE: Washington
ESTABLISHED: 12/1/1926
JURISDICTION LICENSE(S): 11

A" Unsurpassed
Financial Stability Rating®
Demotech, Inc.

NAIC Number: 50970

PACIFIC NORTHWEST

NAIC Group: FIRST AMERICAN

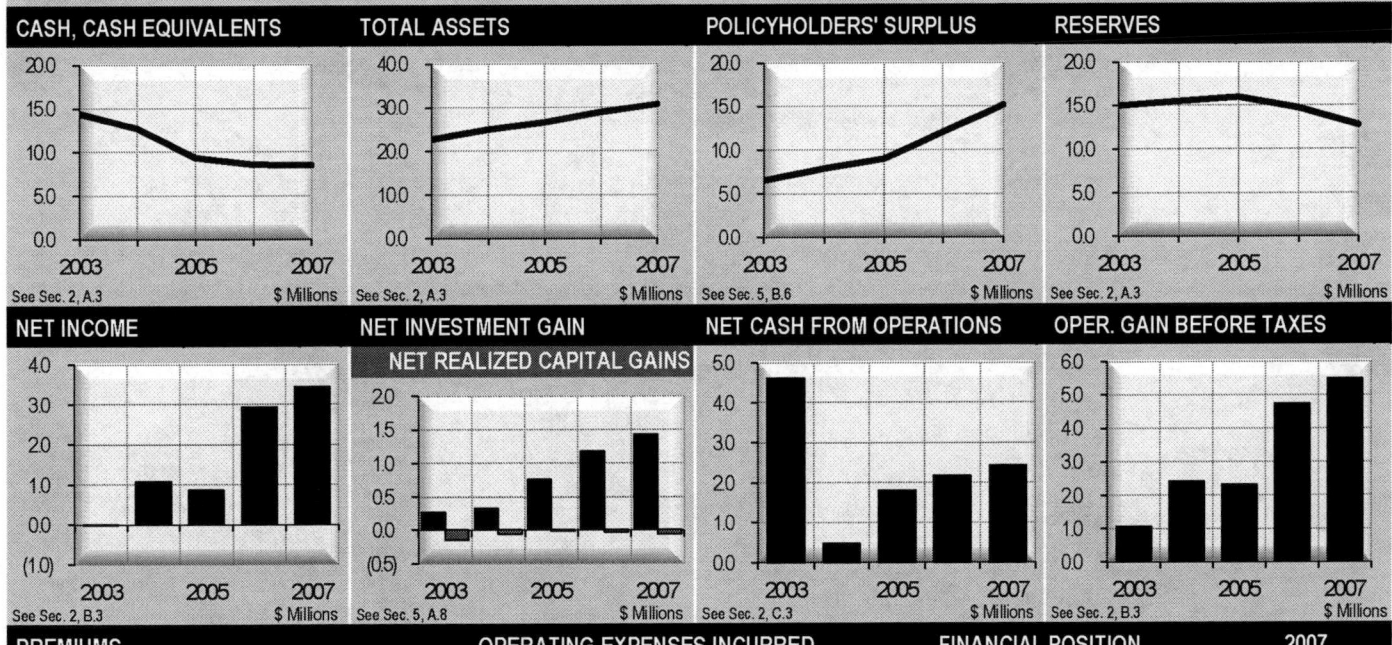

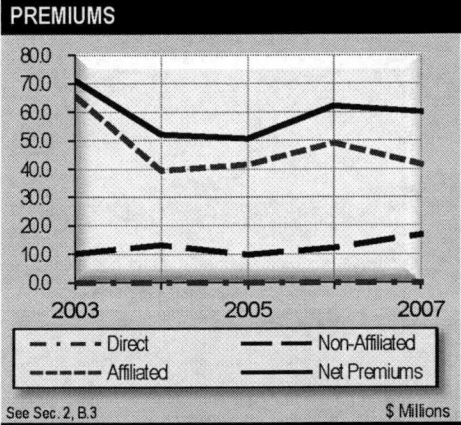

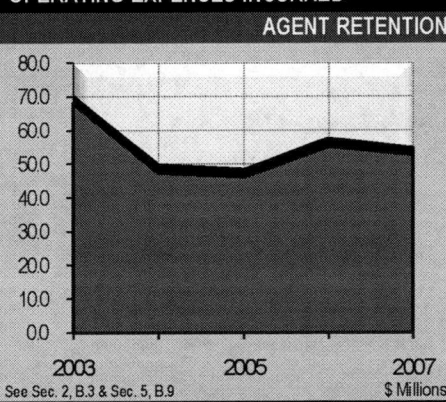

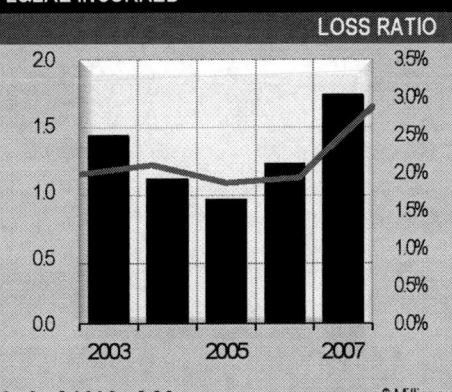

FINANCIAL POSITION 2007

Cash, Cash Equivalents & Short-Term Investments	$8,473,681
Total Assets	$30,705,791
Policyholders' Surplus	$15,156,843
Reserves	$12,754,953

OPERATING RESULTS

Net Income	$3,443,316
Net Investment Gain	$1,430,401
Net Realized Capital Gains	($59,411)
Net Cash from Operations	$2,431,799
Oper. Gain Before Taxes	$5,487,545

UNDERWRITING RESULTS

Direct	$0
Non-Affiliated	$16,794,834
Affiliated	$41,667,730
Direct Premiums Written	$58,462,564
Net Premiums Earned	$60,092,709
Operating Expenses Incurred	$54,680,163
Agent Retention	$52,730,302
L&LAE Incurred	$1,737,205
Loss Ratio	2.89%

6

Penn Attorneys Title Insurance Company

900 State St., Ste. 320
Erie, PA 16501

(814) 454-8278

WEBSITE:	STATE OF DOMICILE:
www.pennattorneys.com	Pennsylvania

PRESIDENT:	ESTABLISHED:	JURISDICTION LICENSE(S):
Josephine K. Subotnik-Lubiejewski	12/1/1980	1

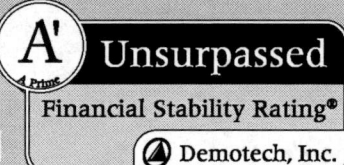

A' Unsurpassed
Financial Stability Rating®
Demotech, Inc.

NAIC Number:
51497

PENN ATTORNEYS

NAIC Group:
FIRST AMERICAN

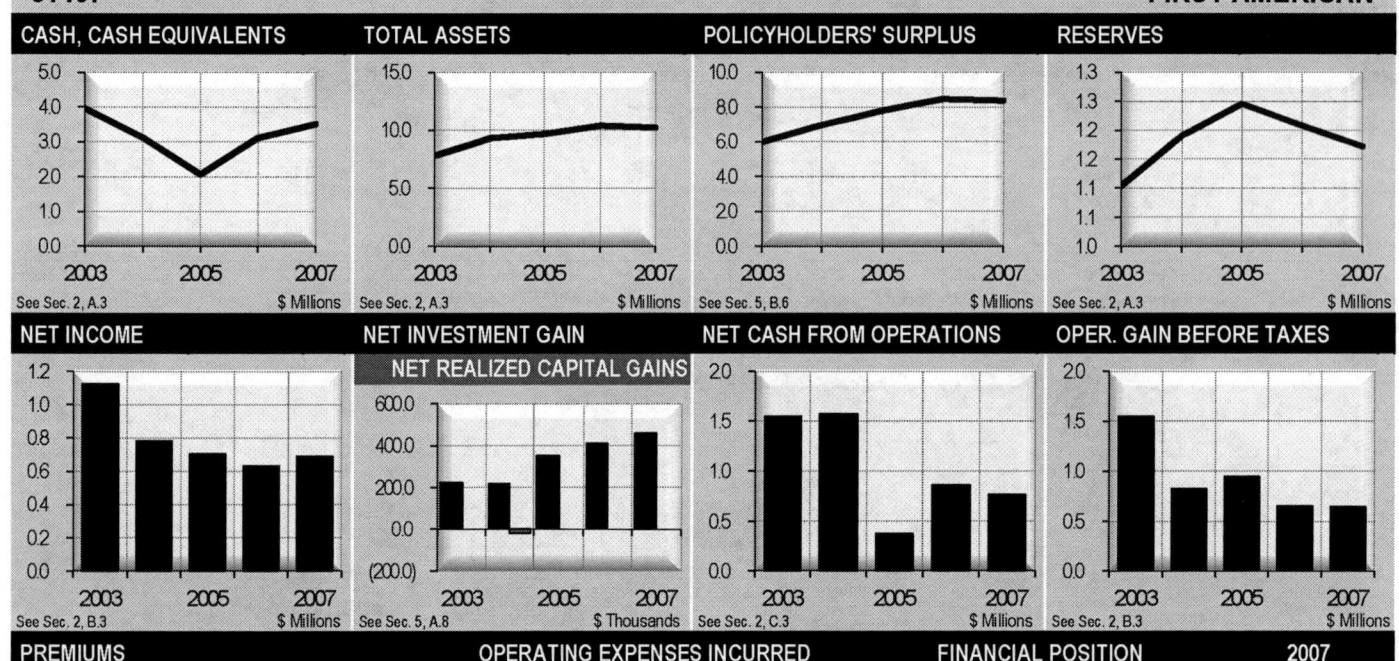

CASH, CASH EQUIVALENTS — See Sec. 2, A.3 — $ Millions

TOTAL ASSETS — See Sec. 2, A.3 — $ Millions

POLICYHOLDERS' SURPLUS — See Sec. 5, B.6 — $ Millions

RESERVES — See Sec. 2, A.3 — $ Millions

NET INCOME — See Sec. 2, B.3 — $ Millions

NET INVESTMENT GAIN / NET REALIZED CAPITAL GAINS — See Sec. 5, A.8 — $ Thousands

NET CASH FROM OPERATIONS — See Sec. 2, C.3 — $ Millions

OPER. GAIN BEFORE TAXES — See Sec. 2, B.3 — $ Millions

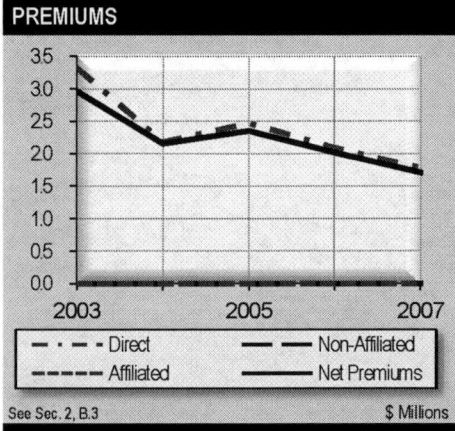

PREMIUMS — See Sec. 2, B.3 — $ Millions
- · - Direct
- - - - Affiliated
- - - Non-Affiliated
——— Net Premiums

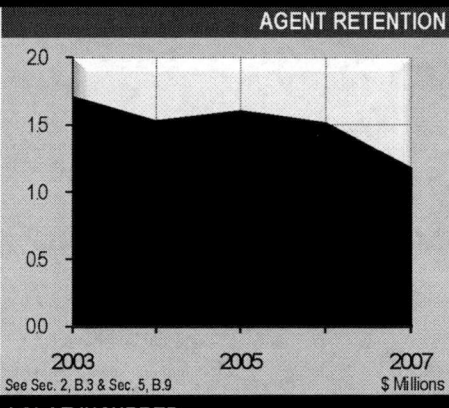

OPERATING EXPENSES INCURRED / AGENT RETENTION — See Sec. 2, B.3 & Sec. 5, B.9 — $ Millions

DIRECT PREMIUMS WRITTEN - YE 2007 — See Sec. 3, B.4
□ Direct ■ Non-Affiliated ■ Affiliated

L&LAE INCURRED / LOSS RATIO — See Sec. 5, A.3 & Sec. 5, C.2 — $ Thousands

FINANCIAL POSITION	2007
Cash, Cash Equivalents & Short-Term Investments	$3,497,188
Total Assets	$10,186,417
Policyholders' Surplus	$8,351,671
Reserves	$1,171,707
OPERATING RESULTS	
Net Income	$691,887
Net Investment Gain	$459,407
Net Realized Capital Gains	$0
Net Cash from Operations	$764,173
Oper. Gain Before Taxes	$649,964
UNDERWRITING RESULTS	
Direct	$1,777,598
Non-Affiliated	$0
Affiliated	$0
Direct Premiums Written	**$1,777,598**
Net Premiums Earned	**$1,710,517**
Operating Expenses Incurred	$1,173,159
Agent Retention	$0
L&LAE Incurred	$44,947
Loss Ratio	2.47%

Port Lawrence Title & Trust Company

616 Madison Ave.
Toledo, OH 43604

(419) 244-4605

WEBSITE:	STATE OF DOMICILE:
www.portlawrence.com	Ohio
PRESIDENT:	**ESTABLISHED:**
Margretta Renz Laskey	8/7/1937

JURISDICTION LICENSE(S): 3

A Exceptional
Financial Stability Rating®
Demotech, Inc.

NAIC Number:
50202

PORT LAWRENCE

NAIC Group:
FIRST AMERICAN

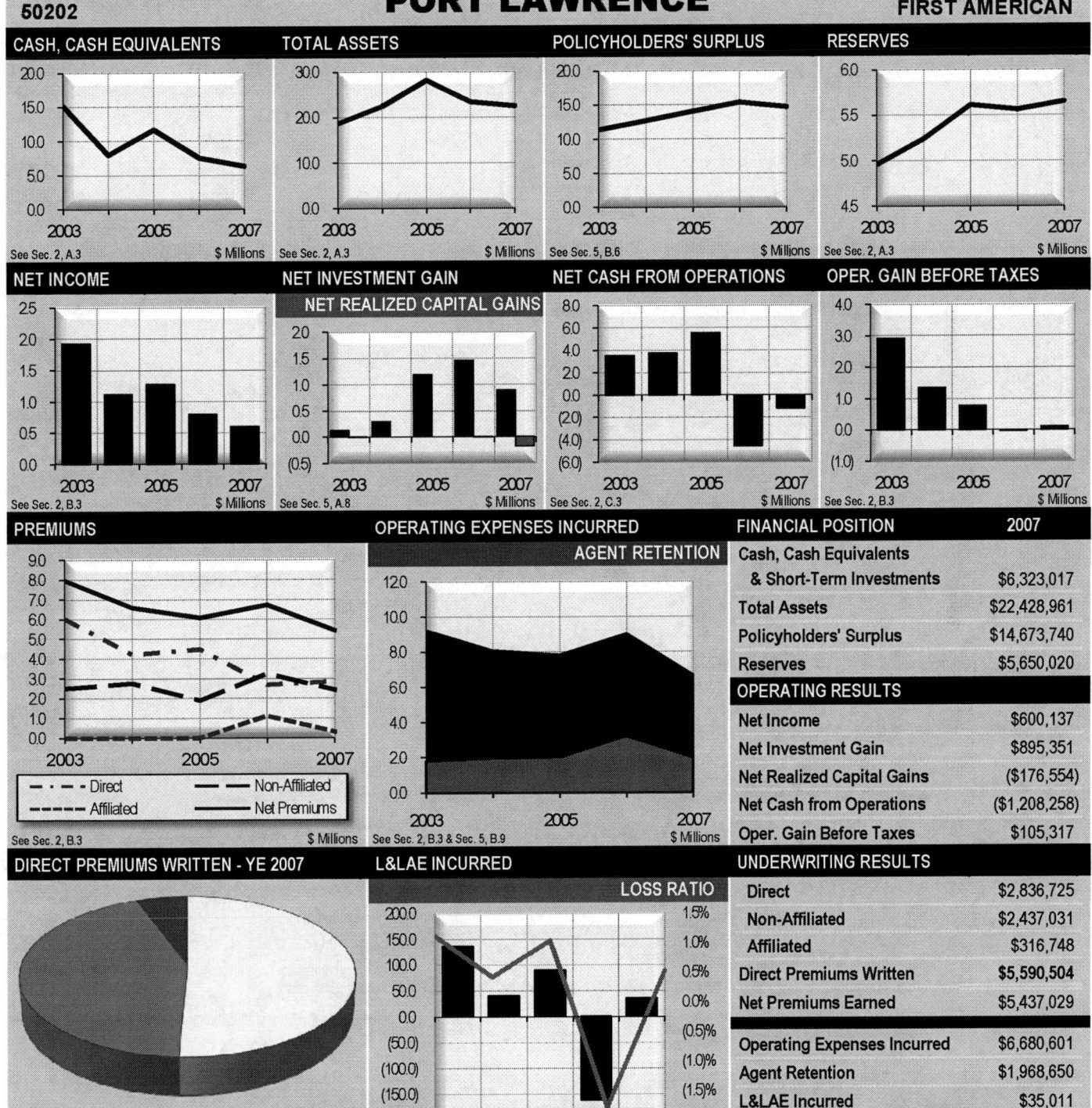

FINANCIAL POSITION	2007
Cash, Cash Equivalents & Short-Term Investments	$6,323,017
Total Assets	$22,428,961
Policyholders' Surplus	$14,673,740
Reserves	$5,650,020
OPERATING RESULTS	
Net Income	$600,137
Net Investment Gain	$895,351
Net Realized Capital Gains	($176,554)
Net Cash from Operations	($1,208,258)
Oper. Gain Before Taxes	$105,317
UNDERWRITING RESULTS	
Direct	$2,836,725
Non-Affiliated	$2,437,031
Affiliated	$316,748
Direct Premiums Written	$5,590,504
Net Premiums Earned	$5,437,029
Operating Expenses Incurred	$6,680,601
Agent Retention	$1,968,650
L&LAE Incurred	$35,011
Loss Ratio	0.52%

6

Public Title Insurance Company

16 W Main St.
Rochester, NY 14614

(585) 987-4950

| WEBSITE: | STATE OF DOMICILE: |
| www.firstam.com | New York |

| PRESIDENT: | ESTABLISHED: | JURISDICTION LICENSE(S): |
| James M. Orphanides | 4/15/2005 | |

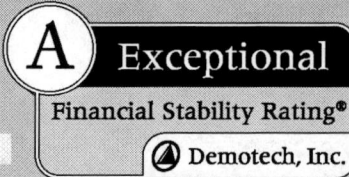

A Exceptional
Financial Stability Rating®
Demotech, Inc.

NAIC Number:
12518

PUBLIC

NAIC Group:
FIRST AMERICAN

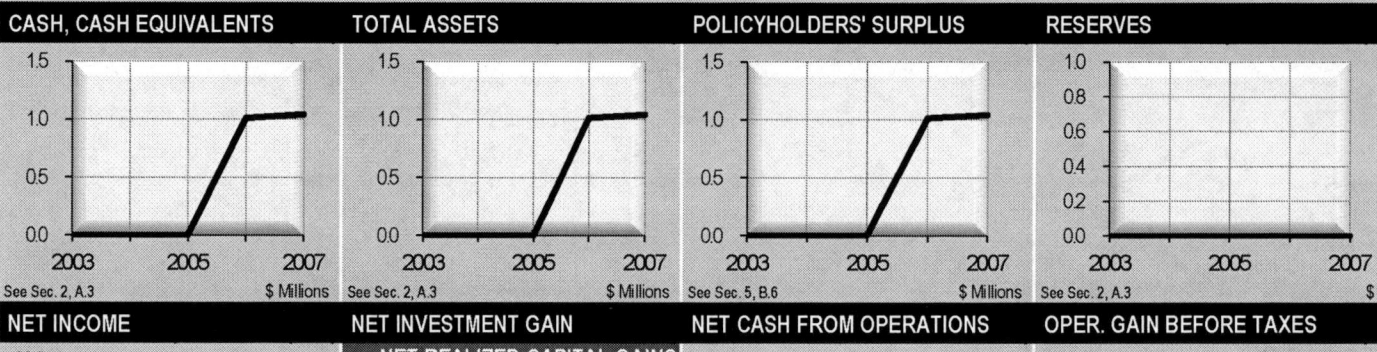

CASH, CASH EQUIVALENTS — See Sec. 2, A.3 — $ Millions
TOTAL ASSETS — See Sec. 2, A.3 — $ Millions
POLICYHOLDERS' SURPLUS — See Sec. 5, B.6 — $ Millions
RESERVES — See Sec. 2, A.3 — $

NET INCOME — See Sec. 2, B.3 — $ Thousands
NET INVESTMENT GAIN / NET REALIZED CAPITAL GAINS — See Sec. 5, A.8 — $ Thousands
NET CASH FROM OPERATIONS — See Sec. 2, C.3 — $ Thousands
OPER. GAIN BEFORE TAXES — See Sec. 2, B.3 — $ Thousands

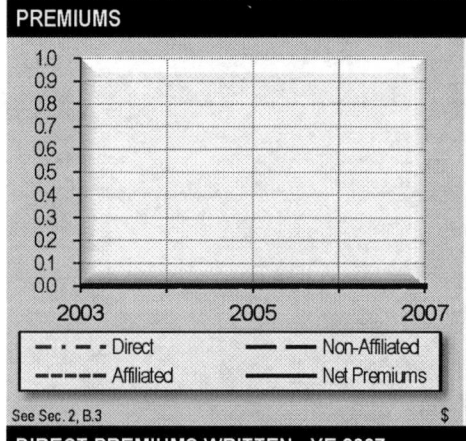

PREMIUMS
- · - Direct
-------- Affiliated
— Non-Affiliated
— Net Premiums
See Sec. 2, B.3 — $

OPERATING EXPENSES INCURRED / AGENT RETENTION
See Sec. 2, B.3 & Sec. 5, B.9 — $ Thousands

FINANCIAL POSITION	2007
Cash, Cash Equivalents & Short-Term Investments	$1,038,244
Total Assets	$1,038,244
Policyholders' Surplus	$1,038,244
Reserves	$0
OPERATING RESULTS	
Net Income	$27,843
Net Investment Gain	$35,090
Net Realized Capital Gains	$0
Net Cash from Operations	$30,343
Oper. Gain Before Taxes	($7,247)

DIRECT PREMIUMS WRITTEN - YE 2007
□ Direct ▨ Non-Affiliated ■ Affiliated
See Sec. 3, B.4

L&LAE INCURRED / LOSS RATIO
See Sec. 5, A.3 & Sec. 5, C.2 — $

UNDERWRITING RESULTS	
Direct	$0
Non-Affiliated	$0
Affiliated	$0
Direct Premiums Written	$0
Net Premiums Earned	$0
Operating Expenses Incurred	$7,247
Agent Retention	$0
L&LAE Incurred	$0
Loss Ratio	--

Seagate Title & Abstract Company, Inc.

626 Madison Ave.
Toledo, OH 43604

(419) 248-4611

WEBSITE:	STATE OF DOMICILE:
–	Ohio

PRESIDENT:	ESTABLISHED:	JURISDICTION LICENSE(S):
John W. Martin	6/29/1984	1

S Substantial
Financial Stability Rating®
Demotech, Inc.

NAIC Number: **50270**

SEAGATE

NAIC Group: **UNAFFILIATED**

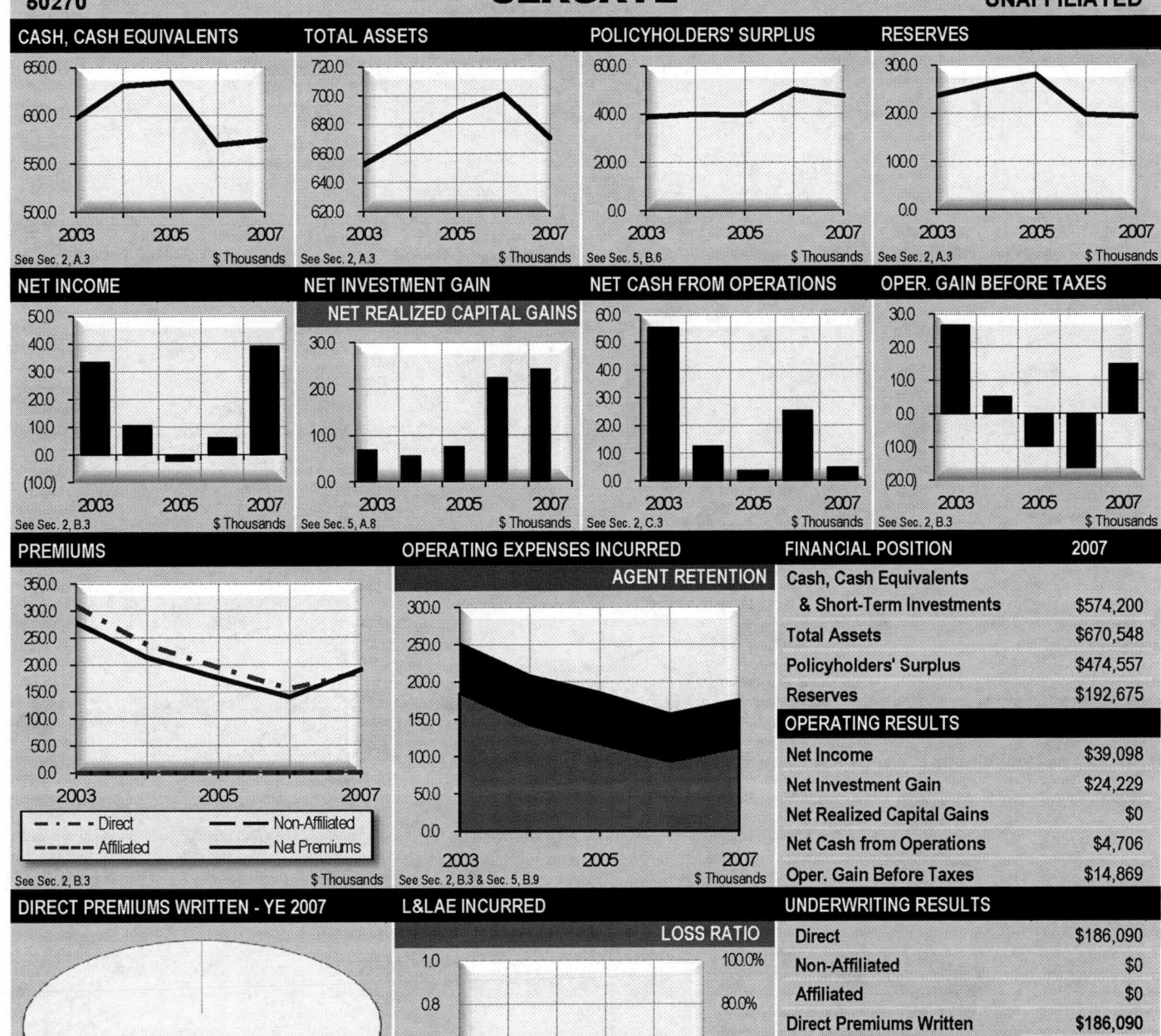

FINANCIAL POSITION	2007
Cash, Cash Equivalents & Short-Term Investments	$574,200
Total Assets	$670,548
Policyholders' Surplus	$474,557
Reserves	$192,675
OPERATING RESULTS	
Net Income	$39,098
Net Investment Gain	$24,229
Net Realized Capital Gains	$0
Net Cash from Operations	$4,706
Oper. Gain Before Taxes	$14,869
UNDERWRITING RESULTS	
Direct	$186,090
Non-Affiliated	$0
Affiliated	$0
Direct Premiums Written	$186,090
Net Premiums Earned	$190,389
Operating Expenses Incurred	$175,520
Agent Retention	$111,654
L&LAE Incurred	$0
Loss Ratio	0.00%

6

Security Title Guarantee Corporation of Baltimore (The)

6 S Calvert St.
Baltimore, MD 21202-1388

(410) 727-4456

WEBSITE:	STATE OF DOMICILE:
www.esecuritytitle.com	Maryland

PRESIDENT:	ESTABLISHED:	JURISDICTION LICENSE(S):
Theodore Clemens Rogers	12/15/1952	19

A' Unsurpassed
Financial Stability Rating®
Demotech, Inc.

NAIC Number:
50784

SECURITY TG (BALTIMORE)

NAIC Group:
UNAFFILIATED

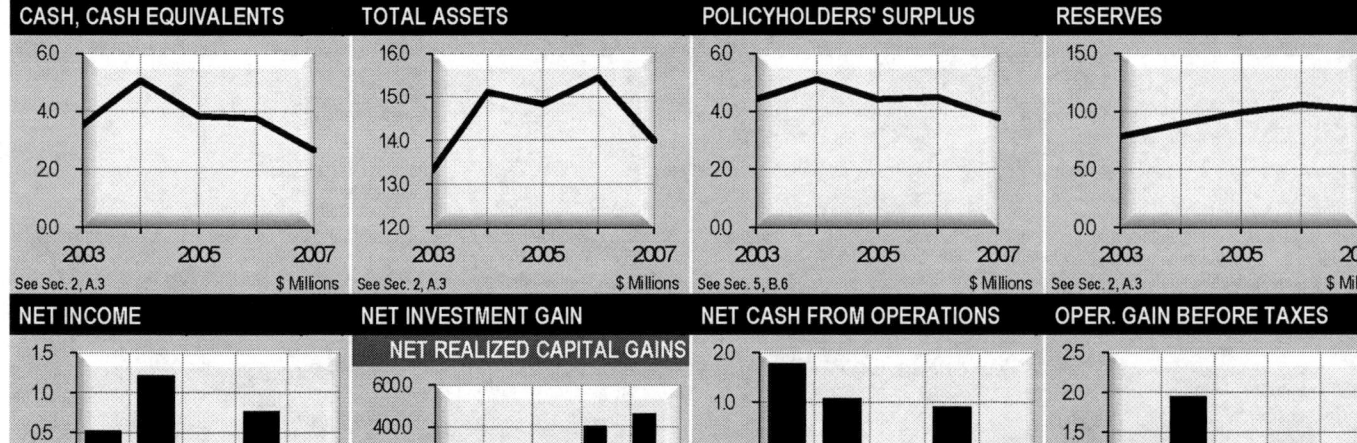

CASH, CASH EQUIVALENTS — See Sec. 2, A.3 — $ Millions
TOTAL ASSETS — See Sec. 2, A.3 — $ Millions
POLICYHOLDERS' SURPLUS — See Sec. 5, B.6 — $ Millions
RESERVES — See Sec. 2, A.3 — $ Millions

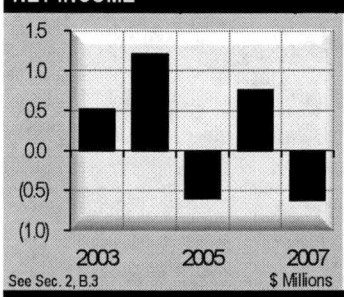

NET INCOME — See Sec. 2, B.3 — $ Millions

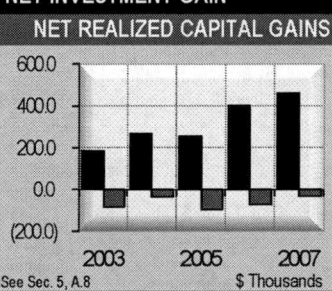

NET INVESTMENT GAIN / NET REALIZED CAPITAL GAINS — See Sec. 5, A.8 — $ Thousands

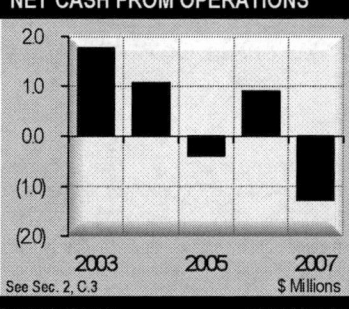

NET CASH FROM OPERATIONS — See Sec. 2, C.3 — $ Millions

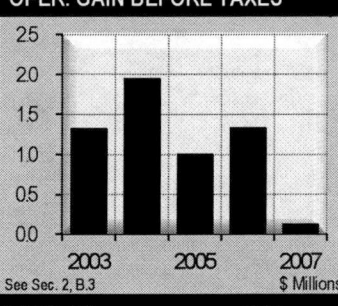

OPER. GAIN BEFORE TAXES — See Sec. 2, B.3 — $ Millions

PREMIUMS

- · - Direct
- - - - - Affiliated
- — - Non-Affiliated
- —— Net Premiums

See Sec. 2, B.3 — $ Millions

OPERATING EXPENSES INCURRED / AGENT RETENTION
See Sec. 2, B.3 & Sec. 5, B.9 — $ Millions

FINANCIAL POSITION	2007
Cash, Cash Equivalents & Short-Term Investments	$2,659,079
Total Assets	$13,992,506
Policyholders' Surplus	$3,764,091
Reserves	$10,107,172
OPERATING RESULTS	
Net Income	($628,282)
Net Investment Gain	$460,064
Net Realized Capital Gains	($33,925)
Net Cash from Operations	($1,275,899)
Oper. Gain Before Taxes	$118,588

DIRECT PREMIUMS WRITTEN - YE 2007

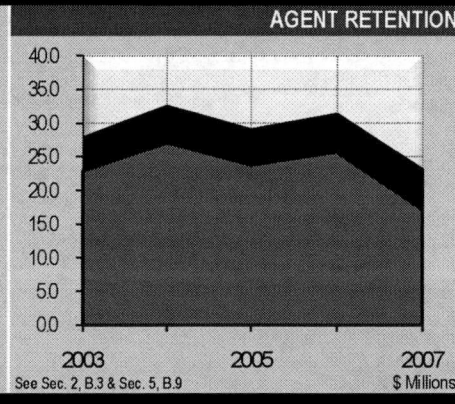

☐ Direct ▨ Non-Affiliated ▪ Affiliated

See Sec. 3, B.4

L&LAE INCURRED / LOSS RATIO
See Sec. 5, A.3 & Sec. 5, C.2 — $ Millions

UNDERWRITING RESULTS	
Direct	$413,934
Non-Affiliated	$20,943,251
Affiliated	$568,301
Direct Premiums Written	$21,925,486
Net Premiums Earned	$22,255,342
Operating Expenses Incurred	$23,029,482
Agent Retention	$17,165,336
L&LAE Incurred	$1,643,655
Loss Ratio	7.10%

Security Union Title Insurance Company

601 Riverside Ave.
Jacksonville, FL 32204

(904) 854-8100

WEBSITE:	STATE OF DOMICILE:
www.fnf.com	California

CHAIRMAN, PRESIDENT & CEO:	ESTABLISHED:	JURISDICTION LICENSE(S):
Raymond Randall Quirk	3/5/1962	42

A' A Prime — Unsurpassed
Financial Stability Rating®
Demotech, Inc.

NAIC Number:
50857

SECURITY UNION

NAIC Group:
CHICAGO / FIDELITY

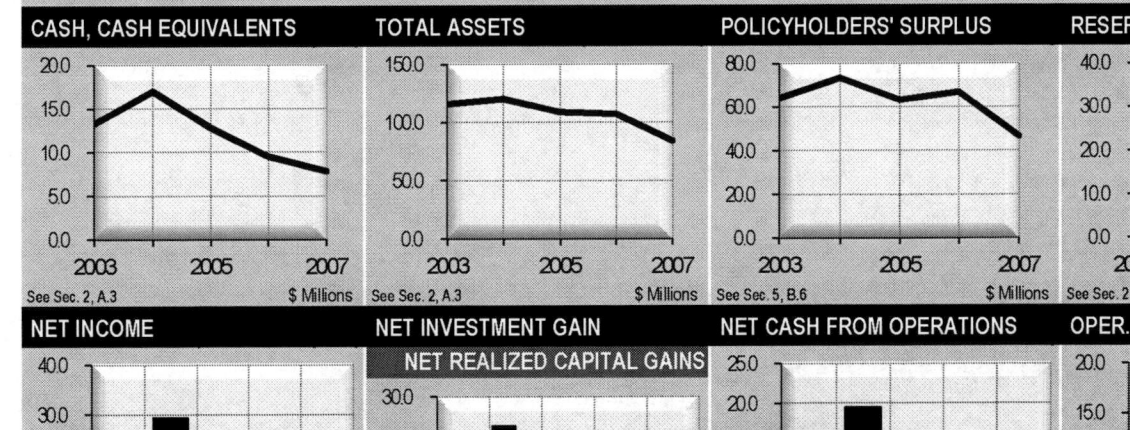

CASH, CASH EQUIVALENTS — See Sec. 2, A.3 — $ Millions
TOTAL ASSETS — See Sec. 2, A.3 — $ Millions
POLICYHOLDERS' SURPLUS — See Sec. 5, B.6 — $ Millions
RESERVES — See Sec. 2, A.3 — $ Millions

NET INCOME — See Sec. 2, B.3 — $ Millions
NET INVESTMENT GAIN / NET REALIZED CAPITAL GAINS — See Sec. 5, A.8 — $ Millions
NET CASH FROM OPERATIONS — See Sec. 2, C.3 — $ Millions
OPER. GAIN BEFORE TAXES — See Sec. 2, B.3 — $ Millions

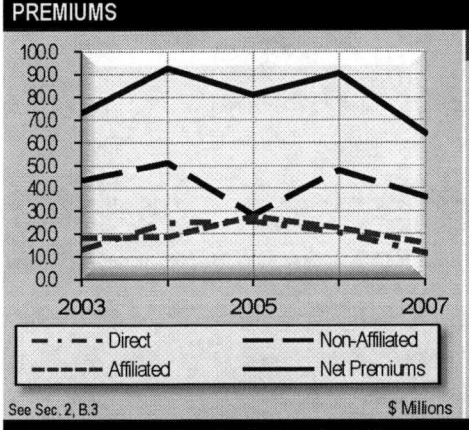

PREMIUMS
- · - Direct
- - - - Affiliated
—— Non-Affiliated
—— Net Premiums
See Sec. 2, B.3 — $ Millions

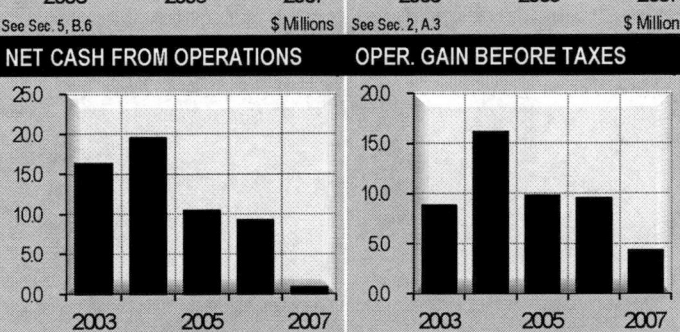

OPERATING EXPENSES INCURRED / AGENT RETENTION — See Sec. 2, B.3 & Sec. 5, B.9 — $ Millions

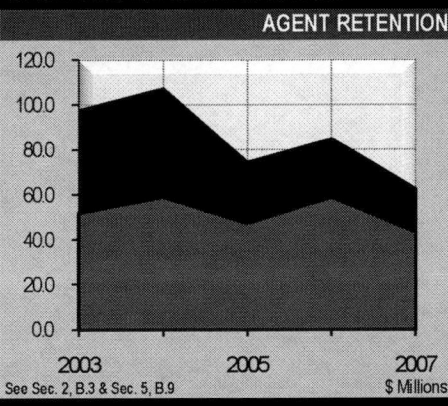

DIRECT PREMIUMS WRITTEN - YE 2007
☐ Direct ■ Non-Affiliated ■ Affiliated
See Sec. 3, B.4

L&LAE INCURRED / LOSS RATIO — See Sec. 5, A.3 & Sec. 5, C.2 — $ Millions

FINANCIAL POSITION	2007
Cash, Cash Equivalents & Short-Term Investments	$7,805,923
Total Assets	$83,985,606
Policyholders' Surplus	$46,565,183
Reserves	$32,390,155
OPERATING RESULTS	
Net Income	$3,611,420
Net Investment Gain	$8,237,091
Net Realized Capital Gains	$868,864
Net Cash from Operations	$895,463
Oper. Gain Before Taxes	$4,294,625
UNDERWRITING RESULTS	
Direct	$11,530,727
Non-Affiliated	$36,182,556
Affiliated	$15,844,405
Direct Premiums Written	$63,557,688
Net Premiums Earned	$64,329,252
Operating Expenses Incurred	$62,327,142
Agent Retention	$43,306,336
L&LAE Incurred	$10,051,219
Loss Ratio	15.09%

6

Sierra Title Insurance Guaranty Company

3409 N Tenth St.
McAllen, TX 78501

(956) 687-6294

WEBSITE:	STATE OF DOMICILE:
www.sierratitle.com	Texas

CHIEF EXECUTIVE OFFICER:	ESTABLISHED:	JURISDICTION LICENSE(S):
John R. King	6/2/2006	1

A Exceptional
Financial Stability Rating®
Demotech, Inc.

NAIC Number: **12591**

SIERRA

NAIC Group: **UNAFFILIATED**

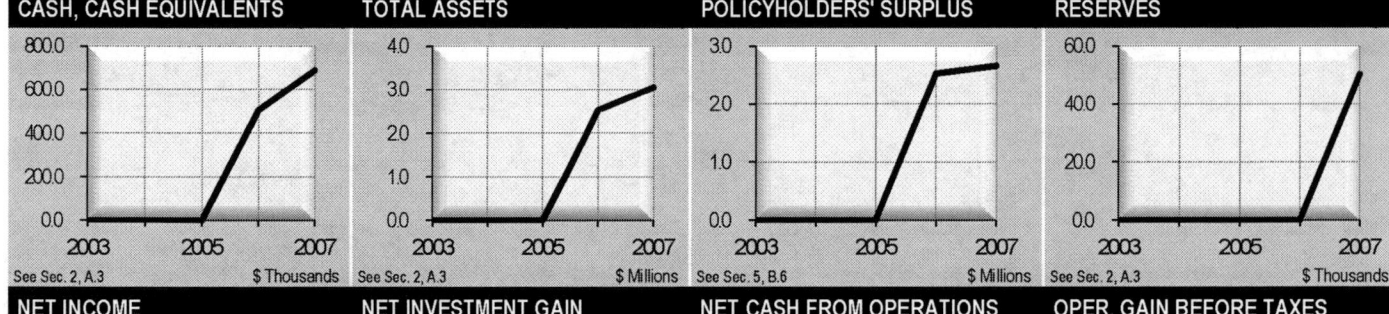

CASH, CASH EQUIVALENTS — See Sec. 2, A.3 — $ Thousands
TOTAL ASSETS — See Sec. 2, A.3 — $ Millions
POLICYHOLDERS' SURPLUS — See Sec. 5, B.6 — $ Millions
RESERVES — See Sec. 2, A.3 — $ Thousands

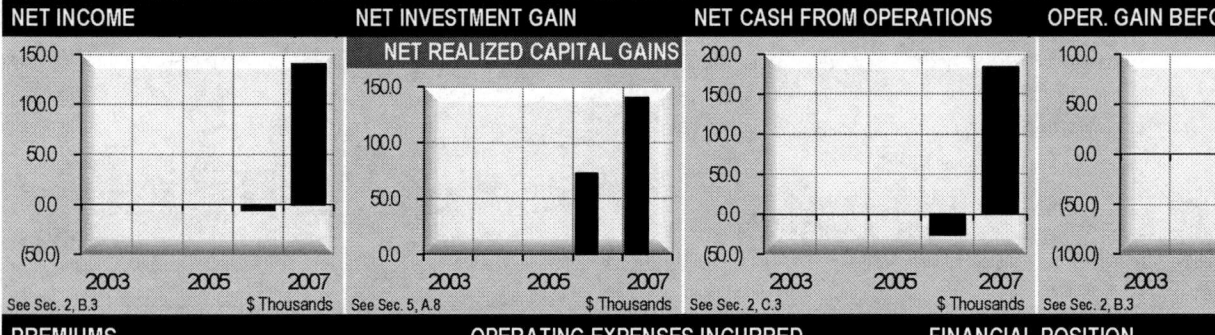

NET INCOME — See Sec. 2, B.3 — $ Thousands
NET INVESTMENT GAIN / NET REALIZED CAPITAL GAINS — See Sec. 5, A.8 — $ Thousands
NET CASH FROM OPERATIONS — See Sec. 2, C.3 — $ Thousands
OPER. GAIN BEFORE TAXES — See Sec. 2, B.3 — $ Thousands

FINANCIAL POSITION	2007
Cash, Cash Equivalents & Short-Term Investments	**$688,196**
Total Assets	$3,048,943
Policyholders' Surplus	$2,657,562
Reserves	$50,118
OPERATING RESULTS	
Net Income	$140,486
Net Investment Gain	$140,652
Net Realized Capital Gains	$0
Net Cash from Operations	$184,080
Oper. Gain Before Taxes	$60,798

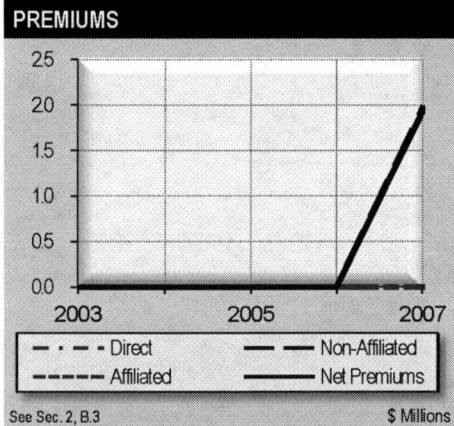

PREMIUMS — See Sec. 2, B.3 — $ Millions

- · - Direct
—— Non-Affiliated
---- Affiliated
—— Net Premiums

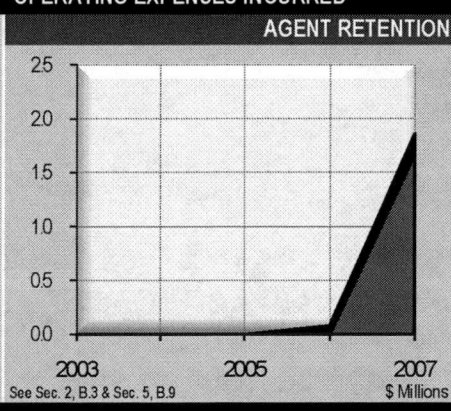

OPERATING EXPENSES INCURRED / AGENT RETENTION — See Sec. 2, B.3 & Sec. 5, B.9 — $ Millions

UNDERWRITING RESULTS	
Direct	$0
Non-Affiliated	$1,966,565
Affiliated	$0
Direct Premiums Written	**$1,966,565**
Net Premiums Earned	$1,923,075
Operating Expenses Incurred	$1,862,277
Agent Retention	$1,671,695
L&LAE Incurred	$0
Loss Ratio	0.00%

DIRECT PREMIUMS WRITTEN - YE 2007

☐ Direct   ▨ Non-Affiliated   ■ Affiliated

See Sec. 3, B.4

L&LAE INCURRED / LOSS RATIO — See Sec. 5, A.3 & Sec. 5, C.2 — $

6

Southern Title Insurance Corporation

1051 E Cary St., Ste. 700
Three James Ctr.
Richmond, VA 23219

(804) 648-6000

WEBSITE:	STATE OF DOMICILE:
www.southerntitle.com	Virginia

PRESIDENT:	ESTABLISHED:	JURISDICTION LICENSE(S):
Dennis Michael Reeves	9/25/1925	21

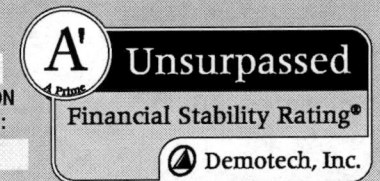

A' **Unsurpassed**
Financial Stability Rating®
Demotech, Inc.

NAIC Number:
50792

SOUTHERN TI CORP

NAIC Group:
OHIO FARMERS

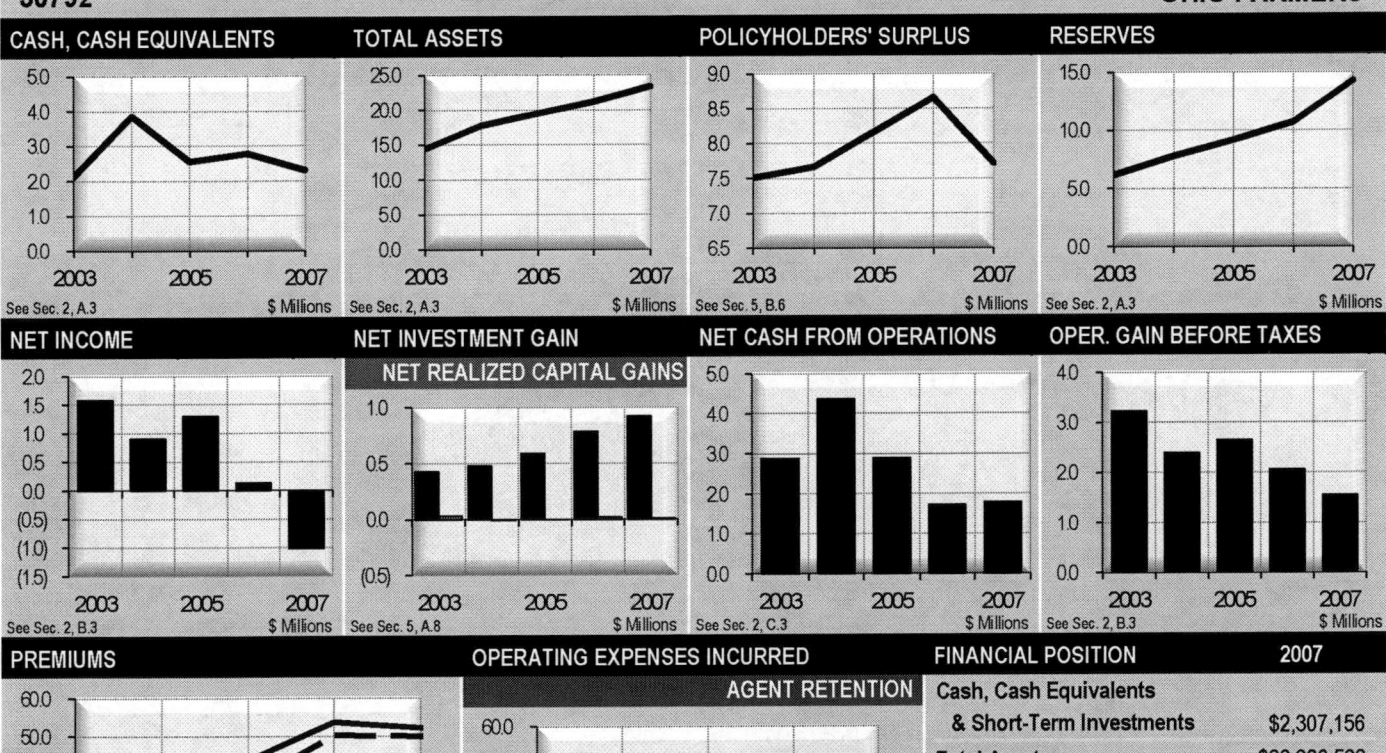

CASH, CASH EQUIVALENTS — See Sec. 2, A.3 — $ Millions

TOTAL ASSETS — See Sec. 2, A.3 — $ Millions

POLICYHOLDERS' SURPLUS — See Sec. 5, B.6 — $ Millions

RESERVES — See Sec. 2, A.3 — $ Millions

NET INCOME — See Sec. 2, B.3 — $ Millions

NET INVESTMENT GAIN / NET REALIZED CAPITAL GAINS — See Sec. 5, A.8 — $ Millions

NET CASH FROM OPERATIONS — See Sec. 2, C.3 — $ Millions

OPER. GAIN BEFORE TAXES — See Sec. 2, B.3 — $ Millions

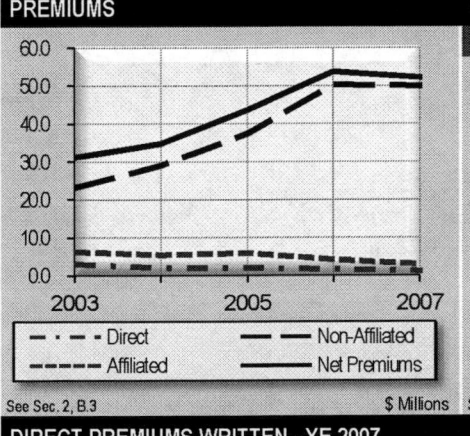

PREMIUMS

- · - Direct
- - - Affiliated
— Non-Affiliated
— Net Premiums

See Sec. 2, B.3 — $ Millions

OPERATING EXPENSES INCURRED / AGENT RETENTION — See Sec. 2, B.3 & Sec. 5, B.9 — $ Millions

FINANCIAL POSITION	2007
Cash, Cash Equivalents & Short-Term Investments	$2,307,156
Total Assets	$23,386,522
Policyholders' Surplus	$7,715,606
Reserves	$14,276,208
OPERATING RESULTS	
Net Income	($1,021,001)
Net Investment Gain	$922,249
Net Realized Capital Gains	$8,609
Net Cash from Operations	$1,788,724
Oper. Gain Before Taxes	$1,544,805

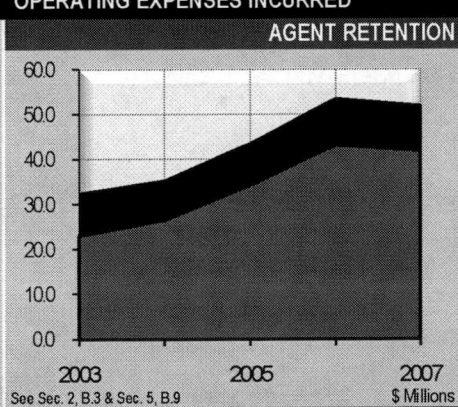

DIRECT PREMIUMS WRITTEN - YE 2007

☐ Direct ■ Non-Affiliated ■ Affiliated

See Sec. 3, B.4

L&LAE INCURRED / LOSS RATIO — See Sec. 5, A.3 & Sec. 5, C.2 — $ Millions

UNDERWRITING RESULTS	
Direct	$1,173,787
Non-Affiliated	$49,984,569
Affiliated	$3,022,358
Direct Premiums Written	**$54,180,714**
Net Premiums Earned	$52,180,887
Operating Expenses Incurred	$51,859,442
Agent Retention	$41,851,861
L&LAE Incurred	$3,737,323
Loss Ratio	7.00%

6

Stewart Title Guaranty Company

1980 Post Oak Blvd.
PO Box 2029
Houston, TX 77056

(713) 625-8100

WEBSITE:	STATE OF DOMICILE:
www.stewart.com	Texas

PRESIDENT:	ESTABLISHED:	JURISDICTION LICENSE(S):
Michael B. Skalka	2/20/1908	54

A" Unsurpassed
Financial Stability Rating®
Demotech, Inc.

NAIC Number: **50121**

STEWART TGC

NAIC Group: **STEWART**

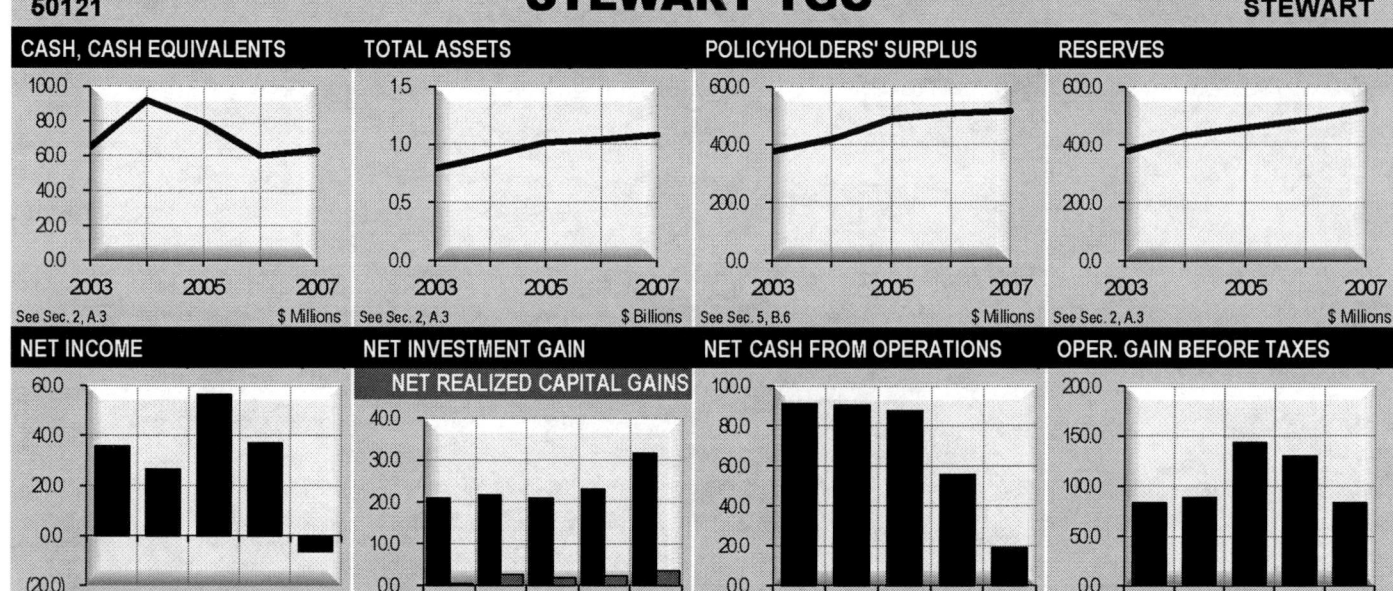

CASH, CASH EQUIVALENTS — See Sec. 2, A.3 — $ Millions

TOTAL ASSETS — See Sec. 2, A.3 — $ Billions

POLICYHOLDERS' SURPLUS — See Sec. 5, B.6 — $ Millions

RESERVES — See Sec. 2, A.3 — $ Millions

NET INCOME — See Sec. 2, B.3 — $ Millions

NET INVESTMENT GAIN / NET REALIZED CAPITAL GAINS — See Sec. 5, A.8 — $ Millions

NET CASH FROM OPERATIONS — See Sec. 2, C.3 — $ Millions

OPER. GAIN BEFORE TAXES — See Sec. 2, B.3 — $ Millions

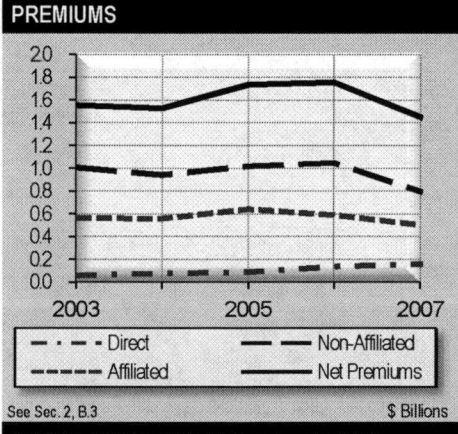

PREMIUMS — See Sec. 2, B.3 — $ Billions
- – · – Direct
- – – Non-Affiliated
- – – – Affiliated
- —— Net Premiums

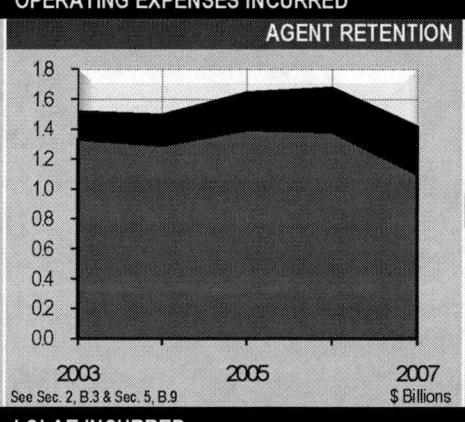

OPERATING EXPENSES INCURRED / AGENT RETENTION — See Sec. 2, B.3 & Sec. 5, B.9 — $ Billions

FINANCIAL POSITION	2007
Cash, Cash Equivalents & Short-Term Investments	$62,968,304
Total Assets	$1,082,024,546
Policyholders' Surplus	$515,901,015
Reserves	$519,864,058
OPERATING RESULTS	
Net Income	($6,458,657)
Net Investment Gain	$31,583,539
Net Realized Capital Gains	$3,445,843
Net Cash from Operations	$19,052,490
Oper. Gain Before Taxes	$83,215,808

DIRECT PREMIUMS WRITTEN - YE 2007 — See Sec. 3, B.4

☐ Direct   ▨ Non-Affiliated   ■ Affiliated

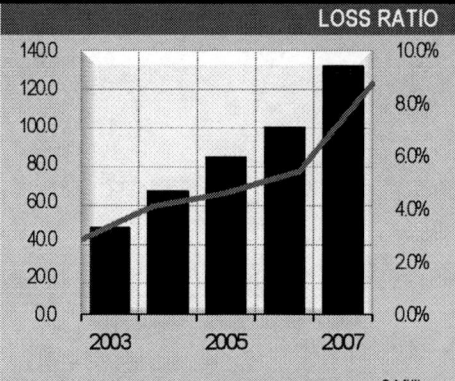

L&LAE INCURRED / LOSS RATIO — See Sec. 5, A.3 & Sec. 5, C.2 — $ Millions

UNDERWRITING RESULTS	
Direct	$157,750,939
Non-Affiliated	$796,976,776
Affiliated	$500,732,921
Direct Premiums Written	$1,455,460,636
Net Premiums Earned	$1,453,129,953
Operating Expenses Incurred	$1,416,388,898
Agent Retention	$1,099,768,492
L&LAE Incurred	$131,848,241
Loss Ratio	8.79%

6

Stewart Title Insurance Company

300 E 42nd St., 10th Fl.
New York, NY 10017

(212) 922-0050

WEBSITE: www.stewart.com	**STATE OF DOMICILE:** New York
PRESIDENT: John F. Welling	**ESTABLISHED:** 10/26/1987
	JURISDICTION LICENSE(S): 2

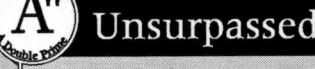

A" Unsurpassed
Financial Stability Rating®
Demotech, Inc.

NAIC Number: **51420**

STEWART TIC

NAIC Group: **STEWART**

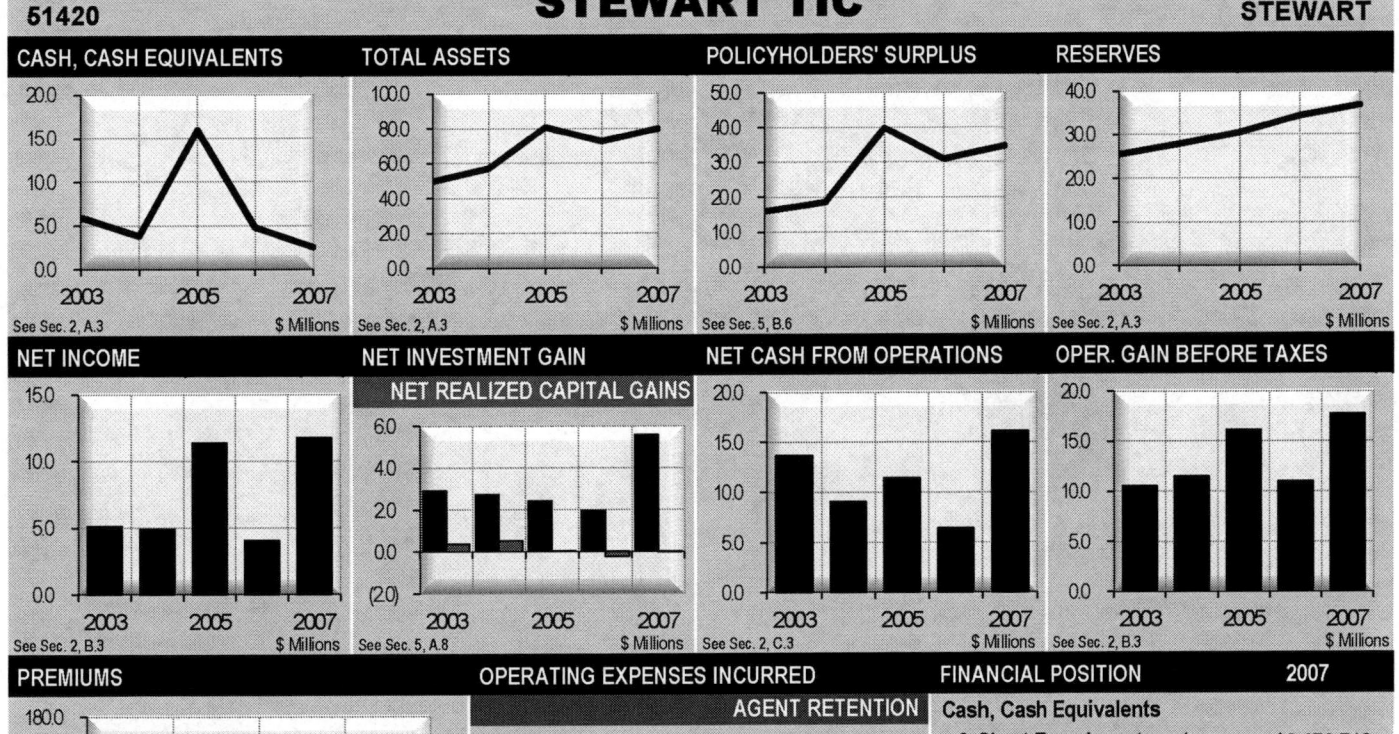

CASH, CASH EQUIVALENTS — See Sec. 2, A.3 — $ Millions

TOTAL ASSETS — See Sec. 2, A.3 — $ Millions

POLICYHOLDERS' SURPLUS — See Sec. 5, B.6 — $ Millions

RESERVES — See Sec. 2, A.3 — $ Millions

NET INCOME — See Sec. 2, B.3 — $ Millions

NET INVESTMENT GAIN / NET REALIZED CAPITAL GAINS — See Sec. 5, A.8 — $ Millions

NET CASH FROM OPERATIONS — See Sec. 2, C.3 — $ Millions

OPER. GAIN BEFORE TAXES — See Sec. 2, B.3 — $ Millions

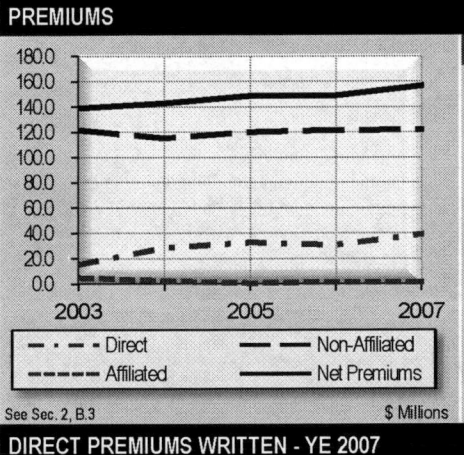

PREMIUMS
- · – · – Direct
- – – – Non-Affiliated
- – – – – Affiliated
- ——— Net Premiums

See Sec. 2, B.3 — $ Millions

DIRECT PREMIUMS WRITTEN - YE 2007
☐ Direct ■ Non-Affiliated ■ Affiliated
See Sec. 3, B.4

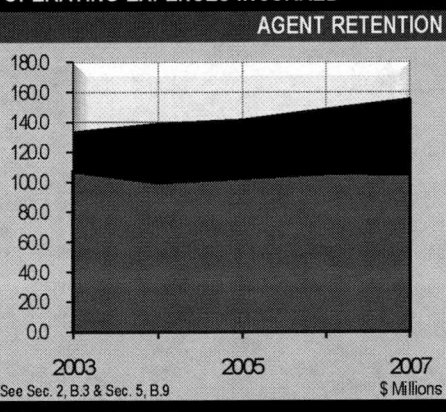

OPERATING EXPENSES INCURRED / AGENT RETENTION — See Sec. 2, B.3 & Sec. 5, B.9 — $ Millions

L&LAE INCURRED / LOSS RATIO — See Sec. 5, A.3 & Sec. 5, C.2 — $ Millions

FINANCIAL POSITION	2007
Cash, Cash Equivalents & Short-Term Investments	$2,478,713
Total Assets	$79,740,865
Policyholders' Surplus	$34,515,499
Reserves	$36,838,465
OPERATING RESULTS	
Net Income	$11,724,163
Net Investment Gain	$5,582,811
Net Realized Capital Gains	$8,233
Net Cash from Operations	$16,083,286
Oper. Gain Before Taxes	$17,745,873
UNDERWRITING RESULTS	
Direct	$38,951,627
Non-Affiliated	$121,926,620
Affiliated	$1,373,640
Direct Premiums Written	$162,251,887
Net Premiums Earned	$156,456,715
Operating Expenses Incurred	$154,836,415
Agent Retention	$105,287,815
L&LAE Incurred	$5,470,985
Loss Ratio	3.17%

6

Stewart Title Insurance Company of Oregon

1980 Post Oak Blvd.
PO Box 2029
Houston, TX 77056
(713) 625-8100

WEBSITE:	STATE OF DOMICILE:
www.stewart.com	Oregon

			JURISDICTION
PRESIDENT:	ESTABLISHED:	LICENSE(S):	
Craig M. Chisholm	4/3/1997	1	

NR Not Rated
Financial Stability Rating®
Demotech, Inc.

NAIC Number:
50036

STEWART (OR)

NAIC Group:
STEWART

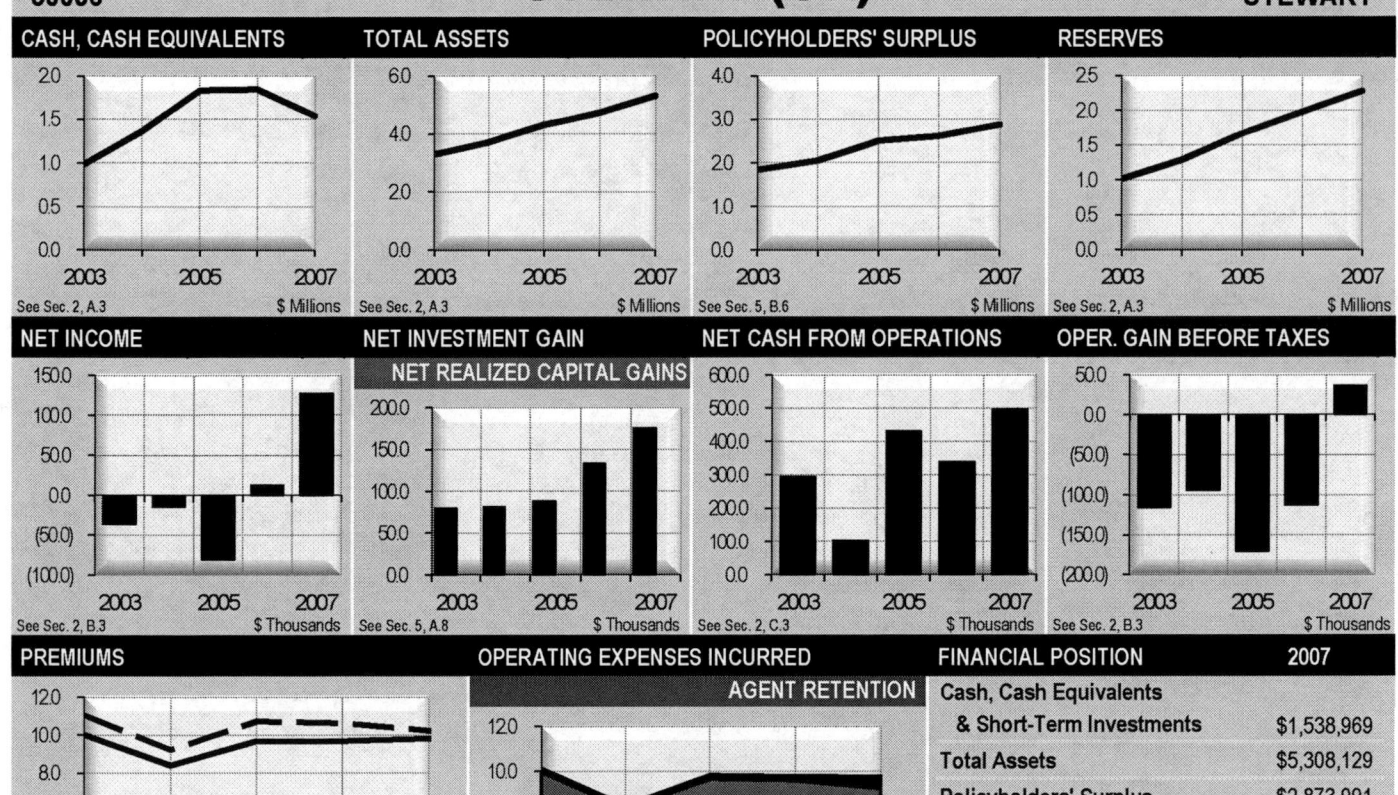

CASH, CASH EQUIVALENTS — See Sec. 2, A.3 — $ Millions
TOTAL ASSETS — See Sec. 2, A.3 — $ Millions
POLICYHOLDERS' SURPLUS — See Sec. 5, B.6 — $ Millions
RESERVES — See Sec. 2, A.3 — $ Millions

NET INCOME — See Sec. 2, B.3 — $ Thousands
NET INVESTMENT GAIN / NET REALIZED CAPITAL GAINS — See Sec. 5, A.8 — $ Thousands
NET CASH FROM OPERATIONS — See Sec. 2, C.3 — $ Thousands
OPER. GAIN BEFORE TAXES — See Sec. 2, B.3 — $ Thousands

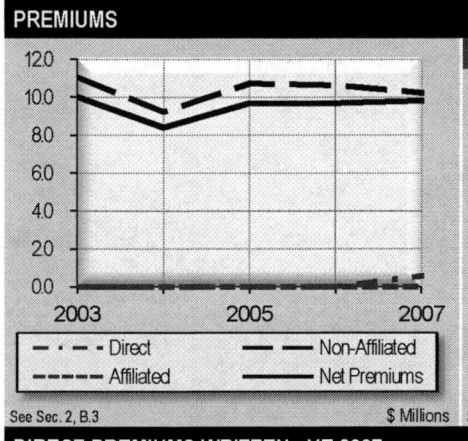

PREMIUMS — See Sec. 2, B.3 — $ Millions
Direct, Affiliated, Non-Affiliated, Net Premiums

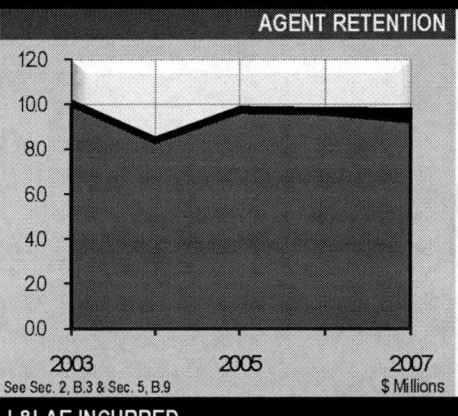

OPERATING EXPENSES INCURRED / AGENT RETENTION — See Sec. 2, B.3 & Sec. 5, B.9 — $ Millions

FINANCIAL POSITION	2007
Cash, Cash Equivalents & Short-Term Investments	$1,538,969
Total Assets	$5,308,129
Policyholders' Surplus	$2,873,991
Reserves	$2,274,776
OPERATING RESULTS	
Net Income	$127,290
Net Investment Gain	$175,981
Net Realized Capital Gains	$0
Net Cash from Operations	$496,235
Oper. Gain Before Taxes	$36,707

DIRECT PREMIUMS WRITTEN - YE 2007 — See Sec. 3, B.4
Direct, Non-Affiliated, Affiliated

L&LAE INCURRED / LOSS RATIO — See Sec. 5, A.3 & Sec. 5, C.2 — $

UNDERWRITING RESULTS	
Direct	$567,888
Non-Affiliated	$10,237,613
Affiliated	$0
Direct Premiums Written	$10,805,501
Net Premiums Earned	$9,836,516
Operating Expenses Incurred	$9,799,809
Agent Retention	$9,221,086
L&LAE Incurred	$0
Loss Ratio	0.00%

T.A. Title Insurance Company

620 Freedom Business Center Dr.
King of Prussia, PA 19406

(610) 892-8100

WEBSITE:	STATE OF DOMICILE:
www.tatitle.com	Pennsylvania

CHIEF EXECUTIVE OFFICER:	ESTABLISHED:	JURISDICTION LICENSE(S):
Patti Jean DeGennaro	5/9/1979	6

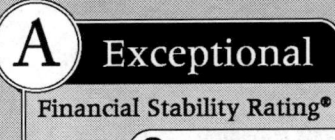

A Exceptional
Financial Stability Rating®
Demotech, Inc.

NAIC Number:
51403

T.A. TITLE

NAIC Group:
FIRST AMERICAN

CASH, CASH EQUIVALENTS
See Sec. 2, A.3 — $ Millions

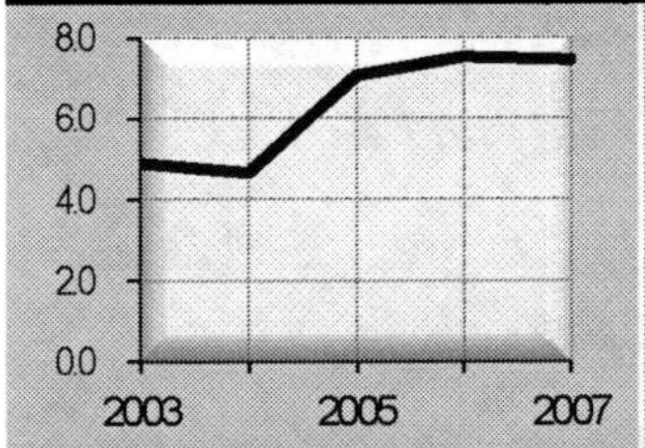

TOTAL ASSETS
See Sec. 2, A.3 — $ Millions

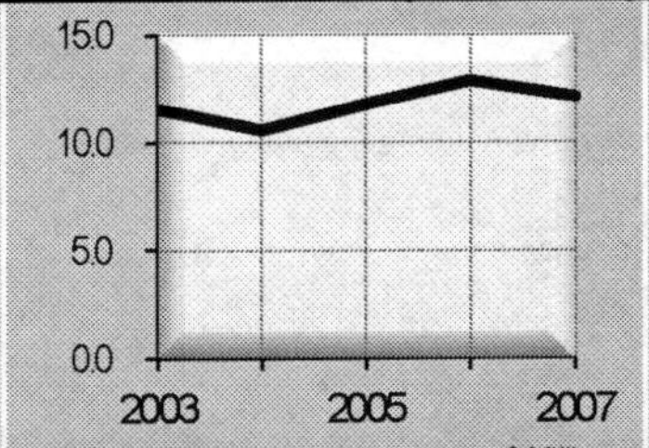

POLICYHOLDERS' SURPLUS
See Sec. 5, B.6 — $ Millions

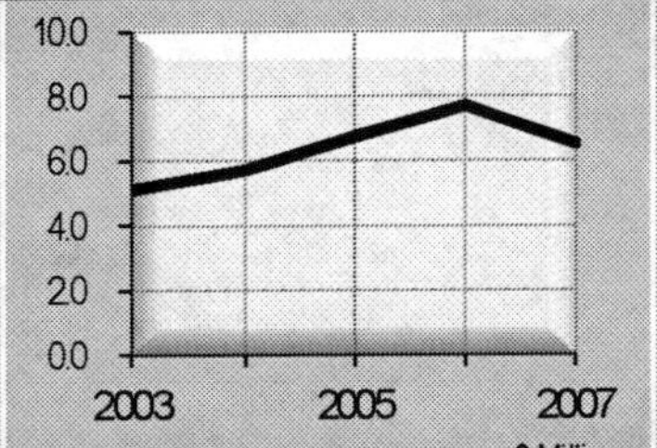

RESERVES
See Sec. 2, A.3 — $ Millions

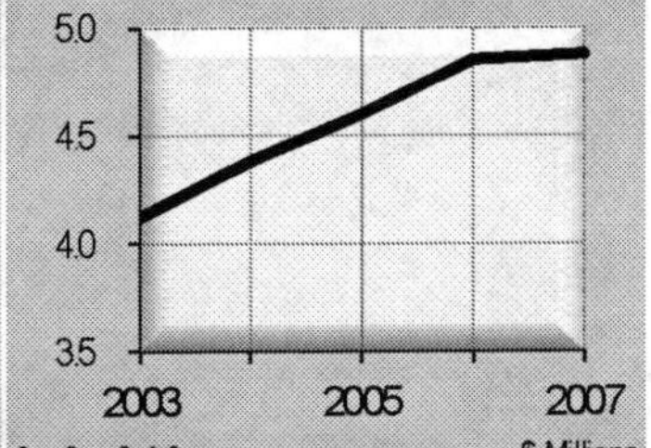

NET INCOME
See Sec. 2, B.3 — $ Millions

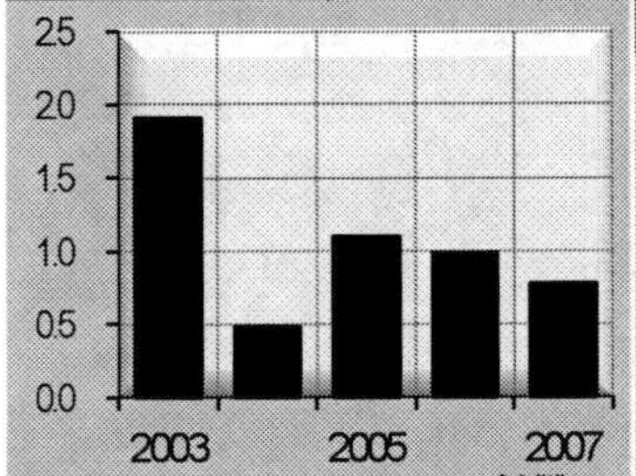

NET INVESTMENT GAIN
NET REALIZED CAPITAL GAINS
See Sec. 5, A.8 — $ Millions

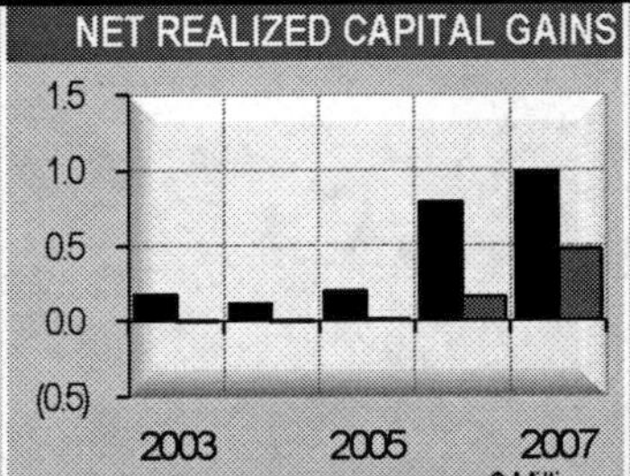

NET CASH FROM OPERATIONS
See Sec. 2, C.3 — $ Millions

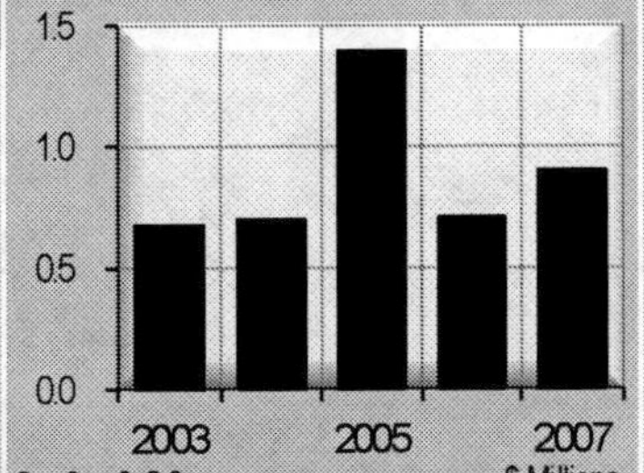

OPER. GAIN BEFORE TAXES
See Sec. 2, B.3 — $ Millions

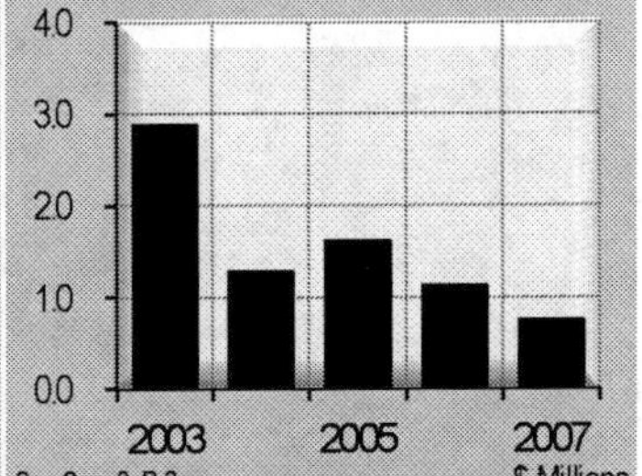

PREMIUMS

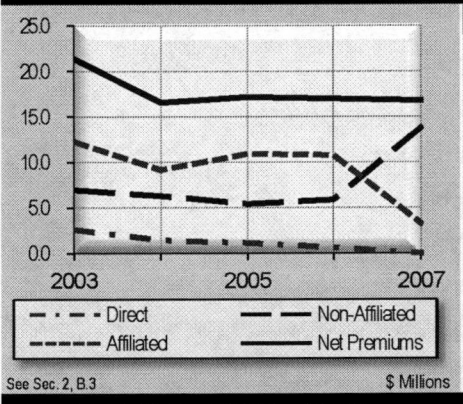

- - - Direct
- - - - Affiliated
——— Non-Affiliated
——— Net Premiums

See Sec. 2, B.3 — $ Millions

OPERATING EXPENSES INCURRED
AGENT RETENTION
See Sec. 2, B.3 & Sec. 5, B.9 — $ Millions

FINANCIAL POSITION	2007
Cash, Cash Equivalents & Short-Term Investments	$7,462,687
Total Assets	$12,091,518
Policyholders' Surplus	$6,503,339
Reserves	$4,877,495
OPERATING RESULTS	
Net Income	$779,522
Net Investment Gain	$992,698
Net Realized Capital Gains	$475,814
Net Cash from Operations	$899,743
Oper. Gain Before Taxes	$750,779

DIRECT PREMIUMS WRITTEN - YE 2007

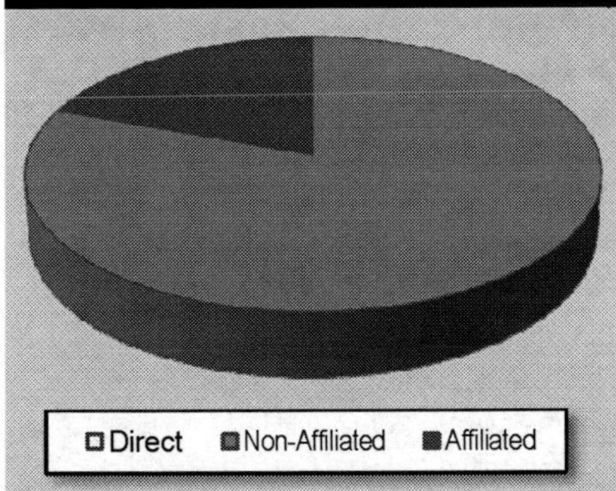

☐ Direct ◼ Non-Affiliated ◼ Affiliated

See Sec. 3, B.4

L&LAE INCURRED
LOSS RATIO

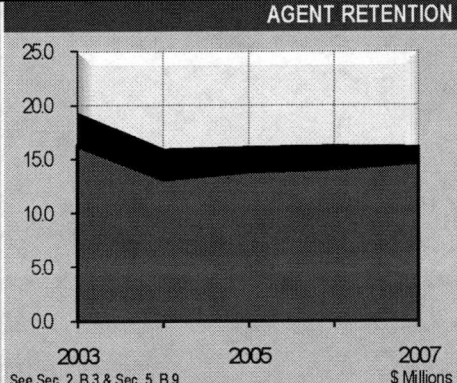

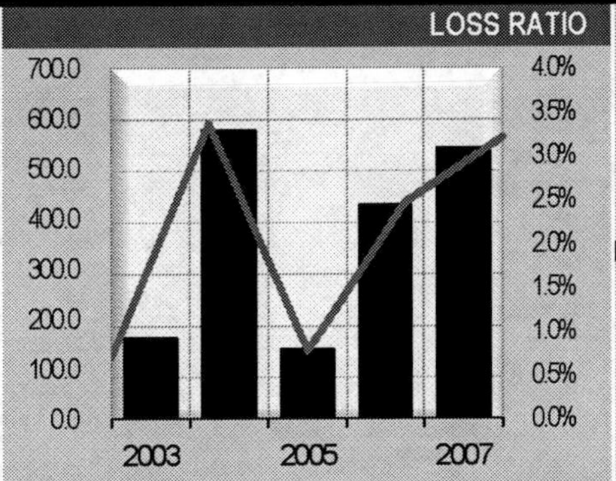

See Sec. 5, A.3 & Sec. 5, C.2 — $ Thousands

UNDERWRITING RESULTS	
Direct	$0
Non-Affiliated	$13,742,041
Affiliated	$3,297,800
Direct Premiums Written	$17,039,841
Net Premiums Earned	$16,770,422
Operating Expenses Incurred	$16,101,842
Agent Retention	$14,655,368
L&LAE Incurred	$544,743
Loss Ratio	3.23%

6

Ticor Title Insurance Company

601 Riverside Ave.
Jacksonville, FL 32204

(904) 854-8100

WEBSITE:	STATE OF DOMICILE:
www.fnf.com	California

	ESTABLISHED:	JURISDICTION LICENSE(S):
CHAIRMAN, PRESIDENT & CEO:		
Raymond Randall Quirk	11/18/1965	53

A' Unsurpassed
Financial Stability Rating®
Demotech, Inc.

NAIC Number:
50067

TICOR

NAIC Group:
CHICAGO / FIDELITY

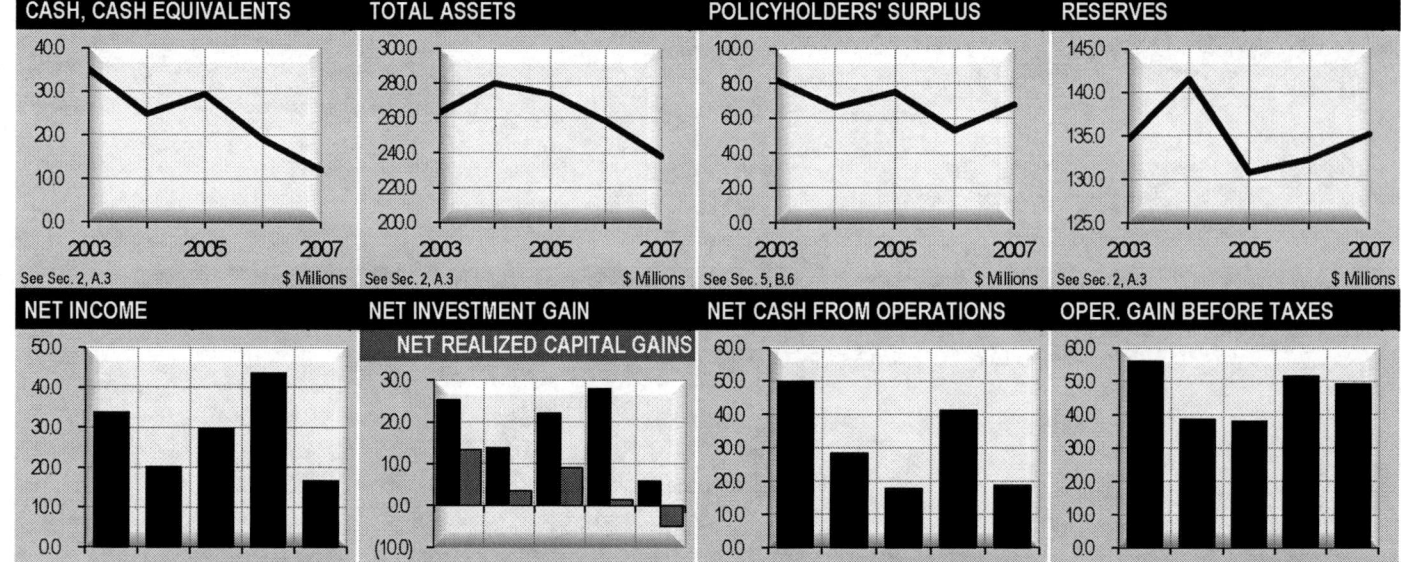

CASH, CASH EQUIVALENTS — See Sec. 2, A.3 — $ Millions
TOTAL ASSETS — See Sec. 2, A.3 — $ Millions
POLICYHOLDERS' SURPLUS — See Sec. 5, B.6 — $ Millions
RESERVES — See Sec. 2, A.3 — $ Millions
NET INCOME — See Sec. 2, B.3 — $ Millions
NET INVESTMENT GAIN / NET REALIZED CAPITAL GAINS — See Sec. 5, A.8 — $ Millions
NET CASH FROM OPERATIONS — See Sec. 2, C.3 — $ Millions
OPER. GAIN BEFORE TAXES — See Sec. 2, B.3 — $ Millions

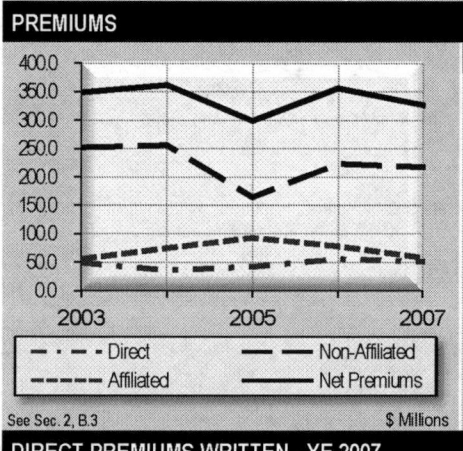

PREMIUMS — See Sec. 2, B.3 — $ Millions
- · - Direct
- - - Affiliated
- — Non-Affiliated
- — Net Premiums

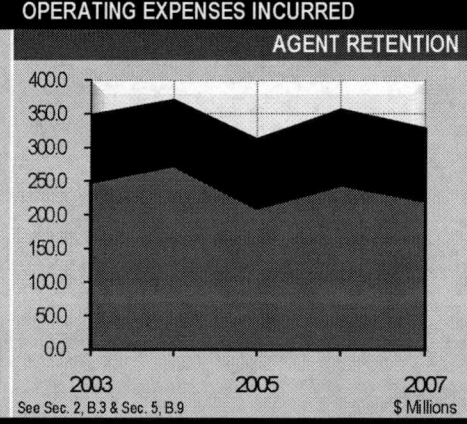

OPERATING EXPENSES INCURRED / AGENT RETENTION — See Sec. 2, B.3 & Sec. 5, B.9 — $ Millions

DIRECT PREMIUMS WRITTEN - YE 2007 — See Sec. 3, B.4
☐ Direct ▨ Non-Affiliated ▪ Affiliated

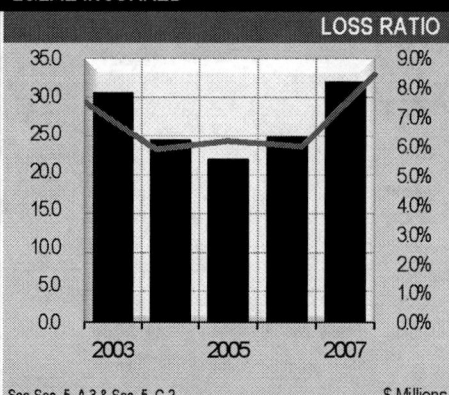

L&LAE INCURRED / LOSS RATIO — See Sec. 5, A.3 & Sec. 5, C.2 — $ Millions

FINANCIAL POSITION	2007
Cash, Cash Equivalents & Short-Term Investments	$11,935,844
Total Assets	$237,995,198
Policyholders' Surplus	$67,686,913
Reserves	$135,148,093
OPERATING RESULTS	
Net Income	$16,674,343
Net Investment Gain	$5,841,529
Net Realized Capital Gains	($5,044,091)
Net Cash from Operations	$18,848,841
Oper. Gain Before Taxes	$49,097,851
UNDERWRITING RESULTS	
Direct	$51,058,558
Non-Affiliated	$218,064,012
Affiliated	$58,074,930
Direct Premiums Written	$327,197,500
Net Premiums Earned	$326,846,416
Operating Expenses Incurred	$327,993,550
Agent Retention	$221,138,248
L&LAE Incurred	$31,901,304
Loss Ratio	8.46%

Ticor Title Insurance Company of Florida

601 Riverside Ave.
Jacksonville, FL 32204

(904) 854-8100

Formerly American Pioneer Title Insurance Company

WEBSITE:	STATE OF DOMICILE:
www.fnf.com	Nebraska

PRESIDENT & CEO:	ESTABLISHED:	JURISDICTION LICENSE(S):
Raymond Randall Quirk	2/4/1980	46

A Exceptional
Financial Stability Rating®
⬩ Demotech, Inc.

NAIC Number:
51535

TICOR (FL)

NAIC Group:
CHICAGO / FIDELITY

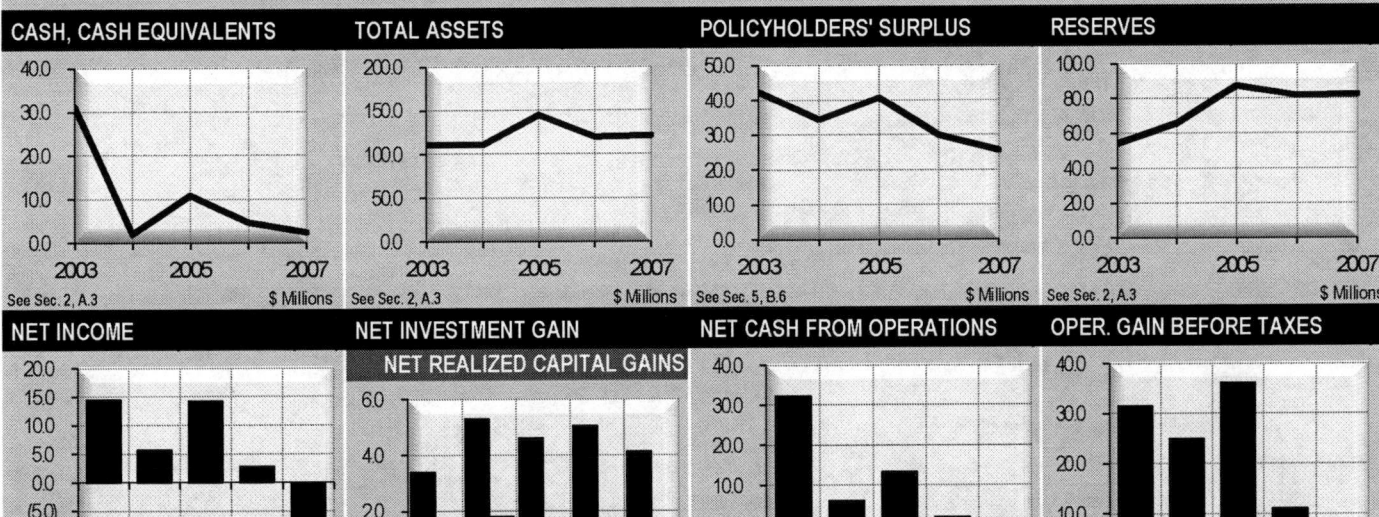

CASH, CASH EQUIVALENTS — See Sec. 2, A.3 — $ Millions
TOTAL ASSETS — See Sec. 2, A.3 — $ Millions
POLICYHOLDERS' SURPLUS — See Sec. 5, B.6 — $ Millions
RESERVES — See Sec. 2, A.3 — $ Millions

NET INCOME — See Sec. 2, B.3 — $ Millions
NET INVESTMENT GAIN / NET REALIZED CAPITAL GAINS — See Sec. 5, A.8 — $ Millions
NET CASH FROM OPERATIONS — See Sec. 2, C.3 — $ Millions
OPER. GAIN BEFORE TAXES — See Sec. 2, B.3 — $ Millions

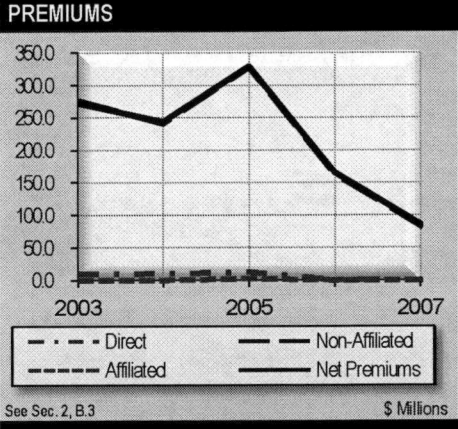

PREMIUMS
- – - Direct
----- Affiliated
— — Non-Affiliated
— Net Premiums
See Sec. 2, B.3 — $ Millions

OPERATING EXPENSES INCURRED / AGENT RETENTION
See Sec. 2, B.3 & Sec. 5, B.9 — $ Millions

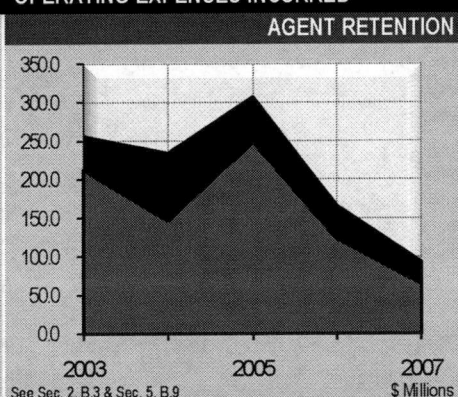

DIRECT PREMIUMS WRITTEN - YE 2007
☐ Direct ▩ Non-Affiliated ▪ Affiliated
See Sec. 3, B.4

L&LAE INCURRED / LOSS RATIO
See Sec. 5, A.3 & Sec. 5, C.2 — $ Millions

FINANCIAL POSITION	2007
Cash, Cash Equivalents & Short-Term Investments	$2,296,791
Total Assets	$120,872,364
Policyholders' Surplus	$25,586,476
Reserves	$82,107,499
OPERATING RESULTS	
Net Income	($10,924,391)
Net Investment Gain	$4,123,733
Net Realized Capital Gains	$84,093
Net Cash from Operations	($5,443,236)
Oper. Gain Before Taxes	$336,464
UNDERWRITING RESULTS	
Direct	$0
Non-Affiliated	$83,543,448
Affiliated	$0
Direct Premiums Written	$83,543,448
Net Premiums Earned	$85,830,997
Operating Expenses Incurred	$93,268,161
Agent Retention	$63,996,950
L&LAE Incurred	$24,844,212
Loss Ratio	26.54%

6

Title Guaranty and Trust Company of Chattanooga

617 Walnut St.
Chattanooga, TN 37402

(423) 266-5751

WEBSITE:	STATE OF DOMICILE:
www.titleguarantyandtrust.com	Tennessee

PRESIDENT:	ESTABLISHED:	JURISDICTION LICENSE(S):
Brian F. Kopet	12/31/1891	1

S Substantial
Financial Stability Rating®
Demotech, Inc.

NAIC Number:
50261

TITLE G&TC

NAIC Group:
UNAFFILIATED

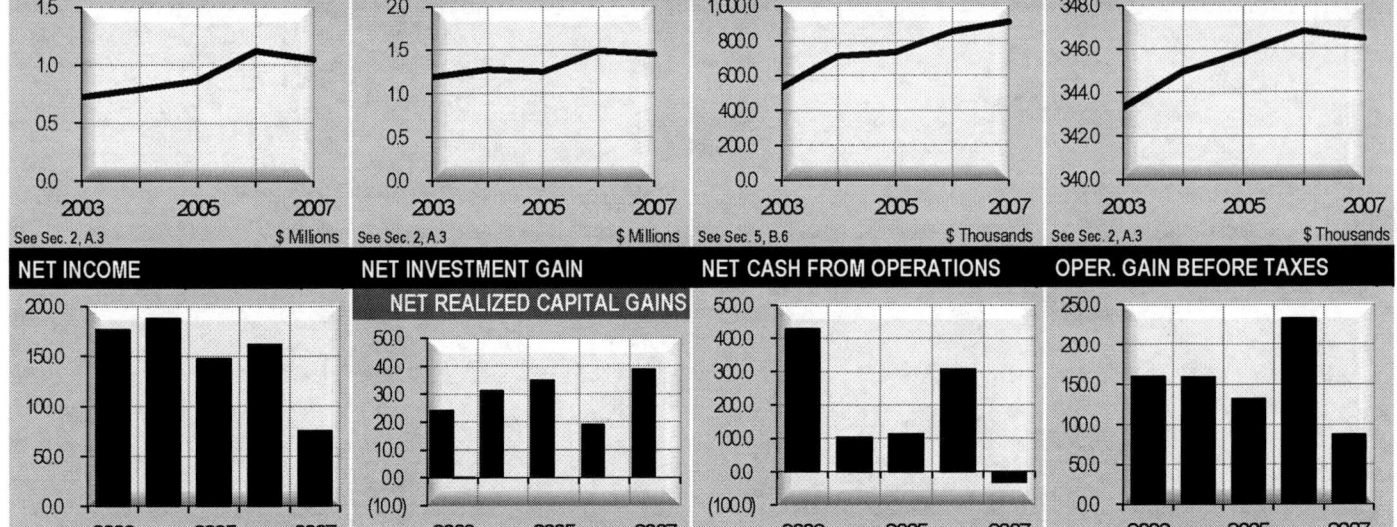

CASH, CASH EQUIVALENTS — See Sec. 2, A.3 — $ Millions
TOTAL ASSETS — See Sec. 2, A.3 — $ Millions
POLICYHOLDERS' SURPLUS — See Sec. 5, B.6 — $ Thousands
RESERVES — See Sec. 2, A.3 — $ Thousands

NET INCOME — See Sec. 2, B.3 — $ Thousands
NET INVESTMENT GAIN / NET REALIZED CAPITAL GAINS — See Sec. 5, A.8 — $ Thousands
NET CASH FROM OPERATIONS — See Sec. 2, C.3 — $ Thousands
OPER. GAIN BEFORE TAXES — See Sec. 2, B.3 — $ Thousands

PREMIUMS
- · - Direct
------ Affiliated
— — Non-Affiliated
—— Net Premiums
See Sec. 2, B.3 — $ Thousands

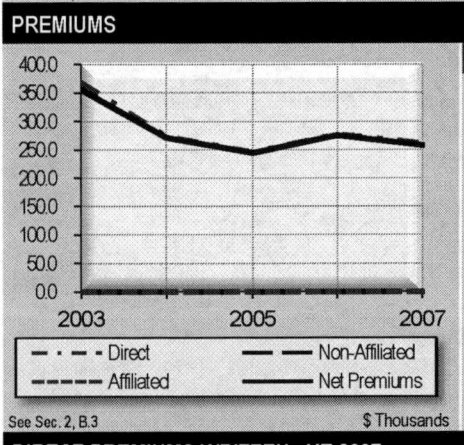

DIRECT PREMIUMS WRITTEN - YE 2007
☐ Direct ▦ Non-Affiliated ■ Affiliated
See Sec. 3, B.4

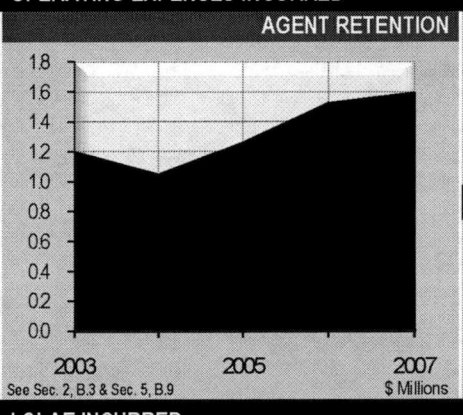

OPERATING EXPENSES INCURRED / AGENT RETENTION
See Sec. 2, B.3 & Sec. 5, B.9 — $ Millions

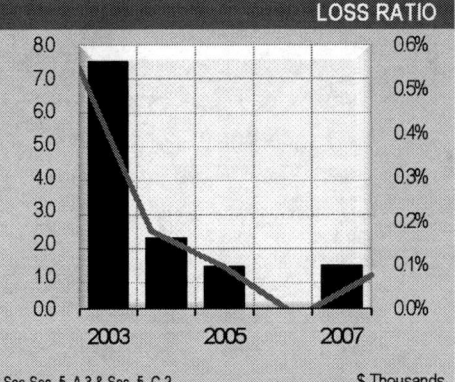

L&LAE INCURRED / LOSS RATIO
See Sec. 5, A.3 & Sec. 5, C.2 — $ Thousands

FINANCIAL POSITION	2007
Cash, Cash Equivalents & Short-Term Investments	$1,044,756
Total Assets	$1,448,651
Policyholders' Surplus	$907,607
Reserves	$346,463
OPERATING RESULTS	
Net Income	$75,149
Net Investment Gain	$38,802
Net Realized Capital Gains	$0
Net Cash from Operations	($34,035)
Oper. Gain Before Taxes	$87,016
UNDERWRITING RESULTS	
Direct	$260,893
Non-Affiliated	$0
Affiliated	$0
Direct Premiums Written	$260,893
Net Premiums Earned	$257,994
Operating Expenses Incurred	$1,589,008
Agent Retention	$0
L&LAE Incurred	$1,500
Loss Ratio	0.09%

Title Guaranty Division of the Iowa Finance Authority

2015 Grand Ave.
Des Moines, IA 50312

(515) 725-4357

WEBSITE:	STATE OF DOMICILE:
www.iowafinanceauthority.gov	Iowa

EXECUTIVE DIRECTOR:	ESTABLISHED:	JURISDICTION LICENSE(S):
Bret L. Mills	7/1/1985	1

A' A Prime Unsurpassed
Financial Stability Rating®
Demotech, Inc.

NAIC Number:

TITLE GUARANTY DIV (IA)

NAIC Group:
UNAFFILIATED

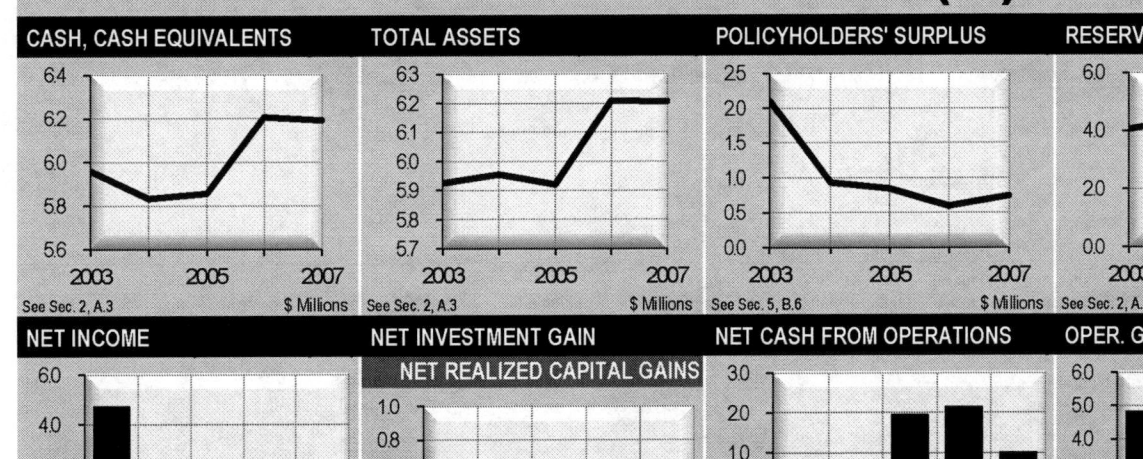

CASH, CASH EQUIVALENTS — See Sec. 2, A.3 — $ Millions
TOTAL ASSETS — See Sec. 2, A.3 — $ Millions
POLICYHOLDERS' SURPLUS — See Sec. 5, B.6 — $ Millions
RESERVES — See Sec. 2, A.3 — $ Millions

NET INCOME — See Sec. 2, B.3 — $ Millions
NET INVESTMENT GAIN / NET REALIZED CAPITAL GAINS — See Sec. 5, A.8 — $
NET CASH FROM OPERATIONS — See Sec. 2, C.3 — $ Millions
OPER. GAIN BEFORE TAXES — See Sec. 2, B.3 — $ Millions

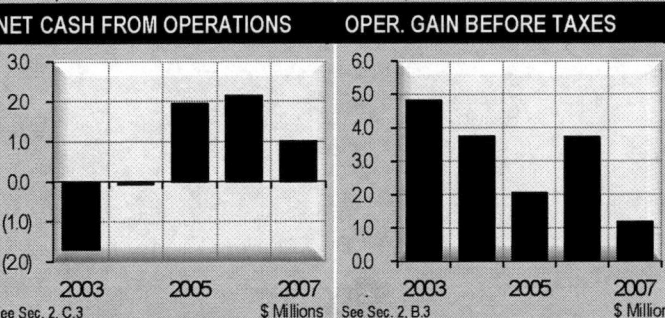

PREMIUMS — See Sec. 2, B.3 — $ Millions
- · - Direct
- - - - Affiliated
—— Non-Affiliated
—— Net Premiums

OPERATING EXPENSES INCURRED / AGENT RETENTION — See Sec. 2, B.3 & Sec. 5, B.9 — $ Millions

FINANCIAL POSITION	2007
Cash, Cash Equivalents & Short-Term Investments	$6,191,804
Total Assets	$6,205,381
Policyholders' Surplus	$739,705
Reserves	$5,009,535
OPERATING RESULTS	
Net Income	$145,733
Net Investment Gain	$0
Net Realized Capital Gains	$0
Net Cash from Operations	$1,006,732
Oper. Gain Before Taxes	$1,166,733
UNDERWRITING RESULTS	
Direct	$3,724,743
Non-Affiliated	$0
Affiliated	$0
Direct Premiums Written	$3,724,743
Net Premiums Earned	$3,590,882
Operating Expenses Incurred	$2,481,484
Agent Retention	$0
L&LAE Incurred	$0
Loss Ratio	0.00%

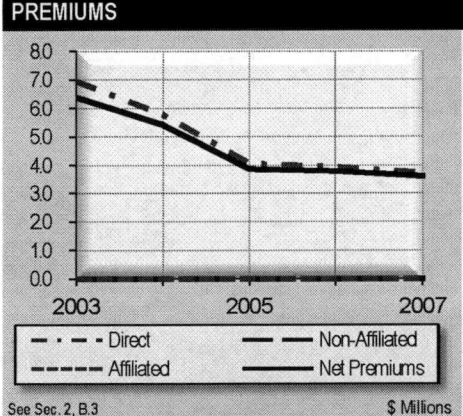

DIRECT PREMIUMS WRITTEN - YE 2007 — See Sec. 3, B.4
☐ Direct ☐ Non-Affiliated ☐ Affiliated

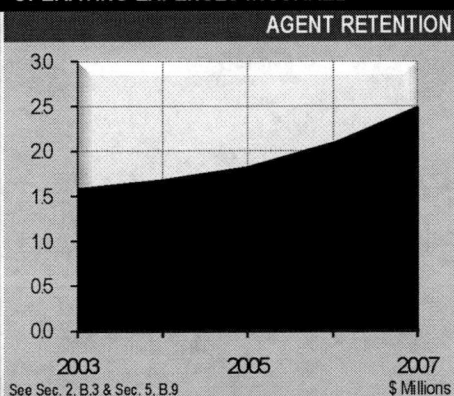

L&LAE INCURRED / LOSS RATIO — See Sec. 5, A.3 & Sec. 5, C.2 — $ Thousands

6

Title Insurance Company of America

7557 Rambler Rd., Ste. 1200
Dallas, TX 75231

(888) 842-2545

WEBSITE:	STATE OF DOMICILE:
www.landam.com	Nebraska

PRESIDENT:	ESTABLISHED:	JURISDICTION LICENSE(S):
William Benton James	1/30/1934	25

A Exceptional
Financial Stability Rating®
Demotech, Inc.

NAIC Number:
50245

TITLE IC AMERICA

NAIC Group:
LAND AMERICA

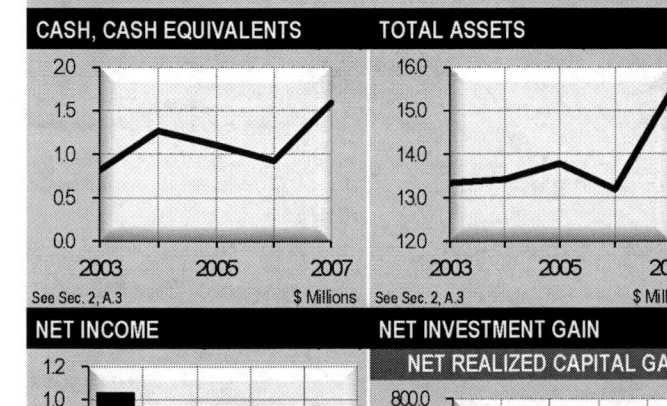

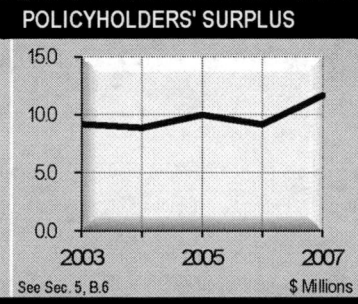

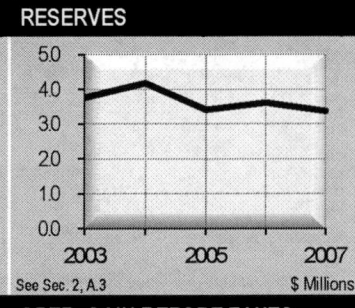

CASH, CASH EQUIVALENTS — See Sec. 2, A.3 — $ Millions
TOTAL ASSETS — See Sec. 2, A.3 — $ Millions
POLICYHOLDERS' SURPLUS — See Sec. 5, B.6 — $ Millions
RESERVES — See Sec. 2, A.3 — $ Millions

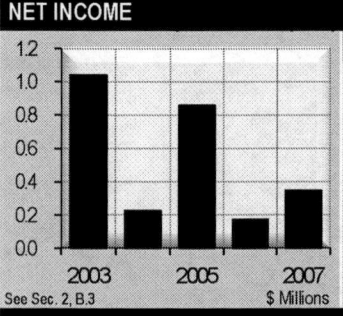

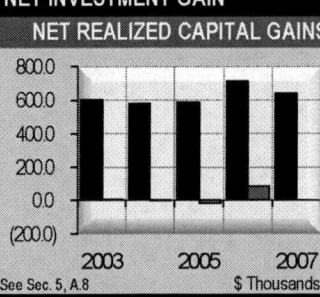

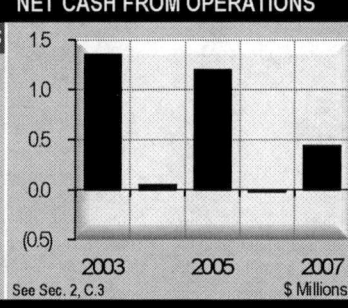

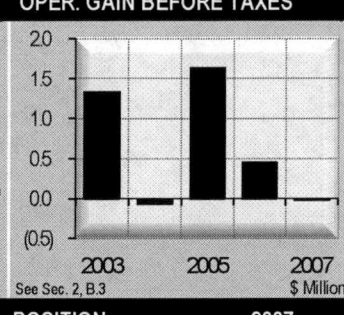

NET INCOME — See Sec. 2, B.3 — $ Millions
NET INVESTMENT GAIN / NET REALIZED CAPITAL GAINS — See Sec. 5, A.8 — $ Thousands
NET CASH FROM OPERATIONS — See Sec. 2, C.3 — $ Millions
OPER. GAIN BEFORE TAXES — See Sec. 2, B.3 — $ Millions

PREMIUMS

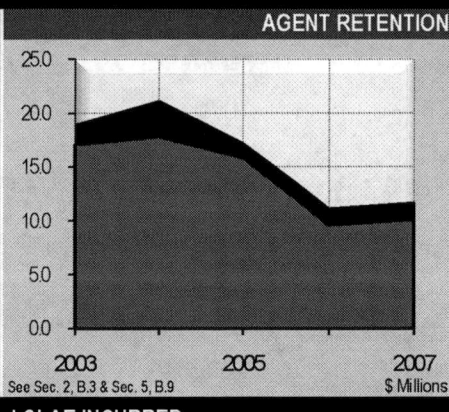

OPERATING EXPENSES INCURRED / AGENT RETENTION

- · - · Direct
- - - - Affiliated
- — — Non-Affiliated
- —— Net Premiums

See Sec. 2, B.3 — $ Millions
See Sec. 2, B.3 & Sec. 5, B.9 — $ Millions

FINANCIAL POSITION	2007
Cash, Cash Equivalents & Short-Term Investments	$1,590,032
Total Assets	$15,413,940
Policyholders' Surplus	$11,666,575
Reserves	$3,372,565
OPERATING RESULTS	
Net Income	$348,514
Net Investment Gain	$640,317
Net Realized Capital Gains	$1,835
Net Cash from Operations	$442,125
Oper. Gain Before Taxes	($15,281)

DIRECT PREMIUMS WRITTEN - YE 2007

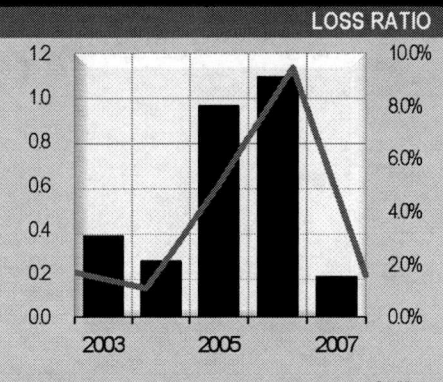

□ Direct ▨ Non-Affiliated ■ Affiliated

See Sec. 3, B.4

L&LAE INCURRED / LOSS RATIO

See Sec. 5, A.3 & Sec. 5, C.2 — $ Millions

UNDERWRITING RESULTS	
Direct	$0
Non-Affiliated	$11,954,125
Affiliated	$0
Direct Premiums Written	$11,954,125
Net Premiums Earned	$11,614,622
Operating Expenses Incurred	$11,629,474
Agent Retention	$10,137,288
L&LAE Incurred	$211,989
Loss Ratio	1.83%

6

Title Resources Guaranty Company

8111 LBJ Freeway, Ste. 1200
Dallas, TX 75251

(972) 644-6500

WEBSITE:	STATE OF DOMICILE:
www.trgctx.com	Texas

PRESIDENT:	ESTABLISHED:	JURISDICTION LICENSE(S):
Albert Frawley Jackson III	3/14/1984	16

A' Unsurpassed
Financial Stability Rating®
Demotech, Inc.

NAIC Number: **50016**	**TITLE RESOURCES**	NAIC Group: **UNAFFILIATED**

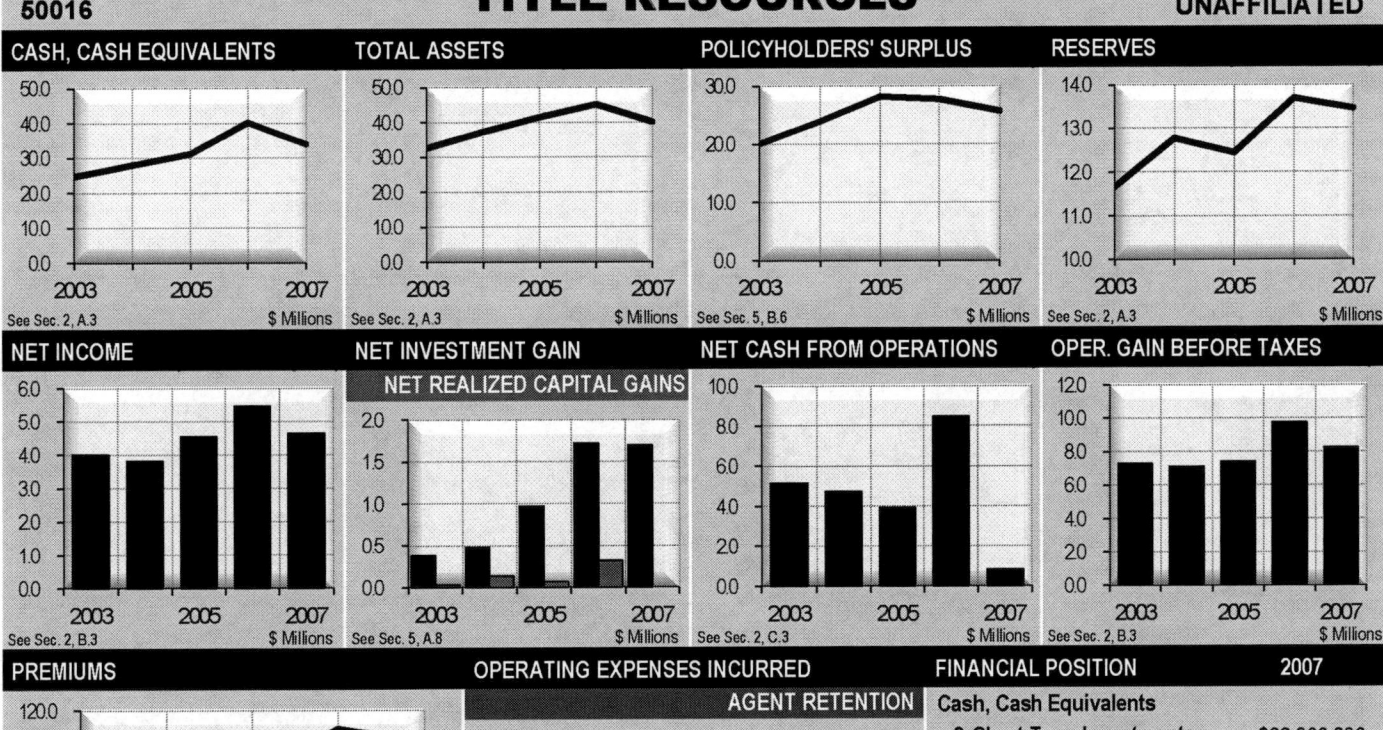

CASH, CASH EQUIVALENTS — See Sec. 2, A.3 — $ Millions

TOTAL ASSETS — See Sec. 2, A.3 — $ Millions

POLICYHOLDERS' SURPLUS — See Sec. 5, B.6 — $ Millions

RESERVES — See Sec. 2, A.3 — $ Millions

NET INCOME — See Sec. 2, B.3 — $ Millions

NET INVESTMENT GAIN / NET REALIZED CAPITAL GAINS — See Sec. 5, A.8 — $ Millions

NET CASH FROM OPERATIONS — See Sec. 2, C.3 — $ Millions

OPER. GAIN BEFORE TAXES — See Sec. 2, B.3 — $ Millions

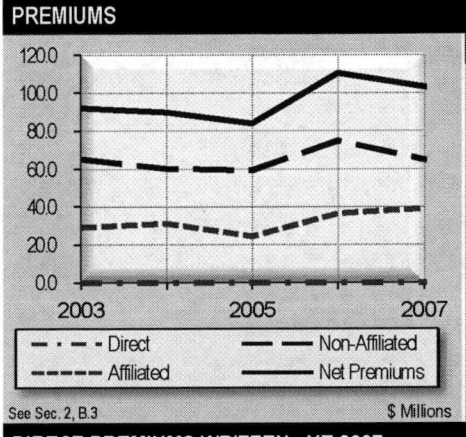

PREMIUMS
- · – · Direct
- - - - Affiliated
- — — Non-Affiliated
- —— Net Premiums

See Sec. 2, B.3 — $ Millions

DIRECT PREMIUMS WRITTEN - YE 2007
☐ Direct ■ Non-Affiliated ■ Affiliated
See Sec. 3, B.4

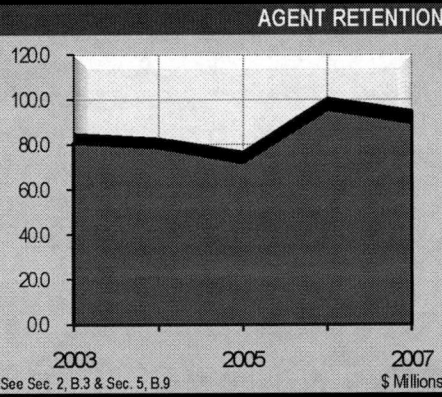

OPERATING EXPENSES INCURRED / AGENT RETENTION
See Sec. 2, B.3 & Sec. 5, B.9 — $ Millions

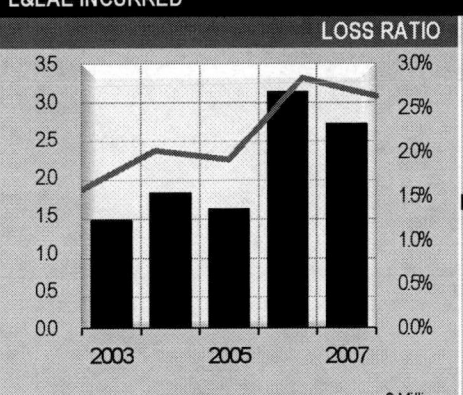

L&LAE INCURRED / LOSS RATIO
See Sec. 5, A.3 & Sec. 5, C.2 — $ Millions

FINANCIAL POSITION	2007
Cash, Cash Equivalents & Short-Term Investments	$33,966,806
Total Assets	$40,058,907
Policyholders' Surplus	$25,711,604
Reserves	$13,461,881
OPERATING RESULTS	
Net Income	$4,648,067
Net Investment Gain	$1,697,987
Net Realized Capital Gains	$0
Net Cash from Operations	$833,984
Oper. Gain Before Taxes	$8,241,145
UNDERWRITING RESULTS	
Direct	$0
Non-Affiliated	$64,857,278
Affiliated	$38,990,484
Direct Premiums Written	**$103,847,762**
Net Premiums Earned	$103,117,424
Operating Expenses Incurred	$94,876,281
Agent Retention	$89,704,496
L&LAE Incurred	$2,723,051
Loss Ratio	2.64%

6

Titledge Insurance Company of New York

654 Sharrotts Rd.
Staten Island, NY 10309

(718) 701-6094

WEBSITE:
www.titledgeinsurancecompany.com

CHIEF EXECUTIVE OFFICER:
Jonathan Boxman

STATE OF DOMICILE:
New York

ESTABLISHED:
8/22/2006

JURISDICTION LICENSE(S):
1

S Substantial
Financial Stability Rating®
Demotech, Inc.

NAIC Number:
12935

TITLEDGE

NAIC Group:
UNAFFILIATED

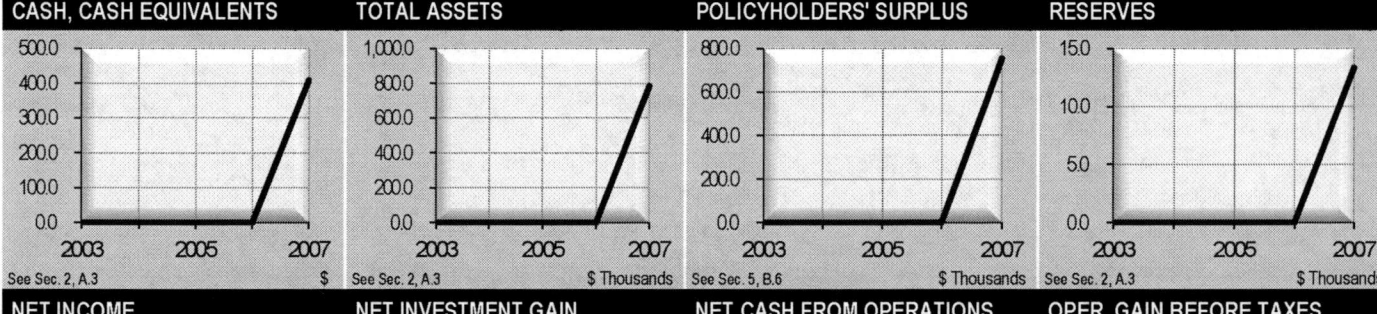

CASH, CASH EQUIVALENTS — See Sec. 2, A.3 — $
TOTAL ASSETS — See Sec. 2, A.3 — $ Thousands
POLICYHOLDERS' SURPLUS — See Sec. 5, B.6 — $ Thousands
RESERVES — See Sec. 2, A.3 — $ Thousands

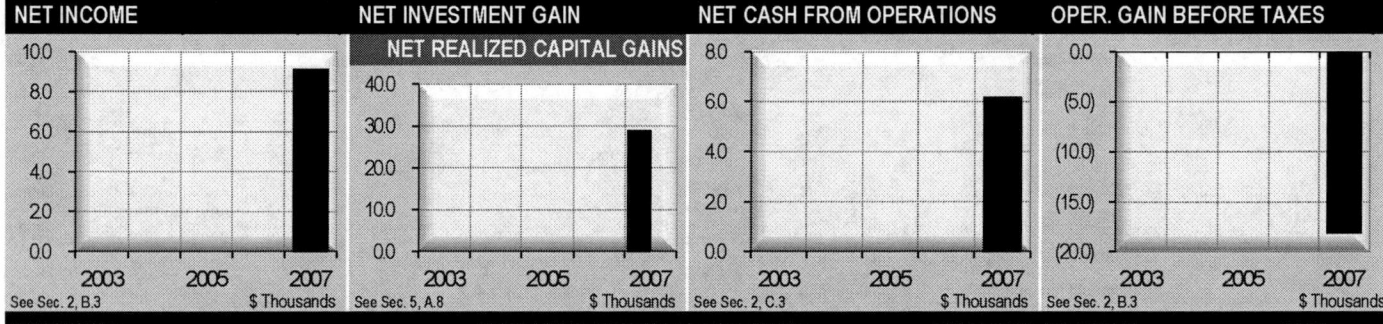

NET INCOME — See Sec. 2, B.3 — $ Thousands
NET INVESTMENT GAIN / NET REALIZED CAPITAL GAINS — See Sec. 5, A.8 — $ Thousands
NET CASH FROM OPERATIONS — See Sec. 2, C.3 — $ Thousands
OPER. GAIN BEFORE TAXES — See Sec. 2, B.3 — $ Thousands

PREMIUMS

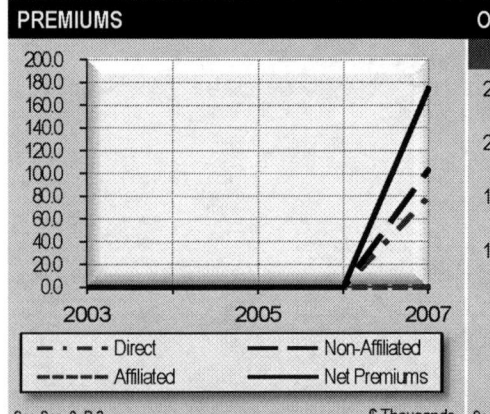

- · - Direct
- — — Non-Affiliated
- ---- Affiliated
- —— Net Premiums

See Sec. 2, B.3 — $ Thousands

OPERATING EXPENSES INCURRED

AGENT RETENTION

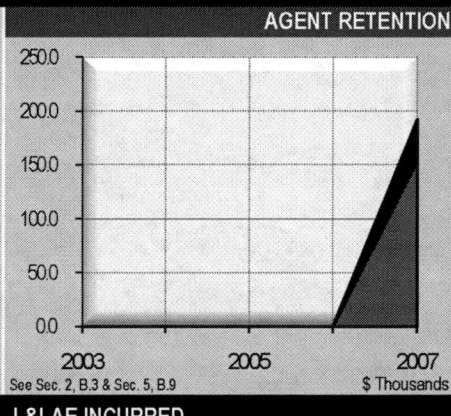

See Sec. 2, B.3 & Sec. 5, B.9 — $ Thousands

FINANCIAL POSITION — 2007

Cash, Cash Equivalents & Short-Term Investments	$408
Total Assets	$783,283
Policyholders' Surplus	$753,085
Reserves	$13,315
OPERATING RESULTS	
Net Income	$9,125
Net Investment Gain	$28,862
Net Realized Capital Gains	$0
Net Cash from Operations	$6,163
Oper. Gain Before Taxes	($18,148)

DIRECT PREMIUMS WRITTEN - YE 2007

□ Direct ▨ Non-Affiliated ▪ Affiliated

See Sec. 3, B.4

L&LAE INCURRED

LOSS RATIO

See Sec. 5, A.3 & Sec. 5, C.2 — $

UNDERWRITING RESULTS

Direct	$78,917
Non-Affiliated	$102,655
Affiliated	$0
Direct Premiums Written	**$181,572**
Net Premiums Earned	**$174,297**
Operating Expenses Incurred	$192,445
Agent Retention	$153,755
L&LAE Incurred	$0
Loss Ratio	0.00%

Transnation Title Insurance Company

5600 Cox Rd.
Glen Allen, VA 23060

(804) 267-8000

Formerly Transamerica Title Insurance Company

WEBSITE:	STATE OF DOMICILE:
www.landam.com	Nebraska

PRESIDENT & CEO:	ESTABLISHED:	JURISDICTION LICENSE(S):
Theodore Lindy Chandler, Jr.	9/15/1992	45

A Exceptional
Financial Stability Rating®
◢ Demotech, Inc.

NAIC Number:
50012

TRANSNATION

NAIC Group:
LAND AMERICA

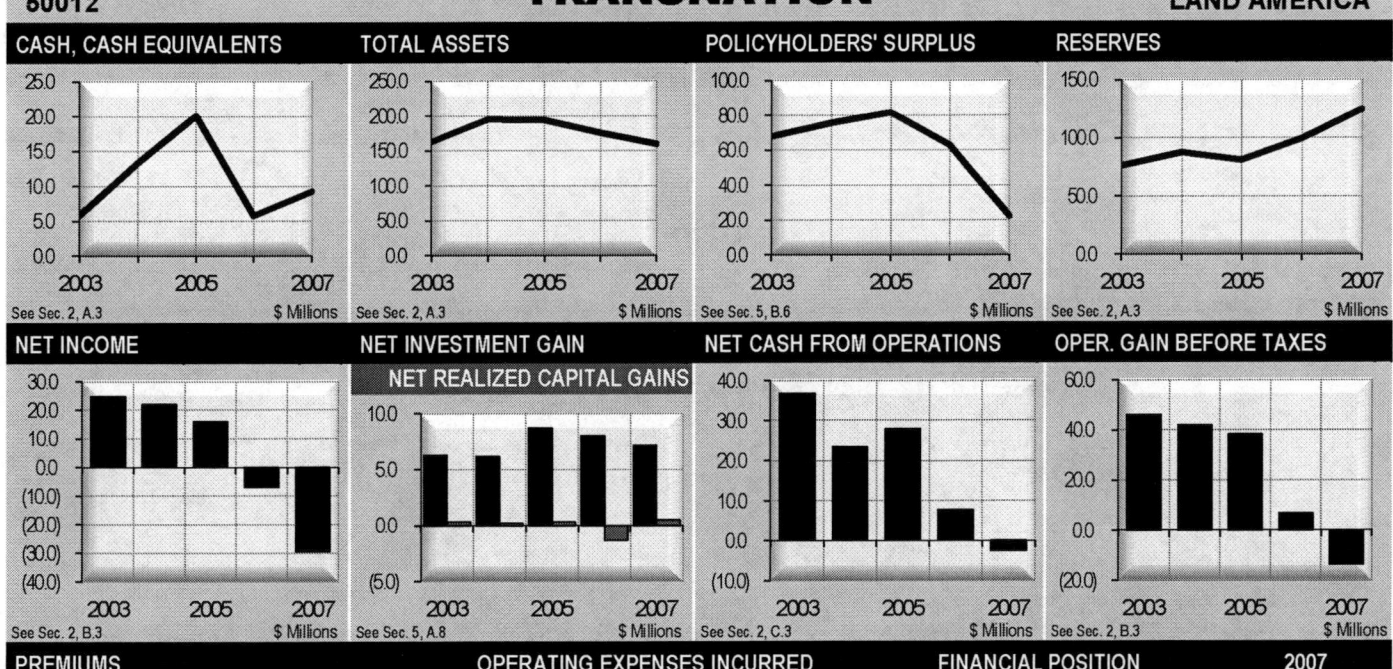

CASH, CASH EQUIVALENTS — See Sec. 2, A.3 — $ Millions
TOTAL ASSETS — See Sec. 2, A.3 — $ Millions
POLICYHOLDERS' SURPLUS — See Sec. 5, B.6 — $ Millions
RESERVES — See Sec. 2, A.3 — $ Millions

NET INCOME — See Sec. 2, B.3 — $ Millions
NET INVESTMENT GAIN / NET REALIZED CAPITAL GAINS — See Sec. 5, A.8 — $ Millions
NET CASH FROM OPERATIONS — See Sec. 2, C.3 — $ Millions
OPER. GAIN BEFORE TAXES — See Sec. 2, B.3 — $ Millions

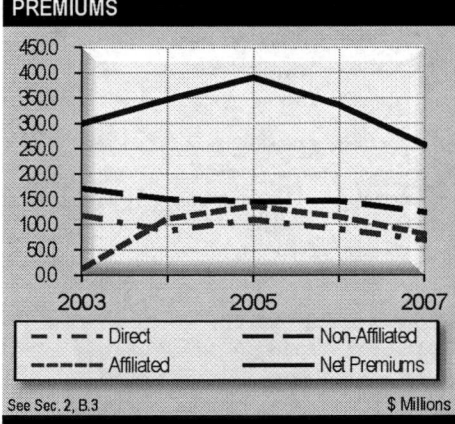

PREMIUMS
- · - Direct
- - - Affiliated
— Non-Affiliated
— Net Premiums
See Sec. 2, B.3 — $ Millions

OPERATING EXPENSES INCURRED / AGENT RETENTION
See Sec. 2, B.3 & Sec. 5, B.9 — $ Millions

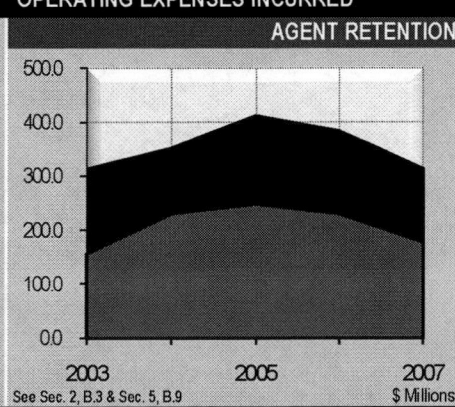

DIRECT PREMIUMS WRITTEN - YE 2007
☐ Direct ▨ Non-Affiliated ■ Affiliated
See Sec. 3, B.4

L&LAE INCURRED / LOSS RATIO
See Sec. 5, A.3 & Sec. 5, C.2 — $ Millions

FINANCIAL POSITION	2007
Cash, Cash Equivalents & Short-Term Investments	$9,192,210
Total Assets	$159,577,693
Policyholders' Surplus	$22,334,782
Reserves	$124,551,750

OPERATING RESULTS	
Net Income	($29,527,216)
Net Investment Gain	$7,150,419
Net Realized Capital Gains	$494,234
Net Cash from Operations	($2,527,784)
Oper. Gain Before Taxes	($13,635,368)

UNDERWRITING RESULTS	
Direct	$69,584,981
Non-Affiliated	$124,240,351
Affiliated	$81,004,543
Direct Premiums Written	**$274,829,875**
Net Premiums Earned	$257,711,742
Operating Expenses Incurred	$313,225,196
Agent Retention	$178,625,661
L&LAE Incurred	$36,073,084
Loss Ratio	12.04%

6

TransUnion National Title Insurance Company

2711 Middleburg Dr., Ste. 312
Columbia, SC 29204

(803) 799-4747

Formerly Atlantic Title Insurance Company

WEBSITE:	STATE OF DOMICILE:
–	South Carolina

PRESIDENT:	ESTABLISHED:	JURISDICTION LICENSE(S):
Joseph Vincent McCabe	6/18/1974	31

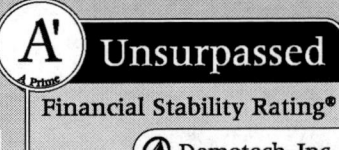

A' Unsurpassed
Financial Stability Rating®
Demotech, Inc.

NAIC Number: **51152**

TRANSUNION NATIONAL

NAIC Group: **TRANSUNION**

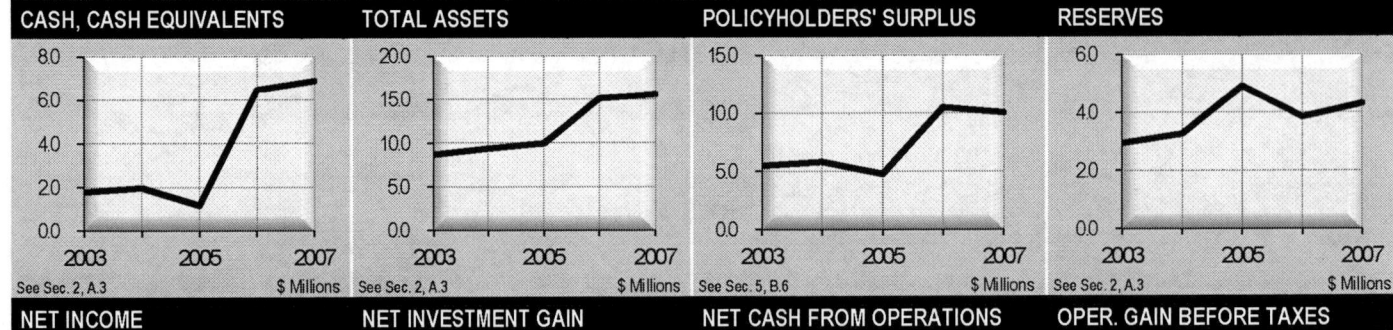

CASH, CASH EQUIVALENTS — See Sec. 2, A.3 — $ Millions
TOTAL ASSETS — See Sec. 2, A.3 — $ Millions
POLICYHOLDERS' SURPLUS — See Sec. 5, B.6 — $ Millions
RESERVES — See Sec. 2, A.3 — $ Millions

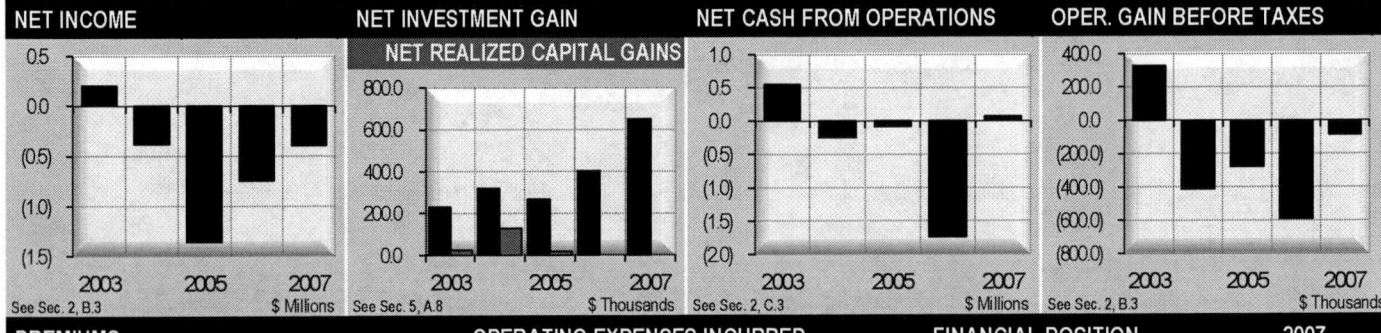

NET INCOME — See Sec. 2, B.3 — $ Millions
NET INVESTMENT GAIN / NET REALIZED CAPITAL GAINS — See Sec. 5, A.8 — $ Thousands
NET CASH FROM OPERATIONS — See Sec. 2, C.3 — $ Millions
OPER. GAIN BEFORE TAXES — See Sec. 2, B.3 — $ Thousands

PREMIUMS

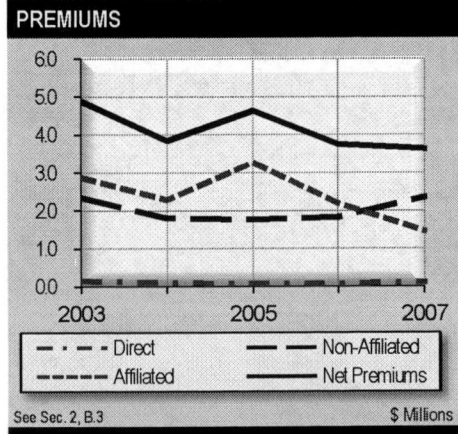

- – · – Direct
- – – Non-Affiliated
- ---- Affiliated
- —— Net Premiums

See Sec. 2, B.3 — $ Millions

OPERATING EXPENSES INCURRED

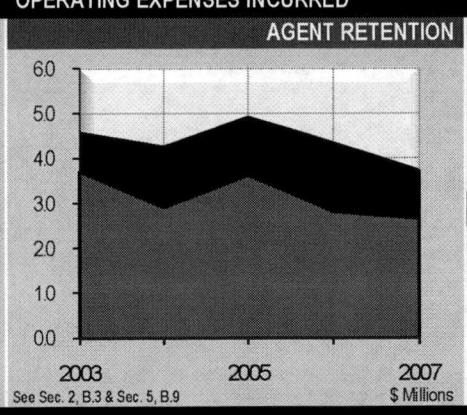

AGENT RETENTION

See Sec. 2, B.3 & Sec. 5, B.9 — $ Millions

FINANCIAL POSITION 2007

Cash, Cash Equivalents & Short-Term Investments	$6,866,625
Total Assets	$15,575,501
Policyholders' Surplus	$10,048,532
Reserves	$4,303,549

OPERATING RESULTS

Net Income	($397,344)
Net Investment Gain	$650,881
Net Realized Capital Gains	$0
Net Cash from Operations	$69,657
Oper. Gain Before Taxes	($85,805)

DIRECT PREMIUMS WRITTEN - YE 2007

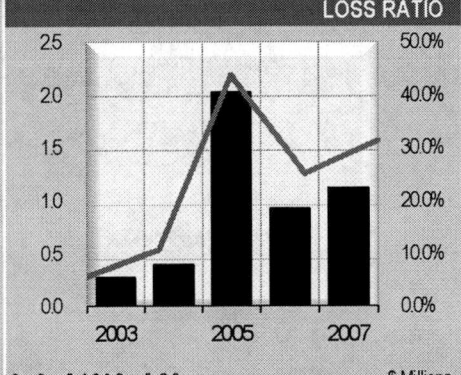

☐ Direct   ▨ Non-Affiliated   ■ Affiliated

See Sec. 3, B.4

L&LAE INCURRED

LOSS RATIO

See Sec. 5, A.3 & Sec. 5, C.2 — $ Millions

UNDERWRITING RESULTS

Direct	$109,890
Non-Affiliated	$2,344,872
Affiliated	$1,458,631
Direct Premiums Written	$3,913,393
Net Premiums Earned	$3,631,141
Operating Expenses Incurred	$3,722,389
Agent Retention	$2,660,897
L&LAE Incurred	$1,156,258
Loss Ratio	31.80%

TransUnion Title Insurance Company

16700 Valley View Ave.
Ste. 275
La Mirada, CA 90638

(626) 307-3180

Formerly Diversified Title Insurance Company

WEBSITE:	STATE OF DOMICILE:
–	California

PRESIDENT:	ESTABLISHED:	JURISDICTION LICENSE(S):
Joseph Vincent McCabe	12/22/1925	1

A Exceptional
Financial Stability Rating®
Demotech, Inc.

NAIC Number:
50849

TRANSUNION TIC

NAIC Group:
TRANSUNION

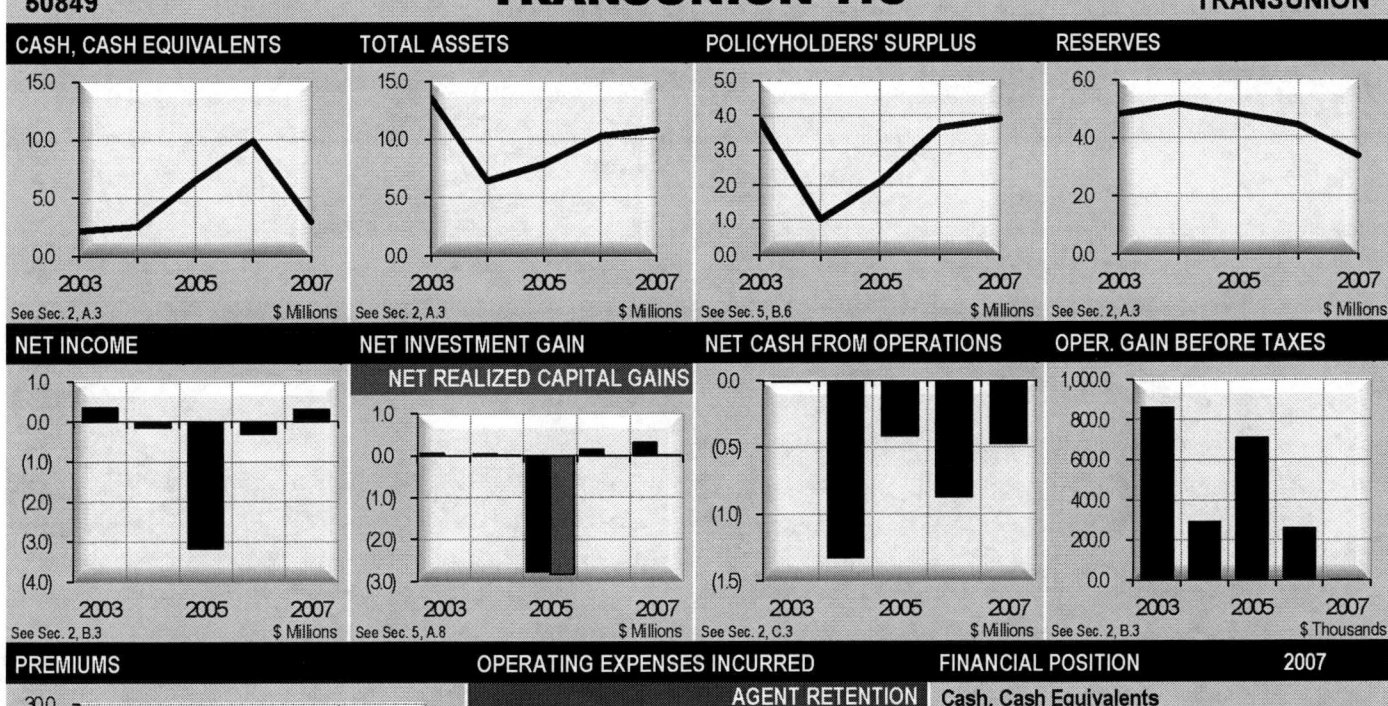

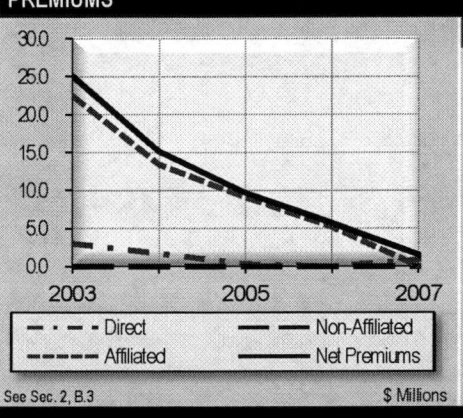

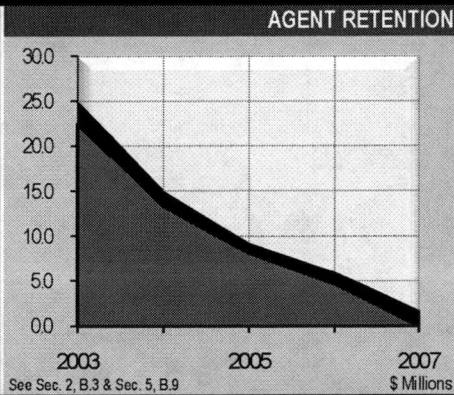

FINANCIAL POSITION	2007
Cash, Cash Equivalents & Short-Term Investments	$2,979,351
Total Assets	$10,769,048
Policyholders' Surplus	$3,880,844
Reserves	$3,369,219
OPERATING RESULTS	
Net Income	$299,381
Net Investment Gain	$314,916
Net Realized Capital Gains	$10,850
Net Cash from Operations	($475,439)
Oper. Gain Before Taxes	$2,091
UNDERWRITING RESULTS	
Direct	$882,460
Non-Affiliated	$0
Affiliated	$0
Direct Premiums Written	$882,460
Net Premiums Earned	$1,517,626
Operating Expenses Incurred	$1,551,230
Agent Retention	$0
L&LAE Incurred	$80,642
Loss Ratio	5.19%

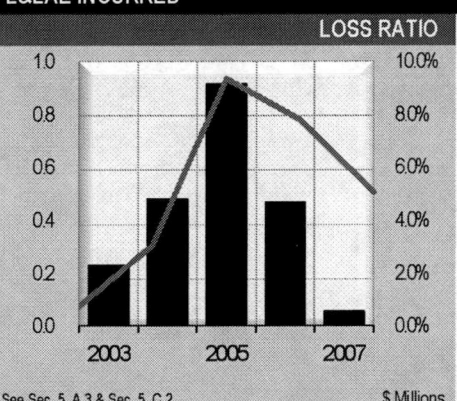

6

United Capital Title Insurance Company

3250 Wilshire Ave., 18th Fl.
Los Angeles, CA 90010

(213) 385-3600

WEBSITE:	STATE OF DOMICILE:
www.landam.com	California

PRESIDENT & CEO:	ESTABLISHED:	JURISDICTION LICENSE(S):
Jerome M. Smolar	3/21/1991	7

A' Unsurpassed
A Prime
Financial Stability Rating®
Demotech, Inc.

NAIC Number:
50041

UNITED CAPITAL

NAIC Group:
LAND AMERICA

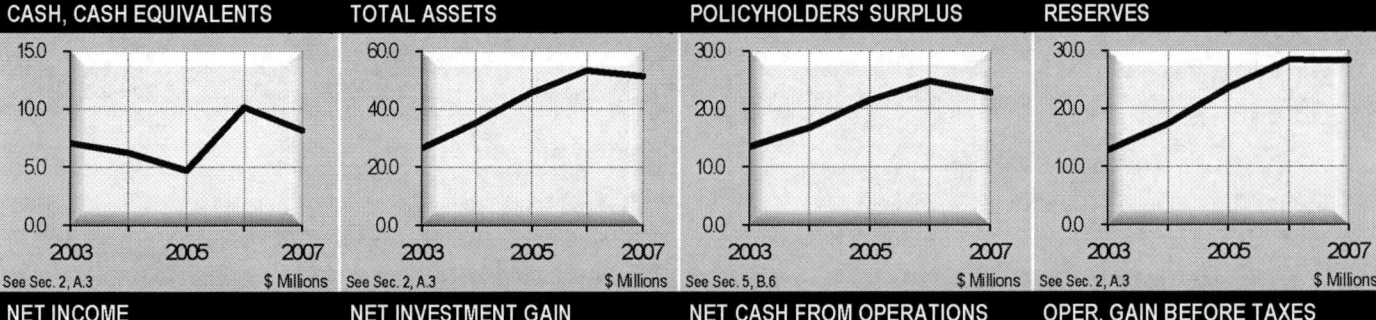

CASH, CASH EQUIVALENTS — See Sec. 2, A.3 — $ Millions
TOTAL ASSETS — See Sec. 2, A.3 — $ Millions
POLICYHOLDERS' SURPLUS — See Sec. 5, B.6 — $ Millions
RESERVES — See Sec. 2, A.3 — $ Millions

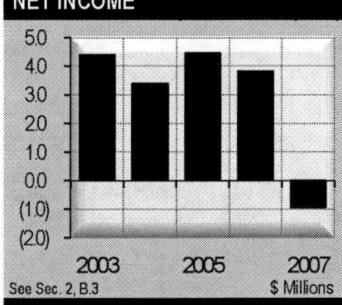
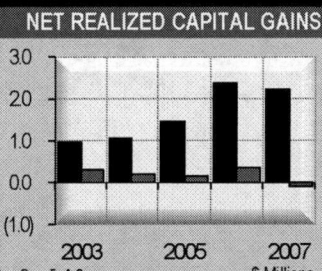
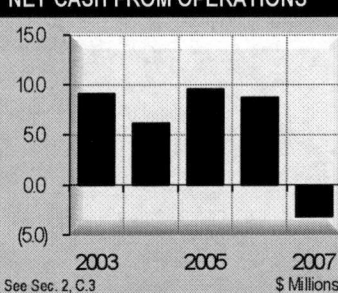
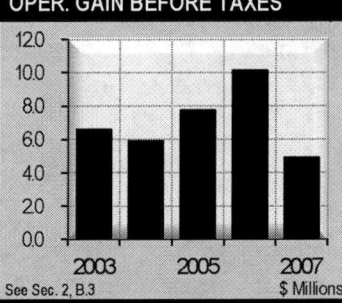

NET INCOME — See Sec. 2, B.3 — $ Millions
NET INVESTMENT GAIN / NET REALIZED CAPITAL GAINS — See Sec. 5, A.8 — $ Millions
NET CASH FROM OPERATIONS — See Sec. 2, C.3 — $ Millions
OPER. GAIN BEFORE TAXES — See Sec. 2, B.3 — $ Millions

PREMIUMS — See Sec. 2, B.3 — $ Millions
Legend: Direct, Affiliated, Non-Affiliated, Net Premiums

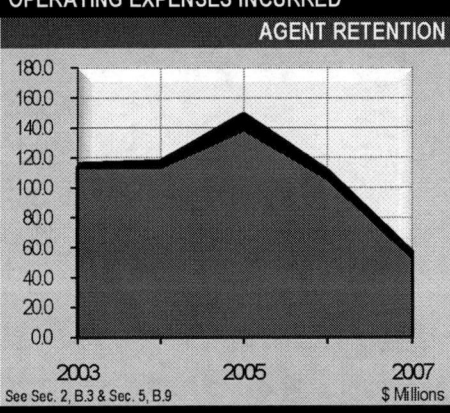

OPERATING EXPENSES INCURRED / AGENT RETENTION — See Sec. 2, B.3 & Sec. 5, B.9 — $ Millions

FINANCIAL POSITION	2007
Cash, Cash Equivalents & Short-Term Investments	$8,132,189
Total Assets	$51,191,665
Policyholders' Surplus	$22,767,542
Reserves	$28,210,811
OPERATING RESULTS	
Net Income	($942,258)
Net Investment Gain	$2,224,269
Net Realized Capital Gains	($108,525)
Net Cash from Operations	($3,226,126)
Oper. Gain Before Taxes	$4,914,966

DIRECT PREMIUMS WRITTEN - YE 2007 — See Sec. 3, B.4
Legend: Direct, Non-Affiliated, Affiliated

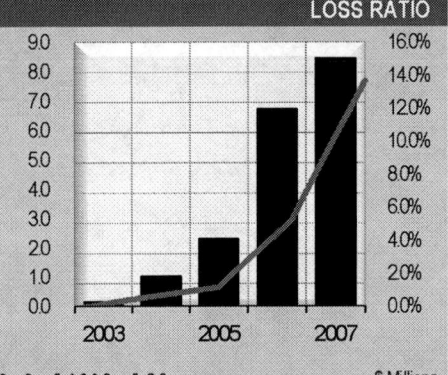

L&LAE INCURRED / LOSS RATIO — See Sec. 5, A.3 & Sec. 5, C.2 — $ Millions

UNDERWRITING RESULTS	
Direct	$2,264,749
Non-Affiliated	$0
Affiliated	$59,156,995
Direct Premiums Written	$61,421,744
Net Premiums Earned	$61,872,009
Operating Expenses Incurred	$56,853,636
Agent Retention	$52,866,551
L&LAE Incurred	$8,465,810
Loss Ratio	13.71%

6

United General Title Insurance Company

8310 S Valley Hwy, Ste. 130
Engelwood, CO 80112

(303) 292-4848

WEBSITE:	STATE OF DOMICILE:
www.ugtic.com	California

PRESIDENT & CEO:	ESTABLISHED:	JURISDICTION LICENSE(S):
Gary Lewis Kermott	9/2/1983	50

A' Unsurpassed
A Prime
Financial Stability Rating®
Demotech, Inc.

NAIC Number:
51624

UNITED GENERAL

NAIC Group:
FIRST AMERICAN

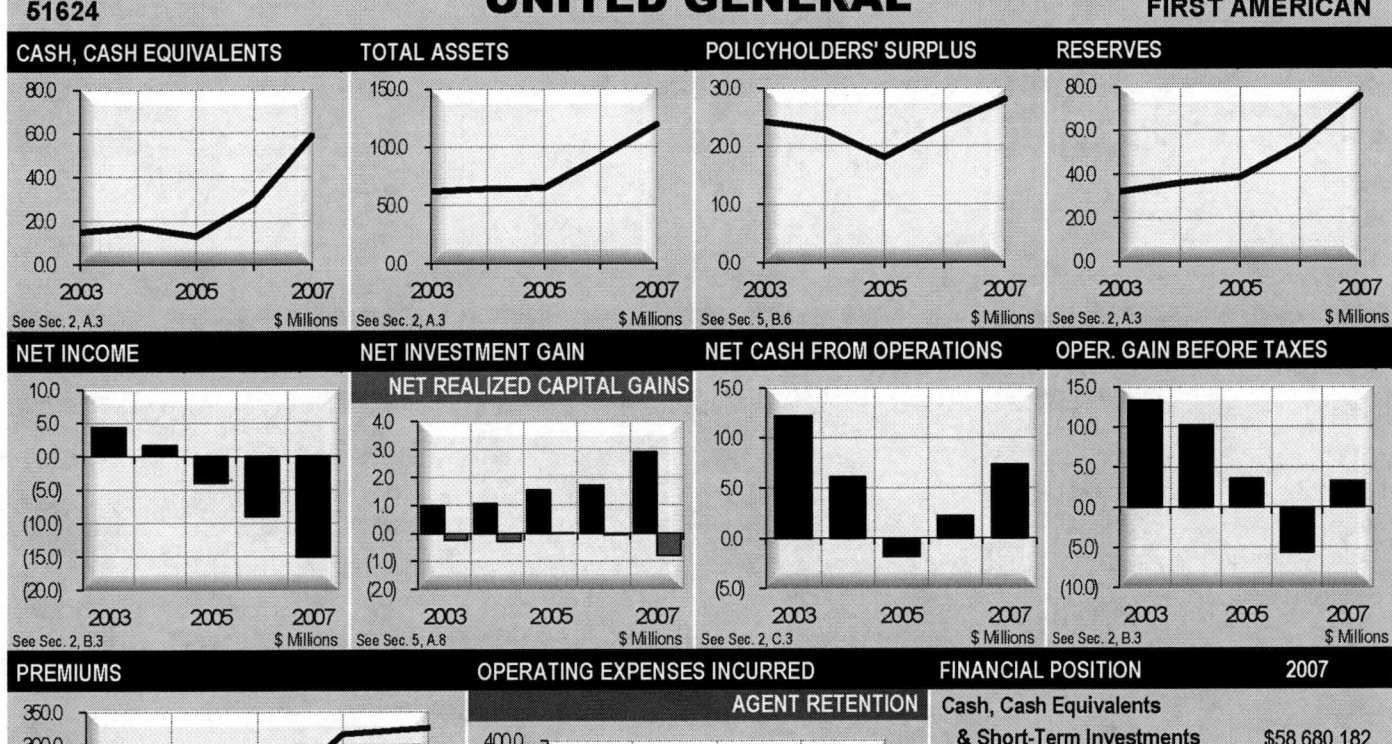

CASH, CASH EQUIVALENTS — See Sec. 2, A.3 — $ Millions

TOTAL ASSETS — See Sec. 2, A.3 — $ Millions

POLICYHOLDERS' SURPLUS — See Sec. 5, B.6 — $ Millions

RESERVES — See Sec. 2, A.3 — $ Millions

NET INCOME — See Sec. 2, B.3 — $ Millions

NET INVESTMENT GAIN / NET REALIZED CAPITAL GAINS — See Sec. 5, A.8 — $ Millions

NET CASH FROM OPERATIONS — See Sec. 2, C.3 — $ Millions

OPER. GAIN BEFORE TAXES — See Sec. 2, B.3 — $ Millions

PREMIUMS — See Sec. 2, B.3 — $ Millions
- – · – Direct
- – – – Non-Affiliated
- – – – – Affiliated
- —— Net Premiums

OPERATING EXPENSES INCURRED / AGENT RETENTION — See Sec. 2, B.3 & Sec. 5, B.9 — $ Millions

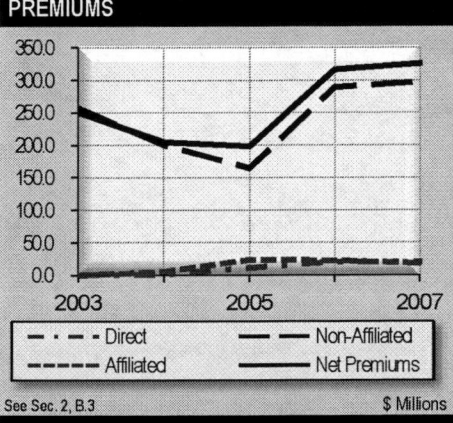

DIRECT PREMIUMS WRITTEN - YE 2007 — See Sec. 3, B.4
- □ Direct ▨ Non-Affiliated ■ Affiliated

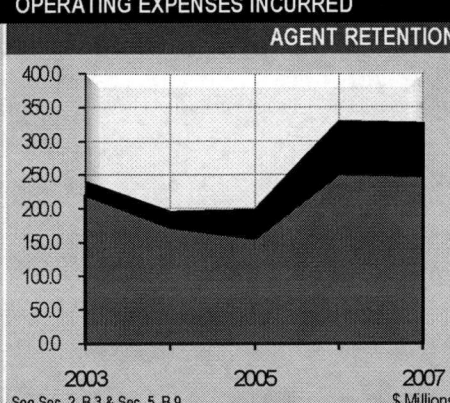

L&LAE INCURRED / LOSS RATIO — See Sec. 5, A.3 & Sec. 5, C.2 — $ Millions

FINANCIAL POSITION	2007
Cash, Cash Equivalents & Short-Term Investments	$58,680,182
Total Assets	$119,101,390
Policyholders' Surplus	$27,974,272
Reserves	$75,893,792
OPERATING RESULTS	
Net Income	($15,142,798)
Net Investment Gain	$2,905,508
Net Realized Capital Gains	($818,526)
Net Cash from Operations	$7,329,890
Oper. Gain Before Taxes	$3,311,262
UNDERWRITING RESULTS	
Direct	$20,969,887
Non-Affiliated	$297,148,060
Affiliated	$18,484,272
Direct Premiums Written	**$336,602,219**
Net Premiums Earned	$324,795,874
Operating Expenses Incurred	$325,885,020
Agent Retention	$248,281,918
L&LAE Incurred	$27,244,717
Loss Ratio	8.28%

6

Washington Title Insurance Company

31 Stewart St.
Floral Park, NY 11001

(516) 488-7100

WEBSITE:	STATE OF DOMICILE:
www.washtitle.com	New York

PRESIDENT:	ESTABLISHED:	JURISDICTION LICENSE(S):
David Gelbard	10/14/1992	1

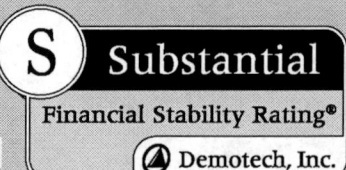

S Substantial
Financial Stability Rating®
Demotech, Inc.

NAIC Number:
50029

WASHINGTON TIC

NAIC Group:
UNAFFILIATED

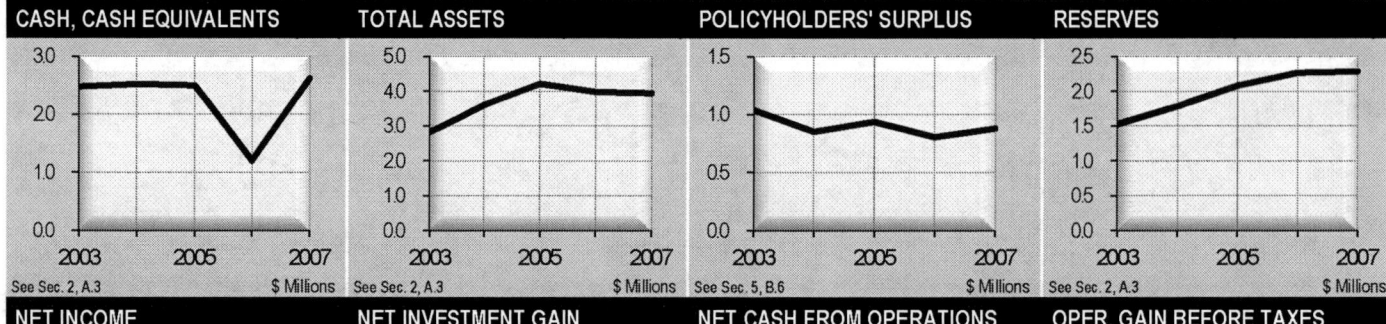

CASH, CASH EQUIVALENTS — See Sec. 2, A.3 — $ Millions
TOTAL ASSETS — See Sec. 2, A.3 — $ Millions
POLICYHOLDERS' SURPLUS — See Sec. 5, B.6 — $ Millions
RESERVES — See Sec. 2, A.3 — $ Millions

NET INCOME — See Sec. 2, B.3 — $ Thousands
NET INVESTMENT GAIN / NET REALIZED CAPITAL GAINS — See Sec. 5, A.8 — $ Thousands
NET CASH FROM OPERATIONS — See Sec. 2, C.3 — $ Thousands
OPER. GAIN BEFORE TAXES — See Sec. 2, B.3 — $ Thousands

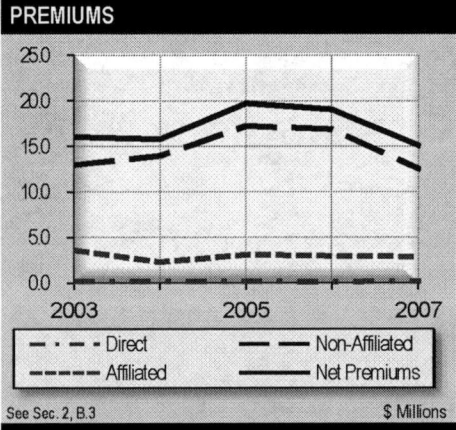

PREMIUMS

--- - Direct
------- Affiliated
—— Non-Affiliated
—— Net Premiums

See Sec. 2, B.3 — $ Millions

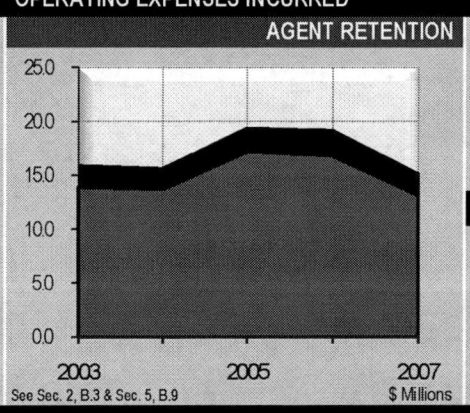

OPERATING EXPENSES INCURRED
AGENT RETENTION

See Sec. 2, B.3 & Sec. 5, B.9 — $ Millions

FINANCIAL POSITION	2007
Cash, Cash Equivalents & Short-Term Investments	$2,616,188
Total Assets	$3,945,060
Policyholders' Surplus	$876,497
Reserves	$2,284,409
OPERATING RESULTS	
Net Income	($110,400)
Net Investment Gain	$144,124
Net Realized Capital Gains	$1,299
Net Cash from Operations	($58,325)
Oper. Gain Before Taxes	$94,311

DIRECT PREMIUMS WRITTEN - YE 2007

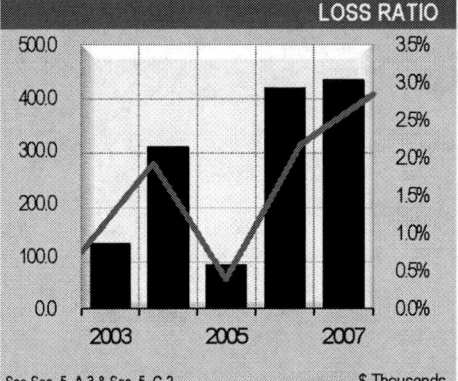

☐ Direct ◼ Non-Affiliated ◼ Affiliated

See Sec. 3, B.4

L&LAE INCURRED
LOSS RATIO

See Sec. 5, A.3 & Sec. 5, C.2 — $ Thousands

UNDERWRITING RESULTS	
Direct	$172,102
Non-Affiliated	$12,559,065
Affiliated	$2,893,006
Direct Premiums Written	$15,624,173
Net Premiums Earned	$15,135,803
Operating Expenses Incurred	$15,093,282
Agent Retention	$13,090,616
L&LAE Incurred	$433,920
Loss Ratio	2.86%

6

Westcor Land Title Insurance Company

201 N New York Ave., Ste. 200
Winter Park, FL 32789

(407) 629-5842

Formerly Nevada Title Insurance Company

WEBSITE:	STATE OF DOMICILE:
www.wltic.com	California

PRESIDENT:	ESTABLISHED:	JURISDICTION LICENSE(S):
Mary O'Donnell	1/11/1993	23

A' Unsurpassed
Financial Stability Rating®
Demotech, Inc.

NAIC Number:
50050

WESTCOR

NAIC Group:
UNAFFILIATED

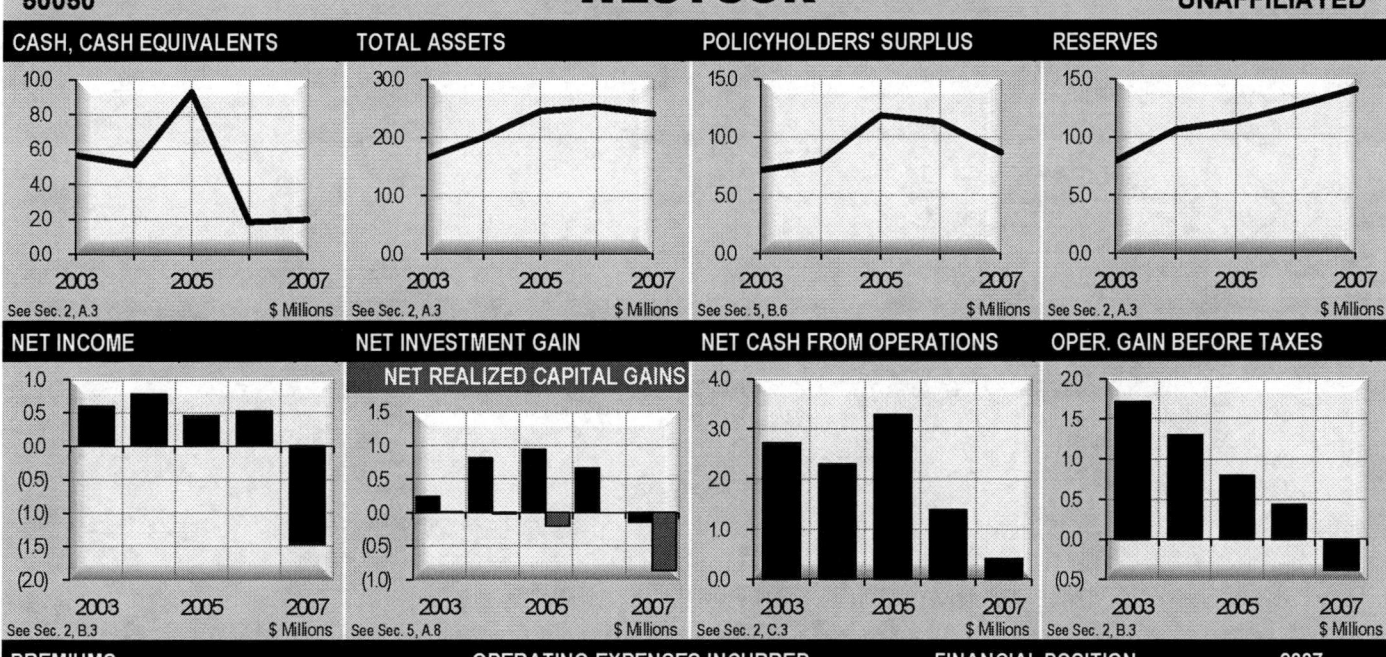

CASH, CASH EQUIVALENTS — See Sec. 2, A.3 — $ Millions

TOTAL ASSETS — See Sec. 2, A.3 — $ Millions

POLICYHOLDERS' SURPLUS — See Sec. 5, B.6 — $ Millions

RESERVES — See Sec. 2, A.3 — $ Millions

NET INCOME — See Sec. 2, B.3 — $ Millions

NET INVESTMENT GAIN / NET REALIZED CAPITAL GAINS — See Sec. 5, A.8 — $ Millions

NET CASH FROM OPERATIONS — See Sec. 2, C.3 — $ Millions

OPER. GAIN BEFORE TAXES — See Sec. 2, B.3 — $ Millions

PREMIUMS

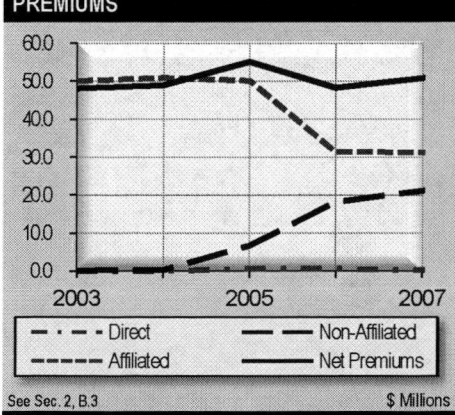

- – · – Direct
- – – – Non-Affiliated
- ----- Affiliated
- —— Net Premiums

See Sec. 2, B.3 — $ Millions

OPERATING EXPENSES INCURRED / AGENT RETENTION

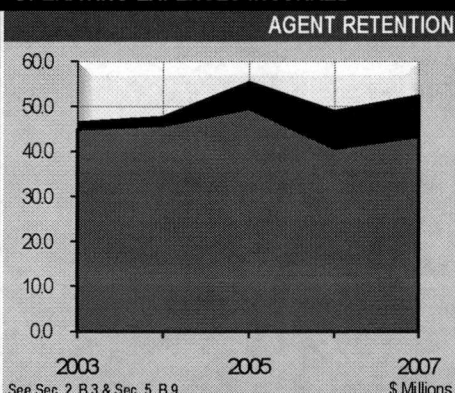

See Sec. 2, B.3 & Sec. 5, B.9 — $ Millions

DIRECT PREMIUMS WRITTEN - YE 2007

☐ Direct ▧ Non-Affiliated ■ Affiliated

See Sec. 3, B.4

L&LAE INCURRED / LOSS RATIO

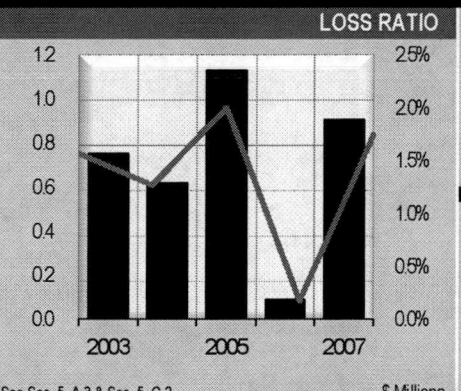

See Sec. 5, A.3 & Sec. 5, C.2 — $ Millions

FINANCIAL POSITION	2007
Cash, Cash Equivalents & Short-Term Investments	$1,971,897
Total Assets	$24,062,681
Policyholders' Surplus	$8,662,482
Reserves	$14,086,905
OPERATING RESULTS	
Net Income	($1,471,179)
Net Investment Gain	($142,361)
Net Realized Capital Gains	($867,387)
Net Cash from Operations	$407,912
Oper. Gain Before Taxes	($386,787)
UNDERWRITING RESULTS	
Direct	$288,117
Non-Affiliated	$21,121,593
Affiliated	$31,217,018
Direct Premiums Written	**$52,626,728**
Net Premiums Earned	$50,819,516
Operating Expenses Incurred	$52,354,461
Agent Retention	$43,363,579
L&LAE Incurred	$912,036
Loss Ratio	1.76%

6

Western National Title Insurance Company

560 S 300 East
Salt Lake City, UT 84111

(801) 578-8888

WEBSITE:	STATE OF DOMICILE:
www.firstam.com	Utah

PRESIDENT:	ESTABLISHED:	JURISDICTION LICENSE(S):
Chester Charles (Chip) Carmer	11/5/1987	1

A Exceptional
Financial Stability Rating®
Demotech, Inc.

NAIC Number: **51225**

WESTERN NATIONAL

NAIC Group: **FIRST AMERICAN**

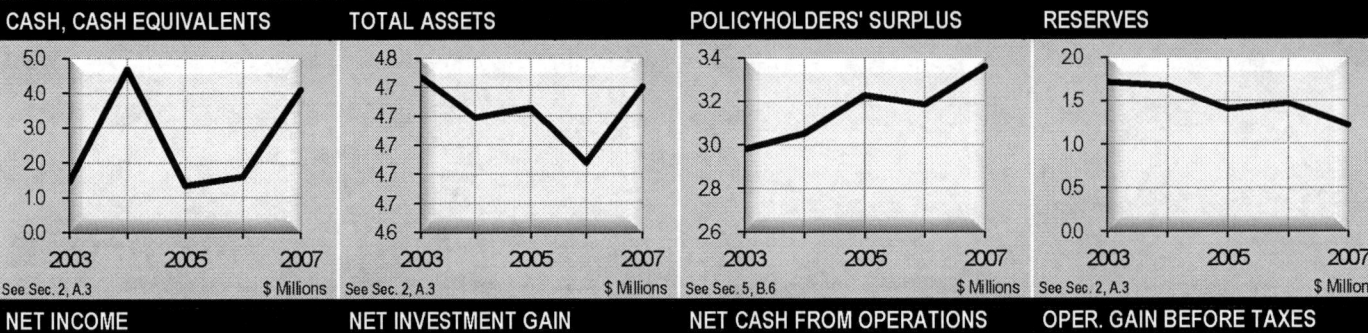

CASH, CASH EQUIVALENTS — See Sec. 2, A.3 — $ Millions
TOTAL ASSETS — See Sec. 2, A.3 — $ Millions
POLICYHOLDERS' SURPLUS — See Sec. 5, B.6 — $ Millions
RESERVES — See Sec. 2, A.3 — $ Millions

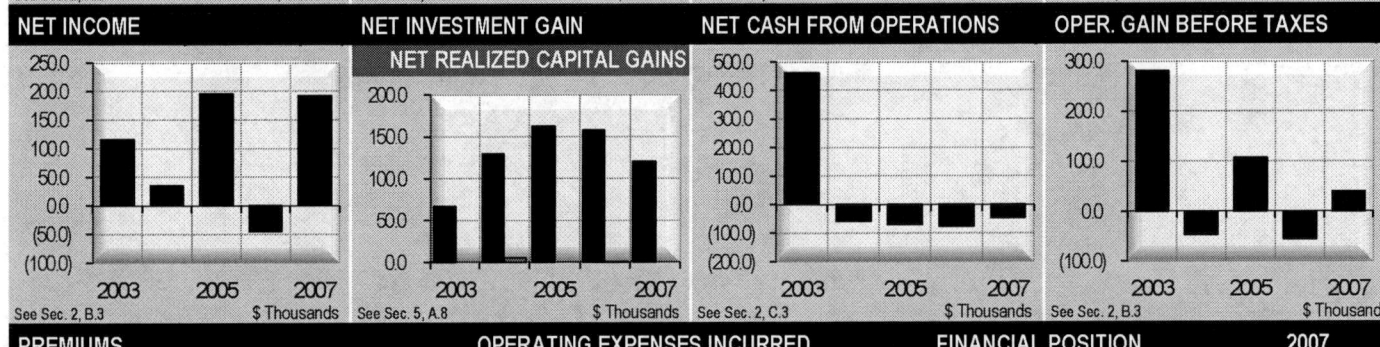

NET INCOME — See Sec. 2, B.3 — $ Thousands
NET INVESTMENT GAIN / NET REALIZED CAPITAL GAINS — See Sec. 5, A.8 — $ Thousands
NET CASH FROM OPERATIONS — See Sec. 2, C.3 — $ Thousands
OPER. GAIN BEFORE TAXES — See Sec. 2, B.3 — $ Thousands

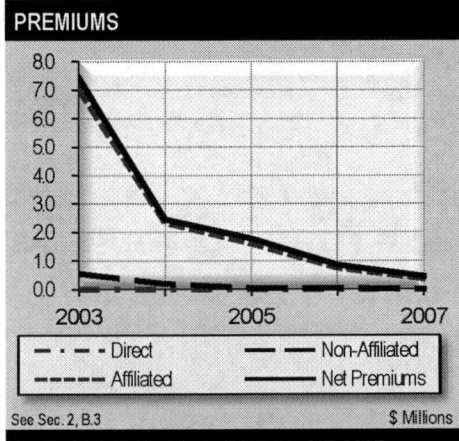

PREMIUMS
Direct / Affiliated / Non-Affiliated / Net Premiums
See Sec. 2, B.3 — $ Millions

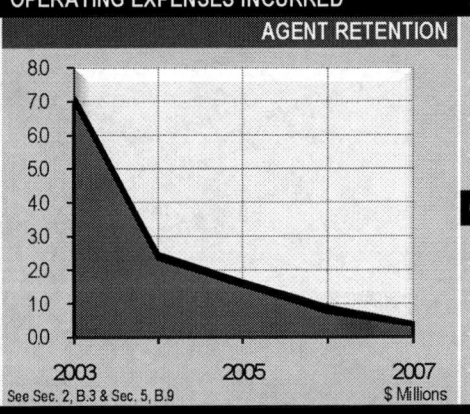

OPERATING EXPENSES INCURRED — AGENT RETENTION
See Sec. 2, B.3 & Sec. 5, B.9 — $ Millions

FINANCIAL POSITION	2007
Cash, Cash Equivalents & Short-Term Investments	$4,081,426
Total Assets	$4,740,303
Policyholders' Surplus	$3,358,552
Reserves	$1,212,643
OPERATING RESULTS	
Net Income	$192,113
Net Investment Gain	$120,546
Net Realized Capital Gains	$0
Net Cash from Operations	($44,950)
Oper. Gain Before Taxes	$40,030

DIRECT PREMIUMS WRITTEN - YE 2007

Direct / Non-Affiliated / Affiliated
See Sec. 3, B.4

L&LAE INCURRED — LOSS RATIO
See Sec. 5, A.3 & Sec. 5, C.2 — $ Thousands

UNDERWRITING RESULTS	
Direct	$0
Non-Affiliated	$8,580
Affiliated	$362,141
Direct Premiums Written	$370,721
Net Premiums Earned	$453,266
Operating Expenses Incurred	$413,236
Agent Retention	$342,509
L&LAE Incurred	($65,757)
Loss Ratio	(14.51)%

6

B.1 JURISDICTION DASHBOARDS - *NEW!*

6

Jurisdiction Dashboards

New for 2008, Jurisdiction Dashboards present a consolidated reference point for jurisdiction resources, market share and trends. These reports provide historical premium and loss activity, along with information regarding the jurisdiction marketplace, including department of insurance contact information and associated Land Title Association where available.

Jurisdiction Dashboards include:

1. **Department of Insurance Information**[1] – Mailing address, phone number, website and executive contact information for the jurisdiction.

2. **Land Title Association**[1] – Mailing address, phone number, website and executive contact for the jurisdiction.

3. **Statutory Premium Reserve (SPR) Requirement**[1] – The current reserve and release to income requirements where available and verifiable for the jurisdiction.

4. **Licensed Underwriters** – Number of Title underwriters licensed in the jurisdiction.
   Note, licensed jurisdictions, which is determined using the Schedule T from the underwriters' collected Form 9 Annual Statement, does not necessarily reflect or limit business activity within the jurisdiction.

5. **Domiciled Underwriters** – Title underwriters domiciled in the jurisdiction.

6. **Market Share by Underwriter** – Direct Premium Written for each Title underwriter with premiums or loss activity in the jurisdiction for either of the prior two years, with their market share within the jurisdiction.

7. **Loss Ratio by Underwriter** – Loss Ratio for each Title underwriter with premiums or loss activity in the jurisdiction for either of the prior two years. The Loss Ratio considers both Losses Incurred and Loss Adjustment Expenses (LAE) Incurred, net of reinsurance recoveries. Unless otherwise noted, all future references to the Loss Ratio include both Losses Incurred and Loss Adjustment Expenses Incurred. See *Section 5, Financial Ratios and Analysis, A.3 Loss Ratio* for further explanation.

8. **Historical Premium Volume** – Historical summarization of Direct Written Premium results for the prior 10 years, with graphic representation for enhanced interpretation.

9. **Historical Loss Ratio** – Historical summarization of Loss Ratio results for the prior 10 years, with graphic representation for enhanced interpretation.

[1]**Source:** Insurance Department, State and Land Title Association websites.

ALABAMA

DEPARTMENT OF INSURANCE INFORMATION	LAND TITLE ASSOCIATION	DOMICILED UNDERWRITERS See Sec. 1	

Alabama Department of Insurance

Dixie Land Title Association, Inc.

Underwriter	NAIC #

Mr. Walter A. Bell
Commissioner of Insurance
201 Monroe St., Ste. 1700
Montgomery, AL 36104
Phone: (334) 269-3550
Fax: (334) 241-4192
www.aldoi.gov

P.O. Box 14806
Baton Rouge, LA 70816
www.dlta.net

None

■ 25 Licensed Underwriters   See Sec. 1

STATUTORY PREMIUM RESERVE (SPR) REQUIREMENTS

Inception:	10% of risk premiums written		
Max Years:	20	Release:	5% per year

MARKET SHARE BY UNDERWRITER   See Sec. 3

2007

	TOTAL DPW	MARKET SHARE	LOSSES INCURRED	MARKET SHARE	LOSS RATIO
1. FIRST AMERICAN TIC	$21.626.004	19.74%	$1.498.066	18.91%	6.50%
2. STEWART TGC	$17.787.058	16.23%	$1.238.423	15.63%	6.96%
3. LAWYERS	$15.913.562	14.52%	$2.809	0.04%	0.02%
4. CHICAGO TIC	$15.474.481	14.12%	$804.269	10.15%	5.12%
5. MISSISSIPPI VALLEY	$13.415.105	12.24%	$682.516	8.61%	5.38%
6. COMMONWEALTH LAND	$9.124.362	8.33%	$1.186.139	14.97%	12.69%
7. FIDELITY NATIONAL	$5.345.457	4.88%	$1.180.536	14.90%	22.11%
8. SOUTHERN TI CORP	$2.459.609	2.24%	$55.597	0.70%	2.38%
9. UNITED GENERAL	$2.298.924	2.10%	$134.694	1.70%	5.60%
10. TICOR (FL)	$1.962.179	1.79%	$254.096	3.21%	13.75%
11. SECURITY UNION	$1.079.032	0.98%	$101.673	1.28%	9.75%
12. TRANSNATION	$647.020	0.59%	$35.500	0.45%	6.18%
13. INVESTORS TIC	$493.747	0.45%	$61.937	0.78%	12.51%
14. SECURITY TG (BALTIMORE)	$490.222	0.45%	$255.723	3.23%	52.43%
15. CONESTOGA	$372.869	0.34%	$0	--	--
16. TICOR	$355.922	0.32%	$102.949	1.30%	22.00%
17. TRANSUNION NATIONAL	$286.370	0.26%	$199.950	2.52%	77.38%
18. NATIONAL LAND	$188.470	0.17%	$0	--	--
19. OLD REPUBLIC NATIONAL	$143.774	0.13%	$128.775	1.63%	35.09%
20. NATIONAL	$82.307	0.08%	$0	--	--
21. WESTCOR	$22.598	0.02%	$0	--	--
22. ATTORNEYS TIF (FL)	$12.139	0.01%	$0	--	--
23. GUARANTEE T&T	$0	--	$0	--	--
24. NORTHEAST INVESTORS	$0	--	$0	--	--
COMPOSITE	$109,581,211	100.00%	$7,923,652	100.00%	7.03%
AVERAGE	$4,565,884		$330,152		

2006

	TOTAL DPW	MARKET SHARE	LOSSES INCURRED	MARKET SHARE	LOSS RATIO
1. FIRST AMERICAN TIC	$21.920.699	19.65%	$1.176.002	14.30%	5.10%
2. STEWART TGC	$17.845.994	16.00%	$3.091.202	37.60%	17.50%
3. LAWYERS	$16.772.492	15.04%	$1.195.317	14.54%	6.65%
4. CHICAGO TIC	$16.543.392	14.83%	$558.572	6.79%	3.35%
5. MISSISSIPPI VALLEY	$13.634.516	12.22%	$588.574	7.16%	4.65%
6. COMMONWEALTH LAND	$9.618.211	8.62%	$569.468	6.93%	5.30%
7. FIDELITY NATIONAL	$4.952.171	4.44%	$900.034	10.95%	18.19%
8. TICOR (FL)	$2.557.593	2.29%	$319.765	3.89%	13.43%
9. SOUTHERN TI CORP	$2.103.221	1.89%	$126.622	1.54%	6.33%
10. UNITED GENERAL	$1.727.862	1.55%	$121.264	1.48%	7.48%
11. SECURITY UNION	$939.354	0.84%	$0	--	--
12. INVESTORS TIC	$824.008	0.74%	$39.216	0.48%	4.91%
13. TRANSNATION	$762.277	0.68%	$10.000	0.12%	1.45%
14. TICOR	$430.038	0.39%	$118.327	1.44%	19.66%
15. SECURITY TG (BALTIMORE)	$332.187	0.30%	($740.177)	(9.00)%	(215.22)%
16. TRANSUNION NATIONAL	$216.558	0.19%	$103.531	1.26%	52.92%
17. OLD REPUBLIC NATIONAL	$132.873	0.12%	$43.287	0.53%	16.84%
18. NATIONAL	$81.878	0.07%	$0	--	--
19. NATIONAL LAND	$77.496	0.07%	$0	--	--
20. CONESTOGA	$57.230	0.05%	$0	--	--
21. ATTORNEYS TIF (FL)	$5.113	0.00%	$0	--	--
22. COMMONWEALTH LAND (NJ	$0	--	$0	--	--
23. NORTHEAST INVESTORS	$0	--	$0	--	--
COMPOSITE	$111,535,163	100.00%	$8,221,004	100.00%	7.23%
AVERAGE	$4,849,355		$357,435		

10-YEAR - DIRECT PREMIUMS WRITTEN (DPW) BY CHANNEL   See Sec. 3

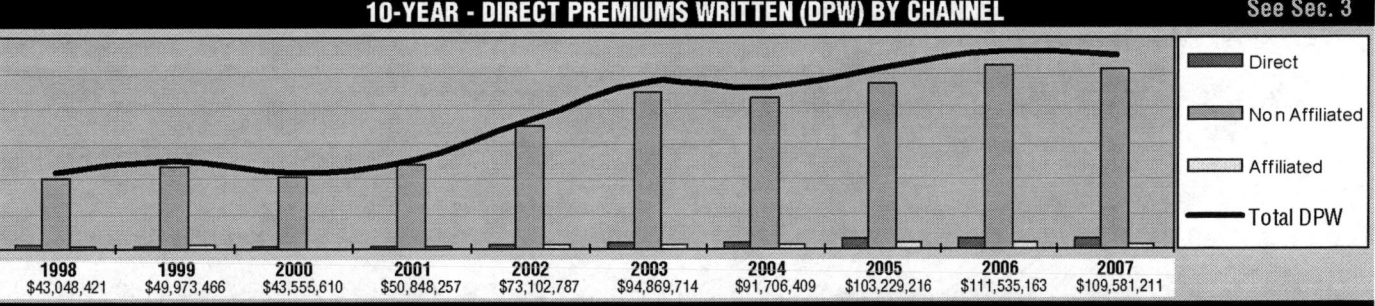

1998	1999	2000	2001	2002	2003	2004	2005	2006	2007
$43,048,421	$49,973,466	$43,555,610	$50,848,257	$73,102,787	$94,869,714	$91,706,409	$103,229,216	$111,535,163	$109,581,211

Legend: Direct / Non Affiliated / Affiliated / Total DPW

10-YEAR - LOSS RATIO   See Sec. 5, A.2

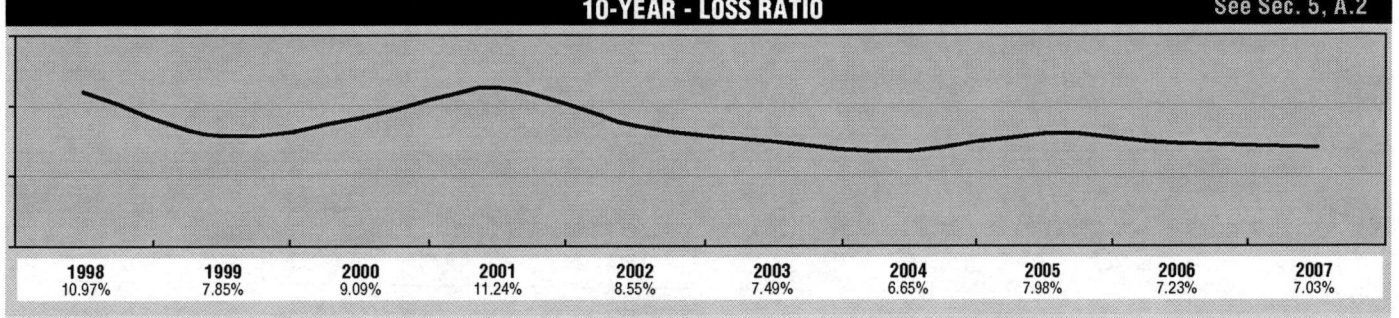

1998	1999	2000	2001	2002	2003	2004	2005	2006	2007
10.97%	7.85%	9.09%	11.24%	8.55%	7.49%	6.65%	7.98%	7.23%	7.03%

6

ALASKA

DEPARTMENT OF INSURANCE INFORMATION	LAND TITLE ASSOCIATION	DOMICILED UNDERWRITERS See Sec. 1	
Alaska Division of Insurance	Alaska Land Title Association	Underwriter	NAIC #

Ms. Linda Hall
Director of Insurance
550 W 7th Ave., Ste. 1560
Robert B. Atwood Building
Anchorage, AK 99501-3567

Phone: (907) 269-7900
Fax: (907) 269-7910
www.dced.state.ak.us/insurance

P.O. Box 241811
Anchorage, AK 99524
www.alaskalandtitle.com

None

■ 11 Licensed Underwriters See Sec. 1

STATUTORY PREMIUM RESERVE (SPR) REQUIREMENTS

Inception:	Not Available		
Max Years:	Not Available	Release:	Not Available

MARKET SHARE BY UNDERWRITER   See Sec. 3

	2007						2006				
	TOTAL DPW	MARKET SHARE	LOSSES INCURRED	MARKET SHARE	LOSS RATIO		TOTAL DPW	MARKET SHARE	LOSSES INCURRED	MARKET SHARE	LOSS RATIO
1. FIRST AMERICAN TIC	$10.814.051	32.80%	$256.495	11.65%	2.28%	1. STEWART TGC	$10.795.880	30.03%	$487.138	53.72%	4.50%
2. STEWART TGC	$8.623.111	26.15%	($35.667)	(1.62)%	(0.41)%	2. FIRST AMERICAN TIC	$10.704.489	29.78%	$131.871	14.54%	1.24%
3. PACIFIC NORTHWEST	$5.533.438	16.78%	$1.622	0.07%	0.03%	3. PACIFIC NORTHWEST	$6.262.198	17.42%	$196.922	21.72%	3.09%
4. OLD REPUBLIC NATIONAL	$3.661.225	11.10%	$81.537	3.70%	2.18%	4. OLD REPUBLIC NATIONAL	$4.455.538	12.39%	$15.050	1.66%	0.33%
5. FIDELITY NATIONAL	$2.662.915	8.08%	$175.277	7.96%	6.61%	5. FIDELITY NATIONAL	$2.008.369	5.59%	($7.048)	(0.78)%	(0.36)%
6. CHICAGO TIC	$1.250.615	3.79%	($5.783)	(0.26)%	(0.28)%	6. CHICAGO TIC	$1.303.440	3.63%	$7.039	0.78%	0.51%
7. LAWYERS	$314.258	0.95%	$1.729.403	78.58%	362.37%	7. LAWYERS	$341.923	0.95%	$61.654	6.80%	13.36%
8. COMMONWEALTH LAND	$75.256	0.23%	$7.500	0.34%	8.35%	8. COMMONWEALTH LAND	$72.463	0.20%	$0	--	--
9. TICOR	$19.276	0.06%	($9.990)	(0.45)%	(30.86)%	9. SECURITY UNION	$2.884	0.00%	$0	--	--
10. UNITED GENERAL	$19.098	0.06%	$0	--	--	10. TICOR	$2.239	0.00%	$8.905	0.98%	51.13%
11. SECURITY UNION	$989	0.00%	$0	--	--	11. TRANSNATION	$693	0.00%	$5.261	0.58%	14.80%
12. TRANSNATION	$0	--	$458	0.02%	11.55%	**COMPOSITE**	$35.950.116	100.00%	$906.792	100.00%	2.49%
COMPOSITE	$32.974.232	100.00%	$2.200.852	100.00%	6.32%	**AVERAGE**	$3.268.192		$82.436		
AVERAGE	$2.747.853		$183.404								

10-YEAR - DIRECT PREMIUMS WRITTEN (DPW) BY CHANNEL   See Sec. 3

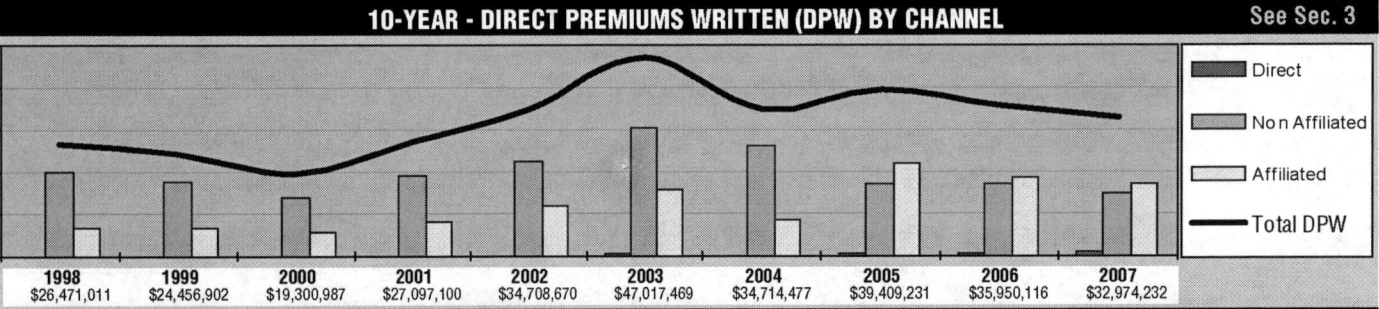

1998	1999	2000	2001	2002	2003	2004	2005	2006	2007
$26,471,011	$24,456,902	$19,300,987	$27,097,100	$34,708,670	$47,017,469	$34,714,477	$39,409,231	$35,950,116	$32,974,232

Legend: Direct, Non Affiliated, Affiliated, Total DPW

10-YEAR - LOSS RATIO   See Sec. 5, A.2

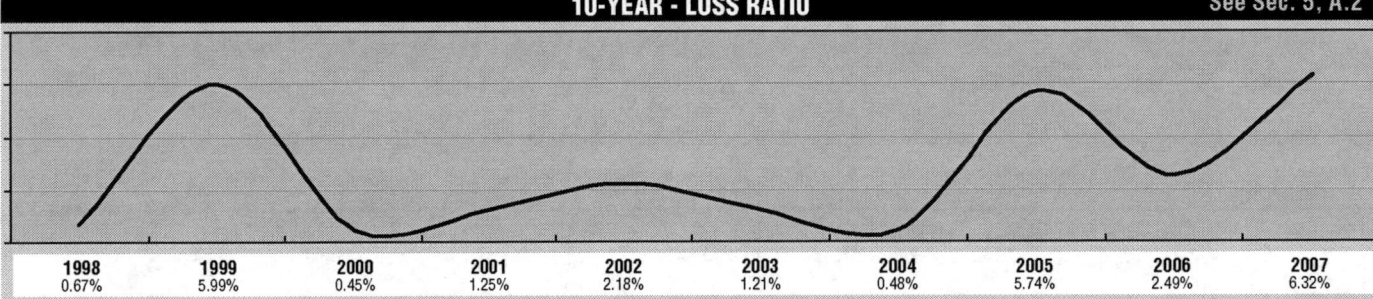

1998	1999	2000	2001	2002	2003	2004	2005	2006	2007
0.67%	5.99%	0.45%	1.25%	2.18%	1.21%	0.48%	5.74%	2.49%	6.32%

6

ARIZONA

DEPARTMENT OF INSURANCE INFORMATION

Arizona Department of Insurance

Ms. Christina Urias
Director of Insurance
2910 N 44th St., Ste. 210
Phoenix, AZ 85018-7256

Phone: (602) 364-3100
Fax: (602) 364-3470
www.id.state.az.us

LAND TITLE ASSOCIATION

Land Title Association of Arizona

7225 W Oakland St.
Chandler, AZ 85226
www.ltaaonline.org

DOMICILED UNDERWRITERS   See Sec. 1

Underwriter	NAIC #
None	

■ 29 | Licensed Underwriters | See Sec. 1

STATUTORY PREMIUM RESERVE (SPR) REQUIREMENTS

Inception:	10 cents per $1,000 of the face amount of net retained liability
Max Years: 20	**Release:** 35% year 1; 15% years 2-3; 10% year 4; 3% years 5-7; 2% years 8-10; 1% years 11-20

MARKET SHARE BY UNDERWRITER   See Sec. 3

2007

	TOTAL DPW	MARKET SHARE	LOSSES INCURRED	MARKET SHARE	LOSS RATIO
1. FIRST AMERICAN TIC	$161,175,326	32.18%	$9,690,896	34.02%	5.06%
2. FIDELITY NATIONAL	$65,926,174	13.16%	$3,758,432	13.19%	4.57%
3. LAWYERS	$51,313,680	10.24%	$238,552	0.84%	0.46%
4. TRANSNATION	$41,510,707	8.29%	$3,133,190	11.00%	5.79%
5. CHICAGO TIC	$33,725,550	6.73%	$2,455,709	8.62%	5.45%
6. COMMONWEALTH LAND	$32,026,902	6.39%	$1,860,075	6.53%	6.30%
7. STEWART TGC	$21,222,189	4.24%	$351,812	1.23%	1.65%
8. TICOR	$18,859,206	3.77%	$4,013,400	14.09%	21.28%
9. SECURITY UNION	$15,997,668	3.19%	$588,071	2.06%	3.68%
10. TITLE RESOURCES	$15,856,339	3.17%	$580,576	2.04%	3.64%
11. UNITED CAPITAL	$15,002,635	3.00%	$668,010	2.34%	4.42%
12. OLD REPUBLIC NATIONAL	$10,045,855	2.01%	$34,500	0.12%	0.33%
13. UNITED GENERAL	$6,618,322	1.32%	$58,693	0.21%	0.90%
14. NORTH AMERICAN	$4,679,454	0.93%	$275,612	0.97%	5.82%
15. WESTCOR	$3,280,714	0.65%	$0	--	--
16. COMMERCE	$1,623,786	0.32%	$0	--	--
17. GUARANTEE T&T	$1,506,068	0.30%	$4,187	0.01%	0.28%
18. TICOR (FL)	$443,037	0.09%	$776,852	2.73%	118.76%
19. TRANSUNION NATIONAL	$81,056	0.02%	$0	--	--
20. INVESTORS TIC	$0	--	$0	--	--
COMPOSITE	**$500,894,668**	**100.00%**	**$28,488,567**	**100.00%**	**4.99%**
AVERAGE	**$25,044,733**		**$1,424,428**		

2006

	TOTAL DPW	MARKET SHARE	LOSSES INCURRED	MARKET SHARE	LOSS RATIO
1. FIRST AMERICAN TIC	$205,378,793	31.70%	$6,883,152	37.63%	2.78%
2. FIDELITY NATIONAL	$78,360,638	12.10%	$5,607,212	30.66%	5.60%
3. LAWYERS	$66,451,110	10.26%	$1,099,010	6.01%	1.65%
4. TRANSNATION	$56,149,825	8.67%	$1,222,935	6.69%	1.78%
5. CHICAGO TIC	$43,249,721	6.68%	$1,588,576	8.69%	2.80%
6. COMMONWEALTH LAND	$34,938,962	5.39%	$749,871	4.10%	1.95%
7. STEWART TGC	$33,445,986	5.16%	($125,523)	(0.69)%	(0.38)%
8. TICOR	$25,713,457	3.97%	$279,631	1.53%	1.11%
9. TITLE RESOURCES	$23,919,927	3.69%	$470,214	2.57%	1.99%
10. SECURITY UNION	$22,559,559	3.48%	$290,129	1.59%	1.31%
11. UNITED CAPITAL	$18,914,399	2.92%	$569,840	3.12%	3.09%
12. OLD REPUBLIC NATIONAL	$12,154,859	1.88%	($320,559)	(1.75)%	(2.57)%
13. UNITED GENERAL	$8,615,514	1.33%	$64,916	0.35%	0.78%
14. NORTH AMERICAN	$7,254,073	1.12%	$112,174	0.61%	1.56%
15. WESTCOR	$4,464,021	0.69%	($22,463)	(0.12)%	(0.59)%
16. TICOR (FL)	$2,298,391	0.35%	($178,882)	(0.98)%	(7.46)%
17. COMMERCE	$2,066,888	0.32%	$0	--	--
18. GUARANTEE T&T	$1,865,334	0.29%	$0	--	--
19. COMMONWEALTH LAND (NJ	$0	--	$0	--	--
20. INVESTORS TIC	$0	--	$0	--	--
COMPOSITE	**$647,801,457**	**100.00%**	**$18,290,233**	**100.00%**	**2.48%**
AVERAGE	**$32,390,073**		**$914,512**		

10-YEAR - DIRECT PREMIUMS WRITTEN (DPW) BY CHANNEL   See Sec. 3

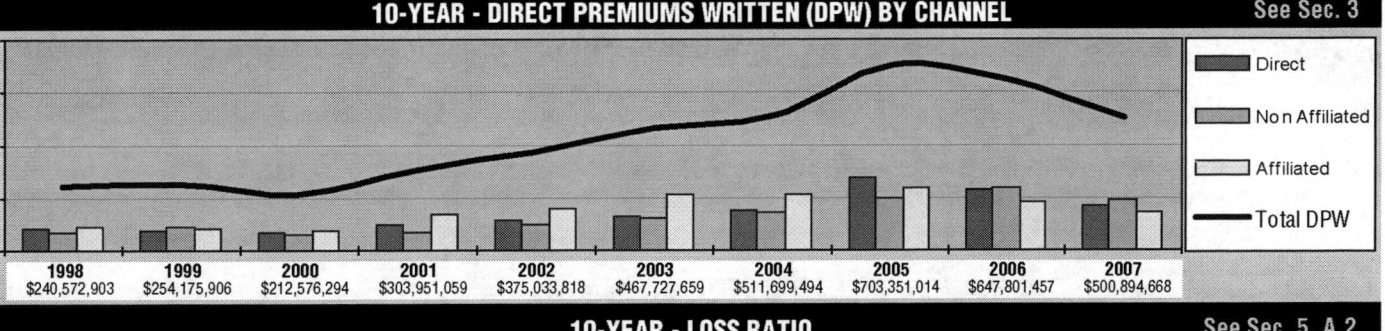

Legend: Direct / Non Affiliated / Affiliated / Total DPW

1998	1999	2000	2001	2002	2003	2004	2005	2006	2007
$240,572,903	$254,175,906	$212,576,294	$303,951,059	$375,033,818	$467,727,659	$511,699,494	$703,351,014	$647,801,457	$500,894,668

10-YEAR - LOSS RATIO   See Sec. 5, A.2

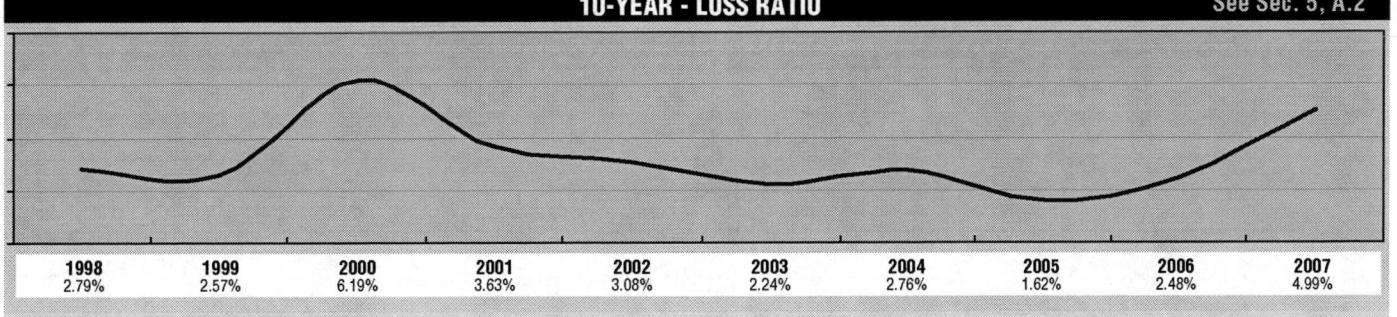

1998	1999	2000	2001	2002	2003	2004	2005	2006	2007
2.79%	2.57%	6.19%	3.63%	3.08%	2.24%	2.76%	1.62%	2.48%	4.99%

6

ARKANSAS

DEPARTMENT OF INSURANCE INFORMATION	LAND TITLE ASSOCIATION	DOMICILED UNDERWRITERS See Sec. 1

Arkansas Department of Insurance

Ms. Julie Benafield Bowman
Insurance Commissioner
1200 W 3rd St.
Little Rock, AR 72201-1904
Phone: (501) 371-2600
Fax: (501) 371-2618
www.insurance.arkansas.gov

Arkansas Land Title Association

P.O. Box 241956
Little Rock, AR 72223
Phone: (501) 228-8237
www.arlta.org

Underwriter	NAIC #
ARKANSAS TIC	50725
25 Licensed Underwriters	See Sec. 1

STATUTORY PREMIUM RESERVE (SPR) REQUIREMENTS

Inception:	10% of risk premium written		
Max Years:	20	Release:	5% per year

MARKET SHARE BY UNDERWRITER　　　　See Sec. 3

2007

	TOTAL DPW	MARKET SHARE	LOSSES INCURRED	MARKET SHARE	LOSS RATIO
1. CHICAGO TIC	$8,923,543	18.22%	$741,364	12.52%	8.18%
2. ARKANSAS TIC	$8,286,400	16.92%	$155,822	2.63%	1.94%
3. LAWYERS	$8,249,937	16.85%	$2,168,901	36.62%	25.48%
4. FIRST AMERICAN TIC	$6,912,956	14.12%	$1,358,850	22.94%	11.04%
5. FIDELITY NATIONAL	$5,185,652	10.59%	$352,380	5.95%	6.96%
6. STEWART TGC	$3,551,730	7.25%	$539,670	9.11%	14.47%
7. OLD REPUBLIC NATIONAL	$2,700,354	5.51%	$260,420	4.40%	8.96%
8. UNITED GENERAL	$2,121,937	4.33%	$242,412	4.09%	11.55%
9. COMMONWEALTH LAND	$715,950	1.46%	$15,138	0.26%	1.92%
10. TICOR	$664,850	1.36%	($151)	0.00%	(0.02)%
11. SOUTHERN TI CORP	$498,173	1.02%	$20,000	0.34%	4.21%
12. SECURITY TG (BALTIMORE)	$415,609	0.85%	$4,932	0.08%	1.18%
13. CENSTAR	$353,239	0.72%	$8,868	0.15%	2.68%
14. GUARANTEE T&T	$176,978	0.36%	$0	--	--
15. TICOR (FL)	$164,642	0.34%	$49,126	0.83%	33.07%
16. SECURITY UNION	$73,416	0.15%	$0	--	--
17. INVESTORS TIC	$31,908	0.07%	$0	--	--
18. ATTORNEYS TIF (FL)	$10,298	0.02%	$0	--	--
19. TRANSUNION NATIONAL	$8,889	0.02%	$0	--	--
20. ALAMO	$0	--	$0	--	--
21. NATIONAL OF NY	$0	--	$0	--	--
22. TRANSNATION	($71,521)	(0.15)%	$5,231	0.09%	(9.32)%
COMPOSITE	**$48,974,940**	**100.00%**	**$5,922,963**	**100.00%**	**10.80%**
AVERAGE	**$2,226,134**		**$269,226**		

2006

	TOTAL DPW	MARKET SHARE	LOSSES INCURRED	MARKET SHARE	LOSS RATIO
1. FIRST AMERICAN TIC	$12,615,672	21.14%	$1,438,323	43.23%	11.52%
2. CHICAGO TIC	$11,704,092	19.61%	$490,532	14.74%	4.26%
3. LAWYERS	$9,660,327	16.19%	$512,376	15.40%	5.18%
4. ARKANSAS TIC	$7,503,726	12.57%	$260,867	7.84%	3.59%
5. FIDELITY NATIONAL	$4,883,058	8.18%	($664)	(0.02)%	(0.01)%
6. STEWART TGC	$4,049,697	6.79%	$296,381	8.91%	7.07%
7. OLD REPUBLIC NATIONAL	$3,152,571	5.28%	$240,775	7.24%	7.18%
8. UNITED GENERAL	$2,231,519	3.74%	$40,423	1.21%	1.88%
9. COMMONWEALTH LAND	$1,544,498	2.59%	($3,990)	(0.12)%	(0.22)%
10. SOUTHERN TI CORP	$964,823	1.62%	$53,795	1.62%	6.11%
11. SECURITY TG (BALTIMORE)	$442,391	0.74%	$0	--	--
12. SECURITY UNION	$310,334	0.52%	$0	--	--
13. CENSTAR	$217,368	0.36%	$0	--	--
14. TICOR (FL)	$212,711	0.36%	$40,635	1.22%	19.51%
15. TRANSNATION	$119,042	0.20%	$10,000	0.30%	8.86%
16. TICOR	$19,139	0.03%	($50,606)	(1.52)%	(64.37)%
17. ATTORNEYS TIF (FL)	$18,479	0.03%	($9,141)	(0.27)%	(50.67)%
18. INVESTORS TIC	$18,105	0.03%	$7,353	0.22%	34.53%
19. COLUMBIAN NATIONAL	$4,265	0.00%	$0	--	--
20. GUARANTEE T&T	$120	0.00%	$0	--	--
21. NORTHEAST INVESTORS	$0	--	$0	--	--
COMPOSITE	**$59,671,937**	**100.00%**	**$3,327,059**	**100.00%**	**5.57%**
AVERAGE	**$2,841,521**		**$158,431**		

10-YEAR - DIRECT PREMIUMS WRITTEN (DPW) BY CHANNEL　　　See Sec. 3

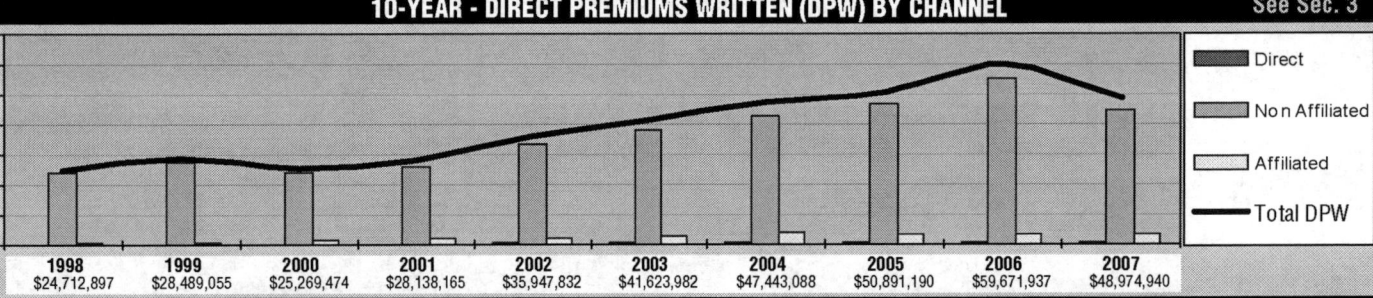

- Direct
- Non Affiliated
- Affiliated
- Total DPW

1998	1999	2000	2001	2002	2003	2004	2005	2006	2007
$24,712,897	$28,489,055	$25,269,474	$28,138,165	$35,947,832	$41,623,982	$47,443,088	$50,891,190	$59,671,937	$48,974,940

10-YEAR - LOSS RATIO　　　See Sec. 5, A.2

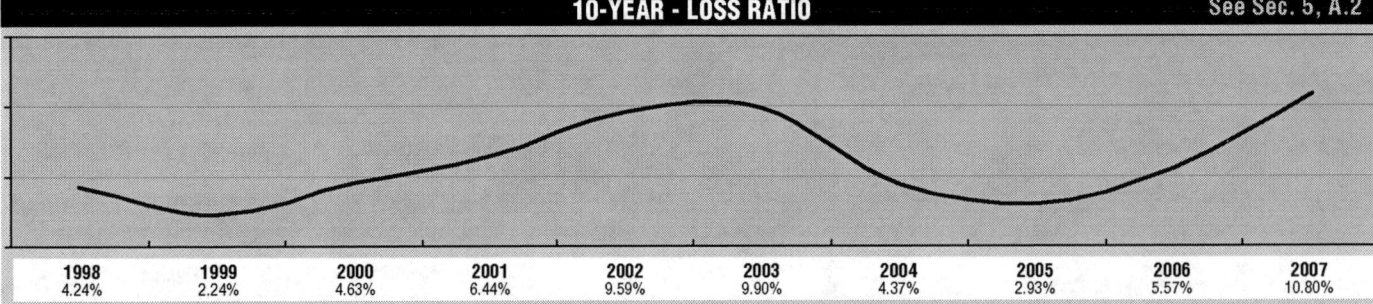

1998	1999	2000	2001	2002	2003	2004	2005	2006	2007
4.24%	2.24%	4.63%	6.44%	9.59%	9.90%	4.37%	2.93%	5.57%	10.80%

CALIFORNIA

DEPARTMENT OF INSURANCE INFORMATION	LAND TITLE ASSOCIATION	DOMICILED UNDERWRITERS See Sec. 1	
California Department of Insurance	California Land Title Association	**Underwriter**	**NAIC #**

California Department of Insurance

Mr. Steve Poizner
Insurance Commissioner
300 Capitol Mall, Ste. 1700
Sacramento, CA 95814
Phone: (916) 492-3500
Fax: (916) 445-5280
www.insurance.ca.gov

California Land Title Association

P.O. Box 13968
Sacramento, CA 95853-3968
Phone: (916) 444-2647
www.clta.org

Underwriter	NAIC #
BRIDGE	50008
COMMERCE	50026
FIDELITY NATIONAL	51586
FIRST AMERICAN TIC	50814
NORTH AMERICAN	50130
SECURITY UNION	50857
TICOR	50067
TRANSUNION TIC	50849
UNITED CAPITAL	50041
UNITED GENERAL	51624
WESTCOR	50050
21 Licensed Underwriters	See Sec. 1

STATUTORY PREMIUM RESERVE (SPR) REQUIREMENTS

Inception:	4.5% of direct premiums written, other income, and reinsurance premiums written less reinsurance premiums ceded
Max Years: 20	Release: 10% years 1-5; 9% years 6-10; 1/2% years 11-20

MARKET SHARE BY UNDERWRITER See Sec. 3

2007

	TOTAL DPW	MARKET SHARE	LOSSES INCURRED	MARKET SHARE	LOSS RATIO
1. FIRST AMERICAN TIC	$714,853,020	35.49%	$72,618,320	29.61%	9.81%
2. CHICAGO TIC	$347,456,053	17.25%	$72,685,545	29.64%	20.57%
3. FIDELITY NATIONAL	$266,779,065	13.24%	$18,986,478	7.74%	7.21%
4. STEWART TGC	$158,458,480	7.87%	$27,844,842	11.35%	17.08%
5. COMMONWEALTH LAND	$103,227,810	5.12%	$11,883,453	4.85%	11.33%
6. OLD REPUBLIC NATIONAL	$90,638,207	4.50%	$5,283,316	2.15%	5.74%
7. TRANSNATION	$69,813,423	3.47%	$16,300,897	6.65%	22.54%
8. LAWYERS	$69,603,607	3.46%	$94,461	0.04%	0.14%
9. NORTH AMERICAN	$58,807,977	2.92%	$1,277,554	0.52%	2.18%
10. UNITED CAPITAL	$43,828,653	2.18%	$5,400,422	2.20%	12.26%
11. UNITED GENERAL	$36,120,568	1.79%	$4,192,315	1.71%	9.99%
12. WESTCOR	$17,766,204	0.88%	$8,566	0.00%	0.05%
13. COMMERCE	$13,971,736	0.69%	($191,146)	(0.08%)	(1.40%)
14. SECURITY UNION	$11,300,377	0.56%	$4,966,456	2.02%	35.74%
15. NATIONAL OF NY	$9,776,776	0.49%	($247,948)	(0.10%)	(2.69%)
16. TICOR	$960,694	0.05%	$4,193,823	1.71%	275.78%
17. TRANSUNION TIC	$882,460	0.04%	($20,659)	0.00%	(1.33%)
18. TICOR (FL)	$0	--	($14,045)	0.00%	(21.98%)
19. COMMONWEALTH LAND (NJ	$0	--	$0	--	--
20. GUARANTEE T&T	$0	--	$0	--	--
21. INVESTORS TIC	$0	--	$0	--	--
22. NATIONS OF NY	$0	--	($780)	0.00%	--
COMPOSITE	**$2,014,245,110**	**100.00%**	**$245,261,870**	**100.00%**	**11.90%**
AVERAGE	**$91,556,596**		**$11,148,267**		

2006

	TOTAL DPW	MARKET SHARE	LOSSES INCURRED	MARKET SHARE	LOSS RATIO
1. FIRST AMERICAN TIC	$885,895,337	33.95%	$32,738,721	26.72%	3.63%
2. CHICAGO TIC	$442,762,472	16.97%	$21,928,562	17.90%	4.98%
3. FIDELITY NATIONAL	$345,418,482	13.24%	$12,875,447	10.51%	3.79%
4. STEWART TGC	$244,049,615	9.35%	$10,531,773	8.60%	4.32%
5. COMMONWEALTH LAND	$114,714,249	4.40%	$12,023,627	9.81%	9.61%
6. TRANSNATION	$101,023,576	3.87%	$9,231,690	7.54%	8.74%
7. OLD REPUBLIC NATIONAL	$100,663,704	3.86%	$2,178,144	1.78%	2.14%
8. UNITED CAPITAL	$100,311,820	3.84%	$5,820,846	4.75%	5.92%
9. LAWYERS	$75,422,298	2.89%	$5,482,794	4.48%	7.31%
10. NORTH AMERICAN	$73,729,782	2.83%	$1,839,281	1.50%	2.53%
11. UNITED GENERAL	$63,087,951	2.42%	$1,422,943	1.16%	2.15%
12. SECURITY UNION	$20,528,991	0.79%	$4,753,144	3.88%	19.63%
13. COMMERCE	$18,098,314	0.69%	$596,800	0.49%	3.44%
14. WESTCOR	$16,761,650	0.64%	$133,804	0.11%	1.23%
15. TRANSUNION TIC	$5,227,050	0.20%	$375,531	0.31%	6.12%
16. TICOR	$1,758,487	0.07%	$516,636	0.42%	23.83%
17. LAND	$71,171	0.00%	$0	--	--
18. NATIONS OF NY	$0	--	$2,000	0.00%	--
19. TICOR (FL)	$0	--	$52,982	0.04%	61.58%
20. ALAMO	$0	--	$0	--	--
21. INVESTORS TIC	$0	--	$0	--	--
22. TITLE IC AMERICA	$0	--	$0	--	--
COMPOSITE	**$2,609,524,949**	**100.00%**	**$122,504,725**	**100.00%**	**4.66%**
AVERAGE	**$118,614,770**		**$5,568,397**		

10-YEAR - DIRECT PREMIUMS WRITTEN (DPW) BY CHANNEL See Sec. 3

Legend: Direct, Non Affiliated, Affiliated, Total DPW

1998	1999	2000	2001	2002	2003	2004	2005	2006	2007
$1,470,604,822	$1,406,648,872	$1,289,489,822	$1,907,198,073	$2,551,408,717	$3,336,797,413	$3,068,170,086	$3,198,269,135	$2,609,524,949	$2,014,245,110

10-YEAR - LOSS RATIO See Sec. 5, A.2

1998	1999	2000	2001	2002	2003	2004	2005	2006	2007
5.21%	5.06%	4.18%	3.70%	3.56%	3.00%	3.83%	4.85%	4.66%	11.90%

COLORADO

DEPARTMENT OF INSURANCE INFORMATION	LAND TITLE ASSOCIATION	DOMICILED UNDERWRITERS See Sec. 1

Colorado Division of Insurance

Ms. Marcy Morrison
Insurance Commissioner
1560 Broadway, Ste. 850
Denver, CO 80202

Phone: (303) 894-7425
Fax: (303) 894-7455
www.dora.state.co.us/insurance

Land Title Association of Colorado

527 Oriole Dr.
P.O. Box 4604
Grand Junction, CO 81502-4604

Phone: (800) 479-3089
www.ltac.org

Underwriter	NAIC #
ALLIANT	12309
ATTORNEYS TGF (CO)	51560
LAND CORP (CO)	50002
29 Licensed Underwriters	See Sec. 1

STATUTORY PREMIUM RESERVE (SPR) REQUIREMENTS

Inception:	$1.00 per policy and 15 cents per $1,000 of the face amount of net retained liability
Max Years:	20	Release:	10% years 1-5; 3.33% years 6-20

MARKET SHARE BY UNDERWRITER   See Sec. 3

2007

	TOTAL DPW	MARKET SHARE	LOSSES INCURRED	MARKET SHARE	LOSS RATIO
1. FIRST AMERICAN TIC	$107,416,152	34.89%	$9,273,596	31.68%	8.53%
2. STEWART TGC	$37,568,983	12.20%	$2,878,391	9.83%	7.81%
3. OLD REPUBLIC NATIONAL	$27,429,019	8.91%	$1,219,789	4.17%	4.39%
4. CHICAGO TIC	$24,933,926	8.10%	$5,028,912	17.18%	19.53%
5. LAND CORP (CO)	$19,602,608	6.37%	$229,149	0.78%	1.16%
6. LAWYERS	$15,625,891	5.08%	$4,905,680	16.76%	27.13%
7. FIDELITY NATIONAL	$12,948,961	4.21%	$942,450	3.22%	4.95%
8. TRANSNATION	$10,286,579	3.34%	$838,305	2.86%	6.22%
9. COMMONWEALTH LAND	$8,099,112	2.63%	$138,092	0.47%	1.45%
10. TITLE RESOURCES	$8,004,091	2.60%	$5,832	0.02%	0.08%
11. ATTORNEYS TGF (CO)	$6,864,905	2.23%	$239,145	0.82%	3.63%
12. UNITED GENERAL	$6,525,501	2.12%	$1,752,607	5.99%	26.19%
13. NORTH AMERICAN	$6,097,041	1.98%	$300,024	1.02%	4.78%
14. ALLIANT	$3,453,141	1.12%	$947,752	3.24%	28.26%
15. SOUTHERN TI CORP	$3,293,782	1.07%	$56,502	0.19%	1.81%
16. WESTCOR	$2,208,182	0.72%	$0	--	--
17. TICOR	$1,820,585	0.59%	$15,787	0.05%	0.81%
18. TITLE IC AMERICA	$1,419,017	0.46%	$152,303	0.52%	11.34%
19. DAKOTA HOMESTEAD	$1,269,727	0.41%	$0	--	--
20. TICOR (FL)	$1,267,698	0.41%	$227,403	0.78%	17.42%
21. SECURITY UNION	$1,034,162	0.34%	($48,364)	(0.17)%	(4.57)%
22. COMMERCE	$340,950	0.11%	$0	--	--
23. CENSTAR	$330,763	0.11%	$12,858	0.04%	3.86%
24. AMERICAN GUARANTY	$350	0.00%	$0	--	--
25. SECURITY TG (BALTIMORE)	$0	--	($1,333)	0.00%	--
26. ALAMO	$0	--	$0	--	--
27. ATTORNEYS TIF (FL)	$0	--	$157,825	0.54%	--
28. CHICAGO TIC (OR)	$0	--	$0	--	--
29. COMMONWEALTH LAND (NJ	$0	--	$0	--	--
30. GUARANTEE T&T	$0	--	$0	--	--
31. INVESTORS TIC	$0	--	$0	--	--
32. NATIONAL OF NY	$0	--	$0	--	--
33. NATIONS OF NY	$0	--	$0	--	--
COMPOSITE	$307,841,126	100.00%	$29,272,705	100.00%	9.12%
AVERAGE	$9,328,519		$887,052		

2006

	TOTAL DPW	MARKET SHARE	LOSSES INCURRED	MARKET SHARE	LOSS RATIO
1. FIRST AMERICAN TIC	$122,365,889	36.64%	$7,210,181	38.61%	5.96%
2. STEWART TGC	$36,977,148	11.07%	$3,001,615	16.07%	8.07%
3. OLD REPUBLIC NATIONAL	$27,137,543	8.12%	$275,154	1.47%	1.01%
4. CHICAGO TIC	$25,946,301	7.77%	$2,415,277	12.93%	9.34%
5. LAND CORP (CO)	$23,128,736	6.92%	($397,160)	(2.13)%	(1.72)%
6. LAWYERS	$16,875,213	5.05%	$1,220,796	6.54%	5.85%
7. FIDELITY NATIONAL	$12,346,815	3.70%	$277,312	1.48%	1.61%
8. UNITED GENERAL	$10,847,387	3.25%	$374,119	2.00%	3.45%
9. TRANSNATION	$10,374,036	3.11%	$656,429	3.51%	5.03%
10. ATTORNEYS TGF (CO)	$9,308,433	2.79%	$465,312	2.49%	5.49%
11. COMMONWEALTH LAND	$8,826,688	2.64%	$615,516	3.30%	5.34%
12. NORTH AMERICAN	$7,275,224	2.18%	$153,539	0.82%	2.08%
13. SOUTHERN TI CORP	$4,149,460	1.24%	$172,969	0.93%	4.42%
14. CENSTAR	$2,892,148	0.87%	$25,539	0.14%	0.93%
15. DAKOTA HOMESTEAD	$2,804,882	0.84%	$0	--	--
16. SECURITY UNION	$2,563,030	0.77%	$24,800	0.13%	0.98%
17. ALLIANT	$2,232,590	0.67%	$0	--	--
18. TICOR (FL)	$1,948,098	0.58%	$92,912	0.50%	4.44%
19. TITLE RESOURCES	$1,921,584	0.58%	$1,090	0.00%	0.06%
20. TITLE IC AMERICA	$1,805,768	0.54%	$910,241	4.87%	49.97%
21. TICOR	$1,781,680	0.53%	$118,096	0.63%	6.28%
22. COMMERCE	$494,890	0.15%	$0	--	--
23. ATTORNEYS TIF (FL)	$0	--	$1,066,361	5.71%	--
24. COMMONWEALTH LAND (NJ	$0	--	$0	--	--
25. INVESTORS TIC	$0	--	$0	--	--
26. SECURITY TG (BALTIMORE)	$0	--	($4,037)	(0.02)%	--
COMPOSITE	$334,003,543	100.00%	$18,676,061	100.00%	5.47%
AVERAGE	$12,846,290		$718,310		

10-YEAR - DIRECT PREMIUMS WRITTEN (DPW) BY CHANNEL   See Sec. 3

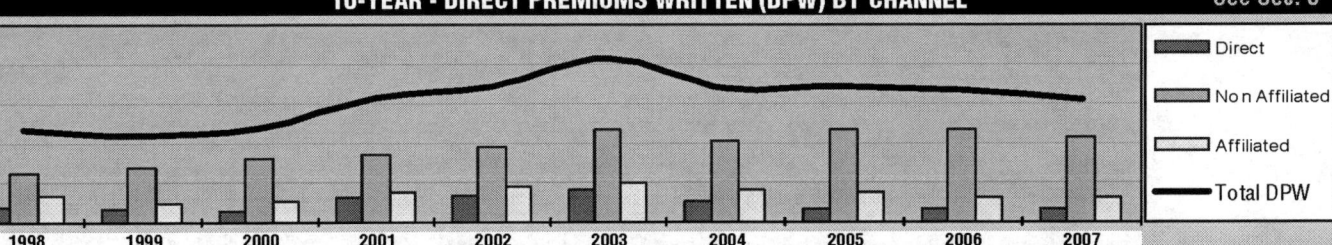

- Direct
- Non Affiliated
- Affiliated
- Total DPW

1998	1999	2000	2001	2002	2003	2004	2005	2006	2007
$231,141,049	$221,352,455	$240,306,480	$314,132,325	$344,373,500	$415,206,787	$338,451,849	$341,762,376	$334,003,543	$307,841,126

10-YEAR - LOSS RATIO   See Sec. 5, A.2

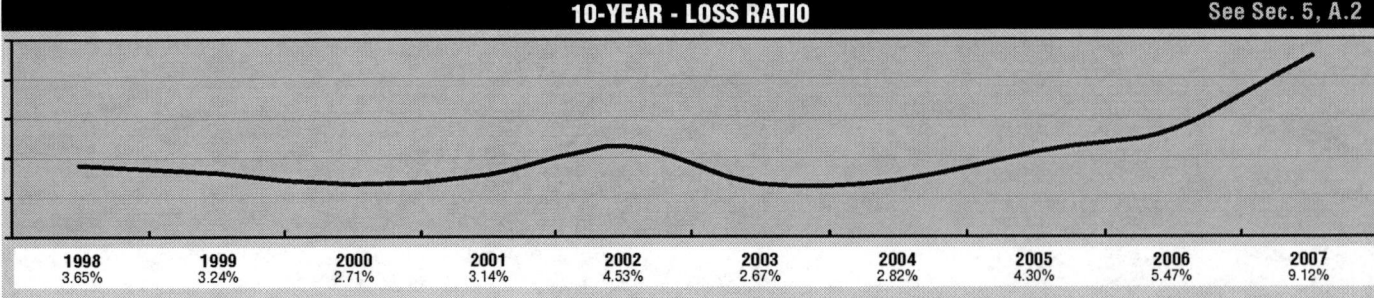

1998	1999	2000	2001	2002	2003	2004	2005	2006	2007
3.65%	3.24%	2.71%	3.14%	4.53%	2.67%	2.82%	4.30%	5.47%	9.12%

6

CONNECTICUT

DEPARTMENT OF INSURANCE INFORMATION	LAND TITLE ASSOCIATION	DOMICILED UNDERWRITERS See Sec. 1

Connecticut Insurance Department — **New England Land Title Association**

Underwriter	NAIC #
CT ATTORNEYS	51268

Mr. Thomas R. Sullivan
Insurance Commissioner
153 Market St.
Hartford, CT 06103
Phone: (860) 297-3800
Fax: (860) 566-7410
www.ct.gov/cid

P.O. Box 743
Norwalk, CT 06852-0743
Phone: (203) 847-6885
www.nelta.org

| | 18 | Licensed Underwriters | See Sec. 1 |

STATUTORY PREMIUM RESERVE (SPR) REQUIREMENTS

Inception:	15 cents per $1,000 of net retained liability
Max Years:	20	Release:	10% years 1-5; 3.33% years 6-20

MARKET SHARE BY UNDERWRITER · See Sec. 3

2007

	TOTAL DPW	MARKET SHARE	LOSSES INCURRED	MARKET SHARE	LOSS RATIO
1. FIRST AMERICAN TIC	$42,442,352	27.51%	$6,253,143	47.11%	14.63%
2. CT ATTORNEYS	$35,170,487	22.79%	$1,525,534	11.49%	4.11%
3. CHICAGO TIC	$14,549,366	9.43%	$4,117,027	31.02%	24.11%
4. FIDELITY NATIONAL	$14,293,633	9.26%	($821,969)	(6.19)%	(5.18)%
5. COMMONWEALTH LAND	$9,866,967	6.39%	$633,898	4.78%	6.10%
6. UNITED GENERAL	$9,830,894	6.37%	$4,194	0.03%	0.05%
7. LAWYERS	$9,257,619	6.00%	$226,117	1.70%	2.09%
8. TICOR	$7,996,243	5.18%	$749,284	5.65%	8.74%
9. STEWART TGC	$5,924,045	3.84%	$154,446	1.16%	2.47%
10. OLD REPUBLIC NATIONAL	$3,443,051	2.23%	($30,013)	(0.23)%	(0.78)%
11. NATIONAL OF NY	$982,520	0.64%	$0	--	--
12. TICOR (FL)	$430,647	0.28%	$461,578	3.48%	101.06%
13. CENSTAR	$86,924	0.06%	$0	--	--
14. TRANSNATION	$21,183	0.01%	$0	--	--
15. AMERICAN GUARANTY	$4,270	0.00%	$0	--	--
16. SECURITY UNION	$659	0.00%	$1,475	0.01%	150.66%
17. EQUITY NATIONAL	$0	--	$0	--	--
18. GUARANTEE T&T	$0	--	$0	--	--
19. INVESTORS TIC	$0	--	$0	--	--
20. NATIONS OF NY	$0	--	($2,000)	(0.02)%	--
COMPOSITE	**$154,300,860**	**100.00%**	**$13,272,714**	**100.00%**	**8.11%**
AVERAGE	**$7,715,043**		**$663,636**		

2006

	TOTAL DPW	MARKET SHARE	LOSSES INCURRED	MARKET SHARE	LOSS RATIO
1. FIRST AMERICAN TIC	$48,376,115	28.83%	$1,839,712	22.68%	3.82%
2. CT ATTORNEYS	$39,559,604	23.57%	$1,978,766	24.39%	4.74%
3. CHICAGO TIC	$17,265,469	10.29%	$1,963,462	24.20%	8.79%
4. FIDELITY NATIONAL	$15,589,610	9.29%	$956,401	11.79%	5.50%
5. COMMONWEALTH LAND	$11,011,429	6.56%	$400,121	4.93%	3.24%
6. LAWYERS	$10,899,589	6.50%	$423,715	5.22%	3.42%
7. TICOR	$9,183,938	5.47%	$152,617	1.88%	1.57%
8. STEWART TGC	$7,234,325	4.31%	$146,901	1.81%	1.90%
9. UNITED GENERAL	$4,977,752	2.97%	$0	--	--
10. OLD REPUBLIC NATIONAL	$2,930,272	1.75%	$366,133	4.51%	10.07%
11. TICOR (FL)	$754,336	0.45%	($41,037)	(0.51)%	(5.15)%
12. TRANSNATION	$24,884	0.01%	$0	--	--
13. SECURITY UNION	$0	--	$3,558	0.04%	912.31%
14. ALAMO	$0	--	$0	--	--
15. EQUITY NATIONAL	$0	--	$0	--	--
16. INVESTORS TIC	$0	--	$0	--	--
17. NATIONS OF NY	$0	--	($77,000)	(0.95)%	--
COMPOSITE	**$167,807,323**	**100.00%**	**$8,113,349**	**100.00%**	**4.47%**
AVERAGE	**$9,871,019**		**$477,256**		

10-YEAR - DIRECT PREMIUMS WRITTEN (DPW) BY CHANNEL · See Sec. 3

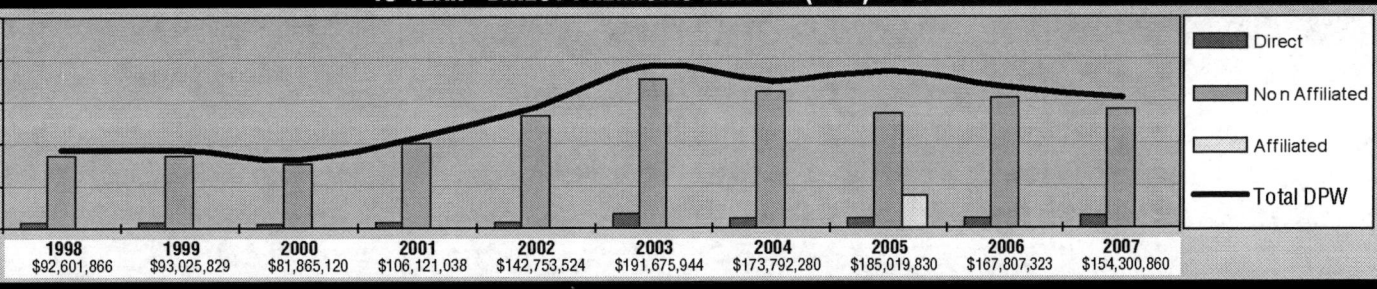

- Direct
- Non Affiliated
- Affiliated
- Total DPW

1998	1999	2000	2001	2002	2003	2004	2005	2006	2007
$92,601,866	$93,025,829	$81,865,120	$106,121,038	$142,753,524	$191,675,944	$173,792,280	$185,019,830	$167,807,323	$154,300,860

10-YEAR - LOSS RATIO · See Sec. 5, A.2

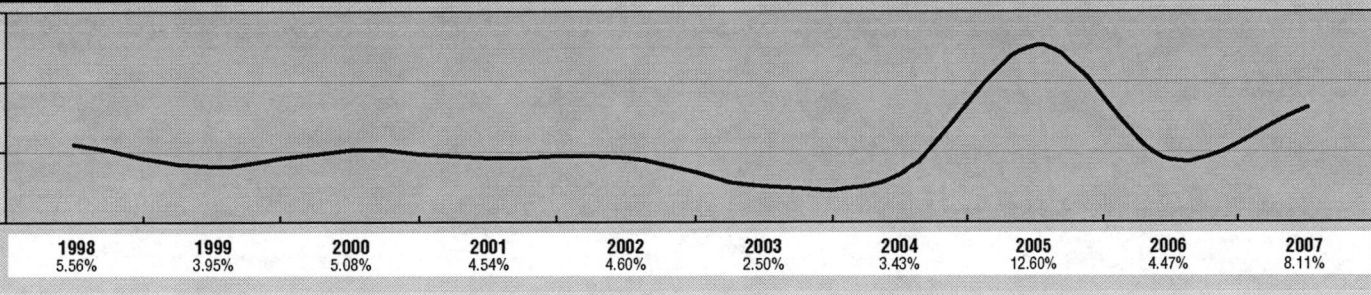

1998	1999	2000	2001	2002	2003	2004	2005	2006	2007
5.56%	3.95%	5.08%	4.54%	4.60%	2.50%	3.43%	12.60%	4.47%	8.11%

6

DELAWARE

DEPARTMENT OF INSURANCE INFORMATION	LAND TITLE ASSOCIATION	DOMICILED UNDERWRITERS See Sec. 1	
		Underwriter	**NAIC #**

Delaware Department of Insurance

Mr. Matthew Denn
Insurance Commissioner
841 Silver Lake Blvd.
Dover, DE 19904

Phone: (302) 674-7300
Fax: (302) 739-5280
www.delawareinsurance.gov

Delaware Title Insurance Rating Bureau

150 Strafford Ave., Ste. 215
Wayne, PA 19087-0393
Phone: (302) 777-4757

None

26 | Licensed Underwriters | See Sec. 1

STATUTORY PREMIUM RESERVE (SPR) REQUIREMENTS

Inception:	10% of risk portion of premiums written	
Max Years:	20	**Release:** 5% per year

MARKET SHARE BY UNDERWRITER
See Sec. 3

2007

	TOTAL DPW	MARKET SHARE	LOSSES INCURRED	MARKET SHARE	LOSS RATIO
1. CHICAGO TIC	$20.675.341	28.50%	$10.287	0.47%	0.07%
2. FIRST AMERICAN TIC	$17.930.230	24.71%	$218.084	9.96%	1.01%
3. COMMONWEALTH LAND	$8.764.984	12.08%	$0	--	--
4. LAWYERS	$7.302.818	10.07%	$1.126.647	51.44%	16.43%
5. TRANSNATION	$6.108.383	8.42%	$287.220	13.11%	4.08%
6. OLD REPUBLIC NATIONAL	$4.092.512	5.64%	$145.469	6.64%	3.00%
7. STEWART TGC	$4.056.812	5.59%	$144.503	6.60%	3.50%
8. SECURITY TG (BALTIMORE)	$1.091.559	1.50%	$31.265	1.43%	2.83%
9. FIDELITY NATIONAL	$755.693	1.04%	$65.785	3.00%	8.62%
10. TICOR	$722.721	1.00%	$29.751	1.36%	2.68%
11. UNITED GENERAL	$438.994	0.61%	$88.536	4.04%	22.30%
12. TICOR (FL)	$184.668	0.25%	$43.304	1.98%	24.14%
13. CONESTOGA	$183.053	0.25%	$0	--	--
14. NORTH AMERICAN	$144.470	0.20%	$0	--	--
15. CENSTAR	$61.996	0.09%	$0	--	--
16. T.A. TITLE	$26.273	0.04%	$0	--	--
17. TRANSUNION NATIONAL	$8.475	0.01%	$0	--	--
18. SECURITY UNION	$362	0.00%	$0	--	--
19. GUARANTEE T&T	$0	--	$0	--	--
20. INVESTORS TIC	$0	--	$0	--	--
21. NATIONAL OF NY	$0	--	$0	--	--
22. NATIONS OF NY	$0	--	($500)	(0.02)%	--
COMPOSITE	**$72,549,344**	**100.00%**	**$2,190,351**	**100.00%**	**3.11%**
AVERAGE	**$3,297,697**		**$99,561**		

2006

	TOTAL DPW	MARKET SHARE	LOSSES INCURRED	MARKET SHARE	LOSS RATIO
1. FIRST AMERICAN TIC	$17.315.734	26.73%	$97.342	17.55%	0.48%
2. STEWART TGC	$9.415.402	14.54%	$63.804	11.51%	0.69%
3. CHICAGO TIC	$9.319.744	14.39%	$49.177	8.87%	0.52%
4. TRANSNATION	$8.754.998	13.52%	$55.063	9.93%	0.56%
5. COMMONWEALTH LAND	$5.660.329	8.74%	($3.327)	(0.60)%	(0.06)%
6. LAWYERS	$5.351.805	8.26%	($21.383)	(3.86)%	(0.48)%
7. OLD REPUBLIC NATIONAL	$4.670.354	7.21%	$14.900	2.69%	0.27%
8. SECURITY TG (BALTIMORE)	$1.497.182	2.31%	$6.833	1.23%	0.48%
9. FIDELITY NATIONAL	$917.743	1.42%	$27.670	4.99%	3.04%
10. TICOR	$770.508	1.19%	$99.193	17.89%	8.11%
11. UNITED GENERAL	$414.268	0.64%	$0	--	--
12. TICOR (FL)	$297.469	0.46%	$166.135	29.96%	58.20%
13. CONESTOGA	$271.594	0.42%	($837)	(0.15)%	(0.32)%
14. CENSTAR	$52.592	0.08%	$0	--	--
15. T.A. TITLE	$47.755	0.07%	$0	--	--
16. SECURITY UNION	$9.079	0.01%	$0	--	--
17. TRANSUNION NATIONAL	$6.067	0.00%	$0	--	--
18. ALAMO	$0	--	$0	--	--
19. INVESTORS TIC	$0	--	$0	--	--
COMPOSITE	**$64,772,623**	**100.00%**	**$554,570**	**100.00%**	**0.80%**
AVERAGE	**$3,409,085**		**$29,188**		

10-YEAR - DIRECT PREMIUMS WRITTEN (DPW) BY CHANNEL
See Sec. 3

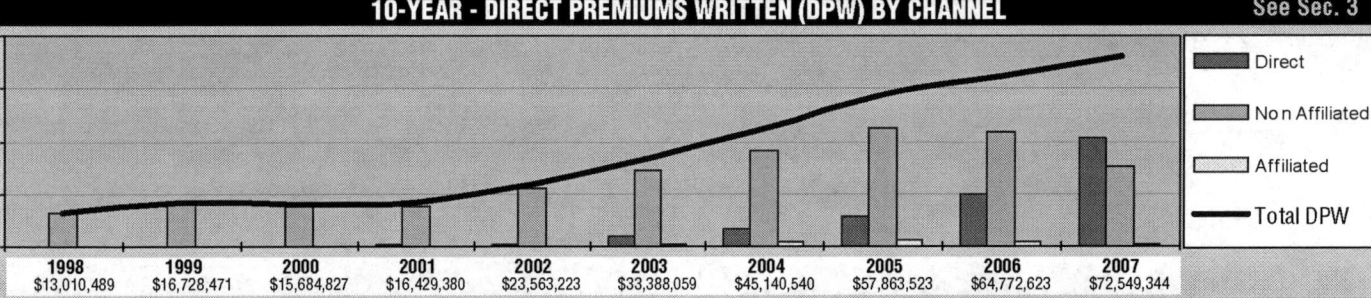

Legend: Direct, Non Affiliated, Affiliated, Total DPW

1998	1999	2000	2001	2002	2003	2004	2005	2006	2007
$13,010,489	$16,728,471	$15,684,827	$16,429,380	$23,563,223	$33,388,059	$45,140,540	$57,863,523	$64,772,623	$72,549,344

10-YEAR - LOSS RATIO
See Sec. 5, A.2

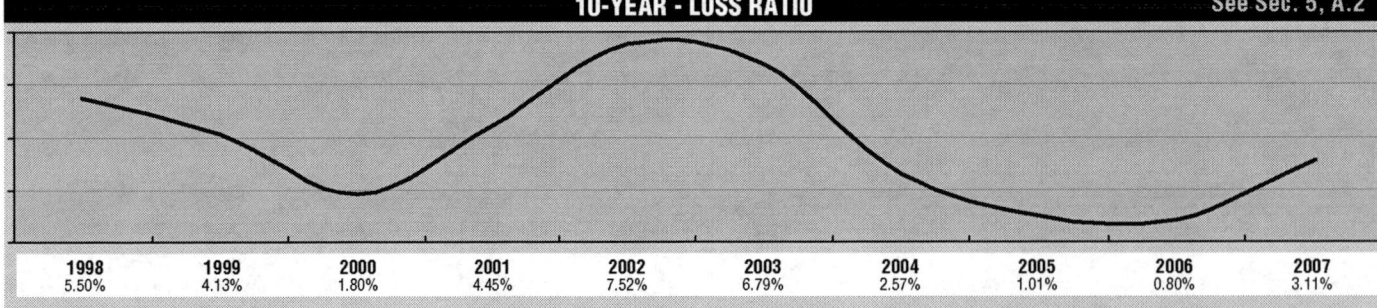

1998	1999	2000	2001	2002	2003	2004	2005	2006	2007
5.50%	4.13%	1.80%	4.45%	7.52%	6.79%	2.57%	1.01%	0.80%	3.11%

6

DISTRICT OF COLUMBIA

DEPARTMENT OF INSURANCE INFORMATION	LAND TITLE ASSOCIATION	DOMICILED UNDERWRITERS See Sec. 1

DEPARTMENT OF INSURANCE INFORMATION

Washington D.C. Department of Insurance, Securities and Banking

Mr. Thomas E. Hampton
Insurance Commissioner
810 First St. NE, Ste. 701
Washington, DC 20002
Phone: (202) 727-8000
Fax: (202) 535-1196
www.disr.dc.gov

LAND TITLE ASSOCIATION

District of Columbia Land Title Association

1015 15th St. NW, Ste. 300
Washington, DC 20005
Phone: (202) 312-5112
www.dclta.com

DOMICILED UNDERWRITERS See Sec. 1

Underwriter	NAIC #
None	
26 Licensed Underwriters	See Sec. 1

STATUTORY PREMIUM RESERVE (SPR) REQUIREMENTS

Inception:	Not Available		
Max Years:	Not Available	Release:	Not Available

MARKET SHARE BY UNDERWRITER See Sec. 3

2007

	TOTAL DPW	MARKET SHARE	LOSSES INCURRED	MARKET SHARE	LOSS RATIO
1. FIRST AMERICAN TIC	$27,406,570	48.24%	$3,084,961	52.78%	10.39%
2. COMMONWEALTH LAND	$8,774,939	15.44%	($105,567)	(1.81)%	(1.16)%
3. CHICAGO TIC	$4,850,180	8.54%	$997,863	17.07%	27.96%
4. LAWYERS	$4,363,742	7.68%	$699,659	11.97%	15.37%
5. STEWART TGC	$4,117,165	7.25%	$127,551	2.18%	2.98%
6. FIDELITY NATIONAL	$2,350,643	4.14%	$389,342	6.66%	16.53%
7. OLD REPUBLIC NATIONAL	$1,557,956	2.74%	($792)	(0.01)%	(0.05)%
8. UNITED GENERAL	$964,754	1.70%	$215,149	3.68%	23.50%
9. CENSTAR	$766,381	1.35%	$31,000	0.53%	4.28%
10. SECURITY TG (BALTIMORE)	$442,689	0.78%	$16,718	0.29%	3.96%
11. TICOR	$368,721	0.65%	$192,213	3.29%	45.29%
12. NORTH AMERICAN	$340,063	0.60%	$0	--	--
13. CONESTOGA	$237,966	0.42%	($1,828)	(0.03)%	(0.77)%
14. SOUTHERN TI CORP	$131,579	0.23%	$161,300	2.76%	128.87%
15. TICOR (FL)	$41,023	0.07%	$33,252	0.57%	87.43%
16. GUARANTEE T&T	$37,974	0.07%	$0	--	--
17. TRANSNATION	$30,396	0.05%	$0	--	--
18. INVESTORS TIC	$27,142	0.05%	$3,803	0.07%	14.53%
19. TRANSUNION NATIONAL	$6,951	0.01%	$0	--	--
20. AMERICAN GUARANTY	$1,640	0.00%	$0	--	--
21. CHICAGO T&T	$0	--	$0	--	--
22. COMMONWEALTH LAND (NJ	$0	--	$0	--	--
23. SECURITY UNION	$0	--	$0	--	--
COMPOSITE	**$56,818,474**	**100.00%**	**$5,844,624**	**100.00%**	**10.00%**
AVERAGE	**$2,470,368**		**$254,114**		

2006

	TOTAL DPW	MARKET SHARE	LOSSES INCURRED	MARKET SHARE	LOSS RATIO
1. FIRST AMERICAN TIC	$27,773,396	47.49%	$1,671,766	41.83%	5.59%
2. COMMONWEALTH LAND	$9,402,731	16.08%	$721,168	18.05%	6.78%
3. CHICAGO TIC	$6,441,160	11.01%	$121,352	3.04%	2.12%
4. LAWYERS	$4,956,429	8.47%	$561,251	14.04%	10.85%
5. STEWART TGC	$4,510,386	7.71%	$389,695	9.75%	9.68%
6. FIDELITY NATIONAL	$2,238,901	3.83%	$193,232	4.84%	8.74%
7. OLD REPUBLIC NATIONAL	$988,291	1.69%	$250,362	6.27%	24.99%
8. UNITED GENERAL	$838,314	1.43%	($6,313)	(0.16)%	(0.81)%
9. TICOR	$324,325	0.55%	$65,000	1.63%	18.57%
10. CONESTOGA	$268,025	0.46%	$27,067	0.68%	10.50%
11. CENSTAR	$263,057	0.45%	$0	--	--
12. NORTH AMERICAN CORP	$216,713	0.37%	$0	--	--
13. SECURITY TG (BALTIMORE)	$157,348	0.27%	$0	--	--
14. SOUTHERN TI CORP	$57,685	0.10%	$0	--	--
15. TRANSUNION NATIONAL	$16,612	0.03%	$0	--	--
16. INVESTORS TIC	$15,043	0.03%	$1,858	0.05%	13.11%
17. TICOR (FL)	$14,706	0.03%	$0	--	--
18. GUARANTEE T&T	$3,215	0.00%	$0	--	--
19. TRANSNATION	$585	0.00%	$0	--	--
20. COMMONWEALTH LAND (NJ	$0	--	$0	--	--
21. NATIONS OF NY	$0	--	($307)	0.00%	--
22. SECURITY UNION	$0	--	$0	--	--
COMPOSITE	**$58,486,922**	**100.00%**	**$3,996,131**	**100.00%**	**6.56%**
AVERAGE	**$2,658,496**		**$181,642**		

10-YEAR - DIRECT PREMIUMS WRITTEN (DPW) BY CHANNEL See Sec. 3

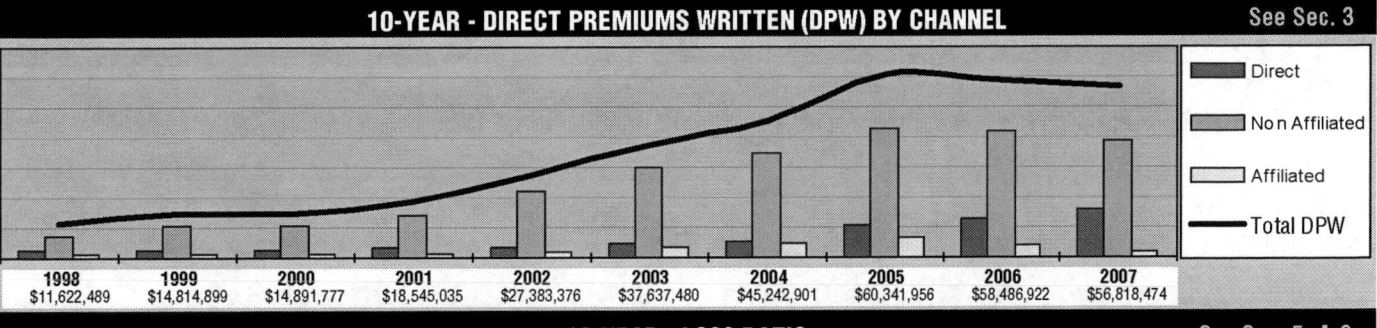

Legend: Direct, Non Affiliated, Affiliated, Total DPW

1998	1999	2000	2001	2002	2003	2004	2005	2006	2007
$11,622,489	$14,814,899	$14,891,777	$18,545,035	$27,383,376	$37,637,480	$45,242,901	$60,341,956	$58,486,922	$56,818,474

10-YEAR - LOSS RATIO See Sec. 5, A.2

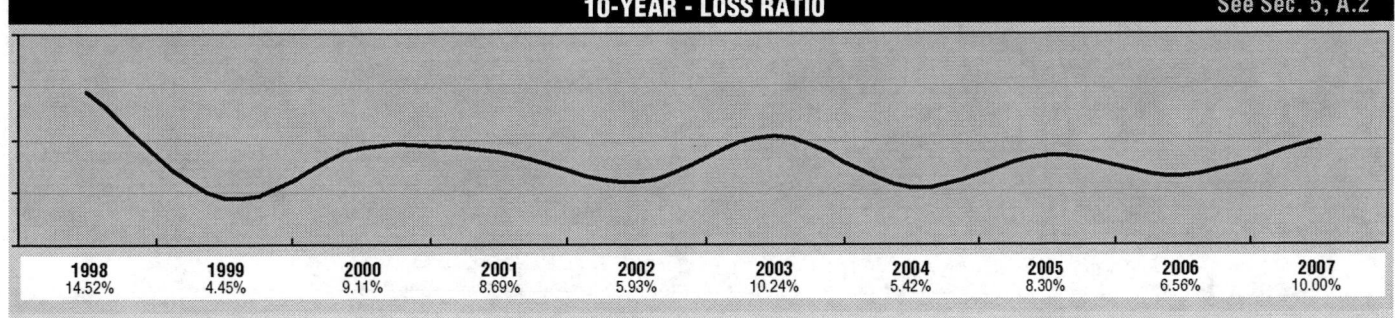

1998	1999	2000	2001	2002	2003	2004	2005	2006	2007
14.52%	4.45%	9.11%	8.69%	5.93%	10.24%	5.42%	8.30%	6.56%	10.00%

6

FLORIDA

DEPARTMENT OF INSURANCE INFORMATION	LAND TITLE ASSOCIATION	DOMICILED UNDERWRITERS See Sec. 1	
Florida Office of Insurance Regulation	**Florida Land Title Association**	**Underwriter**	**NAIC #**

Florida Office of Insurance Regulation

Mr. Kevin McCarty
Commissioner of Insurance Regulation
200 E Gaines St.
Tallahassee, FL 32399-0300
Phone: (850) 413-3100
Fax: (840) 413-2950
www.floir.com

Florida Land Title Association

249 E Virginia St.
Tallahassee, FL 32301
Phone: (850) 681-6422
www.flta.org

Underwriter	NAIC #
ALLIANCE	50035
ATTORNEYS TIF (FL)	50687
K.E.L.	12953
MASON	12550
NATIONAL	50695
31 Licensed Underwriters	See Sec. 1

STATUTORY PREMIUM RESERVE (SPR) REQUIREMENTS

Inception:	30 cents per $1,000 of net retained liability	
Max Years:	20	**Release:** 30% first year; 15% year 2; 10% years 3-4; 5% years 5-6; 3% years 7-8; 2% for years 9-15; 1% years 16-20

MARKET SHARE BY UNDERWRITER　　See Sec. 3

2007

	TOTAL DPW	MARKET SHARE	LOSSES INCURRED	MARKET SHARE	LOSS RATIO
1. FIRST AMERICAN TIC	$334,112,512	19.17%	$36,767,747	24.92%	9.88%
2. ATTORNEYS TIF (FL)	$332,905,096	19.10%	$41,487,066	28.12%	12.33%
3. CHICAGO TIC	$197,274,244	11.32%	$14,144,283	9.59%	6.78%
4. STEWART TGC	$165,292,781	9.49%	$13,288,068	9.01%	7.82%
5. COMMONWEALTH LAND	$156,905,485	9.00%	$10,033,885	6.80%	6.20%
6. FIDELITY NATIONAL	$142,727,205	8.19%	$9,700,689	6.57%	6.33%
7. OLD REPUBLIC NATIONAL	$134,310,695	7.71%	$12,646,201	8.57%	9.11%
8. LAWYERS	$104,776,822	6.01%	$1,052,786	0.71%	0.95%
9. TICOR (FL)	$41,670,435	2.39%	$3,824,993	2.59%	7.46%
10. UNITED GENERAL	$32,391,025	1.86%	$2,384,831	1.62%	7.38%
11. TICOR	$30,485,437	1.75%	$1,364,277	0.92%	4.38%
12. WESTCOR	$18,395,800	1.06%	$142,842	0.10%	0.77%
13. CENSTAR	$17,369,262	1.00%	$137,890	0.09%	0.82%
14. NORTH AMERICAN	$13,503,109	0.77%	$21,470	0.01%	0.16%
15. COMMERCE	$6,789,026	0.39%	$205,714	0.14%	3.11%
16. SOUTHERN TI CORP	$3,831,398	0.22%	$153,450	0.10%	4.11%
17. NATIONAL	$3,328,080	0.19%	($9,014)	0.00%	(0.27)%
18. MASON	$1,552,282	0.09%	$12,200	0.00%	0.80%
19. INVESTORS TIC	$1,428,570	0.08%	($3,810)	0.00%	(0.28)%
20. TITLE RESOURCES	$1,252,864	0.07%	$0	--	--
21. TRANSUNION NATIONAL	$1,195,363	0.07%	$0	--	--
22. K.E.L.	$583,915	0.03%	$0	--	--
23. TRANSNATION	$472,431	0.03%	$11,061	0.00%	2.82%
24. SECURITY UNION	$59,799	0.00%	($574)	0.00%	(0.65)%
25. UNITED CAPITAL	$35,543	0.00%	$35,000	0.02%	73.11%
26. NATIONAL OF NY	$4,027	0.00%	$65,772	0.04%	134.36%
27. AMERICAN GUARANTY	$4,020	0.00%	$0	--	--
28. GUARANTEE T&T	$2,530	0.00%	$731	0.00%	0.05%
29. ALLIANCE	$1,196	0.00%	$66,579	0.05%	122.53%
30. NATIONS OF NY	$0	--	$20,636	0.01%	7,558.97%
31. COMMONWEALTH LAND (NJ	$0	--	$0	--	--
32. EQUITY NATIONAL	$0	--	$0	--	--
33. NORTHEAST INVESTORS	$0	--	$0	--	--
34. SECURITY TG (BALTIMORE)	$0	--	($2,500)	0.00%	--
COMPOSITE	**$1,742,660,952**	**100.00%**	**$147,552,273**	**100.00%**	**8.03%**
AVERAGE	**$51,254,734**		**$4,339,773**		

2006

	TOTAL DPW	MARKET SHARE	LOSSES INCURRED	MARKET SHARE	LOSS RATIO
1. ATTORNEYS TIF (FL)	$460,764,165	18.65%	$22,975,551	24.34%	5.12%
2. FIRST AMERICAN TIC	$442,209,597	17.90%	$12,402,199	13.14%	2.58%
3. CHICAGO TIC	$299,294,534	12.11%	$6,670,396	7.07%	2.14%
4. STEWART TGC	$256,695,399	10.39%	$13,184,386	13.97%	5.09%
5. COMMONWEALTH LAND	$220,699,511	8.93%	$13,654,939	14.46%	5.82%
6. FIDELITY NATIONAL	$211,124,175	8.54%	$5,124,074	5.43%	2.26%
7. OLD REPUBLIC NATIONAL	$186,768,972	7.56%	$12,496,335	13.24%	6.69%
8. LAWYERS	$145,357,690	5.88%	($204,569)	(0.22)%	(0.13)%
9. TICOR (FL)	$93,631,113	3.79%	$2,773,435	2.94%	2.61%
10. UNITED GENERAL	$43,194,714	1.75%	$2,011,157	2.13%	4.83%
11. TICOR	$30,908,912	1.25%	$2,852,561	3.02%	9.34%
12. CENSTAR	$20,864,412	0.84%	$70,541	0.07%	0.35%
13. NORTH AMERICAN CORP	$20,799,790	0.84%	$20,346	0.02%	0.10%
14. WESTCOR	$18,650,121	0.75%	$9,672	0.01%	0.05%
15. COMMERCE	$11,033,480	0.45%	$3,896	0.00%	0.04%
16. SOUTHERN TI CORP	$4,153,524	0.17%	$83,418	0.09%	2.07%
17. NATIONAL	$2,681,567	0.11%	$50,000	0.05%	1.83%
18. INVESTORS TIC	$967,412	0.04%	$24,979	0.03%	2.71%
19. TRANSUNION NATIONAL	$718,401	0.03%	$0	--	--
20. MASON	$482,801	0.02%	$0	--	--
21. TRANSNATION	$25,496	0.00%	$33,886	0.04%	27.18%
22. SECURITY UNION	$3,702	0.00%	$593	0.00%	3.90%
23. ALLIANCE	$1,575	0.00%	$60,972	0.06%	86.08%
24. GUARANTEE T&T	$0	--	$83,210	0.09%	8.77%
25. NATIONS OF NY	$0	--	$28,155	0.03%	--
26. COMMONWEALTH LAND (NJ	$0	--	$0	--	--
27. EQUITY NATIONAL	$0	--	$0	--	--
28. NORTHEAST INVESTORS	$0	--	$0	--	--
29. T.A. TITLE	$0	--	($3,164)	0.00%	--
COMPOSITE	**$2,471,031,063**	**100.00%**	**$94,406,968**	**100.00%**	**3.68%**
AVERAGE	**$85,207,968**		**$3,255,413**		

10-YEAR - DIRECT PREMIUMS WRITTEN (DPW) BY CHANNEL　　See Sec. 3

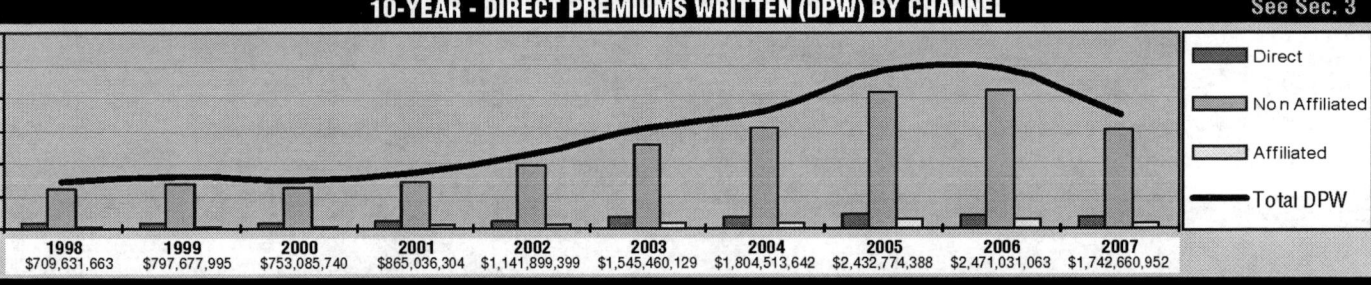

Legend: Direct, Non Affiliated, Affiliated, Total DPW

1998	1999	2000	2001	2002	2003	2004	2005	2006	2007
$709,631,663	$797,677,995	$753,085,740	$865,036,304	$1,141,899,399	$1,545,460,129	$1,804,513,642	$2,432,774,388	$2,471,031,063	$1,742,660,952

10-YEAR - LOSS RATIO　　See Sec. 5, A.2

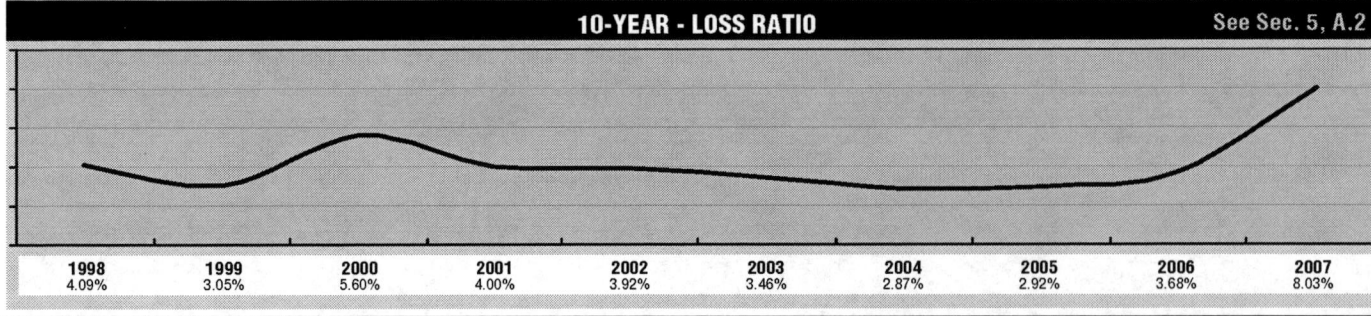

1998	1999	2000	2001	2002	2003	2004	2005	2006	2007
4.09%	3.05%	5.60%	4.00%	3.92%	3.46%	2.87%	2.92%	3.68%	8.03%

6

GEORGIA

DEPARTMENT OF INSURANCE INFORMATION	LAND TITLE ASSOCIATION	DOMICILED UNDERWRITERS See Sec. 1
Georgia Department of Insurance	Dixie Land Title Association, Inc.	Underwriter NAIC #

Mr. John W. Oxendine
Insurance Commissioner
2 Martin Luther King Jr. Dr., Ste. 704
West Tower
Atlanta, GA 30334

Phone: (404) 656-2070
Fax: (404) 657-8542
www.gainsurance.org

P.O. Box 14806
Baton Rouge, LA 70816
Phone: (866) 894-0209
www.dlta.net

None

■ 27   Licensed Underwriters   See Sec. 1

STATUTORY PREMIUM RESERVE (SPR) REQUIREMENTS

Inception:	10% of risk premiums		
Max Years:	20	Release:	5% per year

MARKET SHARE BY UNDERWRITER   See Sec. 3

2007

	TOTAL DPW	MARKET SHARE	LOSSES INCURRED	MARKET SHARE	LOSS RATIO
1. CHICAGO TIC	$51,376,868	18.97%	$6,974,220	22.61%	12.36%
2. FIRST AMERICAN TIC	$47,530,189	17.55%	$5,339,896	17.31%	10.17%
3. LAWYERS	$35,994,238	13.29%	($19,337)	(0.06)%	(0.05)%
4. FIDELITY NATIONAL	$34,403,067	12.70%	$3,837,957	12.44%	10.67%
5. STEWART TGC	$33,816,248	12.49%	$1,864,793	6.05%	5.70%
6. OLD REPUBLIC NATIONAL	$23,598,125	8.71%	$5,350,729	17.35%	21.07%
7. COMMONWEALTH LAND	$12,480,241	4.61%	$1,590,060	5.16%	12.25%
8. UNITED GENERAL	$10,285,618	3.80%	$1,716,922	5.57%	17.06%
9. TICOR	$7,239,747	2.67%	$198,872	0.64%	2.79%
10. SECURITY UNION	$6,036,696	2.23%	$281,394	0.91%	4.84%
11. CENSTAR	$3,121,377	1.15%	$51,049	0.17%	1.76%
12. TICOR (FL)	$2,469,530	0.91%	$2,168,417	7.03%	88.16%
13. SOUTHERN TI CORP	$682,019	0.25%	$134,675	0.44%	21.18%
14. ATTORNEYS TIF (FL)	$633,526	0.23%	$574,982	1.86%	90.22%
15. TITLE IC AMERICA	$398,791	0.15%	$1,930	0.00%	0.52%
16. NATIONAL	$262,162	0.10%	$0	--	--
17. TRANSUNION NATIONAL	$213,280	0.08%	$218,433	0.71%	100.10%
18. TRANSNATION	$166,966	0.06%	$226,996	0.74%	101.33%
19. INVESTORS TIC	$98,634	0.04%	$226,680	0.73%	217.78%
20. AMERICAN GUARANTY	$1,050	0.00%	$0	--	--
21. NATIONAL OF NY	$0	--	$103,974	0.34%	3,215.03%
22. ALAMO	$0	--	$0	--	--
23. BRIDGE	$0	--	$0	--	--
24. COMMONWEALTH LAND (NJ	$0	--	$0	--	--
25. GUARANTEE T&T	$0	--	$0	--	--
26. NATIONS OF NY	$0	--	$0	--	--
27. SECURITY TG (BALTIMORE)	$0	--	$0	--	--
COMPOSITE	**$270,808,372**	**100.00%**	**$30,842,642**	**100.00%**	**10.83%**
AVERAGE	**$10,029,940**		**$1,142,320**		

2006

	TOTAL DPW	MARKET SHARE	LOSSES INCURRED	MARKET SHARE	LOSS RATIO
1. CHICAGO TIC	$60,553,083	19.91%	$4,348,511	18.44%	7.07%
2. FIRST AMERICAN TIC	$49,885,825	16.40%	$3,051,956	12.94%	5.79%
3. FIDELITY NATIONAL	$38,460,772	12.64%	$1,392,988	5.91%	3.53%
4. LAWYERS	$36,901,752	12.13%	$4,848,605	20.56%	12.70%
5. STEWART TGC	$35,312,789	11.61%	$2,785,376	11.81%	7.92%
6. OLD REPUBLIC NATIONAL	$30,680,098	10.09%	$2,520,695	10.69%	7.86%
7. COMMONWEALTH LAND	$17,651,466	5.80%	$1,623,963	6.89%	8.25%
8. UNITED GENERAL	$9,675,041	3.18%	$1,063,978	4.51%	11.69%
9. TICOR	$7,317,134	2.41%	$255,004	1.08%	3.56%
10. SECURITY UNION	$6,074,776	2.00%	$18,567	0.08%	0.32%
11. TICOR (FL)	$4,763,832	1.57%	$952,665	4.04%	20.67%
12. CENSTAR	$3,572,080	1.17%	$0	--	--
13. ATTORNEYS TIF (FL)	$1,035,106	0.34%	$547,719	2.32%	56.17%
14. TITLE IC AMERICA	$753,040	0.25%	($5,173)	(0.02)%	(0.68)%
15. TRANSUNION NATIONAL	$521,669	0.17%	$50,862	0.22%	10.58%
16. TRANSNATION	$410,828	0.14%	$198,354	0.84%	40.78%
17. SOUTHERN TI CORP	$401,478	0.13%	($57,500)	(0.24)%	(15.52)%
18. NATIONAL	$198,063	0.07%	$0	--	--
19. BRIDGE	$7,105	0.00%	$25,000	0.11%	330.82%
20. SECURITY TG (BALTIMORE)	$675	0.00%	$0	--	--
21. ALAMO	$0	--	$0	--	--
22. NORTHEAST INVESTORS	$0	--	$0	--	--
23. INVESTORS TIC	($3,279)	0.00%	($40,299)	(0.17)%	(280.85)%
COMPOSITE	**$304,173,333**	**100.00%**	**$23,581,271**	**100.00%**	**7.56%**
AVERAGE	**$13,224,928**		**$1,025,273**		

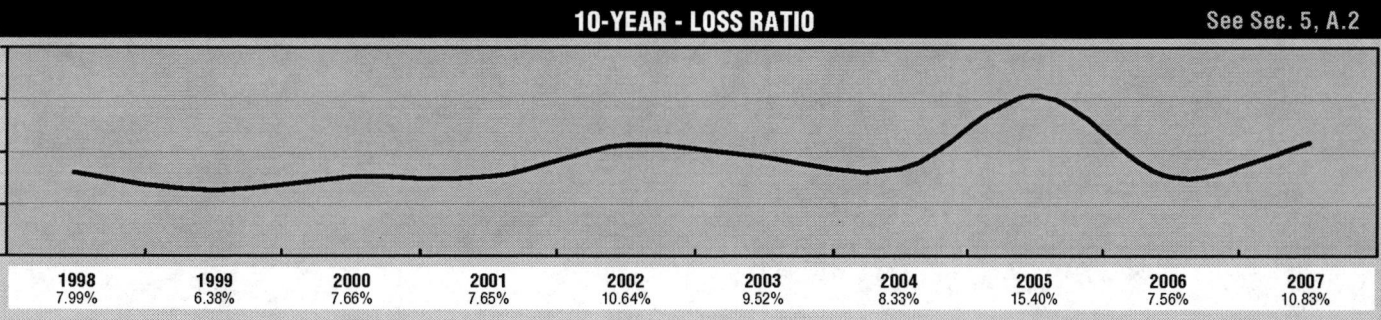

10-YEAR - DIRECT PREMIUMS WRITTEN (DPW) BY CHANNEL   See Sec. 3

Legend: Direct, Non Affiliated, Affiliated, Total DPW

1998	1999	2000	2001	2002	2003	2004	2005	2006	2007
$107,458,211	$132,445,809	$126,884,593	$155,941,826	$199,698,332	$256,064,585	$244,787,827	$273,640,744	$304,173,333	$270,808,372

10-YEAR - LOSS RATIO   See Sec. 5, A.2

1998	1999	2000	2001	2002	2003	2004	2005	2006	2007
7.99%	6.38%	7.66%	7.65%	10.64%	9.52%	8.33%	15.40%	7.56%	10.83%

6

HAWAII

DEPARTMENT OF INSURANCE INFORMATION	LAND TITLE ASSOCIATION	DOMICILED UNDERWRITERS See Sec. 1

Hawaii Insurance Division

Mr. Jeffrey P. Schmidt
Insurance Commissioner
335 Merchant St., Room 213
King Kalakaua Building
Honolulu, HI 96813

Phone: (808) 586-2790
Fax: (808) 586-2806
hawaii.gov/dcca/areas/ins

LAND TITLE ASSOCIATION

No information at time of publication.

DOMICILED UNDERWRITERS See Sec. 1

Underwriter	NAIC #
None	
15 Licensed Underwriters	See Sec. 1

STATUTORY PREMIUM RESERVE (SPR) REQUIREMENTS

Inception:	20 cents per $1,000 of net retained liability	
Max Years:	20	Release: 10% years 1-5; 3.33% years 6-20

MARKET SHARE BY UNDERWRITER   See Sec. 3

2007

	TOTAL DPW	MARKET SHARE	LOSSES INCURRED	MARKET SHARE	LOSS RATIO
1. FIRST AMERICAN TIC	$28,939,729	35.89%	$1,965,452	15.86%	6.84%
2. TICOR	$17,289,315	21.44%	$1,065,493	8.60%	6.14%
3. FIDELITY NATIONAL	$11,584,623	14.37%	$1,907,478	15.39%	16.46%
4. OLD REPUBLIC NATIONAL	$8,815,864	10.93%	$488,819	3.94%	5.45%
5. COMMONWEALTH LAND	$5,876,066	7.29%	$188,981	1.52%	3.21%
6. STEWART TGC	$5,153,738	6.39%	$146,336	1.18%	2.80%
7. CHICAGO TIC	$2,628,833	3.26%	$338,168	2.73%	12.58%
8. LAWYERS	$262,309	0.33%	$6,255,702	50.47%	1,144.37%
9. UNITED GENERAL	$80,980	0.10%	$0	--	--
10. SECURITY UNION	$0	--	$3,871	0.03%	1,325.68%
11. TRANSNATION	$0	--	$35,000	0.28%	1,275.51%
12. GUARANTEE T&T	$0	--	$0	--	--
13. NATIONAL	$0	--	$0	--	--
COMPOSITE	$80,631,457	100.00%	$12,395,300	100.00%	15.29%
AVERAGE	$6,202,420		$953,485		

2006

	TOTAL DPW	MARKET SHARE	LOSSES INCURRED	MARKET SHARE	LOSS RATIO
1. FIRST AMERICAN TIC	$37,303,213	37.13%	$1,485,546	29.76%	4.09%
2. TICOR	$21,216,665	21.12%	$692,113	13.87%	3.29%
3. FIDELITY NATIONAL	$13,997,489	13.93%	$1,233,361	24.71%	8.86%
4. OLD REPUBLIC NATIONAL	$9,705,029	9.66%	$666,794	13.36%	6.71%
5. STEWART TGC	$7,700,869	7.66%	($45,079)	(0.90)%	(0.59)%
6. COMMONWEALTH LAND	$6,334,152	6.30%	$163,133	3.27%	2.35%
7. CHICAGO TIC	$3,727,303	3.71%	$300,943	6.03%	8.44%
8. LAWYERS	$483,934	0.48%	$470,000	9.42%	74.30%
9. SECURITY UNION	$0	--	$24,277	0.49%	761.99%
10. TRANSNATION	$0	--	$0	--	--
COMPOSITE	$100,468,654	100.00%	$4,991,088	100.00%	4.99%
AVERAGE	$10,046,865		$499,109		

10-YEAR - DIRECT PREMIUMS WRITTEN (DPW) BY CHANNEL   See Sec. 3

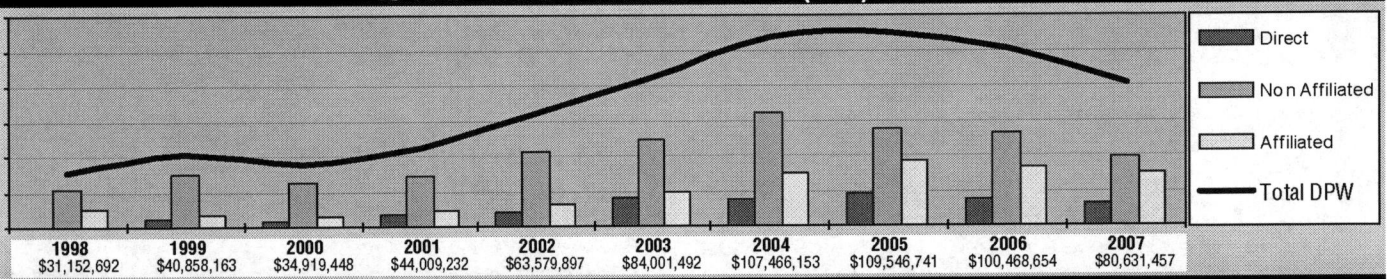

Legend: Direct, Non Affiliated, Affiliated, Total DPW

1998	1999	2000	2001	2002	2003	2004	2005	2006	2007
$31,152,692	$40,858,163	$34,919,448	$44,009,232	$63,579,897	$84,001,492	$107,466,153	$109,546,741	$100,468,654	$80,631,457

10-YEAR - LOSS RATIO   See Sec. 5, A.2

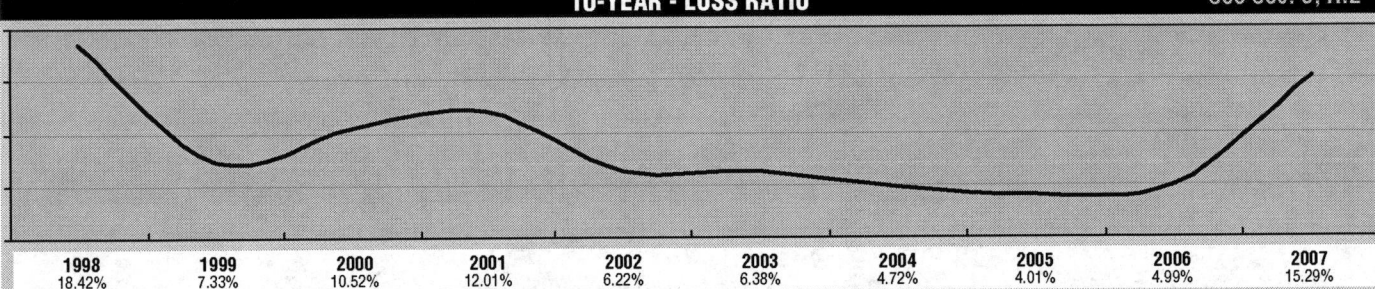

1998	1999	2000	2001	2002	2003	2004	2005	2006	2007
18.42%	7.33%	10.52%	12.01%	6.22%	6.38%	4.72%	4.01%	4.99%	15.29%

6

IDAHO

DEPARTMENT OF INSURANCE INFORMATION	LAND TITLE ASSOCIATION	DOMICILED UNDERWRITERS See Sec. 1

Idaho Department of Insurance | No information at time of publication. | Underwriter   NAIC #

Mr. William W. Deal
Director of Insurance
700 W State St., P.O. Box 83720
Boise, ID 83720-0043
Phone: (208) 334-4250
Fax: (208) 334-4398
www.doi.idaho.gov

None

■ 18   Licensed Underwriters   See Sec. 1

STATUTORY PREMIUM RESERVE (SPR) REQUIREMENTS

Inception:	10% of risk portion of the gross premium or fees received		
Max Years:	10	Release:	All released after 10 years or at policy termination

MARKET SHARE BY UNDERWRITER   See Sec. 3

2007

	TOTAL DPW	MARKET SHARE	LOSSES INCURRED	MARKET SHARE	LOSS RATIO
1. FIRST AMERICAN TIC	$39,780,390	32.85%	$1,107,748	11.93%	2.68%
2. COMMONWEALTH LAND	$16,834,280	13.90%	$181,873	1.96%	1.07%
3. CHICAGO TIC	$15,812,891	13.06%	$937,615	10.10%	5.89%
4. TRANSNATION	$13,292,435	10.98%	$1,047,274	11.28%	7.87%
5. STEWART TGC	$12,822,724	10.59%	$159,264	1.72%	1.25%
6. OLD REPUBLIC NATIONAL	$7,610,543	6.28%	$393,796	4.24%	4.88%
7. TICOR	$5,006,553	4.13%	$120,655	1.30%	2.37%
8. FIDELITY NATIONAL	$4,858,507	4.01%	$57,270	0.62%	1.18%
9. LAWYERS	$3,256,657	2.69%	$4,916,501	52.95%	149.26%
10. UNITED GENERAL	$1,763,322	1.46%	$24,110	0.26%	1.35%
11. PACIFIC NORTHWEST	$65,695	0.05%	$0	--	--
12. SECURITY UNION	$1,721	0.00%	$339,922	3.66%	6,703.25%
13. GUARANTEE T&T	$0	--	$0	--	--
COMPOSITE	**$121,105,718**	**100.00%**	**$9,286,028**	**100.00%**	**7.52%**
AVERAGE	**$9,315,824**		**$714,310**		

2006

	TOTAL DPW	MARKET SHARE	LOSSES INCURRED	MARKET SHARE	LOSS RATIO
1. FIRST AMERICAN TIC	$42,530,189	29.73%	$842,210	23.43%	1.98%
2. CHICAGO TIC	$18,211,705	12.73%	$1,138,626	31.68%	6.33%
3. COMMONWEALTH LAND	$16,393,653	11.46%	$75,704	2.11%	0.44%
4. TRANSNATION	$16,346,310	11.43%	$536,747	14.93%	3.34%
5. STEWART TGC	$16,128,730	11.27%	($11,142)	(0.31%)	(0.07%)
6. OLD REPUBLIC NATIONAL	$13,409,590	9.37%	$598,538	16.65%	4.48%
7. FIDELITY NATIONAL	$7,244,019	5.06%	$30,956	0.86%	0.44%
8. LAWYERS	$5,164,505	3.61%	$70,709	1.97%	1.30%
9. TICOR	$4,655,889	3.25%	$181,410	5.05%	3.88%
10. UNITED GENERAL	$2,907,231	2.03%	$125,091	3.48%	4.35%
11. PACIFIC NORTHWEST	$83,087	0.06%	$0	--	--
12. SECURITY UNION	$0	--	$5,434	0.15%	106.44%
COMPOSITE	**$143,074,908**	**100.00%**	**$3,594,283**	**100.00%**	**2.51%**
AVERAGE	**$11,922,909**		**$299,524**		

10-YEAR - DIRECT PREMIUMS WRITTEN (DPW) BY CHANNEL   See Sec. 3

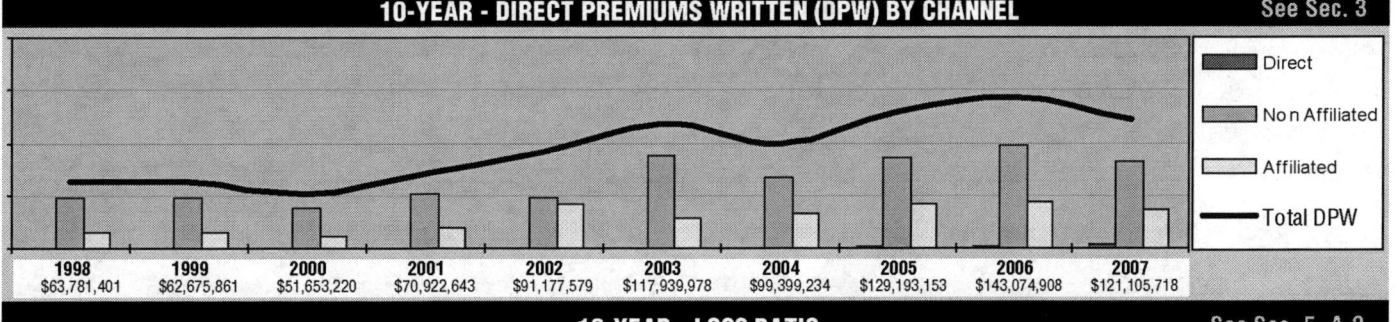

Legend: Direct, Non Affiliated, Affiliated, Total DPW

1998	1999	2000	2001	2002	2003	2004	2005	2006	2007
$63,781,401	$62,675,861	$51,653,220	$70,922,643	$91,177,579	$117,939,978	$99,399,234	$129,193,153	$143,074,908	$121,105,718

10-YEAR - LOSS RATIO   See Sec. 5, A.2

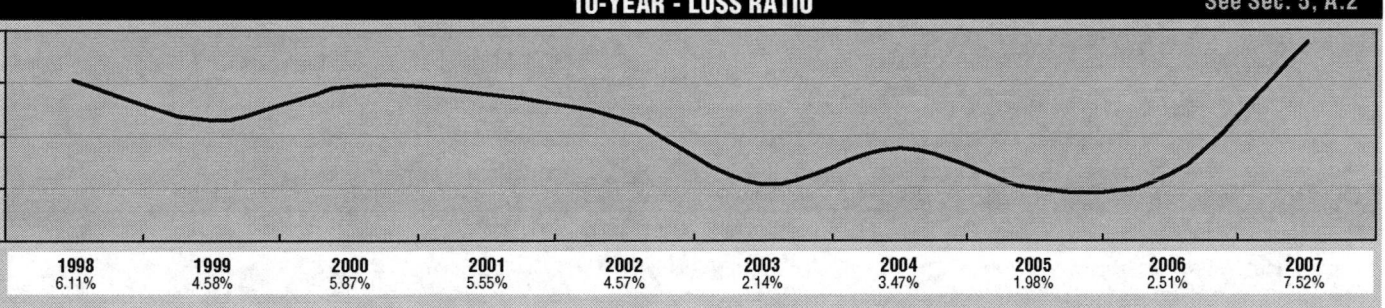

1998	1999	2000	2001	2002	2003	2004	2005	2006	2007
6.11%	4.58%	5.87%	5.55%	4.57%	2.14%	3.47%	1.98%	2.51%	7.52%

6

ILLINOIS

DEPARTMENT OF INSURANCE INFORMATION	LAND TITLE ASSOCIATION	DOMICILED UNDERWRITERS See Sec. 1	

Illinois Division of Insurance

Mr. Michael T. McRaith
Director of Insurance
100 W Randolph, Ste. 9-301
James R. Thompson Center
Chicago, IL 60601-3395

Phone: (312) 814-2420
Fax: (312) 814-5416
www.idfpr.com

Illinois Land Title Association

225 E Cook St.
Springfield, IL 62704
www.illinoislandtitle.org

Underwriter	NAIC #
ATTORNEYS TGF (IL)	50004
CHICAGO T&T	
NATIONAL LAND	50156
26 Licensed Underwriters	See Sec. 1

STATUTORY PREMIUM RESERVE (SPR) REQUIREMENTS

Inception:	12.5 cents per $1,000 of net retained liability
Max Years:	20	Release:	10% years 1-5; 3.33% years 6-20

MARKET SHARE BY UNDERWRITER — See Sec. 3

2007

	TOTAL DPW	MARKET SHARE	LOSSES INCURRED	MARKET SHARE	LOSS RATIO
1. CHICAGO TIC	$97,494,256	31.95%	$14,255,658	40.47%	9.12%
2. FIRST AMERICAN TIC	$83,479,858	27.36%	$8,306,532	23.58%	8.89%
3. STEWART TGC	$30,464,505	9.98%	$2,074,592	5.89%	6.83%
4. TICOR	$25,116,054	8.23%	$2,699,500	7.66%	6.06%
5. LAWYERS	$17,248,318	5.65%	$757,009	2.15%	3.15%
6. ATTORNEYS TGF (IL)	$10,633,487	3.48%	$1,605,519	4.56%	7.98%
7. FIDELITY NATIONAL	$10,550,473	3.46%	$1,211,777	3.44%	11.47%
8. UNITED GENERAL	$5,603,186	1.84%	$264,674	0.75%	4.96%
9. COMMONWEALTH LAND	$5,428,712	1.78%	$1,343,213	3.81%	22.65%
10. ATTORNEYS TIF (FL)	$5,356,039	1.76%	$582,180	1.65%	10.17%
11. OLD REPUBLIC NATIONAL	$3,964,891	1.30%	$1,035,256	2.94%	22.74%
12. SECURITY UNION	$1,844,466	0.60%	$207,663	0.59%	10.74%
13. INVESTORS TIC	$1,655,763	0.54%	$21,999	0.06%	1.43%
14. GUARANTEE T&T	$1,628,557	0.53%	$559,736	1.59%	30.14%
15. NATIONAL LAND	$1,346,879	0.44%	$31,000	0.09%	2.38%
16. PACIFIC NORTHWEST	$974,387	0.32%	$1,554	0.00%	0.16%
17. TRANSNATION	$890,298	0.29%	$180,308	0.51%	23.57%
18. COMMERCE	$868,058	0.28%	$0	--	--
19. NORTH AMERICAN	$456,432	0.15%	$7,500	0.02%	1.78%
20. TRANSUNION NATIONAL	$116,440	0.04%	$22,364	0.06%	22.10%
21. TITLE IC AMERICA	$3,859	0.00%	$10,000	0.03%	274.20%
22. AMERICAN GUARANTY	$3,768	0.00%	$0	--	--
23. TICOR (FL)	$3,527	0.00%	$50,525	0.14%	152.40%
24. CHICAGO T&T	$0	--	$0	--	--
25. COMMONWEALTH LAND (NJ	$0	--	$0	--	--
26. NATIONAL OF NY	$0	--	$0	--	--
27. NORTHEAST INVESTORS	$0	--	$0	--	--
COMPOSITE	$305,132,213	100.00%	$35,228,559	100.00%	7.72%
AVERAGE	$11,301,193		$1,304,761		

2006

	TOTAL DPW	MARKET SHARE	LOSSES INCURRED	MARKET SHARE	LOSS RATIO
1. CHICAGO TIC	$122,525,873	34.84%	$8,964,316	26.97%	4.73%
2. FIRST AMERICAN TIC	$84,071,692	23.90%	$8,372,973	25.19%	9.27%
3. STEWART TGC	$34,846,270	9.91%	($488,769)	(1.47%)	(1.38%)
4. TICOR	$27,896,377	7.93%	$4,175,994	12.56%	8.47%
5. LAWYERS	$20,333,111	5.78%	$4,086,850	12.30%	15.25%
6. FIDELITY NATIONAL	$12,929,671	3.68%	$1,239,852	3.73%	9.69%
7. ATTORNEYS TGF (IL)	$11,910,157	3.39%	$2,237,360	6.73%	10.13%
8. ATTORNEYS TIF (FL)	$10,745,894	3.06%	$1,039,052	3.13%	10.13%
9. COMMONWEALTH LAND	$6,682,553	1.90%	$1,480,243	4.45%	17.36%
10. UNITED GENERAL	$4,926,290	1.40%	$417,011	1.25%	8.90%
11. OLD REPUBLIC NATIONAL	$4,009,721	1.14%	$997,998	3.00%	20.55%
12. GUARANTEE T&T	$2,826,181	0.80%	$191,352	0.58%	6.99%
13. SECURITY UNION	$2,403,221	0.68%	$34,743	0.10%	1.40%
14. LAW	$1,525,580	0.43%	$100,000	0.30%	6.68%
15. NORTH AMERICAN CORP	$1,258,461	0.36%	$0	--	--
16. INVESTORS TIC	$1,118,463	0.32%	$20,331	0.06%	1.95%
17. TRANSNATION	$821,109	0.23%	$77,894	0.23%	10.22%
18. NATIONAL LAND	$379,574	0.11%	$56,691	0.17%	--
19. PACIFIC NORTHWEST	$250,726	0.07%	$0	--	--
20. COMMERCE	$197,824	0.06%	$0	--	--
21. TRANSUNION NATIONAL	$30,840	0.00%	$0	--	--
22. TITLE IC AMERICA	$11,717	0.00%	$0	--	--
23. TICOR (FL)	$4,765	0.00%	$233,148	0.70%	456.18%
24. CHICAGO T&T	$0	--	$0	--	--
25. NORTHEAST INVESTORS	$0	--	$0	--	--
COMPOSITE	$351,706,070	100.00%	$33,237,039	100.00%	6.44%
AVERAGE	$14,068,243		$1,329,482		

10-YEAR - DIRECT PREMIUMS WRITTEN (DPW) BY CHANNEL — See Sec. 3

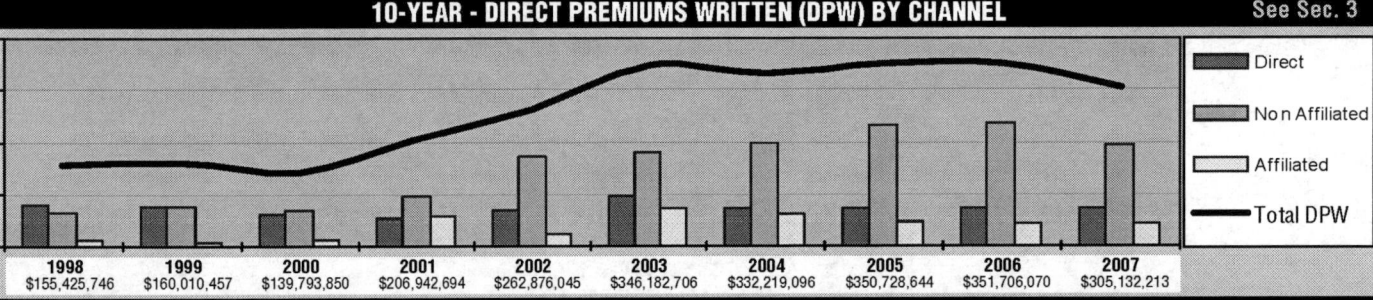

- Direct
- Non Affiliated
- Affiliated
- Total DPW

1998	1999	2000	2001	2002	2003	2004	2005	2006	2007
$155,425,746	$160,010,457	$139,793,850	$206,942,694	$262,876,045	$346,182,706	$332,219,096	$350,728,644	$351,706,070	$305,132,213

10-YEAR - LOSS RATIO — See Sec. 5, A.2

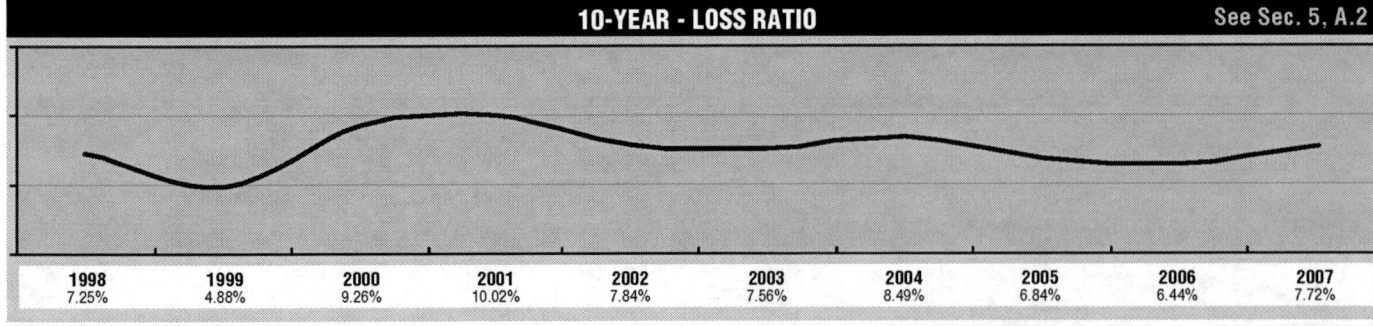

1998	1999	2000	2001	2002	2003	2004	2005	2006	2007
7.25%	4.88%	9.26%	10.02%	7.84%	7.56%	8.49%	6.84%	6.44%	7.72%

INDIANA

DEPARTMENT OF INSURANCE INFORMATION	LAND TITLE ASSOCIATION	DOMICILED UNDERWRITERS See Sec. 1	

Indiana Department of Insurance

Indiana Land Title Association, Inc.

Underwriter	NAIC #
ARSENAL	11865
DREIBELBISS	51381
NATIONAL ATTORNEYS	50938
34 Licensed Underwriters	See Sec. 1

Mr. Jim Atterholt
Insurance Commissioner
311 W Washington St.
Indianapolis, IN 46204-2787
Phone: (317) 232-2385
Fax: (317) 232-5251
www.in.gov/idoi

P.O. Box 20896
Indianapolis, IN 46220
Phone: (800) 929-4582
www.indianalandtitle.org

STATUTORY PREMIUM RESERVE (SPR) REQUIREMENTS

Inception:	10% of the actual premiums collected, until reserve of $50,000 reached
Max Years:	Not Available	Release:	Not Available

MARKET SHARE BY UNDERWRITER See Sec. 3

2007

	TOTAL DPW	MARKET SHARE	LOSSES INCURRED	MARKET SHARE	LOSS RATIO
1. FIRST AMERICAN TIC	$29,411,011	28.75%	$3,147,178	29.43%	8.55%
2. CHICAGO TIC	$17,311,219	16.92%	$1,591,971	14.89%	5.56%
3. STEWART TGC	$14,776,562	14.44%	$2,393,293	22.38%	15.55%
4. LAWYERS	$11,029,630	10.78%	$129,819	1.21%	0.61%
5. TICOR	$9,812,306	9.59%	$740,941	6.93%	5.41%
6. OLD REPUBLIC NATIONAL	$4,044,896	3.95%	$313,877	2.94%	6.35%
7. COMMONWEALTH LAND	$3,697,512	3.61%	$329,928	3.09%	8.36%
8. FIDELITY NATIONAL	$2,657,929	2.60%	$96,027	0.90%	3.55%
9. ARSENAL	$1,583,908	1.55%	$649	0.00%	--
10. CONESTOGA	$1,531,150	1.50%	$368,111	3.44%	23.82%
11. TRANSNATION	$1,522,950	1.49%	$144,168	1.35%	10.59%
12. NATIONAL ATTORNEYS	$831,940	0.81%	$475,150	4.44%	35.54%
13. CENSTAR	$797,369	0.78%	$0	--	--
14. GUARANTEE T&T	$764,529	0.75%	$40,614	0.38%	4.68%
15. UNITED GENERAL	$751,227	0.73%	$64,483	0.60%	7.82%
16. DREIBELBISS	$632,980	0.62%	$0	--	--
17. TICOR (FL)	$505,294	0.49%	$395,759	3.70%	86.98%
18. COMMERCE	$267,698	0.26%	$0	--	--
19. PACIFIC NORTHWEST	$106,959	0.10%	$321,254	3.00%	292.21%
20. ATTORNEYS TGF (IL)	$74,220	0.07%	$58,769	0.55%	62.09%
21. DAKOTA HOMESTEAD	$70,880	0.07%	$0	--	--
22. SECURITY UNION	$42,342	0.04%	$7,471	0.07%	8.62%
23. INVESTORS TIC	$40,938	0.04%	$20,989	0.20%	42.68%
24. OHIO BAR	$23,301	0.02%	$0	--	--
25. TRANSUNION NATIONAL	$17,703	0.02%	$0	--	--
26. TITLE IC AMERICA	$6,710	0.00%	$1,607	0.02%	24.59%
27. GENERAL T&T	$1,000	0.00%	$0	--	--
28. AMERICAN GUARANTY	$300	0.00%	$0	--	--
29. NATIONAL OF NY	$0	--	($5,880)	(0.05)%	(711.00)%
30. ALAMO	$0	--	$0	--	--
31. ATTORNEYS TIF (FL)	$0	--	$58,000	0.54%	--
32. CHICAGO T&T	$0	--	$0	--	--
33. NATIONS OF NY	$0	--	$0	--	--
COMPOSITE	**$102,314,463**	**100.00%**	**$10,694,178**	**100.00%**	**7.81%**
AVERAGE	**$3,100,438**		**$324,066**		

2006

	TOTAL DPW	MARKET SHARE	LOSSES INCURRED	MARKET SHARE	LOSS RATIO
1. FIRST AMERICAN TIC	$31,382,225	28.63%	$2,554,719	28.17%	6.79%
2. CHICAGO TIC	$19,107,533	17.43%	$148,229	1.63%	0.52%
3. STEWART TGC	$14,100,863	12.86%	$2,160,609	23.82%	14.47%
4. LAWYERS	$11,217,210	10.23%	$861,289	9.50%	3.84%
5. TICOR	$10,493,778	9.57%	$707,765	7.80%	4.76%
6. OLD REPUBLIC NATIONAL	$5,689,384	5.19%	$324,146	3.57%	5.16%
7. COMMONWEALTH LAND	$3,771,800	3.44%	$758,142	8.36%	16.91%
8. FIDELITY NATIONAL	$3,412,563	3.11%	$600,884	6.63%	17.94%
9. ARSENAL	$2,389,734	2.18%	$2,554	0.03%	0.11%
10. CONESTOGA	$1,946,764	1.78%	$24,083	0.27%	1.28%
11. TRANSNATION	$1,301,956	1.19%	$261,692	2.89%	22.09%
12. GUARANTEE T&T	$952,204	0.87%	($1,324)	(0.01)%	(0.12)%
13. NATIONAL ATTORNEYS	$871,393	0.79%	$103,813	1.14%	7.70%
14. TICOR (FL)	$763,986	0.70%	$437,154	4.82%	63.57%
15. DREIBELBISS	$755,784	0.69%	$0	--	--
16. UNITED GENERAL	$593,956	0.54%	($61,337)	(0.68)%	(10.68)%
17. CENSTAR	$275,245	0.25%	$0	--	--
18. COMMERCE	$272,540	0.25%	$0	--	--
19. OHIO BAR	$128,191	0.12%	$0	--	--
20. SECURITY UNION	$102,271	0.09%	$13,000	0.14%	9.35%
21. ATTORNEYS TGF (IL)	$58,617	0.05%	$7,397	0.08%	9.41%
22. TRANSUNION NATIONAL	$10,746	0.00%	$0	--	--
23. TITLE IC AMERICA	$9,760	0.00%	$0	--	--
24. INVESTORS TIC	$8,689	0.00%	$16,634	0.18%	75.07%
25. ATTORNEYS TIF (FL)	$0	--	$150,000	1.65%	--
COMPOSITE	**$109,617,192**	**100.00%**	**$9,069,449**	**100.00%**	**6.26%**
AVERAGE	**$4,384,688**		**$362,778**		

10-YEAR - DIRECT PREMIUMS WRITTEN (DPW) BY CHANNEL See Sec. 3

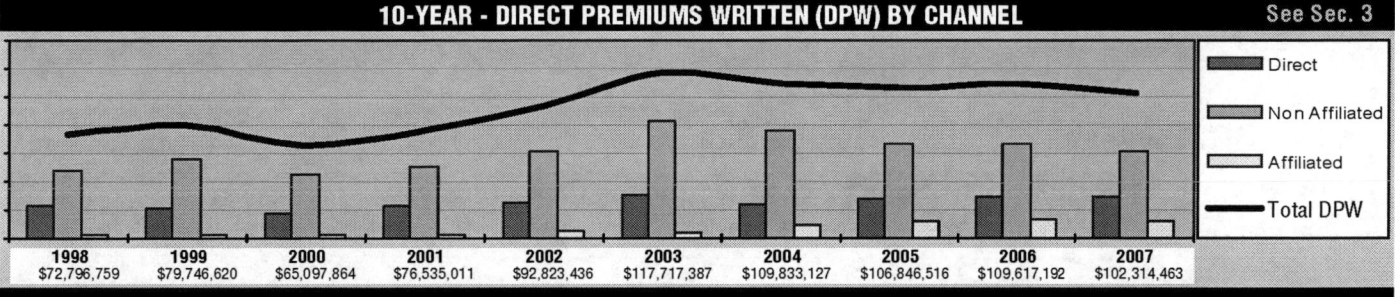

Legend: Direct, Non Affiliated, Affiliated, Total DPW

1998	1999	2000	2001	2002	2003	2004	2005	2006	2007
$72,796,759	$79,746,620	$65,097,864	$76,535,011	$92,823,436	$117,717,387	$109,833,127	$106,846,516	$109,617,192	$102,314,463

10-YEAR - LOSS RATIO See Sec. 5, A.2

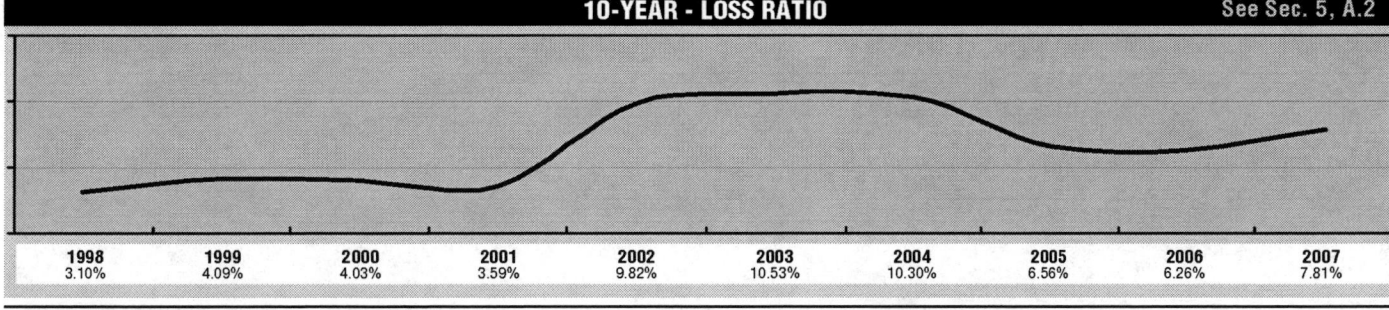

1998	1999	2000	2001	2002	2003	2004	2005	2006	2007
3.10%	4.09%	4.03%	3.59%	9.82%	10.53%	10.30%	6.56%	6.26%	7.81%

6

IOWA

DEPARTMENT OF INSURANCE INFORMATION	LAND TITLE ASSOCIATION	DOMICILED UNDERWRITERS	See Sec. 1

Iowa Division of Insurance | **Iowa Land Title Association** | **Underwriter** | **NAIC #**

Ms. Susan Voss
Insurance Commissioner
330 E Maple St.
Des Moines, IA 50319-0065
Phone: (515) 281-5705
Fax: (515) 281-3059
www.iid.state.ia.us

P.O. Box 444
Carroll, IA 51401
www.iowalandtitle.org

TITLE GUARANTY DIV (IA)

☐ 1 | Licensed Underwriters | See Sec. 1

STATUTORY PREMIUM RESERVE (SPR) REQUIREMENTS

Inception:	Not Available		
Max Years:	Not Available	Release:	Not Available

MARKET SHARE BY UNDERWRITER | See Sec. 3

2007

	TOTAL DPW	MARKET SHARE	LOSSES INCURRED	MARKET SHARE	LOSS RATIO
1. TITLE GUARANTY DIV (IA)	$3,724,743	48.07%	$0	--	--
2. COMMONWEALTH LAND	$1,790,099	23.10%	$16,196	3.11%	0.73%
3. LAWYERS	$1,231,449	15.89%	$64,778	12.45%	3.99%
4. STEWART TGC	$463,149	5.98%	$5,264	1.01%	0.69%
5. CHICAGO TIC	$241,775	3.12%	$232,937	44.77%	32.38%
6. TICOR	$144,951	1.87%	$149,843	28.80%	61.98%
7. FIDELITY NATIONAL	$108,327	1.40%	$110,431	21.22%	94.65%
8. TRANSNATION	$21,294	0.27%	$0	--	--
9. INVESTORS TIC	$14,405	0.19%	$0	--	--
10. PACIFIC NORTHWEST	$4,099	0.05%	$0	--	--
11. SECURITY UNION	$3,900	0.05%	$0	--	--
12. TICOR (FL)	$0	--	($59,327)	(11.40)%	(1,380.34)%
13. GUARANTEE T&T	$0	--	$214	0.04%	0.53%
14. OLD REPUBLIC NATIONAL	$0	--	$0	--	--
COMPOSITE	**$7,748,191**	**100.00%**	**$520,336**	**100.00%**	**9.04%**
AVERAGE	**$553,442**		**$37,167**		

2006

	TOTAL DPW	MARKET SHARE	LOSSES INCURRED	MARKET SHARE	LOSS RATIO
1. TITLE GUARANTY DIV (IA)	$3,940,490	50.85%	$0	--	--
2. COMMONWEALTH LAND	$1,800,061	23.23%	$106,292	19.21%	4.62%
3. LAWYERS	$1,138,989	14.70%	$63,627	11.50%	4.11%
4. STEWART TGC	$561,862	7.25%	$41,105	7.43%	6.70%
5. CHICAGO TIC	$222,713	2.87%	$58,117	10.50%	18.09%
6. FIDELITY NATIONAL	$65,537	0.85%	$36,687	6.63%	119.94%
7. INVESTORS TIC	$6,384	0.08%	$0	--	--
8. PACIFIC NORTHWEST	$6,270	0.08%	$0	--	--
9. TICOR	$3,900	0.05%	$166,141	30.02%	1,492.73%
10. TRANSNATION	$2,562	0.03%	$0	--	--
11. TICOR (FL)	$173	0.00%	$81,462	14.72%	1,104.42%
12. OLD REPUBLIC NATIONAL	$0	--	$0	--	--
13. SECURITY UNION	$0	--	$0	--	--
COMPOSITE	**$7,748,941**	**100.00%**	**$553,431**	**100.00%**	**11.38%**
AVERAGE	**$596,072**		**$42,572**		

10-YEAR - DIRECT PREMIUMS WRITTEN (DPW) BY CHANNEL | See Sec. 3

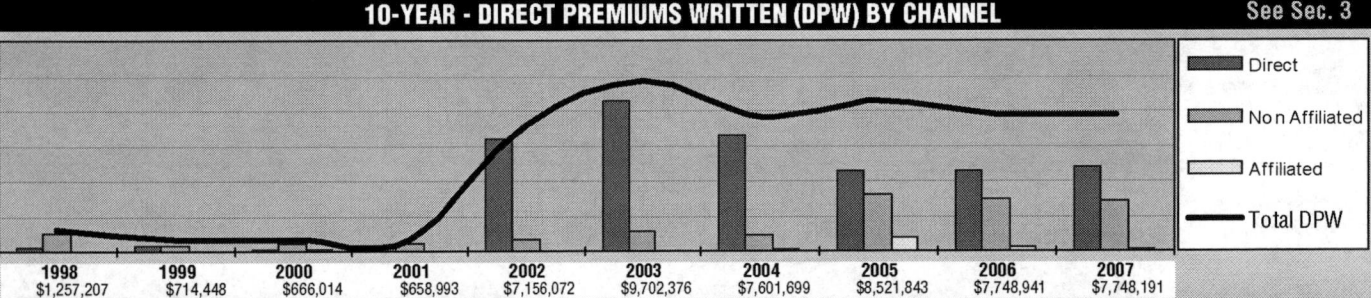

- Direct
- Non Affiliated
- Affiliated
- Total DPW

1998	1999	2000	2001	2002	2003	2004	2005	2006	2007
$1,257,207	$714,448	$666,014	$658,993	$7,156,072	$9,702,376	$7,601,699	$8,521,843	$7,748,941	$7,748,191

10-YEAR - LOSS RATIO | See Sec. 5, A.2

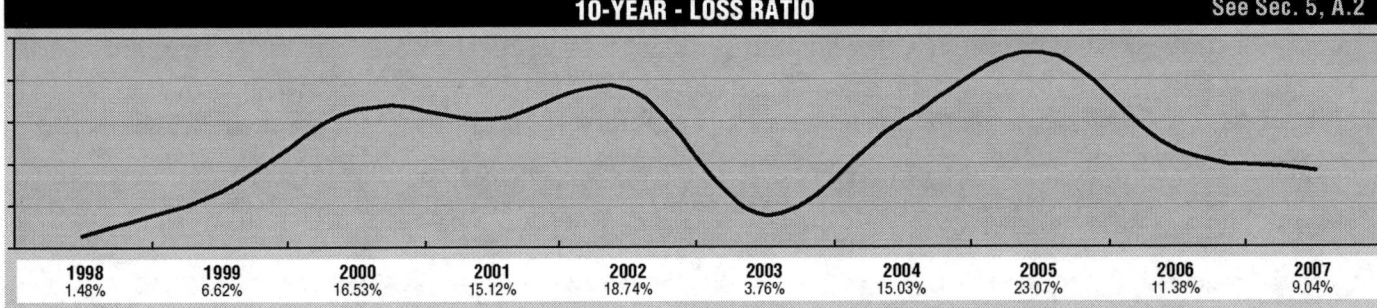

1998	1999	2000	2001	2002	2003	2004	2005	2006	2007
1.48%	6.62%	16.53%	15.12%	18.74%	3.76%	15.03%	23.07%	11.38%	9.04%

6

KANSAS

DEPARTMENT OF INSURANCE INFORMATION

Kansas Department of Insurance

Ms. Sandy Praeger
Insurance Commissioner
420 SW Ninth St.
Topeka, KS 66612-1678

Phone: (785) 296-3071
Fax: (785) 296-2283
www.ksinsurance.org

LAND TITLE ASSOCIATION

Kansas Land Title Association

7321 NW Rochester Rd.
Topeka, KS 66617

www.klta.org

DOMICILED UNDERWRITERS   See Sec. 1

Underwriter	NAIC #
COLUMBIAN NATIONAL	51373
FIRST AMERICAN (KS)	50043
23 Licensed Underwriters	See Sec. 1

STATUTORY PREMIUM RESERVE (SPR) REQUIREMENTS

Inception:	Not Available		
Max Years:	Not Available	Release:	Not Available

MARKET SHARE BY UNDERWRITER   See Sec. 3

2007

	TOTAL DPW	MARKET SHARE	LOSSES INCURRED	MARKET SHARE	LOSS RATIO
1. FIRST AMERICAN (KS)	$14,763,680	33.86%	$351,652	5.28%	2.45%
2. CHICAGO TIC	$7,944,597	18.22%	$207,224	3.11%	2.00%
3. STEWART TGC	$5,636,985	12.93%	$560,968	8.43%	9.76%
4. LAWYERS	$3,645,527	8.36%	$5,199,642	78.13%	105.15%
5. OLD REPUBLIC NATIONAL	$3,415,242	7.83%	$285,318	4.29%	7.83%
6. COMMONWEALTH LAND	$3,360,709	7.71%	$36,995	0.56%	0.94%
7. FIDELITY NATIONAL	$2,357,356	5.41%	($12,965)	(0.19)%	(0.55)%
8. UNITED GENERAL	$1,505,269	3.45%	$19,538	0.29%	1.35%
9. TICOR	$537,934	1.23%	($57,942)	(0.87)%	(9.55)%
10. SECURITY UNION	$179,594	0.41%	$1,562	0.02%	0.90%
11. GUARANTEE	$179,005	0.41%	$21,655	0.33%	13.89%
12. TICOR (FL)	$80,288	0.18%	$41,357	0.62%	34.46%
13. NATIONAL LAND	$1,048	0.00%	$0	--	--
14. GUARANTEE T&T	$0	--	$0	--	--
15. INVESTORS TIC	$0	--	$0	--	--
16. NATIONAL OF NY	$0	--	$0	--	--
17. TITLE RESOURCES	$0	--	$0	--	--
18. TRANSNATION	$0	--	$0	--	--
COMPOSITE	$43,607,234	100.00%	$6,655,004	100.00%	14.12%
AVERAGE	$2,422,624		$369,722		

2006

	TOTAL DPW	MARKET SHARE	LOSSES INCURRED	MARKET SHARE	LOSS RATIO
1. FIRST AMERICAN (KS)	$14,451,423	31.37%	$166,115	8.71%	1.11%
2. CHICAGO TIC	$9,367,468	20.33%	$327,667	17.18%	2.88%
3. STEWART TGC	$5,406,474	11.74%	$184,631	9.68%	3.29%
4. OLD REPUBLIC NATIONAL	$4,455,873	9.67%	$175,298	9.19%	3.77%
5. COMMONWEALTH LAND	$3,833,831	8.32%	$196,201	10.29%	4.04%
6. LAWYERS	$3,814,331	8.28%	$228,619	11.99%	4.78%
7. UNITED GENERAL	$1,568,139	3.40%	$37,108	1.95%	2.41%
8. FIDELITY NATIONAL	$1,385,799	3.01%	$243,540	12.77%	17.91%
9. TICOR	$703,330	1.53%	$153,809	8.06%	20.10%
10. SECURITY UNION	$359,818	0.78%	$4,846	0.25%	1.40%
11. TICOR (FL)	$294,563	0.64%	$183,303	9.61%	56.16%
12. COLUMBIAN NATIONAL	$192,390	0.42%	$0	--	--
13. FIRST AMERICAN (NY)	$148,657	0.32%	$0	--	--
14. GUARANTEE	$84,707	0.18%	$0	--	--
15. TITLE RESOURCES	$0	--	$6,311	0.33%	740.73%
16. INVESTORS TIC	$0	--	$0	--	--
17. TRANSNATION	$0	--	$0	--	--
COMPOSITE	$46,066,803	100.00%	$1,907,448	100.00%	3.75%
AVERAGE	$2,709,812		$112,203		

10-YEAR - DIRECT PREMIUMS WRITTEN (DPW) BY CHANNEL   See Sec. 3

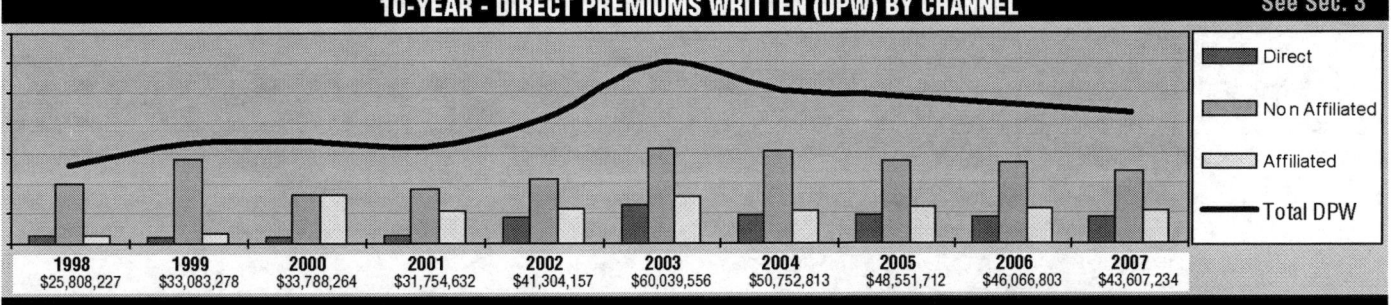

Legend: Direct | Non Affiliated | Affiliated | Total DPW

1998	1999	2000	2001	2002	2003	2004	2005	2006	2007
$25,808,227	$33,083,278	$33,788,264	$31,754,632	$41,304,157	$60,039,556	$50,752,813	$48,551,712	$46,066,803	$43,607,234

10-YEAR - LOSS RATIO   See Sec. 5, A.2

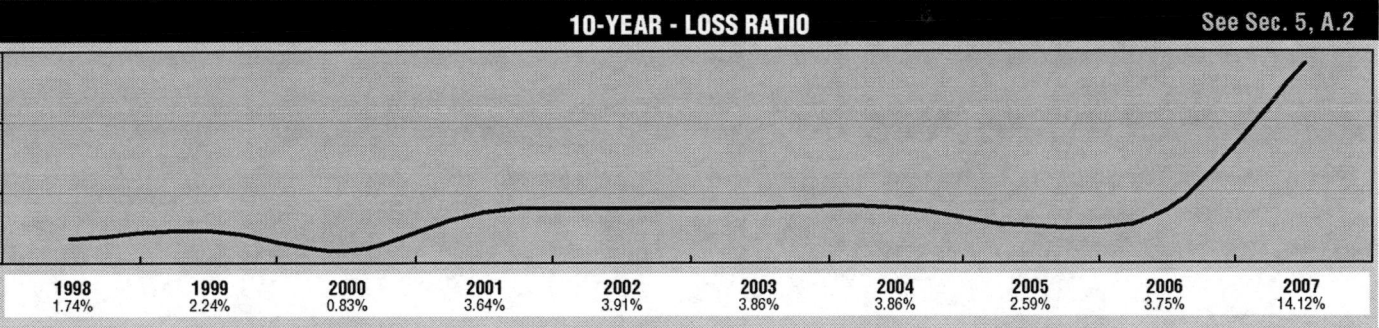

1998	1999	2000	2001	2002	2003	2004	2005	2006	2007
1.74%	2.24%	0.83%	3.64%	3.91%	3.86%	3.86%	2.59%	3.75%	14.12%

6

KENTUCKY

DEPARTMENT OF INSURANCE INFORMATION	LAND TITLE ASSOCIATION	DOMICILED UNDERWRITERS See Sec. 1	
Kentucky Office of Insurance	**Kentucky Land Title Association**	**Underwriter**	**NAIC #**

Mr. Tim LeDonne
Acting Executive Director
215 W Main St.
Frankfort, KY 40601

Phone: (800) 595-6053
Fax: (502) 564-1453
doi.ppr.ky.gov/kentucky

2220 Nicholasville Rd. #10, PMB 289
Lexington, KY 40503
Phone: (866) 610-5582
www.kentuckylandtitle.org

None

| 25 | Licensed Underwriters | See Sec. 1 |

STATUTORY PREMIUM RESERVE (SPR) REQUIREMENTS

Inception:	10% of risk portion of premiums written		
Max Years:	20	Release:	5% per year

MARKET SHARE BY UNDERWRITER — See Sec. 3

2007

	TOTAL DPW	MARKET SHARE	LOSSES INCURRED	MARKET SHARE	LOSS RATIO
1. FIRST AMERICAN TIC	$14,288,063	22.38%	$1,655,622	29.20%	8.88%
2. COMMONWEALTH LAND	$12,328,371	19.31%	$1,465,828	25.85%	11.20%
3. CHICAGO TIC	$9,790,783	15.33%	$515,431	9.09%	4.59%
4. STEWART TGC	$9,605,516	15.04%	$745,177	13.14%	7.46%
5. OLD REPUBLIC NATIONAL	$8,066,079	12.63%	$38,727	0.68%	0.48%
6. LAWYERS	$3,460,209	5.42%	$871,279	15.37%	19.43%
7. INVESTORS TIC	$2,564,401	4.02%	$103,128	1.82%	4.28%
8. FIDELITY NATIONAL	$1,410,285	2.21%	($13,143)	(0.23)%	(0.93)%
9. CENSTAR	$733,946	1.15%	$1,628	0.03%	0.23%
10. UNITED GENERAL	$697,019	1.09%	$35,384	0.62%	5.23%
11. CONESTOGA	$415,379	0.65%	$7,458	0.13%	1.79%
12. OHIO BAR	$171,109	0.27%	$0	--	--
13. TICOR (FL)	$160,475	0.25%	$159,345	2.81%	99.69%
14. TICOR	$97,283	0.15%	$111,491	1.97%	74.15%
15. SECURITY UNION	$37,916	0.06%	$0	--	--
16. TRANSNATION	$12,185	0.02%	$2,743	0.05%	14.84%
17. TRANSUNION NATIONAL	$10,162	0.02%	$0	--	--
18. SECURITY TG (BALTIMORE)	$2,748	0.00%	($50,000)	(0.88)%	(971.44)%
19. AMERICAN GUARANTY	$275	0.00%	$0	--	--
20. GUARANTEE T&T	$150	0.00%	$0	--	--
21. NATIONAL OF NY	$0	--	$15,200	0.27%	0.00%
22. NATIONS OF NY	$0	--	$5,000	0.09%	--
23. NORTHEAST INVESTORS	$0	--	$0	--	--
COMPOSITE	**$63,852,354**	**100.00%**	**$5,670,298**	**100.00%**	**7.91%**
AVERAGE	**$2,776,189**		**$246,535**		

2006

	TOTAL DPW	MARKET SHARE	LOSSES INCURRED	MARKET SHARE	LOSS RATIO
1. FIRST AMERICAN TIC	$13,749,084	22.29%	$1,638,223	23.59%	9.92%
2. COMMONWEALTH LAND	$12,221,173	19.81%	$1,496,175	21.55%	10.89%
3. STEWART TGC	$11,116,088	18.02%	$1,578,015	22.72%	13.89%
4. CHICAGO TIC	$8,601,383	13.95%	$450,959	6.49%	5.04%
5. OLD REPUBLIC NATIONAL	$8,169,041	13.24%	$1,498,878	21.58%	19.15%
6. LAWYERS	$2,680,358	4.35%	($42,089)	(0.61)%	(1.37)%
7. INVESTORS TIC	$2,291,652	3.72%	$76,967	1.11%	3.59%
8. FIDELITY NATIONAL	$1,037,524	1.68%	($60,539)	(0.87)%	(5.95)%
9. CONESTOGA	$478,895	0.78%	$8,240	0.12%	1.79%
10. CENSTAR	$404,095	0.66%	$0	--	--
11. TICOR (FL)	$305,039	0.49%	$221,911	3.20%	75.22%
12. UNITED GENERAL	$225,018	0.36%	$23,495	0.34%	11.42%
13. OHIO BAR	$144,572	0.23%	$0	--	--
14. SECURITY UNION	$90,348	0.15%	$0	--	--
15. TRANSNATION	$75,870	0.12%	$36,262	0.52%	50.92%
16. TICOR	$44,699	0.07%	$130,217	1.88%	192.17%
17. SECURITY TG (BALTIMORE)	$26,233	0.04%	($136,416)	(1.96)%	(536.23)%
18. TRANSUNION NATIONAL	$17,352	0.03%	$0	--	--
19. NATIONS OF NY	$0	--	$24,000	0.35%	--
20. NORTHEAST INVESTORS	$0	--	$0	--	--
COMPOSITE	**$61,678,424**	**100.00%**	**$6,944,298**	**100.00%**	**10.46%**
AVERAGE	**$3,083,921**		**$347,215**		

10-YEAR - DIRECT PREMIUMS WRITTEN (DPW) BY CHANNEL — See Sec. 3

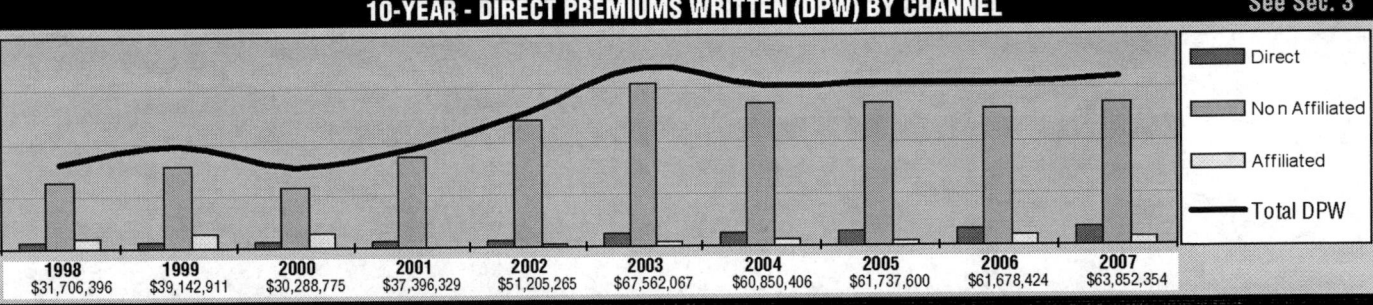

Legend: Direct, Non Affiliated, Affiliated, Total DPW

1998	1999	2000	2001	2002	2003	2004	2005	2006	2007
$31,706,396	$39,142,911	$30,288,775	$37,396,329	$51,205,265	$67,562,067	$60,850,406	$61,737,600	$61,678,424	$63,852,354

10-YEAR - LOSS RATIO — See Sec. 5, A.2

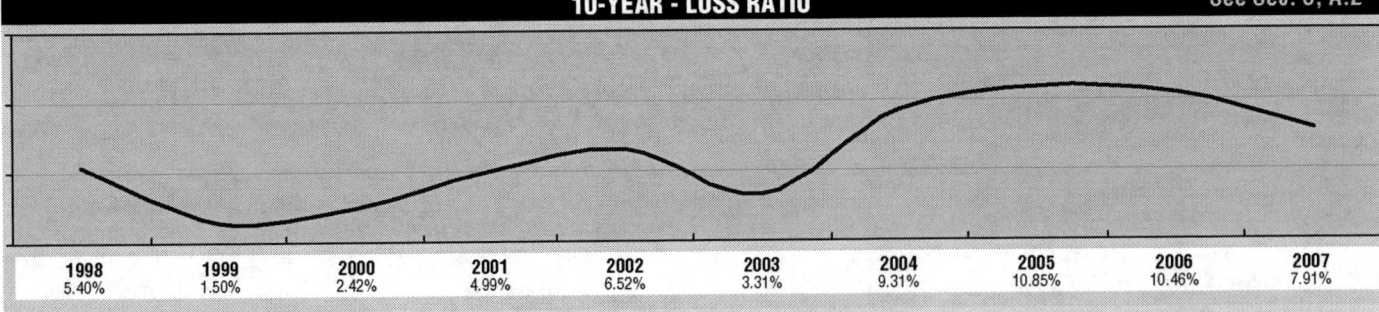

1998	1999	2000	2001	2002	2003	2004	2005	2006	2007
5.40%	1.50%	2.42%	4.99%	6.52%	3.31%	9.31%	10.85%	10.46%	7.91%

6

LOUISIANA

DEPARTMENT OF INSURANCE INFORMATION	LAND TITLE ASSOCIATION	DOMICILED UNDERWRITERS See Sec. 1

Louisiana Department of Insurance

Mr. James Donelon
Insurance Commissioner
1702 N Third St.
Baton Rouge, LA 70802
Phone: (225) 342-5900
Fax: (225) 342-1993
www.ldi.state.la.us

Louisiana Land Title Association

P.O. Box 14806
Baton Rouge, LA 70898
Phone: (225) 291-2806
www.llta.org

Underwriter	NAIC #
FIRST AMERICAN (LA)	50199
FIRST AMERICAN TRANS	51527
22 Licensed Underwriters	See Sec. 1

STATUTORY PREMIUM RESERVE (SPR) REQUIREMENTS

Inception:	Not Available		
Max Years:	Not Available	Release:	Not Available

MARKET SHARE BY UNDERWRITER — See Sec. 3

2007

	TOTAL DPW	MARKET SHARE	LOSSES INCURRED	MARKET SHARE	LOSS RATIO
1. FIRST AMERICAN TIC	$45,695,841	37.61%	($352,369)	(9.40)%	(0.76)%
2. COMMONWEALTH LAND	$23,969,029	19.73%	$2,333,655	62.26%	9.35%
3. STEWART TGC	$15,746,852	12.96%	$392,226	10.46%	2.48%
4. FIDELITY NATIONAL	$11,757,018	9.68%	$644,204	17.19%	5.49%
5. CHICAGO TIC	$9,549,491	7.86%	$122,489	3.27%	1.20%
6. LAWYERS	$7,845,656	6.46%	$82,799	2.21%	0.94%
7. SECURITY TG (BALTIMORE)	$2,343,439	1.93%	$46,098	1.23%	1.92%
8. UNITED GENERAL	$1,652,146	1.36%	$127,110	3.39%	7.48%
9. OLD REPUBLIC NATIONAL	$1,597,351	1.31%	$65,923	1.76%	3.88%
10. TICOR (FL)	$536,084	0.44%	$294,820	7.87%	54.45%
11. INVESTORS TIC	$321,368	0.26%	$0	--	--
12. FIRST AMERICAN TRANS	$256,694	0.21%	($16,063)	(0.43)%	(6.24)%
13. TICOR	$205,045	0.17%	($636)	(0.02)%	(0.24)%
14. SOUTHERN TI CORP	$10,825	0.00%	$0	--	--
15. SECURITY UNION	$939	0.00%	$8,188	0.22%	89.56%
16. TRANSNATION	$467	0.00%	$0	--	--
17. ALAMO	$0	--	$0	--	--
18. CHICAGO T&T	$0	--	$0	--	--
19. GUARANTEE T&T	$0	--	$0	--	--
20. NATIONAL OF NY	$0	--	$0	--	--
21. NATIONS OF NY	$0	--	$0	--	--
COMPOSITE	$121,488,245	100.00%	$3,748,444	100.00%	3.00%
AVERAGE	$5,785,155		$178,497		

2006

	TOTAL DPW	MARKET SHARE	LOSSES INCURRED	MARKET SHARE	LOSS RATIO
1. FIRST AMERICAN TIC	$39,418,486	34.92%	$1,492,623	30.90%	3.75%
2. COMMONWEALTH LAND	$23,934,920	21.21%	$1,239,665	25.66%	4.86%
3. STEWART TGC	$14,270,651	12.64%	$204,430	4.23%	1.43%
4. FIDELITY NATIONAL	$10,464,728	9.27%	$448,515	9.29%	4.23%
5. CHICAGO TIC	$9,513,082	8.43%	$4,691	0.10%	0.05%
6. LAWYERS	$7,568,299	6.71%	$324,975	6.73%	3.82%
7. SECURITY TG (BALTIMORE)	$3,484,410	3.09%	$354,820	7.35%	10.75%
8. UNITED GENERAL	$1,408,318	1.25%	($16,202)	(0.34)%	(1.14)%
9. OLD REPUBLIC NATIONAL	$1,241,607	1.10%	$297,137	6.15%	21.07%
10. TICOR (FL)	$704,488	0.62%	$241,844	5.01%	33.37%
11. FIRST AMERICAN TRANS	$459,341	0.41%	$220,338	4.56%	47.97%
12. INVESTORS TIC	$251,547	0.22%	$0	--	--
13. TICOR	$99,330	0.09%	$0	--	--
14. TRANSNATION	$50,792	0.05%	$0	--	--
15. SECURITY UNION	$584	0.00%	$17,594	0.36%	119.58%
16. ALAMO	$0	--	$0	--	--
COMPOSITE	$112,870,683	100.00%	$4,830,430	100.00%	4.16%
AVERAGE	$7,054,418		$301,902		

10-YEAR - DIRECT PREMIUMS WRITTEN (DPW) BY CHANNEL — See Sec. 3

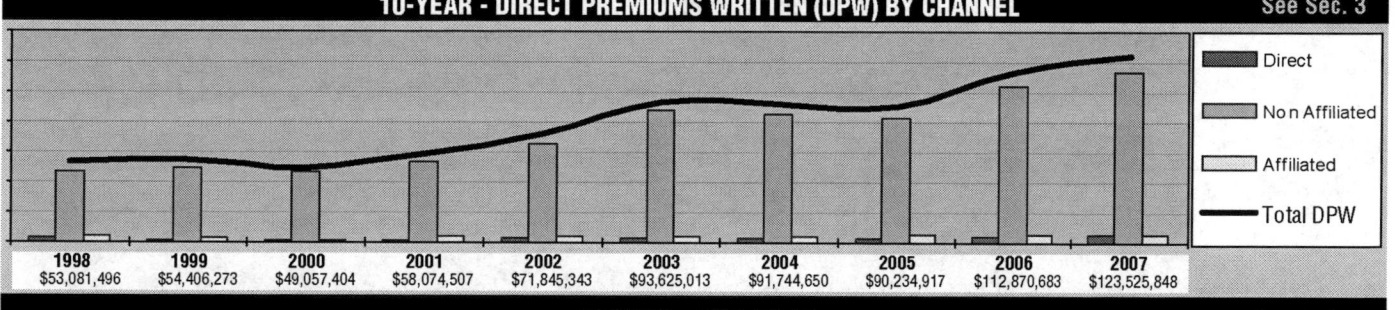

Legend: Direct; Non Affiliated; Affiliated; Total DPW

1998	1999	2000	2001	2002	2003	2004	2005	2006	2007
$53,081,496	$54,406,273	$49,057,404	$58,074,507	$71,845,343	$93,625,013	$91,744,650	$90,234,917	$112,870,683	$123,525,848

10-YEAR - LOSS RATIO — See Sec. 5, A.2

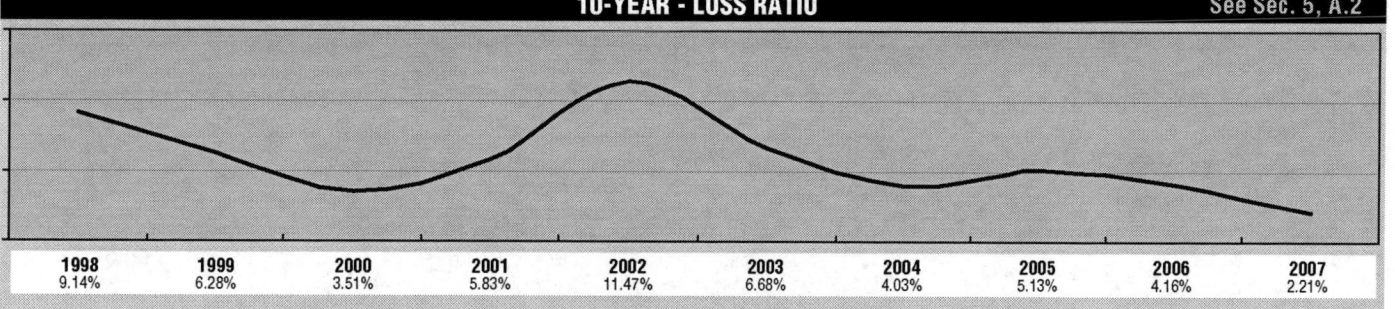

1998	1999	2000	2001	2002	2003	2004	2005	2006	2007
9.14%	6.28%	3.51%	5.83%	11.47%	6.68%	4.03%	5.13%	4.16%	2.21%

6

MAINE

DEPARTMENT OF INSURANCE INFORMATION	LAND TITLE ASSOCIATION	DOMICILED UNDERWRITERS See Sec. 1
Maine Bureau of Insurance	New England Land Title Association	Underwriter / NAIC #

Ms. Mila Kofman
Superintendent
34 State House Station
Augusta, ME 04333-0034
Phone: (207) 624-8475
Fax: (207) 624-8599
www.maine.gov/pfr/insurance

P.O. Box 743
Norwalk, CT 06852-0743
Phone: (203) 847-6885
www.nelta.org

None

19 Licensed Underwriters   See Sec. 1

STATUTORY PREMIUM RESERVE (SPR) REQUIREMENTS

Inception:	Not Available		
Max Years:	Not Available	Release:	Not Available

MARKET SHARE BY UNDERWRITER — See Sec. 3

2007

	TOTAL DPW	MARKET SHARE	LOSSES INCURRED	MARKET SHARE	LOSS RATIO
1. FIRST AMERICAN TIC	$16,303,783	49.89%	$1,377,283	41.39%	8.42%
2. CHICAGO TIC	$4,677,606	14.31%	$1,122,131	33.72%	23.20%
3. LAWYERS	$3,515,368	10.76%	$135,369	4.07%	3.12%
4. TICOR	$2,751,052	8.42%	$65,266	1.96%	2.41%
5. STEWART TGC	$2,301,944	7.04%	$343,811	10.33%	12.70%
6. COMMONWEALTH LAND	$1,527,724	4.67%	$86,917	2.61%	5.66%
7. OLD REPUBLIC NATIONAL	$556,552	1.70%	$142,367	4.28%	23.34%
8. FIDELITY NATIONAL	$425,525	1.30%	$66,906	2.01%	15.46%
9. UNITED GENERAL	$412,771	1.26%	$0	--	--
10. TICOR (FL)	$173,838	0.53%	($14,071)	(0.42)%	(8.75)%
11. TITLE RESOURCES	$14,476	0.04%	$0	--	--
12. GUARANTEE T&T	$10,566	0.03%	$0	--	--
13. CT ATTORNEYS	$8,326	0.03%	$0	--	--
14. NATIONS OF NY	$0	--	$1,411	0.04%	--
15. TRANSNATION	$0	--	$100	0.00%	2.53%
16. EQUITY NATIONAL	$0	--	$0	--	--
17. NATIONAL OF NY	$0	--	$0	--	--
18. SECURITY TG (BALTIMORE)	$0	--	$0	--	--
19. SECURITY UNION	$0	--	$0	--	--
COMPOSITE	$32,679,531	100.00%	$3,327,490	100.00%	9.71%
AVERAGE	$1,719,975		$175,131		

2006

	TOTAL DPW	MARKET SHARE	LOSSES INCURRED	MARKET SHARE	LOSS RATIO
1. FIRST AMERICAN TIC	$18,881,277	48.81%	$834,324	29.61%	4.47%
2. CHICAGO TIC	$5,279,607	13.65%	$628,482	22.30%	11.95%
3. STEWART TGC	$5,084,333	13.14%	$542,203	19.24%	11.17%
4. TICOR	$3,209,443	8.30%	$234,371	8.32%	7.51%
5. LAWYERS	$3,205,499	8.29%	$291,575	10.35%	7.98%
6. COMMONWEALTH LAND	$1,744,626	4.51%	$184,837	6.56%	9.87%
7. OLD REPUBLIC NATIONAL	$509,885	1.32%	$53,019	1.88%	8.77%
8. FIDELITY NATIONAL	$366,515	0.95%	$14,976	0.53%	4.17%
9. TICOR (FL)	$204,446	0.53%	$29,965	1.06%	15.11%
10. UNITED GENERAL	$200,084	0.52%	$0	--	--
11. SECURITY UNION	$890	0.00%	$0	--	--
12. NATIONS OF NY	$0	--	$4,076	0.14%	--
13. EQUITY NATIONAL	$0	--	$0	--	--
14. TRANSNATION	$0	--	$0	--	--
15. SECURITY TG (BALTIMORE)	($6,352)	(0.02)%	$0	--	--
COMPOSITE	$38,680,253	100.00%	$2,817,828	100.00%	7.22%
AVERAGE	$2,578,684		$187,855		

10-YEAR - DIRECT PREMIUMS WRITTEN (DPW) BY CHANNEL — See Sec. 3

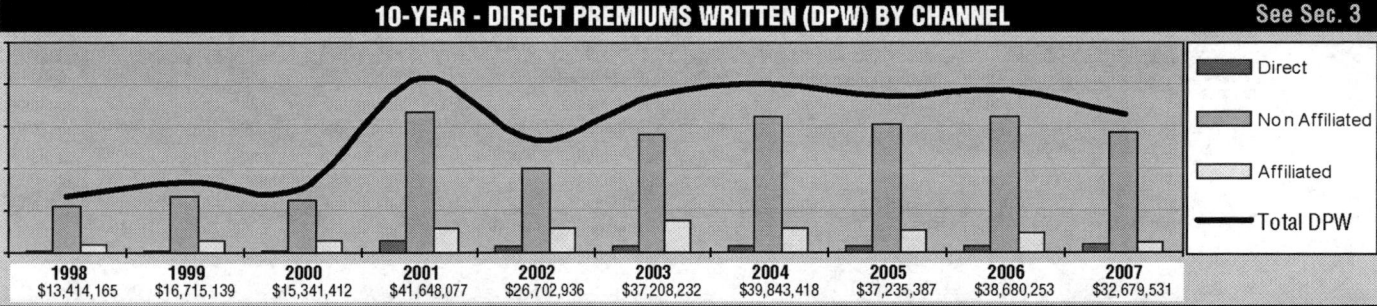

Legend: Direct, Non Affiliated, Affiliated, Total DPW

1998	1999	2000	2001	2002	2003	2004	2005	2006	2007
$13,414,165	$16,715,139	$15,341,412	$41,648,077	$26,702,936	$37,208,232	$39,843,418	$37,235,387	$38,680,253	$32,679,531

10-YEAR - LOSS RATIO — See Sec. 5, A.2

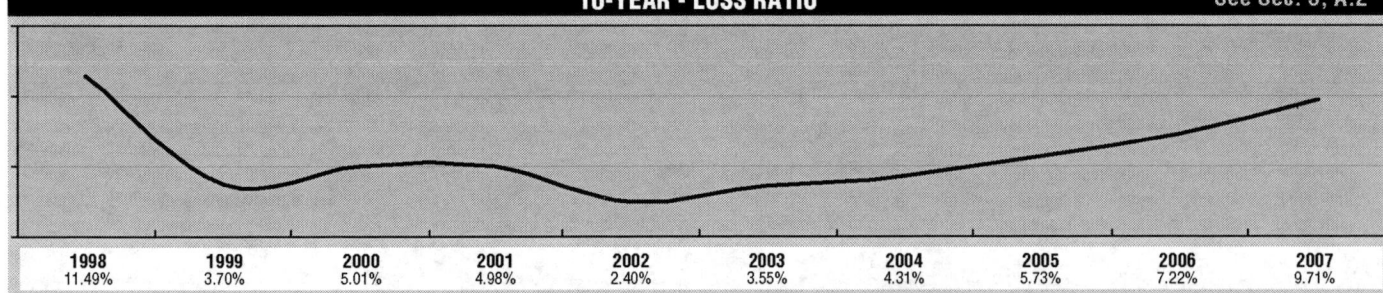

1998	1999	2000	2001	2002	2003	2004	2005	2006	2007
11.49%	3.70%	5.01%	4.98%	2.40%	3.55%	4.31%	5.73%	7.22%	9.71%

6

MARYLAND

DEPARTMENT OF INSURANCE INFORMATION	LAND TITLE ASSOCIATION	DOMICILED UNDERWRITERS See Sec. 1	
Maryland Insurance Administration	**Maryland Land Title Association**	**Underwriter**	**NAIC #**
Mr. Ralph S. Tyler	2485 Manakin Town Ferry Rd.	SECURITY TG (BALTIMORE)	50784
Insurance Commissioner	Midlothian, VA 23113-9106		
525 St. Paul Pl.		**30** Licensed Underwriters	See Sec. 1
Baltimore, MD 21202-2272	Phone: (804) 794-4750		
Phone: (410) 468-2000	www.mdlta.org		
Fax: (410) 468-2020			
www.mdinsurance.state.md.us			

STATUTORY PREMIUM RESERVE (SPR) REQUIREMENTS

Inception:	10% of risk premiums written	
Max Years:	20	Release: 35% for year 1; 15% for years 2-3; 10% for year 4; 3% for years 5-7; 2% for years 8-10; 1% for years 11-20

MARKET SHARE BY UNDERWRITER   See Sec. 3

2007

	TOTAL DPW	MARKET SHARE	LOSSES INCURRED	MARKET SHARE	LOSS RATIO
1. FIRST AMERICAN TIC	$76,728,353	24.93%	$4,117,860	19.57%	5.11%
2. CHICAGO TIC	$51,167,105	16.62%	$4,076,717	19.37%	7.70%
3. COMMONWEALTH LAND	$44,305,573	14.39%	$963,015	4.58%	2.12%
4. STEWART TGC	$40,148,442	13.04%	$2,625,850	12.48%	6.46%
5. LAWYERS	$25,810,327	8.39%	$262,809	1.25%	0.95%
6. FIDELITY NATIONAL	$23,977,552	7.79%	$2,402,656	11.42%	9.75%
7. OLD REPUBLIC NATIONAL	$11,685,145	3.80%	$3,069,718	14.59%	25.78%
8. UNITED GENERAL	$8,847,064	2.87%	$639,138	3.04%	7.49%
9. SECURITY TG (BALTIMORE)	$7,654,791	2.49%	$460,216	2.19%	5.57%
10. TICOR (FL)	$3,443,114	1.12%	$422,075	2.01%	11.63%
11. SOUTHERN TI CORP	$2,774,103	0.90%	$546,711	2.60%	20.48%
12. NORTH AMERICAN	$2,532,497	0.82%	$7,125	0.03%	0.29%
13. TICOR	$2,209,423	0.72%	$582,676	2.77%	22.18%
14. CONESTOGA	$2,170,802	0.71%	$56,278	0.27%	2.60%
15. CENSTAR	$1,657,830	0.54%	$108	0.00%	0.00%
16. INVESTORS TIC	$1,176,007	0.38%	$431,226	2.05%	31.50%
17. COMMERCE	$509,871	0.17%	$0	--	--
18. T.A. TITLE	$353,847	0.11%	$0	--	--
19. TITLE RESOURCES	$340,737	0.11%	$0	--	--
20. TRANSNATION	$246,388	0.08%	$59,090	0.28%	25.97%
21. TRANSUNION NATIONAL	$70,722	0.02%	$0	--	--
22. AMERICAN GUARANTY	$2,165	0.00%	$0	--	--
23. NATIONAL OF NY	$0	--	$168,402	0.80%	8,441.20%
24. NATIONS OF NY	$0	--	$37,407	0.18%	0.00%
25. SECURITY UNION	$0	--	$113,051	0.54%	4,021.74%
26. ALAMO	$0	--	$0	--	--
27. ATTORNEYS TIF (FL)	$0	--	$0	--	--
28. EQUITY NATIONAL	$0	--	$0	--	--
29. GUARANTEE T&T	$0	--	$0	--	--
30. NORTHEAST INVESTORS	$0	--	$0	--	--
COMPOSITE	**$307,811,858**	**100.00%**	**$21,042,128**	**100.00%**	**6.60%**
AVERAGE	**$10,260,395**		**$701,404**		

2006

	TOTAL DPW	MARKET SHARE	LOSSES INCURRED	MARKET SHARE	LOSS RATIO
1. FIRST AMERICAN TIC	$79,297,563	20.96%	$5,349,408	31.49%	6.61%
2. CHICAGO TIC	$72,550,487	19.18%	$3,049,214	17.95%	4.15%
3. STEWART TGC	$59,108,702	15.63%	$3,339,157	19.65%	5.76%
4. COMMONWEALTH LAND	$48,756,323	12.89%	$50,073	0.29%	0.09%
5. LAWYERS	$33,403,673	8.83%	$1,571,458	9.25%	4.60%
6. FIDELITY NATIONAL	$29,859,128	7.89%	$447,107	2.63%	1.49%
7. SECURITY TG (BALTIMORE)	$12,693,006	3.36%	$1,140,471	6.71%	8.93%
8. OLD REPUBLIC NATIONAL	$10,885,536	2.88%	($33,676)	(0.20)%	(0.29)%
9. UNITED GENERAL	$8,140,493	2.15%	$450,734	2.65%	6.06%
10. TICOR (FL)	$7,530,175	1.99%	$1,042,225	6.13%	13.95%
11. CENSTAR	$3,202,014	0.85%	$4,077	0.02%	0.13%
12. CONESTOGA	$3,196,767	0.85%	($13,247)	(0.08)%	(0.43)%
13. TICOR	$2,494,002	0.66%	$369,189	2.17%	13.21%
14. SOUTHERN TI CORP	$2,305,295	0.61%	$9,401	0.06%	0.42%
15. NORTH AMERICAN CORP	$2,081,730	0.55%	$12,000	0.07%	0.60%
16. INVESTORS TIC	$1,519,073	0.40%	$125,423	0.74%	7.39%
17. COMMERCE	$676,588	0.18%	$0	--	--
18. T.A. TITLE	$445,548	0.12%	$83,500	0.49%	19.70%
19. TRANSUNION NATIONAL	$120,702	0.03%	$0	--	--
20. TRANSNATION	$15,466	0.00%	$0	--	--
21. NATIONS OF NY	$0	--	($28,775)	(0.17)%	--
22. SECURITY UNION	$0	--	$21,499	0.13%	3,681.34%
23. ALAMO	$0	--	$0	--	--
24. ATTORNEYS TIF (FL)	$0	--	$0	--	--
25. EQUITY NATIONAL	$0	--	$0	--	--
26. NORTHEAST INVESTORS	$0	--	$0	--	--
COMPOSITE	**$378,282,271**	**100.00%**	**$16,989,238**	**100.00%**	**4.41%**
AVERAGE	**$14,549,318**		**$653,432**		

10-YEAR - DIRECT PREMIUMS WRITTEN (DPW) BY CHANNEL   See Sec. 3

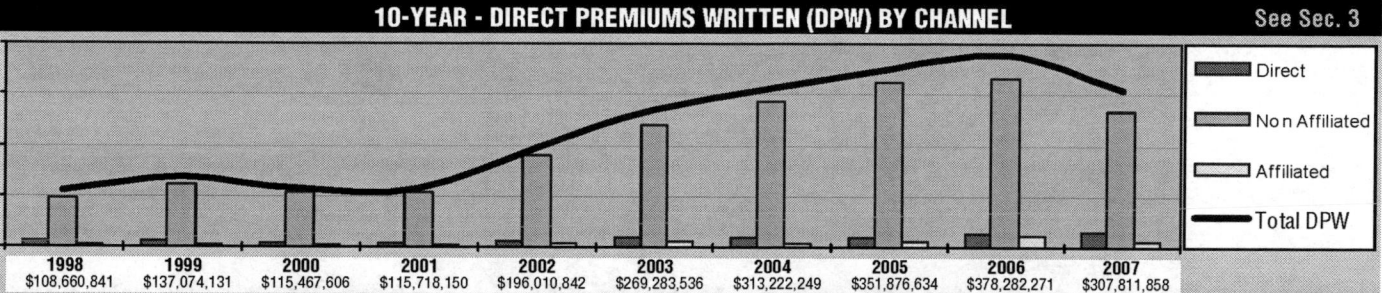

Legend: Direct, Non Affiliated, Affiliated, Total DPW

1998	1999	2000	2001	2002	2003	2004	2005	2006	2007
$108,660,841	$137,074,131	$115,467,606	$115,718,150	$196,010,842	$269,283,536	$313,222,249	$351,876,634	$378,282,271	$307,811,858

10-YEAR - LOSS RATIO   See Sec. 5, A.2

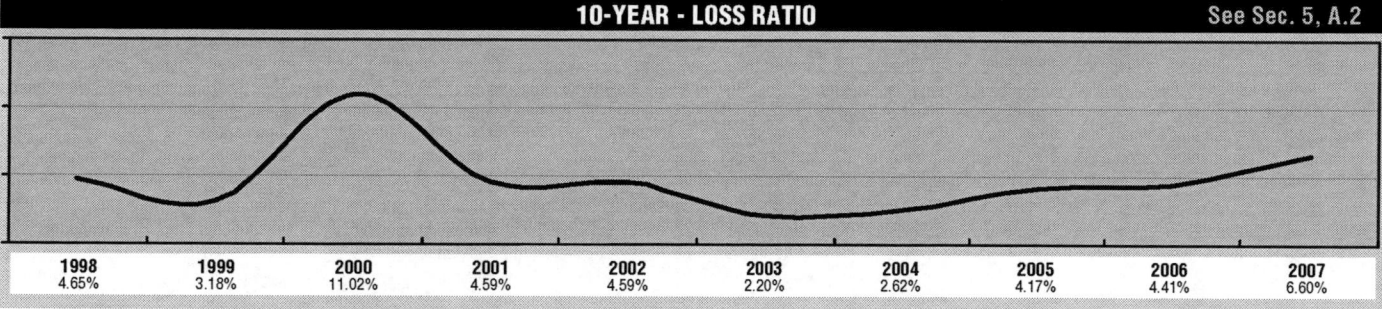

1998	1999	2000	2001	2002	2003	2004	2005	2006	2007
4.65%	3.18%	11.02%	4.59%	4.59%	2.20%	2.62%	4.17%	4.41%	6.60%

6

MASSACHUSETTS

DEPARTMENT OF INSURANCE INFORMATION	LAND TITLE ASSOCIATION	DOMICILED UNDERWRITERS See Sec. 1	

		Underwriter	NAIC #
Massachusetts Division of Insurance	New England Land Title Association	EQUITY NATIONAL	12234
		MASSACHUSETTS TIC	50989

Ms. Nonnie S. Burnes
Commissioner of Insurance
One South Station, 5th Fl.
Boston, MA 02210-2208

Phone: (617) 521-7794
Fax: (617) 521-7575
www.mass.gov/doi

P.O. Box 743
Norwalk, CT 06852-0743

Phone: (203) 847-6885
www.nelta.org

23	Licensed Underwriters	See Sec. 1

STATUTORY PREMIUM RESERVE (SPR) REQUIREMENTS

Inception:	Not Available		
Max Years:	Not Available	Release:	Not Available

MARKET SHARE BY UNDERWRITER See Sec. 3

2007

	TOTAL DPW	MARKET SHARE	LOSSES INCURRED	MARKET SHARE	LOSS RATIO
1. FIRST AMERICAN TIC	$89,222,622	36.98%	$6,043,763	26.89%	6.59%
2. STEWART TGC	$25,238,607	10.46%	$2,724,849	12.12%	10.97%
3. OLD REPUBLIC NATIONAL	$21,834,369	9.05%	$2,307,353	10.27%	9.95%
4. COMMONWEALTH LAND	$21,573,872	8.94%	$1,570,762	6.99%	7.11%
5. FIDELITY NATIONAL	$19,834,650	8.22%	$1,976,272	8.79%	9.48%
6. CHICAGO TIC	$19,779,491	8.20%	$2,429,285	10.81%	12.15%
7. LAWYERS	$18,584,882	7.70%	$2,161,543	9.62%	10.93%
8. CT ATTORNEYS	$8,093,908	3.36%	$1,580,050	7.03%	19.54%
9. TICOR	$7,538,072	3.12%	$1,409,380	6.27%	18.35%
10. UNITED GENERAL	$6,779,820	2.81%	($39,385)	(0.18)%	(0.62)%
11. CENSTAR	$1,047,048	0.43%	$0	--	--
12. NATIONAL OF NY	$576,997	0.24%	$65,765	0.29%	12.51%
13. TICOR (FL)	$566,618	0.23%	$257,288	1.14%	41.84%
14. EQUITY NATIONAL	$280,228	0.12%	$0	--	--
15. TRANSNATION	$250,447	0.10%	$37,767	0.17%	14.81%
16. TITLE RESOURCES	$44,660	0.02%	$0	--	--
17. SECURITY UNION	$0	--	($37,745)	(0.17)%	(676.55)%
18. NATIONS OF NY	$0	--	($11,095)	(0.05)%	--
19. GUARANTEE T&T	$0	--	$0	--	--
20. INVESTORS TIC	$0	--	$0	--	--
21. MASSACHUSETTS TIC	($254)	0.00%	$0	--	--
COMPOSITE	$241,246,037	100.00%	$22,475,852	100.00%	9.08%
AVERAGE	$11,487,907		$1,070,279		

2006

	TOTAL DPW	MARKET SHARE	LOSSES INCURRED	MARKET SHARE	LOSS RATIO
1. FIRST AMERICAN TIC	$112,236,730	41.21%	$5,919,903	23.56%	5.24%
2. OLD REPUBLIC NATIONAL	$26,750,820	9.82%	$1,716,817	6.83%	6.10%
3. COMMONWEALTH LAND	$24,411,394	8.96%	$2,180,079	8.68%	8.06%
4. FIDELITY NATIONAL	$24,122,384	8.86%	$713,132	2.84%	2.91%
5. CHICAGO TIC	$23,691,829	8.70%	$897,963	3.57%	3.59%
6. STEWART TGC	$22,893,527	8.41%	$5,790,504	23.05%	25.15%
7. LAWYERS	$20,840,982	7.65%	$3,372,091	13.42%	16.28%
8. CT ATTORNEYS	$9,248,002	3.40%	$3,073,118	12.23%	33.22%
9. TICOR	$2,740,356	1.01%	$1,244,946	4.96%	39.29%
10. UNITED GENERAL	$2,689,078	0.99%	$0	--	--
11. TICOR (FL)	$1,177,454	0.43%	$67,253	0.27%	5.54%
12. TRANSNATION	$562,625	0.21%	($5,960)	(0.02)%	(1.00)%
13. CENSTAR	$539,766	0.20%	$0	--	--
14. EQUITY NATIONAL	$449,983	0.17%	$0	--	--
15. MASSACHUSETTS TIC	$1,705	0.00%	$0	--	--
16. DAKOTA HOMESTEAD	$540	0.00%	$0	--	--
17. SECURITY UNION	$300	0.00%	$60,379	0.24%	502.11%
18. NATIONS OF NY	$0	--	$94,322	0.38%	0.00%
19. ALAMO	$0	--	$0	--	--
20. INVESTORS TIC	$0	--	$0	--	--
COMPOSITE	$272,357,475	100.00%	$25,124,547	100.00%	9.00%
AVERAGE	$13,617,874		$1,256,227		

10-YEAR - DIRECT PREMIUMS WRITTEN (DPW) BY CHANNEL See Sec. 3

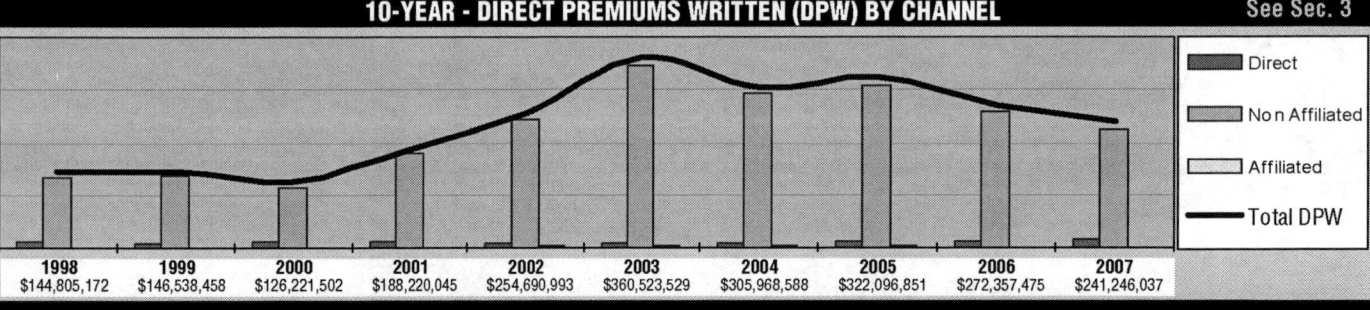

Legend: Direct / Non Affiliated / Affiliated / Total DPW

1998	1999	2000	2001	2002	2003	2004	2005	2006	2007
$144,805,172	$146,538,458	$126,221,502	$188,220,045	$254,690,993	$360,523,529	$305,968,588	$322,096,851	$272,357,475	$241,246,037

10-YEAR - LOSS RATIO See Sec. 5, A.2

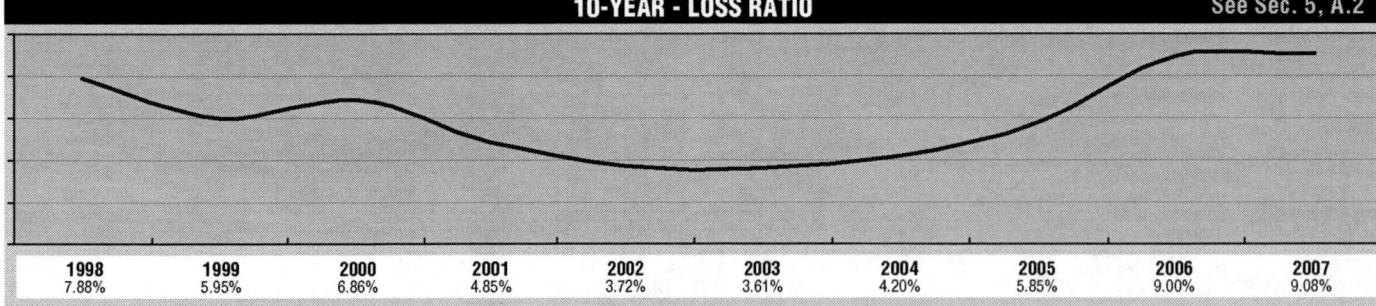

1998	1999	2000	2001	2002	2003	2004	2005	2006	2007
7.88%	5.95%	6.86%	4.85%	3.72%	3.61%	4.20%	5.85%	9.00%	9.08%

6

MICHIGAN

DEPARTMENT OF INSURANCE INFORMATION	LAND TITLE ASSOCIATION	DOMICILED UNDERWRITERS

Michigan Department of Labor & Economic Growth — **Michigan Land Title Association**

		Underwriter	NAIC #

Mr. Ken Ross
Acting Commissioner
611 W Ottawa, Ottawa Building, 3rd Fl.
Office of Financial & Insurance Services
Lansing, MI 48933-1070
Phone: (517) 373-0220
Fax: (517) 335-4978
www.michigan.gov/ofis

1000 W St. Joseph Hwy., Ste. 200
Lansing, MI 48915
Phone: (517) 374-2728
www.milta.org

None

21 | Licensed Underwriters | See Sec. 1

STATUTORY PREMIUM RESERVE (SPR) REQUIREMENTS

Inception:	5% of gross premiums received
Max Years:	20	Release:	0% years 1-10; 10% years 11-20

MARKET SHARE BY UNDERWRITER   See Sec. 3

2007

	TOTAL DPW	MARKET SHARE	LOSSES INCURRED	MARKET SHARE	LOSS RATIO
1. FIRST AMERICAN TIC	$120.166.701	38.17%	$19.875.770	35.83%	14.49%
2. TRANSNATION	$34.119.199	10.84%	$5.974.140	10.77%	15.94%
3. CHICAGO TIC	$31.961.665	10.15%	$846.989	1.53%	2.56%
4. FIDELITY NATIONAL	$31.838.639	10.11%	$5.865.956	10.57%	16.46%
5. LAWYERS	$27.390.596	8.70%	$1.748.802	3.15%	5.17%
6. STEWART TGC	$20.494.008	6.51%	$3.443.832	6.21%	16.05%
7. OLD REPUBLIC NATIONAL	$15.289.359	4.86%	$5.633.471	10.16%	35.46%
8. COMMONWEALTH LAND	$10.316.594	3.28%	$1.610.410	2.90%	13.53%
9. TICOR	$6.183.776	1.96%	$4.583.231	8.26%	68.17%
10. SECURITY UNION	$5.207.848	1.65%	$1.109.741	2.00%	20.34%
11. UNITED GENERAL	$3.205.285	1.02%	$223.579	0.40%	6.57%
12. INVESTORS TIC	$3.094.830	0.98%	$96.749	0.17%	2.95%
13. GUARANTEE T&T	$2.797.453	0.89%	$475.118	0.86%	16.13%
14. TICOR (FL)	$1.868.554	0.59%	$3.566.400	6.43%	162.39%
15. COMMERCE	$498.233	0.16%	$0	--	--
16. CENSTAR	$278.957	0.09%	$0	--	--
17. ATTORNEYS TIF (FL)	$81.020	0.03%	$419.457	0.76%	516.01%
18. AMERICAN GUARANTY	$650	0.00%	$0	--	--
19. COMMONWEALTH LAND (NJ	$0	--	$0	--	--
20. NATIONS OF NY	$0	--	($1.486)	0.00%	--
21. NORTHEAST INVESTORS	$0	--	$0	--	--
COMPOSITE	**$314.793.367**	**100.00%**	**$55.472.159**	**100.00%**	**15.79%**
AVERAGE	**$14.990.160**		**$2.641.531**		

2006

	TOTAL DPW	MARKET SHARE	LOSSES INCURRED	MARKET SHARE	LOSS RATIO
1. FIRST AMERICAN TIC	$156.416.553	39.55%	$14.730.076	23.09%	8.60%
2. TRANSNATION	$45.122.553	11.41%	$8.015.844	12.57%	16.20%
3. LAWYERS	$37.363.515	9.45%	$6.878.792	10.78%	16.13%
4. CHICAGO TIC	$34.895.886	8.82%	$3.889.619	6.10%	11.06%
5. FIDELITY NATIONAL	$30.505.391	7.71%	$6.580.485	10.32%	20.05%
6. STEWART TGC	$30.491.164	7.71%	$7.605.333	11.92%	24.62%
7. OLD REPUBLIC NATIONAL	$15.994.601	4.04%	$7.134.952	11.19%	43.40%
8. COMMONWEALTH LAND	$14.265.044	3.61%	$1.688.140	2.65%	9.72%
9. SECURITY UNION	$8.976.770	2.27%	$842.879	1.32%	9.30%
10. TICOR	$7.868.704	1.99%	$3.184.217	4.99%	38.48%
11. TICOR (FL)	$5.848.259	1.48%	$1.542.545	2.42%	25.11%
12. INVESTORS TIC	$3.475.934	0.88%	$570.581	0.89%	15.52%
13. GUARANTEE T&T	$2.708.413	0.68%	$806.892	1.26%	31.39%
14. COMMERCE	$629.039	0.16%	$0	--	--
15. UNITED GENERAL	$541.746	0.14%	$0	--	--
16. CENSTAR	$229.925	0.06%	$0	--	--
17. ATTORNEYS TIF (FL)	$168.942	0.04%	$315.285	0.49%	197.43%
18. COMMONWEALTH LAND (NJ	$0	--	$0	--	--
19. NORTHEAST INVESTORS	$0	--	$0	--	--
20. NATIONS OF NY	$0	--	$1.358	0.00%	--
COMPOSITE	**$395.502.439**	**100.00%**	**$63.786.998**	**100.00%**	**14.93%**
AVERAGE	**$19.775.122**		**$3.189.350**		

10-YEAR - DIRECT PREMIUMS WRITTEN (DPW) BY CHANNEL   See Sec. 3

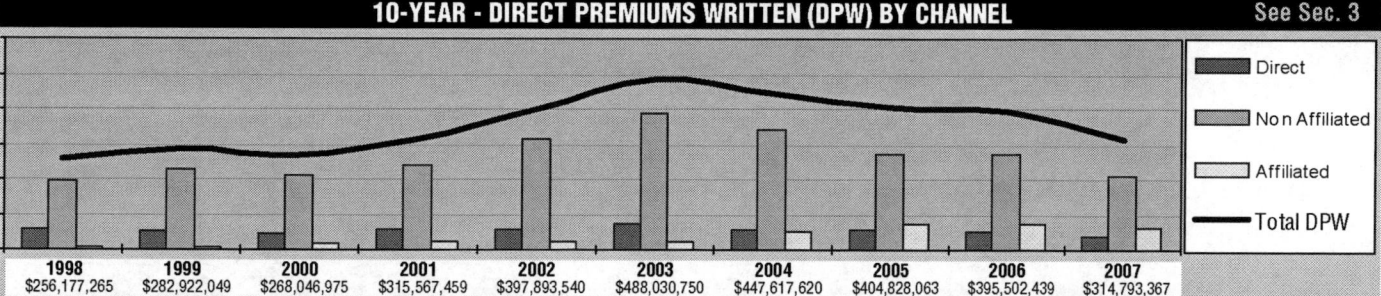

- Direct
- Non Affiliated
- Affiliated
- — Total DPW

1998	1999	2000	2001	2002	2003	2004	2005	2006	2007
$256,177,265	$282,922,049	$268,046,975	$315,567,459	$397,893,540	$488,030,750	$447,617,620	$404,828,063	$395,502,439	$314,793,367

10-YEAR - LOSS RATIO   See Sec. 5, A.2

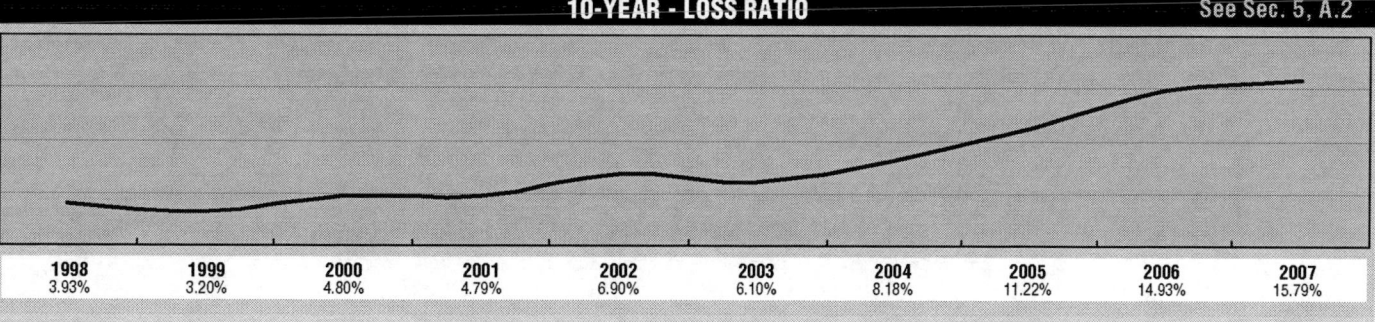

1998	1999	2000	2001	2002	2003	2004	2005	2006	2007
3.93%	3.20%	4.80%	4.79%	6.90%	6.10%	8.18%	11.22%	14.93%	15.79%

6

MINNESOTA

DEPARTMENT OF INSURANCE INFORMATION

Minnesota Department of Commerce

Mr. Glenn Wilson
Insurance Commissioner
85 7th Pl. East, Ste. 500
St. Paul, MN 55101-2198
Phone: (651) 296-6025
Fax: (651) 282-2568
www.commerce.state.mn.us

LAND TITLE ASSOCIATION

Minnesota Land Title Association

1250 N Frontage Rd.
P.O. Box 456
Hastings, MN 55033
www.mlta.org

DOMICILED UNDERWRITERS
See Sec. 1

Underwriter	NAIC #
OLD REPUBLIC NATIONAL	50520

25	Licensed Underwriters	See Sec. 1

STATUTORY PREMIUM RESERVE (SPR) REQUIREMENTS

Inception:	8% of direct risk premiums written, premiums for reinsurance assumed less premiums for reinsurance ceded, and other income
Max Years:	20 **Release:** 35% year 1; 15% years 2-3; 10% year 4; 3% years 5-7; 2% years 8-10; 1% years 11-20

MARKET SHARE BY UNDERWRITER
See Sec. 3

2007

	TOTAL DPW	MARKET SHARE	LOSSES INCURRED	MARKET SHARE	LOSS RATIO
1. COMMONWEALTH LAND	$21,249,720	17.77%	$3,973,519	14.61%	15.98%
2. CHICAGO TIC	$20,605,583	17.23%	$4,340,428	15.96%	18.72%
3. FIRST AMERICAN TIC	$19,094,758	15.97%	$5,512,833	20.27%	21.76%
4. STEWART TGC	$16,605,803	13.89%	$2,977,182	10.95%	17.40%
5. OLD REPUBLIC NATIONAL	$12,081,637	10.11%	$1,703,086	6.26%	8.33%
6. LAWYERS	$11,005,213	9.20%	$145,102	0.53%	1.22%
7. FIDELITY NATIONAL	$6,022,824	5.04%	$5,660,575	20.81%	94.65%
8. TICOR	$5,651,306	4.73%	$1,183,037	4.35%	21.08%
9. ATTORNEYS TIF (FL)	$3,696,692	3.09%	$142,652	0.52%	3.73%
10. UNITED GENERAL	$1,231,375	1.03%	$660,532	2.43%	57.22%
11. TICOR (FL)	$1,178,054	0.99%	$949,870	3.49%	79.33%
12. INVESTORS TIC	$482,025	0.40%	($136,450)	(0.50)%	(26.30)%
13. COMMERCE	$358,903	0.30%	$0	--	--
14. DAKOTA HOMESTEAD	$85,114	0.07%	$0	--	--
15. LAND TIC (ST LOUIS)	$84,302	0.07%	$0	--	--
16. CENSTAR	$60,157	0.05%	$0	--	--
17. NORTH AMERICAN	$36,986	0.03%	$0	--	--
18. NATIONAL LAND	$23,828	0.02%	$0	--	--
19. TRANSNATION	$5,167	0.00%	$10,000	0.04%	68.33%
20. ATTORNEYS TGF (CO)	$0	--	$51,597	0.19%	--
21. NATIONS OF NY	$0	--	$22,069	0.08%	--
22. GUARANTEE T&T	$0	--	$0	--	--
23. SECURITY UNION	$0	--	$0	--	--
COMPOSITE	$119,559,447	100.00%	$27,196,032	100.00%	19.19%
AVERAGE	$5,198,237		$1,182,436		

2006

	TOTAL DPW	MARKET SHARE	LOSSES INCURRED	MARKET SHARE	LOSS RATIO
1. CHICAGO TIC	$32,299,822	20.85%	$2,108,012	15.18%	6.14%
2. STEWART TGC	$27,337,351	17.65%	$1,414,091	10.18%	5.21%
3. COMMONWEALTH LAND	$21,878,634	14.12%	$2,424,768	17.46%	8.71%
4. FIRST AMERICAN TIC	$21,390,258	13.81%	$2,221,328	15.99%	7.21%
5. OLD REPUBLIC NATIONAL	$16,202,894	10.46%	$2,086,599	15.02%	8.07%
6. LAWYERS	$14,252,762	9.20%	$1,191,436	8.58%	7.77%
7. FIDELITY NATIONAL	$8,510,587	5.49%	$1,147,709	8.26%	13.70%
8. TICOR	$5,313,781	3.43%	$545,224	3.93%	10.35%
9. ATTORNEYS TIF (FL)	$4,967,292	3.21%	($64,309)	(0.46)%	(1.29)%
10. TICOR (FL)	$1,401,051	0.90%	$305,778	2.20%	19.44%
11. INVESTORS TIC	$1,052,515	0.68%	$361,067	2.60%	34.96%
12. TRANSNATION	$73,471	0.05%	$6,482	0.05%	11.65%
13. DAKOTA HOMESTEAD	$71,344	0.05%	$0	--	--
14. UNITED GENERAL	$70,047	0.05%	$0	--	--
15. COMMERCE	$51,282	0.03%	$0	--	--
16. CENSTAR	$24,033	0.02%	$0	--	--
17. NATIONS OF NY	$0	--	$107,250	0.77%	--
18. ATTORNEYS TGF (CO)	$0	--	$35,497	0.26%	--
19. COMMONWEALTH LAND (NJ	$0	--	$0	--	--
20. SECURITY UNION	$0	--	$0	--	--
COMPOSITE	$154,897,124	100.00%	$13,890,932	100.00%	7.60%
AVERAGE	$7,744,856		$694,547		

10-YEAR - DIRECT PREMIUMS WRITTEN (DPW) BY CHANNEL
See Sec. 3

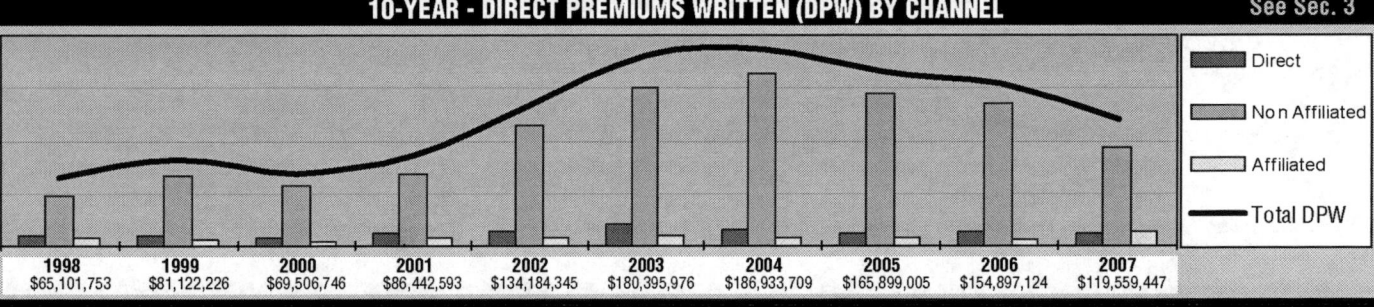

- Direct
- Non Affiliated
- Affiliated
- Total DPW

1998	1999	2000	2001	2002	2003	2004	2005	2006	2007
$65,101,753	$81,122,226	$69,506,746	$86,442,593	$134,184,345	$180,395,976	$186,933,709	$165,899,005	$154,897,124	$119,559,447

10-YEAR - LOSS RATIO
See Sec. 5, A.2

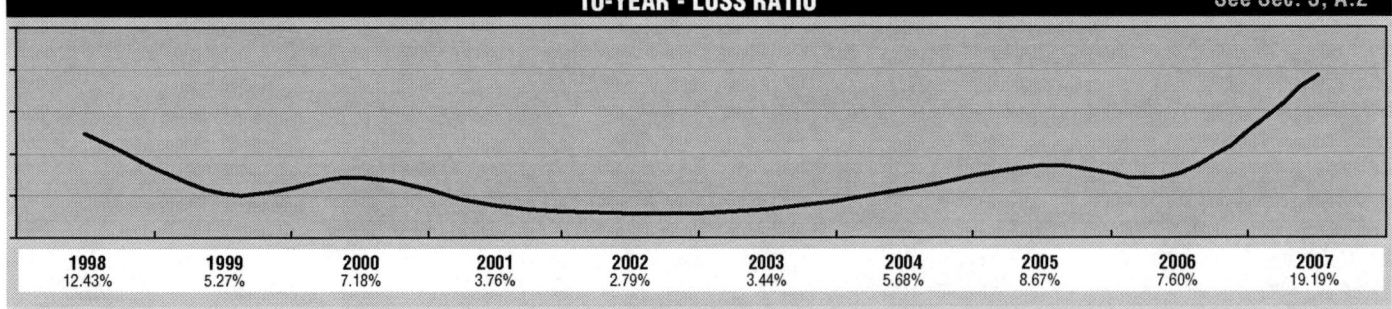

1998	1999	2000	2001	2002	2003	2004	2005	2006	2007
12.43%	5.27%	7.18%	3.76%	2.79%	3.44%	5.68%	8.67%	7.60%	19.19%

MISSISSIPPI

DEPARTMENT OF INSURANCE INFORMATION	LAND TITLE ASSOCIATION	DOMICILED UNDERWRITERS See Sec. 1	

Mississippi Insurance Department | **Dixie Land Title Association, Inc.** | **Underwriter** | **NAIC #**

		MISSISSIPPI GUARANTY	50030
		MISSISSIPPI VALLEY	51004

Mr. Mike Chaney
Commissioner of Insurance
1001 Woolfork State Office Building, 501 N. West St.
Jackson, MS 39201
Phone: (601) 359-3569
Fax: (601) 359-2474
www.mid.state.ms.us/

P.O. Box 14806
Baton Rouge, LA 70816
Phone: (866) 894-0209
www.dlta.net

28	Licensed Underwriters	See Sec. 1

STATUTORY PREMIUM RESERVE (SPR) REQUIREMENTS

Inception:	10% of premiums received		
Max Years:	15	Release:	All released after 180 months

MARKET SHARE BY UNDERWRITER   See Sec. 3

2007

	TOTAL DPW	MARKET SHARE	LOSSES INCURRED	MARKET SHARE	LOSS RATIO
1. FIRST AMERICAN TIC	$12,995,035	27.48%	$1,968,374	13.39%	10.35%
2. MISSISSIPPI VALLEY	$11,567,326	24.46%	$2,528,089	17.20%	21.20%
3. CHICAGO TIC	$4,983,247	10.54%	$253,164	1.72%	4.76%
4. LAWYERS	$4,934,513	10.43%	$8,036,384	54.67%	150.83%
5. STEWART TGC	$3,763,822	7.96%	$319,207	2.17%	7.21%
6. SECURITY TG (BALTIMORE)	$2,917,899	6.17%	$113,161	0.77%	3.84%
7. FIDELITY NATIONAL	$2,286,101	4.83%	$276,227	1.88%	12.03%
8. COMMONWEALTH LAND	$1,476,184	3.12%	$39,076	0.27%	2.41%
9. INVESTORS TIC	$916,453	1.94%	$33,412	0.23%	3.82%
10. MISSISSIPPI GUARANTY	$309,646	0.65%	$0	--	--
11. UNITED GENERAL	$240,378	0.51%	$460,034	3.13%	154.46%
12. SOUTHERN TI CORP	$223,884	0.47%	$0	--	--
13. TICOR	$154,244	0.33%	$28,622	0.19%	15.78%
14. GUARANTEE T&T	$151,012	0.32%	$22	0.00%	0.01%
15. CENSTAR	$132,640	0.28%	$0	--	--
16. TICOR (FL)	$88,536	0.19%	$176,634	1.20%	221.09%
17. OLD REPUBLIC NATIONAL	$67,260	0.14%	$39,718	0.27%	25.65%
18. SECURITY UNION	$52,619	0.11%	$0	--	--
19. TRANSUNION NATIONAL	$15,223	0.03%	$0	--	--
20. AMERICAN GUARANTY	$6,995	0.01%	$0	--	--
21. TRANSNATION	$6,290	0.01%	$0	--	--
22. WESTCOR	$4,790	0.01%	$0	--	--
23. CONESTOGA	$1,015	0.00%	$0	--	--
24. NATIONAL OF NY	$0	--	$428,310	2.91%	0.00%
25. CHICAGO T&T	$0	--	$0	--	--
26. NATIONS OF NY	$0	--	$0	--	--
27. NORTHEAST INVESTORS	$0	--	$0	--	--
COMPOSITE	$47,295,112	100.00%	$14,700,434	100.00%	26.55%
AVERAGE	$1,751,671		$544,461		

2006

	TOTAL DPW	MARKET SHARE	LOSSES INCURRED	MARKET SHARE	LOSS RATIO
1. FIRST AMERICAN TIC	$12,045,601	26.89%	$1,661,185	67.35%	8.38%
2. MISSISSIPPI VALLEY	$11,332,578	25.30%	$567,509	23.01%	4.87%
3. LAWYERS	$4,100,731	9.15%	$204,916	8.31%	4.72%
4. CHICAGO TIC	$4,086,038	9.12%	$181,636	7.36%	4.29%
5. SECURITY TG (BALTIMORE)	$3,545,676	7.92%	($514,561)	(20.86)%	(15.18)%
6. STEWART TGC	$3,356,416	7.49%	$227,772	9.23%	6.02%
7. FIDELITY NATIONAL	$2,579,839	5.76%	$35,780	1.45%	1.42%
8. COMMONWEALTH LAND	$1,451,038	3.24%	$51,815	2.10%	3.09%
9. INVESTORS TIC	$619,028	1.38%	$3,739	0.15%	0.61%
10. MISSISSIPPI GUARANTY	$499,243	1.11%	$0	--	--
11. TICOR	$455,369	1.02%	$87,369	3.54%	17.96%
12. GUARANTEE T&T	$212,713	0.47%	$0	--	--
13. UNITED GENERAL	$168,856	0.38%	($197,300)	(8.00)%	(119.36)%
14. TICOR (FL)	$144,305	0.32%	$187,818	7.61%	144.61%
15. SOUTHERN TI CORP	$82,191	0.18%	$0	--	--
16. OLD REPUBLIC NATIONAL	$54,603	0.12%	($31,193)	(1.26)%	(17.81)%
17. SECURITY UNION	$34,397	0.08%	$0	--	--
18. CENSTAR	$21,026	0.05%	$0	--	--
19. TRANSUNION NATIONAL	$3,880	0.00%	$0	--	--
20. TRANSNATION	$209	0.00%	$0	--	--
21. NORTHEAST INVESTORS	$0	--	$0	--	--
COMPOSITE	$44,793,737	100.00%	$2,466,485	100.00%	4.58%
AVERAGE	$2,133,035		$117,452		

10-YEAR - DIRECT PREMIUMS WRITTEN (DPW) BY CHANNEL   See Sec. 3

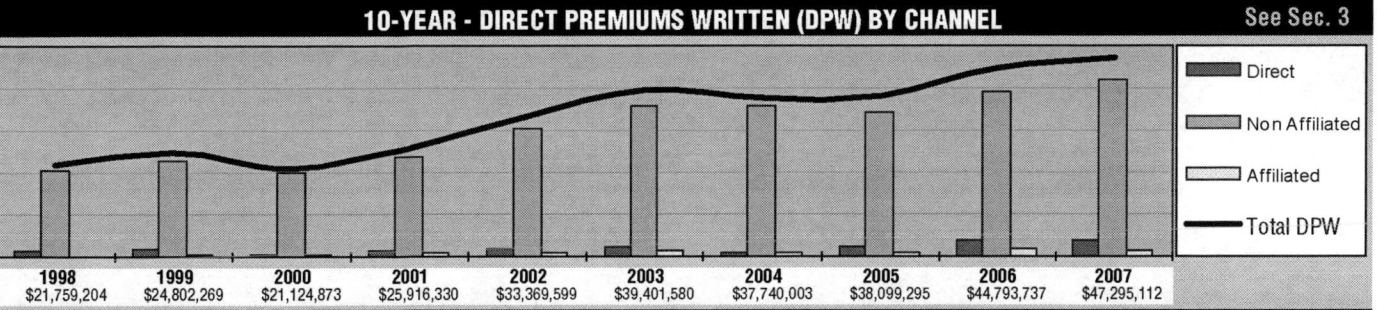

- Direct
- Non Affiliated
- Affiliated
- Total DPW

1998	1999	2000	2001	2002	2003	2004	2005	2006	2007
$21,759,204	$24,802,269	$21,124,873	$25,916,330	$33,369,599	$39,401,580	$37,740,003	$38,099,295	$44,793,737	$47,295,112

10-YEAR - LOSS RATIO   See Sec. 5, A.2

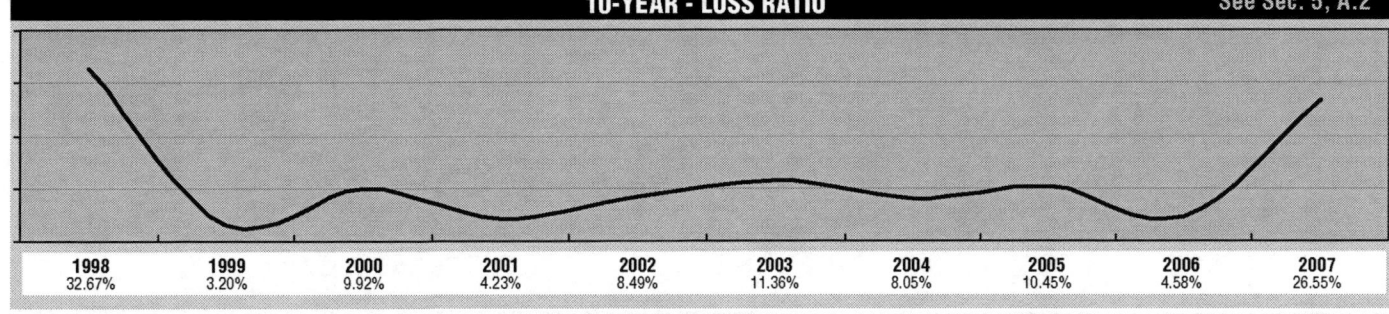

1998	1999	2000	2001	2002	2003	2004	2005	2006	2007
32.67%	3.20%	9.92%	4.23%	8.49%	11.36%	8.05%	10.45%	4.58%	26.55%

6

MISSOURI

DEPARTMENT OF INSURANCE INFORMATION

Missouri Department of Insurance, Financial Institutions & Professional Registration

Mr. Douglas Ommen
Director of Insurance

301 W High St., Ste. 530
Jefferson City, MO 65102-0690

Phone: (573) 751-4126
Fax: (573) 751-1165
www.insurance.mo.gov

LAND TITLE ASSOCIATION

Missouri Land Title Association

P.O. Box 620
Bonne Terre, MO 63628

Phone: (573) 760-3264
www.mlta.com

DOMICILED UNDERWRITERS   See Sec. 1

Underwriter	NAIC #
FARMERS NATIONAL	12522
GUARANTEE	50034
LAND TIC (ST LOUIS)	50237
24 Licensed Underwriters	See Sec. 1

STATUTORY PREMIUM RESERVE (SPR) REQUIREMENTS

Inception:	15 cents per $1,000 of net retained liability	
Max Years:	**20**	**Release:** 10% for years 1-5; 3.33% for years 6-20

MARKET SHARE BY UNDERWRITER   See Sec. 3

2007

	TOTAL DPW	MARKET SHARE	LOSSES INCURRED	MARKET SHARE	LOSS RATIO
1. STEWART TGC	$11.820.652	15.75%	$1.498.469	8.07%	13.17%
2. CHICAGO TIC	$10.942.001	14.58%	$627.565	3.38%	4.45%
3. FIRST AMERICAN TIC	$9.761.459	13.00%	$1.531.860	8.25%	10.49%
4. COMMONWEALTH LAND	$8.810.131	11.74%	$4.622.975	24.91%	22.17%
5. UNITED GENERAL	$6.837.315	9.11%	$210.603	1.13%	3.46%
6. FIDELITY NATIONAL	$6.153.944	8.20%	$1.978.002	10.66%	32.05%
7. OLD REPUBLIC NATIONAL	$4.199.612	5.59%	$2.531.037	13.64%	48.19%
8. LAWYERS	$3.743.995	4.99%	$1.555.498	8.38%	30.90%
9. TRANSNATION	$3.510.657	4.68%	$1.615.831	8.71%	59.41%
10. LAND TIC (ST LOUIS)	$2.173.014	2.90%	$0	--	--
11. GUARANTEE	$1.506.390	2.01%	$844.920	4.55%	64.41%
12. TICOR (FL)	$1.250.066	1.67%	$832.622	4.49%	67.99%
13. FARMERS NATIONAL	$1.138.404	1.52%	$68.819	0.37%	8.57%
14. TICOR	$1.115.837	1.49%	$107.885	0.58%	8.60%
15. NATIONAL OF NY	$698.400	0.93%	$0	--	--
16. SECURITY UNION	$595.021	0.79%	$534.372	2.88%	88.14%
17. COMMERCE	$322.242	0.43%	$0	--	--
18. NATIONAL LAND	$177.820	0.24%	$0	--	--
19. INVESTORS TIC	$161.893	0.22%	$803	0.00%	0.53%
20. CENSTAR	$141.144	0.19%	$0	--	--
21. AMERICAN GUARANTY	$730	0.00%	$0	--	--
22. ALAMO	$0	--	$0	--	--
23. CHICAGO T&T	$0	--	$0	--	--
24. EQUITY NATIONAL	$0	--	$0	--	--
25. GUARANTEE T&T	$0	--	$0	--	--
26. NATIONS OF NY	$0	--	$0	--	--
COMPOSITE	$75,060,727	100.00%	$18,561,261	100.00%	19.57%
AVERAGE	$2,886,951		$713,895		

2006

	TOTAL DPW	MARKET SHARE	LOSSES INCURRED	MARKET SHARE	LOSS RATIO
1. CHICAGO TIC	$12.577.931	16.05%	$1.374.283	6.91%	7.62%
2. FIRST AMERICAN TIC	$10.601.482	13.53%	$7.848.636	39.45%	59.98%
3. STEWART TGC	$10.240.856	13.07%	$1.511.015	7.59%	15.53%
4. COMMONWEALTH LAND	$9.769.008	12.47%	$3.639.443	18.29%	15.57%
5. UNITED GENERAL	$8.167.901	10.43%	$93.917	0.47%	1.53%
6. FIDELITY NATIONAL	$6.109.178	7.80%	$930.211	4.68%	15.50%
7. OLD REPUBLIC NATIONAL	$4.353.617	5.56%	$1.507.192	7.58%	26.38%
8. LAWYERS	$3.825.407	4.88%	$439.679	2.21%	9.19%
9. TRANSNATION	$3.782.731	4.83%	$922.470	4.64%	29.80%
10. TICOR (FL)	$2.403.760	3.07%	($5.570)	(0.03)%	(0.24)%
11. GUARANTEE	$2.160.978	2.76%	$1.290.776	6.49%	71.76%
12. TICOR	$1.316.532	1.68%	($4.861)	(0.02)%	(0.34)%
13. SECURITY UNION	$950.117	1.21%	$335.554	1.69%	35.58%
14. LAND TIC (ST LOUIS)	$721.764	0.92%	$0	--	--
15. COMMERCE	$551.923	0.70%	$0	--	--
16. FARMERS NATIONAL	$507.308	0.65%	$1.221	0.00%	0.24%
17. COLUMBIAN NATIONAL	$199.900	0.26%	$0	--	--
18. INVESTORS TIC	$79.233	0.10%	$11.969	0.06%	15.51%
19. CENSTAR	$25.534	0.03%	$0	--	--
COMPOSITE	$78,345,160	100.00%	$19,895,935	100.00%	20.20%
AVERAGE	$4,123,429		$1,047,154		

10-YEAR - DIRECT PREMIUMS WRITTEN (DPW) BY CHANNEL   See Sec. 3

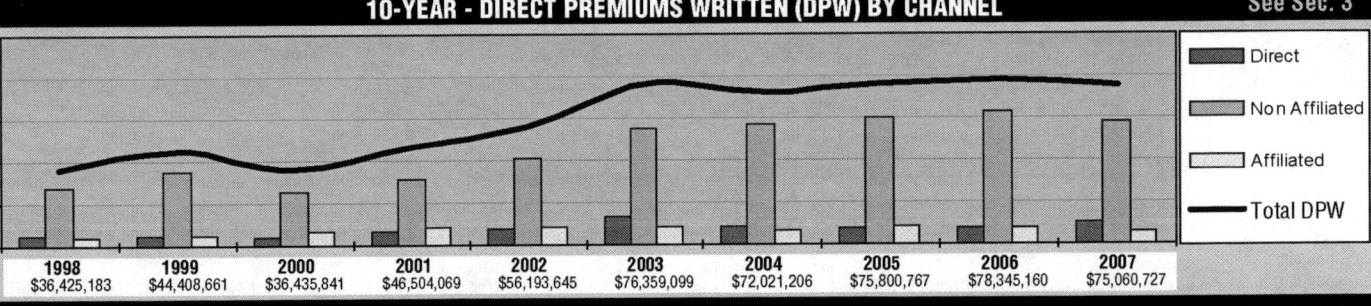

	Direct
	Non Affiliated
	Affiliated
	Total DPW

1998	1999	2000	2001	2002	2003	2004	2005	2006	2007
$36,425,183	$44,408,661	$36,435,841	$46,504,069	$56,193,645	$76,359,099	$72,021,206	$75,800,767	$78,345,160	$75,060,727

10-YEAR - LOSS RATIO   See Sec. 5, A.2

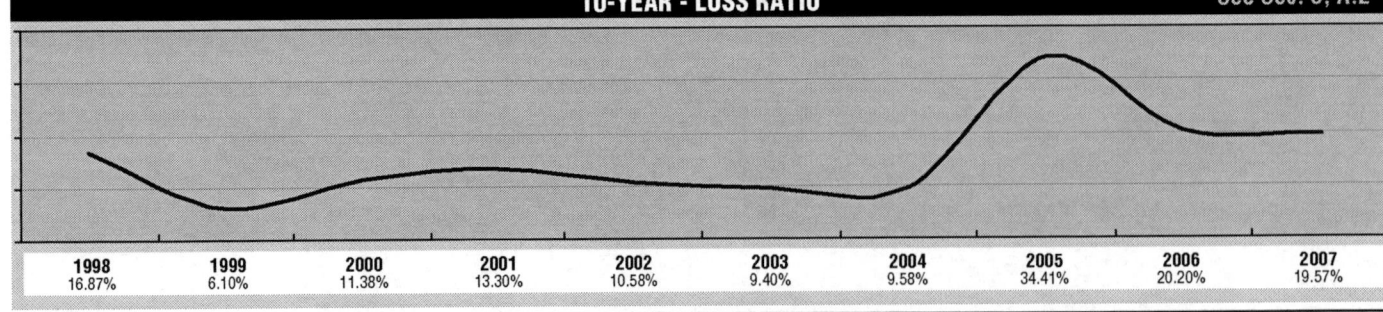

1998	1999	2000	2001	2002	2003	2004	2005	2006	2007
16.87%	6.10%	11.38%	13.30%	10.58%	9.40%	9.58%	34.41%	20.20%	19.57%

6

MONTANA

DEPARTMENT OF INSURANCE INFORMATION	LAND TITLE ASSOCIATION	DOMICILED UNDERWRITERS See Sec. 1

Montana State Auditor's Office	Montana Land and Title Association	Underwriter	NAIC #

Mr. John Morrison
Commissioner of Insurance & Securities
840 Helena Ave.
Helena, MT 59601
Phone: (406) 444-2040
Fax: (406) 444-3497
www.sao.mt.gov

P.O. Box 6322
Helena, MT 59604
www.mtlandtitle.com

None

■ 21 Licensed Underwriters   See Sec. 1

STATUTORY PREMIUM RESERVE (SPR) REQUIREMENTS

Inception:	10% of risk premiums written		
Max Years:	20	Release:	5% per year

MARKET SHARE BY UNDERWRITER   See Sec. 3

2007

	TOTAL DPW	MARKET SHARE	LOSSES INCURRED	MARKET SHARE	LOSS RATIO
1. FIRST AMERICAN TIC	$23,463,875	43.08%	$813,473	35.96%	3.45%
2. STEWART TGC	$8,659,397	15.90%	$156,092	6.90%	1.82%
3. CHICAGO TIC	$7,461,741	13.70%	$287,312	12.70%	3.39%
4. COMMONWEALTH LAND	$5,254,397	9.65%	$243,470	10.76%	4.59%
5. TICOR	$2,979,070	5.47%	($84,990)	(3.76)%	(2.92)%
6. LAWYERS	$2,755,528	5.06%	$691,422	30.57%	23.97%
7. OLD REPUBLIC NATIONAL	$1,485,679	2.73%	$18,528	0.82%	1.18%
8. FIDELITY NATIONAL	$1,360,916	2.50%	$141,882	6.27%	10.47%
9. TRANSNATION	$536,849	0.99%	$0	--	--
10. UNITED GENERAL	$328,572	0.60%	$0	--	--
11. NATIONAL LAND	$121,482	0.22%	$0	--	--
12. TICOR (FL)	$52,941	0.10%	$0	--	--
13. SECURITY UNION	$1,282	0.00%	($5,264)	(0.23)%	(210.06)%
14. GUARANTEE T&T	$0	--	$0	--	--
15. INVESTORS TIC	$0	--	$0	--	--
16. NATIONAL OF NY	$0	--	$0	--	--
COMPOSITE	$54,461,729	100.00%	$2,261,925	100.00%	4.06%
AVERAGE	$3,403,858		$141,370		

2006

	TOTAL DPW	MARKET SHARE	LOSSES INCURRED	MARKET SHARE	LOSS RATIO
1. FIRST AMERICAN TIC	$21,517,397	39.59%	$721,437	34.63%	3.40%
2. STEWART TGC	$9,204,908	16.94%	$154,601	7.42%	1.71%
3. CHICAGO TIC	$8,246,954	15.17%	$369,180	17.72%	3.98%
4. COMMONWEALTH LAND	$5,789,293	10.65%	$176,782	8.48%	2.90%
5. TICOR	$3,443,549	6.34%	$156,551	7.51%	4.67%
6. LAWYERS	$2,327,370	4.28%	$143,112	6.87%	5.72%
7. FIDELITY NATIONAL	$1,555,995	2.86%	$90,768	4.36%	5.94%
8. OLD REPUBLIC NATIONAL	$1,351,572	2.49%	$218,694	10.50%	14.68%
9. TRANSNATION	$607,927	1.12%	$0	--	--
10. UNITED GENERAL	$182,007	0.33%	$0	--	--
11. TICOR (FL)	$119,417	0.22%	$0	--	--
12. SECURITY UNION	$0	--	$52,417	2.52%	1,852.19%
13. INVESTORS TIC	$0	--	$0	--	--
COMPOSITE	$54,346,389	100.00%	$2,083,542	100.00%	3.76%
AVERAGE	$4,180,491		$160,272		

10-YEAR - DIRECT PREMIUMS WRITTEN (DPW) BY CHANNEL   See Sec. 3

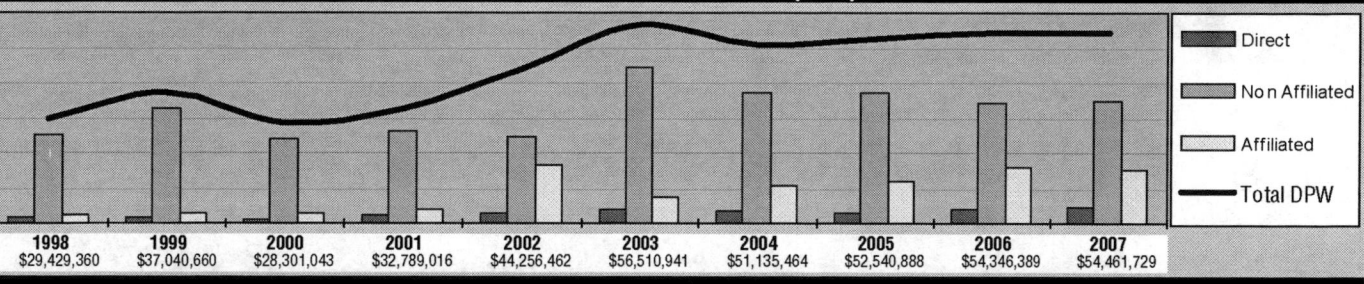

	Direct
	Non Affiliated
	Affiliated
	Total DPW

1998	1999	2000	2001	2002	2003	2004	2005	2006	2007
$29,429,360	$37,040,660	$28,301,043	$32,789,016	$44,256,462	$56,510,941	$51,135,464	$52,540,888	$54,346,389	$54,461,729

10-YEAR - LOSS RATIO   See Sec. 5, A.2

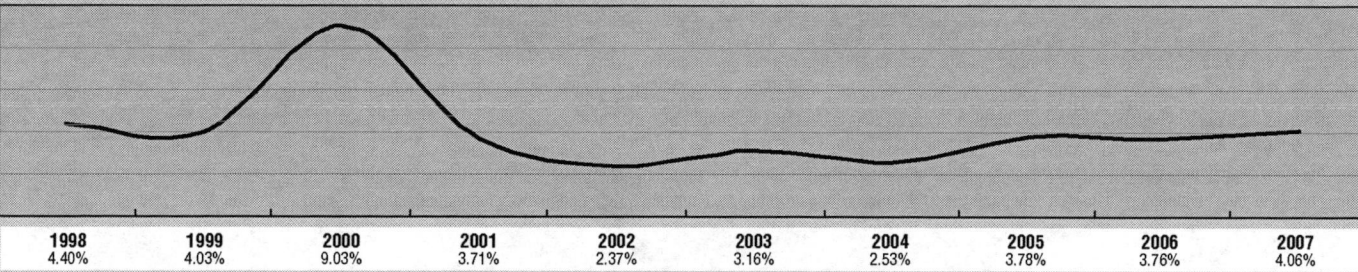

1998	1999	2000	2001	2002	2003	2004	2005	2006	2007
4.40%	4.03%	9.03%	3.71%	2.37%	3.16%	2.53%	3.78%	3.76%	4.06%

6

NEBRASKA

DEPARTMENT OF INSURANCE INFORMATION	LAND TITLE ASSOCIATION	DOMICILED UNDERWRITERS See Sec. 1	
Nebraska Department of Insurance	New England Land Title Association	Underwriter	NAIC #

Nebraska Department of Insurance

Ms. Ann Frohman
Director of Insurance
941 "O" St., Ste. 400
Terminal Building
Lincoln, NE 68508-3639

Phone: (402) 471-2201
Fax: (402) 471-2990
www.doi.ne.gov

New England Land Title Association

P.O. Box 743
Norwalk, CT 06852-0743

Phone: (203) 847-6885
www.nelta.org

Underwriter	NAIC #
CHICAGO TIC	50229
COMMONWEALTH LAND	50083
LAWYERS	50024
TICOR (FL)	51535
TITLE IC AMERICA	50245
TRANSNATION	50012
20 Licensed Underwriters	See Sec. 1

STATUTORY PREMIUM RESERVE (SPR) REQUIREMENTS

Inception:	17 cents per $1,000 of net retained liability		
Max Years:	20	Release:	30% first year; 15% year 2; 10% years 3-4; 5% years 5-6; 3% years 7-8; 2% years 9-15; 1% years 16-20

MARKET SHARE BY UNDERWRITER
See Sec. 3

2007

	TOTAL DPW	MARKET SHARE	LOSSES INCURRED	MARKET SHARE	LOSS RATIO
1. OLD REPUBLIC NATIONAL	$10,389,787	26.71%	$514,570	26.12%	4.91%
2. FIRST AMERICAN TIC	$8,153,795	20.96%	$225,179	11.43%	2.58%
3. COMMONWEALTH LAND	$5,213,864	13.41%	$100,790	5.12%	1.88%
4. CHICAGO TIC	$4,964,312	12.76%	$207,996	10.56%	4.88%
5. LAWYERS	$2,310,782	5.94%	$334,830	17.00%	13.20%
6. STEWART TGC	$1,916,221	4.93%	$242,829	12.33%	11.98%
7. FIDELITY NATIONAL	$1,749,242	4.50%	$221,046	11.22%	12.74%
8. TICOR	$1,068,466	2.75%	$116,293	5.90%	9.59%
9. UNITED GENERAL	$1,038,829	2.67%	$37,283	1.89%	3.72%
10. INVESTORS TIC	$726,417	1.87%	($47,185)	(2.40)%	(5.80)%
11. TICOR (FL)	$704,217	1.81%	$16,163	0.82%	2.44%
12. SECURITY UNION	$377,935	0.97%	$0	--	--
13. TRANSNATION	$182,102	0.47%	($72)	0.00%	(0.04)%
14. DAKOTA HOMESTEAD	$87,386	0.22%	$0	--	--
15. WESTCOR	$9,362	0.02%	$0	--	--
16. GUARANTEE T&T	$0	--	$0	--	--
17. NATIONAL OF NY	$0	--	$0	--	--
18. NORTHEAST INVESTORS	$0	--	$0	--	--
COMPOSITE	$38,892,717	100.00%	$1,969,722	100.00%	5.00%
AVERAGE	$2,160,707		$109,429		

2006

	TOTAL DPW	MARKET SHARE	LOSSES INCURRED	MARKET SHARE	LOSS RATIO
1. OLD REPUBLIC NATIONAL	$10,021,933	24.17%	$129,403	4.59%	1.28%
2. FIRST AMERICAN TIC	$9,166,289	22.11%	$284,971	10.11%	3.10%
3. CHICAGO TIC	$6,073,243	14.65%	$31,453	1.12%	0.52%
4. COMMONWEALTH LAND	$5,152,582	12.43%	$59,646	2.12%	1.06%
5. LAWYERS	$2,804,944	6.77%	$102,675	3.64%	3.43%
6. STEWART TGC	$2,479,771	5.98%	$52,652	1.87%	1.92%
7. FIDELITY NATIONAL	$1,709,562	4.12%	$2,177,527	77.24%	129.68%
8. TICOR	$1,068,761	2.58%	($36,622)	(1.30)%	(3.03)%
9. TICOR (FL)	$910,075	2.19%	$16,871	0.60%	1.88%
10. UNITED GENERAL	$705,956	1.70%	$3,524	0.13%	0.52%
11. INVESTORS TIC	$659,583	1.59%	$0	--	--
12. SECURITY UNION	$446,824	1.08%	$0	--	--
13. TRANSNATION	$261,846	0.63%	($2,920)	(0.10)%	(1.11)%
14. NORTHEAST INVESTORS	$0	--	$0	--	--
COMPOSITE	$41,461,369	100.00%	$2,819,180	100.00%	6.61%
AVERAGE	$2,961,526		$201,370		

10-YEAR - DIRECT PREMIUMS WRITTEN (DPW) BY CHANNEL
See Sec. 3

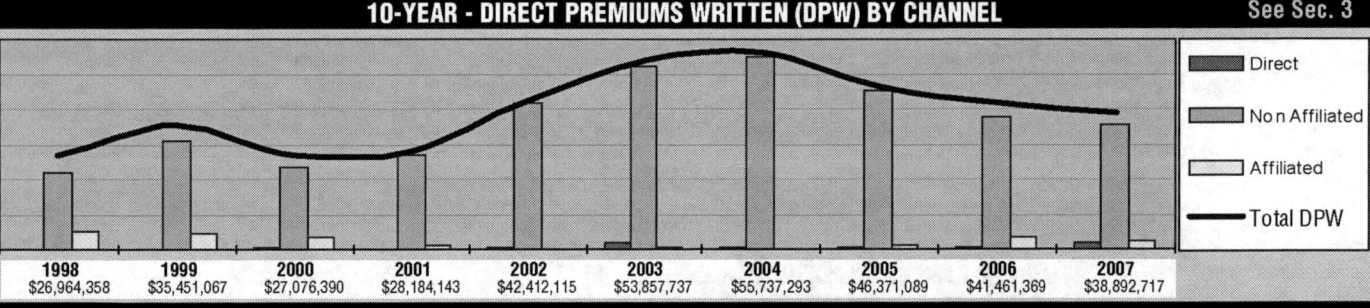

Legend: Direct, Non Affiliated, Affiliated, Total DPW

1998	1999	2000	2001	2002	2003	2004	2005	2006	2007
$26,964,358	$35,451,067	$27,076,390	$28,184,143	$42,412,115	$53,857,737	$55,737,293	$46,371,089	$41,461,369	$38,892,717

10-YEAR - LOSS RATIO
See Sec. 5, A.2

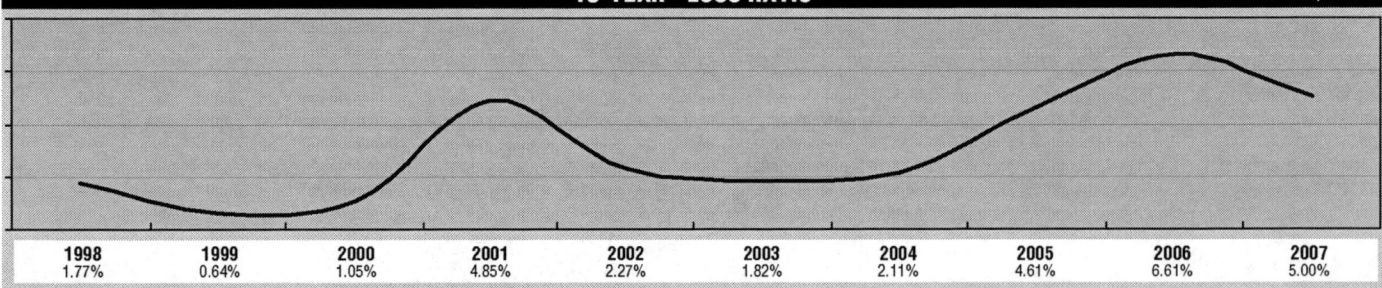

1998	1999	2000	2001	2002	2003	2004	2005	2006	2007
1.77%	0.64%	1.05%	4.85%	2.27%	1.82%	2.11%	4.61%	6.61%	5.00%

6

NEVADA

DEPARTMENT OF INSURANCE INFORMATION	LAND TITLE ASSOCIATION	DOMICILED UNDERWRITERS See Sec. 1
Nevada Division of Insurance	No information at time of publication.	**Underwriter** **NAIC #**

Ms. Alice A. Molasky-Arman
Insurance Commissioner
788 Fairview Dr., Ste. 300
Carson City, NV 89701
Phone: (775) 687-4270
Fax: (775) 687-3937
www.doi.state.nv.us

None

☐ 24   Licensed Underwriters   See Sec. 1

STATUTORY PREMIUM RESERVE (SPR) REQUIREMENTS

Inception:	5% of title insurance premiums collected		
Max Years:	20	Release:	5% per year

MARKET SHARE BY UNDERWRITER   See Sec. 3

2007

	TOTAL DPW	MARKET SHARE	LOSSES INCURRED	MARKET SHARE	LOSS RATIO
1. FIRST AMERICAN TIC	$60,537,745	28.35%	$2,592,836	24.05%	3.53%
2. CHICAGO TIC	$35,745,955	16.74%	$2,132,679	19.78%	6.21%
3. COMMONWEALTH LAND	$21,445,565	10.04%	$562,830	5.22%	2.37%
4. LAWYERS	$20,313,510	9.51%	$34,849	0.32%	0.17%
5. STEWART TGC	$18,894,158	8.85%	$633,207	5.87%	3.24%
6. FIDELITY NATIONAL	$15,229,025	7.13%	$1,587,384	14.73%	10.28%
7. TICOR	$13,002,102	6.09%	$930,787	8.63%	7.17%
8. WESTCOR	$10,300,496	4.82%	$130,009	1.21%	1.31%
9. OLD REPUBLIC NATIONAL	$7,527,602	3.53%	$1,025,252	9.51%	13.39%
10. NORTH AMERICAN	$3,313,273	1.55%	$29,499	0.27%	0.91%
11. UNITED GENERAL	$3,059,080	1.43%	$248,061	2.30%	8.14%
12. UNITED CAPITAL	$2,554,913	1.20%	$899,416	8.34%	34.95%
13. COMMERCE	$1,366,533	0.64%	$0	--	--
14. TRANSNATION	$116,922	0.05%	$4,000	0.04%	1.88%
15. TICOR (FL)	$91,471	0.04%	$207	0.00%	0.24%
16. SECURITY UNION	$13,952	0.00%	$0	--	--
17. TRANSUNION NATIONAL	$8,651	0.00%	$0	--	--
18. AMERICAN GUARANTY	$2,746	0.00%	$0	--	--
19. NATIONAL OF NY	$0	--	($31,055)	(0.29)%	(261.93)%
20. ALAMO	$0	--	$0	--	--
21. CHICAGO T&T	$0	--	$0	--	--
22. GUARANTEE T&T	$0	--	$0	--	--
23. INVESTORS TIC	$0	--	$0	--	--
24. NATIONS OF NY	$0	--	$0	--	--
COMPOSITE	$213,523,699	100.00%	$10,779,961	100.00%	4.71%
AVERAGE	$8,896,821		$449,165		

2006

	TOTAL DPW	MARKET SHARE	LOSSES INCURRED	MARKET SHARE	LOSS RATIO
1. FIRST AMERICAN TIC	$88,624,831	30.92%	$76,007	2.43%	0.07%
2. CHICAGO TIC	$35,395,028	12.35%	$1,908,367	61.13%	5.47%
3. LAWYERS	$31,177,904	10.88%	$1,404,555	44.99%	4.56%
4. COMMONWEALTH LAND	$26,280,238	9.17%	$1,954,457	62.60%	6.51%
5. STEWART TGC	$24,416,305	8.52%	$627,080	20.09%	2.57%
6. FIDELITY NATIONAL	$22,821,777	7.96%	($3,481,669)	(111.52)%	(15.49)%
7. TICOR	$17,997,456	6.28%	($204,949)	(6.56)%	(1.18)%
8. OLD REPUBLIC NATIONAL	$11,834,107	4.13%	$341,767	10.95%	2.84%
9. WESTCOR	$9,904,809	3.46%	($1,540)	(0.05)%	(0.03)%
10. NORTH AMERICAN	$5,893,880	2.06%	$62,901	2.01%	1.11%
11. UNITED CAPITAL	$5,507,864	1.92%	$390,785	12.52%	7.27%
12. UNITED GENERAL	$3,959,984	1.38%	$43,188	1.38%	1.11%
13. COMMERCE	$2,559,513	0.89%	$0	--	--
14. TICOR (FL)	$201,760	0.07%	$947	0.03%	0.51%
15. TRANSNATION	$61,842	0.02%	$0	--	--
16. TITLE IC AMERICA	$19,500	0.00%	$0	--	--
17. SECURITY UNION	$0	--	$0	--	--
18. INVESTORS TIC	$0	--	$0	--	--
COMPOSITE	$286,656,798	100.00%	$3,121,896	100.00%	1.04%
AVERAGE	$15,925,378		$173,439		

10-YEAR - DIRECT PREMIUMS WRITTEN (DPW) BY CHANNEL   See Sec. 3

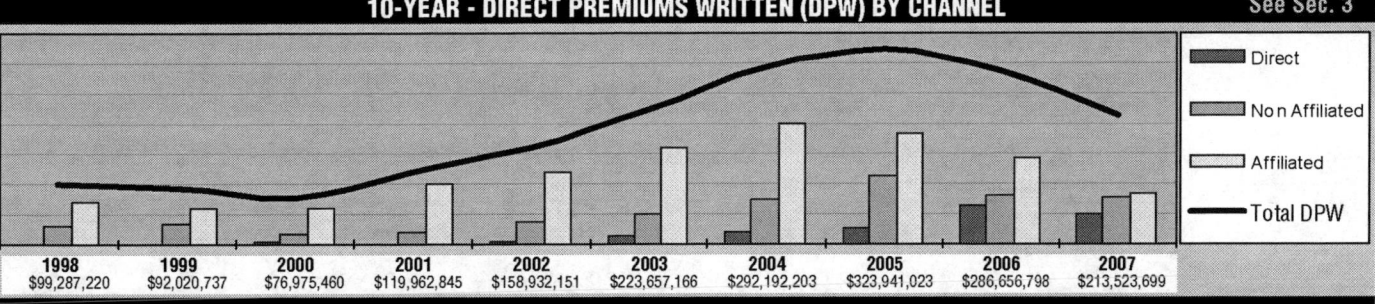

Legend: Direct · Non Affiliated · Affiliated · Total DPW

1998	1999	2000	2001	2002	2003	2004	2005	2006	2007
$99,287,220	$92,020,737	$76,975,460	$119,962,845	$158,932,151	$223,657,166	$292,192,203	$323,941,023	$286,656,798	$213,523,699

10-YEAR - LOSS RATIO   See Sec. 5, A.2

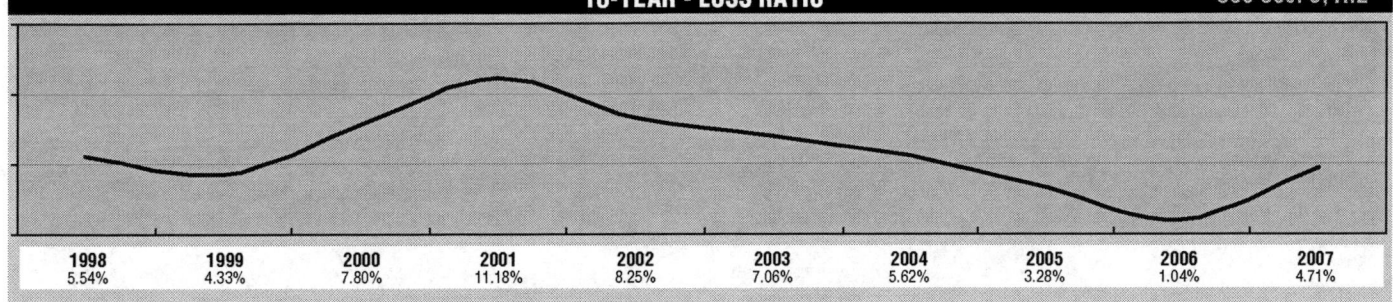

1998	1999	2000	2001	2002	2003	2004	2005	2006	2007
5.54%	4.33%	7.80%	11.18%	8.25%	7.06%	5.62%	3.28%	1.04%	4.71%

6

NEW HAMPSHIRE

DEPARTMENT OF INSURANCE INFORMATION	LAND TITLE ASSOCIATION	DOMICILED UNDERWRITERS See Sec. 1	
New Hampshire Insurance Department	**New England Land Title Association**	**Underwriter**	**NAIC #**

New Hampshire Insurance Department

Mr. Roger A. Sevigny
Insurance Commissioner
21 South Fruit St., Ste. 14
Concord, NH 03301

Phone: (603) 271-2261
Fax: (603) 271-1406
www.nh.gov/insurance

New England Land Title Association

P.O. Box 743
Norwalk, CT 06852-0743

Phone: (203) 847-6885
www.nelta.org

DOMICILED UNDERWRITERS   See Sec. 1

Underwriter	NAIC #
None	
17 Licensed Underwriters	See Sec. 1

STATUTORY PREMIUM RESERVE (SPR) REQUIREMENTS

Inception:	$1.00 per policy & 15 cents per $1,000 of the face amount of net retained liability		
Max Years:	20	Release:	10% years 1-5; 3.33% years 6-20

MARKET SHARE BY UNDERWRITER   See Sec. 3

2007

	TOTAL DPW	MARKET SHARE	LOSSES INCURRED	MARKET SHARE	LOSS RATIO
1. FIRST AMERICAN TIC	$13,273,415	38.40%	$840,419	22.93%	6.32%
2. CHICAGO TIC	$5,322,963	15.40%	$1,146,132	31.27%	20.08%
3. STEWART TGC	$4,307,159	12.46%	$462,821	12.63%	10.51%
4. COMMONWEALTH LAND	$3,269,279	9.46%	$191,105	5.21%	5.71%
5. OLD REPUBLIC NATIONAL	$2,737,993	7.92%	$318,472	8.69%	9.99%
6. LAWYERS	$2,480,247	7.18%	$115,000	3.14%	4.20%
7. TRANSNATION	$1,104,954	3.20%	$62,203	1.70%	5.95%
8. FIDELITY NATIONAL	$804,391	2.33%	$91,552	2.50%	11.25%
9. UNITED GENERAL	$567,535	1.64%	$2,000	0.05%	0.34%
10. CT ATTORNEYS	$402,407	1.16%	$405	0.01%	0.10%
11. TICOR (FL)	$212,697	0.62%	$182,769	4.99%	93.36%
12. TICOR	$83,901	0.24%	$251,963	6.88%	153.46%
13. EQUITY NATIONAL	$0	--	$0	--	--
14. GUARANTEE T&T	$0	--	$0	--	--
15. NATIONAL OF NY	$0	--	$0	--	--
16. SECURITY TG (BALTIMORE)	$0	--	$0	--	--
17. SECURITY UNION	$0	--	$0	--	--
COMPOSITE	$34,566,941	100.00%	$3,664,841	100.00%	10.18%
AVERAGE	$2,033,349		$215,579		

2006

	TOTAL DPW	MARKET SHARE	LOSSES INCURRED	MARKET SHARE	LOSS RATIO
1. FIRST AMERICAN TIC	$15,610,444	37.35%	$868,341	39.23%	5.59%
2. CHICAGO TIC	$8,796,358	21.05%	$522,998	23.63%	5.98%
3. STEWART TGC	$5,354,210	12.81%	$22,618	1.02%	0.42%
4. COMMONWEALTH LAND	$4,669,106	11.17%	$78,402	3.54%	1.54%
5. OLD REPUBLIC NATIONAL	$2,826,240	6.76%	($12,671)	(0.57)%	(0.33)%
6. LAWYERS	$2,270,629	5.43%	$446,574	20.18%	18.20%
7. FIDELITY NATIONAL	$968,938	2.32%	$168,434	7.61%	17.72%
8. TRANSNATION	$413,531	0.99%	$65,000	2.94%	16.78%
9. CT ATTORNEYS	$323,975	0.78%	$0	--	--
10. UNITED GENERAL	$232,159	0.56%	$0	--	--
11. TICOR (FL)	$221,225	0.53%	$15,580	0.70%	7.18%
12. TICOR	$101,205	0.24%	$37,949	1.71%	20.47%
13. SECURITY TG (BALTIMORE)	$2,494	0.00%	$0	--	--
14. SECURITY UNION	$300	0.00%	$0	--	--
15. EQUITY NATIONAL	$0	--	$0	--	--
COMPOSITE	$41,790,814	100.00%	$2,213,225	100.00%	5.08%
AVERAGE	$2,786,054		$147,548		

10-YEAR - DIRECT PREMIUMS WRITTEN (DPW) BY CHANNEL   See Sec. 3

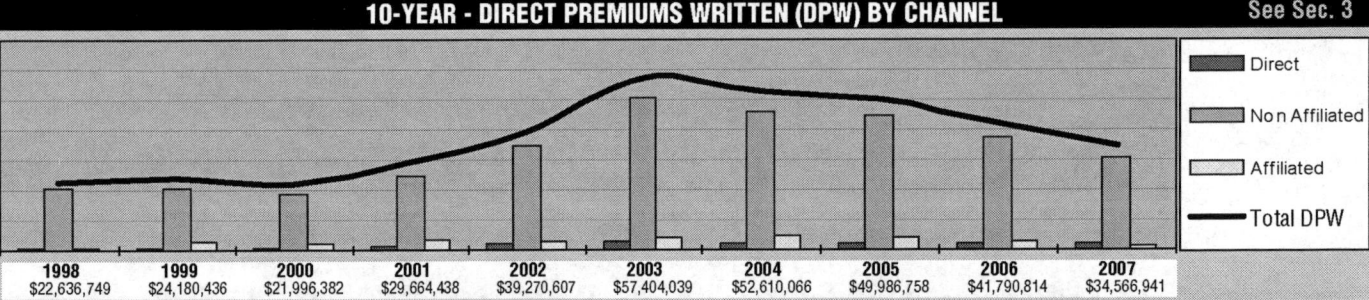

Legend: Direct · Non Affiliated · Affiliated · — Total DPW

1998	1999	2000	2001	2002	2003	2004	2005	2006	2007
$22,636,749	$24,180,436	$21,996,382	$29,664,438	$39,270,607	$57,404,039	$52,610,066	$49,986,758	$41,790,814	$34,566,941

10-YEAR - LOSS RATIO   See Sec. 5, A.2

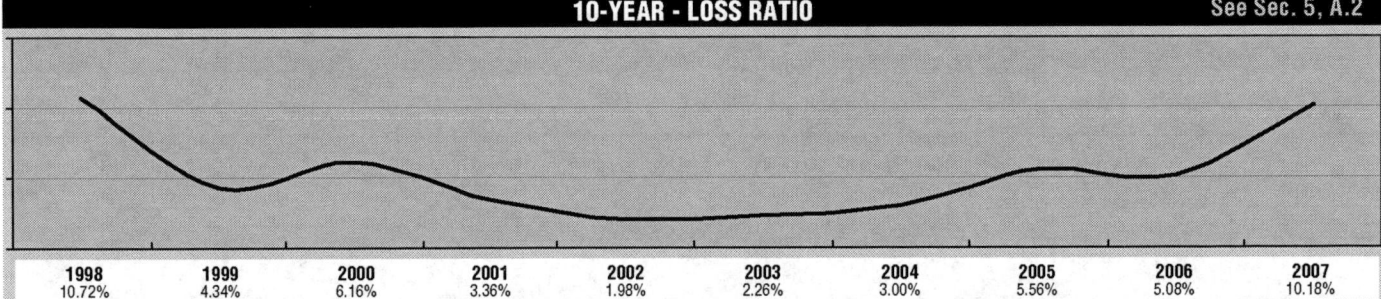

1998	1999	2000	2001	2002	2003	2004	2005	2006	2007
10.72%	4.34%	6.16%	3.36%	1.98%	2.26%	3.00%	5.56%	5.08%	10.18%

NEW JERSEY

DEPARTMENT OF INSURANCE INFORMATION	LAND TITLE ASSOCIATION	DOMICILED UNDERWRITERS See Sec. 1

DEPARTMENT OF INSURANCE INFORMATION
New Jersey Department of Banking and Insurance

Mr. Steven M. Goldman
Insurance Commissioner
20 W State St., P.O. Box 325
Trenton, NJ 08625
Phone: (609) 292-7272
Fax: (609) 292-5273
www.state.nj.us/dobi

LAND TITLE ASSOCIATION
New Jersey Land Title Association

100 Willowbrook Rd.
Monmouth Executive Center, Building 1
Freehold, NJ 07728

Phone: (732) 683-9660
www.njlta.org

DOMICILED UNDERWRITERS See Sec. 1

Underwriter	NAIC #
COMMONWEALTH LAND (NJ)	51195
NEW JERSEY TIC	51187
29 Licensed Underwriters	See Sec. 1

STATUTORY PREMIUM RESERVE (SPR) REQUIREMENTS

Inception:	$1.50 per policy & 12.5 cents per $1,000 of the face amount of net retained liability
Max Years:	20 Release: 5% per year

MARKET SHARE BY UNDERWRITER   See Sec. 3

2007

	TOTAL DPW	MARKET SHARE	LOSSES INCURRED	MARKET SHARE	LOSS RATIO
1. FIRST AMERICAN TIC	$87,728,252	18.53%	$8,618,259	28.01%	9.39%
2. CHICAGO TIC	$71,092,764	15.02%	$5,153,142	16.75%	6.57%
3. STEWART TGC	$62,962,536	13.30%	$5,283,502	17.17%	8.43%
4. FIDELITY NATIONAL	$50,619,874	10.69%	$3,607,945	11.73%	6.49%
5. OLD REPUBLIC NATIONAL	$42,372,773	8.95%	$3,683,846	11.97%	8.49%
6. LAWYERS	$39,798,281	8.41%	$2,286,336	7.43%	5.49%
7. COMMONWEALTH LAND (NJ)	$35,387,441	7.47%	$1,787,925	5.81%	5.05%
8. UNITED GENERAL	$18,267,201	3.86%	$752,336	2.44%	4.45%
9. NEW JERSEY TIC	$16,413,857	3.47%	$1,212,393	3.94%	7.34%
10. COMMONWEALTH LAND	$15,351,173	3.24%	$369,592	1.20%	2.09%
11. TICOR	$9,580,061	2.02%	($3,123,333)	(10.15)%	(31.35)%
12. TRANSNATION	$6,848,756	1.45%	$515,787	1.68%	7.84%
13. TITLE RESOURCES	$5,516,811	1.17%	$0	--	--
14. CENSTAR	$5,150,323	1.09%	$34,940	0.11%	0.72%
15. TICOR (FL)	$3,293,530	0.70%	$216,006	0.70%	6.80%
16. T.A. TITLE	$2,334,985	0.49%	$0	--	--
17. NORTH AMERICAN	$339,499	0.07%	$0	--	--
18. CONESTOGA	$200,402	0.04%	$2,753	0.00%	1.35%
19. SECURITY TG (BALTIMORE)	$162,389	0.03%	$9,163	0.03%	5.11%
20. SECURITY UNION	$9,986	0.00%	$200,431	0.65%	1,430.42%
21. AMERICAN GUARANTY	$716	0.00%	$0	--	--
22. NATIONS OF NY	$0	--	$158,616	0.52%	0.00%
23. SOUTHERN TI CORP	$0	--	$899	0.00%	--
24. CHICAGO T&T	$0	--	$0	--	--
25. EQUITY NATIONAL	$0	--	$0	--	--
26. GUARANTEE T&T	$0	--	$0	--	--
27. INVESTORS TIC	$0	--	$0	--	--
28. NATIONAL OF NY	$0	--	$0	--	--
COMPOSITE	**$473,431,610**	**100.00%**	**$30,770,538**	**100.00%**	**6.24%**
AVERAGE	**$16,908,272**		**$1,098,948**		

2006

	TOTAL DPW	MARKET SHARE	LOSSES INCURRED	MARKET SHARE	LOSS RATIO
1. FIRST AMERICAN TIC	$118,591,657	21.27%	$6,897,448	21.74%	5.82%
2. CHICAGO TIC	$91,859,921	16.47%	$3,800,333	11.98%	3.94%
3. STEWART TGC	$74,067,103	13.28%	$1,990,838	6.28%	2.72%
4. FIDELITY NATIONAL	$54,836,172	9.83%	$3,325,873	10.48%	5.33%
5. LAWYERS	$48,963,337	8.78%	$1,749,543	5.51%	3.47%
6. OLD REPUBLIC NATIONAL	$46,411,494	8.32%	$5,621,651	17.72%	11.87%
7. COMMONWEALTH LAND (NJ)	$44,382,394	7.96%	$2,552,765	8.05%	5.74%
8. COMMONWEALTH LAND	$18,905,074	3.39%	$2,619,113	8.26%	11.11%
9. NEW JERSEY TIC	$18,501,828	3.32%	$994,737	3.14%	5.36%
10. UNITED GENERAL	$14,062,436	2.52%	$511,438	1.61%	4.03%
11. CENSTAR	$7,868,620	1.41%	$0	--	--
12. TRANSNATION	$7,266,035	1.30%	$397,082	1.25%	5.62%
13. TICOR	$6,428,551	1.15%	$495,262	1.56%	7.29%
14. T.A. TITLE	$2,582,221	0.46%	$80,387	0.25%	3.22%
15. TICOR (FL)	$2,340,668	0.42%	$216,424	0.68%	8.94%
16. SECURITY TG (BALTIMORE)	$376,708	0.07%	$60,458	0.19%	14.23%
17. CONESTOGA	$235,244	0.04%	$14,930	0.05%	6.49%
18. AMERICAN GUARANTY	$3,697	0.00%	$0	--	--
19. NATIONS OF NY	$0	--	$88,088	0.28%	--
20. SECURITY UNION	$0	--	$309,911	0.98%	0.00%
21. EQUITY NATIONAL	$0	--	$0	--	--
22. INVESTORS TIC	$0	--	$0	--	--
COMPOSITE	**$557,683,160**	**100.00%**	**$31,726,281**	**100.00%**	**5.51%**
AVERAGE	**$25,349,235**		**$1,442,104**		

10-YEAR - DIRECT PREMIUMS WRITTEN (DPW) BY CHANNEL   See Sec. 3

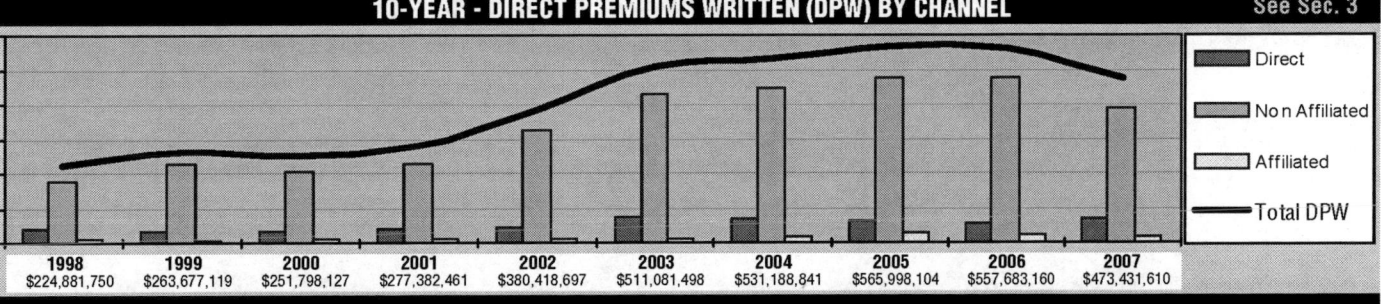

Legend: Direct, Non Affiliated, Affiliated, Total DPW

1998	1999	2000	2001	2002	2003	2004	2005	2006	2007
$224,881,750	$263,677,119	$251,798,127	$277,382,461	$380,418,697	$511,081,498	$531,188,841	$565,998,104	$557,683,160	$473,431,610

10-YEAR - LOSS RATIO   See Sec. 5, A.2

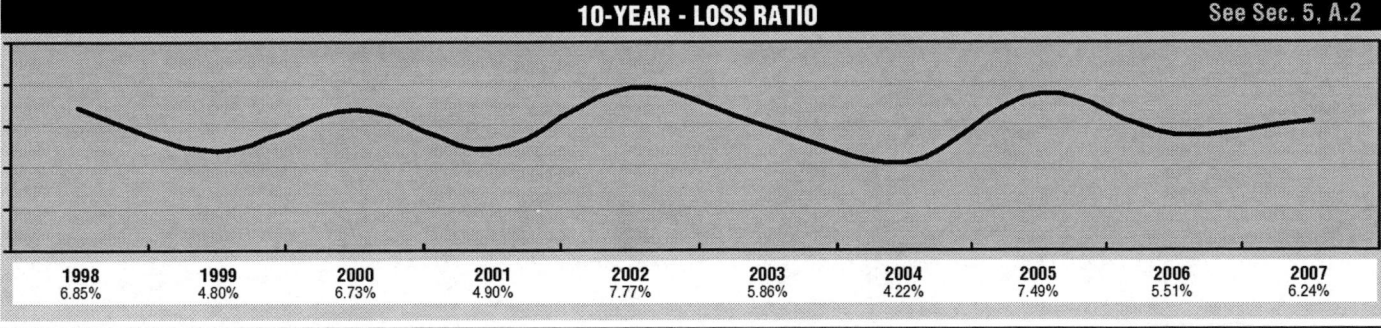

1998	1999	2000	2001	2002	2003	2004	2005	2006	2007
6.85%	4.80%	6.73%	4.90%	7.77%	5.86%	4.22%	7.49%	5.51%	6.24%

6

NEW MEXICO

DEPARTMENT OF INSURANCE INFORMATION	LAND TITLE ASSOCIATION	DOMICILED UNDERWRITERS See Sec. 1	
New Mexico Department of Insurance	New Mexico Land Title Association	Underwriter	NAIC #

Mr. Morris J. Chavez
Superintendent of Insurance
1120 Paseo De Peralta
PERA Building
Santa Fe, NM 87501
Phone: (505) 827-4299
Fax: (505) 827-4106
www.nmprc.state.nm.us

201 Third NW, Ste. 1180
Albuquerque, NM 87102
Phone: (505) 883-2683
www.nmlta.org

None

■ 26 Licensed Underwriters See Sec. 1

STATUTORY PREMIUM RESERVE (SPR) REQUIREMENTS

Inception:	10% of gross risk premium		
Max Years:	20	Release:	5% per year

MARKET SHARE BY UNDERWRITER — See Sec. 3

2007

	TOTAL DPW	MARKET SHARE	LOSSES INCURRED	MARKET SHARE	LOSS RATIO
1. FIRST AMERICAN TIC	$28,994,285	25.60%	$1,077,784	38.18%	3.32%
2. LAWYERS	$21,914,956	19.35%	$53,884	1.91%	0.23%
3. FIDELITY NATIONAL	$19,982,561	17.64%	$666,748	23.62%	2.71%
4. COMMONWEALTH LAND	$17,477,601	15.43%	$422,564	14.97%	2.32%
5. STEWART TGC	$12,854,550	11.35%	$23,571	0.84%	0.19%
6. CHICAGO TIC	$5,153,783	4.55%	$105,935	3.75%	1.86%
7. UNITED GENERAL	$2,625,189	2.32%	$23,753	0.84%	0.92%
8. OLD REPUBLIC NATIONAL	$2,175,598	1.92%	$329,031	11.66%	13.61%
9. COMMERCE	$724,207	0.64%	$0	--	--
10. TICOR	$707,410	0.62%	$98,113	3.48%	13.11%
11. TRANSNATION	$290,683	0.26%	$5,000	0.18%	1.31%
12. TITLE IC AMERICA	$264,573	0.23%	($10,608)	(0.38)%	(4.16)%
13. SECURITY UNION	$54,921	0.05%	$0	--	--
14. ALAMO	$52,471	0.05%	($3,647)	(0.13)%	(5.59)%
15. TITLE RESOURCES	$0	--	$30,711	1.09%	134.87%
16. GUARANTEE T&T	$0	--	$0	--	--
17. INVESTORS TIC	$0	--	$0	--	--
COMPOSITE	$113,272,788	100.00%	$2,822,839	100.00%	2.27%
AVERAGE	$6,663,105		$166,049		

2006

	TOTAL DPW	MARKET SHARE	LOSSES INCURRED	MARKET SHARE	LOSS RATIO
1. FIRST AMERICAN TIC	$31,963,854	23.93%	$2,667,018	32.81%	7.44%
2. LAWYERS	$26,531,539	19.86%	$1,638,738	20.16%	5.73%
3. COMMONWEALTH LAND	$22,662,005	16.96%	$812,642	10.00%	3.34%
4. FIDELITY NATIONAL	$21,652,644	16.21%	$1,007,278	12.39%	3.64%
5. STEWART TGC	$16,222,169	12.14%	$181,389	2.23%	1.13%
6. CHICAGO TIC	$7,504,708	5.62%	$814,801	10.02%	10.34%
7. OLD REPUBLIC NATIONAL	$3,190,970	2.39%	$69,501	0.86%	2.04%
8. UNITED GENERAL	$1,398,608	1.05%	$227,102	2.79%	16.12%
9. COMMERCE	$1,302,453	0.98%	$0	--	--
10. TITLE IC AMERICA	$455,808	0.34%	$256,703	3.16%	55.34%
11. TICOR	$348,825	0.26%	$198,661	2.44%	47.53%
12. TRANSNATION	$311,021	0.23%	($2,808)	(0.03)%	(0.69)%
13. ALAMO	$39,183	0.03%	($11,915)	(0.15)%	(24.43)%
14. TITLE RESOURCES	$0	--	$268,752	3.31%	1,567.71%
15. COMMONWEALTH LAND (NJ	$0	--	$0	--	--
16. SECURITY UNION	$0	--	$0	--	--
COMPOSITE	$133,583,787	100.00%	$8,127,862	100.00%	5.50%
AVERAGE	$8,348,987		$507,991		

10-YEAR - DIRECT PREMIUMS WRITTEN (DPW) BY CHANNEL — See Sec. 3

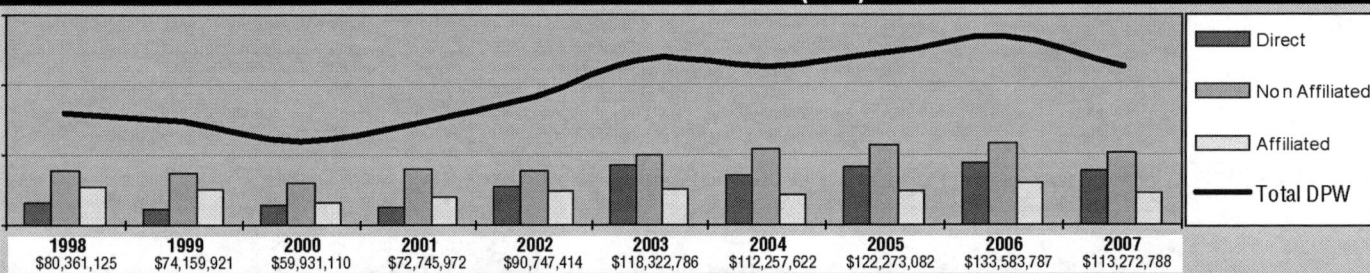

Legend: Direct, Non Affiliated, Affiliated, Total DPW

1998	1999	2000	2001	2002	2003	2004	2005	2006	2007
$80,361,125	$74,159,921	$59,931,110	$72,745,972	$90,747,414	$118,322,786	$112,257,622	$122,273,082	$133,583,787	$113,272,788

10-YEAR - LOSS RATIO — See Sec. 5, A.2

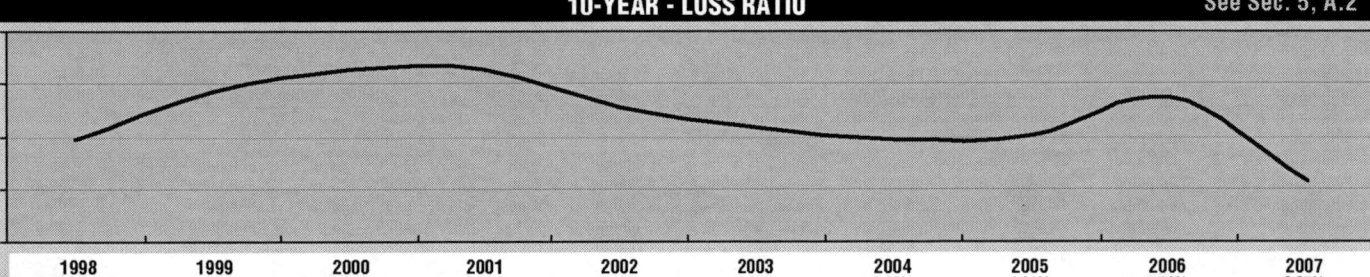

1998	1999	2000	2001	2002	2003	2004	2005	2006	2007
3.92%	5.68%	6.58%	6.54%	5.10%	4.37%	3.86%	4.01%	5.50%	2.27%

6

NEW YORK

DEPARTMENT OF INSURANCE INFORMATION	LAND TITLE ASSOCIATION	DOMICILED UNDERWRITERS See Sec. 1	
New York Department of Insurance	**New York Land Title Association, Inc.**	**Underwriter**	**NAIC #**
Mr. Eric R. Dinallo	Phone: (212) 964-3701	FIRST AMERICAN (NY)	51039
Superintendent of Insurance	www.nyslta.org	MONROE	51063
25 Beaver St.		NATIONAL OF NY	51020
New York, NY 10004-2319		NATIONS OF NY	51101
Phone: (212) 480-6400		PUBLIC	12518
Fax: (212) 480-2310		STEWART TIC	51420
www.ins.state.ny.us		TITLEDGE	12935
		WASHINGTON TIC	50029
		25 Licensed Underwriters	See Sec. 1

STATUTORY PREMIUM RESERVE (SPR) REQUIREMENTS

Inception:	$1.50 per policy, 1/80% of face amount of insurance, and 3% of gross fees & premiums received	
Max Years:	20	**Release:** 5% per year

MARKET SHARE BY UNDERWRITER
See Sec. 3

2007

	TOTAL DPW	MARKET SHARE	LOSSES INCURRED	MARKET SHARE	LOSS RATIO
1. FIRST AMERICAN (NY)	$239,255,687	20.38%	$9,060,184	17.38%	3.33%
2. COMMONWEALTH LAND	$199,392,548	16.98%	$7,467,530	14.32%	3.57%
3. STEWART TIC	$162,251,887	13.82%	$5,470,986	10.49%	3.18%
4. FIDELITY NATIONAL	$141,043,376	12.01%	$8,597,724	16.49%	4.96%
5. CHICAGO TIC	$110,274,965	9.39%	$5,111,157	9.80%	3.66%
6. LAWYERS	$100,947,525	8.60%	$61,152	0.12%	0.06%
7. OLD REPUBLIC NATIONAL	$73,536,152	6.26%	$1,783,212	3.42%	2.42%
8. UNITED GENERAL	$58,270,435	4.96%	$7,241,049	13.89%	12.65%
9. TICOR	$48,550,552	4.13%	$2,079,151	3.99%	3.83%
10. WASHINGTON TIC	$15,624,173	1.33%	$433,920	0.83%	2.86%
11. MONROE	$12,996,679	1.11%	$415,723	0.80%	2.14%
12. TICOR (FL)	$4,570,975	0.39%	$3,565,704	6.84%	78.77%
13. CONESTOGA	$2,480,602	0.21%	$109,306	0.21%	4.41%
14. NORTHEAST INVESTORS	$2,414,626	0.21%	$149,328	0.29%	6.32%
15. T.A. TITLE	$2,362,989	0.20%	$0	--	--
16. TITLEDGE	$181,572	0.02%	$0	--	--
17. TRANSNATION	$2,019	0.00%	$0	--	--
18. NATIONAL OF NY	$0	--	$89,849	0.17%	73.62%
19. NATIONS OF NY	$0	--	$103,886	0.20%	11.85%
20. ALAMO	$0	--	$0	--	--
21. ATTORNEYS TIF (FL)	$0	--	$400,000	0.77%	--
22. EQUITY NATIONAL	$0	--	$0	--	--
23. GUARANTEE T&T	$0	--	$0	--	--
24. INVESTORS TIC	$0	--	$0	--	--
25. SECURITY UNION	$0	--	$0	--	--
26. STEWART TGC	$0	--	$0	--	--
COMPOSITE	**$1,174,156,762**	**100.00%**	**$52,139,861**	**100.00%**	**4.00%**
AVERAGE	**$45,159,875**		**$2,005,379**		

2006

	TOTAL DPW	MARKET SHARE	LOSSES INCURRED	MARKET SHARE	LOSS RATIO
1. FIRST AMERICAN (NY)	$234,836,101	19.95%	$8,782,858	19.69%	3.36%
2. COMMONWEALTH LAND	$183,126,389	15.56%	$7,700,069	17.26%	3.86%
3. FIDELITY NATIONAL	$169,981,318	14.44%	$4,653,907	10.43%	2.42%
4. STEWART TIC	$153,902,843	13.07%	$6,246,430	14.00%	3.92%
5. CHICAGO TIC	$134,807,907	11.45%	$3,051,719	6.84%	2.08%
6. OLD REPUBLIC NATIONAL	$75,523,505	6.42%	$4,622,782	10.36%	6.14%
7. LAWYERS	$74,800,416	6.35%	$1,965,912	4.41%	2.57%
8. UNITED GENERAL	$53,713,919	4.56%	$1,595,375	3.58%	3.01%
9. TICOR	$48,978,607	4.16%	$1,417,815	3.18%	2.58%
10. WASHINGTON TIC	$19,995,288	1.70%	$419,448	0.94%	2.20%
11. MONROE	$13,814,675	1.17%	$242,993	0.54%	1.22%
12. TICOR (FL)	$7,904,883	0.67%	$3,684,754	8.26%	47.16%
13. NORTHEAST INVESTORS	$2,427,563	0.21%	$30,554	0.07%	1.29%
14. CONESTOGA	$2,244,553	0.19%	$9,521	0.02%	0.44%
15. T.A. TITLE	$1,210,465	0.10%	$0	--	--
16. TRANSNATION	$1,380	0.00%	$0	--	--
17. NATIONS OF NY	$0	--	$187,874	0.42%	19.38%
18. ALAMO	$0	--	$0	--	--
19. COMMONWEALTH LAND (NJ	$0	--	$0	--	--
20. EQUITY NATIONAL	$0	--	$0	--	--
21. INVESTORS TIC	$0	--	$0	--	--
22. SECURITY UNION	$0	--	$0	--	--
23. STEWART TGC	$0	--	$0	--	--
COMPOSITE	**$1,177,269,812**	**100.00%**	**$44,612,011**	**100.00%**	**3.49%**
AVERAGE	**$51,185,644**		**$1,939,653**		

10-YEAR - DIRECT PREMIUMS WRITTEN (DPW) BY CHANNEL
See Sec. 3

Legend: Direct, Non Affiliated, Affiliated, Total DPW

1998	1999	2000	2001	2002	2003	2004	2005	2006	2007
$510,302,342	$562,585,890	$500,603,534	$583,623,084	$826,271,755	$1,081,421,303	$1,146,752,301	$1,220,447,404	$1,177,269,812	$1,174,156,762

10-YEAR - LOSS RATIO
See Sec. 5, A.2

1998	1999	2000	2001	2002	2003	2004	2005	2006	2007
5.27%	3.87%	5.01%	4.37%	3.96%	3.40%	3.53%	3.91%	3.49%	4.00%

6

NORTH CAROLINA

DEPARTMENT OF INSURANCE INFORMATION	LAND TITLE ASSOCIATION	DOMICILED UNDERWRITERS

DEPARTMENT OF INSURANCE INFORMATION

North Carolina Department of Insurance

Mr. Jim Long
Insurance Commissioner
1201 Mail Service Ctr.
Raleigh, NC 27699-1201

Phone: (919) 807-6750
Fax: (919) 733-6495
www.ncdoi.com

LAND TITLE ASSOCIATION

North Carolina Land Title Association

1500 Sunday Dr., Ste. 102
Raleigh, NC 27607
Phone: (919) 861-5584
www.nclta.org

DOMICILED UNDERWRITERS See Sec. 1

Underwriter	NAIC #
INVESTORS TIC	50369

| 23 | Licensed Underwriters | See Sec. 1 |

STATUTORY PREMIUM RESERVE (SPR) REQUIREMENTS

Inception:	10% of direct premiums written and premiums for reinsurance assumed less premiums for reinsurance ceded
Max Years:	20	Release:	20% first year; 10% years 2-3; 5% years 4-10; 3% years 11-15; 2% years 16-20

MARKET SHARE BY UNDERWRITER   See Sec. 3

2007

	TOTAL DPW	MARKET SHARE	LOSSES INCURRED	MARKET SHARE	LOSS RATIO
1. INVESTORS TIC	$34,266,316	19.29%	$6,780,856	25.76%	20.19%
2. UNITED GENERAL	$32,270,633	18.16%	$411,651	1.56%	1.53%
3. CHICAGO TIC	$30,310,951	17.06%	$5,997,210	22.78%	18.38%
4. FIRST AMERICAN TIC	$25,825,427	14.54%	$4,557,646	17.31%	14.20%
5. STEWART TGC	$12,990,141	7.31%	$3,507,320	13.32%	26.99%
6. FIDELITY NATIONAL	$12,577,601	7.08%	$2,504,908	9.51%	19.65%
7. LAWYERS	$11,353,368	6.39%	$190,683	0.72%	1.43%
8. OLD REPUBLIC NATIONAL	$10,528,796	5.93%	$918,557	3.49%	8.24%
9. SOUTHERN TI CORP	$2,774,668	1.56%	($34,257)	(0.13)%	(1.35)%
10. TRANSNATION	$1,517,332	0.85%	$98,079	0.37%	6.88%
11. TICOR (FL)	$1,394,889	0.79%	$269,573	1.02%	20.91%
12. TICOR	$621,631	0.35%	$151,102	0.57%	20.69%
13. COMMONWEALTH LAND	$603,992	0.34%	$841,283	3.20%	88.44%
14. ATTORNEYS TIF (FL)	$416,568	0.23%	$0	--	--
15. TRANSUNION NATIONAL	$171,377	0.10%	$205,919	0.78%	113.55%
16. SECURITY UNION	$31,527	0.02%	($73,657)	(0.28)%	(42.22)%
17. BRIDGE	$0	--	$509	0.00%	3.17%
18. GUARANTEE T&T	$0	--	$0	--	--
19. NATIONS OF NY	$0	--	$0	--	--
20. NORTHEAST INVESTORS	$0	--	$0	--	--
COMPOSITE	**$177,655,217**	**100.00%**	**$26,327,382**	**100.00%**	**14.37%**
AVERAGE	**$8,882,761**		**$1,316,369**		

2006

	TOTAL DPW	MARKET SHARE	LOSSES INCURRED	MARKET SHARE	LOSS RATIO
1. INVESTORS TIC	$34,823,535	20.47%	$4,027,291	23.18%	11.94%
2. CHICAGO TIC	$33,027,850	19.41%	$4,583,072	26.38%	14.50%
3. FIRST AMERICAN TIC	$26,207,012	15.40%	$2,524,093	14.53%	8.85%
4. UNITED GENERAL	$15,898,596	9.34%	$38,943	0.22%	0.32%
5. FIDELITY NATIONAL	$13,786,518	8.10%	$1,238,456	7.13%	9.02%
6. STEWART TGC	$12,386,939	7.28%	$489,590	2.82%	3.89%
7. OLD REPUBLIC NATIONAL	$12,194,368	7.17%	$996,736	5.74%	7.79%
8. LAWYERS	$11,827,916	6.95%	$1,116,812	6.43%	9.24%
9. COMMONWEALTH LAND	$4,239,424	2.49%	$1,141,758	6.57%	22.27%
10. SOUTHERN TI CORP	$1,947,048	1.14%	$353,802	2.04%	20.07%
11. TICOR (FL)	$1,422,081	0.84%	$314,868	1.81%	22.40%
12. TRANSNATION	$1,204,466	0.71%	$206,857	1.19%	17.89%
13. TICOR	$424,985	0.25%	$129,923	0.75%	22.84%
14. TRANSUNION NATIONAL	$412,066	0.24%	$43,590	0.25%	11.28%
15. ATTORNEYS TIF (FL)	$274,331	0.16%	$0	--	--
16. SECURITY UNION	$54,129	0.03%	$152,844	0.88%	76.01%
17. BRIDGE	$0	--	$20,762	0.12%	127.92%
18. NATIONS OF NY	$0	--	($3,829)	(0.02)%	--
19. NORTHEAST INVESTORS	$0	--	$0	--	--
COMPOSITE	**$170,131,264**	**100.00%**	**$17,375,568**	**100.00%**	**10.33%**
AVERAGE	**$8,954,277**		**$914,504**		

10-YEAR - DIRECT PREMIUMS WRITTEN (DPW) BY CHANNEL   See Sec. 3

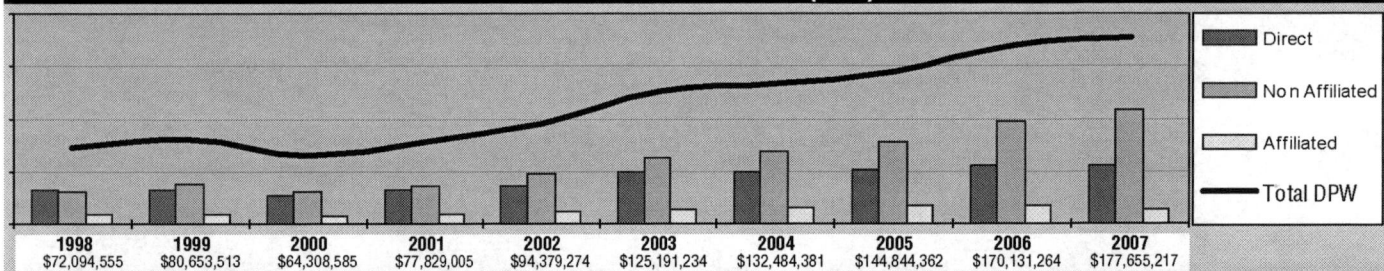

Legend: Direct, Non Affiliated, Affiliated, Total DPW

1998	1999	2000	2001	2002	2003	2004	2005	2006	2007
$72,094,555	$80,653,513	$64,308,585	$77,829,005	$94,379,274	$125,191,234	$132,484,381	$144,844,362	$170,131,264	$177,655,217

10-YEAR - LOSS RATIO   See Sec. 5, A.2

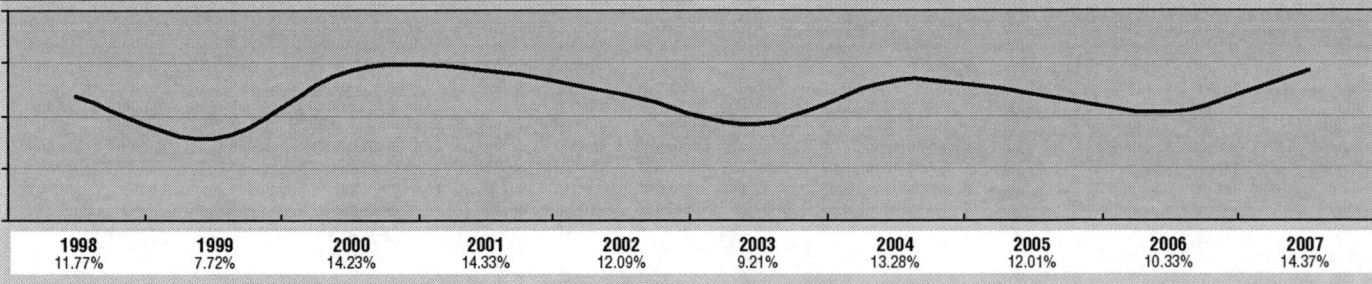

1998	1999	2000	2001	2002	2003	2004	2005	2006	2007
11.77%	7.72%	14.23%	14.33%	12.09%	9.21%	13.28%	12.01%	10.33%	14.37%

6

NORTH DAKOTA

| DEPARTMENT OF INSURANCE INFORMATION | LAND TITLE ASSOCIATION | DOMICILED UNDERWRITERS | See Sec. 1 |

| **North Dakota Department of Insurance** | **North Dakota Land Title Association** | **Underwriter** | **NAIC #** |

Mr. Adam W. Hamm
Insurance Commissioner
600 E Boulevard Ave., 5th Fl.
State Capitol
Bismarck, ND 58505-0320

Phone: (701) 328-2440
Fax: (701) 328-4880
www.state.nd.us/ndins

North Dakota Land Title Association
www.ndlta.org

Domiciled Underwriters: None

18 Licensed Underwriters — See Sec. 1

STATUTORY PREMIUM RESERVE (SPR) REQUIREMENTS

| Inception: | Not Available | | |
| Max Years: | Not Available | Release: | Not Available |

MARKET SHARE BY UNDERWRITER — See Sec. 3

2007

	TOTAL DPW	MARKET SHARE	LOSSES INCURRED	MARKET SHARE	LOSS RATIO
1. FIRST AMERICAN TIC	$1,550,425	26.85%	$20,671	0.61%	1.16%
2. STEWART TGC	$1,190,940	20.63%	($15,383)	(0.45)%	(1.24)%
3. CHICAGO TIC	$949,549	16.45%	($18,392)	(0.54)%	(2.02)%
4. OLD REPUBLIC NATIONAL	$762,043	13.20%	$20,000	0.59%	2.44%
5. COMMONWEALTH LAND	$549,297	9.51%	$3,473	0.10%	0.61%
6. FIDELITY NATIONAL	$248,791	4.31%	$3,980	0.12%	1.60%
7. LAWYERS	$176,806	3.06%	$3,395,836	99.46%	1,409.01%
8. ATTORNEYS TIF (FL)	$169,925	2.94%	$0	--	--
9. TICOR	$140,024	2.43%	$0	--	--
10. UNITED GENERAL	$31,877	0.55%	$0	--	--
11. TICOR (FL)	$4,402	0.08%	$4,141	0.12%	63.58%
12. GUARANTEE T&T	$0	--	$0	--	--
13. SECURITY UNION	$0	--	$0	--	--
14. TRANSNATION	$0	--	$0	--	--
COMPOSITE	**$5,774,179**	**100.00%**	**$3,414,326**	**100.00%**	**55.76%**
AVERAGE	**$412,441**		**$243,880**		

2006

	TOTAL DPW	MARKET SHARE	LOSSES INCURRED	MARKET SHARE	LOSS RATIO
1. STEWART TGC	$2,089,350	28.76%	$15,000	11.07%	0.75%
2. FIRST AMERICAN TIC	$1,340,036	18.45%	$29,837	22.01%	2.24%
3. CHICAGO TIC	$1,337,382	18.41%	$55,069	40.63%	4.30%
4. OLD REPUBLIC NATIONAL	$1,024,337	14.10%	$83	0.06%	0.00%
5. COMMONWEALTH LAND	$542,413	7.47%	$33,004	24.35%	5.42%
6. FIDELITY NATIONAL	$504,886	6.95%	$2,559	1.89%	0.52%
7. TICOR	$193,070	2.66%	$0	--	--
8. LAWYERS	$163,121	2.25%	$0	--	--
9. DAKOTA HOMESTEAD	$49,768	0.69%	$0	--	--
10. UNITED GENERAL	$10,538	0.15%	$0	--	--
11. TICOR (FL)	$8,991	0.12%	$0	--	--
12. SECURITY UNION	$0	--	$0	--	--
COMPOSITE	**$7,263,892**	**100.00%**	**$135,552**	**100.00%**	**1.87%**
AVERAGE	**$605,324**		**$11,296**		

10-YEAR - DIRECT PREMIUMS WRITTEN (DPW) BY CHANNEL — See Sec. 3

Legend: Direct, Non Affiliated, Affiliated, Total DPW

1998	1999	2000	2001	2002	2003	2004	2005	2006	2007
$3,386,998	$3,725,274	$2,819,966	$3,596,669	$4,619,316	$5,989,279	$6,744,855	$5,091,038	$7,263,892	$5,774,179

10-YEAR - LOSS RATIO — See Sec. 5, A.2

1998	1999	2000	2001	2002	2003	2004	2005	2006	2007
2.02%	0.14%	0.15%	2.04%	0.30%	1.03%	1.56%	1.23%	1.87%	55.76%

6

NORTHERN MARIANA ISLANDS

DEPARTMENT OF INSURANCE INFORMATION	LAND TITLE ASSOCIATION	DOMICILED UNDERWRITERS See Sec. 1	
Office of the Insurance Commissioner	No information at time of publication.	Underwriter	NAIC #
		None	

Mr. James A. Santos
Acting Insurance Commissioner
Department of Commerce, Capital Hill
Saipan, MP 96950

Phone: (670) 664-3064
Fax: (670) 664-3067
www.commerce.gov.mp

	0	Licensed Underwriters	See Sec. 1

STATUTORY PREMIUM RESERVE (SPR) REQUIREMENTS

Inception:	Not Available		
Max Years:	Not Available	Release:	Not Available

MARKET SHARE BY UNDERWRITER   See Sec. 3

2007

	TOTAL DPW	MARKET SHARE	LOSSES INCURRED	MARKET SHARE	LOSS RATIO
1. STEWART TGC	$779,364	100.00%	$21,413	66.63%	2.78%
2. INVESTORS TIC	$0	--	$0	--	--
3. LAWYERS	$0	--	$10,723	33.37%	--
COMPOSITE	$779,364	100.00%	$32,136	100.00%	4.18%
AVERAGE	$259,788		$10,712		

2006

	TOTAL DPW	MARKET SHARE	LOSSES INCURRED	MARKET SHARE	LOSS RATIO
1. STEWART TGC	$239,502	100.00%	$116,451	100.00%	49.87%
COMPOSITE	$239,502	100.00%	$116,451	100.00%	49.87%
AVERAGE	$239,502		$116,451		

10-YEAR - DIRECT PREMIUMS WRITTEN (DPW) BY CHANNEL   See Sec. 3

10-YEAR - LOSS RATIO   See Sec. 5, A.2

OHIO

DEPARTMENT OF INSURANCE INFORMATION
Ohio Department of Insurance

Ms. Mary Jo Hudson
Director of Insurance
50 W Town St., Ste. 300
3rd Fl.
Columbus, OH 43215
Phone: (614) 644-2658
Fax: (614) 644-3743
www.ohioinsurance.gov

LAND TITLE ASSOCIATION
Ohio Land Title Association

1100-H Brandywine Blvd.
Zanesville, OH 43701-7303
Phone: (740) 450-1315
www.olta.org

DOMICILED UNDERWRITERS   See Sec. 1

Underwriter	NAIC #
BANKERS GUARANTEE	50164
GENERAL T&T	50172
GUARANTEE T&T	50180
GUARDIAN NATIONAL	51632
OHIO BAR	51330
OLD REPUBLIC GENERAL	50005
OLYMPIC	50440
PORT LAWRENCE	50202
SEAGATE	50270
37	**Licensed Underwriters** See Sec. 1

STATUTORY PREMIUM RESERVE (SPR) REQUIREMENTS

Inception:	10% of premiums received or receivable
Max Years:	20 **Release:** 5% per year

MARKET SHARE BY UNDERWRITER   See Sec. 3

2007

	TOTAL DPW	MARKET SHARE	LOSSES INCURRED	MARKET SHARE	LOSS RATIO
1. FIRST AMERICAN TIC	$99,430,207	27.92%	$5,609,054	27.07%	5.03%
2. CHICAGO TIC	$70,240,769	19.72%	$2,714,975	13.10%	3.43%
3. STEWART TGC	$36,381,328	10.21%	$2,198,486	10.61%	5.86%
4. LAWYERS	$34,506,077	9.69%	$906,047	4.37%	2.06%
5. OLD REPUBLIC NATIONAL	$34,170,186	9.59%	$1,796,816	8.67%	5.15%
6. COMMONWEALTH LAND	$22,548,137	6.33%	$1,519,969	7.33%	6.49%
7. OHIO BAR	$12,878,476	3.62%	$1,445,381	6.97%	11.32%
8. FIDELITY NATIONAL	$10,931,608	3.07%	$1,351,349	6.52%	12.31%
9. PORT LAWRENCE	$5,590,504	1.57%	$35,011	0.17%	0.52%
10. TRANSNATION	$4,568,415	1.28%	$121,814	0.59%	2.63%
11. GUARDIAN NATIONAL	$3,873,893	1.09%	$0	--	--
12. SECURITY UNION	$2,973,981	0.84%	$435,760	2.10%	14.48%
13. UNITED GENERAL	$2,949,008	0.83%	$639,459	3.09%	21.83%
14. TICOR	$2,872,208	0.81%	$299,728	1.45%	9.29%
15. GENERAL T&T	$2,776,191	0.78%	$457,564	2.21%	17.04%
16. CONESTOGA	$2,235,748	0.63%	$192,964	0.93%	8.37%
17. TICOR (FL)	$2,018,384	0.57%	$672,184	3.24%	35.21%
18. GUARANTEE T&T	$1,782,434	0.50%	$256,968	1.24%	14.88%
19. SOUTHERN TI CORP	$1,514,991	0.43%	($2,004)	0.00%	(0.13)%
20. TRANSUNION NATIONAL	$690,568	0.19%	$43,024	0.21%	7.18%
21. CENSTAR	$339,072	0.10%	$0	--	--
22. COMMERCE	$275,558	0.08%	$0	--	--
23. NATIONAL LAND	$186,348	0.05%	$36,550	0.18%	13.57%
24. SEAGATE	$186,090	0.05%	$0	--	--
25. INVESTORS TIC	$141,259	0.04%	$0	--	--
26. SECURITY TG (BALTIMORE)	$89,742	0.03%	$49,452	0.24%	40.72%
27. T.A. TITLE	$4,745	0.00%	$0	--	--
28. AMERICAN GUARANTY	$1,345	0.00%	$0	--	--
29. OLYMPIC	$0	--	$16,293	0.08%	--
30. NATIONS OF NY	$0	--	$4,413	0.02%	--
31. NATIONAL OF NY	$0	--	($78,351)	(0.38)%	(7,308.86)%
COMPOSITE	**$356,157,272**	**100.00%**	**$20,722,906**	**100.00%**	**5.36%**
AVERAGE	**$11,488,944**		**$668,481**		

2006

	TOTAL DPW	MARKET SHARE	LOSSES INCURRED	MARKET SHARE	LOSS RATIO
1. FIRST AMERICAN TIC	$113,298,934	26.59%	$2,643,245	14.11%	2.28%
2. CHICAGO TIC	$77,869,522	18.28%	$1,101,409	5.88%	1.25%
3. STEWART TGC	$52,508,994	12.32%	$4,085,893	21.81%	7.85%
4. LAWYERS	$43,821,350	10.28%	$2,464,486	13.15%	4.74%
5. OLD REPUBLIC NATIONAL	$38,337,648	9.00%	$3,013,574	16.08%	7.75%
6. COMMONWEALTH LAND	$26,660,911	6.26%	$2,694,551	14.38%	9.22%
7. OHIO BAR	$14,782,755	3.47%	$436,133	2.33%	3.02%
8. FIDELITY NATIONAL	$11,190,914	2.63%	$318,117	1.70%	2.84%
9. PORT LAWRENCE	$7,055,071	1.66%	($161,059)	(0.86)%	(1.79)%
10. GENERAL T&T	$6,473,211	1.52%	$607,568	3.24%	10.32%
11. SECURITY UNION	$4,914,577	1.15%	$152,556	0.81%	3.13%
12. GUARDIAN NATIONAL	$4,553,818	1.07%	$0	--	--
13. TICOR	$4,404,587	1.03%	$318,322	1.70%	6.89%
14. CONESTOGA	$4,386,162	1.03%	$180,923	0.97%	4.28%
15. TRANSNATION	$3,545,624	0.83%	$73,591	0.39%	2.13%
16. UNITED GENERAL	$3,437,144	0.81%	$4,461	0.02%	0.13%
17. TICOR (FL)	$3,434,902	0.81%	$428,920	2.29%	13.39%
18. GUARANTEE T&T	$2,162,763	0.51%	$242,177	1.29%	6.36%
19. SOUTHERN TI CORP	$1,751,869	0.41%	($29,266)	(0.16)%	(1.69)%
20. COMMERCE	$453,486	0.11%	$0	--	--
21. SECURITY TG (BALTIMORE)	$431,761	0.10%	$164,032	0.88%	35.57%
22. NATIONAL LAND	$239,016	0.06%	$11,832	0.06%	--
23. SEAGATE	$155,277	0.04%	$0	--	--
24. T.A. TITLE	$97,857	0.02%	($16,758)	(0.09)%	(17.42)%
25. INVESTORS TIC	$62,118	0.01%	$0	--	--
26. CENSTAR	$40,489	0.00%	$0	--	--
27. TRANSUNION NATIONAL	$23,416	0.00%	$0	--	--
28. OLYMPIC	$0	--	$0	--	--
29. TITLE IC AMERICA	$0	--	$1,238	0.00%	--
COMPOSITE	**$426,094,176**	**100.00%**	**$18,735,945**	**100.00%**	**4.18%**
AVERAGE	**$14,692,903**		**$646,067**		

10-YEAR - DIRECT PREMIUMS WRITTEN (DPW) BY CHANNEL   See Sec. 3

Legend: Direct, Non Affiliated, Affiliated, Total DPW

1998	1999	2000	2001	2002	2003	2004	2005	2006	2007
$227,839,703	$250,388,341	$205,645,867	$254,882,429	$345,719,761	$490,954,810	$455,474,464	$438,668,372	$426,094,176	$356,168,857

10-YEAR - LOSS RATIO   See Sec. 5, A.2

1998	1999	2000	2001	2002	2003	2004	2005	2006	2007
1.76%	3.78%	3.95%	4.94%	4.44%	3.05%	2.49%	4.21%	4.18%	5.36%

6

OKLAHOMA

DEPARTMENT OF INSURANCE INFORMATION	LAND TITLE ASSOCIATION	DOMICILED UNDERWRITERS See Sec. 1

Oklahoma Department of Insurance

Ms. Kim Holland
Commissioner of Insurance
2401 NW 23rd St., Ste. 28
Oklahoma City, OK 73107
Phone: (405) 521-2828
Fax: (405) 521-6635
www.oid.state.ok.us

Oklahoma Land Title Association

P.O. Box 720240
Norman, OK 73070
Phone: (405) 227-8101
www.oklahomalandtitle.com

Underwriter	NAIC #
AMERICAN EAGLE	50001
AMERICAN GUARANTY	51411
AMERICAN LAND & AIRCRAFT	11450
AMERICAN SECURITY	51365
FIRST AMERICAN T&T	50037
28 Licensed Underwriters	See Sec. 1

STATUTORY PREMIUM RESERVE (SPR) REQUIREMENTS

Inception:	Not Available		
Max Years:	Not Available	Release:	Not Available

MARKET SHARE BY UNDERWRITER   See Sec. 3

2007

	TOTAL DPW	MARKET SHARE	LOSSES INCURRED	MARKET SHARE	LOSS RATIO
1. FIRST AMERICAN TIC	$16,322,325	26.10%	$218,261	7.99%	1.26%
2. CHICAGO TIC	$7,929,241	12.68%	$347,806	12.73%	4.20%
3. FIRST AMERICAN T&T	$6,291,430	10.06%	$131,073	4.80%	0.54%
4. STEWART TGC	$6,053,949	9.68%	$36,317	1.33%	0.59%
5. LAWYERS	$5,133,606	8.21%	$1,867,727	68.36%	33.27%
6. FIDELITY NATIONAL	$4,130,074	6.60%	($460,922)	(16.87)%	(11.26)%
7. AMERICAN GUARANTY	$3,412,912	5.46%	$98,291	3.60%	3.01%
8. AMERICAN EAGLE	$3,049,169	4.87%	$48,338	1.77%	1.06%
9. AMERICAN SECURITY	$2,940,198	4.70%	$2,283	0.08%	0.08%
10. COMMONWEALTH LAND	$1,495,464	2.39%	$69,787	2.55%	4.46%
11. FIRST AMERICAN TRANS	$1,326,322	2.12%	$0	--	--
12. TICOR	$1,134,152	1.81%	$72,822	2.67%	6.29%
13. UNITED GENERAL	$989,456	1.58%	$35,275	1.29%	3.92%
14. GUARANTEE	$683,390	1.09%	$0	--	--
15. AMERICAN LAND & AIRCRA	$659,156	1.05%	$0	--	--
16. TICOR (FL)	$373,190	0.60%	$184,834	6.77%	49.35%
17. OLD REPUBLIC NATIONAL	$263,463	0.42%	$39,336	1.44%	11.13%
18. SECURITY UNION	$256,272	0.41%	$7,838	0.29%	3.13%
19. TRANSNATION	$103,738	0.17%	$33,539	1.23%	32.11%
20. GUARANTEE T&T	$0	--	$0	--	--
21. INVESTORS TIC	$0	--	$0	--	--
22. NATIONAL OF NY	$0	--	$0	--	--
23. NATIONS OF NY	$0	--	$0	--	--
24. TITLE RESOURCES	$0	--	($577)	(0.02)%	(70.45)%
COMPOSITE	**$62,547,507**	**100.00%**	**$2,732,028**	**100.00%**	**3.26%**
AVERAGE	**$2,606,146**		**$113,835**		

2006

	TOTAL DPW	MARKET SHARE	LOSSES INCURRED	MARKET SHARE	LOSS RATIO
1. FIRST AMERICAN TIC	$15,874,158	26.03%	$677,197	34.61%	4.14%
2. CHICAGO TIC	$9,097,385	14.92%	$210,568	10.76%	2.27%
3. STEWART TGC	$5,898,911	9.67%	$4,478	0.23%	0.07%
4. FIRST AMERICAN T&T	$4,630,569	7.59%	$109,269	5.58%	0.75%
5. FIDELITY NATIONAL	$4,177,205	6.85%	$472,244	24.14%	11.51%
6. LAWYERS	$4,024,693	6.60%	$69,746	3.56%	1.59%
7. AMERICAN GUARANTY	$3,485,137	5.72%	$51,214	2.62%	1.54%
8. AMERICAN EAGLE	$2,751,669	4.51%	$0	--	--
9. AMERICAN SECURITY	$2,476,836	4.06%	$48,890	2.50%	1.97%
10. TICOR	$1,998,187	3.28%	$65,615	3.35%	3.31%
11. COMMONWEALTH LAND	$1,904,856	3.12%	$59,072	3.02%	2.77%
12. FIRST AMERICAN TRANS	$1,438,629	2.36%	$6,295	0.32%	0.46%
13. TRANSNATION	$843,496	1.38%	$34,256	1.75%	4.24%
14. AMERICAN LAND & AIRCRA	$575,017	0.94%	$0	--	--
15. UNITED GENERAL	$552,418	0.91%	$3,812	0.19%	0.68%
16. TICOR (FL)	$397,151	0.65%	$161,243	8.24%	36.44%
17. GUARANTEE	$386,559	0.63%	$0	--	--
18. SECURITY UNION	$268,746	0.44%	$0	--	--
19. OLD REPUBLIC NATIONAL	$160,426	0.26%	($16,982)	(0.87)%	(6.25)%
20. COLUMBIAN NATIONAL	$31,342	0.05%	$0	--	--
21. INVESTORS TIC	$0	--	$0	--	--
22. TITLE RESOURCES	$0	--	($303)	(0.02)%	(29.82)%
COMPOSITE	**$60,973,390**	**100.00%**	**$1,956,614**	**100.00%**	**2.67%**
AVERAGE	**$2,771,518**		**$88,937**		

10-YEAR - DIRECT PREMIUMS WRITTEN (DPW) BY CHANNEL   See Sec. 3

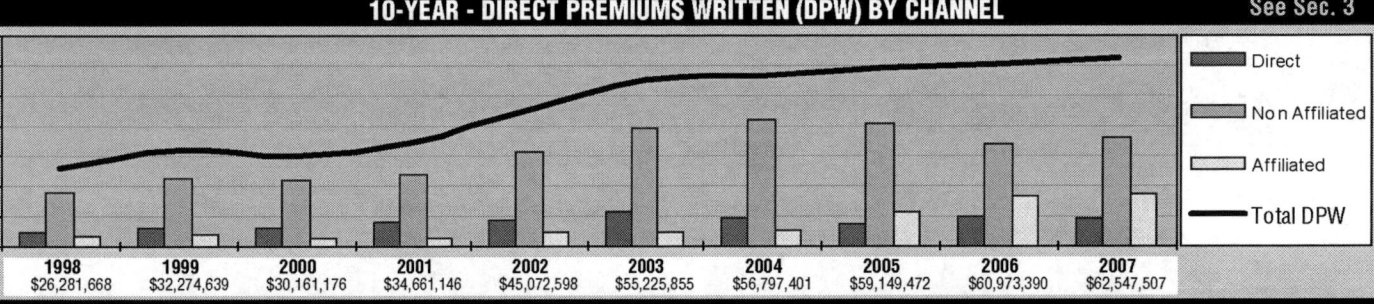

Legend: Direct, Non Affiliated, Affiliated, Total DPW

1998	1999	2000	2001	2002	2003	2004	2005	2006	2007
$26,281,668	$32,274,639	$30,161,176	$34,661,146	$45,072,598	$55,225,855	$56,797,401	$59,149,472	$60,973,390	$62,547,507

10-YEAR - LOSS RATIO   See Sec. 5, A.2

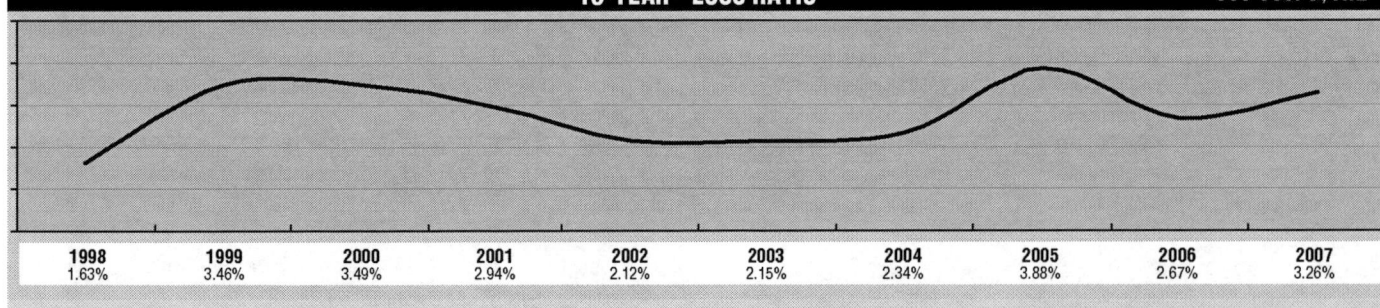

1998	1999	2000	2001	2002	2003	2004	2005	2006	2007
1.63%	3.46%	3.49%	2.94%	2.12%	2.15%	2.34%	3.88%	2.67%	3.26%

6

OREGON

DEPARTMENT OF INSURANCE INFORMATION	LAND TITLE ASSOCIATION	DOMICILED UNDERWRITERS See Sec. 1

Oregon Insurance Division

Mr. Scott Kipper
Insurance Administrator
350 Winter St. NE, Room 440
Salem, OR 97301-3883

Phone: (503) 947-7980
Fax: (503) 378-4351
www.insurance.oregon.gov

Oregon Land Title Association

9020 SW Washington Square Rd., Ste. 120
Tigard, OR 97223

Phone: (503) 356-8385
www.oregonlandtitle.com

Underwriter	NAIC #
CHICAGO TIC (OR)	50490
FIRST AMERICAN (OR)	50504
STEWART (OR)	50036
15 Licensed Underwriters	See Sec. 1

STATUTORY PREMIUM RESERVE (SPR) REQUIREMENTS

Inception:	7% of gross premiums		
Max Years:	Not Available	Release:	All released after 15 years

MARKET SHARE BY UNDERWRITER — See Sec. 3

2007

	TOTAL DPW	MARKET SHARE	LOSSES INCURRED	MARKET SHARE	LOSS RATIO
1. FIRST AMERICAN (OR)	$52,995,662	23.81%	$2,654,467	34.42%	3.06%
2. FIDELITY NATIONAL	$31,956,493	14.36%	$572,613	7.43%	1.81%
3. TICOR	$28,915,061	12.99%	$427,570	5.54%	1.00%
4. CHICAGO TIC (OR)	$26,283,884	11.81%	$626,138	8.12%	1.88%
5. LAWYERS	$21,767,677	9.78%	$1,705,487	22.11%	5.03%
6. TRANSNATION	$21,009,564	9.44%	$917,136	11.89%	4.59%
7. PACIFIC NORTHWEST	$12,647,637	5.68%	$42,450	0.55%	0.33%
8. FIRST AMERICAN TIC	$11,107,672	4.99%	$252,855	3.28%	3.51%
9. STEWART (OR)	$10,805,501	4.85%	$0	--	--
10. CHICAGO TIC	$2,774,995	1.25%	$228,942	2.97%	6.96%
11. COMMONWEALTH LAND	$1,932,310	0.87%	$40,329	0.52%	1.68%
12. UNITED GENERAL	$169,649	0.08%	$0	--	--
13. STEWART TGC	$154,970	0.07%	$219,551	2.85%	20.68%
14. OLD REPUBLIC NATIONAL	$67,301	0.03%	$0	--	--
15. SECURITY UNION	$0	--	$24,382	0.32%	0.00%
16. GUARANTEE T&T	$0	--	$0	--	--
17. INVESTORS TIC	$0	--	$0	--	--
COMPOSITE	$222,588,376	100.00%	$7,711,920	100.00%	2.70%
AVERAGE	$13,093,434		$453,642		

2006

	TOTAL DPW	MARKET SHARE	LOSSES INCURRED	MARKET SHARE	LOSS RATIO
1. FIRST AMERICAN (OR)	$65,082,261	26.44%	$2,061,613	36.40%	2.11%
2. FIDELITY NATIONAL	$34,301,493	13.94%	($268,216)	(4.74)%	(0.80)%
3. TICOR	$33,788,088	13.73%	$1,774,342	31.33%	3.62%
4. CHICAGO TIC (OR)	$33,550,465	13.63%	$305,708	5.40%	0.75%
5. TRANSNATION	$26,412,936	10.73%	$433,271	7.65%	1.71%
6. LAWYERS	$25,319,108	10.29%	$731,533	12.92%	1.83%
7. STEWART (OR)	$10,647,009	4.33%	$0	--	--
8. PACIFIC NORTHWEST	$10,615,016	4.31%	$20,285	0.36%	0.19%
9. FIRST AMERICAN TIC	$4,353,140	1.77%	$320,542	5.66%	6.39%
10. COMMONWEALTH LAND	$1,095,501	0.45%	$0	--	--
11. CHICAGO TIC	$841,104	0.34%	($7,516)	(0.13)%	(0.61)%
12. STEWART TGC	$79,908	0.03%	$187,556	3.31%	19.96%
13. OLD REPUBLIC NATIONAL	$16,306	0.00%	$0	--	--
14. UNITED GENERAL	$4,575	0.00%	$0	--	--
15. SECURITY UNION	$0	--	$104,573	1.85%	0.00%
COMPOSITE	$246,106,910	100.00%	$5,663,691	100.00%	1.79%
AVERAGE	$16,407,127		$377,579		

10-YEAR - DIRECT PREMIUMS WRITTEN (DPW) BY CHANNEL — See Sec. 3

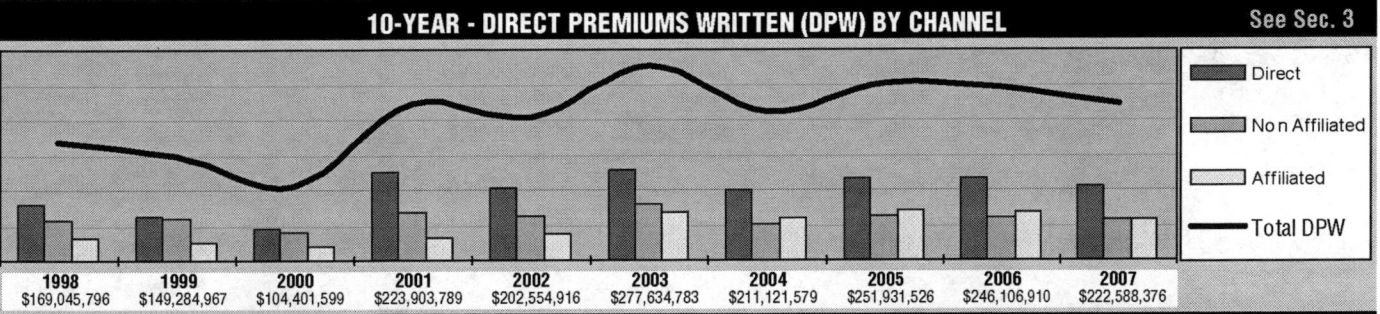

Legend: Direct, Non Affiliated, Affiliated, Total DPW

1998	1999	2000	2001	2002	2003	2004	2005	2006	2007
$169,045,796	$149,284,967	$104,401,599	$223,903,789	$202,554,916	$277,634,783	$211,121,579	$251,931,526	$246,106,910	$222,588,376

10-YEAR - LOSS RATIO — See Sec. 5, A.2

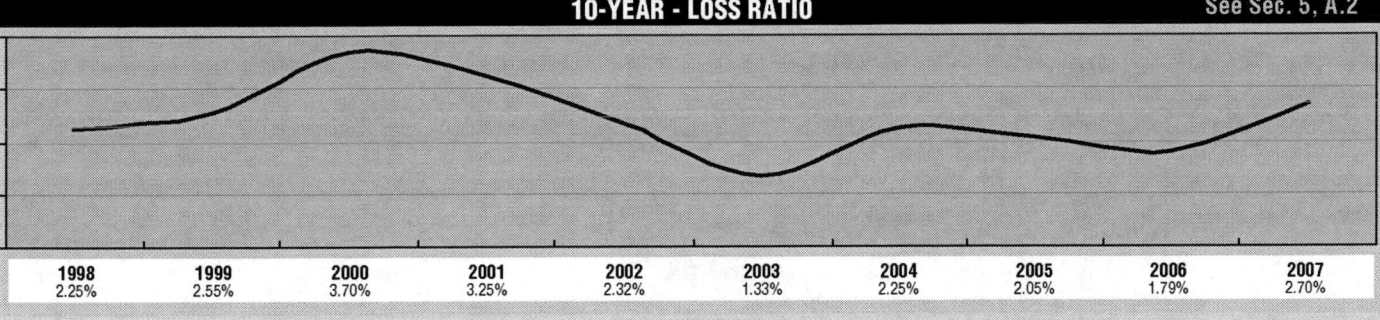

1998	1999	2000	2001	2002	2003	2004	2005	2006	2007
2.25%	2.55%	3.70%	3.25%	2.32%	1.33%	2.25%	2.05%	1.79%	2.70%

6

PENNSYLVANIA

DEPARTMENT OF INSURANCE INFORMATION

Pennsylvania Insurance Department

Mr. Joel Ario
Acting Insurance Commissioner
1326 Strawberry Sq.
Harrisburg, PA 17120
Phone: (717) 783-0442
Fax: (717) 772-1969
www.ins.state.pa.us

LAND TITLE ASSOCIATION

Pennsylvania Land Title Association

1005 West 9th Ave., Ste. B
King of Prussia, PA 19406

Phone: (610) 265-5980
www.plta.org

DOMICILED UNDERWRITERS   See Sec. 1

Underwriter	NAIC #
CONESTOGA	51209
MANITO	51446
PENN ATTORNEYS	51497
T.A. TITLE	51403
36 Licensed Underwriters	See Sec. 1

STATUTORY PREMIUM RESERVE (SPR) REQUIREMENTS

Inception:	Not Available			
Max Years:	Not Available	Release:	Not Available	

MARKET SHARE BY UNDERWRITER   See Sec. 3

2007

	TOTAL DPW	MARKET SHARE	LOSSES INCURRED	MARKET SHARE	LOSS RATIO
1. FIRST AMERICAN TIC	$117,283,411	22.37%	$4,211,302	16.23%	3.35%
2. LAWYERS	$94,057,517	17.94%	$3,526,425	13.59%	3.53%
3. COMMONWEALTH LAND	$88,730,012	16.92%	$2,439,151	9.40%	2.58%
4. CHICAGO TIC	$43,211,791	8.24%	$1,889,524	7.28%	3.94%
5. OLD REPUBLIC NATIONAL	$42,447,114	8.10%	$1,012,227	3.90%	2.35%
6. FIDELITY NATIONAL	$40,801,096	7.78%	$2,142,981	8.26%	4.84%
7. STEWART TGC	$34,034,235	6.49%	$6,574,436	25.34%	11.06%
8. UNITED GENERAL	$16,408,163	3.13%	$1,756,900	6.77%	10.89%
9. T.A. TITLE	$11,957,002	2.28%	$544,743	2.10%	4.58%
10. TICOR	$8,664,031	1.65%	$925,036	3.57%	10.54%
11. TICOR (FL)	$5,114,023	0.98%	$237,487	0.92%	4.68%
12. SECURITY TG (BALTIMORE)	$4,841,486	0.92%	$174,907	0.67%	3.55%
13. CENSTAR	$4,624,937	0.88%	$32,527	0.13%	0.72%
14. CONESTOGA	$3,761,458	0.72%	$137,864	0.53%	3.52%
15. PENN ATTORNEYS	$1,777,598	0.34%	$44,947	0.17%	2.47%
16. GUARANTEE T&T	$1,536,672	0.29%	$203,638	0.79%	10.36%
17. INVESTORS TIC	$1,510,325	0.29%	$2,325	0.00%	0.14%
18. TRANSNATION	$1,174,892	0.22%	$26,179	0.10%	2.26%
19. MANITO	$788,476	0.15%	$39,324	0.15%	4.99%
20. NEW JERSEY TIC	$717,721	0.14%	$3,701	0.01%	0.46%
21. TITLE RESOURCES	$467,688	0.09%	$0	--	--
22. SOUTHERN TI CORP	$394,211	0.08%	($2,901)	(0.01)%	(0.74)%
23. SECURITY UNION	$2,574	0.00%	$20,228	0.08%	576.79%
24. AMERICAN GUARANTY	$909	0.00%	$0	--	--
25. COMMONWEALTH LAND (NJ	$0	--	($2,000)	0.00%	(122.70)%
26. EQUITY NATIONAL	$0	--	$0	--	--
27. NATIONAL OF NY	$0	--	$0	--	--
28. NATIONS OF NY	$0	--	$0	--	--
29. NORTHEAST INVESTORS	$0	--	$0	--	--
30. WESTCOR	$0	--	$0	--	--
COMPOSITE	**$524,307,342**	**100.00%**	**$25,940,951**	**100.00%**	**4.48%**
AVERAGE	**$17,476,911**		**$864,698**		

2006

	TOTAL DPW	MARKET SHARE	LOSSES INCURRED	MARKET SHARE	LOSS RATIO
1. FIRST AMERICAN TIC	$129,240,566	22.62%	$1,912,930	10.92%	1.39%
2. LAWYERS	$108,913,973	19.06%	$3,609,550	20.61%	3.19%
3. COMMONWEALTH LAND	$95,590,760	16.73%	$1,918,638	10.95%	1.85%
4. FIDELITY NATIONAL	$48,940,147	8.57%	$2,607,903	14.89%	4.85%
5. CHICAGO TIC	$43,949,560	7.69%	$1,799,931	10.27%	3.80%
6. OLD REPUBLIC NATIONAL	$40,511,971	7.09%	$1,253,093	7.15%	3.05%
7. STEWART TGC	$39,323,600	6.88%	$2,787,724	15.91%	4.07%
8. UNITED GENERAL	$15,143,135	2.65%	$119,260	0.68%	0.81%
9. T.A. TITLE	$12,877,635	2.25%	$236,293	1.35%	1.81%
10. SECURITY TG (BALTIMORE)	$7,282,319	1.27%	$360,977	2.06%	4.97%
11. TICOR	$6,510,601	1.14%	$202,999	1.16%	3.09%
12. TICOR (FL)	$6,394,694	1.12%	$98,646	0.56%	1.56%
13. CONESTOGA	$4,636,522	0.81%	$110,209	0.63%	2.36%
14. CENSTAR	$3,411,481	0.60%	$3,162	0.02%	0.10%
15. GUARANTEE T&T	$2,187,975	0.38%	$347,477	1.98%	15.13%
16. PENN ATTORNEYS	$2,094,251	0.37%	$100,627	0.57%	4.65%
17. INVESTORS TIC	$1,473,028	0.26%	$6,700	0.04%	0.44%
18. TRANSNATION	$1,151,858	0.20%	$50,000	0.29%	4.39%
19. MANITO	$887,535	0.16%	$14,525	0.08%	1.74%
20. SOUTHERN TI CORP	$511,272	0.09%	($7,861)	(0.04)%	(1.56)%
21. NEW JERSEY TIC	$303,115	0.05%	$0	--	--
22. SECURITY UNION	$968	0.00%	$0	--	--
23. NATIONS OF NY	$0	--	$11,292	0.06%	--
24. ALAMO	$0	--	$0	--	--
25. AMERICAN GUARANTY	$0	--	$0	--	--
26. EQUITY NATIONAL	$0	--	$0	--	--
27. LAND	$0	--	$0	--	--
28. TITLE IC AMERICA	$0	--	$0	--	--
29. WESTCOR	$0	--	$0	--	--
30. COMMONWEALTH LAND (NJ	$0	--	($26,261)	(0.15)%	293.98%
COMPOSITE	**$571,336,966**	**100.00%**	**$17,517,814**	**100.00%**	**2.78%**
AVERAGE	**$19,044,566**		**$583,927**		

10-YEAR - DIRECT PREMIUMS WRITTEN (DPW) BY CHANNEL   See Sec. 3

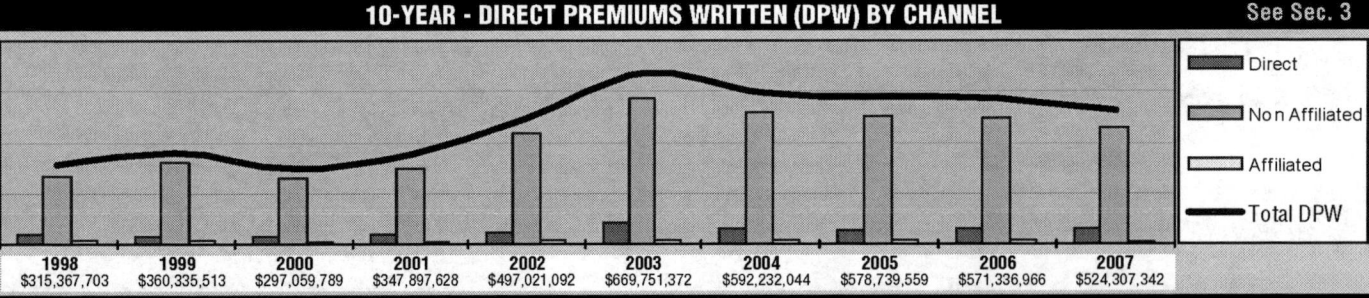

Legend: ■ Direct ■ Non Affiliated □ Affiliated — Total DPW

1998	1999	2000	2001	2002	2003	2004	2005	2006	2007
$315,367,703	$360,335,513	$297,059,789	$347,897,628	$497,021,092	$669,751,372	$592,232,044	$578,739,559	$571,336,966	$524,307,342

10-YEAR - LOSS RATIO   See Sec. 5, A.2

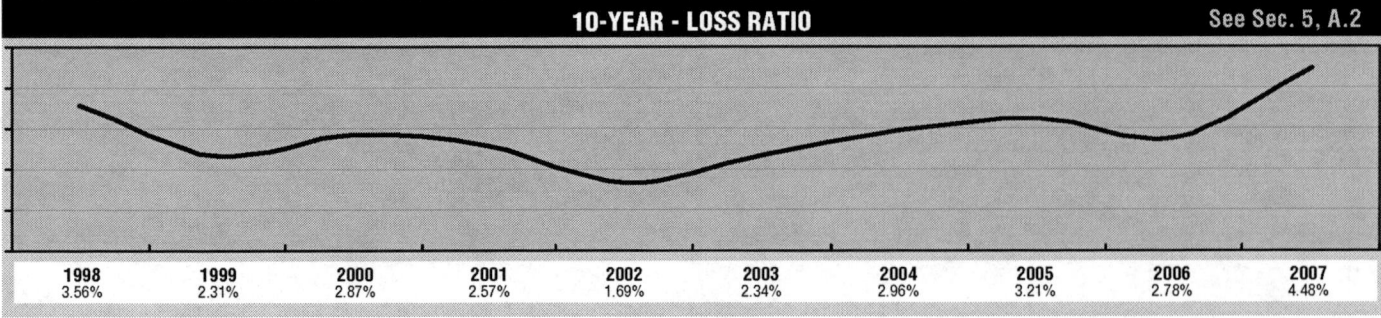

1998	1999	2000	2001	2002	2003	2004	2005	2006	2007
3.56%	2.31%	2.87%	2.57%	1.69%	2.34%	2.96%	3.21%	2.78%	4.48%

6

PUERTO RICO

DEPARTMENT OF INSURANCE INFORMATION
Office of the Commissioner of Insurances

Ms. Dorelisse Juarbe-Jimènez
Commissioner of Insurance
B5 Tabonuco St., Ste. 216
PMB 356
Guaynabo, PR 00968-3029

Phone: (787) 722-8686
Fax: (787) 273-6082
www.ocs.gobierno.pr

LAND TITLE ASSOCIATION
No information at time of publication.

DOMICILED UNDERWRITERS   See Sec. 1

Underwriter	NAIC #
None	

9 **Licensed Underwriters**	See Sec. 1

STATUTORY PREMIUM RESERVE (SPR) REQUIREMENTS

Inception:	Not Available		
Max Years:	Not Available	Release:	Not Available

MARKET SHARE BY UNDERWRITER   See Sec. 3

	TOTAL DPW	MARKET SHARE	LOSSES INCURRED	MARKET SHARE	LOSS RATIO		TOTAL DPW	MARKET SHARE	LOSSES INCURRED	MARKET SHARE	LOSS RATIO
	2007						**2006**				
1. STEWART TGC	$12.779.579	42.08%	$732.304	22.31%	5.75%	1. STEWART TGC	$16.074.137	42.24%	$983.009	32.09%	5.42%
2. FIRST AMERICAN TIC	$5.364.029	17.66%	$712.478	21.70%	13.47%	2. FIRST AMERICAN TIC	$8.011.999	21.05%	$581.263	18.98%	7.40%
3. CHICAGO TIC	$5.067.002	16.68%	$548.998	16.72%	11.38%	3. COMMONWEALTH LAND	$7.745.656	20.35%	$546.632	17.85%	6.61%
4. COMMONWEALTH LAND	$3.391.378	11.17%	$260.568	7.94%	7.38%	4. CHICAGO TIC	$2.671.648	7.02%	$790.098	25.79%	29.55%
5. LAWYERS	$2.085.328	6.87%	$504.094	15.36%	25.74%	5. OLD REPUBLIC NATIONAL	$1.789.799	4.70%	$48.207	1.57%	2.67%
6. OLD REPUBLIC NATIONAL	$1.074.393	3.54%	$153.540	4.68%	13.50%	6. LAWYERS	$1.509.192	3.97%	$115.574	3.77%	7.96%
7. FIDELITY NATIONAL	$363.583	1.20%	$370.688	11.29%	102.90%	7. FIDELITY NATIONAL	$135.319	0.36%	($1.750)	(0.06)%	(1.32)%
8. ATTORNEYS TIF (FL)	$245.518	0.81%	$0	--	--	8. ATTORNEYS TIF (FL)	$118.639	0.31%	$0	--	--
9. INVESTORS TIC	$0	--	$0	--	--	9. INVESTORS TIC	$0	--	$0	--	--
10. TICOR	$0	--	$0	--	--	10. TICOR	$0	--	$0	--	--
11. TRANSNATION	$0	--	$0	--	--	11. TRANSNATION	$0	--	$0	--	--
COMPOSITE	$30,370,810	100.00%	$3,282,670	100.00%	10.92%	**COMPOSITE**	$38,056,389	100.00%	$3,063,033	100.00%	7.58%
AVERAGE	$2,760,983		$298,425			**AVERAGE**	$3,459,672		$278,458		

10-YEAR - DIRECT PREMIUMS WRITTEN (DPW) BY CHANNEL   See Sec. 3

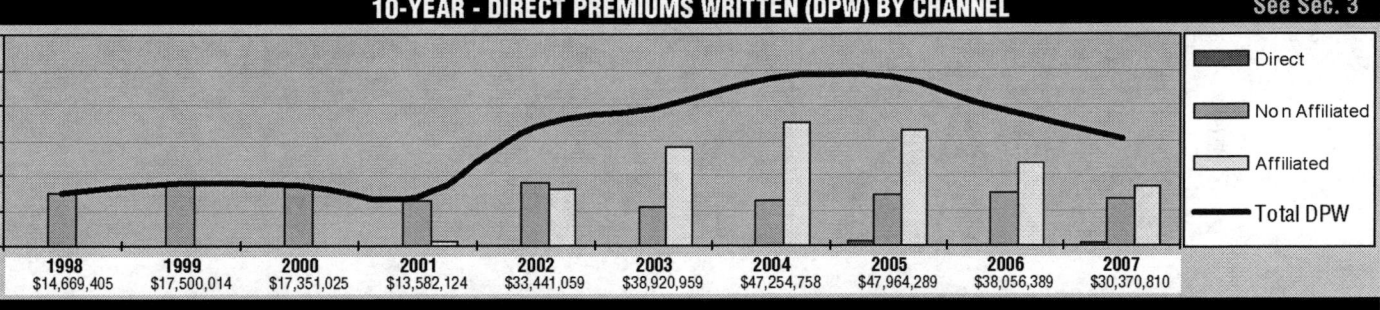

Legend: Direct, Non Affiliated, Affiliated, Total DPW

1998	1999	2000	2001	2002	2003	2004	2005	2006	2007
$14,669,405	$17,500,014	$17,351,025	$13,582,124	$33,441,059	$38,920,959	$47,254,758	$47,964,289	$38,056,389	$30,370,810

10-YEAR - LOSS RATIO   See Sec. 5, A.2

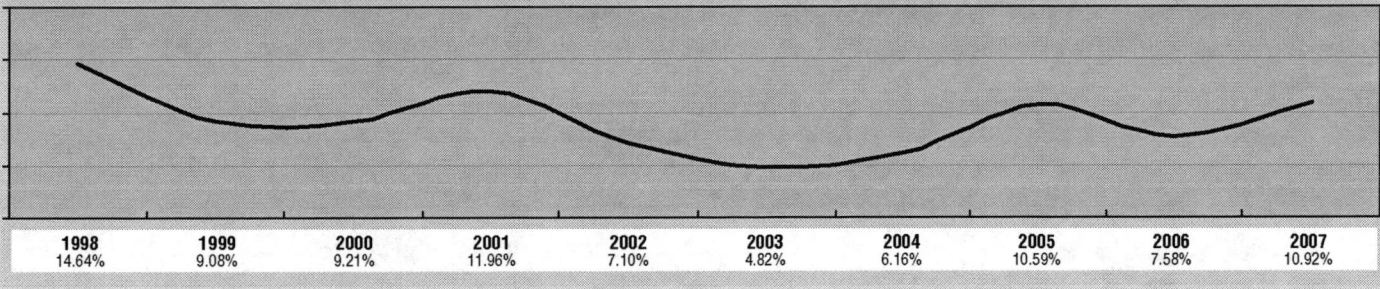

1998	1999	2000	2001	2002	2003	2004	2005	2006	2007
14.64%	9.08%	9.21%	11.96%	7.10%	4.82%	6.16%	10.59%	7.58%	10.92%

RHODE ISLAND

DEPARTMENT OF INSURANCE INFORMATION	LAND TITLE ASSOCIATION	DOMICILED UNDERWRITERS See Sec. 1

Rhode Island Division of Insurance	New England Land Title Association	Underwriter	NAIC #

Mr. Joseph Torti, III
Superintendent of Insurance
233 Richmond St., Ste. 233
Providence, RI 02903-4233

Phone: (401) 222-2223
Fax: (401) 222-5475
www.dbr.state.ri.us

P.O. Box 743
Norwalk, CT 06852-0743
Phone: (203) 847-6885
www.nelta.org

MORTGAGE GUARANTEE
PILGRIM

| 16 | Licensed Underwriters | See Sec. 1 |

STATUTORY PREMIUM RESERVE (SPR) REQUIREMENTS

Inception:	Not Available		
Max Years:	Not Available	Release:	Not Available

MARKET SHARE BY UNDERWRITER See Sec. 3

2007

	TOTAL DPW	MARKET SHARE	LOSSES INCURRED	MARKET SHARE	LOSS RATIO
1. COMMONWEALTH LAND	$8,120,887	32.60%	$939,700	24.20%	11.16%
2. CHICAGO TIC	$3,575,785	14.35%	$228,400	5.88%	5.94%
3. STEWART TGC	$3,306,901	13.27%	$1,788,824	46.06%	53.16%
4. UNITED GENERAL	$3,115,354	12.50%	$2,967	0.08%	0.10%
5. FIDELITY NATIONAL	$2,159,410	8.67%	$227,701	5.86%	10.62%
6. CT ATTORNEYS	$1,565,764	6.28%	$300,704	7.74%	19.12%
7. LAWYERS	$1,440,416	5.78%	$38,533	0.99%	2.37%
8. FIRST AMERICAN TIC	$1,139,898	4.58%	$390,226	10.05%	28.43%
9. OLD REPUBLIC NATIONAL	$262,722	1.05%	($3,749)	(0.10)%	(1.13)%
10. TICOR (FL)	$113,092	0.45%	($49,144)	(1.27)%	(43.40)%
11. TICOR	$100,912	0.41%	$19,665	0.51%	17.70%
12. TRANSNATION	$13,138	0.05%	$0	--	--
13. EQUITY NATIONAL	$0	--	$0	--	--
14. GUARANTEE T&T	$0	--	$0	--	--
15. SECURITY UNION	$0	--	$0	--	--
COMPOSITE	$24,914,279	100.00%	$3,883,827	100.00%	14.90%
AVERAGE	$1,660,952		$258,922		

2006

	TOTAL DPW	MARKET SHARE	LOSSES INCURRED	MARKET SHARE	LOSS RATIO
1. MORTGAGE GUARANTEE	$12,435,110	29.40%	$172,125	9.12%	1.34%
2. COMMONWEALTH LAND	$10,210,526	24.14%	$236,011	12.51%	2.10%
3. STEWART TGC	$5,315,330	12.57%	$173,809	9.21%	3.27%
4. CHICAGO TIC	$5,054,324	11.95%	$450,451	23.88%	8.69%
5. UNITED GENERAL	$2,438,783	5.77%	$0	--	--
6. FIDELITY NATIONAL	$2,142,233	5.07%	$18,886	1.00%	0.90%
7. CT ATTORNEYS	$1,670,073	3.95%	$220,928	11.71%	13.15%
8. LAWYERS	$1,641,265	3.88%	$4,529	0.24%	0.26%
9. OLD REPUBLIC NATIONAL	$613,669	1.45%	$518,214	27.47%	78.02%
10. FIRST AMERICAN TIC	$492,007	1.16%	$89,529	4.75%	13.88%
11. TICOR (FL)	$150,578	0.36%	$6,953	0.37%	4.55%
12. TICOR	$118,753	0.28%	($4,777)	(0.25)%	(3.86)%
13. TRANSNATION	$6,633	0.02%	$0	--	--
14. EQUITY NATIONAL	$0	--	$0	--	--
15. SECURITY UNION	$0	--	$0	--	--
COMPOSITE	$42,289,284	100.00%	$1,886,658	100.00%	4.23%
AVERAGE	$2,819,286		$125,777		

10-YEAR - DIRECT PREMIUMS WRITTEN (DPW) BY CHANNEL See Sec. 3

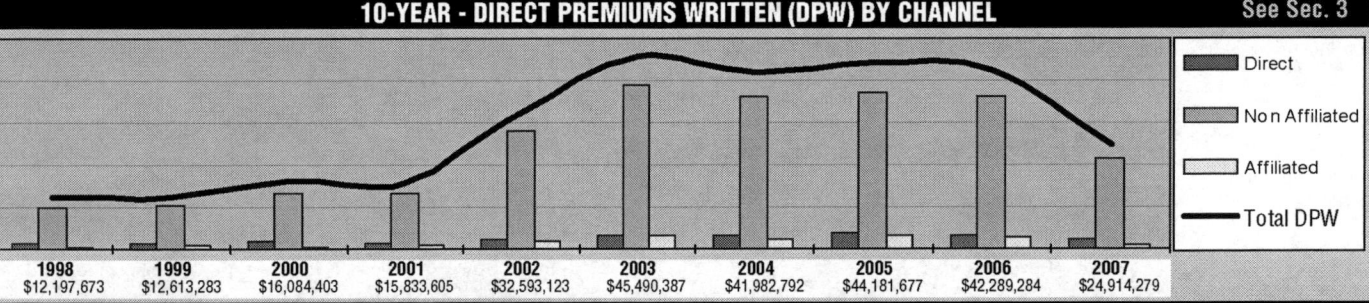

■ Direct
■ Non Affiliated
□ Affiliated
— Total DPW

1998	1999	2000	2001	2002	2003	2004	2005	2006	2007
$12,197,673	$12,613,283	$16,084,403	$15,833,605	$32,593,123	$45,490,387	$41,982,792	$44,181,677	$42,289,284	$24,914,279

10-YEAR - LOSS RATIO See Sec. 5, A.2

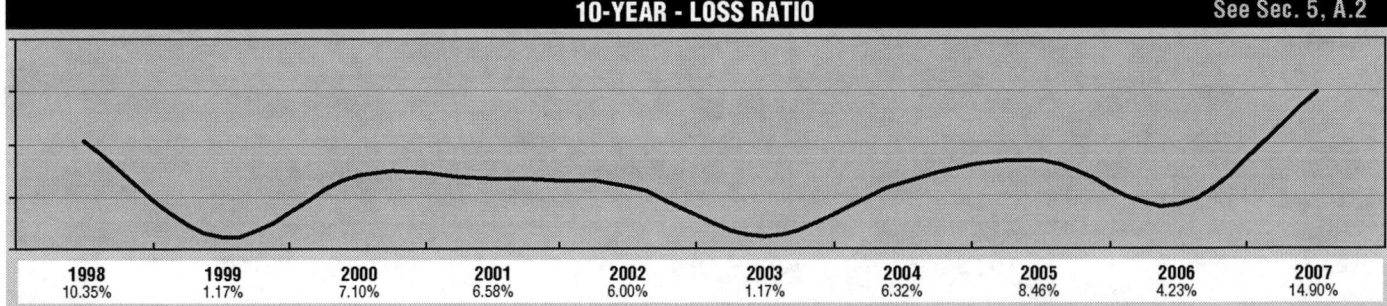

1998	1999	2000	2001	2002	2003	2004	2005	2006	2007
10.35%	1.17%	7.10%	6.58%	6.00%	1.17%	6.32%	8.46%	4.23%	14.90%

6

SOUTH CAROLINA

DEPARTMENT OF INSURANCE INFORMATION

South Carolina Department of Insurance

Mr. Scott H. Richardson
Director of Insurance
1201 Main St., Ste. 1000
Columbia, SC 29201

Phone: (803) 737-6160
Fax: (803) 737-6205
www.doi.sc.gov

LAND TITLE ASSOCIATION

Palmetto Land Title Association

P.O. Box 11372
Columbia, SC 29211

Phone: (803) 892-5582
www.scplta.org

DOMICILED UNDERWRITERS   See Sec. 1

Underwriter	NAIC #
NORTHEAST INVESTORS	50377
TRANSUNION NATIONAL	51152
30 Licensed Underwriters	See Sec. 1

STATUTORY PREMIUM RESERVE (SPR) REQUIREMENTS

Inception:	$1.50 per policy & 12.5 cents per $1,000 of net retained liability
Max Years:	20 Release: 10% years 1-5; 3.33% years 6-20

MARKET SHARE BY UNDERWRITER   See Sec. 3

2007

	TOTAL DPW	MARKET SHARE	LOSSES INCURRED	MARKET SHARE	LOSS RATIO
1. CHICAGO TIC	$39,669,921	28.37%	$1,660,151	16.96%	4.37%
2. FIRST AMERICAN TIC	$23,976,464	17.15%	$1,947,112	19.89%	7.75%
3. LAWYERS	$23,712,950	16.96%	$835,681	8.54%	3.38%
4. STEWART TGC	$17,606,163	12.59%	$1,816,112	18.55%	10.21%
5. FIDELITY NATIONAL	$10,349,742	7.40%	$520,704	5.32%	4.97%
6. INVESTORS TIC	$7,574,228	5.42%	$192,577	1.97%	2.64%
7. OLD REPUBLIC NATIONAL	$6,536,153	4.67%	$809,267	8.27%	11.54%
8. COMMONWEALTH LAND	$2,190,681	1.57%	$673,291	6.88%	29.23%
9. ATTORNEYS TIF (FL)	$1,893,029	1.35%	$456,465	4.66%	25.23%
10. SECURITY TG (BALTIMORE)	$1,429,635	1.02%	($24,304)	(0.25%)	(1.37%)
11. COMMERCE	$1,092,087	0.78%	$0	--	--
12. UNITED GENERAL	$955,841	0.68%	$49,506	0.51%	5.38%
13. TRANSUNION NATIONAL	$826,376	0.59%	$403,276	4.12%	47.67%
14. SOUTHERN TI CORP	$761,782	0.54%	$17,237	0.18%	2.39%
15. TICOR (FL)	$522,993	0.37%	$181,286	1.85%	33.54%
16. TICOR	$355,951	0.25%	$28,809	0.29%	5.20%
17. GUARANTEE T&T	$162,067	0.12%	$33,846	0.35%	16.61%
18. CENSTAR	$117,867	0.08%	$0	--	--
19. TRANSNATION	$45,008	0.03%	$3,000	0.03%	4.63%
20. TITLE IC AMERICA	$33,021	0.02%	$4,197	0.04%	13.55%
21. AMERICAN GUARANTY	$24,483	0.02%	$0	--	--
22. SECURITY UNION	$5,062	0.00%	$0	--	--
23. BRIDGE	$462	0.00%	$182,192	1.86%	7,100.23%
24. NATIONAL OF NY	$0	--	$0	--	--
25. NATIONS OF NY	$0	--	$0	--	--
26. NORTHEAST INVESTORS	$0	--	$0	--	--
COMPOSITE	**$139,841,966**	**100.00%**	**$9,790,405**	**100.00%**	**6.92%**
AVERAGE	**$5,378,537**		**$376,554**		

2006

	TOTAL DPW	MARKET SHARE	LOSSES INCURRED	MARKET SHARE	LOSS RATIO
1. CHICAGO TIC	$48,723,795	33.08%	$1,109,432	13.80%	2.41%
2. FIRST AMERICAN TIC	$22,449,153	15.24%	$1,046,035	13.01%	4.58%
3. LAWYERS	$20,503,160	13.92%	$1,297,971	16.14%	6.32%
4. STEWART TGC	$17,684,794	12.01%	$602,723	7.50%	3.55%
5. FIDELITY NATIONAL	$12,352,392	8.39%	$953,611	11.86%	7.85%
6. INVESTORS TIC	$7,096,557	4.82%	$836,006	10.40%	12.24%
7. OLD REPUBLIC NATIONAL	$6,470,932	4.39%	$581,872	7.24%	8.02%
8. COMMONWEALTH LAND	$2,394,141	1.63%	$417,297	5.19%	15.58%
9. SECURITY TG (BALTIMORE)	$1,833,109	1.24%	($345,260)	(4.29%)	(16.81%)
10. TRANSUNION NATIONAL	$1,750,652	1.19%	$705,919	8.78%	43.26%
11. ATTORNEYS TIF (FL)	$1,540,566	1.05%	$385,977	4.80%	26.27%
12. COMMERCE	$1,417,469	0.96%	$0	--	--
13. TICOR (FL)	$1,028,349	0.70%	$310,865	3.87%	30.70%
14. UNITED GENERAL	$740,981	0.50%	$106,904	1.33%	15.30%
15. SOUTHERN TI CORP	$601,271	0.41%	($5,191)	(0.06%)	(0.91%)
16. GUARANTEE T&T	$310,177	0.21%	$0	--	--
17. TICOR	$212,675	0.14%	($1,792)	(0.02%)	(0.48%)
18. TITLE IC AMERICA	$146,297	0.10%	($1,548)	(0.02%)	(1.03%)
19. CENSTAR	$32,140	0.02%	$0	--	--
20. TRANSNATION	$20,513	0.01%	$0	--	--
21. SECURITY UNION	$300	0.00%	$0	--	--
22. BRIDGE	$0	--	$40,119	0.50%	1,245.54%
23. NORTHEAST INVESTORS	$0	--	$0	--	--
COMPOSITE	**$147,309,423**	**100.00%**	**$8,040,940**	**100.00%**	**5.55%**
AVERAGE	**$6,404,758**		**$349,606**		

10-YEAR - DIRECT PREMIUMS WRITTEN (DPW) BY CHANNEL   See Sec. 3

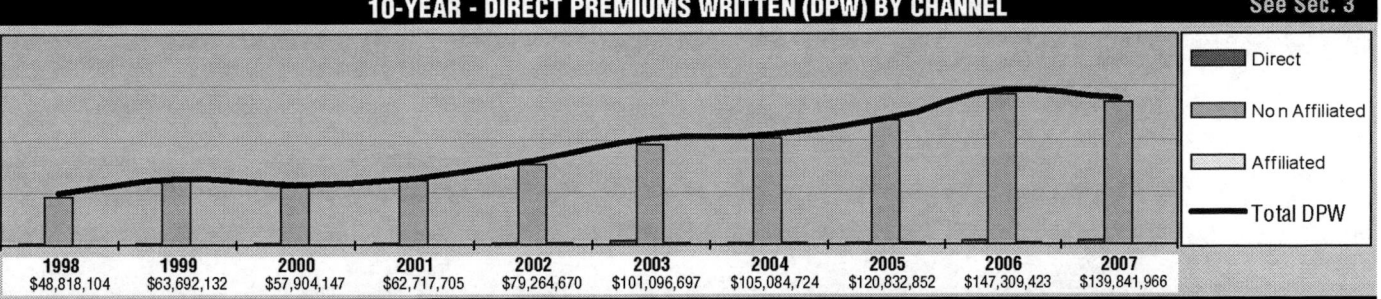

Legend: Direct · Non Affiliated · Affiliated · Total DPW

1998	1999	2000	2001	2002	2003	2004	2005	2006	2007
$48,818,104	$63,692,132	$57,904,147	$62,717,705	$79,264,670	$101,096,697	$105,084,724	$120,832,852	$147,309,423	$139,841,966

10-YEAR - LOSS RATIO   See Sec. 5, A.2

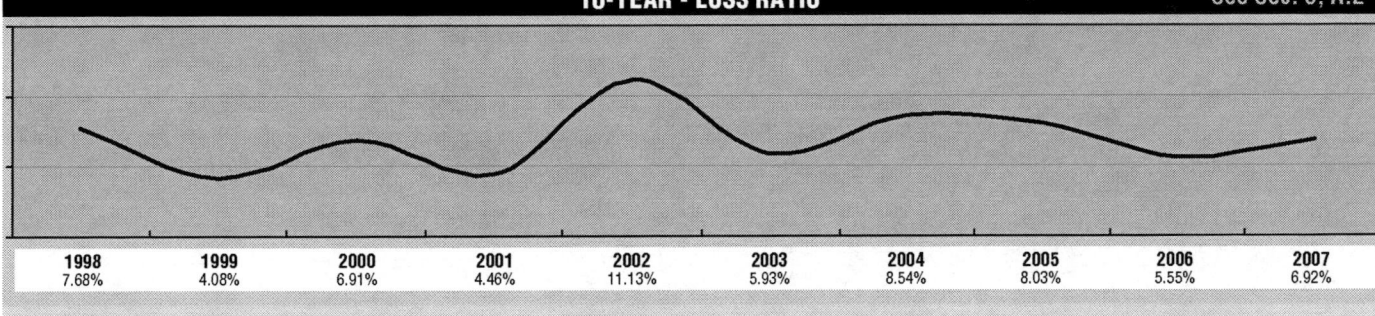

1998	1999	2000	2001	2002	2003	2004	2005	2006	2007
7.68%	4.08%	6.91%	4.46%	11.13%	5.93%	8.54%	8.03%	5.55%	6.92%

SOUTH DAKOTA

DEPARTMENT OF INSURANCE INFORMATION	LAND TITLE ASSOCIATION	DOMICILED UNDERWRITERS See Sec. 1	

South Dakota Division of Insurance	South Dakota Land Title Association	Underwriter	NAIC #
Mr. Merle D. Scheiber		DAKOTA HOMESTEAD	50020
Director of Insurance			
445 E Capitol Ave.		**20** Licensed Underwriters	See Sec. 1
Pierre, SD 57501			
Phone: (605) 773-3563			
Fax: (605) 773-5369			
www.state.sd.us/drr2/reg/insurance			

STATUTORY PREMIUM RESERVE (SPR) REQUIREMENTS

Inception:	24 cents per $1,000 of net retained liability (policies < $500,000) and 12 cents per $1,000 of net retained liability (policies >= $500,000)
Max Years:	20 **Release:** 35% first year; 15% years 2-3; 10% year 4; 3% years 5-7; 2% years 8-10; 1% years 11-20

MARKET SHARE BY UNDERWRITER   See Sec. 3

2007	TOTAL DPW	MARKET SHARE	LOSSES INCURRED	MARKET SHARE	LOSS RATIO
1. OLD REPUBLIC NATIONAL	$2,859,506	19.46%	$41,751	1.05%	1.43%
2. DAKOTA HOMESTEAD	$2,600,461	17.70%	$0	--	--
3. FIRST AMERICAN TIC	$2,440,207	16.60%	$36,709	0.93%	1.42%
4. CHICAGO TIC	$2,107,617	14.34%	$142,481	3.60%	6.60%
5. STEWART TGC	$1,966,721	13.38%	$59,173	1.49%	3.01%
6. COMMONWEALTH LAND	$1,636,841	11.14%	$61,990	1.56%	3.84%
7. SECURITY UNION	$828,139	5.64%	($390)	0.00%	(0.05)%
8. TICOR	$196,941	1.34%	$17,505	0.44%	8.12%
9. LAWYERS	$29,508	0.20%	$3,602,681	90.93%	2,316.15%
10. FIDELITY NATIONAL	$29,140	0.20%	$0	--	--
11. UNITED GENERAL	$788	0.00%	$0	--	--
12. GUARANTEE T&T	$0	--	$0	--	--
13. TRANSNATION	$0	--	$0	--	--
COMPOSITE	**$14,695,869**	**100.00%**	**$3,961,900**	**100.00%**	**31.74%**
AVERAGE	**$1,130,451**		**$304,762**		

2006	TOTAL DPW	MARKET SHARE	LOSSES INCURRED	MARKET SHARE	LOSS RATIO
1. FIRST AMERICAN TIC	$3,916,764	20.84%	$41,379	47.16%	1.06%
2. OLD REPUBLIC NATIONAL	$2,873,510	15.29%	($2,570)	(2.93)%	(0.09)%
3. STEWART TGC	$2,791,205	14.85%	$75,205	85.72%	2.79%
4. DAKOTA HOMESTEAD	$2,731,755	14.54%	$0	--	--
5. COMMONWEALTH LAND	$2,685,223	14.29%	$45,829	52.24%	1.61%
6. CHICAGO TIC	$2,327,962	12.39%	($178,497)	(203.45)%	(7.82)%
7. SECURITY UNION	$1,208,348	6.43%	$390	0.44%	0.03%
8. TICOR	$187,091	1.00%	$13,500	15.39%	6.91%
9. LAWYERS	$45,715	0.24%	$92,500	105.43%	51.63%
10. FIDELITY NATIONAL	$23,460	0.12%	$0	--	--
11. TRANSNATION	$0	--	$0	--	--
COMPOSITE	**$18,791,033**	**100.00%**	**$87,736**	**100.00%**	**0.54%**
AVERAGE	**$1,708,276**		**$7,976**		

10-YEAR - DIRECT PREMIUMS WRITTEN (DPW) BY CHANNEL   See Sec. 3

Legend: Direct, Non Affiliated, Affiliated, Total DPW

1998	1999	2000	2001	2002	2003	2004	2005	2006	2007
$8,482,596	$9,895,205	$9,833,563	$8,950,256	$13,419,890	$16,068,509	$17,212,698	$16,411,316	$18,791,033	$14,695,869

10-YEAR - LOSS RATIO   See Sec. 5, A.2

1998	1999	2000	2001	2002	2003	2004	2005	2006	2007
3.78%	0.37%	0.80%	1.21%	2.41%	0.11%	1.36%	3.87%	0.54%	31.74%

6

TENNESSEE

DEPARTMENT OF INSURANCE INFORMATION	LAND TITLE ASSOCIATION	DOMICILED UNDERWRITERS See Sec. 1

Tennessee Department of Commerce and Insurance

Ms. Leslie A. Newman
Insurance Commissioner
500 James Robertson Pkwy.
Davy Crockett Tower
Nashville, TN 37243-0565

Phone: (615) 741-2241
Fax: (615) 532-6934
www.state.tn.us/commerce/insurance

Tennessee Land Title Association

P.O. Box 125
Watertown, TN 37184
Phone: (615) 286-1600
www.tnlta.org

Underwriter	NAIC #
TITLE G&TC	50261

| 28 | Licensed Underwriters | See Sec. 1 |

STATUTORY PREMIUM RESERVE (SPR) REQUIREMENTS

Inception:	10% of risk rate charge	
Max Years:	25	Release: 10% years 1-5; 2.5% years 6-25

MARKET SHARE BY UNDERWRITER — See Sec. 3

2007

	TOTAL DPW	MARKET SHARE	LOSSES INCURRED	MARKET SHARE	LOSS RATIO
1. CHICAGO TIC	$29,893,129	18.39%	$421,486	6.51%	1.27%
2. FIRST AMERICAN TIC	$27,870,027	17.15%	$1,414,822	21.86%	4.43%
3. LAWYERS	$23,998,657	14.77%	$295,718	4.57%	1.14%
4. OLD REPUBLIC NATIONAL	$23,478,895	14.45%	$1,374,819	21.24%	5.89%
5. STEWART TGC	$17,856,123	10.99%	$1,652,194	25.52%	9.22%
6. FIDELITY NATIONAL	$12,204,580	7.51%	($836,716)	(12.93)%	(6.42)%
7. SOUTHERN TI CORP	$7,024,297	4.32%	($193,588)	(2.99)%	(2.94)%
8. COMMONWEALTH LAND	$6,390,490	3.93%	$736,640	11.38%	11.29%
9. INVESTORS TIC	$2,623,083	1.61%	$100,699	1.56%	3.99%
10. SECURITY UNION	$2,383,695	1.47%	$152,012	2.35%	6.55%
11. TICOR	$2,376,835	1.46%	$385,188	5.95%	15.69%
12. UNITED GENERAL	$2,319,836	1.43%	$139,089	2.15%	5.26%
13. TICOR (FL)	$1,242,405	0.76%	$413,357	6.39%	32.60%
14. MISSISSIPPI VALLEY	$939,463	0.58%	$47,130	0.73%	3.53%
15. CENSTAR	$863,668	0.53%	$0	--	--
16. TRANSNATION	$385,780	0.24%	$111,921	1.73%	29.66%
17. TITLE G&TC	$260,893	0.16%	$1,500	0.02%	0.57%
18. GUARANTEE	$228,810	0.14%	$6,700	0.10%	3.36%
19. CONESTOGA	$114,712	0.07%	$0	--	--
20. TRANSUNION NATIONAL	$59,287	0.04%	$0	--	--
21. AMERICAN GUARANTY	$1,924	0.00%	$0	--	--
22. NATIONAL	$1,367	0.00%	$0	--	--
23. NATIONAL OF NY	$0	--	$269,761	4.17%	1,438.04%
24. TITLE IC AMERICA	$0	--	$4,000	0.06%	--
25. ALAMO	$0	--	$0	--	--
26. CHICAGO TIC (OR)	$0	--	$0	--	--
27. GUARANTEE T&T	$0	--	$0	--	--
28. NATIONS OF NY	$0	--	($3,445)	(0.05)%	(401.05)%
29. NORTHEAST INVESTORS	$0	--	$0	--	--
30. SECURITY TG (BALTIMORE)	($9,209)	0.00%	($20,167)	(0.31)%	420.23%
COMPOSITE	**$162,508,747**	**100.00%**	**$6,473,120**	**100.00%**	**3.74%**
AVERAGE	**$5,416,958**		**$215,771**		

2006

	TOTAL DPW	MARKET SHARE	LOSSES INCURRED	MARKET SHARE	LOSS RATIO
1. CHICAGO TIC	$30,970,157	19.04%	$543,656	6.67%	1.61%
2. FIRST AMERICAN TIC	$26,146,458	16.08%	$976,962	11.99%	3.31%
3. LAWYERS	$25,703,553	15.80%	$800,251	9.82%	2.93%
4. OLD REPUBLIC NATIONAL	$20,208,621	12.43%	$1,064,548	13.06%	5.28%
5. STEWART TGC	$20,174,059	12.40%	$1,697,929	20.83%	8.44%
6. FIDELITY NATIONAL	$12,675,935	7.79%	$1,827,049	22.41%	13.43%
7. COMMONWEALTH LAND	$6,663,012	4.10%	$315,872	3.88%	4.35%
8. SOUTHERN TI CORP	$6,631,313	4.08%	$513,193	6.30%	8.35%
9. SECURITY UNION	$3,210,516	1.97%	$89,618	1.10%	2.89%
10. INVESTORS TIC	$2,452,590	1.51%	$188,872	2.32%	8.02%
11. UNITED GENERAL	$1,805,252	1.11%	($5,336)	(0.07)%	(0.31)%
12. TICOR	$1,505,317	0.93%	$261,452	3.21%	16.22%
13. TICOR (FL)	$1,440,810	0.89%	$49,374	0.61%	3.27%
14. MISSISSIPPI VALLEY	$899,272	0.55%	($173,994)	(2.13)%	(12.01)%
15. CENSTAR	$856,552	0.53%	$0	--	--
16. GUARANTEE	$436,149	0.27%	$0	--	--
17. TRANSNATION	$435,825	0.27%	$0	--	--
18. TITLE G&TC	$276,536	0.17%	$0	--	--
19. TRANSUNION NATIONAL	$70,968	0.04%	$3,922	0.05%	5.79%
20. CONESTOGA	$43,265	0.03%	$0	--	--
21. SECURITY TG (BALTIMORE)	$36,581	0.02%	$52,212	0.64%	143.96%
22. TITLE IC AMERICA	$0	--	($54,295)	(0.67)%	--
23. NORTHEAST INVESTORS	$0	--	$0	--	--
COMPOSITE	**$162,642,741**	**100.00%**	**$8,151,285**	**100.00%**	**4.76%**
AVERAGE	**$7,071,424**		**$354,404**		

10-YEAR - DIRECT PREMIUMS WRITTEN (DPW) BY CHANNEL — See Sec. 3

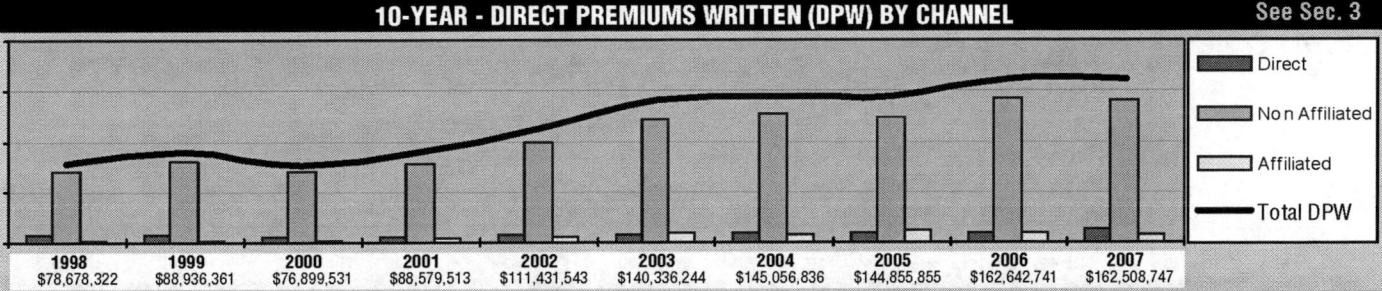

Legend: Direct, Non Affiliated, Affiliated, Total DPW

1998	1999	2000	2001	2002	2003	2004	2005	2006	2007
$78,678,322	$88,936,361	$76,899,531	$88,579,513	$111,431,543	$140,336,244	$145,056,836	$144,855,855	$162,642,741	$162,508,747

10-YEAR - LOSS RATIO — See Sec. 5, A.2

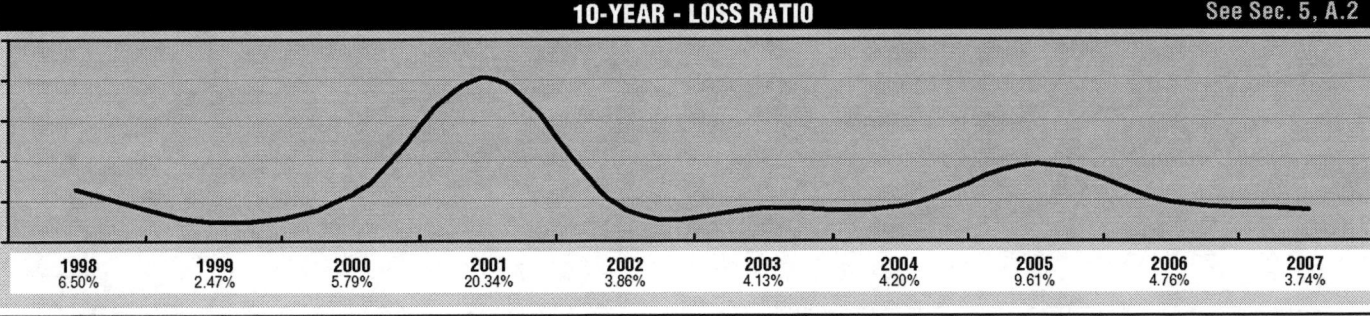

1998	1999	2000	2001	2002	2003	2004	2005	2006	2007
6.50%	2.47%	5.79%	20.34%	3.86%	4.13%	4.20%	9.61%	4.76%	3.74%

6

TEXAS

DEPARTMENT OF INSURANCE INFORMATION	LAND TITLE ASSOCIATION	DOMICILED UNDERWRITERS See Sec. 1	

Texas Department of Insurance

Mr. Mike Geeslin
Insurance Commissioner
333 Guadalupe
Austin, TX 78701
Phone: (512) 463-6169
Fax: (512) 475-2005
www.tdi.state.tx.us

Texas Land Title Association

1717 W 6th St., Ste. 120
Austin, TX 78703
Phone: (512) 472-6593
www.tlta.com

Underwriter	NAIC #
ALAMO	50598
CENSTAR	50636
SIERRA	12591
STEWART TGC	50121
TITLE RESOURCES	50016
32 Licensed Underwriters	See Sec. 1

STATUTORY PREMIUM RESERVE (SPR) REQUIREMENTS

Inception:	18.5 cents per $1,000 net retained liability		
Max Years:	20	Release:	26% year 1; 20% year 2; 10% year 3; 9% year 4; 5% years 5-6; 3% years 7-9; 2% years 10-14; 1% year 15-20

MARKET SHARE BY UNDERWRITER See Sec. 3

2007

	TOTAL DPW	MARKET SHARE	LOSSES INCURRED	MARKET SHARE	LOSS RATIO
1. FIRST AMERICAN TIC	$295,173,624	18.20%	$9,344,177	19.33%	2.90%
2. STEWART TGC	$269,221,833	16.60%	$4,433,545	9.17%	1.64%
3. LAWYERS	$225,537,781	13.91%	$441,663	0.91%	0.18%
4. CHICAGO TIC	$203,087,256	12.52%	$8,493,180	17.57%	3.90%
5. FIDELITY NATIONAL	$149,654,309	9.23%	$6,601,662	13.66%	4.18%
6. COMMONWEALTH LAND	$130,325,662	8.04%	$5,937,142	12.28%	4.19%
7. ALAMO	$94,165,857	5.81%	$4,072,065	8.42%	4.30%
8. TITLE RESOURCES	$72,141,840	4.45%	$2,106,509	4.36%	2.93%
9. OLD REPUBLIC NATIONAL	$48,481,664	2.99%	$2,301,661	4.76%	4.76%
10. UNITED GENERAL	$27,349,669	1.69%	$177,262	0.37%	0.66%
11. TICOR	$26,803,084	1.65%	$1,741,015	3.60%	6.36%
12. NORTH AMERICAN	$17,070,426	1.05%	$28,700	0.06%	0.16%
13. SOUTHERN TI CORP	$14,656,298	0.90%	$2,311,007	4.78%	16.18%
14. COMMERCE	$12,773,712	0.79%	$101,533	0.21%	0.81%
15. ALLIANT	$10,537,510	0.65%	$10,361	0.02%	0.10%
16. TITLE IC AMERICA	$9,828,156	0.61%	$35,818	0.07%	0.37%
17. SECURITY UNION	$5,221,439	0.32%	$99,501	0.21%	1.85%
18. PACIFIC NORTHWEST	$3,515,893	0.22%	$0	--	--
19. TRANSNATION	$2,326,598	0.14%	$43,800	0.09%	1.87%
20. SIERRA	$1,966,566	0.12%	$0	--	--
21. TICOR (FL)	$1,084,339	0.07%	$58,277	0.12%	5.28%
22. NATIONAL LAND	$448,854	0.03%	$0	--	--
23. WESTCOR	$274,717	0.02%	$0	--	--
24. CENSTAR	$0	--	$0	--	--
25. COMMONWEALTH LAND (NJ	$0	--	$0	--	--
26. GUARANTEE T&T	$0	--	$0	--	--
27. INVESTORS TIC	$0	--	$0	--	--
28. NATIONAL OF NY	$0	--	$0	--	--
29. NATIONS OF NY	$0	--	$0	--	--
COMPOSITE	$1,621,647,087	100.00%	$48,338,878	100.00%	2.85%
AVERAGE	$55,918,865		$1,666,858		

2006

	TOTAL DPW	MARKET SHARE	LOSSES INCURRED	MARKET SHARE	LOSS RATIO
1. FIRST AMERICAN TIC	$304,981,167	18.30%	$9,217,761	21.02%	3.03%
2. STEWART TGC	$272,694,535	16.36%	$5,244,849	11.96%	1.93%
3. CHICAGO TIC	$222,156,473	13.33%	$3,679,654	8.39%	1.54%
4. LAWYERS	$215,836,067	12.95%	$7,597,397	17.32%	3.31%
5. FIDELITY NATIONAL	$141,185,668	8.47%	$2,736,174	6.24%	1.83%
6. COMMONWEALTH LAND	$137,863,348	8.27%	$6,792,958	15.49%	4.55%
7. ALAMO	$112,009,711	6.72%	$1,966,194	4.48%	1.74%
8. TITLE RESOURCES	$85,192,430	5.11%	$2,386,105	5.44%	2.81%
9. OLD REPUBLIC NATIONAL	$46,456,763	2.79%	$2,785,742	6.35%	6.06%
10. TICOR	$31,556,919	1.89%	$27,775	0.06%	0.09%
11. UNITED GENERAL	$25,041,059	1.50%	$438,425	1.00%	1.76%
12. NORTH AMERICAN CORP	$20,724,144	1.24%	($21,389)	(0.05)%	(0.11)%
13. COMMERCE	$13,183,066	0.79%	$206,221	0.47%	1.63%
14. SOUTHERN TI CORP	$12,691,857	0.76%	$716,819	1.63%	5.81%
15. TITLE IC AMERICA	$8,221,079	0.49%	($83,505)	(0.19)%	(1.00)%
16. SECURITY UNION	$5,631,733	0.34%	$62,076	0.14%	1.08%
17. ALLIANT	$4,942,923	0.30%	$0	--	--
18. TRANSNATION	$3,787,454	0.23%	($7,007)	(0.02)%	(0.19)%
19. TICOR (FL)	$1,840,685	0.11%	$113,463	0.26%	6.18%
20. NATIONAL LAND	$764,178	0.05%	$0	--	--
21. WESTCOR	$178,264	0.01%	$0	--	--
22. COLUMBIAN NATIONAL	$51,368	0.00%	$0	--	--
23. COMMONWEALTH LAND (NJ	$0	--	$0	--	--
24. INVESTORS TIC	$0	--	$0	--	--
25. NATIONS OF NY	$0	--	$0	--	--
26. CENSTAR	($52,140)	0.00%	$0	--	--
COMPOSITE	$1,666,938,751	100.00%	$43,859,712	100.00%	2.57%
AVERAGE	$64,113,029		$1,686,912		

10-YEAR - DIRECT PREMIUMS WRITTEN (DPW) BY CHANNEL See Sec. 3

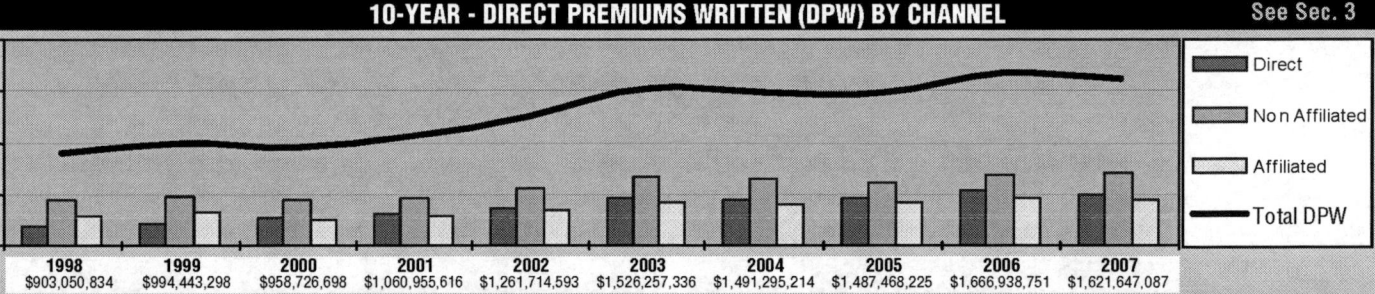

1998	1999	2000	2001	2002	2003	2004	2005	2006	2007
$903,050,834	$994,443,298	$958,726,698	$1,060,955,616	$1,261,714,593	$1,526,257,336	$1,491,295,214	$1,487,468,225	$1,666,938,751	$1,621,647,087

Legend: Direct, Non Affiliated, Affiliated, Total DPW

10-YEAR - LOSS RATIO See Sec. 5, A.2

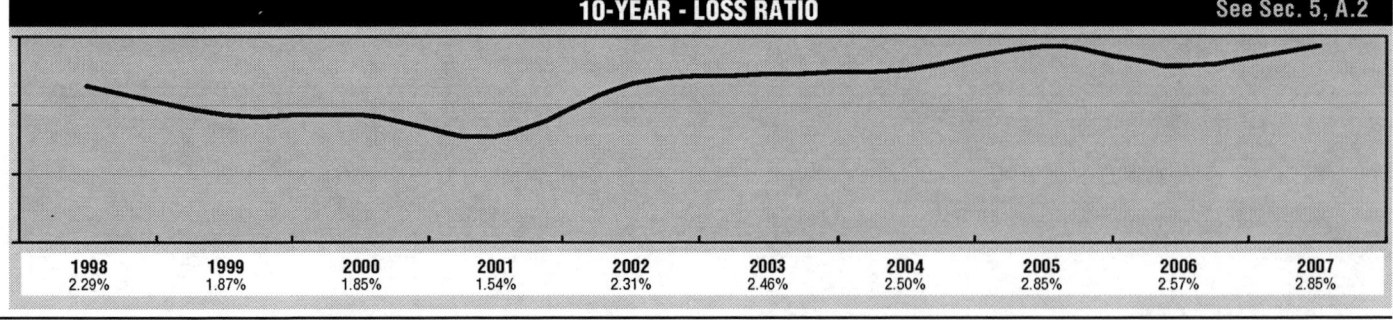

1998	1999	2000	2001	2002	2003	2004	2005	2006	2007
2.29%	1.87%	1.85%	1.54%	2.31%	2.46%	2.50%	2.85%	2.57%	2.85%

6

UTAH

DEPARTMENT OF INSURANCE INFORMATION
Utah Department of Insurance

Mr. Kent Michie
Insurance Commissioner
3110 State Office Building
Salt Lake City, UT 84114-6901
Phone: (801) 538-3800
Fax: (801) 538-3829
www.insurance.utah.gov

LAND TITLE ASSOCIATION
Utah Land Title Association

2131 Gad Way
Sandy, UT 84093
Phone: (801) 947-8453
www.ulta.org

DOMICILED UNDERWRITERS   See Sec. 1

Underwriter	NAIC #
WESTERN NATIONAL	51225

25	Licensed Underwriters	See Sec. 1

STATUTORY PREMIUM RESERVE (SPR) REQUIREMENTS

Inception:	10 cents per $1,000 of the face amount of retained liability
Max Years:	Not Available **Release:** Not Available

MARKET SHARE BY UNDERWRITER   See Sec. 3

2007

	TOTAL DPW	MARKET SHARE	LOSSES INCURRED	MARKET SHARE	LOSS RATIO
1. FIRST AMERICAN TIC	$125,261,686	46.75%	$3,270,448	44.71%	2.53%
2. STEWART TGC	$46,736,613	17.44%	$383,251	5.24%	0.83%
3. FIDELITY NATIONAL	$21,404,757	7.99%	$854,608	11.68%	4.02%
4. LAWYERS	$19,812,137	7.39%	$1,482,988	20.27%	7.09%
5. TRANSNATION	$12,801,335	4.78%	$91,024	1.24%	0.74%
6. COMMONWEALTH LAND	$12,452,270	4.65%	$592,167	8.09%	4.71%
7. CHICAGO TIC	$10,901,946	4.07%	$242,944	3.32%	2.23%
8. UNITED GENERAL	$6,909,726	2.58%	$151,975	2.08%	2.21%
9. OLD REPUBLIC NATIONAL	$3,883,567	1.45%	$197,717	2.70%	4.82%
10. SECURITY UNION	$2,893,646	1.08%	$47,685	0.65%	1.65%
11. ATTORNEYS TGF (CO)	$2,403,171	0.90%	$66,569	0.91%	2.84%
12. GUARANTEE T&T	$761,915	0.28%	$0	--	--
13. PACIFIC NORTHWEST	$439,821	0.16%	$0	--	--
14. WESTERN NATIONAL	$370,721	0.14%	($65,757)	(0.90)%	(14.51)%
15. WESTCOR	$363,865	0.14%	$0	--	--
16. TICOR	$291,877	0.11%	$0	--	--
17. TICOR (FL)	$235,810	0.09%	$0	--	--
18. TRANSUNION NATIONAL	$9,265	0.00%	$0	--	--
19. AMERICAN GUARANTY	$5,005	0.00%	$0	--	--
20. NATIONAL OF NY	$0	--	$0	--	--
COMPOSITE	**$267,939,133**	**100.00%**	**$7,315,619**	**100.00%**	**2.69%**
AVERAGE	**$13,396,957**		**$365,781**		

2006

	TOTAL DPW	MARKET SHARE	LOSSES INCURRED	MARKET SHARE	LOSS RATIO
1. FIRST AMERICAN TIC	$119,278,976	44.30%	$2,482,150	56.63%	2.06%
2. STEWART TGC	$43,134,038	16.02%	$678,768	15.48%	1.59%
3. FIDELITY NATIONAL	$30,466,344	11.32%	($569,892)	(13.00)%	(1.91)%
4. LAWYERS	$18,650,461	6.93%	$1,336,515	30.49%	6.82%
5. TRANSNATION	$17,385,927	6.46%	$119,448	2.72%	0.71%
6. COMMONWEALTH LAND	$13,902,927	5.16%	$344,050	7.85%	2.37%
7. CHICAGO TIC	$9,852,962	3.66%	($224,357)	(5.12)%	(2.31)%
8. UNITED GENERAL	$6,727,826	2.50%	($167,226)	(3.81)%	(2.49)%
9. OLD REPUBLIC NATIONAL	$3,544,534	1.32%	$136,435	3.11%	3.61%
10. SECURITY UNION	$2,627,106	0.98%	$94,133	2.15%	3.58%
11. ATTORNEYS TGF (CO)	$1,447,586	0.54%	($85,525)	(1.95)%	(5.91)%
12. WESTERN NATIONAL	$792,343	0.29%	$238,100	5.43%	27.72%
13. TICOR (FL)	$467,636	0.17%	($6,581)	(0.15)%	(1.45)%
14. TICOR	$346,688	0.13%	$7,427	0.17%	2.28%
15. COLUMBIAN NATIONAL	$275,602	0.10%	$0	--	--
16. PACIFIC NORTHWEST	$137,615	0.05%	$0	--	--
17. WESTCOR	$108,867	0.04%	$0	--	--
18. GUARANTEE T&T	$98,294	0.04%	$0	--	--
COMPOSITE	**$269,245,732**	**100.00%**	**$4,383,445**	**100.00%**	**1.62%**
AVERAGE	**$14,958,096**		**$243,525**		

10-YEAR - DIRECT PREMIUMS WRITTEN (DPW) BY CHANNEL   See Sec. 3

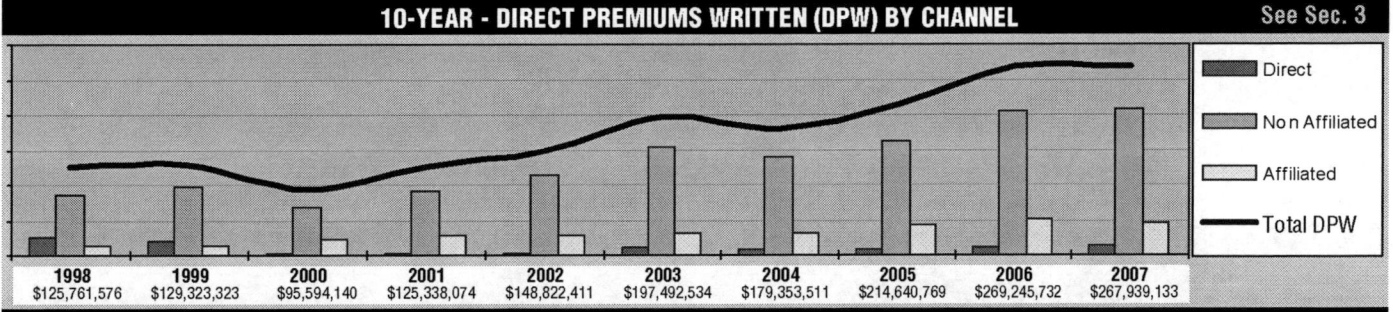

Legend: Direct, Non Affiliated, Affiliated, Total DPW

1998	1999	2000	2001	2002	2003	2004	2005	2006	2007
$125,761,576	$129,323,323	$95,594,140	$125,338,074	$148,822,411	$197,492,534	$179,353,511	$214,640,769	$269,245,732	$267,939,133

10-YEAR - LOSS RATIO   See Sec. 5, A.2

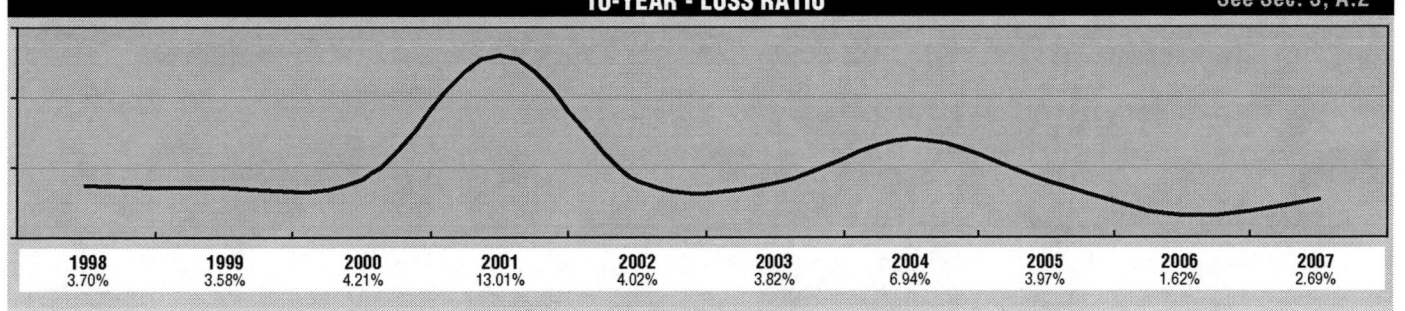

1998	1999	2000	2001	2002	2003	2004	2005	2006	2007
3.70%	3.58%	4.21%	13.01%	4.02%	3.82%	6.94%	3.97%	1.62%	2.69%

6

VERMONT

DEPARTMENT OF INSURANCE INFORMATION	LAND TITLE ASSOCIATION	DOMICILED UNDERWRITERS See Sec. 1

DEPARTMENT OF INSURANCE INFORMATION

Vermont Department of Banking, Insurance, Securities and Health Care Administration

Ms. Paulette Thabault
Commissioner of Insurance
89 Main St., Drawer 20
Montpelier, VT 05620-3101
Phone: (802) 828-3301
Fax: (802) 828-3306
www.bishca.state.vt.us

LAND TITLE ASSOCIATION

New England Land Title Association

P.O. Box 743
Norwalk, CT 06852-0743
Phone: (203) 847-6885
www.nelta.org

DOMICILED UNDERWRITERS See Sec. 1

Underwriter	NAIC #
None	
16 Licensed Underwriters	See Sec. 1

STATUTORY PREMIUM RESERVE (SPR) REQUIREMENTS

Inception:	Not Available		
Max Years:	Not Available	Release:	Not Available

MARKET SHARE BY UNDERWRITER See Sec. 3

2007

	TOTAL DPW	MARKET SHARE	LOSSES INCURRED	MARKET SHARE	LOSS RATIO
1. CT ATTORNEYS	$6,018,064	41.95%	$412,070	46.05%	6.85%
2. FIRST AMERICAN TIC	$3,676,526	25.63%	$393,232	43.94%	10.25%
3. LAWYERS	$1,547,883	10.79%	$0	--	--
4. CHICAGO TIC	$1,127,708	7.86%	$58,683	6.56%	4.46%
5. STEWART TGC	$1,083,614	7.55%	$17,218	1.92%	1.49%
6. COMMONWEALTH LAND	$372,807	2.60%	$3,959	0.44%	1.03%
7. OLD REPUBLIC NATIONAL	$142,949	1.00%	($189,917)	(21.22)%	(117.20)%
8. FIDELITY NATIONAL	$138,901	0.97%	$202,878	22.67%	145.82%
9. TICOR (FL)	$107,951	0.75%	($194)	(0.02)%	(0.20)%
10. UNITED GENERAL	$100,785	0.70%	$0	--	--
11. TICOR	$29,561	0.21%	($3,025)	(0.34)%	(6.63)%
12. SECURITY UNION	$187	0.00%	$0	--	--
13. GUARANTEE T&T	$0	--	$0	--	--
14. NATIONAL OF NY	$0	--	$0	--	--
15. TRANSNATION	$0	--	$0	--	--
COMPOSITE	$14,346,936	100.00%	$894,904	100.00%	6.02%
AVERAGE	$956,462		$59,660		

2006

	TOTAL DPW	MARKET SHARE	LOSSES INCURRED	MARKET SHARE	LOSS RATIO
1. CT ATTORNEYS	$6,351,821	41.75%	$519,444	23.60%	8.18%
2. FIRST AMERICAN TIC	$3,712,685	24.40%	$289,758	13.17%	7.82%
3. LAWYERS	$1,838,348	12.08%	($31,992)	(1.45)%	(1.71)%
4. CHICAGO TIC	$1,182,727	7.77%	$71,923	3.27%	5.84%
5. STEWART TGC	$1,133,898	7.45%	$596,906	27.12%	52.63%
6. COMMONWEALTH LAND	$459,699	3.02%	$4,656	0.21%	0.93%
7. FIDELITY NATIONAL	$175,813	1.16%	$237,675	10.80%	137.25%
8. TICOR (FL)	$112,246	0.74%	$33,988	1.54%	32.78%
9. TICOR	$106,112	0.70%	$153,304	6.97%	136.57%
10. OLD REPUBLIC NATIONAL	$100,596	0.66%	$325,066	14.77%	280.66%
11. UNITED GENERAL	$40,666	0.27%	$0	--	--
12. SECURITY UNION	$760	0.00%	$0	--	--
COMPOSITE	$15,215,371	100.00%	$2,200,728	100.00%	14.35%
AVERAGE	$1,267,948		$183,394		

10-YEAR - DIRECT PREMIUMS WRITTEN (DPW) BY CHANNEL See Sec. 3

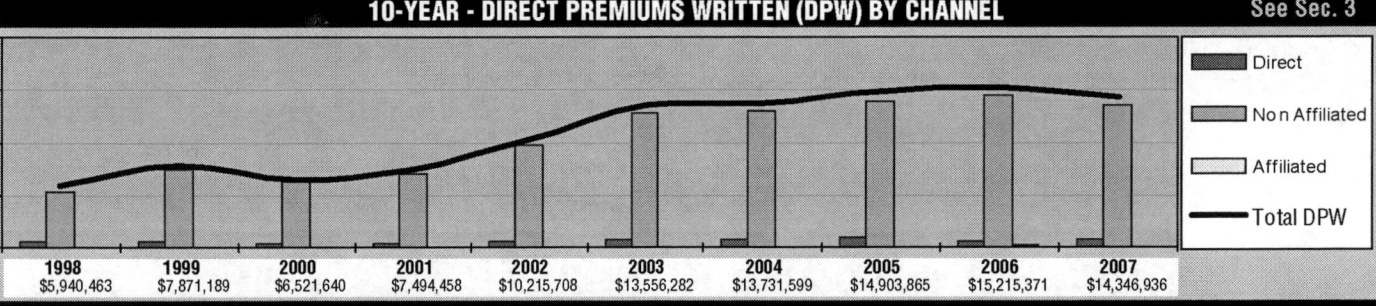

Legend: Direct, Non Affiliated, Affiliated, Total DPW

1998	1999	2000	2001	2002	2003	2004	2005	2006	2007
$5,940,463	$7,871,189	$6,521,640	$7,494,458	$10,215,708	$13,556,282	$13,731,599	$14,903,865	$15,215,371	$14,346,936

10-YEAR - LOSS RATIO See Sec. 5, A.2

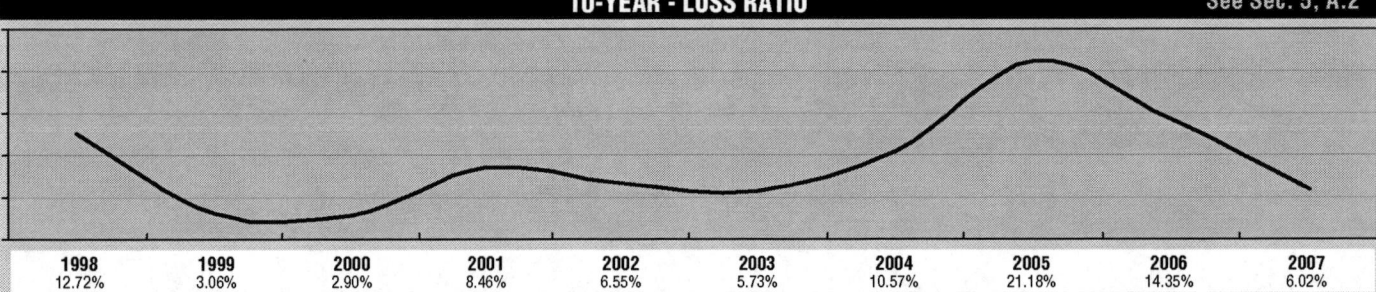

1998	1999	2000	2001	2002	2003	2004	2005	2006	2007
12.72%	3.06%	2.90%	8.46%	6.55%	5.73%	10.57%	21.18%	14.35%	6.02%

6

VIRGINIA

DEPARTMENT OF INSURANCE INFORMATION	LAND TITLE ASSOCIATION	DOMICILED UNDERWRITERS See Sec. 1

Virginia State Corporation Commission Bureau of Insurance

Mr. Alfred W. Gross
Insurance Commissioner
1300 E Main St.
Tyler Building
Richmond, VA 23219
Phone: (804) 371-9741
Fax: (804) 371-9873
www.scc.virginia.gov/division/boi

Virginia Land Title Association
5665 Atlanta Hwy., Ste. 103-140
Alpharetta, GA 30004
Phone: (770) 754-3117
www.vlta.org

Underwriter	NAIC #
SOUTHERN TI CORP	50792
26 Licensed Underwriters	See Sec. 1

STATUTORY PREMIUM RESERVE (SPR) REQUIREMENTS

Inception:	$1.50 per policy & 12.5 cents per $1,000 of net retained liability
Max Years:	20 — Release: 10% years 1-5; 3.33% years 6-20

MARKET SHARE BY UNDERWRITER — See Sec. 3

2007

	TOTAL DPW	MARKET SHARE	LOSSES INCURRED	MARKET SHARE	LOSS RATIO
1. FIRST AMERICAN TIC	$89,287,159	23.85%	$11,214,729	45.46%	12.02%
2. STEWART TGC	$63,429,991	16.94%	$2,788,763	11.31%	4.44%
3. LAWYERS	$59,686,353	15.94%	$1,407,800	5.71%	2.27%
4. CHICAGO TIC	$41,983,327	11.21%	$1,356,941	5.50%	2.91%
5. COMMONWEALTH LAND	$34,901,390	9.32%	$2,082,680	8.44%	6.34%
6. FIDELITY NATIONAL	$28,112,724	7.51%	$2,887,264	11.71%	9.30%
7. SOUTHERN TI CORP	$12,911,755	3.45%	$512,695	2.08%	3.83%
8. UNITED GENERAL	$10,359,693	2.77%	$1,214,151	4.92%	12.63%
9. TRANSNATION	$9,628,708	2.57%	$129,013	0.52%	4.00%
10. OLD REPUBLIC NATIONAL	$8,426,237	2.25%	$436,522	1.77%	4.71%
11. INVESTORS TIC	$6,163,831	1.65%	$207,365	0.84%	3.32%
12. TICOR (FL)	$3,053,509	0.82%	$276,681	1.12%	8.71%
13. COMMERCE	$1,789,931	0.48%	$0	--	--
14. TICOR	$1,510,588	0.40%	$151,349	0.61%	8.33%
15. CENSTAR	$1,252,062	0.33%	$0	--	--
16. NORTH AMERICAN	$1,050,256	0.28%	$0	--	--
17. CONESTOGA	$239,215	0.06%	$0	--	--
18. SECURITY UNION	$227,307	0.06%	$0	--	--
19. TITLE RESOURCES	$208,256	0.06%	$0	--	--
20. TRANSUNION NATIONAL	$117,235	0.03%	$3,000	0.01%	2.64%
21. AMERICAN GUARANTY	$12,149	0.00%	$0	--	--
22. NATIONS OF NY	$0	--	$200	0.00%	42.46%
23. ALAMO	$0	--	$0	--	--
24. BRIDGE	$0	--	($2,297)	0.00%	--
25. EQUITY NATIONAL	$0	--	$0	--	--
26. GUARANTEE T&T	$0	--	$0	--	--
27. NORTHEAST INVESTORS	$0	--	$0	--	--
28. SECURITY TG (BALTIMORE)	$0	--	($61)	0.00%	--
COMPOSITE	**$374,351,676**	**100.00%**	**$24,666,795**	**100.00%**	**6.48%**
AVERAGE	**$13,369,703**		**$880,957**		

2006

	TOTAL DPW	MARKET SHARE	LOSSES INCURRED	MARKET SHARE	LOSS RATIO
1. FIRST AMERICAN TIC	$94,048,057	20.76%	$4,405,162	28.72%	4.58%
2. STEWART TGC	$88,970,090	19.64%	$3,203,886	20.89%	3.63%
3. LAWYERS	$66,492,428	14.68%	$2,578,128	16.81%	3.64%
4. CHICAGO TIC	$58,608,288	12.94%	$1,742,212	11.36%	2.87%
5. COMMONWEALTH LAND	$40,251,680	8.88%	$678,539	4.42%	1.59%
6. FIDELITY NATIONAL	$38,056,201	8.40%	$845,183	5.51%	2.08%
7. SOUTHERN TI CORP	$17,584,665	3.88%	$328,035	2.14%	1.82%
8. OLD REPUBLIC NATIONAL	$11,718,815	2.59%	$668,585	4.36%	5.38%
9. TRANSNATION	$9,228,318	2.04%	$251,549	1.64%	2.68%
10. UNITED GENERAL	$8,739,996	1.93%	$87,694	0.57%	1.18%
11. INVESTORS TIC	$6,633,406	1.46%	$317,890	2.07%	4.82%
12. TICOR (FL)	$6,237,983	1.38%	$511,084	3.33%	8.17%
13. COMMERCE	$2,758,812	0.61%	$0	--	--
14. NORTH AMERICAN CORP	$1,352,995	0.30%	$0	--	--
15. CENSTAR	$887,350	0.20%	$0	--	--
16. TICOR	$772,657	0.17%	$74,007	0.48%	6.83%
17. SECURITY UNION	$294,798	0.07%	$0	--	--
18. CONESTOGA	$246,000	0.05%	$0	--	--
19. TRANSUNION NATIONAL	$174,636	0.04%	$575	0.00%	0.36%
20. BRIDGE	$0	--	$1,564	0.01%	--
21. COMMONWEALTH LAND (NJ	$0	--	$0	--	--
22. EQUITY NATIONAL	$0	--	$0	--	--
23. NORTHEAST INVESTORS	$0	--	$0	--	--
24. TITLE IC AMERICA	$0	--	$0	--	--
25. SECURITY TG (BALTIMORE)	$0	--	($4,845)	(0.03)%	--
26. NATIONS OF NY	$0	--	($348,934)	(2.27)%	--
COMPOSITE	**$453,057,175**	**100.00%**	**$15,340,314**	**100.00%**	**3.29%**
AVERAGE	**$17,425,276**		**$590,012**		

10-YEAR - DIRECT PREMIUMS WRITTEN (DPW) BY CHANNEL — See Sec. 3

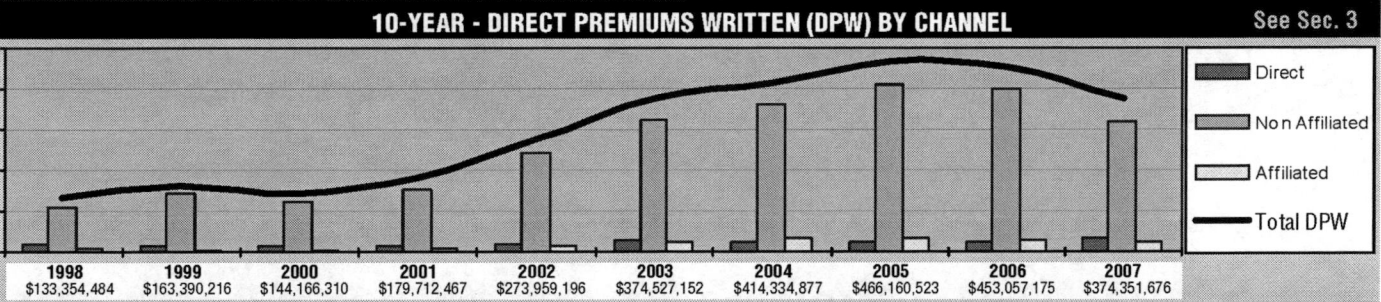

Legend: Direct, Non Affiliated, Affiliated, Total DPW

1998	1999	2000	2001	2002	2003	2004	2005	2006	2007
$133,354,484	$163,390,216	$144,166,310	$179,712,467	$273,959,196	$374,527,152	$414,334,877	$466,160,523	$453,057,175	$374,351,676

10-YEAR - LOSS RATIO — See Sec. 5, A.2

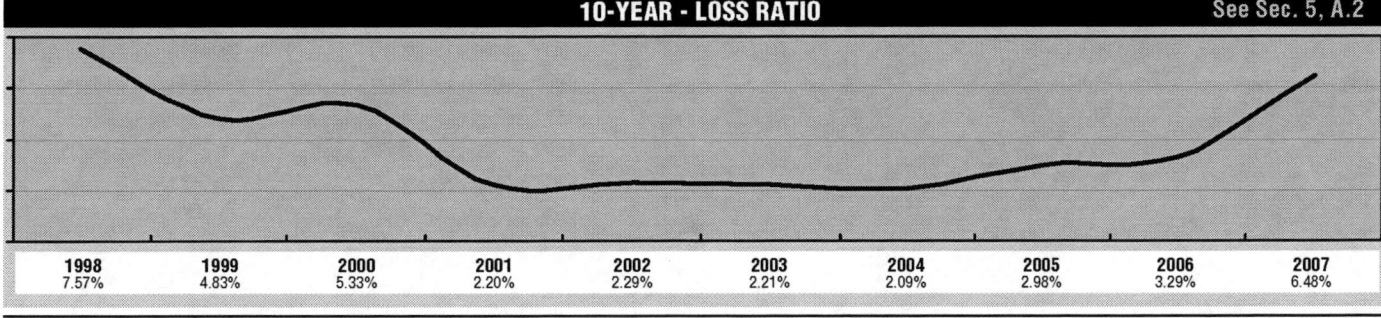

1998	1999	2000	2001	2002	2003	2004	2005	2006	2007
7.57%	4.83%	5.33%	2.20%	2.29%	2.21%	2.09%	2.98%	3.29%	6.48%

WASHINGTON

DEPARTMENT OF INSURANCE INFORMATION	LAND TITLE ASSOCIATION	DOMICILED UNDERWRITERS See Sec. 1

Washington State Department of Insurance

Mr. Mike Bradley Kreidler
Insurance Commissioner
5000 Capitol Blvd.
Tumwater, WA 98501
Phone: (360) 725-7100
Fax: (360) 586-3109
www.insurance.wa.gov

Washington Land Title Association

P.O. Box 2016
Edmonds, WA 98020
Phone: (425) 778-6162
www.wltaonline.org

Underwriter	NAIC #
MASON COUNTY	50962
PACIFIC NORTHWEST	50970
15 Licensed Underwriters	See Sec. 1

STATUTORY PREMIUM RESERVE (SPR) REQUIREMENTS

Inception:	15 cents per $1,000 of net retained liability (policies < $500,000) and 10 cents per $1,000 of net retained liability (policies >= $500,000)
Max Years:	20 **Release:** 35% year 1; 15% years 2-3; 10% year 4; 3% years 5-7; 2% years 8-10; 1% years 11-20

MARKET SHARE BY UNDERWRITER   See Sec. 3

2007

	TOTAL DPW	MARKET SHARE	LOSSES INCURRED	MARKET SHARE	LOSS RATIO
1. CHICAGO TIC	$78,377,891	23.82%	$2,965,453	11.31%	2.65%
2. FIRST AMERICAN TIC	$69,403,953	21.09%	$5,596,879	21.34%	5.07%
3. PACIFIC NORTHWEST	$35,174,635	10.69%	$1,092,672	4.17%	3.02%
4. STEWART TGC	$34,869,622	10.60%	$1,073,711	4.09%	3.12%
5. TRANSNATION	$27,678,501	8.41%	$1,704,990	6.50%	4.36%
6. COMMONWEALTH LAND	$25,220,251	7.67%	$2,864,415	10.92%	11.02%
7. FIDELITY NATIONAL	$18,589,363	5.65%	$1,397,967	5.33%	7.55%
8. TICOR	$15,731,566	4.78%	$201,252	0.77%	1.27%
9. LAWYERS	$13,800,744	4.19%	$8,370,168	31.92%	61.07%
10. OLD REPUBLIC NATIONAL	$9,462,414	2.88%	$577,132	2.20%	5.89%
11. UNITED GENERAL	$354,509	0.11%	$854	0.00%	0.23%
12. SECURITY UNION	$344,444	0.10%	$150,852	0.58%	44.28%
13. TICOR (FL)	$0	--	$225,558	0.86%	0.00%
14. COMMONWEALTH LAND (NJ	$0	--	$0	--	--
15. GUARANTEE T&T	$0	--	$0	--	--
16. INVESTORS TIC	$0	--	$0	--	--
17. NATIONS OF NY	$0	--	$0	--	--
COMPOSITE	$329,007,893	100.00%	$26,221,903	100.00%	6.29%
AVERAGE	$19,353,405		$1,542,465		

2006

	TOTAL DPW	MARKET SHARE	LOSSES INCURRED	MARKET SHARE	LOSS RATIO
1. FIRST AMERICAN TIC	$80,101,269	21.87%	$4,053,071	21.85%	3.30%
2. CHICAGO TIC	$76,373,530	20.85%	$4,185,409	22.57%	3.67%
3. PACIFIC NORTHWEST	$43,867,300	11.98%	$1,013,130	5.46%	2.27%
4. STEWART TGC	$41,854,639	11.43%	$927,910	5.00%	2.22%
5. TRANSNATION	$32,583,880	8.90%	$3,008,573	16.22%	6.36%
6. COMMONWEALTH LAND	$27,962,409	7.64%	$1,608,504	8.67%	5.12%
7. TICOR	$21,534,565	5.88%	$1,132,965	6.11%	5.33%
8. FIDELITY NATIONAL	$18,001,144	4.92%	$1,218,529	6.57%	6.83%
9. LAWYERS	$12,747,855	3.48%	$1,338,380	7.22%	9.93%
10. OLD REPUBLIC NATIONAL	$10,853,334	2.96%	$78,692	0.42%	0.71%
11. SECURITY UNION	$301,999	0.08%	$49,817	0.27%	16.40%
12. UNITED GENERAL	$38,418	0.01%	($11,272)	(0.06)%	(30.62)%
13. CHICAGO TIC (OR)	$0	--	($58,202)	(0.31)%	--
14. INVESTORS TIC	$0	--	$0	--	--
COMPOSITE	$366,220,342	100.00%	$18,545,506	100.00%	3.98%
AVERAGE	$26,158,596		$1,324,679		

10-YEAR - DIRECT PREMIUMS WRITTEN (DPW) BY CHANNEL   See Sec. 3

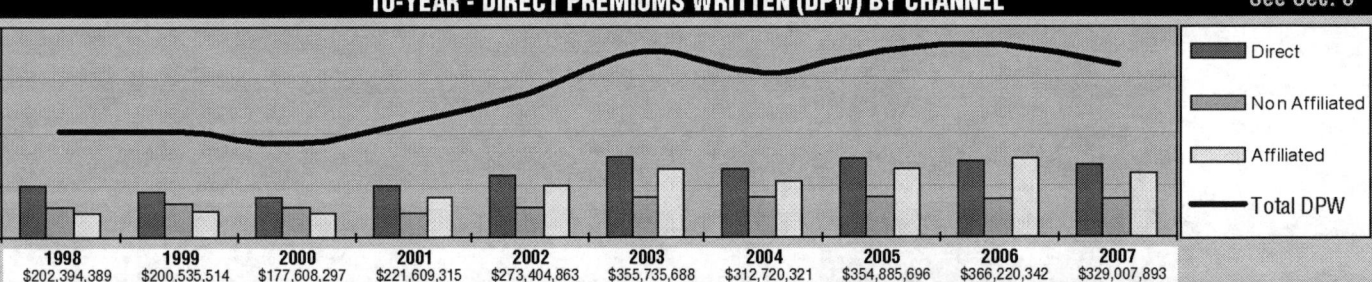

Legend: Direct, Non Affiliated, Affiliated, Total DPW

1998	1999	2000	2001	2002	2003	2004	2005	2006	2007
$202,394,389	$200,535,514	$177,608,297	$221,609,315	$273,404,863	$355,735,688	$312,720,321	$354,885,696	$366,220,342	$329,007,893

10-YEAR - LOSS RATIO   See Sec. 5, A.2

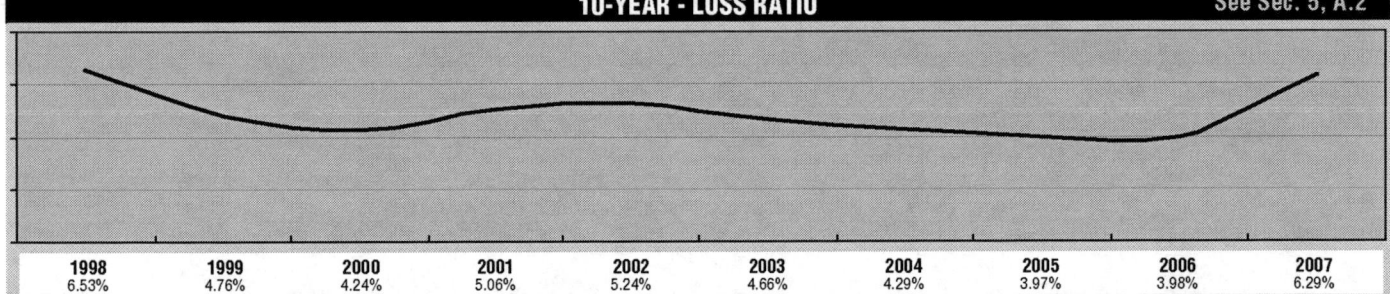

1998	1999	2000	2001	2002	2003	2004	2005	2006	2007
6.53%	4.76%	4.24%	5.06%	5.24%	4.66%	4.29%	3.97%	3.98%	6.29%

6

WEST VIRGINIA

DEPARTMENT OF INSURANCE INFORMATION	LAND TITLE ASSOCIATION	DOMICILED UNDERWRITERS See Sec. 1
West Virginia Insurance Commission	No information at time of publication.	Underwriter / NAIC #

Ms. Jane L. Cline
Insurance Commissioner
1124 Smith St.
Charleston, WV 25301

Phone: (304) 558-3354
Fax: (304) 558-0421
www.wvinsurance.gov

None

22 Licensed Underwriters See Sec. 1

STATUTORY PREMIUM RESERVE (SPR) REQUIREMENTS

Inception:	Not Available		
Max Years:	Not Available	Release:	Not Available

MARKET SHARE BY UNDERWRITER   See Sec. 3

2007

	TOTAL DPW	MARKET SHARE	LOSSES INCURRED	MARKET SHARE	LOSS RATIO
1. FIRST AMERICAN TIC	$6,978,561	28.74%	$238,846	8.75%	2.92%
2. LAWYERS	$3,598,608	14.82%	$1,530,051	56.02%	39.92%
3. STEWART TGC	$3,495,455	14.39%	$159,860	5.85%	4.50%
4. CHICAGO TIC	$2,405,233	9.90%	($77,424)	(2.83)%	(2.65)%
5. OLD REPUBLIC NATIONAL	$2,199,504	9.06%	$256,112	9.38%	11.32%
6. INVESTORS TIC	$2,032,329	8.37%	$61,907	2.27%	3.17%
7. FIDELITY NATIONAL	$1,697,882	6.99%	$109,506	4.01%	4.83%
8. COMMONWEALTH LAND	$1,104,414	4.55%	$223,446	8.18%	18.75%
9. SOUTHERN TI CORP	$237,340	0.98%	$0	--	--
10. TICOR	$151,552	0.62%	$0	--	--
11. UNITED GENERAL	$111,317	0.46%	$0	--	--
12. TRANSNATION	$77,812	0.32%	$0	--	--
13. TICOR (FL)	$71,331	0.29%	$143,677	5.26%	200.24%
14. CENSTAR	$69,567	0.29%	$0	--	--
15. SECURITY TG (BALTIMORE)	$52,488	0.22%	$85,043	3.11%	81.36%
16. AMERICAN GUARANTY	$1,150	0.00%	$0	--	--
17. GUARANTEE T&T	$0	--	$0	--	--
18. NORTHEAST INVESTORS	$0	--	$0	--	--
19. SECURITY UNION	($300)	0.00%	$0	--	--
COMPOSITE	$24,284,243	100.00%	$2,731,024	100.00%	10.11%
AVERAGE	$1,278,118		$143,738		

2006

	TOTAL DPW	MARKET SHARE	LOSSES INCURRED	MARKET SHARE	LOSS RATIO
1. FIRST AMERICAN TIC	$5,961,038	23.95%	$209,749	32.27%	3.45%
2. STEWART TGC	$5,344,752	21.48%	$159,588	24.56%	3.04%
3. LAWYERS	$3,055,183	12.28%	$209,395	32.22%	6.41%
4. CHICAGO TIC	$2,758,622	11.09%	$32,300	4.97%	1.08%
5. OLD REPUBLIC NATIONAL	$2,204,884	8.86%	$10,186	1.57%	0.43%
6. INVESTORS TIC	$2,111,557	8.49%	$4,662	0.72%	0.23%
7. FIDELITY NATIONAL	$1,432,087	5.75%	($62,596)	(9.63)%	(4.44)%
8. COMMONWEALTH LAND	$1,160,712	4.66%	$214,614	33.02%	16.78%
9. SECURITY TG (BALTIMORE)	$460,355	1.85%	$102,610	15.79%	20.58%
10. SOUTHERN TI CORP	$123,113	0.49%	$0	--	--
11. UNITED GENERAL	$85,498	0.34%	$0	--	--
12. TICOR	$76,998	0.31%	($58,000)	(8.92)%	(56.87)%
13. TICOR (FL)	$72,132	0.29%	($172,621)	(26.56)%	(228.55)%
14. TRANSNATION	$27,067	0.11%	$0	--	--
15. CENSTAR	$10,060	0.04%	$0	--	--
16. SECURITY UNION	$701	0.00%	$0	--	--
17. NORTHEAST INVESTORS	$0	--	$0	--	--
COMPOSITE	$24,884,759	100.00%	$649,887	100.00%	2.54%
AVERAGE	$1,463,809		$38,229		

10-YEAR - DIRECT PREMIUMS WRITTEN (DPW) BY CHANNEL   See Sec. 3

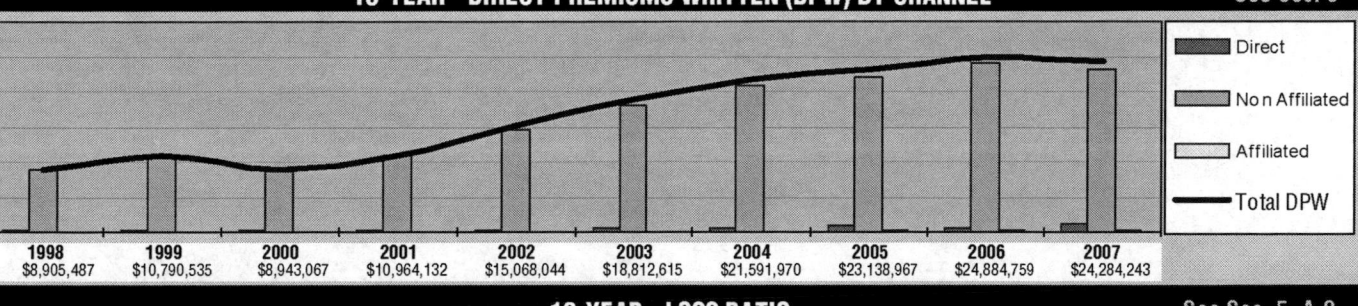

Legend: Direct, Non Affiliated, Affiliated, Total DPW

1998	1999	2000	2001	2002	2003	2004	2005	2006	2007
$8,905,487	$10,790,535	$8,943,067	$10,964,132	$15,068,044	$18,812,615	$21,591,970	$23,138,967	$24,884,759	$24,284,243

10-YEAR - LOSS RATIO   See Sec. 5, A.2

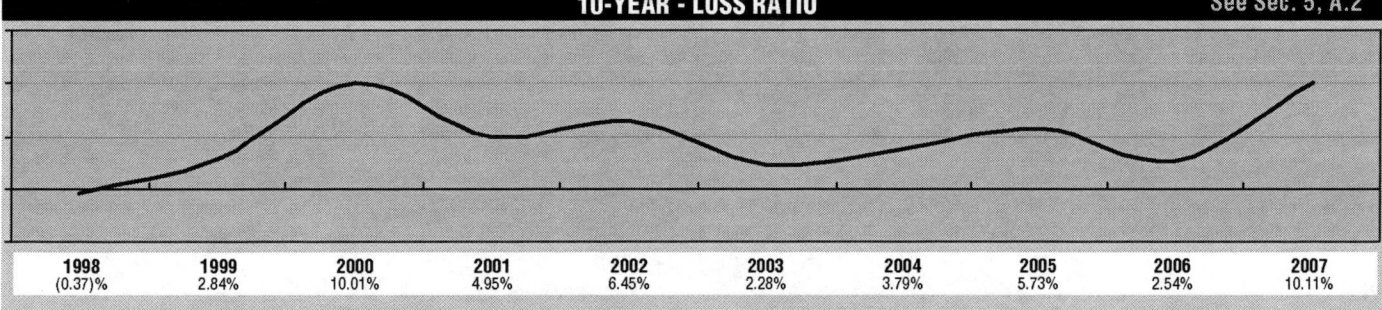

1998	1999	2000	2001	2002	2003	2004	2005	2006	2007
(0.37)%	2.84%	10.01%	4.95%	6.45%	2.28%	3.79%	5.73%	2.54%	10.11%

6

WISCONSIN

DEPARTMENT OF INSURANCE INFORMATION	LAND TITLE ASSOCIATION	DOMICILED UNDERWRITERS See Sec. 1	
Wisconsin Department of Insurance	Wisconsin Land Title Association	Underwriter	NAIC #

Mr. Sean Dilweg
Commissioner of Insurance
125 S Webster St.
Madison, WI 53703-3474
Phone: (608) 266-8517
Fax: (608) 261-8579
www.oci.wi.gov

P.O. Box 873
West Salem, WI 54669
Phone: (608) 786-2336
www.wlta.org

None

| | 21 | Licensed Underwriters | See Sec. 1 |

STATUTORY PREMIUM RESERVE (SPR) REQUIREMENTS

Inception:	Not Available		
Max Years:	Not Available	Release:	Not Available

MARKET SHARE BY UNDERWRITER — See Sec. 3

2007

	TOTAL DPW	MARKET SHARE	LOSSES INCURRED	MARKET SHARE	LOSS RATIO
1. FIRST AMERICAN TIC	$35,976,341	30.76%	$2,931,290	17.73%	6.69%
2. CHICAGO TIC	$23,621,717	20.20%	$2,475,659	14.98%	9.33%
3. STEWART TGC	$15,231,709	13.02%	$5,031,902	30.44%	33.08%
4. LAWYERS	$8,170,324	6.99%	$4,226,673	25.57%	41.57%
5. COMMONWEALTH LAND	$7,922,846	6.77%	$397,530	2.40%	4.90%
6. OLD REPUBLIC NATIONAL	$7,729,393	6.61%	$340,002	2.06%	4.06%
7. TICOR	$6,522,897	5.58%	$674,020	4.08%	9.85%
8. SECURITY UNION	$4,382,113	3.75%	$185,846	1.12%	4.31%
9. FIRST AMERICAN (OR)	$2,068,205	1.77%	$0	--	--
10. FIDELITY NATIONAL	$1,768,503	1.51%	$5,869	0.04%	0.49%
11. TRANSNATION	$1,553,425	1.33%	$92,102	0.56%	7.07%
12. UNITED GENERAL	$818,770	0.70%	$8,192	0.05%	0.99%
13. TICOR (FL)	$792,991	0.68%	$123,889	0.75%	14.78%
14. ATTORNEYS TGF (IL)	$291,071	0.25%	$36,795	0.22%	12.24%
15. CENSTAR	$103,509	0.09%	$0	--	--
16. AMERICAN GUARANTY	$374	0.00%	$0	--	--
17. GUARANTEE T&T	$0	--	$0	--	--
18. INVESTORS TIC	$0	--	$0	--	--
19. NATIONAL OF NY	$0	--	$0	--	--
COMPOSITE	$116,954,188	100.00%	$16,529,769	100.00%	12.74%
AVERAGE	$6,155,484		$869,988		

2006

	TOTAL DPW	MARKET SHARE	LOSSES INCURRED	MARKET SHARE	LOSS RATIO
1. FIRST AMERICAN TIC	$39,137,795	28.57%	$1,566,693	25.25%	3.58%
2. CHICAGO TIC	$29,089,553	21.23%	$1,876,270	30.24%	5.50%
3. STEWART TGC	$14,885,434	10.86%	$564,463	9.10%	3.71%
4. OLD REPUBLIC NATIONAL	$11,555,395	8.43%	$618,179	9.96%	5.14%
5. COMMONWEALTH LAND	$10,100,189	7.37%	$419,772	6.77%	3.73%
6. LAWYERS	$8,476,908	6.19%	$379,294	6.11%	3.51%
7. TICOR	$7,939,013	5.79%	$318,005	5.12%	3.95%
8. SECURITY UNION	$6,096,864	4.45%	$132,308	2.13%	2.23%
9. FIDELITY NATIONAL	$3,140,682	2.29%	($26,153)	(0.42)%	(0.85)%
10. FIRST AMERICAN (OR)	$2,013,100	1.47%	$0	--	--
11. TICOR (FL)	$1,705,783	1.25%	$197,132	3.18%	11.14%
12. TRANSNATION	$1,696,300	1.24%	$67,932	1.09%	4.56%
13. UNITED GENERAL	$760,263	0.55%	$3,971	0.06%	0.52%
14. ATTORNEYS TGF (IL)	$318,409	0.23%	$87,189	1.41%	26.33%
15. CENSTAR	$92,873	0.07%	$0	--	--
16. INVESTORS TIC	$0	--	$0	--	--
COMPOSITE	$137,008,561	100.00%	$6,205,055	100.00%	4.13%
AVERAGE	$8,563,035		$387,816		

10-YEAR - DIRECT PREMIUMS WRITTEN (DPW) BY CHANNEL — See Sec. 3

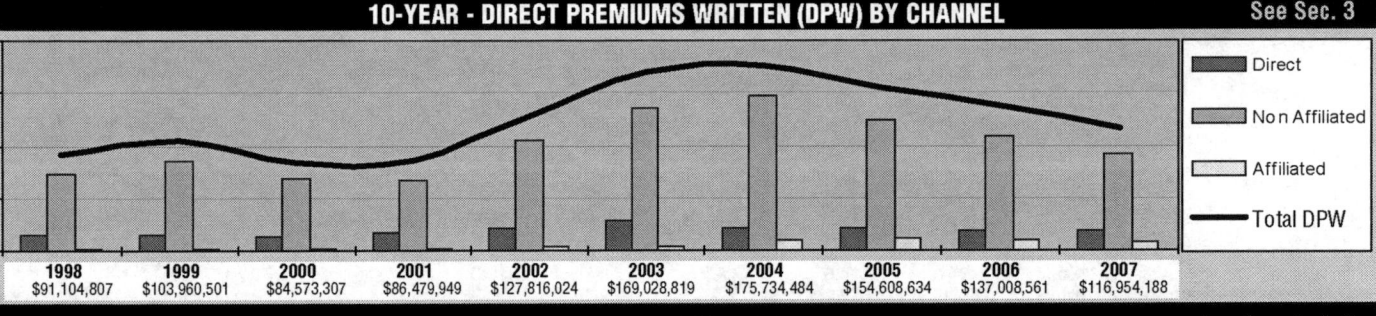

- Direct
- Non Affiliated
- Affiliated
- Total DPW

1998	1999	2000	2001	2002	2003	2004	2005	2006	2007
$91,104,807	$103,960,501	$84,573,307	$86,479,949	$127,816,024	$169,028,819	$175,734,484	$154,608,634	$137,008,561	$116,954,188

10-YEAR - LOSS RATIO — See Sec. 5, A.2

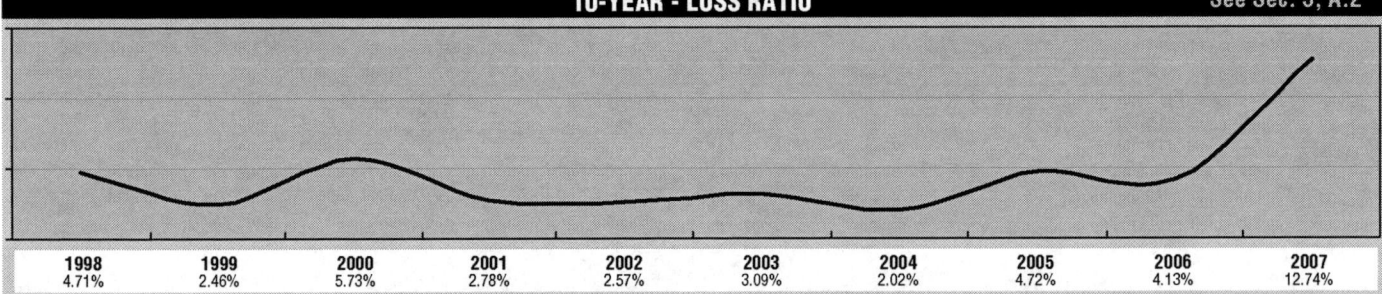

1998	1999	2000	2001	2002	2003	2004	2005	2006	2007
4.71%	2.46%	5.73%	2.78%	2.57%	3.09%	2.02%	4.72%	4.13%	12.74%

6

WYOMING

DEPARTMENT OF INSURANCE INFORMATION	LAND TITLE ASSOCIATION	DOMICILED UNDERWRITERS See Sec. 1	
Wyoming Department of Insurance	**Wyoming Land Title Association**	**Underwriter**	**NAIC #**

Mr. Ken Vines
Insurance Commissioner
106 E 6th Ave.
Cheyenne, WY 82002

Phone: (307) 777-7401
Fax: (307) 777-2446
insurance.state.wy.us

DOMICILED UNDERWRITERS	
FOUNDERS	11974
16 Licensed Underwriters See Sec. 1	

STATUTORY PREMIUM RESERVE (SPR) REQUIREMENTS

Inception:	20 cents per $1,000 of net retained liability
Max Years:	20	Release:	35% year 1; 15% years 2-3; 10% year 4; 3% years 5-7; 2% years 8-10; 1% years 11-20

MARKET SHARE BY UNDERWRITER   See Sec. 3

2007

	TOTAL DPW	MARKET SHARE	LOSSES INCURRED	MARKET SHARE	LOSS RATIO
1. FIRST AMERICAN TIC	$16.302.227	48.85%	$187.521	23.35%	1.13%
2. STEWART TGC	$7.107.136	21.30%	$249.715	31.10%	3.57%
3. CHICAGO TIC	$3.502.314	10.50%	$16.396	2.04%	0.46%
4. LAWYERS	$2.912.071	8.73%	$92.477	11.52%	3.06%
5. OLD REPUBLIC NATIONAL	$1.675.569	5.02%	$98.633	12.28%	5.68%
6. COMMONWEALTH LAND	$1.331.706	3.99%	$129.632	16.14%	9.66%
7. FIDELITY NATIONAL	$333.319	1.00%	$28.660	3.57%	8.62%
8. FOUNDERS	$178.276	0.53%	$0	--	--
9. TICOR	$20.434	0.06%	($10)	0.00%	(0.04)%
10. UNITED GENERAL	$7.512	0.02%	$0	--	--
11. GUARANTEE T&T	$0	--	$0	--	--
12. NATIONAL OF NY	$0	--	$0	--	--
13. SECURITY UNION	$0	--	$0	--	--
14. TRANSNATION	$0	--	$0	--	--
COMPOSITE	$33,370,564	100.00%	$803,024	100.00%	2.37%
AVERAGE	$2,383,612		$57,359		

2006

	TOTAL DPW	MARKET SHARE	LOSSES INCURRED	MARKET SHARE	LOSS RATIO
1. FIRST AMERICAN TIC	$15.875.967	53.64%	$260.687	102.59%	1.64%
2. STEWART TGC	$3.892.195	13.15%	$4.535	1.78%	0.12%
3. CHICAGO TIC	$2.811.955	9.50%	($7.070)	(2.78)%	(0.25)%
4. LAWYERS	$2.735.219	9.24%	($20.481)	(8.06)%	(0.72)%
5. OLD REPUBLIC NATIONAL	$1.966.071	6.64%	$7.970	3.14%	0.40%
6. COMMONWEALTH LAND	$1.695.343	5.73%	($500)	(0.20)%	(0.03)%
7. FIDELITY NATIONAL	$411.256	1.39%	$40.144	15.80%	9.92%
8. FOUNDERS	$196.515	0.66%	$0	--	--
9. TICOR	$10.829	0.04%	($31.176)	(12.27)%	(228.68)%
10. UNITED GENERAL	$430	0.00%	$0	--	--
11. SECURITY UNION	$0	--	$0	--	--
12. TRANSNATION	$0	--	$0	--	--
COMPOSITE	$29,595,780	100.00%	$254,109	100.00%	0.85%
AVERAGE	$2,466,315		$21,176		

10-YEAR - DIRECT PREMIUMS WRITTEN (DPW) BY CHANNEL   See Sec. 3

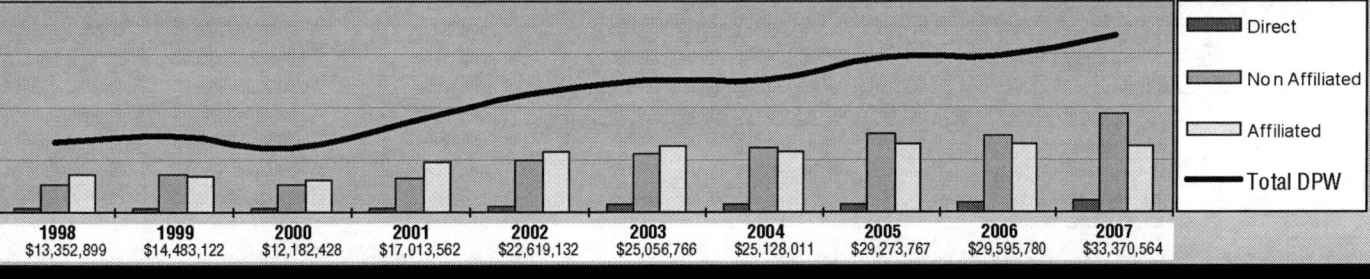

Legend: Direct, Non Affiliated, Affiliated, Total DPW

1998	1999	2000	2001	2002	2003	2004	2005	2006	2007
$13,352,899	$14,483,122	$12,182,428	$17,013,562	$22,619,132	$25,056,766	$25,128,011	$29,273,767	$29,595,780	$33,370,564

10-YEAR - LOSS RATIO   See Sec. 5, A.2

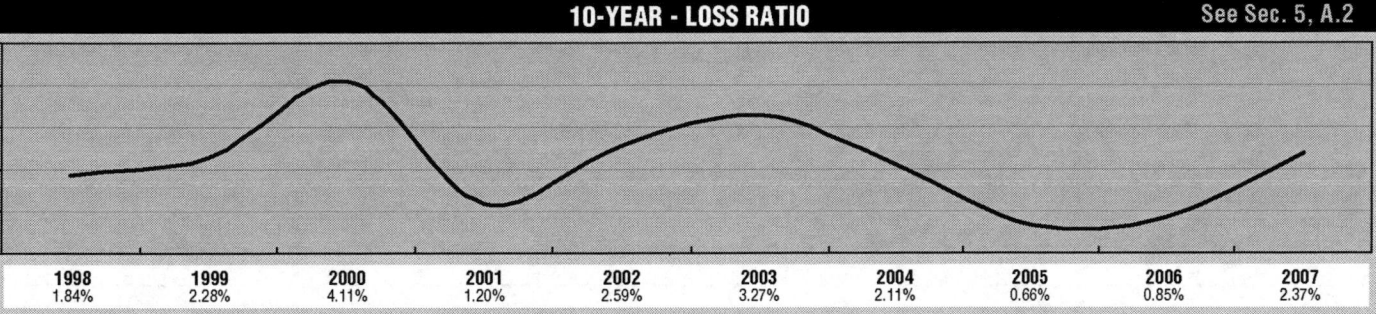

1998	1999	2000	2001	2002	2003	2004	2005	2006	2007
1.84%	2.28%	4.11%	1.20%	2.59%	3.27%	2.11%	0.66%	0.85%	2.37%

Notes

SERIOUS ABOUT SOLVENCY®

About Demotech, Inc.

Demotech, Inc. is a Columbus, Ohio based financial analysis and actuarial services firm providing a wide range of services including pricing analysis, state filings assistance, Financial Stability Ratings® (FSR) and support for other required regulatory reporting. Having worked with insurers of all sizes, Demotech possesses broad experience addressing actuarial and financial analysis issues, whether the issue is unique to a particular insurer or prevalent throughout the industry.

Offering an Individualized Approach to Industry Challenges

Demotech understands the industry is fluid and that every company has unique challenges and objectives. We offer an individualized approach, learning an organization's needs and goals to offer a customized solution.

Working within the Property and Casualty and Title insurance sectors, Demotech provides a variety of solutions, including actuarial consulting, market analysis, loss and loss adjustment expense reserve analysis and Financial Stability Ratings®. Each of our services has continually adapted to address our clients' challenges.

Proactively Responding to Market Needs

Since our beginning in 1985, Demotech has proactively responded to the market with our clients in mind. Starting in 1989, Demotech gained acceptance from the secondary mortgage marketplace, including the Federal National Mortgage Association (Fannie Mae) and later the Federal Home Loan Mortgage Corporation (Freddie Mac) and the United States Department of Housing and Urban Development (HUD), for Financial Stability Ratings® to facilitate activities for financially stable clients.

In 1992, we were the first to analyze the financial position for each Title underwriter. More recently, in 2004 Demotech obtained direct access to personal, farm and commercial umbrella coverage for qualified Property and Casualty insurers with an acceptable Financial Stability Rating®.

In 2005, Demotech was approved to provide Financial Stability Ratings® for regional insurance companies, captive insurance entities, risk retention groups and risk sharing entities providing professional liability insurance under HUD Notice H04-15, Professional Liability Insurance for Section 232 and 223(f) Programs.

Solutions as Unique as Your Company

Demotech continues to assess the market with our clients' interests in mind. Since 1985, clients have looked to Demotech to provide information, analysis and proactive solutions. We continue to evolve along with the industry through the development of innovative solutions, driven by our commitment to our clients.

About *Demotech Performance of Title Insurance Companies*

For twenty years, *Performance of Title Insurance Companies* has analyzed the Title insurance industry and its competitive landscape with industry-wide underwriter and group level benchmarks. Representing more than 99% of the Title industry, *Demotech Performance of Title Insurance Companies* is the most complete and thorough industry analysis available.

For additional information, contact us at:

Demotech, Inc.
2715 Tuller Parkway
Dublin, Ohio 43017-2310
Tel: (614) 761-8602
(800) 354-7207
Fax: (614) 761-0906
www.demotech.com
inquiry@demotech.com

 Demotech, Inc.

Demotech, Inc. Milestones

1985 Founded by Joseph L. Petrelli and Sharon M. Romano to offer actuarial services.

1986 First to issue Financial Stability Ratings® (FSRs) for health maintenance organizations (HMOs).

1987 First to issue FSRs for public entity liability self-insured pools through the development of our Management Audit Process.

1989 First to have Property and Casualty insurance company rating process formally reviewed and accepted by Fannie Mae. An FSR of A or better eliminates the need for property insurance cut-through endorsements.

1990 First to have Property and Casualty insurance company rating process formally reviewed and accepted by Freddie Mac.

Began offering Property and Casualty insurance companies and Title underwriters loss cost analysis and rate, rule and form filing assistance.

Responded to the National Association of Insurance Commissioners (NAIC) requirements for Property and Casualty insurers to submit Statements of Actuarial Opinion related to loss and loss adjustment expense reserves concurrent with the 1990 Property and Casualty annual statement.

1992 First to analyze the financial position for each Title underwriter.

1993 First to have Property and Casualty insurance company rating process formally reviewed and accepted by HUD.

1994 Fannie Mae issued Title underwriting guidelines, naming Demotech as an approved Title underwriter rating service.

1995 First to promulgate Commercial Real Estate Recommendations (CRERs) to provide additional financial due diligence of Title underwriters involved in larger real estate transactions.

1996 Contacted by the Florida Office of Insurance Regulation (OIR) when the property insurance market encountered newly established insurers that did not meet traditional rating requirements. Working with the Florida OIR, Demotech developed evaluation procedures for the assignment of FSRs to newly formed Property and Casualty companies.

Coordinated the first seminar regarding the implementation of Statements of Actuarial Opinion for Title insurance companies on behalf of the Conference of Consulting Actuaries and in cooperation with the American Land Title Association (ALTA).

1999 Co-authored the Commerce Clearing House publication describing the evolution of the Canadian Title insurance industry.

2001 Completed the initial loss and loss adjustment expense review of the Iowa Finance Authority – Title Guaranty Division.

2002 Revitalized the Ohio Title Insurance Rating Bureau (OTIRB).

2003 Assisted the North Carolina Title Insurance Rating Bureau with the development and filing of Closing Services insurance product.

Assisted the OTIRB with its first rate revision since 1980.

2004 Introduced *Demotech Performance of Title Insurance Companies* and *Quarterly Updates*.

Published *Serious about Solvency – Financial Stability Rating® Survival Rates 1989 through 2004*. This article outlines the description of our analysis process, the assignment of FSRs and the survival rates of those ratings. This retrospective analysis indicates that insurers earning FSRs of A or better had survival rates at or above expectations.

2005 Celebrated 20th anniversary, continuing to grow and serve Property and Casualty insurers and Title underwriters throughout the industry.

HUD approved Demotech's rating process for professional liability insurance under Notice H04-15, Professional Liability Insurance for Section 232 and 223(f) Programs.

2006 Joseph L. Petrelli, ACAS, MAAA, FCA, authored *What We've Got Here Is a Failure to Communicate – How Traditional Financial Reporting Contributes to Misunderstanding of Title Insurance Loss Activity*. This discussion expounds upon the ramifications of Title underwriters' required conformance with Property and Casualty financial reporting standards and how industry comparisons fail to recognize fundamental differences between Title and Property and Casualty coverage characteristics.

2007 Designated as the "Official Research Partner" of *Insurance Journal*, providing research, actuarial and statistical support and collaborating on special joint reports pertaining to insurance industry performance and financial results.

Expanded operations into a new facility reflecting our increased capacity to serve the industry and our clients.